Handbook of U.S. Labor Statistics

Employment, Earnings, Prices, Productivity, and Other Labor Data

Fifth Edition, 2001

Handbook of U.S. Labor Statistics

Employment, Earnings, Prices, Productivity, and Other Labor Data

Fifth Edition, 2001

EDITOR
Eva E. Jacobs

ASSOCIATE EDITOR
Sohair M. Abu-Aish

ISBN: 0-89059-567-4

ISSN: 1526-2553

Printed by Automated Graphic Systems, Inc., White Plains, MD, on acid-free paper that meets the American National Standards Institute Z39-48 standard.

2002 2001 4 3 2 1

Bernan Press
4611-F Assembly Drive
Lanham, MD 20706
email: info@bernan.com

CONTENTS

LIST OF TABLES

Work Experience

Labor Force and Employment Characteristics of Selected Family Types

Labor Force and Employment Characteristics by Education

Contingent and Alternative Work Arrangements

Employer-Provided Training

Employment by Industry

Hours and Earnings by Industry

Employment, Hours, and Earnings by State

PART 6: PRICES AND LIVING CONDITIONS 301

PRODUCER PRICE INDEX

CONSUMER PRICE INDEX

EXPORT AND IMPORT PRICE INDEXES

PART 7: CONSUMER EXPENDITURES 341

ABOUT THE EDITORS

Eva E. Jacobs, editor of *Handbook of U.S. Labor Statistics* since the first edition, served as Chief of the Division of Consumer Expenditure Surveys at the U.S. Bureau of Labor Statistics (BLS) for over 20 years. As manager of this division, Ms. Jacobs was responsible for the BLS Family Budget Program, and held positions in the Productivity Division and the Economic Growth Division. More recently, she acted as advisor on cost-of-living projects for both government and private consultants. Currently, Ms. Jacobs serves as chair of a panel advising the Safe Harbor Working Group on issues related to cost-of-living adjustments for federal employees in Alaska, Hawaii, Guam, Puerto Rico, and the Virgin Islands. Ms. Jacobs was the 1998 recipient of the Julius Shiskin Award, given by the National Association of Business Economists and the Washington Statistical Society for distinguished contributions to Economic Statistics.

Sohair M. Abu-Aish, a Bernan Data Analyst, worked for the U.S. Bureau of the Census and taught economics at Zagazig University and Cairo University, Egypt, for over 10 years. Ms. Abu-Aish, an associate editor of the fourth edition of *Handbook of U.S. Labor Statistics*, and a co-editor of the latest edition of *Foreign Trade of the United States,* holds an M.S. in Economics from Zagazig University and a Diploma in Computer Programming from Strayer University.

PREFACE

What industries are expected to show the greatest growth in the next decade? Which occupations are expected to grow with these industries? How is the work environment changing? How do the changing demographics of the population affect the labor force?

Our changing society and our dynamic economy raise different questions over time. The answers are crucial to making public and private decisions. Recent areas of public policy debate involve health care costs, energy costs and education quality. An important factor in both the health care policy and energy debates has been the rate of increase in the price of prescription drugs and medical services and fuel. An important question for education policy is whether we are preparing young people for the occupations required by our increasing technological society. Among other questions requiring policy attention by both government and private business result from the increasing number of women with children in the labor force, the changing face of the future labor force, and the changing structure of benefits provided to workers.

Answering questions such as these for the future requires information about the present and the past. The U.S. Bureau of Labor Statistics (BLS) provides a treasure trove of historical information about the labor market, prices and productivity. Bernan Associates is pleased to present this fifth edition of it's award-winning *Handbook of U.S. Labor Statistics* containing a compilation of such BLS data. The current publication maintains and updates the content of the previous edition and adds additional data and new features.

FEATURES OF THE PUBLICATION

- Over 160 tables presenting authoritative data on workers, industries and prices.
- An introductory article which calls attention to new surveys or major restructuring of existing surveys. The current edition describes the new National Compensation Survey which combines three previous separate surveys. Earlier articles have included a description of the new Standard Occupational Classification (SOC) and the latest revision of the Consumer Price Index.
- An introduction to each part highlighting some salient data in the following numerous tables. Also included is a chart showing a particularly noteworthy trend.
- Each major section is preceded by a concise description of the data sources, definitions and methodology from which the tables are derived.
- The introductory notes also contain references to more comprehensive reports.

NEW IN THIS EDITION

In addition to updating the series published in earlier editions, new tables are introduced as they become available. New tables in this edition are:

- Employment status of the population by region and state.
- Occupational employment and wages according to the new SOC.
- State and local Government employee compensation costs and benefits.
- New data on employee characteristics with nonfatal injuries and illnesses.
- Union affiliation by state.
- Labor force status and earnings by citizenship status.

SOURCES OF ADDITIONAL INFORMATION

BLS data for the most part are derived from surveys conducted by the federal government or through federal-state cooperative arrangements. The comparability of data over time can be affected by the changes in the surveys that are needed to keep pace with the current structure of economic institutions or to take advantage of improved survey techniques. In addition, revisions of current data are made periodically as a result of the availability of new information. The introductory notes to each chapter summarize the specific factors that may affect the data in that chapter. In the tables, the ellipsis character ("...") has been used to indicate data that are not available, not applicable or equal to zero.

More extensive methodological information, including sampling and estimation procedures for all BLS programs, is contained in *The BLS Handbook of Methods* (BLS Bulletin 2490, April 1997). Other sources of current data and analytical articles are the *Monthly Labor Review* and *The Report on the American Workforce,* a biennial publication of BLS, and a daily internet publication, TED, from The Editor's Desk. The Internet address for the BLS home page is <http://stats.bls.gov>.

ACKNOWLEDGEMENTS

Preparation of this book was very much a team activity. The Associate Editor, Sohair M. Abu-Aish, made important contributions to the highlights in addition to ably preparing the tables. Dr. Cornelia Strawser reviewed the tables and the text and made many useful suggestions on the content. Deirdre Gaquin prepared the special tabulations of data from the Current Population Survey. Lorrent Smith prepared all graphics and layout. Copy editing was done by Jacalyn Houston. Special thanks go to Tamera L.Wells-Lee and Dan Parham for directing all editorial and production aspects. Profound appreciations are due to each of these individuals for skills, professionalism and cooperative effort which made this publication possible.

Particular thanks go to the BLS staff members too numerous to mention by name who patiently answered questions and provided material.

BERNAN'S U.S. DATABOOK SERIES

The *Handbook of U.S. Labor Statistics* is one of a number of Bernan publications providing the public with statistical information from official government sources. Other titles in the Bernan U.S. Databook series include *Business Statistics of the United States, Education Statistics of the United States, Health and Healthcare in the United States, Housing Statistics of the United States,* and *Foreign Trade of the United States.* In each of these publications, intense efforts have been made to provide a useful, accurate, and up-to-date selection of information.

We welcome you to the world of government statistics and urge you to provide us with your suggestions on how we may make future editions even more useful. Please contact us by email at bpress@bernan.com or write us at Bernan Press, 4611-F Assembly Dr., Lanham, MD 20706. Visit our Web site at <http://www.bernan.com>.

Eva E. Jacobs, Editor

THE NATIONAL COMPENSATION SURVEY: STATISTICS COMPENSATION FOR THE 21ST CENTURY

The following article, adapted from the winter 2000 issue of the Bureau of Labor Statistics publication, ***Compensation and Working Conditions,*** *describes the background of the National Compensation Survey. This survey is designed to integrate the wage levels, benefit costs and detailed benefit provisions data that are currently available in Part 5 of this volume.*[1]

This article describes new compensation data produced by the Bureau of Labor Statistics (BLS)—the National Compensation Survey (NCS). The NCS will combine three BLS programs and take them in new directions: the Employment Cost Index, the Employee Benefits Survey and the Occupational Compensation Survey. The NCS provides statistically valid, comprehensive, and interrelated data on wages and employee benefits for all American workers. Compensation data are used by a variety of individuals and groups—academics, government policymakers, labor unions, employers, researchers, and individuals. Data are needed to answer questions as diverse as how much to pay registered nurses in Dallas or what is a competitive dental care plan for clerical workers. The box below provides examples of the types of questions that compensation professionals and others might be asking, along with the answers that NCS data can provide now, or will provide in the future. The remainder of this article discusses the origins and structure of the NCS program.

Compensation question? Ask NCS

Below are some examples of the types of information that the NCS is designed to provide:

Q. A manufacturer estimated that its benefit costs increased 3 percent during 1999. Is that comparable to the experience of other employers in the manufacturing industry?

A. Employer-paid benefit costs in manufacturing rose 3.4 percent for the 12 months ending December 1999. These data are from the Employment Cost Index, one of the products of the NCS.

Q. Our employees are asking for dental coverage as part of our health benefits. Is that a common benefit among large employers in the northeast?

A. NCS benefits data indicate that 58 percent of full-time employees in larger private establishments (those with 100 workers or more) in the northeast received dental care benefits in 1997.

Q. We are negotiating with the union cost-of-living increases in our defined benefit pension plans. How widespread are such features in private sector pension plans and how do they typically work?

A. The NCS benefits survey of larger private establishments indicates that 50 percent of full-time workers have a defined benefit pension plan, and of those participants, only 3 percent have a cost-of-living increase. Such increases are found more often among state and local government plans. Where cost-of-living adjustments do exist, they typically are tied to an inflation indicator, such as the BLS Consumer Price Index (CPI). Such plans may provide an annual pension increase equal to the percent increase in the CPI, but often capped at a specified amount, such as 3 percent per year.

A HISTORICAL PERSPECTIVE

Since it was established in the late 19th century, BLS has been conducting compensation surveys. Among the earliest BLS surveys were those designed to gather wage information for a specific purpose, such as to determine the effect of the 1890 tariff on wages in certain industries. Surveys of employee benefits date to the early 20th century, and typically took the form of case studies of new practices undertaken by small numbers of employers. Compensation studies up through the first half of the last century were designed to meet short-term needs; there was little relationship between one study and the next, and there were little or no trend data.

In the 1950s, BLS began the first Occupational Wage Surveys, a program that is a direct ancestor of the National Compensation Survey. These surveys typically were conducted in metropolitan areas throughout the country. Wage data were collected and published for selected jobs (such as secretary or truck driver) and for work levels within those jobs (used to differentiate duties and responsibilities). Over time, this program was expanded to cover specialty jobs in selected industries and white-collar jobs nationwide. A benefit component, the Employee Benefits Survey, was added to the national pay survey in the late 1970s. This program provided the Bureau's first-ever comprehensive set of statistics on the availability and details of employer-provided benefits. Previous benefit studies typically were case studies of plans or their features.

Interest in measures of change in employer costs for wages and benefits in the 1970s led to the development of the Employment Cost Index (ECI), a quarterly measure of compensation cost changes. Previous studies had examined the levels of employer wage and benefit costs. The ECI, introduced in 1975, was the Bureau's first attempt to provide a single measure of change in employer compensation costs. Since 1986, these data on employer cost trends also have been used to produce annual levels of employer compensation costs and estimates of the proportion of those costs attributable to various types of compensation.

There are some seemingly similar data in these various compensation series, but there is a lack of coordination among these products that can limit their usefulness for certain types of analysis. The NCS is designed to coordinate these compensation statistics.

The design of the National Compensation Survey focuses on three basic components: A selection of geographic areas; a selection of establishments within those areas; and a selection of occupations within those establishments. Data for the NCS are captured from a fixed set of geographic areas, rather than from all areas of the country. Within each area, a scientific sample of establishments is chosen to represent all establishments in the area. Within each sampled establishment, a probability sample of occupations is selected. Occupations are classified based on duties and responsibilities. A factor evaluation also is conducted to determine the level of work within the occupation. Compensation is collected only for these sampled occupations.

For each occupation, data will be available on wage rates, employer benefit costs, benefit availability, and detailed benefit provisions. These data will be used to produce new tabulations that relate these variables to each other. For example, wage data and benefit provisions can be related to provide insight as to the richness of benefit plans for those earning differing wage levels. Are higher-paid employees also given more generous benefit plans? Employer benefit cost data also will be linked to benefit provisions to permit comparisons of costs for different plan types. For example, what is the trend in employer costs for fee-for-service plans versus health maintenance organizations? Finally, all of these data will be combined into a database to allow more sophisticated analyses of compensation trends, including regressions of benefit plan provisions against employer cost. For instance, do second surgical opinion features really reduce employer health care premiums?

All NCS compensation data will be available by various useful categories, such as industry, occupation, union status, location, size of establishment, full-time/part-time status, and profit versus nonprofit organizations. NCS data will be available through a variety of media, including traditional news releases and bulletins as well as electronic access via the BLS Internet site. More detailed analyses of NCS data are published in two BLS periodicals—the *Monthly Labor Review* and *Compensation and Working Conditions.*

The Bureau of Labor Statistics has provided data on wages since it was established in the late 19th century, and has provided data on benefits since the early 20th century. Series that provide a consistent look at wages by occupation date from the 1950s and detailed benefits data date from the 1970s. Now for the first time, BLS has combined many of its compensation measures into a single, integrated, comprehensive program detailing the wages, benefits, and establishment practices available to American workers. Interrelated data on wage levels, benefit costs, rates of change in employer costs for compensation, benefit availability, and benefit plan details will now be available from a single source—the National Compensation Survey.

[1] The original article was by William J. Wiatrowski, an economist in the Bureau of Labor Statistics.

PART ONE

POPULATION, LABOR FORCE, AND EMPLOYMENT STATUS

POPULATION, LABOR FORCE, AND EMPLOYMENT STATUS

HIGHLIGHTS

This part presents detailed historical information on the employment status of the population collected in a survey of households, the Current Population Survey (CPS). Basic data on labor force, employment and unemployment are shown for various characteristics of the population such as age, sex, race, and marital status.

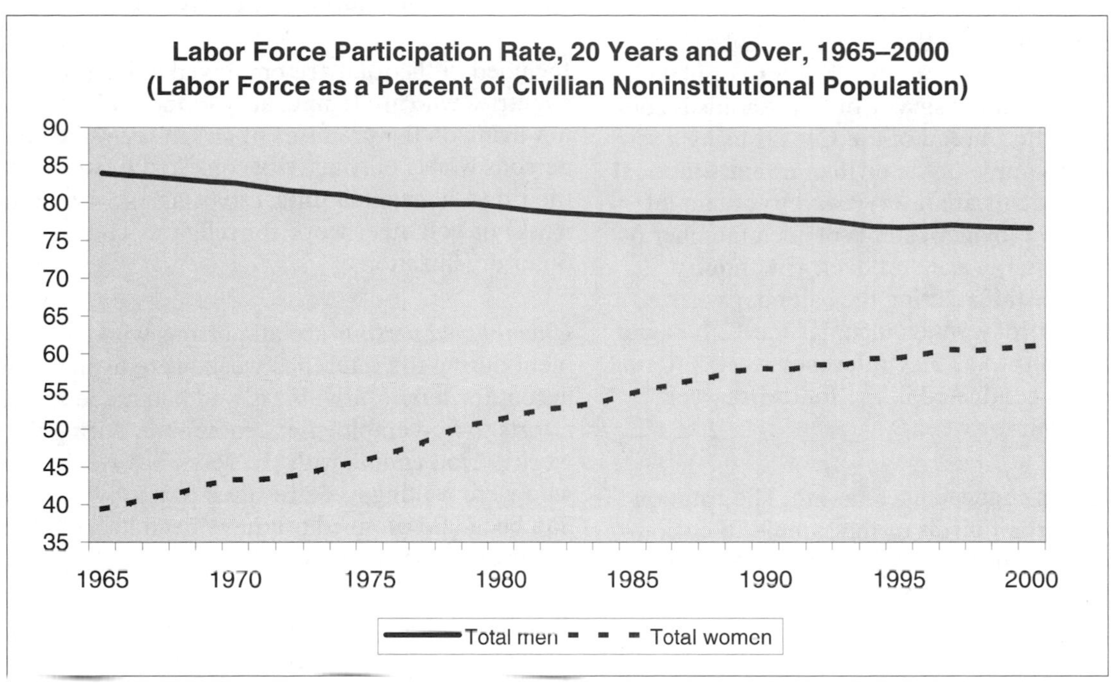

The dramatic increase in women's labor force participation has slowed in recent years and the rate for men has stabilized, decreasing the difference in the trend between the two.

OTHER HIGHLIGHTS:

- Job creation was an outstanding feature of the U.S. economy in the last decade with employment increasing about 14 percent during the period. Since 1993, employment has increased about 2 million per year. The corresponding unemployment rate declined to its lowest level since the late 1960s at 4.0 percent in 2000. (Table 1-1)
- Average duration of unemployment declined from 18.8 weeks in 1994 to 12.5 weeks in 2000. (Table 1-30)
- During the period 1990–2000, the average labor force participation rate for Hispanic men (80 percent) was the highest of all men (75 percent), while that of Hispanic women (54 percent) was the lowest of all women (59 percent). In contrast, the average labor force participation rate of Black men (69 percent) was the lowest of all men, while that of Black women (60 percent) was the highest of all women. (Table 1-7)
- The unemployment rate for Black men age 20–24 continues to be substantially higher than that of young White men, 16.2 percent compared to 6.5 percent in the year 2000. (Table 1-27)
- The labor force participation rate for mothers with children under 6 was 65 percent in the year 2000. The participation rate for married mothers with spouse present and children under one year of age shows some recent decline. (Tables 1-23, 1-24)
- Among states, Virginia reported the lowest annual average unemployment rate for 2000 at 2.2 percent, while Alaska recorded the highest rate at 6.6 percent. (Table 1-5)
- Women increased their share of managerial occupations from 43 to 45 percent from 1995 to 2000, while Blacks only experienced a 0.4 percent gain, increasing from 7.2 to 7.6 percent of total managers. (Table 1-13)

NOTES AND DEFINITIONS

CURRENT POPULATION SURVEY OF HOUSEHOLDS

Collection and Coverage

Statistics on the employment status of the population and related data are compiled by the Bureau of Labor Statistics (BLS) using data from the Current Population Survey (CPS). This monthly survey of households is conducted for BLS by the Bureau of the Census using a scientifically selected sample of the civilian noninstitutional population. Respondents are interviewed to obtain information about the employment status of each member of the household 16 years of age and over. The inquiry relates to activity or status during the calendar week, Sunday through Saturday, which includes the 12th day of the month. This is known as the "reference week." Actual field interviewing is conducted in the following week, referred to as the "survey week."

Part of the sample is changed each month. The rotation plan provides for three-fourths of the sample to be common from one month to the next, and one-half to be common with the same month a year earlier.

Concepts and Definitions

The concepts and definitions underlying labor force data have been modified, but not substantially altered, since the inception of the survey in 1940. Current definitions of some of the major concepts used in the CPS are given below.

The civilian noninstitutional population includes persons 16 years of age and older residing in the 50 states and the District of Columbia who are not inmates of institutions (such as penal and mental facilities, homes for the aged), and who are not on active duty in the armed forces.

Employed persons are all persons who, during the reference week, (a) did any work at all (at least one hour) as paid employees, worked in their own business, profession, or on their own farm, or who worked 15 hours or more as unpaid workers in an enterprise operated by a member of the family, and (b) all those who were not working but who had jobs or businesses from which they were temporarily absent because of vacation, illness, bad weather, child-care problems, maternity or paternity leave, labor-management disputes, job training, or other family or personal reasons, whether or not they were paid for the time off or were seeking other jobs.

Each employed person is counted only once, even if he or she holds more than one job. For purposes of occupation and industry classification, multiple jobholders are counted in the job at which they worked the greatest number of hours during the reference week.

Included in the total are employed citizens of foreign countries who are temporarily in the United States but not living on the premises of an embassy. Excluded are persons whose only activity consisted of work around their own house (painting, repairing, or own home housework) or volunteer work for religious, charitable, and other organizations.

Unemployed persons are all persons who had no employment during the reference week, were available for work, except for temporary illness, and had made specific efforts to find employment some time during the four-week period ending with the reference week. Persons who were waiting to be recalled to a job from which they had been laid off need not have been looking for work to be classified as unemployed.

Duration of unemployment represents the length of time (through the current reference week) that persons classified as unemployed had been looking for work. For persons on layoff, duration of unemployment represents the number of full weeks they had been on layoff. Mean duration is the arithmetic average computed from single weeks of unemployment; median duration is the midpoint of a distribution of weeks of unemployment.

Reason for unemployment is determined by the status of individuals at the time they began to look for work. The reasons for unemployment are divided into five major groups: (1) Job losers, comprised of (a) persons on temporary layoff, who have been given a date to return to work or who expect to return within six months (persons on layoff need not be looking for work to qualify as unemployed), and (b) permanent job losers, whose employment ended involuntarily and who began looking for work; (2) Job leavers, persons who quit or otherwise terminated their employment voluntarily and immediately began looking for work; (3) Persons who completed temporary jobs and immediately began looking for work; (4) Reentrants, persons who previously worked but were out of the labor force prior to beginning their job search; and (5) New entrants, persons who have never worked. Each of these categories of the unemployed can be expressed as a proportion of the entire civilian labor force; the sum of the rates thus equals the unemployment rate for all civilian workers.

The civilian labor force comprises all civilians classified as employed or unemployed.

The unemployment rate is the number unemployed as a percent of the civilian labor force.

The participation rate represents the proportion of the civilian noninstitutional population that is in the labor force.

The employment to population ratio represents the proportion of the population that is employed.

Persons not in the labor force are all persons in the civilian noninstitutional population who are neither employed nor unemployed. Information is collected on their desire for and availability to take a job at the time of the CPS interview, job search activity in the prior year, and reason for not looking in the four-week period prior to the survey week. This group includes discouraged workers.

Discouraged workers are defined as persons not in the labor force who want and are available for a job and who have looked for work sometime in the past 12 months (or since the end of their last job if they held one within the past 12 months), but are not currently looking, because they believe there are no jobs available or there are none for which they would qualify.

Usual full- or part-time status refers to hours usually worked per week. Full-time workers are those who usually worked 35 hours or more. This group includes some individuals who worked less than 35 hours in the reference week for either economic or noneconomic reasons. Part-time workers are those who usually work less than 35 hours per week (at all jobs), regardless of the number of hours worked in the reference week. These concepts are used to differentiate a person's normal schedule from their specific activity during the reference week. Unemployed persons who are looking for full-time work or are on layoff from full-time jobs are counted as part of the full-time labor force; unemployed persons who are seeking or who are on layoff from part-time jobs are counted as part of the part-time labor force. Unemployment rates for full- and part-time workers are calculated using the concepts of the full- and part-time labor force.

Occupation, industry, and class of worker for the employed is determined by the job held in the reference week. Persons with two or more jobs are classified in the job at which they worked the greatest number of hours. The unemployed are classified according to their last job. The occupational and industrial classification of CPS data is based on the coding systems used in the 1990 Census. The class-of-worker breakdown assigns workers to the following categories: private and government wage and salary workers; self-employed workers; and unpaid family workers. Wage and salary workers receive wages, salaries, commissions, tips, or pay in kind from a private employer or from a government unit. Self-employed persons are those who work for profit or fees in their own business, profession, trade, or farm. Only the unincorporated self-employed are included in the self-employed category in the class-of-worker typology. Self-employed persons who respond that their businesses are incorporated are included among wage and salary workers, because technically, they are paid employees of a corporation. Unpaid family workers are persons working without pay for 15 hours a week or more on a farm or in a business operated by a member of the household to whom they are related by birth or marriage.

Multiple jobholders are employed persons who, during the reference week, had two or more jobs as a wage and salary worker, were self-employed and also held a wage and salary job, or worked as an unpaid family worker and also held a wage and salary job. A person employed only in private households (cleaner, gardener, babysitter, etc.) who worked for two or more employers during the reference week is not counted as a multiple jobholder, since working for several employers is considered an inherent characteristic of private household work. Also excluded are self-employed persons with multiple businesses and persons with multiple jobs as unpaid family workers.

At work part-time for economic reasons, sometimes referred to as involuntary part-time, refers to individuals who gave an economic reason for working one to 34 hours during the reference week. Economic reasons include slack work or unfavorable business conditions, inability to find full-time work, and seasonal declines in demand. Those who usually work part-time must also indicate that they want and are available to work full-time to be classified as on part-time for economic reasons.

At work part-time for noneconomic reasons refers to persons who usually work part-time and were at work one to 34 hours during the reference week for a noneconomic reason. Noneconomic reasons include, for example: illness or other medical limitations; childcare problems or other family or personal obligations; school or training; retirement or Social Security limits on earnings; and being in a job where full-time work is less than 35 hours. The group also includes those who gave an economic reason for usually working one to 34 hours but said they do not want to work full-time or were unavailable for such work.

White, Black, and Other are terms used to describe the race of persons. Included in the "Other" group are Native Americans, Alaskan Natives, and Asians and Pacific Islanders. Because of the relatively small sample size, data for "Other" races are not published. In the enumeration process, race is determined by the household respondent.

Hispanic origin refers to persons who identified themselves in the enumeration process as Mexican, Puerto Rican, Cuban, Central or South American, or of other Hispanic origin or descent. Persons of Hispanic origin may be of any race; thus some are included in the White, some in the Black, and possibly some in the Other population groups.

Single, never married; married, spouse present; and other marital status are the terms used to define the marital status of individuals at the time of interview. Married, spouse present, applies to husband and wife if both were living in the same household, even though one may be temporarily absent on business, vacation, on a visit, in a hospital, etc. Other marital status applies to persons who are married, spouse absent; widowed; or divorced. Married, spouse absent relates to persons who are separated due to marital problems, as well as husbands and wives who are living apart because one or the other was employed elsewhere, on duty with the armed forces, or any other reasons.

A household consists of all persons—related family members and all unrelated persons—who occupy a housing unit and have no other usual address. A house, an apartment, a group of rooms, or a single room is regarded as a housing unit when occupied or intended for occupancy as separate living quarters. A householder is the person (or one of the persons) in whose name the housing unit is owned or rented. The term is not applied to either husbands or wives in married-couple families but only to persons in families maintained by either men or women without a spouse.

Family is defined as a group of two or more persons residing together who are related by birth, marriage, or adoption; all such persons are considered as members of one family. Families are classified either as married-couple families or as families maintained by women or men without spouses. A family maintained by a woman or a man is one in which the householder is single; widowed; divorced; or married, spouse absent.

The annual CPS data on the employment characteristics of families and family members begin with data for 1995. These data are not strictly comparable with family data derived from the March CPS. The annual data are derived by averaging the data for each month of the year, whereas the March data refer to that month. The annual average data provide a larger sample size, while the March family data provide a longer historical series.

Additional Concepts and Definitions: CPS Supplements

In addition to the above concepts and definitions, the definitions below apply to the special labor force data collected annually in the March supplement to the monthly CPS, and the data on tenure usually collected in a February supplement.

Persons with work experience are civilians who worked at any time during the preceding calendar year at full- or part-time jobs for pay or profit (including paid vacations and sick leave) or worked without pay on a farm or in a business that was family operated. From 1989 forward, these supplementary tables also include members of the armed forces within the United States.

Tenure refers to length of time a worker has been continuously employed by the current employer. The data were collected through a supplement to the CPS. The question asked of all employed persons was how long the person has been working continuously for their present employer and, if one or two years, the exact number of months. The follow-up question was asked for the first time in the 1998 February supplement. Prior to 1983 the question was asked differently; data prior to 1983 are not strictly comparable to data for subsequent years.

Year-round full-time workers are workers who worked primarily at full-time jobs for 50 weeks or more during the preceding calendar year. *Part-year workers* worked either full or part-time for one to 49 weeks.

Spell of unemployment is a continuous period of unemployment of at least one week's duration. A spell is terminated by employment or withdrawal from the labor force.

Extent of unemployment refers to the number and proportion of the labor force that were unemployed at some time during the year. The number of weeks unemployed is the total number of weeks accumulated during the entire year.

Children refers to "own" children of the husband, wife, or person maintaining the family, including sons and daughters, stepchildren, and adopted children. Excluded are other related children, such as grandchildren, nieces, nephews, and cousins, and unrelated children.

Earnings are all money income of $1 or more from wages and salaries and net money income of $1 or more from farm and nonfarm self-employment.

Educational attainment refers to years of school completed in regular schools, which include graded public, private, and parochial elementary and high schools, whether day or night school; also college, university, or professional school.

Minimum wages. The prevailing federal minimum wage was $5.15 per hour in 1999. Data are for wage and salary workers who are paid hourly rates. They refer to a person's earnings on their sole or principal job.

Absences are defined as instances when persons who usually work 35 or more hours a week worked less than that during the reference period for reasons of illness or family obligations. Excluded are situations in which work was missed for vacation, holidays or other reasons. The estimates are based on one-fourth of the sample only.

Historical Comparability

While current survey concepts and methods are very similar to those introduced at the inception of the survey in 1940, a number of changes have been made over the years to improve the accuracy and usefulness of the data. Only the latest changes are described here.

In 1994, major changes to the CPS were introduced, which included a complete redesign of the questionnaire and the use of computer-assisted interviewing for the entire survey. In addition, there were revisions to some of the labor force concepts and definitions, including the implementation of some changes recommended in 1979 by the National Commission on Employment and Unemployment Statistics (NCEUS, also known as the Levitan Commission). Some of the major changes to the survey were:

a) The introduction of a redesigned and automated questionnaire. The CPS questionnaire was totally redesigned in order to obtain more accurate, comprehensive, and relevant information, and to take advantage of state-of-the-art computer interviewing techniques.

b) The addition of two, more objective, criteria to the definition of discouraged workers. Beginning in 1994, persons classified as discouraged must also have looked for a job within the past year (or since their last job, if they worked during the year), and must have been available for work during the reference week (a direct question on availability was added in 1994). These changes were made because the NCEUS and others felt that the previous definition of discouraged workers was too subjective, relying mainly on an individual's stated desire for a job and not on prior testing of the labor market.

c) Similarly, the identification of persons employed part-time for economic reasons (working less than 35 hours in the reference week because of poor business conditions or because of an inability to find full-time work) was tightened by adding two new criteria for persons who usually work part-time: They must want and be available for full-time work. (Persons who usually work full-time but worked part-time for an economic reason during the reference week are assumed to meet these criteria.)

d) Specific questions were added about the expectation of recall for persons who indicate that they are on layoff. To be classified as "on temporary layoff," persons must expect to be recalled to their jobs.

e) Persons volunteering that they were waiting to start a new job within 30 days must have looked for work in the four weeks prior to the survey in order to be classified as unemployed.

Comparability of Labor Force Levels

In addition to the refinements in concepts, definitions, and methods made over the years, other changes—made to improve the accuracy of the estimates—have also affected the comparability of the labor force data. The most important of these is the adjustment of the population totals as a result of new information from the decennial censuses and to correct for estimating errors during the intercensal years. Those affecting the most recent decade are described below.

Beginning in January 1994, 1990 census-based population controls were introduced, adjusted for the undercount as measured by the Census Bureau's Post-Enumeration

Survey. In February 1996, these population controls were introduced into the estimates for 1990–1993 as well. This change increased the civilian non-institutional population for 1990 by about 1.1 million, employment by about 880,000, and unemployment by about 175,000. The overall unemployment rate rose by about 0.1 percentage point.

In the case of data from the March supplement to the CPS, the 1990 controls were introduced in 1994 and have not been carried back to 1990.

Beginning in January 1997, updated information on the demographic characteristics of immigrants and emigrants was introduced. This raised the overall population by about 470,000, labor force by 320,000, and employment by 290,000, with similar upward adjustments for Hispanics. Unemployment and other percentage rates were not affected.

Beginning in January 1998, new estimating procedures were introduced, which reduced labor force by about 229,000 and employment by 256,000 but raised unemployment by 27,000. New information about immigration and emigration was also incorporated which increased the Hispanic population by about 57,000. Unemployment rates were not significantly affected.

Beginning in January 1999, new information on immigration raised the population by about 310,000, with differing impacts on different demographic groups. The population of men was lowered by about 185,000, but of women was raised by 490,000. The Hispanic population was lowered by about 165,000 while the rest of the population was raised by about 470,000. Hispanic labor force and employment estimates were each reduced by over 200,000. The impact on unemployment rates and other percentages was small.

Beginning in January 2000, the population controls used in the survey were revised to reflect newly updated information on immigration and an upward revision in the number of deaths. As a result, the civilian noninstitutional population 16 years and over was lowered by about 215,000. The labor force and employment levels were decreased by about 125,000 and 120,000, respectively. Overall and subgroup unemployment rates and other percentages of labor market participation were not significantly affected.

Changes in the Occupational and Industrial Classification System

Beginning in January 1983, the occupational and industrial classification systems used in the 1980 Census were introduced into the CPS. The 1980 Census occupational classification system was so radically different in concepts and nomenclature from the 1970 system that comparisons of historical data are not possible without major adjustments.

The industrial classification system used in the 1980 Census was based on the 1972 Standard Industrial Classification (SIC) system, as modified in 1977. The adoption of the new industrial system had much less of an adverse effect on historical comparability than did the new occupational system.

Beginning in January 1992, the occupational and industrial classification systems used in the 1990 Census were introduced into the CPS. There were a few breaks in comparability between the 1980 and 1990 census-based systems, particularly within the "technical, sales, and administrative support" categories. The most notable changes in industry classification were the shift of several industries from "business services" to "professional services" and the splitting of some industries into smaller, more detailed categories.

Future Plans

Expansion of CPS: The CPS sample has been increased to 60,000 households from 50,000. The new sample was introduced beginning September 2, 2000. However, the estimates of the national labor force from the additional sample were not introduced at that time in order to evaluate the impact of the change. The estimates from the two samples were virtually the same, BLS plans to incorporate the additional sample into the July 2001 official national estimates.

Industries: The new North American Industry Classification System (NAICS), published by the Office of Management and Budget in July 1998, will be introduced over the next several years to supplant the current SIC system. The NAICS classifications incorporate major changes. A number of new major sectors are created and a new 6-digit industry numbering system is used.

Occupations: A new system for classifying occupations will be introduced into the CPS in 2003. (The new system is already in use in the Occupational Wage Survey, see Part 5 of this book.) The Standard Occupational Classification (SOC) reflects the many changes in recent decades to the types of jobs workers perform, especially the shift towards more service-oriented and high technology jobs.

Source of Additional Information

Descriptions of sampling and estimation procedures and further information on the impact of the historical changes in the survey can be found in the *Monthly Labor Review,* September, 1993; *Employment and Earnings,* February 1994, March 1996, and subsequent February issues of that publication; and the *BLS Handbook of Methods,* BLS Bulletin 2490, April 1997. Technical Paper 63, Design and Methodology of the *Current Population Survey.*

Table 1-1. Employment Status of the Civilian Noninstitutional Population, 1947–2000

(Thousands of persons, percent.)

Year	Civilian noninstitutional population	Civilian labor force								Not in labor force
		Total	Participation rate	Employed				Unemployed		
				Total	Percent of population	Agriculture	Non-agricultural industries	Number	Unemploy-ment rate	
1947	101 827	59 350	58.3	57 038	56.0	7 890	49 148	2 311	3.9	42 477
1948	103 068	60 621	58.8	58 343	56.6	7 629	50 714	2 276	3.8	42 447
1949	103 994	61 286	58.9	57 651	55.4	7 658	49 993	3 637	5.9	42 708
1950	104 995	62 208	59.2	58 918	56.1	7 160	51 758	3 288	5.3	42 787
1951	104 621	62 017	59.2	59 961	57.3	6 726	53 235	2 055	3.3	42 604
1952	105 231	62 138	59.0	60 250	57.3	6 500	53 749	1 883	3.0	43 093
1953	107 056	63 015	58.9	61 179	57.1	6 260	54 919	1 834	2.9	44 041
1954	108 321	63 643	58.8	60 109	55.5	6 205	53 904	3 532	5.5	44 678
1955	109 683	65 023	59.3	62 170	56.7	6 450	55 722	2 852	4.4	44 660
1956	110 954	66 552	60.0	63 799	57.5	6 283	57 514	2 750	4.1	44 402
1957	112 265	66 929	59.6	64 071	57.1	5 947	58 123	2 859	4.3	45 336
1958	113 727	67 639	59.5	63 036	55.4	5 586	57 450	4 602	6.8	46 088
1959	115 329	68 369	59.3	64 630	56.0	5 565	59 065	3 740	5.5	46 960
1960	117 245	69 628	59.4	65 778	56.1	5 458	60 318	3 852	5.5	47 617
1961	118 771	70 459	59.3	65 746	55.4	5 200	60 546	4 714	6.7	48 312
1962	120 153	70 614	58.8	66 702	55.5	4 944	61 759	3 911	5.5	49 539
1963	122 416	71 833	58.7	67 762	55.4	4 687	63 076	4 070	5.7	50 583
1964	124 485	73 091	58.7	69 305	55.7	4 523	64 782	3 786	5.2	51 394
1965	126 513	74 455	58.9	71 088	56.2	4 361	66 726	3 366	4.5	52 058
1966	128 058	75 770	59.2	72 895	56.9	3 979	68 915	2 875	3.8	52 288
1967	129 874	77 347	59.6	74 372	57.3	3 844	70 527	2 975	3.8	52 527
1968	132 028	78 737	59.6	75 920	57.5	3 817	72 103	2 817	3.6	53 291
1969	134 335	80 734	60.1	77 902	58.0	3 606	74 296	2 832	3.5	53 602
1970	137 085	82 771	60.4	78 678	57.4	3 463	75 215	4 093	4.9	54 315
1971	140 216	84 382	60.2	79 367	56.6	3 394	75 972	5 016	5.9	55 834
1972	144 126	87 034	60.4	82 153	57.0	3 484	78 669	4 882	5.6	57 091
1973	147 096	89 429	60.8	85 064	57.8	3 470	81 594	4 365	4.9	57 667
1974	150 120	91 949	61.3	86 794	57.8	3 515	83 279	5 156	5.6	58 171
1975	153 153	93 775	61.2	85 846	56.1	3 408	82 438	7 929	8.5	59 377
1976	156 150	96 158	61.6	88 752	56.8	3 331	85 421	7 406	7.7	59 991
1977	159 033	99 009	62.3	92 017	57.9	3 283	88 734	6 991	7.1	60 025
1978	161 910	102 251	63.2	96 048	59.3	3 387	92 661	6 202	6.1	59 659
1979	164 863	104 962	63.7	98 824	59.9	3 347	95 477	6 137	5.8	59 900
1980	167 745	106 940	63.8	99 303	59.2	3 364	95 938	7 637	7.1	60 806
1981	170 130	108 670	63.9	100 397	59.0	3 368	97 030	8 273	7.6	61 460
1982	172 271	110 204	64.0	99 526	57.8	3 401	96 125	10 678	9.7	62 067
1983	174 215	111 550	64.0	100 834	57.9	3 383	97 450	10 717	9.6	62 665
1984	176 383	113 544	64.4	105 005	59.5	3 321	101 685	8 539	7.5	62 839
1985	178 206	115 461	64.8	107 150	60.1	3 179	103 971	8 312	7.2	62 744
1986	180 587	117 834	65.3	109 597	60.7	3 163	106 434	8 237	7.0	62 752
1987	182 753	119 865	65.6	112 440	61.5	3 208	109 232	7 425	6.2	62 888
1988	184 613	121 669	65.9	114 968	62.3	3 169	111 800	6 701	5.5	62 944
1989	186 393	123 869	66.5	117 342	63.0	3 199	114 142	6 528	5.3	62 523
1990	189 164	125 840	66.5	118 793	62.8	3 223	115 570	7 047	5.6	63 324
1991	190 925	126 346	66.2	117 718	61.7	3 269	114 449	8 628	6.8	64 578
1992	192 805	128 105	66.4	118 492	61.5	3 247	115 245	9 613	7.5	64 700
1993	194 838	129 200	66.3	120 259	61.7	3 115	117 144	8 940	6.9	65 638
1994	196 814	131 056	66.6	123 060	62.5	3 409	119 651	7 996	6.1	65 758
1995	198 584	132 304	66.6	124 900	62.9	3 440	121 460	7 404	5.6	66 280
1996	200 591	133 943	66.8	126 708	63.2	3 443	123 264	7 236	5.4	66 647
1997	203 133	136 297	67.1	129 558	63.8	3 399	126 159	6 739	4.9	66 837
1998	205 220	137 673	67.1	131 463	64.1	3 378	128 085	6 210	4.5	67 547
1999	207 753	139 368	67.1	133 488	64.3	3 281	130 207	5 880	4.2	68 385
2000	209 699	140 863	67.2	135 208	64.5	3 305	131 903	5 655	4.0	68 836

Note: See "Notes and Definitions" for information on historical comparability.

Table 1-2. Employment Status of the Civilian Noninstitutional Population by Sex, 1965–2000

(Thousands of persons, percent.)

Year	Civilian noninstitutional population	Civilian labor force								Not in labor force
		Total	Participation rate	Employed				Unemployed		
				Total	Percent of population	Agriculture	Non-agricultural industries	Number	Unemploy-ment rate	
MEN										
1965	59 782	48 255	80.7	46 340	77.5	3 547	42 792	1 914	4.0	11 527
1966	60 262	48 471	80.4	46 919	77.9	3 243	43 675	1 551	3.2	11 792
1967	60 905	48 987	80.4	47 479	78.0	3 164	44 315	1 508	3.1	11 919
1968	61 847	49 533	80.1	48 114	77.8	3 157	44 957	1 419	2.9	12 315
1969	62 898	50 221	79.8	48 818	77.6	2 963	45 855	1 403	2.8	12 677
1970	64 304	51 228	79.7	48 990	76.2	2 862	46 128	2 238	4.4	13 076
1971	65 942	52 180	79.1	49 390	74.9	2 795	46 595	2 789	5.3	13 762
1972	67 835	53 555	78.9	50 896	75.0	2 849	48 047	2 659	5.0	14 280
1973	69 292	54 624	78.8	52 349	75.5	2 847	49 502	2 275	4.2	14 667
1974	70 808	55 739	78.7	53 024	74.9	2 919	50 105	2 714	4.9	15 069
1975	72 291	56 299	77.9	51 857	71.7	2 824	49 032	4 442	7.9	15 993
1976	73 759	57 174	77.5	53 138	72.0	2 744	50 394	4 036	7.1	16 585
1977	75 193	58 396	77.7	54 728	72.8	2 671	52 057	3 667	6.3	16 797
1978	76 576	59 620	77.9	56 479	73.8	2 718	53 761	3 142	5.3	16 956
1979	78 020	60 726	77.8	57 607	73.8	2 686	54 921	3 120	5.1	17 293
1980	79 398	61 453	77.4	57 186	72.0	2 709	54 477	4 267	6.9	17 945
1981	80 511	61 974	77.0	57 397	71.3	2 700	54 697	4 577	7.4	18 537
1982	81 523	62 450	76.6	56 271	69.0	2 736	53 534	6 179	9.9	19 073
1983	82 531	63 047	76.4	56 787	68.8	2 704	54 083	6 260	9.9	19 484
1984	83 605	63 835	76.4	59 091	70.7	2 668	56 423	4 744	7.4	19 771
1985	84 469	64 411	76.3	59 891	70.9	2 535	57 356	4 521	7.0	20 058
1986	85 798	65 422	76.3	60 892	71.0	2 511	58 381	4 530	6.9	20 376
1987	86 899	66 207	76.2	62 107	71.5	2 543	59 564	4 101	6.2	20 692
1988	87 857	66 927	76.2	63 273	72.0	2 493	60 780	3 655	5.5	20 930
1989	88 762	67 840	76.4	64 315	72.5	2 513	61 802	3 525	5.2	20 923
1990	90 377	69 011	76.4	65 104	72.0	2 546	62 559	3 906	5.7	21 367
1991	91 278	69 168	75.8	64 223	70.4	2 589	61 634	4 946	7.2	22 110
1992	92 270	69 964	75.8	64 440	69.8	2 575	61 866	5 523	7.9	22 306
1993	93 332	70 404	75.4	65 349	70.0	2 478	62 871	5 055	7.2	22 027
1994	94 355	70 817	75.1	66 450	70.4	2 554	63 896	4 367	6.2	23 538
1995	95 178	71 360	75.0	67 377	70.8	2 559	64 818	3 983	5.6	23 818
1996	96 206	72 087	74.9	68 207	70.9	2 573	65 634	3 880	5.4	24 119
1997	97 715	73 261	75.0	69 685	71.3	2 552	67 133	3 577	4.9	24 454
1998	98 758	73 959	74.9	70 693	71.6	2 550	68 140	3 266	4.4	24 799
1999	99 722	74 512	74.7	71 446	71.6	2 432	69 014	3 066	4.1	25 210
2000	100 731	75 247	74.7	72 293	71.8	2 434	69 859	2 954	3.9	25 484
WOMEN										
1965	66 731	26 200	39.3	24 748	37.1	814	23 934	1 452	5.5	40 531
1966	67 795	27 299	40.3	25 976	38.3	736	25 240	1 324	4.8	40 496
1967	68 968	28 360	41.1	26 893	39.0	680	26 212	1 468	5.2	40 608
1968	70 179	29 204	41.6	27 807	39.6	660	27 147	1 397	4.8	40 976
1969	71 436	30 513	42.7	29 084	40.7	643	28 441	1 429	4.7	40 924
1970	72 782	31 543	43.3	29 688	40.8	601	29 087	1 855	5.9	41 239
1971	74 274	32 202	43.4	29 976	40.4	599	29 377	2 227	6.9	42 072
1972	76 290	33 479	43.9	31 257	41.0	635	30 622	2 222	6.6	42 811
1973	77 804	34 804	44.7	32 715	42.0	622	32 093	2 089	6.0	43 000
1974	79 312	36 211	45.7	33 769	42.6	596	33 173	2 441	6.7	43 101
1975	80 860	37 475	46.3	33 989	42.0	584	33 404	3 486	9.3	43 386
1976	82 390	38 983	47.3	35 615	43.2	588	35 027	3 369	8.6	43 406
1977	83 840	40 613	48.4	37 289	44.5	612	36 677	3 324	8.2	43 227
1978	85 334	42 631	50.0	39 569	46.4	669	38 900	3 061	7.2	42 703
1979	86 843	44 235	50.9	41 217	47.5	661	40 556	3 018	6.8	42 608
1980	88 348	45 487	51.5	42 117	47.7	656	41 461	3 370	7.4	42 861
1981	89 618	46 696	52.1	43 000	48.0	667	42 333	3 696	7.9	42 922
1982	90 748	47 755	52.6	43 256	47.7	665	42 591	4 499	9.4	42 993
1983	91 684	48 503	52.9	44 047	48.0	680	43 367	4 457	9.2	43 181
1984	92 778	49 709	53.6	45 915	49.5	653	45 262	3 794	7.6	43 068
1985	93 736	51 050	54.5	47 259	50.4	644	46 615	3 791	7.4	42 686
1986	94 789	52 413	55.3	48 706	51.4	652	48 054	3 707	7.1	42 376
1987	95 853	53 658	56.0	50 334	52.5	666	49 668	3 324	6.2	42 195
1988	96 756	54 742	56.6	51 696	53.4	676	51 020	3 046	5.6	42 014
1989	97 630	56 030	57.4	53 027	54.3	687	52 341	3 003	5.4	41 601
1990	98 787	56 829	57.5	53 689	54.3	678	53 011	3 140	5.5	41 957
1991	99 646	57 178	57.4	53 496	53.7	680	52 815	3 683	6.4	42 468
1992	100 535	58 141	57.8	54 052	53.8	672	53 380	4 090	7.0	42 394
1993	101 506	58 795	57.9	54 910	54.1	637	54 273	3 885	6.6	42 711
1994	102 460	60 239	58.8	56 610	55.3	855	55 755	3 629	6.0	42 221
1995	103 406	60 944	58.9	57 523	55.6	881	56 642	3 421	5.6	42 462
1996	104 385	61 857	59.3	58 501	56.0	871	57 630	3 356	5.4	42 528
1997	105 418	63 036	59.8	59 873	56.8	847	59 026	3 162	5.0	42 382
1998	106 462	63 714	59.8	60 771	57.1	825	59 945	2 944	4.6	42 748
1999	108 031	64 855	60.0	62 042	57.4	849	61 193	2 814	4.3	43 175
2000	108 968	65 616	60.2	62 915	57.7	871	62 044	2 701	4.1	43 352

Note: See "Notes and Definitions" for information on historical comparability.

Table 1-3. Employment Status of the Civilian Noninstitutional Population by Sex, Race, Hispanic Origin, and Age, 1981–2000

(Thousands of persons.)

Employment status, sex, and age	1981	1982	1983	1984	1985	1986	1987	1988	1989	1990
TOTAL CIVILIAN NONINSTITUTIONAL POPULATION										
Population	170 130	172 271	174 215	176 383	178 206	180 587	182 753	184 613	186 393	189 164
Civilian labor force	108 670	110 204	111 550	113 544	115 461	117 834	119 865	121 669	123 869	125 840
Employed	100 397	99 526	100 834	105 005	107 150	109 597	112 440	114 968	117 342	118 793
Agriculture	3 368	3 401	3 383	3 321	3 179	3 163	3 208	3 169	3 199	3 223
Nonagriculture	97 030	96 125	97 450	101 685	103 971	106 434	109 232	111 800	114 142	115 570
Unemployed	8 273	10 678	10 717	8 539	8 312	8 237	7 425	6 701	6 528	7 047
Not in labor force	61 460	62 067	62 665	62 839	62 744	62 752	62 888	62 944	62 523	63 324
MEN, 16 YEARS AND OVER										
Population	80 511	81 523	82 531	83 605	84 469	85 798	86 899	87 857	88 762	90 377
Civilian labor force	61 974	62 450	63 047	63 835	64 411	65 422	66 207	66 927	67 840	69 011
Employed	57 397	56 271	56 787	59 091	59 891	60 892	62 107	63 273	64 315	65 104
Agriculture	2 700	2 736	2 704	2 668	2 535	2 511	2 543	2 493	2 513	2 546
Nonagriculture	54 697	53 534	54 083	56 423	57 356	58 381	59 564	60 780	61 802	62 559
Unemployed	4 577	6 179	6 260	4 744	4 521	4 530	4 101	3 655	3 525	3 906
Not in labor force	18 537	19 073	19 484	19 771	20 058	20 376	20 692	20 930	20 923	21 367
MEN, 20 YEARS AND OVER										
Population	72 419	73 644	74 872	76 219	77 195	78 523	79 565	80 553	81 619	83 030
Civilian labor force	57 197	57 980	58 744	59 701	60 277	61 320	62 095	62 768	63 704	64 916
Employed	53 582	52 891	53 487	55 769	56 562	57 569	58 726	59 781	60 837	61 678
Agriculture	2 384	2 422	2 429	2 418	2 278	2 292	2 329	2 271	2 307	2 329
Nonagriculture	51 199	50 469	51 058	53 351	54 284	55 277	56 397	57 510	58 530	59 349
Unemployed	3 615	5 089	5 257	3 932	3 715	3 751	3 369	2 987	2 867	3 239
Not in labor force	15 222	15 664	16 129	16 518	16 918	17 203	17 470	17 785	17 915	18 114
WOMEN, 16 YEARS AND OVER										
Population	89 618	90 748	91 684	92 778	93 736	94 789	95 853	96 756	97 630	98 787
Civilian labor force	46 696	47 755	48 503	49 709	51 050	52 413	53 658	54 742	56 030	56 829
Employed	43 000	43 256	44 047	45 915	47 259	48 706	50 334	51 696	53 027	53 689
Agriculture	667	665	680	653	644	652	666	676	687	678
Nonagriculture	42 333	42 591	43 367	45 262	46 615	48 054	49 668	51 020	52 341	53 011
Unemployed	3 696	4 499	4 457	3 794	3 791	3 707	3 324	3 046	3 003	3 140
Not in labor force	42 922	42 993	43 181	43 068	42 686	42 376	42 195	42 014	41 601	41 957
WOMEN, 20 YEARS AND OVER										
Population	81 497	82 864	84 069	85 429	86 506	87 567	88 583	89 532	90 550	91 614
Civilian labor force	42 485	43 699	44 636	45 900	47 283	48 589	49 783	50 870	52 212	53 131
Employed	39 590	40 086	41 004	42 793	44 154	45 556	47 074	48 383	49 745	50 535
Agriculture	604	601	620	595	596	614	622	625	642	631
Nonagriculture	38 986	39 485	40 384	42 198	43 558	44 943	46 453	47 757	49 103	49 904
Unemployed	2 895	3 613	3 632	3 107	3 129	3 032	2 709	2 487	2 467	2 596
Not in labor force	39 012	39 165	39 433	39 529	39 222	38 979	38 800	38 662	38 339	38 483
BOTH SEXES, 16-19 YEARS										
Population	16 214	15 763	15 274	14 735	14 506	14 496	14 606	14 527	14 223	14 520
Civilian labor force	8 988	8 526	8 171	7 943	7 901	7 926	7 988	8 031	7 954	7 792
Employed	7 225	6 549	6 342	6 444	6 434	6 472	6 640	6 805	6 759	6 581
Agriculture	380	378	334	309	305	258	258	273	250	264
Nonagriculture	6 845	6 171	6 008	6 135	6 129	6 215	6 382	6 532	6 510	6 317
Unemployed	1 763	1 977	1 829	1 499	1 468	1 454	1 347	1 226	1 194	1 212
Not in labor force	7 226	7 238	7 104	6 791	6 604	6 570	6 618	6 497	6 270	6 727

See *Note* at end of table.

Table 1-3. Employment Status of the Civilian Noninstitutional Population by Sex, Race, Hispanic Origin, and Age, 1981–2000—*Continued*

(Thousands of persons.)

Employment status, sex, and age	1991	1992	1993	1994	1995	1996	1997	1998	1999	2000
TOTAL CIVILIAN NONINSTITUTIONAL POPULATION										
Population	190 925	192 805	194 838	196 814	198 584	200 591	203 133	205 220	207 753	209 699
Civilian labor force	126 346	128 105	129 200	131 056	132 304	133 943	136 297	137 673	139 368	140 863
Employed	117 718	118 492	120 259	123 060	124 900	126 708	129 558	131 463	133 488	135 208
Agriculture	3 269	3 247	3 115	3 409	3 440	3 443	3 399	3 378	3 281	3 305
Nonagriculture	114 449	115 245	117 144	119 651	121 460	123 264	126 159	128 085	130 207	131 903
Unemployed	8 628	9 613	8 940	7 996	7 404	7 236	6 739	6 210	5 880	5 655
Not in labor force	64 578	64 700	65 638	65 758	66 280	66 647	66 837	67 547	68 385	68 836
MEN, 16 YEARS AND OVER										
Population	91 278	92 270	93 332	94 355	95 178	96 206	97 715	98 758	99 722	100 731
Civilian labor force	69 168	69 964	70 404	70 817	71 360	72 087	73 261	73 959	74 512	75 247
Employed	64 223	64 440	65 349	66 450	67 377	68 207	69 685	70 693	71 446	72 293
Agriculture	2 589	2 575	2 478	2 554	2 559	2 573	2 552	2 553	2 432	2 434
Nonagriculture	61 634	61 866	62 871	63 896	64 818	65 634	67 133	68 140	69 014	69 859
Unemployed	4 946	5 523	5 055	4 367	3 983	3 880	3 577	3 266	3 066	2 954
Not in labor force	22 110	22 306	22 927	23 538	23 818	24 119	24 454	24 799	25 210	25 484
MEN, 20 YEARS AND OVER										
Population	84 144	85 247	86 256	87 151	87 811	88 606	89 879	90 790	91 555	92 580
Civilian labor force	65 374	66 213	66 642	66 921	67 324	68 044	69 166	69 715	70 194	70 930
Employed	61 178	61 496	62 355	63 294	64 085	64 897	66 284	67 135	67 761	68 580
Agriculture	2 383	2 385	2 293	2 351	2 335	2 356	2 356	2 350	2 244	2 252
Nonagriculture	58 795	59 111	60 063	60 943	61 750	62 541	63 927	64 785	65 517	66 328
Unemployed	4 195	4 717	4 287	3 627	3 239	3 146	2 882	2 580	2 433	2 350
Not in labor force	18 770	19 034	19 613	20 230	20 487	20 563	20 713	21 075	21 362	21 650
WOMEN, 16 YEARS AND OVER										
Population	99 646	100 535	101 506	102 460	103 406	104 385	105 418	106 462	108 031	108 968
Civilian labor force	57 178	58 141	58 795	60 239	60 944	61 857	63 036	63 714	64 855	65 616
Employed	53 496	54 052	54 910	56 610	57 523	58 501	59 873	60 771	62 042	62 915
Agriculture	680	672	637	855	881	871	847	826	849	871
Nonagriculture	52 815	53 380	54 273	55 755	56 642	57 630	59 026	59 945	61 193	62 044
Unemployed	3 683	4 090	3 885	3 629	3 421	3 356	3 162	2 944	2 814	2 701
Not in labor force	42 468	42 394	42 711	42 221	42 462	42 528	42 382	42 748	43 175	43 352
WOMEN, 20 YEARS AND OVER										
Population	92 708	93 718	94 647	95 467	96 262	97 050	97 889	98 786	100 158	101 078
Civilian labor force	53 708	54 796	55 388	56 655	57 215	58 094	59 198	59 702	60 840	61 565
Employed	50 634	51 328	52 099	53 606	54 396	55 311	56 613	57 278	58 555	59 352
Agriculture	639	625	598	809	830	827	798	768	803	818
Nonagriculture	49 995	50 702	51 501	52 796	53 566	54 484	55 815	56 510	57 752	58 535
Unemployed	3 074	3 469	3 288	3 049	2 819	2 783	2 585	2 424	2 285	2 212
Not in labor force	39 000	38 922	39 260	38 813	39 047	38 956	38 691	39 084	39 318	39 513
BOTH SEXES, 16-19 YEARS										
Population	14 073	13 840	13 935	14 196	14 511	14 934	15 365	15 644	16 040	16 042
Civilian labor force	7 265	7 096	7 170	7 481	7 765	7 806	7 932	8 256	8 333	8 369
Employed	5 906	5 669	5 805	6 161	6 419	6 500	6 661	7 051	7 172	7 276
Agriculture	247	237	224	249	275	261	244	261	234	235
Nonagriculture	5 659	5 432	5 580	5 912	6 144	6 239	6 417	6 790	6 938	7 041
Unemployed	1 359	1 427	1 365	1 320	1 346	1 306	1 271	1 205	1 162	1 093
Not in labor force	6 808	6 745	6 765	6 715	6 746	7 128	7 433	7 388	7 706	7 673

See *Note* at end of table.

Table 1-3. Employment Status of the Civilian Noninstitutional Population by Sex, Race, Hispanic Origin, and Age, 1981–2000—*Continued*

(Thousands of persons.)

Employment status, sex, and age	1981	1982	1983	1984	1985	1986	1987	1988	1989	1990
TOTAL, WHITE										
Population	147 908	149 441	150 805	152 347	153 679	155 432	156 958	158 194	159 338	160 625
Civilian labor force	95 052	96 143	97 021	98 492	99 926	101 801	103 290	104 756	106 355	107 447
Employed	88 709	87 903	88 893	92 120	93 736	95 660	97 789	99 812	101 584	102 261
Agriculture	3 109	3 142	3 119	3 057	2 936	2 958	2 986	2 965	2 996	2 998
Nonagriculture	85 600	84 761	85 774	89 063	90 799	92 703	94 803	96 846	98 588	99 263
Unemployed	6 343	8 241	8 128	6 372	6 191	6 140	5 501	4 944	4 770	5 186
Not in labor force	52 856	53 298	53 784	53 855	53 753	53 631	53 669	53 439	52 983	53 178
WHITE MEN, 16 YEARS AND OVER										
Population	70 480	71 211	71 922	72 723	73 373	74 390	75 189	75 855	76 468	77 369
Civilian labor force	54 895	55 133	55 480	56 062	56 472	57 217	57 779	58 317	58 988	59 638
Employed	51 315	50 287	50 621	52 462	53 046	53 785	54 647	55 550	56 352	56 703
Agriculture	2 481	2 518	2 484	2 437	2 325	2 340	2 354	2 318	2 345	2 353
Nonagriculture	48 833	47 770	48 138	50 025	50 720	51 444	52 293	53 232	54 007	54 350
Unemployed	3 580	4 846	4 859	3 600	3 426	3 433	3 132	2 766	2 636	2 935
Not in labor force	15 585	16 078	16 441	16 661	16 901	17 173	17 410	17 538	17 480	17 731
WHITE MEN, 20 YEARS AND OVER										
Population	63 715	64 655	65 581	66 610	67 386	68 413	69 175	69 887	70 654	71 457
Civilian labor force	50 671	51 200	51 716	52 453	52 895	53 675	54 232	54 734	55 441	56 116
Employed	47 846	47 209	47 618	49 461	50 061	50 818	51 649	52 466	53 292	53 685
Agriculture	2 183	2 218	2 225	2 201	2 085	2 131	2 150	2 104	2 149	2 148
Nonagriculture	45 663	44 990	45 393	47 260	47 976	48 687	49 499	50 362	51 143	51 537
Unemployed	2 825	3 991	4 098	2 992	2 834	2 857	2 584	2 268	2 149	2 431
Not in labor force	13 044	13 455	13 865	14 157	14 490	14 738	14 942	15 153	15 213	15 340
WHITE WOMEN, 16 YEARS AND OVER										
Population	77 428	78 230	78 884	79 624	80 306	81 042	81 769	82 340	82 871	83 256
Civilian labor force	40 157	41 010	41 541	42 431	43 455	44 584	45 510	46 439	47 367	47 809
Employed	37 394	37 615	38 272	39 659	40 690	41 876	43 142	44 262	45 232	45 558
Agriculture	628	624	635	620	611	617	632	648	651	645
Nonagriculture	36 767	36 991	37 636	39 038	40 079	41 259	42 509	43 614	44 581	44 913
Unemployed	2 762	3 395	3 270	2 772	2 765	2 708	2 369	2 177	2 135	2 251
Not in labor force	37 272	37 220	37 342	37 193	36 852	36 458	36 258	35 901	35 504	35 447
WHITE WOMEN, 20 YEARS AND OVER										
Population	70 677	71 711	72 601	73 590	74 394	75 140	75 845	76 470	77 154	77 539
Civilian labor force	36 418	37 425	38 119	39 087	40 190	41 264	42 164	43 081	44 105	44 648
Employed	34 275	34 710	35 476	36 823	37 907	39 050	40 242	41 316	42 346	42 796
Agriculture	567	565	580	564	566	580	590	599	608	598
Nonagriculture	33 708	34 144	34 896	36 259	37 341	38 471	39 652	40 717	41 738	42 198
Unemployed	2 143	2 715	2 643	2 264	2 283	2 213	1 922	1 766	1 758	1 852
Not in labor force	34 258	34 286	34 482	34 503	34 204	33 876	33 681	33 389	33 050	32 891
WHITE BOTH SEXES, 16-19 YEARS										
Population	13 516	13 076	12 623	12 147	11 900	11 879	11 939	11 838	11 530	11 630
Civilian labor force	7 962	7 518	7 186	6 952	6 841	6 862	6 893	6 940	6 809	6 683
Employed	6 588	5 984	5 799	5 836	5 768	5 792	5 898	6 030	5 946	5 779
Agriculture	359	358	314	292	285	247	246	263	239	252
Nonagriculture	6 229	5 626	5 485	5 544	5 483	5 545	5 652	5 767	5 707	5 528
Unemployed	1 374	1 534	1 387	1 116	1 074	1 070	995	910	863	903
Not in labor force	5 554	5 557	5 436	5 195	5 058	5 017	5 045	4 897	4 721	4 947

See *Note* at end of table.

Table 1-3. Employment Status of the Civilian Noninstitutional Population by Sex, Race, Hispanic Origin, and Age, 1981–2000—*Continued*

(Thousands of persons.)

Employment status, sex, and age	1991	1992	1993	1994	1995	1996	1997	1998	1999	2000
TOTAL, WHITE										
Population	161 759	162 972	164 289	165 555	166 914	168 317	169 993	171 478	173 085	174 428
Civilian labor force	107 743	108 837	109 700	111 082	111 950	113 108	114 693	115 415	116 509	117 574
Employed	101 182	101 669	103 045	105 190	106 490	107 808	109 856	110 931	112 235	113 475
Agriculture	3 026	3 018	2 895	3 162	3 194	3 276	3 208	3 160	3 083	3 099
Nonagriculture	98 157	98 650	100 150	102 027	103 296	104 532	106 648	107 770	109 152	110 376
Unemployed	6 560	7 169	6 655	5 892	5 459	5 300	4 836	4 484	4 273	4 099
Not in labor force	54 016	54 135	54 589	54 473	54 965	55 209	55 301	56 064	56 577	56 854
WHITE MEN, 16 YEARS AND OVER										
Population	77 977	78 651	79 371	80 059	80 733	81 489	82 577	83 352	83 930	84 647
Civilian labor force	59 656	60 168	60 484	60 727	61 146	61 783	62 639	63 034	63 413	63 861
Employed	55 797	55 959	56 656	57 452	58 146	58 888	59 998	60 604	61 139	61 696
Agriculture	2 384	2 378	2 286	2 347	2 347	2 436	2 389	2 376	2 273	2 266
Nonagriculture	53 413	53 580	54 370	55 104	55 800	56 452	57 608	58 228	58 866	59 429
Unemployed	3 859	4 209	3 828	3 275	2 999	2 896	2 641	2 431	2 274	2 165
Not in labor force	18 321	18 484	18 887	19 332	19 587	19 706	19 938	20 317	20 517	20 786
WHITE MEN, 20 YEARS AND OVER										
Population	72 274	73 040	73 721	74 311	74 879	75 454	76 320	76 966	77 432	78 151
Civilian labor force	56 387	56 976	57 284	57 411	57 719	58 340	59 126	59 421	59 747	60 182
Employed	53 103	53 357	54 021	54 676	55 254	55 977	56 986	57 500	57 934	58 469
Agriculture	2 192	2 197	2 114	2 151	2 132	2 224	2 201	2 182	2 094	2 092
Nonagriculture	50 912	51 160	51 907	52 525	53 122	53 753	54 785	55 319	55 839	56 377
Unemployed	3 284	3 620	3 263	2 735	2 465	2 363	2 140	1 920	1 813	1 713
Not in labor force	15 887	16 064	16 436	16 900	17 161	17 114	17 194	17 545	17 685	17 969
WHITE WOMEN, 16 YEARS AND OVER										
Population	83 781	84 321	84 918	85 496	86 181	86 828	87 417	88 126	89 156	89 781
Civilian labor force	48 087	48 669	49 216	50 356	50 804	51 325	52 054	52 380	53 096	53 714
Employed	45 385	45 710	46 390	47 738	48 344	48 920	49 859	50 327	51 096	51 780
Agriculture	641	640	609	815	847	840	819	784	810	833
Nonagriculture	44 744	45 070	45 780	46 923	47 497	48 080	49 040	49 543	50 286	50 947
Unemployed	2 701	2 959	2 827	2 617	2 460	2 404	2 195	2 053	1 999	1 934
Not in labor force	35 695	35 651	35 702	35 141	35 377	35 503	35 363	35 746	36 060	36 068
WHITE WOMEN, 20 YEARS AND OVER										
Population	78 285	78 928	79 490	79 980	80 567	81 041	81 492	82 073	82 053	83 570
Civilian labor force	45 111	45 839	46 311	47 314	47 686	48 162	48 847	49 029	49 714	50 318
Employed	42 862	43 327	43 910	45 116	45 643	46 164	47 063	47 342	48 098	48 736
Agriculture	601	594	572	772	799	798	771	729	765	784
Nonagriculture	42 261	42 733	43 339	44 344	44 844	45 366	46 292	46 612	47 333	47 953
Unemployed	2 248	2 512	2 400	2 197	2 042	1 998	1 784	1 688	1 616	1 581
Not in labor force	33 174	33 089	33 179	32 666	32 881	32 879	32 645	33 044	33 239	33 253
WHITE BOTH SEXES, 16-19 YEARS										
Population	11 200	11 004	11 078	11 264	11 468	11 822	12 181	12 439	12 700	12 707
Civilian labor force	6 245	6 022	6 105	6 357	6 545	6 607	6 720	6 965	7 048	7 075
Employed	5 216	4 985	5 113	5 398	5 593	5 667	5 807	6 089	6 204	6 270
Agriculture	233	228	209	239	262	254	236	250	224	224
Nonagriculture	4 984	4 757	4 904	5 158	5 331	5 413	5 571	5 839	5 980	6 046
Unemployed	1 029	1 037	992	960	952	939	912	876	844	805
Not in labor force	4 955	4 982	4 973	4 907	4 923	5 215	5 462	5 475	5 652	5 632

See *Note* at end of table.

Table 1-3. Employment Status of the Civilian Noninstitutional Population by Sex, Race, Hispanic Origin, and Age, 1981–2000—*Continued*

(Thousands of persons.)

Employment status, sex, and age	1981	1982	1983	1984	1985	1986	1987	1988	1989	1990
TOTAL, BLACK										
Population	18 219	18 584	18 925	19 348	19 664	19 989	20 352	20 692	21 021	21 477
Civilian labor force	11 086	11 331	11 647	12 033	12 364	12 654	12 993	13 205	13 497	13 740
Employed	9 355	9 189	9 375	10 119	10 501	10 814	11 309	11 658	11 953	12 175
Agriculture	184	188	193	196	189	155	164	153	150	142
Nonagriculture	9 171	9 001	9 182	9 923	10 312	10 659	11 145	11 505	11 803	12 034
Unemployed	1 731	2 142	2 272	1 914	1 864	1 840	1 684	1 547	1 544	1 565
Not in labor force	7 134	7 254	7 278	7 315	7 299	7 335	7 359	7 487	7 524	7 737
BLACK MEN, 16 YEARS AND OVER										
Population	8 117	8 283	8 447	8 654	8 790	8 956	9 128	9 289	9 439	9 573
Civilian labor force	5 685	5 804	5 966	6 126	6 220	6 373	6 486	6 596	6 701	6 802
Employed	4 794	4 637	4 753	5 124	5 270	5 428	5 661	5 824	5 928	5 995
Agriculture	162	163	165	174	167	133	142	133	127	124
Nonagriculture	4 632	4 474	4 587	4 950	5 103	5 295	5 519	5 691	5 802	5 872
Unemployed	891	1 167	1 213	1 003	951	946	826	771	773	806
Not in labor force	2 433	2 481	2 482	2 528	2 570	2 583	2 642	2 694	2 738	2 772
BLACK MEN, 20 YEARS AND OVER										
Population	7 007	7 186	7 360	7 599	7 731	7 907	8 063	8 215	8 364	8 479
Civilian labor force	5 223	5 368	5 533	5 686	5 749	5 915	6 023	6 127	6 221	6 357
Employed	4 520	4 414	4 531	4 871	4 992	5 150	5 357	5 509	5 602	5 692
Agriculture	148	150	152	161	154	125	135	129	119	117
Nonagriculture	4 372	4 264	4 379	4 710	4 837	5 025	5 222	5 381	5 483	5 576
Unemployed	703	954	1 002	815	757	765	666	617	619	664
Not in labor force	1 785	1 819	1 828	1 913	1 982	1 991	2 040	2 089	2 143	2 122
BLACK WOMEN, 16 YEARS AND OVER										
Population	10 102	10 300	10 477	10 694	10 873	11 033	11 224	11 402	11 582	11 904
Civilian labor force	5 401	5 527	5 681	5 907	6 144	6 281	6 507	6 609	6 796	6 938
Employed	4 561	4 552	4 622	4 995	5 231	5 386	5 648	5 834	6 025	6 180
Agriculture	22	25	28	22	22	22	22	20	24	18
Nonagriculture	4 539	4 527	4 595	4 973	5 209	5 364	5 626	5 814	6 001	6 162
Unemployed	840	975	1 059	911	913	894	858	776	772	758
Not in labor force	4 701	4 773	4 796	4 787	4 729	4 752	4 717	4 793	4 786	4 965
BLACK WOMEN, 20 YEARS AND OVER										
Population	8 924	9 146	9 340	9 588	9 773	9 945	10 126	10 298	10 482	10 760
Civilian labor force	5 001	5 140	5 306	5 520	5 727	5 855	6 071	6 190	6 352	6 517
Employed	4 329	4 347	4 428	4 773	4 977	5 128	5 365	5 548	5 727	5 884
Agriculture	19	21	25	21	19	22	20	18	23	18
Nonagriculture	4 310	4 326	4 403	4 752	4 959	5 106	5 345	5 530	5 703	5 867
Unemployed	671	793	878	747	750	728	706	642	625	633
Not in labor force	3 923	4 006	4 034	4 069	4 046	4 090	4 054	4 108	4 130	4 243
BLACK, BOTH SEXES, 16-19 YEARS										
Population	2 288	2 252	2 225	2 161	2 160	2 137	2 163	2 179	2 176	2 238
Civilian labor force	862	824	809	827	889	883	899	889	925	866
Employed	505	428	416	474	532	536	587	601	625	598
Agriculture	17	16	16	13	16	8	9	7	8	7
Nonagriculture	489	412	400	460	516	529	578	594	617	591
Unemployed	357	396	392	353	357	347	312	288	300	268
Not in labor force	1 426	1 429	1 416	1 334	1 271	1 254	1 264	1 291	1 251	1 372

See *Note* at end of table.

Table 1-3. Employment Status of the Civilian Noninstitutional Population by Sex, Race, Hispanic Origin, and Age, 1981–2000—*Continued*

(Thousands of persons.)

Employment status, sex, and age	1991	1992	1993	1994	1995	1996	1997	1998	1999	2000
TOTAL, BLACK										
Population	21 799	22 147	22 521	22 879	23 246	23 604	24 003	24 373	24 855	25 218
Civilian labor force	13 797	14 162	14 225	14 502	14 817	15 134	15 529	15 982	16 365	16 603
Employed	12 074	12 151	12 382	12 835	13 279	13 542	13 969	14 556	15 056	15 334
Agriculture	160	153	143	136	101	98	117	138	117	138
Nonagriculture	11 914	11 997	12 239	12 699	13 178	13 444	13 852	14 417	14 939	15 196
Unemployed	1 723	2 011	1 844	1 666	1 538	1 592	1 560	1 426	1 309	1 269
Not in labor force	8 002	7 985	8 296	8 377	8 429	8 470	8 474	8 391	8 490	8 615
BLACK MEN, 16 YEARS AND OVER										
Population	9 725	9 896	10 083	10 258	10 411	10 575	10 763	10 927	11 143	11 320
Civilian labor force	6 851	6 997	7 019	7 089	7 183	7 264	7 354	7 542	7 652	7 816
Employed	5 961	5 930	6 047	6 241	6 422	6 456	6 607	6 871	7 027	7 180
Agriculture	139	138	128	118	93	86	103	118	99	116
Nonagriculture	5 822	5 791	5 919	6 122	6 329	6 371	6 504	6 752	6 928	7 064
Unemployed	890	1 067	971	848	762	808	747	671	626	636
Not in labor force	2 874	2 899	3 064	3 169	3 228	3 311	3 409	3 386	3 491	3 504
BLACK MEN, 20 YEARS AND OVER										
Population	8 652	8 840	9 008	9 171	9 280	9 414	9 575	9 727	9 926	10 107
Civilian labor force	6 451	6 568	6 594	6 646	6 730	6 806	6 910	7 053	7 182	7 343
Employed	5 706	5 681	5 793	5 964	6 137	6 167	6 325	6 530	6 702	6 832
Agriculture	131	131	120	115	89	83	101	112	96	111
Nonagriculture	5 575	5 550	5 673	5 849	6 048	6 084	6 224	6 418	6 606	6 720
Unemployed	745	886	801	682	593	639	585	524	480	511
Not in labor force	2 202	2 272	2 413	2 525	2 550	2 608	2 665	2 673	2 743	2 765
BLACK WOMEN, 16 YEARS AND OVER										
Population	12 074	12 251	12 438	12 621	12 835	13 029	13 241	13 446	13 711	13 898
Civilian labor force	6 946	7 166	7 206	7 413	7 634	7 869	8 175	8 441	8 713	8 787
Employed	6 113	6 221	6 334	6 595	6 857	7 086	7 362	7 685	8 029	8 154
Agriculture	21	15	13	19	8	13	14	20	18	21
Nonagriculture	6 092	6 206	6 320	6 577	6 849	7 073	7 340	7 665	8 011	8 133
Unemployed	833	944	872	818	777	784	813	756	684	633
Not in labor force	5 129	5 086	5 231	5 208	5 201	5 159	5 066	5 005	4 999	5 111
BLACK WOMEN, 20 YEARS AND OVER										
Population	10 959	11 152	11 332	11 496	11 682	11 833	12 010	12 203	12 451	12 643
Civilian labor force	6 572	6 778	6 824	7 004	7 175	7 405	7 686	7 912	8 224	8 293
Employed	5 874	5 978	6 095	6 320	6 556	6 762	7 013	7 290	7 663	7 774
Agriculture	20	15	14	17	7	12	13	19	17	20
Nonagriculture	5 853	5 963	6 081	6 303	6 548	6 749	7 000	7 272	7 646	7 754
Unemployed	698	800	729	685	620	643	673	622	561	519
Not in labor force	4 388	4 374	4 508	4 492	4 507	4 428	4 330	4 291	4 226	4 350
BLACK, BOTH SEXES, 16-19 YEARS										
Population	2 187	2 155	2 181	2 211	2 284	2 356	2 412	2 443	2 479	2 468
Civilian labor force	774	816	807	852	911	923	933	1 017	959	967
Employed	494	492	494	552	586	613	631	736	691	729
Agriculture	8	7	9	1	5	3	3	8	4	7
Nonagriculture	486	485	485	547	581	611	628	728	687	722
Unemployed	280	324	313	300	325	310	302	281	268	239
Not in labor force	1 413	1 339	1 374	1 360	1 372	1 434	1 479	1 427	1 520	1 500

See *Note* at end of table.

Table 1-3. Employment Status of the Civilian Noninstitutional Population by Sex, Race, Hispanic Origin, and Age, 1981–2000—*Continued*

(Thousands of persons.)

Employment status, sex, and age	1981	1982	1983	1984	1985	1986	1987	1988	1989	1990
TOTAL, HISPANIC										
Population	10 120	10 580	11 029	11 478	11 915	12 344	12 867	13 325	13 791	15 904
Civilian labor force	6 492	6 734	7 033	7 451	7 698	8 076	8 541	8 982	9 323	10 720
Employed	5 813	5 805	6 072	6 651	6 888	7 219	7 790	8 250	8 573	9 845
Agriculture	273	285	316	341	302	329	398	407	440	517
Nonagriculture	5 540	5 521	5 756	6 310	6 586	6 890	7 391	7 843	8 133	9 328
Unemployed	678	929	961	800	811	857	751	732	750	876
Not in labor force	3 628	3 846	3 997	4 027	4 217	4 268	4 327	4 342	4 468	5 184
HISPANIC MEN, 16 YEARS AND OVER										
Population	4 968	5 203	5 432	5 661	5 885	6 106	6 371	6 604	6 825	8 041
Civilian labor force	4 005	4 148	4 362	4 563	4 729	4 948	5 163	5 409	5 595	6 546
Employed	3 597	3 583	3 771	4 083	4 245	4 428	4 713	4 972	5 172	6 021
Agriculture	229	243	271	296	264	287	351	356	393	449
Nonagriculture	3 369	3 340	3 499	3 787	3 981	4 140	4 361	4 616	4 779	5 572
Unemployed	408	565	591	480	483	520	451	437	423	524
Not in labor force	963	1 055	1 070	1 098	1 157	1 158	1 208	1 195	1 230	1 495
HISPANIC MEN, 20 YEARS AND OVER										
Population	4 306	4 539	4 771	5 005	5 232	5 451	5 700	5 921	6 114	7 126
Civilian labor force	3 647	3 815	4 014	4 218	4 395	4 612	4 818	5 031	5 195	6 034
Employed	3 325	3 354	3 523	3 825	3 994	4 174	4 444	4 680	4 853	5 609
Agriculture	205	222	246	271	239	263	327	327	366	415
Nonagriculture	3 120	3 132	3 276	3 554	3 754	3 911	4 118	4 353	4 487	5 195
Unemployed	321	461	491	393	401	438	374	351	342	425
Not in labor force	659	724	758	787	837	839	882	890	919	1 092
HISPANIC WOMEN, 16 YEARS AND OVER										
Population	5 151	5 377	5 597	5 816	6 029	6 238	6 496	6 721	6 965	7 863
Civilian labor force	2 486	2 586	2 671	2 888	2 970	3 128	3 377	3 573	3 728	4 174
Employed	2 216	2 222	2 301	2 568	2 642	2 791	3 077	3 278	3 401	3 823
Agriculture	44	42	44	46	38	42	47	51	48	68
Nonagriculture	2 172	2 180	2 257	2 522	2 604	2 749	3 030	3 227	3 353	3 755
Unemployed	269	364	369	320	327	337	300	296	327	351
Not in labor force	2 665	2 792	2 927	2 929	3 059	3 110	3 119	3 147	3 237	3 689
HISPANIC WOMEN, 20 YEARS AND OVER										
Population	4 513	4 734	4 954	5 173	5 385	5 591	5 835	6 050	6 278	7 041
Civilian labor force	2 242	2 333	2 429	2 615	2 725	2 893	3 112	3 281	3 448	3 857
Employed	2 029	2 040	2 127	2 357	2 456	2 615	2 872	3 047	3 172	3 567
Agriculture	37	35	40	37	31	39	45	49	44	62
Nonagriculture	1 992	2 006	2 086	2 320	2 424	2 576	2 827	2 998	3 128	3 505
Unemployed	212	293	302	258	269	278	241	234	276	289
Not in labor force	2 271	2 401	2 525	2 558	2 660	2 698	2 723	2 769	2 830	3 184
HISPANIC, BOTH SEXES, 16-19 YEARS										
Population	1 301	1 307	1 304	1 300	1 298	1 302	1 332	1 354	1 399	1 737
Civilian labor force	603	585	590	618	579	571	610	671	680	829
Employed	459	410	423	468	438	430	474	523	548	668
Agriculture	31	28	29	34	31	27	27	32	31	40
Nonagriculture	428	382	394	435	407	403	447	492	517	628
Unemployed	144	175	167	149	141	141	136	148	132	161
Not in labor force	697	722	714	682	719	730	722	683	719	907

See *Note* at end of table.

Table 1-3. Employment Status of the Civilian Noninstitutional Population by Sex, Race, Hispanic Origin, and Age, 1981–2000—*Continued*

(Thousands of persons.)

Employment status, sex, and age	1991	1992	1993	1994	1995	1996	1997	1998	1999	2000
TOTAL, HISPANIC										
Population	16 425	16 961	17 532	18 117	18 629	19 213	20 321	21 070	21 650	22 393
Civilian labor force	10 920	11 338	11 610	11 975	12 267	12 774	13 796	14 317	14 665	15 368
Employed	9 828	10 027	10 361	10 788	11 127	11 642	12 726	13 291	13 720	14 492
Agriculture	512	524	523	560	604	609	660	742	734	745
Nonagriculture	9 315	9 503	9 838	10 227	10 524	11 033	12 067	12 549	12 986	13 747
Unemployed	1 092	1 311	1 248	1 187	1 140	1 132	1 069	1 026	945	876
Not in labor force	5 506	5 623	5 922	6 142	6 362	6 439	6 526	6 753	6 985	7 025
HISPANIC MEN, 16 YEARS AND OVER										
Population	8 296	8 553	8 824	9 104	9 329	9 604	10 368	10 734	10 713	11 064
Civilian labor force	6 664	6 900	7 076	7 210	7 376	7 646	8 309	8 571	8 546	8 919
Employed	5 979	6 093	6 328	6 530	6 725	7 039	7 728	8 018	8 067	8 478
Agriculture	453	468	469	494	527	537	571	651	642	639
Nonagriculture	5 526	5 625	5 860	6 036	6 198	6 502	7 157	7 367	7 425	7 839
Unemployed	685	807	747	680	651	607	582	552	480	441
Not in labor force	1 632	1 654	1 749	1 894	1 952	1 957	2 059	2 164	2 167	2 145
HISPANIC MEN, 20 YEARS AND OVER										
Population	7 392	7 655	7 930	8 178	8 375	8 611	9 250	9 573	9 523	9 859
Civilian labor force	6 198	6 432	6 621	6 747	6 898	7 150	7 779	8 005	7 950	8 306
Employed	5 623	5 757	5 992	6 189	6 367	6 655	7 307	7 570	7 576	7 961
Agriculture	419	437	441	466	501	510	544	621	602	601
Nonagriculture	5 204	5 320	5 551	5 722	5 866	6 145	6 763	6 949	6 974	7 360
Unemployed	575	675	629	558	530	495	471	436	374	345
Not in labor force	1 194	1 223	1 309	1 431	1 477	1 461	1 471	1 568	1 573	1 554
HISPANIC WOMEN, 16 YEARS AND OVER										
Population	8 130	8 408	8 708	9 014	9 300	9 610	9 953	10 335	10 937	11 329
Civilian labor force	4 256	4 439	4 534	4 765	4 891	5 128	5 486	5 746	6 119	6 449
Employed	3 848	3 934	4 033	4 258	4 403	4 602	4 999	5 273	5 653	6 014
Agriculture	59	57	55	[illegible]	76	72	89	91	92	106
Nonagriculture	3 789	3 877	3 978	4 191	4 320	4 531	4 910	5 182	5 561	5 908
Unemployed	407	504	501	508	488	525	488	473	466	435
Not in labor force	3 874	3 969	4 174	4 248	4 409	4 482	4 466	4 589	4 819	4 880
HISPANIC WOMEN, 20 YEARS AND OVER										
Population	7 301	7 569	7 846	8 122	8 382	8 651	8 950	9 292	9 821	10 193
Civilian labor force	3 941	4 110	4 218	4 421	4 520	4 779	5 106	5 304	5 666	5 979
Employed	3 603	3 693	3 800	3 989	4 116	4 341	4 705	4 928	5 290	5 629
Agriculture	53	51	49	61	72	69	83	85	88	100
Nonagriculture	3 549	3 642	3 751	3 928	4 044	4 272	4 622	4 843	5 202	5 529
Unemployed	339	418	418	431	404	438	401	376	376	350
Not in labor force	3 360	3 459	3 628	3 701	3 863	3 875	3 845	3 988	4 155	4 214
HISPANIC, BOTH SEXES, 16-19 YEARS										
Population	1 732	1 737	1 756	1 818	1 872	1 948	2 121	2 204	2 307	2 341
Civilian labor force	781	796	771	807	850	845	911	1 007	1 049	1 083
Employed	602	577	570	609	645	646	714	793	854	902
Agriculture	41	36	33	32	31	29	33	36	45	44
Nonagriculture	562	541	537	577	614	617	682	757	809	858
Unemployed	179	219	201	198	205	199	197	214	196	181
Not in labor force	951	941	985	1 010	1 022	1 103	1 210	1 197	1 257	1 258

Note: Detail for the above race and Hispanic-origin groups will not sum to totals because data for the Other races group are not presented and Hispanics are included in both the White and Black population groups. See "Notes and Definitions" for information on historical comparability.

Table 1-4. Employment Status of the Civilian Noninstitutional Population by Marital Status, Sex, and Race, 1982–2000

(Thousands of persons.)

TOTAL: SINGLE

Year	Men				Women			
	Civilian noninstitutional population	Civilian labor force			Civilian noninstitutional population	Civilian labor force		
		Total	Employed	Unemployed		Total	Employed	Unemployed
1982	22 410	16 157	13 304	2 853	19 135	12 460	10 765	1 694
1983	22 965	16 657	13 783	2 874	19 479	12 659	10 996	1 663
1984	23 233	16 997	14 699	2 298	19 628	12 867	11 444	1 423
1985	23 328	17 208	15 022	2 186	19 768	13 163	11 758	1 404
1986	23 662	17 553	15 407	2 146	20 113	13 512	12 071	1 442
1987	23 947	17 772	15 794	1 978	20 596	13 885	12 561	1 323
1988	24 572	18 345	16 521	1 824	20 961	14 194	12 979	1 215
1989	24 831	18 738	16 936	1 801	21 141	14 377	13 175	1 202
1990	25 870	19 357	17 405	1 952	21 901	14 612	13 336	1 276
1991	26 197	19 411	17 011	2 400	22 173	14 681	13 198	1 482
1992	26 436	19 709	17 098	2 611	22 475	14 872	13 263	1 609
1993	26 570	19 706	17 261	2 445	22 713	15 031	13 484	1 547
1994	26 786	19 786	17 604	2 181	23 000	15 333	13 847	1 486
1995	26 918	19 841	17 833	2 007	23 151	15 467	14 053	1 413
1996	27 387	20 071	18 055	2 016	23 623	15 842	14 403	1 439
1997	28 311	20 689	18 783	1 906	24 285	16 492	15 037	1 455
1998	28 693	21 037	19 240	1 798	24 941	17 087	15 755	1 332
1999	29 104	21 351	19 686	1 665	25 576	17 575	16 267	1 308
2000	30 232	21 641	19 823	1 818	25 863	17 750	16 446	1 303

TOTAL: MARRIED, SPOUSE PRESENT

Year	Men				Women			
	Civilian noninstitutional population	Civilian labor force			Civilian noninstitutional population	Civilian labor force		
		Total	Employed	Unemployed		Total	Employed	Unemployed
1982	50 891	40 706	38 074	2 632	50 783	25 971	24 053	1 918
1983	51 118	40 601	37 967	2 634	51 084	26 468	24 603	1 865
1984	51 732	40 952	39 056	1 896	51 557	27 199	25 636	1 562
1985	52 128	41 014	39 248	1 767	51 832	27 894	26 336	1 558
1986	52 769	41 477	39 658	1 819	52 158	28 623	27 144	1 479
1987	53 223	41 889	40 265	1 625	52 532	29 381	28 107	1 273
1988	53 246	41 832	40 472	1 360	52 775	29 921	28 756	1 166
1989	53 530	42 036	40 760	1 276	52 885	30 548	29 404	1 145
1990	53 793	42 275	40 829	1 446	52 917	30 901	29 714	1 188
1991	54 158	42 303	40 429	1 875	53 169	31 112	29 698	1 415
1992	54 509	42 491	40 341	2 150	53 501	31 700	30 100	1 600
1993	55 178	42 834	40 935	1 899	53 838	31 980	30 499	1 482
1994	55 560	43 005	41 414	1 592	54 155	32 888	31 536	1 352
1995	56 100	43 472	42 048	1 424	54 716	33 359	32 063	1 296
1996	56 363	43 739	42 417	1 322	54 970	33 618	32 406	1 211
1997	56 396	43 808	42 642	1 167	54 915	33 802	32 755	1 047
1998	56 670	43 957	42 923	1 034	55 331	33 857	32 872	985
1999	57 089	44 244	43 254	990	56 178	34 372	33 450	921
2000	55 897	43 254	42 261	993	56 432	34 960	33 998	961

TOTAL: DIVORCED, WIDOWED, OR SEPARATED

Year	Men				Women			
	Civilian noninstitutional population	Civilian labor force			Civilian noninstitutional population	Civilian labor force		
		Total	Employed	Unemployed		Total	Employed	Unemployed
1982	8 222	5 587	4 892	695	20 831	9 324	8 438	886
1983	8 448	5 788	5 036	752	21 121	9 376	8 447	929
1984	8 640	5 886	5 335	551	21 592	9 644	8 835	809
1985	9 013	6 190	5 621	568	22 136	9 993	9 165	828
1986	9 367	6 392	5 827	565	22 518	10 277	9 491	787
1987	9 729	6 546	6 048	498	22 726	10 393	9 665	727
1988	10 039	6 751	6 280	471	23 020	10 627	9 962	665
1989	10 401	7 066	6 618	448	23 604	11 104	10 448	656
1990	10 714	7 378	6 871	508	23 968	11 315	10 639	676
1991	10 924	7 454	6 783	671	24 304	11 385	10 600	786
1992	11 325	7 763	7 001	762	24 559	11 570	10 689	881
1993	11 584	7 864	7 153	711	24 955	11 784	10 927	856
1994	12 008	8 026	7 432	594	25 304	12 018	11 227	791
1995	12 160	8 047	7 496	551	25 539	12 118	11 407	712
1996	12 456	8 277	7 735	541	25 791	12 397	11 691	706
1997	13 009	8 764	8 260	504	26 218	12 742	12 082	660
1998	13 394	8 965	8 530	435	26 190	12 771	12 143	628
1999	13 528	8 918	8 507	411	26 276	12 909	12 324	585
2000	14 290	9 623	9 152	470	26 354	13 227	12 656	571

See *Note* at end of table.

Table 1-4. Employment Status of the Civilian Noninstitutional Population by Marital Status, Sex, and Race, 1982–2000—*Continued*

(Thousands of persons.)

WHITE: SINGLE

Year	Men				Women			
	Civilian noninstitutional population	Civilian labor force			Civilian noninstitutional population	Civilian labor force		
		Total	Employed	Unemployed		Total	Employed	Unemployed
1982	18 521	13 723	11 609	2 114	15 189	10 334	9 201	1 134
1983	18 934	14 074	11 991	2 084	15 342	10 413	9 352	1 061
1984	19 034	14 281	12 677	1 605	15 365	10 528	9 622	906
1985	19 100	14 426	12 875	1 550	15 472	10 705	9 828	877
1986	19 316	14 672	13 162	1 510	15 686	10 965	10 060	906
1987	19 526	14 850	13 449	1 401	15 990	11 196	10 382	815
1988	19 966	15 279	13 982	1 297	16 218	11 428	10 674	754
1989	20 076	15 511	14 249	1 263	16 289	11 474	10 741	734
1990	20 746	15 993	14 617	1 376	16 555	11 522	10 729	794
1991	20 899	15 989	14 233	1 756	16 569	11 497	10 557	939
1992	21 025	16 129	14 285	1 844	16 684	11 502	10 526	976
1993	20 974	16 033	14 303	1 730	16 768	11 613	10 633	980
1994	21 071	16 074	14 539	1 535	16 936	11 805	10 885	920
1995	21 132	16 080	14 674	1 406	17 046	11 830	10 967	864
1996	21 454	16 285	14 891	1 394	17 282	11 977	11 099	878
1997	22 236	16 810	15 507	1 303	17 728	12 322	11 443	879
1998	22 513	17 007	15 746	1 261	18 247	12 742	11 945	797
1999	22 788	17 272	16 116	1 157	18 635	13 029	12 206	823
2000	23 501	17 353	16 047	1 307	18 701	13 102	12 293	809

WHITE: MARRIED, SPOUSE PRESENT

Year	Men				Women			
	Civilian noninstitutional population	Civilian labor force			Civilian noninstitutional population	Civilian labor force		
		Total	Employed	Unemployed		Total	Employed	Unemployed
1982	46 019	36 809	34 600	2 209	45 982	23 140	21 532	1 609
1983	46 099	36 631	34 416	2 215	46 226	23 585	22 018	1 567
1984	46 616	36 905	35 318	1 588	46 599	24 196	22 888	1 308
1985	46 925	36 934	35 472	1 462	46 728	24 777	23 468	1 308
1986	47 399	37 230	35 727	1 503	46 892	25 368	24 141	1 226
1987	47 600	37 486	36 127	1 359	47 180	26 014	24 969	1 045
1988	47 685	37 429	36 304	1 125	47 004	26 499	25 540	959
1989	47 883	37 589	36 545	1 044	47 382	27 030	26 083	947
1990	47 841	37 515	36 338	1 177	47 240	27 271	26 285	986
1991	48 137	37 507	35 923	1 585	47 456	27 479	26 290	1 189
1992	48 416	37 671	35 886	1 785	47 705	27 951	26 623	1 329
1993	48 937	37 953	36 396	1 557	47 944	28 221	26 993	1 228
1994	49 169	38 008	36 719	1 288	48 120	29 017	27 888	1 129
1995	49 597	38 376	37 211	1 165	48 497	29 360	28 290	1 070
1996	49 800	38 616	37 522	1 094	48 684	29 517	28 496	1 020
1997	49 719	38 593	37 636	957	48 542	29 664	28 809	855
1998	49 901	38 629	37 793	836	48 722	29 534	28 727	808
1999	50 091	38 765	37 968	797	49 296	29 806	29 056	749
2000	49 183	38 057	37 231	826	49 534	30 356	29 547	810

WHITE: DIVORCED, WIDOWED, OR SEPARATED

Year	Men				Women			
	Civilian noninstitutional population	Civilian labor force			Civilian noninstitutional population	Civilian labor force		
		Total	Employed	Unemployed		Total	Employed	Unemployed
1982	6 671	4 600	4 078	522	17 059	7 535	6 883	653
1983	6 889	4 775	4 214	560	17 316	7 543	6 902	642
1984	7 073	4 875	4 467	407	17 660	7 706	7 148	558
1985	7 348	5 112	4 698	414	18 106	7 973	7 393	580
1986	7 675	5 315	4 896	420	18 463	8 251	7 675	576
1987	7 974	5 443	5 070	373	18 599	8 300	7 791	509
1988	8 204	5 608	5 265	344	18 758	8 512	8 047	464
1989	8 509	5 887	5 558	329	19 200	8 863	8 409	454
1990	8 782	6 131	5 748	382	19 461	9 016	8 544	471
1991	8 941	6 159	5 641	518	19 757	9 111	8 538	573
1992	9 210	6 368	5 788	580	19 931	9 216	8 561	654
1993	9 459	6 498	5 957	541	20 206	9 382	8 764	618
1994	9 819	6 644	6 193	451	20 439	9 533	8 965	569
1995	10 005	6 689	6 261	428	20 638	9 613	9 087	526
1996	10 234	6 883	6 474	408	20 862	9 831	9 325	506
1997	10 622	7 236	6 855	382	21 147	10 068	9 607	461
1998	10 937	7 398	7 064	334	21 157	10 104	9 656	449
1999	11 050	7 375	7 056	320	21 225	10 261	9 834	427
2000	11 614	7 880	7 522	358	21 335	10 526	10 113	412

See *Note* at end of table.

Table 1-4. Employment Status of the Civilian Noninstitutional Population by Marital Status, Sex, and Race, 1982–2000—*Continued*

(Thousands of persons.)

BLACK AND OTHER: SINGLE

Year	Men				Women			
	Civilian noninstitutional population	Civilian labor force			Civilian noninstitutional population	Civilian labor force		
		Total	Employed	Unemployed		Total	Employed	Unemployed
1982	3 890	2 433	1 695	738	3 946	2 126	1 565	561
1983	4 031	2 583	1 793	790	4 138	2 246	1 644	602
1984	4 199	2 716	2 023	693	4 263	2 338	1 821	517
1985	4 228	2 782	2 147	635	4 297	2 458	1 930	528
1986	4 345	2 881	2 245	636	4 427	2 547	2 011	536
1987	4 421	2 922	2 345	577	4 606	2 688	2 179	509
1988	4 606	3 066	2 539	527	4 743	2 766	2 304	461
1989	4 755	3 227	2 687	538	4 852	2 903	2 434	468
1990	5 124	3 364	2 788	576	5 346	3 090	2 607	482
1991	5 298	3 422	2 778	644	5 604	3 184	2 641	543
1992	5 411	3 580	2 813	767	5 791	3 370	2 737	633
1993	5 596	3 673	2 958	715	5 945	3 418	2 851	567
1994	5 715	3 712	3 065	646	6 064	3 528	2 962	566
1995	5 786	3 761	3 159	601	6 105	3 637	3 086	549
1996	5 933	3 786	3 164	622	6 341	3 865	3 304	561
1997	6 075	3 879	3 276	603	6 557	4 170	3 594	576
1998	6 180	4 030	3 494	537	6 694	4 345	3 810	535
1999	6 316	4 079	3 570	508	6 941	4 546	4 061	485
2000	8 880	6 095	5 390	705	8 764	5 635	5 013	622

BLACK AND OTHER: MARRIED, SPOUSE PRESENT

Year	Men				Women			
	Civilian noninstitutional population	Civilian labor force			Civilian noninstitutional population	Civilian labor force		
		Total	Employed	Unemployed		Total	Employed	Unemployed
1982	4 872	3 897	3 474	422	4 800	2 830	2 521	309
1983	5 019	3 970	3 551	419	4 858	2 883	2 585	298
1984	5 116	4 046	3 739	308	4 958	3 002	2 748	254
1985	5 203	4 080	3 775	305	5 104	3 118	2 868	250
1986	5 370	4 247	3 931	316	5 266	3 255	3 003	253
1987	5 534	4 403	4 137	266	5 352	3 367	3 138	228
1988	5 560	4 403	4 168	234	5 411	3 422	3 215	207
1989	5 647	4 447	4 215	232	5 503	3 518	3 321	198
1990	5 952	4 760	4 491	269	5 677	3 630	3 429	202
1991	6 021	4 796	4 506	290	5 713	3 633	3 408	226
1992	6 093	4 820	4 455	365	5 796	3 749	3 477	271
1993	6 241	4 881	4 539	342	5 894	3 759	3 506	254
1994	6 391	4 997	4 695	304	6 035	3 871	3 648	223
1995	6 503	5 096	4 837	259	6 219	3 999	3 773	226
1996	6 563	5 123	4 895	228	6 286	4 101	3 910	191
1997	6 677	5 215	5 006	210	6 373	4 138	3 946	192
1998	6 769	5 328	5 130	198	6 609	4 323	4 145	177
1999	6 998	5 479	5 286	193	6 882	4 566	4 394	172
2000	9 708	7 862	7 589	273	9 744	6 020	5 742	278

BLACK AND OTHER: DIVORCED, WIDOWED, OR SEPARATED

Year	Men				Women			
	Civilian noninstitutional population	Civilian labor force			Civilian noninstitutional population	Civilian labor force		
		Total	Employed	Unemployed		Total	Employed	Unemployed
1982	1 551	987	814	173	3 772	1 788	1 555	234
1983	1 559	1 014	822	192	3 805	1 833	1 546	287
1984	1 568	1 011	868	143	3 932	1 938	1 687	251
1985	1 665	1 078	923	155	4 030	2 020	1 772	248
1986	1 692	1 076	931	146	4 055	2 026	1 816	210
1987	1 755	1 103	977	125	4 127	2 093	1 875	218
1988	1 836	1 142	1 015	127	4 262	2 115	1 914	201
1989	1 892	1 179	1 060	119	4 404	2 241	2 039	202
1990	1 932	1 247	1 123	126	4 507	2 299	2 095	205
1991	1 983	1 295	1 142	153	4 547	2 274	2 062	213
1992	2 115	1 395	1 213	182	4 628	2 354	2 128	227
1993	2 125	1 366	1 196	170	4 749	2 402	2 163	238
1994	2 189	1 382	1 239	143	4 865	2 485	2 262	222
1995	2 155	1 358	1 235	123	4 901	2 505	2 320	186
1996	2 222	1 394	1 261	133	4 929	2 566	2 366	200
1997	2 387	1 528	1 405	122	5 071	2 674	2 475	199
1998	2 457	1 567	1 466	101	5 033	2 667	2 487	179
1999	2 478	1 543	1 451	91	5 051	2 648	2 490	158
2000	3 645	2 535	2 347	187	6 533	3 539	3 295	243

Note: See "Notes and Definitions" for information on historical comparability.

Table 1-5. Employment Status of the Civilian Noninstitutional Population by Region, Division, and State, 1999–2000

(Thousands of persons, percent.)

Region, division, and state	1999						2000					
	Civilian noninstitutional population	Civilian labor force					Civilian noninstitutional population	Civilian labor force				
		Total	Participation rate	Employed	Unemployed	Unemploy-ment rate		Total	Participation rate	Employed	Unemployed	Unemploy-ment rate
UNITED STATES [1]	207 753	139 368	64.3	133 488	5 880	4.2	209 699	140 863	64.5	135 208	5 655	4.0
Northeast	40 105	26 234	62.5	25 083	1 151	4.4	40 247	26 295	62.8	25 281	1 014	3.9
New England	10 439	7 171	66.4	6 935	236	3.3	10 502	7 194	66.6	6 995	199	2.8
Connecticut	2 530	1 708	65.4	1 654	54	3.2	2 537	1 746	67.3	1 707	39	2.3
Maine	987	670	65.1	642	27	4.1	998	689	66.6	665	24	3.5
Massachusetts	4 781	3 284	66.5	3 179	105	3.2	4 804	3 237	65.6	3 151	86	2.6
New Hampshire	924	668	70.3	650	18	2.7	939	686	71.0	666	19	2.8
Rhode Island	751	504	64.4	484	21	4.1	753	505	64.3	484	21	4.1
Vermont	466	336	69.9	326	10	3.0	471	332	68.3	322	10	2.9
Middle Atlantic	29 666	19 063	61.2	18 148	915	4.8	29 745	19 101	61.5	18 286	815	4.3
New Jersey	6 264	4 205	64.1	4 012	193	4.6	6 292	4 188	64.1	4 030	157	3.8
New York	14 120	8 882	59.7	8 423	459	5.2	14 163	8 941	60.3	8 533	408	4.6
Pennsylvania	9 282	5 976	61.6	5 713	263	4.4	9 290	5 972	61.6	5 722	250	4.2
Midwest	47 946	33 442	67.3	32 244	1 198	3.6	48 222	33 729	67.4	32 493	1 236	3.7
East North Central	33 764	23 242	66.2	22 348	894	3.8	33 931	23 422	66.4	22 517	905	3.9
Illinois	9 155	6 378	66.7	6 105	273	4.3	9 199	6 419	66.7	6 140	279	4.4
Indiana	4 504	3 076	66.2	2 983	93	3.0	4 529	3 084	65.9	2 984	100	3.2
Michigan	7 505	5 144	66.0	4 950	194	3.8	7 548	5 201	66.5	5 016	185	3.6
Ohio	8 605	5 754	64.0	5 508	246	4.3	8 624	5 783	64.3	5 546	237	4.1
Wisconsin	3 995	2 890	70.1	2 802	88	3.0	4 031	2 935	70.2	2 831	104	3.5
West North Central	14 182	10 200	69.8	9 896	303	3.0	14 291	10 307	69.8	9 976	331	3.2
Iowa	2 187	1 573	70.1	1 533	40	2.5	2 193	1 563	69.4	1 522	41	2.6
Kansas	1 988	1 434	70.0	1 392	43	3.0	2 001	1 411	67.9	1 359	52	3.7
Minnesota	3 600	2 703	73.0	2 627	76	2.8	3 648	2 739	72.6	2 649	90	3.3
Missouri	4 135	2 841	66.4	2 745	96	3.4	4 166	2 930	67.9	2 828	101	3.5
Nebraska	1 248	912	71.0	886	26	2.9	1 254	924	71.5	897	28	3.0
North Dakota	478	337	68.1	325	11	3.4	477	339	68.9	329	10	3.0
South Dakota	546	400	71.1	388	12	2.9	552	401	71.0	392	9	2.3
South	73 427	40 400	63.2	46 412	1 994	4.1	74 337	49 035	63.4	47 104	1 931	3.9
South Atlantic	38 033	25 060	65.4	24 123	937	3.7	38 528	25 534	66.0	24 624	910	3.6
Delaware	581	390	64.7	376	14	3.5	588	409	66.8	393	16	4.0
District Of Columbia	415	281	63.4	263	18	6.3	413	279	63.6	263	16	5.8
Florida	11 783	7 361	60.1	7 077	284	3.9	11 960	7 490	60.4	7 221	269	3.6
Georgia	5 859	4 078	66.8	3 916	162	4.0	5 967	4 173	67.4	4 019	154	3.7
Maryland	3 975	2 775	67.3	2 676	98	3.5	4 015	2 805	67.2	2 697	108	3.9
North Carolina	5 755	3 868	65.1	3 746	122	3.2	5 809	3 958	65.7	3 814	144	3.6
South Carolina	2 992	1 963	62.7	1 875	88	4.5	3 032	1 905	63.0	1 909	77	3.9
Virginia	5 226	3 528	65.6	3 430	98	2.8	5 299	3 610	66.6	3 530	80	2.2
West Virginia	1 447	816	52.7	763	54	6.6	1 445	825	53.9	779	46	5.5
East South Central	12 763	8 190	61.3	7 823	368	4.5	12 853	8 261	61.4	7 895	366	4.4
Alabama	3 384	2 141	60.3	2 039	102	4.8	3 401	2 154	60.4	2 055	99	4.6
Kentucky	3 057	1 967	61.5	1 879	88	4.5	3 082	1 982	61.7	1 900	82	4.1
Mississippi	2 073	1 268	58.0	1 203	65	5.1	2 086	1 326	60.0	1 251	75	5.7
Tennessee	4 249	2 816	63.6	2 702	113	4.0	4 284	2 798	62.7	2 688	110	3.9
West South Central	22 631	15 155	63.9	14 466	688	4.5	22 956	15 240	63.5	14 585	655	4.3
Arkansas	1 957	1 229	60.0	1 174	55	4.5	1 977	1 238	59.8	1 183	55	4.4
Louisiana	3 278	2 052	59.4	1 948	104	5.1	3 289	2 030	58.3	1 917	112	5.5
Oklahoma	2 540	1 655	62.9	1 598	57	3.4	2 558	1 648	62.5	1 598	50	3.0
Texas	14 856	10 219	65.6	9 747	472	4.6	15 132	10 325	65.3	9 887	437	4.2
West	46 129	31 191	64.3	29 658	1 533	4.9	46 891	31 806	64.7	30 333	1 473	4.6
Mountain	12 802	8 847	66.2	8 478	369	4.2	13 033	8 949	66.1	8 614	336	3.8
Arizona	3 563	2 359	63.3	2 255	104	4.4	3 626	2 347	62.2	2 256	91	3.9
Colorado	3 080	2 264	71.4	2 198	66	2.9	3 141	2 276	70.5	2 213	63	2.7
Idaho	934	651	66.1	617	34	5.2	951	658	65.8	626	32	4.9
Montana	685	474	65.6	449	25	5.2	691	479	65.9	456	24	4.9
Nevada	1 363	942	66.0	900	42	4.4	1 408	986	67.2	946	40	4.1
New Mexico	1 300	809	58.5	764	45	5.6	1 318	833	60.1	792	40	4.9
Utah	1 503	1 086	69.6	1 046	41	3.7	1 527	1 104	70.0	1 068	36	3.2
Wyoming	368	262	67.8	249	13	4.9	371	267	69.2	257	10	3.9
Pacific	33 327	22 344	63.6	21 180	1 164	5.2	33 858	22 856	64.1	21 719	1 137	5.0
Alaska	434	319	68.8	299	20	6.4	438	322	68.6	301	21	6.6
California	25 044	16 596	62.8	15 732	865	5.2	25 489	17 091	63.7	16 246	845	4.9
Hawaii	885	593	63.2	560	33	5.6	889	595	64.1	570	26	4.3
Oregon	2 583	1 761	64.3	1 661	100	5.7	2 608	1 803	65.8	1 715	87	4.9
Washington	4 381	3 075	66.9	2 929	145	4.7	4 434	3 045	65.1	2 888	158	5.2
Puerto Rico [2]	2 803	1 302	41.0	1 149	153	11.7	2 834	1 306	41.4	1 174	132	10.1

Note: Region and division data are derived from summing the component states.

1. Because of separate processing and weighing procedures, totals for the United States differ from the results obtained by aggregating data for regions, divisions, or states.
2. The source of these data is the Puerto Rico Department of Labor and Human Resources.

Table 1-6. Civilian Noninstitutional Population by Race, Hispanic Origin, Sex, and Age, 1948–2000

(Thousands of persons.)

Year, race, Hispanic origin, and sex	16 years and over	16 to 19 years			20 years and over						
		Total	16 to 17 years	18 to 19 years	Total	20 to 24 years	25 to 34 years	35 to 44 years	45 to 54 years	55 to 64 years	65 years and over
TOTAL											
1948	103 068	8 449	4 265	4 185	94 618	11 530	22 610	20 097	16 771	12 885	10 720
1949	103 994	8 215	4 139	4 079	95 778	11 312	22 822	20 401	17 002	13 201	11 035
1950	104 995	8 143	4 076	4 068	96 851	11 080	23 013	20 681	17 240	13 469	11 363
1951	104 621	7 865	4 096	3 771	96 755	10 167	22 843	20 863	17 464	13 692	11 724
1952	105 231	7 922	4 234	3 689	97 305	9 389	23 044	21 137	17 716	13 889	12 126
1953	107 056	8 014	4 241	3 773	99 041	8 960	23 266	21 922	17 991	13 830	13 075
1954	108 321	8 224	4 336	3 889	100 095	8 885	23 304	22 135	18 305	14 085	13 375
1955	109 683	8 364	4 440	3 925	101 318	9 036	23 249	22 348	18 643	14 309	13 728
1956	110 954	8 434	4 482	3 953	102 518	9 271	23 072	22 567	19 012	14 516	14 075
1957	112 265	8 612	4 587	4 026	103 653	9 486	22 849	22 786	19 424	14 727	14 376
1958	113 727	8 986	4 872	4 114	104 737	9 733	22 563	23 025	19 832	14 923	14 657
1959	115 329	9 618	5 337	4 282	105 711	9 975	22 201	23 207	20 203	15 134	14 985
1960	117 245	10 187	5 573	4 615	107 056	10 273	21 998	23 437	20 601	15 409	15 336
1961	118 771	10 513	5 462	5 052	108 255	10 583	21 829	23 585	20 893	15 675	15 685
1962	120 153	10 652	5 503	5 150	109 500	10 852	21 503	23 797	20 916	15 874	16 554
1963	122 416	11 370	6 301	5 070	111 045	11 464	21 400	23 948	21 144	16 138	16 945
1964	124 485	12 111	6 974	5 139	112 372	12 017	21 367	23 940	21 452	16 442	17 150
1965	126 513	12 930	6 936	5 995	113 582	12 442	21 417	23 832	21 728	16 727	17 432
1966	128 058	13 592	6 914	6 679	114 463	12 638	21 543	23 579	21 977	17 007	17 715
1967	129 874	13 480	7 003	6 480	116 391	13 421	22 057	23 313	22 256	17 310	18 029
1968	132 028	13 698	7 200	6 499	118 328	13 891	22 912	23 036	22 534	17 614	18 338
1969	134 335	14 095	7 422	6 673	120 238	14 488	23 645	22 709	22 806	17 930	18 657
1970	137 085	14 519	7 643	6 876	122 566	15 323	24 435	22 489	23 059	18 250	19 007
1971	140 216	15 022	7 849	7 173	125 193	16 345	25 337	22 274	23 244	18 581	19 406
1972	144 126	15 510	8 076	7 435	128 614	17 143	26 740	22 358	23 338	19 007	20 023
1973	147 096	15 840	8 227	7 613	131 253	17 692	28 172	22 287	23 431	19 281	20 389
1974	150 120	16 180	8 373	7 809	133 938	17 994	29 439	22 461	23 578	19 517	20 945
1975	153 153	16 418	8 419	7 999	136 733	18 595	30 710	22 526	23 535	19 844	21 525
1976	156 150	16 614	8 442	8 171	139 536	19 109	31 953	22 796	23 409	20 185	22 083
1977	159 033	16 688	8 482	8 206	142 345	19 582	33 117	23 296	23 197	20 557	22 597
1978	161 910	16 695	8 484	8 211	145 216	20 007	34 091	24 099	22 977	20 875	23 166
1979	164 863	16 657	8 389	8 268	148 205	20 353	35 261	24 861	22 752	21 210	23 767
1980	167 745	16 543	8 279	8 264	151 202	20 635	36 558	25 578	22 563	21 520	24 350
1981	170 130	16 214	8 068	8 145	153 916	20 820	37 777	26 291	22 422	21 756	24 850
1982	172 271	15 763	7 714	8 049	156 508	20 845	38 492	27 611	22 264	21 909	25 387
1983	174 215	15 274	7 385	7 889	158 941	20 799	39 147	28 932	22 167	22 003	25 892
1984	176 383	14 735	7 196	7 538	161 648	20 688	39 999	30 251	22 226	22 052	26 433
1985	178 206	14 506	7 232	7 274	163 700	20 097	40 670	31 379	22 418	22 140	26 997
1986	180 587	14 496	7 386	7 110	166 091	19 569	41 731	32 550	22 732	22 011	27 497
1987	182 753	14 606	7 501	7 104	168 147	18 970	42 297	33 755	23 183	21 835	28 108
1988	184 613	14 527	7 284	7 243	170 085	18 434	42 611	34 784	24 004	21 641	28 612
1989	186 393	14 223	6 886	7 338	172 169	18 025	42 845	35 977	24 744	21 406	29 173
1990	189 164	14 520	6 893	7 626	174 644	18 902	42 976	37 719	25 081	20 719	29 247
1991	190 925	14 073	6 901	7 173	176 852	18 963	42 688	39 116	25 709	20 675	29 700
1992	192 805	13 840	6 907	6 933	178 965	18 846	42 278	39 852	27 206	20 604	30 179
1993	194 838	13 935	7 010	6 925	180 903	18 642	41 771	40 733	28 549	20 574	30 634
1994	196 814	14 196	7 245	6 951	182 619	18 353	41 306	41 534	29 778	20 635	31 012
1995	198 584	14 511	7 407	7 104	184 073	17 864	40 798	42 254	30 974	20 735	31 448
1996	200 591	14 934	7 678	7 256	185 656	17 409	40 252	43 086	32 167	20 990	31 751
1997	203 133	15 365	7 861	7 504	187 769	17 442	39 559	43 883	33 391	21 505	31 989
1998	205 220	15 644	7 895	7 749	189 576	17 593	38 778	44 299	34 373	22 296	32 237
1999	207 753	16 040	8 060	7 979	191 714	17 968	37 976	44 635	35 587	23 064	32 484
2000	209 699	16 042	8 003	8 038	193 657	18 411	37 417	44 605	36 904	23 615	32 705

See *Note* at end of table.

Table 1-6. Civilian Noninstitutional Population by Race, Hispanic Origin, Sex, and Age, 1948–2000—*Continued*

(Thousands of persons.)

Year, race, Hispanic origin, and sex	16 years and over	16 to 19 years			20 years and over						
		Total	16 to 17 years	18 to 19 years	Total	20 to 24 years	25 to 34 years	35 to 44 years	45 to 54 years	55 to 64 years	65 years and over
WHITE											
1954	97 705	7 180	3 786	3 394	90 524	7 794	20 818	19 915	16 569	12 993	12 438
1955	98 880	7 292	3 874	3 419	91 586	7 912	20 742	20 110	16 869	13 169	12 785
1956	99 976	7 346	3 908	3 438	92 629	8 106	20 564	20 314	17 198	13 341	13 105
1957	101 119	7 505	4 007	3 498	93 612	8 293	20 342	20 514	17 562	13 518	13 383
1958	102 392	7 843	4 271	3 573	94 547	8 498	20 063	20 734	17 924	13 681	13 645
1959	103 803	8 430	4 707	3 725	95 370	8 697	19 715	20 893	18 257	13 858	13 951
1960	105 282	8 924	4 909	4 016	96 355	8 927	19 470	21 049	18 578	14 070	14 260
1961	106 604	9 211	4 785	4 427	97 390	9 203	19 289	21 169	18 845	14 304	14 581
1962	107 715	9 343	4 818	4 526	98 371	9 484	18 974	21 293	18 872	14 450	15 297
1963	109 705	9 978	5 549	4 430	99 725	10 069	18 867	21 398	19 082	14 681	15 629
1964	111 534	10 616	6 137	4 481	100 916	10 568	18 838	21 375	19 360	14 957	15 816
1965	113 284	11 319	6 049	5 271	101 963	10 935	18 882	21 258	19 604	15 215	16 070
1966	114 566	11 862	5 993	5 870	102 702	11 094	18 989	21 005	19 822	15 469	16 322
1967	116 100	11 682	6 051	5 632	104 417	11 797	19 464	20 745	20 067	15 745	16 602
1968	117 948	11 840	6 225	5 616	106 107	12 184	20 245	20 474	20 310	16 018	16 875
1969	119 913	12 179	6 418	5 761	107 733	12 677	20 892	20 156	20 546	16 305	17 156
1970	122 174	12 521	6 591	5 931	109 652	13 359	21 546	19 929	20 760	16 591	17 469
1971	124 758	12 937	6 750	6 189	111 821	14 208	22 295	19 694	20 907	16 884	17 833
1972	127 906	13 301	6 910	6 392	114 603	14 897	23 555	19 673	20 950	17 250	18 278
1973	130 097	13 533	7 021	6 512	116 563	15 264	24 685	19 532	20 991	17 484	18 607
1974	132 417	13 784	7 114	6 671	118 632	15 502	25 711	19 628	21 061	17 645	19 085
1975	134 790	13 941	7 132	6 808	120 849	15 980	26 746	19 641	20 981	17 918	19 587
1976	137 106	14 055	7 125	6 930	123 050	16 368	27 757	19 827	20 816	18 220	20 064
1977	139 380	14 095	7 150	6 944	125 285	16 728	28 703	20 231	20 575	18 540	20 508
1978	141 612	14 060	7 132	6 928	127 552	17 038	29 453	20 932	20 322	18 799	21 007
1979	143 894	13 994	7 029	6 964	129 900	17 204	30 371	21 579	20 058	19 071	21 538
1980	146 122	13 854	6 912	6 943	132 268	17 484	31 407	22 174	19 837	19 316	22 050
1981	147 908	13 516	6 704	6 813	134 392	17 609	32 367	22 778	19 666	19 485	22 487
1982	149 441	13 076	6 383	6 693	136 366	17 579	32 863	23 910	19 478	19 591	22 945
1983	150 805	12 623	6 089	6 534	138 183	17 492	33 286	25 027	19 349	19 625	23 403
1984	152 347	12 147	5 918	6 228	140 200	17 304	33 889	26 124	19 348	19 629	23 906
1985	153 679	11 900	5 922	5 978	141 780	16 853	34 450	27 100	19 405	19 620	24 352
1986	155 432	11 879	6 036	5 843	143 553	16 353	35 293	28 062	19 587	19 477	24 780
1987	156 958	11 939	6 110	5 829	145 020	15 808	35 667	29 036	19 905	19 242	25 301
1988	158 194	11 838	5 893	5 945	146 357	15 276	35 876	29 818	20 652	18 996	25 739
1989	159 338	11 530	5 506	6 023	147 809	14 879	35 951	30 774	21 287	18 743	26 175
1990	160 625	11 630	5 464	6 166	148 996	15 538	35 661	31 739	21 535	18 204	26 319
1991	161 759	11 200	5 451	5 749	150 558	15 516	35 342	32 854	22 052	18 074	26 721
1992	162 972	11 004	5 478	5 526	151 968	15 354	34 885	33 305	23 364	17 951	27 108
1993	164 289	11 078	5 562	5 516	153 210	15 087	34 365	33 919	24 456	17 892	27 493
1994	165 555	11 264	5 710	5 554	154 291	14 708	33 865	34 582	25 435	17 924	27 776
1995	166 914	11 468	5 822	5 646	155 446	14 313	33 355	35 222	26 418	17 986	28 153
1996	168 317	11 822	6 026	5 796	156 495	13 907	32 852	35 810	27 403	18 136	28 387
1997	169 993	12 181	6 213	5 968	157 812	13 983	32 091	36 325	28 388	18 511	28 514
1998	171 478	12 439	6 264	6 176	159 039	14 138	31 286	36 610	29 132	19 231	28 642
1999	173 085	12 700	6 342	6 358	160 385	14 394	30 516	36 755	30 048	19 855	28 818
2000	174 428	12 707	6 312	6 395	161 721	14 721	29 951	36 688	31 091	20 324	28 947

See *Note* at end of table.

Table 1-6. Civilian Noninstitutional Population by Race, Hispanic Origin, Sex, and Age, 1948–2000—*Continued*

(Thousands of persons.)

Year, race, Hispanic origin, and sex	16 years and over	16 to 19 years			20 years and over						
		Total	16 to 17 years	18 to 19 years	Total	20 to 24 years	25 to 34 years	35 to 44 years	45 to 54 years	55 to 64 years	65 years and over
BLACK											
1972	14 526	2 018	1 061	956	12 508	2 027	2 809	2 329	2 139	1 601	1 605
1973	14 917	2 095	1 095	1 000	12 823	2 132	2 957	2 333	2 156	1 616	1 628
1974	15 329	2 137	1 122	1 014	13 192	2 137	3 103	2 382	2 202	1 679	1 689
1975	15 751	2 191	1 146	1 046	13 560	2 228	3 258	2 395	2 211	1 717	1 755
1976	16 196	2 264	1 165	1 098	13 932	2 303	3 412	2 435	2 220	1 736	1 826
1977	16 605	2 273	1 175	1 097	14 332	2 400	3 566	2 493	2 225	1 765	1 883
1978	16 970	2 270	1 169	1 101	14 701	2 483	3 717	2 547	2 226	1 794	1 932
1979	17 397	2 276	1 167	1 109	15 121	2 556	3 899	2 615	2 240	1 831	1 980
1980	17 824	2 289	1 171	1 119	15 535	2 606	4 095	2 687	2 249	1 870	2 030
1981	18 219	2 288	1 161	1 127	15 931	2 642	4 290	2 758	2 260	1 913	2 069
1982	18 584	2 252	1 119	1 134	16 332	2 697	4 438	2 887	2 263	1 935	2 113
1983	18 925	2 225	1 092	1 133	16 700	2 734	4 607	2 999	2 260	1 964	2 135
1984	19 348	2 161	1 056	1 105	17 187	2 783	4 789	3 167	2 288	1 977	2 183
1985	19 664	2 160	1 083	1 077	17 504	2 649	4 873	3 290	2 372	2 060	2 259
1986	19 989	2 137	1 090	1 048	17 852	2 625	5 026	3 410	2 413	2 079	2 298
1987	20 352	2 163	1 123	1 040	18 189	2 578	5 139	3 563	2 460	2 097	2 352
1988	20 692	2 179	1 130	1 049	18 513	2 527	5 234	3 716	2 524	2 110	2 402
1989	21 021	2 176	1 116	1 060	18 846	2 479	5 308	3 900	2 587	2 118	2 454
1990	21 477	2 238	1 101	1 138	19 239	2 554	5 407	4 328	2 618	1 970	2 362
1991	21 799	2 187	1 085	1 102	19 612	2 585	5 419	4 538	2 682	1 985	2 403
1992	22 147	2 155	1 086	1 069	19 992	2 615	5 404	4 722	2 809	1 996	2 446
1993	22 521	2 181	1 113	1 069	20 339	2 600	5 409	4 886	2 941	2 016	2 487
1994	22 879	2 211	1 168	1 044	20 668	2 616	5 362	5 038	3 084	2 045	2 524
1995	23 246	2 284	1 198	1 086	20 962	2 554	5 337	5 178	3 244	2 079	2 571
1996	23 604	2 356	1 238	1 118	21 248	2 519	5 311	5 290	3 408	2 110	2 609
1997	24 003	2 412	1 255	1 158	21 591	2 515	5 279	5 410	3 571	2 164	2 653
1998	24 373	2 443	1 241	1 202	21 930	2 546	5 221	5 510	3 735	2 224	2 695
1999	24 855	2 479	1 250	1 229	22 376	2 615	5 197	5 609	3 919	2 295	2 741
2000	25 218	2 468	1 246	1 222	22 750	2 690	5 145	5 669	4 117	2 351	2 778
HISPANIC											
1973	6 104	867	. . .	. . .	5 238	. . .	. . .	. . .	. . .	. . .	. . .
1974	6 564	926	. . .	. . .	5 645	. . .	. . .	. . .	. . .	. . .	. . .
1975	6 862	962	. . .	. . .	5 900	. . .	. . .	. . .	. . .	. . .	. . .
1976	6 910	953	494	480	6 075	1 053	1 775	1 261	936	570	479
1977	7 362	1 024	513	508	6 376	1 163	1 869	1 283	989	587	485
1978	7 912	1 076	561	515	6 836	1 265	2 004	1 378	1 033	627	529
1979	8 207	1 095	544	551	7 113	1 296	2 117	1 458	1 015	659	566
1980	9 598	1 281	638	643	8 317	1 564	2 508	1 575	1 190	782	698
1981	10 120	1 301	641	660	8 819	1 650	2 698	1 680	1 231	832	728
1982	10 580	1 307	639	668	9 273	1 724	2 871	1 779	1 264	880	755
1983	11 029	1 304	635	670	9 725	1 790	3 045	1 883	1 298	928	781
1984	11 478	1 300	633	667	10 178	1 839	3 224	1 996	1 336	973	810
1985	11 915	1 298	638	661	10 617	1 864	3 401	2 117	1 377	1 015	843
1986	12 344	1 302	658	644	11 042	1 899	3 510	2 239	1 496	1 023	875
1987	12 867	1 332	651	681	11 536	1 910	3 714	2 464	1 492	1 061	895
1988	13 325	1 354	662	692	11 970	1 948	3 807	2 565	1 571	1 159	920
1989	13 791	1 399	672	727	12 392	1 950	3 953	2 658	1 649	1 182	1 001
1990	15 904	1 737	821	915	14 167	2 428	4 589	3 001	1 817	1 247	1 084
1991	16 425	1 732	819	913	14 693	2 481	4 674	3 243	1 879	1 283	1 134
1992	16 961	1 737	836	901	15 224	2 444	4 806	3 458	1 980	1 321	1 216
1993	17 532	1 756	855	901	15 776	2 487	4 887	3 632	2 094	1 324	1 353
1994	18 117	1 818	902	916	16 300	2 518	5 000	3 756	2 223	1 401	1 401
1995	18 629	1 872	903	969	16 757	2 528	5 050	3 965	2 294	1 483	1 437
1996	19 213	1 948	962	986	17 265	2 524	5 181	4 227	2 275	1 546	1 512
1997	20 321	2 121	1 088	1 033	18 200	2 623	5 405	4 453	2 581	1 580	1 558
1998	21 070	2 204	1 070	1 135	18 865	2 731	5 447	4 636	2 775	1 615	1 662
1999	21 650	2 307	1 113	1 194	19 344	2 700	5 512	4 833	2 868	1 713	1 718
2000	22 393	2 341	1 120	1 221	20 052	2 775	5 627	5 007	3 033	1 819	1 791

See *Note* at end of table.

Table 1-6. Civilian Noninstitutional Population by Race, Hispanic Origin, Sex, and Age, 1948–2000—*Continued*

(Thousands of persons.)

Year, race, Hispanic origin, and sex	16 years and over	16 to 19 years			20 years and over						
		Total	16 to 17 years	18 to 19 years	Total	20 to 24 years	25 to 34 years	35 to 44 years	45 to 54 years	55 to 64 years	65 years and over
MEN											
1948	49 996	4 078	2 128	1 951	45 918	5 527	10 767	9 798	8 290	6 441	5 093
1949	50 321	3 946	2 062	1 884	46 378	5 405	10 871	9 926	8 379	6 568	5 226
1950	50 725	3 962	2 043	1 920	46 763	5 270	10 963	10 034	8 472	6 664	5 357
1951	49 727	3 725	2 039	1 687	46 001	4 451	10 709	10 049	8 551	6 737	5 503
1952	49 700	3 767	2 121	1 647	45 932	3 788	10 855	10 164	8 655	6 798	5 670
1953	50 750	3 823	2 122	1 701	46 927	3 482	11 020	10 632	8 878	6 798	6 119
1954	51 395	3 953	2 174	1 780	47 441	3 509	11 067	10 718	9 018	6 885	6 241
1955	52 109	4 022	2 225	1 798	48 086	3 708	11 068	10 804	9 164	6 960	6 380
1956	52 723	4 020	2 238	1 783	48 704	3 970	10 983	10 889	9 322	7 032	6 505
1957	53 315	4 083	2 284	1 800	49 231	4 166	10 889	10 965	9 499	7 109	6 602
1958	54 033	4 293	2 435	1 858	49 740	4 339	10 787	11 076	9 675	7 179	6 683
1959	54 793	4 652	2 681	1 971	50 140	4 488	10 625	11 149	9 832	7 259	6 785
1960	55 662	4 963	2 805	2 159	50 698	4 679	10 514	11 230	10 000	7 373	6 901
1961	56 286	5 112	2 742	2 371	51 173	4 844	10 440	11 286	10 112	7 483	7 006
1962	56 831	5 150	2 764	2 386	51 681	4 925	10 207	11 389	10 162	7 610	7 386
1963	57 921	5 496	3 162	2 334	52 425	5 240	10 165	11 476	10 274	7 740	7 526
1964	58 847	5 866	3 503	2 364	52 981	5 520	10 144	11 466	10 402	7 873	7 574
1965	59 782	6 318	3 488	2 831	53 463	5 701	10 182	11 427	10 512	7 990	7 649
1966	60 262	6 658	3 478	3 180	53 603	5 663	10 224	11 294	10 598	8 099	7 723
1967	60 905	6 537	3 528	3 010	54 367	5 977	10 495	11 161	10 705	8 218	7 809
1968	61 847	6 683	3 634	3 049	55 165	6 127	10 944	11 040	10 819	8 336	7 897
1969	62 898	6 928	3 741	3 187	55 969	6 379	11 309	10 890	10 935	8 464	7 990
1970	64 304	7 145	3 848	3 299	57 157	6 861	11 750	10 810	11 052	8 590	8 093
1971	65 942	7 430	3 954	3 477	58 511	7 511	12 227	10 721	11 129	8 711	8 208
1972	67 835	7 706	4 081	3 624	60 130	8 061	12 911	10 762	11 167	8 895	8 330
1973	69 292	7 855	4 160	3 703	61 436	8 429	13 641	10 746	11 202	8 990	8 426
1974	70 808	8 012	4 231	3 781	62 796	8 000	14 282	10 884	11 315	9 140	8 641
1975	72 291	8 134	4 252	3 882	64 158	8 950	14 899	10 874	11 298	9 286	8 852
1976	73 759	8 244	4 266	3 978	65 515	9 237	15 528	11 010	11 243	9 444	9 053
1977	75 193	8 288	4 290	4 000	66 904	9 477	16 108	11 260	11 144	9 616	9 297
1978	76 576	8 309	4 295	4 014	68 268	9 693	16 598	11 665	11 045	9 758	9 509
1979	78 020	8 310	4 251	4 060	69 709	9 873	17 193	12 046	10 944	9 907	9 746
1980	79 398	8 260	4 195	4 064	71 138	10 023	17 833	12 400	10 861	10 042	9 979
1981	80 511	8 092	4 087	4 005	72 419	10 116	18 427	12 750	10 797	10 151	10 170
1982	81 523	7 879	3 911	3 968	73 644	10 136	18 787	13 410	10 726	10 215	10 371
1983	82 531	7 659	3 750	3 908	74 872	10 140	19 143	14 067	10 689	10 261	10 573
1984	83 605	7 386	3 655	3 731	76 219	10 108	19 596	14 719	10 724	10 285	10 788
1985	84 469	7 275	3 689	3 586	77 195	9 746	19 864	15 265	10 844	10 392	11 084
1986	85 798	7 275	3 768	3 507	78 523	9 498	20 498	15 858	10 986	10 336	11 347
1987	86 899	7 335	3 824	3 510	79 565	9 195	20 781	16 475	11 215	10 267	11 632
1988	87 857	7 304	3 715	3 588	80 553	8 931	20 937	17 008	11 625	10 193	11 859
1989	88 762	7 143	3 524	3 619	81 619	8 743	21 080	17 590	11 981	10 092	12 134
1990	90 377	7 347	3 534	3 813	83 030	9 320	21 117	18 529	12 238	9 778	12 049
1991	91 278	7 134	3 548	3 586	84 144	9 367	20 977	19 213	12 554	9 780	12 254
1992	92 270	7 023	3 542	3 481	85 247	9 326	20 792	19 585	13 271	9 776	12 496
1993	93 332	7 076	3 595	3 481	86 256	9 216	20 569	20 037	13 944	9 773	12 717
1994	94 355	7 203	3 718	3 486	87 151	9 074	20 361	20 443	14 545	9 810	12 918
1995	95 178	7 367	3 794	3 573	87 811	8 835	20 079	20 800	15 111	9 856	13 130
1996	96 206	7 600	3 955	3 645	88 606	8 611	19 775	21 222	15 674	9 997	13 327
1997	97 715	7 836	4 053	3 783	89 879	8 706	19 478	21 669	16 276	10 282	13 469
1998	98 758	7 968	4 059	3 909	90 790	8 804	19 094	21 857	16 773	10 649	13 613
1999	99 722	8 167	4 143	4 024	91 555	8 899	18 565	21 969	17 335	11 008	13 779
2000	100 731	8 151	4 108	4 043	92 580	9 154	18 289	21 951	18 004	11 257	13 925

See *Note* at end of table.

Table 1-6. Civilian Noninstitutional Population by Race, Hispanic Origin, Sex, and Age, 1948–2000—*Continued*

(Thousands of persons.)

Year, race, Hispanic origin, and sex	16 years and over	16 to 19 years			20 years and over						
		Total	16 to 17 years	18 to 19 years	Total	20 to 24 years	25 to 34 years	35 to 44 years	45 to 54 years	55 to 64 years	65 years and over
WOMEN											
1948	53 071	4 371	2 137	2 234	48 700	6 003	11 843	10 299	8 481	6 444	5 627
1949	53 670	4 269	2 077	2 195	49 400	5 907	11 951	10 475	8 623	6 633	5 809
1950	54 270	4 181	2 033	2 148	50 088	5 810	12 050	10 647	8 768	6 805	6 006
1951	54 895	4 140	2 057	2 084	50 754	5 716	12 134	10 814	8 913	6 955	6 221
1952	55 529	4 155	2 113	2 042	51 373	5 601	12 189	10 973	9 061	7 091	6 456
1953	56 305	4 191	2 119	2 072	52 114	5 478	12 246	11 290	9 113	7 032	6 956
1954	56 925	4 271	2 162	2 109	52 654	5 376	12 237	11 417	9 287	7 200	7 134
1955	57 574	4 342	2 215	2 127	53 232	5 328	12 181	11 544	9 479	7 349	7 348
1956	58 228	4 414	2 244	2 170	53 814	5 301	12 089	11 678	9 690	7 484	7 570
1957	58 951	4 529	2 303	2 226	54 421	5 320	11 960	11 821	9 925	7 618	7 774
1958	59 690	4 693	2 437	2 256	54 997	5 394	11 776	11 949	10 157	7 744	7 974
1959	60 534	4 966	2 656	2 311	55 570	5 487	11 576	12 058	10 371	7 875	8 200
1960	61 582	5 224	2 768	2 456	56 358	5 594	11 484	12 207	10 601	8 036	8 435
1961	62 484	5 401	2 720	2 681	57 082	5 739	11 389	12 299	10 781	8 192	8 679
1962	63 321	5 502	2 739	2 764	57 819	5 927	11 296	12 408	10 754	8 264	9 168
1963	64 494	5 874	3 139	2 736	58 620	6 224	11 235	12 472	10 870	8 398	9 419
1964	65 637	6 245	3 471	2 775	59 391	6 497	11 223	12 474	11 050	8 569	9 576
1965	66 731	6 612	3 448	3 164	60 119	6 741	11 235	12 405	11 216	8 737	9 783
1966	67 795	6 934	3 436	3 499	60 860	6 975	11 319	12 285	11 379	8 908	9 992
1967	68 968	6 943	3 475	3 470	62 026	7 445	11 562	12 152	11 551	9 092	10 220
1968	70 179	7 015	3 566	3 450	63 164	7 764	11 968	11 996	11 715	9 278	10 441
1969	71 436	7 167	3 681	3 486	64 269	8 109	12 336	11 819	11 871	9 466	10 667
1970	72 782	7 373	3 796	3 578	65 408	8 462	12 684	11 679	12 008	9 659	10 914
1971	74 274	7 591	3 895	3 697	66 682	8 834	13 110	11 553	12 115	9 870	11 198
1972	76 290	7 805	3 994	3 811	68 484	9 082	13 829	11 597	12 171	10 113	11 693
1973	77 804	7 985	4 076	3 909	69 819	9 263	14 531	11 541	12 229	10 290	11 963
1974	79 312	8 168	4 142	4 028	71 144	9 393	15 177	11 627	12 263	10 377	12 304
1975	80 860	8 285	4 168	4 117	72 576	9 645	15 811	11 652	12 237	10 558	12 673
1976	82 390	8 370	4 176	4 194	74 020	9 872	16 425	11 786	12 166	10 742	13 030
1977	83 840	8 400	4 193	4 206	75 441	10 103	17 008	12 036	12 053	10 940	13 300
1978	85 334	8 386	4 189	4 197	76 948	10 315	17 493	12 435	11 932	11 118	13 658
1979	86 843	8 347	4 139	4 208	78 496	10 480	18 070	12 815	11 808	11 303	14 021
1980	88 348	8 283	4 083	4 200	80 065	10 612	18 725	13 177	11 701	11 478	14 372
1981	89 618	8 121	3 981	4 140	81 497	10 705	19 350	13 533	11 625	11 605	14 680
1982	90 748	7 884	3 804	4 081	82 864	10 709	19 705	14 201	11 538	11 694	15 017
1983	91 684	7 616	3 635	3 981	84 069	10 660	20 004	14 865	11 478	11 742	15 319
1984	92 778	7 349	3 542	3 807	85 429	10 580	20 403	15 532	11 501	11 768	15 645
1985	93 736	7 231	3 543	3 688	86 506	10 351	20 805	16 114	11 574	11 748	15 913
1986	94 789	7 221	3 618	3 603	87 567	10 072	21 233	16 692	11 746	11 675	16 150
1987	95 853	7 271	3 677	3 594	88 583	9 776	21 516	17 279	11 968	11 567	16 476
1988	96 756	7 224	3 569	3 655	89 532	9 503	21 674	17 776	12 378	11 448	16 753
1989	97 630	7 080	3 361	3 719	90 550	9 282	21 765	18 387	12 763	11 314	17 039
1990	98 787	7 173	3 359	3 813	91 614	9 582	21 859	19 190	12 843	10 941	17 198
1991	99 646	6 939	3 353	3 586	92 708	9 597	21 711	19 903	13 155	10 895	17 446
1992	100 535	6 818	3 366	3 452	93 718	9 520	21 486	20 267	13 935	10 828	17 682
1993	101 506	6 859	3 415	3 444	94 647	9 426	21 202	20 696	14 605	10 801	17 917
1994	102 460	6 993	3 528	3 465	95 467	9 279	20 945	21 091	15 233	10 825	18 094
1995	103 406	7 144	3 613	3 531	96 262	9 029	20 719	21 454	15 862	10 879	18 318
1996	104 385	7 335	3 723	3 612	97 050	8 798	20 477	21 865	16 493	10 993	18 424
1997	105 418	7 528	3 808	3 721	97 889	8 736	20 081	22 214	17 115	11 224	18 520
1998	106 462	7 676	3 835	3 840	98 786	8 790	19 683	22 442	17 600	11 646	18 625
1999	108 031	7 873	3 917	3 955	100 158	9 069	19 411	22 666	18 251	12 056	18 705
2000	108 968	7 890	3 895	3 995	101 079	9 257	19 128	22 655	18 901	12 358	18 780

See *Note* at end of table.

Table 1-6. Civilian Noninstitutional Population by Race, Hispanic Origin, Sex, and Age, 1948–2000—*Continued*

(Thousands of persons.)

Year, race, Hispanic origin, and sex	16 years and over	16 to 19 years			20 years and over						
		Total	16 to 17 years	18 to 19 years	Total	20 to 24 years	25 to 34 years	35 to 44 years	45 to 54 years	55 to 64 years	65 years and over
WHITE MEN											
1954	46 462	3 455	1 902	1 553	43 007	3 074	9 948	9 688	8 172	6 341	5 787
1955	47 076	3 507	1 945	1 563	43 569	3 241	9 936	9 768	8 303	6 398	5 923
1956	47 602	3 500	1 955	1 546	44 102	3 464	9 851	9 848	8 446	6 455	6 038
1957	48 119	3 556	2 000	1 557	44 563	3 638	9 758	9 917	8 605	6 518	6 127
1958	48 745	3 747	2 140	1 607	44 998	3 783	9 656	10 018	8 765	6 574	6 203
1959	49 408	4 079	2 370	1 710	45 329	3 903	9 499	10 081	8 909	6 639	6 298
1960	50 065	4 349	2 476	1 874	45 716	4 054	9 373	10 131	9 042	6 721	6 395
1961	50 608	4 479	2 407	2 073	46 129	4 204	9 290	10 178	9 148	6 819	6 490
1962	51 054	4 520	2 426	2 094	46 534	4 306	9 080	10 239	9 191	6 917	6 801
1963	52 031	4 827	2 792	2 036	47 204	4 610	9 039	10 309	9 297	7 031	6 919
1964	52 869	5 148	3 090	2 059	47 721	4 862	9 024	10 301	9 417	7 153	6 963
1965	53 681	5 541	3 050	2 492	48 140	5 017	9 056	10 262	9 516	7 261	7 028
1966	54 061	5 820	3 023	2 798	48 241	4 974	9 085	10 136	9 592	7 362	7 092
1967	54 608	5 671	3 058	2 613	48 937	5 257	9 339	10 013	9 688	7 474	7 167
1968	55 434	5 787	3 153	2 635	49 647	5 376	9 752	9 902	9 790	7 585	7 242
1969	56 348	6 005	3 246	2 759	50 343	5 589	10 074	9 760	9 895	7 705	7 320
1970	57 516	6 179	3 329	2 851	51 336	5 988	10 441	9 678	9 999	7 822	7 409
1971	58 900	6 420	3 412	3 008	52 481	6 546	10 841	9 578	10 066	7 933	7 517
1972	60 473	6 627	3 503	3 125	53 845	7 042	11 495	9 568	10 078	8 089	7 573
1973	61 577	6 737	3 555	3 182	54 842	7 312	12 075	9 514	10 099	8 178	7 664
1974	62 791	6 851	3 604	3 247	55 942	7 476	12 599	9 564	10 165	8 288	7 849
1975	63 981	6 929	3 609	3 320	57 052	7 766	13 131	9 578	10 134	8 413	8 031
1976	65 132	6 993	3 609	3 384	58 138	7 987	13 655	9 674	10 063	8 556	8 203
1977	66 301	7 024	3 625	3 399	59 278	8 175	14 139	9 880	9 957	8 708	8 420
1978	67 401	7 022	3 619	3 404	60 378	8 335	14 528	10 236	9 845	8 826	8 608
1979	68 547	7 007	3 568	3 439	61 540	8 470	15 008	10 563	9 730	8 949	8 820
1980	69 634	6 941	3 508	3 433	62 694	8 581	15 520	10 867	9 636	9 059	9 027
1981	70 480	6 764	3 401	3 363	63 715	8 644	16 005	11 171	9 560	9 139	9 195
1982	71 211	6 556	3 249	3 307	64 655	8 621	16 260	11 756	9 463	9 188	9 367
1983	71 922	6 340	3 098	3 242	65 581	8 597	16 499	12 314	9 408	9 208	9 556
1984	72 723	6 113	3 019	3 094	66 610	8 522	16 816	12 853	9 434	9 217	9 768
1985	73 373	5 987	3 026	2 961	67 386	8 246	17 042	13 337	9 488	9 262	10 010
1986	74 390	5 977	3 084	2 894	68 413	8 002	17 564	13 840	9 578	9 201	10 229
1987	75 189	6 015	3 125	2 890	69 175	7 720	17 754	14 338	9 771	9 101	10 481
1988	75 855	5 968	3 015	2 953	69 887	7 473	17 867	14 743	10 114	9 001	10 688
1989	76 468	5 813	2 817	2 996	70 654	7 279	17 908	15 237	10 434	8 900	10 897
1990	77 369	5 913	2 809	3 103	71 457	7 764	17 766	15 770	10 598	8 680	10 879
1991	77 977	5 704	2 805	2 899	72 274	7 748	17 615	16 340	10 856	8 640	11 074
1992	78 651	5 611	2 819	2 792	73 040	7 676	17 403	16 579	11 513	8 602	11 268
1993	79 371	5 650	2 862	2 788	73 721	7 545	17 158	16 900	12 058	8 590	11 470
1994	80 059	5 748	2 938	2 810	74 311	7 357	16 915	17 247	12 545	8 618	11 629
1995	80 733	5 854	2 995	2 859	74 879	7 163	16 653	17 567	13 028	8 653	11 815
1996	81 489	6 035	3 099	2 936	75 454	6 971	16 395	17 868	13 518	8 734	11 968
1997	82 577	6 257	3 209	3 048	76 320	7 087	16 043	18 163	14 030	8 929	12 067
1998	83 352	6 386	3 233	3 153	76 966	7 170	15 644	18 310	14 400	9 286	12 155
1999	83 930	6 498	3 266	3 232	77 432	7 244	15 150	18 340	14 834	9 581	12 283
2000	84 647	6 496	3 250	3 246	78 151	7 420	14 870	18 304	15 356	9 811	12 390

See *Note* at end of table.

Table 1-6. Civilian Noninstitutional Population by Race, Hispanic Origin, Sex, and Age, 1948–2000—*Continued*

(Thousands of persons.)

Year, race, Hispanic origin, and sex	16 years and over	16 to 19 years			20 years and over						
		Total	16 to 17 years	18 to 19 years	Total	20 to 24 years	25 to 34 years	35 to 44 years	45 to 54 years	55 to 64 years	65 years and over
WHITE WOMEN											
1954	51 242	3 725	1 884	1 841	47 517	4 720	10 870	10 227	8 397	6 652	6 651
1955	51 802	3 785	1 929	1 856	48 017	4 671	10 806	10 342	8 566	6 771	6 862
1956	52 373	3 846	1 953	1 892	48 527	4 642	10 713	10 466	8 752	6 886	7 067
1957	52 998	3 949	2 007	1 941	49 049	4 655	10 584	10 597	8 957	7 000	7 256
1958	53 645	4 096	2 131	1 966	49 549	4 715	10 407	10 716	9 159	7 107	7 442
1959	54 392	4 351	2 337	2 015	50 041	4 794	10 216	10 812	9 348	7 219	7 653
1960	55 214	4 575	2 433	2 142	50 639	4 873	10 097	10 918	9 536	7 349	7 865
1961	55 993	4 732	2 378	2 354	51 261	4 999	9 999	10 991	9 697	7 485	8 091
1962	56 660	4 823	2 392	2 432	51 837	5 178	9 894	11 054	9 681	7 533	8 496
1963	57 672	5 151	2 757	2 394	52 521	5 459	9 828	11 089	9 785	7 650	8 710
1964	58 663	5 468	3 047	2 422	53 195	5 706	9 814	11 074	9 943	7 804	8 853
1965	59 601	5 778	2 999	2 779	53 823	5 918	9 826	10 996	10 088	7 954	9 042
1966	60 503	6 042	2 970	3 072	54 461	6 120	9 904	10 869	10 230	8 107	9 230
1967	61 491	6 011	2 993	3 019	55 480	6 540	10 125	10 732	10 379	8 271	9 435
1968	62 512	6 053	3 072	2 981	56 460	6 809	10 493	10 572	10 520	8 433	9 633
1969	63 563	6 174	3 172	3 002	57 390	7 089	10 818	10 396	10 651	8 600	9 836
1970	64 656	6 342	3 262	3 080	58 315	7 370	11 105	10 251	10 761	8 769	10 060
1971	65 857	6 518	3 338	3 180	59 340	7 662	11 454	10 117	10 841	8 951	10 315
1972	67 431	6 673	3 407	3 267	60 758	7 855	12 060	10 105	10 872	9 161	10 705
1973	68 517	6 796	3 466	3 331	61 721	7 951	12 610	10 018	10 891	9 306	10 943
1974	69 623	6 933	3 510	3 424	62 690	8 026	13 112	10 064	10 896	9 356	11 236
1975	70 810	7 011	3 523	3 488	63 798	8 214	13 615	10 063	10 847	9 505	11 556
1976	71 974	7 062	3 516	3 546	64 912	8 381	14 102	10 153	10 752	9 664	11 860
1977	73 077	7 071	3 525	3 545	66 007	8 553	14 564	10 351	10 618	9 832	12 088
1978	74 213	7 038	3 513	3 524	67 174	8 704	14 926	10 696	10 476	9 974	12 399
1979	75 347	6 987	3 460	3 527	68 360	8 815	15 363	11 017	10 327	10 122	12 717
1980	76 489	6 914	3 403	3 511	69 575	8 904	15 878	11 313	10 201	10 256	13 022
1981	77 428	6 752	3 303	3 449	70 677	8 965	16 362	11 606	10 106	10 346	13 292
1982	78 230	6 519	3 134	3 385	71 711	8 959	16 603	12 154	10 015	10 402	13 579
1983	78 884	6 282	2 991	3 292	72 601	8 895	16 788	12 714	9 941	10 418	13 847
1984	79 624	6 034	2 899	3 135	73 590	8 782	17 073	13 271	9 914	10 412	14 138
1985	80 306	5 912	2 895	3 017	74 394	8 607	17 409	13 762	9 917	10 358	14 342
1986	81 042	5 902	2 953	2 949	75 140	8 351	17 728	14 223	10 009	10 277	14 551
1987	81 769	5 924	2 985	2 939	75 845	8 079	17 913	14 698	10 194	10 141	14 820
1988	82 340	5 869	2 878	2 991	76 470	7 804	18 009	15 074	10 537	9 994	15 052
1989	82 871	5 716	2 690	3 027	77 154	7 600	18 043	15 537	10 853	9 843	15 278
1990	83 256	5 717	2 654	3 063	77 539	7 774	17 895	15 969	10 937	9 524	15 440
1991	83 781	5 497	2 646	2 850	78 285	7 768	17 726	16 514	11 196	9 435	15 647
1992	84 321	5 393	2 659	2 734	78 928	7 678	17 482	16 727	11 851	9 350	15 841
1993	84 918	5 428	2 700	2 728	79 490	7 542	17 206	17 019	12 398	9 302	16 023
1994	85 496	5 516	2 772	2 744	79 980	7 351	16 950	17 335	12 890	9 306	16 148
1995	86 181	5 614	2 827	2 787	80 567	7 150	16 702	17 654	13 390	9 333	16 337
1996	86 828	5 787	2 927	2 860	81 041	6 936	16 457	17 943	13 884	9 402	16 419
1997	87 417	5 924	3 004	2 920	81 492	6 896	16 047	18 162	14 357	9 582	16 447
1998	88 126	6 053	3 031	3 023	82 073	6 969	15 642	18 300	14 732	9 944	16 486
1999	89 156	6 202	3 076	3 127	82 953	7 150	15 366	18 415	15 214	10 274	16 536
2000	89 781	6 211	3 062	3 149	83 570	7 300	15 081	18 384	15 736	10 513	16 557

See *Note* at end of table.

Table 1-6. Civilian Noninstitutional Population by Race, Hispanic Origin, Sex, and Age, 1948–2000—*Continued*

(Thousands of persons.)

Year, race, Hispanic origin, and sex	16 years and over	16 to 19 years			20 years and over						
		Total	16 to 17 years	18 to 19 years	Total	20 to 24 years	25 to 34 years	35 to 44 years	45 to 54 years	55 to 64 years	65 years and over
BLACK MEN											
1972	6 538	978	525	453	5 559	921	1 251	1 027	963	720	680
1973	6 704	1 007	539	468	5 697	979	1 326	1 027	962	718	684
1974	6 875	1 027	555	472	5 848	956	1 380	1 055	996	753	708
1975	7 060	1 051	565	486	6 009	1 002	1 452	1 061	998	769	730
1976	7 265	1 099	580	518	6 167	1 037	1 522	1 078	1 000	774	756
1977	7 431	1 102	585	516	6 329	1 080	1 588	1 103	997	786	775
1978	7 577	1 093	580	513	6 484	1 120	1 656	1 128	995	795	789
1979	7 761	1 100	581	520	6 661	1 151	1 739	1 160	998	809	804
1980	7 944	1 110	584	526	6 834	1 171	1 828	1 191	999	825	822
1981	8 117	1 110	577	534	7 007	1 189	1 914	1 224	1 003	844	835
1982	8 283	1 097	556	542	7 186	1 225	1 983	1 282	1 003	848	846
1983	8 447	1 087	542	545	7 360	1 254	2 068	1 333	1 000	857	847
1984	8 654	1 055	524	531	7 599	1 292	2 164	1 411	1 012	858	861
1985	8 790	1 059	543	517	7 731	1 202	2 180	1 462	1 060	924	902
1986	8 956	1 049	548	503	7 907	1 195	2 264	1 517	1 072	934	924
1987	9 128	1 065	566	499	8 063	1 173	2 320	1 587	1 092	944	947
1988	9 289	1 074	569	505	8 215	1 151	2 367	1 656	1 121	951	970
1989	9 439	1 075	575	501	8 364	1 128	2 403	1 741	1 146	956	990
1990	9 573	1 094	555	540	8 479	1 144	2 412	1 968	1 183	856	916
1991	9 725	1 072	546	526	8 652	1 168	2 416	2 060	1 211	864	933
1992	9 896	1 056	544	512	8 840	1 194	2 409	2 149	1 267	869	951
1993	10 083	1 075	559	517	9 008	1 181	2 426	2 227	1 330	874	969
1994	10 258	1 087	586	501	9 171	1 206	2 399	2 300	1 392	889	986
1995	10 411	1 131	601	530	9 280	1 162	2 389	2 362	1 462	901	1 006
1996	10 575	1 161	623	538	9 414	1 155	2 373	2 413	1 534	914	1 025
1997	10 763	1 188	635	554	9 575	1 153	2 363	2 471	1 607	936	1 045
1998	10 927	1 201	623	578	9 727	1 166	2 335	2 519	1 682	956	1 069
1999	11 143	1 218	628	589	9 926	1 197	2 321	2 566	1 765	986	1 091
2000	11 320	1 213	626	587	10 107	1 235	2 300	2 597	1 856	1 015	1 105
BLACK WOMEN											
1972	7 988	1 040	536	503	6 948	1 106	1 558	1 302	1 176	881	925
1973	8 214	1 088	556	532	7 126	1 153	1 631	1 306	1 194	898	944
1974	8 454	1 110	567	542	7 344	1 181	1 723	1 327	1 206	926	981
1975	8 691	1 141	581	560	7 550	1 226	1 806	1 334	1 213	948	1 025
1976	8 931	1 165	585	580	7 765	1 266	1 890	1 357	1 220	962	1 070
1977	9 174	1 171	590	581	8 003	1 320	1 978	1 390	1 228	979	1 108
1978	9 394	1 177	589	588	8 217	1 363	2 061	1 419	1 231	999	1 143
1979	9 636	1 176	586	589	8 460	1 405	2 160	1 455	1 242	1 022	1 176
1980	9 880	1 180	587	593	8 700	1 435	2 267	1 496	1 250	1 045	1 208
1981	10 102	1 178	584	593	8 924	1 453	2 376	1 534	1 257	1 069	1 234
1982	10 300	1 155	563	592	9 146	1 472	2 455	1 605	1 260	1 087	1 267
1983	10 477	1 138	550	588	9 340	1 480	2 539	1 666	1 260	1 107	1 288
1984	10 694	1 106	532	574	9 588	1 491	2 625	1 756	1 276	1 119	1 322
1985	10 873	1 101	540	560	9 773	1 447	2 693	1 828	1 312	1 136	1 357
1986	11 033	1 088	542	545	9 945	1 430	2 762	1 893	1 341	1 145	1 374
1987	11 224	1 098	557	541	10 126	1 405	2 819	1 976	1 368	1 153	1 405
1988	11 402	1 105	561	544	10 298	1 376	2 867	2 060	1 403	1 159	1 432
1989	11 582	1 100	541	559	10 482	1 351	2 905	2 159	1 441	1 162	1 464
1990	11 904	1 144	546	598	10 760	1 410	2 995	2 360	1 435	1 114	1 446
1991	12 074	1 115	539	576	10 959	1 417	3 003	2 478	1 471	1 121	1 470
1992	12 251	1 099	542	557	11 152	1 421	2 995	2 573	1 542	1 127	1 495
1993	12 438	1 106	554	552	11 332	1 419	2 983	2 659	1 611	1 142	1 518
1994	12 621	1 125	582	543	11 496	1 410	2 963	2 738	1 692	1 156	1 538
1995	12 835	1 153	597	556	11 682	1 392	2 948	2 816	1 782	1 178	1 565
1996	13 029	1 195	615	580	11 833	1 364	2 938	2 877	1 874	1 196	1 584
1997	13 241	1 225	620	604	12 016	1 362	2 916	2 939	1 964	1 228	1 608
1998	13 446	1 243	618	624	12 203	1 380	2 886	2 991	2 053	1 268	1 626
1999	13 711	1 261	621	640	12 451	1 418	2 876	3 043	2 153	1 310	1 650
2000	13 898	1 255	620	634	12 643	1 455	2 844	3 072	2 262	1 336	1 673

See *Note* at end of table.

Table 1-6. Civilian Noninstitutional Population by Race, Hispanic Origin, Sex, and Age, 1948–2000—*Continued*

(Thousands of persons.)

Year, race, Hispanic origin, and sex	16 years and over	16 to 19 years			20 years and over						
		Total	16 to 17 years	18 to 19 years	Total	20 to 24 years	25 to 34 years	35 to 44 years	45 to 54 years	55 to 64 years	65 years and over
HISPANIC MEN											
1973	2 891	. . .	. . .	. . .	2 472	. . .	. . .	. . .	. . .	. . .	. . .
1974	3 130	. . .	. . .	. . .	2 680	. . .	. . .	. . .	. . .	. . .	. . .
1975	3 219	. . .	. . .	. . .	2 741	. . .	. . .	. . .	. . .	. . .	. . .
1976	3 241	485	251	234	2 764	494	824	579	444	260	211
1977	3 483	495	247	248	2 982	561	884	601	465	271	216
1978	3 750	525	287	238	3 228	621	934	655	484	293	240
1979	3 917	555	285	271	3 362	623	1 001	690	495	299	253
1980	4 689	653	326	327	4 036	792	1 245	760	570	367	301
1981	4 968	663	327	336	4 306	842	1 354	816	591	392	312
1982	5 203	664	324	340	4 539	882	1 450	865	607	414	321
1983	5 432	661	321	340	4 771	918	1 548	916	623	436	330
1984	5 661	656	319	337	5 005	944	1 649	973	641	457	341
1985	5 885	654	322	332	5 232	956	1 750	1 036	660	476	354
1986	6 106	655	330	325	5 451	1 006	1 787	1 088	735	466	368
1987	6 371	671	336	335	5 700	985	1 925	1 205	741	463	383
1988	6 604	683	319	364	5 921	1 003	1 963	1 268	775	516	397
1989	6 825	711	343	368	6 114	1 005	2 017	1 311	810	538	434
1990	8 041	915	431	484	7 126	1 319	2 369	1 512	890	573	463
1991	8 296	904	425	479	7 392	1 358	2 441	1 632	890	594	477
1992	8 553	899	436	463	7 655	1 306	2 547	1 728	972	603	499
1993	8 824	894	437	457	7 930	1 306	2 602	1 812	1 032	600	579
1994	9 104	926	472	454	8 178	1 346	2 627	1 871	1 076	644	614
1995	9 329	954	481	473	8 375	1 337	2 657	1 966	1 127	668	619
1996	9 604	992	485	507	8 611	1 321	2 692	2 144	1 111	712	630
1997	10 368	1 119	585	534	9 250	1 439	2 872	2 275	1 266	747	651
1998	10 734	1 161	586	575	9 573	1 462	2 907	2 377	1 342	771	714
1999	10 713	1 190	571	619	9 523	1 398	2 805	2 407	1 397	767	749
2000	11 064	1 205	575	631	9 859	1 457	2 820	2 506	1 491	826	759
HISPANIC WOMEN											
1973	3 213	. . .	. . .	. . .	2 766	. . .	. . .	. . .	. . .	. . .	. . .
1974	3 434	. . .	. . .	. . .	2 959	. . .	. . .	. . .	. . .	. . .	. . .
1975	3 644	. . .	. . .	. . .	3 161	. . .	. . .	. . .	. . .	. . .	. . .
1976	3 669	490	244	246	3 263	559	952	682	493	310	268
1977	3 879	526	266	259	3 377	602	984	682	524	317	269
1978	4 159	551	274	277	3 608	642	1 069	723	548	335	289
1979	4 291	540	259	281	3 751	674	1 117	767	520	361	313
1980	4 909	628	312	316	4 281	771	1 263	815	619	415	398
1981	5 151	638	314	324	4 513	808	1 344	864	640	441	417
1982	5 377	643	314	329	4 734	842	1 421	914	657	466	434
1983	5 597	644	313	330	4 954	872	1 497	967	675	492	451
1984	5 816	644	313	330	5 173	895	1 575	1 022	695	516	469
1985	6 029	644	316	328	5 385	908	1 652	1 081	716	539	489
1986	6 238	647	328	319	5 591	893	1 723	1 151	760	557	507
1987	6 496	661	316	345	5 835	925	1 789	1 259	751	598	513
1988	6 721	671	343	328	6 050	945	1 844	1 297	796	643	524
1989	6 965	687	329	359	6 278	945	1 936	1 347	839	644	567
1990	7 863	822	391	431	7 041	1 109	2 220	1 489	927	675	621
1991	8 130	828	394	435	7 301	1 122	2 233	1 611	989	689	657
1992	8 408	839	400	439	7 569	1 138	2 259	1 729	1 008	718	716
1993	8 708	862	418	444	7 846	1 182	2 285	1 820	1 062	724	774
1994	9 014	892	430	462	8 122	1 173	2 373	1 885	1 147	757	787
1995	9 300	918	422	496	8 382	1 191	2 393	1 999	1 167	815	818
1996	9 610	956	477	479	8 654	1 203	2 489	2 082	1 164	834	882
1997	9 953	1 003	503	500	8 950	1 184	2 533	2 178	1 315	833	907
1998	10 335	1 044	483	560	9 292	1 269	2 539	2 259	1 433	844	948
1999	10 937	1 116	542	575	9 821	1 302	2 707	2 425	1 470	947	969
2000	11 329	1 136	545	590	10 193	1 319	2 806	2 501	1 542	993	1 032

Note: Detail for the above race and Hispanic-origin groups will not sum to totals because data for the Other races group are not presented and Hispanics are included in both the White and Black population groups. See "Notes and Definitions" for information on historical comparability.

Table 1-7. Civilian Labor Force by Race, Hispanic Origin, Sex, and Age, 1948–2000

(Thousands of persons.)

Year, race, Hispanic origin, and sex	16 years and over	16 to 19 years			20 years and over						
		Total	16 to 17 years	18 to 19 years	Total	20 to 24 years	25 to 34 years	35 to 44 years	45 to 54 years	55 to 64 years	65 years and over
TOTAL											
1948	60 621	4 435	1 780	2 654	56 187	7 392	14 258	13 397	10 914	7 329	2 897
1949	61 286	4 288	1 704	2 583	57 000	7 340	14 415	13 711	11 107	7 426	3 010
1950	62 208	4 216	1 659	2 557	57 994	7 307	14 619	13 954	11 444	7 633	3 036
1951	62 017	4 103	1 743	2 360	57 914	6 594	14 668	14 100	11 739	7 796	3 020
1952	62 138	4 064	1 806	2 257	58 075	5 840	14 904	14 383	11 961	7 980	3 005
1953	63 015	4 027	1 727	2 299	58 989	5 481	14 898	15 099	12 249	8 024	3 236
1954	63 643	3 976	1 643	2 300	59 666	5 475	14 983	15 221	12 524	8 269	3 192
1955	65 023	4 092	1 711	2 382	60 931	5 666	15 058	15 400	12 992	8 513	3 305
1956	66 552	4 296	1 878	2 418	62 257	5 940	14 961	15 694	13 407	8 830	3 423
1957	66 929	4 275	1 843	2 433	62 653	6 071	14 826	15 847	13 768	8 853	3 290
1958	67 639	4 260	1 818	2 442	63 377	6 272	14 668	16 028	14 179	9 031	3 199
1959	68 369	4 492	1 971	2 522	63 876	6 413	14 435	16 127	14 518	9 227	3 158
1960	69 628	4 841	2 095	2 747	64 788	6 702	14 382	16 269	14 852	9 385	3 195
1961	70 459	4 936	1 984	2 951	65 524	6 950	14 319	16 402	15 071	9 636	3 146
1962	70 614	4 916	1 919	2 997	65 699	7 082	14 023	16 589	15 096	9 757	3 154
1963	71 833	5 139	2 171	2 966	66 695	7 473	14 050	16 788	15 338	10 006	3 041
1964	73 091	5 388	2 449	2 940	67 702	7 963	14 056	16 771	15 637	10 182	3 090
1965	74 455	5 910	2 486	3 425	68 543	8 259	14 233	16 840	15 756	10 350	3 108
1966	75 770	6 558	2 664	3 893	69 219	8 410	14 458	16 738	15 984	10 575	3 053
1967	77 347	6 521	2 734	3 786	70 825	9 010	15 055	16 703	16 172	10 792	3 097
1968	78 737	6 619	2 817	3 803	72 118	9 305	15 708	16 591	16 397	10 964	3 153
1969	80 734	6 970	3 009	3 959	73 763	9 879	16 336	16 458	16 730	11 135	3 227
1970	82 771	7 249	3 135	4 115	75 521	10 597	17 036	16 437	16 949	11 283	3 222
1971	84 382	7 470	3 192	4 278	76 913	11 331	17 714	16 305	17 024	11 390	3 149
1972	87 034	8 054	3 420	4 636	78 980	12 130	18 960	16 398	16 967	11 412	3 114
1973	89 429	8 507	3 665	4 839	80 924	12 846	20 376	16 492	16 983	11 256	2 974
1974	91 949	8 871	3 810	5 059	83 080	13 314	21 654	16 763	17 131	11 284	2 934
1975	93 775	8 870	3 740	5 131	84 904	13 750	22 804	16 003	17 084	11 346	2 956
1976	96 158	9 056	3 767	5 288	87 103	14 284	24 203	17 317	16 982	11 422	2 895
1977	99 009	9 351	3 919	5 431	89 658	14 825	25 500	17 943	16 878	11 577	2 934
1978	102 251	9 652	4 127	5 526	92 598	15 370	26 703	18 821	16 891	11 744	3 070
1979	104 962	9 638	4 079	5 559	95 325	15 769	27 938	19 685	16 897	11 931	3 104
1980	106 940	9 378	3 883	5 496	97 561	15 922	29 227	20 463	16 910	11 985	3 054
1981	108 670	8 988	3 647	5 340	99 682	16 099	30 392	21 211	16 970	11 969	3 042
1982	110 204	8 526	3 330	5 189	101 679	16 082	31 186	22 431	16 889	12 062	3 030
1983	111 550	8 171	3 073	5 098	103 379	16 052	31 834	23 611	16 851	11 992	3 040
1984	113 544	7 943	3 050	4 894	105 601	16 046	32 723	24 933	17 006	11 961	2 933
1985	115 461	7 901	3 154	4 747	107 560	15 718	33 550	26 073	17 322	11 991	2 907
1986	117 834	7 926	3 287	4 639	109 908	15 441	34 591	27 232	17 739	11 894	3 010
1987	119 865	7 988	3 384	4 604	111 878	14 977	35 233	28 460	18 210	11 877	3 119
1988	121 669	8 031	3 286	4 745	113 638	14 505	35 503	29 435	19 104	11 808	3 284
1989	123 869	7 954	3 125	4 828	115 916	14 180	35 896	30 601	19 916	11 877	3 446
1990	125 840	7 792	2 937	4 856	118 047	14 700	35 929	32 145	20 248	11 575	3 451
1991	126 346	7 265	2 789	4 476	119 082	14 548	35 507	33 312	20 828	11 473	3 413
1992	128 105	7 096	2 769	4 327	121 009	14 521	35 369	33 899	22 160	11 587	3 473
1993	129 200	7 170	2 831	4 338	122 030	14 354	34 780	34 562	23 296	11 599	3 439
1994	131 056	7 481	3 134	4 347	123 576	14 131	34 353	35 226	24 318	11 713	3 834
1995	132 304	7 765	3 225	4 540	124 539	13 688	34 198	35 751	25 223	11 860	3 819
1996	133 943	7 806	3 263	4 543	126 137	13 377	33 833	36 556	26 397	12 146	3 828
1997	136 297	7 932	3 237	4 695	128 365	13 532	33 380	37 326	27 574	12 665	3 887
1998	137 673	8 256	3 335	4 921	129 417	13 638	32 813	37 536	28 368	13 215	3 847
1999	139 368	8 333	3 337	4 996	131 034	13 933	32 143	37 882	29 388	13 682	4 005
2000	140 863	8 369	3 284	5 085	132 495	14 346	31 669	37 838	30 467	13 974	4 200

See *Note* at end of table.

Table 1-7. Civilian Labor Force by Race, Hispanic Origin, Sex, and Age, 1948–2000—*Continued*

(Thousands of persons.)

Year, race, Hispanic origin, and sex	16 years and over	16 to 19 years			20 years and over						
		Total	16 to 17 years	18 to 19 years	Total	20 to 24 years	25 to 34 years	35 to 44 years	45 to 54 years	55 to 64 years	65 years and over
WHITE											
1954	56 816	3 501	1 448	2 054	53 315	4 752	13 226	13 540	11 258	7 591	2 946
1955	58 085	3 598	1 511	2 087	54 487	4 941	13 267	13 729	11 680	7 810	3 062
1956	59 428	3 771	1 656	2 113	55 657	5 194	13 154	14 000	12 061	8 080	3 166
1957	59 754	3 775	1 637	2 135	55 979	5 283	13 044	14 117	12 382	8 091	3 049
1958	60 293	3 757	1 615	2 144	56 536	5 449	12 884	14 257	12 727	8 254	2 964
1959	60 952	4 000	1 775	2 225	56 952	5 544	12 670	14 355	13 048	8 411	2 925
1960	61 915	4 275	1 871	2 405	57 640	5 787	12 594	14 450	13 322	8 522	2 964
1961	62 656	4 362	1 767	2 594	58 294	6 026	12 503	14 557	13 517	8 773	2 917
1962	62 750	4 354	1 709	2 645	58 396	6 164	12 218	14 695	13 551	8 856	2 912
1963	63 830	4 559	1 950	2 608	59 271	6 537	12 229	14 859	13 789	9 067	2 790
1964	64 921	4 784	2 211	2 572	60 137	6 952	12 235	14 852	14 043	9 239	2 817
1965	66 137	5 267	2 221	3 044	60 870	7 189	12 391	14 900	14 162	9 392	2 839
1966	67 276	5 827	2 367	3 460	61 449	7 324	12 591	14 785	14 370	9 583	2 793
1967	68 699	5 749	2 432	3 318	62 950	7 886	13 123	14 765	14 545	9 817	2 821
1968	69 976	5 839	2 519	3 320	64 137	8 109	13 740	14 683	14 756	9 968	2 884
1969	71 778	6 168	2 698	3 470	65 611	8 614	14 289	14 564	15 057	10 132	2 954
1970	73 556	6 442	2 824	3 617	67 113	9 238	14 896	14 525	15 269	10 255	2 930
1971	74 963	6 681	2 894	3 787	68 282	9 889	15 445	14 374	15 343	10 351	2 880
1972	77 275	7 193	3 096	4 098	70 082	10 605	16 584	14 399	15 283	10 402	2 809
1973	79 151	7 579	3 320	4 260	71 572	11 182	17 764	14 440	15 256	10 240	2 687
1974	81 281	7 899	3 441	4 459	73 381	11 600	18 862	14 644	15 375	10 241	2 656
1975	82 831	7 899	3 375	4 525	74 932	12 019	19 897	14 753	15 308	10 287	2 668
1976	84 767	8 088	3 410	4 679	76 678	12 444	20 990	15 088	15 187	10 371	2 599
1977	87 141	8 352	3 562	4 790	78 789	12 892	22 099	15 604	15 053	10 495	2 647
1978	89 634	8 555	3 715	4 839	81 079	13 309	23 067	16 353	15 004	10 602	2 745
1979	91 923	8 548	3 668	4 881	83 375	13 632	24 101	17 123	14 965	10 767	2 787
1980	93 600	8 312	3 485	4 827	85 286	13 769	25 181	17 811	14 956	10 812	2 759
1981	95 052	7 962	3 274	4 688	87 089	13 926	26 208	18 445	14 993	10 764	2 753
1982	96 143	7 518	3 001	4 518	88 625	13 866	26 814	19 491	14 879	10 832	2 742
1983	97 021	7 186	2 765	4 421	89 835	13 816	27 237	20 488	14 798	10 732	2 766
1984	98 492	6 952	2 720	4 232	91 540	13 733	27 958	21 588	14 899	10 701	2 660
1985	99 926	6 841	2 777	4 065	93 085	13 469	28 640	22 591	15 101	10 679	2 605
1986	101 801	6 862	2 895	3 967	94 939	13 176	29 497	23 571	15 379	10 583	2 732
1987	103 290	6 893	2 963	3 931	96 396	12 764	29 956	24 581	15 792	10 497	2 806
1988	104 756	6 940	2 861	4 079	97 815	12 311	30 167	25 358	16 573	10 462	2 943
1989	106 355	6 809	2 685	4 124	99 546	11 940	30 388	26 312	17 278	10 533	3 094
1990	107 447	6 683	2 543	4 140	100 764	12 397	30 174	27 265	17 515	10 290	3 123
1991	107 743	6 245	2 432	3 813	101 498	12 248	29 794	28 213	18 028	10 129	3 086
1992	108 837	6 022	2 388	3 633	102 815	12 187	29 518	28 580	19 200	10 196	3 135
1993	109 700	6 105	2 458	3 647	103 595	11 987	29 027	29 056	20 181	10 215	3 129
1994	111 082	6 357	2 681	3 677	104 725	11 688	28 580	29 626	21 026	10 319	3 486
1995	111 950	6 545	2 749	3 796	105 404	11 266	28 325	30 112	21 804	10 432	3 466
1996	113 108	6 607	2 780	3 826	106 502	11 003	27 901	30 683	22 781	10 648	3 485
1997	114 693	6 720	2 779	3 941	107 973	11 127	27 362	31 171	23 709	11 086	3 517
1998	115 415	6 965	2 860	4 105	108 450	11 244	26 707	31 221	24 282	11 548	3 448
1999	116 509	7 048	2 849	4 199	109 461	11 436	25 978	31 391	25 102	11 960	3 595
2000	117 574	7 075	2 800	4 275	110 499	11 762	25 482	31 346	25 968	12 192	3 749

See *Note* at end of table.

Table 1-7. Civilian Labor Force by Race, Hispanic Origin, Sex, and Age, 1948–2000—*Continued*

(Thousands of persons.)

Year, race, Hispanic origin, and sex	16 years and over	16 to 19 years			20 years and over						
		Total	16 to 17 years	18 to 19 years	Total	20 to 24 years	25 to 34 years	35 to 44 years	45 to 54 years	55 to 64 years	65 years and over
BLACK											
1972	8 707	788	293	496	7 919	1 393	2 107	1 735	1 496	909	281
1973	8 976	833	307	525	8 143	1 489	2 242	1 741	1 513	901	258
1974	9 167	851	317	534	8 317	1 492	2 358	1 777	1 517	917	253
1975	9 263	838	312	524	8 426	1 477	2 466	1 775	1 519	929	258
1976	9 561	837	304	532	8 724	1 544	2 646	1 824	1 518	925	268
1977	9 932	861	304	557	9 072	1 641	2 798	1 894	1 530	943	267
1978	10 432	930	341	589	9 501	1 739	2 961	1 975	1 560	978	289
1979	10 678	912	340	572	9 766	1 793	3 094	2 039	1 584	974	281
1980	10 865	891	326	565	9 975	1 802	3 259	2 081	1 596	978	257
1981	11 086	862	308	554	10 224	1 828	3 365	2 164	1 608	1 009	249
1982	11 331	824	268	556	10 507	1 849	3 492	2 303	1 610	1 012	243
1983	11 647	809	248	561	10 838	1 871	3 675	2 406	1 630	1 032	224
1984	12 033	827	268	558	11 206	1 926	3 800	2 565	1 671	1 020	224
1985	12 364	889	311	578	11 476	1 854	3 888	2 681	1 742	1 059	252
1986	12 654	883	322	562	11 770	1 881	4 028	2 793	1 793	1 051	224
1987	12 993	899	336	563	12 094	1 818	4 147	2 942	1 838	1 098	251
1988	13 205	889	344	545	12 316	1 782	4 226	3 069	1 894	1 069	276
1989	13 497	925	353	572	12 573	1 789	4 295	3 227	1 954	1 023	285
1990	13 740	866	306	560	12 874	1 758	4 307	3 566	2 003	977	262
1991	13 797	774	266	508	13 023	1 750	4 254	3 719	2 042	1 001	256
1992	14 162	816	285	532	13 346	1 763	4 309	3 843	2 142	1 029	259
1993	14 225	807	283	524	13 418	1 764	4 232	3 960	2 212	1 013	237
1994	14 502	852	351	501	13 650	1 800	4 199	4 068	2 308	1 007	267
1995	14 817	911	366	545	13 906	1 754	4 267	4 165	2 404	1 046	271
1996	15 134	923	366	556	14 211	1 738	4 305	4 287	2 553	1 073	255
1997	15 529	933	352	580	14 596	1 783	4 329	4 401	2 724	1 093	265
1998	15 982	1 017	370	646	14 966	1 797	4 332	4 531	2 863	1 163	278
1999	[illegible]	959	352	607	15 406	1 866	4 430	4 653	2 992	1 180	285
2000	16 603	967	366	602	15 635	1 932	4 328	4 665	3 101	1 227	[illegible]
HISPANIC											
1973	3 673	407	...	...	...	...	...	...	...	...	...
1974	4 012	442	...	...	...	...	...	...	...	...	...
1975	4 171	444	...	...	...	...	...	...	...	...	...
1976	4 205	447	176	285	3 820	729	1 248	875	625	294	48
1977	4 536	493	184	305	4 059	813	1 325	916	656	293	55
1978	4 979	533	221	312	4 446	901	1 446	1 008	701	323	67
1979	5 219	551	207	343	4 668	960	1 532	1 062	704	339	72
1980	6 146	645	241	404	5 502	1 136	1 843	1 163	860	414	85
1981	6 492	603	215	388	5 888	1 231	2 015	1 239	886	430	87
1982	6 734	585	192	393	6 148	1 251	2 163	1 313	891	444	85
1983	7 033	590	189	401	6 442	1 282	2 267	1 380	931	495	86
1984	7 451	618	209	409	6 833	1 325	2 436	1 509	954	524	84
1985	7 698	579	199	379	7 119	1 358	2 571	1 595	985	527	82
1986	8 076	571	203	368	7 505	1 414	2 685	1 713	1 097	511	84
1987	8 541	610	206	404	7 931	1 425	2 890	1 904	1 086	545	81
1988	8 982	671	234	437	8 311	1 486	2 957	1 996	1 147	621	103
1989	9 323	680	224	456	8 643	1 483	3 118	2 092	1 205	625	120
1990	10 720	829	276	554	9 891	1 839	3 590	2 386	1 320	647	110
1991	10 920	781	249	532	10 139	1 835	3 596	2 539	1 376	681	111
1992	11 338	796	263	533	10 542	1 815	3 740	2 735	1 442	687	122
1993	11 610	771	246	525	10 839	1 811	3 800	2 865	1 534	684	145
1994	11 975	807	285	522	11 168	1 863	3 865	2 965	1 626	698	151
1995	12 267	850	291	559	11 417	1 818	3 943	3 113	1 671	720	152
1996	12 774	845	284	561	11 929	1 845	4 054	3 361	1 697	806	166
1997	13 796	911	315	596	12 884	2 004	4 298	3 601	1 945	850	186
1998	14 317	1 007	320	688	13 310	2 077	4 372	3 707	2 090	894	169
1999	14 665	1 049	333	717	13 616	2 052	4 330	3 929	2 178	927	199
2000	15 368	1 083	338	745	14 285	2 155	4 485	4 086	2 357	983	218

See *Note* at end of table.

Table 1-7. Civilian Labor Force by Race, Hispanic Origin, Sex, and Age, 1948–2000—*Continued*

(Thousands of persons.)

Year, race, Hispanic origin, and sex	16 years and over	16 to 19 years			20 years and over						
		Total	16 to 17 years	18 to 19 years	Total	20 to 24 years	25 to 34 years	35 to 44 years	45 to 54 years	55 to 64 years	65 years and over
MEN											
1948	43 286	2 600	1 109	1 490	40 687	4 673	10 327	9 596	7 943	5 764	2 384
1949	43 498	2 477	1 056	1 420	41 022	4 682	10 418	9 722	8 008	5 748	2 454
1950	43 819	2 504	1 048	1 456	41 316	4 632	10 527	9 793	8 117	5 794	2 453
1951	43 001	2 347	1 081	1 266	40 655	3 935	10 375	9 799	8 205	5 873	2 469
1952	42 869	2 312	1 101	1 210	40 558	3 338	10 585	9 945	8 326	5 949	2 416
1953	43 633	2 320	1 070	1 249	41 315	3 053	10 736	10 437	8 570	5 975	2 543
1954	43 965	2 295	1 023	1 272	41 669	3 051	10 771	10 513	8 702	6 105	2 526
1955	44 475	2 369	1 070	1 299	42 106	3 221	10 806	10 595	8 838	6 122	2 526
1956	45 091	2 433	1 142	1 291	42 658	3 485	10 685	10 663	9 002	6 220	2 602
1957	45 197	2 415	1 127	1 289	42 780	3 629	10 571	10 731	9 153	6 222	2 477
1958	45 521	2 428	1 133	1 295	43 092	3 771	10 475	10 843	9 320	6 304	2 378
1959	45 886	2 596	1 206	1 390	43 289	3 940	10 346	10 899	9 438	6 345	2 322
1960	46 388	2 787	1 290	1 496	43 603	4 123	10 251	10 967	9 574	6 399	2 287
1961	46 653	2 794	1 210	1 583	43 860	4 253	10 176	11 012	9 668	6 530	2 220
1962	46 600	2 770	1 178	1 592	43 831	4 279	9 920	11 115	9 715	6 560	2 241
1963	47 129	2 907	1 321	1 586	44 222	4 514	9 876	11 187	9 836	6 675	2 135
1964	47 679	3 074	1 499	1 575	44 604	4 754	9 876	11 156	9 956	6 741	2 124
1965	48 255	3 397	1 532	1 866	44 857	4 894	9 903	11 120	10 045	6 763	2 132
1966	48 471	3 685	1 609	2 075	44 788	4 820	9 948	10 983	10 100	6 847	2 089
1967	48 987	3 634	1 658	1 976	45 354	5 043	10 207	10 859	10 189	6 937	2 118
1968	49 533	3 681	1 687	1 995	45 852	5 070	10 610	10 725	10 267	7 026	2 154
1969	50 221	3 870	1 770	2 100	46 351	5 202	10 941	10 556	10 344	7 058	2 170
1970	51 228	4 008	1 810	2 199	47 220	5 717	11 327	10 469	10 417	7 126	2 165
1971	52 180	4 172	1 856	2 315	48 009	6 233	11 731	10 347	10 451	7 155	2 090
1972	53 555	4 476	1 955	2 522	49 079	6 766	12 350	10 372	10 412	7 155	2 026
1973	54 624	4 693	2 073	2 618	49 932	7 183	13 056	10 338	10 416	7 028	1 913
1974	55 739	4 861	2 138	2 721	50 879	7 387	13 665	10 401	10 431	7 063	1 932
1975	56 299	4 805	2 065	2 740	51 494	7 565	14 192	10 398	10 401	7 023	1 914
1976	57 174	4 886	2 069	2 817	52 288	7 866	14 784	10 500	10 293	7 020	1 826
1977	58 396	5 048	2 155	2 893	53 348	8 109	15 353	10 771	10 158	7 100	1 857
1978	59 620	5 149	2 227	2 923	54 471	8 327	15 814	11 159	10 083	7 151	1 936
1979	60 726	5 111	2 192	2 919	55 615	8 535	16 387	11 531	10 008	7 212	1 943
1980	61 453	4 999	2 102	2 897	56 455	8 607	16 971	11 836	9 905	7 242	1 893
1981	61 974	4 777	1 957	2 820	57 197	8 648	17 479	12 166	9 868	7 170	1 866
1982	62 450	4 470	1 776	2 694	57 980	8 604	17 793	12 781	9 784	7 174	1 845
1983	63 047	4 303	1 621	2 682	58 744	8 601	18 038	13 398	9 746	7 119	1 842
1984	63 835	4 134	1 591	2 542	59 701	8 594	18 488	14 037	9 776	7 050	1 755
1985	64 411	4 134	1 663	2 471	60 277	8 283	18 808	14 506	9 870	7 060	1 750
1986	65 422	4 102	1 707	2 395	61 320	8 148	19 383	15 029	9 994	6 954	1 811
1987	66 207	4 112	1 745	2 367	62 095	7 837	19 656	15 587	10 176	6 940	1 899
1988	66 927	4 159	1 714	2 445	62 768	7 594	19 742	16 074	10 566	6 831	1 960
1989	67 840	4 136	1 630	2 505	63 704	7 458	19 905	16 622	10 919	6 783	2 017
1990	69 011	4 094	1 537	2 557	64 916	7 866	19 872	17 481	11 103	6 627	1 967
1991	69 168	3 795	1 452	2 343	65 374	7 820	19 641	18 077	11 362	6 550	1 924
1992	69 964	3 751	1 453	2 297	66 213	7 770	19 495	18 347	12 040	6 551	2 010
1993	70 404	3 762	1 497	2 265	66 642	7 671	19 214	18 713	12 562	6 502	1 980
1994	70 817	3 896	1 630	2 266	66 921	7 540	18 854	18 966	12 962	6 423	2 176
1995	71 360	4 036	1 668	2 368	67 324	7 338	18 670	19 189	13 421	6 504	2 201
1996	72 087	4 043	1 665	2 378	68 044	7 104	18 430	19 602	13 967	6 693	2 247
1997	73 261	4 095	1 676	2 419	69 166	7 184	18 110	20 058	14 564	6 952	2 298
1998	73 959	4 244	1 728	2 516	69 715	7 221	17 796	20 242	14 963	7 253	2 240
1999	74 512	4 318	1 732	2 587	70 194	7 291	17 318	20 382	15 394	7 477	2 333
2000	75 247	4 317	1 688	2 629	70 930	7 558	17 073	20 334	15 951	7 574	2 439

See *Note* at end of table.

Table 1-7. Civilian Labor Force by Race, Hispanic Origin, Sex, and Age, 1948–2000—*Continued*

(Thousands of persons.)

Year, race, Hispanic origin, and sex	16 years and over	16 to 19 years			20 years and over						
		Total	16 to 17 years	18 to 19 years	Total	20 to 24 years	25 to 34 years	35 to 44 years	45 to 54 years	55 to 64 years	65 years and over
WOMEN											
1948	17 335	1 835	671	1 164	15 500	2 719	3 931	3 801	2 971	1 565	513
1949	17 788	1 811	648	1 163	15 978	2 658	3 997	3 989	3 099	1 678	556
1950	18 389	1 712	611	1 101	16 678	2 675	4 092	4 161	3 327	1 839	583
1951	19 016	1 756	662	1 094	17 259	2 659	4 293	4 301	3 534	1 923	551
1952	19 269	1 752	705	1 047	17 517	2 502	4 319	4 438	3 635	2 031	589
1953	19 382	1 707	657	1 050	17 674	2 428	4 162	4 662	3 679	2 049	693
1954	19 678	1 681	620	1 028	17 997	2 424	4 212	4 708	3 822	2 164	666
1955	20 548	1 723	641	1 083	18 825	2 445	4 252	4 805	4 154	2 391	779
1956	21 461	1 863	736	1 127	19 599	2 455	4 276	5 031	4 405	2 610	821
1957	21 732	1 860	716	1 144	19 873	2 442	4 255	5 116	4 615	2 631	813
1958	22 118	1 832	685	1 147	20 285	2 501	4 193	5 185	4 859	2 727	821
1959	22 483	1 896	765	1 132	20 587	2 473	4 089	5 228	5 080	2 882	836
1960	23 240	2 054	805	1 251	21 185	2 579	4 131	5 302	5 278	2 986	908
1961	23 806	2 142	774	1 368	21 664	2 697	4 143	5 390	5 403	3 106	926
1962	24 014	2 146	741	1 405	21 868	2 803	4 103	5 474	5 381	3 197	913
1963	24 704	2 232	850	1 380	22 473	2 959	4 174	5 601	5 502	3 331	906
1964	25 412	2 314	950	1 365	23 098	3 209	4 180	5 615	5 681	3 441	966
1965	26 200	2 513	954	1 559	23 686	3 365	4 330	5 720	5 711	3 587	976
1966	27 299	2 873	1 055	1 818	24 431	3 590	4 510	5 755	5 884	3 728	964
1967	28 360	2 887	1 076	1 810	25 475	3 966	4 848	5 844	5 983	3 855	979
1968	29 204	2 938	1 130	1 808	26 266	4 235	5 098	5 866	6 130	3 939	999
1969	30 513	3 100	1 239	1 859	27 413	4 597	5 395	5 902	6 386	4 077	1 057
1970	31 543	3 241	1 325	1 916	28 301	4 880	5 708	5 968	6 532	4 157	1 056
1971	32 202	3 298	1 336	1 963	28 904	5 098	5 983	5 957	6 573	4 234	1 059
1972	33 479	3 578	1 464	2 114	29 901	5 364	6 610	6 027	6 555	4 257	1 089
1973	34 804	3 814	1 592	2 221	30 991	5 663	7 320	6 154	6 567	4 228	1 061
1974	36 211	4 010	1 672	2 338	32 201	5 926	7 989	6 362	6 699	4 221	1 002
1975	37 475	4 065	1 674	2 391	33 410	6 185	8 870	6 505	6 683	4 323	1 042
1976	38 983	4 170	1 698	2 470	34 814	6 418	9 419	6 817	6 689	4 402	1 000
1977	40 613	4 303	1 765	2 538	36 310	6 717	10 149	7 171	6 720	4 477	1 078
1978	42 631	4 503	1 900	2 603	38 128	7 043	10 888	7 662	6 807	4 593	1 134
1979	44 235	4 527	1 887	2 639	39 708	7 234	11 551	8 154	6 889	4 719	1 161
1980	45 487	4 381	1 781	2 599	41 106	7 315	12 257	8 627	7 004	4 742	1 161
1981	46 696	4 211	1 691	2 520	42 485	7 451	12 912	9 045	7 101	4 708	1 170
1982	47 755	4 056	1 561	2 495	43 699	7 477	13 393	9 651	7 105	4 888	1 185
1983	48 503	3 868	1 452	2 416	44 636	7 451	13 796	10 213	7 105	4 873	1 198
1984	49 709	3 810	1 458	2 351	45 900	7 451	14 234	10 896	7 230	4 911	1 177
1985	51 050	3 767	1 491	2 276	47 283	7 434	14 742	11 567	7 452	4 932	1 156
1986	52 413	3 824	1 580	2 244	48 589	7 293	15 208	12 204	7 746	4 940	1 199
1987	53 658	3 875	1 638	2 237	49 783	7 140	15 577	12 873	8 034	4 937	1 221
1988	54 742	3 872	1 572	2 300	50 870	6 910	15 761	13 361	8 537	4 977	1 324
1989	56 030	3 818	1 495	2 323	52 212	6 721	15 990	13 980	8 997	5 095	1 429
1990	56 829	3 698	1 400	2 298	53 131	6 834	16 058	14 663	9 145	4 948	1 483
1991	57 178	3 470	1 337	2 133	53 708	6 728	15 867	15 235	9 465	4 924	1 489
1992	58 141	3 345	1 316	2 030	54 796	6 750	15 875	15 552	10 120	5 035	1 464
1993	58 795	3 408	1 335	2 073	55 388	6 683	15 566	15 849	10 733	5 097	1 459
1994	60 239	3 585	1 504	2 081	56 655	6 592	15 499	16 259	11 357	5 289	1 658
1995	60 944	3 729	1 557	2 172	57 215	6 349	15 528	16 562	11 801	5 356	1 618
1996	61 857	3 763	1 599	2 164	58 094	6 273	15 403	16 954	12 430	5 452	1 581
1997	63 036	3 837	1 561	2 277	59 198	6 348	15 271	17 268	13 010	5 713	1 590
1998	63 714	4 012	1 607	2 405	59 702	6 418	15 017	17 294	13 405	5 962	1 607
1999	64 855	4 015	1 606	2 410	60 840	6 643	14 826	17 501	13 994	6 204	1 673
2000	65 616	4 051	1 596	2 456	61 565	6 788	14 596	17 504	14 515	6 400	1 762

See *Note* at end of table.

Table 1-7. Civilian Labor Force by Race, Hispanic Origin, Sex, and Age, 1948–2000—*Continued*

(Thousands of persons.)

Year, race, Hispanic origin, and sex	16 years and over	16 to 19 years			20 years and over						
		Total	16 to 17 years	18 to 19 years	Total	20 to 24 years	25 to 34 years	35 to 44 years	45 to 54 years	55 to 64 years	65 years and over
WHITE MEN											
1954	39 759	1 989	896	1 095	37 770	2 654	9 695	9 516	7 913	5 653	2 339
1955	40 197	2 056	935	1 121	38 141	2 803	9 721	9 597	8 025	5 654	2 343
1956	40 734	2 114	1 002	1 110	38 620	3 036	9 595	9 661	8 175	5 736	2 417
1957	40 826	2 108	992	1 114	38 718	3 152	9 483	9 719	8 317	5 735	2 307
1958	41 080	2 116	1 001	1 116	38 964	3 278	9 386	9 822	8 465	5 800	2 213
1959	41 397	2 279	1 077	1 202	39 118	3 409	9 261	9 876	8 581	5 833	2 158
1960	41 743	2 433	1 140	1 293	39 310	3 559	9 153	9 919	8 689	5 861	2 129
1961	41 986	2 439	1 067	1 372	39 547	3 681	9 072	9 961	8 776	5 988	2 068
1962	41 931	2 432	1 041	1 391	39 499	3 726	8 846	10 029	8 820	5 995	2 082
1963	42 404	2 563	1 183	1 380	39 841	3 955	8 805	10 079	8 944	6 090	1 967
1964	42 894	2 716	1 345	1 371	40 178	4 166	8 800	10 055	9 053	6 161	1 942
1965	43 400	2 999	1 359	1 639	40 401	4 279	8 824	10 023	9 130	6 188	1 959
1966	43 572	3 253	1 423	1 830	40 319	4 200	8 859	9 892	9 189	6 250	1 928
1967	44 041	3 191	1 464	1 727	40 851	4 416	9 102	9 785	9 260	6 348	1 944
1968	44 553	3 236	1 504	1 732	41 318	4 432	9 477	9 662	9 340	6 427	1 981
1969	45 185	3 413	1 583	1 830	41 772	4 615	9 773	9 509	9 413	6 467	1 996
1970	46 035	3 551	1 629	1 922	42 483	4 988	10 099	9 414	9 487	6 517	1 978
1971	46 904	3 719	1 681	2 039	43 185	5 448	10 444	9 294	9 528	6 550	1 922
1972	48 118	3 980	1 758	2 223	44 138	5 937	11 039	9 278	9 473	6 562	1 846
1973	48 920	4 174	1 875	2 300	44 747	6 274	11 621	9 212	9 445	6 452	1 740
1974	49 843	4 312	1 922	2 391	45 532	6 470	12 135	9 246	9 455	6 464	1 759
1975	50 324	4 290	1 871	2 418	46 034	6 642	12 579	9 231	9 415	6 425	1 742
1976	51 033	4 357	1 869	2 489	46 675	6 890	13 092	9 289	9 310	6 437	1 657
1977	52 033	4 496	1 949	2 548	47 537	7 097	13 575	9 509	9 175	6 492	1 688
1978	52 955	4 565	2 002	2 563	48 390	7 274	13 939	9 858	9 068	6 508	1 744
1979	53 856	4 537	1 974	2 563	49 320	7 421	14 415	10 183	8 968	6 571	1 761
1980	54 473	4 424	1 881	2 543	50 049	7 479	14 893	10 455	8 877	6 618	1 727
1981	54 895	4 224	1 751	2 473	50 671	7 521	15 340	10 740	8 836	6 530	1 704
1982	55 133	3 933	1 602	2 331	51 200	7 438	15 549	11 289	8 727	6 520	1 677
1983	55 480	3 764	1 452	2 312	51 716	7 406	15 707	11 817	8 649	6 446	1 691
1984	56 062	3 609	1 420	2 189	52 453	7 370	16 037	12 348	8 683	6 410	1 606
1985	56 472	3 576	1 467	2 109	52 895	7 122	16 306	12 767	8 730	6 376	1 595
1986	57 217	3 542	1 502	2 040	53 675	6 986	16 769	13 207	8 791	6 260	1 663
1987	57 779	3 547	1 524	2 023	54 232	6 717	16 963	13 674	8 945	6 200	1 733
1988	58 317	3 583	1 487	2 095	54 734	6 468	17 018	14 068	9 285	6 108	1 787
1989	58 988	3 546	1 401	2 146	55 441	6 316	17 077	14 516	9 615	6 082	1 835
1990	59 638	3 522	1 333	2 189	56 116	6 688	16 920	15 026	9 713	5 957	1 811
1991	59 656	3 269	1 266	2 003	56 387	6 619	16 709	15 523	9 926	5 847	1 763
1992	60 168	3 192	1 260	1 932	56 976	6 542	16 512	15 701	10 570	5 821	1 830
1993	60 484	3 200	1 292	1 908	57 284	6 449	16 244	15 971	11 010	5 784	1 825
1994	60 727	3 315	1 403	1 912	57 411	6 294	15 879	16 188	11 327	5 726	1 998
1995	61 146	3 427	1 429	1 998	57 719	6 096	15 669	16 414	11 730	5 809	2 000
1996	61 783	3 444	1 421	2 023	58 340	5 922	15 475	16 728	12 217	5 943	2 054
1997	62 639	3 513	1 440	2 073	59 126	6 029	15 120	17 019	12 710	6 154	2 094
1998	63 034	3 614	1 487	2 127	59 421	6 063	14 770	17 157	13 003	6 415	2 013
1999	63 413	3 666	1 478	2 188	59 747	6 151	14 292	17 201	13 368	6 618	2 117
2000	63 861	3 679	1 439	2 240	60 182	6 308	14 043	17 158	13 783	6 692	2 198

See *Note* at end of table.

Table 1-7. Civilian Labor Force by Race, Hispanic Origin, Sex, and Age, 1948–2000—*Continued*

(Thousands of persons.)

Year, race, Hispanic origin, and sex	16 years and over	16 to 19 years			20 years and over						
		Total	16 to 17 years	18 to 19 years	Total	20 to 24 years	25 to 34 years	35 to 44 years	45 to 54 years	55 to 64 years	65 years and over
WHITE WOMEN											
1954	17 057	1 512	552	959	15 545	2 098	3 531	4 024	3 345	1 938	607
1955	17 888	1 542	576	966	16 346	2 138	3 546	4 132	3 655	2 156	719
1956	18 694	1 657	654	1 003	17 037	2 158	3 559	4 339	3 886	2 344	749
1957	18 928	1 667	645	1 021	17 261	2 131	3 561	4 398	4 065	2 356	742
1958	19 213	1 641	614	1 028	17 572	2 171	3 498	4 435	4 262	2 454	751
1959	19 555	1 721	698	1 023	17 834	2 135	3 409	4 479	4 467	2 578	767
1960	20 172	1 842	731	1 112	18 330	2 228	3 441	4 531	4 633	2 661	835
1961	20 670	1 923	700	1 222	18 747	2 345	3 431	4 596	4 741	2 785	849
1962	20 819	1 922	668	1 254	18 897	2 438	3 372	4 666	4 731	2 861	830
1963	21 426	1 996	767	1 228	19 430	2 582	3 424	4 780	4 845	2 977	823
1964	22 027	2 068	866	1 201	19 959	2 786	3 435	4 797	4 990	3 078	875
1965	22 737	2 268	862	1 405	20 469	2 910	3 567	4 877	5 032	3 204	880
1966	23 704	2 574	944	1 630	21 130	3 124	3 732	4 893	5 181	3 333	865
1967	24 658	2 558	968	1 591	22 100	3 471	4 021	4 980	5 285	3 469	877
1968	25 423	2 603	1 015	1 588	22 821	3 677	4 263	5 021	5 416	3 541	903
1969	26 593	2 755	1 115	1 640	23 839	3 999	4 516	5 055	5 644	3 665	958
1970	27 521	2 891	1 195	1 695	24 630	4 250	4 797	5 111	5 781	3 738	952
1971	28 060	2 962	1 213	1 748	25 097	4 441	5 001	5 080	5 816	3 801	958
1972	29 157	3 213	1 338	1 875	25 945	4 668	5 544	5 121	5 810	3 839	963
1973	30 231	3 405	1 445	1 960	26 825	4 908	6 143	5 228	5 811	3 788	947
1974	31 437	3 588	1 520	2 068	27 850	5 131	6 727	5 399	5 920	3 777	897
1975	32 508	3 610	1 504	2 107	28 898	5 378	7 318	5 522	5 892	3 862	926
1976	33 735	3 731	1 541	2 189	30 004	5 554	7 898	5 799	5 877	3 935	940
1977	35 108	3 856	1 614	2 243	31 253	5 795	8 523	6 095	5 877	4 003	959
1978	36 679	3 990	1 713	2 276	32 689	6 035	9 128	6 495	5 936	4 094	1 001
1979	38 067	4 011	1 694	2 318	34 056	6 211	9 687	6 940	5 997	4 196	1 024
1980	39 127	3 888	1 605	2 284	35 239	6 290	10 289	7 356	6 079	4 194	1 032
1981	40 157	3 735	1 520	2 216	36 418	6 406	10 868	7 704	6 157	4 235	1 049
1982	41 010	3 585	1 399	2 186	37 425	6 428	11 264	8 202	6 152	4 312	1 065
1983	41 541	3 422	1 314	2 109	38 119	6 410	11 530	8 670	6 149	4 285	1 074
1984	42 431	3 343	1 300	2 043	39 087	6 363	11 922	9 240	6 217	4 292	1 054
1985	43 455	3 265	1 310	1 955	40 190	6 348	12 334	9 824	6 371	4 303	1 010
1986	44 584	3 320	1 393	1 927	41 264	6 191	12 729	10 364	6 588	4 323	1 069
1987	45 510	3 347	1 439	1 908	42 164	6 047	12 993	10 907	6 847	4 297	1 073
1988	46 439	3 358	1 374	1 984	43 081	5 844	13 149	11 291	7 288	4 354	1 156
1989	47 367	3 262	1 284	1 978	44 105	5 625	13 311	11 796	7 663	4 451	1 259
1990	47 809	3 161	1 210	1 951	44 648	5 709	13 254	12 239	7 802	4 333	1 312
1991	48 087	2 976	1 166	1 810	45 111	5 629	13 085	12 689	8 101	4 282	1 324
1992	48 669	2 830	1 128	1 702	45 839	5 645	13 006	12 879	8 630	4 375	1 305
1993	49 216	2 905	1 167	1 739	46 311	5 539	12 783	13 085	9 171	4 430	1 304
1994	50 356	3 042	1 278	1 764	47 314	5 394	12 702	13 439	9 699	4 593	1 487
1995	50 804	3 118	1 320	1 798	47 686	5 170	12 656	13 697	10 074	4 622	1 466
1996	51 325	3 163	1 360	1 803	48 162	5 081	12 426	13 955	10 563	4 706	1 431
1997	52 054	3 207	1 339	1 867	48 847	5 099	12 242	14 153	10 999	4 932	1 422
1998	52 380	3 351	1 373	1 977	49 029	5 180	11 937	14 064	11 279	5 133	1 435
1999	53 096	3 382	1 371	2 010	49 714	5 285	11 685	14 190	11 734	5 342	1 478
2000	53 714	3 396	1 360	2 035	50 318	5 455	11 439	14 188	12 186	5 500	1 550

See *Note* at end of table.

Table 1-7. Civilian Labor Force by Race, Hispanic Origin, Sex, and Age, 1948–2000—*Continued*

(Thousands of persons.)

Year, race, Hispanic origin, and sex	16 years and over	16 to 19 years			20 years and over						
		Total	16 to 17 years	18 to 19 years	Total	20 to 24 years	25 to 34 years	35 to 44 years	45 to 54 years	55 to 64 years	65 years and over
BLACK MEN											
1972	4 816	453	180	272	4 364	761	1 158	935	824	522	165
1973	4 924	460	175	286	4 464	819	1 217	935	842	499	153
1974	5 020	480	189	291	4 540	798	1 279	953	838	519	152
1975	5 016	447	168	279	4 569	790	1 328	948	833	520	150
1976	5 101	454	168	285	4 648	820	1 383	969	824	504	149
1977	5 263	476	178	299	4 787	856	1 441	1 003	818	515	154
1978	5 435	491	186	306	4 943	883	1 504	1 022	829	540	166
1979	5 559	480	179	301	5 079	928	1 577	1 049	844	524	156
1980	5 612	479	181	298	5 134	935	1 659	1 061	830	509	138
1981	5 685	462	169	293	5 223	940	1 702	1 093	829	524	134
1982	5 804	436	137	300	5 368	964	1 769	1 152	824	525	135
1983	5 966	433	134	300	5 533	997	1 840	1 196	845	536	119
1984	6 126	440	141	299	5 686	1 022	1 924	1 270	847	505	118
1985	6 220	471	162	310	5 749	950	1 937	1 313	879	544	125
1986	6 373	458	164	294	5 915	957	2 029	1 359	901	552	116
1987	6 486	463	179	284	6 023	914	2 074	1 406	915	586	130
1988	6 596	469	186	283	6 127	913	2 114	1 459	936	565	139
1989	6 701	480	190	291	6 221	904	2 157	1 544	945	530	141
1990	6 802	445	161	284	6 357	879	2 142	1 733	988	496	119
1991	6 851	400	140	260	6 451	896	2 111	1 806	1 010	507	122
1992	6 997	429	149	280	6 568	900	2 121	1 859	1 037	521	130
1993	7 019	425	154	270	6 594	875	2 118	1 918	1 065	506	112
1994	7 089	443	176	266	6 646	891	2 068	1 975	1 102	484	125
1995	7 183	453	184	269	6 730	866	2 089	1 987	1 148	490	150
1996	7 264	458	182	276	6 806	848	2 077	2 036	1 204	509	132
1997	7 354	444	178	266	6 910	832	2 052	2 096	1 287	508	134
1998	7 542	488	181	307	7 053	837	2 034	2 142	1 343	548	150
1999	7 652	470	180	291	7 182	835	2 069	2 206	1 387	547	138
2000	7 816	473	187	286	7 343	906	2 019	2 214	1 467	580	157
BLACK WOMEN											
1972	3 890	335	113	224	3 555	632	949	800	672	387	116
1973	4 052	373	133	240	3 678	670	1 026	806	670	402	105
1974	4 148	371	128	243	3 777	694	1 079	824	679	398	100
1975	4 247	391	144	245	3 857	687	1 138	827	686	409	108
1976	4 460	384	136	247	4 076	723	1 264	855	694	421	119
1977	4 670	385	127	258	4 286	785	1 357	891	712	429	113
1978	4 997	439	155	283	4 558	856	1 456	953	731	439	124
1979	5 119	432	161	271	4 687	865	1 517	990	740	451	124
1980	5 253	412	144	267	4 841	867	1 600	1 020	767	469	119
1981	5 401	400	139	261	5 001	888	1 663	1 071	779	485	115
1982	5 527	387	131	256	5 140	885	1 723	1 151	786	487	108
1983	5 681	375	114	261	5 306	874	1 835	1 210	785	496	105
1984	5 907	387	127	260	5 520	904	1 876	1 294	823	515	106
1985	6 144	417	149	268	5 727	904	1 951	1 368	862	515	127
1986	6 281	425	157	268	5 855	924	1 999	1 434	892	499	107
1987	6 507	435	157	278	6 071	904	2 073	1 537	924	512	121
1988	6 609	419	158	262	6 190	869	2 112	1 610	958	504	137
1989	6 796	445	163	281	6 352	885	2 138	1 683	1 009	493	144
1990	6 938	421	145	276	6 517	879	2 165	1 833	1 015	481	143
1991	6 946	374	126	248	6 572	854	2 143	1 913	1 032	494	135
1992	7 166	387	135	252	6 778	863	2 188	1 985	1 105	508	129
1993	7 206	383	129	254	6 824	889	2 115	2 042	1 147	506	125
1994	7 413	409	174	235	7 004	909	2 131	2 093	1 206	523	142
1995	7 634	458	182	276	7 175	887	2 177	2 178	1 256	556	121
1996	7 869	464	184	280	7 405	890	2 228	2 251	1 349	565	122
1997	8 175	489	175	314	7 686	951	2 277	2 305	1 437	585	131
1998	8 441	528	189	339	7 912	960	2 298	2 390	1 520	615	128
1999	8 713	489	172	316	8 224	1 031	2 360	2 447	1 606	633	147
2000	8 787	494	179	315	8 293	1 026	2 310	2 451	1 694	647	165

See *Note* at end of table.

Table 1-7. Civilian Labor Force by Race, Hispanic Origin, Sex, and Age, 1948–2000—*Continued*

(Thousands of persons.)

Year, race, Hispanic origin, and sex	16 years and over	16 to 19 years			20 years and over						
		Total	16 to 17 years	18 to 19 years	Total	20 to 24 years	25 to 34 years	35 to 44 years	45 to 54 years	55 to 64 years	65 years and over
HISPANIC MEN											
1973	2 356	...	...	...	2 124	...	...	...	...	...	...
1974	2 556	...	...	...	2 306	...	...	...	...	...	...
1975	2 597	...	...	...	2 343	...	...	...	...	...	...
1976	2 580	260	104	155	2 326	433	771	541	398	189	34
1977	2 817	285	105	179	2 530	485	828	567	416	197	42
1978	3 041	299	129	171	2 742	546	882	620	425	217	52
1979	3 184	315	121	194	2 869	562	941	648	445	216	56
1980	3 818	392	147	245	3 426	697	1 161	713	522	270	62
1981	4 005	359	130	229	3 647	747	1 269	756	535	278	61
1982	4 148	333	111	221	3 815	759	1 361	808	539	290	58
1983	4 362	348	109	239	4 014	789	1 447	852	557	311	58
1984	4 563	345	113	232	4 218	822	1 540	910	570	325	51
1985	4 729	334	116	218	4 395	835	1 629	957	591	331	53
1986	4 948	336	114	222	4 612	888	1 669	1 015	661	323	56
1987	5 163	345	112	233	4 818	865	1 801	1 121	652	325	55
1988	5 409	378	123	255	5 031	897	1 834	1 189	686	355	69
1989	5 595	400	129	271	5 195	909	1 899	1 221	719	375	71
1990	6 546	512	165	346	6 034	1 182	2 230	1 403	775	380	65
1991	6 664	466	141	325	6 198	1 202	2 260	1 487	780	401	67
1992	6 900	468	154	314	6 432	1 141	2 366	1 593	844	414	74
1993	7 076	455	145	310	6 621	1 147	2 417	1 675	900	394	88
1994	7 210	463	163	300	6 747	1 184	2 430	1 713	922	410	89
1995	7 376	479	168	311	6 898	1 153	2 469	1 795	965	417	98
1996	7 646	496	156	340	7 150	1 132	2 510	1 966	967	469	105
1997	8 309	531	177	354	7 779	1 267	2 684	2 091	1 112	511	113
1998	8 571	565	188	377	8 005	1 288	2 733	2 173	1 164	541	106
1999	8 546	596	181	415	7 950	1 231	2 633	2 219	1 205	526	136
2000	8 919	613	183	431	8 306	1 299	2 650	2 338	1 305	573	138
HISPANIC WOMEN											
1973	1 317	...	...	...	1 142	...	...	...	...	...	...
1974	1 456	...	...	...	1 264	...	...	...	...	...	...
1975	1 574	...	...	...	1 384	...	...	...	...	...	...
1976	1 625	201	71	130	1 454	295	479	334	227	105	13
1977	1 720	204	80	125	1 523	327	497	349	240	96	13
1978	1 938	233	93	142	1 704	354	564	388	275	106	16
1979	2 035	235	86	149	1 800	397	590	413	258	124	15
1980	2 328	252	93	159	2 076	439	682	450	337	144	22
1981	2 486	244	85	159	2 242	484	745	483	351	152	27
1982	2 586	252	81	172	2 333	492	802	504	352	155	28
1983	2 671	242	80	162	2 429	493	820	529	374	184	29
1984	2 888	273	96	177	2 615	503	896	599	384	199	34
1985	2 970	245	84	161	2 725	524	943	639	394	196	29
1986	3 128	236	89	147	2 893	526	1 016	698	436	189	28
1987	3 377	265	94	171	3 112	559	1 090	783	434	220	27
1988	3 573	293	111	182	3 281	589	1 123	806	461	267	34
1989	3 728	280	95	185	3 448	574	1 219	871	486	251	49
1990	4 174	318	110	207	3 857	657	1 360	983	545	268	45
1991	4 256	315	107	207	3 941	633	1 336	1 052	596	279	44
1992	4 439	328	110	219	4 110	674	1 374	1 142	599	273	48
1993	4 534	316	101	215	4 218	664	1 383	1 190	633	290	57
1994	4 765	345	122	222	4 421	679	1 435	1 252	704	288	62
1995	4 891	371	123	249	4 520	666	1 473	1 318	706	303	54
1996	5 128	349	128	221	4 779	713	1 544	1 395	729	338	61
1997	5 486	381	138	242	5 106	737	1 614	1 510	833	338	73
1998	5 746	442	132	310	5 304	789	1 639	1 533	927	353	62
1999	6 119	453	151	302	5 666	821	1 698	1 710	973	401	63
2000	6 449	470	155	315	5 979	856	1 833	1 748	1 053	410	80

Note: Detail for the above race and Hispanic-origin groups will not sum to totals because data for the Other races group are not presented and Hispanics are included in both the White and Black population groups. See "Notes and Definitions" for information on historical comparability.

Table 1-8. Civilian Labor Force Participation Rates by Race, Hispanic Origin, Sex, and Age, 1948–2000

(Percent.)

Year, race, Hispanic origin, and sex	16 years and over	16 to 19 years	20 years and over						
			Total	20 to 24 years	25 to 34 years	35 to 44 years	45 to 54 years	55 to 64 years	65 years and over
TOTAL									
1948	58.8	52.5	59.4	64.1	63.1	66.7	65.1	56.9	27.0
1949	58.9	52.2	59.5	64.9	63.2	67.2	65.3	56.2	27.3
1950	59.2	51.8	59.9	65.9	63.5	67.5	66.4	56.7	26.7
1951	59.2	52.2	59.8	64.8	64.2	67.6	67.2	56.9	25.8
1952	59.0	51.3	59.7	62.2	64.7	68.0	67.5	57.5	24.8
1953	58.9	50.2	59.6	61.2	64.0	68.9	68.1	58.0	24.8
1954	58.8	48.3	59.6	61.6	64.3	68.8	68.4	58.7	23.9
1955	59.3	48.9	60.1	62.7	64.8	68.9	69.7	59.5	24.1
1956	60.0	50.9	60.7	64.1	64.8	69.5	70.5	60.8	24.3
1957	59.6	49.6	60.4	64.0	64.9	69.5	70.9	60.1	22.9
1958	59.5	47.4	60.5	64.4	65.0	69.6	71.5	60.5	21.8
1959	59.3	46.7	60.4	64.3	65.0	69.5	71.9	61.0	21.1
1960	59.4	47.5	60.5	65.2	65.4	69.4	72.2	60.9	20.8
1961	59.3	46.9	60.5	65.7	65.6	69.5	72.1	61.5	20.1
1962	58.8	46.1	60.0	65.3	65.2	69.7	72.2	61.5	19.1
1963	58.7	45.2	60.1	65.1	65.6	70.1	72.5	62.0	17.9
1964	58.7	44.5	60.2	66.3	65.8	70.0	72.9	61.9	18.0
1965	58.9	45.7	60.3	66.4	66.4	70.7	72.5	61.9	17.8
1966	59.2	48.2	60.5	66.5	67.1	71.0	72.7	62.2	17.2
1967	59.6	48.4	60.9	67.1	68.2	71.6	72.7	62.3	17.2
1968	59.6	48.3	60.9	67.0	68.6	72.0	72.8	62.2	17.2
1969	60.1	49.4	61.3	68.2	69.1	72.5	73.4	62.1	17.3
1970	60.4	49.9	61.6	69.2	69.7	73.1	73.5	61.8	17.0
1971	60.2	49.7	61.4	69.3	69.9	73.2	73.2	61.3	16.2
1972	60.4	51.9	61.4	70.8	70.9	73.3	72.7	60.0	15.6
1973	60.8	53.7	61.7	72.6	72.3	74.0	72.5	58.4	14.6
1974	61.3	54.8	62.0	74.0	73.6	74.6	72.7	57.8	14.0
1975	61.2	54.0	62.1	73.9	74.4	75.0	72.6	57.2	13.7
1976	61.6	54.5	62.4	74.7	75.7	76.0	72.5	56.6	13.1
1977	62.3	56.0	63.0	75.7	77.0	77.0	72.8	56.3	13.0
1978	63.2	57.8	63.8	76.8	78.3	78.1	73.5	56.3	13.3
1979	63.7	57.9	64.3	77.5	79.2	79.2	74.3	56.2	13.1
1980	63.8	56.7	64.5	77.2	79.9	80.0	74.9	55.7	12.5
1981	63.9	55.4	64.8	77.3	80.5	80.7	75.7	55.0	12.2
1982	64.0	54.1	65.0	77.1	81.0	81.2	75.9	55.1	11.9
1983	64.0	53.5	65.0	77.2	81.3	81.6	76.0	54.5	11.7
1984	64.4	53.9	65.3	77.6	81.8	82.4	76.5	54.2	11.1
1985	64.8	54.5	65.7	78.2	82.5	83.1	77.3	54.2	10.8
1986	65.3	54.7	66.2	78.9	82.9	83.7	78.0	54.0	10.9
1987	65.6	54.7	66.5	78.9	83.3	84.3	78.6	54.4	11.1
1988	65.9	55.3	66.8	78.7	83.3	84.6	79.6	54.6	11.5
1989	66.5	55.9	67.3	78.7	83.8	85.1	80.5	55.5	11.8
1990	66.5	53.7	67.6	77.8	83.6	85.2	80.7	55.9	11.8
1991	66.2	51.6	67.3	76.7	83.2	85.2	81.0	55.5	11.5
1992	66.4	51.3	67.6	77.0	83.7	85.1	81.5	56.2	11.5
1993	66.3	51.5	67.5	77.0	83.3	84.9	81.6	56.4	11.2
1994	66.6	52.7	67.7	77.0	83.2	84.8	81.7	56.8	12.4
1995	66.6	53.5	67.7	76.6	83.8	84.6	81.4	57.2	12.1
1996	66.8	52.3	67.9	76.8	84.1	84.8	82.1	57.9	12.1
1997	67.1	51.6	68.4	77.6	84.4	85.1	82.6	58.9	12.2
1998	67.1	52.8	68.3	77.5	84.6	84.7	82.5	59.3	11.9
1999	67.1	52.0	68.3	77.5	84.6	84.9	82.6	59.3	12.3
2000	67.2	52.2	68.4	77.9	84.6	84.8	82.6	59.2	12.8

See *Note* at end of table.

Table 1-8. Civilian Labor Force Participation Rates by Race, Hispanic Origin, Sex, and Age, 1948–2000—*Continued*

(Percent.)

Year, race, Hispanic origin, and sex	16 years and over	16 to 19 years	20 years and over						
			Total	20 to 24 years	25 to 34 years	35 to 44 years	45 to 54 years	55 to 64 years	65 years and over
WHITE									
1954	58.2	48.8	58.9	61.0	63.5	68.0	67.9	58.4	23.7
1955	58.7	49.3	59.5	62.4	64.0	68.3	69.2	59.3	23.9
1956	59.4	51.3	60.1	64.1	64.0	68.9	70.1	60.6	24.2
1957	59.1	50.3	59.8	63.7	64.1	68.8	70.5	59.9	22.8
1958	58.9	47.9	59.8	64.1	64.2	68.8	71.0	60.3	21.7
1959	58.7	47.4	59.7	63.7	64.3	68.7	71.5	60.7	21.0
1960	58.8	47.9	59.8	64.8	64.7	68.6	71.7	60.6	20.8
1961	58.8	47.4	59.9	65.5	64.8	68.8	71.7	61.3	20.0
1962	58.3	46.6	59.4	65.0	64.4	69.0	71.8	61.3	19.0
1963	58.2	45.7	59.4	64.9	64.8	69.4	72.3	61.8	17.9
1964	58.2	45.1	59.6	65.8	64.9	69.5	72.5	61.8	17.8
1965	58.4	46.5	59.7	65.7	65.6	70.1	72.2	61.7	17.7
1966	58.7	49.1	59.8	66.0	66.3	70.4	72.5	61.9	17.1
1967	59.2	49.2	60.3	66.8	67.4	71.2	72.5	62.3	17.0
1968	59.3	49.3	60.4	66.6	67.9	71.7	72.7	62.2	17.1
1969	59.9	50.6	60.9	67.9	68.4	72.3	73.3	62.1	17.2
1970	60.2	51.4	61.2	69.2	69.1	72.9	73.5	61.8	16.8
1971	60.1	51.6	61.1	69.6	69.3	73.0	73.4	61.3	16.1
1972	60.4	54.1	61.2	71.2	70.4	73.2	72.9	60.3	15.4
1973	60.8	56.0	61.4	73.3	72.0	73.9	72.7	58.6	14.4
1974	61.4	57.3	61.9	74.8	73.4	74.6	73.0	58.0	13.9
1975	61.5	56.7	62.0	75.2	74.4	75.1	73.0	57.4	13.6
1976	61.8	57.5	62.3	76.0	75.6	76.1	73.0	56.9	13.0
1977	62.5	59.3	62.9	77.1	77.0	77.1	73.2	56.6	12.9
1978	63.0	60.8	63.6	78.1	78.3	78.1	73.8	56.4	13.1
1979	63.9	61.1	64.2	78.9	79.4	79.3	74.6	56.5	12.9
1980	64.1	60.0	64.5	78.7	80.2	80.3	75.4	56.0	12.5
1981	64.3	58.9	64.8	79.1	81.0	81.0	76.2	55.2	12.2
1982	64.3	57.5	65.0	78.9	81.6	81.5	76.4	55.3	12.0
1983	64.3	56.9	65.0	79.0	81.8	81.9	76.5	54.7	11.8
1984	64.6	57.2	65.3	79.4	82.5	82.6	77.0	54.5	11.1
1985	65.0	57.5	65.7	79.9	83.1	83.4	77.8	54.4	10.7
1986	65.5	57.8	66.1	80.6	83.6	84.0	78.5	54.3	11.0
1987	65.8	57.7	66.5	80.7	84.0	84.7	79.1	54.6	11.1
1988	66.2	58.6	66.8	80.6	84.1	85.0	80.3	55.1	11.4
1989	66.7	59.1	67.3	80.2	84.5	85.5	81.2	56.2	11.8
1990	66.9	57.5	67.6	79.8	84.6	85.9	81.3	56.5	11.9
1991	66.6	55.8	67.4	78.9	84.3	85.9	81.8	56.0	11.6
1992	66.8	54.7	67.7	79.4	84.6	85.8	82.2	56.8	11.6
1993	66.8	55.1	67.6	79.5	84.5	85.7	82.5	57.1	11.4
1994	67.1	56.4	67.9	79.5	84.4	85.7	82.7	57.6	12.5
1995	67.1	57.1	67.8	78.7	84.9	85.5	82.5	58.0	12.3
1996	67.2	55.9	68.1	79.1	84.9	85.7	83.1	58.7	12.3
1997	67.5	55.2	68.4	79.6	85.3	85.8	83.5	59.9	12.3
1998	67.3	56.0	68.2	79.5	85.4	85.3	83.4	60.1	12.0
1999	67.3	55.5	68.2	79.5	85.1	85.4	83.5	60.2	12.5
2000	67.4	55.7	68.3	79.9	85.1	85.4	83.5	60.0	13.0

See *Note* at end of table.

Table 1-8. Civilian Labor Force Participation Rates by Race, Hispanic Origin, Sex, and Age, 1948–2000—*Continued*

(Percent.)

Year, race, Hispanic origin, and sex	16 years and over	16 to 19 years	20 years and over						
			Total	20 to 24 years	25 to 34 years	35 to 44 years	45 to 54 years	55 to 64 years	65 years and over
BLACK									
1972	59.9	39.0	63.3	68.7	75.0	74.5	69.9	56.8	17.5
1973	60.2	39.8	63.4	69.8	75.8	74.6	70.2	55.8	15.8
1974	59.8	39.8	63.0	69.8	76.0	74.6	68.9	54.6	15.0
1975	58.8	38.2	62.0	66.3	75.7	74.1	68.7	54.1	14.7
1976	59.0	37.0	62.5	67.0	77.5	74.9	68.4	53.3	14.7
1977	59.8	37.9	63.2	68.4	78.5	76.0	68.8	53.4	14.2
1978	61.5	41.0	64.5	70.0	79.7	77.5	70.1	54.5	15.0
1979	61.4	40.1	64.5	70.1	79.4	78.0	70.7	53.2	14.2
1980	61.0	38.9	64.1	69.1	79.6	77.4	71.0	52.3	12.7
1981	60.8	37.7	64.2	69.2	78.4	78.5	71.2	52.7	12.0
1982	61.0	36.6	64.3	68.6	78.7	79.8	71.1	52.3	11.5
1983	61.5	36.4	64.9	68.4	79.8	80.2	72.1	52.5	10.5
1984	62.2	38.3	65.2	69.2	79.3	81.0	73.0	51.6	10.3
1985	62.9	41.2	65.6	70.0	79.8	81.5	73.4	51.4	11.2
1986	63.3	41.3	65.9	71.7	80.1	81.9	74.3	50.6	9.7
1987	63.8	41.6	66.5	70.5	80.7	82.6	74.7	52.4	10.7
1988	63.8	40.8	66.5	70.5	80.7	82.6	75.0	50.7	11.5
1989	64.2	42.5	66.7	72.2	80.9	82.7	75.5	48.3	11.6
1990	64.0	38.7	66.9	68.8	79.7	82.4	76.5	49.6	11.1
1991	63.3	35.4	66.4	67.7	78.5	82.0	76.1	50.4	10.7
1992	63.9	37.9	66.8	67.4	79.7	81.4	76.3	51.6	10.6
1993	63.2	37.0	66.0	67.8	78.2	81.0	75.2	50.2	9.5
1994	63.4	38.5	66.0	68.8	78.3	80.7	74.8	49.2	10.6
1995	63.7	39.9	66.3	68.7	80.0	80.4	74.1	50.3	10.5
1996	64.1	39.2	66.9	69.0	81.1	81.0	74.9	50.9	9.8
1997	64.7	38.7	67.6	70.9	82.0	81.3	76.3	50.5	10.0
1998	65.6	41.6	68.2	70.6	83.0	82.2	76.7	52.3	10.3
1999	65.8	38.7	68.9	71.4	85.2	83.0	76.4	51.4	10.4
2000	65.8	39.2	68.7	71.8	84.1	82.3	76.8	52.2	11.6
HISPANIC									
1980	64.0	50.3	66.2	72.6	73.5	73.8	72.3	52.9	12.2
1981	64.2	46.4	66.8	74.6	74.7	73.8	72.0	51.7	12.0
1982	63.6	44.8	66.3	72.6	75.3	73.8	70.5	50.5	11.3
1983	63.8	45.3	66.2	71.6	74.4	73.3	71.7	53.3	11.0
1984	64.9	47.5	67.1	72.1	75.6	75.6	71.4	53.9	10.4
1985	64.6	44.6	67.1	72.9	75.6	75.3	71.5	51.9	9.7
1986	65.4	43.9	68.0	74.5	76.5	76.5	73.3	50.0	9.6
1987	66.4	45.8	68.8	74.6	77.8	77.3	72.8	51.4	9.1
1988	67.4	49.6	69.4	76.3	77.7	77.8	73.0	53.6	11.2
1989	67.6	48.6	69.7	76.1	78.9	78.7	73.1	52.9	12.0
1990	67.4	47.8	69.8	75.7	78.2	79.5	72.6	51.9	10.1
1991	66.5	45.1	69.0	74.0	76.9	78.3	73.2	53.1	9.8
1992	66.8	45.8	69.2	74.3	77.8	79.1	72.8	52.0	10.0
1993	66.2	43.9	68.7	72.8	77.8	78.9	73.3	51.7	10.7
1994	66.1	44.4	68.5	74.0	77.3	78.9	73.1	49.8	10.8
1995	65.8	45.4	68.1	71.9	78.1	78.5	72.8	48.6	10.6
1996	66.5	43.4	69.1	73.1	78.2	79.5	74.6	52.1	11.0
1997	67.9	43.0	70.8	76.4	79.5	80.9	75.4	53.8	11.9
1998	67.9	45.7	70.6	76.1	80.3	80.0	75.3	55.4	10.2
1999	67.7	45.5	70.4	76.0	78.6	81.3	75.9	54.1	11.6
2000	68.6	46.3	71.2	77.7	79.7	81.6	77.7	54.1	12.2

See *Note* at end of table.

Table 1-8. Civilian Labor Force Participation Rates by Race, Hispanic Origin, Sex, and Age, 1948–2000—*Continued*

(Percent.)

Year, race, Hispanic origin, and sex	16 years and over	16 to 19 years	20 years and over						
			Total	20 to 24 years	25 to 34 years	35 to 44 years	45 to 54 years	55 to 64 years	65 years and over
MEN									
1948	86.6	63.7	88.6	84.6	95.9	97.9	95.8	89.5	46.8
1949	86.4	62.8	88.5	86.6	95.8	97.9	95.6	87.5	47.0
1950	86.4	63.2	88.4	87.9	96.0	97.6	95.8	86.9	45.8
1951	86.3	63.0	88.2	88.4	96.9	97.5	95.9	87.2	44.9
1952	86.3	61.3	88.3	88.1	97.5	97.8	96.2	87.5	42.6
1953	86.0	60.7	88.0	87.7	97.4	98.2	96.5	87.9	41.6
1954	85.5	58.0	87.8	86.9	97.3	98.1	96.5	88.7	40.5
1955	85.4	58.9	87.6	86.9	97.6	98.1	96.4	87.9	39.6
1956	85.5	60.5	87.6	87.8	97.3	97.9	96.6	88.5	40.0
1957	84.8	59.1	86.9	87.1	97.1	97.9	96.3	87.5	37.5
1958	84.2	56.6	86.6	86.9	97.1	97.9	96.3	87.8	35.6
1959	83.7	55.8	86.3	87.8	97.4	97.8	96.0	87.4	34.2
1960	83.3	56.1	86.0	88.1	97.5	97.7	95.7	86.8	33.1
1961	82.9	54.6	85.7	87.8	97.5	97.6	95.6	87.3	31.7
1962	82.0	53.8	84.8	86.9	97.2	97.6	95.6	86.2	30.3
1963	81.4	52.9	84.4	86.1	97.1	97.5	95.7	86.2	28.4
1964	81.0	52.4	84.2	86.1	97.3	97.3	95.7	85.6	28.0
1965	80.7	53.8	83.9	85.8	97.2	97.3	95.6	84.6	27.9
1966	80.4	55.3	83.6	85.1	97.3	97.2	95.3	84.5	27.1
1967	80.4	55.6	83.4	84.4	97.2	97.3	95.2	84.4	27.1
1968	80.1	55.1	83.1	82.8	96.9	97.1	94.9	84.3	27.3
1969	79.8	55.9	82.8	82.8	96.7	96.9	94.6	83.4	27.2
1970	79.7	56.1	82.6	83.3	96.4	96.9	94.3	83.0	26.8
1971	79.1	56.1	82.1	83.0	95.9	96.5	93.9	82.1	25.5
1972	78.9	58.1	81.6	83.9	95.7	96.4	93.2	80.4	24.3
1973	78.8	59.7	81.3	85.2	95.7	96.2	93.0	78.2	22.7
1974	78.7	60.7	81.0	85.9	95.8	96.0	92.2	77.3	22.4
1975	77.9	59.1	80.3	84.5	95.2	95.6	92.1	75.6	21.6
1976	77.5	59.3	79.8	85.2	95.2	95.4	91.6	74.3	20.2
1977	77.7	60.9	79.7	85.6	95.3	95.7	91.1	73.8	20.0
1978	77.9	62.0	79.8	85.9	95.3	95.7	91.3	73.3	20.4
1979	77.8	61.5	79.8	86.4	95.3	95.7	91.4	72.8	19.9
1980	77.4	60.5	79.4	85.9	95.2	95.5	91.2	72.1	19.0
1981	77.0	59.0	79.0	85.5	94.9	95.4	91.4	70.6	18.4
1982	76.6	56.7	78.7	84.9	94.7	95.3	91.2	70.2	17.8
1983	76.4	56.2	78.5	84.8	94.2	95.2	91.2	69.4	17.4
1984	76.4	56.0	78.3	85.0	94.4	95.4	91.2	68.5	16.3
1985	76.3	56.8	78.1	85.0	94.7	95.0	91.0	67.9	15.8
1986	76.3	56.4	78.1	85.8	94.6	94.8	91.0	67.3	16.0
1987	76.2	56.1	78.0	85.2	94.6	94.6	90.7	67.6	16.3
1988	76.2	56.9	77.9	85.0	94.3	94.5	90.9	67.0	16.5
1989	76.4	57.9	78.1	85.3	94.4	94.5	91.1	67.2	16.6
1990	76.4	55.7	78.2	84.4	94.1	94.3	90.7	67.8	16.3
1991	75.8	53.2	77.7	83.5	93.6	94.1	90.5	67.0	15.7
1992	75.8	53.4	77.7	83.3	93.8	93.7	90.7	67.0	16.1
1993	75.4	53.2	77.3	83.2	93.4	93.4	90.1	66.5	15.6
1994	75.1	54.1	76.8	83.1	92.6	92.8	89.1	65.5	16.8
1995	75.0	54.8	76.7	83.1	93.0	92.3	88.8	66.0	16.8
1996	74.9	53.2	76.8	82.5	93.2	92.4	89.1	67.0	16.9
1997	75.0	52.3	77.0	82.5	93.0	92.6	89.5	67.6	17.1
1998	74.9	53.3	76.8	82.0	93.2	92.6	89.2	68.1	16.5
1999	74.7	52.9	76.7	81.9	93.3	92.8	88.8	67.9	16.9
2000	74.7	53.0	76.6	82.6	93.4	92.6	88.6	67.3	17.5

See *Note* at end of table.

Table 1-8. Civilian Labor Force Participation Rates by Race, Hispanic Origin, Sex, and Age, 1948–2000—*Continued*

(Percent.)

Year, race, Hispanic origin, and sex	16 years and over	16 to 19 years	20 years and over						
			Total	20 to 24 years	25 to 34 years	35 to 44 years	45 to 54 years	55 to 64 years	65 years and over
WOMEN									
1948	32.7	42.0	31.8	45.3	33.2	36.9	35.0	24.3	9.1
1949	33.1	42.4	32.3	45.0	33.4	38.1	35.9	25.3	9.6
1950	33.9	41.0	33.3	46.0	34.0	39.1	37.9	27.0	9.7
1951	34.6	42.4	34.0	46.5	35.4	39.8	39.7	27.6	8.9
1952	34.7	42.2	34.1	44.7	35.4	40.4	40.1	28.7	9.1
1953	34.4	40.7	33.9	44.3	34.0	41.3	40.4	29.1	10.0
1954	34.6	39.4	34.2	45.1	34.4	41.2	41.2	30.0	9.3
1955	35.7	39.7	35.4	45.9	34.9	41.6	43.8	32.5	10.6
1956	36.9	42.2	36.4	46.3	35.4	43.1	45.5	34.9	10.8
1957	36.9	41.1	36.5	45.9	35.6	43.3	46.5	34.5	10.5
1958	37.1	39.0	36.9	46.3	35.6	43.4	47.8	35.2	10.3
1959	37.1	38.2	37.1	45.1	35.3	43.4	49.0	36.6	10.2
1960	37.7	39.3	37.6	46.1	36.0	43.4	49.9	37.2	10.8
1961	38.1	39.7	38.0	47.0	36.4	43.8	50.1	37.9	10.7
1962	37.9	39.0	37.8	47.3	36.3	44.1	50.0	38.7	10.0
1963	38.3	38.0	38.3	47.5	37.2	44.9	50.6	39.7	9.6
1964	38.7	37.0	38.9	49.4	37.2	45.0	51.4	40.2	10.1
1965	39.3	38.0	39.4	49.9	38.5	46.1	50.9	41.1	10.0
1966	40.3	41.4	40.1	51.5	39.8	46.8	51.7	41.8	9.6
1967	41.1	41.6	41.1	53.3	41.9	48.1	51.8	42.4	9.6
1968	41.6	41.9	41.6	54.5	42.6	48.9	52.3	42.4	9.6
1969	42.7	43.2	42.7	56.7	43.7	49.9	53.8	43.1	9.9
1970	43.3	44.0	43.3	57.7	45.0	51.1	54.4	43.0	9.7
1971	43.4	43.4	43.3	57.7	45.6	51.6	54.3	42.9	9.5
1972	43.9	45.8	43.7	59.1	47.8	52.0	53.9	42.1	9.3
1973	44.7	47.8	44.4	61.1	50.4	53.3	53.7	41.1	8.9
1974	45.7	49.1	45.3	63.1	52.6	54.7	54.6	40.7	8.1
1975	46.3	49.1	46.0	64.1	54.9	55.8	54.6	40.9	8.2
1976	47.3	49.8	47.0	65.0	57.3	57.8	55.0	41.0	8.2
1977	48.4	51.2	48.1	66.5	59.7	59.6	55.8	40.9	8.1
1978	50.0	53.7	49.6	68.3	62.2	61.6	57.1	41.3	8.3
1979	50.9	54.2	50.6	69.0	63.9	63.6	58.3	41.7	8.3
1980	51.5	52.9	51.3	68.9	65.5	65.5	59.9	41.3	8.1
1981	52.1	51.8	52.1	69.6	66.7	66.8	61.1	41.4	8.0
1982	52.6	51.4	52.7	69.8	68.0	68.0	61.6	41.8	7.9
1983	52.9	50.8	53.1	69.9	69.0	68.7	61.9	41.5	7.8
1984	53.6	51.8	53.7	70.4	69.8	70.1	62.9	41.7	7.5
1985	54.5	52.1	54.7	71.8	70.9	71.8	64.4	42.0	7.3
1986	55.3	53.0	55.5	72.4	71.6	73.1	65.9	42.3	7.4
1987	56.0	53.3	56.2	73.0	72.4	74.5	67.1	42.7	7.4
1988	56.6	53.6	56.8	72.7	72.7	75.2	69.0	43.5	7.9
1989	57.4	53.9	57.7	72.4	73.5	76.0	70.5	45.0	8.4
1990	57.5	51.6	58.0	71.3	73.5	76.4	71.2	45.2	8.6
1991	57.4	50.0	57.9	70.1	73.1	76.5	72.0	45.2	8.5
1992	57.8	49.1	58.5	70.9	73.9	76.7	72.6	46.5	8.3
1993	57.9	49.7	58.5	70.9	73.4	76.6	73.5	47.2	8.1
1994	58.8	51.3	59.3	71.0	74.0	77.1	74.6	48.9	9.2
1995	58.9	52.2	59.4	70.3	74.9	77.2	74.4	49.2	8.8
1996	59.3	51.3	59.9	71.3	75.2	77.5	75.4	49.6	8.6
1997	59.8	51.0	60.5	72.7	76.0	77.7	76.0	50.9	8.6
1998	59.8	52.3	60.4	73.0	76.3	77.1	76.2	51.2	8.6
1999	60.0	51.0	60.7	73.2	76.4	77.2	76.7	51.5	8.9
2000	60.2	51.3	60.9	73.3	76.3	77.3	76.8	51.8	9.4

See *Note* at end of table.

Table 1-8. Civilian Labor Force Participation Rates by Race, Hispanic Origin, Sex, and Age, 1948–2000—*Continued*

(Percent.)

Year, race, Hispanic origin, and sex	16 years and over	16 to 19 years	20 years and over						
			Total	20 to 24 years	25 to 34 years	35 to 44 years	45 to 54 years	55 to 64 years	65 years and over
WHITE MEN									
1954	85.6	57.6	87.8	86.3	97.5	98.2	96.8	89.1	40.4
1955	85.4	58.6	87.5	86.5	97.8	98.2	96.7	88.4	39.6
1956	85.6	60.4	87.6	87.6	97.4	98.1	96.8	88.9	40.0
1957	84.8	59.2	86.9	86.6	97.2	98.0	96.7	88.0	37.7
1958	84.3	56.5	86.6	86.7	97.2	98.0	96.6	88.2	35.7
1959	83.8	55.9	86.3	87.3	97.5	98.0	96.3	87.9	34.3
1960	83.4	55.9	86.0	87.8	97.7	97.9	96.1	87.2	33.3
1961	83.0	54.5	85.7	87.6	97.7	97.9	95.9	87.8	31.9
1962	82.1	53.8	84.9	86.5	97.4	97.9	96.0	86.7	30.6
1963	81.5	53.1	84.4	85.8	97.4	97.8	96.2	86.6	28.4
1964	81.1	52.7	84.2	85.7	97.5	97.6	96.1	86.1	27.9
1965	80.8	54.1	83.9	85.3	97.4	97.7	95.9	85.2	27.9
1966	80.6	55.9	83.6	84.4	97.5	97.6	95.8	84.9	27.2
1967	80.6	56.3	83.5	84.0	97.5	97.7	95.6	84.9	27.1
1968	80.4	55.9	83.2	82.4	97.2	97.6	95.4	84.7	27.4
1969	80.2	56.8	83.0	82.6	97.0	97.4	95.1	83.9	27.3
1970	80.0	57.5	82.8	83.3	96.7	97.3	94.9	83.3	26.7
1971	79.6	57.9	82.3	83.2	96.3	97.0	94.7	82.6	25.6
1972	79.6	60.1	82.0	84.3	96.0	97.0	94.0	81.1	24.4
1973	79.4	62.0	81.6	85.8	96.2	96.8	93.5	78.9	22.7
1974	79.4	62.9	81.4	86.6	96.3	96.7	93.0	78.0	22.4
1975	78.7	61.9	80.7	85.5	95.8	96.4	92.9	76.4	21.7
1976	78.4	62.3	80.3	86.3	95.9	96.0	92.5	75.2	20.2
1977	78.5	64.0	80.2	86.8	96.0	96.2	92.1	74.6	20.0
1978	78.6	65.0	80.1	87.3	95.9	96.3	92.1	73.7	20.3
1979	78.6	64.8	80.1	87.6	96.0	96.4	92.2	73.4	20.0
1980	78.2	63.7	79.8	87.2	95.9	96.2	92.1	70.1	19.1
1981	77.9	62.4	79.5	87.0	95.8	96.1	92.4	71.5	18.5
1982	77.4	60.0	79.2	86.3	95.6	96.0	92.2	71.0	17.9
1983	77.1	59.4	78.9	86.1	95.2	96.0	91.9	70.0	17.7
1984	77.1	59.0	78.7	86.5	95.4	96.1	92.0	69.5	16.4
1985	77.0	59.7	78.5	86.4	95.7	95.7	92.0	68.8	15.9
1986	76.9	59.3	78.5	87.3	95.5	95.4	91.8	68.0	16.3
1987	76.8	59.0	78.4	86.9	95.5	95.4	91.6	68.1	16.5
1988	76.9	60.0	78.3	86.6	95.2	95.4	91.8	67.9	16.7
1989	77.1	61.0	78.5	86.8	95.4	95.3	92.2	68.3	16.8
1990	77.1	59.6	78.5	86.2	95.2	95.3	91.7	68.6	16.6
1991	76.5	57.3	78.0	85.4	94.9	95.0	91.4	67.7	15.9
1992	76.5	56.9	78.0	85.2	94.9	94.7	91.8	67.7	16.2
1993	76.2	56.6	77.7	85.5	94.7	94.5	91.3	67.3	15.9
1994	75.9	57.7	77.3	85.5	93.9	93.9	90.3	66.4	17.2
1995	75.7	58.5	77.1	85.1	94.1	93.4	90.0	67.1	16.9
1996	75.8	57.1	77.3	85.0	94.4	93.6	90.4	68.0	17.2
1997	75.9	56.1	77.5	85.1	94.2	93.7	90.6	68.9	17.4
1998	75.6	56.6	77.2	84.6	94.4	93.7	90.3	69.1	16.6
1999	75.6	56.4	77.2	84.9	94.3	93.8	90.1	69.1	17.2
2000	75.4	56.6	77.0	85.0	94.4	93.7	89.8	68.2	17.7

See *Note* at end of table.

Table 1-8. Civilian Labor Force Participation Rates by Race, Hispanic Origin, Sex, and Age, 1948–2000—*Continued*

(Percent.)

Year, race, Hispanic origin, and sex	16 years and over	16 to 19 years	20 years and over						
			Total	20 to 24 years	25 to 34 years	35 to 44 years	45 to 54 years	55 to 64 years	65 years and over
WHITE WOMEN									
1954	33.3	40.6	32.7	44.4	32.5	39.3	39.8	29.1	9.1
1955	34.5	40.7	34.0	45.8	32.8	40.0	42.7	31.8	10.5
1956	35.7	43.1	35.1	46.5	33.2	41.5	44.4	34.0	10.6
1957	35.7	42.2	35.2	45.8	33.6	41.5	45.4	33.7	10.2
1958	35.8	40.1	35.5	46.0	33.6	41.4	46.5	34.5	10.1
1959	36.0	39.6	35.6	44.5	33.4	41.4	47.8	35.7	10.0
1960	36.5	40.3	36.2	45.7	34.1	41.5	48.6	36.2	10.6
1961	36.9	40.6	36.6	46.9	34.3	41.8	48.9	37.2	10.5
1962	36.7	39.8	36.5	47.1	34.1	42.2	48.9	38.0	9.8
1963	37.2	38.7	37.0	47.3	34.8	43.1	49.5	38.9	9.4
1964	37.5	37.8	37.5	48.8	35.0	43.3	50.2	39.4	9.9
1965	38.1	39.2	38.0	49.2	36.3	44.4	49.9	40.3	9.7
1966	39.2	42.6	38.8	51.0	37.7	45.0	50.6	41.1	9.4
1967	40.1	42.5	39.8	53.1	39.7	46.4	50.9	41.9	9.3
1968	40.7	43.0	40.4	54.0	40.6	47.5	51.5	42.0	9.4
1969	41.8	44.6	41.5	56.4	41.7	48.6	53.0	42.6	9.7
1970	42.6	45.6	42.2	57.7	43.2	49.9	53.7	42.6	9.5
1971	42.6	45.4	42.3	58.0	43.7	50.2	53.6	42.5	9.3
1972	43.2	48.1	42.7	59.4	46.0	50.7	53.4	41.9	9.0
1973	44.1	50.1	43.5	61.7	48.7	52.2	53.4	40.7	8.7
1974	45.2	51.7	44.4	63.9	51.3	53.6	54.3	40.4	8.0
1975	45.9	51.5	45.3	65.5	53.8	54.9	54.3	40.6	8.0
1976	46.9	52.8	46.2	66.3	56.0	57.1	54.7	40.7	7.9
1977	48.0	54.5	47.3	67.8	58.5	58.9	55.3	40.7	7.9
1978	49.4	56.7	48.7	69.3	61.2	60.7	56.7	41.1	8.1
1979	50.5	57.4	49.8	70.5	63.1	63.0	58.1	41.5	8.1
1980	51.2	56.2	50.6	70.6	64.8	65.0	59.6	40.9	7.9
1981	51.9	55.4	51.5	71.5	66.4	66.4	60.9	40.9	7.9
1982	52.4	55.0	52.2	71.8	67.8	67.5	61.4	41.5	7.8
1983	52.7	54.5	52.5	72.1	68.7	68.2	61.9	41.1	7.8
1984	53.3	55.4	53.1	72.5	69.8	69.6	62.7	41.2	7.5
1985	54.1	55.2	54.0	73.8	70.9	71.4	64.2	41.5	7.0
1986	55.0	56.3	54.9	74.1	71.8	72.9	65.8	42.1	7.3
1987	55.7	56.5	55.6	74.8	72.5	74.2	67.2	42.4	7.2
1988	56.4	57.2	56.3	74.9	73.0	74.9	69.2	43.6	7.7
1989	57.2	57.1	57.2	74.0	73.8	75.9	70.6	45.2	8.2
1990	57.4	55.3	57.6	73.4	74.1	76.6	71.3	45.5	8.5
1991	57.4	54.1	57.6	72.5	73.8	76.8	72.4	45.4	8.5
1992	57.7	52.5	58.1	73.5	74.4	77.0	72.8	46.8	8.2
1993	58.0	53.5	58.3	73.4	74.3	76.9	74.0	47.6	8.1
1994	58.9	55.1	59.2	73.4	74.9	77.5	75.2	49.4	9.2
1995	59.0	55.5	59.2	72.3	75.8	77.6	75.2	49.5	9.0
1996	59.1	54.7	59.4	73.3	75.5	77.8	76.1	50.1	8.7
1997	59.5	54.1	59.9	73.9	76.3	77.9	76.6	51.5	8.6
1998	59.4	55.4	59.7	74.3	76.3	76.9	76.6	51.6	8.7
1999	59.6	54.5	59.9	73.9	76.0	77.1	77.1	52.0	8.9
2000	59.8	54.7	60.2	74.7	75.9	77.2	77.4	52.3	9.4

See *Note* at end of table.

Table 1-8. Civilian Labor Force Participation Rates by Race, Hispanic Origin, Sex, and Age, 1948–2000—*Continued*

(Percent.)

Year, race, Hispanic origin, and sex	16 years and over	16 to 19 years	20 years and over						
			Total	20 to 24 years	25 to 34 years	35 to 44 years	45 to 54 years	55 to 64 years	65 years and over
BLACK MEN									
1972	73.7	46.3	78.5	82.6	92.6	91.0	85.6	72.5	24.3
1973	73.4	45.7	78.4	83.7	91.8	91.0	87.5	69.5	22.4
1974	73.0	46.7	77.6	83.5	92.7	90.3	84.1	68.9	21.5
1975	71.0	42.5	76.0	78.8	91.5	89.3	83.5	67.6	20.5
1976	70.2	41.3	75.4	79.1	90.9	89.9	82.4	65.1	19.7
1977	70.8	43.2	75.6	79.3	90.7	90.9	82.0	65.5	19.9
1978	71.7	44.9	76.2	78.8	90.8	90.6	83.3	67.9	21.0
1979	71.6	43.6	76.3	80.6	90.7	90.4	84.6	64.8	19.4
1980	70.6	43.2	75.1	79.8	90.8	89.1	83.1	61.7	16.8
1981	70.0	41.6	74.5	79.1	88.9	89.3	82.7	62.1	16.0
1982	70.1	39.7	74.7	78.7	89.2	89.9	82.2	61.9	16.0
1983	70.6	39.8	75.2	79.5	89.0	89.7	84.5	62.5	14.0
1984	70.8	41.7	74.8	79.1	88.9	90.0	83.7	58.9	13.7
1985	70.8	44.5	74.4	79.0	88.9	89.8	82.9	58.9	13.9
1986	71.2	43.7	74.8	80.1	89.6	89.6	84.0	59.1	12.6
1987	71.1	43.5	74.7	77.9	89.4	88.6	83.8	62.1	13.7
1988	71.0	43.7	74.6	79.3	89.3	88.1	83.5	59.4	14.3
1989	71.0	44.7	74.4	80.1	89.8	88.7	82.5	55.4	14.2
1990	71.1	40.7	75.0	76.8	88.8	88.1	83.5	57.9	13.0
1991	70.4	37.3	74.6	76.7	87.4	87.7	83.4	58.7	13.1
1992	70.7	40.6	74.3	75.4	88.0	86.5	81.8	60.0	13.7
1993	69.6	39.5	73.2	74.1	87.3	86.1	80.1	57.9	11.6
1994	69.1	40.8	72.5	73.9	86.2	85.9	79.2	54.4	12.7
1995	69.0	40.1	72.5	74.5	87.4	84.1	78.5	54.4	14.9
1996	68.7	39.4	72.3	73.4	87.5	84.4	78.5	55.7	12.9
1997	68.3	37.4	72.2	72.2	86.8	84.8	80.1	54.3	12.8
1998	69.0	40.0	72.5	71.8	87.1	85.0	79.8	57.3	14.0
1999	68.7	38.6	72.4	69.8	89.2	86.0	78.5	55.5	12.7
2000	69.0	39.0	72.6	73.4	87.7	85.3	79.1	57.1	14.2
BLACK WOMEN									
1972	48.7	32.2	51.2	57.1	60.9	61.4	57.1	43.9	12.5
1973	49.3	34.3	51.6	58.1	62.9	61.7	56.1	44.8	11.1
1974	49.1	33.4	51.4	58.8	62.6	62.1	56.3	43.0	10.2
1975	48.9	34.3	51.1	56.0	63.0	62.0	56.6	43.1	10.5
1976	49.9	33.0	52.5	57.1	66.9	63.0	56.9	43.8	11.1
1977	50.9	32.9	53.6	59.5	68.6	64.1	58.0	43.8	10.2
1978	53.2	37.3	55.5	62.8	70.6	67.2	59.4	43.9	10.8
1979	53.1	36.7	55.4	61.6	70.2	68.0	59.6	44.1	10.5
1980	53.2	34.9	55.6	60.4	70.6	68.2	61.4	44.9	9.9
1981	53.5	34.0	56.0	61.1	70.0	69.8	62.0	45.4	9.3
1982	53.7	33.5	56.2	60.1	70.2	71.7	62.4	44.8	8.5
1983	54.2	33.0	56.8	59.1	72.3	72.6	62.3	44.8	8.2
1984	55.2	35.0	57.6	60.6	71.5	73.7	64.5	46.0	8.0
1985	56.5	37.9	58.6	62.5	72.4	74.8	65.7	45.3	9.4
1986	56.9	39.1	58.9	64.6	72.4	75.8	66.5	43.6	7.8
1987	58.0	39.6	60.0	64.3	73.5	77.8	67.5	44.4	8.6
1988	58.0	37.9	60.1	63.2	73.7	78.2	68.3	43.5	9.6
1989	58.7	40.5	60.6	65.5	73.6	78.0	70.0	42.4	9.8
1990	58.3	36.8	60.6	62.3	72.3	77.7	70.7	43.2	9.9
1991	57.5	33.5	60.0	60.3	71.4	77.2	70.2	44.1	9.2
1992	58.5	35.2	60.8	60.7	73.1	77.1	71.7	45.1	8.6
1993	57.9	34.6	60.2	62.6	70.9	76.8	71.2	44.3	8.2
1994	58.7	36.4	60.9	64.5	71.9	76.4	71.3	45.2	9.2
1995	59.5	39.7	61.4	63.7	73.8	77.3	70.5	47.2	7.7
1996	60.4	38.8	62.6	65.2	75.8	78.2	72.0	47.2	7.7
1997	61.7	39.9	64.0	69.8	78.1	78.4	73.2	47.6	8.1
1998	62.8	42.5	64.8	69.6	79.6	79.9	74.0	48.5	7.9
1999	63.5	38.8	66.1	72.7	82.1	80.4	74.6	48.4	8.9
2000	63.2	39.4	65.6	70.5	81.2	79.8	74.9	48.4	9.9

See *Note* at end of table.

Table 1-8. Civilian Labor Force Participation Rates by Race, Hispanic Origin, Sex, and Age, 1948–2000—*Continued*

(Percent.)

Year, race, Hispanic origin, and sex	16 years and over	16 to 19 years	20 years and over						
			Total	20 to 24 years	25 to 34 years	35 to 44 years	45 to 54 years	55 to 64 years	65 years and over
HISPANIC MEN									
1980	81.4	60.0	84.9	88.0	93.3	93.8	91.6	73.6	20.6
1981	80.6	54.1	84.7	88.7	93.7	92.6	90.5	70.9	19.6
1982	79.7	50.2	84.0	86.1	93.9	93.4	88.8	70.0	18.1
1983	80.3	52.6	84.1	85.9	93.5	93.0	89.4	71.3	17.6
1984	80.6	52.6	84.3	87.1	93.4	93.5	88.9	71.1	15.0
1985	80.4	51.1	84.0	87.3	93.1	92.4	89.5	69.5	15.0
1986	81.0	51.3	84.6	88.3	93.4	93.3	89.9	69.3	15.2
1987	81.0	51.4	84.5	87.8	93.6	93.0	88.0	70.2	14.4
1988	81.9	55.3	85.0	89.4	93.4	93.8	88.5	68.8	17.4
1989	82.0	56.3	85.0	90.4	94.1	93.1	88.8	69.7	16.4
1990	81.4	56.0	84.7	89.6	94.1	92.8	87.1	66.3	14.0
1991	80.3	51.5	83.8	88.5	92.6	91.1	87.6	67.5	14.0
1992	80.7	52.1	84.0	87.4	92.9	92.2	86.8	68.7	14.8
1993	80.2	50.9	83.5	87.8	92.9	92.4	87.2	65.7	15.2
1994	79.2	50.0	82.5	88.0	92.5	91.6	85.7	63.7	14.5
1995	79.1	50.2	82.4	86.2	92.9	91.3	85.6	62.4	15.8
1996	79.6	50.0	83.0	85.7	93.2	91.7	87.0	65.9	16.7
1997	80.1	47.5	84.1	88.0	93.5	91.9	87.8	68.4	17.4
1998	79.8	48.7	83.6	88.1	94.0	91.4	86.7	70.2	14.8
1999	79.8	50.1	83.5	88.1	93.9	92.2	86.2	68.6	18.2
2000	80.6	50.9	84.2	89.2	94.0	93.3	87.5	69.4	18.2
HISPANIC WOMEN									
1980	47.4	40.1	48.5	56.9	54.0	55.2	54.4	34.7	5.5
1981	48.3	38.2	49.7	59.9	55.4	55.9	54.8	34.5	6.5
1982	48.1	39.2	49.3	58.4	56.4	55.1	53.6	33.3	6.5
1983	47.7	37.6	49.0	56.5	54.8	54.7	55.4	37.4	6.4
1984	49.7	42.4	50.5	56.2	56.9	58.6	55.3	38.6	7.2
1985	49.3	38.0	50.6	57.7	57.1	59.1	55.0	36.4	5.9
1986	50.1	36.5	51.7	58.9	59.0	60.6	57.4	33.9	5.5
1987	52.0	40.1	53.3	60.4	60.9	62.2	57.8	36.8	5.3
1988	53.2	43.7	54.2	62.3	60.9	62.1	57.9	41.5	6.5
1989	53.5	40.8	54.9	60.7	63.0	64.7	57.9	39.0	8.6
1990	53.1	38.7	54.8	59.2	61.3	66.0	58.8	39.7	7.2
1991	52.3	38.0	54.0	56.4	59.8	65.3	60.3	40.5	6.7
1992	52.8	39.1	54.3	59.2	60.8	66.0	59.4	38.0	6.7
1993	52.1	36.7	53.8	56.2	60.5	65.4	59.6	40.1	7.4
1994	52.9	38.7	54.4	57.9	60.5	66.4	61.4	38.0	7.9
1995	52.6	40.4	53.9	55.9	61.6	65.9	60.5	37.2	6.6
1996	53.4	36.5	55.2	59.3	62.0	67.0	62.6	40.5	6.9
1997	55.1	38.0	57.0	62.2	63.7	69.3	63.3	40.6	8.0
1998	55.6	42.3	57.1	62.2	64.6	67.9	64.7	41.8	6.5
1999	55.9	40.6	57.7	63.0	62.7	70.5	66.2	42.4	6.5
2000	56.9	41.4	58.7	64.9	65.3	69.9	68.3	41.3	7.7

Note: Detail for the above race and Hispanic-origin groups will not sum to totals because data for the Other races group are not presented and Hispanics are included in both the White and Black population groups. See "Notes and Definitions" for information on historical comparability.

Table 1-9. Employed and Unemployed Full- and Part-Time Workers by Age, Sex, and Race, 1994–2000

(Thousands of persons.)

Year, age, sex, and race	Employed[1]								Unemployed	
	Full-time workers				Part-time workers					
	Total	At work: 35 hours or more	At work: 1 to 34 hours for economic or noneconomic reasons	Not at work	Total	At work[2]: Part-time for economic reasons	At work[2]: Part-time for noneconomic reasons	Not at work	Looking for full-time work	Looking for part-time work
TOTAL, 16 YEARS AND OVER										
1994	99 772	85 686	9 980	4 106	23 288	3 453	18 321	1 513	6 513	1 483
1995	101 679	87 736	9 924	4 020	23 220	3 215	18 443	1 562	5 909	1 495
1996	103 537	89 020	10 381	4 137	23 170	3 080	18 459	1 631	5 803	1 433
1997	106 334	92 399	9 922	4 013	23 224	2 826	18 856	1 542	5 395	1 344
1998	108 202	91 880	12 260	4 062	23 261	2 497	19 239	1 524	4 916	1 293
1999	110 302	96 276	10 079	3 947	23 186	2 216	19 509	1 461	4 669	1 211
2000	112 291	99 136	9 020	4 135	22 917	1 985	19 451	1 481	4 502	1 153
TOTAL, 20 YEARS AND OVER										
1994	97 890	84 126	9 711	4 052	19 010	3 094	14 580	1 337	5 865	811
1995	99 651	86 043	9 643	3 965	18 830	2 853	14 613	1 365	5 253	806
1996	101 496	87 344	10 070	4 083	18 712	2 733	14 556	1 423	5 157	773
1997	104 168	90 613	9 601	3 954	18 729	2 500	14 872	1 357	4 748	719
1998	105 882	89 966	11 915	4 001	18 530	2 197	15 007	1 326	4 332	672
1999	107 917	94 270	9 754	3 893	18 399	1 939	15 187	1 273	4 094	624
2000	109 769	97 019	8 678	4 073	18 163	1 726	15 148	1 290	3 936	626
MEN, 16 YEARS AND OVER										
1994	58 832	51 615	5 144	2 073	7 617	1 524	5 691	403	3 745	622
1995	59 936	52 833	5 120	1 984	7 441	1 401	5 626	414	3 374	609
1996	60 762	53 425	5 290	2 047	7 445	1 322	5 692	431	3 276	604
1997	62 258	55 216	5 040	2 001	7 427	1 187	5 821	418	3 012	564
1998	62 189	55 080	6 130	1 973	7 504	1 063	6 026	416	2 707	559
1999	63 930	57 034	4 971	1 924	7 616	946	6 178	302	2 548	518
2000	64 938	58 440	4 495	2 003	7 355	845	6 099	412	2 465	489
MEN, 20 YEARS AND OVER										
1994	57 707	50 678	4 989	2 040	5 587	1 351	3 908	329	3 359	269
1995	58 707	51 793	4 960	1 955	5 377	1 228	3 828	322	2 988	251
1996	5 275	4 676	490	109	1 390	307	1 027	56	595	78
1996	59 543	52 411	5 117	2 015	5 354	1 155	3 850	341	2 899	248
1997	60 974	54 148	4 857	1 969	5 310	1 023	3 944	343	2 644	239
1998	61 837	53 947	5 950	1 940	5 297	925	4 050	322	2 366	214
1999	62 514	55 827	4 790	1 897	5 247	809	4 127	311	2 222	211
2000	63 458	57 179	4 307	1 972	5 122	721	4 076	325	2 138	212
WOMEN, 16 YEARS AND OVER										
1994	40 940	34 071	4 836	2 033	15 670	1 929	12 631	1 111	2 768	861
1995	41 743	34 903	4 805	2 036	15 779	1 814	12 817	1 148	2 535	886
1996	42 776	35 594	5 091	2 090	15 725	1 758	12 767	1 200	2 527	829
1997	44 076	37 183	4 882	2 011	15 797	1 638	13 035	1 124	2 383	779
1998	45 014	36 800	6 124	2 090	15 757	1 435	13 214	1 108	2 210	734
1999	46 372	39 242	5 108	2 022	15 670	1 270	13 330	1 069	2 121	693
2000	47 353	40 696	4 526	2 131	15 562	1 140	13 352	1 069	2 037	663
WOMEN, 20 YEARS AND OVER										
1994	40 183	33 449	4 722	2 012	13 423	1 743	10 672	1 008	2 506	543
1995	40 943	34 250	4 683	2 010	13 453	1 623	10 785	1 043	2 265	554
1996	41 953	34 933	4 953	2 068	13 357	1 579	10 697	1 082	2 258	525
1997	43 194	36 465	4 744	1 985	13 419	1 477	10 927	1 015	2 105	480
1998	44 045	36 019	5 965	2 061	13 233	1 272	10 957	1 004	1 966	458
1999	45 403	38 443	4 964	1 996	13 152	1 131	11 059	962	1 872	413
2000	46 312	39 840	4 371	2 101	13 041	1 005	11 072	964	1 798	414

See footnotes and *Note* at end of table.

Table 1-9. Employed and Unemployed Full- and Part-Time Workers by Age, Sex, and Race, 1994–2000—*Continued*

(Thousands of persons.)

Year, age, sex, and race	Employed[1]								Unemployed	
	Full-time workers				Part-time workers					
	Total	At work		Not at work	Total	At work[2]		Not at work	Looking for full-time work	Looking for part-time work
		35 hours or more	1 to 34 hours for economic or noneconomic reasons			Part-time for economic reasons	Part-time for noneconomic reasons			
WHITE MEN, 16 YEARS AND OVER										
1994	50 964	44 750	4 431	1 783	6 487	1 192	4 946	350	2 800	475
1995	51 768	45 634	4 406	1 728	6 378	1 100	4 921	357	2 525	475
1996	52 527	46 208	4 547	1 772	6 361	1 046	4 941	374	2 426	470
1997	53 640	47 563	4 358	1 719	6 358	909	5 084	365	2 202	440
1998	54 206	47 239	5 257	1 709	6 398	829	5 209	360	1 999	432
1999	54 756	48 834	4 274	1 647	6 383	730	5 314	339	1 883	391
2000	55 455	49 877	3 859	1 720	6 241	650	5 240	351	1 783	382
WHITE MEN, 20 YEARS AND OVER										
1994	49 959	43 912	4 291	1 756	4 717	1 048	3 382	287	2 533	203
1995	50 691	44 726	4 263	1 702	4 563	958	3 330	275	2 260	204
1996	51 442	45 300	4 397	1 745	4 534	907	3 330	297	2 167	197
1997	52 498	46 609	4 199	1 691	4 488	771	3 419	298	1 946	194
1998	53 017	46 240	5 095	1 682	4 483	716	3 487	280	1 756	164
1999	53 513	47 764	4 124	1 626	4 420	618	3 534	268	1 651	162
2000	54 146	48 762	3 692	1 691	4 323	550	3 496	277	1 547	165
WHITE WOMEN, 16 YEARS AND OVER										
1994	33 906	28 170	4 031	1 705	13 832	1 517	11 316	1 000	1 935	682
1995	34 422	28 685	4 039	1 697	13 922	1 431	11 448	1 043	1 755	705
1996	35 057	29 124	4 196	1 737	13 863	1 388	11 398	1 077	1 749	656
1997	35 965	30 286	4 036	1 643	13 894	1 260	11 623	1 011	1 587	608
1998	36 553	29 792	5 039	1 722	13 774	1 089	11 695	990	1 481	572
1999	37 417	31 577	4 157	1 684	13 679	947	11 768	964	1 469	530
2000	38 126	32 674	3 703	1 750	13 653	865	11 833	955	1 413	521
WHITE WOMEN, 20 YEARS AND OVER										
1994	33 250	27 628	3 936	1 686	11 866	1 359	9 596	912	1 754	443
1995	33 728	28 116	3 938	1 674	11 916	1 277	9 690	949	1 579	463
1996	34 350	28 553	4 078	1 719	11 814	1 243	9 598	973	1 570	427
1997	35 216	29 677	3 919	1 620	11 847	1 136	9 788	923	1 396	388
1998	35 738	29 130	4 910	1 698	11 604	953	9 749	902	1 318	370
1999	36 602	30 905	4 036	1 662	11 496	839	9 789	867	1 297	319
2000	37 258	31 960	3 572	1 726	11 479	750	9 865	864	1 245	337

See footnotes and *Note* at end of table.

Table 1-9. Employed and Unemployed Full- and Part-Time Workers by Age, Sex, and Race, 1994–2000—*Continued*

(Thousands of persons.)

Year, age, sex, and race	Employed[1]								Unemployed	
	Full-time workers				Part-time workers					
	Total	At work: 35 hours or more	At work: 1 to 34 hours for economic or noneconomic reasons	Not at work	Total	At work[2]: Part-time for economic reasons	At work[2]: Part-time for noneconomic reasons	Not at work	Looking for full-time work	Looking for part-time work
BLACK MEN, 16 YEARS AND OVER										
1994	5 452	4 723	520	209	788	247	504	38	738	111
1995	5 685	4 995	513	177	737	216	479	43	660	101
1996	5 723	4 971	547	206	733	199	494	40	705	103
1997	5 894	5 193	490	211	713	203	474	36	648	98
1998	6 148	5 322	637	189	723	168	520	34	572	99
1999	6 263	5 574	494	196	764	163	568	33	528	97
2000	6 434	5 780	450	204	746	146	559	41	555	80
BLACK MEN, 20 YEARS AND OVER										
1994	5 369	4 655	509	205	595	223	343	29	634	47
1995	5 582	4 906	502	175	554	193	326	36	558	35
1996	5 622	4 892	528	201	545	177	338	30	602	37
1997	5 790	5 111	471	208	535	179	326	30	549	35
1998	6 023	5 218	620	185	507	147	334	25	487	37
1999	6 140	5 477	471	192	561	142	392	27	446	35
2000	6 303	5 668	434	201	529	126	369	33	479	32
BLACK WOMEN, 16 YEARS AND OVER										
1994	5 289	4 408	627	253	1 306	319	906	79	678	140
1995	5 542	4 679	594	268	1 315	290	952	74	637	140
1996	5 776	4 785	710	280	1 310	289	933	88	652	132
1997	6 026	5 005	652	289	1 336	305	952	79	677	136
1998	6 281	5 166	[illegible]	288	1 404	278	1 045	81	624	131
1999	6 641	5 651	734	256	1 308	257	1 059	72	654	130
2000	6 845	5 918	638	289	1 309	214	1 017	78	524	109
BLACK WOMEN, 20 YEARS AND OVER										
1994	5 211	4 346	612	251	1 108	300	740	69	608	76
1995	5 469	4 623	580	266	1 087	263	757	66	553	66
1996	5 684	4 714	693	277	1 078	263	737	79	570	73
1997	5 921	5 001	634	286	1 092	273	755	64	603	70
1998	6 159	5 073	803	283	1 131	256	807	68	555	66
1999	6 519	5 549	717	252	1 145	230	850	65	486	75
2000	6 711	5 805	621	285	1 062	199	796	68	462	57

Note: See "Notes and Definitions" for information on historical comparability.

1. Employed persons are classified as full- or part-time workers based on their usual weekly hours at all jobs regardless of the number of hours they are at work during the reference week. Persons absent from work also are classified according to their usual status.
2. Includes some persons at work 35 hours or more classified by their reason for working part-time.

Table 1-10. Persons Not in the Labor Force by Desire and Availability for Work, Age, and Sex, 1995–2000

(Thousands of persons.)

Category	Total		Age: 16 to 24 years		Age: 25 to 54 years		Age: 55 years and over		Sex: Men		Sex: Women	
	1995	1996	1995	1996	1995	1996	1995	1996	1995	1996	1995	1996
TOTAL, NOT IN THE LABOR FORCE	66 280	66 647	10 922	11 160	18 854	18 720	36 503	36 768	23 818	24 119	42 462	42 528
Do Not Want A Job Now [1]	60 610	61 197	8 807	9 110	16 246	16 205	35 557	35 882	21 536	21 929	39 704	39 267
Want A Job [1]	5 670	5 451	2 115	2 050	2 608	2 514	947	886	2 282	2 190	3 388	3 261
Did not search for work in the previous year	3 286	3 161	1 153	1 100	1 436	1 407	697	654	1 231	1 185	2 054	1 976
Searched for work in the previous year [2]	2 384	2 290	963	950	1 172	1 108	250	232	1 050	1 005	1 334	1 285
Not available to work now	791	732	397	365	350	328	45	40	302	277	490	455
Available to work now	1 593	1 558	556	585	822	780	205	192	749	728	844	830
Reason not currently looking:												
Discouragement over job prospects [3]	410	397	108	115	231	225	72	58	245	233	166	164
Reasons other than discouragement	1 182	1 160	458	471	591	555	133	135	504	495	679	666
Family responsibilities	185	177	39	35	131	125	15	17	26	31	159	146
In school or training	245	257	199	211	44	43	2	3	131	138	114	119
Ill health or disability	131	121	19	22	84	73	28	27	60	49	71	72
Other [4]	621	605	201	203	331	314	89	88	287	277	334	328

Category	Total		Age: 16 to 24 years		Age: 25 to 54 years		Age: 55 years and over		Sex: Men		Sex: Women	
	1997	1998	1997	1998	1997	1998	1997	1998	1997	1998	1997	1998
TOTAL, NOT IN THE LABOR FORCE	66 837	67 547	11 343	11 343	18 552	18 732	36 942	37 472	24 454	24 799	42 382	42 748
Do Not Want A Job Now [1]	61 895	62 735	9 434	9 491	16 311	16 580	36 151	36 664	22 420	22 790	39 475	39 945
Want A Job [1]	4 941	4 812	1 909	1 852	2 241	2 152	791	807	2 034	2 008	2 907	2 803
Did not search for work in the previous year	2 857	2 859	1 034	1 011	1 245	1 240	579	608	1 118	1 134	1 739	1 725
Searched for work in the previous year [2]	2 084	1 953	875	841	997	912	212	200	917	875	1 168	1 078
Not available to work now	669	643	346	332	289	275	34	36	257	250	412	392
Available to work now	1 416	1 310	529	509	708	637	178	164	659	624	756	686
Reason not currently looking:												
Discouragement over job prospects [3]	343	331	107	108	184	170	52	53	200	198	143	133
Reasons other than discouragement	1 073	979	423	401	524	467	126	111	460	427	613	552
Family responsibilities	139	143	26	37	97	93	16	13	21	23	117	120
In school or training	235	206	188	173	45	32	2	1	113	105	121	102
Ill health or disability	116	104	17	14	71	69	28	21	52	52	64	52
Other [4]	583	525	191	177	311	273	81	75	273	247	311	278

Category	Total		Age: 16 to 24 years		Age: 25 to 54 years		Age: 55 years and over		Sex: Men		Sex: Women	
	1999	2000	1999	2000	1999	2000	1999	2000	1999	2000	1999	2000
TOTAL, NOT IN THE LABOR FORCE	68 385	68 836	11 740	11 738	18 785	18 953	37 861	38 146	25 210	25 484	43 175	43 352
Do Not Want A Job Now [1]	63 818	64 459	9 938	10 107	16 814	17 007	37 066	37 345	23 307	23 627	40 511	40 832
Want A Job [1]	4 568	4 377	1 802	1 631	1 971	1 945	795	801	1 903	1 856	2 665	2 521
Did not search for work in the previous year	2 723	2 675	981	903	1 144	1 143	599	629	1 083	1 068	1 640	1 607
Searched for work in the previous year [2]	1 844	1 703	822	728	827	802	196	172	820	788	1 024	914
Not available to work now	644	550	345	280	258	237	41	33	249	217	395	334
Available to work now	1 201	1 152	477	448	569	565	155	139	571	572	629	581
Reason not currently looking:												
Discouragement over job prospects [3]	273	260	86	79	146	143	41	39	161	160	113	100
Reasons other than discouragement	927	892	391	369	423	422	114	101	411	412	517	481
Family responsibilities	132	118	29	26	92	83	11	10	29	23	103	96
In school or training	214	185	176	158	34	26	4	1	110	97	104	88
Ill health or disability	97	95	13	15	57	58	26	22	39	49	58	46
Other [4]	485	493	173	171	239	255	73	68	234	243	251	250

Note: See "Notes and Definitions" for information on historical comparability.

1. Includes some persons who are not asked if they want a job.
2. Persons who had a job in the prior 12 months must have searched since the end of that job.
3. Includes believes no work available, could not find work, lacks necessary schooling or training, employer thinks too young or old, and other types of discrimination.
4. Includes those who did not actively look for work in the prior 4 weeks for such reasons as child-care and transportation problems, as well as a small number for which reason for nonparticipation was not ascertained.

Table 1-11. Employed Civilians by Race, Hispanic Origin, Sex, and Age, 1948–2000

(Thousands of persons.)

Year, race, Hispanic origin, and sex	16 years and over	16 to 19 years			20 years and over						
		Total	16 to 17 years	18 to 19 years	Total	20 to 24 years	25 to 34 years	35 to 44 years	45 to 54 years	55 to 64 years	65 years and over
TOTAL											
1948	58 343	4 026	1 600	2 426	54 318	6 937	13 801	13 050	10 624	7 103	2 804
1949	57 651	3 712	1 466	2 246	53 940	6 660	13 639	13 108	10 636	7 042	2 864
1950	58 918	3 703	1 433	2 270	55 218	6 746	13 917	13 424	10 966	7 265	2 899
1951	59 961	3 767	1 575	2 192	56 196	6 321	14 233	13 746	11 421	7 558	2 917
1952	60 250	3 719	1 626	2 092	56 536	5 572	14 515	14 058	11 687	7 785	2 919
1953	61 179	3 720	1 577	2 142	57 460	5 225	14 519	14 774	11 969	7 806	3 166
1954	60 109	3 475	1 422	2 053	56 634	4 971	14 190	14 541	11 976	7 895	3 060
1955	62 170	3 642	1 500	2 143	58 528	5 270	14 481	14 879	12 556	8 158	3 185
1956	63 799	3 818	1 647	2 171	59 983	5 545	14 407	15 218	12 978	8 519	3 314
1957	64 071	3 778	1 613	2 167	60 291	5 641	14 253	15 348	13 320	8 553	3 179
1958	63 036	3 582	1 519	2 063	59 454	5 571	13 675	15 157	13 448	8 559	3 045
1959	64 630	3 838	1 670	2 168	60 791	5 870	13 709	15 454	13 915	8 822	3 023
1960	65 778	4 129	1 770	2 360	61 648	6 119	13 630	15 598	14 238	8 989	3 073
1961	65 746	4 108	1 621	2 486	61 638	6 227	13 429	15 552	14 320	9 120	2 987
1962	66 702	4 195	1 607	2 588	62 508	6 446	13 311	15 901	14 491	9 346	3 013
1963	67 762	4 255	1 751	2 504	63 508	6 815	13 318	16 114	14 749	9 596	2 915
1964	69 305	4 516	2 013	2 503	64 789	7 303	13 449	16 166	15 094	9 804	2 973
1965	71 088	5 036	2 075	2 962	66 052	7 702	13 704	16 294	15 320	10 028	3 005
1966	72 895	5 721	2 269	3 452	67 178	7 964	14 017	16 312	15 615	10 310	2 961
1967	74 372	5 682	2 334	3 348	68 690	8 499	14 575	16 281	15 789	10 536	3 011
1968	75 920	5 781	2 403	3 377	70 141	8 762	15 265	16 220	16 083	10 745	3 065
1969	77 902	6 117	2 573	3 543	71 785	9 319	15 883	16 100	16 410	10 919	3 155
1970	78 678	6 144	2 598	3 546	72 534	9 731	16 318	15 922	16 473	10 974	3 118
1971	79 367	6 208	2 596	3 613	73 158	10 201	16 781	15 675	16 451	11 009	3 040
1972	82 153	6 746	2 787	3 959	75 407	10 999	18 082	15 822	16 457	11 044	3 003
1973	85 064	7 271	3 032	4 239	77 793	11 839	19 509	16 041	16 553	10 966	2 886
1974	86 794	7 418	3 111	4 338	79 347	12 101	20 610	16 203	16 633	10 964	2 835
1975	85 846	7 104	2 941	4 162	78 744	11 885	21 087	15 953	16 190	10 027	2 801
1976	88 752	7 336	2 972	4 363	81 416	12 570	22 493	16 468	16 224	10 912	2 747
1977	92 017	7 688	3 138	4 550	84 329	13 196	23 850	17 157	16 212	11 126	2 787
1978	96 048	8 070	3 330	4 739	87 979	13 887	25 281	18 128	16 338	11 400	2 946
1979	98 824	8 083	3 340	4 743	90 741	14 327	26 492	18 981	16 357	11 585	2 999
1980	99 303	7 710	3 106	4 605	91 593	14 087	27 204	19 523	16 234	11 586	2 960
1981	100 397	7 225	2 866	4 359	93 172	14 122	28 180	20 145	16 255	11 525	2 945
1982	99 526	6 549	2 505	4 044	92 978	13 690	28 149	20 879	15 923	11 414	2 923
1983	100 834	6 342	2 320	4 022	94 491	13 722	28 756	21 960	15 812	11 315	2 927
1984	105 005	6 444	2 404	4 040	98 562	14 207	30 348	23 598	16 178	11 395	2 835
1985	107 150	6 434	2 492	3 941	100 716	13 980	31 208	24 732	16 509	11 474	2 813
1986	109 597	6 472	2 622	3 850	103 125	13 790	32 201	25 861	16 949	11 405	2 919
1987	112 440	6 640	2 736	3 905	105 800	13 524	33 105	27 179	17 487	11 465	3 041
1988	114 968	6 805	2 713	4 092	108 164	13 244	33 574	28 269	18 447	11 433	3 197
1989	117 342	6 759	2 588	4 172	110 582	12 962	34 045	29 443	19 279	11 499	3 355
1990	118 793	6 581	2 410	4 171	112 213	13 401	33 935	30 817	19 525	11 189	3 346
1991	117 718	5 906	2 202	3 704	111 812	12 975	33 061	31 593	19 882	11 001	3 300
1992	118 492	5 669	2 128	3 540	112 824	12 872	32 667	31 923	21 022	10 998	3 341
1993	120 259	5 805	2 226	3 579	114 455	12 840	32 385	32 666	22 175	11 058	3 331
1994	123 060	6 161	2 510	3 651	116 899	12 758	32 286	33 599	23 348	11 228	3 681
1995	124 900	6 419	2 573	3 846	118 481	12 443	32 356	34 202	24 378	11 435	3 666
1996	126 708	6 500	2 646	3 853	120 208	12 138	32 077	35 051	25 514	11 739	3 690
1997	129 558	6 661	2 648	4 012	122 897	12 380	31 809	35 908	26 744	12 296	3 761
1998	131 463	7 051	2 762	4 289	124 413	12 557	31 394	36 278	27 587	12 872	3 725
1999	133 488	7 172	2 793	4 379	126 316	12 891	30 865	36 728	28 635	13 315	3 882
2000	135 208	7 276	2 778	4 498	127 933	13 321	30 501	36 697	29 717	13 627	4 070

See *Note* at end of table.

Table 1-11. Employed Civilians by Race, Hispanic Origin, Sex, and Age, 1948–2000—*Continued*

(Thousands of persons.)

Year, race, Hispanic origin, and sex	16 years and over	16 to 19 years			20 years and over						
		Total	16 to 17 years	18 to 19 years	Total	20 to 24 years	25 to 34 years	35 to 44 years	45 to 54 years	55 to 64 years	65 years and over
WHITE											
1954	53 957	3 078	1 257	1 822	50 879	4 358	12 616	13 000	10 811	7 262	2 831
1955	55 833	3 225	1 330	1 896	52 608	4 637	12 855	13 327	11 322	7 510	2 957
1956	57 269	3 389	1 465	1 922	53 880	4 897	12 748	13 637	11 706	7 822	3 068
1957	57 465	3 374	1 442	1 931	54 091	4 952	12 619	13 716	12 009	7 829	2 951
1958	56 613	3 216	1 370	1 847	53 397	4 908	12 128	13 571	12 113	7 849	2 828
1959	58 006	3 475	1 520	1 955	54 531	5 138	12 144	13 830	12 552	8 063	2 805
1960	58 850	3 700	1 598	2 103	55 150	5 331	12 021	13 930	12 820	8 192	2 855
1961	58 913	3 693	1 472	2 220	55 220	5 460	11 835	13 905	12 906	8 335	2 778
1962	59 698	3 774	1 447	2 327	55 924	5 676	11 703	14 173	13 066	8 511	2 795
1963	60 622	3 851	1 600	2 250	56 771	6 036	11 689	14 341	13 304	8 718	2 683
1964	61 922	4 076	1 846	2 230	57 846	6 444	11 794	14 380	13 596	8 916	2 717
1965	63 446	4 562	1 892	2 670	58 884	6 752	11 992	14 473	13 804	9 116	2 748
1966	65 021	5 176	2 052	3 124	59 845	6 986	12 268	14 449	14 072	9 356	2 713
1967	66 361	5 114	2 121	2 993	61 247	7 493	12 763	14 429	14 224	9 596	2 746
1968	67 750	5 195	2 193	3 002	62 555	7 687	13 410	14 386	14 487	9 781	2 804
1969	69 518	5 508	2 347	3 161	64 010	8 182	13 935	14 270	14 788	9 947	2 888
1970	70 217	5 571	2 386	3 185	64 645	8 559	14 326	14 092	14 854	9 979	2 835
1971	70 878	5 670	2 404	3 266	65 208	9 000	14 713	13 858	14 843	10 014	2 780
1972	73 370	6 173	2 581	3 592	67 197	9 718	15 904	13 940	14 845	10 077	2 714
1973	75 708	6 623	2 806	3 816	69 086	10 424	17 099	14 083	14 886	9 983	2 610
1974	77 184	6 796	2 881	3 916	70 388	10 676	18 040	14 196	14 948	9 958	2 568
1975	76 411	6 487	2 721	3 770	69 924	10 546	18 485	13 979	14 555	9 827	2 533
1976	78 853	6 724	2 762	3 962	72 129	11 119	19 662	14 407	14 549	9 923	2 470
1977	81 700	7 068	2 926	4 142	74 632	11 696	20 844	14 984	14 483	10 107	2 518
1978	84 936	7 367	3 085	4 282	77 569	12 251	22 008	15 809	14 550	10 311	2 642
1979	87 259	7 356	3 079	4 278	79 904	12 594	23 033	16 578	14 522	10 477	2 699
1980	87 715	7 021	2 861	4 161	80 694	12 405	23 653	17 071	14 405	10 475	2 684
1981	88 709	6 588	2 645	3 943	82 121	12 477	24 551	17 617	14 414	10 386	2 676
1982	87 903	5 984	2 317	3 667	81 918	12 097	24 531	18 268	14 083	10 283	2 656
1983	88 893	5 799	2 156	3 643	83 094	12 138	24 955	19 194	13 961	10 169	2 678
1984	92 120	5 836	2 209	3 627	86 284	12 451	26 235	20 552	14 239	10 227	2 580
1985	93 736	5 768	2 270	3 498	87 968	12 235	26 945	21 552	14 459	10 247	2 530
1986	95 660	5 792	2 386	3 406	89 869	12 027	27 746	22 515	14 750	10 176	2 654
1987	97 789	5 898	2 468	3 431	91 890	11 748	28 429	23 596	15 216	10 164	2 738
1988	99 812	6 030	2 424	3 606	93 782	11 438	28 796	24 468	16 054	10 153	2 874
1989	101 584	5 946	2 278	3 668	95 638	11 084	29 091	25 442	16 775	10 223	3 024
1990	102 261	5 779	2 141	3 638	96 481	11 498	28 773	26 282	16 933	9 960	3 035
1991	101 182	5 216	1 971	3 246	95 966	11 116	27 989	26 883	17 269	9 719	2 990
1992	101 669	4 985	1 904	3 081	96 684	11 031	27 552	27 097	18 285	9 701	3 019
1993	103 045	5 113	1 990	3 123	97 932	10 931	27 274	27 645	19 273	9 772	3 037
1994	105 190	5 398	2 210	3 188	99 792	10 736	27 101	28 442	20 247	9 912	3 354
1995	106 490	5 593	2 273	3 320	100 897	10 400	27 014	28 951	21 127	10 070	3 335
1996	107 808	5 667	2 325	3 343	102 141	10 149	26 678	29 566	22 071	10 313	3 364
1997	109 856	5 807	2 341	3 466	104 049	10 362	26 294	30 137	23 061	10 785	3 411
1998	110 931	6 089	2 436	3 653	104 842	10 512	25 729	30 320	23 662	11 272	3 347
1999	112 235	6 204	2 435	3 769	106 032	10 716	25 113	30 548	24 507	11 657	3 491
2000	113 475	6 270	2 411	3 859	107 205	11 078	24 678	30 522	25 384	11 901	3 643

See *Note* at end of table.

Table 1-11. Employed Civilians by Race, Hispanic Origin, Sex, and Age, 1948–2000—*Continued*

(Thousands of persons.)

Year, race, Hispanic origin, and sex	16 years and over	16 to 19 years			20 years and over						
		Total	16 to 17 years	18 to 19 years	Total	20 to 24 years	25 to 34 years	35 to 44 years	45 to 54 years	55 to 64 years	65 years and over
BLACK											
1972	7 802	509	180	329	7 292	1 166	1 924	1 629	1 434	872	269
1973	8 128	570	194	378	7 559	1 258	2 062	1 659	1 460	872	249
1974	8 203	554	190	364	7 649	1 231	2 157	1 682	1 452	884	243
1975	7 894	507	183	325	7 386	1 115	2 145	1 617	1 393	874	241
1976	8 227	508	170	338	7 719	1 193	2 309	1 679	1 416	870	252
1977	8 540	508	169	339	8 031	1 244	2 443	1 754	1 448	892	251
1978	9 102	571	191	380	8 531	1 359	2 641	1 848	1 479	932	273
1979	9 359	579	204	376	8 780	1 424	2 759	1 902	1 502	927	266
1980	9 313	547	192	356	8 765	1 376	2 827	1 910	1 487	925	239
1981	9 355	505	170	335	8 849	1 346	2 872	1 957	1 489	954	231
1982	9 189	428	138	290	8 761	1 283	2 830	2 025	1 469	928	225
1983	9 375	416	123	294	8 959	1 280	2 976	2 107	1 456	937	204
1984	10 119	474	146	328	9 645	1 423	3 223	2 311	1 533	945	209
1985	10 501	532	175	356	9 969	1 399	3 325	2 427	1 598	985	235
1986	10 814	536	183	353	10 278	1 429	3 464	2 524	1 666	982	214
1987	11 309	587	203	385	10 722	1 421	3 614	2 695	1 714	1 036	241
1988	11 658	601	223	378	11 057	1 433	3 725	2 839	1 783	1 018	261
1989	11 953	625	237	388	11 328	1 467	3 801	2 981	1 844	970	265
1990	12 175	598	194	404	11 577	1 409	3 803	3 287	1 897	933	248
1991	12 074	494	161	334	11 580	1 373	3 714	3 401	1 892	957	243
1992	12 151	492	157	335	11 659	1 343	3 699	3 441	1 964	965	246
1993	12 382	494	171	323	11 888	1 377	3 700	3 584	2 059	941	226
1994	12 835	552	224	328	12 284	1 449	3 732	3 722	2 178	953	251
1995	13 279	586	223	363	12 693	1 443	3 844	3 861	2 288	1 004	253
1996	13 542	613	233	380	12 929	1 411	3 851	3 974	2 426	1 025	241
1997	13 969	631	229	401	13 339	1 456	3 903	4 094	2 588	1 048	249
1998	14 556	736	246	490	13 820	1 496	3 967	4 238	2 739	1 118	262
1999	15 056	691	243	448	14 365	1 594	4 091	4 404	2 872	1 134	271
2000	15 334	729	266	462	14 606	1 642	4 036	4 404	3 031	1 190	302
HISPANIC											
1973	3 396	. . .	. . .	. . .	3 070	. . .	. . .	. . .	. . .	. . .	. . .
1974	3 687	. . .	. . .	. . .	3 331	. . .	. . .	. . .	. . .	. . .	. . .
1975	3 663	. . .	. . .	. . .	3 341	. . .	. . .	. . .	. . .	. . .	. . .
1976	3 720	341	124	230	3 436	614	1 135	803	573	269	42
1977	4 079	381	135	245	3 715	715	1 212	860	608	269	50
1978	4 527	423	159	264	4 104	803	1 330	942	661	307	62
1979	4 785	445	152	292	4 340	860	1 430	996	666	319	69
1980	5 527	500	174	325	5 028	998	1 675	1 074	811	389	80
1981	5 813	459	155	304	5 354	1 060	1 837	1 147	829	399	82
1982	5 805	410	119	291	5 394	1 030	1 896	1 173	816	399	80
1983	6 072	423	125	297	5 649	1 068	1 997	1 224	837	441	81
1984	6 651	468	148	320	6 182	1 160	2 201	1 385	883	474	79
1985	6 888	438	144	294	6 449	1 187	2 316	1 473	913	486	75
1986	7 219	430	146	284	6 789	1 231	2 427	1 570	1 011	474	76
1987	7 790	474	149	325	7 316	1 273	2 668	1 775	1 010	512	76
1988	8 250	523	171	353	7 727	1 341	2 749	1 876	1 078	585	97
1989	8 573	548	165	383	8 025	1 325	2 900	1 968	1 129	589	114
1990	9 845	668	208	460	9 177	1 672	3 327	2 229	1 235	611	103
1991	9 828	602	169	433	9 225	1 622	3 264	2 333	1 266	637	103
1992	10 027	577	169	408	9 450	1 575	3 350	2 468	1 316	628	112
1993	10 361	570	160	410	9 792	1 574	3 446	2 605	1 402	630	135
1994	10 788	609	195	415	10 178	1 643	3 517	2 737	1 495	647	139
1995	11 127	645	194	450	10 483	1 609	3 618	2 889	1 565	666	135
1996	11 642	646	199	447	10 996	1 628	3 758	3 115	1 595	748	152
1997	12 726	714	228	487	12 012	1 798	4 029	3 371	1 846	794	173
1998	13 291	793	230	563	12 498	1 883	4 113	3 504	1 994	846	158
1999	13 720	854	254	600	12 866	1 881	4 097	3 738	2 074	886	190
2000	14 492	902	261	641	13 590	1 994	4 270	3 903	2 278	939	206

See *Note* at end of table.

Table 1-11. Employed Civilians by Race, Hispanic Origin, Sex, and Age, 1948–2000—*Continued*

(Thousands of persons.)

Year, race, Hispanic origin, and sex	16 years and over	16 to 19 years			20 years and over						
		Total	16 to 17 years	18 to 19 years	Total	20 to 24 years	25 to 34 years	35 to 44 years	45 to 54 years	55 to 64 years	65 years and over
MEN											
1948	41 725	2 344	996	1 348	39 382	4 349	10 038	9 363	7 742	5 587	2 303
1949	40 925	2 124	911	1 213	38 803	4 197	9 879	9 308	7 661	5 438	2 329
1950	41 578	2 186	909	1 277	39 394	4 255	10 060	9 445	7 790	5 508	2 336
1951	41 780	2 156	979	1 177	39 626	3 780	10 134	9 607	8 012	5 711	2 382
1952	41 682	2 107	985	1 121	39 578	3 183	10 352	9 753	8 144	5 804	2 343
1953	42 430	2 136	976	1 159	40 296	2 901	10 500	10 229	8 374	5 808	2 483
1954	41 619	1 985	881	1 104	39 634	2 724	10 254	10 082	8 330	5 830	2 414
1955	42 621	2 095	936	1 159	40 526	2 973	10 453	10 267	8 553	5 857	2 424
1956	43 379	2 164	1 008	1 156	41 216	3 245	10 337	10 385	8 732	6 004	2 512
1957	43 357	2 115	987	1 130	41 239	3 346	10 222	10 427	8 851	6 002	2 394
1958	42 423	2 012	948	1 064	40 411	3 293	9 790	10 291	8 828	5 955	2 254
1959	43 466	2 198	1 015	1 183	41 267	3 597	9 862	10 492	9 048	6 058	2 210
1960	43 904	2 361	1 090	1 271	41 543	3 754	9 759	10 552	9 182	6 105	2 191
1961	43 656	2 315	989	1 325	41 342	3 795	9 591	10 505	9 195	6 155	2 098
1962	44 177	2 362	990	1 372	41 815	3 898	9 475	10 711	9 333	6 260	2 138
1963	44 657	2 406	1 073	1 334	42 251	4 118	9 431	10 801	9 478	6 385	2 038
1964	45 474	2 587	1 242	1 345	42 886	4 370	9 531	10 832	9 637	6 478	2 039
1965	46 340	2 918	1 285	1 634	43 422	4 583	9 611	10 837	9 792	6 542	2 057
1966	46 919	3 253	1 389	1 863	43 668	4 599	9 709	10 764	9 904	6 668	2 024
1967	47 479	3 186	1 417	1 769	44 294	4 809	9 988	10 674	9 990	6 774	2 058
1968	48 114	3 255	1 453	1 802	44 859	4 812	10 405	10 554	10 102	6 893	2 093
1969	48 818	3 430	1 526	1 904	45 388	5 012	10 736	10 401	10 187	6 931	2 122
1970	48 990	3 409	1 504	1 905	45 581	5 237	10 936	10 216	10 170	6 928	2 094
1971	49 390	3 478	1 510	1 968	45 912	5 593	11 218	10 028	10 139	6 916	2 019
1972	50 896	3 765	1 598	2 167	47 130	6 138	11 884	10 088	10 139	6 929	1 953
1973	52 349	4 039	1 721	2 318	48 310	6 655	12 617	10 126	10 197	6 857	1 856
1974	53 024	4 103	1 744	2 359	48 922	6 739	13 119	10 135	10 181	6 880	1 869
1975	51 857	3 839	1 621	2 219	48 018	6 484	13 205	9 891	9 902	6 722	1 811
1976	53 138	3 947	1 626	2 321	49 190	6 915	13 869	10 069	9 881	6 724	1 732
1977	54 728	4 174	1 733	2 441	50 555	7 232	14 483	10 399	9 832	6 848	1 761
1978	56 479	4 336	1 800	2 535	52 143	7 559	15 124	10 845	9 806	6 954	1 855
1979	57 607	4 300	1 799	2 501	53 308	7 791	15 688	11 202	9 735	7 015	1 876
1980	57 186	4 085	1 672	2 412	53 101	7 532	15 832	11 355	9 548	6 999	1 835
1981	57 397	3 815	1 526	2 289	53 582	7 504	16 266	11 613	9 478	6 909	1 812
1982	56 271	3 379	1 307	2 072	52 891	7 197	16 002	11 902	9 234	6 781	1 776
1983	56 787	3 300	1 213	2 087	53 487	7 232	16 216	12 450	9 133	6 686	1 770
1984	59 091	3 322	1 244	2 078	55 769	7 571	17 166	13 309	9 326	6 694	1 703
1985	59 891	3 328	1 300	2 029	56 562	7 339	17 564	13 800	9 411	6 753	1 695
1986	60 892	3 323	1 352	1 971	57 569	7 250	18 092	14 266	9 554	6 654	1 753
1987	62 107	3 381	1 393	1 988	58 726	7 058	18 487	14 898	9 750	6 682	1 850
1988	63 273	3 492	1 403	2 089	59 781	6 918	18 702	15 457	10 201	6 591	1 911
1989	64 315	3 477	1 327	2 150	60 837	6 799	18 952	16 002	10 569	6 548	1 968
1990	65 104	3 427	1 254	2 173	61 678	7 151	18 779	16 771	10 690	6 378	1 909
1991	64 223	3 044	1 135	1 909	61 178	6 909	18 265	17 086	10 813	6 245	1 860
1992	64 440	2 944	1 096	1 848	61 496	6 819	17 966	17 230	11 365	6 173	1 943
1993	65 349	2 994	1 155	1 839	62 355	6 805	17 877	17 665	11 927	6 166	1 916
1994	66 450	3 156	1 288	1 868	63 294	6 771	17 741	18 111	12 439	6 142	2 089
1995	67 377	3 292	1 316	1 977	64 085	6 665	17 709	18 374	12 958	6 272	2 108
1996	68 207	3 310	1 318	1 992	64 897	6 429	17 527	18 816	13 483	6 470	2 172
1997	69 685	3 401	1 355	2 045	66 284	6 548	17 338	19 327	14 107	6 735	2 229
1998	70 693	3 558	1 398	2 161	67 135	6 638	17 097	19 634	14 544	7 052	2 171
1999	71 446	3 685	1 437	2 249	67 761	6 729	16 694	19 811	14 991	7 274	2 263
2000	72 293	3 713	1 405	2 308	68 580	7 009	16 494	19 770	15 561	7 389	2 357

See *Note* at end of table.

Table 1-11. Employed Civilians by Race, Hispanic Origin, Sex, and Age, 1948–2000—*Continued*

(Thousands of persons.)

Year, race, Hispanic origin, and sex	16 years and over	16 to 19 years			20 years and over						
		Total	16 to 17 years	18 to 19 years	Total	20 to 24 years	25 to 34 years	35 to 44 years	45 to 54 years	55 to 64 years	65 years and over
WOMEN											
1948	16 617	1 682	604	1 078	14 936	2 588	3 763	3 687	2 882	1 516	501
1949	16 723	1 588	555	1 033	15 137	2 463	3 760	3 800	2 975	1 604	535
1950	17 340	1 517	524	993	15 824	2 491	3 857	3 979	3 176	1 757	563
1951	18 181	1 611	596	1 015	16 570	2 541	4 099	4 139	3 409	1 847	535
1952	18 568	1 612	641	971	16 958	2 389	4 163	4 305	3 543	1 981	576
1953	18 749	1 584	601	983	17 164	2 324	4 019	4 545	3 595	1 998	683
1954	18 490	1 490	541	949	17 000	2 247	3 936	4 459	3 646	2 065	646
1955	19 551	1 547	564	984	18 002	2 297	4 028	4 612	4 003	2 301	761
1956	20 419	1 654	639	1 015	18 767	2 300	4 070	4 833	4 246	2 515	802
1957	20 714	1 663	626	1 037	19 052	2 295	4 031	4 921	4 469	2 551	785
1958	20 613	1 570	571	999	19 043	2 278	3 885	4 866	4 620	2 604	791
1959	21 164	1 640	655	985	19 524	2 273	3 847	4 962	4 867	2 764	813
1960	21 874	1 768	680	1 089	20 105	2 365	3 871	5 046	5 056	2 884	882
1961	22 090	1 793	632	1 161	20 296	2 432	3 838	5 047	5 125	2 965	889
1962	22 525	1 833	617	1 216	20 693	2 548	3 836	5 190	5 158	3 086	875
1963	23 105	1 849	678	1 170	21 257	2 697	3 887	5 313	5 271	3 211	877
1964	23 831	1 929	771	1 158	21 903	2 933	3 918	5 334	5 457	3 326	934
1965	24 748	2 118	790	1 328	22 630	3 119	4 093	5 457	5 528	3 486	948
1966	25 976	2 468	880	1 589	23 510	3 365	4 308	5 548	5 711	3 642	937
1967	26 893	2 496	917	1 579	24 397	3 690	4 587	5 607	5 799	3 762	953
1968	27 807	2 526	950	1 575	25 281	3 950	4 860	5 666	5 981	3 852	972
1969	29 084	2 687	1 047	1 639	26 397	4 307	5 147	5 699	6 223	3 988	1 033
1970	29 688	2 735	1 094	1 641	26 952	4 492	5 382	5 706	6 303	4 046	1 023
1971	29 976	2 730	1 086	1 645	27 246	4 609	5 563	5 647	6 313	4 093	1 021
1972	31 257	2 980	1 188	1 792	28 276	4 861	6 197	5 734	6 318	4 115	1 051
1973	32 715	3 231	1 310	1 920	29 484	5 184	6 893	5 915	6 356	4 109	1 029
1974	33 769	3 345	1 367	1 978	30 424	5 363	7 492	6 068	6 451	4 084	966
1975	33 989	3 263	1 320	1 943	30 726	5 401	7 882	6 061	6 288	4 105	989
1976	35 615	3 389	1 346	2 043	32 226	5 655	8 624	6 400	6 430	4 100	1 017
1977	37 289	3 514	1 403	2 110	33 775	5 965	9 367	6 758	6 380	4 279	1 027
1978	39 569	3 734	1 530	2 204	35 836	6 328	10 157	7 282	6 532	4 446	1 091
1979	41 217	3 783	1 541	2 242	37 434	6 538	10 802	7 779	6 622	4 569	1 124
1980	42 117	3 625	1 433	2 192	38 492	6 555	11 370	8 168	6 686	4 587	1 125
1981	43 000	3 411	1 340	2 070	39 590	6 618	11 914	8 532	6 777	4 616	1 133
1982	43 256	3 170	1 198	1 972	40 086	6 492	12 147	8 977	6 689	4 634	1 147
1983	44 047	3 043	1 107	1 935	41 004	6 490	12 540	9 510	6 678	4 629	1 157
1984	45 915	3 122	1 161	1 962	42 793	6 636	13 182	10 289	6 852	4 700	1 133
1985	47 259	3 105	1 193	1 913	44 154	6 640	13 644	10 933	7 097	4 721	1 118
1986	48 706	3 149	1 270	1 879	45 556	6 540	14 109	11 595	7 395	4 751	1 165
1987	50 334	3 260	1 343	1 917	47 074	6 466	14 617	12 281	7 737	4 783	1 191
1988	51 696	3 313	1 310	2 003	48 383	6 326	14 872	12 811	8 246	4 841	1 286
1989	53 027	3 282	1 261	2 021	49 745	6 163	15 093	13 440	8 711	4 950	1 388
1990	53 689	3 154	1 156	1 998	50 535	6 250	15 155	14 046	8 835	4 811	1 437
1991	53 496	2 862	1 067	1 794	50 634	6 066	14 796	14 507	9 069	4 756	1 440
1992	54 052	2 724	1 032	1 692	51 328	6 053	14 701	14 693	9 657	4 825	1 398
1993	54 910	2 811	1 071	1 740	52 099	6 035	14 508	15 002	10 248	4 892	1 414
1994	56 610	3 005	1 222	1 783	53 606	5 987	14 545	15 488	10 908	5 085	1 592
1995	57 523	3 127	1 258	1 869	54 396	5 779	14 647	15 828	11 421	5 163	1 558
1996	58 501	3 190	1 328	1 862	55 311	5 709	14 549	16 235	12 031	5 269	1 518
1997	59 873	3 260	1 293	1 967	56 613	5 831	14 471	16 581	12 637	5 561	1 532
1998	60 771	3 493	1 364	2 128	57 278	5 919	14 298	16 644	13 043	5 820	1 554
1999	62 042	3 487	1 357	2 130	58 555	6 163	14 171	16 917	13 644	6 041	1 619
2000	62 915	3 563	1 373	2 190	59 352	6 312	14 006	16 927	14 156	6 238	1 713

See *Note* at end of table.

Table 1-11. Employed Civilians by Race, Hispanic Origin, Sex, and Age, 1948–2000—*Continued*

(Thousands of persons.)

Year, race, Hispanic origin, and sex	16 years and over	16 to 19 years			20 years and over						
		Total	16 to 17 years	18 to 19 years	Total	20 to 24 years	25 to 34 years	35 to 44 years	45 to 54 years	55 to 64 years	65 years and over
WHITE MEN											
1954	37 846	1 723	771	953	36 123	2 394	9 287	9 175	7 614	5 412	2 241
1955	38 719	1 824	821	1 004	36 895	2 607	9 461	9 351	7 792	5 431	2 254
1956	39 368	1 893	890	1 002	37 475	2 850	9 330	9 449	7 950	5 559	2 336
1957	39 349	1 865	874	990	37 484	2 930	9 226	9 480	8 067	5 542	2 234
1958	38 591	1 783	852	932	36 808	2 896	8 861	9 386	8 061	5 501	2 103
1959	39 494	1 961	915	1 046	37 533	3 153	8 911	9 560	8 261	5 588	2 060
1960	39 755	2 092	973	1 119	37 663	3 264	8 777	9 589	8 372	5 618	2 043
1961	39 588	2 055	891	1 164	37 533	3 311	8 630	9 566	8 394	5 670	1 961
1962	40 016	2 098	883	1 215	37 918	3 426	8 514	9 718	8 512	5 749	1 998
1963	40 428	2 156	972	1 184	38 272	3 646	8 463	9 782	8 650	5 844	1 887
1964	41 115	2 316	1 128	1 188	38 799	3 856	8 538	9 800	8 787	5 945	1 872
1965	41 844	2 612	1 159	1 453	39 232	4 025	8 598	9 795	8 924	5 998	1 892
1966	42 331	2 913	1 245	1 668	39 418	4 028	8 674	9 719	9 029	6 096	1 871
1967	42 833	2 849	1 278	1 571	39 985	4 231	8 931	9 632	9 093	6 208	1 892
1968	43 411	2 908	1 319	1 589	40 503	4 226	9 315	9 522	9 198	6 316	1 926
1969	44 048	3 070	1 385	1 685	40 978	4 401	9 608	9 379	9 279	6 359	1 953
1970	44 178	3 066	1 374	1 692	41 112	4 601	9 784	9 202	9 271	6 340	1 914
1971	44 595	3 157	1 393	1 764	41 438	4 935	10 026	9 026	9 256	6 339	1 856
1972	45 944	3 416	1 470	1 947	42 528	5 431	10 664	9 047	9 236	6 363	1 786
1973	47 085	3 660	1 590	2 071	43 424	5 863	11 268	9 046	9 257	6 299	1 689
1974	47 674	3 728	1 611	2 117	43 946	5 965	11 701	9 027	9 242	6 304	1 706
1975	46 697	3 505	1 502	2 002	43 192	5 770	11 783	8 818	9 005	6 160	1 656
1976	47 775	3 604	1 501	2 103	44 171	6 140	12 362	8 944	8 968	6 176	1 579
1977	49 150	3 824	1 607	2 217	45 326	6 437	12 893	9 212	8 898	6 279	1 605
1978	50 544	3 950	1 664	2 286	46 594	6 717	13 413	9 608	8 840	6 339	1 677
1979	51 452	3 904	1 654	2 250	47 546	6 868	13 888	9 930	8 748	6 406	1 707
1980	51 127	3 708	1 534	2 174	47 419	6 652	14 009	10 077	8 586	6 412	1 684
1981	51 315	3 469	1 402	2 066	47 846	6 652	14 398	10 307	8 518	6 309	1 662
1982	50 287	3 079	1 214	1 865	47 209	6 372	14 164	10 593	8 267	6 188	1 624
1983	50 621	3 003	1 124	1 879	47 618	6 386	14 297	11 062	8 152	6 084	1 637
1984	52 462	3 001	1 140	1 861	49 461	6 647	15 045	11 776	8 320	6 108	1 564
1985	53 046	2 985	1 185	1 800	50 061	6 428	15 374	12 214	8 374	6 118	1 552
1986	53 785	2 966	1 225	1 741	50 818	6 340	15 790	12 620	8 442	6 012	1 612
1987	54 647	2 999	1 252	1 747	51 649	6 150	16 084	13 138	8 596	5 991	1 690
1988	55 550	3 084	1 248	1 836	52 466	5 987	16 241	13 590	8 992	5 909	1 748
1989	56 352	3 060	1 171	1 889	53 292	5 839	16 383	14 046	9 335	5 891	1 797
1990	56 703	3 018	1 119	1 899	53 685	6 179	16 124	14 496	9 383	5 744	1 760
1991	55 797	2 694	1 017	1 677	53 103	5 942	15 644	14 743	9 488	5 578	1 707
1992	55 959	2 602	990	1 612	53 357	5 855	15 357	14 842	10 027	5 503	1 772
1993	56 656	2 634	1 031	1 603	54 021	5 830	15 230	15 178	10 497	5 514	1 772
1994	57 452	2 776	1 144	1 632	54 676	5 738	15 052	15 562	10 910	5 490	1 925
1995	58 146	2 892	1 169	1 723	55 254	5 613	14 958	15 793	11 359	5 609	1 921
1996	58 888	2 911	1 161	1 750	55 977	5 444	14 820	16 136	11 834	5 755	1 987
1997	59 998	3 011	1 206	1 806	56 986	5 590	14 567	16 470	12 352	5 972	2 037
1998	60 604	3 103	1 233	1 870	57 500	5 659	14 259	16 715	12 661	6 251	1 955
1999	61 139	3 205	1 254	1 951	57 934	5 753	13 851	16 781	13 046	6 447	2 056
2000	61 696	3 227	1 220	2 007	58 469	5 939	13 634	16 749	13 484	6 532	2 130

See *Note* at end of table.

Table 1-11. Employed Civilians by Race, Hispanic Origin, Sex, and Age, 1948–2000—*Continued*

(Thousands of persons.)

Year, race, Hispanic origin, and sex	16 years and over	16 to 19 years			20 years and over						
		Total	16 to 17 years	18 to 19 years	Total	20 to 24 years	25 to 34 years	35 to 44 years	45 to 54 years	55 to 64 years	65 years and over
WHITE WOMEN											
1954	16 111	1 355	486	869	14 756	1 964	3 329	3 825	3 197	1 850	590
1955	17 114	1 401	509	892	15 713	2 030	3 394	3 976	3 530	2 079	703
1956	17 901	1 496	575	920	16 405	2 047	3 418	4 188	3 756	2 263	732
1957	18 116	1 509	568	941	16 607	2 022	3 393	4 236	3 942	2 287	717
1958	18 022	1 433	518	915	16 589	2 012	3 267	4 185	4 052	2 348	725
1959	18 512	1 514	605	909	16 998	1 985	3 233	4 270	4 291	2 475	745
1960	19 095	1 608	625	984	17 487	2 067	3 244	4 341	4 448	2 574	812
1961	19 325	1 638	581	1 056	17 687	2 149	3 205	4 339	4 512	2 665	817
1962	19 682	1 676	564	1 112	18 006	2 250	3 189	4 455	4 554	2 762	797
1963	20 194	1 695	628	1 066	18 499	2 390	3 226	4 559	4 654	2 874	796
1964	20 807	1 760	718	1 042	19 047	2 588	3 256	4 580	4 809	2 971	845
1965	21 602	1 950	733	1 217	19 652	2 727	3 394	4 678	4 880	3 118	856
1966	22 690	2 263	807	1 456	20 427	2 958	3 594	4 730	5 043	3 260	842
1967	23 528	2 265	843	1 422	21 263	3 262	3 832	4 797	5 131	3 388	854
1968	24 339	2 287	874	1 413	22 052	3 461	4 095	4 864	5 289	3 465	878
1969	25 470	2 438	962	1 476	23 032	3 781	4 327	4 891	5 509	3 588	935
1970	26 039	2 505	1 012	1 493	23 534	3 959	4 542	4 890	5 582	3 640	921
1971	26 283	2 513	1 011	1 502	23 770	4 065	4 687	4 831	5 588	3 675	924
1972	27 426	2 755	1 111	1 645	24 669	4 286	5 240	4 893	5 608	3 714	928
1973	28 623	2 962	1 217	1 746	25 661	4 562	5 831	5 036	5 628	3 684	920
1974	29 511	3 069	1 269	1 799	26 442	4 711	6 340	5 169	5 706	3 654	862
1975	29 714	2 983	1 215	1 767	26 731	4 775	6 701	5 161	5 550	3 667	877
1976	31 078	3 120	1 260	1 860	27 958	4 978	7 300	5 462	5 580	3 746	891
1977	32 550	3 244	1 319	1 923	29 306	5 259	7 950	5 772	5 585	3 829	912
1978	34 392	3 416	1 420	1 996	30 975	5 535	8 595	6 201	5 710	3 972	964
1979	35 807	3 451	1 423	2 027	32 357	5 726	9 145	6 648	5 773	4 071	993
1980	36 587	3 314	1 327	1 986	33 275	5 753	9 644	6 994	5 818	4 064	1 001
1981	37 394	3 119	1 242	1 877	34 275	5 826	10 153	7 311	5 896	4 077	1 013
1982	37 615	2 905	1 103	1 802	34 710	5 724	10 367	7 070	5 916	4 095	1 032
1983	38 272	2 796	1 032	1 764	35 476	5 751	10 659	8 132	5 809	4 084	1 041
1984	39 659	2 835	1 069	1 766	36 823	5 804	11 190	8 776	5 920	4 118	1 015
1985	40 690	2 783	1 085	1 698	37 907	5 807	11 571	9 338	6 084	4 128	978
1986	41 876	2 825	1 160	1 665	39 050	5 687	11 956	9 895	6 307	4 164	1 042
1987	43 142	2 900	1 216	1 684	40 242	5 508	12 345	10 459	6 620	4 172	1 047
1988	44 262	2 946	1 176	1 770	41 316	5 450	12 555	10 878	7 062	4 244	1 126
1989	45 232	2 886	1 107	1 779	42 346	5 245	12 708	11 395	7 440	4 332	1 227
1990	45 558	2 762	1 023	1 739	42 796	5 319	12 649	11 785	7 551	4 217	1 275
1991	45 385	2 523	954	1 569	42 862	5 174	12 344	12 139	7 781	4 141	1 283
1992	45 710	2 383	915	1 468	43 327	5 176	12 195	12 254	8 258	4 198	1 246
1993	46 390	2 479	959	1 520	43 910	5 101	12 044	12 467	8 776	4 258	1 265
1994	47 738	2 622	1 066	1 556	45 116	4 997	12 049	12 880	9 338	4 423	1 429
1995	48 344	2 701	1 104	1 597	45 643	4 787	12 056	13 157	9 768	4 461	1 415
1996	48 920	2 756	1 164	1 592	46 164	4 705	11 858	13 430	10 237	4 558	1 376
1997	49 859	2 796	1 136	1 660	47 063	4 773	11 727	13 667	10 709	4 813	1 374
1998	50 327	2 986	1 203	1 783	47 342	4 853	11 470	13 604	11 001	5 021	1 392
1999	51 096	2 999	1 181	1 817	48 098	4 963	11 262	13 767	11 461	5 211	1 435
2000	51 780	3 043	1 191	1 852	48 736	5 140	11 043	13 772	11 899	5 369	1 512

See *Note* at end of table.

Table 1-11. Employed Civilians by Race, Hispanic Origin, Sex, and Age, 1948–2000—*Continued*

(Thousands of persons.)

Year, race, Hispanic origin, and sex	16 years and over	16 to 19 years			20 years and over						
		Total	16 to 17 years	18 to 19 years	Total	20 to 24 years	25 to 34 years	35 to 44 years	45 to 54 years	55 to 64 years	65 years and over
BLACK MEN											
1972	4 368	309	114	195	4 058	648	1 074	890	793	499	156
1973	4 527	330	112	220	4 197	711	1 142	898	816	483	148
1974	4 527	322	114	209	4 204	668	1 176	912	803	500	145
1975	4 275	276	98	179	3 998	595	1 159	865	755	487	137
1976	4 404	283	100	184	4 120	635	1 217	897	763	472	137
1977	4 565	291	105	186	4 273	659	1 271	940	777	484	143
1978	4 796	312	106	206	4 483	697	1 357	969	788	516	155
1979	4 923	316	111	205	4 606	754	1 425	983	801	498	147
1980	4 798	299	109	191	4 498	713	1 438	975	770	478	126
1981	4 794	273	95	178	4 520	693	1 457	991	764	492	123
1982	4 637	223	65	158	4 414	660	1 414	997	750	471	122
1983	4 753	222	64	158	4 531	684	1 483	1 034	749	477	105
1984	5 124	252	79	173	4 871	750	1 635	1 138	780	460	108
1985	5 270	278	92	186	4 992	726	1 669	1 187	795	501	114
1986	5 428	278	96	182	5 150	732	1 756	1 211	831	507	112
1987	5 661	304	109	195	5 357	728	1 821	1 283	853	547	124
1988	5 824	316	122	193	5 509	736	1 881	1 348	878	536	131
1989	5 928	327	124	202	5 602	742	1 931	1 415	886	498	131
1990	5 995	303	99	204	5 692	702	1 895	1 586	926	469	114
1991	5 961	255	85	170	5 706	695	1 859	1 634	923	481	114
1992	5 930	249	78	170	5 681	679	1 819	1 650	930	478	124
1993	6 047	254	88	166	5 793	674	1 858	1 717	978	461	106
1994	6 241	276	107	169	5 964	718	1 850	1 795	1 030	455	115
1995	6 422	285	111	174	6 137	714	1 895	1 836	1 085	468	138
1996	6 456	289	109	180	6 167	685	1 867	1 878	1 129	482	126
1997	6 607	282	108	174	6 325	668	1 874	1 955	1 215	487	127
1998	6 871	341	120	221	6 530	686	1 886	2 008	1 284	524	142
1999	7 027	325	120	205	6 702	700	1 926	2 092	1 327	525	131
2000	7 180	348	133	215	6 832	755	1 882	2 087	1 396	564	147
BLACK WOMEN											
1972	3 433	200	65	134	3 233	519	850	739	641	373	113
1973	3 601	239	81	158	3 362	546	920	761	644	389	101
1974	3 677	232	77	155	3 445	562	981	770	649	383	98
1975	3 618	231	85	146	3 388	520	985	752	638	387	104
1976	3 823	224	70	154	3 599	558	1 092	782	653	398	115
1977	3 975	217	64	153	3 758	585	1 172	814	671	408	109
1978	4 307	260	85	175	4 047	662	1 283	879	691	416	118
1979	4 436	263	92	171	4 174	670	1 333	919	702	428	119
1980	4 515	248	82	165	4 267	663	1 389	936	717	448	113
1981	4 561	232	75	157	4 329	653	1 415	966	725	462	108
1982	4 552	205	73	132	4 347	623	1 416	1 028	719	457	103
1983	4 622	194	59	136	4 428	596	1 493	1 073	707	460	99
1984	4 995	222	67	155	4 773	673	1 588	1 173	753	485	101
1985	5 231	254	83	171	4 977	673	1 656	1 240	804	484	121
1986	5 386	259	87	171	5 128	696	1 708	1 313	835	475	102
1987	5 648	283	93	190	5 365	693	1 793	1 412	860	489	117
1988	5 834	285	101	184	5 548	697	1 844	1 491	905	482	129
1989	6 025	298	113	185	5 727	725	1 870	1 566	959	472	134
1990	6 180	296	96	200	5 884	707	1 907	1 701	971	464	135
1991	6 113	239	76	164	5 874	677	1 855	1 768	969	476	129
1992	6 221	243	79	164	5 978	664	1 880	1 791	1 034	487	123
1993	6 334	239	82	157	6 095	703	1 842	1 867	1 081	480	121
1994	6 595	275	117	158	6 320	731	1 882	1 926	1 147	497	136
1995	6 857	301	112	189	6 556	729	1 949	2 025	1 202	536	114
1996	7 086	324	124	200	6 762	726	1 984	2 096	1 297	543	115
1997	7 362	349	122	227	7 013	789	2 029	2 139	1 373	561	122
1998	7 685	395	126	268	7 290	810	2 081	2 230	1 455	594	120
1999	8 029	366	123	243	7 663	893	2 165	2 312	1 545	609	139
2000	8 154	380	133	247	7 774	887	2 154	2 317	1 635	626	155

See *Note* at end of table.

Table 1-11. Employed Civilians by Race, Hispanic Origin, Sex, and Age, 1948–2000—*Continued*

(Thousands of persons.)

Year, race, Hispanic origin, and sex	16 years and over	16 to 19 years			20 years and over						
		Total	16 to 17 years	18 to 19 years	Total	20 to 24 years	25 to 34 years	35 to 44 years	45 to 54 years	55 to 64 years	65 years and over
HISPANIC MEN											
1973	2 198	. . .	. . .	. . .	2 010	. . .	. . .	. . .	. . .	. . .	. . .
1974	2 369	. . .	. . .	. . .	2 165	. . .	. . .	. . .	. . .	. . .	. . .
1975	2 301	. . .	. . .	. . .	2 117	. . .	. . .	. . .	. . .	. . .	. . .
1976	2 303	199	74	125	2 109	364	708	504	369	173	30
1977	2 564	225	78	147	2 335	427	763	540	394	184	37
1978	2 808	241	93	147	2 568	494	824	590	405	207	47
1979	2 962	260	93	168	2 701	511	891	615	427	205	53
1980	3 448	306	109	198	3 142	611	1 065	662	491	254	58
1981	3 597	272	90	182	3 325	642	1 157	707	504	259	56
1982	3 583	229	66	162	3 354	621	1 192	729	498	261	53
1983	3 771	248	71	177	3 523	655	1 280	760	499	275	53
1984	4 083	258	78	180	3 825	718	1 398	841	530	292	46
1985	4 245	251	82	169	3 994	727	1 473	888	550	308	48
1986	4 428	254	82	172	4 174	773	1 510	929	614	297	51
1987	4 713	268	81	188	4 444	777	1 664	1 044	606	303	50
1988	4 972	292	87	205	4 680	815	1 706	1 120	645	331	64
1989	5 172	319	94	225	4 853	821	1 787	1 152	676	350	67
1990	6 021	412	126	286	5 609	1 083	2 076	1 312	722	355	61
1991	5 979	356	94	263	5 623	1 063	2 050	1 360	719	369	62
1992	6 093	336	97	238	5 757	985	2 127	1 437	768	372	69
1993	6 328	337	95	242	5 992	1 003	2 200	1 527	822	360	80
1994	6 530	341	109	233	6 189	1 056	2 227	1 600	847	379	80
1995	6 725	358	110	248	6 367	1 030	2 284	1 675	908	384	86
1996	7 039	384	107	277	6 655	1 015	2 345	1 842	918	438	97
1997	7 728	420	130	290	7 307	1 142	2 547	1 978	1 059	477	104
1998	8 018	449	133	315	7 570	1 173	2 592	2 077	1 115	512	101
1999	8 067	491	139	352	7 576	1 135	2 524	2 135	1 151	502	130
2000	8 478	517	142	375	7 961	1 214	2 554	2 249	1 264	550	130
HISPANIC WOMEN											
1973	1 198	. . .	. . .	. . .	1 060	. . .	. . .	. . .	. . .	. . .	. . .
1974	1 319	. . .	. . .	. . .	1 166	. . .	. . .	. . .	. . .	. . .	. . .
1975	1 362	. . .	. . .	. . .	1 224	. . .	. . .	. . .	. . .	. . .	. . .
1976	1 417	155	50	106	1 288	249	427	300	204	96	12
1977	1 516	155	57	98	1 370	288	449	320	214	86	13
1978	1 719	182	65	117	1 537	308	506	352	256	99	15
1979	1 824	185	60	125	1 638	349	539	381	241	115	15
1980	2 079	193	65	128	1 886	387	610	412	320	136	22
1981	2 216	187	65	122	2 029	418	680	440	326	139	26
1982	2 222	181	52	129	2 040	409	704	444	318	139	26
1983	2 301	175	54	120	2 127	413	717	464	338	166	28
1984	2 568	211	71	140	2 357	442	804	544	354	181	33
1985	2 642	187	62	125	2 456	460	843	585	362	178	27
1986	2 791	176	64	112	2 615	458	917	641	397	177	25
1987	3 077	206	69	137	2 872	496	1 004	732	405	209	26
1988	3 278	231	84	147	3 047	526	1 042	756	434	254	33
1989	3 401	229	71	158	3 172	504	1 114	816	453	239	46
1990	3 823	256	82	174	3 567	588	1 251	917	513	256	42
1991	3 848	246	76	170	3 603	559	1 214	972	548	268	41
1992	3 934	242	72	170	3 693	591	1 223	1 031	548	256	43
1993	4 033	233	65	168	3 800	571	1 246	1 077	581	269	55
1994	4 258	268	86	182	3 989	587	1 290	1 137	648	268	59
1995	4 403	287	85	202	4 116	579	1 334	1 213	657	282	50
1996	4 602	261	92	169	4 341	612	1 412	1 273	677	310	56
1997	4 999	294	98	196	4 705	656	1 482	1 393	787	318	69
1998	5 273	345	97	247	4 928	710	1 521	1 428	879	334	57
1999	5 653	363	115	248	5 290	746	1 574	1 603	923	384	60
2000	6 014	385	120	265	5 629	780	1 716	1 654	1 015	389	152

Note: Detail for the above race and Hispanic-origin groups will not sum to totals because data for the Other races group are not presented and Hispanics are included in both the White and Black population groups. See "Notes and Definitions" for information on historical comparability.

Table 1-12. Civilian Employment to Population Ratios by Sex, Race, Hispanic Origin, and Age, 1948–2000

(Percent.)

Year, race, and Hispanic origin	Total			Men			Women		
	16 years and over	16 to 19 years	20 years and over	16 years and over	16 to 19 years	20 years and over	16 years and over	16 to 19 years	20 years and over
TOTAL									
1948	56.6	47.7	57.4	83.5	57.5	85.8	31.3	38.5	30.7
1949	55.4	45.2	56.3	81.3	53.8	83.7	31.2	37.2	30.6
1950	56.1	45.5	57.0	82.0	55.2	84.2	32.0	36.3	31.6
1951	57.3	47.9	58.1	84.0	57.9	86.1	33.1	38.9	32.6
1952	57.3	46.9	58.1	83.9	55.9	86.2	33.4	38.8	33.0
1953	57.1	46.4	58.0	83.6	55.9	85.9	33.3	37.8	32.9
1954	55.5	42.3	56.6	81.0	50.2	83.5	32.5	34.9	32.3
1955	56.7	43.5	57.8	81.8	52.1	84.3	34.0	35.6	33.8
1956	57.5	45.3	58.5	82.3	53.8	84.6	35.1	37.5	34.9
1957	57.1	43.9	58.2	81.3	51.8	83.8	35.1	36.7	35.0
1958	55.4	39.9	56.8	78.5	46.9	81.2	34.5	33.5	34.6
1959	56.0	39.9	57.5	79.3	47.2	82.3	35.0	33.0	35.1
1960	56.1	40.5	57.6	78.9	47.6	81.9	35.5	33.8	35.7
1961	55.4	39.1	56.9	77.6	45.3	80.8	35.4	33.2	35.6
1962	55.5	39.4	57.1	77.7	45.9	80.9	35.6	33.3	35.8
1963	55.4	37.4	57.2	77.1	43.8	80.6	35.8	31.5	36.3
1964	55.7	37.3	57.7	77.3	44.1	80.9	36.3	30.9	36.9
1965	56.2	38.9	58.2	77.5	46.2	81.2	37.1	32.0	37.6
1966	56.9	42.1	58.7	77.9	48.9	81.5	38.3	35.6	38.6
1967	57.3	42.2	59.0	78.0	48.7	81.5	39.0	35.9	39.3
1968	57.5	42.2	59.3	77.8	48.7	81.3	39.6	36.0	40.0
1969	58.0	43.4	59.7	77.6	49.5	81.1	40.7	37.5	41.1
1970	57.4	42.3	59.2	76.2	47.7	79.7	40.8	37.1	41.2
1971	56.6	41.3	58.4	74.9	46.8	78.5	40.4	36.0	40.9
1972	57.0	43.5	58.6	75.0	48.9	78.4	41.0	38.2	41.3
1973	57.8	45.9	59.3	75.5	51.4	78.6	42.0	40.5	42.2
1974	57.8	46.0	59.2	74.9	51.2	77.9	42.6	41.0	42.8
1975	56.1	43.3	57.6	71.7	47.2	74.8	42.0	39.4	42.3
1976	56.8	44.2	58.3	72.0	47.9	75.1	43.2	40.5	43.5
1977	57.9	46.1	59.2	72.8	50.4	75.6	44.5	41.8	44.8
1978	59.3	48.3	60.6	73.8	52.2	76.4	46.4	44.5	46.6
1979	59.9	48.5	61.2	73.8	51.7	76.5	47.5	45.3	47.7
1980	59.2	46.6	60.6	72.0	49.5	74.6	47.7	43.8	48.1
1981	59.0	44.6	60.5	71.3	47.1	74.0	48.0	42.0	48.6
1982	57.8	41.5	59.4	69.0	42.9	71.8	47.7	40.2	48.4
1983	57.9	41.5	59.5	68.8	43.1	71.4	48.0	40.0	48.8
1984	59.5	43.7	61.0	70.7	45.0	73.2	49.5	42.5	50.1
1985	60.1	44.4	61.5	70.9	45.7	73.3	50.4	42.9	51.0
1986	60.7	44.6	62.1	71.0	45.7	73.3	51.4	43.6	52.0
1987	61.5	45.5	62.9	71.5	46.1	73.8	52.5	44.8	53.1
1988	62.3	46.8	63.6	72.0	47.8	74.2	53.4	45.9	54.0
1989	63.0	47.5	64.2	72.5	48.7	74.5	54.3	46.4	54.9
1990	62.8	45.3	64.3	72.0	46.6	74.3	54.3	44.0	55.2
1991	61.7	42.0	63.2	70.4	42.7	72.7	53.7	41.2	54.6
1992	61.5	41.0	63.0	69.8	41.9	72.1	53.8	40.0	54.8
1993	61.7	41.7	63.3	70.0	42.3	72.3	54.1	41.0	55.0
1994	62.5	43.4	64.0	70.4	43.8	72.6	55.3	43.0	56.2
1995	62.9	44.2	64.4	70.8	44.7	73.0	55.6	43.8	56.5
1996	63.2	43.5	64.7	70.9	43.6	73.2	56.0	43.5	57.0
1997	63.8	43.4	65.5	71.3	43.4	73.7	56.8	43.3	57.8
1998	64.1	45.1	65.6	71.6	44.7	73.9	57.1	45.5	58.0
1999	64.3	44.7	65.9	71.6	45.1	74.0	57.4	44.3	58.5
2000	64.5	45.4	66.1	71.8	45.6	74.1	57.7	45.2	58.7

See *Note* at end of table.

Table 1-12. Civilian Employment to Population Ratios by Sex, Race, Hispanic Origin, and Age, 1948–2000—*Continued*

(Percent.)

Year, race, and Hispanic origin	Total			Men			Women		
	16 years and over	16 to 19 years	20 years and over	16 years and over	16 to 19 years	20 years and over	16 years and over	16 to 19 years	20 years and over
WHITE									
1954	55.2	42.9	56.2	81.5	49.9	84.0	31.4	36.4	31.1
1955	56.5	44.2	57.4	82.2	52.0	84.7	33.0	37.0	32.7
1956	57.3	46.1	58.2	82.7	54.1	85.0	34.2	38.9	33.8
1957	56.8	45.0	57.8	81.8	52.4	84.1	34.2	38.2	33.9
1958	55.3	41.0	56.5	79.2	47.6	81.8	33.6	35.0	33.5
1959	55.9	41.2	57.2	79.9	48.1	82.8	34.0	34.8	34.0
1960	55.9	41.5	57.2	79.4	48.1	82.4	34.6	35.1	34.5
1961	55.3	40.1	56.7	78.2	45.9	81.4	34.5	34.6	34.5
1962	55.4	40.4	56.9	78.4	46.4	81.5	34.7	34.8	34.7
1963	55.3	38.6	56.9	77.7	44.7	81.1	35.0	32.9	35.2
1964	55.5	38.4	57.3	77.8	45.0	81.3	35.5	32.2	35.8
1965	56.0	40.3	57.8	77.9	47.1	81.5	36.2	33.7	36.5
1966	56.8	43.6	58.3	78.3	50.1	81.7	37.5	37.5	37.5
1967	57.2	43.8	58.7	78.4	50.2	81.7	38.3	37.7	38.3
1968	57.4	43.9	59.0	78.3	50.3	81.6	38.9	37.8	39.1
1969	58.0	45.2	59.4	78.2	51.1	81.4	40.1	39.5	40.1
1970	57.5	44.5	59.0	76.8	49.6	80.1	40.3	39.5	40.4
1971	56.8	43.8	58.3	75.7	49.2	79.0	39.9	38.6	40.1
1972	57.4	46.4	58.6	76.0	51.5	79.0	40.7	41.3	40.6
1973	58.2	48.9	59.3	76.5	54.3	79.2	41.8	43.6	41.6
1974	58.3	49.3	59.3	75.9	54.4	78.6	42.4	44.3	42.2
1975	56.7	46.5	57.9	73.0	50.6	75.7	42.0	42.5	41.9
1976	57.5	47.8	58.6	73.4	51.5	76.0	43.2	44.2	43.1
1977	58.6	50.1	59.6	74.1	54.4	76.5	44.5	45.9	44.4
1978	60.0	52.4	60.8	75.0	56.3	77.2	46.3	48.5	46.1
1979	60.6	52.6	61.5	75.1	55.7	77.3	47.5	49.4	47.3
1980	60.0	50.7	61.0	73.4	53.4	75.6	47.8	47.9	47.8
1981	60.0	48.7	61.1	72.8	51.3	75.1	48.3	46.2	48.5
1982	58.8	45.8	60.1	70.6	47.0	73.0	48.1	44.6	48.4
1983	58.9	45.9	60.1	70.4	47.4	72.6	48.5	44.5	48.9
1984	60.5	48.0	61.5	72.1	49.1	74.3	49.8	47.0	50.0
1985	61.0	48.5	62.0	72.3	49.9	74.0	50.7	47.1	51.0
1986	61.5	48.8	62.6	72.3	49.6	74.3	51.7	47.9	52.0
1987	62.3	49.4	63.4	72.7	49.9	74.7	52.8	49.0	53.1
1988	63.1	50.9	64.1	73.2	51.7	75.1	53.8	50.2	54.0
1989	63.8	51.6	64.7	73.7	52.6	75.4	54.6	50.5	54.9
1990	63.7	49.7	64.8	73.3	51.0	75.1	54.7	48.3	55.2
1991	62.6	46.6	63.7	71.6	47.2	73.5	54.2	45.9	54.8
1992	62.4	45.3	63.6	71.1	46.4	73.1	54.2	44.2	54.9
1993	62.7	46.2	63.9	71.4	46.6	73.3	54.6	45.7	55.2
1994	63.5	47.9	64.7	71.8	48.3	73.6	55.8	47.5	56.4
1995	63.8	48.8	64.9	72.0	49.4	73.8	56.1	48.1	56.7
1996	64.1	47.9	65.3	72.3	48.2	74.2	56.3	47.6	57.0
1997	64.6	47.7	65.9	72.7	48.1	74.7	57.0	47.2	57.8
1998	64.7	48.9	65.9	72.7	48.6	74.7	57.1	49.3	57.7
1999	64.8	48.8	66.1	72.8	49.3	74.8	57.3	48.3	58.0
2000	65.1	49.3	66.3	72.9	49.7	74.8	57.7	49.0	58.3

See *Note* at end of table.

Table 1-12. Civilian Employment to Population Ratios by Sex, Race, Hispanic Origin, and Age, 1948–2000—*Continued*

(Percent.)

Year, race, and Hispanic origin	Total			Men			Women		
	16 years and over	16 to 19 years	20 years and over	16 years and over	16 to 19 years	20 years and over	16 years and over	16 to 19 years	20 years and over
BLACK									
1972	53.7	25.2	58.3	66.8	31.6	73.0	43.0	19.2	46.5
1973	54.5	27.2	58.9	67.5	32.8	73.7	43.8	22.0	47.2
1974	53.5	25.9	58.0	65.8	31.4	71.9	43.5	20.9	46.9
1975	50.1	23.1	54.5	60.6	26.3	66.5	41.6	20.2	44.9
1976	50.8	22.4	55.4	60.6	25.8	66.8	42.8	19.2	46.4
1977	51.4	22.3	56.0	61.4	26.4	67.5	43.3	18.5	47.0
1978	53.6	25.2	58.0	63.3	28.5	69.1	45.8	22.1	49.3
1979	53.8	25.4	58.1	63.4	28.7	69.1	46.0	22.4	49.3
1980	52.3	23.9	56.4	60.4	27.0	65.8	45.7	21.0	49.1
1981	51.3	22.1	55.5	59.1	24.6	64.5	45.1	19.7	48.5
1982	49.4	19.0	53.6	56.0	20.3	61.4	44.2	17.7	47.5
1983	49.5	18.7	53.6	56.3	20.4	61.6	44.1	17.0	47.4
1984	52.3	21.9	56.1	59.2	23.9	64.1	46.7	20.1	49.8
1985	53.4	24.6	57.0	60.0	26.3	64.6	48.1	23.1	50.9
1986	54.1	25.1	57.6	60.6	26.5	65.1	48.8	23.8	51.6
1987	55.6	27.1	58.9	62.0	28.5	66.4	50.3	25.8	53.0
1988	56.3	27.6	59.7	62.7	29.4	67.1	51.2	25.8	53.9
1989	56.9	28.7	60.1	62.8	30.4	67.0	52.0	27.1	54.6
1990	56.7	26.7	60.2	62.6	27.7	67.1	51.9	25.8	54.7
1991	55.4	22.6	59.0	61.3	23.8	65.9	50.6	21.5	53.6
1992	54.9	22.8	58.3	59.9	23.6	64.3	50.8	22.1	53.6
1993	55.0	22.6	58.4	60.0	23.6	64.3	50.9	21.6	53.8
1994	56.1	24.9	59.4	60.8	25.4	65.0	52.3	24.5	55.0
1995	57.1	25.7	60.5	61.7	25.2	66.1	53.4	26.1	56.1
1996	57.4	26.0	60.8	61.1	24.9	65.5	54.4	27.1	57.1
1997	58.2	26.1	61.8	61.4	23.7	66.1	55.6	28.5	58.4
1998	59.7	30.1	63.0	62.9	28.4	67.1	57.2	31.8	59.7
1999	60.6	27.9	64.2	63.1	26.7	67.5	58.6	29.0	61.5
2000	60.8	29.5	64.2	63.4	28.7	67.6	58.7	30.3	61.5
HISPANIC									
1973	55.6	. . .	58.6	76.0	. . .	81.3	37.3	. . .	38.3
1974	56.2	. . .	59.0	75.7	. . .	80.8	38.4	. . .	39.4
1975	53.4	. . .	56.6	71.5	. . .	77.2	37.4	. . .	38.7
1976	53.8	35.8	56.6	71.1	41.0	76.3	38.6	31.6	39.5
1977	55.4	37.2	58.3	73.6	45.5	78.3	39.1	29.5	40.6
1978	57.2	39.3	60.0	74.9	45.9	79.6	41.3	33.0	42.6
1979	58.3	40.6	61.0	75.6	46.8	80.3	42.5	34.3	43.7
1980	57.6	39.0	60.5	73.5	46.9	77.8	42.4	30.7	44.1
1981	57.4	35.3	60.7	72.4	41.0	77.2	43.0	29.3	45.0
1982	54.9	31.4	58.2	68.9	34.5	73.9	41.3	28.1	43.1
1983	55.1	32.4	58.1	69.4	37.5	73.8	41.1	27.2	42.9
1984	57.9	36.0	60.7	72.1	39.3	76.4	44.2	32.8	45.6
1985	57.8	33.7	60.7	72.1	38.4	76.3	43.8	29.0	45.6
1986	58.5	33.0	61.5	72.5	38.8	76.6	44.7	27.2	46.8
1987	60.5	35.6	63.4	74.0	39.9	78.0	47.4	31.2	49.2
1988	61.9	38.6	64.6	75.3	42.8	79.0	48.8	34.4	50.4
1989	62.2	39.2	64.8	75.8	44.9	79.4	48.8	33.3	50.5
1990	61.9	38.5	64.8	74.9	45.0	78.7	48.6	31.1	50.7
1991	59.8	34.8	62.8	72.1	39.4	76.1	47.3	29.7	49.3
1992	59.1	33.2	62.1	71.2	37.4	75.2	46.8	28.8	48.8
1993	59.1	32.5	62.1	71.7	37.7	75.6	46.3	27.0	48.4
1994	59.5	33.5	62.4	71.7	36.8	75.7	47.2	30.0	49.1
1995	59.7	34.5	62.6	72.1	37.5	76.0	47.3	31.3	49.1
1996	60.6	33.2	63.7	73.3	38.7	77.3	47.9	27.0	50.2
1997	62.6	33.7	66.0	74.5	37.5	79.0	50.2	29.3	52.6
1998	63.1	36.0	66.2	74.7	38.7	79.1	51.0	33.0	53.0
1999	63.4	37.0	66.5	75.3	41.2	79.6	51.7	32.5	53.9
2000	64.7	38.5	67.8	76.6	42.9	80.7	53.1	33.9	56.0

Note: Detail for the above race and Hispanic-origin groups will not sum to totals because data for the Other races group are not presented and Hispanics are included in both the White and Black population groups. See "Notes and Definitions" for information on historical comparability.

Table 1-13. Employed Civilians by Occupation, Sex, Race, and Hispanic Origin, 1983–2000

(Thousands of persons.)

Occupation	1983						1984					
	Total	Men	Women	White	Black	Hispanic	Total	Men	Women	White	Black	Hispanic
TOTAL	100 834	56 787	44 047	88 893	9 375	6 072	105 005	59 091	45 915	92 120	10 119	6 651
Managerial and professional specialty	23 592	13 933	9 659	21 608	1 324	716	24 858	14 529	10 329	22 702	1 422	797
Executive, administrative, and managerial	10 772	7 282	3 490	10 016	504	349	11 571	7 683	3 889	10 704	582	417
Professional specialty	12 820	6 651	6 169	11 592	820	366	13 286	6 846	6 440	11 998	840	379
Technical, sales, and administrative support	31 265	11 078	20 187	28 159	2 380	1 539	32 476	11 556	20 920	29 082	2 592	1 677
Technicians and related support	3 053	1 582	1 471	2 689	251	108	3 172	1 646	1 527	2 783	262	142
Sales occupations	11 818	6 201	5 617	10 999	558	499	12 582	6 550	6 032	11 673	627	584
Administrative support, including clerical	16 395	3 295	13 100	14 471	1 571	933	16 722	3 361	13 361	14 626	1 703	951
Service occupations	13 857	5 530	8 326	11 123	2 295	1 073	14 151	5 545	8 607	11 214	2 478	1 174
Private household	980	38	942	686	272	95	993	38	955	667	301	107
Protective service	1 672	1 457	215	1 419	228	89	1 678	1 461	217	1 395	252	85
Other services	11 205	4 035	7 170	9 019	1 795	889	11 481	4 046	7 435	9 152	1 925	982
Precision production, craft, and repair	12 328	11 328	1 000	11 219	841	873	13 057	11 945	1 112	11 844	939	967
Operation, fabricators, and laborers	16 091	11 809	4 282	13 444	2 256	1 521	16 864	12 479	4 385	14 036	2 411	1 655
Machine operators, assemblers, and inspectors	7 744	4 484	3 259	6 414	1 081	829	7 984	4 702	3 282	6 600	1 132	888
Transportation and material moving occupations	4 201	3 875	326	3 592	547	285	4 467	4 098	369	3 782	625	304
Handlers, equipment cleaners, helpers, and laborers	4 147	3 450	697	3 438	628	408	4 413	3 679	734	3 655	654	463
Farming, forestry, and fishing	3 700	3 108	592	3 339	279	349	3 600	3 037	562	3 242	277	381

Occupation	1985						1986					
	Total	Men	Women	White	Black	Hispanic	Total	Men	Women	White	Black	Hispanic
TOTAL	107 150	59 891	47 259	93 736	10 501	6 888	109 597	60 892	48 706	95 660	10 814	7 219
Managerial and professional specialty	25 851	14 802	11 049	23 561	1 514	871	26 554	15 029	11 525	24 134	1 594	923
Executive, administrative, and managerial	12 221	7 871	4 351	11 256	649	442	12 642	7 990	4 653	11 649	658	466
Professional specialty	13 630	6 932	6 699	12 305	865	429	13 911	7 039	6 872	12 485	936	457
Technical, sales, and administrative support	33 231	11 725	21 507	29 553	2 785	1 705	34 354	12 130	22 223	30 497	2 923	1 812
Technicians and related support	3 255	1 719	1 537	2 823	291	134	3 364	1 783	1 581	2 953	277	134
Sales occupations	12 667	6 579	6 088	11 669	696	575	13 245	6 862	6 383	12 168	750	646
Administrative support, including clerical	17 309	3 427	13 882	15 061	1 798	995	17 745	3 485	14 260	15 377	1 896	1 032
Service occupations	14 441	5 695	8 747	11 432	2 522	1 211	14 680	5 775	8 905	11 685	2 480	1 298
Private household	1 006	38	968	692	291	101	981	39	942	721	235	127
Protective service	1 718	1 491	227	1 428	259	103	1 787	1 566	221	1 487	268	99
Other services	11 718	4 166	7 552	9 312	1 972	1 006	11 913	4 170	7 742	9 478	1 977	1 071
Precision production, craft, and repair	13 340	12 213	1 127	12 107	946	1 025	13 405	12 256	1 150	12 083	1 009	1 031
Operation, fabricators, and laborers	16 816	12 539	4 277	13 951	2 465	1 737	17 160	12 805	4 355	14 107	2 583	1 795
Machine operators, assemblers, and inspectors	7 840	4 681	3 159	6 483	1 120	944	7 911	4 725	3 187	6 462	1 167	956
Transportation and material moving occupations	4 535	4 160	375	3 849	620	328	4 564	4 158	406	3 847	641	344
Handlers, equipment cleaners, helpers, and laborers	4 441	3 697	744	3 618	725	466	4 685	3 923	762	3 798	776	494
Farming, forestry, and fishing	3 470	2 917	552	3 132	269	337	3 444	2 896	548	3 154	224	360

Occupation	1987						1988					
	Total	Men	Women	White	Black	Hispanic	Total	Men	Women	White	Black	Hispanic
TOTAL	112 440	62 107	50 334	97 789	11 309	7 790	114 968	63 273	51 696	99 812	11 658	8 250
Managerial and professional specialty	27 742	15 457	12 286	25 107	1 712	1 018	29 190	16 139	13 050	26 408	1 794	1 086
Executive, administrative, and managerial	13 316	8 263	5 053	12 200	741	509	14 216	8 626	5 590	13 022	789	570
Professional specialty	14 426	7 194	7 232	12 907	972	509	14 974	7 513	7 460	13 386	1 005	516
Technical, sales, and administrative support	35 082	12 378	22 704	30 949	3 099	1 969	35 532	12 494	23 038	31 178	3 239	2 064
Technicians and related support	3 346	1 721	1 624	2 914	283	130	3 521	1 833	1 688	3 019	329	152
Sales occupations	13 480	7 015	6 465	12 295	806	713	13 747	7 025	6 722	12 495	839	730
Administrative support, including clerical	18 256	3 642	14 614	15 740	2 010	1 126	18 264	3 636	14 628	15 664	2 071	1 182
Service occupations	15 054	5 924	9 130	11 916	2 614	1 369	15 332	6 056	9 275	12 105	2 698	1 560
Private household	934	34	900	703	211	120	909	34	875	687	205	152
Protective service	1 907	1 637	271	1 558	316	111	1 944	1 664	279	1 584	324	122
Other services	12 213	4 253	7 960	9 655	2 087	1 139	12 479	4 358	8 121	9 834	2 169	1 286
Precision production, craft, and repair	13 568	12 416	1 153	12 262	996	1 083	13 664	12 474	1 190	12 305	1 029	1 116
Operation, fabricators, and laborers	17 486	12 978	4 508	14 340	2 659	1 890	17 814	13 234	4 580	14 665	2 672	1 975
Machine operators, assemblers, and inspectors	7 994	4 699	3 295	6 498	1 195	1 001	8 117	4 806	3 311	6 642	1 197	1 079
Transportation and material moving occupations	4 712	4 317	395	3 934	699	360	4 831	4 397	434	4 027	719	343
Handlers, equipment cleaners, helpers, and laborers	4 779	3 962	817	3 909	765	528	4 866	4 031	835	3 997	755	552
Farming, forestry, and fishing	3 507	2 954	554	3 214	229	461	3 437	2 875	562	3 150	226	448

See *Note* at end of table.

Table 1-13. Employed Civilians by Occupation, Sex, Race, and Hispanic Origin, 1983–2000—*Continued*

(Thousands of persons.)

Occupation	1989						1990					
	Total	Men	Women	White	Black	Hispanic	Total	Men	Women	White	Black	Hispanic
TOTAL	117 342	64 315	53 027	101 584	11 953	8 573	118 793	65 104	53 689	102 261	12 175	9 845
Managerial and professional specialty	30 398	16 652	13 746	27 459	1 862	1 126	30 602	16 601	14 001	27 416	1 945	1 208
Executive, administrative, and managerial	14 848	8 944	5 904	13 555	840	599	14 802	8 872	5 931	13 432	869	630
Professional specialty	15 550	7 708	7 842	13 903	1 022	527	15 800	7 729	8 071	13 984	1 076	578
Technical, sales, and administrative support	36 127	12 687	23 440	31 619	3 346	2 057	36 913	13 054	23 859	32 136	3 465	2 366
Technicians and related support	3 645	1 887	1 759	3 125	347	157	3 866	1 973	1 893	3 298	357	182
Sales occupations	14 065	7 124	6 941	12 741	906	730	14 285	7 247	7 038	12 871	937	848
Administrative support, including clerical	18 416	3 676	14 741	15 752	2 094	1 169	18 762	3 834	14 928	15 967	2 170	1 336
Service occupations	15 556	6 164	9 391	12 237	2 731	1 684	16 012	6 470	9 543	12 565	2 757	1 984
Private household	872	36	836	628	219	138	792	29	763	571	191	168
Protective service	1 960	1 654	305	1 594	329	113	2 000	1 708	293	1 618	334	131
Other services	12 724	4 474	8 250	10 016	2 184	1 433	13 220	4 732	8 488	10 376	2 233	1 685
Precision production, craft, and repair	13 818	12 627	1 190	12 369	1 089	1 173	13 745	12 580	1 166	12 255	1 083	1 301
Operation, fabricators, and laborers	18 022	13 327	4 695	14 752	2 714	2 059	18 071	13 494	4 577	14 732	2 715	2 436
Machine operators, assemblers, and inspectors	8 248	4 878	3 370	6 721	1 202	1 121	8 200	4 931	3 269	6 668	1 184	1 249
Transportation and material moving occupations	4 886	4 436	450	4 080	712	371	4 886	4 449	436	4 010	757	466
Handlers, equipment cleaners, helpers, and laborers	4 888	4 013	875	3 950	800	567	4 985	4 114	871	4 054	775	721
Farming, forestry, and fishing	3 421	2 857	565	3 149	210	474	3 450	2 907	544	3 157	209	550

Occupation	1991						1992					
	Total	Men	Women	White	Black	Hispanic	Total	Men	Women	White	Black	Hispanic
TOTAL	117 718	64 223	53 496	101 182	12 074	9 828	118 492	64 440	54 052	101 669	12 151	10 027
Managerial and professional specialty	30 934	16 623	14 311	27 706	1 972	1 259	31 085	16 387	14 698	27 719	2 044	1 322
Executive, administrative, and managerial	14 904	8 858	6 046	13 513	875	653	14 722	8 612	6 110	13 327	872	683
Professional specialty	16 030	7 765	8 265	14 193	1 097	606	16 363	7 775	8 588	14 393	1 172	639
Technical, sales, and administrative support	36 318	12 852	23 466	31 524	3 443	2 413	37 048	13 379	23 669	32 167	3 423	2 492
Technicians and related support	3 814	1 937	1 877	3 257	344	196	4 277	2 185	2 092	3 620	418	216
Sales occupations	14 052	7 180	6 872	12 590	955	867	14 014	7 286	6 728	12 576	891	882
Administrative support, including clerical	18 452	3 735	14 717	15 677	2 145	1 349	18 757	3 908	14 849	15 971	2 114	1 395
Service occupations	16 254	6 610	9 644	12 739	2 783	2 005	16 377	6 676	9 701	12 778	2 843	2 037
Private household	799	33	766	608	162	179	891	37	854	695	162	187
Protective service	2 083	1 765	318	1 682	351	144	2 114	1 760	354	1 669	383	168
Other services	13 372	4 812	8 560	10 449	2 270	1 682	13 373	4 879	8 493	10 414	2 298	1 682
Precision production, craft, and repair	13 250	12 112	1 138	11 824	1 039	1 269	13 225	12 087	1 137	11 798	1 016	1 345
Operation, fabricators, and laborers	17 456	13 075	4 380	14 205	2 613	2 311	17 247	12 954	4 294	14 018	2 599	2 243
Machine operators, assemblers, and inspectors	7 820	4 693	3 127	6 284	1 159	1 142	7 658	4 623	3 035	6 141	1 153	1 130
Transportation and material moving occupations	4 913	4 476	437	4 022	774	462	4 908	4 482	426	4 069	730	460
Handlers, equipment cleaners, helpers, and laborers	4 723	3 906	816	3 899	680	707	4 682	3 850	832	3 808	716	653
Farming, forestry, and fishing	3 506	2 951	556	3 184	224	570	3 510	2 957	553	3 188	226	588

Occupation	1993						1994					
	Total	Men	Women	White	Black	Hispanic	Total	Men	Women	White	Black	Hispanic
TOTAL	120 259	65 349	54 910	103 045	12 382	10 361	123 060	66 450	56 610	105 190	12 835	10 788
Managerial and professional specialty	32 231	16 811	15 419	28 647	2 181	1 437	33 847	17 583	16 264	30 045	2 405	1 517
Executive, administrative, and managerial	15 338	8 897	6 441	13 783	977	762	16 312	9 298	7 014	14 605	1 103	807
Professional specialty	16 893	7 915	8 978	14 863	1 204	675	17 536	8 285	9 250	15 439	1 302	709
Technical, sales, and administrative support	37 058	13 417	23 641	32 096	3 501	2 578	37 306	13 322	23 984	32 232	3 637	2 639
Technicians and related support	4 039	2 000	2 039	3 433	395	223	3 869	1 856	2 013	3 301	376	205
Sales occupations	14 342	7 418	6 924	12 824	974	940	14 817	7 543	7 273	13 235	1 056	1 010
Administrative support, including clerical	18 677	3 999	14 679	15 839	2 132	1 415	18 620	3 923	14 697	15 696	2 205	1 424
Service occupations	16 821	6 867	9 953	13 145	2 901	2 069	16 912	6 840	10 072	13 207	2 890	2 131
Private household	928	45	883	735	154	214	817	30	787	643	136	223
Protective service	2 165	1 792	373	1 729	380	160	2 249	1 873	376	1 778	407	167
Other services	13 727	5 030	8 697	10 681	2 367	1 695	13 847	4 938	8 909	10 787	2 346	1 741
Precision production, craft, and repair	13 429	12 279	1 150	11 990	1 006	1 372	13 489	12 241	1 248	11 974	1 040	1 407
Operation, fabricators, and laborers	17 341	13 109	4 232	14 090	2 580	2 310	17 876	13 535	4 341	14 416	2 677	2 474
Machine operators, assemblers, and inspectors	7 553	4 642	2 911	6 066	1 117	1 140	7 754	4 800	2 954	6 166	1 167	1 151
Transportation and material moving occupations	5 036	4 570	465	4 195	706	481	5 136	4 654	483	4 227	749	511
Handlers, equipment cleaners, helpers, and laborers	4 753	3 897	856	3 829	757	689	4 986	4 081	904	4 023	760	811
Farming, forestry, and fishing	3 379	2 864	515	3 078	212	596	3 629	2 928	701	3 315	187	620

See *Note* at end of table.

Table 1-13. Employed Civilians by Occupation, Sex, Race, and Hispanic Origin, 1983–2000—*Continued*

(Thousands of persons.)

Occupation	1995						1996					
	Total	Men	Women	White	Black	Hispanic	Total	Men	Women	White	Black	Hispanic
TOTAL	124 900	67 377	57 523	106 490	13 279	11 127	126 708	68 207	58 501	107 808	13 542	11 642
Managerial and professional specialty	35 318	18 378	16 940	31 323	2 651	1 548	36 497	18 744	17 754	32 116	2 706	1 654
Executive, administrative, and managerial	17 186	9 840	7 346	15 398	1 233	821	17 746	9 979	7 767	15 807	1 218	854
Professional specialty	18 132	8 539	9 593	15 924	1 418	727	18 752	8 764	9 987	16 309	1 488	799
Technical, sales, and administrative support	37 417	13 310	24 107	32 184	3 808	2 719	37 683	13 489	24 194	32 177	3 877	2 849
Technicians and related support	3 909	1 900	2 009	3 361	378	240	3 926	1 865	2 061	3 334	368	248
Sales occupations	15 119	7 634	7 485	13 366	1 183	1 048	15 404	7 782	7 622	13 519	1 218	1 085
Administrative support, including clerical	18 389	3 776	14 613	15 457	2 248	1 431	18 353	3 842	14 511	15 323	2 291	1 516
Service occupations	16 930	6 774	10 155	13 208	2 880	2 195	17 177	6 967	10 210	13 447	2 962	2 349
Private household	821	37	784	638	137	204	804	41	764	637	139	211
Protective service	2 237	1 881	356	1 772	406	166	2 187	1 811	375	1 748	389	175
Other services	13 872	4 857	9 015	10 799	2 337	1 825	14 186	5 115	9 071	11 062	2 435	1 963
Precision production, craft, and repair	13 524	12 323	1 201	11 949	1 073	1 430	13 587	12 368	1 219	12 020	1 069	1 498
Operation, fabricators, and laborers	18 068	13 675	4 393	14 496	2 712	2 577	18 197	13 750	4 447	14 697	2 789	2 607
Machine operators, assemblers, and inspectors	7 907	4 958	2 949	6 221	1 218	1 250	7 874	4 902	2 972	6 270	1 193	1 295
Transportation and material moving occupations	5 171	4 682	490	4 254	760	512	5 302	4 799	504	4 412	772	548
Handlers, equipment cleaners, helpers, and laborers	4 990	4 035	955	4 022	734	816	5 021	4 049	971	4 016	824	764
Farming, forestry, and fishing	3 642	2 916	726	3 330	154	658	3 566	2 889	677	3 350	139	685

Occupation	1997						1998					
	Total	Men	Women	White	Black	Hispanic	Total	Men	Women	White	Black	Hispanic
TOTAL	129 558	69 685	59 873	109 856	13 969	12 726	131 463	70 693	60 771	110 931	14 556	13 291
Managerial and professional specialty	37 686	19 249	18 437	33 089	2 764	1 867	38 937	19 867	19 070	34 063	2 947	1 933
Executive, administrative, and managerial	18 440	10 271	8 170	16 420	1 267	1 001	19 054	10 585	8 469	16 903	1 368	1 028
Professional specialty	19 245	8 978	10 267	16 669	1 497	866	19 883	9 282	10 602	17 160	1 579	905
Technical, sales, and administrative support	38 309	13 760	24 549	32 624	4 032	3 026	38 521	13 792	24 728	32 490	4 264	3 186
Technicians and related support	4 214	2 028	2 186	3 571	410	256	4 261	1 976	2 285	3 557	441	283
Sales occupations	15 734	7 040	7 894	13 730	1 271	1 198	15 850	7 875	7 975	13 704	1 415	1 245
Administrative support, including clerical	18 361	3 892	14 469	15 323	2 352	1 572	18 410	3 941	14 469	15 229	2 408	1 657
Service occupations	17 537	7 122	10 416	13 604	3 092	2 560	17 836	7 222	10 614	13 807	3 148	2 670
Private household	795	37	758	642	129	212	847	46	801	704	116	262
Protective service	2 300	1 890	411	1 800	430	202	2 417	1 986	431	1 892	463	204
Other services	14 442	5 195	9 247	11 162	2 533	2 146	14 572	5 190	9 382	11 211	2 569	2 204
Precision production, craft, and repair	14 124	12 868	1 256	12 472	1 144	1 714	14 411	13 208	1 203	12 729	1 158	1 793
Operation, fabricators, and laborers	18 399	13 858	4 540	14 813	2 781	2 839	18 256	13 769	4 487	14 609	2 866	2 917
Machine operators, assemblers, and inspectors	7 962	4 962	3 000	6 322	1 178	1 426	7 791	4 882	2 909	6 146	1 200	1 340
Transportation and material moving occupations	5 389	4 872	518	4 435	810	592	5 363	4 818	545	4 351	872	640
Handlers, equipment cleaners, helpers, and laborers	5 048	4 025	1 023	4 057	784	821	5 102	4 069	1 033	4 112	795	938
Farming, forestry, and fishing	3 503	2 828	675	3 254	156	721	3 502	2 835	668	3 233	172	792

Occupation	1999						2000					
	Total	Men	Women	White	Black	Hispanic	Total	Men	Women	White	Black	Hispanic
TOTAL	133 488	71 446	62 042	112 235	15 056	13 720	135 208	72 293	62 915	113 475	15 334	14 492
Managerial and professional specialty	40 467	20 446	20 021	35 125	3 233	2 040	40 887	20 543	20 345	35 304	3 349	2 036
Executive, administrative, and managerial	19 584	10 744	8 840	17 235	1 484	1 097	19 774	10 814	8 960	17 372	1 512	1 072
Professional specialty	20 883	9 702	11 181	17 890	1 749	943	21 113	9 728	11 385	17 932	1 836	964
Technical, sales, and administrative support	38 921	14 079	24 842	32 779	4 356	3 286	39 442	14 288	25 154	33 146	4 497	3 504
Technicians and related support	4 355	2 094	2 261	3 622	467	279	4 385	2 118	2 267	3 611	492	303
Sales occupations	16 118	8 049	8 069	13 956	1 405	1 267	16 340	8 231	8 110	14 169	1 436	1 385
Administrative support, including clerical	18 448	3 936	14 512	15 201	2 484	1 740	18 717	3 939	14 778	15 366	2 570	1 816
Service occupations	17 915	7 093	10 822	13 725	3 275	2 716	18 278	7 245	11 034	14 066	3 301	2 867
Private household	831	40	791	670	126	244	792	35	757	631	118	251
Protective service	2 440	1 980	460	1 886	484	200	2 399	1 944	455	1 860	471	208
Other services	14 644	5 074	9 570	11 168	2 666	2 271	15 087	5 265	9 822	11 575	2 712	2 408
Precision production, craft, and repair	14 593	13 286	1 307	12 908	1 174	1 871	14 882	13 532	1 351	13 133	1 191	2 075
Operation, fabricators, and laborers	18 167	13 793	4 374	14 535	2 847	3 014	18 319	13 988	4 331	14 680	2 830	3 202
Machine operators, assemblers, and inspectors	7 386	4 637	2 749	5 824	1 143	1 364	7 319	4 622	2 697	5 802	1 080	1 416
Transportation and material moving occupations	5 516	4 968	548	4 488	879	659	5 557	5 003	554	4 476	915	662
Handlers, equipment cleaners, helpers, and laborers	5 265	4 188	1 077	4 223	825	992	5 443	4 363	1 080	4 402	835	1 125
Farming, forestry, and fishing	3 426	2 749	676	3 165	172	793	3 399	2 698	701	3 146	166	807

Note: Detail for the above race and Hispanic-origin groups will not sum to totals because data for the Other races group are not presented and Hispanics are included in both the White and Black population groups. See "Notes and Definitions" for information on historical comparability.

Table 1-14. Employed Civilians by Industry and Occupation, 1989–2000

(Thousands of persons.)

Industry	Total employed	Managerial and professional specialty		Technical, sales, and administrative support			Service occupations		Precision production, craft, and repair	Operators, fabricators, and laborers			Farming, forestry, and fishing
		Executive, administrative, and managerial	Professional specialty	Technicians and related support	Sales	Administrative support, including clerical	Private household	Other services, including protective		Machine operators, assemblers, and inspectors	Transportation and material moving	Handlers, equipment cleaners, helpers, and laborers	
1989													
Agriculture	3 199	78	72	29	21	114	...	18	45	11	51	22	2 738
Mining	719	105	63	31	9	81	...	9	232	34	123	30	1
Construction	7 680	1 024	145	54	66	444	...	35	4 410	114	533	837	17
Manufacturing	21 652	2 576	1 807	739	758	2 394	...	350	4 109	6 774	846	1 208	91
Durable goods	12 805	1 550	1 222	519	321	1 322	...	193	2 830	3 729	445	590	84
Nondurable goods	8 847	1 026	586	220	437	1 072	...	157	1 279	3 045	401	619	7
Transportation and public utilities	8 094	934	477	276	349	2 162	...	269	1 260	122	1 748	483	13
Wholesale trade	4 611	510	89	40	1 844	798	...	44	322	136	472	343	14
Retail trade	19 618	1 535	352	78	8 237	1 587	...	4 426	1 226	190	500	1 463	23
Finance, insurance, and real estate	7 989	2 115	205	140	1 865	3 121	...	274	142	20	16	25	65
Services	38 227	4 748	11 560	2 008	890	6 243	872	7 899	1 833	817	533	421	403
Services, except private households	37 118	4 744	11 553	2 003	889	6 233	...	7 813	1 820	816	528	400	319
Professional services	24 609	2 640	10 215	1 624	142	4 490	...	4 397	391	226	295	100	90
Public administration	5 553	1 222	780	250	24	1 473	...	1 359	239	30	63	56	56
1990													
Agriculture	3 223	95	85	30	23	108	...	17	42	13	49	21	2 740
Mining	724	110	63	32	9	72	...	9	243	26	123	36	2
Construction	7 764	1 034	133	64	75	426	...	35	4 445	114	524	890	23
Manufacturing	21 346	2 530	1 794	765	779	2 363	...	374	3 964	6 696	805	1 173	102
Durable goods	12 630	1 521	1 225	533	326	1 363	...	197	2 721	3 685	416	552	91
Nondurable goods	8 717	1 010	569	232	453	1 000	...	178	1 243	3 011	389	621	11
Transportation and public utilities	8 168	915	459	306	340	2 166	...	293	1 259	122	1 812	481	14
Wholesale trade	4 669	528	88	50	1 862	788	...	39	323	138	464	380	10
Retail trade	19 953	1 557	379	89	8 295	1 633	...	4 584	1 181	197	512	1 498	27
Finance, insurance, and real estate	8 051	2 087	225	155	1 904	3 097	...	296	155	19	17	25	71
Services	39 267	4 745	11 786	2 125	971	6 561	792	8 194	1 898	831	521	436	408
Services, except private households	38 231	4 742	11 773	2 121	969	6 552	...	8 098	1 881	829	514	417	336
Professional services	25 351	2 642	10 425	1 719	162	4 763	...	4 545	400	228	276	101	91
Public administration	5 627	1 199	788	251	26	1 549	...	1 380	235	43	60	44	53
1991													
Agriculture	3 269	91	78	31	22	102	...	18	41	12	54	16	2 803
Mining	732	112	65	37	8	81	...	12	244	24	115	34	1
Construction	7 140	969	137	53	71	386	...	29	4 077	100	497	797	24
Manufacturing	20 580	2 499	1 777	749	729	2 283	...	355	3 837	6 402	780	1 076	92
Durable goods	12 015	1 489	1 178	512	292	1 260	...	185	2 630	3 459	404	525	80
Nondurable goods	8 565	1 010	599	237	437	1 023	...	170	1 207	2 943	376	551	13
Transportation and public utilities	8 234	973	474	301	331	2 170	...	262	1 285	125	1 833	465	16
Wholesale trade	4 660	537	77	37	1 868	776	...	36	319	135	490	374	11
Retail trade	19 758	1 591	372	103	8 181	1 589	...	4 605	1 142	173	530	1 450	23
Finance, insurance, and real estate	7 806	2 027	216	133	1 849	3 022	...	270	167	18	14	20	69
Services	39 884	4 873	12 035	2 148	967	6 534	799	8 455	1 884	792	537	444	416
Services, except private households	38 868	4 871	12 029	2 144	966	6 522	...	8 375	1 870	791	531	422	346
Professional services	25 853	2 706	10 629	1 742	162	4 788	...	4 749	393	211	295	87	92
Public administration	5 655	1 231	798	223	27	1 508	...	1 414	253	41	62	46	51
1992													
Agriculture	3 247	91	74	44	21	118	...	17	45	10	44	19	2 764
Mining	666	100	58	31	7	79	...	12	214	28	106	31	1
Construction	7 063	892	147	67	73	410	...	34	4 073	99	480	762	28
Manufacturing	20 124	2 401	1 640	758	768	2 268	...	330	3 808	6 244	749	1 074	84
Durable goods	11 561	1 405	1 069	525	306	1 251	...	158	2 569	3 344	374	485	75
Nondurable goods	8 563	996	571	234	462	1 017	...	172	1 239	2 901	375	589	8
Transportation and public utilities	8 284	946	461	375	250	2 281	...	274	1 227	114	1 874	464	18
Wholesale trade	4 783	556	85	46	1 883	820	...	42	302	118	490	405	38
Retail trade	19 938	1 603	374	146	8 229	1 591	...	4 717	1 117	180	530	1 428	25
Finance, insurance, and real estate	7 780	1 966	224	162	1 851	2 991	...	290	171	19	13	22	73
Services	40 967	4 937	12 473	2 379	908	6 728	891	9 259	2 022	810	563	440	449
Services, except private households	39 821	4 933	12 463	2 373	906	6 714	...	8 368	2 007	807	555	421	372
Professional services	27 713	3 150	11 168	2 040	175	5 032	...	5 017	411	208	314	102	95
Public administration	5 640	1 231	829	268	25	1 472	...	1 404	246	37	59	38	31

See *Note* at end of table.

Table 1-14. Employed Civilians by Industry and Occupation, 1989–2000—*Continued*

(Thousands of persons.)

Industry	Total employed	Managerial and professional specialty		Technical, sales, and administrative support			Service occupations			Precision produc-tion, craft, and repair	Operators, fabricators, and laborers			Farming, forestry, and fishing
		Executive, adminis-trative, and man-agerial	Profes-sional specialty	Techni-cians and related support	Sales	Adminis-trative support, including clerical	Private household	Other services, including protective		Machine operators, assem-blers, and inspectors	Transpor-tation and material moving	Handlers, equip-ment cleaners, helpers, and laborers	
1993													
Agriculture	3 115	99	87	39	14	114	...	15	45	8	53	20	2 621
Mining	672	102	75	24	4	73	...	8	233	25	103	25	...
Construction	7 276	928	137	46	74	390	...	35	4 292	79	517	753	25
Manufacturing	19 711	2 432	1 688	693	739	2 161	...	312	3 744	6 124	710	1 012	95
Durable goods	11 385	1 415	1 085	463	282	1 181	...	161	2 553	3 352	361	446	87
Nondurable goods	8 326	1 017	603	231	457	981	...	151	1 191	2 772	349	566	9
Transportation and public utilities	8 526	975	500	329	241	2 318	...	266	1 271	131	2 000	479	18
Wholesale trade	4 622	533	85	49	1 819	771	...	40	296	115	492	378	44
Retail trade	20 521	1 652	351	129	8 543	1 571	...	4 873	1 095	179	543	1 563	23
Finance, insurance, and real estate	7 975	2 089	244	161	1 918	2 967	...	290	183	21	13	19	70
Services	42 059	5 234	12 864	2 300	963	6 841	928	8 579	2 047	831	551	467	453
Services, except private households	40 924	5 231	12 857	2 298	961	6 830	...	8 497	2 035	831	547	446	392
Professional services	28 365	3 299	11 476	1 969	176	5 111	...	5 163	419	223	314	108	105
Public administration	5 782	1 294	862	270	26	1 469	...	1 475	224	39	54	39	31
1994													
Agriculture	3 409	97	88	38	14	145	...	18	42	5	45	19	2 897
Mining	669	110	76	22	10	67	...	9	222	21	109	21	1
Construction	7 493	1 055	138	60	59	429	...	34	4 263	86	529	818	22
Manufacturing	20 157	2 588	1 814	611	745	2 093	...	290	3 803	6 298	744	1 082	89
Durable goods	11 792	1 555	1 170	412	310	1 146	...	152	2 622	3 415	416	514	80
Nondurable goods	8 365	1 033	644	200	435	946	...	138	1 181	2 883	328	569	9
Transportation and public utilities	8 692	1 065	486	329	248	2 337	...	246	1 270	120	2 049	528	15
Wholesale trade	4 713	531	89	37	1 880	775	...	34	296	150	464	398	60
Retail trade	20 986	1 704	402	119	8 772	1 555	...	4 948	1 145	197	548	1 569	27
Finance, insurance, and real estate	8 141	2 198	272	160	2 029	2 915	...	282	167	18	17	18	66
Services	42 986	5 649	13 319	2 274	1 032	6 864	817	8 654	2 071	826	567	493	421
Services, except private households	42 009	5 645	13 311	2 272	1 031	6 855	...	8 584	2 063	825	564	480	380
Professional services	29 030	3 559	11 888	1 968	193	5 083	...	5 134	470	222	314	94	105
Public administration	5 814	1 315	853	221	28	1 440	...	1 579	211	32	64	39	30
1995													
Agriculture	3 440	105	92	45	15	145	...	16	35	17	45	19	2 907
Mining	627	100	60	22	4	53	...	5	228	28	101	25	2
Construction	7 668	1 117	145	43	63	431	...	33	4 362	85	513	858	18
Manufacturing	20 493	2 804	1 787	615	756	2 108	...	294	3 837	6 386	728	1 067	111
Durable goods	12 015	1 683	1 160	404	311	1 117	...	156	2 660	3 498	390	535	100
Nondurable goods	8 478	1 121	627	211	445	991	...	138	1 177	2 888	338	532	11
Transportation and public utilities	8 709	1 124	510	310	259	2 337	...	247	1 223	121	2 079	487	12
Wholesale trade	4 986	554	108	48	1 979	792	...	37	308	187	488	423	62
Retail trade	21 086	1 740	425	141	8 949	1 501	...	4 844	1 111	214	578	1 548	34
Finance, insurance, and real estate	7 983	2 258	268	148	1 985	2 757	...	269	183	14	14	19	68
Services	43 953	6 029	13 755	2 307	1 086	6 848	821	8 788	2 008	824	572	510	405
Services, except private households	42 982	6 023	13 746	2 305	1 086	6 838	...	8 719	2 002	822	569	497	374
Professional services	29 661	3 721	12 233	1 974	199	5 114	...	5 284	465	178	312	87	94
Public administration	5 957	1 356	981	230	24	1 417	...	1 577	229	32	52	35	25
1996													
Agriculture	3 443	108	88	40	19	174	...	28	41	11	34	13	2 888
Mining	569	90	44	21	10	47	...	7	208	21	105	17	1
Construction	7 943	1 221	165	45	65	452	...	32	4 442	96	513	890	21
Manufacturing	20 518	2 840	1 882	631	766	2 033	...	264	3 814	6 350	767	1 069	101
Durable goods	12 202	1 690	1 204	425	337	1 131	...	144	2 677	3 561	425	518	90
Nondurable goods	8 316	1 150	678	206	429	903	...	120	1 137	2 789	342	551	11
Transportation and public utilities	8 817	1 159	529	332	288	2 319	...	251	1 185	132	2 126	489	7
Wholesale trade	4 956	563	100	52	2 005	749	...	48	320	142	515	400	62
Retail trade	21 541	1 818	410	123	9 055	1 577	...	4 983	1 137	204	614	1 583	39
Finance, insurance, and real estate	8 076	2 274	271	162	2 052	2 744	...	298	165	15	13	28	54
Services	45 043	6 347	14 312	2 312	1 120	6 905	804	8 876	2 055	875	573	496	367
Services, except private households	44 107	6 343	14 302	2 310	1 119	6 900	...	8 821	2 048	875	572	484	335
Professional services	30 085	3 853	12 592	1 941	204	5 090	...	5 340	417	190	301	88	69
Public administration	5 802	1 325	951	208	25	1 353	...	1 585	221	28	43	37	25

See *Note* at end of table.

Table 1-14. Employed Civilians by Industry and Occupation, 1989–2000—*Continued*

(Thousands of persons.)

Industry	Total employed	Managerial and professional specialty		Technical, sales, and administrative support			Service occupations		Precision production, craft, and repair	Operators, fabricators, and laborers			Farming, forestry, and fishing
		Executive, administrative, and managerial	Professional specialty	Technicians and related support	Sales	Administrative support, including clerical	Private household	Other services, including protective		Machine operators, assemblers, and inspectors	Transportation and material moving	Handlers, equipment cleaners, helpers, and laborers	
1997													
Agriculture	3 399	124	83	48	19	160	. . .	24	34	10	51	26	2 821
Mining	634	92	51	25	10	66	. . .	4	236	24	101	24	1
Construction	8 302	1 274	158	45	72	425	. . .	35	4 731	97	558	884	22
Manufacturing	20 835	2 882	1 938	689	785	2 029	. . .	268	3 887	6 471	762	1 027	96
Durable goods	12 437	1 699	1 261	441	316	1 133	. . .	145	2 753	3 685	406	512	87
Nondurable goods	8 399	1 183	677	249	469	896	. . .	123	1 134	2 786	356	515	9
Transportation and public utilities	9 182	1 230	562	342	283	2 297	. . .	301	1 257	133	2 230	531	16
Wholesale trade	4 907	589	110	47	1 928	740	. . .	56	326	133	520	393	66
Retail trade	21 869	1 893	427	155	9 303	1 480	. . .	5 048	1 173	202	572	1 580	36
Finance, insurance, and real estate	8 297	2 428	308	151	2 092	2 749	. . .	307	175	12	11	28	38
Services	46 393	6 642	14 677	2 490	1 210	7 113	795	9 055	2 115	854	537	521	384
Services, except private households	45 472	6 638	14 671	2 485	1 210	7 107	. . .	8 988	2 109	853	537	514	359
Professional services	30 935	4 057	12 846	2 110	225	5 177	. . .	5 432	420	207	279	89	93
Public administration	5 738	1 287	932	221	32	1 303	. . .	1 644	191	27	46	33	23
1998													
Agriculture	3 378	110	105	51	23	136	. . .	21	39	20	42	19	2 814
Mining	620	101	63	19	11	53	. . .	8	208	31	105	18	1
Construction	8 518	1 380	144	47	56	415	. . .	28	4 889	94	535	910	21
Manufacturing	20 733	3 008	2 007	646	764	1 982	. . .	291	3 956	6 219	765	1 019	76
Durable goods	12 566	1 796	1 351	430	318	1 127	. . .	150	2 807	3 594	415	509	71
Nondurable goods	8 168	1 212	656	217	446	856	. . .	141	1 150	2 625	350	510	5
Transportation and public utilities	9 307	1 307	561	324	273	2 349	. . .	296	1 285	135	2 243	522	13
Wholesale trade	5 090	622	131	43	2 054	756	. . .	57	346	137	493	380	71
Retail trade	22 113	1 916	459	188	9 306	1 438	. . .	5 125	1 177	230	575	1 670	30
Finance, insurance, and real estate	8 605	2 489	356	166	2 143	2 860	. . .	323	177	12	13	17	49
Services	47 212	6 793	15 090	2 541	1 197	7 118	847	9 117	2 154	887	551	516	399
Services, except private households	46 244	6 787	15 084	2 540	1 196	7 109	. . .	9 061	2 151	887	548	509	374
Professional services	31 392	4 164	13 122	2 132	213	5 132	. . .	5 485	473	195	294	99	85
Public administration	5 887	1 329	968	234	25	1 302	. . .	1 722	182	27	40	30	27
1999													
Agriculture	3 281	118	97	53	15	149	. . .	15	36	10	48	18	2 722
Mining	565	83	69	19	7	35	. . .	6	198	24	102	21	1
Construction	8 987	1 379	159	60	67	406	. . .	33	5 224	108	543	984	22
Manufacturing	20 070	2 955	1 981	645	736	1 883	. . .	242	3 883	5 896	726	1 035	88
Durable goods	12 283	1 799	1 286	440	351	1 067	. . .	125	2 715	3 504	394	520	82
Nondurable goods	7 787	1 156	694	205	385	816	. . .	117	1 168	2 391	332	515	7
Transportation and public utilities	9 554	1 340	557	359	275	2 386	. . .	304	1 335	123	2 318	546	14
Wholesale trade	5 189	630	158	50	2 047	819	. . .	52	324	118	523	406	62
Retail trade	22 383	1 967	461	207	9 489	1 495	. . .	5 122	1 108	229	625	1 643	38
Finance, insurance, and real estate	8 815	2 664	380	200	2 224	2 780	. . .	294	177	10	12	23	50
Services	48 687	7 061	16 031	2 533	1 230	7 242	831	9 275	2 119	847	575	547	395
Services, except private households	47 747	7 056	16 026	2 530	1 230	7 234	. . .	9 219	2 116	847	573	535	382
Professional services	32 370	4 307	13 796	2 074	210	5 333	. . .	5 536	463	167	301	91	90
Public administration	5 958	1 386	992	229	28	1 253	. . .	1 741	189	22	42	42	34
2000													
Agriculture	3 305	106	105	60	13	145	. . .	15	54	17	55	18	2 718
Mining	521	79	52	15	5	41	. . .	7	194	19	87	22	. . .
Construction	9 433	1 302	182	60	94	435	. . .	30	5 555	120	546	1 093	17
Manufacturing	19 940	3 016	1 920	621	749	1 917	. . .	271	3 785	5 850	681	1 045	85
Durable goods	12 168	1 834	1 282	438	319	1 059	. . .	148	2 659	3 450	380	525	74
Nondurable goods	7 772	1 182	639	182	430	858	. . .	123	1 126	2 399	301	520	12
Transportation and public utilities	9 740	1 356	614	339	286	2 445	. . .	318	1 327	99	2 355	584	16
Wholesale trade	5 421	642	165	66	2 184	800	. . .	63	354	148	526	415	58
Retail trade	22 411	1 925	496	211	9 378	1 479	. . .	5 316	1 117	205	613	1 643	27
Finance, insurance, and real estate	8 727	2 571	380	194	2 288	2 751	. . .	298	157	10	12	20	45
Services	49 695	7 413	16 178	2 602	1 313	7 367	792	9 459	2 144	822	635	564	406
Services, except private households	48 801	7 410	16 172	2 600	1 312	7 361	. . .	9 410	2 142	822	633	559	380
Professional services	32 784	4 450	13 812	2 113	230	5 390	. . .	5 658	449	165	335	93	89
Public administration	6 015	1 364	1 021	219	29	1 336	. . .	1 709	196	29	47	38	27

Note: See "Notes and Definitions" for information on historical comparability.

Table 1-15. Employed Civilians in Agriculture and Nonagricultural Industries by Class of Worker and Sex, 1978–2000

(Thousands of persons.)

Year and sex	Total employed	Agriculture				Nonagricultural industries						
		Total	Wage and salary workers	Self-employed workers	Unpaid family workers	Total	Wage and salary workers				Self-employed workers	Unpaid family workers
							Total	Govern-ment	Private household	Other private		
TOTAL												
1978	96 048	3 387	1 452	1 618	316	92 661	85 753	15 525	1 384	68 844	6 429	479
1979	98 824	3 347	1 451	1 593	304	95 477	88 222	15 635	1 264	71 323	6 791	463
1980	99 302	3 364	1 425	1 642	297	95 938	88 525	15 912	1 192	71 421	7 000	413
1981	100 398	3 368	1 464	1 638	266	97 030	89 543	15 689	1 208	72 646	7 097	390
1982	99 526	3 401	1 505	1 636	261	96 125	88 462	15 516	1 207	71 739	7 262	401
1983	100 833	3 383	1 579	1 565	240	97 450	89 500	15 537	1 244	72 719	7 575	376
1984	105 006	3 321	1 555	1 553	213	101 685	93 565	15 770	1 238	76 557	7 785	335
1985	107 150	3 179	1 535	1 458	185	103 971	95 871	16 031	1 249	78 591	7 811	289
1986	109 597	3 163	1 547	1 447	169	106 434	98 299	16 342	1 235	80 722	7 881	255
1987	112 440	3 208	1 632	1 423	153	109 232	100 771	16 800	1 208	82 763	8 201	260
1988	114 969	3 169	1 621	1 398	150	111 800	103 021	17 114	1 153	84 754	8 519	260
1989	117 341	3 199	1 665	1 403	131	114 142	105 259	17 469	1 101	86 689	8 605	279
1990	118 793	3 223	1 740	1 378	105	115 570	106 598	17 769	1 027	87 802	8 719	253
1991	117 718	3 269	1 729	1 423	118	114 449	105 373	17 934	1 010	86 429	8 851	226
1992	118 492	3 247	1 750	1 385	112	115 245	106 437	18 136	1 135	87 166	8 575	233
1993	120 259	3 115	1 689	1 320	106	117 144	107 966	18 579	1 126	88 261	8 959	218
1994	123 060	3 409	1 715	1 645	49	119 651	110 517	18 293	966	91 258	9 003	131
1995	124 900	3 440	1 814	1 580	45	121 460	112 448	18 362	963	93 123	8 902	110
1996	126 707	3 443	1 869	1 518	56	123 264	114 171	18 217	928	95 026	8 971	122
1997	129 558	3 399	1 890	1 457	51	126 159	116 983	18 131	915	97 937	9 056	120
1998	131 463	3 378	2 000	1 341	38	128 085	119 019	18 383	962	99 674	8 962	103
1999	133 488	3 281	1 944	1 297	40	130 207	121 323	18 903	933	101 487	8 790	95
2000	135 208	3 305	2 034	1 233	38	131 903	123 128	19 053	890	103 186	8 674	101
MEN												
1978	56 479	2 718	1 162	1 465	91	53 761	49 103	7 836	181	41 086	4 614	44
1979	57 607	2 686	1 160	1 429	98	54 921	50 068	7 790	159	42 119	4 810	43
1980	57 186	2 709	1 149	1 458	101	54 477	49 517	7 822	149	41 546	4 904	56
1981	57 397	2 700	1 168	1 442	91	54 697	49 745	7 676	192	41 877	4 905	47
1982	56 270	2 736	1 208	1 433	95	53 534	48 529	7 598	188	40 743	4 954	52
1983	56 787	2 704	1 265	1 355	84	54 083	48 896	7 623	208	41 065	5 136	51
1984	59 091	2 668	1 254	1 350	65	56 423	51 151	7 720	178	43 253	5 219	52
1985	59 891	2 535	1 230	1 244	60	57 356	52 111	7 757	170	44 184	5 207	38
1986	60 892	2 511	1 230	1 227	54	58 381	53 075	7 805	180	45 090	5 271	35
1987	62 107	2 543	1 290	1 194	58	59 564	54 102	8 013	180	45 909	5 423	39
1988	63 273	2 493	1 268	1 174	50	60 780	55 177	8 074	157	46 946	5 564	39
1989	64 315	2 513	1 302	1 167	44	61 802	56 202	8 116	156	47 930	5 562	38
1990	65 105	2 546	1 355	1 151	39	62 559	56 913	8 245	149	48 519	5 597	48
1991	64 223	2 589	1 359	1 185	45	61 634	55 899	8 300	143	47 456	5 700	35
1992	64 441	2 575	1 371	1 164	40	61 866	56 212	8 348	156	47 708	5 613	41
1993	65 349	2 478	1 323	1 117	39	62 871	56 926	8 435	146	48 345	5 894	50
1994	66 450	2 554	1 330	1 197	27	63 896	58 300	8 327	99	49 874	5 560	37
1995	67 377	2 559	1 395	1 138	26	64 818	59 332	8 267	96	50 969	5 461	25
1996	68 207	2 573	1 418	1 124	31	65 634	60 133	8 110	99	51 924	5 465	36
1997	69 685	2 552	1 439	1 084	29	67 133	61 595	8 015	81	53 499	5 506	31
1998	70 693	2 553	1 526	1 005	23	68 140	62 630	8 178	86	54 366	5 480	29
1999	71 446	2 432	1 450	962	20	69 014	63 624	8 278	74	55 272	5 366	25
2000	72 293	2 434	1 512	898	24	69 859	64 574	8 215	67	56 292	5 256	29
WOMEN												
1978	39 569	669	290	155	225	38 900	36 651	7 689	1 204	27 758	1 814	435
1979	41 217	661	290	165	206	40 556	38 154	7 845	1 105	29 204	1 982	419
1980	42 117	656	275	184	197	41 461	39 007	8 090	1 044	29 873	2 097	357
1981	43 000	667	296	196	176	42 333	39 798	8 013	1 016	30 769	2 192	343
1982	43 256	665	296	203	166	42 591	39 934	7 918	1 019	30 997	2 309	348
1983	44 047	680	314	210	156	43 367	40 603	7 913	1 036	31 654	2 439	325
1984	45 915	653	301	203	148	45 262	42 413	8 050	1 061	33 302	2 566	283
1985	47 259	644	305	214	125	46 615	43 761	8 274	1 078	34 409	2 603	251
1986	48 706	652	317	220	115	48 054	45 225	8 537	1 055	35 633	2 610	219
1987	50 334	666	342	229	95	49 668	46 669	8 788	1 029	36 852	2 778	221
1988	51 696	676	353	224	99	51 020	47 844	9 039	996	37 809	2 955	220
1989	53 028	687	363	236	87	52 341	49 057	9 353	945	38 759	3 043	240
1990	53 689	678	385	227	66	53 011	49 685	9 524	879	39 282	3 122	205
1991	53 495	680	369	237	73	52 815	49 474	9 635	867	38 972	3 150	191
1992	54 052	672	379	221	73	53 380	50 225	9 788	979	39 458	2 963	192
1993	54 910	637	367	204	67	54 273	51 040	10 144	980	39 916	3 065	168
1994	56 610	855	384	448	23	55 755	52 217	9 965	867	41 385	3 443	95
1995	57 523	881	419	442	20	56 642	53 115	10 095	867	42 153	3 440	86
1996	58 501	871	452	394	25	57 630	54 037	10 107	830	43 100	3 506	87
1997	59 873	847	451	373	23	59 026	55 388	10 116	834	44 438	3 550	89
1998	60 770	825	474	336	15	59 945	56 389	10 205	876	45 308	3 482	74
1999	62 042	849	494	335	20	61 193	57 699	10 625	859	46 215	3 424	70
2000	62 915	871	521	336	14	62 044	58 554	10 838	823	46 894	3 417	72

Note: See "Notes and Definitions" for information on historical comparabilty.

Table 1-16. Number of Employed Persons 25 Years and Over by Educational Attainment, Race, Hispanic Origin, and Sex, 1992–2000

(Thousands of persons.)

Year, race, Hispanic origin, and sex	Total	Less than a high school diploma	High school graduates, no college	Some college, no degree	Associate degree	College graduates	
						Total	Bachelor's degree only
TOTAL							
1992	99 947	11 843	35 305	18 007	7 519	27 273	17 662
1993	101 615	11 201	35 395	18 729	8 174	28 115	18 300
1994	104 141	11 053	35 135	19 861	8 834	29 257	19 225
1995	106 037	10 945	34 999	20 436	9 245	30 412	19 924
1996	108 070	11 317	36 300	20 590	9 404	31 459	20 742
1997	110 518	11 546	36 163	20 678	9 643	32 488	21 524
1998	111 855	11 673	35 976	20 626	9 850	33 730	22 260
1999	113 425	11 294	36 017	21 129	10 079	34 905	22 973
2000	114 612	11 283	35 886	21 374	10 591	35 478	23 382
WHITE							
1992	85 649	9 531	30 282	15 420	6 502	23 914	15 441
1993	87 001	9 109	30 242	15 987	7 052	24 613	15 962
1994	89 057	8 879	30 004	16 893	7 622	25 658	16 719
1995	90 498	8 690	29 776	17 265	7 970	26 796	17 434
1996	91 992	9 258	30 042	17 249	8 072	27 371	17 978
1997	93 687	9 414	30 552	17 302	8 271	28 148	18 801
1998	94 330	9 510	30 249	17 101	8 426	29 044	19 107
1999	95 316	9 235	30 211	17 388	8 556	29 925	19 668
2000	96 127	9 232	30 015	17 615	8 995	30 270	19 943
BLACK							
1992	10 313	1 781	4 011	2 017	744	1 760	1 219
1993	10 511	1 580	4 075	2 180	815	1 862	1 315
1994	10 834	1 543	4 016	2 340	902	2 034	1 483
1995	11 249	1 482	4 142	2 517	960	2 149	1 538
1996	11 518	1 534	4 192	2 640	969	2 183	1 539
1997	11 882	1 578	4 409	2 681	984	2 230	1 591
1998	12 324	1 579	4 504	2 776	1 020	2 446	1 741
1999	12 771	1 488	4 631	2 924	1 108	2 621	1 814
2000	12 964	1 490	4 609	2 949	1 176	2 741	1 889
HISPANIC							
1992	7 875	2 964	2 349	1 153	458	952	644
1993	8 218	2 996	2 422	1 276	514	1 009	697
1994	8 535	3 078	2 503	1 353	530	1 071	740
1995	8 873	3 204	2 624	1 427	534	1 084	759
1996	9 368	3 450	2 746	1 453	568	1 151	813
1997	10 214	3 738	2 945	1 603	611	1 316	926
1998	10 615	3 889	3 018	1 622	660	1 427	1 007
1999	10 985	3 926	3 213	1 696	660	1 491	1 034
2000	11 596	4 190	3 410	1 706	706	1 585	1 111
MEN							
1992	54 672	7 299	18 422	9 549	3 652	15 751	9 864
1993	55 550	6 977	18 575	9 878	4 012	16 109	10 170
1994	56 523	6 851	18 418	10 402	4 184	16 668	10 672
1995	57 420	6 691	18 426	10 653	4 394	17 255	10 983
1996	58 468	7 058	18 639	10 759	4 416	17 596	11 266
1997	59 736	7 210	19 124	10 876	4 517	18 010	11 587
1998	60 497	7 238	19 188	10 684	4 731	18 656	12 028
1999	61 032	6 921	19 125	10 941	4 838	19 208	12 343
2000	61 571	6 889	19 086	11 133	4 960	19 503	12 576
WOMEN							
1992	45 275	4 544	16 883	8 458	3 868	11 522	7 798
1993	46 064	4 224	16 820	8 851	4 163	12 006	8 130
1994	47 618	4 202	16 717	9 459	4 650	12 589	8 553
1995	48 617	4 254	16 573	9 783	4 851	13 157	8 941
1996	49 602	4 259	16 661	9 831	4 988	13 863	9 475
1997	50 782	4 336	17 039	9 802	5 126	14 478	9 937
1998	51 359	4 435	16 788	9 943	5 119	15 074	10 231
1999	52 392	4 372	16 893	10 189	5 242	15 697	10 630
2000	53 041	4 394	16 799	10 240	5 631	15 975	10 806

See *Note* at end of table.

Table 1-16. Number of Employed Persons 25 Years and Over by Educational Attainment, Race, Hispanic Origin, and Sex, 1992–2000—*Continued*

(Thousands of persons.)

Year, race, Hispanic origin, and sex	Total	Less than a high school diploma	High school graduates, no college	Some college, no degree	Associate degree	College graduates	
						Total	Bachelor's degree only
WHITE MEN							
1992	47 497	6 030	15 962	8 303	3 200	14 002	8 778
1993	48 191	5 807	16 002	8 581	3 514	14 288	9 020
1994	48 938	5 633	15 833	8 990	3 667	14 814	9 435
1995	49 641	5 444	15 760	9 155	3 856	15 426	9 780
1996	50 533	5 920	15 995	9 197	3 861	15 559	9 965
1997	51 397	6 049	16 330	9 245	3 941	15 832	10 191
1998	51 842	6 123	16 308	9 009	4 118	16 284	10 490
1999	52 180	5 883	16 193	9 182	4 160	16 763	10 806
2000	52 530	5 833	16 145	9 350	4 284	16 919	10 962
WHITE WOMEN							
1992	38 152	3 500	14 321	7 117	3 302	9 912	6 663
1993	38 810	3 301	14 240	7 406	3 538	10 325	6 941
1994	40 119	3 246	14 171	7 902	3 955	10 844	7 285
1995	40 857	3 246	14 016	8 110	4 115	11 370	7 655
1996	41 459	3 337	14 046	8 052	4 211	11 812	8 012
1997	42 290	3 365	14 222	8 058	4 330	12 316	8 410
1998	42 488	3 387	13 941	8 092	4 308	12 760	8 618
1999	43 135	3 352	14 018	8 207	4 396	13 162	8 862
2000	43 597	3 399	13 870	8 265	4 711	13 351	8 981
BLACK MEN							
1992	5 002	976	1 955	940	320	809	554
1993	5 119	875	2 014	998	353	879	617
1994	5 246	844	2 001	1 057	373	970	712
1995	5 423	778	2 101	1 142	393	1 010	717
1996	5 483	861	2 104	1 177	382	960	666
1997	5 658	868	2 181	1 241	385	983	710
1998	5 844	811	2 248	1 267	413	1 104	802
1999	6 001	741	2 030	1 313	469	1 140	789
2000	6 077	749	2 280	1 348	475	1 226	841
BLACK WOMEN							
1992	5 312	805	2 056	1 077	424	951	665
1993	5 392	705	2 060	1 182	462	983	698
1994	5 589	699	2 015	1 283	529	1 064	771
1995	5 826	704	2 042	1 375	566	1 139	822
1996	6 035	673	2 088	1 463	587	1 224	873
1997	6 225	710	2 229	1 439	600	1 247	882
1998	6 480	768	2 256	1 509	607	1 341	939
1999	6 770	746	2 292	1 612	639	1 481	1 025
2000	6 887	741	2 329	1 601	701	1 515	1 048
HISPANIC MEN							
1992	4 773	1 982	1 337	660	245	549	364
1993	4 989	2 019	1 365	742	281	582	401
1994	5 133	2 059	1 416	761	287	610	413
1995	5 337	2 125	1 501	818	279	615	408
1996	5 640	2 320	1 588	790	271	671	456
1997	6 165	2 502	1 714	899	302	747	502
1998	6 397	2 594	1 764	913	336	790	547
1999	6 441	2 554	1 839	917	334	797	540
2000	6 747	2 695	1 939	907	364	841	577
HISPANIC WOMEN							
1992	3 102	982	1 012	493	214	402	279
1993	3 229	977	1 057	535	233	428	296
1994	3 402	1 019	1 087	592	242	461	327
1995	3 536	1 079	1 123	609	255	470	351
1996	3 729	1 131	1 159	663	297	480	357
1997	4 049	1 236	1 231	704	309	569	425
1998	4 219	1 295	1 254	708	325	637	459
1999	4 544	1 372	1 373	778	327	694	494
2000	4 850	1 495	1 470	798	342	744	534

Note: Detail for the above race and Hispanic-origin groups will not sum to totals because data for the Other races group are not presented and Hispanics are included in both the White and Black population groups. See "Notes and Definitions" for information on historical comparability.

Table 1-17. Multiple Jobholders and Multiple Jobholding Rates by Selected Characteristics, May of Selected Years, 1970–2000

(Thousands of persons, percent, not seasonally adjusted.)

Year	Multiple jobholders				Multiple jobholding rate [1]				
	Total	Men	Women		Total	Men	Women	White	Black [2]
			Number	Percent of all multiple jobholders					
1970	4 048	3 412	636	15.7	5.2	7.0	2.2	5.3	4.4
1971	4 035	3 270	765	19.0	5.1	6.7	2.6	5.3	3.8
1972	3 770	3 035	735	19.5	4.6	6.0	2.4	4.8	3.7
1973	4 262	3 393	869	20.4	5.1	6.6	2.7	5.1	4.7
1974	3 889	3 022	867	22.3	4.5	5.8	2.6	4.6	3.8
1975	3 918	2 962	956	24.4	4.7	5.8	2.9	4.8	3.7
1976	3 948	3 037	911	23.1	4.5	5.8	2.6	4.7	2.8
1977	4 558	3 317	1 241	27.2	5.0	6.2	3.4	5.3	2.6
1978	4 493	3 212	1 281	28.5	4.8	5.8	3.3	5.0	3.1
1979	4 724	3 317	1 407	29.8	4.9	5.9	3.5	5.1	3.0
1980	4 759	3 210	1 549	32.5	4.9	5.8	3.8	5.1	3.2
1985	5 730	3 537	2 192	38.3	5.4	5.9	4.7	5.7	3.2
1989	7 225	4 115	3 109	43.0	6.2	6.4	5.9	6.5	4.3
1991	7 183	4 054	3 129	43.6	6.2	6.4	5.9	6.4	4.9
1994	7 316	3 973	3 343	45.7	6.0	6.0	5.9	6.1	4.9
1995	7 952	4 225	3 727	46.9	6.4	6.3	6.5	6.6	5.2
1996	7 846	4 352	3 494	44.5	6.2	6.4	6.0	6.4	5.1
1997	8 197	4 398	3 800	46.4	6.3	6.3	6.4	6.5	5.7
1998	8 126	4 438	3 688	45.4	6.2	6.3	6.1	6.3	5.5
1999	7 895	4 117	3 778	47.9	5.9	5.8	6.1	6.0	5.5
2000	7 710	4 059	3 650	47.3	5.7	5.6	5.8	5.9	4.9

Note: Comprehensive surveys of multiple jobholders were not conducted in 1981–84, 1986–88, 1990, and 1992–93. See "Notes and Definitions" for information on historical comparability.

1. Multiple jobholders as a percent of all employed persons in specified group.
2. Data for years prior to 1977 refer to the Black-and-Other population group.

Table 1-18. Multiple Jobholders by Sex, Age, Marital Status, Race, Hispanic Origin, and Job Status, 1997–2000

(Thousands of persons, percent.)

Characteristic	Both sexes				Men				Women			
	Number		Rate [1]		Number		Rate [1]		Number		Rate [1]	
	1997	1998	1997	1998	1997	1998	1997	1998	1997	1998	1997	1998
AGE												
Total, 16 years and over [2]	7 955	7 926	6.1	6.0	4 237	4 178	6.1	5.9	3 718	3 748	6.2	6.2
16 to 19 years	331	335	5.0	4.8	144	138	4.2	3.9	187	198	5.7	5.7
20 to 24 years	809	788	6.5	6.3	385	363	5.9	5.5	424	425	7.3	7.2
25 to 34 years	1 935	1 939	6.1	6.2	1 073	1 082	6.2	6.3	862	857	6.0	6.0
35 to 44 years	2 378	2 285	6.6	6.3	1 301	1 238	6.7	6.3	1 078	1 048	6.5	6.3
45 to 54 years	1 763	1 787	6.6	6.5	904	908	6.4	6.2	859	878	6.8	6.7
55 to 64 years	625	682	5.1	5.3	356	378	5.3	5.4	268	303	4.8	5.2
65 years and over	115	109	3.1	2.9	74	71	3.3	3.3	40	39	2.6	2.5
MARITAL STATUS												
Single	2 133	2 127	6.3	6.1	1 067	1 016	5.7	5.3	1 067	1 110	7.1	7.0
Married, spouse present	4 434	4 414	5.9	5.8	2 675	2 664	6.3	6.2	1 758	1 750	5.4	5.3
Widowed, divorced or separated	1 388	1 385	6.8	6.7	495	498	6.0	5.8	893	887	7.4	7.3
RACE AND HISPANIC ORIGIN												
White	6 909	6 832	6.3	6.2	3 693	3 622	6.2	6.0	3 216	3 210	6.4	6.4
Black	758	802	5.4	5.5	388	406	5.9	5.9	370	396	5.0	5.2
Hispanic origin	494	503	3.9	3.8	305	299	3.9	3.7	190	204	3.8	3.9
FULL- OR PART-TIME STATUS												
Primary job full-time, secondary job part-time	4 488	4 478	...	...	2 661	2 608	...	...	1 827	1 870	...	...
Primary and secondary jobs both part-time	1 689	1 635	...	...	521	512	...	...	1 168	1 124	...	...
Primary and secondary jobs both full-time	237	266	...	...	169	188	...	...	68	78	...	...
Hours vary on primary or secondary job	1 509	1 504	...	...	869	848	...	...	640	656	...	...

Characteristic	Both sexes				Men				Women			
	Number		Rate [1]		Number		Rate [1]		Number		Rate [1]	
	1999	2000	1999	2000	1999	2000	1999	2000	1999	2000	1999	2000
AGE												
Total, 16 years and over [2]	7 802	7 556	5.8	5.6	4 104	3 968	5.7	5.5	3 698	3 588	6.0	5.7
16 to 19 years	343	346	4.8	4.8	153	145	4.1	3.9	190	201	5.5	5.6
20 to 24 years	751	752	5.8	5.6	341	337	5.1	4.8	410	415	6.7	6.6
25 to 34 years	1 843	1 715	6.0	5.6	1 013	929	6.1	5.6	830	786	5.9	5.6
35 to 44 years	2 268	2 130	6.2	5.8	1 238	1 170	6.3	5.9	1 029	960	6.1	5.7
45 to 54 years	1 775	1 770	6.2	6.0	895	912	6.0	5.9	880	858	6.5	6.1
55 to 64 years	701	695	5.3	5.1	387	379	5.3	5.1	314	317	5.2	5.1
65 years and over	122	148	3.1	3.6	77	95	3.4	4.1	45	52	2.7	3.1
MARITAL STATUS												
Single	2 137	2 101	5.9	5.7	1 048	1 000	5.3	5.0	1 089	1 102	6.7	6.6
Married, spouse present	4 309	4 156	5.6	5.4	2 566	2 499	5.9	5.8	1 744	1 656	5.2	4.9
Widowed, divorced or separated	1 356	1 299	6.5	6.1	490	469	5.8	5.3	866	830	7.0	6.6
RACE AND HISPANIC ORIGIN												
White	6 674	6 462	5.9	5.7	3 514	3 433	5.7	5.6	3 159	3 029	6.2	5.8
Black	831	818	5.5	5.3	442	396	6.3	5.5	389	422	4.8	5.2
Hispanic origin	490	490	3.6	3.4	280	298	3.5	3.5	210	192	3.7	3.2
FULL- OR PART-TIME STATUS												
Primary job full-time, secondary job part-time	4 293	4 173	...	...	2 497	2 409	...	...	1 796	1 764	...	...
Primary and secondary jobs both part-time	1 657	1 595	...	...	519	518	...	...	1 138	1 077	...	...
Primary and secondary jobs both full-time	298	317	...	...	204	210	...	...	94	106	...	...
Hours vary on primary or secondary job	1 513	1 429	...	...	861	811	...	...	652	618	...	...

Note: Detail for the above race and Hispanic-origin groups will not sum to totals because data for the Other races group are not presented and Hispanics are included in both the White and Black population groups. See "Notes and Definitions" for information on historical comparability.

1. Multiple jobholders as a percent of all employed persons in specified group.
2. Includes a small number of persons who work part time on their primary job and full time on their secondary job(s), not shown separately.

Table 1-19. Multiple Jobholders by Industry of Principal Secondary Job, and Sex, 1999–2000, Annual Averages

(Thousands of persons.)

Industry of secondary job	Total	Men	Women
1999			
Nonagricultural Wage And Salary Workers	5 147	2 520	2 628
Mining	5	3	2
Construction	128	97	32
Manufacturing	207	143	63
Durable goods	81	61	20
Nondurable goods	125	82	43
Transportation, communications, and other public utilities	246	173	73
Transportation	201	140	61
Communications and other public utilities	45	33	12
Wholesale and retail trade	1 566	741	825
Wholesale trade	103	72	31
Retail trade	1 464	669	794
Finance, insurance, and real estate	208	115	93
Services	2 592	1 107	1 484
Private household	93	10	83
Miscellaneous services	2 499	1 097	1 401
Business, auto, and repair services	362	223	139
Personal services, except private households	174	80	93
Entertainment and recreation services	336	175	161
Professional and related services	1 624	617	1 008
Hospitals	160	46	114
Health services, except hospitals	368	88	279
Educational services	604	263	341
Social services	141	41	100
Other professional services	351	178	173
Forestry and fisheries	3	3	. . .
Public administration	195	140	55
2000			
Nonagricultural Wage And Salary Workers	5 284	2 538	2 746
Mining	7	5	2
Construction	134	98	36
Manufacturing	226	154	72
Durable goods	95	66	29
Nondurable goods	131	88	43
Transportation, communications, and other public utilities	245	170	75
Transportation	189	131	58
Communications and other public utilities	56	39	17
Wholesale and retail trade	1 576	689	886
Wholesale trade	106	72	34
Retail trade	1 470	618	853
Finance, insurance, and real estate	240	127	113
Services	2 630	1 138	1 491
Private household	92	9	84
Miscellaneous services	2 538	1 130	1 408
Business, auto, and repair services	392	244	148
Personal services, except private households	170	70	99
Entertainment and recreation services	344	186	158
Professional and related services	1 631	628	1 002
Hospitals	184	66	118
Health services, except hospitals	344	75	268
Educational services	595	270	325
Social services	167	53	114
Other professional services	341	164	177
Forestry and fisheries	2	2	. . .
Public administration	226	156	70

Table 1-20. Employment and Unemployment in Families by Race and Hispanic Origin, 1995–2000, Annual Averages

(Thousands of persons, percent.)

Characteristic	1995	1996	1997	1998	1999	2000
TOTAL						
Total Families	68 552	69 203	69 714	70 218	71 250	71 680
With employed member(s)	55 633	56 342	57 289	57 986	59 185	59 626
As percent of total families	81.2	81.4	82.2	82.6	83.1	83.2
Some usually work full time [1]	51 473	52 249	53 226	53 945	55 123	55 683
With no employed member	12 919	12 860	12 425	12 232	12 065	12 054
As percent of total families	18.8	18.6	17.8	17.4	16.9	16.8
With unemployed member(s)	5 404	5 270	4 913	4 503	4 260	4 110
As percent of total families	7.9	7.6	7.0	6.4	6.0	5.7
Some member(s) employed	3 795	3 678	3 445	3 177	3 091	2 973
As percent of families with unemployed member(s)	70.2	69.8	70.1	70.6	72.6	72.3
Some usually work full time [1]	3 334	3 265	3 070	2 830	2 771	2 675
As percent of families with unemployed member(s)	61.7	62.0	62.5	62.8	65.0	65.1
WHITE						
Total Families	57 650	58 315	58 514	58 930	59 661	59 918
With employed member(s)	47 216	47 882	48 378	48 850	49 632	49 877
As percent of total families	81.9	82.1	82.7	82.9	83.2	83.2
Some usually work full time [1]	43 804	44 522	45 069	45 567	46 333	46 639
With no employed member	10 433	10 434	10 135	10 080	10 029	10 042
As percent of total families	18.1	17.9	17.3	17.1	16.8	16.8
With unemployed member(s)	4 002	3 896	3 566	3 299	3 134	3 010
As percent of total families	6.9	6.7	6.1	5.6	5.3	5.0
Some member(s) employed	2 934	2 875	2 632	2 463	2 374	2 276
As percent of families with unemployed member(s)	73.3	73.8	73.8	74.7	75.8	75.6
Some usually work full time [1]	2 579	2 557	2 353	2 204	2 132	2 052
As percent of families with unemployed member(s)	64.4	65.6	66.0	66.8	68.0	68.2
BLACK						
Total Families	8 015	8 149	8 308	8 317	8 498	8 600
With employed member(s)	5 991	6 137	6 409	6 554	6 847	6 964
As percent of total families	74.7	75.3	77.1	78.8	80.6	81.0
Some usually work full time [1]	5 419	5 563	5 810	5 953	6 249	6 401
With no employed member	2 024	2 012	1 899	1 763	1 652	1 636
As percent of total families	25.3	24.7	22.9	21.2	19.4	19.0
With unemployed member(s)	1 080	1 121	1 104	984	905	881
As percent of total families	13.5	13.8	13.3	11.8	10.6	10.2
Some member(s) employed	631	627	631	555	551	535
As percent of families with unemployed member(s)	58.4	55.9	57.2	56.4	60.8	60.8
Some usually work full time [1]	556	553	553	485	486	476
As percent of families with unemployed member(s)	51.5	49.3	50.1	49.3	53.7	54.1
HISPANIC						
Total Families	6 233	6 465	6 779	7 025	7 403	7 581
With employed member(s)	5 086	5 312	5 701	5 947	6 405	6 633
As percent of total families	81.6	82.2	84.1	84.7	86.5	87.5
Some usually work full time [1]	4 673	4 917	5 285	5 545	6 017	6 255
With no employed member	1 147	1 153	1 078	1 078	998	947
As percent of total families	18.4	17.8	15.9	15.3	13.5	12.5
With unemployed member(s)	841	841	789	744	715	679
As percent of total families	13.5	13.0	11.6	10.6	9.7	9.0
Some member(s) employed	568	563	532	522	518	493
As percent of families with unemployed member(s)	67.5	66.9	67.4	70.2	72.5	72.7
Some usually work full time [1]	490	497	473	467	467	446
As percent of families with unemployed member(s)	58.3	59.1	59.9	62.8	65.3	65.8

Note: Detail for the above race and Hispanic-origin groups will not sum to totals because data for the Other races group are not presented and Hispanics are included in both the White and Black population groups. See "Notes and Definitions" for information on historical comparability.

1. Usually work 35 hours or more a week at all jobs.

Table 1-21. Families by Presence and Relationship of Employed Members and Family Type, 1995–2000, Annual Averages

(Thousands of persons, percent.)

Characteristic	Number						Percent distribution					
	1995	1996	1997	1998	1999	2000	1995	1996	1997	1998	1999	2000
MARRIED-COUPLE FAMILIES												
Total	52 929	53 214	53 248	53 689	54 468	54 704	100.0	100.0	100.0	100.0	100.0	100.0
Member(s) employed, total	44 194	44 448	44 641	45 061	45 800	45 967	83.5	83.5	83.8	83.9	84.1	84.0
Husband only	10 113	10 103	9 959	10 285	10 533	10 500	19.1	19.0	18.7	19.2	19.3	19.2
Wife only	2 956	2 846	2 839	2 843	2 980	2 946	5.6	5.3	5.3	5.3	5.5	5.4
Husband and wife	27 617	28 077	28 422	28 531	28 882	29 128	52.2	52.8	53.4	53.1	53.0	53.2
Other employment combinations	3 509	3 422	3 421	3 402	3 404	3 394	6.6	6.4	6.4	6.3	6.3	6.2
No member(s) employed	8 734	8 766	8 607	8 628	8 668	8 737	16.5	16.5	16.2	16.1	15.9	16.0
FAMILIES MAINTAINED BY WOMEN [1]												
Total	12 165	12 264	12 524	12 447	12 625	12 775	100.0	100.0	100.0	100.0	100.0	100.0
Member(s) employed, total	8 546	8 788	9 263	9 417	9 797	10 026	70.3	71.7	74.0	75.7	77.6	78.5
Householder only	4 757	4 964	5 282	5 322	5 566	5 581	39.1	40.5	42.2	42.8	44.1	43.7
Householder and other member(s)	2 401	2 385	2 484	2 582	2 663	2 806	19.7	19.4	19.8	20.7	21.1	22.0
Other member(s), not householder	1 388	1 438	1 497	1 513	1 568	1 639	11.4	11.7	12.0	12.2	12.4	12.8
No member(s) employed	3 620	3 477	3 261	3 029	2 827	2 749	29.8	28.4	26.0	24.3	22.4	21.5
FAMILIES MAINTAINED BY MEN [1]												
Total	3 458	3 724	3 942	4 083	4 158	4 200	100.0	100.0	100.0	100.0	100.0	100.0
Member(s) employed, total	2 893	3 106	3 385	3 509	3 588	3 632	83.7	83.4	85.9	85.9	86.3	86.5
Householder only	1 459	1 614	1 703	1 746	1 718	1 761	42.2	43.3	43.2	42.8	41.3	41.9
Householder and other member(s)	1 035	1 076	1 228	1 283	1 353	1 358	29.9	28.9	31.2	31.4	32.5	32.3
Other member(s), not householder	399	416	455	480	517	514	11.5	11.2	11.5	11.8	12.4	12.2
No member(s) employed	566	618	557	574	569	567	16.4	16.6	14.1	14.1	13.7	13.5

Note: See "Notes and Definitions" for information on historical comparability.

1. No spouse present.

Table 1-22. Unemployment in Families by Presence and Relationship of Employed Members and Family Type, 1995–2000, Annual Averages

(Thousands of persons, percent.)

Characteristic	Number						Percent distribution					
	1995	1996	1997	1998	1999	2000	1995	1996	1997	1998	1999	2000
MARRIED-COUPLE FAMILIES												
With Unemployed Member(s), Total	3 587	3 378	3 056	2 815	2 705	2 584	100.0	100.0	100.0	100.0	100.0	100.0
No member employed	670	601	530	471	440	411	18.7	17.8	17.3	16.7	16.3	15.9
Some member(s) employed	2 917	2 777	2 526	2 343	2 265	2 174	81.3	82.2	82.7	83.2	83.7	84.1
Husband unemployed	1 292	1 207	1 048	948	924	836	36.0	35.7	34.3	33.7	34.2	32.3
Wife employed	756	746	651	594	589	531	21.1	22.1	21.3	21.1	21.8	20.5
Wife unemployed	1 110	1 016	906	844	790	789	30.9	30.1	29.6	30.0	29.2	30.5
Husband employed	977	891	787	745	696	694	27.2	26.4	25.8	26.5	25.8	26.8
Other family member unemployed	1 186	1 155	1 102	1 023	991	959	33.1	34.2	36.1	36.3	36.6	37.1
FAMILIES MAINTAINED BY WOMEN [1]												
With Unemployed Member(s), Total	1 437	1 485	1 456	1 301	1 222	1 194	100.0	100.0	100.0	100.0	100.0	100.0
No member employed	772	809	782	696	613	587	53.7	54.5	53.7	53.5	50.2	49.1
Some member(s) employed	666	676	674	605	609	607	46.3	45.5	46.3	46.5	49.8	50.9
Householder unemployed	633	670	694	612	560	522	44.1	45.1	47.7	47.0	45.8	43.7
Other member(s) employed	103	102	122	99	110	102	7.2	6.9	8.4	7.6	9.0	8.5
Other member(s) unemployed	531	569	572	689	662	672	37.0	38.3	39.3	53.0	54.2	56.3
FAMILIES MAINTAINED BY MEN [1]												
With Unemployed Member(s), Total	380	407	400	388	333	331	100.0	100.0	100.0	100.0	100.0	100.0
No member employed	168	182	156	158	115	139	44.2	44.7	39.0	40.7	34.6	42.0
Some member(s) employed	212	224	244	229	218	192	55.8	55.0	61.0	59.0	65.4	58.0
Householder unemployed	181	200	197	186	154	173	47.6	49.1	49.2	47.9	46.4	52.2
Other member(s) employed	57	67	77	69	71	67	15.0	16.5	19.2	17.8	21.4	20.4
Other member(s) unemployed	198	206	204	202	178	158	52.1	50.6	51.0	52.1	53.6	47.8

Note: Detail may not sum to totals due to rounding. See "Notes and Definitions" for information on historical comparability.

1. No spouse present

Table 1-23. Employment Status of the Population by Sex, Marital Status, and Presence and Age of Own Children Under 18, 1995–2000, Annual Averages

(Thousands of persons, percent.)

Characteristic	1995			1996			1997		
	Total	Men	Women	Total	Men	Women	Total	Men	Women
WITH OWN CHILDREN UNDER 18 YEARS, TOTAL									
Civilian Noninstitutional Population	62 037	26 882	35 155	62 733	27 319	35 415	62 787	27 349	35 438
Civilian labor force	49 841	25 306	24 535	50 866	25 803	25 063	51 343	25 877	25 466
Participation rate	80.3	94.1	69.8	81.1	94.5	70.8	81.8	94.6	71.9
Employed	47 390	24 372	23 018	48 521	24 933	23 588	49 178	25 111	24 067
Employment-population ratio	76.4	90.7	65.5	77.3	91.3	66.6	78.3	91.8	67.9
Full-time workers [1]	40 100	23 535	16 566	41 164	24 085	17 080	41 934	24 306	17 628
Part-time workers [2]	7 290	838	6 452	7 356	848	6 508	7 244	806	6 439
Unemployed	2 451	934	1 517	2 345	870	1 475	2 165	766	1 399
Unemployment rate	4.9	3.7	6.2	4.6	3.4	5.9	4.2	3.0	5.5
MARRIED, SPOUSE PRESENT									
Civilian Noninstitutional Population	50 685	25 097	25 589	51 128	25 349	25 779	50 995	25 292	25 704
Civilian labor force	41 624	23 724	17 900	42 185	24 043	18 141	42 192	24 027	18 165
Participation rate	82.1	94.5	70.0	82.5	94.8	70.4	82.7	95.0	70.7
Employed	40 026	22 913	17 112	40 743	23 305	17 438	40 918	23 383	17 535
Employment-population ratio	79.0	91.3	66.9	79.7	91.9	67.6	80.2	92.5	68.2
Full-time workers [1]	33 988	22 163	11 825	34 732	22 559	12 173	35 042	22 685	12 357
Part-time workers [2]	6 037	750	5 287	6 011	747	5 265	5 877	698	5 179
Unemployed	1 598	810	788	1 441	738	703	1 273	644	630
Unemployment rate	3.8	3.4	4.4	3.4	3.1	3.9	3.0	2.7	3.5
OTHER MARITAL STATUS [3]									
Civilian Noninstitutional Population	11 352	1 785	9 566	11 606	1 970	9 636	11 791	2 057	9 734
Civilian labor force	8 217	1 582	6 635	8 680	1 759	6 921	9 151	1 850	7 301
Participation rate	72.4	88.6	69.4	74.8	89.3	71.8	77.6	89.9	75.0
Employed	7 364	1 459	5 905	7 777	1 628	6 149	8 259	1 728	6 531
Employment-population ratio	64.9	81.7	61.7	67.0	82.6	63.8	70.0	84.0	67.1
Full-time workers [1]	6 112	1 372	4 740	6 432	1 526	4 907	6 893	1 621	5 272
Part-time workers [2]	1 253	87	1 165	1 344	101	1 244	1 367	107	1 261
Unemployed	853	124	730	903	132	772	891	123	770
Unemployment rate	10.4	7.8	11.0	10.4	7.5	11.2	9.7	6.6	10.5
WITH OWN CHILDREN 6 TO 17 YEARS, NONE YOUNGER									
Civilian Noninstitutional Population	32 678	14 207	18 471	33 411	14 601	18 809	33 997	14 822	19 175
Civilian labor force	27 350	13 207	14 143	28 221	13 645	14 576	28 812	13 877	14 935
Participation rate	83.7	93.0	76.6	84.5	93.5	77.5	84.7	93.6	77.9
Employed	26 182	12 756	13 426	27 123	13 229	13 894	27 752	13 480	14 273
Employment-population ratio	80.1	89.8	72.7	81.2	90.6	73.9	81.6	90.9	74.4
Full-time workers [1]	22 434	12 358	10 076	23 267	12 810	10 456	23 885	13 071	10 814
Part-time workers [2]	3 748	398	3 350	3 857	418	3 438	3 868	409	3 459
Unemployed	1 168	451	716	1 097	416	681	1 060	397	662
Unemployment rate	4.3	3.4	5.1	3.9	3.0	4.7	3.7	2.9	4.4
WITH OWN CHILDREN UNDER 6 YEARS									
Civilian Noninstitutional Population	29 359	12 675	16 684	29 323	12 718	16 605	28 789	12 526	16 263
Civilian labor force	22 492	12 099	10 392	22 645	12 158	10 487	22 530	12 000	10 531
Participation rate	76.6	95.5	62.3	77.2	95.6	63.2	78.3	95.8	64.8
Employed	21 208	11 617	9 591	21 398	11 704	9 694	21 426	11 632	9 794
Employment-population ratio	72.2	91.6	57.5	73.0	92.0	58.4	74.4	92.9	60.2
Full-time workers [1]	17 666	11 177	6 489	17 898	11 274	6 623	18 049	11 235	6 814
Part-time workers [2]	3 542	440	3 102	3 500	430	3 070	3 376	397	2 980
Unemployed	1 284	482	801	1 247	454	794	1 105	368	737
Unemployment rate	5.7	4.0	7.7	5.5	3.7	7.6	4.9	3.1	7.0
WITH NO OWN CHILDREN UNDER 18 YEARS									
Civilian Noninstitutional Population	135 902	66 283	68 251	135 902	66 931	68 970	138 365	68 385	69 980
Civilian labor force	80 950	44 426	36 524	81 618	44 736	36 882	83 524	45 847	37 677
Participation rate	60.2	67.0	53.5	60.1	66.8	53.5	60.4	67.0	53.8
Employed	75 984	41 405	34 578	76 717	41 748	34 969	78 917	43 045	35 873
Employment-population ratio	56.5	62.5	50.7	56.5	62.4	50.7	57.0	62.9	51.3
Full-time workers [1]	60 053	34 839	25 214	60 920	35 200	25 719	62 902	36 452	26 449
Part-time workers [2]	15 930	6 566	9 364	15 797	6 548	9 250	16 016	6 592	9 424
Unemployed	4 967	3 021	1 946	4 901	2 988	1 913	4 606	2 802	1 804
Unemployment rate	6.1	6.8	5.3	6.0	6.7	5.2	5.5	6.1	4.8

See footnotes and *Note* at end of table.

Table 1-23. Employment Status of the Population by Sex, Marital Status, and Presence and Age of Own Children Under 18, 1995–2000, Annual Averages—*Continued*

(Thousands of persons, percent.)

Characteristic	1998			1999			2000		
	Total	Men	Women	Total	Men	Women	Total	Men	Women
WITH OWN CHILDREN UNDER 18 YEARS, TOTAL									
Civilian Noninstitutional Population	62 912	27 489	35 423	63 158	27 573	35 585	63 267	27 673	35 595
Civilian labor force	51 462	26 018	25 443	51 778	26 092	25 686	51 944	26 202	25 742
Participation rate	81.8	94.6	71.8	82.0	94.6	72.2	82.1	94.7	72.3
Employed	49 480	25 333	24 147	50 010	25 472	24 538	50 259	25 622	24 637
Employment-population ratio	78.6	92.2	68.2	79.2	92.4	69.0	79.4	92.6	69.2
Full-time workers [1]	42 372	24 562	17 811	43 033	24 712	18 321	43 365	24 922	18 443
Part-time workers [2]	7 108	771	6 337	6 977	761	6 216	6 894	699	6 195
Unemployed	1 981	686	1 296	1 768	620	1 149	1 685	581	1 104
Unemployment rate	3.8	2.6	5.1	3.4	2.4	4.5	3.2	2.2	4.3
MARRIED, SPOUSE PRESENT									
Civilian Noninstitutional Population	51 061	25 325	25 737	51 302	25 462	25 840	51 415	25 540	25 874
Civilian labor force	42 088	24 080	18 009	42 260	24 222	18 038	42 361	24 290	18 072
Participation rate	82.4	95.1	70.0	82.4	95.1	69.8	82.4	95.1	69.8
Employed	40 914	23 506	17 408	41 193	23 688	17 505	41 357	23 816	17 541
Employment-population ratio	80.1	92.8	67.6	80.3	93.0	67.7	80.4	93.2	67.8
Full-time workers [1]	35 197	22 839	12 357	35 568	23 024	12 544	35 793	23 212	12 581
Part-time workers [2]	5 718	667	5 051	5 625	664	4 961	5 564	604	4 960
Unemployed	1 174	573	601	1 067	534	533	1 004	474	531
Unemployment rate	2.8	2.4	3.3	2.5	2.2	3.0	2.4	2.0	2.9
OTHER MARITAL STATUS [3]									
Civilian Noninstitutional Population	11 851	2 166	9 686	11 856	2 110	9 746	11 853	2 132	9 720
Civilian labor force	9 374	1 939	7 434	9 518	1 870	7 648	9 583	1 913	7 670
Participation rate	79.1	89.5	76.7	80.3	88.6	78.5	80.8	89.7	78.9
Employed	8 565	1 826	6 739	8 817	1 784	7 032	8 902	1 806	7 096
Employment-population ratio	72.3	84.3	69.6	74.4	84.6	72.2	75.1	84.7	73.0
Full-time workers [1]	7 177	1 724	5 453	7 465	1 687	5 777	7 572	1 710	5 862
Part-time workers [2]	1 391	104	1 286	1 352	97	1 255	1 330	96	1 234
Unemployed	807	113	695	702	86	616	681	107	574
Unemployment rate	8.6	5.8	0.3	7.4	4.6	8.1	7.1	5.6	7.5
WITH OWN CHILDREN 6 TO 17 YEARS, NONE YOUNGER									
Civilian Noninstitutional Population	34 329	14 947	19 383	34 662	15 090	19 572	34 737	15 165	19 572
Civilian labor force	29 003	13 969	15 033	29 403	14 092	15 311	29 576	14 178	15 398
Participation rate	84.5	93.5	77.6	84.8	93.4	78.2	85.1	93.5	78.7
Employed	28 046	13 629	14 417	28 528	13 782	14 747	28 744	13 877	14 868
Employment-population ratio	81.7	91.2	74.4	82.3	91.3	75.3	82.7	91.5	76.0
Full-time workers [1]	24 286	13 238	11 048	24 807	13 385	11 422	25 042	13 513	11 529
Part-time workers [2]	3 760	391	3 369	3 722	397	3 325	3 703	364	3 339
Unemployed	957	340	617	875	310	564	832	302	530
Unemployment rate	3.3	2.4	4.1	3.0	2.2	3.7	2.8	2.1	3.4
WITH OWN CHILDREN UNDER 6 YEARS									
Civilian Noninstitutional Population	28 583	12 543	16 040	28 496	12 482	16 014	28 530	12 508	16 022
Civilian labor force	22 459	12 049	10 410	22 375	12 000	10 375	22 368	12 024	10 344
Participation rate	78.6	96.1	64.9	78.5	96.1	64.8	78.4	96.1	64.6
Employed	21 434	11 703	9 731	21 482	11 691	9 791	21 515	11 745	9 770
Employment-population ratio	75.0	93.3	60.7	75.4	93.7	61.1	75.4	93.9	61.0
Full-time workers [1]	18 086	11 323	6 763	18 227	11 327	6 900	18 323	11 410	6 914
Part-time workers [2]	3 348	380	2 968	3 255	364	2 891	3 191	335	2 856
Unemployed	1 025	346	679	894	310	584	853	279	574
Unemployment rate	4.6	2.9	6.5	4.0	2.6	5.6	3.8	2.3	5.6
WITH NO OWN CHILDREN UNDER 18 YEARS									
Civilian Noninstitutional Population	140 436	69 396	71 040	143 160	70 714	72 446	145 199	71 825	73 374
Civilian labor force	84 735	46 464	38 271	86 424	47 255	39 169	88 014	48 140	39 874
Participation rate	60.3	67.0	53.9	60.4	66.8	54.1	60.6	67.0	54.3
Employed	80 545	43 922	36 623	82 333	44 828	37 504	84 058	45 781	38 278
Employment-population ratio	57.4	63.3	51.6	57.5	63.4	51.8	57.9	63.7	52.2
Full-time workers [1]	64 429	37 226	27 203	66 136	38 086	28 051	68 046	39 136	28 910
Part-time workers [2]	16 116	6 696	9 420	16 196	6 743	9 454	16 012	6 645	9 367
Unemployed	4 190	2 542	1 648	4 091	2 426	1 665	3 956	2 359	1 596
Unemployment rate	4.9	5.5	4.3	4.7	5.1	4.3	4.5	4.9	4.0

Note: Own children include sons, daughters, step-children, and adopted children. Not included are nieces, nephews, grandchildren, and other related and unrelated children. Detail may not sum to totals due to rounding. See "Notes and Definitions" for information on historical comparability.

1. Usually work 35 hours or more a week at all jobs.
2. Usually work less than 35 hours a week at all jobs.
3. Includes never-married, divorced, separated, and widowed persons.

Table 1-24. Employment Status of Mothers with Own Children Under 3 Years Old by Single Year of Age of Youngest Child, and Marital Status, 1996–2000, Annual Averages

(Thousands of persons, percent.)

Year and characteristic	Civilian noninstitutional population	Civilian labor force: Total	Civilian labor force: Percent of population	Employed: Total	Employed: Percent of population	Employed: Full-time workers[1]	Employed: Part-time workers[2]	Unemployed: Number	Unemployed: Percent of labor force
1996									
Total Mothers With Own Children Under 3 Years	9 610	5 710	59.4	5 252	54.7	3 543	1 708	458	8.0
2 years	2 899	1 836	63.3	1 694	58.4	1 168	526	142	7.7
1 year	3 333	2 040	61.2	1 885	56.6	1 268	617	155	7.6
Under 1 year	3 378	1 834	54.3	1 673	49.5	1 107	565	161	8.8
Married, Spouse Present With Own Children Under 3 Years	7 203	4 343	60.3	4 143	57.5	2 762	1 381	201	4.6
2 years	2 150	1 362	63.3	1 303	60.6	876	427	60	4.4
1 year	2 500	1 555	62.2	1 489	59.6	993	496	66	4.2
Under 1 year	2 553	1 426	55.9	1 351	52.9	893	458	75	5.3
Other Marital Status With Own Children Under 3 Years[3]	2 407	1 367	56.8	1 111	46.2	782	328	256	18.7
2 years	749	473	63.2	391	52.2	292	99	82	17.3
1 year	833	486	58.3	397	47.7	275	121	89	18.3
Under 1 year	825	408	49.5	323	39.2	215	108	85	20.8
1997									
Total Mothers With Own Children Under 3 Years	9 347	5 738	61.4	5 306	56.8	3 560	1 746	432	7.5
2 years	2 871	1 890	65.8	1 763	61.4	1 208	555	127	6.7
1 year	3 306	2 012	60.9	1 851	56.0	1 205	646	161	8.0
Under 1 year	3 170	1 836	57.9	1 692	53.4	1 147	545	144	7.8
Married, Spouse Present With Own Children Under 3 Years	7 049	4 296	60.9	4 105	58.2	2 718	1 387	191	4.4
2 years	2 142	1 380	64.4	1 327	62.0	883	444	53	3.8
1 year	2 459	1 468	59.7	1 399	56.9	890	509	69	4.7
Under 1 year	2 448	1 448	59.2	1 379	56.3	945	434	69	4.8
Other Marital Status With Own Children Under 3 Years[3]	2 297	1 445	62.9	1 201	52.3	842	361	241	16.7
2 years	729	511	70.1	436	59.8	325	112	74	14.5
1 year	847	545	64.3	452	53.4	315	138	92	16.9
Under 1 year	721	389	54.0	313	43.4	202	111	75	19.3
1998									
Total Mothers With Own Children Under 3 Years	9 333	5 779	61.9	5 384	57.7	3 626	1 758	395	6.8
2 years	2 772	1 786	64.4	1 673	60.4	1 149	524	113	6.3
1 year	3 213	2 055	64.0	1 917	59.7	1 281	636	138	6.7
Under 1 year	3 348	1 938	57.9	1 794	53.6	1 196	598	144	7.4
Married, Spouse Present With Own Children Under 3 Years	7 110	4 316	60.7	4 145	58.3	2 765	1 380	171	4.0
2 years	2 073	1 291	62.3	1 244	60.0	831	413	47	3.6
1 year	2 493	1 560	62.6	1 497	60.0	989	508	63	4.0
Under 1 year	2 544	1 465	57.6	1 404	55.2	945	459	61	4.2
Other Marital Status With Own Children Under 3 Years[3]	2 225	1 463	65.8	1 238	55.6	860	379	223	15.2
2 years	700	495	70.7	429	61.3	318	111	65	13.1
1 year	721	495	68.7	420	58.3	292	129	75	15.2
Under 1 year	804	473	58.8	389	48.4	250	139	83	17.5
1999									
Total Mothers With Own Children Under 3 Years	9 339	5 742	61.5	5 389	57.7	3 692	1 697	353	6.1
2 years	2 890	1 888	65.3	1 788	61.9	1 257	530	101	5.3
1 year	3 283	2 062	62.8	1 934	58.9	1 298	635	128	6.2
Under 1 year	3 166	1 792	56.6	1 668	52.7	1 137	531	124	6.9
Married, Spouse Present With Own Children Under 3 Years	7 089	4 224	59.6	4 078	57.5	2 744	1 334	147	3.5
2 years	2 175	1 356	62.4	1 316	60.5	898	419	40	2.9
1 year	2 522	1 532	60.8	1 477	58.6	964	513	56	3.6
Under 1 year	2 392	1 336	55.8	1 285	53.7	882	403	51	3.8
Other Marital Status With Own Children Under 3 Years[3]	2 251	1 517	67.4	1 311	58.3	949	362	206	13.6
2 years	715	532	74.4	472	65.9	360	112	61	11.4
1 year	761	529	69.5	457	60.0	334	123	72	13.7
Under 1 year	774	456	58.8	383	49.5	255	128	73	16.0
2000									
Total Mothers With Own Children Under 3 Years	9 356	5 653	60.4	5 311	56.8	3 614	1 697	342	6.0
2 years	2 803	1 807	64.5	1 712	61.1	1 193	519	95	5.3
1 year	3 300	2 069	62.7	1 939	58.8	1 310	629	130	6.3
Under 1 year	3 253	1 777	54.6	1 660	51.0	1 112	548	117	6.6
Married, Spouse Present With Own Children Under 3 Years	7 056	4 090	58.0	3 940	55.8	2 613	1 327	150	3.7
2 years	2 096	1 276	60.9	1 233	58.9	823	411	42	3.3
1 year	2 499	1 503	60.1	1 448	57.9	953	495	55	3.6
Under 1 year	2 461	1 312	53.3	1 259	51.1	837	421	53	4.1
Other Marital Status With Own Children Under 3 Years[3]	2 300	1 563	67.9	1 371	59.6	1 002	370	191	12.2
2 years	707	531	75.1	478	67.6	370	108	53	9.9
1 year	801	566	70.7	491	61.3	357	134	75	13.2
Under 1 year	792	465	58.8	402	50.7	275	127	64	13.7

Note: Own children include sons, daughters, step-children, and adopted children. Not included are nieces, nephews, grandchildren, and other related and unrelated children. Detail may not sum to totals due to rounding. See "Notes and Definitions" for information on historical comparability.

1. Usually work 35 hours or more a week at all jobs.
2. Usually work less than 35 hours a week at all jobs.
3. Includes never-married, divorced, separated, and widowed persons.

Table 1-25. Major Unemployment Indicators, 1948–2000

(Unemployment as a percent of civilian labor force.)

Year	All civilian workers	Men 20 years and over	Women 20 years and over	Both sexes 16 to 19 years	Both sexes 25 years and over	White	Black	Hispanic	Full-time workers	Part-time workers	Women who maintain families	Married men, spouse present
1948	3.8	3.2	3.6	9.2	2.9	...	...	...	...	...	...	...
1949	5.9	5.4	5.3	13.4	4.8	...	...	...	...	...	...	...
1950	5.3	4.7	5.1	12.2	4.4	...	...	...	...	...	...	...
1951	3.3	2.5	4.0	8.2	2.8	...	...	...	...	...	...	...
1952	3.0	2.4	3.2	8.5	2.4	...	...	...	...	...	...	...
1953	2.9	2.5	2.9	7.6	2.4	...	...	...	...	...	...	...
1954	5.5	4.9	5.5	12.6	4.7	5.0	...	...	...	...	...	...
1955	4.4	3.8	4.4	11.0	3.6	3.9	...	...	...	...	...	2.6
1956	4.1	3.4	4.2	11.1	3.3	3.6	...	...	...	...	...	2.3
1957	4.3	3.6	4.1	11.6	3.4	3.8	...	...	...	...	...	2.8
1958	6.8	6.2	6.1	15.9	5.6	6.1	...	...	...	...	...	5.1
1959	5.5	4.7	5.2	14.6	4.4	4.8	...	...	...	...	...	3.6
1960	5.5	4.7	5.1	14.7	4.4	5.0	...	...	...	...	...	3.7
1961	6.7	5.7	6.3	16.8	5.4	6.0	...	...	...	...	...	4.6
1962	5.5	4.6	5.4	14.7	4.4	4.9	...	...	...	...	...	3.6
1963	5.7	4.5	5.4	17.2	4.3	5.0	...	...	5.5	7.3	...	3.4
1964	5.2	3.9	5.2	16.2	3.8	4.6	...	...	4.9	7.2	...	2.8
1965	4.5	3.2	4.5	14.8	3.2	4.1	...	...	4.2	6.7	...	2.4
1966	3.8	2.5	3.8	12.8	2.6	3.4	...	...	3.5	6.2	...	1.9
1967	3.8	2.3	4.2	12.9	2.6	3.4	...	...	3.4	6.9	4.9	1.8
1968	3.6	2.2	3.8	12.7	2.3	3.2	...	...	3.2	6.0	4.4	1.6
1969	3.5	2.1	3.7	12.2	2.2	3.1	...	...	3.1	5.7	4.4	1.5
1970	4.9	3.5	4.8	15.3	3.3	4.5	...	...	4.6	6.9	5.4	2.6
1971	5.9	4.4	5.7	16.9	4.0	5.4	...	...	5.6	7.8	7.3	3.2
1972	5.6	4.0	5.4	16.2	3.6	5.1	10.4	...	5.2	7.7	7.2	2.8
1973	4.9	3.3	4.9	14.5	3.1	4.3	9.4	7.5	4.4	7.2	7.1	2.3
1974	5.6	3.8	5.5	16.0	3.6	5.0	10.5	8.1	5.2	7.7	7.0	2.7
1975	8.5	6.8	8.0	19.9	6.0	7.8	14.8	12.2	8.4	9.0	10.0	5.1
1976	7.7	5.9	7.4	19.0	5.5	7.0	14.0	11.5	7.5	8.8	10.1	4.2
1977	7.1	5.2	7.0	17.8	4.9	6.2	14.0	10.1	6.8	8.6	9.4	3.6
1978	6.1	4.3	6.0	16.4	4.1	5.2	12.8	9.1	5.7	7.9	8.5	2.8
1979	5.8	4.2	5.7	16.1	3.9	5.1	12.3	8.3	5.5	7.7	8.3	2.8
1980	7.1	5.9	6.4	17.8	5.1	6.3	14.3	10.1	7.1	7.6	9.2	4.2
1981	7.6	6.3	6.8	19.6	5.4	6.7	15.6	10.4	7.5	7.9	10.4	4.3
1982	9.7	8.8	8.3	23.2	7.4	8.6	18.9	13.8	10.0	8.5	11.7	6.5
1983	9.6	8.9	8.1	22.4	7.5	8.4	19.5	13.7	9.9	8.1	12.2	6.5
1984	7.5	6.6	6.8	18.9	5.8	6.5	15.9	10.7	7.5	7.4	10.3	4.6
1985	7.2	6.2	6.6	18.6	5.6	6.2	15.1	10.5	7.1	7.5	10.4	4.3
1986	7.0	6.1	6.2	18.3	5.4	6.0	14.5	10.6	6.9	7.4	9.8	4.4
1987	6.2	5.4	5.4	16.9	4.8	5.3	13.0	8.8	6.0	6.9	9.2	3.9
1988	5.5	4.8	4.9	15.3	4.3	4.7	11.7	8.2	5.3	6.4	8.1	3.3
1989	5.3	4.5	4.7	15.0	4.0	4.5	11.4	8.0	5.1	6.2	8.1	3.0
1990	5.6	5.0	4.9	15.5	4.4	4.8	11.4	8.2	5.4	6.4	8.3	3.4
1991	6.8	6.4	5.7	18.7	5.4	6.1	12.5	10.0	6.8	7.0	9.3	4.4
1992	7.5	7.1	6.3	20.1	6.1	6.6	14.2	11.6	7.5	7.5	10.0	5.1
1993	6.9	6.4	5.9	19.0	5.6	6.1	13.0	10.8	6.9	7.2	9.7	4.4
1994	6.1	5.4	5.4	17.6	4.8	5.3	11.5	9.9	6.1	6.0	8.9	3.7
1995	5.6	4.8	4.9	17.3	4.3	4.9	10.4	9.3	5.5	6.0	8.0	3.3
1996	5.4	4.6	4.8	16.7	4.2	4.7	10.5	8.9	5.3	5.8	8.2	3.0
1997	4.9	4.2	4.4	16.0	3.8	4.2	10.0	7.7	4.8	5.5	8.1	2.7
1998	4.5	3.7	4.1	14.6	3.4	3.9	8.9	7.2	4.3	5.3	7.2	2.4
1999	4.2	3.5	3.8	13.9	3.1	3.7	8.0	6.4	4.1	5.0	6.4	2.2
2000	4.0	3.3	3.6	13.1	3.0	3.5	7.6	5.7	3.9	4.8	5.9	2.0

Note: Data for the Other races group are not presented and Hispanics are included in both the White and Black population groups. See "Notes and Definitions" for information on historical comparability.

Table 1-26. Unemployed Persons by Race, Hispanic Origin, Sex, and Age, 1948–2000

(Thousands of persons.)

Year, race, Hispanic origin, and sex	16 years and over	16 to 19 years			20 years and over						
		Total	16 to 17 years	18 to 19 years	Total	20 to 24 years	25 to 34 years	35 to 44 years	45 to 54 years	55 to 64 years	65 years and over
TOTAL											
1948	2 276	409	180	228	1 869	455	457	347	290	226	93
1949	3 637	576	238	337	3 060	680	776	603	471	384	146
1950	3 288	513	226	287	2 776	561	702	530	478	368	137
1951	2 055	336	168	168	1 718	273	435	354	318	238	103
1952	1 883	345	180	165	1 539	268	389	325	274	195	86
1953	1 834	307	150	157	1 529	256	379	325	280	218	70
1954	3 532	501	221	247	3 032	504	793	680	548	374	132
1955	2 852	450	211	239	2 403	396	577	521	436	355	120
1956	2 750	478	231	247	2 274	395	554	476	429	311	109
1957	2 859	497	230	266	2 362	430	573	499	448	300	111
1958	4 602	678	299	379	3 923	701	993	871	731	472	154
1959	3 740	654	301	354	3 085	543	726	673	603	405	135
1960	3 852	712	325	387	3 140	583	752	671	614	396	122
1961	4 714	828	363	465	3 886	723	890	850	751	516	159
1962	3 911	721	312	409	3 191	636	712	688	605	411	141
1963	4 070	884	420	462	3 187	658	732	674	589	410	126
1964	3 786	872	436	437	2 913	660	607	605	543	378	117
1965	3 366	874	411	463	2 491	557	529	546	436	322	103
1966	2 875	837	395	441	2 041	446	441	426	369	265	92
1967	2 975	839	400	438	2 140	511	480	422	383	256	86
1968	2 817	838	414	426	1 978	543	443	371	314	219	88
1969	2 832	853	436	416	1 978	560	453	358	320	216	72
1970	4 093	1 106	537	569	2 987	866	718	515	476	309	104
1971	5 016	1 262	596	665	3 755	1 130	933	630	573	381	109
1972	4 882	1 308	633	676	3 573	1 132	878	576	510	368	111
1973	4 365	1 235	634	600	3 130	1 008	866	451	430	290	88
1974	5 156	1 422	699	722	3 733	1 212	1 044	559	498	321	99
1975	7 929	1 767	799	968	6 161	1 865	1 776	951	893	520	155
1976	7 406	1 719	796	924	5 687	1 714	1 710	849	758	510	147
1977	6 991	1 663	781	881	5 330	1 629	1 650	785	666	450	147
1978	6 202	1 583	796	787	4 620	1 483	1 422	694	552	345	123
1979	6 137	1 555	739	816	4 583	1 442	1 446	705	540	346	104
1980	7 637	1 669	778	890	5 969	1 835	2 024	940	676	399	94
1981	8 273	1 763	781	981	6 510	1 976	2 211	1 065	715	444	98
1982	10 678	1 977	831	1 145	8 701	2 392	3 037	1 552	966	647	107
1983	10 717	1 829	753	1 076	8 888	2 330	3 078	1 650	1 039	677	114
1984	8 539	1 499	646	854	7 039	1 838	2 374	1 335	828	566	97
1985	8 312	1 468	662	806	6 844	1 738	2 341	1 340	813	518	93
1986	8 237	1 454	665	789	6 783	1 651	2 390	1 371	790	489	91
1987	7 425	1 347	648	700	6 077	1 453	2 129	1 281	723	412	78
1988	6 701	1 226	573	653	5 475	1 261	1 929	1 166	657	375	87
1989	6 528	1 194	537	657	5 333	1 218	1 851	1 159	637	379	91
1990	7 047	1 212	527	685	5 835	1 299	1 995	1 328	723	386	105
1991	8 628	1 359	587	772	7 269	1 573	2 447	1 719	946	473	113
1992	9 613	1 427	641	787	8 186	1 649	2 702	1 976	1 138	589	132
1993	8 940	1 365	606	759	7 575	1 514	2 395	1 896	1 121	541	108
1994	7 996	1 320	624	696	6 676	1 373	2 067	1 627	971	485	153
1995	7 404	1 346	652	695	6 058	1 244	1 841	1 549	844	425	153
1996	7 236	1 306	617	689	5 929	1 239	1 757	1 505	883	406	139
1997	6 739	1 271	589	683	5 467	1 152	1 571	1 418	830	369	127
1998	6 210	1 205	573	632	5 005	1 081	1 419	1 258	782	343	122
1999	5 880	1 162	544	618	4 718	1 042	1 278	1 154	753	367	124
2000	5 655	1 093	506	587	4 562	1 025	1 168	1 141	749	347	131

See *Note* at end of table.

Table 1-26. Unemployed Persons by Race, Hispanic Origin, Sex, and Age, 1948–2000—*Continued*

(Thousands of persons.)

Year, race, Hispanic origin, and sex	16 years and over	16 to 19 years			20 years and over						
		Total	16 to 17 years	18 to 19 years	Total	20 to 24 years	25 to 34 years	35 to 44 years	45 to 54 years	55 to 64 years	65 years and over
WHITE											
1954	2 859	423	191	232	2 436	394	610	540	447	329	115
1955	2 252	373	181	191	1 879	304	412	402	358	300	105
1956	2 159	382	191	191	1 777	297	406	363	355	258	98
1957	2 289	401	195	204	1 888	331	425	401	373	262	98
1958	3 680	541	245	297	3 139	541	756	686	614	405	136
1959	2 946	525	255	270	2 421	406	526	525	496	348	120
1960	3 065	575	273	302	2 490	456	573	520	502	330	109
1961	3 743	669	295	374	3 074	566	668	652	611	438	139
1962	3 052	580	262	318	2 472	488	515	522	485	345	117
1963	3 208	708	350	358	2 500	501	540	518	485	349	107
1964	2 999	708	365	342	2 291	508	441	472	447	323	100
1965	2 691	705	329	374	1 986	437	399	427	358	276	91
1966	2 255	651	315	336	1 604	338	323	336	298	227	80
1967	2 338	635	311	325	1 703	393	360	336	321	221	75
1968	2 226	644	326	318	1 582	422	330	297	269	187	80
1969	2 260	660	351	309	1 601	432	354	294	269	185	66
1970	3 339	871	438	432	2 468	679	570	433	415	275	95
1971	4 085	1 011	491	521	3 074	887	732	517	500	338	100
1972	3 906	1 021	515	506	2 885	887	679	459	439	324	95
1973	3 442	955	513	443	2 486	758	664	358	371	257	77
1974	4 097	1 104	561	544	2 993	925	821	448	427	283	88
1975	6 421	1 413	657	755	5 007	1 474	1 413	774	753	460	136
1976	5 914	1 364	649	715	4 550	1 326	1 329	682	637	448	128
1977	5 441	1 284	636	648	4 157	1 195	1 255	621	569	388	129
1978	4 698	1 189	631	558	3 509	1 059	1 059	543	453	290	104
1979	4 664	1 193	589	603	3 472	1 038	1 068	545	443	290	87
1980	5 884	1 291	625	666	4 593	1 364	1 520	740	550	335	74
1981	6 343	1 374	629	745	4 968	1 449	1 658	827	579	379	77
1982	8 241	1 534	683	851	6 707	1 770	2 283	1 223	796	549	86
1983	8 128	1 387	609	778	6 741	1 678	2 282	1 294	837	563	88
1984	6 372	1 116	510	605	5 256	1 282	1 723	1 036	660	475	81
1985	6 191	1 074	507	567	5 117	1 235	1 695	1 039	642	432	75
1986	6 140	1 070	509	561	5 070	1 149	1 751	1 056	629	407	78
1987	5 501	995	495	500	4 506	1 017	1 527	984	576	333	68
1988	4 944	910	437	473	4 033	874	1 371	890	520	309	69
1989	4 770	863	407	456	3 908	856	1 297	871	503	311	70
1990	5 186	903	401	502	4 283	899	1 401	983	582	330	88
1991	6 560	1 029	461	568	5 532	1 132	1 805	1 330	759	410	96
1992	7 169	1 037	484	553	6 132	1 156	1 967	1 483	915	495	116
1993	6 655	992	468	523	5 663	1 057	1 754	1 411	907	442	92
1994	5 892	960	471	489	4 933	952	1 479	1 184	779	407	132
1995	5 459	952	476	476	4 507	866	1 311	1 161	676	362	131
1996	5 300	939	456	484	4 361	854	1 223	1 117	709	336	122
1997	4 836	912	438	475	3 924	765	1 068	1 035	648	302	106
1998	4 484	876	424	451	3 608	731	978	901	620	276	101
1999	4 273	844	414	430	3 429	720	865	843	595	303	104
2000	4 099	805	389	416	3 294	684	804	825	585	290	106

See *Note* at end of table.

Table 1-26. Unemployed Persons by Race, Hispanic Origin, Sex, and Age, 1948–2000—*Continued*

(Thousands of persons.)

Year, race, Hispanic origin, and sex	16 years and over	16 to 19 years			20 years and over						
		Total	16 to 17 years	18 to 19 years	Total	20 to 24 years	25 to 34 years	35 to 44 years	45 to 54 years	55 to 64 years	65 years and over
BLACK											
1972	906	279	113	167	627	226	183	106	62	37	12
1973	846	262	114	148	584	231	181	82	53	29	9
1974	965	297	127	170	666	261	201	95	65	33	10
1975	1 369	330	130	200	1 040	362	321	157	126	54	17
1976	1 334	330	134	195	1 005	350	338	145	101	54	16
1977	1 393	354	135	218	1 040	397	355	140	81	51	16
1978	1 330	360	150	210	972	379	320	127	82	47	17
1979	1 319	333	137	197	986	369	335	137	82	48	15
1980	1 553	343	134	210	1 209	426	433	171	109	53	18
1981	1 731	357	138	219	1 374	483	493	207	119	55	17
1982	2 142	396	130	266	1 747	565	662	278	141	84	17
1983	2 272	392	125	267	1 879	591	700	299	174	95	21
1984	1 914	353	122	230	1 561	504	577	253	138	75	15
1985	1 864	357	135	221	1 507	455	562	254	143	74	18
1986	1 840	347	138	209	1 493	453	564	269	127	69	10
1987	1 684	312	134	178	1 373	397	533	247	124	62	10
1988	1 547	288	121	167	1 259	349	502	230	111	51	15
1989	1 544	300	116	184	1 245	322	494	246	109	53	20
1990	1 565	268	112	156	1 297	349	505	278	106	44	14
1991	1 723	280	105	175	1 443	378	539	318	151	44	13
1992	2 011	324	127	197	1 687	421	610	402	178	64	13
1993	1 844	313	112	201	1 530	387	532	376	153	72	11
1994	1 666	300	127	173	1 366	351	468	346	130	55	16
1995	1 538	325	143	182	1 213	311	423	303	116	42	18
1996	1 592	310	133	177	1 282	327	454	313	127	48	13
1997	1 560	302	123	179	1 258	327	426	307	136	45	16
1998	1 426	281	124	156	1 146	301	366	294	125	45	16
1999	1 309	268	109	159	1 041	273	339	249	121	46	14
2000	1 269	239	100	139	1 030	290	292	261	130	37	20
HISPANIC											
1976	485	106	51	55	385	116	113	72	53	26	6
1977	456	113	50	60	344	98	114	56	48	24	5
1978	452	110	63	47	342	98	116	65	41	16	5
1979	434	106	54	51	329	100	102	65	37	20	4
1980	620	145	66	79	474	138	168	90	49	24	5
1981	678	144	60	84	533	171	178	92	57	31	5
1982	929	175	73	102	754	221	267	140	75	45	5
1983	961	167	64	104	793	214	270	156	93	54	5
1984	800	149	60	88	651	164	235	124	71	51	5
1985	811	141	55	85	670	171	256	123	73	41	7
1986	857	141	57	84	716	183	258	143	85	38	9
1987	751	136	57	79	615	152	222	128	75	33	5
1988	732	148	63	84	585	145	209	120	69	36	6
1989	750	132	59	73	618	158	218	124	76	36	6
1990	876	161	68	94	714	167	263	156	85	36	7
1991	1 092	179	79	99	913	214	332	206	110	44	8
1992	1 311	219	94	124	1 093	240	390	267	126	59	10
1993	1 248	201	86	115	1 047	237	354	261	132	54	10
1994	1 187	198	90	108	989	220	348	227	132	51	12
1995	1 140	205	96	109	934	209	325	224	106	54	16
1996	1 132	199	85	114	933	217	296	246	101	59	14
1997	1 069	197	87	110	872	206	269	229	99	56	13
1998	1 026	214	89	125	812	194	260	203	96	48	11
1999	945	196	79	117	750	171	233	190	104	42	10
2000	876	181	77	105	695	162	215	183	79	44	12

See *Note* at end of table.

Table 1-26. Unemployed Persons by Race, Hispanic Origin, Sex, and Age, 1948–2000—*Continued*

(Thousands of persons.)

Year, race, Hispanic origin, and sex	16 years and over	16 to 19 years			20 years and over						
		Total	16 to 17 years	18 to 19 years	Total	20 to 24 years	25 to 34 years	35 to 44 years	45 to 54 years	55 to 64 years	65 years and over
MEN											
1948	1 559	256	113	142	1 305	324	289	233	201	177	81
1949	2 572	353	145	207	2 219	485	539	414	347	310	125
1950	2 239	318	139	179	1 922	377	467	348	327	286	117
1951	1 221	191	102	89	1 029	155	241	192	193	162	87
1952	1 185	205	116	89	980	155	233	192	182	145	73
1953	1 202	184	94	90	1 019	152	236	208	196	167	60
1954	2 344	310	142	168	2 035	327	517	431	372	275	112
1955	1 854	274	134	140	1 580	248	353	328	285	265	102
1956	1 711	269	134	135	1 442	240	348	278	270	216	90
1957	1 841	300	140	159	1 541	283	349	304	302	220	83
1958	3 098	416	185	231	2 681	478	685	552	492	349	124
1959	2 420	398	191	207	2 022	343	484	407	390	287	112
1960	2 486	426	200	225	2 060	369	492	415	392	294	96
1961	2 997	479	221	258	2 518	458	585	507	473	375	122
1962	2 423	408	188	220	2 016	381	445	404	382	300	103
1963	2 472	501	248	252	1 971	396	445	386	358	290	97
1964	2 205	487	257	230	1 718	384	345	324	319	263	85
1965	1 914	479	247	232	1 435	311	292	283	253	221	75
1966	1 551	432	220	212	1 120	221	239	219	196	179	65
1967	1 508	448	241	207	1 060	235	219	185	199	163	60
1968	1 419	426	234	193	993	258	205	171	165	132	61
1969	1 403	440	244	196	963	270	205	155	157	127	48
1970	2 238	599	306	294	1 638	479	391	253	247	198	71
1971	2 789	693	346	347	2 097	640	513	320	313	239	71
1972	2 659	711	357	355	1 948	628	466	284	272	227	73
1973	2 275	653	352	300	1 624	528	439	211	219	171	57
1974	2 714	757	394	362	1 957	649	546	266	250	183	63
1975	4 442	966	445	521	3 476	1 081	986	507	499	302	103
1976	4 036	939	443	496	3 098	951	914	431	411	296	94
1977	3 667	874	421	453	2 794	877	869	373	326	252	97
1978	3 142	813	426	388	2 328	768	691	314	277	198	81
1979	3 120	811	393	418	2 308	744	699	329	272	196	67
1980	4 267	913	429	485	3 353	1 076	1 137	482	357	243	58
1981	4 577	902	431	531	3 615	1 144	1 213	552	390	261	55
1982	6 179	1 090	469	621	5 089	1 407	1 791	879	550	393	69
1983	6 260	1 003	408	595	5 257	1 369	1 822	947	613	433	73
1984	4 744	812	348	464	3 932	1 023	1 322	728	450	356	53
1985	4 521	806	363	443	3 715	944	1 244	706	459	307	55
1986	4 530	779	355	424	3 751	899	1 291	763	440	301	58
1987	4 101	732	353	379	3 369	779	1 169	689	426	258	49
1988	3 655	667	311	356	2 987	676	1 040	617	366	240	49
1989	3 525	658	303	355	2 867	660	953	619	351	234	49
1990	3 906	667	283	384	3 239	715	1 092	711	413	249	59
1991	4 946	751	317	433	4 195	911	1 375	990	550	305	64
1992	5 523	806	357	449	4 717	951	1 529	1 118	675	378	67
1993	5 055	768	342	426	4 287	865	1 338	1 049	636	336	64
1994	4 367	740	342	398	3 627	768	1 113	855	522	281	88
1995	3 983	744	352	391	3 239	673	961	815	464	233	94
1996	3 880	733	347	387	3 146	675	903	786	484	223	76
1997	3 577	694	321	373	2 882	636	772	732	457	217	69
1998	3 266	686	330	355	2 580	583	699	609	420	201	69
1999	3 066	633	295	338	2 433	562	624	571	403	203	70
2000	2 954	604	283	321	2 350	549	579	564	391	185	82

See *Note* at end of table.

Table 1-26. Unemployed Persons by Race, Hispanic Origin, Sex, and Age, 1948–2000—*Continued*

(Thousands of persons.)

Year, race, Hispanic origin, and sex	16 years and over	16 to 19 years			20 years and over						
		Total	16 to 17 years	18 to 19 years	Total	20 to 24 years	25 to 34 years	35 to 44 years	45 to 54 years	55 to 64 years	65 years and over
WOMEN											
1948	717	153	67	86	564	131	168	114	89	49	12
1949	1 065	223	93	130	841	195	237	189	124	74	21
1950	1 049	195	87	108	854	184	235	182	151	82	20
1951	834	145	66	79	689	118	194	162	125	76	16
1952	698	140	64	76	559	113	156	133	92	50	13
1953	632	123	56	67	510	104	143	117	84	51	10
1954	1 188	191	79	79	997	177	276	249	176	99	20
1955	998	176	77	99	823	148	224	193	151	90	18
1956	1 039	209	97	112	832	155	206	198	159	95	19
1957	1 018	197	90	107	821	147	224	195	146	80	28
1958	1 504	262	114	148	1 242	223	308	319	239	123	30
1959	1 320	256	110	147	1 063	200	242	266	213	118	23
1960	1 366	286	125	162	1 080	214	260	256	222	102	26
1961	1 717	349	142	207	1 368	265	305	343	278	141	37
1962	1 488	313	124	189	1 175	255	267	284	223	111	38
1963	1 598	383	172	210	1 216	262	287	288	231	120	29
1964	1 581	385	179	207	1 195	276	262	281	224	115	32
1965	1 452	395	164	231	1 056	246	237	263	183	101	28
1966	1 324	405	175	229	921	225	202	207	173	86	27
1967	1 468	391	159	231	1 078	277	261	237	184	93	26
1968	1 397	412	180	233	985	285	238	200	149	87	27
1969	1 429	413	192	220	1 015	290	248	203	163	89	24
1970	1 855	506	231	275	1 349	387	327	262	229	111	33
1971	2 227	568	250	318	1 658	489	420	310	260	142	38
1972	2 222	598	276	322	1 625	503	413	293	237	141	38
1973	2 089	583	282	301	1 507	480	427	240	212	119	31
1974	2 441	665	305	360	1 777	564	497	294	248	137	36
1975	3 486	802	355	447	2 684	783	791	444	395	219	52
1976	3 369	780	352	429	2 588	763	795	417	346	214	53
1977	3 324	789	361	428	2 535	752	782	412	340	198	50
1978	3 061	769	370	399	2 292	714	731	381	275	148	43
1979	3 018	743	346	396	2 276	697	748	375	268	150	38
1980	3 370	755	349	407	2 615	760	886	459	318	155	36
1981	3 696	800	350	450	2 895	833	998	513	325	184	43
1982	4 499	886	362	524	3 613	985	1 246	673	416	254	38
1983	4 457	825	344	481	3 632	961	1 255	703	427	244	41
1984	3 794	687	298	390	3 107	815	1 052	607	378	211	45
1985	3 791	661	298	363	3 129	794	1 098	634	355	211	39
1986	3 707	675	310	365	3 032	752	1 099	609	350	189	33
1987	3 324	616	295	321	2 709	674	960	592	298	155	30
1988	3 046	558	262	297	2 487	585	889	550	291	136	38
1989	3 003	536	234	302	2 467	558	897	540	286	144	41
1990	3 140	544	243	301	2 596	584	902	617	310	137	46
1991	3 683	608	270	338	3 074	662	1 071	728	396	168	49
1992	4 090	621	283	338	3 469	698	1 173	858	463	210	66
1993	3 885	597	264	333	3 288	648	1 058	847	485	205	45
1994	3 629	580	282	298	3 049	605	954	772	449	204	66
1995	3 421	602	299	303	2 819	571	880	735	381	193	60
1996	3 356	573	270	303	2 783	564	854	720	399	183	63
1997	3 162	577	268	310	2 585	516	800	686	373	152	58
1998	2 944	519	242	277	2 424	498	720	650	362	141	53
1999	2 814	529	249	280	2 285	480	654	584	350	163	54
2000	2 701	489	223	266	2 212	476	590	577	359	162	49

See *Note* at end of table.

Table 1-26. Unemployed Persons by Race, Hispanic Origin, Sex, and Age, 1948–2000—*Continued*

(Thousands of persons.)

Year, race, Hispanic origin, and sex	16 years and over	16 to 19 years: Total	16 to 19 years: 16 to 17 years	16 to 19 years: 18 to 19 years	20 years and over: Total	20 to 24 years	25 to 34 years	35 to 44 years	45 to 54 years	55 to 64 years	65 years and over
WHITE MEN											
1954	1 913	266	125	142	1 647	260	408	341	299	241	98
1955	1 478	232	114	117	1 246	196	260	246	233	223	89
1956	1 366	221	112	108	1 145	186	265	212	225	177	81
1957	1 477	243	118	124	1 234	222	257	239	250	193	73
1958	2 489	333	149	184	2 156	382	525	436	404	299	110
1959	1 903	318	162	156	1 585	256	350	316	320	245	98
1960	1 988	341	167	174	1 647	295	376	330	317	243	86
1961	2 398	384	176	208	2 014	370	442	395	382	318	107
1962	1 915	334	158	176	1 581	300	332	311	308	246	84
1963	1 976	407	211	196	1 569	309	342	297	294	246	80
1964	1 779	400	217	183	1 379	310	262	255	266	216	70
1965	1 556	387	200	186	1 169	254	226	228	206	190	67
1966	1 241	340	178	162	901	172	185	173	160	154	57
1967	1 208	342	186	156	866	185	171	153	167	140	52
1968	1 142	328	185	143	814	206	162	140	142	111	55
1969	1 137	343	198	145	794	214	165	130	134	108	43
1970	1 857	485	255	230	1 372	388	316	212	216	177	64
1971	2 309	562	288	275	1 747	513	418	268	272	211	66
1972	2 173	564	288	276	1 610	506	375	231	237	199	60
1973	1 836	513	284	229	1 323	411	353	166	188	153	51
1974	2 169	584	311	274	1 585	505	434	218	213	161	53
1975	3 627	785	369	416	2 841	871	796	412	411	265	86
1976	3 258	754	368	385	2 504	750	730	346	341	259	78
1977	2 883	672	342	330	2 211	660	682	297	276	213	82
1978	2 411	615	338	277	1 797	558	525	250	227	169	68
1979	2 405	633	319	313	1 773	553	526	253	220	165	56
1980	3 345	716	347	309	2 629	827	884	378	291	206	44
1981	3 580	755	349	406	2 825	[illegible]	943	433	[illegible]	221	42
1982	4 846	854	387	467	3 991	1 066	1 385	696	460	331	53
1983	4 859	761	328	433	4 098	1 019	1 410	755	497	362	54
1984	3 600	608	280	328	2 992	722	991	572	363	302	42
1985	3 426	592	282	310	2 834	694	931	553	356	257	43
1986	3 433	576	276	299	2 857	645	978	586	349	248	51
1987	3 132	548	272	276	2 584	568	879	536	350	209	43
1988	2 766	499	239	260	2 268	480	777	477	293	200	40
1989	2 636	487	230	257	2 149	476	694	470	280	191	38
1990	2 935	504	214	290	2 431	510	796	530	330	214	51
1991	3 859	575	249	327	3 284	677	1 064	780	438	269	55
1992	4 209	590	270	319	3 620	686	1 155	858	543	318	58
1993	3 828	565	261	305	3 263	619	1 015	793	512	270	53
1994	3 275	540	259	280	2 735	555	827	626	417	236	74
1995	2 999	535	260	275	2 465	483	711	621	371	200	79
1996	2 896	532	260	273	2 363	478	655	592	383	188	67
1997	2 641	502	234	268	2 140	439	553	549	358	182	58
1998	2 431	510	254	257	1 920	405	512	441	342	164	58
1999	2 274	461	223	237	1 813	398	441	419	322	172	61
2000	2 165	452	219	233	1 713	369	409	409	298	159	68

See *Note* at end of table.

Table 1-26. Unemployed Persons by Race, Hispanic Origin, Sex, and Age, 1948–2000—*Continued*

(Thousands of persons.)

Year, race, Hispanic origin, and sex	16 years and over	16 to 19 years			20 years and over						
		Total	16 to 17 years	18 to 19 years	Total	20 to 24 years	25 to 34 years	35 to 44 years	45 to 54 years	55 to 64 years	65 years and over
WHITE WOMEN											
1954	946	157	66	90	789	134	202	199	148	88	17
1955	774	141	67	74	633	108	152	156	125	77	16
1956	793	161	79	83	632	111	141	151	130	81	17
1957	812	158	77	80	654	109	168	162	123	69	25
1958	1 191	208	96	113	983	159	231	250	210	106	26
1959	1 043	207	93	114	836	150	176	209	176	103	22
1960	1 077	234	106	128	843	161	197	190	185	87	23
1961	1 345	285	119	166	1 060	196	226	257	229	120	32
1962	1 137	246	104	142	891	188	183	211	177	99	33
1963	1 232	301	139	162	931	192	198	221	191	103	27
1964	1 220	308	148	159	912	198	179	217	181	107	30
1965	1 135	318	129	188	817	183	173	199	152	86	24
1966	1 014	311	137	174	703	166	138	163	138	73	23
1967	1 130	293	125	169	837	209	189	183	154	81	23
1968	1 084	316	141	175	768	216	168	157	127	76	25
1969	1 123	317	153	164	806	218	189	164	135	77	23
1970	1 482	386	183	202	1 096	291	254	221	199	98	31
1971	1 777	449	203	246	1 328	376	314	249	228	126	34
1972	1 733	457	227	230	1 275	381	304	227	202	125	35
1973	1 606	442	228	214	1 164	347	311	192	183	104	26
1974	1 927	519	250	270	1 408	420	387	230	214	122	35
1975	2 794	628	288	340	2 166	602	617	362	342	195	49
1976	2 656	611	280	330	2 045	577	598	336	296	188	49
1977	2 558	612	294	318	1 946	536	573	323	293	175	47
1978	2 287	574	292	281	1 713	500	533	294	226	122	37
1979	2 260	560	270	290	1 699	485	542	293	223	125	32
1980	2 540	576	278	298	1 964	537	645	362	259	129	31
1981	2 762	620	281	339	2 143	580	715	394	261	158	36
1982	3 395	680	296	384	2 715	704	898	527	337	217	33
1983	3 270	626	282	345	2 643	659	872	539	340	201	33
1984	2 772	508	231	277	2 264	559	731	464	297	173	39
1985	2 765	482	225	257	2 283	541	763	486	286	175	32
1986	2 708	495	233	262	2 213	504	773	470	281	159	27
1987	2 369	447	223	224	1 922	449	648	448	227	124	25
1988	2 177	412	198	214	1 766	393	594	413	227	110	30
1989	2 135	376	177	199	1 758	380	603	401	223	120	32
1990	2 251	399	187	212	1 852	389	605	453	251	116	37
1991	2 701	453	212	241	2 248	455	741	550	320	141	41
1992	2 959	447	214	233	2 512	469	811	625	372	177	58
1993	2 827	426	208	219	2 400	438	739	618	395	172	39
1994	2 617	420	211	208	2 197	397	652	558	361	170	58
1995	2 460	418	216	201	2 042	384	600	540	306	162	52
1996	2 404	407	196	211	1 998	376	568	525	326	148	55
1997	2 195	411	204	207	1 784	326	515	486	290	119	49
1998	2 053	365	171	195	1 688	327	467	460	279	112	43
1999	1 999	383	190	193	1 616	322	423	423	273	131	43
2000	1 934	353	170	183	1 581	315	396	415	286	131	38

See *Note* at end of table.

Table 1-26. Unemployed Persons by Race, Hispanic Origin, Sex, and Age, 1948–2000—*Continued*

(Thousands of persons.)

Year, race, Hispanic origin, and sex	16 years and over	16 to 19 years			20 years and over						
		Total	16 to 17 years	18 to 19 years	Total	20 to 24 years	25 to 34 years	35 to 44 years	45 to 54 years	55 to 64 years	65 years and over
BLACK MEN											
1972	448	143	66	77	305	113	84	45	31	23	9
1973	395	128	62	66	267	108	75	37	27	16	5
1974	494	159	75	82	336	129	103	41	35	19	8
1975	741	170	71	100	571	195	169	83	78	33	13
1976	698	170	69	103	528	185	166	73	60	32	13
1977	698	187	73	114	512	197	170	63	40	31	12
1978	641	180	80	101	462	185	148	53	40	24	11
1979	636	164	68	97	473	174	152	66	44	27	10
1980	815	179	72	108	636	222	222	88	60	32	12
1981	891	188	73	115	703	248	245	102	65	32	10
1982	1 167	213	72	141	954	304	355	154	74	54	12
1983	1 213	211	70	142	1 002	313	358	162	96	59	14
1984	1 003	188	62	126	815	272	289	132	67	45	9
1985	951	193	69	124	757	224	268	127	85	43	11
1986	946	180	68	112	765	225	273	148	70	44	5
1987	826	160	70	90	666	186	253	122	61	39	6
1988	771	154	64	90	617	177	233	111	58	30	8
1989	773	153	65	88	619	162	226	129	59	33	10
1990	806	142	62	80	664	177	247	146	62	27	6
1991	890	145	54	91	745	201	252	172	87	25	7
1992	1 067	180	71	109	886	221	301	208	107	42	6
1993	971	170	66	104	801	201	260	201	87	46	7
1994	848	167	69	97	682	173	218	180	72	29	10
1995	762	168	73	95	593	153	195	150	63	21	11
1996	808	169	73	96	639	163	210	158	75	26	7
1997	747	162	70	92	585	165	178	141	72	22	7
1998	671	147	61	86	524	151	148	133	60	24	8
1999	626	145	60	85	480	135	143	114	60	22	7
2000	636	125	54	71	511	151	136	127	71	16	10
BLACK WOMEN											
1972	458	136	47	90	322	113	99	61	31	14	3
1973	451	134	51	82	317	123	105	45	26	13	4
1974	470	139	51	87	331	132	98	55	30	14	2
1975	629	160	60	100	469	167	153	75	48	22	4
1976	637	160	66	93	477	165	172	73	41	23	3
1977	695	167	63	104	528	200	185	77	41	21	4
1978	690	179	70	110	510	194	173	74	41	23	6
1979	683	169	69	100	513	195	183	71	38	21	5
1980	738	164	62	102	574	204	211	83	49	21	6
1981	840	169	65	104	671	235	248	105	54	23	7
1982	975	182	58	124	793	261	307	123	67	29	5
1983	1 059	181	56	125	878	278	342	137	77	36	7
1984	911	165	60	104	747	231	288	121	71	30	5
1985	913	164	66	98	750	231	295	127	58	31	7
1986	894	167	70	97	728	228	291	121	57	25	5
1987	858	152	64	88	706	211	280	125	63	23	4
1988	776	134	57	78	642	172	269	118	53	22	7
1989	772	147	51	96	625	160	267	118	50	21	9
1990	758	126	49	76	633	172	258	132	44	17	8
1991	833	135	51	84	698	177	288	145	64	19	6
1992	944	144	56	88	800	200	308	194	71	22	6
1993	872	143	46	97	729	186	272	175	66	26	5
1994	818	133	57	76	685	178	249	166	59	26	6
1995	777	157	...	87	620	158	228	153	53	20	...
1996	784	141	60	80	643	164	244	155	52	21	7
1997	813	140	53	87	673	163	248	166	64	24	9
1998	756	134	63	71	622	150	218	160	65	21	8
1999	684	123	49	74	561	138	196	135	61	25	7
2000	633	114	46	68	519	139	156	134	59	21	10

See *Note* at end of table.

Table 1-26. Unemployed Persons by Race, Hispanic Origin, Sex, and Age, 1948–2000—*Continued*

(Thousands of persons.)

Year, race, Hispanic origin, and sex	16 years and over	16 to 19 years			20 years and over						
		Total	16 to 17 years	18 to 19 years	Total	20 to 24 years	25 to 34 years	35 to 44 years	45 to 54 years	55 to 64 years	65 years and over
HISPANIC MEN											
1976	278	60	30	31	217	69	63	38	29	16	4
1977	253	60	27	33	195	57	65	28	22	15	4
1978	234	59	35	24	175	51	59	30	20	10	4
1979	223	55	29	27	168	52	50	33	19	11	3
1980	370	86	39	47	284	85	96	51	31	16	5
1981	408	87	40	47	321	105	113	49	31	19	4
1982	565	104	45	59	461	138	169	80	40	29	4
1983	591	100	38	62	491	134	168	92	57	36	4
1984	480	87	36	51	393	103	142	69	41	33	4
1985	483	82	34	49	401	108	156	69	40	23	5
1986	520	82	33	50	438	115	159	86	46	26	5
1987	451	77	32	45	374	88	137	77	46	22	4
1988	437	86	36	50	351	83	128	70	42	24	5
1989	423	81	36	45	342	88	113	69	43	25	4
1990	524	100	40	60	425	99	154	91	53	25	4
1991	685	110	47	62	575	139	210	126	62	33	5
1992	807	132	56	75	675	156	239	156	75	42	6
1993	747	118	50	68	629	144	217	148	79	33	8
1994	680	121	54	67	558	128	203	113	75	30	9
1995	651	121	59	63	530	123	185	120	57	33	13
1996	607	112	49	63	495	117	165	124	49	31	9
1997	582	110	47	63	471	125	137	113	54	35	8
1998	552	117	54	62	436	115	142	97	49	29	5
1999	480	106	42	63	374	96	109	83	54	24	7
2000	441	96	41	55	345	85	98	89	41	23	9
HISPANIC WOMEN											
1976	207	45	22	24	166	47	52	33	22	10	2
1977	204	50	23	27	153	40	49	28	25	11	1
1978	219	51	28	23	168	46	58	36	20	8	1
1979	211	50	26	24	160	48	52	32	18	10	1
1980	249	59	28	31	190	53	72	39	18	8	...
1981	269	57	20	37	212	65	65	43	25	13	1
1982	364	71	28	43	293	83	98	60	35	16	1
1983	369	68	26	42	302	80	102	65	36	18	1
1984	320	62	25	37	258	61	93	55	30	17	1
1985	327	58	22	37	269	63	100	54	32	18	2
1986	337	59	25	35	278	68	99	57	39	12	3
1987	300	59	25	34	241	64	85	51	29	11	1
1988	296	62	27	34	234	63	81	50	27	12	1
1989	327	51	23	28	276	70	105	55	33	11	2
1990	351	62	28	34	289	68	109	65	32	11	3
1991	407	69	32	37	339	74	122	80	48	12	3
1992	504	87	38	49	418	84	151	111	51	17	4
1993	501	83	36	47	418	93	136	113	53	21	1
1994	508	77	36	40	431	92	145	115	57	21	2
1995	488	84	38	46	404	86	140	104	50	21	3
1996	525	88	36	52	438	100	131	122	52	27	5
1997	488	87	40	46	401	81	132	117	46	21	4
1998	473	98	35	63	376	80	118	106	48	19	5
1999	466	90	36	54	376	75	124	107	50	17	3
2000	435	85	36	49	350	77	117	94	38	21	4

Note: Detail for the above race and Hispanic-origin groups will not sum to totals because data for the Other races group are not presented and Hispanics are included in both the White and Black population groups. See "Notes and Definitions" for information on historical comparability.

Table 1-27. Unemployment Rates of Civilian Workers by Race, Hispanic Origin, Sex, and Age, 1948–2000

(Percent of labor force.)

Year, race, Hispanic origin, and sex	16 years and over	16 to 19 years			20 years and over						
		Total	16 to 17 years	18 to 19 years	Total	20 to 24 years	25 to 34 years	35 to 44 years	45 to 54 years	55 to 64 years	65 years and over
TOTAL											
1948	3.8	9.2	10.1	8.6	3.3	6.2	3.2	2.6	2.7	3.1	3.2
1949	5.9	13.4	14.0	13.0	5.4	9.3	5.4	4.4	4.2	5.2	4.9
1950	5.3	12.2	13.6	11.2	4.8	7.7	4.8	3.8	4.2	4.8	4.5
1951	3.3	8.2	9.6	7.1	3.0	4.1	3.0	2.5	2.7	3.1	3.4
1952	3.0	8.5	10.0	7.3	2.7	4.6	2.6	2.3	2.3	2.4	2.9
1953	2.9	7.6	8.7	6.8	2.6	4.7	2.5	2.2	2.3	2.7	2.2
1954	5.5	12.6	13.5	10.7	5.1	9.2	5.3	4.5	4.4	4.5	4.1
1955	4.4	11.0	12.3	10.0	3.9	7.0	3.8	3.4	3.4	4.2	3.6
1956	4.1	11.1	12.3	10.2	3.7	6.6	3.7	3.0	3.2	3.5	3.2
1957	4.3	11.6	12.5	10.9	3.8	7.1	3.9	3.1	3.3	3.4	3.4
1958	6.8	15.9	16.4	15.5	6.2	11.2	6.8	5.4	5.2	5.2	4.8
1959	5.5	14.6	15.3	14.0	4.8	8.5	5.0	4.2	4.2	4.4	4.3
1960	5.5	14.7	15.5	14.1	4.8	8.7	5.2	4.1	4.1	4.2	3.8
1961	6.7	16.8	18.3	15.8	5.9	10.4	6.2	5.2	5.0	5.4	5.1
1962	5.5	14.7	16.3	13.6	4.9	9.0	5.1	4.1	4.0	4.2	4.5
1963	5.7	17.2	19.3	15.6	4.8	8.8	5.2	4.0	3.8	4.1	4.1
1964	5.2	16.2	17.8	14.9	4.3	8.3	4.3	3.6	3.5	3.7	3.8
1965	4.5	14.8	16.5	13.5	3.6	6.7	3.7	3.2	2.8	3.1	3.3
1966	3.8	12.8	14.8	11.3	2.9	5.3	3.1	2.5	2.3	2.5	3.0
1967	3.8	12.9	14.6	11.6	3.0	5.7	3.2	2.5	2.4	2.4	2.8
1968	3.6	12.7	14.7	11.2	2.7	5.8	2.8	2.2	1.9	2.0	2.8
1969	3.5	12.2	14.5	10.5	2.7	5.7	2.8	2.2	1.9	1.9	2.2
1970	4.9	15.3	17.1	13.8	4.0	8.2	4.2	3.1	2.8	2.7	3.2
1971	5.9	16.9	18.7	15.5	4.9	10.0	5.3	3.9	3.4	3.3	3.5
1972	5.6	16.2	18.5	14.6	4.5	9.3	4.6	3.5	3.0	3.2	3.6
1973	4.0	14.5	17.3	12.4	3.9	7.8	4.2	2.7	2.5	2.6	3.0
1974	5.6	16.0	18.3	14.3	4.5	9.1	4.8	3.3	2.9	2.8	3.4
1975	8.5	19.9	21.4	18.9	7.3	13.6	7.8	5.6	5.2	4.6	5.2
1976	7.7	19.0	21.1	17.5	6.5	12.0	7.1	4.9	4.5	4.5	5.1
1977	7.1	17.8	19.9	16.2	5.9	11.0	6.5	4.4	3.9	3.9	5.0
1978	6.1	16.4	19.3	14.2	5.0	9.6	5.3	3.7	3.3	2.9	4.0
1979	5.8	16.1	10.1	14.7	4.8	9.1	5.2	3.6	3.2	2.9	3.4
1980	7.1	17.8	20.0	16.2	6.1	11.5	6.9	4.6	4.0	3.3	3.1
1981	7.6	19.6	21.4	18.4	6.5	12.3	7.3	5.0	4.2	3.7	3.2
1982	9.7	23.2	24.9	22.1	8.6	14.9	9.7	6.9	5.7	5.4	3.5
1983	9.6	22.4	24.5	21.1	8.6	14.5	9.7	7.0	6.2	5.6	3.7
1984	7.5	18.9	21.2	17.4	6.7	11.5	7.3	5.4	4.9	4.7	3.3
1985	7.2	18.6	21.0	17.0	6.4	11.1	7.0	5.1	4.7	4.3	3.2
1986	7.0	18.3	20.2	17.0	6.2	10.7	6.9	5.0	4.5	4.1	3.0
1987	6.2	16.9	19.1	15.2	5.4	9.7	6.0	4.5	4.0	3.5	2.5
1988	5.5	15.3	17.4	13.8	4.8	8.7	5.4	4.0	3.4	3.2	2.7
1989	5.3	15.0	17.2	13.6	4.6	8.6	5.2	3.8	3.2	3.2	2.6
1990	5.6	15.5	17.9	14.1	4.9	8.8	5.6	4.1	3.6	3.3	3.0
1991	6.8	18.7	21.0	17.2	6.1	10.8	6.9	5.2	4.5	4.1	3.3
1992	7.5	20.1	23.1	18.2	6.8	11.4	7.6	5.8	5.1	5.1	3.8
1993	6.9	19.0	21.4	17.5	6.2	10.5	6.9	5.5	4.8	4.7	3.2
1994	6.1	17.6	19.9	16.0	5.4	9.7	6.0	4.6	4.0	4.1	4.0
1995	5.6	17.3	20.2	15.3	4.9	9.1	5.4	4.3	3.3	3.6	4.0
1996	5.4	16.7	18.9	15.2	4.7	9.3	5.2	4.1	3.3	3.3	3.6
1997	4.9	16.0	18.2	14.5	4.3	8.5	4.7	3.8	3.0	2.9	3.3
1998	4.5	14.6	17.2	12.8	3.9	7.9	4.3	3.4	2.8	2.6	3.2
1999	4.2	13.9	16.3	12.4	3.6	7.5	4.0	3.0	2.6	2.7	3.1
2000	4.0	13.1	15.4	11.5	3.4	7.1	3.7	3.0	2.5	2.5	3.1

See *Note* at end of table.

Table 1-27. Unemployment Rates of Civilian Workers by Race, Hispanic Origin, Sex, and Age, 1948–2000—*Continued*

(Percent of labor force.)

Year, race, Hispanic origin, and sex	16 years and over	16 to 19 years			20 years and over						
		Total	16 to 17 years	18 to 19 years	Total	20 to 24 years	25 to 34 years	35 to 44 years	45 to 54 years	55 to 64 years	65 years and over
WHITE											
1954	5.0	12.1	13.2	11.3	4.6	8.3	4.6	4.0	4.0	4.3	3.9
1955	3.9	10.4	12.0	9.2	3.4	6.2	3.1	2.9	3.1	3.8	3.4
1956	3.6	10.1	11.5	9.0	3.2	5.7	3.1	2.6	2.9	3.2	3.1
1957	3.8	10.6	11.9	9.6	3.4	6.3	3.3	2.8	3.0	3.2	3.2
1958	6.1	14.4	15.2	13.9	5.6	9.9	5.9	4.8	4.8	4.9	4.6
1959	4.8	13.1	14.4	12.1	4.3	7.3	4.2	3.7	3.8	4.1	4.1
1960	5.0	13.5	14.6	12.6	4.3	7.9	4.5	3.6	3.8	3.9	3.7
1961	6.0	15.3	16.7	14.4	5.3	9.4	5.3	4.5	4.5	5.0	4.8
1962	4.9	13.3	15.3	12.0	4.2	7.9	4.2	3.6	3.6	3.9	4.0
1963	5.0	15.5	17.9	13.7	4.2	7.7	4.4	3.5	3.5	3.8	3.8
1964	4.6	14.8	16.5	13.3	3.8	7.3	3.6	3.2	3.2	3.5	3.5
1965	4.1	13.4	14.8	12.3	3.3	6.1	3.2	2.9	2.5	2.9	3.2
1966	3.4	11.2	13.3	9.7	2.6	4.6	2.6	2.3	2.1	2.4	2.9
1967	3.4	11.0	12.8	9.8	2.7	5.0	2.7	2.3	2.2	2.3	2.7
1968	3.2	11 0	12.9	9.6	2.5	5.2	2.4	2.0	1.8	1.9	2.8
1969	3.1	10.7	13.0	8.9	2.4	5.0	2.5	2.0	1.8	1.8	2.2
1970	4.5	13.5	15.5	11.9	3.7	7.3	3.8	3.0	2.7	2.7	3.2
1971	5.4	15.1	17.0	13.8	4.5	9.0	4.7	3.6	3.3	3.3	3.5
1972	5.1	14.2	16.6	12.3	4.1	8.4	4.1	3.2	2.9	3.1	3.4
1973	4.3	12.6	15.4	10.4	3.5	6.8	3.7	2.5	2.4	2.5	2.9
1974	5.0	14.0	16.3	12.2	4.1	8.0	4.4	3.1	2.8	2.8	3.3
1975	7.8	17.9	19.5	16.7	6.7	12.3	7.1	5.2	4.9	4.5	5.1
1976	7.0	16.9	19.0	15.3	5.9	10.7	6.3	4.5	4.2	4.3	4.9
1977	6.2	15.4	17.9	13.5	5.3	9.3	5.7	4.0	3.8	3.7	4.9
1978	5.2	13.9	17.0	11.5	4.3	8.0	4.6	3.3	3.0	2.7	3.8
1979	5.1	14.0	16.1	12.4	4.2	7.6	4.4	3.2	3.0	2.7	3.1
1980	6.3	15.5	17.9	13.8	5.4	9.9	6.1	4.2	3.7	3.1	2.7
1981	6.7	17.3	19.2	15.9	5.7	10.4	6.3	4.5	3.9	3.5	2.8
1982	8.6	20.4	22.8	18.8	7.6	12.8	8.5	6.3	5.4	5.1	3.1
1983	8.4	19.3	22.0	17.6	7.5	12.1	8.4	6.3	5.7	5.2	3.2
1984	6.5	16.0	18.8	14.3	5.7	9.3	6.2	4.8	4.4	4.4	3.0
1985	6.2	15.7	18.3	13.9	5.5	9.2	5.9	4.6	4.3	4.0	2.9
1986	6.0	15.6	17.6	14.1	5.3	8.7	5.9	4.5	4.1	3.8	2.9
1987	5.3	14.4	16.7	12.7	4.7	8.0	5.1	4.0	3.7	3.2	2.4
1988	4.7	13.1	15.3	11.6	4.1	7.1	4.5	3.5	3.1	3.0	2.4
1989	4.5	12.7	15.2	11.1	3.9	7.2	4.3	3.3	2.9	3.0	2.3
1990	4.8	13.5	15.8	12.1	4.3	7.3	4.6	3.6	3.3	3.2	2.8
1991	6.1	16.5	19.0	14.9	5.5	9.2	6.1	4.7	4.2	4.0	3.1
1992	6.6	17.2	20.3	15.2	6.0	9.5	6.7	5.2	4.8	4.9	3.7
1993	6.1	16.2	19.0	14.4	5.5	8.8	6.0	4.9	4.5	4.3	3.0
1994	5.3	15.1	17.6	13.3	4.7	8.1	5.2	4.0	3.7	3.9	3.8
1995	4.9	14.5	17.3	12.5	4.3	7.7	4.6	3.9	3.1	3.5	3.8
1996	4.7	14.2	16.4	12.6	4.1	7.8	4.4	3.6	3.1	3.2	3.5
1997	4.2	13.6	15.8	12.0	3.6	6.9	3.9	3.3	2.7	2.7	3.0
1998	3.9	12.6	14.8	11.0	3.3	6.5	3.7	2.9	2.6	2.4	2.9
1999	3.7	12.0	14.5	10.2	3.1	6.3	3.3	2.7	2.4	2.5	2.9
2000	3.5	11.4	13.9	9.7	3.0	5.8	3.2	2.6	2.3	2.4	2.8

See *Note* at end of table.

Table 1-27. Unemployment Rates of Civilian Workers by Race, Hispanic Origin, Sex, and Age, 1948–2000—*Continued*

(Percent of labor force.)

Year, race, Hispanic origin, and sex	16 years and over	16 to 19 years			20 years and over						
		Total	16 to 17 years	18 to 19 years	Total	20 to 24 years	25 to 34 years	35 to 44 years	45 to 54 years	55 to 64 years	65 years and over
BLACK											
1972	10.4	35.4	38.7	33.6	7.9	16.3	8.7	6.1	4.2	4.1	4.3
1973	9.4	31.5	37.0	28.1	7.2	15.5	8.1	4.7	3.5	3.2	3.5
1974	10.5	35.0	40.0	31.8	8.0	17.5	8.5	5.4	4.3	3.6	3.9
1975	14.8	39.5	41.6	38.1	12.3	24.5	13.0	8.9	8.3	5.9	6.6
1976	14.0	39.3	44.2	36.7	11.5	22.7	12.8	8.0	6.7	5.9	5.9
1977	14.0	41.1	44.5	39.2	11.5	24.2	12.7	7.4	5.3	5.5	5.9
1978	12.8	38.7	43.9	35.7	10.2	21.8	10.8	6.4	5.2	4.8	5.8
1979	12.3	36.5	40.2	34.4	10.1	20.6	10.8	6.7	5.2	4.9	5.3
1980	14.3	38.5	41.1	37.1	12.1	23.6	13.3	8.2	6.8	5.4	6.9
1981	15.6	41.4	44.8	39.5	13.4	26.4	14.7	9.5	7.4	5.5	7.0
1982	18.9	48.0	48.6	47.8	16.6	30.6	19.0	12.1	8.7	8.3	7.1
1983	19.5	48.5	50.5	47.6	17.3	31.6	19.0	12.4	10.7	9.2	9.2
1984	15.9	42.7	45.7	41.2	13.9	26.1	15.2	9.9	8.2	7.4	6.5
1985	15.1	40.2	43.6	38.3	13.1	24.5	14.5	9.5	8.2	7.0	7.0
1986	14.5	39.3	43.0	37.2	12.7	24.1	14.0	9.6	7.1	6.6	4.5
1987	13.0	34.7	39.7	31.6	11.3	21.8	12.8	8.4	6.8	5.6	3.9
1988	11.7	32.4	35.1	30.7	10.2	19.6	11.9	7.5	5.9	4.8	5.5
1989	11.4	32.4	32.9	32.2	9.9	18.0	11.5	7.6	5.6	5.2	6.9
1990	11.4	30.9	36.5	27.8	10.1	19.9	11.7	7.8	5.3	4.6	5.3
1991	12.5	36.1	39.5	34.4	11.1	21.6	12.7	8.5	7.4	4.4	5.2
1992	14.2	39.7	44.7	37.1	12.6	23.8	14.2	10.5	8.3	6.2	4.9
1993	13.0	38.8	39.7	38.4	11.4	21.9	12.6	9.5	6.9	7.1	4.7
1994	11.5	35.2	36.1	34.6	10.0	19.5	11.1	8.5	5.6	5.4	6.2
1995	10.4	35.7	39.1	33.4	8.7	17.7	9.9	7.3	4.8	4.0	6.7
1996	10.5	33.6	36.3	31.7	9.0	18.8	10.5	7.3	5.0	4.4	5.3
1997	10.0	32.4	35.0	30.8	8.6	18.3	9.9	7.0	5.0	4.2	6.1
1998	8.9	27.6	33.6	24.2	7.7	16.8	8.4	6.5	4.4	3.9	5.6
1999	8.0	27.9	31.0	26.2	7.0	14.6	7.6	5.3	4.0	3.0	5.0
2000	7.6	24.7	27.2	23.2	6.6	15.0	6.8	5.6	4.1	3.0	6.1
HISPANIC											
1973	7.5	19.7	23.4	17.3	6.0	8.5	5.7	5.6	4.7	5.5	3.9
1974	8.1	19.8	23.5	17.2	6.6	9.8	6.3	5.9	4.6	6.1	6.3
1975	12.2	27.7	30.0	26.5	10.3	16.7	9.9	8.6	8.1	7.7	9.9
1976	11.5	23.8	29.2	19.2	10.1	15.9	9.1	8.2	8.4	8.8	12.6
1977	10.1	22.9	27.0	19.6	8.5	12.0	8.6	6.1	7.3	8.2	9.2
1978	9.1	20.7	28.3	15.1	7.7	10.9	8.0	6.5	5.8	5.0	7.5
1979	8.3	19.2	26.0	14.9	7.0	10.4	6.7	6.2	5.2	6.0	5.7
1980	10.1	22.5	27.6	19.5	8.6	12.1	9.1	7.7	5.7	5.9	6.0
1981	10.4	23.9	28.0	21.7	9.1	13.9	8.8	7.4	6.4	7.3	5.4
1982	13.8	29.9	38.1	25.9	12.3	17.7	12.3	10.7	8.4	10.1	6.5
1983	13.7	28.4	33.8	25.8	12.3	16.7	11.9	11.3	10.0	10.9	5.8
1984	10.7	24.1	28.9	21.6	9.5	12.4	9.7	8.2	7.5	9.7	6.1
1985	10.5	24.3	27.8	22.5	9.4	12.6	9.9	7.7	7.4	7.8	8.1
1986	10.6	24.7	28.1	22.9	9.5	12.9	9.6	8.4	7.8	7.3	10.1
1987	8.8	22.3	27.7	19.5	7.8	10.6	7.7	6.7	6.9	6.0	6.5
1988	8.2	22.0	27.1	19.3	7.0	9.8	7.1	6.0	6.0	5.8	5.6
1989	8.0	19.4	26.4	16.0	7.2	10.7	7.0	5.9	6.3	5.8	5.3
1990	8.2	19.5	24.5	16.9	7.2	9.1	7.3	6.6	6.4	5.6	6.0
1991	10.0	22.9	31.9	18.7	9.0	11.6	9.2	8.1	8.0	6.5	7.0
1992	11.6	27.5	35.7	23.4	10.4	13.2	10.4	9.8	8.8	8.6	8.1
1993	10.8	26.1	35.1	21.8	9.7	13.1	9.3	9.1	8.6	8.0	6.6
1994	9.9	24.5	31.7	20.6	8.9	11.8	9.0	7.7	8.1	7.3	7.9
1995	9.3	24.1	33.1	19.5	8.2	11.5	8.2	7.2	6.4	7.5	10.6
1996	8.9	23.6	30.0	20.3	7.8	11.8	7.3	7.3	6.0	7.3	8.2
1997	7.7	21.6	27.7	18.4	6.8	10.3	6.3	6.4	5.1	6.5	6.8
1998	7.2	21.3	28.0	18.1	6.1	9.4	5.9	5.5	4.6	5.3	6.4
1999	6.4	18.6	23.7	16.3	5.5	8.3	5.4	4.8	4.8	4.5	5.0
2000	5.7	16.7	22.7	14.0	4.9	7.5	4.8	4.5	3.3	4.5	5.7

See *Note* at end of table.

Table 1-27. Unemployment Rates of Civilian Workers by Race, Hispanic Origin, Sex, and Age, 1948–2000—*Continued*

(Percent of labor force.)

Year, race, Hispanic origin, and sex	16 years and over	16 to 19 years			20 years and over						
		Total	16 to 17 years	18 to 19 years	Total	20 to 24 years	25 to 34 years	35 to 44 years	45 to 54 years	55 to 64 years	65 years and over
MEN											
1948	3.6	9.8	10.2	9.5	3.2	6.9	2.8	2.4	2.5	3.1	3.4
1949	5.9	14.3	13.7	14.6	5.4	10.4	5.2	4.3	4.3	5.4	5.1
1950	5.1	12.7	13.3	12.3	4.7	8.1	4.4	3.6	4.0	4.9	4.8
1951	2.8	8.1	9.4	7.0	2.5	3.9	2.3	2.0	2.4	2.8	3.5
1952	2.8	8.9	10.5	7.4	2.4	4.6	2.2	1.9	2.2	2.4	3.0
1953	2.8	7.9	8.8	7.2	2.5	5.0	2.2	2.0	2.3	2.8	2.4
1954	5.3	13.5	13.9	13.2	4.9	10.7	4.8	4.1	4.3	4.5	4.4
1955	4.2	11.6	12.5	10.8	3.8	7.7	3.3	3.1	3.2	4.3	4.0
1956	3.8	11.1	11.7	10.5	3.4	6.9	3.3	2.6	3.0	3.5	3.5
1957	4.1	12.4	12.4	12.3	3.6	7.8	3.3	2.8	3.3	3.5	3.4
1958	6.8	17.1	16.3	17.8	6.2	12.7	6.5	5.1	5.3	5.5	5.2
1959	5.2	15.3	15.8	14.9	4.7	8.7	4.7	3.7	4.1	4.5	4.8
1960	5.4	15.3	15.5	15.0	4.7	8.9	4.8	3.8	4.1	4.6	4.2
1961	6.4	17.1	18.3	16.3	5.7	10.8	5.7	4.6	4.9	5.7	5.5
1962	5.2	14.7	16.0	13.8	4.6	8.9	4.5	3.6	3.9	4.6	4.6
1963	5.2	17.2	18.8	15.9	4.5	8.8	4.5	3.5	3.6	4.3	4.5
1964	4.6	15.8	17.1	14.6	3.9	8.1	3.5	2.9	3.2	3.9	4.0
1965	4.0	14.1	16.1	12.4	3.2	6.4	2.9	2.5	2.5	3.3	3.5
1966	3.2	11.7	13.7	10.2	2.5	4.6	2.4	2.0	1.9	2.6	3.1
1967	3.1	12.3	14.5	10.5	2.3	4.7	2.1	1.7	2.0	2.3	2.8
1968	2.9	11.6	13.9	9.7	2.2	5.1	1.9	1.6	1.6	1.9	2.8
1969	2.8	11.4	13.8	9.3	2.1	5.1	1.9	1.5	1.5	1.8	2.2
1970	4.4	15.0	16.9	13.4	3.5	8.4	3.5	2.4	2.4	2.8	3.3
1971	5.3	16.6	18.7	15.0	4.4	10.3	4.4	3.1	3.0	3.3	3.4
1972	5.0	15.9	18.3	14.1	4.0	9.3	3.8	2.7	2.6	3.2	3.6
1973	4.2	13.9	17.0	11.4	3.3	7.3	3.4	2.0	2.1	2.4	3.0
1974	4.9	15.6	18.4	13.3	3.8	8.8	4.0	2.6	2.4	2.6	3.3
1975	7.9	20.1	21.6	19.0	6.8	14.3	6.9	4.9	4.8	4.3	5.4
1976	7.1	19.2	21.4	17.6	5.9	12.1	6.2	4.1	4.0	4.2	5.1
1977	6.3	17.3	19.5	15.6	5.2	10.8	5.7	3.5	3.2	3.6	5.2
1978	5.3	15.8	19.1	13.3	4.3	9.2	4.4	2.8	2.7	2.8	4.2
1979	5.1	15.9	17.9	14.3	4.2	8.7	4.3	2.9	2.7	2.7	3.4
1980	6.9	18.3	20.4	16.7	5.9	12.5	6.7	4.1	3.6	3.4	3.1
1981	7.4	20.1	22.0	18.8	6.3	13.2	6.9	4.5	4.0	3.6	2.9
1982	9.9	24.4	26.4	23.1	8.8	16.4	10.1	6.9	5.6	5.5	3.7
1983	9.9	23.3	25.2	22.2	8.9	15.9	10.1	7.1	6.3	6.1	3.9
1984	7.4	19.6	21.9	18.3	6.6	11.9	7.2	5.2	4.6	5.0	3.0
1985	7.0	19.5	21.9	17.9	6.2	11.4	6.6	4.9	4.6	4.3	3.1
1986	6.9	19.0	20.8	17.7	6.1	11.0	6.7	5.1	4.4	4.3	3.2
1987	6.2	17.8	20.2	16.0	5.4	9.9	5.9	4.4	4.2	3.7	2.6
1988	5.5	16.0	18.2	14.6	4.8	8.9	5.3	3.8	3.5	3.5	2.5
1989	5.2	15.9	18.6	14.2	4.5	8.8	4.8	3.7	3.2	3.5	2.4
1990	5.7	16.3	18.4	15.0	5.0	9.1	5.5	4.1	3.7	3.8	3.0
1991	7.2	19.8	21.8	18.5	6.4	11.6	7.0	5.5	4.8	4.6	3.3
1992	7.9	21.5	24.6	19.5	7.1	12.2	7.8	6.1	5.6	5.8	3.3
1993	7.2	20.4	22.9	18.8	6.4	11.3	7.0	5.6	5.1	5.2	3.2
1994	6.2	19.0	21.0	17.6	5.4	10.2	5.9	4.5	4.0	4.4	4.0
1995	5.6	18.4	21.1	16.5	4.8	9.2	5.1	4.2	3.5	3.6	4.3
1996	5.4	18.1	20.8	16.3	4.6	9.5	4.9	4.0	3.5	3.3	3.4
1997	4.9	16.9	19.1	15.4	4.2	8.9	4.3	3.6	3.1	3.1	3.0
1998	4.4	16.2	19.1	14.1	3.7	8.1	3.9	3.0	2.8	2.8	3.1
1999	4.1	14.7	17.0	13.1	3.5	7.7	3.6	2.8	2.6	2.7	3.0
2000	3.9	14.0	16.8	12.2	3.3	7.3	3.4	2.8	2.4	2.4	3.4

See *Note* at end of table.

Table 1-27. Unemployment Rates of Civilian Workers by Race, Hispanic Origin, Sex, and Age, 1948–2000—*Continued*

(Percent of labor force.)

Year, race, Hispanic origin, and sex	16 years and over	16 to 19 years			20 years and over						
		Total	16 to 17 years	18 to 19 years	Total	20 to 24 years	25 to 34 years	35 to 44 years	45 to 54 years	55 to 64 years	65 years and over
WOMEN											
1948	4.1	8.3	10.0	7.4	3.6	4.8	4.3	3.0	3.0	3.1	2.3
1949	6.0	12.3	14.4	11.2	5.3	7.3	5.9	4.7	4.0	4.4	3.8
1950	5.7	11.4	14.2	9.8	5.1	6.9	5.7	4.4	4.5	4.5	3.4
1951	4.4	8.3	10.0	7.2	4.0	4.4	4.5	3.8	3.5	4.0	2.9
1952	3.6	8.0	9.1	7.3	3.2	4.5	3.6	3.0	2.5	2.5	2.2
1953	3.3	7.2	8.5	6.4	2.9	4.3	3.4	2.5	2.3	2.5	1.4
1954	6.0	11.4	12.7	7.7	5.5	7.3	6.6	5.3	4.6	4.6	3.0
1955	4.9	10.2	12.0	9.1	4.4	6.1	5.3	4.0	3.6	3.8	2.3
1956	4.8	11.2	13.2	9.9	4.2	6.3	4.8	3.9	3.6	3.6	2.3
1957	4.7	10.6	12.6	9.4	4.1	6.0	5.3	3.8	3.2	3.0	3.4
1958	6.8	14.3	16.6	12.9	6.1	8.9	7.3	6.2	4.9	4.5	3.7
1959	5.9	13.5	14.4	13.0	5.2	8.1	5.9	5.1	4.2	4.1	2.8
1960	5.9	13.9	15.5	12.9	5.1	8.3	6.3	4.8	4.2	3.4	2.9
1961	7.2	16.3	18.3	15.1	6.3	9.8	7.4	6.4	5.1	4.5	4.0
1962	6.2	14.6	16.7	13.5	5.4	9.1	6.5	5.2	4.1	3.5	4.2
1963	6.5	17.2	20.2	15.2	5.4	8.9	6.9	5.1	4.2	3.6	3.2
1964	6.2	16.6	18.8	15.2	5.2	8.6	6.3	5.0	3.9	3.3	3.3
1965	5.5	15.7	17.2	14.8	4.5	7.3	5.5	4.6	3.2	2.8	2.9
1966	4.8	14.1	16.6	12.6	3.8	6.3	4.5	3.6	2.9	2.3	2.8
1967	5.2	13.5	14.8	12.8	4.2	7.0	5.4	4.1	3.1	2.4	2.7
1968	4.8	14.0	15.9	12.9	3.8	6.7	4.7	3.4	2.4	2.2	2.7
1969	4.7	13.3	15.5	11.8	3.7	6.3	4.6	3.4	2.6	2.2	2.3
1970	5.9	15.6	17.4	14.4	4.8	7.9	5.7	4.4	3.5	2.7	3.1
1971	6.9	17.2	18.7	16.2	5.7	9.6	7.0	5.2	4.0	3.3	3.6
1972	6.6	16.7	18.8	15.2	5.4	9.4	6.2	4.9	3.6	3.3	3.5
1973	6.0	15.3	17.7	10.5	4.9	8.5	5.8	3.9	3.2	2.8	2.9
1974	6.7	16.6	18.2	15.4	5.5	9.5	6.2	4.6	3.7	3.2	3.6
1975	9.3	19.7	21.2	18.7	8.0	12.7	9.1	6.8	5.9	5.1	5.0
1976	8.6	18.7	20.8	17.4	7.4	11.9	8.4	6.1	5.2	4.9	5.0
1977	8.2	18.3	20.5	16.9	7.0	11.2	7.7	5.7	5.1	4.4	4.7
1978	7.2	17.1	19.5	15.3	6.0	10.1	6.7	5.0	4.0	3.2	3.8
1979	6.8	16.4	18.3	15.0	5.7	9.6	6.5	4.6	3.9	3.2	3.3
1980	7.4	17.2	19.6	15.6	6.4	10.4	7.2	5.3	4.5	3.3	3.1
1981	7.9	19.0	20.7	17.9	6.8	11.2	7.7	5.7	4.6	3.8	3.6
1982	9.4	21.9	23.2	21.0	8.3	13.2	9.3	7.0	5.9	5.2	3.2
1983	9.2	21.3	23.7	19.9	8.1	12.9	9.1	6.9	6.0	5.0	3.4
1984	7.6	18.0	20.4	16.6	6.8	10.9	7.4	5.6	5.2	4.3	3.8
1985	7.4	17.6	20.0	16.0	6.6	10.7	7.4	5.5	4.8	4.3	3.3
1986	7.1	17.6	19.6	16.3	6.2	10.3	7.2	5.0	4.5	3.8	2.8
1987	6.2	15.9	18.0	14.3	5.4	9.4	6.2	4.6	3.7	3.1	2.4
1988	5.6	14.4	16.6	12.9	4.9	8.5	5.6	4.1	3.4	2.7	2.9
1989	5.4	14.0	15.7	13.0	4.7	8.3	5.6	3.9	3.2	2.8	2.9
1990	5.5	14.7	17.4	13.1	4.9	8.5	5.6	4.2	3.4	2.8	3.1
1991	6.4	17.5	20.2	15.9	5.7	9.8	6.8	4.8	4.2	3.4	3.3
1992	7.0	18.6	21.5	16.6	6.3	10.3	7.4	5.5	4.6	4.2	4.5
1993	6.6	17.5	19.8	16.1	5.9	9.7	6.8	5.3	4.5	4.0	3.1
1994	6.0	16.2	18.7	14.3	5.4	9.2	6.2	4.7	4.0	3.9	4.0
1995	5.6	16.1	19.2	14.0	4.9	9.0	5.7	4.4	3.2	3.6	3.7
1996	5.4	15.2	16.9	14.0	4.8	9.0	5.5	4.2	3.2	3.4	4.0
1997	5.0	15.0	17.2	13.6	4.4	8.1	5.2	4.0	2.9	2.7	3.6
1998	4.6	12.9	15.1	11.5	4.1	7.8	4.8	3.8	2.7	2.4	3.3
1999	4.3	13.2	15.5	11.6	3.8	7.2	4.4	3.3	2.5	2.6	3.2
2000	4.1	12.1	14.0	10.8	3.6	7.0	4.0	3.3	2.5	2.5	2.8

See *Note* at end of table.

Table 1-27. Unemployment Rates of Civilian Workers by Race, Hispanic Origin, Sex, and Age, 1948–2000—*Continued*

(Percent of labor force.)

Year, race, Hispanic origin, and sex	16 years and over	16 to 19 years			20 years and over						
		Total	16 to 17 years	18 to 19 years	Total	20 to 24 years	25 to 34 years	35 to 44 years	45 to 54 years	55 to 64 years	65 years and over
WHITE MEN											
1954	4.8	13.4	14.0	13.0	4.4	9.8	4.2	3.6	3.8	4.3	4.2
1955	3.7	11.3	12.2	10.4	3.3	7.0	2.7	2.6	2.9	3.9	3.8
1956	3.4	10.5	11.2	9.7	3.0	6.1	2.8	2.2	2.8	3.1	3.4
1957	3.6	11.5	11.9	11.1	3.2	7.0	2.7	2.5	3.0	3.4	3.2
1958	6.1	15.7	14.9	16.5	5.5	11.7	5.6	4.4	4.8	5.2	5.0
1959	4.6	14.0	15.0	13.0	4.1	7.5	3.8	3.2	3.7	4.2	4.5
1960	4.8	14.0	14.6	13.5	4.2	8.3	4.1	3.3	3.6	4.1	4.0
1961	5.7	15.7	16.5	15.2	5.1	10.1	4.9	4.0	4.4	5.3	5.2
1962	4.6	13.7	15.2	12.7	4.0	8.1	3.8	3.1	3.5	4.1	4.0
1963	4.7	15.9	17.8	14.2	3.9	7.8	3.9	2.9	3.3	4.0	4.1
1964	4.1	14.7	16.1	13.3	3.4	7.4	3.0	2.5	2.9	3.5	3.6
1965	3.6	12.9	14.7	11.3	2.9	5.9	2.6	2.3	2.3	3.1	3.4
1966	2.8	10.5	12.5	8.9	2.2	4.1	2.1	1.7	1.7	2.5	3.0
1967	2.7	10.7	12.7	9.0	2.1	4.2	1.9	1.6	1.8	2.2	2.7
1968	2.6	10.1	12.3	8.3	2.0	4.6	1.7	1.4	1.5	1.7	2.8
1969	2.5	10.0	12.5	7.9	1.9	4.6	1.7	1.4	1.4	1.7	2.2
1970	4.0	13.7	15.7	12.0	3.2	7.8	3.1	2.3	2.3	2.7	3.2
1971	4.9	15.1	17.1	13.5	4.0	9.4	4.0	2.9	2.9	3.2	3.4
1972	4.5	14.2	16.4	12.4	3.6	8.5	3.4	2.5	2.5	3.0	3.3
1973	3.8	12.3	15.2	10.0	3.0	6.6	3.0	1.8	2.0	2.4	2.9
1974	4.4	13.5	16.2	11.5	3.5	7.8	3.6	2.4	2.2	2.5	3.0
1975	7.2	18.3	19.7	17.2	6.2	13.1	6.3	4.5	4.4	4.1	5.0
1976	6.4	17.3	19.7	15.5	5.4	10.9	5.6	3.7	3.7	4.0	4.7
1977	5.5	15.0	17.6	13.0	4.7	9.3	5.0	3.1	3.0	3.3	4.9
1978	4.6	13.5	16.9	10.8	3.7	7.7	3.8	2.5	2.5	2.6	3.9
1979	4.5	13.9	16.1	12.2	3.6	7.5	3.7	2.5	2.5	2.5	3.2
1980	6.1	16.2	18.5	14.5	5.3	11.1	5.9	3.6	3.3	3.1	2.5
1981	6.5	17.9	19.9	16.4	5.6	11.6	6.1	4.0	3.6	3.4	2.4
1982	8.8	21.7	24.2	20.0	7.8	14.3	8.9	6.2	5.3	5.1	3.2
1983	8.8	20.2	22.6	18.7	7.9	13.8	9.0	6.4	5.7	5.6	3.2
1984	6.4	16.8	19.7	15.0	5.7	9.8	6.2	4.6	4.2	4.7	2.6
1985	6.1	16.5	19.2	14.7	5.4	9.7	5.7	4.3	4.1	4.0	2.7
1986	6.0	16.3	18.4	14.7	5.3	9.2	5.8	4.4	4.0	4.0	3.0
1987	5.4	15.5	17.9	13.7	4.8	8.4	5.2	3.9	3.9	3.4	2.5
1988	4.7	13.9	16.1	12.4	4.1	7.4	4.6	3.4	3.2	3.3	2.2
1989	4.5	13.7	16.4	12.0	3.9	7.5	4.1	3.2	2.9	3.1	2.1
1990	4.9	14.3	16.1	13.2	4.3	7.6	4.7	3.5	3.4	3.6	2.8
1991	6.5	17.6	19.7	16.3	5.8	10.2	6.4	5.0	4.4	4.6	3.1
1992	7.0	18.5	21.5	16.5	6.4	10.5	7.0	5.5	5.1	5.5	3.2
1993	6.3	17.7	20.2	16.0	5.7	9.6	6.2	5.0	4.7	4.7	2.9
1994	5.4	16.3	18.5	14.7	4.8	8.8	5.2	3.9	3.7	4.1	3.7
1995	4.9	15.6	18.2	13.8	4.3	7.9	4.5	3.8	3.2	3.4	4.0
1996	4.7	15.5	18.3	13.5	4.1	8.1	4.2	3.5	3.1	3.2	3.2
1997	4.2	14.3	16.3	12.9	3.6	7.3	3.7	3.2	2.8	3.0	2.7
1998	3.9	14.1	17.1	12.1	3.2	6.7	3.5	2.6	2.6	2.6	2.9
1999	3.6	12.6	15.1	10.8	3.0	6.5	3.1	2.4	2.4	2.6	2.9
2000	3.4	12.3	15.2	10.4	2.8	5.9	2.9	2.4	2.2	2.4	3.1

See *Note* at end of table.

Table 1-27. Unemployment Rates of Civilian Workers by Race, Hispanic Origin, Sex, and Age, 1948–2000—*Continued*

(Percent of labor force.)

Year, race, Hispanic origin, and sex	16 years and over	16 to 19 years			20 years and over						
		Total	16 to 17 years	18 to 19 years	Total	20 to 24 years	25 to 34 years	35 to 44 years	45 to 54 years	55 to 64 years	65 years and over
WHITE WOMEN											
1954	5.5	10.4	12.0	9.4	5.1	6.4	5.7	4.9	4.4	4.5	2.8
1955	4.3	9.1	11.6	7.7	3.9	5.1	4.3	3.8	3.4	3.6	2.2
1956	4.2	9.7	12.1	8.3	3.7	5.1	4.0	3.5	3.3	3.5	2.3
1957	4.3	9.5	11.9	7.8	3.8	5.1	4.7	3.7	3.0	2.9	3.4
1958	6.2	12.7	15.6	11.0	5.6	7.3	6.6	5.6	4.9	4.3	3.5
1959	5.3	12.0	13.3	11.1	4.7	7.0	5.2	4.7	3.9	4.0	2.9
1960	5.3	12.7	14.5	11.5	4.6	7.2	5.7	4.2	4.0	3.3	2.8
1961	6.5	14.8	17.0	13.6	5.7	8.4	6.6	5.6	4.8	4.3	3.8
1962	5.5	12.8	15.6	11.3	4.7	7.7	5.4	4.5	3.7	3.5	4.0
1963	5.8	15.1	18.1	13.2	4.8	7.4	5.8	4.6	3.9	3.5	3.3
1964	5.5	14.9	17.1	13.2	4.6	7.1	5.2	4.5	3.6	3.5	3.4
1965	5.0	14.0	15.0	13.4	4.0	6.3	4.9	4.1	3.0	2.7	2.7
1966	4.3	12.1	14.5	10.7	3.3	5.3	3.7	3.3	2.7	2.2	2.7
1967	4.6	11.5	12.9	10.6	3.8	6.0	4.7	3.7	2.9	2.3	2.6
1968	4.3	12.1	13.9	11.0	3.4	5.9	3.9	3.1	2.3	2.1	2.8
1969	4.2	11.5	13.7	10.0	3.4	5.5	4.2	3.2	2.4	2.1	2.4
1970	5.4	13.4	15.3	11.9	4.4	6.9	5.3	4.3	3.4	2.6	3.3
1971	6.3	15.1	16.7	14.1	5.3	8.5	[illegible]	4.9	3.9	3.3	3.6
1972	5.9	14.2	17.0	12.3	4.9	8.2	[illegible]	4.4	3.5	3.3	3.7
1973	5.3	13.0	15.8	10.9	4.3	7.1	5.1	3.7	3.2	2.7	2.8
1974	6.1	14.5	16.4	13.0	5.1	8.2	5.8	4.3	3.6	3.2	3.9
1975	8.6	17.4	19.2	16.1	7.5	11.2	8.4	6.5	5.8	5.0	5.3
1976	7.9	16.4	18.2	15.1	6.8	10.4	7.6	5.8	5.0	4.8	5.3
1977	7.3	15.9	18.2	14.2	6.2	9.3	6.7	5.3	5.0	4.4	4.9
1978	6.2	14.4	17.1	12.4	5.2	8.3	5.8	4.5	3.8	3.0	3.7
1979	5.9	14.0	15.9	12.5	5.0	7.8	5.6	4.2	3.7	3.0	3.1
1980	6.5	14.8	17.3	13.1	5.6	8.5	6.3	4.9	4.3	3.1	3.0
1981	6.9	16.6	18.4	15.3	5.9	9.1	6.6	5.1	4.2	3.7	3.4
1982	8.3	19.0	21.2	17.6	7.3	10.9	8.0	6.4	5.5	5.0	3.1
1983	7.9	18.3	21.4	16.4	6.9	10.3	7.6	6.2	5.5	4.7	3.1
1984	6.5	15.2	17.8	13.0	5.8	8.8	6.1	5.0	4.8	4.0	3.7
1985	6.4	14.8	17.2	13.1	5.7	8.5	6.2	4.9	4.5	4.1	3.1
1986	6.1	14.9	16.7	13.6	5.4	8.1	6.1	4.5	4.3	3.7	2.6
1987	5.2	13.4	15.5	11.7	4.6	7.4	5.0	4.1	3.3	2.9	2.4
1988	4.7	12.3	14.4	10.8	4.1	6.7	4.5	3.7	3.1	2.5	2.6
1989	4.5	11.5	13.8	10.1	4.0	6.8	4.5	3.4	2.9	2.7	2.5
1990	4.7	12.6	15.5	10.9	4.1	6.8	4.6	3.7	3.2	2.7	2.8
1991	5.6	15.2	18.2	13.3	5.0	8.1	5.7	4.3	4.0	3.3	3.1
1992	6.1	15.8	18.9	13.7	5.5	8.3	6.2	4.9	4.3	4.0	4.5
1993	5.7	14.7	17.8	12.6	5.2	7.9	5.8	4.7	4.3	3.9	3.0
1994	5.2	13.8	16.6	11.8	4.6	7.4	5.1	4.2	3.7	3.7	3.9
1995	4.8	13.4	16.4	11.2	4.3	7.4	4.7	3.9	3.0	3.5	3.5
1996	4.7	12.9	14.4	11.7	4.1	7.4	4.6	3.8	3.1	3.1	3.8
1997	4.2	12.8	15.2	11.1	3.7	6.4	4.2	3.4	2.6	2.4	3.4
1998	3.9	10.9	12.4	9.8	3.4	6.3	3.9	3.3	2.5	2.2	3.0
1999	3.8	11.3	13.9	9.6	3.3	6.1	3.6	3.0	2.3	2.5	2.9
2000	3.6	10.4	12.5	9.0	3.1	5.8	3.5	2.9	2.3	2.4	2.4

See *Note* at end of table.

Table 1-27. Unemployment Rates of Civilian Workers by Race, Hispanic Origin, Sex, and Age, 1948–2000—*Continued*

(Percent of labor force.)

Year, race, Hispanic origin, and sex	16 years and over	16 to 19 years			20 years and over						
		Total	16 to 17 years	18 to 19 years	Total	20 to 24 years	25 to 34 years	35 to 44 years	45 to 54 years	55 to 64 years	65 years and over
BLACK MEN											
1972	9.3	31.7	36.7	28.4	7.0	14.9	7.2	4.8	3.8	4.4	5.4
1973	8.0	27.8	35.7	23.0	6.0	13.2	6.2	3.9	3.2	3.2	3.3
1974	9.8	33.1	39.9	28.3	7.4	16.2	8.1	4.3	4.2	3.6	5.3
1975	14.8	38.1	41.9	35.9	12.5	24.7	12.7	8.7	9.3	6.3	8.7
1976	13.7	37.5	40.8	36.0	11.4	22.6	12.0	7.5	7.3	6.3	8.7
1977	13.3	39.2	41.0	38.2	10.7	23.0	11.8	6.2	4.9	6.0	7.8
1978	11.8	36.7	43.0	32.9	9.3	21.0	9.8	5.1	4.9	4.4	6.6
1979	11.4	34.2	37.9	32.2	9.3	18.7	9.6	6.3	5.2	5.1	6.4
1980	14.5	37.5	39.7	36.2	12.4	23.7	13.4	8.2	7.2	6.2	8.7
1981	15.7	40.7	43.2	39.2	13.5	26.4	14.4	9.3	7.8	6.1	7.5
1982	20.1	48.9	52.7	47.1	17.8	31.5	20.1	13.4	9.0	10.3	9.3
1983	20.3	48.8	52.2	47.3	18.1	31.4	19.4	13.5	11.4	11.0	11.8
1984	16.4	42.7	44.0	42.2	14.3	26.6	15.0	10.4	7.9	8.9	7.9
1985	15.3	41.0	42.9	40.0	13.2	23.5	13.8	9.6	9.7	7.9	8.9
1986	14.8	39.3	41.4	38.2	12.9	23.5	13.5	10.9	7.8	8.0	4.3
1987	12.7	34.4	39.0	31.6	11.1	20.3	12.2	8.7	6.7	6.6	4.3
1988	11.7	32.7	34.4	31.7	10.1	19.4	11.0	7.6	6.2	5.2	5.6
1989	11.5	31.9	34.4	30.3	10.0	17.9	10.5	8.4	6.2	6.2	7.4
1990	11.9	31.9	38.8	28.0	10.4	20.1	11.5	8.4	6.3	5.4	4.6
1991	13.0	36.3	39.0	34.8	11.5	22.4	11.9	9.5	8.6	5.0	6.1
1992	15.2	42.0	47.5	39.1	13.5	24.6	14.2	11.2	10.3	8.1	4.9
1993	13.8	40.1	42.7	38.6	12.1	23.0	12.3	10.5	8.1	9.0	5.8
1994	12.0	37.6	39.3	36.5	10.3	19.4	10.6	9.1	6.5	6.0	8.2
1995	10.6	37.1	39.7	35.4	8.8	17.6	9.3	7.6	5.5	4.4	7.6
1996	11.1	36.9	39.9	34.9	9.4	19.2	10.1	7.8	6.3	5.2	5.0
1997	10.2	36.5	39.5	34.4	8.5	19.8	8.7	6.7	5.6	4.2	5.5
1998	8.9	30.1	33.9	27.9	7.4	18.0	7.3	6.2	4.4	4.5	5.2
1999	8.2	30.9	33.3	29.4	6.7	16.2	6.9	5.2	4.3	3.9	5.0
2000	8.1	26.4	28.6	25.0	7.0	16.7	6.8	5.7	4.8	2.7	6.3
BLACK WOMEN											
1972	11.8	40.5	42.0	40.1	9.0	17.9	10.5	7.6	4.6	3.7	2.6
1973	11.1	36.1	38.6	34.2	8.6	18.4	10.3	5.6	3.9	3.3	3.7
1974	11.3	37.4	40.2	36.0	8.8	19.0	9.0	6.6	4.4	3.6	1.9
1975	14.8	41.0	41.2	40.6	12.2	24.3	13.4	9.0	7.0	5.3	3.6
1976	14.3	41.6	48.4	37.6	11.7	22.8	13.6	8.5	5.9	5.4	2.4
1977	14.9	43.4	49.5	40.4	12.3	25.5	13.6	8.7	5.8	4.8	3.4
1978	13.8	40.8	45.0	38.7	11.2	22.7	11.9	7.8	5.6	5.2	4.7
1979	13.3	39.1	42.7	36.9	10.9	22.6	12.1	7.2	5.2	4.7	3.9
1980	14.0	39.8	42.9	38.2	11.9	23.5	13.2	8.2	6.4	4.5	4.9
1981	15.6	42.2	46.5	39.8	13.4	26.4	14.9	9.8	6.9	4.7	6.0
1982	17.6	47.1	44.2	48.6	15.4	29.6	17.8	10.7	8.5	6.1	4.5
1983	18.6	48.2	48.6	48.0	16.5	31.8	18.6	11.4	9.9	7.3	6.3
1984	15.4	42.6	47.5	40.2	13.5	25.6	15.4	9.4	8.6	5.9	4.9
1985	14.9	39.2	44.3	36.4	13.1	25.6	15.1	9.3	6.8	6.0	5.2
1986	14.2	39.2	44.6	36.1	12.4	24.7	14.6	8.5	6.4	5.0	4.9
1987	13.2	34.9	40.5	31.7	11.6	23.3	13.5	8.1	6.9	4.5	3.4
1988	11.7	32.0	35.9	29.6	10.4	19.8	12.7	7.4	5.6	4.3	5.4
1989	11.4	33.0	31.1	34.0	9.8	18.1	12.5	7.0	5.0	4.2	6.4
1990	10.9	29.9	34.1	27.6	9.7	19.6	11.9	7.2	4.3	3.6	5.9
1991	12.0	36.0	40.1	33.9	10.6	20.7	13.4	7.6	6.2	3.8	4.4
1992	13.2	37.2	41.7	34.8	11.8	23.1	14.1	9.8	6.4	4.2	5.0
1993	12.1	37.4	36.1	38.1	10.7	20.9	12.9	8.6	5.8	5.1	3.6
1994	11.0	32.6	32.9	32.5	9.8	19.6	11.7	8.0	4.9	4.9	4.4
1995	10.2	34.3	...	31.5	8.6	17.8	10.5	7.0	4.2	3.6	...
1996	10.0	30.3	32.8	28.6	8.7	18.4	11.0	6.9	3.8	3.8	5.6
1997	9.9	28.7	30.3	27.8	8.8	17.1	10.9	7.2	4.4	4.1	6.6
1998	9.0	25.3	33.2	20.9	7.9	15.7	9.5	6.7	4.3	3.4	6.1
1999	7.8	25.1	28.5	23.3	6.8	13.4	8.3	5.5	3.8	3.9	5.0
2000	7.2	23.0	25.7	21.5	6.3	13.5	6.8	5.5	3.5	3.3	6.0

See *Note* at end of table.

Table 1-27. Unemployment Rates of Civilian Workers by Race, Hispanic Origin, Sex, and Age, 1948–2000—*Continued*

(Percent of labor force.)

Year, race, Hispanic origin, and sex	16 years and over	16 to 19 years			20 years and over						
		Total	16 to 17 years	18 to 19 years	Total	20 to 24 years	25 to 34 years	35 to 44 years	45 to 54 years	55 to 64 years	65 years and over
HISPANIC MEN											
1973	6.7	19.0	20.9	17.7	5.4	8.2	5.0	4.2	4.5	5.4	5.5
1974	7.3	19.0	22.0	17.1	6.0	9.9	5.5	5.0	4.3	5.4	5.3
1975	11.4	27.6	29.3	26.5	9.6	16.3	9.6	7.9	7.0	6.8	11.0
1976	10.8	23.3	28.7	19.7	9.4	16.0	8.1	7.0	7.4	8.7	12.1
1977	9.0	20.9	25.9	18.2	7.7	11.7	7.9	4.9	5.4	7.4	9.7
1978	7.7	19.7	27.5	13.9	6.4	9.4	6.6	4.8	4.8	4.4	7.8
1979	7.0	17.5	23.5	13.8	5.8	9.2	5.3	5.1	4.4	5.0	5.5
1980	9.7	21.9	26.2	19.3	8.3	12.2	8.3	7.1	6.0	5.9	7.6
1981	10.2	24.3	30.9	20.3	8.8	14.1	8.9	6.5	5.9	6.7	6.7
1982	13.6	31.3	40.2	26.8	12.1	18.2	12.4	9.9	7.5	10.0	7.4
1983	13.6	28.7	34.7	25.9	12.2	17.0	11.6	10.8	10.3	11.7	6.8
1984	10.5	25.2	31.5	22.2	9.3	12.5	9.2	7.6	7.2	10.2	8.2
1985	10.2	24.7	29.1	22.4	9.1	12.9	9.6	7.2	6.8	7.0	9.4
1986	10.5	24.5	28.5	22.4	9.5	13.0	9.5	8.5	7.0	8.0	9.6
1987	8.7	22.2	28.2	19.3	7.8	10.2	7.6	6.9	7.1	6.7	7.9
1988	8.1	22.7	29.5	19.5	7.0	9.2	7.0	5.9	6.1	6.7	6.9
1989	7.6	20.2	27.6	16.8	6.6	9.7	5.9	5.7	6.0	6.6	5.6
1990	8.0	19.5	24.0	17.4	7.0	8.4	6.9	6.5	6.8	6.5	5.8
1991	10.3	23.5	33.6	19.2	9.3	11.6	9.3	8.5	7.9	8.1	7.0
1992	11.7	28.2	36.6	24.0	10.5	13.7	10.1	9.8	8.9	10.2	7.7
1993	10.6	25.9	34.5	21.9	9.5	12.6	9.0	8.8	8.8	8.5	9.5
1994	9.4	26.3	33.3	22.5	8.3	10.8	8.4	6.6	8.1	7.4	10.5
1995	8.8	25.3	34.8	20.2	7.7	10.6	7.5	6.7	5.9	7.9	12.9
1996	7.9	22.5	31.5	18.4	6.9	10.3	6.6	6.3	5.1	6.7	8.3
1997	7.0	20.8	26.5	17.9	6.1	9.8	5.1	5.4	4.8	6.8	7.2
1998	6.4	20.6	29.0	16.4	5.4	8.9	5.2	4.5	4.2	5.3	5.0
1999	5.6	17.0	22.4	15.3	4.7	7.8	4.1	3.8	4.5	4.6	5.0
2000	4.9	15.7	22.5	12.8	4.2	6.5	3.7	3.8	3.1	4.1	6.3
HISPANIC WOMEN											
1973	9.0	20.7	26.8	16.7	7.3	9.0	6.9	8.3	5.1	5.6	. . .
1974	9.4	20.8	25.3	17.4	7.7	9.7	7.7	7.6	5.3	7.5	9.5
1975	13.5	27.9	31.0	26.4	11.5	17.2	10.5	9.9	10.0	9.3	6.5
1976	12.7	22.2	30.3	18.7	11.4	15.8	10.8	10.0	9.8	9.0	14.7
1977	11.9	24.4	28.5	21.9	10.1	12.1	9.8	8.2	10.6	11.0	7.1
1978	11.3	21.8	29.9	16.6	9.8	13.0	10.3	9.2	7.4	7.2	5.7
1979	10.3	21.2	30.0	15.8	8.9	12.1	8.0	7.7	7.1	7.9	6.0
1980	10.7	23.4	29.7	19.8	9.2	12.0	10.6	8.6	5.3	5.8	1.1
1981	10.8	23.4	23.5	23.4	9.5	13.5	8.7	8.9	7.2	8.4	2.5
1982	14.1	28.2	35.1	25.0	12.5	16.8	12.2	11.9	9.9	10.4	4.8
1983	13.8	28.0	32.5	25.7	12.4	16.2	12.5	12.2	9.7	9.6	3.5
1984	11.1	22.8	26.1	21.0	9.9	12.2	10.3	9.1	7.9	8.8	3.4
1985	11.0	23.8	26.2	22.6	9.9	12.1	10.6	8.5	8.1	9.2	5.5
1986	10.8	25.1	27.6	23.6	9.6	12.9	9.8	8.2	8.9	6.2	11.2
1987	8.9	22.4	27.1	19.9	7.7	11.4	7.8	6.5	6.7	5.0	3.7
1988	8.3	21.0	24.5	18.9	7.1	10.7	7.2	6.2	5.9	4.6	3.0
1989	8.8	18.2	24.7	14.9	8.0	12.2	8.6	6.3	6.7	4.5	4.7
1990	8.4	19.4	25.4	16.2	7.5	10.4	8.0	6.7	6.0	4.3	6.4
1991	9.6	21.9	29.6	17.9	8.6	11.7	9.1	7.6	8.1	4.1	6.9
1992	11.4	26.4	34.5	22.4	10.2	12.4	11.0	9.7	8.5	6.2	8.7
1993	11.0	26.3	36.0	21.7	9.9	14.0	9.9	9.5	8.3	7.2	2.2
1994	10.7	22.2	29.7	18.1	9.8	13.5	10.1	9.2	8.0	7.1	3.6
1995	10.0	22.6	30.7	18.7	8.9	13.0	9.5	7.9	7.0	6.8	6.4
1996	10.2	25.1	28.2	23.3	9.2	14.1	8.5	8.7	7.2	8.1	8.0
1997	8.9	22.7	29.2	19.1	7.9	11.0	8.2	7.7	5.5	6.1	6.0
1998	8.2	22.1	26.4	20.2	7.1	10.1	7.2	6.9	5.1	5.4	8.8
1999	7.6	19.8	24.0	17.7	6.6	9.1	7.3	6.3	5.1	4.3	4.8
2000	6.7	18.1	22.9	15.7	5.9	8.9	6.4	5.4	3.6	5.1	4.8

Note: Detail for the above race and Hispanic-origin groups will not sum to totals because data for the Other races group are not presented and Hispanics are included in both the White and Black population groups. See "Notes and Definitions" for information on historical comparability.

Table 1-28. Unemployed Persons and Unemployment Rates by Occupation, 1986–2000

(Thousands of persons, percent of civilian labor force.)

Occupation	1986	1987	1988	1989	1990	1991	1992	1993	1994	1995	1996	1997	1998	1999	2000
UNEMPLOYED PERSONS, TOTAL, 16 YEARS AND OVER [1]	8 237	7 425	6 701	6 528	7 047	8 628	9 613	8 940	7 996	7 404	7 236	6 739	6 210	5 880	5 655
Managerial and professional specialty	653	650	577	614	666	889	1 009	984	907	880	869	761	722	770	725
Executive, administrative, and managerial	336	350	311	348	350	494	576	527	454	420	431	359	343	376	356
Professional specialty	317	300	266	265	316	395	433	457	453	460	438	403	380	394	369
Technical, sales, and administrative support	1 700	1 595	1 479	1 470	1 641	1 977	2 308	2 111	1 962	1 744	1 766	1 646	1 550	1 477	1 464
Technicians and related support	114	104	95	90	116	133	176	165	127	113	114	104	96	101	97
Sales occupations	718	691	652	643	720	857	985	927	907	795	843	814	745	714	684
Administrative support, including clerical	868	799	732	738	804	988	1 147	1 020	928	836	810	728	710	662	684
Service occupations	1 381	1 259	1 136	1 088	1 139	1 330	1 461	1 401	1 471	1 378	1 334	1 255	1 216	1 081	1 023
Private household	69	55	54	55	47	56	66	65	91	99	79	73	74	67	58
Protective service	90	94	81	74	74	101	108	108	96	86	84	89	85	72	65
Service, except private household and protective	1 223	1 110	1 000	960	1 018	1 172	1 287	1 228	1 285	1 193	1 170	1 093	1 057	943	900
Precision production, craft, and repair	1 038	875	773	762	861	1 149	1 294	1 155	910	860	795	719	630	607	554
Mechanics and repairers	226	191	166	161	175	246	281	258	201	182	174	167	149	136	129
Construction trades	522	470	405	428	483	655	730	631	518	501	456	406	338	330	312
Other precision production, craft, and repair	290	214	202	173	202	248	284	266	191	177	165	145	143	142	113
Operators, fabricators, and laborers	2 089	1 820	1 620	1 578	1 714	2 062	2 151	1 926	1 761	1 618	1 570	1 490	1 304	1 207	1 228
Machine operators, assemblers, and inspectors	907	777	673	678	727	903	922	816	672	629	654	551	494	440	455
Transportation and material moving occupations	431	366	317	306	329	398	428	404	364	329	292	306	279	235	253
Handlers, equipment cleaners, helpers, and laborers	752	677	630	594	657	761	802	706	725	660	625	633	531	532	520
Construction laborers	198	189	192	152	177	204	200	172	172	179	158	167	136	140	133
Other handlers, equipment cleaners, helpers, and laborers	554	488	439	442	481	556	601	534	552	481	467	467	395	392	387
Farming, forestry, and fishing	293	268	260	234	237	299	320	310	333	311	293	267	244	249	215
UNEMPLOYMENT RATE, TOTAL, 16 YEARS AND OVER [1]	7.0	6.2	5.5	5.3	5.6	6.8	7.5	6.9	6.1	5.6	5.4	4.9	4.5	4.2	4.0
Managerial and professional specialty	2.4	2.3	1.9	2.0	2.1	2.8	3.1	3.0	2.6	2.4	2.3	2.0	1.8	1.9	1.7
Executive, administrative, and managerial	2.6	2.6	2.1	2.3	2.3	3.2	3.8	3.3	2.7	2.4	2.4	1.9	1.8	1.9	1.8
Professional specialty	2.2	2.0	1.7	1.7	2.0	2.4	2.6	2.6	2.5	2.5	2.3	2.1	1.9	1.9	1.7
Technical, sales, and administrative support	4.7	4.3	4.0	3.9	4.3	5.2	5.9	5.4	5.0	4.5	4.5	4.1	3.9	3.7	3.6
Technicians and related support	3.3	3.0	2.6	2.4	2.9	3.4	4.0	3.9	3.2	2.8	2.8	2.4	2.2	2.3	2.2
Sales occupations	5.1	4.9	4.5	4.4	4.8	5.7	6.6	6.1	5.8	5.0	5.2	4.9	4.5	4.2	4.0
Administrative support, including clerical	4.7	4.2	3.9	3.9	4.1	5.1	5.8	5.2	4.7	4.3	4.2	3.8	3.7	3.5	3.5
Service occupations	8.6	7.7	6.9	6.5	6.6	7.6	8.2	7.7	8.0	7.5	7.2	6.7	6.4	5.7	5.3
Private household	6.5	5.6	5.7	5.9	5.6	6.5	6.9	6.5	10.0	10.7	9.0	8.4	8.0	7.4	6.9
Protective service	4.8	4.7	4.0	3.6	3.6	4.6	4.9	4.7	4.1	3.7	3.7	3.7	3.4	2.9	2.6
Service, except private household and protective	9.3	8.3	7.4	7.0	7.1	8.1	8.8	8.2	8.5	7.9	7.6	7.0	6.8	6.0	5.6
Precision production, craft, and repair	7.2	6.1	5.4	5.2	5.9	8.0	8.9	7.9	6.3	6.0	5.5	4.8	4.2	4.0	3.6
Mechanics and repairers	4.9	4.1	3.6	3.4	3.8	5.2	5.9	5.5	4.3	4.0	3.7	3.5	3.0	2.7	2.6
Construction trades	9.6	8.6	7.4	7.7	8.5	11.9	13.1	11.1	9.4	9.0	8.2	7.0	5.7	5.4	4.9
Other precision production, craft, and repair	6.6	5.0	4.7	4.0	4.7	5.9	6.7	6.3	4.5	4.2	4.0	3.4	3.4	3.5	2.8
Operators, fabricators, and laborers	10.9	9.4	8.3	8.0	8.7	10.6	11.1	10.0	9.0	8.2	7.9	7.5	6.7	6.2	6.3
Machine operators, assemblers, and inspectors	10.3	8.9	7.7	7.6	8.1	10.4	10.7	9.7	8.0	7.4	7.7	6.5	6.0	5.6	5.9
Transportation and material moving occupations	8.6	7.2	6.2	5.9	6.3	7.5	8.0	7.4	6.6	6.0	5.2	5.4	4.9	4.1	4.4
Handlers, equipment cleaners, helpers, and laborers	13.8	12.4	11.5	10.8	11.6	13.9	14.6	12.9	12.7	11.7	11.1	11.1	9.4	9.2	8.7
Construction laborers	21.0	19.8	19.4	16.8	18.1	22.1	22.9	20.3	18.9	18.7	16.3	17.1	14.2	13.2	11.6
Other handlers, equipment cleaners, helpers, and laborers	12.3	10.8	9.7	9.7	10.3	12.2	13.0	11.6	11.5	10.3	10.0	9.9	8.4	8.3	8.0
Farming, forestry, and fishing	7.8	7.1	7.0	6.4	6.4	7.9	8.3	8.4	8.4	7.9	7.6	7.1	6.5	6.8	6.0

Note: See "Notes and Definitions" for information on historical comparability.

1. Includes a small number of persons whose last job was in the Armed Forces.

Table 1-29. Unemployed Persons by Industry and Class of Worker, 1948–2000

(Thousands of persons.)

Year	All civilian workers [1]	Experienced wage and salary workers												
		Total [2]	Agriculture	Wage and salary workers in private nonagricultural industries, except private households										Govern-ment
				Total	Mining	Construc-tion	Manufacturing			Transpor-tation and public utilities	Wholesale and retail trade	Finance, insurance, and real estate	Services, except private house-holds	
							Total	Durable goods	Nondura-ble goods					
1948	2 276	2 046	96	1 756	28	232	678	339	339	149	415	30	224	118
1949	3 637	3 310	132	2 871	73	380	1 242	652	590	252	578	36	310	175
1950	3 288	2 990	162	2 512	61	348	981	466	515	189	580	40	313	178
1951	2 055	1 857	71	1 578	36	218	637	271	366	95	373	27	192	111
1952	1 883	1 707	73	1 453	35	218	573	266	307	95	326	33	173	103
1953	1 834	1 671	81	1 419	45	227	536	253	283	90	315	34	172	100
1954	3 532	3 230	133	2 827	106	386	1 232	720	512	231	549	46	277	151
1955	2 852	2 568	124	2 188	69	337	821	436	385	163	464	49	285	140
1956	2 750	2 443	126	2 081	50	313	832	448	384	127	459	39	261	118
1957	2 859	2 542	118	2 181	41	349	901	502	399	139	461	42	248	139
1958	4 602	4 096	180	3 584	72	523	1 605	1 036	569	246	705	68	365	190
1959	3 740	3 252	158	2 782	59	466	1 055	611	444	178	617	63	344	175
1960	3 852	3 337	159	2 847	59	463	1 103	626	477	193	637	63	329	191
1961	4 714	4 061	173	3 516	67	544	1 376	835	541	218	783	91	437	212
1962	3 911	3 342	127	2 889	46	466	1 045	575	470	166	678	82	406	188
1963	4 070	3 415	158	2 916	41	456	1 061	573	488	170	689	75	424	201
1964	3 786	3 134	158	2 643	37	390	941	498	443	143	649	75	408	198
1965	3 366	2 732	114	2 320	29	364	775	382	393	118	585	70	379	191
1966	2 875	2 331	89	1 957	20	286	651	325	326	88	528	62	322	194
1967	2 975	2 489	96	2 098	19	257	775	418	357	100	521	80	346	210
1968	2 817	2 356	86	1 971	16	247	691	368	323	87	513	74	343	218
1969	2 832	2 372	76	1 997	15	225	705	382	323	99	530	73	350	229
1970	4 093	3 526	94	3 070	16	380	1 195	719	475	150	732	102	495	282
1971	5 010	4 300	100	3 731	23	428	1 401	841	559	178	948	128	625	388
1972	4 882	4 122	103	3 537	19	450	1 154	653	501	168	994	138	613	409
1973	4 365	3 646	95	3 091	19	407	939	500	439	143	890	117	570	385
1974	5 156	4 391	110	3 769	20	486	1 257	703	554	162	1 058	139	648	442
1975	7 929	6 970	151	6 110	31	807	2 333	1 431	902	278	1 493	217	952	620
1976	7 406	6 387	180	5 421	37	694	1 700	987	714	246	1 527	200	1 017	698
1977	6 991	5 015	171	4 087	33	593	1 474	805	669	242	1 473	180	986	677
1978	6 202	5 220	142	4 359	37	530	1 244	661	583	201	1 295	161	891	637
1979	6 137	5 217	148	4 391	45	541	1 306	702	603	206	1 250	165	879	608
1980	7 637	6 634	175	5 710	65	740	1 991	1 254	736	280	1 443	188	1 004	681
1981	8 273	7 129	201	6 089	70	809	1 915	1 139	777	304	1 609	199	1 182	767
1982	10 678	9 275	260	8 128	154	1 031	2 771	1 788	983	397	2 066	276	1 433	799
1983	10 717	9 276	300	7 985	182	1 005	2 454	1 562	892	424	2 109	272	1 539	875
1984	8 539	7 236	243	6 145	103	817	1 654	955	699	330	1 710	232	1 299	739
1985	8 312	7 074	233	6 088	96	778	1 694	1 004	690	316	1 679	228	1 297	651
1986	8 237	7 019	222	6 097	134	809	1 559	910	650	313	1 706	239	1 336	603
1987	7 425	6 313	191	5 434	87	724	1 305	749	556	277	1 582	225	1 234	603
1988	6 701	5 718	192	4 943	62	669	1 161	653	508	246	1 433	221	1 151	497
1989	6 528	5 616	176	4 866	42	634	1 140	634	506	251	1 412	230	1 157	493
1990	7 047	6 104	190	5 354	36	718	1 289	762	527	252	1 551	221	1 287	492
1991	8 628	7 512	231	6 593	60	946	1 572	950	621	353	1 851	290	1 522	611
1992	9 613	8 361	251	7 344	56	1 020	1 663	979	685	373	2 097	332	1 802	675
1993	8 940	7 708	224	6 751	52	874	1 487	842	645	352	1 964	303	1 719	641
1994	7 996	7 092	218	6 113	37	724	1 154	630	524	340	1 899	271	1 688	645
1995	7 404	6 533	225	5 636	34	737	1 030	534	496	314	1 682	240	1 599	552
1996	7 236	6 389	213	5 532	30	666	1 013	563	450	291	1 679	201	1 653	547
1997	6 739	5 900	190	5 131	24	623	885	445	440	260	1 645	229	1 465	485
1998	6 210	5 477	180	4 781	20	532	816	426	390	254	1 493	197	1 470	424
1999	5 880	5 202	189	4 511	33	520	739	434	305	235	1 422	191	1 371	423
2000	5 655	5 022	165	4 610	21	499	733	413	320	243	1 381	185	1 314	413

Note: See "Notes and Definitions" for information on historical comparability.

1. Includes self-employed, unpaid family workers, and persons with no previous work experience, not shown separately.
2. Includes private household members, not shown separately.

Table 1-30. Unemployment Rates by Industry and Class of Worker, 1948–2000

(Percent of civilian labor force.)

Year	All civilian workers[1]	Experienced wage and salary workers												
		Total[2]	Agriculture	Wage and salary workers in private nonagricultural industries, except private households										Government
				Total	Mining	Construction	Manufacturing			Transportation and public utilities	Wholesale and retail trade	Finance, insurance, and real estate	Services, except private households	
							Total	Durable goods	Nondurable goods					
1948	3.8	4.3	5.5	4.5	3.1	8.7	4.2	4.0	4.4	3.5	4.7	1.8	5.0	2.2
1949	5.9	6.8	7.1	7.3	8.9	14.0	8.0	8.1	7.8	5.9	6.2	2.1	6.5	3.1
1950	5.3	6.0	9.0	6.2	6.9	12.2	6.2	5.7	6.7	4.6	6.0	2.2	6.2	3.0
1951	3.3	3.7	4.4	3.9	4.0	7.2	3.9	3.1	4.7	2.3	3.9	1.5	4.0	1.8
1952	3.0	3.4	4.8	3.6	3.8	6.7	3.5	3.0	4.1	2.3	3.5	1.8	3.4	1.6
1953	2.9	3.2	5.6	3.4	4.6	7.2	3.1	2.6	3.8	2.2	3.4	1.8	3.3	1.5
1954	5.5	6.2	9.0	6.7	14.4	12.9	7.1	7.3	6.9	5.6	5.7	2.3	5.2	2.2
1955	4.4	4.8	7.2	5.1	9.1	10.9	4.7	4.4	5.2	4.0	4.7	2.4	5.1	2.0
1956	4.1	4.4	7.4	4.7	6.8	10.0	4.7	4.4	5.2	3.0	4.5	1.8	4.4	1.7
1957	4.3	4.6	6.9	4.9	5.9	10.9	5.1	4.9	5.3	3.3	4.5	1.8	4.0	1.9
1958	6.8	7.3	10.3	8.0	11.0	15.3	9.3	10.6	7.7	6.1	6.8	2.9	5.6	2.5
1959	5.5	5.7	9.1	6.2	9.7	13.4	6.1	6.2	6.0	4.4	5.8	2.5	5.1	2.2
1960	5.5	5.7	8.3	6.2	9.7	13.5	6.2	6.4	6.1	4.6	5.9	2.4	4.8	2.4
1961	6.7	6.8	9.6	7.5	11.1	15.7	7.8	8.5	6.8	5.3	7.3	3.3	6.0	2.5
1962	5.5	5.6	7.5	6.2	7.8	13.5	5.8	5.7	6.0	4.1	6.3	3.0	5.4	2.1
1963	5.7	5.6	9.2	6.1	7.2	13.3	5.7	5.5	6.0	4.2	6.2	2.7	5.6	2.2
1964	5.2	5.0	9.7	5.4	6.7	11.2	5.0	4.7	5.4	3.5	5.7	2.6	5.2	2.1
1965	4.5	4.3	7.6	4.6	5.4	10.1	4.0	3.5	4.7	2.9	5.0	2.3	4.6	1.9
1966	3.8	3.5	6.6	3.8	3.7	8.0	3.2	2.8	3.8	2.1	4.4	2.1	3.8	1.8
1967	3.8	3.6	6.9	3.9	3.4	7.4	3.7	3.4	4.1	2.4	4.2	2.5	3.9	1.8
1968	3.6	3.4	6.3	3.6	3.1	6.9	3.3	3.0	3.7	2.0	4.0	2.2	3.7	1.8
1969	3.5	3.3	6.1	3.5	2.9	6.0	3.3	3.0	3.7	2.2	4.1	2.1	3.5	1.9
1970	4.9	4.8	7.5	5.3	3.1	9.7	5.6	5.7	5.4	3.2	5.3	2.8	4.7	2.2
1971	5.9	5.7	7.9	6.3	4.0	10.4	6.8	7.0	6.5	3.8	6.4	3.3	5.8	2.9
1972	5.6	5.3	7.7	5.8	3.2	10.3	5.6	5.5	5.8	3.5	6.4	3.4	5.4	3.0
1973	4.9	4.5	7.0	4.9	2.9	8.9	4.4	3.9	5.0	3.0	5.7	2.7	4.8	2.7
1974	5.6	5.3	7.5	5.8	3.0	10.7	5.8	5.4	6.3	3.3	6.5	3.1	5.2	3.0
1975	8.5	8.2	10.4	9.2	4.1	18.0	10.9	11.3	10.4	5.6	8.7	4.9	7.2	4.1
1976	7.7	7.3	11.8	8.0	4.6	15.5	7.9	7.7	8.2	5.0	8.6	4.3	7.3	4.4
1977	7.1	6.6	11.2	7.1	3.8	12.7	6.7	6.2	7.4	4.7	8.0	3.8	6.8	4.2
1978	6.1	5.6	8.9	6.0	4.2	10.6	5.5	5.0	6.3	3.7	6.9	3.1	5.8	3.9
1979	5.8	5.5	9.3	5.8	4.9	10.3	5.6	5.0	6.5	3.7	6.5	3.0	5.5	3.7
1980	7.1	6.9	11.0	7.4	6.4	14.1	8.5	8.9	7.9	4.9	7.4	3.4	6.0	4.1
1981	7.6	7.3	12.1	7.7	6.0	15.6	8.3	8.2	8.4	5.2	8.1	3.5	6.7	4.7
1982	9.7	9.3	14.7	10.2	13.4	20.0	12.3	13.3	10.8	6.8	10.0	4.7	7.7	4.9
1983	9.6	9.2	16.0	9.9	17.0	18.4	11.2	12.1	10.0	7.4	10.0	4.5	7.9	5.3
1984	7.5	7.1	13.5	7.4	10.0	14.3	7.5	7.2	7.8	5.5	8.0	3.7	6.5	4.5
1985	7.2	6.8	13.2	7.2	9.5	13.1	7.7	7.6	7.8	5.1	7.6	3.5	6.2	3.9
1986	7.0	6.6	12.5	7.0	13.5	13.1	7.1	6.9	7.4	5.1	7.6	3.5	6.1	3.6
1987	6.2	5.8	10.5	6.2	10.0	11.6	6.0	5.8	6.3	4.5	6.9	3.1	5.4	3.5
1988	5.5	5.2	10.6	5.5	7.9	10.6	5.3	5.0	5.7	3.9	6.2	3.0	4.8	2.8
1989	5.3	5.0	9.6	5.3	5.8	10.0	5.1	4.8	5.5	3.9	6.0	3.1	4.7	2.7
1990	5.6	5.3	9.8	5.7	4.8	11.1	5.8	5.8	5.8	3.9	6.4	3.0	5.0	2.7
1991	6.8	6.6	11.8	7.1	7.8	15.5	7.3	7.5	6.9	5.3	7.6	4.0	5.8	3.3
1992	7.5	7.2	12.5	7.8	8.0	16.8	7.8	8.0	7.6	5.5	8.4	4.6	6.5	3.6
1993	6.9	6.6	11.7	7.1	7.4	14.4	7.2	7.1	7.4	5.1	7.8	4.1	6.1	3.3
1994	6.1	5.9	11.3	6.3	5.4	11.8	5.6	5.2	6.0	4.8	7.4	3.6	5.7	3.4
1995	5.6	5.4	11.1	5.7	5.2	11.5	4.9	4.4	5.7	4.5	6.5	3.3	5.2	2.9
1996	5.4	5.2	10.2	5.5	5.1	10.1	4.8	4.5	5.2	4.1	6.4	2.7	5.2	2.9
1997	4.9	4.7	9.1	5.0	3.8	9.0	4.2	3.5	5.1	3.5	6.2	3.0	4.5	2.6
1998	4.5	4.3	8.3	4.6	3.2	7.5	3.9	3.4	4.7	3.4	5.5	2.5	4.4	2.3
1999	4.2	4.0	8.9	4.3	5.7	7.0	3.6	3.5	3.9	3.0	5.2	2.3	4.0	2.2
2000	4.0	3.9	7.5	4.2	3.9	6.4	3.6	3.4	4.0	3.1	5.0	2.3	3.7	2.1

Note: See "Notes and Definitions" for information on historical comparability.

1. Includes self-employed, unpaid family workers, and persons with no previous work experience, not shown separately.
2. Includes private household members, not shown separately.

Table 1-31. Unemployed Persons by Duration of Unemployment, 1948–2000

(Thousands of persons.)

Year	Total	Less than 5 weeks	5 to 14 weeks	15 weeks and over			Average duration, in weeks	Median duration, in weeks
				Total	15 to 26 weeks	27 weeks and over		
1948	2 276	1 300	669	309	193	116	8.6	. . .
1949	3 637	1 756	1 194	684	428	256	10.0	. . .
1950	3 288	1 450	1 055	782	425	357	12.1	. . .
1951	2 055	1 177	574	303	166	137	9.7	. . .
1952	1 883	1 135	516	232	148	84	8.4	. . .
1953	1 834	1 142	482	210	132	78	8.0	. . .
1954	3 532	1 605	1 116	812	495	317	11.8	. . .
1955	2 852	1 335	815	702	366	336	13.0	. . .
1956	2 750	1 412	805	533	301	232	11.3	. . .
1957	2 859	1 408	891	560	321	239	10.5	. . .
1958	4 602	1 753	1 396	1 452	785	667	13.9	. . .
1959	3 740	1 585	1 114	1 040	469	571	14.4	. . .
1960	3 852	1 719	1 176	957	503	454	12.8	. . .
1961	4 714	1 806	1 376	1 532	728	804	15.6	. . .
1962	3 911	1 663	1 134	1 119	534	585	14.7	. . .
1963	4 070	1 751	1 231	1 088	535	553	14.0	. . .
1964	3 786	1 697	1 117	973	491	482	13.3	. . .
1965	3 366	1 628	983	755	404	351	11.8	. . .
1966	2 875	1 573	779	526	287	239	10.4	. . .
1967	2 975	1 634	893	448	271	177	8.7	2.3
1968	2 817	1 594	810	412	256	156	8.4	4.5
1969	2 832	1 629	827	375	242	133	7.8	4.4
1970	4 093	2 139	1 290	663	428	235	8.6	4.9
1971	5 016	2 245	1 585	1 187	668	519	11.3	6.3
1972	4 882	2 242	1 472	1 167	601	566	12.0	6.2
1973	4 365	2 224	1 314	826	483	343	10.0	5.2
1974	5 156	2 604	1 597	955	574	381	9.8	5.2
1975	7 929	2 940	2 484	2 505	1 303	1 203	14.2	8.4
1976	7 406	2 844	2 196	2 366	1 018	1 348	15.8	8.2
1977	6 991	2 919	2 132	1 942	913	1 028	14.3	7.0
1978	6 202	2 865	1 923	1 414	766	648	11.9	5.9
1979	6 137	2 950	1 946	1 241	706	535	10.8	5.4
1980	7 637	3 295	2 470	1 871	1 052	820	11.9	6.5
1981	8 273	3 449	2 539	2 285	1 122	1 162	13.7	6.9
1982	10 678	3 883	3 311	3 485	1 708	1 776	15.6	8.7
1983	10 717	3 570	2 937	4 210	1 652	2 559	20.0	10.1
1984	8 539	3 350	2 451	2 737	1 104	1 634	18.2	7.9
1985	8 312	3 498	2 509	2 305	1 025	1 280	15.6	6.8
1986	8 237	3 448	2 557	2 232	1 045	1 187	15.0	6.9
1987	7 425	3 246	2 196	1 983	943	1 040	14.5	6.5
1988	6 701	3 084	2 007	1 610	801	809	13.5	5.9
1989	6 528	3 174	1 978	1 375	730	646	11.9	4.8
1990	7 047	3 265	2 257	1 525	822	703	12.0	5.3
1991	8 628	3 480	2 791	2 357	1 246	1 111	13.7	6.8
1992	9 613	3 376	2 830	3 408	1 453	1 954	17.7	8.7
1993	8 940	3 262	2 584	3 094	1 297	1 798	18.0	8.3
1994	7 996	2 728	2 408	2 860	1 237	1 623	18.8	9.2
1995	7 404	2 700	2 342	2 363	1 085	1 278	16.6	8.3
1996	7 236	2 633	2 287	2 316	1 053	1 262	16.7	8.3
1997	6 739	2 538	2 138	2 062	995	1 067	15.8	8.0
1998	6 210	2 622	1 950	1 637	763	875	14.5	6.7
1999	5 880	2 568	1 832	1 480	755	725	13.4	6.4
2000	5 655	2 543	1 803	1 309	665	644	12.6	5.9

Note: See "Notes and Definitions" for information on historical comparability.

Table 1-32. Long-Term Unemployment by Industry and Occupation, 1986–2000

(Thousands of persons.)

Industry and occupation	1986	1987	1988	1989	1990	1991	1992	1993	1994	1995	1996	1997	1998	1999	2000
UNEMPLOYED 15 WEEKS AND OVER															
Total	2 232	1 983	1 610	1 375	1 525	2 357	3 408	3 094	2 860	2 363	2 316	2 062	1 637	1 480	1 309
WAGE AND SALARY WORKERS BY INDUSTRY [1]															
Agriculture	51	42	39	32	31	47	57	56	72	58	65	50	44	41	35
Mining	57	42	28	15	11	23	25	27	21	13	11	9	3	...	...
Construction	234	209	169	153	162	285	402	330	238	233	208	171	134	127	102
Manufacturing	547	449	361	299	353	525	725	655	482	371	374	309	230	221	203
Durable goods	354	273	228	177	221	334	457	394	283	198	207	155	115	137	102
Nondurable goods	193	176	133	123	132	192	268	262	199	172	168	154	115	84	101
Transportation and public utilities	114	99	86	74	75	130	190	171	171	135	118	103	80	74	73
Wholesale and retail trade	423	387	295	268	303	448	699	630	628	493	486	456	359	318	287
Finance and services	501	457	405	350	403	615	921	840	825	711	729	645	533	460	419
Public administration	69	79	55	42	36	66	71	85	79	57	63	50	44	45	39
EXPERIENCED WORKERS BY OCCUPATION															
Managerial and professional specialty	190	202	164	156	184	310	473	429	371	320	316	258	211	214	191
Technical, sales, and administrative support	419	403	338	281	352	543	858	773	699	553	558	487	393	347	337
Service occupations	345	293	232	209	215	308	427	404	470	407	396	376	320	271	225
Precision production, craft, and repair	335	266	215	193	211	363	533	460	335	287	262	222	161	147	123
Operators, fabricators, and laborers	667	576	462	376	413	618	810	722	640	517	516	457	341	322	290
Farming, forestry, fishing	73	65	63	48	43	62	75	82	113	81	91	75	63	57	48
UNEMPLOYED 27 WEEKS AND OVER															
Total	1 187	1 040	809	646	703	1 111	1 954	1 798	1 623	1 278	1 262	1 067	875	725	644
WAGE AND SALARY WORKERS BY INDUSTRY [1]															
Agriculture	26	19	16	13	13	17	26	26	36	27	29	25	20	17	15
Mining	32	28	17	8	5	13	19	16	14	9	7	4	2	...	...
Construction	114	101	78	66	69	125	219	188	125	125	105	78	66	55	43
Manufacturing	318	249	194	146	168	255	455	392	282	203	207	167	113	108	109
Durable goods	209	159	128	85	102	160	294	237	170	108	116	84	58	67	49
Nondurable goods	109	90	66	62	65	95	162	155	113	95	90	83	56	41	60
Transportation and public utilities	57	52	46	39	34	67	120	102	107	77	62	53	49	38	36
Wholesale and retail trade	212	189	154	120	139	203	378	368	350	259	251	218	191	151	130
Finance and services	264	239	191	160	179	293	527	492	452	380	409	333	282	228	205
Public administration	37	43	28	22	20	32	45	53	50	32	37	30	27	24	23
EXPERIENCED WORKERS BY OCCUPATION															
Managerial and professional specialty	97	107	73	73	86	153	290	266	214	181	177	143	112	107	91
Technical, sales, and administrative support	201	198	162	119	152	247	498	460	389	289	295	232	206	157	158
Service occupations	190	157	125	97	104	146	231	234	268	228	220	209	177	148	118
Precision production, craft, and repair	191	143	108	98	95	169	308	270	184	156	144	108	84	66	59
Operators, fabricators, and laborers	362	312	247	183	197	302	480	416	373	276	280	234	177	156	140
Farming, forestry, fishing	36	33	29	22	17	25	33	39	57	41	42	39	27	26	24

Note: See "Notes and Definitions" for information on historical comparability.

1. Includes wage and salary workers only.

Table 1-33. Unemployed Persons and Unemployment Rates by Sex, Age, and Reason for Unemployment, 1968–2000

(Thousands of persons, percent.)

Year and sex	Number of unemployed					Unemployed as a percent of the total civilian labor force			
	Total	Job losers	Job leavers	Entrants		Job losers	Job leavers	Entrants	
				Reentrants	New entrants			Reentrants	New entrants
TOTAL									
1968	2 817	1 070	431	909	407	1.4	0.5	1.2	0.5
1969	2 832	1 017	436	965	413	1.3	0.5	1.2	0.5
1970	4 093	1 811	550	1 228	504	2.2	0.7	1.5	0.6
1971	5 016	2 323	590	1 472	630	2.8	0.7	1.7	0.7
1972	4 882	2 108	641	1 456	677	2.4	0.7	1.7	0.8
1973	4 365	1 694	683	1 340	649	1.9	0.8	1.5	0.7
1974	5 156	2 242	768	1 463	681	2.4	0.8	1.6	0.7
1975	7 929	4 386	827	1 892	823	4.7	0.9	2.0	0.9
1976	7 406	3 679	903	1 928	895	3.8	0.9	2.0	0.9
1977	6 991	3 166	909	1 963	953	3.2	0.9	2.0	1.0
1978	6 202	2 585	874	1 857	885	2.5	0.9	1.8	0.9
1979	6 137	2 635	880	1 806	817	2.5	0.8	1.7	0.8
1980	7 637	3 947	891	1 927	872	3.7	0.8	1.8	0.8
1981	8 273	4 267	923	2 102	981	3.9	0.8	1.9	0.9
1982	10 678	6 268	840	2 384	1 185	5.7	0.8	2.2	1.1
1983	10 717	6 258	830	2 412	1 216	5.6	0.7	2.2	1.1
1984	8 539	4 421	823	2 184	1 110	3.9	0.7	1.9	1.0
1985	8 312	4 139	877	2 256	1 039	3.6	0.8	2.0	0.9
1986	8 237	4 033	1 015	2 160	1 029	3.4	0.9	1.8	0.9
1987	7 425	3 566	965	1 974	920	3.0	0.8	1.6	0.8
1988	6 701	3 092	983	1 809	816	2.5	0.8	1.5	0.7
1989	6 528	2 983	1 024	1 843	677	2.4	0.8	1.5	0.5
1990	7 047	3 387	1 041	1 930	688	2.7	0.8	1.5	0.5
1991	8 628	4 694	1 004	2 139	792	3.7	0.8	1.7	0.6
1992	9 613	5 389	1 002	2 285	937	4.2	0.8	1.8	0.7
1993	8 940	4 848	976	2 198	919	3.8	0.8	1.7	0.7
1994	7 996	3 815	791	2 786	604	2.9	0.6	2.1	0.5
1995	7 404	3 476	824	2 525	579	2.6	0.6	1.9	0.4
1996	7 236	3 370	774	2 512	580	2.5	0.6	1.9	0.4
1997	6 739	3 037	795	2 338	569	2.2	0.6	1.7	0.4
1998	6 210	2 822	734	2 132	520	2.1	0.5	1.5	0.4
1999	5 880	2 622	783	2 005	469	1.9	0.6	1.4	0.3
2000	5 655	2 492	775	1 957	431	1.8	0.6	1.4	0.3
MEN, 20 YEARS AND OVER									
1968	993	599	167	205	22	1.3	0.4	0.4	0.1
1969	963	556	164	216	27	1.2	0.4	0.5	0.1
1970	1 638	1 066	209	318	44	2.2	0.4	0.7	0.1
1971	2 097	1 301	239	411	57	2.9	0.5	0.9	0.1
1972	1 948	1 219	248	420	60	2.5	0.5	0.9	0.1
1973	1 624	959	258	350	56	1.9	0.5	0.7	0.1
1974	1 957	1 276	276	356	48	2.5	0.5	0.7	0.1
1975	3 476	2 598	298	506	70	5.0	0.6	1.0	0.1
1976	3 098	2 167	323	521	86	4.1	0.6	1.0	0.2
1977	2 794	1 816	335	540	103	3.4	0.6	1.0	0.2
1978	2 328	1 433	337	471	86	2.6	0.6	0.9	0.2
1979	2 308	1 464	325	446	73	2.6	0.6	0.8	0.1
1980	3 353	2 389	359	516	90	4.2	0.6	0.9	0.2
1981	3 615	2 565	356	592	102	4.5	0.6	1.0	0.2
1982	5 089	3 965	327	678	119	6.8	0.6	1.2	0.2
1983	5 257	4 088	336	695	138	6.9	0.6	1.2	0.2
1984	3 932	2 800	324	663	146	4.7	0.5	1.1	0.2
1985	3 715	2 568	352	671	124	4.3	0.6	1.1	0.2
1986	3 751	2 568	444	611	128	4.1	0.7	1.0	0.2
1987	3 369	2 289	413	558	108	3.7	0.7	0.9	0.2
1988	2 987	1 939	416	534	98	3.1	0.7	0.9	0.2
1989	2 867	1 843	394	541	88	2.9	0.6	0.8	0.1
1990	3 239	2 100	431	626	82	3.2	0.7	1.0	0.1
1991	4 195	2 982	411	698	105	4.6	0.6	1.1	0.2
1992	4 717	3 420	421	765	111	5.2	0.6	1.2	0.2
1993	4 287	2 996	429	747	114	4.5	0.6	1.1	0.2
1994	3 627	2 296	367	898	65	3.4	0.5	1.3	0.1
1995	3 239	2 051	356	775	57	3.0	0.5	1.2	0.1
1996	3 146	2 043	322	731	51	3.0	0.5	1.1	0.1
1997	2 882	1 795	358	675	55	2.6	0.5	1.0	0.1
1998	2 580	1 588	318	611	63	2.3	0.5	0.9	0.1
1999	2 433	1 459	336	592	46	2.1	0.5	0.8	0.1
2000	2 350	1 398	324	574	54	2.0	0.5	0.8	0.1

See *Note* at end of table.

Table 1-33. Unemployed Persons and Unemployment Rates by Sex, Age, and Reason for Unemployment, 1968–2000— *Continued*

(Thousands of persons, percent.)

Year and sex	Number of unemployed					Unemployed as a percent of the total civilian labor force			
	Total	Job losers	Job leavers	Entrants		Job losers	Job leavers	Entrants	
				Reentrants	New entrants			Reentrants	New entrants
WOMEN, 20 YEARS AND OVER									
1968	985	341	167	422	55	1.3	0.6	1.6	0.2
1969	1 015	335	171	455	55	1.2	0.6	1.7	0.2
1970	1 349	546	214	531	58	1.9	0.8	1.9	0.2
1971	1 658	700	235	651	72	2.5	0.8	2.3	0.2
1972	1 625	641	264	641	80	2.2	0.9	2.1	0.3
1973	1 507	522	280	625	80	1.6	0.9	2.0	0.3
1974	1 777	685	319	673	100	2.1	1.0	2.1	0.3
1975	2 684	1 339	375	858	114	4.0	1.1	2.6	0.3
1976	2 588	1 124	427	912	126	3.2	1.2	2.6	0.4
1977	2 535	1 031	419	945	140	2.8	1.2	2.6	0.4
1978	2 292	852	371	930	138	2.2	1.0	2.4	0.4
1979	2 276	851	370	908	145	2.1	0.9	2.3	0.4
1980	2 615	1 170	376	930	139	2.8	0.9	2.3	0.3
1981	2 895	1 317	404	1 023	151	3.1	1.0	2.4	0.4
1982	3 613	1 844	379	1 197	192	4.2	0.9	2.7	0.4
1983	3 632	1 801	384	1 235	212	4.0	0.9	2.8	0.5
1984	3 107	1 350	386	1 151	220	2.9	0.8	2.5	0.5
1985	3 129	1 296	412	1 195	227	2.7	0.9	2.5	0.5
1986	3 032	1 225	426	1 175	206	2.5	0.9	2.4	0.4
1987	2 709	1 067	406	1 041	194	2.2	0.8	2.1	0.4
1988	2 487	946	408	965	168	1.9	0.8	1.9	0.3
1989	2 467	942	430	958	137	1.8	0.8	1.8	0.3
1990	2 596	1 054	429	966	146	2.0	0.8	1.8	0.3
1991	3 074	1 423	413	1 075	163	2.6	0.8	2.0	0.3
1992	3 469	1 710	433	1 142	183	3.1	0.8	2.1	0.3
1993	3 288	1 619	395	1 098	176	2.9	0.7	2.0	0.3
1994	3 049	1 334	339	1 253	122	2.4	0.6	2.2	0.2
1995	2 819	1 211	366	1 135	107	2.1	0.6	2.0	0.2
1996	2 783	1 145	361	1 156	120	2.0	0.6	2.0	0.2
1997	2 585	1 069	333	1 057	126	1.8	0.6	1.8	0.2
1998	2 424	1 053	330	944	97	1.8	0.6	1.6	0.2
1999	2 285	990	333	866	96	1.6	0.5	1.4	0.2
2000	2 212	934	340	860	78	1.5	0.6	1.4	0.1
BOTH SEXES, 16 TO 19 YEARS									
1968	838	130	97	281	330	2.0	1.5	4.2	5.0
1969	853	127	101	295	331	1.8	1.5	4.2	4.8
1970	1 106	200	126	378	401	2.8	1.7	5.2	5.5
1971	1 262	233	117	410	501	3.1	1.6	5.5	6.7
1972	1 308	248	129	395	536	3.1	1.6	4.9	6.6
1973	1 235	212	146	364	513	2.4	1.7	4.3	6.0
1974	1 422	280	173	436	533	3.1	2.0	4.9	6.0
1975	1 767	450	155	529	634	5.1	1.7	6.0	7.1
1976	1 719	387	153	496	683	4.3	1.7	5.5	7.5
1977	1 663	318	156	477	711	3.4	1.7	5.1	7.6
1978	1 583	300	167	455	660	3.1	1.7	4.7	6.8
1979	1 555	319	184	452	599	3.3	1.9	4.7	6.2
1980	1 669	388	156	481	643	4.1	1.7	5.1	6.9
1981	1 763	385	162	487	728	4.3	1.8	5.4	8.1
1982	1 977	460	134	509	874	5.4	1.6	6.0	10.2
1983	1 829	370	110	482	867	4.6	1.3	5.9	10.6
1984	1 499	271	114	370	745	3.4	1.4	4.7	9.4
1985	1 468	275	113	390	689	3.5	1.4	4.9	8.7
1986	1 454	240	145	374	695	3.0	1.8	4.7	8.8
1987	1 347	210	146	375	617	2.7	1.8	4.7	7.7
1988	1 226	207	159	310	550	2.6	2.0	3.9	6.8
1989	1 194	198	200	345	452	2.5	2.5	4.3	5.7
1990	1 212	233	181	338	460	3.0	2.3	4.3	5.9
1991	1 359	289	180	365	524	4.0	2.5	5.0	7.2
1992	1 427	259	149	377	643	3.6	2.1	5.3	9.1
1993	1 365	233	151	353	628	3.3	2.1	4.9	8.8
1994	1 320	185	84	634	416	2.5	1.1	8.5	5.6
1995	1 346	214	102	615	415	2.8	1.3	7.9	5.3
1996	1 306	182	91	625	409	2.3	1.2	8.0	5.2
1997	1 271	174	104	606	388	2.2	1.3	7.6	4.9
1998	1 205	181	86	577	361	2.2	1.0	7.0	4.4
1999	1 162	173	114	547	328	2.1	1.4	6.6	3.9
2000	1 093	160	111	522	300	1.9	1.3	6.2	3.6

Note: See "Notes and Definitions" for information on historical comparability.

Table 1-34. Percent of the Population with Work Experience During the Year by Sex and Age, 1987–1999

Year	Total	16 to 17 years	18 to 19 years	20 to 24 years	25 to 34 years	35 to 44 years	45 to 54 years	55 to 59 years	60 to 64 years	65 to 69 years	70 years and over
TOTAL											
1987	69.7	51.8	76.6	85.5	85.7	86.1	81.6	69.4	51.3	26.2	10.2
1988	70.2	50.6	75.5	85.7	86.0	86.8	82.2	70.5	52.2	27.9	10.3
1989	70.5	51.9	75.4	84.9	86.6	86.9	82.8	70.4	52.5	28.4	10.0
1990	70.2	48.6	74.2	84.1	86.2	87.0	82.8	70.9	53.4	28.3	10.2
1991	69.5	43.4	70.8	83.4	85.9	86.6	83.0	70.3	52.9	27.2	9.8
1992	69.1	43.8	69.9	82.7	85.2	85.9	82.8	70.8	53.5	25.5	9.8
1993	69.2	42.1	70.4	82.0	85.0	85.3	82.8	71.6	51.6	27.5	10.7
1994	69.6	44.1	71.5	82.5	85.5	85.6	83.8	72.2	52.8	27.5	10.0
1995	69.6	44.4	71.2	82.0	85.6	85.9	83.4	72.2	53.3	28.0	10.2
1996	69.9	43.3	70.5	83.1	86.1	85.7	84.3	73.3	54.3	27.8	10.4
1997	70.1	43.6	70.5	83.0	87.1	85.9	84.4	73.8	53.8	28.5	10.0
1998	70.1	42.1	69.9	82.9	86.7	86.3	84.2	73.7	54.5	29.2	10.6
1999	70.7	43.7	71.2	82.7	87.3	86.9	85.0	72.3	55.8	30.5	11.6
MEN											
1987	78.9	52.4	77.4	90.4	94.3	94.1	91.9	83.3	63.2	34.2	15.4
1988	79.1	51.8	78.9	90.7	94.3	94.6	91.6	82.1	63.1	35.6	15.6
1989	79.4	53.2	77.7	89.9	94.7	94.7	91.9	82.0	64.2	35.4	15.1
1990	78.9	50.3	76.7	88.7	94.4	94.7	91.3	82.0	65.8	35.8	14.0
1991	77.9	45.4	72.2	87.9	93.5	93.6	91.3	81.5	63.6	35.0	14.4
1992	77.4	46.6	73.7	87.1	93.3	92.8	89.9	80.9	63.2	32.4	14.3
1993	76.8	43.9	71.4	86.6	92.5	92.0	89.3	79.8	59.1	34.3	15.3
1994	77.2	44.4	74.7	87.2	92.9	92.0	90.0	81.3	61.4	33.9	14.8
1995	77.0	43.7	73.6	86.4	92.6	92.2	89.7	81.5	62.1	34.5	14.9
1996	77.2	44.1	71.8	86.7	93.4	92.1	90.4	81.8	62.5	33.6	15.2
1997	77.1	43.4	70.3	86.6	94.1	92.3	90.7	81.4	62.9	33.8	13.9
1998	70.0	40.4	71.6	86.4	93.5	92.7	90.1	81.7	63.5	35.5	14.7
1999	77.3	44.7	70.0	85.5	93.9	90.2	89.9	79.2	65.1	37.4	16.5
WOMEN											
1987	61.3	51.1	75.8	81.0	77.3	78.5	71.9	56.7	41.0	19.6	6.8
1988	62.1	49.3	72.2	81.0	78.1	79.4	73.5	60.0	42.5	21.4	6.8
1989	62.3	50.6	73.1	80.2	78.6	79.3	74.2	59.9	42.4	22.5	6.7
1990	62.2	46.8	71.7	79.6	78.0	79.6	74.9	60.4	42.5	22.1	7.7
1991	61.8	41.4	69.4	79.0	78.3	79.9	75.3	59.9	43.6	20.6	6.7
1992	61.5	40.9	66.1	78.4	77.2	79.1	76.1	61.5	44.4	20.0	6.7
1993	62.1	40.3	69.4	77.5	77.6	78.7	76.5	63.9	44.7	22.1	7.7
1994	62.5	43.7	68.4	77.8	78.1	79.4	78.0	63.9	45.0	22.2	6.8
1995	62.8	45.2	68.7	77.7	78.8	79.8	77.6	63.2	45.6	22.4	7.1
1996	63.2	42.5	69.2	79.5	78.9	79.5	78.4	65.4	46.9	23.0	7.1
1997	63.6	43.9	70.7	79.5	80.1	79.6	78.4	66.7	45.6	24.0	7.3
1998	63.7	44.1	68.2	79.4	80.1	80.0	78.6	66.3	46.2	23.8	7.8
1999	64.5	42.6	70.1	79.9	80.9	80.7	80.3	66.2	47.3	24.4	8.2

Note: See "Notes and Definitions" for information on historical comparability.

Table 1-35. Persons with Work Experience During the Year by Industry and Class of Worker of Job Held the Longest, 1987–1999

(Thousands of persons.)

Industry and class of worker	1987	1988	1989	1990	1991	1992	1993	1994	1995	1996	1997	1998	1999
TOTAL	128 316	130 450	132 817	133 534	133 410	133 912	136 354	138 469	139 723	142 200	143 967	145 566	148 295
Agriculture	3 832	3 754	3 770	3 743	3 555	3 793	3 844	3 924	3 918	3 624	3 422	3 608	3 679
Wage and salary workers	2 238	2 262	2 197	2 149	2 150	2 286	2 186	2 364	2 448	2 262	2 344	2 308	2 430
Self-employed workers	1 419	1 359	1 453	1 458	1 313	1 398	1 591	1 502	1 419	1 333	1 057	1 269	1 215
Unpaid family workers	176	133	120	136	92	109	67	58	51	29	20	32	34
Nonagricultural Industries	124 484	126 696	129 047	129 791	129 856	130 118	132 510	134 544	135 805	138 575	140 545	141 958	148 295
Wage and salary workers	115 594	117 757	120 019	120 416	120 734	120 924	123 314	125 567	126 916	129 232	132 140	133 039	138 315
Mining	769	807	735	858	775	718	709	683	612	643	703	606	558
Construction	6 937	7 235	7 491	7 236	6 888	6 607	6 690	7 134	7 226	7 720	7 996	8 103	8 211
Manufacturing	22 563	22 957	22 764	22 435	21 624	21 174	21 198	21 488	21 475	22 130	21 652	21 268	21 737
Durable goods	13 268	13 196	13 379	13 155	12 353	11 983	12 309	12 082	12 552	12 988	12 943	13 056	13 172
Lumber and wood products	770	789	840	797	639	632	653	752	891	860	800	767	822
Furniture and fixtures	670	727	683	621	600	694	757	651	647	684	694	632	667
Stone, clay, and glass products	694	628	721	691	594	549	629	656	664	637	521	649	651
Primary metal industries	764	768	892	852	830	823	784	733	845	801	706	802	809
Fabricated metal products	1 402	1 367	1 386	1 348	1 375	1 293	1 325	1 339	1 265	1 469	1 443	1 419	1 310
Machinery, except electrical	2 600	2 778	2 601	2 631	2 442	2 264	2 445	2 557	2 502	2 603	2 659	2 707	2 739
Electrical equipment	2 295	2 231	2 280	2 281	2 142	1 925	1 857	1 945	1 966	1 996	2 047	2 149	2 068
Transportation equipment	2 745	2 693	2 669	2 661	2 483	2 460	2 476	2 124	2 262	2 399	2 520	2 432	2 546
Automobiles	1 278	1 284	1 273	1 206	1 157	1 214	1 205	1 102	1 258	1 361	1 446	1 342	1 447
Other transportation equipment	1 467	1 409	1 396	1 455	1 326	1 246	1 271	1 022	1 004	1 038	1 074	1 090	1 099
Other durable goods	1 329	1 215	1 307	1 274	1 248	1 344	1 383	1 324	1 510	1 539	1 552	1 499	1 562
Nondurable goods	9 295	9 761	9 385	9 280	9 271	9 191	8 889	9 406	8 923	9 142	8 709	8 212	8 565
Food and kindred products	2 033	2 083	2 048	2 000	1 920	2 028	1 879	1 906	1 952	1 952	1 846	1 808	1 863
Textile mill products	797	785	747	800	716	639	694	807	695	716	624	642	568
Apparel and related products	1 321	1 343	1 214	1 174	1 172	1 290	1 189	1 235	1 138	1 066	973	857	800
Printing and publishing	1 874	1 951	2 018	1 880	2 013	1 933	1 905	2 053	1 882	1 883	1 862	1 840	2 041
Chemicals and allied products	1 270	1 533	1 404	1 356	1 405	1 276	1 396	1 402	1 373	1 496	1 306	1 160	1 431
Other nondurable goods	1 999	2 066	1 953	2 069	2 046	2 025	1 827	2 002	1 881	2 029	2 098	1 904	1 863
Transportation and public utilities	8 188	8 195	8 267	8 364	8 490	8 495	8 639	8 567	8 586	9 114	9 487	9 536	9 786
Transportation	4 778	4 856	4 952	5 021	5 066	5 219	5 411	5 373	5 430	5 888	6 079	6 087	6 125
Communications and utilities	3 410	3 339	3 315	3 343	3 425	3 276	3 227	3 194	3 155	3 226	3 408	3 449	3 661
Wholesale and retail trade	26 069	26 078	26 387	26 879	26 846	26 943	27 328	27 837	28 563	28 852	29 193	29 593	30 155
Wholesale trade	4 599	4 454	4 642	4 809	4 822	4 583	4 509	4 933	4 954	4 841	4 906	5 224	5 466
Retail trade	21 470	21 624	21 745	22 070	22 025	22 360	22 819	22 904	23 609	24 011	24 287	24 370	24 689
Finance and services	44 919	46 321	47 370	47 587	49 117	49 786	51 659	52 360	53 402	54 141	56 263	56 704	58 323
Finance, insurance, and real estate	7 937	7 980	8 091	7 760	7 730	7 629	7 971	7 869	7 911	8 000	8 508	8 619	8 535
Business and repair services	6 299	6 646	6 985	7 040	6 135	6 308	6 849	7 002	7 547	8 035	8 282	8 547	8 856
Private households	1 493	1 535	1 238	1 161	1 266	1 395	1 254	1 241	1 171	1 038	1 131	1 067	1 213
Personal services, except private households	2 943	3 019	3 196	3 177	3 110	2 999	3 272	3 181	3 219	3 099	3 209	3 227	3 186
Entertainment and recreation	1 575	1 568	1 673	1 752	2 235	2 294	2 371	2 407	2 571	2 705	2 904	2 908	2 947
Medical and other health services	8 843	9 247	9 389	9 904	10 457	10 573	10 979	11 029	11 412	11 788	11 756	11 680	11 842
Social services	2 083	2 092	2 264	2 335	2 479	2 606	2 752	2 632	3 038	3 016	3 068	3 198	3 292
Educational services	9 622	9 895	10 094	9 976	10 328	10 705	10 882	11 454	11 064	11 076	11 539	11 627	12 167
Other professional services	4 018	4 181	4 270	4 296	5 251	5 079	5 144	5 398	5 326	5 241	5 729	5 692	6 119
Forestry and fisheries	107	160	169	186	125	198	184	148	144	145	137	139	165
Public administration	6 147	6 163	7 005	7 057	6 917	7 097	7 088	7 498	7 053	6 630	6 846	7 229	7 115
Self-employed workers	8 588	8 580	8 717	9 120	8 855	8 965	8 992	8 843	8 753	9 235	8 257	8 806	9 833
Unpaid family workers	302	359	312	255	267	229	204	135	137	109	147	114	146

Note: See "Notes and Definitions" for information on historical comparability.

Table 1-36. Number of Persons with Work Experience During the Year by Sex and Extent of Employment, 1987–1999

(Thousands of persons.)

Year and sex	Total	Full-time				Part-time			
		Total	50 to 52 weeks	27 to 49 weeks	1 to 26 weeks	Total	50 to 52 weeks	27 to 49 weeks	1 to 26 weeks
TOTAL									
1987	128 315	100 288	77 015	13 361	9 912	28 027	10 973	6 594	10 460
1988	130 451	102 131	79 627	12 875	9 629	28 320	11 384	6 624	10 312
1989	132 817	104 876	81 117	14 271	9 488	27 941	11 275	6 987	9 679
1990	133 535	105 323	80 932	14 758	9 633	28 212	11 507	7 012	9 693
1991	133 410	104 472	80 385	14 491	9 596	28 938	11 946	7 003	9 989
1992	133 912	104 813	81 523	13 587	9 703	29 099	12 326	6 841	9 932
1993	136 354	106 299	83 384	13 054	9 861	30 055	12 818	6 777	10 460
1994	138 468	108 141	85 764	13 051	9 326	30 327	12 936	6 956	10 435
1995	139 724	110 063	88 173	12 970	8 920	29 661	12 725	6 831	10 105
1996	142 201	112 313	90 252	12 997	9 064	29 888	13 382	6 643	9 863
1997	143 968	113 879	92 631	12 508	8 740	30 089	13 810	6 565	9 714
1998	145 566	116 412	95 772	12 156	8 484	29 155	13 538	6 480	9 137
1999	148 295	119 096	97 941	12 294	8 861	29 199	13 680	6 317	9 202
MEN									
1987	69 144	59 736	47 040	7 503	5 193	9 408	3 260	2 191	3 957
1988	70 021	60 504	48 299	7 329	4 876	9 517	3 468	2 199	3 850
1989	71 640	62 108	49 693	7 642	4 773	9 532	3 619	2 254	3 659
1990	71 953	62 319	49 175	8 188	4 956	9 634	3 650	2 322	3 662
1991	71 700	61 636	47 895	8 324	5 417	10 064	3 820	2 342	3 902
1992	72 007	61 722	48 300	7 965	5 457	10 285	3 864	2 354	4 067
1993	72 872	62 513	49 832	7 317	5 364	10 359	4 005	2 144	4 210
1994	73 958	63 634	51 582	7 094	4 958	10 324	3 948	2 358	4 018
1995	74 001	64 145	52 671	6 973	4 501	10 236	4 034	2 257	3 945
1996	75 760	65 356	53 795	6 891	4 670	10 404	4 321	2 136	3 947
1997	76 408	66 089	54 918	6 638	4 533	10 319	4 246	2 274	3 799
1998	76 918	67 250	56 953	6 208	4 089	9 669	4 197	2 090	3 382
1999	78 145	68 347	57 520	6 401	4 426	9 797	4 297	2 062	3 438
WOMEN									
1987	59 171	40 552	29 975	5 858	4 719	18 619	7 713	4 403	6 503
1988	60 430	41 627	31 328	5 546	4 753	18 803	7 916	4 425	6 462
1989	61 178	42 768	31 424	6 629	4 715	18 410	7 656	4 733	6 021
1990	61 582	43 004	31 757	6 570	4 677	18 578	7 857	4 690	6 031
1991	61 712	42 837	32 491	6 167	4 179	18 875	8 126	4 662	6 087
1992	61 904	43 090	33 223	5 621	4 246	18 814	8 462	4 487	5 865
1993	63 481	43 785	33 552	5 736	4 497	19 696	8 813	4 633	6 250
1994	64 511	44 508	34 182	5 957	4 369	20 003	8 988	4 598	6 417
1995	65 342	45 917	35 502	5 997	4 418	19 425	8 691	4 574	6 160
1996	66 439	46 955	36 457	6 105	4 393	19 484	9 061	4 507	5 916
1997	67 559	47 790	37 713	5 870	4 207	19 769	9 564	4 291	5 914
1998	68 648	49 162	38 819	5 948	4 395	19 486	9 341	4 390	5 755
1999	70 150	50 748	40 421	5 892	4 435	19 402	9 383	4 255	5 764

Note: See "Notes and Definitions" for information on historical comparability.

Table 1-37. Percent Distribution of the Population with Work Experience During the Year by Sex and Extent of Employment, 1987–1999

(Percent of total persons with work experience.)

Year and sex	Total	Full-time				Part-time			
		Total	50 to 52 weeks	27 to 49 weeks	1 to 26 weeks	Total	50 to 52 weeks	27 to 49 weeks	1 to 26 weeks
TOTAL									
1987	100.0	78.1	60.0	10.4	7.7	21.9	8.6	5.1	8.2
1988	100.0	78.3	61.0	9.9	7.4	21.7	8.7	5.1	7.9
1989	100.0	78.9	61.1	10.7	7.1	21.1	8.5	5.3	7.3
1990	100.0	78.9	60.6	11.1	7.2	21.2	8.6	5.3	7.3
1991	100.0	78.4	60.3	10.9	7.2	21.7	9.0	5.2	7.5
1992	100.0	78.2	60.9	10.1	7.2	21.7	9.2	5.1	7.4
1993	100.0	78.0	61.2	9.6	7.2	22.1	9.4	5.0	7.7
1994	100.0	78.0	61.9	9.4	6.7	21.8	9.3	5.0	7.5
1995	100.0	78.8	63.1	9.3	6.4	21.2	9.1	4.9	7.2
1996	100.0	79.0	63.5	9.1	6.4	21.0	9.4	4.7	6.9
1997	100.0	79.1	64.3	8.7	6.1	20.9	9.6	4.6	6.7
1998	100.0	80.0	65.8	8.4	5.8	20.1	9.3	4.5	6.3
1999	100.0	80.3	66.0	8.3	6.0	19.7	9.2	4.3	6.2
MEN									
1987	100.0	86.4	68.0	10.9	7.5	13.6	4.7	3.2	5.7
1988	100.0	86.5	69.0	10.5	7.0	13.6	5.0	3.1	5.5
1989	100.0	86.8	69.4	10.7	6.7	13.3	5.1	3.1	5.1
1990	100.0	86.6	68.3	11.4	6.9	13.4	5.1	3.2	5.1
1991	100.0	86.0	66.8	11.6	7.6	14.0	5.3	3.3	5.4
1992	100.0	85.8	67.1	11.1	7.6	14.3	5.4	3.3	5.6
1993	100.0	85.8	68.4	10.0	7.4	14.2	5.5	2.9	5.8
1994	100.0	86.0	69.7	9.6	6.7	13.9	5.3	3.2	5.4
1995	100.0	86.3	70.8	9.4	6.1	13.7	5.4	3.0	5.3
1996	100.0	86.3	71.0	9.1	6.2	13.7	5.7	2.8	5.2
1997	100.0	86.5	71.9	8.7	5.9	13.6	5.6	3.0	5.0
1998	100.0	87.4	74.0	8.1	5.3	12.6	5.5	2.7	4.4
1999	100.0	87.5	73.6	8.2	5.7	12.5	5.5	2.6	4.4
WOMEN									
1987	100.0	68.6	50.7	9.9	8.0	31.4	13.0	7.4	11.0
1988	100.0	68.9	51.8	9.2	7.9	31.1	13.1	7.3	10.7
1989	100.0	69.9	51.4	10.8	7.7	30.0	12.5	7.7	9.8
1990	100.0	69.9	51.6	10.7	7.6	30.2	12.8	7.6	9.8
1991	100.0	69.4	52.6	10.0	6.8	30.7	13.2	7.6	9.9
1992	100.0	69.7	53.7	9.1	6.9	30.4	13.7	7.2	9.5
1993	100.0	69.0	52.9	9.0	7.1	31.0	13.9	7.3	9.8
1994	100.0	69.0	53.0	9.2	6.8	30.9	13.9	7.1	9.9
1995	100.0	70.3	54.3	9.2	6.8	29.7	13.3	7.0	9.4
1996	100.0	70.7	54.9	9.2	6.6	29.3	13.6	6.8	8.9
1997	100.0	70.7	55.8	8.7	6.2	29.4	14.2	6.4	8.8
1998	100.0	71.6	56.5	8.7	6.4	28.4	13.6	6.4	8.4
1999	100.0	72.3	57.6	8.4	6.3	27.7	13.4	6.1	8.2

Note: See "Notes and Definitions" for information on historical comparability.

Table 1-38. Extent of Unemployment During the Year by Sex, 1987–1999

(Thousands of persons, percent.)

Sex and extent of unemployment	1987	1988	1989	1990	1991	1992	1993	1994	1995	1996	1997	1998	1999
TOTAL													
Total Who Worked Or Looked For Work	130 353	132 185	134 394	135 408	135 826	136 654	139 786	141 325	142 413	144 528	146 096	147 295	149 798
Percent with unemployment	14.1	12.9	12.9	14.6	15.7	15.7	14.7	13.4	12.7	11.6	10.7	9.5	8.7
Total With Unemployment	18 399	17 096	17 273	19 809	21 276	21 455	20 527	18 966	18 067	16 789	15 637	14 044	13 068
Did not work but looked for work	2 037	1 735	1 577	1 874	2 415	2 742	3 432	2 857	2 690	2 329	2 129	1 729	1 503
Worked during the year	16 362	15 362	15 697	17 936	18 861	18 714	17 094	16 109	15 377	14 460	13 508	12 316	11 566
Year-round workers with 1 or 2 weeks of unemployment	792	830	833	1 056	966	871	688	746	715	589	611	630	562
Part-year workers with unemployment	15 570	14 532	14 864	16 880	17 895	17 843	16 406	15 363	14 662	13 871	12 897	11 686	11 004
1 to 4 weeks	3 363	3 256	3 489	3 645	3 224	2 944	2 626	2 788	2 812	2 550	2 582	2 323	2 361
5 to 10 weeks	3 191	3 148	3 359	3 669	3 655	3 496	2 898	2 983	2 725	2 671	2 601	2 495	2 218
11 to 14 weeks	2 258	2 128	2 235	2 501	2 587	2 574	2 300	2 265	2 147	2 020	1 822	1 701	1 594
15 to 26 weeks	3 904	3 479	3 600	4 316	4 927	4 877	4 549	4 158	4 013	3 662	3 378	3 019	2 803
27 weeks or more	2 854	2 521	2 181	2 749	3 502	3 952	4 033	3 169	2 965	2 968	2 514	2 148	2 028
With two spells or more of unemployment	5 149	5 136	5 073	5 811	5 864	5 734	5 338	4 783	4 468	4 237	4 044	3 628	3 225
2 spells	2 442	2 460	2 460	2 855	2 738	2 698	2 572	2 207	1 963	1 982	1 853	1 650	1 449
3 spells or more	2 707	2 676	2 613	2 956	3 126	3 036	2 766	2 576	2 505	2 255	2 191	1 978	1 776
MEN													
Total Who Worked Or Looked For Work	69 995	70 738	72 362	72 844	72 909	73 387	74 516	75 244	75 698	76 786	77 385	77 704	78 905
Percent with unemployment	15.0	13.7	13.5	15.5	17.3	17.5	15.7	14.1	13.2	11.9	11.1	9.4	9.0
Total With Unemployment	10 504	9 696	9 792	11 307	12 642	12 844	11 723	10 582	9 996	9 157	8 604	7 284	7 091
Did not work but looked for work	852	717	723	891	1 210	1 379	1 641	1 286	1 317	1 026	978	787	760
Worked during the year	9 653	8 978	9 071	10 415	11 432	11 466	10 082	9 296	8 679	8 130	7 626	6 497	6 332
Year-round workers with 1 or 2 weeks of unemployment	536	585	568	711	612	567	449	527	462	395	382	386	373
Part-year workers with unemployment	9 117	8 393	8 503	9 704	10 820	10 899	9 633	8 769	8 217	7 735	7 244	6 111	5 959
1 to 4 weeks	1 561	1 633	1 742	1 819	1 591	1 563	1 343	1 365	1 398	1 272	1 275	1 085	1 166
5 to 10 weeks	1 824	1 808	1 890	2 041	2 111	2 039	1 647	1 666	1 434	1 478	1 474	1 363	1 168
11 to 14 weeks	1 415	1 279	1 365	1 462	1 659	1 615	1 354	1 370	1 253	1 258	1 068	980	937
15 to 26 weeks	2 514	2 124	2 188	2 645	3 206	3 165	2 862	2 449	2 439	2 076	1 949	1 585	1 655
27 weeks or more	1 803	1 549	1 318	1 737	2 253	2 517	2 427	1 919	1 693	1 651	1 478	1 098	1 033
With two spells or more of unemployment	3 300	3 366	3 178	3 689	3 886	3 889	3 451	2 940	2 793	2 554	2 437	2 014	1 845
2 spells	1 488	1 560	1 517	1 676	1 742	1 781	1 580	1 266	1 110	1 109	1 078	880	707
3 spells or more	1 812	1 806	1 661	2 013	2 144	2 108	1 871	1 674	1 683	1 445	1 359	1 134	1 058
WOMEN													
Total Who Worked Or Looked For Work	60 357	61 447	62 032	62 564	62 917	63 267	65 270	66 081	66 716	67 742	68 710	69 591	70 893
Percent with unemployment	13.1	12.0	12.1	13.6	13.7	13.6	13.5	12.7	12.1	11.3	10.2	9.7	8.4
Total With Unemployment	7 895	7 400	7 481	8 502	8 634	8 611	8 804	8 383	8 070	7 632	7 033	6 760	5 976
Did not work but looked for work	1 185	1 017	854	982	1 205	1 363	1 791	1 570	1 373	1 303	1 151	942	743
Worked during the year	6 710	6 382	6 628	7 520	7 427	7 247	7 014	6 813	6 696	6 330	5 882	5 816	5 234
Year-round workers with 1 or 2 weeks of unemployment	255	244	265	344	354	304	239	219	253	194	229	243	189
Part-year workers with unemployment	6 455	6 138	6 363	7 176	7 073	6 943	6 775	6 594	6 443	6 136	5 653	5 573	5 045
1 to 4 weeks	1 802	1 623	1 747	1 827	1 633	1 380	1 284	1 422	1 413	1 279	1 307	1 237	1 194
5 to 10 weeks	1 368	1 340	1 469	1 627	1 544	1 457	1 252	1 317	1 291	1 192	1 127	1 131	1 050
11 to 14 weeks	844	849	870	1 038	927	959	946	896	893	762	754	721	657
15 to 26 weeks	1 391	1 354	1 413	1 671	1 720	1 712	1 687	1 708	1 574	1 586	1 429	1 434	1 148
27 weeks or more	1 050	972	864	1 013	1 249	1 435	1 606	1 251	1 272	1 317	1 036	1 050	996
With two spells or more of unemployment	1 848	1 769	1 895	2 122	1 979	1 844	1 887	1 843	1 675	1 682	1 607	1 614	1 379
2 spells	954	899	943	1 179	997	916	992	941	853	872	775	770	662
3 spells or more	895	870	952	943	982	928	895	902	822	810	832	844	717

Note: See "Notes and Definitions" for information on historical comparability.

Table 1-39. Percent Distribution of Persons with Unemployment During the Year by Sex and Extent of Unemployment, 1987–1999

Sex and extent of unemployment	1987	1988	1989	1990	1991	1992	1993	1994	1995	1996	1997	1998	1999
TOTAL													
Total With Unemployment Who Worked During The Year	100.0	100.0	100.0	100.0	100.0	100.0	100.0	100.0	100.0	100.0	100.0	100.0	100.0
Year-round workers with 1 or 2 weeks of unemployment	4.8	5.4	5.3	5.9	5.1	4.7	4.0	4.6	4.6	4.1	4.5	5.1	4.9
Part-year workers with unemployment	95.2	94.5	94.6	94.1	94.8	95.4	96.1	95.4	95.4	96.0	95.5	95.0	95.1
1 to 4 weeks	20.6	21.2	22.2	20.3	17.1	15.7	15.4	17.3	18.3	17.6	19.1	18.9	20.4
5 to 10 weeks	19.5	20.5	21.4	20.5	19.4	18.7	17.0	18.5	17.7	18.5	19.3	20.3	19.2
11 to 14 weeks	13.8	13.8	14.2	13.9	13.7	13.8	13.5	14.1	14.0	14.0	13.5	13.8	13.8
15 to 26 weeks	23.9	22.6	22.9	24.1	26.1	26.1	26.6	25.8	26.1	25.3	25.0	24.5	24.2
27 weeks or more	17.4	16.4	13.9	15.3	18.5	21.1	23.6	19.7	19.3	20.6	18.6	17.5	17.5
With two spells or more of unemployment	31.4	33.4	32.3	32.4	31.1	30.6	31.2	29.7	29.1	29.3	29.9	29.5	27.9
2 spells	14.9	16.0	15.7	15.9	14.5	14.4	15.0	13.7	12.8	13.7	13.7	13.4	12.5
3 spells or more	16.5	17.4	16.6	16.5	16.6	16.2	16.2	16.0	16.3	15.6	16.2	16.1	15.4
MEN													
Total With Unemployment Who Worked During The Year	100.0	100.0	100.0	100.0	100.0	100.0	100.0	100.0	100.0	100.0	100.0	100.0	100.0
Year-round workers with 1 or 2 weeks of unemployment	5.6	6.5	6.3	6.8	5.4	4.9	4.4	5.7	5.3	4.9	5.0	5.9	5.9
Part-year workers with unemployment	94.5	93.4	93.7	93.2	94.6	95.0	95.5	94.3	94.7	95.1	95.1	94.1	94.0
1 to 4 weeks	16.2	18.2	19.2	17.5	13.9	13.6	13.3	14.7	16.1	15.6	16.7	16.7	18.4
5 to 10 weeks	18.9	20.1	20.8	19.6	18.5	17.8	16.3	17.9	16.5	18.2	19.3	21.0	18.4
11 to 14 weeks	14.7	14.2	15.1	14.0	14.5	14.1	13.4	14.7	14.4	15.5	14.0	15.1	14.8
15 to 26 weeks	26.0	23.7	24.1	25.4	28.0	27.6	28.4	26.4	28.1	25.5	25.6	24.4	26.1
27 weeks or more	18.7	17.2	14.5	16.7	19.7	21.9	24.1	20.6	19.5	20.3	19.4	16.9	16.3
With two spells or more of unemployment	34.2	37.5	35.0	35.4	34.0	33.9	34.3	31.6	32.2	31.4	31.9	31.0	29.1
2 spells	15.4	17.4	16.7	16.1	15.2	15.5	15.7	13.6	12.8	13.6	14.1	13.5	12.4
3 spells or more	18.8	20.1	18.3	19.3	18.8	18.4	18.6	18.0	19.4	17.8	17.8	17.5	16.7
WOMEN													
Total With Unemployment Who Worked During The Year	100.0	100.0	100.0	100.0	100.0	100.0	100.0	100.0	100.0	100.0	100.0	100.0	100.0
Year-round workers with 1or 2 weeks of unemployment	3.8	3.8	4.0	4.6	4.8	4.2	3.4	3.2	3.8	3.1	3.9	4.2	3.6
Part-year workers with unemployment	96.3	96.1	96.0	95.3	95.3	95.7	96.6	96.7	96.2	96.9	96.1	95.8	96.4
1 to 4 weeks	26.9	25.4	26.4	24.3	22.0	19.0	18.3	20.9	21.1	20.2	22.2	21.3	22.8
5 to 10 weeks	20.4	21.0	22.2	21.6	20.8	20.1	17.8	19.3	19.3	18.8	19.2	19.4	20.1
11 to 14 weeks	12.6	13.3	13.1	13.8	12.5	13.2	13.5	13.1	13.3	12.0	12.8	12.4	12.6
15 to 26 weeks	20.7	21.2	21.3	22.2	23.2	23.6	24.1	25.1	23.5	25.1	24.3	24.7	21.9
27 weeks or more	15.7	15.2	13.0	13.4	16.8	19.8	22.9	18.3	19.0	20.8	17.6	18.0	19.0
With two spells or more of unemployment	27.5	27.7	28.6	28.2	26.6	25.4	26.9	27.0	25.0	26.6	27.3	27.7	26.3
2 spells	14.2	14.1	14.2	15.7	13.4	12.6	14.1	13.8	12.7	13.8	13.2	13.2	12.6
3 spells or more	13.3	13.6	14.4	12.5	13.2	12.8	12.8	13.2	12.3	12.8	14.1	14.5	13.7

Note: See "Notes and Definitions" for information on historical comparability.

Table 1-40. Number and Median Annual Earnings of Year-Round Full-Time Wage and Salary Workers by Age, Sex, and Race, 1987–1999

(Thousands of persons, dollars.)

Age, sex and race	1987	1988	1989	1990	1991	1992	1993	1994	1995	1996	1997	1998	1999
NUMBER													
Total, 16 Years And Over	71 069	73 598	74 898	74 728	74 449	75 517	77 427	79 875	83 407	85 611	86 905	89 748	91 722
16 to 24 years	7 563	7 400	7 471	6 978	6 571	6 224	6 685	6 684	6 892	6 809	7 063	7 618	7 631
25 to 44 years	42 211	44 036	45 082	45 086	44 811	45 022	45 951	47 150	48 695	49 225	49 513	50 264	50 532
25 to 34 years	22 884	23 727	23 721	23 201	22 541	22 469	22 637	23 193	23 310	23 071	23 186	23 048	22 952
35 to 44 years	19 327	20 309	21 361	21 885	22 270	22 553	23 314	23 957	25 385	26 154	26 327	27 216	27 580
45 to 54 years	12 764	13 506	13 848	14 070	14 718	15 652	16 424	17 366	18 436	19 714	20 109	21 274	22 375
55 to 64 years	7 406	7 529	7 321	7 458	7 219	7 590	7 208	7 500	8 122	8 455	8 901	9 273	9 594
65 years and over	1 125	1 127	1 177	1 137	1 130	1 029	1 159	1 174	1 263	1 408	1 318	1 318	1 590
Men, 16 Years And Over	42 490	43 785	45 107	44 574	43 523	43 894	45 494	47 255	49 334	50 407	50 772	52 509	53 132
16 to 24 years	4 145	4 165	4 223	3 982	3 596	3 457	3 853	3 918	4 094	3 942	4 021	4 479	4 347
25 to 44 years	25 293	26 246	27 321	27 069	26 353	26 335	27 161	28 000	28 940	29 282	29 453	29 763	29 738
25 to 34 years	13 659	14 163	14 439	13 941	13 303	13 146	13 400	13 749	13 844	13 817	13 735	13 612	13 471
35 to 44 years	11 634	12 083	12 882	13 128	13 050	13 189	13 761	14 251	15 096	15 465	15 718	16 151	16 267
45 to 54 years	7 726	8 086	8 276	8 168	8 479	8 908	9 522	10 120	10 589	11 372	11 388	12 030	12 546
55 to 64 years	4 654	4 616	4 562	4 650	4 403	4 588	4 238	4 460	4 884	4 908	5 133	5 438	5 498
65 years and over	672	672	725	705	694	606	719	757	827	903	775	801	1 003
Women, 16 Years And Over	28 579	29 812	29 791	30 155	30 925	31 622	31 933	32 619	34 073	35 203	36 133	37 239	38 591
16 to 24 years	3 418	3 235	3 249	2 995	2 976	2 767	2 832	2 767	2 798	2 867	3 041	3 140	3 285
25 to 44 years	16 918	17 790	17 760	18 017	18 458	18 688	18 790	19 150	19 755	19 942	20 060	20 503	20 794
25 to 34 years	9 225	9 564	9 282	9 260	9 238	9 323	9 237	9 444	9 467	9 254	9 451	9 437	9 481
35 to 44 years	7 693	8 226	8 478	8 757	9 220	9 365	9 553	9 706	10 288	10 688	10 609	11 066	11 313
45 to 54 years	5 037	5 420	5 572	5 902	6 239	6 744	6 902	7 246	7 847	8 343	8 721	9 244	9 829
55 to 64 years	2 752	2 913	2 758	2 808	2 816	3 002	2 970	3 040	3 238	3 547	3 767	3 836	4 096
65 years and over	453	455	451	433	436	423	439	417	436	505	543	517	586
White, 16 Years And Over	61 546	63 357	64 246	64 128	63 926	64 706	65 656	67 370	70 430	72 068	72 650	75 046	76 203
Men	37 461	38 449	39 430	38 915	38 018	38 267	39 347	40 589	42 608	43 554	43 429	44 901	45 211
Women	24 085	24 908	24 815	25 213	25 908	26 439	26 309	26 782	27 822	28 514	29 221	30 145	30 992
Black, 16 Years And Over	7 440	7 007	8 140	8 027	7 041	7 995	8 478	9 074	9 446	9 706	10 248	10 532	11 145
Men	3 838	3 976	4 219	4 162	[illegible]	4 011	[illegible]	4 598	4 686	[illegible]	5 026	5 202	5 411
Women	3 602	3 931	3 920	3 865	3 940	3 984	4 219	4 476	4 759	5 024	5 222	[illegible]	5 734
MEDIAN ANNUAL EARNINGS													
Total, 16 Years And Over	$21 000	$22 000	$23 000	$24 000	$25 000	$25 871	$26 000	$26 620	$27 000	$28 000	$30 000	$30 000	$31 000
16 to 24 years	13 000	13 500	14 000	14 400	14 100	15 000	15 000	15 000	15 500	15 600	16 000	18 000	18 000
25 to 34 years	20 000	21 000	22 000	22 000	23 000	24 000	24 000	24 480	25 000	25 300	27 000	28 500	30 000
35 to 44 years	25 000	26 000	27 000	27 970	28 000	29 483	30 000	30 000	30 000	31 000	32 000	33 000	34 992
45 to 54 years	25 000	26 000	27 000	28 000	29 000	30 000	30 500	32 343	32 000	33 000	35 000	35 000	36 000
55 to 64 years	23 000	24 000	26 000	26 000	27 000	27 430	28 000	30 000	30 000	30 000	32 000	34 000	35 000
65 years and over	18 000	19 500	23 000	23 841	22 000	24 000	24 000	24 377	29 600	26 496	28 200	26 000	30 000
Men, 16 Years And Over	25 900	26 570	27 300	28 000	29 120	30 000	30 000	30 000	31 000	32 000	34 000	35 000	36 000
16 to 24 years	14 000	14 200	15 000	15 000	15 000	15 000	15 000	15 000	16 000	17 000	17 000	18 720	19 000
25 to 34 years	23 000	24 000	24 000	25 000	25 000	26 000	25 000	26 000	27 000	28 000	29 852	30 000	32 000
35 to 44 years	30 000	31 000	32 000	32 000	33 000	34 000	35 000	35 000	35 000	36 000	37 000	38 000	40 000
45 to 54 years	31 200	32 000	34 000	35 000	36 000	37 000	38 000	40 000	40 000	40 000	41 000	42 000	44 616
55 to 64 years	29 181	30 000	32 000	31 875	33 000	33 000	34 000	36 000	36 000	36 000	39 000	40 000	40 853
65 years and over	24 000	25 000	30 000	29 000	28 000	30 000	28 000	30 000	36 000	33 000	36 400	35 000	36 000
Women, 16 Years And Over	17 000	18 000	18 574	20 000	20 000	21 500	22 000	22 150	23 000	24 000	25 000	25 000	26 000
16 to 24 years	12 000	13 000	13 167	13 392	13 800	14 000	14 872	14 560	15 000	15 000	15 000	17 000	17 000
25 to 34 years	17 000	18 000	19 000	19 500	20 000	21 000	21 000	22 000	22 000	23 000	24 000	25 000	26 000
35 to 44 years	19 000	20 000	20 200	22 000	22 510	23 397	24 000	25 000	25 000	25 000	26 000	27 200	28 000
45 to 54 years	18 148	19 000	20 000	21 000	22 000	24 000	24 000	25 000	25 000	26 000	27 040	28 132	30 000
55 to 64 years	17 000	17 000	18 000	19 000	20 000	22 000	21 500	22 000	22 500	24 000	24 800	25 775	27 000
65 years and over	16 000	15 600	17 566	18 586	17 000	18 500	20 000	19 000	23 290	20 800	24 000	22 000	20 800
White, 16 Years And Over	22 000	23 000	24 000	25 000	25 000	26 200	27 000	28 000	28 000	29 000	30 000	31 000	32 000
Men	26 500	27 489	28 500	29 000	30 000	31 000	30 700	32 000	32 000	33 000	35 000	36 000	37 200
Women	17 000	18 000	19 000	20 000	20 500	22 000	22 000	23 000	23 000	24 000	25 000	26 000	27 000
Black, 16 Years And Over	17 000	18 000	19 000	19 350	20 000	21 000	20 800	21 000	22 000	23 784	24 000	25 000	25 760
Men	18 850	20 000	20 000	20 800	22 000	22 312	23 000	23 500	24 500	26 000	26 000	27 000	30 000
Women	15 500	16 200	17 115	18 000	18 500	20 000	19 843	20 000	20 000	21 000	22 000	23 000	24 000

Note: Detail for the above race groups will not sum to totals because data for the Other races group are not presented. See "Notes and Definitions" for information on historical comparability.

Table 1-41. Number and Median Annual Earnings of Year-Round Full-Time Wage and Salary Workers by Sex and Occupation of Job Held the Longest, 1987–1999

(Thousands of persons, dollars.)

Age, sex and race	1987	1988	1989	1990	1991	1992	1993	1994	1995	1996	1997	1998	1999
TOTAL, NUMBER OF WORKERS													
Managerial and professional specialty	20 802	22 213	21 972	21 996	22 037	23 479	23 682	24 816	26 215	27 377	27 943	29 250	30 033
Executive, administrative, and managerial	10 776	11 715	11 735	11 662	11 644	12 167	12 361	12 954	13 839	14 693	14 592	15 367	15 937
Professional specialty	10 026	10 498	10 237	10 334	10 393	11 312	11 321	11 862	12 376	12 684	13 351	13 883	14 096
Technical, sales, and administrative support	22 010	22 280	23 119	22 889	23 749	23 193	23 353	23 525	24 380	24 575	25 182	25 418	26 108
Technicians and related support	2 594	2 716	2 893	2 842	3 163	2 963	2 972	2 962	2 984	3 179	3 281	3 302	3 478
Sales occupations	7 381	7 565	7 856	7 605	7 665	7 826	8 120	8 484	8 989	9 170	9 186	9 537	9 802
Administrative support, including clerical	12 035	11 999	12 370	12 442	12 921	12 404	12 261	12 079	12 407	12 226	12 715	12 579	12 828
Service occupations	6 651	6 857	7 118	7 264	7 392	7 721	7 823	8 257	8 432	8 874	8 921	9 591	9 858
Private household	194	236	215	192	165	227	206	218	252	266	232	254	339
Protective service	1 398	1 551	1 637	1 639	1 674	1 761	1 748	1 776	1 756	1 746	1 886	2 078	2 002
Service, except private household and protective	5 059	5 070	5 266	5 433	5 553	5 733	5 869	6 263	6 424	6 862	6 803	7 259	7 517
Precision production, craft, and repair	9 348	9 640	9 542	9 373	8 710	8 570	9 226	9 420	9 655	10 225	10 465	10 904	10 785
Mechanics and repairers	3 466	3 550	3 395	3 519	3 345	3 168	3 449	3 420	3 590	3 799	3 751	4 045	3 939
Construction trades	2 693	2 877	2 880	2 850	2 412	2 431	2 540	2 940	3 054	3 270	3 496	3 779	3 724
Other precision production, craft, and repair	3 189	3 213	3 267	3 004	2 953	2 971	3 237	3 060	3 011	3 156	3 218	3 080	3 122
Operators, fabricators, and laborers	11 228	11 584	11 278	11 343	10 790	10 717	11 471	11 887	12 556	12 497	12 425	12 642	13 021
Machine operators, assemblers, and inspectors	5 806	5 989	5 664	5 733	5 341	5 231	5 534	5 821	6 084	6 123	6 022	5 818	5 905
Transportation and material moving occupations	3 017	3 187	3 168	3 165	3 025	3 129	3 364	3 370	3 630	3 711	3 658	3 690	3 933
Handlers, equipment cleaners, helpers, and laborers	2 405	2 408	2 446	2 445	2 424	2 357	2 573	2 696	2 842	2 663	2 745	3 134	3 183
Farming, forestry, and fishing	896	916	993	995	926	1 067	1 059	1 145	1 481	1 373	1 217	1 221	1 238
Armed forces	. . .	. . .	876	869	845	769	813	824	690	691	751	724	679
TOTAL, MEDIAN ANNUAL EARNINGS													
Managerial and professional specialty	$30 000	$30 000	$33 000	$34 000	$35 000	$35 624	$37 000	$38 300	$39 000	$40 000	$40 000	$43 000	$45 000
Executive, administrative, and managerial	30 000	30 000	33 000	33 372	35 000	35 200	36 000	38 000	39 000	39 000	41 000	43 275	45 000
Professional specialty	30 000	30 200	32 645	34 000	35 000	36 000	37 953	38 500	40 000	40 000	40 000	42 000	45 000
Technical, sales, and administrative support	19 000	19 800	20 000	21 000	22 000	23 200	24 000	24 000	24 500	25 000	26 000	27 000	28 000
Technicians and related support	24 200	25 000	25 400	27 000	27 000	28 000	30 000	30 000	30 000	31 000	31 200	34 000	35 000
Sales occupations	22 000	22 000	23 400	24 000	25 000	26 000	26 000	27 000	27 000	28 000	30 000	30 000	31 200
Administrative support, including clerical	17 000	17 500	18 200	19 500	20 000	21 000	21 000	21 700	22 000	23 000	24 000	25 000	25 000
Service occupations	13 050	14 000	15 000	15 000	15 000	16 000	16 000	16 400	17 000	17 616	18 000	18 000	19 600
Private household	6 240	7 600	7 200	7 280	9 100	10 000	8 000	10 000	10 000	10 400	13 000	12 000	11 960
Protective service	25 000	26 000	27 000	26 000	27 000	30 000	30 000	30 700	30 000	33 000	35 800	33 000	36 000
Service, except private household and protective	12 000	12 000	13 000	13 000	13 800	14 000	14 847	15 000	15 000	15 600	16 000	16 000	17 400
Precision production, craft, and repair	24 000	25 000	25 600	26 000	27 000	28 000	27 387	29 000	30 000	30 000	30 000	31 000	33 280
Mechanics and repairers	24 810	25 432	26 000	27 000	28 000	30 000	28 000	30 000	31 000	30 000	32 000	34 000	35 000
Construction trades	24 000	24 000	25 000	25 000	27 000	27 200	26 000	28 343	28 500	29 000	30 000	29 440	32 711
Other precision production, craft, and repair	24 000	25 000	26 000	25 000	27 000	28 000	27 000	28 542	29 000	30 000	30 000	30 000	31 000
Operators, fabricators, and laborers	18 000	18 045	19 500	20 000	20 000	20 770	20 000	21 000	21 000	23 000	24 000	25 000	25 000
Machine operators, assemblers, and inspectors	17 000	17 100	19 000	18 458	19 200	20 000	20 000	20 658	21 000	22 000	23 000	24 960	25 000
Transportation and material moving occupations	22 000	22 700	23 000	24 000	24 000	25 000	25 000	25 000	25 968	27 000	27 395	30 000	30 000
Handlers, equipment cleaners, helpers, and laborers	16 000	16 000	17 200	17 000	17 000	18 000	17 000	17 000	18 000	20 000	20 000	20 000	20 000
Farming, forestry, and fishing	12 000	13 000	13 600	14 000	14 400	15 000	15 600	15 028	17 000	18 000	17 000	19 000	18 200
Armed forces	. . .	. . .	19 700	19 751	20 000	22 000	24 000	25 000	24 103	26 000	27 574	30 000	29 000
MEN, NUMBER OF WORKERS													
Managerial and professional specialty	12 275	12 846	12 860	12 597	12 301	12 860	13 168	13 898	14 464	15 028	15 173	15 774	16 260
Executive, administrative, and managerial	6 656	7 070	7 187	7 061	6 887	7 100	7 166	7 554	8 031	8 406	8 240	8 552	8 978
Professional specialty	5 619	5 776	5 673	5 536	5 414	5 760	6 002	6 344	6 433	6 622	6 933	7 222	7 282
Technical, sales, and administrative support	8 736	8 856	9 320	9 048	9 322	9 306	9 312	9 562	9 965	9 884	9 977	10 281	10 306
Technicians and related support	1 468	1 524	1 561	1 567	1 666	1 585	1 454	1 540	1 454	1 620	1 561	1 698	1 712
Sales occupations	4 622	4 652	4 876	4 671	4 784	4 798	4 950	5 202	5 467	5 409	5 397	5 621	5 720
Administrative support, including clerical	2 646	2 680	2 883	2 810	2 872	2 923	2 908	2 820	3 044	2 855	3 019	2 962	2 874
Service occupations	3 435	3 540	3 804	3 947	3 938	3 933	4 066	4 210	4 310	4 554	4 581	4 762	4 879
Private household	6	13	17	9	22	25	16	13	10	9	7	9	14
Protective service	1 279	1 373	1 459	1 442	1 416	1 528	1 508	1 560	1 526	1 483	1 596	1 728	1 715
Service, except private household and protective	2 150	2 154	2 328	2 496	2 500	2 380	2 542	2 637	2 774	3 062	2 978	3 025	3 150
Precision production, craft, and repair	8 587	8 887	8 749	8 610	8 021	7 891	8 316	8 651	8 882	9 411	9 645	10 008	9 766
Mechanics and repairers	3 334	3 416	3 271	3 385	3 227	3 057	3 280	3 272	3 451	3 638	3 598	3 851	3 722
Construction trades	2 663	2 806	2 825	2 815	2 391	2 410	2 491	2 890	3 018	3 230	3 456	3 715	3 652
Other precision production, craft, and repair	2 590	2 665	2 653	2 410	2 403	2 424	2 545	2 489	2 413	2 543	2 591	2 442	2 392
Operators, fabricators, and laborers	8 525	8 747	8 653	8 699	8 295	8 197	8 940	9 149	9 761	9 700	9 656	9 929	10 213
Machine operators, assemblers, and inspectors	3 612	3 681	3 554	3 657	3 443	3 295	3 608	3 787	4 010	4 002	3 961	3 893	3 966
Transportation and material moving occupations	2 876	3 029	2 990	3 002	2 872	2 935	3 150	3 141	3 403	3 483	3 412	3 440	3 659
Handlers, equipment cleaners, helpers, and laborers	2 037	2 037	2 109	2 040	1 980	1 967	2 182	2 221	2 348	2 215	2 283	2 596	2 588
Farming, forestry, and fishing	810	817	891	887	847	979	948	1 022	1 295	1 207	1 082	1 088	1 095
Armed forces	. . .	. . .	830	787	801	728	745	762	658	625	657	667	612

See *Note* at end of table.

Table 1-41. Number and Median Annual Earnings of Year-Round Full-Time Wage and Salary Workers by Sex and Occupation of Job Held the Longest, 1987–1999—*Continued*

(Thousands of persons, dollars.)

Age, sex and race	1987	1988	1989	1990	1991	1992	1993	1994	1995	1996	1997	1998	1999
MEN, MEDIAN ANNUAL EARNINGS													
Managerial and professional specialty	$36 000	$37 000	$39 500	$40 000	$42 000	$43 000	$44 000	$45 613	$47 000	$48 000	$50 000	$50 700	$55 000
Executive, administrative, and managerial	37 000	37 299	40 000	41 000	42 000	44 000	45 000	46 000	47 500	47 100	50 000	52 000	55 000
Professional specialty	35 000	36 500	38 000	40 000	42 000	42 270	43 995	45 000	47 000	48 000	50 000	50 000	53 250
Technical, sales, and administrative support	26 000	26 050	28 000	29 000	30 000	30 000	31 000	31 197	32 000	33 600	34 000	35 000	37 000
Technicians and related support	29 000	30 000	31 000	30 300	31 100	33 000	34 000	35 000	35 000	36 000	38 000	40 000	41 000
Sales occupations	27 500	27 000	29 000	30 000	30 000	32 000	33 000	34 000	35 000	35 000	35 000	37 800	38 027
Administrative support, including clerical	23 860	24 000	25 000	25 220	27 000	27 000	26 632	27 000	27 286	30 000	29 000	30 000	31 400
Service occupations	17 466	18 000	18 400	18 000	19 315	20 000	20 000	20 500	21 000	20 400	22 000	23 000	24 000
Private household	6 000	11 200	11 000	14 000	9 600	10 800	18 000	5 000	12 318	9 000	10 000	13 000	13 000
Protective service	25 800	27 000	28 000	27 000	28 500	30 000	30 000	32 800	32 400	34 000	37 000	35 000	38 000
Service, except private household and protective	14 000	15 000	15 000	15 000	16 000	15 600	16 000	17 000	17 000	18 000	18 000	18 000	20 000
Precision production, craft, and repair	25 000	25 434	26 000	27 000	28 000	29 000	28 000	30 000	30 000	30 000	31 200	32 000	35 000
Mechanics and repairers	24 403	25 000	26 000	27 000	28 000	30 000	28 000	30 000	31 000	30 000	32 000	34 000	35 000
Construction trades	24 000	24 500	25 000	25 000	27 000	27 116	26 000	28 600	28 500	29 000	30 000	29 097	32 760
Other precision production, craft, and repair	26 000	27 000	29 000	28 000	30 000	30 000	30 000	30 000	31 200	33 000	33 800	35 000	35 000
Operators, fabricators, and laborers	20 000	20 500	21 000	22 000	22 000	23 000	23 000	23 000	23 500	25 000	26 000	26 500	26 400
Machine operators, assemblers, and inspectors	20 246	21 000	22 000	22 000	23 500	24 000	23 400	24 000	24 000	25 000	27 000	27 935	28 600
Transportation and material moving occupations	22 071	23 800	23 200	24 000	24 960	25 000	26 000	25 500	26 000	27 250	28 000	30 000	30 000
Handlers, equipment cleaners, helpers, and laborers	16 500	16 858	18 000	18 000	17 053	18 144	17 623	18 000	18 824	20 000	21 000	21 000	20 800
Farming, forestry, and fishing	12 000	13 400	14 000	14 000	15 000	15 000	15 600	16 000	17 350	18 000	17 000	19 500	19 084
Armed forces	. . .	. . .	20 000	19 200	20 700	22 202	24 748	25 000	24 103	26 000	28 000	30 000	30 000
WOMEN, NUMBER OF WORKERS													
Managerial and professional specialty	8 527	9 367	9 113	9 398	9 736	10 618	10 515	10 918	11 751	12 349	12 769	13 476	13 773
Executive, administrative, and managerial	4 120	4 645	4 548	4 600	4 757	5 067	5 195	5 400	5 808	6 287	6 352	6 815	6 959
Professional specialty	4 407	4 722	4 565	4 798	4 979	5 551	5 320	5 518	5 943	6 062	6 417	6 661	6 814
Technical, sales, and administrative support	13 273	13 425	13 800	13 842	14 427	13 888	14 041	13 962	14 415	14 691	15 206	15 135	15 801
Technicians and related support	1 126	1 192	1 332	1 275	1 497	1 379	1 518	1 422	1 530	1 559	1 721	1 604	1 765
Sales occupations	2 759	2 913	2 981	2 934	2 882	3 028	3 170	3 281	3 522	3 761	3 789	3 915	4 082
Administrative support, including clerical	9 388	9 320	9 487	9 633	10 048	9 481	9 353	9 259	9 363	9 371	9 696	9 616	9 954
Service occupations	3 216	3 318	3 313	3 318	3 455	3 787	3 758	4 048	4 120	4 320	4 340	4 829	4 979
Private household	188	224	197	183	144	202	190	206	241	257	225	245	325
Protective service	119	179	178	197	258	232	241	216	229	263	290	350	287
Service, except private household and protective	2 909	2 915	2 938	2 938	3 050	3 353	3 327	3 626	3 650	3 800	3 825	4 234	4 367
Precision production, craft, and repair	761	753	793	764	689	679	910	770	773	813	821	897	1 019
Mechanics and repairers	132	134	124	134	118	111	169	148	139	160	154	194	217
Construction trades	30	71	55	36	21	21	49	50	36	40	40	64	72
Other precision production, craft, and repair	599	548	614	594	550	547	692	572	598	613	627	639	730
Operators, fabricators, and laborers	2 703	2 836	2 625	2 644	2 495	2 521	2 531	2 738	2 795	2 796	2 769	2 713	2 810
Machine operators, assemblers, and inspectors	2 194	2 308	2 110	2 076	1 898	1 936	1 926	2 034	2 074	2 121	2 061	1 925	1 940
Transportation and material moving occupations	141	157	178	163	153	195	214	229	227	227	246	250	274
Handlers, equipment cleaners, helpers, and laborers	368	371	337	405	444	390	391	475	494	448	462	538	590
Farming, forestry, and fishing	87	99	102	108	79	88	111	123	187	166	135	133	143
Armed forces	. . .	. . .	45	83	45	41	68	62	32	67	94	57	67
WOMEN, MEDIAN ANNUAL EARNINGS													
Managerial and professional specialty	$23 000	$25 000	$26 000	$27 500	$29 000	$29 863	$30 000	$31 000	$32 000	$32 000	$34 500	$35 000	$37 000
Executive, administrative, and managerial	22 000	23 500	24 755	25 400	27 000	28 000	29 000	30 000	30 000	31 000	33 600	35 000	36 000
Professional specialty	24 328	25 000	28 000	29 000	30 000	30 000	32 000	32 000	33 000	34 000	35 000	35 500	38 000
Technical, sales, and administrative support	16 000	16 600	17 594	18 500	19 111	20 000	20 000	21 000	21 000	22 000	23 000	24 000	24 960
Technicians and related support	19 000	20 500	21 800	24 000	22 270	24 353	26 000	27 000	26 000	27 000	27 300	28 000	29 161
Sales occupations	14 263	15 000	15 500	17 000	18 000	18 000	18 720	19 000	20 000	21 000	21 000	23 000	23 000
Administrative support, including clerical	16 000	16 376	17 500	18 000	19 000	20 000	20 000	20 260	20 800	21 840	22 500	24 000	24 000
Service occupations	10 600	11 000	12 000	12 444	12 000	13 000	13 513	13 500	14 749	15 000	15 400	15 000	16 000
Private household	6 240	7 000	7 000	7 280	7 800	9 200	8 000	10 000	10 000	10 400	13 000	12 000	11 960
Protective service	20 000	22 000	21 267	22 314	23 000	23 570	26 000	23 550	24 000	28 000	28 496	26 000	26 052
Service, except private household and protective	10 700	11 000	12 000	12 050	12 000	13 000	13 000	13 200	14 539	15 000	15 000	15 000	16 000
Precision production, craft, and repair	17 500	17 000	17 836	18 852	18 707	20 000	21 000	22 000	21 000	21 000	21 000	24 000	25 000
Mechanics and repairers	26 011	28 000	26 000	26 500	30 000	29 000	30 000	33 000	33 000	22 000	33 000	31 601	32 000
Construction trades	18 000	20 000	29 000	20 000	20 000	42 000	26 000	24 000	29 000	20 000	25 700	35 000	29 000
Other precision production, craft, and repair	15 600	15 000	16 000	17 900	17 000	18 000	20 000	20 000	19 000	20 500	19 000	21 000	22 000
Operators, fabricators, and laborers	13 000	13 000	14 000	14 300	15 000	15 000	15 000	16 000	16 000	17 000	17 200	18 500	18 200
Machine operators, assemblers, and inspectors	13 000	13 000	14 000	14 374	15 000	15 000	15 000	16 000	16 000	17 576	17 839	18 867	18 200
Transportation and material moving occupations	13 300	13 000	15 000	16 100	19 000	20 000	19 000	24 000	18 000	17 500	20 000	21 000	20 000
Handlers, equipment cleaners, helpers, and laborers	13 800	13 500	13 500	13 441	15 000	14 200	14 520	14 600	14 800	16 640	15 800	16 000	18 000
Farming, forestry, and fishing	10 000	10 400	12 000	11 799	12 200	13 000	15 600	10 700	16 000	18 000	17 000	15 600	15 000
Armed forces	. . .	. . .	14 000	22 000	14 000	18 500	18 300	24 000	25 000	22 000	25 000	28 000	26 000

Note: See "Notes and Definitions" for information on historical comparability.

Table 1-42. Wage and Salary Workers Paid Hourly Rates with Earnings at or below the Prevailing Federal Minimum Wage by Selected Characteristics, 1999–2000

(Thousands of persons, percent.)

Characteristic	Workers paid hourly rates				
	Total	Below prevailing federal minimum wage	At prevailing federal minimum wage	Total at or below prevailing federal minimum wage	
				Number	Percent of hourly-paid workers
1999					
Sex And Age					
Total, 16 years and over	72 306	2 194	1 146	3 340	4.6
16 to 24 years	16 636	1 064	632	1 695	10.2
25 years and over	55 670	1 130	514	1 644	3.0
Men, 16 years and over	36 073	768	446	1 214	3.4
16 to 24 years	8 556	410	289	699	8.2
25 years and over	27 517	358	157	515	1.9
Women, 16 years and over	36 233	1 426	700	2 126	5.9
16 to 24 years	8 080	654	343	996	12.3
25 years and over	28 153	772	357	1 129	4.0
Race, Hispanic Origin, And Sex					
White, 16 years and over	58 999	1 803	895	2 698	4.6
Men	29 906	602	356	958	3.2
Women	29 093	1 200	539	1 740	6.0
Black, 16 years and over	10 126	298	217	516	5.1
Men	4 632	126	74	199	4.3
Women	5 494	173	144	316	5.8
Hispanic origin, 16 years and over	9 402	275	238	513	5.5
Men	5 490	126	105	232	4.2
Women	3 913	148	133	281	7.2
Full-And Part-Time Status And Sex[1]					
Full-time workers	54 931	948	372	1 320	2.4
Men	30 582	383	169	552	1.8
Women	24 349	565	203	768	3.2
Part-time workers	17 227	1 238	772	2 011	11.7
Men	5 410	383	276	659	12.2
Women	11 817	855	496	1 351	11.4
2000					
Sex And Age					
Total, 16 years and over	72 744	1 844	866	2 710	3.7
16 to 24 years	16 938	938	510	1 447	8.5
25 years and over	55 806	906	357	1 263	2.3
Men, 16 years and over	36 228	632	322	954	2.6
16 to 24 years	8 743	346	202	548	6.3
25 years and over	27 485	286	120	406	1.5
Women, 16 years and over	36 516	1 212	544	1 757	4.8
16 to 24 years	8 194	592	308	899	11.0
25 years and over	28 321	621	237	857	3.0
Race, Hispanic Origin, And Sex					
White, 16 years and over	59 374	1 555	687	2 242	3.8
Men	29 970	506	246	752	2.5
Women	29 404	1 049	441	1 490	5.1
Black, 16 years and over	10 105	213	148	361	3.6
Men	4 648	94	63	157	3.4
Women	5 457	119	85	204	3.7
Hispanic origin, 16 years and over	9 847	189	129	318	3.2
Men	5 787	91	50	141	2.4
Women	4 060	99	78	177	4.4
Full-And Part-Time Status And Sex[1]					
Full-time workers	55 701	736	289	1 025	1.8
Men	30 856	286	113	400	1.3
Women	24 845	450	176	626	2.5
Part-time workers	16 909	1 096	577	1 673	9.9
Men	5 308	342	208	550	10.4
Women	11 601	754	369	1 123	9.7

Note: Detail for the above race and Hispanic origin groups will not sum to totals because data for the Other races groups are not presented and Hispanics are included in both the White and Black population groups.

1. The distinction between full- and part-time workers is based on the hours usually worked. These data will not sum to totals because full- or part-time status on the principal job is not identifiable for a small number of multiple jobholders.

Table 1-43. Absences from Work of Employed Full-Time Wage and Salary Workers by Age and Sex, 1999–2000

(Thousands of persons, percent.)

Age and sex	Total employed	Absence rate			Lost worktime rate [1]		
		Total	Illness or injury	Other reasons	Total	Illness or injury	Other reasons
1999							
Total, 16 Years And Over	97 740	3.8	2.8	1.0	2.0	1.5	0.6
16 to 19 years	2 256	4.0	3.0	1.0	1.8	1.3	0.5
20 to 24 years	9 131	3.9	2.7	1.2	1.9	1.2	0.7
25 years and over	86 353	3.8	2.8	1.0	2.0	1.5	0.5
25 to 54 years	76 092	3.8	2.7	1.1	2.0	1.4	0.6
55 years and over	10 261	4.2	3.5	0.7	2.6	2.3	0.3
Men, 16 Years And Over	55 161	2.8	2.2	0.6	1.5	1.2	0.3
16 to 19 years	1 352	3.1	2.4	0.7	1.4	1.1	0.3
20 to 24 years	5 112	2.6	2.1	0.5	1.3	1.0	0.2
25 years and over	48 696	2.8	2.3	0.6	1.5	1.3	0.3
25 to 54 years	42 882	2.7	2.1	0.6	1.4	1.2	0.3
55 years and over	5 814	3.6	3.1	0.5	2.2	2.0	0.2
Women, 16 Years And Over	42 579	5.1	3.5	1.6	2.7	1.8	1.0
16 to 19 years	904	5.4	3.9	1.4	2.4	1.6	0.8
20 to 24 years	4 018	5.4	3.4	2.0	2.8	1.5	1.3
25 years and over	37 657	5.1	3.5	1.6	2.7	1.8	0.9
25 to 54 years	33 210	5.1	3.4	1.7	2.7	1.7	1.0
55 years and over	4 447	5.1	4.1	0.9	3.0	2.5	0.4
2000							
Total, 16 Years And Over	99 846	3.8	2.7	1.0	2.0	1.4	0.6
16 to 19 years	2 382	4.2	3.1	1.1	1.9	1.3	0.6
20 to 24 years	9 608	4.0	2.7	1.3	1.9	1.2	0.7
25 years and over	87 856	3.8	2.7	1.0	2.0	1.5	0.5
25 to 54 years	77 120	3.7	2.7	1.1	2.0	1.4	0.6
55 years and over	10 736	3.9	3.2	0.7	2.3	2.0	0.3
Men, 16 Years And Over	56 228	2.8	2.2	0.6	1.5	1.2	0.3
16 to 19 years	1 414	3.2	2.5	0.7	1.5	1.1	0.4
20 to 24 years	5 420	2.8	2.1	0.7	1.3	1.0	0.3
25 years and over	49 394	2.7	2.2	0.6	1.5	1.2	0.3
25 to 54 years	43 353	2.7	2.1	0.6	1.4	1.2	0.3
55 years and over	6 041	3.3	2.7	0.6	2.0	1.7	0.3
Women, 16 Years And Over	43 618	5.1	3.5	1.6	2.7	1.8	1.0
16 to 19 years	908	5.6	3.9	1.7	2.6	1.5	1.1
20 to 24 years	4 188	5.5	3.5	2.0	2.7	1.5	1.2
25 years and over	38 461	5.1	3.5	1.6	2.7	1.8	0.9
25 to 54 years	33 767	5.1	3.4	1.7	2.7	1.7	1.0
55 years and over	4 694	4.8	3.9	0.9	2.6	2.3	0.4

1. Hours absent as a percent of the hours usually worked.

Table 1-44. Median Years of Tenure with Current Employer for Employed Wage and Salary Workers by Age and Sex, Selected Years, 1983–2000

Age and sex	January 1983	January 1987	January 1991	February 1996	February 1998	February 2000
TOTAL						
16 Years And Over	3.5	3.4	3.6	3.8	3.6	3.5
16 to 17 years	0.7	0.6	0.7	0.7	0.6	0.6
18 to 19 years	0.8	0.7	0.8	0.7	0.7	0.7
20 to 24 years	1.5	1.3	1.3	1.2	1.1	1.1
25 years and over	5.0	5.0	4.8	5.0	4.7	4.7
25 to 34 years	3.0	2.9	2.9	2.8	2.7	2.6
35 to 44 years	5.2	5.5	5.4	5.3	5.0	4.8
45 to 54 years	9.5	8.8	8.9	8.3	8.1	8.2
55 to 64 years	12.2	11.6	11.1	10.2	10.1	10.0
65 years and over	9.6	9.5	8.1	8.4	7.8	9.5
MEN						
16 Years And Over	4.1	4.0	4.1	4.0	3.8	3.8
16 to 17 years	0.7	0.6	0.7	0.6	0.6	0.6
18 to 19 years	0.8	0.7	0.8	0.7	0.7	0.7
20 to 24 years	1.5	1.3	1.4	1.2	1.2	1.2
25 years and over	5.9	5.7	5.4	5.3	4.9	5.0
25 to 34 years	3.2	3.1	3.1	3.0	2.8	2.7
35 to 44 years	7.3	7.0	6.5	6.1	5.5	5.4
45 to 54 years	12.8	11.8	11.2	10.1	9.4	9.5
55 to 64 years	15.3	14.5	13.4	10.5	11.2	10.2
65 years and over	8.3	8.3	7.0	8.3	7.1	9.1
WOMEN						
16 Years And Over	3.1	3.0	3.2	3.5	3.4	3.3
16 to 17 years	0.7	0.6	0.7	0.7	0.7	0.6
18 to 19 years	0.8	0.7	0.8	0.7	0.7	0.7
20 to 24 years	1.5	1.3	1.3	1.2	1.1	1.0
25 years and over	4.2	4.3	4.3	4.7	4.4	4.4
25 to 34 years	2.8	2.6	2.7	2.7	2.5	2.5
35 to 44 years	4.1	4.4	4.5	4.8	4.5	4.3
45 to 54 years	6.3	6.8	6.7	7.0	7.2	7.3
55 to 64 years	9.8	9.7	9.9	10.0	9.6	9.9
65 years and over	10.1	9.9	9.5	8.4	8.7	9.7

Note: Data exclude the incorporated and unincorporated self-employed. See "Notes and Definitions" for information on historical comparability.

Table 1-45. Median Years of Tenure with Current Employer for Employed Wage and Salary Workers by Industry, Selected Years, 1983–2000

Industry	January 1983	January 1987	January 1991	February 1996	February 1998	February 2000
TOTAL, 16 YEARS AND OVER	3.5	3.4	3.6	3.8	3.6	3.5
Agriculture	2.2	2.4	2.6	3.4	2.9	3.1
Nonagricultural Industries	3.6	3.4	3.6	3.8	3.6	3.5
Government	5.8	6.5	6.5	6.9	7.3	7.2
Private industries	3.2	3.0	3.2	3.3	3.2	3.2
Mining	3.4	6.1	5.8	6.1	5.6	6.5
Construction	2.0	2.0	2.6	2.9	2.7	2.8
Manufacturing	5.4	5.5	5.2	5.4	4.9	5.0
Durable goods [1]	5.6	6.0	5.8	5.3	4.9	4.9
Lumber and wood products	4.0	3.2	3.6	3.3	3.8	4.0
Furniture and fixtures	4.2	3.2	4.0	4.2	3.9	4.1
Stone, clay, and glass products	7.0	6.8	6.3	5.1	6.1	5.4
Primary metal industries	10.0	10.2	9.7	8.1	8.0	7.0
Fabricated metal products	5.7	5.5	5.5	5.1	4.0	4.7
Machinery and computing equipment	5.8	6.7	5.9	5.2	4.4	4.5
Electrical machinery, equipment, and supplies	4.7	4.8	5.5	4.9	5.0	4.7
Transportation equipment [1]	8.8	8.0	7.6	8.3	7.8	6.4
Motor vehicles and equipment	13.0	11.2	11.7	7.8	6.4	5.8
Aircraft and parts	6.4	6.8	6.3	9.8	9.6	9.7
Professional and photographic equipment and watches	4.7	5.9	5.1	5.1	5.5	5.2
Toys, amusements, and sporting goods	3.6	5.8	3.2	2.7	3.6	3.7
Nondurable goods [1]	5.1	4.9	4.7	5.4	4.9	5.1
Food and kindred products	5.2	4.4	4.2	5.1	5.1	5.0
Textile mill products	7.0	7.0	5.6	5.4	6.7	7.4
Apparel and other finished textile products	3.8	3.2	3.8	3.8	3.8	3.3
Paper and allied products	7.6	8.6	7.6	8.4	7.5	6.1
Printing and publishing	3.2	3.2	3.5	4.3	4.0	4.4
Chemicals and allied products	7.0	7.2	5.7	6.9	5.4	5.8
Petroleum and coal products	6.0	11.7	8.4	10.3	9.4	7.5
Rubber and miscellaneous plastics products	5.4	4.4	4.7	4.7	4.6	4.9
Transportation and public utilities	5.8	5.7	5.8	5.2	4.8	4.4
Transportation	4.6	3.9	4.2	4.1	3.8	3.9
Communications and other public utilities	8.3	8.4	9.9	8.2	8.2	5.2
Wholesale trade	3.8	3.7	3.4	3.9	4.1	3.9
Retail trade	1.9	1.8	1.9	1.9	1.8	2.0
Finance, insurance, and real estate	3.2	0.0	3.4	4.1	3.5	3.6
Banking and other finance	3.3	3.1	3.6	3.9	3.7	3.3
Insurance and real estate	3.0	2.9	3.2	4.2	3.4	3.9
Services [1]	2.5	2.5	2.7	3.0	2.9	2.9
Private households	1.8	1.7	1.9	2.3	2.3	2.9
Services, except private households	2.5	2.5	2.7	3.0	2.9	2.9
Business services	1.5	1.6	1.8	2.0	1.9	1.8
Automobile and repair services	2.3	2.0	2.2	2.9	2.4	2.7
Personal services, except private households	2.0	2.0	2.1	2.3	2.3	2.7
Entertainment and recreation services	1.8	1.8	2.3	1.9	1.9	2.3
Hospitals	3.5	4.6	4.2	5.2	5.2	5.2
Health services, except hospitals	2.5	2.4	2.7	2.9	2.9	3.2
Educational services	2.7	3.1	3.5	3.8	3.5	3.3
Social services	2.2	2.3	2.3	2.8	2.7	2.6
Other professional services	2.9	2.8	3.3	3.5	3.3	3.2

Note: Data exclude the incorporated and unincorporated self-employed. See "Notes and Definitions" for information on historical comparability.

1. Includes other industries, not shown separately.

Table 1-46. Employment Status of the Population by Marital Status and Sex, March 1989–2000

(Thousands of persons, percent.)

Marital status and year	Men						Women					
	Population	Labor force					Population	Labor force				
		Total		Employed	Unemployed			Total		Employed	Unemployed	
		Number	Percent of population		Number	Percent of labor force		Number	Percent of population		Number	Percent of labor force
SINGLE												
1989	25 714	18 867	73.4	16 999	1 868	9.9	21 153	13 969	66.0	12 843	1 126	8.1
1990	25 757	18 829	73.1	16 893	1 936	10.3	21 088	14 003	66.4	12 856	1 147	8.2
1991	26 220	19 014	72.5	16 418	2 596	13.7	21 688	14 125	65.1	12 887	1 238	8.8
1992	26 529	19 229	72.5	16 401	2 828	14.7	21 738	14 072	64.7	12 793	1 279	9.1
1993	26 951	19 625	72.8	16 858	2 767	14.1	21 848	14 091	64.5	12 711	1 380	9.8
1994	28 350	20 365	71.8	17 826	2 539	12.5	22 885	14 903	65.1	13 419	1 484	10.0
1995	28 318	20 449	72.2	18 286	2 163	10.6	22 853	14 974	65.5	13 673	1 301	8.7
1996	28 695	20 561	71.7	18 097	2 464	12.0	23 632	15 417	65.2	14 084	1 333	8.6
1997	29 294	20 942	71.5	18 683	2 259	10.8	24 215	16 178	66.8	14 747	1 431	8.8
1998	29 558	21 255	71.9	19 124	2 131	10.0	24 808	16 885	68.1	15 626	1 259	7.5
1999	29 883	21 329	71.4	19 465	1 864	8.7	25 674	17 486	68.1	16 185	1 301	7.4
2000	30 232	21 641	71.6	19 823	1 818	8.4	25 863	17 749	68.6	16 446	1 303	7.3
MARRIED, SPOUSE PRESENT												
1989	52 155	40 912	78.4	39 516	1 396	3.4	52 889	30 489	57.6	29 446	1 043	3.4
1990	52 464	41 020	78.2	39 562	1 458	3.6	53 207	30 967	58.2	29 870	1 097	3.5
1991	52 460	40 883	77.9	38 843	2 040	5.0	53 176	31 103	58.5	29 668	1 435	4.6
1992	52 780	40 930	77.5	38 650	2 280	5.6	53 464	31 686	59.3	30 130	1 556	4.9
1993	53 488	41 255	77.1	39 069	2 186	5.3	54 146	32 158	59.4	30 757	1 401	4.4
1994	53 436	40 993	76.7	39 085	1 908	4.7	54 198	32 863	60.6	31 397	1 466	4.5
1995	54 166	41 806	77.2	40 262	1 544	3.7	54 902	33 563	61.1	32 267	1 296	3.9
1996	53 996	41 837	77.5	40 356	1 481	3.5	54 640	33 382	61.1	32 258	1 124	3.4
1997	53 981	41 967	77.7	40 628	1 339	3.2	54 611	33 907	62.1	32 836	1 071	3.2
1998	54 685	42 288	77.3	41 039	1 249	3.0	55 241	34 136	61.8	33 028	1 108	3.2
1999	55 256	42 557	77.0	41 476	1 081	2.5	55 801	34 349	61.6	33 403	946	2.8
2000	55 897	43 254	77.4	42 261	993	2.3	56 432	34 959	61.9	33 998	961	2.7
WIDOWED, DIVORCED OR SEPARATED												
1989	10 641	7 108	66.8	6 552	556	7.8	23 346	10 733	46.0	10 119	614	5.7
1990	11 152	7 513	67.4	6 959	554	7.4	23 857	11 168	46.8	10 530	638	5.7
1991	11 588	7 804	67.3	6 985	819	10.5	24 105	11 145	46.2	10 386	759	6.8
1992	11 927	8 049	67.5	7 140	909	11.3	24 582	11 486	46.7	10 610	876	7.6
1993	11 861	7 956	67.1	7 055	901	11.3	24 661	11 308	45.9	10 528	780	6.9
1994	12 239	8 156	66.6	7 382	774	9.5	25 098	11 879	47.3	10 995	884	7.4
1995	12 410	8 315	67.0	7 632	683	8.2	25 373	12 001	47.3	11 308	693	5.8
1996	13 176	8 697	66.0	7 976	721	8.3	25 786	12 430	48.2	11 742	688	5.5
1997	14 113	9 420	66.7	8 715	705	7.5	26 301	12 814	48.7	12 071	743	5.8
1998	14 166	9 482	66.9	8 954	528	5.6	26 092	12 880	49.4	12 235	645	5.0
1999	14 225	9 449	66.4	8 971	478	5.1	26 199	12 951	49.4	12 307	644	5.0
2000	14 289	9 623	67.3	9 152	471	4.9	26 354	13 228	50.2	12 657	571	4.3

See *Note* at end of table.

Table 1-46. Employment Status of the Population by Marital Status and Sex, March 1989–2000—*Continued*

(Thousands of persons, percent.)

Marital status and year	Men						Women					
	Population	Labor force					Population	Labor force				
		Total		Employed	Unemployed			Total		Employed	Unemployed	
		Number	Percent of population		Number	Percent of labor force		Number	Percent of population		Number	Percent of labor force
Widowed												
1989	2 279	536	23.5	521	15	2.8	11 493	2 309	20.1	2 231	78	3.4
1990	2 331	519	22.3	490	29	5.6	11 477	2 243	19.5	2 149	94	4.2
1991	2 385	486	20.4	448	38	7.8	11 288	2 150	19.0	2 044	106	4.9
1992	2 529	566	22.4	501	65	11.5	11 325	2 131	18.8	2 029	102	4.8
1993	2 468	596	24.1	535	61	10.2	11 214	1 961	17.5	1 856	105	5.4
1994	2 220	474	21.4	440	34	7.2	11 073	1 945	17.6	1 825	120	6.2
1995	2 282	496	21.7	469	27	5.4	11 080	1 941	17.5	1 844	97	5.0
1996	2 476	487	19.7	466	21	4.3	11 070	1 916	17.3	1 820	96	5.0
1997	2 686	559	20.8	529	30	5.4	11 058	2 018	18.2	1 926	92	4.6
1998	2 567	563	21.9	551	12	2.1	11 027	2 157	19.6	2 071	86	4.0
1999	2 540	562	22.1	532	30	5.3	10 943	2 039	18.6	1 942	97	4.8
2000	2 601	583	22.4	547	36	6.2	11 061	2 011	18.2	1 911	100	5.0
Divorced												
1989	6 023	4 819	80.0	4 433	386	8.0	8 521	6 396	75.1	6 035	361	5.6
1990	6 256	5 004	80.0	4 639	365	7.3	8 845	6 678	75.5	6 333	345	5.2
1991	6 586	5 262	79.9	4 722	540	10.3	9 152	6 779	74.1	6 365	414	6.1
1992	6 743	5 418	80.3	4 823	595	11.0	9 569	7 076	73.9	6 578	498	7.0
1993	6 770	5 330	78.7	4 736	594	11.1	9 879	7 183	72.7	6 736	447	6.2
1994	7 222	5 548	76.8	5 028	520	9.4	10 113	7 473	73.9	6 962	511	6.8
1995	7 343	5 739	78.2	5 266	473	8.2	10 262	7 559	73.7	7 206	353	4.7
1996	7 734	5 954	77.0	5 468	486	8.2	10 508	7 829	74.5	7 468	361	4.6
1997	8 191	6 298	76.9	5 851	447	7.1	11 102	8 092	72.9	7 666	426	5.3
1998	8 307	6 378	76.8	6 045	333	5.2	11 065	[illegible]	72.6	7 687	351	4.4
1999	8 529	6 481	76.0	6 151	330	5.1	11 130	8 171	73.4	7 841	330	4.0
2000	8 532	6 583	77.2	6 279	304	4.6	11 061	8 505	76.9	8 217	288	3.4
Separated												
1989	2 339	1 753	74.9	1 598	155	8.8	3 332	2 028	60.9	1 853	175	8.6
1990	2 565	1 990	77.6	1 830	160	8.0	3 535	2 247	63.6	2 048	199	8.9
1991	2 616	2 057	78.6	1 816	241	11.7	3 665	2 216	60.5	1 977	239	10.8
1992	2 655	2 065	77.8	1 816	249	12.1	3 688	2 279	61.8	2 003	276	12.1
1993	2 623	2 030	77.4	1 784	246	12.1	3 568	2 165	60.7	1 937	228	10.5
1994	2 797	2 134	76.3	1 914	220	10.3	3 911	2 461	62.9	2 208	253	10.3
1995	2 784	2 081	74.7	1 898	183	8.8	4 031	2 501	62.0	2 258	243	9.7
1996	2 966	2 255	76.0	2 041	214	9.5	4 209	2 684	63.8	2 453	231	8.6
1997	3 236	2 563	79.2	2 335	228	8.9	4 141	2 705	65.3	2 480	225	8.3
1998	3 293	2 542	77.2	2 358	184	7.2	4 000	2 683	67.1	2 476	207	7.7
1999	3 156	2 405	76.2	2 287	118	4.9	4 126	2 740	66.4	2 523	217	7.9
2000	3 157	2 456	77.8	2 326	130	5.3	4 012	2 711	67.6	2 528	183	6.8

Note: See "Notes and Definitions" for information on historical comparability.

Table 1-47. Employment Status of All Women and Single Women by Presence and Age of Children, March 1988–2000

(Thousands of persons, percent.)

Age of children and year	All women							Single women						
	Civilian labor force	Civilian labor force as percent of population	Employed			Unemployed		Civilian labor force	Civilian labor force as percent of population	Employed			Unemployed	
			Number	Percent full-time	Percent part-time	Number	Percent of labor force			Number	Percent full-time	Percent part-time	Number	Percent of labor force
WOMEN WITH NO CHILDREN UNDER 18														
1988	32 490	51.2	30 911	73.6	26.4	1 580	4.9	12 417	67.3	11 538	66.7	33.3	880	7.1
1989	33 255	51.9	31 761	73.7	26.3	1 495	4.5	12 445	67.8	11 643	66.1	33.9	803	6.5
1990	33 942	52.3	32 391	74.4	25.6	1 551	4.6	12 478	68.1	11 611	65.9	34.1	866	6.9
1991	34 047	52.0	32 167	74.0	26.0	1 880	5.5	12 472	67.0	11 529	66.2	33.8	943	7.6
1992	34 487	52.3	32 481	74.3	25.7	2 006	5.8	12 355	66.9	11 374	66.6	33.4	982	7.9
1993	34 495	52.1	32 476	74.6	25.4	2 020	5.9	12 223	66.4	11 201	66.1	33.9	1 022	8.4
1994	35 454	53.1	33 343	72.7	27.3	2 110	6.0	12 737	66.8	11 674	64.5	35.5	1 063	8.3
1995	35 843	52.9	34 054	72.9	27.1	1 789	5.0	12 870	67.1	11 919	64.5	35.5	951	7.4
1996	36 509	53.0	34 698	73.3	26.7	1 811	5.0	13 172	66.1	12 255	64.6	35.4	918	7.0
1997	37 295	53.6	35 572	73.7	26.3	1 723	4.6	13 405	66.5	12 442	64.0	36.0	964	7.2
1998	38 253	54.1	36 680	74.1	25.9	1 573	4.1	13 888	67.2	13 082	64.8	35.2	806	5.8
1999	39 316	54.3	37 589	74.6	25.4	1 727	4.4	14 435	67.1	13 491	65.6	34.4	944	6.5
2000	40 142	54.8	38 408	75.4	24.6	1 733	4.3	14 677	67.6	13 713	66.6	33.4	964	6.6
WOMEN WITH CHILDREN UNDER 18														
1988	21 545	65.1	20 141	73.0	27.0	1 404	6.5	1 375	51.6	1 068	79.8	20.2	308	22.4
1989	20 936	65.7	20 647	72.8	27.2	1 289	6.2	1 524	54.7	1 200	79.0	21.0	324	21.3
1990	22 196	66.7	20 865	73.0	27.0	1 331	6.0	1 525	55.2	1 244	79.1	20.9	280	18.4
1991	22 327	66.6	20 774	73.0	27.0	1 552	7.0	1 654	53.6	1 358	76.4	23.6	296	17.9
1992	22 756	67.2	21 052	73.8	26.2	1 704	7.5	1 716	52.5	1 420	75.9	24.1	297	17.3
1993	23 063	66.9	21 521	73.9	26.1	1 541	6.7	1 869	54.4	1 510	74.8	25.2	359	19.2
1994	24 191	68.4	22 467	70.8	29.2	1 724	7.1	2 166	56.9	1 745	73.9	26.1	421	19.4
1995	24 695	69.7	23 195	71.7	28.3	1 500	6.1	2 104	57.5	1 754	73.6	26.4	350	16.6
1996	24 720	70.2	23 386	72.6	27.4	1 334	5.4	2 245	60.5	1 829	73.5	26.5	416	18.5
1997	25 604	72.1	24 082	74.1	25.9	1 522	5.9	2 772	68.1	2 305	76.6	23.4	467	16.8
1998	25 647	72.3	24 209	74.0	26.0	1 438	5.6	2 997	72.5	2 544	75.6	24.4	453	15.1
1999	25 469	72.1	24 305	74.1	25.9	1 165	4.6	3 051	73.4	2 694	75.8	24.2	357	11.7
2000	25 795	72.9	24 693	74.6	25.4	1 102	4.3	3 073	73.9	2 734	79.7	20.3	339	11.0
Women With Children Under 6														
1988	8 862	56.1	8 099	69.5	30.5	763	8.6	831	44.9	621	78.8	21.2	211	25.4
1989	9 136	56.7	8 478	68.8	31.2	657	7.2	966	48.9	722	79.2	20.8	244	25.3
1990	9 397	58.2	8 732	69.6	30.4	664	7.1	929	48.7	736	75.0	25.0	194	20.9
1991	9 636	58.4	8 758	69.5	30.5	878	9.1	1 050	48.8	819	72.2	27.8	231	22.0
1992	9 573	58.0	8 662	70.2	29.8	911	9.5	1 029	45.8	829	73.2	26.8	200	19.4
1993	9 621	57.9	8 764	70.1	29.9	857	8.9	1 125	47.4	869	70.0	30.0	257	22.8
1994	10 328	60.3	9 394	67.1	32.9	935	9.1	1 379	52.2	1 062	70.0	30.0	317	23.0
1995	10 395	62.3	9 587	67.5	32.5	809	7.8	1 328	53.0	1 069	68.6	31.4	259	19.5
1996	10 293	62.3	9 592	68.4	31.6	701	6.8	1 378	55.1	1 099	67.3	32.7	279	20.2
1997	10 610	65.0	9 800	70.5	29.5	810	7.6	1 755	65.1	1 424	71.6	28.4	330	18.8
1998	10 619	65.2	9 839	69.8	30.2	780	7.3	1 755	67.3	1 448	71.7	28.3	307	17.5
1999	10 322	64.4	9 674	69.0	31.0	648	6.3	1 811	68.1	1 565	71.0	29.0	246	13.6
2000	10 316	65.3	9 763	70.5	29.5	553	5.4	1 835	70.5	1 603	75.3	24.7	232	12.6

Note: See "Notes and Definitions" for information on historical comparability.

Table 1-48. Employment Status of Ever-Married Women and Married Women, Spouse Present, by Presence and Age of Children, March 1988–2000

(Thousands of persons, percent.)

Age of children and year	Ever-married women [1]							Married women, spouse present						
	Civilian labor force	Civilian labor force as percent of population	Employed			Unemployed		Civilian labor force	Civilian labor force as percent of population	Employed			Unemployed	
			Number	Percent full-time	Percent part-time	Number	Percent of labor force			Number	Percent full-time	Percent part-time	Number	Percent of labor force
WOMEN WITH NO CHILDREN UNDER 18														
1988	20 073	44.6	19 373	77.7	22.3	700	3.5	13 460	48.9	13 058	76.3	23.7	401	3.0
1989	20 810	45.6	20 118	78.1	21.9	692	3.3	14 044	50.5	13 633	77.2	22.8	411	2.9
1990	21 464	46.1	20 779	79.1	20.9	685	3.2	14 467	51.1	14 068	77.3	22.7	399	2.8
1991	21 575	46.1	20 637	78.4	21.6	937	4.3	14 529	51.2	13 976	77.6	22.4	552	3.8
1992	22 132	46.6	21 108	78.5	21.5	1 024	4.6	14 851	51.9	14 247	77.8	22.2	604	4.1
1993	22 273	46.6	21 275	79.0	21.0	998	4.5	15 211	52.4	14 630	77.6	22.4	581	3.8
1994	22 716	47.6	21 669	77.1	22.9	1 047	4.6	15 234	53.2	14 641	75.6	24.4	593	3.9
1995	22 973	47.3	22 134	77.4	22.6	839	3.7	15 594	53.2	15 072	76.3	23.7	522	3.3
1996	23 337	47.7	22 444	78.1	21.9	893	3.8	15 628	53.4	15 123	76.8	23.2	506	3.2
1997	23 890	48.3	23 130	78.9	21.1	760	3.2	15 750	54.2	15 315	77.7	22.3	435	2.8
1998	24 366	48.7	23 598	79.3	20.7	767	3.1	16 007	54.1	15 581	78.3	21.7	426	2.7
1999	24 881	48.9	24 098	79.7	20.3	783	3.1	16 484	54.4	16 061	78.2	21.8	423	2.6
2000	25 465	49.4	24 695	80.3	19.7	769	3.0	16 786	54.7	16 357	79.1	20.9	429	2.6
WOMEN WITH CHILDREN UNDER 18														
1988	20 170	66.3	19 074	72.6	27.4	1 096	5.4	16 218	65.0	15 441	69.6	30.4	776	4.8
1989	20 411	66.7	19 446	72.5	27.5	965	4.7	16 445	65.6	15 813	69.6	30.4	632	3.8
1990	20 671	67.8	19 621	72.6	27.4	1 051	5.1	16 500	66.3	15 803	69.8	30.2	698	4.2
1991	20 673	67.9	19 416	72.8	27.2	1 257	6.1	16 575	66.8	15 692	70.1	29.9	883	5.3
1992	21 040	68.8	19 633	73.6	26.4	1 407	6.7	16 835	67.8	15 884	71.3	28.7	952	5.7
1993	21 194	68.3	20 011	73.9	26.1	1 183	5.6	16 947	67.5	16 127	71.4	28.6	820	4.8
1994	22 025	69.8	20 722	70.5	29.5	1 303	5.9	17 628	69.0	16 755	68.0	32.0	873	5.0
1995	22 591	71.1	21 441	71.5	28.5	1 150	5.1	17 905	70.0	17 105	68.8	31.2	774	4.3
1996	22 475	71.4	21 556	72.5	27.5	919	4.1	17 754	70.0	17 136	69.6	30.4	618	3.5
1997	22 831	72.6	21 777	73.9	26.1	1 054	4.6	18 157	71.1	17 521	71.6	28.4	636	3.5
1998	22 650	72.3	21 665	73.8	26.2	985	4.3	18 129	70.6	17 447	71.5	28.5	682	3.8
1999	22 419	71.9	21 611	73.9	26.1	808	3.6	17 865	70.1	17 342	71.5	28.5	523	2.9
2000	22 722	72.7	21 960	74.0	26.0	703	3.4	18 174	70.6	17 641	71.7	28.3	533	2.9
Women With Children Under 6														
1988	8 031	57.6	7 478	68.7	31.3	552	6.9	6 950	57.1	6 527	66.4	33.6	422	6.1
1989	8 169	57.8	7 756	67.8	32.2	413	5.1	7 034	57.4	6 749	66.0	34.0	285	4.1
1990	8 467	59.5	7 996	69.1	30.9	471	5.6	7 247	58.9	6 901	67.4	32.6	346	4.8
1991	8 585	59.9	7 938	69.2	30.8	647	7.5	7 434	59.9	6 933	67.5	32.5	501	6.7
1992	8 544	60.0	7 832	69.9	30.1	711	8.3	7 333	59.9	6 819	68.5	31.5	514	7.0
1993	8 496	59.6	7 895	70.2	29.8	600	7.1	7 289	59.6	6 840	68.8	31.2	450	6.2
1994	8 949	61.8	8 332	66.7	33.3	617	6.9	7 723	61.7	7 291	65.4	34.6	432	5.6
1995	9 067	63.9	8 517	67.4	32.6	550	6.1	7 759	63.5	7 349	66.1	33.9	409	5.3
1996	8 915	63.6	8 493	68.6	31.4	422	4.7	7 590	62.7	7 297	66.5	33.5	293	3.9
1997	8 856	64.9	8 376	70.3	29.7	480	5.4	7 582	63.6	7 252	69.1	30.9	330	4.4
1998	8 864	64.8	8 391	69.5	30.5	473	5.3	7 655	63.7	7 309	68.1	31.9	346	4.5
1999	8 511	63.7	8 109	68.6	31.4	402	4.7	7 246	61.8	6 979	67.1	32.9	267	3.7
2000	8 481	64.3	8 159	69.5	30.5	321	3.8	7 341	62.8	7 087	68.1	31.9	254	3.5

Note: See "Notes and Definitions" for information on historical comparability.

1. Ever-married women are women who are, or have been married.

Table 1-49. Employment Status of Women Who Maintain Families by Marital Status and Presence and Age of Children, March 1988–2000

(Thousands of persons, percent.)

Family status, age of children, and year	Civilian noninstitutional population	Civilian labor force					Not in the labor force
		Number	Percent of the population	Employed	Unemployed		
					Number	Percent of the labor force	
WOMEN WHO MAINTAIN FAMILIES, TOTAL							
1988	11 074	6 851	61.9	6 296	555	8.1	4 222
1989	11 280	6 999	62.0	6 420	579	8.3	4 281
1990	11 309	7 088	62.7	6 471	617	8.7	4 221
1991	11 765	7 329	62.3	6 657	672	9.2	4 436
1992	12 214	7 517	61.5	6 798	719	9.6	4 697
1993	12 489	7 777	62.3	7 093	684	8.8	4 712
1994	12 963	8 214	63.4	7 413	801	9.8	4 750
1995	12 762	8 192	64.2	7 527	665	8.1	4 570
1996	12 993	8 460	65.1	7 832	628	7.4	4 532
1997	13 258	8 998	67.9	8 192	806	9.0	4 260
1998	13 102	8 976	68.5	8 309	667	7.4	4 127
1999	13 191	9 213	69.8	8 596	617	6.7	3 978
2000	13 145	9 226	70.2	8 592	634	6.9	3 918
WOMEN WITH NO CHILDREN UNDER 18							
1988	4 315	2 299	53.3	2 213	86	3.7	2 015
1989	4 375	2 291	52.4	2 213	78	3.4	2 084
1990	4 290	2 227	51.9	2 132	95	4.3	2 062
1991	4 447	2 364	53.2	2 231	133	5.6	2 083
1992	4 651	2 427	52.2	2 307	120	4.9	2 223
1993	4 708	2 466	52.4	2 339	127	5.2	2 242
1994	4 758	2 609	54.8	2 489	120	4.6	2 149
1995	4 610	2 471	53.6	2 394	77	3.1	2 139
1996	4 847	2 552	52.7	2 462	90	3.5	2 295
1997	4 909	2 663	54.2	2 571	92	3.5	2 246
1998	4 952	2 649	53.5	2 578	71	2.7	2 303
1999	4 942	2 667	54.0	2 556	111	4.2	2 275
2000	5 097	2 707	53.1	2 546	161	5.9	2 390
Single Women With No Children Under 18							
1988	609	427	70.1	415	12	2.8	183
1989	665	466	70.1	452	14	3.0	198
1990	642	450	70.1	425	25	5.6	192
1991	682	469	68.8	441	28	6.0	214
1992	745	505	67.8	475	30	5.9	241
1993	752	531	70.6	494	37	7.0	221
1994	704	490	69.6	451	39	8.0	213
1995	779	534	68.5	508	26	4.9	245
1996	895	588	65.7	572	16	2.7	308
1997	860	585	68.0	563	22	3.8	275
1998	893	637	71.3	613	24	3.8	256
1999	969	674	69.6	638	36	5.3	295
2000	1 004	720	71.7	642	78	10.8	284
Widowed, Divorced Or Separated Women With No Children Under 18							
1988	3 705	1 872	50.5	1 798	74	4.0	1 833
1989	3 711	1 825	49.2	1 761	64	3.5	1 886
1990	3 648	1 778	48.7	1 708	70	3.9	1 870
1991	3 765	1 896	50.4	1 791	105	5.5	1 869
1992	3 905	1 923	49.2	1 832	91	4.7	1 982
1993	3 956	1 935	48.9	1 845	90	4.7	2 021
1994	4 054	2 118	52.2	2 037	81	3.8	1 936
1995	3 831	1 938	50.6	1 887	51	2.6	1 894
1996	3 952	1 964	49.7	1 890	74	3.8	1 988
1997	4 049	2 077	51.3	2 008	69	3.3	1 971
1998	4 058	2 011	49.6	1 965	46	2.3	2 047
1999	3 974	1 993	50.2	1 918	75	3.8	1 980
2000	4 093	1 987	48.5	1 904	83	4.2	2 106

See *Note* at end of table.

Table 1-49. Employment Status of Women Who Maintain Families by Marital Status and Presence and Age of Children, March 1988–2000—*Continued*

(Thousands of persons, percent.)

Family status, age of children, and year	Civilian noninstitutional population	Civilian labor force					Not in the labor force
		Number	Percent of the population	Employed	Unemployed		
					Number	Percent of the labor force	
WOMEN WITH CHILDREN UNDER 18							
1988	6 759	4 552	67.3	4 083	469	10.3	2 207
1989	6 905	4 707	68.2	4 206	501	10.6	2 197
1990	7 018	4 860	69.3	4 338	522	10.7	2 159
1991	7 318	4 965	67.8	4 426	539	10.9	2 353
1992	7 564	5 090	67.3	4 491	599	11.8	2 473
1993	7 781	5 311	68.3	4 755	556	10.5	2 470
1994	8 205	5 604	68.3	4 924	680	12.1	2 601
1995	8 152	5 720	70.2	5 132	588	10.3	2 431
1996	8 146	5 908	72.5	5 370	538	9.1	2 237
1997	8 348	6 335	75.9	5 621	714	11.3	2 014
1998	8 151	6 327	77.6	5 731	596	9.4	1 823
1999	8 248	6 546	79.4	6 040	506	7.7	1 702
2000	8 048	6 520	81.0	6 046	474	7.3	1 528
Single Women With Children Under 18							
1988	1 778	950	53.4	754	196	20.6	829
1989	1 921	1 116	58.1	905	211	18.9	805
1990	1 953	1 095	56.1	874	221	20.2	858
1991	2 208	1 187	53.8	985	202	17.0	1 021
1992	2 376	1 256	52.9	1 067	189	15.0	1 120
1993	2 445	1 414	57.8	1 161	253	17.9	1 031
1994	2 790	1 625	58.2	1 328	297	18.3	1 165
1995	2 613	1 510	57.8	1 261	249	16.5	1 102
1996	2 639	1 633	61.9	1 346	287	17.6	1 006
1997	3 012	2 087	69.3	1 749	338	16.2	925
1998	3 083	2 280	74.0	1 960	320	14.0	803
1999	3 163	2 415	76.4	2 146	269	11.1	748
2000	3 167	2 413	76.2	2 151	262	10.9	754
Widowed, Divorced Or Separated Women With Children Under 18							
1988	4 981	3 602	72.3	3 329	273	7.6	1 379
1989	4 983	3 591	72.1	3 302	289	8.0	1 392
1990	5 065	3 765	74.3	3 464	301	8.0	1 301
1991	5 109	3 778	73.9	3 441	337	8.9	1 331
1992	5 187	3 834	73.9	3 424	410	10.7	1 353
1993	5 336	3 897	73.0	3 594	303	7.8	1 439
1994	5 415	3 979	73.5	3 596	383	9.6	1 436
1995	5 539	4 210	76.0	3 871	339	8.1	1 329
1996	5 507	4 275	77.6	4 024	251	5.9	1 231
1997	5 337	4 248	79.6	3 872	376	8.9	1 089
1998	5 068	4 047	79.9	3 771	276	6.8	1 020
1999	5 086	4 131	81.2	3 894	237	5.7	955
2000	4 881	4 107	84.1	3 895	212	5.2	774

Note: See "Notes and Definitions" for information on historical comparability.

Table 1-50. Number and Age of Children in Families by Type of Family and Labor Force Status of Mother, March 1988–2000

(Thousands of children.)

Age of children and year	Total children	Mother in labor force	Mother not in labor force	Married-couple families			Families maintained by women			Families maintained by men
				Total	Mother in labor force	Mother not in labor force	Total	Mother in labor force	Mother not in labor force	
CHILDREN UNDER 16 YEARS										
1988	58 716	35 279	21 799	45 474	28 091	17 384	11 603	7 188	4 415	1 638
1989	59 483	36 050	21 757	45 988	28 673	17 315	11 819	7 377	4 442	1 676
1990	59 596	36 712	21 110	45 898	29 077	16 820	11 925	7 635	4 290	1 774
1991	60 330	36 968	21 526	45 912	29 056	16 856	12 582	7 912	4 670	1 836
1992	61 262	38 081	21 176	45 966	29 882	16 084	13 291	8 199	5 093	2 005
1993	62 020	38 542	21 444	46 499	30 054	16 445	13 487	8 488	4 999	2 034
1994	63 407	40 186	21 188	47 247	31 279	15 968	14 127	8 907	5 220	2 033
1995	63 989	41 365	20 421	47 675	32 190	15 486	14 111	9 176	4 935	2 202
1996	64 506	41 573	20 449	47 484	31 764	15 720	14 538	9 809	4 729	2 484
1997	64 710	42 747	19 223	47 529	32 263	15 265	14 441	10 483	3 958	2 740
1998	65 043	43 156	19 069	47 909	32 533	15 376	14 317	10 623	3 694	2 818
1999	65 191	43 419	19 074	47 945	32 193	15 752	14 547	11 226	3 322	2 699
2000	65 601	44 188	18 674	48 902	33 149	15 753	13 960	11 039	2 921	2 739
CHILDREN FROM 6 TO 17 YEARS										
1988	38 744	24 957	12 614	29 304	19 394	9 910	8 268	5 563	2 705	1 172
1989	39 084	25 421	12 451	29 637	19 861	9 777	8 235	5 561	2 674	1 212
1990	39 095	25 805	12 079	29 726	20 067	9 659	8 157	5 737	2 420	1 211
1991	39 470	25 806	12 392	29 598	19 907	9 691	8 599	5 899	2 701	1 272
1992	40 064	26 666	12 067	29 673	20 586	9 087	9 060	6 079	2 980	1 331
1993	40 622	27 046	12 291	30 233	20 796	9 437	9 104	6 249	2 854	1 285
1994	41 795	28 179	12 287	30 895	21 663	9 233	9 570	6 516	3 054	1 329
1995	42 423	28 931	12 000	31 298	22 239	9 059	9 633	6 692	2 941	1 492
1996	42 964	29 381	11 897	31 231	22 092	9 139	10 047	7 289	2 758	1 685
1997	43 488	30 308	11 400	31 509	22 602	8 906	10 199	7 705	2 493	1 781
1998	43 771	30 579	11 367	31 707	22 706	9 001	10 238	7 873	2 365	1 826
1999	44 110	30 885	11 370	31 975	22 706	9 269	10 281	8 179	2 101	1 855
2000	44 562	31 531	11 198	32 732	23 393	9 339	9 997	8 138	1 859	1 833
CHILDREN UNDER 6 YEARS										
1988	19 972	10 321	9 185	16 171	8 696	7 474	3 335	1 625	1 711	466
1989	20 399	10 628	9 306	16 351	8 812	7 539	3 584	1 816	1 767	465
1990	20 502	10 907	9 031	16 171	9 010	7 161	3 767	1 897	1 870	563
1991	20 860	11 162	9 134	16 313	9 148	7 165	3 983	2 013	1 969	563
1992	21 198	11 415	9 109	16 293	9 296	6 997	4 232	2 119	2 112	674
1993	21 398	11 496	9 153	16 266	9 258	7 008	4 383	2 239	2 145	749
1994	21 612	12 007	8 901	16 352	9 617	6 735	4 556	2 391	2 166	704
1995	21 566	12 435	8 421	16 377	9 951	6 427	4 478	2 484	1 995	710
1996	21 542	12 192	8 552	16 253	9 672	6 581	4 491	2 520	1 971	799
1997	21 222	12 439	7 823	16 020	9 661	6 359	4 243	2 778	1 464	959
1998	21 272	12 577	7 703	16 201	9 827	6 375	4 079	2 751	1 328	992
1999	21 081	12 533	7 704	15 971	9 487	6 484	4 267	3 046	1 220	844
2000	21 039	12 657	7 476	16 170	9 757	6 413	3 963	2 901	1 062	906

Note: See "Notes and Definitions" for information on historical comparability.

Table 1-51. Number of Families and Median Family Income by Type of Family and Earner Status of Members, 1987–1999

(Thousand of families, dollars.)

Number of families and median family income	1987	1988	1989	1990	1991	1992	1993	1994	1995	1996	1997	1998	1999
NUMBER OF FAMILIES													
Married-Couple Families, Total	51 720	52 149	52 385	52 241	52 549	53 254	53 248	53 929	53 621	53 654	54 362	54 829	55 352
No earners	6 648	6 751	6 812	6 765	7 101	7 250	7 281	7 225	7 276	7 145	7 286	7 257	7 160
One earner	12 083	11 938	11 737	11 630	11 553	12 053	11 806	11 715	11 708	11 493	11 700	12 246	12 290
Husband	9 651	9 508	9 196	9 110	8 907	9 182	8 715	8 673	8 792	8 611	8 770	9 173	9 062
Wife	1 765	1 782	1 844	1 816	1 987	2 145	2 405	2 364	2 251	2 207	2 298	2 411	2 585
Other family member	667	648	697	703	659	726	686	678	666	674	632	662	643
Two earners	24 968	25 397	25 681	25 896	26 037	26 344	26 742	27 263	27 180	27 260	27 712	27 593	28 010
Husband and wife	22 623	23 237	23 534	23 697	23 880	24 255	24 543	25 123	25 274	25 274	25 731	25 696	26 134
Husband and other family member	1 826	1 652	1 718	1 711	1 633	1 447	1 582	1 565	1 393	1 483	1 406	1 306	1 325
Husband not an earner	519	509	429	487	524	642	617	574	513	502	575	590	552
Three earners or more	8 020	8 062	8 155	7 950	7 858	7 606	7 419	7 727	7 456	7 756	7 664	7 733	7 892
Husband and wife	7 027	7 140	7 245	7 029	7 052	6 882	6 723	6 987	6 770	7 126	7 023	7 102	7 220
Husband, not wife	823	744	761	756	595	550	535	543	531	479	478	456	528
husband not an earner	170	178	150	165	211	175	162	196	155	150	163	176	144
Families Maintained By Women, Total	11 087	11 288	11 310	11 771	12 214	12 504	12 982	12 771	13 007	13 277	13 115	13 206	13 164
No earners	2 607	2 547	2 496	2 623	2 925	2 968	3 100	2 848	2 664	2 574	2 332	2 143	1 883
One earner	5 141	5 390	5 467	5 672	5 926	6 184	6 407	6 506	6 815	7 027	7 091	7 351	7 441
Householder	4 060	4 300	4 396	4 585	4 812	5 042	5 278	5 415	5 590	5 817	5 841	6 167	6 127
Other family member	1 081	1 090	1 071	1 087	1 114	1 142	1 129	1 091	1 225	1 211	1 251	1 183	1 314
Two earners or more	3 339	3 350	3 347	3 476	3 363	3 352	3 476	3 417	3 527	3 675	3 692	3 712	3 840
Householder and other family member(s)	3 020	3 022	2 975	3 146	3 058	2 998	3 139	3 126	3 225	3 431	3 398	3 399	3 508
Householder not an earner	318	328	372	330	305	354	337	291	302	245	294	313	332
Families Maintained By Men, Total	2 859	2 874	2 929	2 948	3 079	3 094	2 992	3 287	3 557	3 924	3 982	4 041	4 086
No earners	312	296	281	296	310	345	329	383	357	359	344	381	376
One earner	1 288	1 263	1 350	1 396	1 541	1 544	1 593	1 705	1 800	1 972	2 104	2 027	2 044
Householder	1 054	992	1 103	1 133	1 289	1 305	1 352	1 428	1 548	1 667	1 791	1 725	1 721
Other family member	234	271	247	263	253	239	241	277	253	305	313	302	323
Two earners or more	1 258	1 315	1 298	1 257	1 228	1 204	1 070	1 198	1 400	1 593	1 534	1 634	1 666
Householder and other family member(s)	1 173	1 242	1 225	1 180	1 157	1 117	1 002	1 128	1 302	1 469	1 427	1 532	1 522
Householder not an earner	85	73	73	76	71	88	67	71	98	124	107	102	143
MEDIAN FAMILY INCOME													
Married-Couple Families, Total	$34 834	$36 267	$38 415	$39 802	$40 746	$42 000	$43 000	$44 853	$47 000	$49 614	$51 475	$54 043	$56 792
No earners	16 338	17 000	17 820	19 221	20 415	20 023	19 983	20 604	21 888	22 622	23 782	24 525	25 262
One earner	28 000	28 701	30 700	31 020	31 671	32 500	32 084	33 393	35 100	36 468	39 140	40 519	41 261
Husband	29 225	30 030	32 236	32 422	33 208	34 714	34 401	35 000	36 052	38 150	40 300	42 000	44 200
Wife	22 700	23 771	24 000	25 228	26 500	27 343	27 502	28 661	32 098	30 301	34 050	35 625	35 546
Other family member	25 640	27 840	29 992	33 262	33 042	33 622	30 254	32 578	37 784	39 644	40 317	42 414	41 120
Two earners	38 100	40 030	42 208	44 000	45 359	47 737	49 650	51 190	53 500	56 000	58 020	61 300	64 007
Husband and wife	38 074	40 050	42 285	44 031	45 516	48 050	49 980	51 500	53 626	56 392	58 564	61 900	64 950
Husband and other family member	40 400	41 388	43 000	42 602	45 000	45 094	48 862	48 517	52 530	49 610	53 854	57 680	53 541
Husband not an earner	32 184	33 333	35 201	39 494	40 495	40 124	38 800	42 800	47 121	46 990	47 979	50 955	52 466
Three earners or more	53 150	54 556	56 500	59 336	61 120	61 640	63 535	66 172	68 996	70 400	75 593	78 973	81 940
Husband and wife	53 324	54 672	56 980	55 846	61 448	62 674	64 099	66 674	69 371	71 148	76 105	79 907	83 000
Husband, not wife	53 000	56 600	53 928	59 675	60 592	57 015	60 712	63 633	60 360	61 824	68 890	71 001	69 561
Husband not earner	40 500	40 900	47 656	49 107	44 874	47 551	54 805	54 655	61 196	55 495	62 684	63 205	69 275
Families Maintained By Women, Total	14 183	14 935	15 800	16 351	16 054	16 431	16 800	17 600	19 306	19 416	20 470	21 875	23 100
No earners	5 184	5 396	5 618	5 880	6 060	5 964	6 492	6 805	7 440	7 092	7 476	7 737	8 010
One earner	14 000	14 235	15 187	15 987	16 284	16 468	16 745	17 226	18 824	18 500	19 000	20 000	20 092
Householder	13 385	13 754	14 700	15 001	15 542	15 905	15 700	16 603	17 890	18 000	18 000	18 800	19 000
Other family member	15 851	16 580	18 628	20 173	20 220	19 709	20 800	21 300	23 166	21 000	22 870	25 981	26 800
Two earners or more	27 154	28 302	30 038	30 500	31 508	32 705	33 300	33 820	35 000	36 400	39 275	40 000	41 144
Householder and other family member(s)	27 150	28 000	30 000	30 367	31 550	33 280	33 165	33 357	34 674	36 400	39 000	39 713	40 855
Householder not an earner	27 535	33 590	33 524	32 800	29 477	30 460	35 394	37 531	39 444	38 249	47 471	43 725	48 004
Families Maintained By Men, Total	25 000	26 610	27 600	28 493	28 000	27 400	25 856	27 486	30 000	31 500	32 984	35 000	37 000
No earners	10 800	10 200	9 800	11 386	11 196	9 416	10 900	11 293	12 240	12 030	14 252	15 468	13 752
One earner	20 305	22 357	22 732	25 000	23 715	23 020	22 300	24 011	25 337	26 100	26 897	29 125	31 038
Householder	20 391	23 053	23 000	24 150	23 309	23 000	22 079	24 000	25 069	25 874	27 000	29 125	30 483
Other family member	19 681	19 869	21 196	27 620	25 720	24 359	26 916	26 253	27 291	28 584	25 486	28 241	34 756
Two earners or more	33 750	36 500	37 601	40 000	37 700	39 000	38 000	41 439	43 100	44 275	49 900	51 288	51 040
Householder and other family member(s)	33 846	36 525	37 859	40 256	37 550	39 300	38 363	41 534	43 000	43 065	50 000	50 954	50 960
Householder not an earner	32 560	34 335	35 390	34 064	40 000	36 445	33 700	37 386	55 133	47 001	44 786	68 257	57 407

Note: See "Notes and Definitions" for information on historical comparability.

Table 1-52. Employment Status of the Civilian Noninstitutional Population by Citizenship Status and Sex, March 1996–2000

(Thousands of persons, percent.)

Year, employment status, and sex	Total		Citizenship status					
			Native		Naturalized citizen		Not a citizen	
	Number	Percent	Number	Percent	Number	Percent	Number	Percent
1996								
Total, 16 Years And Over								
Civilian labor force	132 324	100.0	118 026	100.0	4 883	100.0	9 416	100.0
Employed	124 513	94.1	111 309	94.3	4 674	95.7	8 530	90.6
Unemployed	7 811	5.9	6 716	5.7	209	4.3	886	9.4
Men, 16 Years And Over								
Civilian labor force	71 095	100.0	62 709	100.0	2 641	100.0	5 745	100.0
Employed	66 429	93.4	58 695	93.6	2 532	95.9	5 203	90.6
Unemployed	4 666	6.6	4 014	6.4	110	4.1	542	9.4
Women, 16 Years And Over								
Civilian labor force	61 229	100.0	55 317	100.0	2 241	100.0	3 671	100.0
Employed	58 084	94.9	52 615	95.1	2 142	95.6	3 327	90.6
Unemployed	3 145	5.1	2 702	4.9	99	4.4	344	9.4
1997								
Total, 16 Years And Over								
Civilian labor force	135 227	100.0	119 635	100.0	5 792	100.0	9 800	100.0
Employed	127 680	94.4	113 156	94.6	5 542	95.7	8 981	91.6
Unemployed	7 547	5.6	6 479	5.4	250	4.3	819	8.4
Men, 16 Years And Over								
Civilian labor force	72 329	100.0	63 069	100.0	3 198	100.0	6 061	100.0
Employed	68 026	94.1	59 367	94.1	3 072	96.1	5 587	92.2
Unemployed	4 302	5.9	3 702	5.9	126	3.9	474	7.8
Women, 16 Years And Over								
Civilian labor force	62 899	100.0	56 565	100.0	2 594	100.0	3 739	100.0
Employed	59 654	94.8	53 789	95.1	2 470	95.2	3 395	90.8
Unemployed	3 245	5.2	2 776	4.9	124	4.8	344	9.2
1998								
Total, 16 Years And Over								
Civilian labor force	136 926	100.0	120 725	100.0	6 160	100.0	10 041	100.0
Employed	130 007	94.9	114 746	95.0	5 927	96.2	9 333	92.9
Unemployed	6 919	5.1	5 979	5.0	232	3.8	708	7.1
Men, 16 Years And Over								
Civilian labor force	73 026	100.0	63 386	100.0	3 424	100.0	6 215	100.0
Employed	69 117	94.6	60 018	94.7	3 315	96.8	5 784	93.1
Unemployed	3 908	5.4	3 368	5.3	110	3.2	431	6.9
Women, 16 Years And Over								
Civilian labor force	63 900	100.0	57 339	100.0	2 735	100.0	3 826	100.0
Employed	60 889	95.3	54 728	95.4	2 613	95.5	3 549	92.8
Unemployed	3 011	4.7	2 611	4.6	123	4.5	277	7.2
1999								
Total, 16 Years And Over								
Civilian labor force	138 120	100.0	122 006	100.0	6 171	100.0	9 943	100.0
Employed	131 806	95.4	116 569	95.5	5 915	95.9	9 322	93.8
Unemployed	6 314	4.6	5 437	4.5	256	4.1	621	6.2
Men, 16 Years And Over								
Civilian labor force	73 334	100.0	63 844	100.0	3 306	100.0	6 183	100.0
Employed	69 912	95.3	60 890	95.4	3 184	96.3	5 838	94.4
Unemployed	3 422	4.7	2 955	4.6	122	3.7	345	5.6
Women, 16 Years And Over								
Civilian labor force	64 786	100.0	58 161	100.0	2 864	100.0	3 760	100.0
Employed	61 894	95.5	55 679	95.7	2 731	95.3	3 485	92.7
Unemployed	2 891	4.5	2 482	4.3	134	4.7	275	7.3
2000								
Total, 16 Years And Over								
Civilian labor force	140 454	100.0	123 070	100.0	6 720	100.0	10 664	100.0
Employed	134 338	95.6	117 806	95.7	6 499	96.7	10 033	94.1
Unemployed	6 116	4.4	5 264	4.3	221	3.3	631	5.9
Men, 16 Years And Over								
Civilian labor force	74 517	100.0	64 183	100.0	3 623	100.0	6 712	100.0
Employed	71 237	95.6	61 364	95.6	3 520	97.2	6 353	94.7
Unemployed	3 281	4.4	2 820	4.4	102	2.8	359	5.3
Women, 16 Years And Over								
Civilian labor force	65 937	100.0	58 886	100.0	3 098	100.0	3 953	100.0
Employed	63 102	95.7	56 442	95.8	2 979	96.2	3 680	93.1
Unemployed	2 835	4.3	2 444	4.2	119	3.8	273	6.9

Table 1-53. Employed Civilians by Occupation, Citizenship Status, and Sex, March 2000

(Thousands of persons, percent.)

Occupation and sex	Total		Citizenship status					
			Native		Naturalized citizen		Not a citizen	
	Number	Percent	Number	Percent	Number	Percent	Number	Percent
TOTAL	134 338	100.0	117 806	100.0	6 499	100.0	10 033	100.0
Managerial and professional specialty	40 493	30.1	36 408	30.9	2 183	33.6	1 902	19.0
Executive, administrative, and managerial	19 764	14.7	18 004	15.3	1 000	15.4	759	7.6
Professional specialty	20 729	15.4	18 404	15.6	1 182	18.2	1 143	11.4
Technical, sales, and administrative support	39 541	29.4	36 093	30.6	1 677	25.8	1 771	17.7
Technicians and related support	4 384	3.3	3 889	3.3	236	3.6	258	2.6
Sales occupations	16 138	12.0	14 580	12.4	714	11.0	843	8.4
Administrative support, including clerical	19 020	14.2	17 624	15.0	727	11.2	669	6.7
Service occupations	18 671	13.9	15 497	13.2	1 002	15.4	2 171	21.6
Private household	884	0.7	572	0.5	75	1.2	237	2.4
Protective service	2 364	1.8	2 233	1.9	65	1.0	66	0.7
Other service occupations	15 423	11.5	12 692	10.8	862	13.3	1 868	18.6
Precision production, craft, and repair	14 386	10.7	12 389	10.5	648	10.0	1 348	13.4
Mechanics and repairers	4 798	3.6	4 335	3.7	192	3.0	272	2.7
Construction trades	5 716	4.3	4 791	4.1	215	3.3	710	7.1
Other precision production, craft, and repair	3 871	2.9	3 263	2.8	242	3.7	366	3.6
Operators, fabricators, and laborers	18 002	13.4	14 914	12.7	867	13.3	2 221	22.1
Operators, assemblers, and inspectors	7 352	5.5	5 844	5.0	440	6.8	1 067	10.6
Transportation and material moving occupations	5 340	4.0	4 712	4.0	205	3.2	423	4.2
Other laborers	5 310	4.0	4 358	3.7	222	3.4	731	7.3
Farming, forestry, and fishing	3 245	2.4	2 503	2.1	122	1.9	620	6.2
Farm operators and managers	1 089	0.8	1 066	0.9	15	0.2	8	0.1
Other farming, forestry, and fishing occupations	2 155	1.6	1 437	1.2	106	1.6	612	6.1
MEN	71 237	53.0	61 364	52.1	3 520	54.2	6 353	63.3
Managerial and professional specialty	20 297	15.1	17 912	15.2	1 206	18.6	1 179	11.8
Executive, administrative, and managerial	10 877	8.1	9 841	8.4	544	8.4	492	4.9
Professional specialty	9 420	7.0	8 071	6.9	662	10.2	687	6.8
Technical, sales, and administrative support	14 174	10.6	12 611	10.7	712	11.0	851	8.5
Technicians and related support	2 060	1.5	1 788	1.5	133	2.0	139	1.4
Sales occupations	8 207	6.1	7 333	6.2	397	6.1	477	4.8
Administrative support, including clerical	3 908	2.9	3 491	3.0	182	2.8	235	2.3
Service occupations	7 459	5.6	6 118	5.2	354	5.4	987	9.8
Private household	40	(1)	31	(1)	5	0.1	3	(1)
Protective service	1 934	1.4	1 822	1.5	53	0.8	50	0.5
Other service occupations	5 485	4.1	4 263	3.6	296	4.6	926	9.2
Precision production, craft, and repair	12 975	9.7	11 239	9.5	531	8.2	1 205	12.0
Mechanics and repairers	4 541	3.4	4 119	3.5	161	2.5	261	2.6
Construction trades	5 557	4.1	4 640	3.9	210	3.2	707	7.0
Other precision production, craft, and repair	2 877	2.1	2 470	2.1	160	2.5	237	2.4
Operators, fabricators, and laborers	13 816	10.3	11 604	9.9	609	9.4	1 603	16.0
Operators, assemblers, and inspectors	4 775	3.6	3 930	3.3	253	3.9	592	5.9
Transportation and material moving occupations	4 786	3.6	4 191	3.6	195	3.0	399	4.0
Other laborers	4 254	3.2	3 483	3.0	161	2.5	611	6.1
Farming, forestry, and fishing	2 515	1.9	1 878	1.6	109	1.7	528	5.3
Farm operators and managers	800	0.6	781	0.7	13	0.2	7	0.1
Other farming, forestry, and fishing occupations	1 715	1.3	1 098	0.9	96	1.5	521	5.2
WOMEN	63 102	47.0	56 442	47.9	2 979	45.8	3 680	36.7
Managerial and professional specialty	20 196	15.0	18 496	15.7	977	15.0	723	7.2
Executive, administrative, and managerial	8 888	6.6	8 163	6.9	457	7.0	268	2.7
Professional specialty	11 309	8.4	10 333	8.8	520	8.0	455	4.5
Technical, sales, and administrative support	25 367	18.9	23 482	19.9	965	14.8	920	9.2
Technicians and related support	2 324	1.7	2 101	1.8	103	1.6	119	1.2
Sales occupations	7 931	5.9	7 248	6.2	317	4.9	367	3.7
Administrative support, including clerical	15 112	11.2	14 133	12.0	545	8.4	434	4.3
Service occupations	11 212	8.3	9 379	8.0	649	10.0	1 185	11.8
Private household	843	0.6	538	0.5	70	1.1	235	2.3
Protective service	431	0.3	411	0.3	12	0.2	7	0.1
Other service occupations	9 938	7.4	8 430	7.2	566	8.7	942	9.4
Precision production, craft, and repair	1 410	1.0	1 151	1.0	117	1.8	143	1.4
Mechanics and repairers	257	0.2	216	0.2	30	0.5	11	0.1
Construction trades	159	0.1	151	0.1	4	0.1	3	(1)
Other precision production, craft, and repair	995	0.7	784	0.7	82	1.3	129	1.3
Operators, fabricators, and laborers	4 187	3.1	3 310	2.8	258	4.0	618	6.2
Operators, assemblers, and inspectors	2 576	1.9	1 914	1.6	187	2.9	475	4.7
Transportation and material moving occupations	554	0.4	521	0.4	10	0.2	24	0.2
Other laborers	1 056	0.8	875	0.7	62	1.0	119	1.2
Farming, forestry, and fishing	729	0.5	624	0.5	13	0.2	92	0.9
Farm operators and managers	289	0.2	285	0.2	2	(1)	1	(1)
Other farming, forestry, and fishing occupations	440	0.3	339	0.3	10	0.2	91	0.9

1. Value less than 0.05.

Table 1-54. Total Money Earnings[1] of Year-Round Full-Time Workers by Citizenship Status and Sex, March 2000

(Thousands of persons, percent.)

Sex and money earnings	Total		Citizenship status					
			Native		Naturalized citizen		Not a citizen	
	Number	Percent	Number	Percent	Number	Percent	Number	Percent
TOTAL	97 914	100.0	85 677	100.0	5 109	100.0	7 128	100.0
$1 to $2,499	1 107	1.1	950	1.1	49	1.0	107	1.5
$2,500 to $4,999	477	0.5	401	0.5	27	0.5	49	0.7
$5,000 to $9,999	2 695	2.8	2 226	2.6	104	2.0	365	5.1
$10,000 to $14,999	7 923	8.1	6 073	7.1	448	8.8	1 402	19.7
$15,000 to $19,999	10 487	10.7	8 588	10.0	559	10.9	1 341	18.8
$20,000 to $24,999	11 409	11.7	9 877	11.5	607	11.9	925	13.0
$25,000 to $34,999	20 403	20.8	18 264	21.3	981	19.2	1 158	16.2
$35,000 to $49,999	19 984	20.4	18 203	21.2	997	19.5	783	11.0
$50,000 to $74,999	14 424	14.7	13 034	15.2	800	15.7	589	8.3
$75,000 and over	9 007	9.2	8 062	9.4	536	10.5	409	5.7
MEN	57 511	100.0	49 659	100.0	3 014	100.0	4 838	100.0
$1 to $2,499	641	1.1	534	1.1	32	1.1	74	1.5
$2,500 to $4,999	181	0.3	149	0.3	14	0.5	19	0.4
$5,000 to $9,999	1 159	2.0	917	1.8	33	1.1	210	4.3
$10,000 to $14,999	3 385	5.9	2 378	4.8	187	6.2	820	16.9
$15,000 to $19,999	4 849	8.4	3 673	7.4	289	9.6	887	18.3
$20,000 to $24,999	5 511	9.6	4 531	9.1	328	10.9	652	13.5
$25,000 to $34,999	10 993	19.1	9 639	19.4	556	18.5	797	16.5
$35,000 to $49,999	12 631	22.0	11 488	23.1	586	19.4	557	11.5
$50,000 to $74,999	10 667	18.5	9 642	19.4	553	18.3	472	9.7
$75,000 and over	7 494	13.0	6 708	13.5	437	14.5	350	7.2
WOMEN	40 404	100.0	36 018	100.0	2 095	100.0	2 290	100.0
$1 to $2,499	466	1.2	416	1.2	17	0.8	33	1.4
$2,500 to $4,999	296	0.7	252	0.7	13	0.6	30	1.3
$5,000 to $9,999	1 536	3.8	1 310	3.6	72	3.4	155	6.7
$10,000 to $14,999	4 537	11.2	3 695	10.3	261	12.4	582	25.4
$15,000 to $19,999	5 639	14.0	4 915	13.6	270	12.9	454	19.8
$20,000 to $24,999	5 898	14.6	5 346	14.8	279	13.3	272	11.9
$25,000 to $34,999	9 410	23.3	8 625	23.9	425	20.3	361	15.8
$35,000 to $49,999	7 353	18.2	6 715	18.6	412	19.7	226	9.9
$50,000 to $74,999	3 757	9.3	3 392	9.4	247	11.8	117	5.1
$75,000 and over	1 512	3.7	1 353	3.8	99	4.7	60	2.6

Note: Age 15 years and over.

1. Income for previous calendar year. Total money income is the algebraic sum of money wages and salaries, net income from self-employment, and income other than earnings.

Table 1-55. Percent Distribution of the Civilian Labor Force 25 to 64 Years of Age by Educational Attainment, Sex, and Race, March 1988–2000

Sex, race, and year	Civilian labor force (thousands)	Percent distribution				
		Total	Less than a high school diploma	Four years of high school only	One to three years of college	Four or more years of college
TOTAL						
1988	94 922	100.0	14.7	39.9	19.7	25.7
1989	97 318	100.0	14.0	39.6	20.0	26.4
1990	99 175	100.0	13.4	39.5	20.7	26.4
1991	100 480	100.0	13.0	39.4	21.1	26.5
1992	102 387	100.0	12.2	36.2	25.2	26.4
1993	103 504	100.0	11.5	35.2	26.3	27.0
1994	104 868	100.0	11.0	34.0	27.7	27.3
1995	106 519	100.0	10.8	33.1	27.8	28.3
1996	108 037	100.0	10.9	32.9	27.7	28.5
1997	110 514	100.0	10.9	33.0	27.4	28.6
1998	111 857	100.0	10.7	32.8	27.4	29.1
1999	112 542	100.0	10.3	32.3	27.4	30.0
2000	114 052	100.0	9.8	31.8	27.9	30.4
MEN						
1988	52 653	100.0	16.5	37.2	18.5	27.7
1989	53 668	100.0	15.7	36.9	19.2	28.2
1990	54 476	100.0	15.1	37.2	19.7	28.0
1991	55 165	100.0	14.7	37.5	20.2	27.6
1992	55 917	100.0	13.9	34.7	23.8	27.5
1993	56 544	100.0	13.2	33.9	24.7	28.1
1994	56 633	100.0	12.7	32.9	25.8	28.6
1995	57 454	100.0	12.2	32.3	25.7	29.7
1996	58 121	100.0	12.7	32.2	26.0	29.1
1997	59 268	100.0	12.8	32.2	25.8	29.2
1998	59 905	100.0	12.3	32.3	25.8	29.6
1999	60 030	100.0	11.7	32.0	25.8	30.5
2000	60 510	100.0	11.1	31.8	26.1	30.9
WOMEN						
1988	42 269	100.0	12.5	43.3	21.1	23.1
1989	43 050	100.0	11.9	42.9	20.9	24.3
1990	44 699	100.0	11.3	42.4	21.9	21.0
1991	45 315	100.0	10.9	41.6	22.2	25.2
1992	46 469	100.0	10.2	37.9	26.9	25.0
1993	46 961	100.0	9.3	36.7	28.2	25.8
1994	48 235	100.0	9.1	35.3	29.8	25.8
1995	49 065	100.0	9.1	34.1	30.2	26.6
1996	49 916	100.0	8.8	33.7	29.7	27.8
1997	51 246	100.0	8.7	34.0	29.3	28.0
1998	51 953	100.0	8.8	33.3	29.3	28.6
1999	52 512	100.0	8.7	32.7	29.2	29.5
2000	53 541	100.0	8.4	31.8	30.0	29.8
WHITE						
1988	81 902	100.0	13.8	40.0	19.7	26.4
1989	83 694	100.0	13.0	39.7	20.0	27.2
1990	85 238	100.0	12.6	39.6	20.6	27.1
1991	86 344	100.0	12.2	39.3	21.1	27.4
1992	87 656	100.0	11.3	36.1	25.5	27.1
1993	88 457	100.0	10.7	35.0	26.4	27.9
1994	89 009	100.0	10.5	33.7	27.7	28.1
1995	90 192	100.0	10.0	32.8	27.8	29.3
1996	91 506	100.0	10.4	32.8	27.5	29.3
1997	93 179	100.0	10.4	32.8	27.3	29.5
1998	93 527	100.0	10.2	32.7	27.4	29.8
1999	94 216	100.0	9.8	32.2	27.2	30.8
2000	95 073	100.0	9.5	31.8	27.7	31.0
BLACK						
1988	10 032	100.0	22.6	43.2	19.2	15.0
1989	10 358	100.0	21.7	42.3	20.5	15.6
1990	10 537	100.0	19.9	42.5	22.1	15.5
1991	10 650	100.0	19.5	42.9	22.1	15.4
1992	10 936	100.0	19.2	40.3	24.9	15.6
1993	11 051	100.0	16.8	39.5	27.6	16.1
1994	11 368	100.0	14.5	39.3	29.2	17.0
1995	11 695	100.0	14.1	38.6	29.6	17.7
1996	11 891	100.0	14.2	37.2	31.2	17.4
1997	12 253	100.0	14.3	37.8	31.3	16.6
1998	12 893	100.0	14.3	37.3	30.1	18.2
1999	12 945	100.0	13.0	37.2	30.4	19.5
2000	13 383	100.0	11.8	36.1	31.5	20.7

Note: Data for the above race groups will not sum to totals because data for the Other races group are not presented. See "Notes and Definitions" for information on historical comparability.

Table 1-56. Labor Force Participation Rates of Persons 25 to 64 Years of Age by Educational Attainment, Sex, and Race, March 1988–2000

(Civilian labor force as a percent of the civilian noninstitutional population.)

Sex, race, and year	Participation rates				
	Total	Less than a high school diploma	Four years of high school only	One to three years of college	Four or more years of college
TOTAL					
1988	77.5	60.9	76.9	82.4	88.4
1989	78.2	60.5	77.9	83.3	88.4
1990	78.6	60.7	78.2	83.3	88.4
1991	78.6	60.7	78.1	83.2	88.4
1992	79.0	60.3	78.3	83.5	88.4
1993	78.9	59.6	77.7	82.9	88.3
1994	78.9	58.3	77.8	83.2	88.2
1995	79.3	59.8	77.3	83.2	88.7
1996	79.4	60.2	77.9	83.7	87.8
1997	80.1	61.7	78.5	83.7	88.5
1998	80.2	63.0	78.4	83.5	88.0
1999	80.0	62.7	78.1	83.0	87.6
2000	80.3	62.7	78.4	83.2	87.8
MEN					
1988	88.6	76.6	89.4	91.2	94.4
1989	88.8	75.9	89.6	91.8	94.5
1990	88.8	75.1	89.9	91.5	94.5
1991	88.6	75.1	89.3	92.0	94.2
1992	88.6	75.1	89.0	91.8	93.7
1993	88.1	74.9	88.1	90.6	93.7
1994	87.0	71.5	86.8	90.3	93.2
1995	87.4	72.0	86.9	90.1	93.8
1996	87.5	74.3	86.9	90.0	92.9
1997	87.7	75.2	86.4	90.6	93.5
1998	87.8	75.3	86.7	90.0	93.4
1999	87.5	74.4	86.6	89.4	93.0
2000	87.5	74.9	86.2	88.9	93.3
WOMEN					
1988	67.1	45.5	66.9	74.6	80.7
1989	68.3	45.5	68.5	75.4	81.1
1990	68.9	46.2	68.7	75.9	81.1
1991	69.1	46.2	68.6	75.2	81.8
1992	70.0	45.6	69.1	76.2	82.2
1993	70.0	44.2	68.8	76.1	82.2
1994	71.1	44.7	70.0	77.0	82.5
1995	71.5	47.2	68.9	77.3	82.8
1996	71.8	45.7	69.8	78.1	82.3
1997	72.8	47.1	71.4	77.6	83.2
1998	73.0	49.8	70.9	77.8	82.3
1999	72.8	50.5	70.4	77.4	81.9
2000	73.5	50.4	71.2	78.3	82.0
WHITE					
1988	78.1	62.3	76.9	82.2	88.6
1989	78.7	61.6	77.8	83.2	88.5
1990	79.2	62.5	78.4	83.3	88.3
1991	79.4	62.5	78.3	83.1	88.6
1992	79.8	61.5	78.7	83.8	88.7
1993	79.7	61.1	78.2	83.1	88.8
1994	79.8	60.3	78.3	83.5	88.5
1995	80.1	61.6	77.9	83.4	88.8
1996	80.4	62.5	78.6	83.9	88.2
1997	81.0	63.8	79.2	83.9	89.0
1998	80.6	63.8	78.6	83.5	88.3
1999	80.6	64.2	78.5	83.3	87.9
2000	80.8	64.2	78.7	83.1	87.9
BLACK					
1988	74.4	56.4	78.0	85.6	90.7
1989	74.9	56.7	78.9	83.9	90.4
1990	74.6	54.5	78.2	84.2	92.0
1991	73.9	53.9	77.1	84.1	90.2
1992	74.4	55.4	76.9	83.4	89.1
1993	73.8	53.4	74.7	83.0	89.6
1994	73.5	49.4	75.2	82.4	89.5
1995	74.2	51.0	74.5	82.8	90.9
1996	73.7	50.1	74.3	83.0	87.9
1997	74.9	52.9	75.0	83.8	89.0
1998	77.7	59.3	77.0	85.0	88.8
1999	76.5	55.1	76.5	82.9	88.6
2000	77.9	55.5	77.0	84.2	90.3

Note: Data for the above race groups will not sum to totals because data for the Other races group are not presented. See "Notes and Definitions" for information on historical comparability.

Table 1-57. Unemployment Rates of Persons 25 to 64 Years of Age by Educational Attainment, Sex, and Race, March 1988–2000

(Unemployment as a percent of the civilian labor force.)

Sex, race, and year	Unemployment rates				
	Total	Less than a high school diploma	Four years of high school only	One to three years of college	Four or more years of college
TOTAL					
1988	4.8	9.5	5.5	3.7	1.8
1989	4.4	8.9	4.8	3.4	2.2
1990	4.5	9.6	4.9	3.7	1.9
1991	6.1	12.3	6.7	5.0	2.9
1992	6.7	13.5	7.7	5.9	2.9
1993	6.4	13.0	7.3	5.5	3.2
1994	5.8	12.6	6.7	5.0	2.9
1995	4.8	10.0	5.2	4.5	2.5
1996	4.8	10.9	5.5	4.1	2.2
1997	4.4	10.4	5.1	3.8	2.0
1998	4.0	8.5	4.8	3.6	1.8
1999	3.5	7.7	4.0	3.1	1.9
2000	3.3	7.9	3.8	3.0	1.5
MEN					
1988	5.2	10.1	6.3	3.9	1.7
1989	4.7	9.4	5.4	3.2	2.3
1990	4.8	9.6	5.3	3.9	2.1
1991	6.8	13.4	7.7	5.2	3.2
1992	7.5	14.8	8.8	6.4	3.2
1993	7.3	14.1	8.7	6.3	3.4
1994	6.2	12.8	7.2	5.3	2.9
1995	5.1	10.9	5.7	4.4	2.6
1996	5.3	11.0	6.4	4.5	2.3
1997	4.7	9.9	5.6	4.0	2.1
1998	4.1	8.0	5.1	3.7	1.7
1999	3.5	7.0	4.1	3.2	1.9
2000	3.3	7.1	3.9	3.1	1.6
WOMEN					
1988	4.2	8.6	4.6	3.5	1.9
1989	4.0	8.1	4.2	3.7	2.0
1990	4.2	9.5	4.6	3.5	1.7
1991	5.2	10.7	5.5	4.8	2.5
1992	5.7	11.4	6.5	5.3	2.5
1993	5.2	11.2	5.8	4.6	2.9
1994	5.4	12.4	6.2	4.7	2.9
1995	4.4	8.6	4.6	4.5	2.4
1996	4.1	10.7	4.4	3.8	2.1
1997	4.1	11.3	4.5	3.6	2.0
1998	3.9	9.3	4.4	3.5	1.9
1999	3.5	8.8	3.9	3.0	1.9
2000	3.2	9.1	3.6	2.9	1.4
WHITE					
1988	4.1	8.5	4.6	3.3	1.5
1989	3.8	7.7	4.2	3.0	2.0
1990	4.0	8.3	4.4	3.3	1.8
1991	5.6	11.6	6.2	4.6	2.7
1992	6.0	12.9	6.8	5.3	2.7
1993	5.8	12.4	6.5	5.0	3.1
1994	5.2	11.7	5.8	4.5	2.6
1995	4.3	9.2	4.6	4.2	2.3
1996	4.2	10.2	4.6	3.7	2.1
1997	3.9	9.4	4.6	3.4	1.8
1998	3.5	7.5	4.2	3.2	1.7
1999	3.1	7.0	3.4	2.8	1.7
2000	3.0	7.5	3.3	2.7	1.4
BLACK					
1988	10.1	14.5	11.3	7.5	3.4
1989	9.2	14.6	9.2	6.9	4.7
1990	8.6	15.9	8.6	6.5	1.9
1991	10.1	15.9	10.3	8.0	5.2
1992	12.4	17.2	14.1	10.7	4.8
1993	10.9	17.3	12.4	8.7	4.1
1994	10.6	17.4	12.2	8.3	4.9
1995	7.7	13.7	8.4	6.3	4.1
1996	8.9	15.3	10.8	6.9	3.3
1997	8.1	16.6	8.2	6.1	4.4
1998	7.3	13.4	8.4	6.4	2.1
1999	6.3	12.0	6.7	5.2	3.3
2000	5.4	10.4	6.3	4.3	2.5

Note: Data for the above race groups will not sum to totals because data for the Other races group are not presented. See "Notes and Definitions" for information on historical comparability.

Table 1-58. Workers Age 25 to 64 by Educational Attainment, Occupation of Longest Held Job, and Sex, 1999

(Thousands of persons with work experience during the year.)

Sex and occupation	Total	Less than a high school diploma	Four years of high school only	One to three years of college	Four or more years of college
TOTAL	118 202	11 613	37 579	33 194	35 815
Managerial and professional specialty	38 228	585	4 729	8 465	24 449
Executive, administrative, and managerial	18 883	453	3 726	5 431	9 273
Professional specialty	19 345	132	1 003	3 034	15 176
Technical, sales, and administrative support	33 164	1 347	11 512	12 459	7 846
Technicians and related support	4 148	60	893	1 975	1 220
Sales occupations	12 803	700	4 085	3 898	4 120
Administrative support, including clerical	16 212	587	6 533	6 586	2 506
Service occupations	14 516	2 902	6 227	4 116	1 271
Private household	716	255	280	132	48
Protective service	2 099	107	676	917	399
Service, except private household and protective	11 701	2 540	5 271	3 066	824
Precision production, craft, and repair	13 301	2 271	6 189	3 896	945
Mechanics and repairers	4 351	564	1 938	1 541	307
Construction trades	5 480	1 160	2 610	1 405	306
Other precision production, craft, and repair	3 470	547	1 641	950	332
Operators, fabricators, and laborers	15 678	3 640	7 815	3 435	787
Machine operators, assemblers, and inspectors	6 763	1 614	3 381	1 447	322
Transportation and material moving occupations	5 018	920	2 581	1 211	307
Handlers, equipment cleaners, helpers, and laborers	3 896	1 106	1 853	778	158
Farming, forestry, and fishing	2 722	865	991	571	295
Armed forces	592	2	116	253	222
MEN	62 231	6 847	19 722	16 438	19 226
Managerial and professional specialty	18 987	320	2 255	3 775	12 638
Executive, administrative, and managerial	10 273	265	1 811	2 590	5 607
Professional specialty	8 714	55	443	1 185	7 031
Technical, sales, and administrative support	11 579	403	3 108	3 981	4 088
Technicians and related support	1 875	29	363	802	681
Sales occupations	6 583	234	1 747	1 937	2 665
Administrative support, including clerical	3 121	140	999	1 241	741
Service occupations	5 394	902	2 090	1 734	667
Private household	34	8	13	9	4
Protective service	1 749	52	557	787	353
Service, except private household and protective	3 612	842	1 521	939	310
Precision production, craft, and repair	11 991	2 013	5 555	3 618	805
Mechanics and repairers	4 101	544	1 828	1 456	274
Construction trades	5 325	1 121	2 535	1 374	295
Other precision production, craft, and repair	2 564	348	1 192	789	236
Operators, fabricators, and laborers	11 680	2 531	5 841	2 686	622
Machine operators, assemblers, and inspectors	4 175	867	2 063	1 024	221
Transportation and material moving occupations	4 509	841	2 335	1 061	272
Handlers, equipment cleaners, helpers, and laborers	2 996	823	1 443	601	129
Farming, forestry, and fishing	2 068	676	766	418	208
Armed forces	532	2	106	225	199
WOMEN	55 970	4 766	17 859	16 757	16 588
Managerial and professional specialty	19 241	265	2 475	4 690	11 812
Executive, administrative, and managerial	8 610	188	1 915	2 841	3 666
Professional specialty	10 631	77	560	1 849	8 145
Technical, sales, and administrative support	21 585	945	8 403	8 478	3 758
Technicians and related support	2 273	32	531	1 172	539
Sales occupations	6 220	466	2 338	1 961	1 454
Administrative support, including clerical	13 091	447	5 534	5 345	1 765
Service occupations	9 123	2 000	4 137	2 381	604
Private household	683	248	268	123	44
Protective service	350	55	119	130	46
Service, except private household and protective	8 090	1 697	3 751	2 128	514
Precision production, craft, and repair	1 311	259	635	278	139
Mechanics and repairers	249	21	111	86	32
Construction trades	155	39	75	31	11
Other precision production, craft, and repair	906	199	449	161	96
Operators, fabricators, and laborers	3 998	1 109	1 974	749	166
Machine operators, assemblers, and inspectors	2 588	746	1 318	422	101
Transportation and material moving occupations	510	79	246	150	35
Handlers, equipment cleaners, helpers, and laborers	900	283	410	177	30
Farming, forestry, and fishing	654	189	225	153	87
Armed forces	60	...	9	28	23

Table 1-59. Percent Distribution of Workers Age 25 to 64 by Educational Attainment, Occupation of Longest Held Job, and Sex, 1999

(Percent of total workers in occupation.)

Sex and occupation	Total	Less than a high school diploma	Four years of high school only	One to three years of college	Four or more years of college
TOTAL	100.0	9.8	31.8	28.1	30.3
Managerial and professional specialty	100.0	1.5	12.4	22.1	64.0
Executive, administrative, and managerial	100.0	2.4	19.7	28.8	49.1
Professional specialty	100.0	0.7	5.2	15.7	78.5
Technical, sales, and administrative support	100.0	4.1	34.7	37.6	23.7
Technicians and related support	100.0	1.5	21.5	47.6	29.4
Sales occupations	100.0	5.5	31.9	30.4	32.2
Administrative support, including clerical	100.0	3.6	40.3	40.6	15.5
Service occupations	100.0	20.0	42.9	28.4	8.8
Private household	100.0	35.7	39.2	18.5	6.7
Protective service	100.0	5.1	32.2	43.7	19.0
Service, except private household and protective	100.0	21.7	45.0	26.2	7.0
Precision production, craft, and repair	100.0	17.1	46.5	29.3	7.1
Mechanics and repairers	100.0	13.0	44.6	35.4	7.0
Construction trades	100.0	21.2	47.6	25.6	5.6
Other precision production, craft, and repair	100.0	15.8	47.3	27.4	9.6
Operators, fabricators, and laborers	100.0	23.2	49.8	21.9	5.0
Machine operators, assemblers, and inspectors	100.0	23.9	50.0	21.4	4.8
Transportation and material moving occupations	100.0	18.3	51.4	24.1	6.1
Handlers, equipment cleaners, helpers, and laborers	100.0	28.4	47.6	20.0	4.1
Farming, forestry, and fishing	100.0	31.8	36.4	21.0	10.8
Armed forces	100.0	0.3	19.6	42.7	37.5
MEN	100.0	11.0	31.7	26.4	30.9
Managerial and professional specialty	100.0	1.7	11.9	19.9	66.6
Executive, administrative, and managerial	100.0	2.6	17.6	25.2	54.6
Professional specialty	100.0	0.6	5.1	13.6	80.7
Technical, sales, and administrative support	100.0	3.5	26.8	34.4	35.3
Technicians and related support	100.0	1.5	19.3	42.8	36.3
Sales occupations	100.0	3.6	26.5	29.4	40.5
Administrative support, including clerical	100.0	4.5	32.0	39.8	23.7
Service occupations	100.0	16.7	38.8	32.2	12.4
Private household	100.0	23.3	37.6	26.5	12.6
Protective service	100.0	3.0	31.9	45.0	20.2
Service, except private household and protective	100.0	23.3	42.1	26.0	8.6
Precision production, craft, and repair	100.0	16.8	46.3	30.2	6.7
Mechanics and repairers	100.0	13.3	44.6	35.5	6.7
Construction trades	100.0	21.1	47.6	25.8	5.5
Other precision production, craft, and repair	100.0	13.6	46.5	30.8	9.2
Operators, fabricators, and laborers	100.0	21.7	50.0	23.0	5.3
Machine operators, assemblers, and inspectors	100.0	20.8	49.4	24.5	5.3
Transportation and material moving occupations	100.0	18.6	51.8	23.5	6.0
Handlers, equipment cleaners, helpers, and laborers	100.0	27.5	48.2	20.0	4.3
Farming, forestry, and fishing	100.0	32.7	37.1	20.2	10.1
Armed forces	100.0	0.3	20.0	42.2	37.5
WOMEN	100.0	8.5	31.9	29.9	29.6
Managerial and professional specialty	100.0	1.4	12.9	24.4	61.4
Executive, administrative, and managerial	100.0	2.2	22.2	33.0	42.6
Professional specialty	100.0	0.7	5.3	17.4	76.6
Technical, sales, and administrative support	100.0	4.4	38.9	39.3	17.4
Technicians and related support	100.0	1.4	23.3	51.6	23.7
Sales occupations	100.0	7.5	37.6	31.5	23.4
Administrative support, including clerical	100.0	3.4	42.3	40.8	13.5
Service occupations	100.0	21.9	45.3	26.1	6.6
Private household	100.0	36.3	39.2	18.1	6.4
Protective service	100.0	15.7	33.9	37.2	13.1
Service, except private household and protective	100.0	21.0	46.4	26.3	6.4
Precision production, craft, and repair	100.0	19.7	48.4	21.2	10.6
Mechanics and repairers	100.0	8.3	44.4	34.3	12.9
Construction trades	100.0	24.9	48.1	20.0	7.0
Other precision production, craft, and repair	100.0	22.0	49.6	17.8	10.6
Operators, fabricators, and laborers	100.0	27.7	49.4	18.7	4.1
Machine operators, assemblers, and inspectors	100.0	28.8	50.9	16.3	3.9
Transportation and material moving occupations	100.0	15.6	48.2	29.4	6.8
Handlers, equipment cleaners, helpers, and laborers	100.0	31.5	45.6	19.7	3.3
Farming, forestry, and fishing	100.0	28.9	34.4	23.4	13.3
Armed forces	100.0	. . .	15.8	46.7	37.5

Table 1-60. Median Annual Earnings by Educational Attainment and Sex, Year-Round Full-Time Wage and Salary Workers, Age 25 to 64, 1996–1999

(Thousands of workers, dollars.)

Year and sex	Total	Less than a high school diploma	Four years of high school only	One to threee years of college	Four or more years of college
1996					
Total					
Number of workers (thousands)	77 394	7 210	25 280	21 737	23 167
Median annual earnings	$30 000	$18 000	$25 000	$30 000	$41 500
Men					
Number of workers (thousands)	45 562	4 919	14 507	12 183	13 954
Median annual earnings	$34 668	$20 000	$30 000	$35 000	$50 000
Women					
Number of workers (thousands)	31 832	2 292	10 773	9 554	9 213
Median annual earnings	$25 000	$15 000	$20 000	$25 000	$35 000
1997					
Total					
Number of workers (thousands)	78 524	7 218	25 432	21 742	24 131
Median annual earnings	$30 000	$19 000	$25 740	$30 000	$44 000
Men					
Number of workers (thousands)	45 976	4 873	14 686	12 126	14 291
Median annual earnings	$35 000	$21 840	$30 000	$35 000	$50 000
Women					
Number of workers (thousands)	32 548	2 345	10 746	9 617	9 840
Median annual earnings	$25 000	$15 000	$21 000	$25 000	$36 000
1998					
Total					
Number of workers (thousands)	80 812	7 353	25 595	22 526	25 338
Median annual earnings	$32 000	$19 000	$26 300	$31 619	$45 000
Men					
Number of workers (thousands)	47 230	4 872	14 744	12 473	15 142
Median annual earnings	$36 400	$22 000	$30 000	$36 000	$52 000
Women					
Number of workers (thousands)	33 582	2 482	10 851	10 053	10 197
Median annual earnings	$27 000	$15 000	$22 000	$26 500	$38 000
1999					
Total					
Number of workers (thousands)	82 501	7 208	25 792	23 380	26 120
Median annual earnings	$33 000	$20 000	$27 000	$33 000	$48 000
Men					
Number of workers (thousands)	47 781	4 693	14 806	12 824	15 459
Median annual earnings	$38 500	$22 000	$32 000	$39 000	$55 600
Women					
Number of workers (thousands)	34 720	2 516	10 986	10 556	10 662
Median annual earnings	$27 040	$15 000	$22 000	$27 280	$40 000

NOTES AND DEFINITIONS

CONTINGENT AND ALTERNATIVE WORK ARRANGEMENTS

Collection and Coverage

The data on contingent and alternative work arrangements were collected through a supplement to the February 1999 Current Population Survey (CPS). The CPS is a monthly survey of about 50,000 households that provides the basic data on employment and unemployment for the nation. This supplement obtained information from workers on whether they held contingent jobs, that is, jobs that were expected to last only a limited period of time. In addition, information was collected on several alternative employment arrangements, namely working as independent contractors and on call, as well as working through temporary help agencies and contract firms. The contingent and alternative work arrangements data will be collected every other year.

Concepts and Definitions

Alternative Work Arrangements

To provide estimates of the number of workers in alternative employment arrangements, the February 1999 CPS supplement included questions about whether individuals were paid by a temporary help agency or contract company, or whether they were on-call workers or independent contractors.

Independent contractors are all those who were identified in the survey as independent contractors, consultants, and free-lance workers, regardless of whether they were identified as wage and salary workers or self-employed in the responses to basic CPS labor force status questions. Workers identified as self-employed (incorporated and unincorporated) in the basic CPS were asked, "Are you self-employed as an independent contractor, independent consultant, free-lance worker, or something else (such as a shop or restaurant owner)?" in order to distinguish those who consider themselves to be independent contractors, consultants, or free-lance workers from those who were business operators such as shop owners. Those identified as wage and salary workers in the basic CPS were asked, "Last week, were you working as an independent contractor, an independent consultant, or a free-lance worker? That is, someone who obtains customers on their own to provide a product or service."

About 88 percent of independent contractors were identified as self-employed in the main questionnaire, while 12 percent were identified as wage and salary workers. Conversely, about half of the self-employed were identified as independent contractors. The self-employed are excluded from the data for workers with other arrangements.

On-call workers are persons who are called into work only when they are needed, although they can be scheduled to work several days or weeks in a row.

Temporary help agency workers were all those who were paid by a temporary help agency, whether or not their job was temporary. To the extent that permanent staff of temporary help agencies indicate that they are paid by their agencies, the estimate of the number of workers whose employment was mediated by temporary help agencies is overstated.

Workers provided by contract firms are those individuals who are employed by a company that provides their services to others under contract, and who usually work for only one customer and usually work at the customer's work site. A few examples of services that can be contracted out include security, landscaping, and computer programming.

Workers with traditional arrangements are those who do not fall into any of the alternative arrangements categories.

Contingent Workers

Contingent workers are defined as those who do not have an explicit or implicit contract for long-term employment. Several pieces of information were collected in the supplement from which the existence of a contingent employment arrangement could be discerned. These include whether the job was temporary or not expected to continue, how long the worker expected to be able to hold the job, and how long the worker had held the job. For workers who had a job with an intermediary, namely a temporary help agency or a contract company, information was collected about their employment at the place they were assigned to work by the intermediary as well as their employment with the intermediary itself.

The key factor used to determine if a worker's job fit the conceptual definition of contingent was whether the job was temporary or not expected to continue. The first questions of the supplement were:

1. Some people are in temporary jobs that last only for a limited time or until the completion of a project. Is your job temporary?

2. Provided the economy does not change and your job performance is adequate, can you continue to work for your current employer as long as you wish?

Respondents who answered "yes" to the first question, or "no" to the second, were then asked a series of questions to distinguish persons who were in temporary jobs from those who, for personal reasons, were temporarily holding jobs that offered the opportunity of ongoing employment.

Workers also were asked how long they expected to stay in their current job and how long they had been with their current employer. The rationale for asking how long an individual expects to remain in his or her current job was that being able to hold a job for a year or more could be taken as evidence of at least an implicit contract for ongoing employment. To assess the impact of the defining factors on the estimated size of the contingent workforce, three measures of contingent employment were developed.

Estimate 1, which is the narrowest, measures contingent workers as wage and salary workers who indicated that they expected to work in their current job for 1 year or less and who had worked for their current employer for 1 year or less. Self-employed workers, both incorporated and unincorporated, and independent contractors are excluded from the count of contingent workers under estimate 1.

Estimate 2 expands the measure of the contingent work force by including the self-employed—both the incorporated and the unincorporated—and independent contractors who expect to be, and had been, in such employment arrangements for 1 year or less.

Estimate 3 expands the count of contingency by removing the 1 year or less requirement on both expected duration of the job and current tenure for wage and salary workers. Thus, the estimate effectively includes all the wage and salary workers who do not expect their employment to last, except for those who, for personal reasons, expect to leave jobs they would otherwise be able to keep.

Non-contingent workers are those who do not fall into any estimate of contingent workers.

Sources of Additional Information

A complete description of the survey and additional tables are available from BLS news release USDL 99 - 362. Several analytical articles appear in the Monthly Labor Review.

Table 1-61. Employed Workers with Alternative and Traditional Work Arrangements by Selected Characteristics, February 1999

(Thousands of persons.)

Characteristic	Total employed	Workers with alternative arrangements				Workers with traditional arrangements
		Independent contractors	On-call workers	Temporary help agency workers	Workers provided by contract firms	
AGE AND SEX						
Total, 16 years and over	131 494	8 247	2 032	1 188	769	119 109
16 to 19 years	6 662	76	179	68	37	6 265
20 to 24 years	12 462	252	202	249	87	11 637
25 to 34 years	30 968	1 479	470	348	235	28 410
35 to 44 years	36 415	2 491	507	231	216	32 960
45 to 54 years	28 144	2 177	303	182	132	25 332
55 to 64 years	13 062	1 212	205	77	47	11 505
65 years and over	3 781	561	167	33	14	3 000
Men, 16 years and over	70 040	5 459	993	501	542	62 464
16 to 19 years	3 339	47	93	38	29	3 116
20 to 24 years	6 489	158	120	114	71	6 005
25 to 34 years	16 617	901	203	145	168	15 179
35 to 44 years	19 603	1 705	235	84	155	17 422
45 to 54 years	14 684	1 406	155	75	72	12 966
55 to 64 years	7 186	814	102	27	35	6 203
65 years and over	2 122	427	84	18	12	1 575
Women, 16 years and over	61 454	2 788	1 040	687	227	56 645
16 to 19 years	3 323	29	86	30	8	3 149
20 to 24 years	5 973	93	81	134	16	5 632
25 to 34 years	14 351	578	266	203	67	13 231
35 to 44 years	16 812	786	272	147	61	15 538
45 to 54 years	13 459	772	149	107	60	12 367
55 to 64 years	5 876	397	103	50	12	5 302
65 years and over	1 659	133	83	15	2	1 426
RACE AND HISPANIC ORIGIN						
White	110 887	7 471	1 711	883	609	100 063
Black	14 620	476	258	252	97	13 542
Hispanic origin	13 356	506	237	161	46	12 355
FULL- OR PART-TIME STATUS						
Full-time workers	107 630	6 195	1 003	933	668	98 766
Part-time workers	23 864	2 053	1 029	255	101	20 343

Note: Detail may not add to totals because the total employed includes day laborers, an alternative arrangement not shown separately, and a small number of workers were both on call and provided by contract firms. Detail for the above race and Hispanic-origin groups will not sum to totals because data for the Other races group are not presented and Hispanics are included in both the White and Black population groups. Detail for other characteristics may not sum to totals due to rounding.

Table 1-62. Employed Contingent and Noncontingent Workers by Occupation and Industry, February 1999

(Thousands of persons, percent.)

Characteristic	Contingent workers			Noncontingent workers
	Estimate 1	Estimate 2	Estimate 3	
OCCUPATION				
Total, 16 years and over (thousands)	2 444	3 038	5 641	125 853
Total, 16 years and over (percent distribution)	100.0	100.0	100.0	100.0
Executive, administrative and managerial	3.8	4.9	6.8	15.1
Professional specialty	20.1	18.2	24.7	15.4
Technicians and related support	3.4	3.5	3.3	3.2
Sales occupations	8.0	8.8	6.8	12.3
Administrative support, including clerical	22.4	20.6	19.2	14.0
Services occupations	16.5	18.2	14.7	13.4
Precision production, craft, and repair	8.4	8.7	8.4	11.1
Operators, fabricators and laborers	14.1	13.9	12.5	13.4
Farming, forestry, and fishing	3.3	3.1	3.7	2.1
INDUSTRY				
Total 16 years and over (thousands)	2 444	3 038	5 641	125 853
Total, 16 years and over (percent distribution)	100.0	100.0	100.0	100.0
Agriculture	3.0	3.0	3.1	2.1
Mining	0.2	0.1	0.2	0.4
Construction	7.5	7.7	7.5	6.1
Manufacturing	6.5	6.7	8.1	15.9
Transportation and public utilities	3.5	3.8	3.4	7.4
Wholesale trade	2.4	2.5	2.5	4.0
Retail trade	14.5	13.0	10.7	17.1
Finance, insurance, and real estate	2.2	3.0	3.0	6.9
Services	57.0	57.4	58.1	35.4
Public administration	3.1	2.7	3.3	4.7

Note: See "Notes and Definitions" for explanation of Estimate 1, 2 and 3. Detail may not sum to totals due to rounding.

Table 1-63. Employed Contingent Workers by Their Preference for Contingent or Noncontingent Work Arrangements, February 1999

(Thousands of persons, percent.)

Preference	Estimate 1	Estimate 2	Estimate 3
TOTAL, 16 YEARS AND OVER	2 444	3 038	5 641
Percent	100.0	100.0	100.0
Prefer noncontingent employment	54.0	53.4	53.1
Prefer contingent employment	39.2	39.8	38.9
It depends	5.1	4.5	5.3
Not available	1.7	2.3	2.7

Note: See "Notes and Definitions" for explanation of Estimate 1, 2 and 3. Detail may not sum to totals due to rounding.

Table 1-64. Employed Contingent and Noncontingent Workers with Alternative and Traditional Work Arrangements by Health Insurance Coverage and Eligibility for Employer-Provided Pension Plans, February 1999

(Thousands of persons, percent.)

Characteristic	Total employed	Percent with heath insurance coverage		Percent eligible for employer-provided pension plan [2]	
		Total	Provided by employer [1]	Total	Included in employer-provided pension plan
BY CONTINGENCY					
Contingent Workers					
Estimate 1	2 444	60.2	12.4	11.9	5.4
Estimate 2	3 038	57.7	11.0	11.6	5.5
Estimate 3	5 641	64.1	20.6	21.4	13.8
Noncontingent Workers	125 853	82.3	54.6	51.3	45.8
BY TYPE OF ARRANGEMENT					
With Alternative Arrangements					
Independent contractors	8 247	73.3	. . .	2.8	1.9
On-call workers	2 032	67.3	21.1	29.0	22.5
Temporary help agency workers	1 188	41.0	8.5	11.8	5.8
Workers provided by contract firms	769	79.9	56.1	53.9	40.2
With Traditional Arrangements	119 109	82.8	57.9	54.1	48.3

Note: See "Notes and Definitions" for explanation of Estimate 1, 2 and 3. Detail may not sum to totals due to rounding.

1. Excludes the self-employed (incorporated and unincorporated) and independent contractors.
2. Excludes the self-employed (incorporated and unincorporated); includes independent contractors who were self-employed.

Table 1-65. Median Usual Weekly Earnings of Workers with Contingent and Alternative Work Arrangements by Selected Characteristics, February 1999

(Dollars.)

Characteristic	By contingency				By type of arrangement				
	Contingent workers			Noncontingent workers	Workers with alternative arrangements				Workers with traditional arrangements
	Estimate 1	Estimate 2	Estimate 3		Independent contractors	On-call workers	Temporary help agency workers	Workers provided by contract firms	
FULL-TIME WORKERS									
Total, 16 years and over	$360	$374	$415	$542	$640	$472	$342	$756	$540
Men	413	434	494	614	689	507	367	770	613
Women	306	314	340	476	441	348	331	690	474
White	378	384	420	564	662	478	338	734	562
Black	265	297	350	447	414	393	354	719	445
Hispanic origin	278	286	313	397	504	308	296	(1)	396
PART-TIME WORKERS									
Total, 16 years and over	111	112	114	160	209	119	187	171	157
Men	116	117	119	150	319	133	192	(1)	146
Women	108	109	112	166	169	114	185	(1)	163
White	111	111	113	161	220	119	183	197	158
Black	115	119	122	150	142	130	(1)	(1)	146
Hispanic origin	116	117	116	159	240	102	(1)	(1)	156

Note: See "Notes and Definitions" for definitions of Estimate 1, 2 and 3. Data for independent contractors include the incorporated and unincorporated self-employed; these groups, however, are excluded from the data for workers with other arrangements. Data for the Other races group are not presented and Hispanics are included in both the White and Black population groups.

1. Data not shown where base number of workers is less than 75,000.

NOTES AND DEFINITIONS

EMPLOYER-PROVIDED TRAINING

Collection and Coverage

The 1995 Survey of Employer-Provided Training was a one time survey conducted by the Bureau of Labor Statistics and was sponsored by the Employment and Training Administration of the U.S. Department of Labor. The survey consisted of two major components: 1) a survey of establishments; and 2) a survey of randomly-selected employees in the survey establishments.

The employer survey focused on the amount of formal training provided and selected costs of formal training. Formal training is defined as training that is planned in advance and has a structured format and defined curriculum. The employee survey obtained information on the amount of formal and informal training received and the wage and salary cost of the time that employees spend in both formal and informal training. Informal training is unstructured, unplanned and easily adapted to situations or individuals.

The kinds of training covered were management training; professional and technical skills; computer procedures, programming, and software; clerical and administrative support skills; sales and customer relations; service-related training; production and construction related training; general skills; basic skills; occupational safety; employee health and wellness; orientation to personnel procedures; awareness; and communication, employee development, and quality.

The employer portion of the 1995 Survey of Employer-Provided Training was carried out over a 6-month period, from May 1995 through October 1995. Two survey instruments were utilized—a questionnaire and a training log. The employer questionnaire focused on training programs and practices of the establishments.

The questionnaire was administered during a personal interview. Questions were included on the selected costs of formal training during 1994 including the wages and salaries of in-house trainers, fees paid to outside training companies, and tuition reimbursement amounts. In addition, information was collected on a variety of establishment characteristics expected to be correlated with the provision of formal training. These included the existence of various workplace practices, types of benefits, extent of contract employment, extent of unionization, and employee turnover rates.

The employer log collected detailed information on all formal training events provided or financed by the establishment over a 2-week period. The requested information included a count of the number of employees in each formal training activity, the hours of training, the type of training, and who conducted the training.

The employee component of the training survey was conducted in tandem with the employer survey. Over 1,000 employees were surveyed from May through October 1995. Each employee had a personal visit interview. Two survey instruments were utilized—an employee questionnaire and an employee log.

The employee questionnaire focused on employment and demographic characteristics. Questions were included on job; employer and occupational tenure; income; weeks and hours worked; education; sex, age, race and ethnicity; marital status; and number of children. In addition, the employee questionnaire included general questions on types of training provided by the employer during the employee's tenure and in the last 12 months and on the benefits of training. The employee log collected detailed information on all training and learning activities the employee participated in over a 10-day period. The requested information on the activity included a description, its duration, who was involved, and what type of training medium was used.

Sources of Additional Information

Additional details on data collection and measurement methods and extensive tables are available in news releases, USDL 96-268 and USDL 96-515.

Table 1-66. Number of Hours of Formal Training per Employee by Type of Formal Training and Industry, May–October 1995, Employer Survey

Characteristic	Total, 50 or more employees	Mining	Construction	Manufacturing		Transportation, communications, and public utilities	Wholesale trade	Retail trade	Finance, insurance, and real estate	Services
				Durable	Nondurable					
TYPE OF FORMAL TRAINING										
Any formal training	10.7	14.4	5.0	11.7	11.9	18.3	8.4	3.7	16.6	11.0
Job skills										
Management training	0.8	0.3	0.1	1.1	...	1.6	0.8	0.3	1.3	0.7
Professional and technical training	1.3	1.1	0.2	1.9	0.9	2.0	0.2	0.1	2.1	1.6
Computer training	2.1	2.3	0.2	1.5	0.9	1.8	1.3	0.4	5.6	3.4
Clerical and administrative training	0.5	0.1	...	...	0.2	1.7	0.1	...	1.4	0.8
Sales and customer relations training	0.8	0.4	0.1	0.5	0.2	1.8	1.2	1.5	1.6	0.4
Service related training	0.6	...	...	...	0.1	2.1	...	0.5	...	0.9
Production and construction training	1.1	1.7	1.2	1.9	2.2	3.6	3.0	0.3	...	0.1
General skills										
Basic skills training	0.1	...	...	0.3	0.4	...	0.1	...	...	...
Occupational safety training	1.2	5.5	2.9	1.5	2.3	1.0	0.5	0.1	...	1.3
Employee health and wellness training	0.2	0.6	...	0.1	0.1	0.1	0.3	...	0.6	0.2
Orientation training	0.6	0.9	0.1	0.3	1.3	0.9	0.2	0.5	0.2	0.7
Awareness training	0.1	...	...	...	0.1	0.1	0.1	...	0.3	...
Communications and quality training	1.4	1.3	0.4	2.6	2.8	1.6	0.5	0.1	3.5	0.8
Other types of formal training	0.1	0.4	...	...	0.1	...	...	...	0.1	0.1

Table 1-67. Selected 1994 Training Expenditures per Employee by Industry, May–October 1995, Employer Survey

(Dollars.)

Characteristic	Establishments with 50 or more employees									
	Total	Mining	Construction	Manufacturing: Durable	Manufacturing: Nondurable	Transportation, communications, and public utilities	Wholesale trade	Retail trade	Finance, insurance, and real estate	Services
Tuition reimbursements	$51	$50	$16	$74	$64	$62	$56	$22	$74	$45
Wages and salaries of in-house trainers	139	299	64	98	188	334	108	31	202	146
Payments to outside trainers	98	160	60	95	157	135	108	21	213	87
Contributions to outside training funds	12	12	102	22	1	7	18	5	. . .	7
Subsidies for training received from outside sources	5	. . .	1	9	7	3	1	. . .	. . .	8

Table 1-68. Percent of Employees Who Received Training by Type of Training, May–October 1995, Employee Survey

Characteristic	Received formal training		Received informal training while with current employer
	While with current employer	Within the last 12 months	
TOTAL			
All employed [1]	84.4	69.8	95.8
JOB SKILLS			
Management	28.4	16.3	32.3
Professional and technical skills	30.9	21.4	27.7
Computer procedures, programming, and software	38.4	23.5	54.3
Clerical and administrative support skills	18.7	8.4	30.1
Sales and customer relations	26.6	15.1	30.9
Service-related	12.5	5.9	14.7
Production and construction-related	21.0	11.3	34.1
GENERAL SKILLS			
Basic skills	6.7	2.3	2.9
Occupational safety	58.0	42.8	47.7
Communications, employee development, and quality training	40.2	22.8	32.6
Other	3.4	1.4	0.8

1. Employees working in establishments of 50 or more employees.

Table 1-69. Percent of Employees Who Received Training by Selected Demographic Characteristics, May–October 1995, Employee Survey

Characteristic	Received formal training		Received informal training while with current employer
	While with current employer	Within the last 12 months	
TOTAL			
All employed [1]	84.4	69.8	95.8
AGE			
24 years and younger	81.6	63.4	100.0
25 to 34 years	91.3	78.5	96.9
35 to 44 years	88.1	74.7	97.7
45 to 54 years	77.9	64.7	93.7
55 years and over	74.4	50.7	89.9
SEX			
Men	81.7	66.5	96.2
Women	87.2	73.1	95.4
RACE AND ORIGIN			
White	85.2	70.4	95.5
Black	82.6	70.6	96.4
Hispanic origin	90.8	73.7	96.9
EDUCATIONAL ATTAINMENT			
High school graduates or less	82.3	60.1	95.0
Some college	79.1	67.8	96.2
Bachelor's degree or higher	96.8	89.7	96.6

1. Employees working in establishments of 50 or more employees.

Table 1-70. Total Wage and Salary Costs of Training by Industry and Size Class, May–October 1995, Employee Survey

(Thousands of dollars.)

Characteristic	Total [1]	Formal training	Informal training
ALL EMPLOYEES [2]	$37 061 259	$12 838 575	$24 221 982
INDUSTRY			
Mining	305 571	172 181	133 390
Construction	1 321 935	345 217	976 718
Manufacturing:			
Durable goods	7 655 647	3 254 112	4 400 978
Nondurable goods	3 668 602	2 192 938	1 475 664
Transportation, communications, and public utilities	1 614 793	811 305	803 444
Wholesale trade	1 278 848	352 234	926 614
Retail trade	6 285 244	666 128	5 619 116
Finance, insurance, and real estate	2 425 810	649 319	1 776 391
Services	12 504 809	4 395 142	8 109 667
ESTABLISHMENT SIZE			
50 to 99 employees	5 652 306	1 348 650	4 303 656
100 to 499 employees	16 781 558	5 521 417	11 260 007
500 employees or more	14 627 394	5 968 508	8 658 319

1. Parts may not add to total because of separate estimates.
2. Employees working in establishments of 50 or more employees.

PART TWO

EMPLOYMENT, HOURS, AND EARNINGS—NONFARM PAYROLLS

EMPLOYMENT, HOURS, AND EARNINGS—NONFARM PAYROLLS

HIGHLIGHTS

The employment, hours, and earnings data by industry and state in this part are derived from a survey of non-farm establishments. The employment numbers differ from Part 1 because of differences in methodology, concepts, definitions and coverage. Since the data are obtained from payroll records, the data are consistent for industry classifications, and the data on hours and earnings are likely to be accurate.

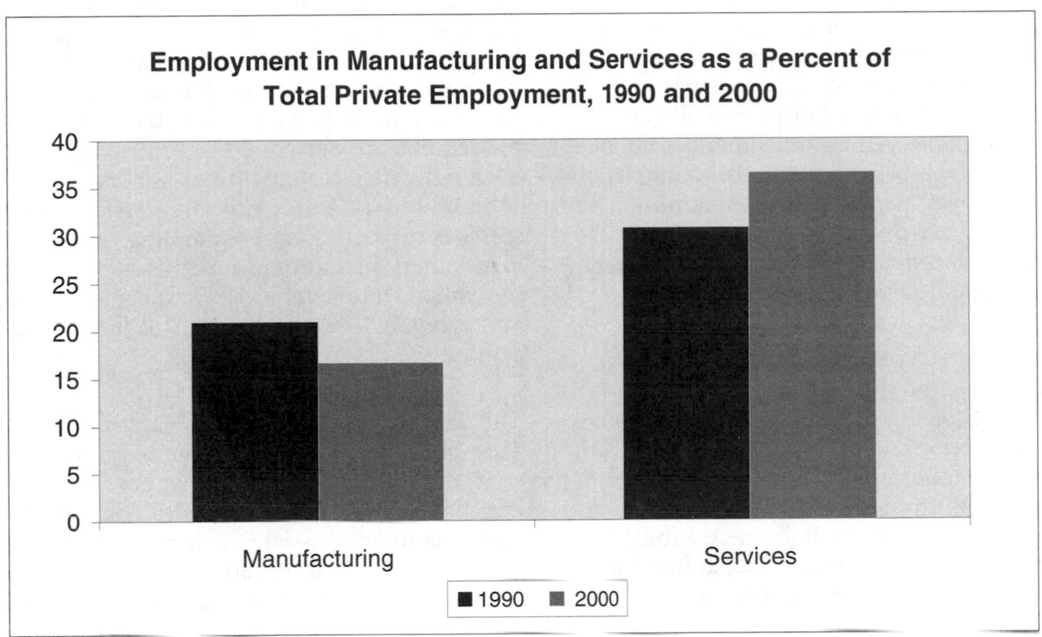

Manufacturing employment continued its slow absolute decline over the past decade, and even more as a share of total private employment. At the same time, employment in the services sector almost doubled, and is now over one-third of private employment.

OTHER HIGHLIGHTS:

- Within the services sector in service-producing industries, the business services industry provided most of the growth, rising 92 percent during the decade. This growth is largely accounted for by growth in the help supply industry as well as computer and data processing, both growing 171 percent. (Table 2-1)
- Growth in health services employment has slowed during the decade from 3.4 percent per year in the early half of the decade to 1.8 percent per year in the last half. (Table 2-1)
- Federal government employment declined over the period 1990–2000 by 10 percent. Employment in education in state and local governments increased 17.5 percent and 23 percent respectively. (Table 2-1)
- Over one-third of employed women are in the services sector, recording an increase of 42 percent during the period 1990–2000. (Table 2-2)

NOTES AND DEFINITIONS

Collection and Coverage

Statistics on employment, hours, and earnings are compiled from payroll records reported monthly on a voluntary basis to the Bureau of Labor Statistics (BLS) and its cooperating state agencies by about 390,000 establishments representing all industries except agriculture. This Current Employment Statistics, or CES, program also is referred to as the "establishment" or "payroll" survey. In most industries, the sampling probabilities are based on the size of the establishment; most large establishments are therefore in the sample. An establishment is not necessarily a firm; it may be a branch plant, for example, or a warehouse. Self-employed persons and others not on a regular civilian payroll are outside the scope of the survey. Persons are considered employed if they receive pay for any part of the specified pay period.

The exclusion from the payroll survey of farm employment, self-employment, and domestic service employment accounts in part for the differences in employment figures between the household and payroll surveys. The payroll survey also excludes persons on leave without pay, who are counted as employed in the household survey. Persons who worked in more than one establishment during the reporting period are counted each time their names appear on payrolls, whereas such persons are only counted once in the household survey.

Industries are classified in accordance with the 1987 Standard Industrial Classification. For an establishment making more than one product or engaging in more than one activity, the entire employment of the establishment is included under the industry indicated by the principal product or activity.

Establishment survey data are adjusted annually to accord with comprehensive counts of employment in March of the preceding year, called "benchmarks." The adjustments are published with the release of May data each year. The benchmarks are derived mainly from employment reports from all employers subject to unemployment insurance. The employment count for the previous March becomes the revised employment number for that month; the difference between it and the previous sample-based March estimate is spread back over the previous 11 months, creating a continuous series. The difference is also projected forward and the "bias factors" that adjust recent sample-based estimates for known systematic biases are recalculated. (The main source of systematic bias is the failure of the sample to pick up newly-created businesses.) Thus, each year's benchmarking results in recalculation of employment data for the current and 2 previous years. The related series on production and nonsupervisory workers, hours, and earnings are recalculated consistent with the employment benchmarks.

For employment, the sum of the state figures will differ from the official U.S. national totals because of the effects of differing industrial and geographic stratifications used in the process of expanding sample totals to universe estimates, as well as differences in the timing of benchmark adjustments. The national estimation procedures used by BLS are designed to produce accurate national data by detailed industry; the state estimation procedures are designed to produce accurate data for each individual state. State estimates are not forced to sum to national totals, nor vice versa. Because each state series is subject to larger sampling and nonsampling errors than the national series, summing them cumulates individual state level errors and can cause distortions at an aggregate level, particularly at turning points for the economy.

The data include Alaska and Hawaii beginning in 1959. This inclusion resulted in an increase of 212,000 (0.4 percent) in total nonfarm employment for the March 1959 benchmark month. In 1996, BLS completed implementation of computer assisted reporting through telephone interviews, touch-tone self-reporting, and voice recognition systems and introduced electronic data interchange.

CES Revision

In June of 1995, the Bureau of Labor Statistics (BLS) announced plans for a comprehensive sample redesign of its monthly payroll survey. The original CES survey was based on a quota sample. The redesign introduces a probability-based sample. In addition, procedures have been developed for regular sample updates of employment from new business births.

The initial research phase for the Current Employment Statistics (CES) sample redesign was completed in 1997, and the Bureau launched a production test of the new sample design at that time. The production test for the wholesale trade industry was concluded in June 2000, when the first estimates from the new design for that industry were published with the 1999 benchmark revisions. With the 2000 benchmark revisions, estimates for the mining, construction and manufacturing industries were published under the new design for the first time. Redesigned samples for the remaining industry divisions will be phased in with the next two benchmark releases. The conversion of the CES series from industry coding based on the 1987 Standard Industrial Classification (SIC) system to industry coding based on the North American Industrial Classification System (NAICS) will take place in 2003.

Concepts and Definitions

An *establishment* is an economic unit that produces goods or services (such as a factory or store) at a single location and is engaged in one type of economic activity.

Employed persons are all persons who received pay (including holiday and sick pay) for any part of the payroll period including the 12th day of the month. Persons holding more than one job (about 5 percent of all persons in the labor force) are counted in each establishment that reports them. The data exclude proprietors, the self-employed, unpaid volunteer or family workers, farm workers, and domestic workers. Salaried officers of corporations are included. Government employment covers only civilian employees and excludes military personnel. Employees of the Central Intelligence Agency and the National Security Agency are also excluded.

Production or nonsupervisory workers are a subgroup of employment accounting for about four-fifths of total employment on private nonagricultural payrolls. They comprise production workers in manufacturing and mining, construction workers in construction, and nonsupervisory employees elsewhere. Separate employment figures are tabulated for this group and the data on hours and earnings refer to this group only.

Manufacturing and mining production workers are working supervisors and nonsupervisory workers closely associated with production operations, including those engaged in fabricating, processing, assembling, inspecting, receiving, storing, handling, packing, warehousing, shipping, trucking, hauling, maintenance, repair, janitorial and guard services, product development, and record keeping.

Construction workers are working supervisors and others engaged in new work, alterations, demolition, repair, maintenance, etc., whether working at the site or in shops or yards at jobs ordinarily performed by members of the construction trades.

Nonsupervisory workers are enumerated in the following industries: transportation and public utilities; wholesale and retail trade; finance, insurance, and real estate; and services. The category includes employees not above the working supervisory level, such as office and clerical workers, repairers, salespersons, operators, drivers, physicians, lawyers, accountants, nurses, social workers, research aides, teachers, drafters, photographers, beauticians, musicians, restaurant workers, custodial workers, attendants, line installers and repairers, laborers, janitors, guards, and other employees at similar occupational levels whose services are closely associated with those of the employees listed.

Earnings of production or nonsupervisory workers are the payments they receive during the survey period, including premium pay for overtime or late-shift work and holiday, vacation, and sick pay paid directly by the firm. Earnings exclude irregular bonuses, retroactive pay, tips, and payments in kind. Earnings also exclude employee benefits such as health or other insurance and contributions to Social Security and other retirement. Payroll earnings are reported before deductions of any kind, e.g., the employee share of Social Security contributions, group insurance, withholding tax, bonds, or union dues. Real earnings are earnings adjusted to reflect the effects of changes in consumer prices using the Consumer Price Index for Urban Wage Earners and Clerical Workers (CPI-W). Real earnings are expressed in 1982 dollars.

Hours are hours paid for during the pay period including the 12th of the month for production or nonsupervisory workers, including hours paid for holidays, vacations, and sick leave.

Average weekly hours for any industry grouping are total production or nonsupervisory hours paid for divided by total reported production or nonsupervisory employment. These are not the same as standard or scheduled weekly hours because hours paid reflect such factors as unpaid absenteeism, labor turnover, part-time work, and work stoppages. Averages for industries and for all production and nonsupervisory workers reflect changes in the workweeks of component industries and shifts in the composition of employment among industries with shorter and longer workweeks. Because the survey reports multiple jobholders separately at each job, average hours refer to jobs and not to individuals. Thus, if a worker with a full-time job takes a part-time job and nothing changes for any other worker, the average workweek will decline, even though every person is working the same or longer hours.

Aggregate weekly hours for individual industries are the products of average hours and production worker or nonsupervisory worker employment. At all higher levels of industry aggregation, hours aggregates are the sum of the component aggregates. They are published in the form of indexes, 1982=100. The indexes are calculated by dividing each year's aggregate by the 1982 average and expressing the result in percentage form. Thus, these indexes measure changes in the labor inputs of production or nonsupervisory workers.

Average overtime hours are the portion of average weekly hours that exceed regular hours and for which overtime premiums were paid.

Average hourly earnings reflect not only changes in basic hourly and incentive wage rates, but also such variable factors as premium pay for overtime and late-shift work and changes in output of workers paid on an incentive plan. They also reflect shifts in the number of employees between relatively high-paid and low-paid work, as well as changes in workers' earnings in individual establishments. Averages for groups and divisions (such as total private industry, total goods-producing, and total service-producing) further reflect shifts among component industries, as well as changes in average hourly earnings for individual industries. Earnings do not measure the level of total labor costs to the employers since many items are not included (see above) nor are the earnings for those employees not covered under production worker, construction worker, or non-supervisory employee definitions.

Average weekly earnings are derived by multiplying average weekly hours estimates by average hourly earnings estimates. Therefore, weekly earnings are affected not only by changes in average hourly earnings but also by changes in the length of the workweek. Average weekly earnings are per job and will not necessarily reflect trends in income per worker (because of multiple jobholders) or per family (because of families with more than one earner).

Sources of Additional Information

For further details on estimation methods and relation to establishment data, see Bureau of Labor Statistics, *Employment and Earnings,* June 1996 and subsequent issues of that monthly publication, as well as the *BLS Handbook of Methods,* BLS Bulletin 2490, April 1997 and occasional articles in the *Monthly Labor Review.* A detailed description of the CES redesign is available from BLS, Office of Employment and Unemployment Statistics. For a complete description of the CES sample redesign see BLS, *Employment and Earnings,* June 2001.

Table 2-1. Employees on Nonfarm Payrolls by Major Industry and Selected Component Groups, 1945–2000

(Thousands of persons.)

Industry	1945	1946	1947	1948	1949	1950	1951	1952	1953	1954	1955	1956	1957	1958
TOTAL	40 374	41 652	43 857	44 866	43 754	45 197	47 819	48 793	50 202	48 990	50 641	52 369	52 855	51 322
TOTAL PRIVATE	34 431	36 056	38 382	39 216	37 897	39 170	41 430	42 185	43 556	42 238	43 727	45 091	45 239	43 483
GOODS-PRODUCING	17 507	17 248	18 509	18 774	17 565	18 506	19 959	20 198	21 074	19 751	20 513	21 104	20 967	19 513
Mining	836	862	955	994	930	901	929	898	866	791	792	822	828	751
Metal mining	89.3	87.8	103.0	104.2	97.7	96.9	101.0	99.8	106.0	99.3	101.5	108.8	111.4	93.2
Coal mining	...	...	...	...	...	...	...	...	...	...	...	...	...	215.1
Oil and gas extraction	215.2	230.6	248.5	274.0	266.3	266.1	284.4	303.4	311.4	318.1	331.9	340.1	344.0	327.5
Nonmetallic minerals, except fuels	74.7	89.5	97.8	99.6	95.0	95.1	102.4	103.8	105.9	105.1	108.3	115.2	114.3	114.9
Construction	1 147	1 683	2 009	2 198	2 194	2 364	2 637	2 668	2 659	2 646	2 839	3 039	2 962	2 817
General building contractors	...	...	...	...	...	...	...	...	...	...	...	...	...	861.4
Heavy construction, except building	...	...	...	...	...	...	...	...	...	...	...	...	...	...
Special trade contractors	...	...	...	...	...	...	...	...	...	...	...	...	...	...
Manufacturing	15 524	14 703	15 545	15 582	14 441	15 241	16 393	16 632	17 549	16 314	16 882	17 243	17 176	15 945
Durable goods	9 108	7 785	8 358	8 298	7 462	8 066	9 059	9 320	10 080	9 101	9 511	9 802	9 825	8 801
Lumber and wood products	...	...	881.6	854.6	775.3	845.9	879.4	830.4	813.4	747.0	780.9	772.8	697.2	655.3
Furniture and fixtures	...	...	319.8	329.2	301.1	346.3	340.1	340.0	352.1	325.6	346.5	357.7	356.5	343.4
Stone, clay, and glass products	385.8	471.8	508.4	519.7	486.0	518.1	555.6	533.9	550.3	523.2	557.0	573.1	563.6	532.5
Primary metal industries	...	...	1 224.8	1 236.2	1 086.5	1 194.0	1 307.0	1 228.3	1 325.1	1 168.1	1 266.9	1 298.4	1 298.4	1 106.5
Fabricated metal products	...	...	1 049.2	1 040.8	935.2	1 042.3	1 158.1	1 173.0	1 286.5	1 171.3	1 221.5	1 239.9	1 267.3	1 169.9
Industrial machinery and equipment	...	...	1 386.1	1 381.9	1 191.5	1 221.0	1 469.6	1 532.5	1 572.7	1 433.7	1 465.4	1 588.5	1 603.3	1 378.2
Computer and office equipment	...	...	...	...	...	...	...	...	...	...	...	...	...	130.0
Electronic and other electrical equipment	819.5	768.7	855.1	819.1	712.6	819.0	926.7	999.0	1 127.7	1 000.9	1 039.3	1 106.1	1 123.3	1 045.1
Electronic components and accessories	...	...	...	...	...	...	...	...	...	...	...	...	...	174.0
Transportation equipment	2 517.1	1 234.7	1 260.9	1 256.0	1 196.4	1 252.6	1 515.5	1 738.9	2 021.5	1 783.7	1 874.1	1 871.1	1 927.8	1 634.5
Motor vehicles and equipment	656.0	655.2	767.8	780.7	751.3	816.2	833.3	777.5	917.3	765.7	891.2	792.5	769.3	606.5
Aircraft and parts	759.1	228.6	230.5	228.9	254.5	272.7	450.7	645.9	766.3	754.2	733.3	806.5	862.9	742.6
Instruments and related products	...	...	451.0	438.6	392.9	426.5	500.9	549.9	610.0	556.7	563.4	591.7	599.8	562.8
Miscellaneous manufacturing industries	...	...	420.8	421.6	384.9	400.2	406.0	393.7	420.9	390.7	306.2	403.0	387.2	373.0
Nondurable goods	6 415	6 918	7 187	7 285	6 979	7 175	7 334	7 313	7 468	7 213	7 370	7 442	7 351	7 144
Food and kindred products	1 691.0	1 767.0	1 799.0	1 801.0	1 778.0	1 790.0	1 823.2	1 827.8	1 838.9	1 818.3	1 824.7	1 841.9	1 805.4	1 772.8
Tobacco products	...	...	118.0	114.0	109.0	103.0	104.1	105.6	103.6	103.3	102.5	99.6	97.0	94.5
Textile mill products	1 139.0	1 264.0	1 298.0	1 332.0	1 187.0	1 256.0	1 237.7	1 163.4	1 154.8	1 042.3	1 050.2	1 032.0	981.1	918.8
Apparel and other textile products	1 060.0	1 146.0	1 154.0	1 190.0	1 173.0	1 202.0	1 207.2	1 216.4	1 248.0	1 183.6	1 219.2	1 223.4	1 210.1	1 171.8
Paper and allied products	389.0	444.0	462.0	469.0	452.0	482.0	507.8	500.4	527.0	527.7	546.4	564.1	566.8	560.4
Printing and publishing	577.0	669.0	721.0	739.0	740.0	748.0	767.6	779.9	802.8	813.9	834.7	862.0	870.0	872.6
Chemicals and allied products	668.0	633.0	649.0	655.0	618.0	640.0	707.0	730.1	768.2	752.7	773.1	796.5	810.0	794.1
Petroleum and coal products	186.0	208.0	221.0	228.0	221.0	218.0	231.3	234.6	241.4	238.1	237.1	235.5	232.2	223.8
Rubber and miscellaneous plastics products	308.0	345.0	353.0	344.0	312.0	342.0	367.9	370.6	394.3	360.0	396.7	403.8	406.0	376.2
Leather and leather products	358.0	408.0	412.0	412.0	389.0	395.0	380.0	384.2	389.2	373.0	385.9	382.7	372.7	359.2
SERVICE-PRODUCING	22 869	24 404	25 348	26 092	26 189	26 691	27 860	28 595	29 128	29 239	30 128	31 264	31 889	31 811
Transportation And Public Utilities	3 906	4 061	4 166	4 189	4 001	4 034	4 226	4 248	4 290	4 084	4 141	4 244	4 241	3 976
Transportation	...	...	...	...	...	...	...	...	...	...	...	...	...	...
Railroad transportation	...	...	1 557.0	1 517.0	1 367.0	1 391.0	1 449.3	1 399.8	1 376.9	1 215.4	1 205.4	1 190.4	1 121.4	957.4
Local and interurban passenger transit	...	...	...	...	...	...	...	...	...	...	...	...	...	284.8
Trucking and warehousing	...	...	...	...	...	...	...	...	...	...	...	...	...	...
Water transportation	...	...	...	...	...	...	...	...	...	...	...	...	...	...
Transportation by air	...	...	...	...	...	...	...	...	...	...	...	...	...	...
Pipelines, except natural gas	...	...	...	...	...	...	...	...	...	...	...	25.9	26.5	25.7
Transportation services	...	...	...	...	...	...	...	...	...	...	...	...	...	...
Communications and public utilities	...	...	...	...	...	...	...	...	...	...	...	...	...	...
Communications	...	...	...	...	...	...	...	...	...	...	...	...	...	860.0
Electric, gas, and sanitary services	...	...	...	...	...	...	...	...	...	...	...	...	...	...
Wholesale Trade	1 955	2 298	2 478	2 612	2 610	2 643	2 735	2 821	2 862	2 875	2 934	3 027	3 037	2 989
Durable goods	...	...	...	...	...	...	...	...	...	...	...	...	...	...
Nondurable goods	...	...	...	...	...	...	...	...	...	...	...	...	...	...

See *Note* at end of table.

Table 2-1. Employees on Nonfarm Payrolls by Major Industry and Selected Component Groups, 1945–2000—*Continued*

(Thousands of persons.)

Industry	1959	1960	1961	1962	1963	1964	1965	1966	1967	1968	1969	1970	1971	1972
TOTAL	53 270	54 189	53 999	55 549	56 653	58 283	60 763	63 901	65 803	67 897	70 384	70 880	71 211	73 675
TOTAL PRIVATE	45 186	45 836	45 404	46 660	47 429	48 686	50 689	53 116	54 413	56 058	58 189	58 325	58 331	60 341
GOODS-PRODUCING	20 411	20 434	19 857	20 451	20 640	21 005	21 926	23 158	23 308	23 737	24 361	23 578	22 935	23 668
Mining	732	712	672	650	635	634	632	627	613	606	619	623	609	628
Metal mining	83.7	93.8	87.4	82.3	79.7	79.5	83.8	86.5	79.2	82.0	89.2	93.3	86.6	82.7
Coal mining	198.2	186.1	161.3	151.9	149.0	147.3	141.4	137.3	138.8	132.3	135.3	145.1	145.6	160.9
Oil and gas extraction	329.5	309.2	303.1	298.0	289.2	291.1	287.1	281.8	275.8	275.6	279.9	270.1	264.2	267.9
Nonmetallic minerals, except fuels	120.4	123.0	119.8	118.1	117.0	116.2	119.6	121.2	119.6	116.2	114.9	114.7	114.8	116.2
Construction	3 004	2 926	2 859	2 948	3 010	3 097	3 232	3 317	3 248	3 350	3 575	3 588	3 704	3 889
General building contractors	927.6	877.1	848.2	857.9	888.5	919.9	961.1	991.7	946.5	975.9	1 071.0	1 065.6	1 102.0	1 164.6
Heavy construction, except building	...	...	...	...	...	...	...	...	...	...	...	...	...	773.5
Special trade contractors	...	...	...	...	...	...	...	...	...	...	...	...	...	1 950.6
Manufacturing	16 675	16 796	16 326	16 853	16 995	17 274	18 062	19 214	19 447	19 781	20 167	19 367	18 623	19 151
Durable goods	9 342	9 429	9 041	9 450	9 586	9 785	10 374	11 250	11 408	11 594	11 862	11 176	10 604	11 022
Lumber and wood products	703.4	670.1	624.3	634.3	641.4	657.8	665.1	677.4	661.5	674.0	690.8	658.1	680.9	740.2
Furniture and fixtures	366.5	364.9	350.0	366.8	371.3	386.5	410.2	439.6	434.1	449.5	461.3	439.9	443.6	483.3
Stone, clay, and glass products	571.9	572.0	551.1	561.0	569.0	581.2	595.1	610.3	595.4	602.1	622.0	609.8	610.6	644.6
Primary metal industries	1 133.2	1 184.8	1 100.1	1 120.9	1 127.3	1 187.8	1 252.8	1 296.5	1 267.0	1 261.0	1 305.0	1 260.4	1 171.0	1 173.3
Fabricated metal products	1 218.9	1 230.0	1 180.9	1 237.7	1 263.8	1 295.0	1 372.1	1 489.0	1 556.1	1 609.2	1 665.0	1 559.1	1 479.4	1 540.9
Industrial machinery and equipment	1 469.1	1 496.1	1 435.4	1 511.2	1 547.5	1 627.0	1 753.9	1 931.1	1 991.1	1 988.2	2 054.7	2 003.0	1 833.7	1 908.8
Computer and office equipment	135.3	143.5	148.9	155.5	159.6	169.1	186.3	213.4	233.8	244.3	269.2	281.0	256.6	252.3
Electronic and other electrical equipment	1 165.6	1 220.9	1 221.6	1 295.9	1 282.4	1 273.1	1 367.6	1 571.3	1 614.6	1 629.1	1 664.3	1 583.6	1 476.7	1 535.0
Electronic components and accessories	207.5	227.1	236.3	258.8	255.4	257.6	298.7	378.1	374.4	371.0	383.3	356.8	320.4	345.1
Transportation equipment	1 714.5	1 668.1	1 574.4	1 682.8	1 748.6	1 732.1	1 853.1	2 031.0	2 058.4	2 132.8	2 120.0	1 832.9	1 743.0	1 776.7
Motor vehicles and equipment	692.3	724.1	632.3	691.7	741.3	752.9	842.7	861.6	815.8	873.7	911.4	799.0	848.5	874.8
Aircraft and parts	694.2	604.8	587.3	615.0	615.7	583.1	601.3	725.6	803.0	820.7	774.8	644.1	509.0	481.3
Instruments and related products	611.3	632.2	624.6	650.3	647.7	646.7	684.3	770.0	801.1	814.4	838.3	803.6	753.1	786.2
Miscellaneous manufacturing industries	387.7	389.9	378.2	389.6	386.8	397.6	419.5	433.7	428.4	433.4	441.0	425.7	411.7	433.3
Nondurable goods	7 333	7 367	7 285	7 403	7 410	7 489	7 688	7 963	8 039	8 187	8 304	8 190	8 019	8 129
Food and kindred products	1 789.6	1 790.0	1 775.2	1 763.0	1 752.0	1 750.4	1 756.7	1 777.2	1 786.3	1 781.5	1 790.8	1 786.2	1 765.6	1 745.2
Tobacco products	94.5	94.0	90.7	90.5	88.6	90.2	86.8	84.3	86.5	84.6	83.0	82.9	77.1	74.9
Textile mill products	945.7	924.4	893.4	902.3	885.4	892.0	925.6	963.5	958.5	993.9	1 002.5	974.8	954.7	985.7
Apparel and other textile products	1 225.9	1 233.2	1 214.5	1 263.7	1 282.8	1 302.5	1 354.2	1 401.9	1 397.5	1 405.8	1 409.1	1 363.8	1 342.6	1 382.7
Paper and allied products	583.3	597.2	597.4	610.4	614.5	621.4	634.9	662.5	674.6	686.7	706.4	700.9	677.4	678.8
Printing and publishing	888.5	911.3	917.3	926.4	930.6	951.5	979.4	1 016.9	1 047.8	1 065.1	1 093.6	1 104.3	1 080.5	1 094.0
Chemicals and allied products	809.2	828.2	828.2	848.5	865.3	878.6	907.8	961.4	1 001.4	1 029.9	1 059.9	1 049.3	1 010.7	1 009.2
Petroleum and coal products	215.5	211.9	201.9	195.3	188.7	183.9	182.9	184.2	183.2	186.8	182.3	191.2	194.2	195.4
Rubber and miscellaneous plastics products	407.0	413.3	408.3	442.0	452.6	470.8	506.5	547.4	552.4	597.5	633.6	616.7	616.9	666.9
Leather and leather products	374.0	363.4	358.2	360.7	349.2	347.6	352.9	363.6	350.9	355.2	343.2	319.5	299.1	296.0
SERVICE-PRODUCING	32 857	33 755	34 142	35 098	36 013	37 278	38 839	40 743	42 495	44 158	46 023	47 302	48 276	50 007
Transportation And Public Utilities	4 011	4 004	3 903	3 906	3 903	3 951	4 036	4 158	4 268	4 318	4 442	4 515	4 476	4 541
Transportation	...	...	...	...	...	2 487	2 530	2 598	2 655	2 680	2 722	2 694	2 639	2 676
Railroad transportation	924.8	885.3	816.8	796.4	771.6	756.1	735.3	725.2	698.1	667.9	649.2	633.8	605.7	581.5
Local and interurban passenger transit	281.3	284.4	276.9	270.7	269.2	266.9	268.8	270.5	279.4	281.5	280.6	280.5	278.9	276.1
Trucking and warehousing	...	...	...	...	...	...	...	...	...	...	...	...	...	...
Water transportation	...	...	...	...	...	229.0	228.4	237.8	240.9	238.9	229.0	212.3	194.1	210.7
Transportation by air	...	...	...	...	...	...	...	...	...	...	...	...	...	...
Pipelines, except natural gas	24.3	23.1	22.2	21.6	20.7	20.0	19.5	18.9	18.7	18.5	17.9	17.6	17.3	16.7
Transportation services	...	...	...	...	...	...	...	...	...	...	...	...	...	...
Communications and public utilities	...	...	...	...	...	1 464	1 506	1 560	1 614	1 638	1 721	1 822	1 841	1 865
Communications	836.8	839.7	828.9	824.1	823.8	847.9	880.8	928.3	969.6	982.3	1 049.3	1 129.4	1 143.4	1 152.0
Electric, gas, and sanitary services	...	...	...	...	...	616.5	625.2	631.3	644.0	655.7	671.7	692.3	698.1	713.2
Wholesale Trade	3 092	3 153	3 142	3 207	3 258	3 347	3 477	3 608	3 700	3 791	3 919	4 006	4 014	4 127
Durable goods	...	...	...	...	...	...	...	...	...	...	...	...	...	2 336
Nondurable goods	...	...	...	...	...	...	...	...	...	...	...	...	...	1 791

See *Note* at end of table.

Table 2-1. Employees on Nonfarm Payrolls by Major Industry and Selected Component Groups, 1945–2000—*Continued*

(Thousands of persons.)

Industry	1973	1974	1975	1976	1977	1978	1979	1980	1981	1982	1983	1984	1985	1986
TOTAL	76 790	78 265	76 945	79 382	82 471	86 697	89 823	90 406	91 152	89 544	90 152	94 408	97 387	99 344
TOTAL PRIVATE	63 058	64 095	62 259	64 511	67 344	71 026	73 876	74 166	75 121	73 707	74 282	78 384	80 992	82 651
GOODS-PRODUCING	24 893	24 794	22 600	23 352	24 346	25 585	26 461	25 658	25 497	23 812	23 330	24 718	24 842	24 533
Mining	642	697	752	779	813	851	958	1 027	1 139	1 128	952	966	927	777
Metal mining	87.4	95.4	93.5	94.1	90.3	93.7	101.0	98.2	103.7	72.9	56.4	55.1	46.4	41.1
Coal mining	161.8	179.5	212.7	225.0	225.3	209.6	258.8	246.3	224.5	236.6	193.5	195.5	187.3	175.9
Oil and gas extraction	273.9	300.2	328.8	345.7	381.4	429.3	474.2	559.7	692.1	708.3	597.8	606.4	582.7	450.3
Nonmetallic minerals, except fuels	118.6	121.8	116.7	114.6	115.9	118.5	123.8	122.7	118.6	109.7	104.3	108.5	110.1	109.6
Construction	4 097	4 020	3 525	3 576	3 851	4 229	4 463	4 346	4 188	3 904	3 946	4 380	4 668	4 810
General building contractors	1 221.1	1 191.7	1 011.9	1 022.4	1 108.4	1 228.5	1 272.0	1 173.0	1 094.2	990.3	1 019.2	1 160.5	1 251.4	1 289.2
Heavy construction, except building	789.6	799.0	733.9	747.3	759.8	827.6	898.1	894.6	865.1	794.7	753.4	757.8	764.6	749.5
Special trade contractors	2 086.7	2 029.0	1 778.8	1 805.8	1 982.7	2 172.6	2 292.6	2 278.3	2 228.6	2 119.2	2 173.6	2 461.7	2 652.2	2 770.6
Manufacturing	20 154	20 077	18 323	18 997	19 682	20 505	21 040	20 285	20 170	18 780	18 432	19 372	19 248	18 947
Durable goods	11 863	11 897	10 662	11 051	11 570	12 245	12 730	12 159	12 082	11 014	10 707	11 476	11 458	11 195
Lumber and wood products	774.1	726.6	626.9	692.5	736.0	769.8	781.8	704.2	679.8	610.3	670.5	717.9	711.1	724.0
Furniture and fixtures	506.8	489.3	416.9	444.3	464.3	494.1	497.8	465.8	464.3	462.0	448.0	486.4	492.9	497.5
Stone, clay, and glass products	680.4	672.8	597.8	612.7	635.7	663.7	673.5	628.9	606.1	547.5	540.7	561.6	557.1	553.9
Primary metal industries	1 259.1	1 288.8	1 139.0	1 154.9	1 181.6	1 214.9	1 253.9	1 142.2	1 122.4	921.9	831.8	857.4	807.9	751.4
Fabricated metal products	1 644.9	1 632.2	1 452.9	1 505.2	1 576.9	1 666.7	1 712.6	1 609.0	1 586.3	1 424.4	1 368.4	1 461.6	1 463.9	1 422.4
Industrial machinery and equipment	2 110.8	2 230.0	2 076.2	2 084.6	2 194.7	2 346.9	2 507.7	2 517.0	2 520.7	2 264.3	2 052.6	2 217.9	2 194.7	2 073.7
Computer and office equipment	276.1	296.2	278.0	278.3	302.5	339.8	385.5	420.1	446.8	460.0	473.8	514.8	500.2	469.1
Electronic and other electrical equipment	1 667.2	1 666.4	1 441.5	1 502.7	1 590.5	1 699.0	1 793.1	1 770.9	1 773.6	1 700.5	1 703.8	1 868.5	1 859.0	1 790.1
Electronic components and accessories	399.5	409.6	329.0	356.1	393.6	444.8	510.4	538.5	542.2	543.0	562.9	657.4	645.1	610.1
Transportation equipment	1 914.5	1 853.0	1 700.4	1 784.8	1 857.1	1 986.6	2 058.9	1 880.5	1 878.9	1 717.6	1 730.4	1 882.8	1 959.6	2 002.6
Motor vehicles and equipment	976.5	907.7	792.4	881.0	947.3	1 004.9	990.4	788.8	788.7	699.3	753.6	861.5	883.1	871.8
Aircraft and parts	510.1	524.1	499.4	473.2	467.3	511.1	592.5	633.1	[illegible]	584.0	561.6	574.9	616.2	655.8
Instruments and related products	650.8	885.4	803.7	839.8	894.9	951.9	1 006.3	1 021.9	1 041.3	1 013.3	990.2	1 040.4	1 044.7	1 018.4
Miscellaneous manufacturing industries	454.4	452.0	406.8	429.1	438.4	451.5	444.8	418.0	408.3	[illegible]	370.3	381.6	380.5	360.7
Nondurable goods	8 291	8 181	7 661	7 946	8 112	8 259	8 310	8 127	8 089	7 766	7 725	7 896	7 790	7 752
Food and kindred products	1 714.8	1 706.7	1 657.5	1 688.9	1 711.0	1 724.1	1 732.5	1 708.0	1 671.1	1 635.8	1 614.4	1 611.4	1 600.9	1 606.7
Tobacco products	77.5	77.1	75.5	76.6	70.7	70.6	70.0	68.9	70.4	68.7	67.9	64.2	63.9	58.5
Textile mill products	1 009.8	965.0	867.9	918.8	910.2	899.1	885.1	847.7	823.0	749.4	741.3	746.1	702.2	702.9
Apparel and other textile products	1 438.1	1 362.6	1 243.3	1 318.1	1 316.3	1 332.3	1 304.3	1 263.5	1 244.4	1 161.1	1 163.2	1 184.8	1 120.4	1 099.6
Paper and allied products	694.4	696.1	633.4	666.4	682.1	688.8	697.3	684.6	680.5	655.4	653.9	673.8	670.9	667.1
Printing and publishing	1 110.7	1 111.3	1 083.4	1 099.2	1 141.4	1 192.0	1 235.1	1 252.1	1 266.3	1 271.8	1 298.2	1 375.2	1 426.1	1 456.0
Chemicals and allied products	1 037.6	1 060.5	1 014.7	1 042.5	1 073.7	1 095.5	1 109.3	1 107.4	1 109.0	1 075.1	1 042.8	1 049.0	1 043.5	1 021.0
Petroleum and coal products	192.9	197.0	194.4	198.5	202.3	207.7	209.8	197.9	214.0	200.8	195.6	188.9	179.3	168.8
Rubber and miscellaneous plastics products	731.1	733.4	642.7	674.7	749.9	792.6	820.6	763.8	772.3	729.3	742.8	813.2	818.2	822.5
Leather and leather products	284.0	271.1	248.2	262.7	254.8	256.8	245.7	232.9	237.7	218.9	204.9	189.4	164.9	149.0
SERVICE-PRODUCING	51 897	53 471	54 345	56 030	58 125	61 113	63 363	64 748	65 655	65 732	66 821	69 690	72 544	74 811
Transportation And Public Utilities	4 656	4 725	4 542	4 582	4 713	4 923	5 136	5 146	5 165	5 081	4 952	5 156	5 233	5 247
Transportation	2 746	2 779	2 634	2 678	2 781	2 905	3 019	2 960	2 920	2 787	2 742	2 914	2 997	3 051
Railroad transportation	579.1	590.4	548.2	537.9	544.9	539.2	556.3	532.1	494.9	429.4	375.9	375.7	359.0	331.5
Local and interurban passenger transit	277.5	278.6	270.3	264.3	261.5	258.2	262.6	264.6	265.1	263.2	256.5	270.3	277.1	286.0
Trucking and warehousing	. . .	. . .	. . .	. . .	. . .	. . .	. . .	. . .	. . .	. . .	. . .	. . .	. . .	. . .
Water transportation	199.1	202.9	193.8	194.0	194.5	207.8	214.2	211.2	217.6	200.3	189.0	190.0	184.5	174.0
Transportation by air	. . .	. . .	. . .	. . .	. . .	. . .	. . .	. . .	. . .	. . .	. . .	. . .	. . .	. . .
Pipelines, except natural gas	16.8	17.3	17.5	17.7	18.5	19.6	20.1	21.3	21.8	21.3	20.1	19.1	18.7	18.2
Transportation services	. . .	. . .	. . .	. . .	. . .	. . .	. . .	. . .	. . .	. . .	. . .	. . .	. . .	. . .
Communications and public utilities	1 910	1 947	1 908	1 904	1 932	2 018	2 116	2 186	2 245	2 294	2 210	2 242	2 235	2 196
Communications	1 179.5	1 202.5	1 175.6	1 169.4	1 185.2	1 239.8	1 309.0	1 357.0	1 390.5	1 417.1	1 323.9	1 340.3	1 318.8	1 274.8
Electric, gas, and sanitary services	730.9	744.2	732.6	734.5	747.2	778.4	807.4	829.1	854.2	877.3	886.3	901.6	916.3	921.4
Wholesale Trade	4 291	4 447	4 430	4 562	4 723	4 985	5 221	5 292	5 375	5 295	5 283	5 568	5 727	5 761
Durable goods	2 457	2 578	2 539	2 615	2 732	2 917	3 098	3 139	3 182	3 107	3 087	3 291	3 402	3 395
Nondurable goods	1 835	1 869	1 891	1 946	1 991	2 068	2 123	2 153	2 193	2 188	2 197	2 277	2 325	2 365

See *Note* at end of table.

Table 2-1. Employees on Nonfarm Payrolls by Major Industry and Selected Component Groups, 1945–2000—*Continued*

(Thousands of persons.)

Industry	1987	1988	1989	1990	1991	1992	1993	1994	1995	1996	1997	1998	1999	2000
TOTAL	101 958	105 209	107 884	109 403	108 249	108 601	110 713	114 163	117 191	119 608	122 690	125 865	128 916	131 759
TOTAL PRIVATE	84 948	87 823	90 105	91 098	89 847	89 956	91 872	95 036	97 885	100 189	103 133	106 042	108 709	111 079
GOODS-PRODUCING	24 674	25 125	25 254	24 905	23 745	23 231	23 352	23 908	24 265	24 493	24 962	25 414	25 507	25 709
Mining	717	713	692	709	689	635	610	601	581	580	596	590	539	543
Metal mining	43.8	49.8	55.7	57.8	55.9	53.2	49.8	48.6	51.3	53.8	53.6	49.3	44.3	40.6
Coal mining	161.8	150.8	143.7	146.5	135.5	126.8	108.6	111.8	104.4	97.7	96.0	91.8	84.6	77.2
Oil and gas extraction	401.5	400.3	381.0	394.7	392.9	352.6	349.8	336.5	320.1	322.0	339.0	339.1	297.4	311.1
Nonmetallic minerals, except fuels	110.0	111.8	111.2	110.3	104.5	101.8	101.5	103.6	105.3	106.2	107.8	109.8	112.8	113.7
Construction	4 958	5 098	5 171	5 120	4 650	4 492	4 668	4 986	5 160	5 418	5 691	6 020	6 415	6 698
General building contractors	1 317.8	1 349.8	1 331.8	1 298.0	1 140.4	1 076.8	1 119.5	1 188.2	1 207.0	1 257.2	1 309.6	1 376.7	1 457.6	1 527.6
Heavy construction, except building	738.6	742.7	767.0	770.4	726.6	711.2	712.6	739.6	752.2	776.8	798.9	839.6	874.0	900.7
Special trade contractors	2 901.4	3 005.2	3 072.1	3 051.0	2 783.3	2 704.1	2 835.6	3 058.4	3 201.1	3 383.6	3 582.3	3 803.6	4 083.7	4 269.4
Manufacturing	18 999	19 314	19 391	19 076	18 406	18 104	18 075	18 321	18 524	18 495	18 675	18 805	18 552	18 469
Durable goods	11 154	11 363	11 394	11 109	10 569	10 277	10 221	10 448	10 683	10 789	11 010	11 205	11 111	11 138
Lumber and wood products	753.8	767.3	756.2	733.3	675.2	679.9	709.1	754.3	769.2	778.4	796.0	813.5	834.3	831.8
Furniture and fixtures	514.8	526.7	524.3	505.8	474.7	477.7	486.9	504.6	509.7	504.3	512.2	532.9	548.2	558.2
Stone, clay, and glass products	554.3	567.4	568.4	556.2	521.5	513.3	517.0	531.6	539.6	543.8	552.4	561.5	566.4	578.9
Primary metal industries	746.2	770.3	771.8	756.2	722.6	694.5	683.1	697.7	712.0	710.5	710.7	714.6	699.1	697.7
Fabricated metal products	1 399.4	1 428.4	1 445.4	1 419.0	1 355.1	1 329.1	1 338.5	1 388.1	1 437.0	1 448.7	1 478.5	1 509.2	1 521.0	1 537.0
Industrial machinery and equipment	2 027.8	2 088.6	2 124.9	2 094.6	1 999.6	1 928.6	1 930.6	1 989.5	2 067.1	2 114.6	2 167.8	2 205.8	2 136.3	2 120.2
Computer and office equipment	461.2	459.1	458.7	437.6	415.3	391.0	363.4	354.2	352.2	361.8	375.9	381.7	367.5	361.4
Electronic and other electrical equipment	1 749.6	1 764.1	1 744.3	1 673.4	1 591.1	1 528.1	1 525.7	1 570.6	1 625.0	1 660.6	1 689.3	1 707.1	1 671.5	1 718.7
Electronic components and accessories	602.3	622.0	611.4	582.3	554.8	527.4	527.7	544.2	580.8	616.6	650.3	659.7	640.8	682.2
Transportation equipment	2 027.5	2 036.1	2 051.5	1 988.9	1 890.0	1 829.6	1 756.2	1 761.1	1 790.2	1 784.9	1 845.2	1 892.5	1 887.6	1 849.0
Motor vehicles and equipment	865.9	856.4	858.5	812.1	788.8	812.5	836.6	909.3	970.9	966.8	985.6	995.3	1 018.3	1 013.0
Aircraft and parts	678.0	683.5	711.0	712.3	669.2	611.7	542.0	481.5	450.5	458.1	500.6	525.1	496.3	465.2
Instruments and related products	1 011.1	1 031.0	1 025.9	1 005.9	974.0	928.5	895.5	861.1	843.4	855.4	866.0	873.1	855.4	852.4
Miscellaneous manufacturing industries	369.5	382.8	381.2	375.3	365.5	367.6	378.3	389.0	389.7	387.8	391.5	394.7	391.3	394.0
Nondurable goods	7 845	7 951	7 997	7 968	7 837	7 827	7 854	7 873	7 841	7 706	7 665	7 600	7 441	7 331
Food and kindred products	1 616.8	1 626.1	1 644.4	1 660.5	1 666.9	1 662.5	1 679.6	1 678.0	1 691.9	1 691.9	1 685.3	1 683.2	1 682.3	1 683.8
Tobacco products	55.0	54.4	49.9	49.1	49.0	47.5	43.7	42.9	42.1	41.4	41.4	40.5	37.4	33.9
Textile mill products	725.3	728.3	719.8	691.4	670.0	674.1	675.1	676.4	663.2	626.5	616.1	597.6	558.9	528.4
Apparel and other textile products	1 096.9	1 085.1	1 075.7	1 036.2	1 006.0	1 007.2	989.1	974.0	935.8	867.7	823.6	765.8	690.1	633.2
Paper and allied products	674.0	688.8	695.7	696.7	687.9	690.3	691.7	692.3	692.8	683.6	683.1	677.2	667.9	656.7
Printing and publishing	1 502.7	1 542.9	1 555.9	1 569.4	1 535.6	1 506.5	1 516.7	1 537.2	1 545.9	1 540.3	1 552.4	1 564.6	1 552.3	1 547.4
Chemicals and allied products	1 024.6	1 057.3	1 073.9	1 086.1	1 075.9	1 084.1	1 080.5	1 057.0	1 038.1	1 033.8	1 035.8	1 042.9	1 035.2	1 037.8
Petroleum and coal products	163.9	160.1	156.0	157.4	160.0	157.6	151.5	149.1	145.2	142.1	141.0	139.1	132.1	127.4
Rubber and miscellaneous plastics products	842.1	865.6	888.0	887.6	861.9	877.6	909.0	953.1	979.9	982.7	906.1	1 004.9	1 008.6	1 010.5
Leather and leather products	143.3	142.6	137.6	133.1	123.7	119.9	117.2	112.9	105.6	95.7	90.5	84.1	76.6	71.4
SERVICE-PRODUCING	77 284	80 084	82 630	84 497	84 504	85 370	87 361	90 256	92 925	95 115	97 727	100 451	103 409	106 050
Transportation And Public Utilities	5 362	5 512	5 614	5 777	5 755	5 718	5 811	5 984	6 132	6 253	6 408	6 611	6 834	7 019
Transportation	3 156	3 301	3 404	3 511	3 495	3 495	3 598	3 761	3 904	4 019	4 123	4 273	4 411	4 529
Railroad transportation	308.7	298.0	292.5	278.6	262.0	254.3	248.3	240.5	238.4	230.9	226.5	230.5	234.5	235.5
Local and interurban passenger transit	294.2	309.3	325.7	337.8	354.1	361.4	379.4	404.0	419.2	436.9	452.4	468.5	477.7	476.2
Trucking and warehousing	. . .	1 351.1	1 379.0	1 395.2	1 377.8	1 384.6	1 443.6	1 526.1	1 587.1	1 636.8	1 676.7	1 744.0	1 809.9	1 855.6
Water transportation	172.2	171.3	171.6	176.6	183.6	173.3	168.2	172.4	174.5	174.1	178.7	181.3	185.5	195.8
Transportation by air	. . .	850.2	897.2	967.6	961.8	964.0	988.2	1 023.0	1 068.3	1 107.4	1 133.9	1 180.6	1 226.7	1 281.3
Pipelines, except natural gas	18.8	18.5	18.5	18.5	19.0	19.2	18.4	17.1	15.1	14.5	14.2	13.8	13.4	13.7
Transportation services	. . .	302.4	319.0	336.1	336.3	338.4	351.7	377.9	401.2	418.2	440.5	454.0	463.3	471.3
Communications and public utilities	2 206	2 211	2 210	2 266	2 260	2 223	2 214	2 223	2 229	2 234	2 285	2 338	2 423	2 490
Communications	1 281.5	1 279.9	1 272.1	1 308.9	1 298.8	1 268.9	1 269.1	1 294.8	1 317.6	1 350.6	1 419.3	1 477.2	1 560.1	1 638.9
Electric, gas, and sanitary services	924.7	931.0	938.1	957.1	961.2	954.0	944.4	928.3	910.9	883.7	865.8	860.7	862.8	851.0
Wholesale Trade	5 848	6 030	6 187	6 173	6 081	5 997	5 981	6 162	6 378	6 482	6 648	6 800	6 911	7 024
Durable goods	3 437	3 564	3 653	3 614	3 531	3 446	3 433	3 559	3 715	3 805	3 927	4 043	4 117	4 193
Nondurable goods	2 411	2 466	2 534	2 559	2 550	2 552	2 549	2 604	2 663	2 677	2 721	2 757	2 793	2 831

See *Note* at end of table.

Table 2-1. Employees on Nonfarm Payrolls by Major Industry and Selected Component Groups, 1945–2000—*Continued*

(Thousands of persons.)

Industry	1945	1946	1947	1948	1949	1950	1951	1952	1953	1954	1955	1956	1957	1958
Retail Trade	5 359	6 077	6 477	6 659	6 654	6 743	7 007	7 184	7 385	7 360	7 601	7 831	7 848	7 761
Building materials and garden supplies	...	...	...	...	...	...	...	...	...	...	...	...	...	...
General merchandise stores	...	...	...	...	...	...	...	...	...	...	...	...	...	...
Department stores	...	...	...	...	...	...	...	...	...	...	...	...	...	867.3
Food stores	...	...	...	...	...	...	...	...	...	...	...	...	...	1 264.5
Automotive dealers and service stations	...	...	...	...	...	...	...	...	...	...	...	...	...	1 207.7
New and used car dealers	...	...	...	...	...	...	...	...	...	...	...	...	...	...
Apparel and accessory stores	...	...	585.2	600.1	585.8	573.4	594.8	608.1	617.9	609.4	616.1	629.9	625.0	610.8
Furniture and home furnishings stores	...	...	...	...	...	...	381.2	383.5	388.4	383.0	396.1	405.9	398.6	388.4
Eating and drinking places	...	...	...	...	...	...	...	...	...	...	...	...	...	1 528.9
Miscellaneous retail establishments	...	...	...	...	...	...	...	...	...	...	...	...	...	...
Finance, Insurance, And Real Estate	1 481	1 675	1 728	1 800	1 828	1 888	1 956	2 035	2 111	2 200	2 298	2 389	2 438	2 481
Finance	...	...	...	...	...	...	...	...	...	...	...	...	...	...
Depository institutions	...	...	...	...	...	...	...	...	...	...	...	...	...	...
Commercial banks	...	...	...	...	...	...	...	...	...	...	...	...	...	...
Savings institutions	...	...	...	...	...	...	...	...	...	...	...	...	...	...
Nondepository institutions	...	...	...	...	...	...	...	...	...	...	...	...	...	...
Mortgage bankers and brokers	...	...	...	...	...	...	...	...	...	...	...	...	...	...
Security and commodity brokers	...	...	62.8	60.7	58.3	62.4	66.7	68.2	68.9	70.7	81.3	86.9	90.3	93.8
Holding and other investment offices	...	...	...	...	...	...	...	...	...	...	...	...	...	...
Insurance	...	...	...	...	...	...	...	...	...	...	...	...	...	...
Insurance carriers	...	...	...	...	...	...	...	...	...	...	...	...	...	813.6
Insurance agents, brokers, and service	...	...	...	...	...	...	...	...	...	...	...	...	...	...
Real estate	...	...	...	...	...	...	...	...	...	...	...	...	...	...
Services	4 222	4 697	5 025	5 181	5 239	5 356	5 547	5 699	5 835	5 969	6 240	6 497	6 708	6 765
Agricultural services	...	...	...	...	...	...	...	...	...	...	...	...	...	...
Hotels and other lodging places	...	...	...	...	...	...	...	...	...	...	...	...	...	...
Personal services	...	...	...	...	...	...	...	...	...	...	...	...	...	796.2
Business services	...	...	...	...	...	...	...	...	...	...	...	...	...	555.0
Services to buildings	...	...	...	...	...	...	...	...	...	...	...	...	...	...
Personnel supply services	...	...	...	...	...	...	...	...	...	...	...	...	...	...
Help supply services	...	...	...	...	...	...	...	...	...	...	...	...	...	...
Computer and data processing services	...	...	...	...	...	...	...	...	...	...	...	...	...	...
Auto repair, services, and parking	...	...	...	...	...	...	...	...	...	...	...	...	...	...
Miscellaneous repair services	...	...	...	...	...	...	...	...	...	...	...	...	...	...
Motion pictures	...	...	...	...	...	...	...	...	...	...	...	...	...	...
Amusement and recreation services	...	...	...	...	...	...	...	...	...	...	...	...	...	...
Health services	...	...	...	...	...	...	...	...	...	...	...	...	...	1 365.2
Offices and clinics of medical doctors	...	...	...	...	...	...	...	...	...	...	...	...	...	...
Nursing and personal care facilities	...	...	...	...	...	...	...	...	...	...	...	...	...	...
Hospitals	...	...	...	...	...	...	...	...	...	...	...	...	...	908.3
Home health care services	...	...	...	...	...	...	...	...	...	...	...	...	...	...
Legal services	...	...	...	...	...	...	...	...	...	...	...	...	...	...
Educational services	...	...	...	...	...	...	...	...	...	...	...	...	...	572.1
Social services	...	...	...	...	...	...	...	...	...	...	...	...	...	...
Child day care services	...	...	...	...	...	...	...	...	...	...	...	...	...	...
Residential care	...	...	...	...	...	...	...	...	...	...	...	...	...	...
Museums and botanical and zoological gardens	...	...	...	...	...	...	...	...	...	...	...	...	...	...
Membership organizations	...	...	...	...	...	...	...	...	...	...	...	...	...	...
Engineering and management services	...	...	...	...	...	...	...	...	...	...	...	...	...	...
Engineering and architectural services	...	...	...	...	...	...	...	...	...	...	...	...	...	173.1
Management and public relations	...	...	...	...	...	...	...	...	...	...	...	...	...	...
Government	5 944	5 595	5 474	5 650	5 856	6 026	6 389	6 609	6 645	6 751	6 914	7 278	7 616	7 839
Federal	2 808	2 254	1 892	1 863	1 908	1 928	2 302	2 420	2 305	2 188	2 187	2 209	2 217	2 191
Federal, except Postal Service	2 372	1 785	1 425	1 369	1 385	1 416	1 784	1 882	1 778	1 658	1 657	1 674	1 666	1 628
State	...	...	...	...	...	...	...	...	...	...	1 168	1 250	1 328	1 415
Education	...	...	...	...	...	...	...	...	...	...	308	334	362	389
Other state government	...	...	...	...	...	...	...	...	...	...	860	916	966	1 027
Local	...	...	...	...	...	...	...	...	...	...	3 558	3 819	4 071	4 230
Education	...	...	...	...	...	...	...	...	...	...	1 792	1 928	2 073	2 165
Other local government	...	...	...	...	...	...	...	...	...	...	1 766	1 891	1 997	2 065

See *Note* at end of table.

Table 2-1. Employees on Nonfarm Payrolls by Major Industry and Selected Component Groups, 1945–2000—*Continued*

(Thousands of persons.)

Industry	1959	1960	1961	1962	1963	1964	1965	1966	1967	1968	1969	1970	1971	1972
Retail Trade	8 035	8 238	8 195	8 359	8 520	8 812	9 239	9 637	9 906	10 308	10 785	11 034	11 338	11 822
Building materials and garden supplies	...	...	...	...	...	...	...	...	...	...	...	...	...	508.4
General merchandise stores	...	...	...	...	...	...	...	...	...	...	...	...	...	2 149.4
Department stores	899.7	920.2	927.6	974.6	1 024.5	1 091.3	1 176.8	1 259.0	1 328.6	1 410.8	1 488.0	1 519.4	1 563.1	1 660.5
Food stores	1 305.4	1 355.8	1 354.6	1 363.6	1 383.8	1 419.4	1 468.6	1 535.5	1 571.6	1 619.9	1 682.8	1 730.6	1 752.4	1 805.1
Automotive dealers and service stations	1 243.6	1 267.2	1 239.8	1 272.6	1 324.4	1 366.8	1 424.2	1 462.3	1 491.7	1 549.0	1 610.9	1 617.4	1 642.3	1 722.6
New and used car dealers	...	...	...	...	...	...	...	...	...	...	...	...	...	775.3
Apparel and accessory stores	624.0	639.3	631.5	636.5	632.0	636.2	660.8	681.1	694.4	725.1	752.8	760.6	778.6	783.8
Furniture and home furnishings stores	395.9	400.1	389.0	388.5	389.0	394.5	409.6	419.9	425.9	440.0	464.2	471.6	487.2	513.2
Eating and drinking places	1 602.9	1 654.3	1 664.8	1 720.5	1 747.9	1 848.1	1 987.9	2 117.9	2 191.4	2 308.8	2 465.7	2 574.6	2 700.4	2 860.2
Miscellaneous retail establishments	...	...	...	...	...	...	...	...	...	...	...	...	...	1 479.7
Finance, Insurance, And Real Estate	2 549	2 628	2 688	2 754	2 830	2 911	2 977	3 058	3 185	3 337	3 512	3 645	3 772	3 908
Finance	...	...	...	...	...	...	...	...	...	...	...	...	...	1 778.0
Depository institutions	...	...	...	...	...	...	...	...	...	...	...	...	...	...
Commercial banks	...	...	...	...	...	...	...	...	...	...	...	...	...	1 012.7
Savings institutions	...	...	...	...	...	...	...	...	...	...	...	...	...	...
Nondepository institutions	...	...	...	...	...	...	...	...	...	...	...	...	...	...
Mortgage bankers and brokers	...	...	...	...	...	...	...	...	...	...	...	...	...	...
Security and commodity brokers	106.7	114.4	128.5	131.8	123.9	125.8	129.0	140.8	156.0	192.1	225.5	204.5	197.7	202.7
Holding and other investment offices	...	...	...	...	...	...	...	...	...	...	...	...	...	72.7
Insurance	...	...	...	...	...	...	...	...	...	...	...	...	...	1 373
Insurance carriers	816.9	831.7	843.7	852.4	871.9	889.5	893.4	908.2	946.8	980.6	998.8	1 029.7	1 046.9	1 054.3
Insurance agents, brokers, and service	...	...	...	...	...	...	...	...	...	...	...	...	...	319.1
Real estate	...	...	...	...	...	...	...	...	...	...	...	...	...	756
Services	7 087	7 378	7 619	7 982	8 277	8 660	9 036	9 498	10 045	10 567	11 169	11 548	11 797	12 276
Agricultural services	...	...	...	...	...	...	...	...	...	...	...	...	...	...
Hotels and other lodging places	...	...	...	...	...	...	...	...	...	...	...	...	...	813.1
Personal services	808.7	812.0	816.4	830.9	845.4	866.1	894.7	923.8	933.2	936.5	930.5	898.0	847.9	828.4
Business services	607.6	655.7	693.2	753.7	813.7	880.8	954.9	1 051.5	1 144.6	1 210.0	1 328.5	1 397.3	1 401.7	1 490.5
Services to buildings	...	...	...	...	...	167.5	182.5	199.7	224.9	241.3	267.9	294.7	308.3	336.2
Personnel supply services	...	...	...	...	...	...	...	...	...	...	...	...	...	213.5
Help supply services	...	...	...	...	...	...	...	...	...	...	...	...	...	...
Computer and data processing services	...	...	...	...	...	...	...	...	...	...	...	...	...	106.7
Auto repair, services, and parking	...	...	...	...	...	...	...	...	...	...	...	...	...	398.6
Miscellaneous repair services	...	...	...	...	...	148.8	155.0	161.4	167.9	174.1	183.5	188.7	193.1	198.9
Motion pictures	...	...	...	...	...	...	...	...	...	...	...	...	...	...
Amusement and recreation services	...	...	...	...	...	...	...	...	...	...	...	...	...	...
Health services	1 453.7	1 547.6	1 640.1	1 739.3	1 837.0	1 963.0	2 079.5	2 204.2	2 434.3	2 638.6	2 862.1	3 052.5	3 238.5	3 411.9
Offices and clinics of medical doctors	...	...	...	...	...	...	...	...	...	...	...	...	...	467.1
Nursing and personal care facilities	...	...	...	...	...	...	...	...	...	...	...	...	...	591.2
Hospitals	967.3	1 030.0	1 087.1	1 144.7	1 217.4	1 295.1	1 356.5	1 419.7	1 554.2	1 653.9	1 769.6	1 863.2	1 934.9	1 980.2
Home health care services	...	...	...	...	...	...	...	...	...	...	...	...	...	...
Legal services	...	...	...	...	...	...	...	...	...	...	...	...	...	271.1
Educational services	598.1	616.1	636.8	678.7	707.5	743.4	772.1	803.9	842.1	891.2	929.7	939.6	947.8	958.4
Social services	...	...	...	...	...	...	...	...	...	...	...	...	...	552.9
Child day care services	...	...	...	...	...	...	...	...	...	...	...	...	...	145.5
Residential care	...	...	...	...	...	...	...	...	...	...	...	...	...	...
Museums and botanical and zoological gardens	...	...	...	...	...	...	...	...	...	...	...	...	...	...
Membership organizations	...	...	...	...	...	...	...	...	...	...	...	...	...	1 402.7
Engineering and management services	...	...	...	...	...	...	...	...	...	...	...	...	...	...
Engineering and architectural services	183.7	190.0	193.3	205.4	216.1	225.9	242.4	266.3	281.2	289.3	306.2	304.0	310.1	339.3
Management and public relations	...	...	...	...	...	...	...	...	...	...	...	...	...	...
Government	8 083	8 353	8 594	8 890	9 225	9 596	10 074	10 784	11 391	11 839	12 195	12 554	12 881	13 334
Federal	2 233	2 270	2 279	2 340	2 358	2 348	2 378	2 564	2 719	2 737	2 758	2 731	2 696	2 684
Federal, except Postal Service	1 658	1 683	1 682	1 743	1 760	1 748	1 764	1 883	2 005	2 013	2 025	1 995	1 969	1 986
State	1 484	1 536	1 607	1 668	1 747	1 856	1 996	2 141	2 302	2 442	2 533	2 664	2 747	2 859
Education	420	448	474	510	557	609	679	775	873	958	1 042	1 104	1 149	1 188
Other state government	1 065	1 088	1 133	1 158	1 190	1 247	1 317	1 366	1 428	1 484	1 491	1 560	1 599	1 672
Local	4 366	4 547	4 708	4 881	5 121	5 392	5 700	6 080	6 371	6 660	6 904	7 158	7 437	7 790
Education	2 250	2 369	2 468	2 581	2 738	2 906	3 102	3 375	3 572	3 736	3 874	4 004	4 188	4 363
Other local government	2 116	2 178	2 240	2 300	2 383	2 486	2 598	2 705	2 799	2 924	3 030	3 154	3 250	3 427

See *Note* at end of table.

Table 2-1. Employees on Nonfarm Payrolls by Major Industry and Selected Component Groups, 1945–2000—*Continued*

(Thousands of persons.)

Industry	1973	1974	1975	1976	1977	1978	1979	1980	1981	1982	1983	1984	1985	1986
Retail Trade	12 315	12 539	12 630	13 193	13 792	14 556	14 972	15 018	15 171	15 158	15 587	16 512	17 315	17 880
Building materials and garden supplies	534.5	542.2	520.9	546.4	575.8	608.1	629.2	617.4	606.8	588.3	615.1	658.8	689.5	703.9
General merchandise stores	2 229.3	2 209.5	2 113.0	2 155.3	2 204.3	2 307.8	2 287.4	2 244.6	2 230.0	2 183.7	2 165.2	2 267.0	2 323.2	2 364.9
Department stores	1 721.5	1 711.3	1 649.0	1 685.5	1 738.4	1 839.5	1 828.4	1 821.6	1 822.3	1 790.1	1 782.3	1 866.4	1 897.0	1 928.7
Food stores	1 855.5	1 947.6	2 007.2	2 038.6	2 106.3	2 198.9	2 296.8	2 383.6	2 448.4	2 477.3	2 555.5	2 635.9	2 773.5	2 896.3
Automotive dealers and service stations	1 777.8	1 665.8	1 677.1	1 743.6	1 800.8	1 860.6	1 812.3	1 688.5	1 653.0	1 631.5	1 673.6	1 797.6	1 888.5	1 941.4
New and used car dealers	802.6	753.3	730.6	769.9	801.9	839.9	835.3	745.2	707.4	694.3	722.1	794.3	856.1	895.7
Apparel and accessory stores	794.7	810.8	805.7	841.7	869.9	909.2	949.4	956.7	968.3	942.4	962.5	1 007.5	1 039.1	1 075.3
Furniture and home furnishings stores	532.5	538.0	516.5	539.8	562.5	594.7	614.9	606.4	595.4	583.4	607.8	677.4	733.2	766.5
Eating and drinking places	3 053.8	3 231.2	3 379.5	3 656.2	3 948.6	4 277.2	4 513.1	4 625.8	4 749.0	4 829.4	5 038.0	5 380.9	5 698.6	5 901.5
Miscellaneous retail establishments	1 537.4	1 594.1	1 609.8	1 671.8	1 724.0	1 799.8	1 868.7	1 894.9	1 920.3	1 922.1	1 969.7	2 087.0	2 169.7	2 230.5
Finance, Insurance, And Real Estate	4 046	4 148	4 165	4 271	4 467	4 724	4 975	5 160	5 298	5 340	5 466	5 684	5 948	6 273
Finance	1 866.0	1 936.0	1 964.0	2 026.0	2 113.0	2 233.0	2 369.0	2 483.0	2 593.0	2 647.0	2 741.0	2 852.0	2 974.0	3 145.0
Depository institutions	. . .	. . .	. . .	. . .	. . .	. . .	. . .	. . .	. . .	. . .	. . .	. . .	. . .	. . .
Commercial banks	1 068.0	1 130.2	1 150.4	1 182.0	1 220.6	1 280.8	1 349.7	1 412.5	1 461.1	1 485.0	1 484.1	1 496.0	1 521.8	1 542.2
Savings institutions	. . .	. . .	. . .	. . .	. . .	. . .	. . .	. . .	. . .	. . .	. . .	. . .	. . .	. . .
Nondepository institutions	. . .	. . .	. . .	. . .	. . .	. . .	. . .	. . .	. . .	. . .	. . .	. . .	. . .	. . .
Mortgage bankers and brokers	. . .	. . .	. . .	. . .	. . .	. . .	. . .	. . .	. . .	61.5	81.3	100.8	116.0	151.2
Security and commodity brokers	192.0	173.5	169.5	176.4	181.8	188.8	204.2	227.4	259.0	273.8	308.4	338.7	354.5	393.2
Holding and other investment offices	77.1	81.9	86.6	90.6	95.4	103.4	111.2	114.6	122.5	134.0	136.3	144.2	165.8	189.5
Insurance	1 401	1 434	1 442	1 468	1 528	1 591	1 643	1 688	1 713	1 723	1 728	1 765	1 840	1 944
Insurance carriers	1 071.0	1 087.2	1 085.3	1 101.3	1 140.9	1 173.6	1 199.8	1 224.1	1 236.9	1 237.3	1 228.9	1 239.7	1 291.6	1 364.8
Insurance agents, brokers, and service	329.6	346.4	356.6	366.9	387.5	417.7	442.8	463.8	475.8	485.9	498.9	525.0	548.2	579.4
Real estate	778	778	760	776	826	900	963	989	992	970	997	1 067	1 135	1 184
Services	12 857	13 441	13 892	14 551	15 302	16 252	17 112	17 890	18 615	19 021	19 664	20 746	21 927	22 957
Agricultural services	. . .	. . .	. . .	184.3	197.3	216.7	234.2	246.2	257.7	266.7	286.6	328.2	361.2	388.6
Hotels and other lodging places	854.2	877.7	898.4	929.4	956.1	988.0	1 059.8	1 075.8	1 118.7	1 132.9	1 171.5	1 262.8	1 331.3	1 377.8
Personal services	823.0	806.6	781.7	790.4	806.4	826.7	820.8	817.8	827.6	844.2	869.1	918.3	956.6	990.7
Business services	1 609.5	1 685.8	1 697.2	1 805.9	1 957.6	2 180.5	2 410.1	2 563.5	2 699.6	2 722.2	2 948.0	3 352.7	3 679.4	3 957.4
Services to buildings	363.9	393.8	390.0	406.1	422.3	451.7	487.0	495.0	511.0	523.5	558.8	608.5	649.8	684.9
Personnel supply services	246.6	256.7	242.0	292.7	357.2	438.1	507.8	543.3	585.0	541.0	618.6	796.7	890.7	990.2
Help supply services	. . .	. . .	. . .	. . .	. . .	. . .	. . .	. . .	. . .	417.0	408.1	642.5	732.0	836.5
Computer and data processing services	119.5	134.6	143.0	159.4	186.6	223.8	270.8	304.3	336.6	364.6	415.6	474.4	541.5	588.1
Auto repair, services, and parking	422.0	429.6	438.8	405.6	497.7	549.2	575.1	570.9	573.6	589.1	618.5	682.3	729.7	761.5
Miscellaneous repair services	205.1	217.1	217.5	227.4	240.7	261.4	281.8	288.8	292.8	280.0	287.4	310.4	318.9	321.8
Motion pictures	. . .	. . .	. . .	. . .	. . .	. . .	. . .	. . .	. . .	. . .	. . .	. . .	. . .	. . .
Amusement and recreation services	. . .	. . .	. . .	. . .	. . .	. . .	. . .	. . .	. . .	. . .	. . .	. . .	. . .	. . .
Health services	3 640.8	3 886.7	4 133.8	4 350.4	4 583.9	4 791.6	4 992.8	5 278.0	5 562.1	5 810.8	5 986.2	6 118.3	6 292.8	6 527.6
Offices and clinics of medical doctors	518.7	567.1	607.9	644.4	680.5	719.7	760.8	801.7	844.9	887.2	933.5	977.2	1 028.2	1 081.4
Nursing and personal care facilities	659.0	708.1	759.3	809.1	860.0	910.6	950.8	996.6	1 028.8	1 066.9	1 106.0	1 147.2	1 197.5	1 244.6
Hospitals	2 051.3	2 160.1	2 273.7	2 363.2	2 465.2	2 538.2	2 608.4	2 750.2	2 904.2	3 014.4	3 036.6	3 003.6	2 996.8	3 037.4
Home health care services	. . .	. . .	. . .	. . .	. . .	. . .	. . .	. . .	. . .	. . .	. . .	. . .	. . .	. . .
Legal services	295.5	325.5	340.9	363.8	394.4	427.1	460.3	498.1	532.3	565.3	601.6	645.1	692.0	746.6
Educational services	974.8	990.1	1 000.9	1 012.5	1 031.0	1 062.4	1 089.7	1 138.2	1 178.5	1 198.5	1 225.2	1 270.4	1 358.9	1 421.3
Social services	552.1	624.9	689.9	763.0	854.6	990.6	1 081.3	1 134.3	1 149.0	1 149.4	1 188.4	1 222.4	1 324.6	1 405.7
Child day care services	151.0	172.0	198.9	214.6	245.2	284.8	303.1	298.9	289.8	282.4	283.8	291.7	310.0	321.9
Residential care	. . .	. . .	. . .	. . .	. . .	. . .	. . .	. . .	. . .	236.0	250.7	269.1	294.0	320.8
Museums and botanical and zoological gardens	. . .	. . .	. . .	. . .	. . .	. . .	. . .	. . .	. . .	. . .	. . .	. . .	. . .	. . .
Membership organizations	1 410.3	1 437.9	1 452.3	1 486.8	1 495.4	1 501.6	1 516.2	1 539.3	1 527.2	1 525.5	1 509.8	1 504.0	1 517.1	1 536.4
Engineering and management services	. . .	. . .	. . .	. . .	. . .	. . .	. . .	. . .	. . .	. . .	. . .	. . .	. . .	. . .
Engineering and architectural services	372.3	394.7	382.3	386.9	424.0	472.6	515.0	544.9	571.9	572.2	575.6	625.0	656.4	681.4
Management and public relations	. . .	. . .	. . .	. . .	. . .	. . .	. . .	. . .	. . .	. . .	. . .	. . .	. . .	. . .
Government	13 732	14 170	14 686	14 871	15 127	15 672	15 947	16 241	16 031	15 837	15 869	16 024	16 394	16 693
Federal	2 663	2 724	2 748	2 733	2 727	2 753	2 773	2 866	2 772	2 739	2 774	2 807	2 875	2 899
Federal, except Postal Service	1 970	2 019	2 051	2 062	2 073	2 104	2 112	2 205	2 111	2 076	2 088	2 104	2 133	2 110
State	2 923	3 039	3 179	3 273	3 377	3 474	3 541	3 610	3 640	3 640	3 662	3 734	3 832	3 893
Education	1 205	1 267	1 323	1 371	1 385	1 367	1 378	1 398	1 420	1 433	1 450	1 488	1 540	1 561
Other state government	1 717	1 772	1 856	1 902	1 992	2 106	2 162	2 212	2 220	2 207	2 212	2 246	2 292	2 332
Local	8 146	8 407	8 758	8 865	9 023	9 446	9 633	9 765	9 619	9 458	9 434	9 482	9 687	9 901
Education	4 537	4 692	4 834	4 899	4 974	5 075	5 107	5 210	5 216	5 169	5 139	5 196	5 344	5 484
Other local government	3 608	3 715	3 924	3 966	4 048	4 370	4 526	4 555	4 403	4 290	4 295	4 286	4 343	4 417

See *Note* at end of table.

Table 2-1. Employees on Nonfarm Payrolls by Major Industry and Selected Component Groups, 1945–2000—*Continued*

(Thousands of persons.)

Industry	1987	1988	1989	1990	1991	1992	1993	1994	1995	1996	1997	1998	1999	2000
Retail Trade	18 422	19 023	19 475	19 601	19 284	19 356	19 773	20 507	21 187	21 597	21 966	22 295	22 848	23 307
Building materials and garden supplies	743.0	779.1	783.4	771.2	746.5	757.7	779.0	833.4	867.5	893.7	929.2	947.7	988.0	1 016.2
General merchandise stores	2 410.7	2 471.6	2 544.3	2 540.0	2 452.8	2 451.0	2 488.3	2 582.8	2 680.5	2 701.8	2 700.8	2 730.1	2 798.0	2 837.0
Department stores	1 959.7	2 010.3	2 116.3	2 149.8	2 073.7	2 080.0	2 140.1	2 246.1	2 345.6	2 367.4	2 379.5	2 415.4	2 458.5	2 490.5
Food stores	2 958.3	3 073.9	3 163.5	3 215.0	3 203.7	3 179.8	3 224.1	3 291.2	3 366.0	3 435.5	3 478.1	3 483.5	3 496.8	3 521.0
Automotive dealers and service stations	2 000.8	2 071.4	2 092.4	2 063.1	1 983.8	1 966.3	2 013.8	2 116.2	2 189.6	2 266.7	2 310.8	2 332.3	2 368.1	2 412.2
New and used car dealers	924.6	958.1	953.7	924.3	879.3	875.4	908.3	962.5	996.0	1 030.5	1 046.1	1 047.4	1 080.1	1 114.3
Apparel and accessory stores	1 122.8	1 164.7	1 196.7	1 183.4	1 150.6	1 130.9	1 143.6	1 144.0	1 125.4	1 098.4	1 108.5	1 140.6	1 171.4	1 193.2
Furniture and home furnishings stores	789.3	802.0	826.4	820.4	801.4	799.8	827.5	889.1	945.5	975.2	998.8	1 025.2	1 086.8	1 133.9
Eating and drinking places	6 085.7	6 258.2	6 401.9	6 509.1	6 476.3	6 609.3	6 821.4	7 077.8	7 354.2	7 516.6	7 645.7	7 767.8	7 960.6	8 113.7
Miscellaneous retail establishments	2 311.1	2 401.9	2 466.8	2 498.6	2 468.4	2 461.4	2 475.5	2 572.5	2 658.3	2 708.5	2 793.9	2 867.9	2 977.9	3 079.6
Finance, Insurance, And Real Estate	6 533	6 630	6 668	6 709	6 646	6 602	6 757	6 896	6 806	6 911	7 109	7 389	7 555	7 560
Finance	3 264.0	3 274.0	3 283.0	3 268.0	3 187.0	3 160.0	3 238.0	3 299.0	3 231.0	3 303.0	3 424.0	3 588.0	3 688.0	3 710.0
Depository institutions	. . .	2 255.0	2 273.4	2 250.5	2 164.2	2 095.7	2 088.8	2 065.7	2 025.1	2 018.6	2 027.2	2 046.0	2 055.6	2 029.3
Commercial banks	1 539.0	1 533.8	1 555.0	1 563.8	1 529.0	1 489.5	1 497.2	1 484.3	1 465.5	1 458.3	1 462.5	1 471.8	1 467.8	1 430.2
Savings institutions	. . .	497.2	481.5	438.0	382.4	345.9	324.1	305.1	275.8	265.8	259.8	256.3	254.2	253.0
Nondepository institutions	. . .	363.3	361.2	372.8	379.4	405.5	454.9	490.6	462.9	522.0	577.3	657.6	709.3	681.2
Mortgage bankers and brokers	174.2	157.2	149.1	152.1	152.4	180.2	224.8	248.9	204.9	233.0	262.7	326.2	352.7	309.0
Security and commodity brokers	442.2	446.5	430.2	424.2	419.6	440.1	471.6	515.5	525.4	553.0	596.0	646.5	688.8	748.3
Holding and other investment offices	201.0	209.3	217.7	220.7	223.6	219.0	222.6	226.5	217.2	209.9	223.2	238.2	234.1	251.1
Insurance	2 027	2 075	2 090	2 126	2 161	2 152	2 197	2 236	2 225	2 226	2 264	2 335	2 368	2 346
Insurance carriers	1 415.0	1 435.4	1 438.4	1 462.2	1 494.6	1 495.6	1 529.0	1 551.9	1 528.8	1 517.1	1 538.8	1 591.1	1 610.0	1 589.4
Insurance agents, brokers, and service	611.8	639.6	651.8	663.3	666.3	656.6	668.0	683.6	695.5	708.6	725.2	744.2	757.8	756.5
Real estate	1 242	1 280	1 296	1 315	1 299	1 290	1 322	1 361	1 351	1 382	1 421	1 465	1 500	1 504
Services	24 110	25 504	26 907	27 934	28 336	29 052	30 197	31 579	33 117	34 454	36 040	37 533	39 055	40 460
Agricultural services	410.9	447.3	464.9	490.1	486.5	489.6	519.0	564.1	581.8	627.2	678.2	707.9	766.0	801.4
Hotels and other lodging places	1 464.2	1 540.1	1 595.8	1 631.1	1 589.4	1 576.4	1 595.7	1 630.9	1 668.1	1 715.0	1 745.7	1 789.4	1 848.1	1 911.8
Personal services	1 027.1	1 055.8	1 085.7	1 103.5	1 111.5	1 116.2	1 137.1	1 140.4	1 162.9	1 180.2	1 185.9	1 201.2	1 225.6	1 250.8
Business services	4 278.3	4 638.3	4 940.6	5 139.3	5 086.2	5 315.3	5 734.7	6 280.7	6 812.4	7 293.0	7 987.5	8 618.0	9 299.9	9 858.4
Services to buildings	724.3	780.2	797.5	806.5	796.0	805.4	823.0	857.3	882.2	906.8	930.2	949.7	983.1	994.1
Personnel supply services	1 176.8	1 350.4	1 454.5	1 534.5	1 484.5	1 629.3	1 906.1	2 271.7	2 475.5	2 653.5	2 985.0	3 278.1	3 615.8	3 887.0
Help supply services	988.9	1 125.9	1 215.8	1 288.2	1 268.4	1 410.6	1 669.2	2 017.1	2 188.8	2 352.4	2 656.3	2 925.8	3 247.8	3 487.1
Computer and data processing services	628.6	673.3	736.3	771.9	797.0	835.5	892.8	958.6	1 089.9	1 227.7	1 409.4	1 615.0	1 875.4	2 094.9
Auto repair, services, and parking	793.6	833.6	884.1	913.7	881.8	881.3	924.7	968.3	1 020.1	1 080.0	1 119.6	1 145.2	1 196.4	1 248.4
Miscellaneous repair services	321.4	350.0	374.3	374.4	341.0	347.0	348.5	338.2	359.1	371.8	374.1	376.1	371.6	365.8
Motion pictures	. . .	340.9	374.7	407.7	410.9	400.9	412.0	441.2	487.6	524.7	550.4	576.0	598.8	593.8
Amusement and recreation services	. . .	976.8	1 033.3	1 076.0	1 122.2	1 188.1	1 258.2	1 334.1	1 417.4	1 476.1	1 552.3	1 594.4	1 651.4	1 728.0
Health services	6 794.2	7 105.4	7 462.8	7 814.3	8 182.9	8 490.0	8 755.9	8 991.9	9 230.4	9 477.9	9 702.7	9 852.5	9 976.6	10 095.2
Offices and clinics of medical doctors	1 139.1	1 199.5	1 267.9	1 338.2	1 404.5	1 463.1	1 506.0	1 544.9	1 608.9	1 678.3	1 739.0	1 805.7	1 875.0	1 924.1
Nursing and personal care facilities	1 282.6	1 310.6	1 355.7	1 415.4	1 492.6	1 532.8	1 585.0	1 648.6	1 691.4	1 730.4	1 756.2	1 771.6	1 786.1	1 795.9
Hospitals	3 142.1	3 293.8	3 438.5	3 548.7	3 655.1	3 749.9	3 779.1	3 763.0	3 772.1	3 811.5	3 860.4	3 930.2	3 973.5	3 990.3
Home health care services	. . .	216.1	243.7	290.6	344.5	397.8	469.0	559.4	628.7	674.6	710.4	666.4	636.1	643.0
Legal services	800.9	844.5	880.4	907.7	911.9	913.5	924.0	924.0	921.4	927.5	944.4	971.4	996.2	1 009.6
Educational services	1 449.2	1 567.3	1 647.0	1 660.7	1 709.7	1 677.6	1 711.3	1 850.0	1 965.2	2 029.9	2 103.6	2 178.3	2 266.6	2 325.0
Social services	1 453.8	1 551.7	1 643.6	1 734.2	1 844.8	1 958.6	2 070.3	2 199.7	2 335.6	2 412.6	2 517.7	2 646.3	2 783.3	2 902.8
Child day care services	333.4	356.3	378.4	391.4	417.2	450.8	473.4	515.1	562.6	564.7	575.9	620.8	680.0	711.9
Residential care	351.6	389.4	422.7	461.1	501.3	533.5	567.2	603.8	642.6	676.8	715.5	743.7	771.3	805.9
Museums and botanical and zoological gardens	. . .	58.0	62.0	66.2	69.1	72.7	75.5	78.6	80.4	85.4	90.1	93.5	99.2	106.4
Membership organizations	1 613.6	1 740.4	1 835.7	1 945.5	1 981.9	1 973.0	2 034.6	2 081.5	2 145.9	2 201.4	2 276.6	2 372.1	2 436.0	2 474.8
Engineering and management services	. . .	2 230.4	2 389.2	2 477.6	2 433.4	2 470.8	2 520.9	2 578.5	2 731.1	2 844.3	2 987.8	3 139.1	3 255.6	3 418.6
Engineering and architectural services	705.7	730.4	770.3	786.3	750.1	742.4	757.1	778.3	814.8	836.2	865.2	908.0	956.2	1 017.2
Management and public relations	. . .	508.1	570.0	610.4	617.1	655.1	688.4	718.7	805.2	869.5	938.8	1 000.2	1 031.1	1 089.7
Government	17 010	17 386	17 779	18 304	18 402	18 645	18 841	19 128	19 305	19 419	19 557	19 823	20 206	20 681
Federal	2 943	2 971	2 988	3 085	2 966	2 969	2 915	2 870	2 822	2 757	2 699	2 686	2 669	2 777
Federal, except Postal Service	2 133	2 140	2 155	2 267	2 159	2 177	2 128	2 053	1 978	1 901	1 842	1 819	1 796	1 917
State	3 967	4 076	4 182	4 305	4 355	4 408	4 488	4 576	4 635	4 606	4 582	4 612	4 709	4 785
Education	1 586	1 620	1 668	1 730	1 768	1 799	1 834	1 882	1 919	1 911	1 904	1 922	1 983	2 032
Other state government	2 381	2 456	2 514	2 574	2 587	2 610	2 654	2 694	2 715	2 695	2 678	2 690	2 726	2 753
Local	10 100	10 339	10 609	10 914	11 081	11 267	11 438	11 682	11 849	12 056	12 276	12 525	12 829	13 119
Education	5 598	5 722	5 875	6 042	6 136	6 220	6 353	6 479	6 606	6 748	6 918	7 084	7 289	7 440
Other local government	4 502	4 617	4 734	4 873	4 945	5 048	5 085	5 202	5 243	5 308	5 357	5 440	5 540	5 679

Note: Data include Alaska and Hawaii beginning in 1959.

Table 2-2. Women Employees on Nonfarm Payrolls by Major Industry, 1959–2000

(Thousands of persons.)

Year	Total	Mining	Construction	Manufacturing			Transportation and public utilities	Wholesale trade	Retail trade	Finance, insurance, and real estate	Services	Government			
				Total	Durable goods	Nondurable goods						Total	Federal	State	Local
1959	. . .	. . .	. . .	4 358	1 692	2 667	. . .	. . .	. . .	. . .	. . .	. . .	. . .	. . .	. . .
1960	. . .	36	. . .	4 371	1 702	2 670	. . .	717	3 579	. . .	. . .	. . .	. . .	. . .	. . .
1961	. . .	35	. . .	4 292	1 662	2 630	. . .	703	3 564	. . .	. . .	. . .	. . .	. . .	. . .
1962	. . .	35	. . .	4 474	1 770	2 705	. . .	712	3 643	. . .	. . .	. . .	. . .	. . .	. . .
1963	. . .	35	. . .	4 482	1 767	2 715	. . .	720	3 708	. . .	. . .	. . .	. . .	. . .	. . .
1964	19 662	34	152	4 537	1 777	2 760	723	741	3 878	1 464	4 415	3 718	530	708	2 480
1965	20 660	34	152	4 768	1 911	2 857	748	768	4 113	1 496	4 611	3 970	542	768	2 660
1966	22 168	34	156	5 213	2 204	3 009	786	809	4 315	1 549	4 931	4 375	610	841	2 924
1967	23 272	35	158	5 353	2 300	3 053	835	832	4 465	1 624	5 267	4 703	674	931	3 099
1968	24 395	36	164	5 490	2 361	3 129	860	857	4 669	1 709	5 632	4 979	710	1 013	3 256
1969	25 595	37	174	5 667	2 469	3 197	911	904	4 937	1 819	5 994	5 153	723	1 087	3 343
1970	26 132	37	186	5 448	2 307	3 141	957	924	5 083	1 907	6 224	5 365	723	1 126	3 517
1971	26 466	37	199	5 229	2 152	3 078	955	917	5 211	1 978	6 438	5 502	715	1 118	3 669
1972	27 541	40	219	5 470	2 280	3 190	953	939	5 410	2 032	6 718	5 759	747	1 162	3 849
1973	28 988	43	241	5 865	2 567	3 298	987	996	5 686	2 138	7 023	6 010	780	1 216	4 014
1974	30 124	49	262	5 849	2 618	3 230	1 018	1 050	5 928	2 245	7 454	6 270	798	1 287	4 185
1975	30 178	55	256	5 257	2 271	2 985	996	1 053	5 998	2 287	7 822	6 454	805	1 373	4 276
1976	31 570	60	281	5 607	2 444	3 163	1 010	1 100	6 301	2 371	8 256	6 586	808	1 448	4 329
1977	33 252	65	304	5 880	2 645	3 235	1 051	1 153	6 611	2 511	8 771	6 907	856	1 510	4 540
1978	35 349	76	331	6 237	2 894	3 343	1 133	1 243	7 036	2 708	9 368	7 216	866	1 537	4 813
1979	37 096	91	355	6 466	3 085	3 380	1 237	1 328	7 369	2 882	9 919	7 450	860	1 572	5 018
1980	38 186	105	372	6 317	3 003	3 314	1 292	1 371	7 480	3 039	10 452	7 759	908	1 632	5 219
1981	39 035	129	380	6 341	3 029	3 312	1 340	1 404	7 585	3 158	10 969	7 730	878	1 659	5 193
1982	39 041	134	377	5 990	2 822	3 168	1 339	1 424	7 653	3 198	11 330	7 595	883	1 637	5 075
1983	39 826	117	388	5 964	2 788	3 176	1 313	1 463	7 912	3 277	11 755	7 637	939	1 584	5 114
1984	42 022	118	427	6 295	3 031	3 265	1 386	1 557	8 519	3 430	12 413	7 878	975	1 678	5 224
1985	43 851	120	463	6 230	3 022	3 208	1 448	1 632	9 037	3 634	13 129	8 159	1 009	1 776	5 374
1986	45 476	106	495	6 181	2 974	3 207	1 480	1 684	9 404	3 886	13 819	8 420	1 031	1 848	5 541
1987	47 188	95	523	6 242	2 987	3 255	1 532	1 736	9 764	4 076	14 549	0 072	1 048	1 919	5 705
1988	49 053	96	539	6 352	3 032	3 320	1 619	1 815	10 113	4 134	15 454	8 931	1 060	2 000	5 870
1989	50 690	94	547	6 399	3 048	3 351	1 643	1 891	10 384	4 188	16 296	9 248	1 105	2 070	6 073
1990	51 894	95	552	6 285	2 969	3 316	1 714	1 892	10 445	4 239	16 958	9 714	1 258	2 141	6 315
1991	52 016	97	532	6 067	2 824	3 243	1 722	1 864	10 304	4 215	17 352	9 862	1 220	2 177	6 460
1992	52 483	93	511	5 964	2 736	3 228	1 711	1 838	10 312	4 192	17 830	10 033	1 226	2 202	6 606
1993	53 560	88	521	5 933	2 710	3 222	1 740	1 826	10 471	4 279	18 507	10 197	1 211	2 245	6 742
1994	55 164	85	546	5 987	2 761	3 226	1 799	1 890	10 834	4 354	19 271	10 397	1 197	2 289	6 911
1995	56 643	81	573	6 010	2 814	3 195	1 857	1 959	11 169	4 295	20 131	10 568	1 184	2 335	7 049
1996	57 855	80	605	5 950	2 845	3 105	1 908	2 000	11 372	4 359	20 883	10 699	1 164	2 326	7 209
1997	59 388	82	632	5 992	2 920	3 073	1 940	2 057	11 567	4 478	21 787	10 853	1 146	2 335	7 372
1998	60 846	84	666	6 001	2 983	3 018	1 989	2 095	11 750	4 639	22 559	11 064	1 139	2 366	7 558
1999	62 383	80	711	5 896	2 963	2 933	2 091	2 132	12 030	4 727	23 370	11 347	1 132	2 425	7 790
2000	63 807	76	743	5 858	2 989	2 870	2 174	2 175	12 237	4 733	24 154	11 656	1 199	2 475	7 982

Note: Data include Alaska and Hawaii beginning in 1959.

Table 2-3. Production or Nonsupervisory Workers on Private Nonfarm Payrolls by Major Industry, 1947–2000

(Thousands of persons.)

	Total private	Mining	Construction	Manufacturing			Transportation and public utilities	Wholesale trade	Retail trade	Finance, insurance, and real estate	Services
				Total	Durable goods	Nondurable goods					
1947	33 747	871	1 786	12 990	7 064	5 926	...	2 248	6 000	1 436	...
1948	34 489	906	1 954	12 910	6 962	5 950	...	2 361	6 275	1 496	...
1949	33 159	839	1 949	11 790	6 158	5 633	...	2 354	6 248	1 517	...
1950	34 349	816	2 101	12 523	6 741	5 781	...	2 382	6 368	1 565	...
1951	36 225	840	2 343	13 368	7 514	5 854	...	2 456	6 642	1 622	...
1952	36 643	801	2 360	13 359	7 583	5 777	...	2 533	6 807	1 683	...
1953	37 694	765	2 341	14 055	8 186	5 869	...	2 554	6 964	1 742	...
1954	36 276	686	2 316	12 817	7 226	5 591	...	2 536	6 928	1 807	...
1955	37 500	680	2 477	13 288	7 580	5 708	...	2 574	7 109	1 889	...
1956	38 495	702	2 653	13 436	7 701	5 735	...	2 645	7 296	1 961	...
1957	38 384	695	2 577	13 189	7 581	5 607	...	2 639	7 292	1 998	...
1958	36 608	611	2 420	11 997	6 611	5 387	...	2 572	7 174	2 029	...
1959	38 080	590	2 577	12 603	7 065	5 538	...	2 661	7 434	2 086	...
1960	38 516	570	2 497	12 586	7 060	5 526	...	2 705	7 618	2 145	...
1961	37 989	532	2 426	12 083	6 650	5 433	...	2 684	7 558	2 189	...
1962	38 979	512	2 500	12 488	6 967	5 521	...	2 726	7 682	2 237	...
1963	39 553	498	2 562	12 555	7 059	5 495	...	2 758	7 811	2 291	...
1964	40 560	497	2 637	12 781	7 245	5 537	3 490	2 832	8 037	2 346	7 939
1965	42 278	494	2 749	13 434	7 746	5 688	3 561	2 932	8 426	2 388	8 295
1966	44 249	487	2 818	14 296	8 400	5 895	3 638	3 033	8 787	2 441	8 749
1967	45 137	469	2 741	14 308	8 396	5 912	3 718	3 095	9 026	2 533	9 246
1968	46 473	461	2 822	14 514	8 489	6 024	3 757	3 164	9 378	2 651	9 727
1969	48 208	472	3 012	14 767	8 683	6 084	3 863	3 271	9 822	2 797	10 205
1970	48 156	473	2 990	14 044	8 088	5 956	3 914	3 340	10 034	2 879	10 481
1971	48 148	455	3 071	13 544	7 697	5 847	3 872	3 327	10 288	2 936	10 655
1972	49 939	475	3 257	14 045	8 025	6 022	3 943	3 418	10 717	3 024	11 059
1973	52 201	486	3 405	14 838	8 699	6 138	4 034	3 560	11 152	3 121	11 606
1974	52 809	530	3 294	14 638	8 634	6 004	4 079	3 683	11 316	3 169	12 100
1975	50 991	571	2 808	13 043	7 532	5 510	3 894	3 650	11 373	3 173	12 479
1976	52 897	592	2 814	13 638	7 888	5 750	3 918	3 759	11 890	3 243	13 043
1977	55 179	618	3 021	14 135	8 280	5 855	4 008	3 892	12 424	3 397	13 683
1978	58 156	638	3 354	14 734	8 777	5 956	4 142	4 109	13 110	3 593	14 476
1979	60 367	719	3 565	15 068	9 082	5 986	4 299	4 290	13 458	3 776	15 193
1980	60 331	762	3 421	14 214	8 416	5 798	4 293	4 328	13 484	3 907	15 921
1981	60 923	841	3 261	14 020	8 270	5 751	4 283	4 375	13 582	3 999	16 562
1982	59 468	821	2 998	12 742	7 290	5 451	4 190	4 261	13 594	3 996	16 867
1983	60 028	673	3 031	12 528	7 095	5 433	4 072	4 239	13 989	4 066	17 429
1984	63 339	686	3 404	13 280	7 715	5 565	4 258	4 466	14 736	4 226	18 284
1985	65 475	658	3 655	13 084	7 618	5 466	4 335	4 607	15 421	4 410	19 305
1986	66 866	545	3 770	12 864	7 399	5 465	4 339	4 623	15 925	4 637	20 163
1987	68 771	511	3 870	12 952	7 409	5 543	4 446	4 685	16 378	4 797	21 132
1988	71 099	512	3 980	13 193	7 582	5 611	4 555	4 858	16 869	4 811	22 323
1989	73 017	493	4 035	13 230	7 594	5 636	4 655	4 981	17 262	4 829	23 532
1990	73 774	509	3 974	12 947	7 363	5 584	4 781	4 959	17 358	4 860	24 387
1991	72 631	489	3 549	12 434	6 967	5 467	4 774	4 872	17 006	4 795	24 712
1992	72 918	448	3 431	12 287	6 822	5 466	4 768	4 817	17 048	4 772	25 347
1993	74 761	431	3 589	12 341	6 849	5 492	4 862	4 823	17 428	4 908	26 380
1994	77 607	427	3 858	12 632	7 104	5 528	5 012	4 972	18 056	5 018	27 632
1995	80 125	424	3 993	12 826	7 317	5 508	5 140	5 163	18 639	4 961	28 979
1996	82 092	430	4 199	12 776	7 386	5 390	5 260	5 238	19 002	5 043	30 144
1997	84 541	450	4 415	12 907	7 553	5 354	5 366	5 355	19 337	5 193	31 518
1998	86 805	447	4 669	12 952	7 666	5 287	5 481	5 449	19 592	5 429	32 786
1999	88 997	406	4 963	12 747	7 596	5 150	5 666	5 527	20 103	5 536	34 049
2000	91 032	417	5 180	12 628	7 591	5 038	5 843	5 599	20 522	5 531	35 311

Note: Data include Alaska and Hawaii beginning in 1959.

Table 2-4. Production Workers on Durable Goods Manufacturing Payrolls by Industry, Selected Years, 1939–2000

(Thousands of persons.)

Year	Total	Lumber and wood products	Furniture and fixtures	Stone, clay, and glass products	Primary metal industries		Fabricated metal products	Industrial machinery and equipment	Electronic and other electrical equipment	Transportation equipment		Instruments and related products	Miscellaneous manufacturing
					Total	Blast furnaces and basic steel products				Total	Motor vehicles and equipment		
1939	3 926	. . .	. . .	297.0	. . .	452.6	. . .	. . .	. . .	539.5	388.3	. . .	. . .
1940	4 506	. . .	. . .	310.7	. . .	519.6	. . .	. . .	. . .	710.7	448.6	. . .	. . .
1945	7 571	. . .	. . .	334.4	. . .	527.3	. . .	. . .	. . .	2 057.4	519.7	. . .	. . .
1950	6 741	777.2	301.8	447.6	1 030.5	586.8	861.5	938.6	. . .	1 016.4	677.1	. . .	343.7
1955	7 580	706.3	292.6	469.1	1 069.4	604.5	974.5	1 082.1	. . .	1 418.1	718.3	. . .	330.4
1956	7 701	696.0	300.6	479.9	1 084.6	595.4	977.0	1 170.9	. . .	1 366.2	619.5	. . .	333.1
1957	7 581	622.0	298.2	466.5	1 071.4	600.1	989.1	1 155.6	. . .	1 394.5	601.7	. . .	315.3
1958	6 611	581.8	284.4	433.5	890.8	486.5	892.2	956.3	. . .	1 128.8	452.5	. . .	299.5
1959	7 065	628.5	305.7	469.7	914.2	470.9	939.5	1 038.9	. . .	1 183.8	537.5	. . .	312.9
1960	7 060	595.8	303.5	465.5	956.9	528.4	943.4	1 047.4	. . .	1 134.6	563.3	. . .	314.3
1961	6 650	551.4	289.5	444.4	880.8	478.4	896.5	987.3	. . .	1 029.2	479.1	. . .	303.5
1962	6 967	562.7	304.5	452.3	901.5	476.3	944.8	1 049.4	. . .	1 096.5	534.0	. . .	313.2
1963	7 059	565.8	308.7	458.1	911.7	479.1	965.4	1 070.9	. . .	1 142.9	573.6	. . .	310.4
1964	7 245	574.8	320.9	467.4	967.1	515.6	992.2	1 131.8	. . .	1 144.7	579.2	. . .	317.9
1965	7 746	579.3	340.3	477.8	1 022.7	538.4	1 059.5	1 227.4	. . .	1 259.2	658.9	. . .	335.5
1966	8 400	587.4	364.4	489.9	1 055.5	530.9	1 158.9	1 358.1	. . .	1 385.3	670.3	. . .	346.1
1967	8 396	570.6	357.6	473.5	1 015.7	509.5	1 204.8	1 383.2	. . .	1 390.9	626.9	. . .	338.3
1968	8 489	581.0	371.5	482.0	1 002.6	506.2	1 243.5	1 357.5	. . .	1 449.9	680.8	. . .	340.4
1969	8 683	594.3	382.9	498.5	1 042.2	513.6	1 283.6	1 397.1	. . .	1 443.3	708.0	. . .	344.6
1970	8 088	563.5	362.4	484.9	999.7	499.7	1 188.3	1 335.8	. . .	1 222.7	605.3	. . .	328.7
1971	7 697	588.4	364.5	485.5	923.3	454.6	1 128.0	1 195.1	. . .	1 196.1	655.4	. . .	317.6
1972	8 025	636.7	400.4	515.5	932.9	452.6	1 189.1	1 258.4	. . .	1 225.7	676.0	. . .	339.9
1973	8 699	664.9	420.0	545.8	1 010.5	484.8	1 276.7	1 415.9	. . .	1 324.1	754.9	. . .	356.4
1974	8 634	618.1	401.9	539.1	1 029.5	487.3	1 255.9	1 494.3	. . .	1 256.3	687.5	. . .	353.8
1975	7 532	525.6	337.3	472.7	886.6	428.1	1 089.0	1 360.2	. . .	1 141.7	602.4	. . .	310.6
1976	7 888	585.4	364.0	486.2	904.4	430.5	1 138.2	1 352.0	. . .	1 222.5	682.4	. . .	328.7
1977	8 280	625.8	381.8	504.6	922.1	432.6	1 197.5	1 434.7	. . .	1 277.0	734.7	. . .	334.2
1978	8 777	656.5	406.3	524.9	954.3	441.7	1 269.3	1 540.0	. . .	1 369.5	781.7	. . .	344.5
1979	9 082	663.7	405.0	529.1	986.4	451.3	1 298.3	1 648.2	. . .	1 408.5	764.4	. . .	338.8
1980	8 416	587.2	375.8	486.0	877.6	395.7	1 194.3	1 614.4	. . .	1 220.3	575.4	. . .	310.1
1981	8 270	562.5	373.8	464.8	861.9	391.6	1 170.6	1 592.4	. . .	1 206.8	586.0	. . .	302.1
1982	7 290	496.7	341.8	412.7	683.4	293.9	1 027.5	1 367.1	. . .	1 067.7	511.9	. . .	276.4
1983	7 095	555.3	356.1	411.6	619.8	256.3	993.6	1 206.9	. . .	1 084.8	568.3	. . .	266.7
1984	7 715	598.2	389.9	431.0	651.4	256.8	1 078.4	1 342.3	. . .	1 202.5	663.9	. . .	277.5
1985	7 618	592.2	393.6	426.7	611.4	231.5	1 082.9	1 319.8	. . .	1 243.6	684.5	. . .	264.0
1986	7 399	605.0	397.4	426.2	565.3	208.7	1 051.0	1 233.7	. . .	1 258.0	670.2	. . .	261.6
1987	7 409	627.8	412.0	428.7	562.2	202.8	1 037.6	1 203.4	. . .	1 278.2	673.1	. . .	269.4
1988	7 582	638.9	420.2	442.7	589.0	215.4	1 061.5	1 256.1	1 112.3	1 272.8	667.4	508.0	280.3
1989	7 594	625.7	417.7	443.6	588.9	215.2	1 070.4	1 281.5	1 101.7	1 277.7	663.8	509.4	277.6
1990	7 363	603.2	399.5	432.1	573.9	211.9	1 044.5	1 260.1	1 054.6	1 223.6	617.1	499.1	272.3
1991	6 967	552.5	372.6	402.5	544.8	199.6	991.0	1 193.2	999.0	1 169.2	601.5	479.4	262.9
1992	6 822	558.0	376.6	396.2	525.1	188.8	975.2	1 151.9	970.8	1 146.6	621.9	456.5	264.7
1993	6 849	583.8	384.7	398.6	520.3	183.2	988.1	1 169.5	974.5	1 120.0	642.0	438.2	270.9
1994	7 104	622.9	399.6	410.7	536.9	182.1	1 037.2	1 233.0	1 010.4	1 154.3	703.9	422.1	276.8
1995	7 317	632.1	403.1	417.9	552.8	184.5	1 079.8	1 294.6	1 044.9	1 200.3	761.4	416.5	275.5
1996	7 386	639.6	398.4	423.1	553.4	184.5	1 088.3	1 320.9	1 056.0	1 209.6	763.6	423.1	273.3
1997	7 553	655.0	406.8	430.9	555.4	180.9	1 114.8	1 364.1	1 068.6	1 255.8	779.1	427.0	274.8
1998	7 666	668.6	424.6	438.5	559.8	180.4	1 137.3	1 392.2	1 070.8	1 264.1	764.4	434.4	275.6
1999	7 596	683.8	437.4	443.4	546.9	176.5	1 143.7	1 345.3	1 044.3	1 250.7	774.0	429.0	271.9
2000	7 591	678.1	445.4	456.1	546.2	175.3	1 157.2	1 321.9	1 068.0	1 220.1	765.8	426.1	271.4

Note: Data include Alaska and Hawaii beginning in 1959.

Table 2-5. Production Workers on Nondurable Goods Manufacturing Payrolls by Industry, Selected Years, 1939–2000

(Thousands of persons.)

Year	Total	Food and kindred products	Tobacco products	Textile mill products	Apparel and other textile products	Paper and allied products	Printing and publishing	Chemicals and allied products	Petroleum and coal products	Rubber and miscellaneous plastics products	Leather and leather products
1939	4 392	989.0	. . .	1 108.0	814.0	264.6	320.0	252.0	100.0	149.0	349.0
1940	4 434	1 003.0	. . .	1 090.0	819.0	276.8	321.0	274.0	105.0	161.0	337.0
1945	5 438	1 380.0	. . .	1 074.0	973.0	342.8	381.0	518.0	148.0	255.0	325.0
1950	5 781	1 331.0	95.0	1 169.0	1 080.0	413.0	494.0	461.0	165.0	279.0	355.0
1955	5 708	1 291.7	94.4	961.6	1 086.4	450.6	539.0	518.1	163.2	316.3	344.0
1956	5 735	1 302.1	90.1	944.3	1 088.1	461.5	559.6	525.7	161.2	319.5	340.9
1957	5 607	1 263.2	85.3	893.3	1 072.0	460.3	563.7	519.7	156.6	318.1	331.0
1958	5 387	1 222.0	84.1	832.5	1 039.5	451.2	563.2	493.7	146.9	290.2	318.2
1959	5 538	1 222.1	83.9	857.4	1 091.4	468.7	575.1	505.6	139.9	317.7	332.9
1960	5 526	1 211.8	83.3	835.1	1 098.2	476.5	588.9	509.9	137.9	320.5	320.9
1961	5 433	1 191.1	79.6	805.0	1 079.6	474.9	591.7	505.0	129.9	314.7	316.4
1962	5 521	1 178.4	78.7	812.1	1 122.9	482.8	594.5	519.3	125.5	343.3	318.9
1963	5 495	1 167.1	76.6	793.4	1 138.0	483.2	590.3	525.3	119.9	349.8	307.8
1964	5 537	1 157.3	78.4	798.2	1 158.3	485.6	602.1	529.4	114.2	364.1	305.5
1965	5 688	1 159.1	74.8	826.7	1 205.6	494.4	620.6	546.1	112.9	394.3	310.0
1966	5 895	1 180.0	71.8	858.8	1 245.7	514.9	646.4	574.3	114.7	427.1	318.5
1967	5 912	1 187.3	73.9	850.2	1 237.2	522.9	661.6	592.3	114.7	425.3	303.7
1968	6 024	1 191.6	71.9	880.7	1 240.1	532.7	667.0	609.9	118.0	463.2	306.3
1969	6 084	1 201.8	69.6	884.0	1 237.9	547.0	681.7	621.9	112.2	491.3	294.4
1970	5 956	1 206.9	69.0	855.0	1 196.4	539.6	679.0	604.0	118.2	472.7	273.4
1971	5 847	1 203.2	63.4	837.2	1 177.5	518.4	658.0	587.8	124.1	478.5	257.1
1972	6 022	1 191.8	62.2	866.6	1 208.0	528.1	665.7	592.8	125.1	524.8	256.4
1973	6 138	1 166.8	64.8	886.2	1 249.7	539.6	672.9	610.5	123.9	579.1	245.0
1974	6 004	1 163.6	63.8	842.2	1 174.9	540.8	660.4	623.0	126.1	576.5	232.3
1975	5 510	1 120.3	62.4	752.4	1 066.6	476.6	624.0	579.6	123.0	492.7	212.6
1976	5 750	1 145.1	63.6	800.4	1 134.3	505.0	624.7	600.1	127.8	521.6	227.0
1977	5 855	1 161.0	57.0	792.3	1 129.4	514.8	646.5	616.0	131.3	587.7	218.4
1978	5 956	1 173.9	56.2	783.1	1 144.6	521.3	671.9	627.6	135.5	622.1	220.4
1979	5 986	1 190.8	55.5	770.9	1 116.8	532.1	697.2	633.3	137.1	643.0	209.1
1980	5 798	1 174.6	53.6	736.9	1 079.4	519.3	698.9	625.8	124.7	588.2	196.6
1981	5 751	1 149.5	54.7	712.5	1 059.5	515.0	699.3	628.3	133.9	596.8	201.1
1982	5 451	1 125.5	53.4	642.1	981.2	490.7	699.1	598.6	119.9	557.8	182.9
1983	5 433	1 113.5	52.0	639.2	983.5	491.2	711.5	578.6	118.0	574.2	171.1
1984	5 565	1 118.9	48.6	645.6	1 002.1	508.1	757.7	582.8	111.3	632.2	158.0
1985	5 466	1 117.0	48.0	606.3	943.9	508.4	787.9	577.4	108.5	631.7	136.6
1986	5 465	1 129.4	44.1	608.1	926.0	507.2	815.7	567.6	105.9	638.5	122.7
1987	5 543	1 145.1	41.5	629.5	921.7	512.3	839.4	574.6	106.8	652.6	119.7
1988	5 611	1 154.8	40.7	631.8	912.4	516.3	863.6	596.0	104.3	673.6	117.8
1989	5 636	1 176.2	37.0	621.9	906.8	520.5	863.2	603.1	101.8	691.5	114.1
1990	5 584	1 193.8	36.3	592.9	868.5	522.3	871.2	599.6	102.9	686.9	109.4
1991	5 467	1 205.2	36.3	574.1	841.1	517.4	847.0	579.7	103.4	662.0	100.2
1992	5 466	1 211.9	35.7	577.1	843.9	519.8	833.1	567.1	103.3	677.1	96.9
1993	5 492	1 227.8	32.8	574.5	828.6	521.6	838.5	572.6	98.9	703.3	93.7
1994	5 528	1 230.9	33.0	574.5	814.7	524.2	845.5	577.5	96.6	741.8	89.6
1995	5 508	1 247.5	32.0	560.2	776.1	525.4	847.6	580.2	93.8	762.7	82.7
1996	5 390	1 253.7	32.0	529.4	711.2	519.0	841.3	575.4	92.0	762.0	73.9
1997	5 354	1 251.7	31.9	522.3	672.6	520.9	847.3	572.7	93.0	772.5	68.8
1998	5 287	1 251.1	31.5	506.2	615.9	516.0	844.6	586.7	91.8	779.4	63.3
1999	5 150	1 254.9	27.9	471.6	548.1	505.4	827.9	582.8	88.9	785.7	57.0
2000	5 038	1 249.5	25.1	442.1	495.7	498.3	817.3	577.2	87.3	791.5	53.5

Note: Data include Alaska and Hawaii beginning in 1959.

Table 2-6. Average Weekly Hours of Production or Nonsupervisory Workers on Private Nonfarm Payrolls by Major Industry, 1947–2000

Year	Total private	Mining	Construction	Manufacturing			Transportation and public utilities	Wholesale trade	Retail trade	Finance, insurance, and real estate	Services
				Total	Durable goods	Nondurable goods					
1947	40.3	40.8	38.2	40.4	40.5	40.2	...	41.1	40.3	37.9	...
1948	40.0	39.4	38.1	40.0	40.4	39.6	...	41.0	40.2	37.9	...
1949	39.4	36.3	37.7	39.1	39.4	38.9	...	40.8	40.4	37.8	...
1950	39.8	37.9	37.4	40.5	41.1	39.7	...	40.7	40.4	37.7	...
1951	39.9	38.4	38.1	40.6	41.5	39.6	...	40.8	40.4	37.7	...
1952	39.9	38.6	38.9	40.7	41.4	39.7	...	40.7	39.8	37.8	...
1953	39.6	38.8	37.9	40.5	41.2	39.6	...	40.6	39.1	37.7	...
1954	39.1	38.6	37.2	39.6	40.1	39.0	...	40.5	39.2	37.6	...
1955	39.6	40.7	37.1	40.7	41.3	39.9	...	40.7	39.0	37.6	...
1956	39.3	40.8	37.5	40.4	41.0	39.6	...	40.5	38.6	36.9	...
1957	38.8	40.1	37.0	39.8	40.3	39.2	...	40.3	38.1	36.7	...
1958	38.5	38.9	36.8	39.2	39.5	38.8	...	40.2	38.1	37.1	...
1959	39.0	40.5	37.0	40.3	40.7	39.7	...	40.6	38.2	37.3	...
1960	38.6	40.4	36.7	39.7	40.1	39.2	...	40.5	38.0	37.2	...
1961	38.6	40.5	36.9	39.8	40.2	39.3	...	40.5	37.6	36.9	...
1962	38.7	41.0	37.0	40.4	40.9	39.7	...	40.6	37.4	37.3	...
1963	38.8	41.6	37.3	40.5	41.1	39.6	...	40.6	37.3	37.5	...
1964	38.7	41.9	37.2	40.7	41.5	39.7	41.1	40.7	37.0	37.3	36.1
1965	38.8	42.3	37.4	41.2	42.0	40.1	41.3	40.8	36.6	37.2	35.9
1966	38.6	42.7	37.6	41.4	42.1	40.2	41.2	40.7	35.9	37.3	35.5
1967	38.0	42.6	37.7	40.6	41.2	39.7	40.5	40.3	35.3	37.1	35.1
1968	37.8	42.6	37.3	40.7	41.4	39.8	40.6	40.1	34.7	37.0	34.7
1969	37.7	43.0	37.9	40.6	41.3	39.7	40.7	40.2	34.2	37.1	34.7
1970	37.1	42.7	37.3	39.8	40.3	39.1	40.5	39.9	33.8	36.7	34.4
1971	36.9	42.4	37.2	39.9	40.3	39.3	40.1	39.4	33.7	36.6	33.9
1972	37.0	42.6	36.5	40.5	41.2	30.7	40.4	39.4	33.4	36.6	33.9
1973	36.9	42.4	36.8	40.7	41.4	39.6	40.5	39.2	30.1	36.6	33.8
1974	36.5	41.9	36.6	40.0	40.6	39.1	40.2	38.8	32.7	36.5	33.6
1975	36.1	41.9	36.4	39.5	39.9	38.8	39.7	38.6	32.4	36.5	33.5
1976	36.1	42.4	36.8	40.1	40.6	39.4	39.8	38.7	32.1	36.4	33.3
1977	36.0	43.4	36.5	40.3	41.0	39.4	39.9	38.8	31.6	36.4	33.0
1978	35.8	43.4	36.8	40.4	41.1	39.4	40.0	38.8	31.0	36.4	32.8
1979	35.7	43.0	37.0	40.2	40.8	39.3	39.9	38.8	30.6	36.2	32.7
1980	35.3	43.3	37.0	39.7	40.1	39.0	39.6	38.4	30.2	36.2	32.6
1981	35.2	43.7	36.9	39.8	40.2	39.2	39.4	38.5	30.1	36.3	32.6
1982	34.8	42.7	36.7	38.9	39.3	38.4	39.0	38.3	29.9	36.2	32.6
1983	35.0	42.5	37.1	40.1	40.7	39.4	39.0	38.5	29.8	36.2	32.7
1984	35.2	43.3	37.8	40.7	41.4	39.7	39.4	38.5	29.8	36.5	32.6
1985	34.9	43.4	37.7	40.5	41.2	39.6	39.5	38.4	29.4	36.4	32.5
1986	34.8	42.2	37.4	40.7	41.3	39.9	39.2	38.3	29.2	36.4	32.5
1987	34.8	42.4	37.8	41.0	41.5	40.2	39.2	38.1	29.2	36.3	32.5
1988	34.7	42.3	37.9	41.1	41.8	40.2	38.2	38.1	29.1	35.9	32.6
1989	34.6	43.0	37.9	41.0	41.6	40.2	38.3	38.0	28.9	35.8	32.6
1990	34.5	44.1	38.2	40.8	41.3	40.0	38.4	38.1	28.8	35.8	32.5
1991	34.3	44.4	38.1	40.7	41.1	40.2	38.1	38.1	28.6	35.7	32.4
1992	34.4	43.9	38.0	41.0	41.5	40.4	38.3	38.2	28.8	35.8	32.5
1993	34.5	44.3	38.5	41.4	42.1	40.6	39.3	38.2	28.8	35.8	32.5
1994	34.7	44.8	38.9	42.0	42.9	40.9	39.7	38.4	28.9	35.8	32.5
1995	34.5	44.7	38.9	41.6	42.4	40.5	39.4	38.3	28.8	35.9	32.4
1996	34.4	45.3	39.0	41.6	42.4	40.5	39.6	38.3	28.8	35.9	32.4
1997	34.6	45.4	39.0	42.0	42.8	40.9	39.7	38.4	28.9	36.1	32.6
1998	34.6	43.9	38.9	41.7	42.3	40.9	39.5	38.3	29.0	36.4	32.6
1999	34.5	43.2	39.1	41.7	42.2	40.9	38.7	38.3	29.0	36.2	32.6
2000	34.5	43.1	39.3	41.6	42.1	40.8	38.6	38.5	28.9	36.3	32.7

Note: Data include Alaska and Hawaii beginning in 1959.

Table 2-7. Average Weekly Hours of Production Workers on Manufacturing Payrolls by Industry, 1947–2000

Year	Durable goods												
	Total	Lumber and wood products	Furniture and fixtures	Stone, clay, and glass products	Primary metal industries		Fabricated metal products	Industrial machinery and equipment	Electronic and other electrical equipment	Transportation equipment		Instruments and related products	Miscellaneous manufacturing
					Total	Blast furnaces and basic steel products				Total	Motor vehicles and equipment		
1947	40.5	40.3	41.5	41.0	39.9	39.0	40.9	41.5	. . .	39.7	39.8	. . .	40.5
1948	40.4	40.0	41.0	40.7	40.2	39.5	40.7	41.3	. . .	39.4	39.2	. . .	40.6
1949	39.4	39.2	40.0	39.7	38.4	38.2	39.7	39.6	. . .	39.6	39.7	. . .	39.6
1950	41.1	39.5	41.8	41.1	40.9	39.9	41.5	41.9	. . .	41.4	42.1	. . .	40.8
1951	41.5	39.3	41.1	41.4	41.6	40.9	41.8	43.5	. . .	41.2	40.4	. . .	40.5
1952	41.4	39.7	41.4	41.1	40.8	40.0	41.7	43.0	. . .	41.8	41.4	. . .	40.7
1953	41.2	39.3	40.9	40.8	41.0	40.5	41.8	42.4	. . .	41.6	42.0	. . .	40.5
1954	40.1	39.1	40.0	40.5	38.8	37.8	40.8	40.7	. . .	40.9	41.5	. . .	39.6
1955	41.3	39.5	41.4	41.4	41.3	40.5	41.7	41.9	. . .	42.3	43.6	. . .	40.3
1956	41.0	38.9	40.7	41.1	41.0	40.5	41.3	42.3	. . .	41.4	41.2	. . .	40.0
1957	40.3	38.4	39.9	40.4	39.6	39.1	40.9	41.1	. . .	40.8	40.9	. . .	39.7
1958	39.5	38.6	39.3	40.0	38.3	37.5	39.9	39.8	. . .	40.0	39.7	. . .	39.2
1959	40.7	39.7	40.7	41.2	40.5	40.1	40.9	41.5	. . .	40.7	41.1	. . .	39.9
1960	40.1	39.1	40.0	40.6	39.0	38.2	40.5	41.0	. . .	40.7	41.0	. . .	39.3
1961	40.2	39.5	40.0	40.7	39.5	38.9	40.5	40.9	. . .	40.5	40.1	. . .	39.5
1962	40.9	39.8	40.7	41.0	40.2	39.2	41.1	41.7	. . .	42.0	42.7	. . .	39.7
1963	41.1	40.2	40.9	41.4	41.0	40.2	41.3	41.8	. . .	42.0	42.8	. . .	39.6
1964	41.5	40.4	41.2	41.7	41.7	41.2	41.7	42.4	. . .	42.1	43.0	. . .	39.6
1965	42.0	40.9	41.5	42.0	42.1	41.2	42.1	43.1	. . .	42.9	44.2	. . .	39.9
1966	42.1	40.8	41.5	42.0	42.1	41.0	42.4	43.8	. . .	42.6	42.8	. . .	40.0
1967	41.2	40.3	40.4	41.6	41.1	40.2	41.5	42.5	. . .	41.4	40.8	. . .	39.4
1968	41.4	40.6	40.6	41.8	41.6	41.0	41.7	42.0	. . .	42.2	43.1	. . .	39.4
1969	41.3	40.2	40.4	41.9	41.8	41.3	41.6	42.5	. . .	41.5	41.7	. . .	39.0
1970	40.3	39.6	39.2	41.2	40.4	40.0	40.7	41.1	. . .	40.3	40.3	. . .	38.7
1971	40.3	39.8	39.8	41.6	40.1	39.6	40.4	40.6	. . .	40.7	41.2	. . .	38.9
1972	41.2	40.4	40.2	42.0	41.4	40.6	41.2	42.1	. . .	41.7	43.0	. . .	39.5
1973	41.4	40.0	40.0	41.9	42.3	41.7	41.6	42.8	. . .	42.1	43.5	. . .	39.0
1974	40.6	39.2	39.1	41.3	41.6	41.3	40.8	42.1	. . .	40.5	40.6	. . .	38.7
1975	39.9	38.8	38.0	40.4	40.0	39.5	40.1	40.8	. . .	40.4	40.3	. . .	38.5
1976	40.6	39.9	38.8	41.1	40.8	40.3	40.8	41.2	. . .	41.7	42.9	. . .	38.8
1977	41.0	39.9	39.0	41.3	41.3	40.5	41.0	41.5	. . .	42.5	44.0	. . .	38.8
1978	41.1	39.8	39.3	41.6	41.8	41.5	41.0	42.0	. . .	42.2	43.3	. . .	38.0
1979	40.8	39.5	38.7	41.5	41.4	41.2	40.7	41.7	. . .	41.1	41.1	. . .	38.8
1980	40.1	30.0	38.1	40.8	40.1	39.4	40.4	41.0	. . .	40.6	40.0	. . .	38.7
1981	40.2	38.7	38.4	40.6	40.5	40.4	40.3	40.9	. . .	40.9	40.9	. . .	38.8
1982	39.3	38.1	37.2	40.1	38.6	37.9	39.2	39.7	. . .	40.5	40.5	. . .	38.4
1983	40.7	40.1	39.4	41.5	40.5	39.5	40.6	40.5	. . .	42.1	43.3	. . .	39.1
1984	41.4	39.9	39.7	42.0	41.7	40.7	41.4	41.9	. . .	42.7	43.8	. . .	39.4
1985	41.2	39.9	39.4	41.9	41.5	41.1	41.3	41.5	. . .	42.6	43.5	. . .	39.4
1986	41.3	40.4	39.8	42.2	41.9	41.7	41.3	41.6	. . .	42.3	42.6	. . .	39.6
1987	41.5	40.6	40.0	42.3	43.1	43.4	41.6	42.2	. . .	42.0	42.2	. . .	39.4
1988	41.8	40.1	39.4	42.3	43.5	44.0	41.9	42.7	41.0	42.7	43.5	41.4	39.2
1989	41.6	40.1	39.5	42.3	43.0	43.4	41.6	42.4	40.8	42.4	43.1	41.1	39.4
1990	41.3	40.2	39.1	42.0	42.7	43.4	41.3	41.9	40.8	42.0	42.4	41.1	39.5
1991	41.1	40.0	38.9	41.7	42.2	42.7	41.2	41.7	40.7	41.9	42.3	41.0	39.7
1992	41.5	40.6	39.7	42.2	43.0	43.5	41.6	42.2	41.2	41.8	42.4	41.1	39.9
1993	42.1	40.8	40.1	42.7	43.7	44.1	42.1	43.0	41.8	43.0	44.3	41.1	39.8
1994	42.9	41.2	40.4	43.4	44.7	44.9	42.9	43.7	42.2	44.3	46.0	41.7	40.0
1995	42.4	40.6	39.6	43.0	44.0	44.4	42.4	43.4	41.6	43.8	44.9	41.4	39.9
1996	42.4	40.8	39.4	43.3	44.2	44.5	42.4	43.1	41.5	44.0	44.9	41.7	39.7
1997	42.8	41.0	40.2	43.2	44.9	44.9	42.6	43.6	42.0	44.5	45.0	42.0	40.4
1998	42.3	41.1	40.5	43.5	44.2	44.6	42.3	42.8	41.4	43.4	43.5	41.3	39.9
1999	42.2	41.1	40.3	43.4	44.5	45.2	42.4	42.1	41.2	43.8	45.0	41.3	39.8
2000	42.1	41.0	40.0	43.1	44.9	46.0	42.6	42.2	41.1	43.4	44.4	41.3	39.0

See *Note* at end of table.

Table 2-7. Average Weekly Hours of Production Workers on Manufacturing Payrolls by Industry, 1947–2000—*Continued*

Year	Nondurable goods										
	Total	Food and kindred products	Tobacco products	Textile mill products	Apparel and other textile products	Paper and allied products	Printing and publishing	Chemicals and allied products	Petroleum and coal products	Rubber and miscellane-ous plastics products	Leather and leather products
1947	40.2	43.2	38.9	39.6	36.0	43.1	40.2	41.2	40.6	40.0	38.6
1948	39.6	42.4	38.3	39.2	35.8	42.8	39.4	41.2	40.6	39.3	37.2
1949	38.9	41.9	37.3	37.7	35.4	41.7	38.8	40.7	40.3	38.5	36.6
1950	39.7	41.9	38.1	39.6	36.0	43.3	38.9	41.2	40.8	41.0	37.6
1951	39.6	42.1	38.5	38.8	35.6	43.1	38.9	41.3	40.8	40.8	36.9
1952	39.7	41.9	38.4	39.1	36.3	42.8	38.9	40.9	40.5	40.9	38.4
1953	39.6	41.5	38.1	39.1	36.1	43.0	39.0	41.0	40.7	40.4	37.7
1954	39.0	41.3	37.6	38.3	35.3	42.3	38.5	40.8	40.7	39.8	36.9
1955	39.9	41.5	38.7	40.1	36.3	43.1	38.9	41.1	40.9	41.7	37.9
1956	39.6	41.3	38.8	39.7	36.0	42.8	38.9	41.1	41.0	40.4	37.6
1957	39.2	40.8	38.4	38.9	35.7	42.3	38.6	40.9	40.8	40.6	37.4
1958	38.8	40.8	39.1	38.6	35.1	41.9	38.0	40.7	40.9	39.3	36.7
1959	39.7	41.0	39.1	40.4	36.3	42.8	38.5	41.4	41.2	41.3	37.9
1960	39.2	40.8	38.2	39.5	35.5	42.1	38.4	41.3	41.1	40.0	36.9
1961	39.3	40.9	39.0	39.9	35.4	42.5	38.2	41.4	41.2	40.4	37.4
1962	39.7	41.0	38.6	40.6	36.2	42.6	38.3	41.6	41.6	41.0	37.6
1963	39.6	41.0	38.7	40.6	36.1	42.7	38.3	41.6	41.7	40.9	37.5
1964	39.7	41.0	38.8	41.0	35.9	42.8	38.5	41.6	41.8	41.3	37.9
1965	40.1	41.1	37.9	41.7	36.4	43.1	38.6	41.9	42.2	42.0	38.2
1966	40.2	41.2	38.9	41.9	36.4	43.4	38.8	42.0	42.4	42.0	38.6
1967	39.7	40.9	38.6	40.9	36.0	42.8	38.4	41.6	42.7	41.4	38.2
1968	39.8	40.8	37.9	41.2	36.1	42.9	38.3	41.8	42.5	41.5	38.3
1969	39.7	40.8	37.4	40.8	35.9	43.0	38.3	41.8	42.6	41.2	37.2
1970	39.1	40.5	37.8	39.9	35.3	41.9	37.7	41.6	42.8	40.3	37.2
1971	39.3	40.3	37.8	40.6	35.6	42.1	37.5	41.6	42.8	40.4	37.7
1972	39.7	40.5	37.6	41.3	36.0	42.8	37.7	41.7	42.7	41.2	38.3
1973	39.6	40.4	38.6	40.9	35.9	42.9	37.7	41.8	42.4	41.2	37.8
1974	39.1	40.4	38.3	39.5	35.2	42.2	37.5	41.5	42.1	40.6	36.9
1975	38.8	40.3	38.2	39.3	35.2	41.6	36.9	41.0	41.2	39.9	37.1
1976	39.4	40.5	37.5	40.1	35.8	42.5	37.5	41.6	42.1	40.7	37.4
1977	39.4	40.0	37.8	40.4	35.6	42.9	37.7	41.7	42.7	41.1	36.9
1978	39.4	39.7	38.1	40.4	35.6	42.9	37.6	41.9	43.6	40.9	37.1
1979	39.3	39.9	38.0	40.4	35.3	42.6	37.5	41.9	43.8	40.6	36.5
1980	39.0	39.7	38.1	40.1	35.4	42.2	37.1	41.5	41.8	40.0	36.7
1981	39.2	39.7	38.8	39.6	35.7	42.5	37.3	41.6	43.2	40.3	36.7
1982	38.4	39.4	37.8	37.5	34.7	41.8	37.1	40.9	43.9	39.6	35.6
1983	39.4	39.5	37.4	40.4	36.2	42.6	37.6	41.6	43.9	41.2	36.8
1984	39.7	39.8	38.9	39.9	36.4	43.1	37.9	41.9	43.7	41.7	36.8
1985	39.6	40.0	37.2	39.7	36.4	43.1	37.8	41.9	43.0	41.1	37.2
1986	39.9	40.0	37.4	41.1	36.7	43.2	38.0	41.9	43.8	41.4	36.9
1987	40.2	40.2	39.0	41.8	37.0	43.4	38.0	42.3	44.0	41.6	38.2
1988	40.2	40.3	39.8	41.0	37.0	43.3	38.0	42.2	44.4	41.7	37.5
1989	40.2	40.7	38.6	40.9	36.9	43.3	37.9	42.4	44.3	41.4	37.9
1990	40.0	40.8	39.2	39.9	36.4	43.3	37.9	42.6	44.6	41.1	37.4
1991	40.2	40.6	39.1	40.6	37.0	43.3	37.7	42.9	44.1	41.1	37.5
1992	40.4	40.6	38.6	41.1	37.2	43.6	38.1	43.1	43.8	41.7	38.0
1993	40.6	40.7	37.4	41.4	37.2	43.6	38.3	43.1	44.2	41.8	38.6
1994	40.9	41.3	39.3	41.6	37.5	43.9	38.6	43.2	44.4	42.2	38.5
1995	40.5	41.1	39.6	40.8	37.0	43.1	38.2	43.2	43.7	41.5	38.0
1996	40.5	41.0	40.0	40.6	37.0	43.3	38.2	43.2	43.6	41.5	38.1
1997	40.9	41.3	38.9	41.4	37.3	43.7	38.5	43.2	43.1	41.8	38.4
1998	40.9	41.7	38.3	41.0	37.3	43.4	38.3	43.2	43.6	41.7	37.6
1999	40.9	41.8	38.4	40.9	37.5	43.4	38.1	43.0	42.4	41.7	37.4
2000	40.8	41.7	40.7	41.2	37.8	42.5	38.3	42.5	42.4	41.4	37.5

Note: Data include Alaska and Hawaii beginning in 1959.

Table 2-8. Average Weekly Overtime Hours of Production Workers on Manufacturing Payrolls by Industry, 1956–2000

Year	Manufac-turing	Durable goods												
		Total	Lumber and wood products	Furniture and fixtures	Stone, clay, and glass products	Primary metal industries		Fabricat-ed metal products	Industrial machin-ery and equip-ment	Electron-ic and other electrical equip-ment	Transportation equipment		Instru-ments and related products	Miscella-neous manufac-turing industries
						Total	Blast furnaces and basic steel products				Total	Motor vehicles and equip-ment		
1956	2.8	3.0	2.6	2.3	3.3	2.8	. . .	3.1	3.9	. . .	3.1	. . .	. . .	2.8
1957	2.3	2.4	2.2	1.9	2.8	2.0	. . .	2.8	2.8	. . .	2.5	. . .	. . .	2.4
1958	2.0	1.9	2.3	2.0	2.8	1.4	0.9	2.1	1.8	. . .	2.1	2.3	. . .	1.9
1959	2.7	2.7	3.2	2.8	3.6	2.6	2.2	2.8	2.9	. . .	2.6	3.1	. . .	2.4
1960	2.5	2.4	2.9	2.5	3.1	1.8	1.3	2.6	2.7	. . .	2.7	3.2	. . .	2.1
1961	2.4	2.4	2.9	2.4	3.2	1.9	1.3	2.4	2.5	. . .	2.5	2.6	. . .	2.2
1962	2.8	2.8	3.2	2.9	3.4	2.2	1.4	2.9	3.1	. . .	3.5	4.1	. . .	2.3
1963	2.8	3.0	3.3	3.0	3.7	2.7	1.9	3.0	3.2	. . .	3.6	4.4	. . .	2.2
1964	3.1	3.3	3.4	3.2	3.9	3.2	2.4	3.4	3.9	. . .	3.9	5.0	. . .	2.4
1965	3.6	3.9	3.8	3.6	4.2	3.8	2.8	4.0	4.6	. . .	4.8	6.2	. . .	2.7
1966	3.9	4.3	4.0	3.8	4.5	4.0	2.7	4.5	5.5	. . .	4.7	4.9	. . .	3.0
1967	3.4	3.5	3.6	3.0	4.2	3.2	2.1	3.8	4.4	. . .	3.7	3.4	. . .	2.6
1968	3.6	3.8	3.9	3.4	4.5	3.8	2.9	4.1	4.0	. . .	4.6	5.8	. . .	2.5
1969	3.6	3.8	3.8	3.3	4.8	4.1	3.2	4.2	4.5	. . .	3.8	4.2	. . .	2.6
1970	3.0	3.0	3.3	2.3	4.2	3.0	2.3	3.3	3.2	. . .	2.9	3.2	. . .	2.2
1971	2.9	2.9	3.6	2.6	4.5	3.0	2.3	2.8	2.6	. . .	3.1	3.6	. . .	2.2
1972	3.5	3.6	4.0	3.1	4.8	3.6	2.6	3.5	3.8	. . .	4.3	5.3	. . .	2.7
1973	3.8	4.1	3.9	3.1	5.0	4.5	3.5	4.1	4.8	. . .	4.9	6.1	. . .	2.6
1974	3.3	3.4	3.3	2.4	4.4	3.9	3.1	3.5	4.2	. . .	3.4	3.5	. . .	2.2
1975	2.6	2.6	2.9	1.8	3.7	2.6	1.9	2.6	2.9	. . .	2.8	2.6	. . .	1.9
1976	3.1	3.2	3.5	2.0	4.1	3.3	2.5	3.2	3.3	. . .	4.2	5.4	. . .	2.2
1977	3.5	3.7	3.7	2.4	4.6	3.7	2.8	3.6	4.0	. . .	5.0	6.4	. . .	2.2
1978	3.6	3.8	3.7	2.7	4.8	4.2	3.5	3.8	4.3	. . .	5.0	6.1	. . .	2.4
1979	3.3	3.5	3.5	2.2	4.5	3.9	3.4	3.4	4.0	. . .	4.2	4.4	. . .	2.2
1980	2.8	2.8	2.8	1.7	3.8	2.8	2.2	2.8	3.4	. . .	3.2	2.6	. . .	1.9
1981	2.8	2.8	2.6	1.8	3.8	3.0	2.7	2.7	3.2	. . .	3.2	3.0	. . .	1.9
1982	2.3	2.2	2.3	1.5	3.5	2.0	1.5	2.0	2.2	. . .	2.7	2.5	. . .	1.6
1983	3.0	3.0	3.1	2.3	4.1	3.0	2.3	2.9	2.7	. . .	3.9	4.8	. . .	2.0
1984	3.4	3.6	3.2	2.5	4.8	3.9	3.1	3.6	3.7	. . .	4.7	5.6	. . .	2.2
1985	3.3	3.5	3.2	2.4	4.8	3.8	3.2	3.5	3.4	. . .	4.8	5.4	. . .	2.2
1986	3.4	3.5	3.5	2.6	4.9	4.1	3.8	3.5	3.4	. . .	4.3	4.4	. . .	2.4
1987	3.7	3.8	3.8	2.8	5.1	4.9	5.0	3.8	4.0	. . .	4.2	4.3	. . .	2.6
1988	3.9	4.1	3.6	2.7	5.2	5.5	5.8	4.1	4.4	3.4	4.7	5.2	3.0	2.5
1989	3.8	3.9	3.5	2.7	5.1	5.2	5.5	3.9	4.3	3.2	4.6	4.7	2.8	2.5
1990	3.6	3.7	3.5	2.4	4.9	5.0	5.6	3.6	3.9	3.1	4.0	4.1	2.8	2.5
1991	3.6	3.5	3.3	2.4	4.6	4.6	4.8	3.5	3.7	3.2	3.8	4.0	2.9	2.6
1992	3.8	3.7	3.8	2.8	4.9	5.0	5.3	3.8	4.0	3.4	3.8	4.1	2.8	2.8
1993	4.1	4.3	4.1	3.1	5.2	5.6	5.8	4.3	4.7	3.9	4.8	5.8	2.8	2.8
1994	4.7	5.0	4.5	3.4	5.8	6.6	6.5	5.1	5.4	4.3	6.2	7.6	3.3	3.1
1995	4.4	4.7	4.1	3.0	5.5	6.1	6.4	4.7	5.1	4.0	5.8	6.6	3.4	3.0
1996	4.5	4.8	4.2	3.1	5.9	6.3	6.4	4.8	5.0	4.0	5.9	6.5	3.7	3.1
1997	4.8	5.1	4.3	3.5	5.9	6.7	6.5	5.1	5.5	4.2	6.4	6.8	3.9	3.3
1998	4.6	4.8	4.4	3.6	6.3	6.3	6.1	4.8	5.0	3.8	5.5	5.6	3.3	3.0
1999	4.6	4.8	4.8	3.8	6.1	6.7	6.4	4.8	4.9	3.8	5.3	5.9	3.3	3.0
2000	4.6	4.7	4.8	3.5	6.1	7.0	7.4	4.8	4.9	3.9	4.9	5.4	3.4	2.3

See *Note* at end of table.

Table 2-8. Average Weekly Overtime Hours of Production Workers on Manufacturing Payrolls by Industry, 1956–2000—*Continued*

Year	Nondurable goods										
	Total	Food and kindred products	Tobacco products	Textile mill products	Apparel and other textile products	Paper and allied products	Printing and publishing	Chemicals and allied products	Petroleum and coal products	Rubber and miscellane-ous plastics products	Leather and leather products
1956	2.4	3.1	1.3	2.6	1.0	4.5	3.1	2.1	2.2	2.2	1.4
1957	2.3	2.9	1.4	2.2	1.0	4.2	2.9	2.0	2.0	2.2	1.3
1958	2.2	3.1	1.3	2.1	1.0	3.9	2.5	1.9	1.8	2.0	1.1
1959	2.7	3.3	1.2	3.1	1.3	4.5	2.8	2.5	2.0	3.5	1.4
1960	2.5	3.3	1.0	2.6	1.2	4.1	2.9	2.3	2.0	2.4	1.2
1961	2.5	3.3	1.1	2.7	1.1	4.2	2.7	2.3	2.0	2.7	1.4
1962	2.7	3.4	1.0	3.2	1.3	4.4	2.8	2.5	2.3	3.1	1.4
1963	2.7	3.4	1.1	3.2	1.3	4.5	2.7	2.5	2.3	3.0	1.4
1964	2.9	3.6	1.6	3.6	1.3	4.7	2.9	2.7	2.5	3.5	1.7
1965	3.2	3.8	1.1	4.2	1.4	5.0	3.1	3.0	2.8	4.1	1.8
1966	3.4	4.0	1.4	4.4	1.5	5.5	3.5	3.3	3.2	4.4	2.1
1967	3.1	4.0	1.8	3.7	1.3	5.0	3.2	3.0	3.5	4.0	1.9
1968	3.3	4.1	1.8	4.1	1.4	5.3	3.1	3.3	3.6	4.2	2.1
1969	3.4	4.2	1.4	3.9	1.3	5.5	3.4	3.4	3.9	4.2	1.8
1970	3.0	4.0	1.7	3.3	1.1	4.6	2.8	3.1	3.8	3.4	1.7
1971	3.0	3.8	1.7	3.8	1.2	4.6	2.6	3.1	3.7	3.3	1.9
1972	3.3	4.0	1.6	4.5	1.5	4.9	2.9	3.2	3.8	4.0	2.3
1973	3.4	4.1	2.4	4.4	1.5	5.2	3.0	3.5	3.9	4.3	2.1
1974	3.0	4.1	2.1	3.3	1.2	4.6	2.7	3.3	3.9	3.5	1.8
1975	2.7	3.9	2.0	3.1	1.2	4.0	2.2	2.7	3.0	2.9	1.9
1976	3.0	4.1	1.3	3.4	1.3	4.8	2.5	3.2	3.5	3.6	1.9
1977	3.2	4.1	1.9	3.5	1.3	4.8	2.8	3.4	4.0	3.7	1.8
1978	3.2	4.0	2.1	3.6	1.3	5.1	3.0	3.5	4.3	3.7	1.8
1979	3.1	4.0	1.3	3.5	1.0	4.8	2.8	3.5	4.3	3.1	1.4
1980	2.8	3.8	1.7	3.2	1.0	4.3	2.5	3.1	3.7	2.7	1.5
1981	2.8	3.7	2.0	3.0	1.1	4.5	2.4	3.3	3.8	3.1	1.4
1982	2.5	3.6	1.4	2.2	1.0	4.1	2.3	2.8	3.9	2.7	1.2
1983	3.0	3.6	1.2	3.5	1.3	4.6	2.6	3.1	4.0	3.5	1.4
1984	3.1	3.8	1.4	3.2	1.4	4.9	2.8	3.4	4.2	3.9	1.4
1985	3.1	3.8	1.1	3.2	1.4	4.7	2.7	3.3	4.2	3.6	1.5
1986	3.3	3.9	1.4	4.0	1.6	4.8	2.9	3.6	4.5	3.8	1.5
1987	3.6	4.1	2.8	4.4	1.8	5.2	3.1	4.0	5.0	4.1	2.2
1988	3.6	4.2	2.6	4.0	1.8	5.0	3.1	4.1	5.5	4.1	2.0
1989	3.6	4.4	2.1	4.0	1.9	4.5	3.0	4.2	5.8	3.8	2.0
1990	3.6	4.5	2.3	3.6	1.6	4.8	3.0	4.4	6.1	3.6	1.8
1991	3.7	4.5	2.0	4.1	1.8	4.9	2.7	4.5	6.2	3.6	1.9
1992	3.8	4.5	2.1	4.3	1.8	5.3	2.9	4.8	6.2	4.1	2.1
1993	4.0	4.6	1.9	4.4	1.8	5.4	3.1	4.8	6.0	4.4	2.3
1994	4.3	4.9	3.7	4.7	2.1	5.6	3.4	5.0	6.4	4.7	2.5
1995	4.0	4.8	4.7	4.2	1.8	5.2	3.1	4.9	6.1	4.1	2.0
1996	4.1	4.8	4.9	4.3	2.0	5.5	3.1	5.0	6.1	4.3	2.0
1997	4.4	5.0	3.1	4.6	2.2	5.7	3.4	5.2	6.2	4.6	2.2
1998	4.3	5.2	2.6	4.5	2.1	5.6	3.2	5.1	6.6	4.4	2.2
1999	4.4	5.5	2.9	4.3	2.4	5.7	3.1	5.0	6.3	4.5	2.0
2000	4.4	5.4	4.1	4.2	2.3	5.6	3.4	4.9	6.1	4.1	2.3

Note: Data include Alaska and Hawaii beginning in 1959.

Table 2-9. Indexes of Aggregate Weekly Hours of Production or Nonsupervisory Workers on Private Nonfarm Payrolls by Industry, 1947–2000

(1982=100.)

Year	Total private	Goods-producing						Service-producing					
		Total	Mining	Construction	Manufacturing			Total	Transportation and public utilities	Wholesale trade	Retail trade	Finance, insurance, and real estate	Services
					Total	Durable goods	Nondurable goods						
1947	. . .	98.0	101.4	62.0	105.8	99.2	114.9	. . .	. . .	56.8	. . .	. . .	. . .
1948	. . .	97.8	101.9	67.6	104.2	97.4	113.8	. . .	. . .	59.5	. . .	. . .	. . .
1949	. . .	88.2	86.8	66.7	93.0	84.0	105.6	. . .	. . .	59.0	. . .	. . .	. . .
1950	. . .	96.1	88.3	71.3	102.2	96.0	110.8	. . .	. . .	59.7	. . .	. . .	. . .
1951	. . .	103.7	91.9	81.0	109.6	108.0	111.7	. . .	. . .	61.7	. . .	. . .	. . .
1952	. . .	103.9	88.2	83.3	109.6	108.9	110.6	. . .	. . .	63.3	. . .	. . .	. . .
1953	. . .	107.3	84.8	80.5	114.8	116.9	112.0	. . .	. . .	63.7	. . .	. . .	. . .
1954	. . .	96.8	75.5	78.2	102.4	100.5	105.3	. . .	. . .	63.1	. . .	. . .	. . .
1955	. . .	103.0	78.9	83.4	109.0	108.5	109.8	. . .	. . .	64.4	. . .	. . .	. . .
1956	. . .	104.7	81.5	90.2	109.5	109.5	109.5	. . .	. . .	65.9	. . .	. . .	. . .
1957	. . .	101.1	79.6	86.6	105.9	105.8	106.0	. . .	. . .	65.4	. . .	. . .	. . .
1958	. . .	90.9	67.9	80.8	94.8	90.4	100.9	. . .	. . .	63.6	. . .	. . .	. . .
1959	. . .	97.8	68.1	86.7	102.3	99.6	106.1	. . .	. . .	66.4	. . .	. . .	. . .
1960	. . .	95.8	65.7	83.2	100.7	98.1	104.4	. . .	. . .	67.3	. . .	. . .	. . .
1961	. . .	92.4	61.5	81.4	97.0	92.8	103.0	. . .	. . .	66.8	. . .	. . .	. . .
1962	. . .	96.3	59.8	83.9	101.6	98.8	105.6	. . .	. . .	68.1	. . .	. . .	. . .
1963	. . .	97.4	59.1	86.8	102.4	100.6	105.0	. . .	. . .	68.8	. . .	. . .	. . .
1964	75.8	99.7	59.4	89.1	104.9	104.1	106.1	65.1	87.7	70.6	73.2	60.4	51.9
1965	79.1	105.6	59.6	93.4	111.5	112.7	109.9	67.3	89.9	73.3	75.9	61.4	54.0
1966	82.5	112.0	59.3	96.3	119.2	122.7	114.4	69.3	91.7	75.7	77.6	62.8	56.4
1967	82.9	109.8	57.0	93.8	117.1	119.8	113.3	70.8	92.1	76.5	78.3	64.8	58.9
1968	84.9	111.7	56.0	95.6	119.2	121.7	115.7	72.8	93.4	77.7	80.1	67.8	61.3
1969	87.7	114.5	57.9	103.6	121.0	124.2	116.5	75.7	96.3	80.6	82.6	71.6	64.2
1970	86.3	107.8	57.6	101.3	112.8	113.0	112.4	76.7	96.9	81.7	83.4	73.0	65.3
1971	85.8	105.0	54.9	103.6	108.8	107.4	110.8	77.2	95.1	80.4	85.3	74.3	65.6
1972	89.2	110.5	57.8	107.9	114.8	115.4	114.1	79.6	97.3	82.5	88.2	76.5	68.0
1973	93.2	116.9	58.8	113.7	121.7	125.8	116.0	82.5	99.9	85.6	90.9	78.9	71.3
1974	93.2	113.7	63.4	109.5	118.1	122.4	112.1	84.0	100.4	87.6	91.0	79.8	73.9
1975	88.8	99.9	68.3	92.7	103.8	104.9	102.1	83.9	94.6	86.4	90.6	79.9	76.0
1976	92.3	105.4	71.5	94.0	110.3	111.9	108.1	86.4	95.5	89.1	93.9	81.5	78.8
1977	96.0	110.3	76.5	100.2	115.0	118.4	110.2	89.5	97.9	92.5	96.5	85.4	82.0
1978	100.7	116.5	79.0	112.2	120.1	125.9	112.0	93.6	101.3	97.7	100.0	90.3	86.3
1979	104.0	119.9	88.2	119.9	122.1	129.1	112.3	96.9	104.9	102.0	101.5	94.4	90.2
1980	102.8	112.9	94.1	115.1	113.8	117.8	108.1	98.3	104.1	101.9	100.1	97.8	94.3
1981	104.1	111.6	104.8	109.3	112.5	116.1	107.6	100.8	103.3	103.3	100.6	105.5	98.2
1982	100.0	100.0	100.0	100.0	100.0	100.0	100.0	100.0	100.0	100.0	100.0	100.0	100.0
1983	101.5	100.5	81.5	102.2	101.4	100.7	102.4	102.0	97.3	99.9	102.7	101.6	103.6
1984	107.7	109.0	84.9	116.8	109.0	111.5	105.5	107.1	102.8	105.3	108.2	106.4	108.2
1985	110.5	108.7	81.4	125.3	106.9	109.5	103.4	111.3	104.6	108.4	111.7	110.9	114.0
1986	112.3	107.3	65.7	128.2	105.7	106.8	104.2	114.6	104.0	108.5	114.3	116.7	119.2
1987	115.6	109.0	61.8	132.7	107.0	107.4	106.6	118.5	106.5	109.4	117.9	120.1	124.9
1988	119.3	111.4	61.7	136.9	109.3	110.5	107.7	122.8	108.2	113.3	121.0	119.2	132.2
1989	122.1	111.7	60.5	138.9	109.3	110.1	108.2	126.8	111.1	116.1	122.9	119.5	139.3
1990	123.0	109.5	63.9	138.0	106.4	106.1	106.8	129.1	114.5	115.7	123.0	120.2	144.2
1991	120.4	103.4	62.0	122.8	102.1	99.3	105.9	128.0	113.4	113.7	119.5	118.3	145.3
1992	121.2	102.1	56.2	118.4	101.7	98.2	106.6	129.7	113.6	112.8	120.6	118.1	149.3
1993	124.6	104.2	54.3	125.4	103.1	100.0	107.4	133.7	118.2	112.8	123.4	121.2	155.4
1994	130.0	109.2	54.6	136.4	107.0	106.2	108.1	139.4	121.8	116.9	128.6	124.0	163.1
1995	133.5	110.3	54.1	140.9	107.5	108.2	106.6	143.9	123.9	121.1	132.2	122.9	170.7
1996	136.7	111.5	55.6	148.7	107.2	109.2	104.3	148.0	127.5	122.9	134.6	125.0	177.4
1997	141.5	114.6	58.3	156.2	109.4	112.9	104.6	153.6	130.5	126.1	137.7	129.6	186.6
1998	145.1	115.6	56.0	164.7	109.0	112.4	104.2	158.3	132.3	127.9	140.0	130.3	194.2
1999	148.2	115.9	50.1	176.1	107.2	111.2	101.6	162.7	134.3	129.6	143.5	138.4	201.5
2000	151.6	116.5	51.3	184.8	105.9	110.8	99.1	167.3	137.9	132.0	146.1	138.5	209.6

Note: Data include Alaska and Hawaii beginning in 1959.

Table 2-10. Indexes of Aggregate Weekly Hours of Production Workers on Manufacturing Payrolls by Industry, 1947–2000

(1982=100.)

Year	Durable goods												
	Total	Lumber and wood products	Furniture and fixtures	Stone, clay, and glass products	Primary metal industries: Total	Primary metal industries: Blast furnaces and basic steel products	Fabricated metal products	Industrial machinery and equipment	Electronic and other electrical equipment	Transportation equipment: Total	Transportation equipment: Motor vehicles and equipment	Instruments and related products	Miscellaneous manufacturing industries
1947	99.2	173.6	92.0	110.4	161.7	201.2	89.1	83.9	. . .	94.3	120.4	. . .	140.1
1948	97.4	167.0	93.3	111.7	163.5	210.8	87.0	82.4	. . .	92.6	119.5	. . .	139.1
1949	84.0	146.9	82.0	100.4	135.0	180.8	74.9	66.3	. . .	88.3	117.7	. . .	121.9
1950	96.0	162.4	99.2	111.1	159.7	210.1	88.8	72.5	. . .	97.4	137.5	. . .	131.8
1951	108.0	167.4	94.5	120.2	177.4	227.4	98.4	91.4	. . .	115.6	132.9	. . .	132.1
1952	108.9	158.2	94.7	112.7	160.7	194.4	97.7	93.1	. . .	130.8	123.8	. . .	127.3
1953	116.9	152.8	96.7	115.3	174.6	225.7	107.8	93.6	. . .	151.5	149.9	. . .	136.0
1954	100.5	139.1	86.3	107.6	143.5	185.5	94.1	79.5	. . .	127.4	120.5	. . .	121.6
1955	108.5	147.5	95.1	117.5	167.3	219.8	100.9	83.7	. . .	138.7	151.2	. . .	125.2
1956	109.5	143.1	96.1	119.2	168.7	216.3	100.2	91.4	. . .	130.8	123.1	. . .	125.4
1957	105.8	126.3	93.5	113.9	161.0	210.7	100.6	87.5	. . .	131.7	118.7	. . .	117.6
1958	90.4	118.9	87.9	104.8	129.1	163.7	88.5	70.2	. . .	104.4	86.8	. . .	110.5
1959	99.6	132.0	97.7	117.0	140.2	169.3	95.6	79.4	. . .	111.4	106.5	. . .	117.6
1960	98.1	123.1	95.4	114.1	141.4	181.1	95.0	79.2	. . .	106.8	111.4	. . .	116.4
1961	92.8	115.2	90.9	109.3	132.0	166.9	90.2	74.5	. . .	96.4	92.8	. . .	113.0
1962	98.8	118.5	97.5	112.0	137.4	167.5	96.5	80.7	. . .	106.6	110.0	. . .	117.1
1963	100.6	120.2	99.2	114.6	141.7	172.7	99.2	82.5	. . .	111.2	118.5	. . .	115.7
1964	104.1	122.8	103.8	117.9	153.0	190.6	102.8	88.5	. . .	111.5	120.3	. . .	118.3
1965	112.7	125.3	111.1	121.2	163.2	199.1	110.8	97.6	. . .	125.0	140.5	. . .	126.0
1966	122.7	126.9	118.8	124.4	168.4	195.2	122.1	109.6	. . .	136.7	138.4	. . .	130.3
1967	119.8	121.5	113.5	119.1	158.1	184.0	124.2	108.5	. . .	133.2	123.4	. . .	125.6
1968	121.7	124.8	110.6	121.9	158.1	186.1	128.8	105.2	. . .	141.7	141.6	. . .	126.1
1969	124.2	126.5	121.5	126.4	165.1	190.5	132.0	100.4	. . .	138.5	142.4	. . .	126.5
1970	113.0	117.9	111.6	120.9	152.9	179.5	120.3	101.2	. . .	114.1	117.7	. . .	119.8
1971	107.4	123.8	114.0	122.2	140.5	161.5	113.2	89.5	. . .	112.6	130.3	. . .	116.2
1972	115.4	136.1	126.0	131.1	146.3	165.1	121.9	97.8	. . .	118.4	140.5	. . .	126.2
1973	125.8	140.6	132.0	138.4	161.8	181.5	131.8	111.0	. . .	129.1	158.5	. . .	130.9
1974	122.4	128.2	123.4	134.5	162.4	180.7	127.4	116.1	. . .	117.9	134.9	. . .	128.8
1975	104.9	107.8	100.7	116.6	134.3	151.8	108.4	101.6	. . .	106.8	117.3	. . .	112.5
1976	111.9	123.5	111.0	120.8	140.0	155.6	115.3	102.0	. . .	117.9	141.2	. . .	120.1
1977	118.4	132.0	117.2	125.9	144.2	157.2	121.9	109.8	. . .	125.6	156.0	. . .	122.2
1978	125.9	138.3	125.6	132.1	151.3	164.6	129.3	119.4	. . .	133.6	163.3	. . .	125.9
1979	129.1	138.6	123.5	132.8	154.8	167.0	131.4	126.9	. . .	134.1	151.8	. . .	123.8
1980	117.8	119.9	112.4	119.8	133.4	139.8	119.8	122.1	. . .	114.6	111.0	. . .	113.9
1981	116.1	115.1	112.7	114.1	132.5	141.9	117.1	120.2	. . .	114.2	115.7	. . .	110.5
1982	100.0	100.0	100.0	100.0	100.0	100.0	100.0	100.0	. . .	100.0	100.0	. . .	100.0
1983	100.7	117.7	110.3	103.2	95.2	90.8	100.3	90.1	. . .	105.7	118.9	. . .	98.1
1984	111.5	126.3	121.6	109.5	102.9	93.7	111.0	103.8	. . .	118.9	140.2	. . .	102.9
1985	109.5	124.9	121.9	108.1	96.1	85.3	111.2	101.0	. . .	122.7	143.6	. . .	97.8
1986	106.8	129.2	124.2	108.7	89.8	78.2	107.8	94.7	. . .	123.3	137.7	. . .	97.5
1987	107.4	134.9	129.5	109.7	91.8	79.0	107.1	93.8	. . .	124.3	137.2	. . .	99.9
1988	110.5	135.6	130.1	113.3	97.2	85.1	110.5	98.8	113.1	125.8	140.0	89.9	103.5
1989	110.1	132.6	129.6	113.5	96.0	83.9	110.6	100.3	111.5	125.3	138.0	89.6	103.0
1990	106.1	128.2	122.8	109.7	93.0	82.6	107.1	97.5	106.5	119.1	126.2	87.6	101.1
1991	99.3	116.9	113.9	101.4	87.2	76.4	101.4	91.8	100.7	113.3	122.9	84.0	98.1
1992	98.2	119.9	117.6	101.2	85.6	73.7	100.7	89.6	99.1	110.9	127.3	80.2	99.4
1993	100.0	126.1	121.3	102.9	86.2	72.6	103.3	92.7	100.9	111.4	137.4	77.0	101.6
1994	106.2	135.8	127.0	107.9	91.0	73.4	110.4	99.3	105.6	118.5	156.2	75.2	104.2
1995	108.2	135.7	125.6	108.7	92.1	73.6	113.6	103.5	107.8	121.6	164.9	73.7	103.4
1996	109.2	138.0	123.4	110.8	92.6	73.6	114.5	105.0	108.5	123.1	165.5	75.4	102.1
1997	112.9	142.1	128.6	112.4	94.5	72.9	118.1	109.6	111.1	129.2	169.2	76.7	104.4
1998	112.4	145.4	135.3	115.4	93.7	72.1	119.5	109.9	109.9	127.0	160.5	76.7	103.5
1999	111.2	148.7	138.6	116.4	92.2	71.6	120.4	104.5	106.7	126.9	168.2	75.8	101.8
2000	110.8	147.0	140.2	118.8	92.9	72.4	122.4	102.8	108.7	122.5	164.1	75.3	99.5

See *Note* at end of table.

Table 2-10. Indexes of Aggregate Weekly Hours of Production Workers on Manufacturing Payrolls by Industry, 1947–2000—*Continued*

(1982=100.)

Year	Nondurable goods										
	Total	Food and kindred products	Tobacco products	Textile mill products	Apparel and other textile products	Paper and allied products	Printing and publishing	Chemicals and allied products	Petroleum and coal products	Rubber and miscellane-ous plastics products	Leather and leather products
1947	114.9	136.0	212.3	200.9	110.6	84.8	75.6	82.2	131.0	52.6	221.8
1948	113.8	131.3	202.2	203.3	112.7	84.6	75.0	81.6	135.3	50.0	211.2
1949	105.6	126.6	186.4	172.6	109.4	78.6	73.1	74.7	129.7	43.8	195.8
1950	110.8	125.7	178.9	192.5	114.0	87.1	74.2	77.6	127.7	51.7	205.0
1951	111.7	127.1	182.8	184.8	113.0	90.9	75.8	84.7	133.9	55.2	193.1
1952	110.6	125.7	184.8	174.5	115.8	87.5	76.6	84.6	130.0	55.0	203.0
1953	112.0	124.5	180.5	172.9	118.2	92.3	78.5	87.6	134.0	57.8	202.2
1954	105.3	120.7	177.2	151.7	109.1	90.4	78.0	83.9	129.1	51.1	188.4
1955	109.8	120.8	180.7	160.3	115.9	94.6	81.0	87.0	127.0	59.8	200.0
1956	109.5	121.2	173.0	155.6	114.9	96.3	84.0	88.2	125.6	58.5	196.9
1957	106.0	116.3	162.2	144.3	112.4	94.9	83.9	86.7	121.6	58.4	190.4
1958	100.9	112.3	162.7	133.7	107.2	92.1	82.6	82.1	114.3	51.6	179.3
1959	106.1	112.8	162.2	144.1	116.3	97.7	85.4	85.6	109.5	59.4	193.6
1960	104.4	111.5	157.6	137.1	114.3	97.9	87.4	86.0	107.7	58.0	181.9
1961	103.0	109.8	153.7	133.4	112.1	98.4	87.3	85.3	101.9	57.5	181.6
1962	105.6	108.8	150.4	137.0	119.4	100.2	87.9	88.1	99.2	63.7	184.4
1963	105.0	107.8	146.5	133.8	120.7	100.7	87.2	89.2	94.9	64.8	177.2
1964	106.1	107.0	150.8	136.1	122.1	101.3	89.4	89.9	90.9	68.2	177.7
1965	109.9	107.4	140.3	143.4	128.7	104.0	92.4	93.5	90.6	75.0	182.0
1966	114.4	109.5	138.2	149.5	133.2	109.0	96.8	98.6	92.4	81.3	188.8
1967	113.3	109.4	141.0	144.4	130.8	109.1	97.9	100.6	93.0	79.7	178.0
1968	115.7	109.5	134.8	150.6	131.3	111.4	98.5	104.1	95.4	87.0	180.0
1969	116.5	110.5	128.8	150.0	130.5	114.6	100.9	106.2	90.9	91.6	168.1
1970	112.4	110.2	129.2	141.8	123.9	110.2	98.9	102.5	96.2	86.3	156.4
1971	110.8	109.3	118.7	141.3	122.9	106.4	95.3	99.8	100.9	87.5	148.7
1972	114.1	108.7	115.9	148.9	127.8	110.3	96.5	100.9	101.5	97.8	150.7
1973	116.0	106.3	124.0	150.7	131.7	112.7	97.4	104.2	99.9	107.9	142.3
1974	112.1	106.0	120.9	138.5	121.3	111.2	95.5	105.7	100.9	105.8	131.8
1975	102.1	101.8	118.1	122.9	110.2	96.8	88.9	97.1	96.3	89.0	121.3
1976	108.1	104.4	118.2	133.3	119.3	104.7	90.3	102.0	102.3	96.1	130.6
1977	110.2	104.6	106.8	132.9	117.9	107.6	94.1	105.0	106.6	109.2	123.9
1978	112.0	105.1	106.1	131.6	119.5	109.0	97.5	107.4	112.2	115.3	125.5
1979	112.3	107.0	104.4	129.3	115.6	110.5	101.0	108.3	114.0	118.2	117.1
1900	108.1	105.1	101.2	122.7	112.2	106.9	100.1	106.0	99.1	106.7	110.7
1981	107.6	102.8	105.1	117.3	111.0	106.8	100.6	106.8	110.0	109.0	113.6
1982	100.0	100.0	100.0	100.0	100.0	100.0	100.0	100.0	100.0	100.0	100.0
1983	102.4	99.1	96.3	107.4	104.5	102.1	103.3	98.3	98.4	107.2	96.8
1984	105.5	100.3	93.5	107.0	107.2	106.8	110.9	99.8	92.5	119.6	89.3
1985	103.4	100.6	88.4	100.1	100.7	106.8	114.9	98.9	88.7	117.6	78.1
1986	104.2	101.7	81.6	103.8	99.7	106.9	119.6	97.3	88.1	119.6	69.5
1987	106.6	103.7	80.1	109.4	100.1	108.5	123.2	99.3	89.4	123.1	70.3
1988	107.7	105.0	80.1	107.7	99.0	108.9	126.7	102.9	88.1	127.3	67.9
1989	108.2	107.8	70.6	105.6	98.3	109.9	126.2	104.5	85.7	129.6	66.4
1990	106.8	109.7	70.6	98.4	92.9	110.4	127.5	104.3	87.2	127.9	62.8
1991	105.9	110.2	70.2	97.0	91.3	109.3	123.3	101.6	86.7	123.2	57.7
1992	106.6	110.9	68.2	98.6	92.2	110.5	122.3	100.0	86.0	127.8	56.6
1993	107.4	112.6	60.7	98.9	90.4	110.9	123.9	100.9	83.1	133.2	55.6
1994	108.1	114.6	64.1	99.3	89.7	112.3	126.0	102.0	81.5	142.0	53.0
1995	106.6	115.5	02.8	94.9	84.2	110.5	125.0	102.5	77.9	143.5	48.3
1996	104.3	115.9	63.3	89.2	77.2	109.5	124.0	101.5	76.3	143.2	43.3
1997	104.6	116.6	61.4	89.8	73.7	111.0	126.0	101.2	76.1	146.4	40.6
1998	104.2	117.5	59.7	86.3	67.4	109.3	124.8	103.4	76.0	147.3	36.5
1999	101.6	118.2	53.2	80.1	60.3	106.9	121.7	102.3	71.6	148.5	32.7
2000	99.1	117.5	50.5	75.7	55.0	103.3	120.7	100.2	70.4	148.2	30.8

Note: Data include Alaska and Hawaii beginning in 1959.

Table 2-11. Average Hourly Earnings of Production or Nonsupervisory Workers on Private Nonfarm Payrolls by Industry, 1947–2000

(Dollars.)

Year	Total private	Mining	Construction	Manufacturing			Transportation and public utilities	Wholesale trade	Retail trade	Finance, insurance, and real estate	Services
				Total	Durable goods	Nondurable goods					
1947	1.13	1.47	1.54	1.22	1.28	1.15	...	1.22	0.84	1.14	...
1948	1.23	1.66	1.71	1.33	1.39	1.25	...	1.31	0.90	1.20	...
1949	1.28	1.72	1.79	1.38	1.45	1.30	...	1.36	0.95	1.26	...
1950	1.34	1.77	1.86	1.44	1.45	1.30	...	1.36	0.98	1.26	...
1951	1.45	1.93	2.02	1.56	1.65	1.45	...	1.52	1.06	1.45	...
1952	1.52	2.01	2.13	1.64	1.74	1.51	...	1.61	1.09	1.51	...
1953	1.61	2.14	2.28	1.74	1.85	1.58	...	1.69	1.16	1.58	...
1954	1.65	2.14	2.38	1.78	1.89	1.62	...	1.76	1.20	1.65	...
1955	1.71	2.20	2.45	1.85	1.98	1.68	...	1.83	1.25	1.70	...
1956	1.80	2.33	2.57	1.95	2.08	1.77	...	1.93	1.30	1.78	...
1957	1.89	2.45	2.71	2.04	2.18	1.85	...	2.02	1.37	1.84	...
1958	1.95	2.47	2.82	2.10	2.25	1.92	...	2.09	1.42	1.89	...
1959	2.02	2.56	2.93	2.19	2.35	1.98	...	2.18	1.47	1.95	...
1960	2.09	2.60	3.07	2.26	2.42	2.05	...	2.24	1.52	2.02	...
1961	2.14	2.64	3.20	2.32	2.48	2.11	...	2.31	1.56	2.09	...
1962	2.22	2.70	3.31	2.39	2.55	2.17	...	2.37	1.63	2.17	...
1963	2.28	2.75	3.41	2.45	2.63	2.22	...	2.45	1.68	2.25	...
1964	2.36	2.81	3.55	2.53	2.70	2.29	2.89	2.52	1.75	2.30	1.94
1965	2.46	2.92	3.70	2.61	2.78	2.36	3.03	2.60	1.82	2.39	2.05
1966	2.56	3.05	3.89	2.71	2.89	2.45	3.11	2.73	1.91	2.47	2.17
1967	2.68	3.19	4.11	2.82	2.99	2.57	3.23	2.87	2.01	2.58	2.29
1968	2.85	3.35	4.41	3.01	3.18	2.74	3.42	3.04	2.16	2.75	2.42
1969	3.04	3.60	4.79	3.19	3.38	2.91	3.63	3.23	2.30	2.93	2.61
1970	3.23	3.85	5.24	3.35	3.55	3.08	3.85	3.43	2.44	3.07	2.81
1971	3.45	4.06	5.69	3.57	3.79	3.27	4.21	3.64	2.60	3.22	3.04
1972	3.70	4.44	6.06	3.82	4.07	3.48	4.65	3.85	2.75	3.36	3.27
1973	3.94	4.75	6.41	4.09	4.35	3.70	5.02	4.07	2.91	3.53	3.47
1974	4.21	5.23	6.81	4.42	4.70	4.01	5.41	4.38	3.14	3.77	3.75
1975	4.53	5.95	7.31	4.83	5.15	4.37	5.88	4.72	3.36	4.06	4.02
1976	4.86	6.46	7.71	5.22	5.57	4.71	6.45	5.02	3.57	4.27	4.31
1977	5.25	6.94	8.10	5.68	6.06	5.11	6.99	5.39	3.85	4.54	4.65
1978	5.69	7.67	8.66	6.17	6.58	5.54	7.57	5.88	4.20	4.89	4.99
1979	6.16	8.49	9.27	6.70	7.12	6.01	8.16	6.39	4.53	5.27	5.36
1980	6.66	9.17	9.94	7.27	7.75	6.56	8.87	6.95	4.88	5.79	5.85
1981	7.25	10.04	10.82	7.99	8.53	7.19	9.70	7.55	5.25	6.31	6.41
1982	7.68	10.77	11.63	8.49	9.03	7.75	10.32	8.08	5.48	6.78	6.92
1983	8.02	11.28	11.94	8.83	9.38	8.09	10.79	8.54	5.74	7.29	7.31
1984	8.32	11.63	12.13	9.19	9.73	8.39	11.12	8.88	5.85	7.63	7.59
1985	8.57	11.98	12.32	9.54	10.09	8.72	11.40	9.15	5.94	7.94	7.90
1986	8.76	12.46	12.48	9.73	10.28	8.95	11.70	9.34	6.03	8.36	8.18
1987	8.98	12.54	12.71	9.91	10.43	9.19	12.03	9.59	6.12	8.73	8.49
1988	9.28	12.80	13.08	10.19	10.71	9.45	12.24	9.98	6.31	9.06	8.88
1989	9.66	13.26	13.54	10.48	11.01	9.75	12.57	10.39	6.53	9.53	9.38
1990	10.01	13.68	13.77	10.83	11.35	10.12	12.92	10.79	6.75	9.97	9.83
1991	10.32	14.19	14.00	11.18	11.75	10.44	13.20	11.15	6.94	10.39	10.23
1992	10.57	14.54	14.15	11.46	12.02	10.73	13.43	11.39	7.12	10.82	10.54
1993	10.83	14.60	14.38	11.74	12.33	10.98	13.55	11.74	7.29	11.35	10.78
1994	11.12	14.88	14.73	12.07	12.68	11.24	13.78	12.06	7.49	11.83	11.04
1995	11.43	15.30	15.09	12.37	12.94	11.58	14.13	12.43	7.69	12.32	11.39
1996	11.82	15.62	15.47	12.77	13.33	11.97	14.45	12.87	7.99	12.80	11.79
1997	12.28	16.15	16.04	13.17	13.73	12.34	14.92	13.45	8.33	13.34	12.28
1998	12.78	16.91	16.61	13.49	13.98	12.76	15.31	14.07	8.74	14.07	12.84
1999	13.24	17.05	17.19	13.90	14.36	13.21	15.69	14.59	9.09	14.62	13.37
2000	13.75	17.24	17.88	14.38	14.82	13.69	16.22	15.20	9.46	15.07	13.91

Note: Data include Alaska and Hawaii beginning in 1959.

Table 2-12. Average Hourly Earnings of Production Workers on Manufacturing Payrolls by Industry, 1947–2000

(Dollars.)

Year	Durable goods												
	Total	Lumber and wood products	Furniture and fixtures	Stone, clay, and glass products	Primary metal industries		Fabricated metal products	Industrial machinery and equipment	Electronic and other electrical equipment	Transportation equipment		Instru-ments and related products	Miscella-neous manufac-turing industries
					Total	Blast furnaces and basic steel products				Total	Motor vehicles and equipment		
1947	1.28	1.09	1.10	1.19	1.39	1.44	1.27	1.34	...	1.44	1.47	...	1.11
1948	1.39	1.19	1.19	1.31	1.52	1.59	1.39	1.46	...	1.57	1.61	...	1.18
1949	1.45	1.23	1.23	1.37	1.59	1.65	1.45	1.52	...	1.64	1.70	...	1.22
1950	1.45	1.30	1.28	1.44	1.65	1.70	1.52	1.60	...	1.72	1.78	...	1.28
1951	1.65	1.41	1.39	1.54	1.81	1.90	1.64	1.75	...	1.84	1.91	...	1.36
1952	1.74	1.49	1.47	1.61	1.90	2.00	1.72	1.85	...	1.95	2.05	...	1.45
1953	1.85	1.56	1.54	1.72	2.06	2.18	1.83	1.95	...	2.05	2.14	...	1.52
1954	1.89	1.57	1.57	1.77	2.10	2.22	1.88	2.00	...	2.11	2.20	...	1.56
1955	1.98	1.62	1.62	1.86	2.24	2.39	1.96	2.08	...	2.21	2.29	...	1.61
1956	2.08	1.69	1.69	1.96	2.37	2.54	2.05	2.20	...	2.29	2.35	...	1.69
1957	2.18	1.74	1.75	2.05	2.50	2.70	2.16	2.29	...	2.39	2.46	...	1.75
1958	2.25	1.80	1.78	2.12	2.64	2.88	2.26	2.37	...	2.51	2.55	...	1.79
1959	2.35	1.87	1.83	2.22	2.77	3.06	2.35	2.48	...	2.64	2.71	...	1.84
1960	2.42	1.90	1.88	2.28	2.81	3.04	2.43	2.55	...	2.74	2.81	...	1.89
1961	2.48	1.95	1.91	2.34	2.90	3.16	2.49	2.62	...	2.80	2.86	...	1.92
1962	2.55	1.99	1.95	2.41	2.98	3.25	2.55	2.71	...	2.91	2.99	...	1.98
1963	2.63	2.05	2.00	2.48	3.04	3.31	2.61	2.78	...	3.01	3.10	...	2.03
1964	2.70	2.12	2.05	2.53	3.11	3.36	2.68	2.87	...	3.09	3.21	...	2.08
1965	2.78	2.18	2.12	2.62	3.18	3.42	2.76	2.95	...	3.21	3.34	...	2.14
1966	2.89	2.26	2.21	2.72	3.28	3.53	2.88	3.08	...	3.33	3.44	...	2.22
1967	2.99	2.38	2.33	2.82	3.34	3.57	2.98	3.19	...	3.44	3.55	...	2.35
1968	3.18	2.58	2.47	2.99	3.55	3.76	3.16	3.36	...	3.69	3.89	...	2.50
1969	3.38	2.75	2.62	3.19	3.79	4.02	3.34	3.58	...	3.89	4.10	...	2.66
1970	3.55	2.97	2.77	3.40	3.93	4.16	3.53	3.77	...	4.06	4.22	...	2.83
1971	3.79	3.18	2.90	3.67	4.23	4.49	3.77	4.02	...	4.45	4.72	...	2.97
1972	4.07	3.34	3.08	3.94	4.66	5.08	4.05	4.32	...	4.81	5.13	...	3.11
1973	4.35	3.62	3.29	4.22	5.04	5.51	4.29	4.60	...	5.15	5.46	...	3.29
1974	4.70	3.90	3.53	4.54	5.60	6.27	4.61	4.94	...	5.54	5.87	...	3.53
1975	5.15	4.28	3.78	4.92	6.18	6.94	5.05	5.37	...	6.07	6.44	...	3.81
1976	5.57	4.74	3.99	5.33	6.77	7.59	5.50	5.79	...	6.62	7.09	...	4.04
1977	6.06	5.11	4.34	5.81	7.40	8.36	5.91	6.26	...	7.29	7.85	...	4.36
1978	6.58	5.62	4.68	6.32	8.20	9.39	6.35	6.78	...	7.91	8.50	...	4.69
1979	7.12	6.08	5.06	6.85	8.98	10.41	6.85	7.32	...	8.53	9.06	...	5.03
1980	7.75	6.57	5.49	7.50	9.77	11.39	7.45	8.00	...	9.35	9.85	...	5.46
1981	8.53	7.02	5.91	8.27	10.81	12.60	8.20	8.81	...	10.39	11.02	...	5.97
1982	9.03	7.46	6.31	8.87	11.33	13.35	8.77	9.26	...	11.11	11.62	...	6.42
1983	9.38	7.82	6.62	9.27	11.35	12.89	9.12	9.56	...	11.67	12.14	...	6.81
1984	9.73	8.05	6.84	9.57	11.47	12.98	9.40	9.97	...	12.20	12.73	...	7.05
1985	10.09	8.25	7.17	9.84	11.67	13.33	9.71	10.30	...	12.71	13.39	...	7.30
1986	10.28	8.37	7.46	10.04	11.86	13.73	9.89	10.58	...	12.81	13.45	...	7.55
1987	10.43	8.43	7.67	10.25	11.94	13.77	10.01	10.73	...	12.94	13.53	...	7.76
1988	10.71	8.59	7.95	10.56	12.16	13.98	10.29	11.08	9.79	13.29	13.99	10.60	8.00
1989	11.01	8.84	8.25	10.82	12.43	14.25	10.57	11.40	10.05	13.67	14.25	10.83	8.29
1990	11.35	9.08	8.52	11.12	12.92	14.82	10.83	11.77	10.30	14.08	14.56	11.29	8.61
1991	11.75	9.24	8.76	11.36	13.33	15.36	11.19	12.15	10.70	14.75	15.23	11.64	8.85
1992	12.02	9.44	9.01	11.60	13.66	15.87	11.42	12.41	11.00	15.20	15.45	11.89	9.15
1993	12.33	9.61	9.27	11.85	13.99	16.36	11.69	12.73	11.24	15.80	16.10	12.23	9.39
1994	12.68	9.84	9.55	12.13	14.34	16.85	11.93	13.00	11.50	16.51	17.02	12.47	9.67
1995	12.94	10.12	9.82	12.41	14.62	17.33	12.13	13.24	11.69	16.74	17.34	12.71	10.05
1996	13.33	10.44	10.15	12.82	14.97	17.80	12.50	13.59	12.18	17.19	17.74	13.13	10.38
1997	13.73	10.76	10.55	13.18	15.22	18.03	12.78	14.07	12.70	17.55	18.04	13.52	10.60
1998	13.98	11.10	10.90	13.59	15.48	18.42	13.07	14.47	13.10	17.51	17.84	13.81	10.88
1999	14.36	11.51	11.29	13.97	15.80	18.84	13.50	15.03	13.43	17.79	18.10	14.08	11.26
2000	14.82	11.93	11.73	14.53	16.42	19.82	13.87	15.55	13.80	18.45	18.79	14.43	11.63

See *Note* at end of table.

Table 2-12. Average Hourly Earnings of Production Workers on Manufacturing Payrolls by Industry, 1947–2000—*Continued*

(Dollars.)

Year	Nondurable goods										
	Total	Food and kindred products	Tobacco products	Textile mill products	Apparel and other textile products	Paper and allied products	Printing and publishing	Chemicals and allied products	Petroleum and coal products	Rubber and miscellaneous plastics products	Leather and leather products
1947	1.15	1.06	0.90	1.04	1.16	1.15	1.48	1.22	1.50	1.29	1.04
1948	1.25	1.15	0.96	1.16	1.22	1.28	1.65	1.34	1.71	1.36	1.11
1949	1.30	1.21	1.00	1.18	1.21	1.33	1.77	1.42	1.80	1.41	1.12
1950	1.30	1.26	1.08	1.23	1.24	1.40	1.83	1.50	1.84	1.47	1.17
1951	1.45	1.35	1.14	1.32	1.31	1.51	1.91	1.62	1.99	1.58	1.25
1952	1.51	1.44	1.18	1.34	1.32	1.59	2.02	1.69	2.10	1.70	1.30
1953	1.58	1.53	1.25	1.36	1.35	1.67	2.11	1.81	2.22	1.79	1.35
1954	1.62	1.59	1.30	1.36	1.37	1.73	2.18	1.89	2.29	1.83	1.36
1955	1.68	1.66	1.34	1.38	1.37	1.81	2.26	1.97	2.37	1.95	1.39
1956	1.77	1.76	1.45	1.44	1.47	1.92	2.33	2.09	2.54	2.02	1.48
1957	1.85	1.85	1.53	1.49	1.51	2.02	2.40	2.20	2.66	2.11	1.52
1958	1.92	1.94	1.59	1.49	1.54	2.10	2.49	2.29	2.73	2.18	1.56
1959	1.98	2.02	1.65	1.56	1.56	2.18	2.59	2.40	2.85	2.27	1.59
1960	2.05	2.11	1.70	1.61	1.59	2.26	2.68	2.50	2.89	2.32	1.64
1961	2.11	2.17	1.78	1.63	1.64	2.34	2.75	2.58	3.01	2.38	1.68
1962	2.17	2.24	1.85	1.68	1.69	2.40	2.82	2.65	3.05	2.44	1.72
1963	2.22	2.30	1.91	1.71	1.73	2.48	2.89	2.72	3.16	2.47	1.76
1964	2.29	2.37	1.95	1.79	1.79	2.56	2.97	2.80	3.20	2.54	1.83
1965	2.36	2.44	2.09	1.87	1.83	2.65	3.06	2.89	3.28	2.61	1.88
1966	2.45	2.52	2.19	1.96	1.89	2.75	3.16	2.98	3.41	2.68	1.94
1967	2.57	2.64	2.27	2.06	2.03	2.87	3.28	3.10	3.58	2.75	2.07
1968	2.74	2.80	2.48	2.21	2.21	3.05	3.48	3.26	3.75	2.93	2.23
1969	2.91	3.06	2.62	2.35	2.31	3.24	3.69	3.47	4.00	3.08	2.36
1970	3.08	3.16	2.91	2.45	2.39	3.44	3.92	3.69	4.28	3.21	2.49
1971	3.27	3.38	3.16	2.57	2.49	3.67	4.20	3.97	4.57	3.41	2.59
1972	3.48	3.60	3.47	2.75	2.60	3.95	4.51	4.26	4.96	3.63	2.68
1973	3.70	3.85	3.76	2.95	2.76	4.20	4.75	4.51	5.28	3.84	2.79
1974	4.01	4.19	4.12	3.20	2.97	4.53	5.03	4.88	5.68	4.09	2.99
1975	4.37	4.61	4.55	3.42	3.17	5.01	5.38	5.39	6.48	4.42	3.21
1976	4.71	4.98	4.98	3.69	3.40	5.47	5.71	5.91	7.21	4.71	3.40
1977	5.11	5.37	5.54	3.99	3.62	5.96	6.12	6.43	7.83	5.21	3.61
1978	5.54	5.80	6.13	4.30	3.94	6.52	6.51	7.02	8.63	5.57	3.89
1979	6.01	6.27	6.67	4.66	4.23	7.13	6.94	7.60	9.36	6.02	4.22
1980	6.56	6.85	7.74	5.07	4.56	7.84	7.53	8.30	10.10	6.58	4.58
1981	7.19	7.44	8.88	5.52	4.97	8.60	8.19	9.12	11.38	7.22	4.99
1982	7.75	7.92	9.79	5.83	5.20	9.32	8.74	9.96	12.46	7.70	5.33
1983	8.09	8.19	10.38	6.18	5.38	9.93	9.11	10.58	13.28	8.06	5.54
1984	8.39	8.39	11.22	6.46	5.55	10.41	9.41	11.07	13.44	8.35	5.71
1985	8.72	8.57	11.96	6.70	5.73	10.83	9.71	11.56	14.06	8.60	5.83
1986	8.95	8.75	12.88	6.93	5.84	11.18	9.99	11.98	14.19	8.79	5.92
1987	9.19	8.93	14.07	7.17	5.94	11.43	10.28	12.37	14.58	8.98	6.08
1988	9.45	9.12	14.67	7.38	6.12	11.69	10.53	12.71	14.97	9.19	6.28
1989	9.75	9.38	15.31	7.67	6.35	11.96	10.88	13.09	15.41	9.46	6.59
1990	10.12	9.62	16.23	8.02	6.57	12.31	11.24	13.54	16.24	9.76	6.91
1991	10.44	9.90	16.77	8.30	6.77	12.72	11.48	14.04	17.04	10.07	7.18
1992	10.73	10.20	16.92	8.60	6.95	13.07	11.74	14.51	17.90	10.36	7.42
1993	10.98	10.45	16.89	8.88	7.09	13.42	11.93	14.82	18.53	10.57	7.63
1994	11.24	10.66	19.07	9.13	7.34	13.77	12.14	15.13	19.07	10.70	7.97
1995	11.58	10.93	19.41	9.41	7.64	14.23	12.33	15.62	19.36	10.91	8.17
1996	11.97	11.20	19.35	9.69	7.96	14.67	12.65	16.17	19.32	11.24	8.57
1997	12.34	11.48	19.24	10.03	8.25	15.05	13.06	16.57	20.20	11.57	8.97
1998	12.76	11.80	18.56	10.39	8.52	15.50	13.46	17.09	20.91	11.89	9.35
1999	13.21	12.11	19.87	10.81	8.92	15.88	13.96	17.42	21.43	12.40	9.71
2000	13.69	12.50	21.57	11.16	9.30	16.25	14.40	18.15	22.00	12.85	10.18

Note: Data include Alaska and Hawaii beginning in 1959.

Table 2-13. Average Weekly Earnings of Production or Nonsupervisory Workers on Nonfarm Payrolls by Industry in Current and Constant Dollars, 1947–2000

Year	Total private		Mining		Construction		Manufacturing		Transportation and public utilities	
	Current dollars	1982 dollars	Current dollars	1982 dollars	Current dollars	1982 dollars	Current dollars	1982 dollars	Current dollars	1982 dollars
1947	45.58	196.47	59.89	258.15	58.83	253.58	49.13	211.77	. . .	. . .
1948	49.00	196.00	65.52	262.08	65.23	260.92	53.08	212.32	. . .	. . .
1949	50.24	202.58	62.33	251.33	67.56	272.42	53.80	216.94	. . .	. . .
1950	53.13	212.52	67.16	268.64	69.68	278.72	58.28	233.12	. . .	. . .
1951	57.86	215.09	74.11	275.50	76.96	286.10	63.34	235.46	. . .	. . .
1952	60.65	219.75	77.59	281.12	82.86	300.22	66.75	241.85	. . .	. . .
1953	63.76	229.35	83.03	298.67	86.41	310.83	70.47	253.49	. . .	. . .
1954	64.52	231.25	82.60	296.06	88.54	317.35	70.49	252.65	. . .	. . .
1955	67.72	243.60	89.54	322.09	90.90	326.98	75.30	270.86	. . .	. . .
1956	70.74	250.85	95.06	337.09	96.38	341.77	78.78	279.36	. . .	. . .
1957	73.33	251.13	98.25	336.47	100.27	343.39	81.19	278.05	. . .	. . .
1958	75.08	250.27	96.08	320.27	103.78	345.93	82.32	274.40	. . .	. . .
1959	78.78	260.86	103.68	343.31	108.41	358.97	88.26	292.25	. . .	. . .
1960	80.67	261.92	105.04	341.04	112.67	365.81	89.72	291.30	. . .	. . .
1961	82.60	265.59	106.92	343.79	118.08	379.68	92.34	296.91	. . .	. . .
1962	85.91	273.60	110.70	352.55	122.47	390.03	96.56	307.52	. . .	. . .
1963	88.46	278.18	114.40	359.75	127.19	399.97	99.23	312.04	. . .	. . .
1964	91.33	283.63	117.74	365.65	132.06	410.12	102.97	319.78	118.78	368.88
1965	95.45	291.90	123.52	377.74	138.38	423.18	107.53	328.84	125.14	382.69
1966	98.82	294.11	130.24	387.62	146.26	435.30	112.19	333.90	128.13	381.34
1967	101.84	293.49	135.89	391.61	154.95	446.54	114.49	329.94	130.82	377.00
1968	107.73	298.42	142.71	395.32	164.49	455.65	122.51	339.36	138.85	384.63
1969	114.61	300.81	154.80	406.30	181.54	476.48	129.51	339.92	147.74	387.77
1970	119.83	298.08	164.40	408.96	195.45	486.19	133.33	331.67	155.93	387.89
1971	127.31	303.12	172.14	409.86	211.67	503.98	142.44	339.14	168.82	401.95
1972	136.90	315.44	189.14	435.81	221.19	509.65	154.71	356.47	187.86	432.86
1973	145.39	315.38	201.40	436.88	235.89	511.69	166.46	361.08	203.31	441.02
1974	154.76	302.27	219.14	428.01	249.25	486.82	176.80	345.31	217.48	424.77
1975	163.53	293.06	249.31	446.79	266.08	476.85	190.79	341.92	233.44	418.35
1976	175.45	297.37	273.90	464.24	283.73	480.90	209.32	354.78	256.71	435.10
1977	189.00	300.96	301.20	479.62	295.65	470.78	228.90	364.49	278.90	444.11
1978	203.70	300.89	332.88	491.70	318.69	470.74	249.27	368.20	302.80	447.27
1979	219.91	291.66	365.07	484.18	342.99	454.89	269.34	357.21	325.58	431.80
1980	235.10	274.65	397.06	463.86	367.78	429.65	288.62	337.17	351.25	410.34
1981	255.20	270.63	438.75	465.27	399.26	423.39	318.00	337.22	382.18	405.28
1982	267.26	267.26	459.88	459.88	426.82	426.82	330.26	330.26	402.48	402.48
1983	280.70	272.52	479.40	465.44	442.97	430.07	354.08	343.77	420.81	408.55
1984	292.86	274.73	503.58	472.40	458.51	430.12	374.03	350.87	438.13	411.00
1985	299.09	271.16	519.93	471.38	464.46	421.09	386.37	350.29	450.30	408.25
1986	304.85	271.94	525.81	469.05	466.75	416.37	396.01	353.26	458.64	409.13
1987	312.50	269.16	531.70	457.97	480.44	413.82	406.31	349.97	471.58	406.18
1988	322.02	266.79	541.44	448.58	495.73	410.71	418.81	346.98	467.57	387.38
1989	334.24	264.22	570.18	450.74	513.17	405.67	429.68	339.67	481.43	380.58
1990	345.35	259.47	603.29	453.26	526.01	395.20	441.86	331.98	496.13	372.75
1991	353.98	255.40	630.04	454.57	533.40	384.85	455.03	328.30	502.92	362.86
1992	363.61	254.99	638.31	447.62	537.70	377.07	469.86	329.50	514.37	360.71
1993	373.64	254.87	646.78	441.19	553.63	377.65	486.04	331.54	532.52	363.25
1994	385.86	256.73	666.62	443.53	573.00	381.24	506.94	337.29	547.07	363.99
1995	394.34	255.07	683.91	442.37	587.00	379.69	514.59	332.85	556.72	360.10
1996	406.61	255.73	707.59	445.03	603.33	379.45	531.23	334.11	572.22	359.89
1997	424.89	261.31	733.21	450.93	625.56	384.72	553.14	340.18	592.32	364.28
1998	442.19	268.32	742.35	450.46	646.13	392.07	562.53	341.34	604.75	366.96
1999	456.78	271.25	736.56	437.39	672.13	399.13	579.63	344.20	607.20	360.57
2000	474.38	272.16	743.04	426.30	702.68	403.14	598.21	343.21	626.09	359.20

See *Note* at end of table.

Table 2-13. Average Weekly Earnings of Production or Nonsupervisory Workers on Nonfarm Payrolls by Industry in Current and Constant Dollars, 1947–2000—*Continued*

Year	Wholesale trade		Retail trade		Finance, insurance, and real estate		Services	
	Current dollars	1982 dollars	Current dollars	1982 dollars	Current dollars	1982 dollars	Current dollars	1982 dollars
1947	50.06	215.95	33.77	145.56	43.21	186.25	...	...
1948	53.59	214.12	36.22	144.88	45.48	181.92	...	...
1949	55.45	223.59	38.42	154.92	47.63	192.06	...	...
1950	55.31	232.40	39.71	158.84	47.50	202.08	...	...
1951	62.02	230.93	42.82	159.18	54.67	203.20	...	...
1952	65.53	237.17	43.38	157.17	57.08	206.81	...	...
1953	68.61	246.94	45.36	163.17	59.57	214.28	...	...
1954	71.28	255.02	47.04	168.60	62.04	222.37	...	...
1955	74.48	268.02	48.75	175.36	63.92	229.93	...	...
1956	78.17	277.77	50.18	177.94	65.68	232.91	...	...
1957	81.41	278.73	52.20	178.77	67.53	231.27	...	...
1958	84.02	280.47	54.10	180.33	70.12	233.73	...	...
1959	88.51	292.78	56.15	185.93	72.74	240.83	...	...
1960	90.72	293.93	57.76	187.53	75.14	243.96	...	...
1961	93.56	299.87	58.66	188.62	77.12	247.97	...	...
1962	96.22	306.43	60.96	194.14	80.94	257.77	...	...
1963	99.47	312.61	62.66	197.04	84.38	265.35	...	...
1964	102.56	317.89	64.75	201.27	85.79	266.37	70.03	217.55
1965	106.08	324.98	66.61	203.82	88.91	271.71	73.60	225.08
1966	111.11	330.60	68.57	203.87	92.13	274.43	77.04	228.93
1967	115.66	333.86	70.95	204.21	95.72	275.79	80.38	231.41
1968	121.90	337.65	74.95	207.56	101.75	281.72	83.97	232.91
1969	129.85	340.52	78.66	206.48	108.70	284.93	90.57	237.85
1970	136.86	340.57	82.47	204.75	112.67	280.57	96.66	240.10
1971	143.42	342.10	87.62	208.30	117.85	281.00	103.06	245.33
1972	151.69	348.89	91.85	212.05	122.98	283.27	110.85	254.88
1973	159.54	346.51	96.32	209.22	129.20	280.56	117.29	254.86
1974	169.94	332.25	102.68	200.29	137.61	268.91	126.00	246.52
1975	182.19	326.92	108.86	194.68	148.19	265.04	134.67	241.45
1976	194.27	329.07	114.60	194.17	155.43	263.58	143.52	243.27
1977	209.13	332.42	121.66	193.54	165.26	263.41	153.45	244.57
1978	228.14	336.59	130.20	192.23	178.00	262.97	163.67	242.08
1979	247.93	328.45	138.62	184.12	190.77	253.21	175.27	232.57
1980	266.88	312.07	147.30	172.01	209.60	244.95	190.71	223.11
1981	290.68	308.25	158.03	167.58	229.05	242.90	208.97	221.60
1982	309.46	309.46	163.85	163.85	245.44	245.44	225.59	225.59
1983	328.79	319.21	171.05	166.07	263.90	256.21	239.04	232.08
1984	341.88	320.71	174.33	163.54	278.50	261.26	247.43	232.11
1985	351.36	318.55	174.64	158.33	289.02	262.03	256.75	232.77
1986	357.72	319.11	176.08	157.07	304.30	271.45	265.85	237.15
1987	365.38	314.71	178.70	153.92	316.90	272.95	275.93	237.67
1988	380.24	315.03	183.62	152.13	325.25	269.47	289.49	239.84
1989	394.82	312.11	188.72	149.19	341.17	269.70	305.79	241.73
1990	411.10	308.87	194.40	146.06	356.93	268.17	319.48	240.03
1991	424.82	306.51	198.48	143.20	370.92	267.62	331.45	239.14
1992	435.10	305.12	205.06	143.80	387.36	271.64	342.55	240.22
1993	448.47	305.91	209.95	143.21	406.33	277.17	350.35	238.98
1994	463.10	308.12	216.46	144.02	423.51	281.78	358.80	238.72
1995	476.07	307.94	221.47	143.25	442.29	286.09	369.04	238.71
1996	492.92	310.01	230.11	144.72	459.52	289.01	382.00	240.25
1997	516.48	317.64	240.74	148.06	481.57	296.17	400.33	246.21
1998	538.88	326.99	253.46	153.80	512.15	310.77	418.58	253.99
1999	558.80	331.83	263.61	156.54	529.24	314.28	435.86	258.82
2000	585.20	335.74	273.39	156.85	547.04	313.85	454.86	260.96

Note: Data include Alaska and Hawaii beginning in 1959.

Table 2-14. Average Weekly Earnings of Production Workers on Manufacturing Payrolls by Industry, 1947–2000

(Dollars.)

Year	Total manufacturing	Durable goods: Total	Lumber and wood products	Furniture and fixtures	Stone, clay, and glass products	Primary metal industries: Total	Primary metal industries: Blast furnaces and basic steel products	Fabricated metal products	Industrial machinery and equipment	Electronic and other electrical equipment	Transportation equipment: Total	Transportation equipment: Motor vehicles and equipment	Instruments and related products	Miscellaneous manufacturing industries
1947	49.13	51.64	43.93	45.53	48.95	55.38	56.51	51.74	55.78	...	56.97	58.63	...	44.75
1948	53.08	56.24	47.64	48.83	53.20	61.14	62.84	56.37	60.38	...	61.70	63.15	...	48.03
1949	53.80	57.13	48.10	49.36	54.27	60.90	63.34	57.45	60.27	...	65.10	67.33	...	48.23
1950	58.28	59.60	51.31	53.55	59.06	67.36	67.95	63.04	67.04	...	71.29	74.85	...	52.02
1951	63.34	68.48	55.41	57.13	63.76	75.30	77.71	68.55	76.13	...	75.81	77.16	...	55.08
1952	66.75	72.04	59.15	60.86	66.17	77.52	80.00	71.72	79.55	...	81.51	84.87	...	59.02
1953	70.47	76.22	61.31	62.99	70.18	84.46	88.29	76.49	82.68	...	85.28	89.88	...	61.56
1954	70.49	75.79	61.39	62.80	71.69	81.48	83.92	76.70	81.40	...	86.30	91.30	...	61.78
1955	75.30	81.77	63.99	67.07	77.00	92.51	96.80	81.73	87.15	...	93.48	99.84	...	64.88
1956	78.78	85.28	65.74	68.78	80.56	97.17	102.87	84.67	93.06	...	94.81	96.82	...	67.60
1957	81.19	87.85	66.82	69.83	82.82	99.00	105.57	88.34	94.12	...	97.51	100.61	...	69.48
1958	82.32	88.88	69.48	69.95	84.80	101.11	108.00	90.17	94.33	...	100.40	101.24	...	70.17
1959	88.26	95.65	74.24	74.48	91.46	112.19	122.71	96.12	102.92	...	107.45	111.38	...	73.42
1960	89.72	97.04	74.29	75.20	92.57	109.59	116.13	98.42	104.55	...	111.52	115.21	...	74.28
1961	92.34	99.70	77.03	76.40	95.24	114.55	122.92	100.85	107.16	...	113.40	114.69	...	75.84
1962	96.56	104.30	79.20	79.37	98.81	119.80	127.40	104.81	113.01	...	122.22	127.67	...	78.61
1963	99.23	108.09	82.41	81.80	102.67	124.64	133.06	107.79	116.20	...	126.42	132.68	...	80.39
1964	102.97	112.05	85.65	84.46	105.50	129.69	138.43	111.76	121.69	...	130.09	138.03	...	82.37
1965	107.53	116.76	89.16	87.98	110.04	133.88	140.90	116.20	127.15	...	137.71	147.63	...	85.39
1966	112.19	121.67	92.21	91.72	114.24	138.09	144.73	122.11	134.90	...	141.86	147.23	...	88.80
1967	114.49	123.19	95.91	94.13	117.31	137.27	143.51	123.67	135.58	...	142.42	144.84	...	92.59
1968	122.51	131.65	104.75	100.28	124.98	147.68	154.16	131.77	141.12	...	155.72	167.66	...	98.50
1969	129.51	139.59	110.55	105.85	133.66	158.42	166.03	138.94	152.15	...	161.44	170.97	...	103.74
1970	133.33	143.07	117.61	108.58	140.08	158.77	166.40	143.67	154.95	...	163.62	170.07	...	109.52
1971	142.44	152.74	126.56	115.42	152.67	169.62	177.80	152.31	163.21	...	181.12	194.46	...	115.53
1972	154.71	167.68	134.94	123.82	165.48	192.92	206.25	166.86	181.87	...	200.58	220.59	...	122.85
1973	166.46	180.09	144.80	131.60	176.82	213.19	229.77	178.46	196.88	...	216.82	237.51	...	128.31
1974	176.80	190.82	152.88	138.02	187.50	232.96	258.95	188.09	207.97	...	224.37	238.32	...	136.61
1975	190.79	205.49	166.06	143.64	198.77	247.20	274.13	202.51	219.10	...	245.23	259.53	...	146.69
1976	209.32	226.14	189.13	154.81	219.06	276.22	305.88	224.40	238.55	...	276.05	304.16	...	156.75
1977	228.90	248.46	203.89	169.26	239.95	305.62	338.58	242.31	259.79	...	309.83	345.40	...	169.17
1978	249.27	270.44	223.68	183.92	262.91	342.76	389.69	260.35	284.76	...	333.80	368.05	...	181.97
1979	269.34	290.50	240.16	195.82	284.28	371.77	428.89	278.80	305.24	...	350.58	372.37	...	195.16
1980	288.62	310.78	253.60	209.17	306.00	391.78	448.77	300.98	328.00	...	379.61	394.00	...	211.30
1981	318.00	342.91	271.67	226.94	335.76	437.81	509.04	330.46	360.33	...	424.95	450.72	...	231.64
1982	330.26	354.88	284.23	234.73	355.69	437.34	505.97	343.78	367.62	...	449.96	470.61	...	246.53
1983	354.08	381.77	313.58	260.83	384.71	459.68	509.16	370.27	387.18	...	491.31	525.66	...	266.27
1984	374.03	402.82	321.20	271.55	401.94	478.30	528.29	389.16	417.74	...	520.94	557.57	...	277.77
1985	386.37	415.71	329.18	282.50	412.30	484.31	547.86	401.02	427.45	...	541.45	582.47	...	287.62
1986	396.01	424.56	338.15	296.91	423.69	496.93	572.54	408.46	440.13	...	541.86	572.97	...	298.98
1987	406.31	432.85	342.26	306.80	433.58	514.61	597.62	416.42	452.81	...	543.48	570.97	...	305.74
1988	418.81	447.68	344.46	313.23	446.69	528.96	615.12	431.15	473.12	401.39	567.48	608.57	438.84	313.60
1989	429.68	458.02	354.48	325.88	457.69	534.49	618.45	439.71	483.36	410.04	579.61	614.18	445.11	326.63
1990	441.86	468.76	365.02	333.13	467.04	551.68	643.19	447.28	493.16	420.24	591.36	617.34	464.02	340.10
1991	455.03	482.93	369.60	340.76	473.71	562.53	655.87	461.03	506.66	435.49	618.03	644.23	477.24	351.35
1992	469.86	498.83	383.26	357.70	489.52	587.38	690.35	475.07	523.70	453.20	635.36	655.08	488.68	365.09
1993	486.04	519.09	392.09	371.73	506.00	611.36	721.48	492.15	547.39	469.83	679.40	713.23	502.65	373.72
1994	506.94	543.97	405.41	385.82	526.44	641.00	756.57	511.80	568.10	485.30	731.39	782.92	520.00	386.80
1995	514.59	548.66	410.87	388.87	533.63	643.28	769.45	514.31	574.62	486.30	733.21	778.57	526.19	401.00
1996	531.23	565.19	425.96	399.91	555.11	661.67	792.10	530.00	585.73	505.47	756.36	796.53	547.52	412.09
1997	553.14	587.64	441.16	424.11	569.38	683.38	809.55	544.43	613.45	533.40	780.98	811.80	567.84	428.24
1998	562.53	591.35	456.21	441.45	591.17	684.22	821.53	552.86	619.32	542.34	759.93	776.04	570.35	434.11
1999	579.63	605.99	473.06	454.99	606.30	703.10	851.57	572.40	632.76	553.32	779.20	814.50	581.50	448.15
2000	598.21	623.92	489.13	469.20	626.24	737.26	911.72	590.86	656.21	567.18	800.73	834.28	595.96	453.57

See *Note* at end of table.

Table 2-14. Average Weekly Earnings of Production Workers on Manufacturing Payrolls by Industry, 1947–2000—*Continued*

(Dollars.)

Year	Nondurable goods										
	Total	Food and kindred products	Tobacco products	Textile mill products	Apparel and other textile products	Paper and allied products	Printing and publishing	Chemicals and allied products	Petroleum and coal products	Rubber and miscella-neous plastics products	Leather and leather products
1947	46.03	45.92	35.17	40.99	41.80	49.69	59.30	50.26	60.94	51.60	40.07
1948	49.54	48.84	36.58	45.28	43.68	54.70	65.13	55.29	69.30	53.29	41.11
1949	50.41	50.49	37.26	44.52	42.76	55.42	68.60	57.67	72.42	54.13	41.03
1950	51.45	52.88	41.00	48.59	44.60	60.53	71.23	61.64	75.11	60.27	43.95
1951	57.42	56.84	43.89	51.22	46.64	65.08	74.30	66.91	81.19	64.46	46.13
1952	59.95	60.34	45.31	52.39	47.92	68.05	78.58	69.12	85.05	69.53	49.92
1953	62.57	63.50	47.63	53.18	48.74	71.81	82.29	74.21	90.35	72.32	50.90
1954	63.18	65.67	48.88	52.09	48.36	73.18	83.93	77.11	93.20	72.83	50.18
1955	67.03	68.89	51.86	55.34	49.73	78.01	87.91	80.97	96.93	81.32	52.68
1956	70.09	72.69	56.26	57.17	52.92	82.18	90.64	85.90	104.14	81.61	55.65
1957	72.52	75.48	58.75	57.96	53.91	85.45	92.64	89.98	108.53	85.67	56.85
1958	74.50	79.15	62.17	57.51	54.05	87.99	94.62	93.20	111.66	85.67	57.25
1959	78.61	82.82	64.52	63.02	56.63	93.30	99.72	99.36	117.42	93.75	60.26
1960	80.36	86.09	64.94	63.60	56.45	95.15	102.91	103.25	118.78	92.80	60.52
1961	82.92	88.75	69.42	65.04	58.06	99.45	105.05	106.81	124.01	96.15	62.83
1962	86.15	91.84	71.41	68.21	61.18	102.24	108.01	110.24	126.88	100.04	64.67
1963	87.91	94.30	73.92	69.43	62.45	105.90	110.69	113.15	131.77	101.02	66.00
1964	90.91	97.17	75.66	73.39	64.26	109.57	114.35	116.48	133.76	104.90	69.36
1965	94.64	100.28	79.21	77.98	66.61	114.22	118.12	121.09	138.42	109.62	71.82
1966	98.49	103.82	85.19	82.12	68.80	119.35	122.61	125.16	144.58	112.56	74.88
1967	102.03	107.98	87.62	84.25	73.08	122.84	125.95	128.96	152.87	113.85	79.07
1968	109.05	114.24	93.99	91.05	79.78	130.85	133.28	136.27	159.38	121.60	85.41
1969	115.53	120.77	97.99	95.88	82.93	139.32	141.33	145.05	170.40	126.90	87.79
1970	120.43	127.98	110.00	97.76	84.37	144.14	147.78	153.50	183.18	129.36	92.63
1971	128.51	136.21	119.45	104.34	88.64	154.51	157.50	165.15	195.60	137.76	97.64
1972	138.16	145.80	130.47	113.58	93.60	169.06	170.03	177.64	211.79	149.56	102.64
1973	146.52	155.54	145.14	120.00	99.08	180.18	179.08	188.52	223.87	158.21	105.46
1974	156.79	169.28	157.80	126.40	104.54	191.17	188.63	202.52	239.13	166.05	110.33
1975	169.56	185.78	173.81	134.41	111.58	208.42	198.52	220.99	266.98	176.36	119.09
1976	185.57	201.69	186.75	147.97	121.72	232.48	214.13	245.86	303.54	191.70	127.16
1977	201.33	214.80	209.41	161.20	128.87	255.68	230.72	268.13	334.34	214.13	133.21
1978	218.28	230.26	233.55	173.72	140.26	279.71	244.78	294.14	376.27	227.81	144.32
1979	236.19	250.17	253.46	188.26	149.32	303.74	260.25	318.44	409.97	244.41	154.03
1980	255.84	271.95	294.89	203.31	161.42	330.85	279.36	344.45	422.18	263.20	168.09
1981	281.85	295.37	344.54	218.59	177.43	365.50	305.49	379.39	491.62	290.97	183.13
1982	297.60	312.05	370.06	218.63	180.44	389.58	324.25	407.36	546.99	304.92	189.75
1983	318.75	323.51	388.21	249.67	194.76	423.02	342.54	440.13	582.99	332.07	203.87
1984	333.08	333.92	436.46	257.75	202.02	448.67	356.64	463.83	587.33	348.20	210.13
1985	345.31	342.80	444.91	265.99	208.57	466.77	367.04	484.36	604.58	353.46	216.88
1986	357.11	350.00	481.71	284.82	214.33	482.98	379.62	501.96	621.52	363.91	218.45
1987	369.44	358.99	548.73	299.71	219.78	496.06	390.64	523.25	641.52	373.57	232.26
1988	379.89	367.54	583.87	302.58	226.44	506.18	400.14	536.36	664.67	383.22	235.50
1989	391.95	381.77	590.97	313.70	234.32	517.87	412.35	555.02	682.66	391.64	249.76
1990	404.80	392.50	636.22	320.00	239.15	533.02	426.00	576.80	724.30	401.14	258.43
1991	419.69	401.94	655.71	336.98	250.49	550.78	432.80	602.32	751.46	413.88	269.25
1992	433.49	414.12	653.11	353.46	258.54	569.85	447.29	625.38	784.02	432.01	281.96
1993	445.79	425.32	631.69	367.63	263.75	585.11	456.92	638.74	819.03	441.83	294.52
1994	459.72	440.26	749.45	379.81	275.25	604.50	468.60	653.62	846.71	451.54	306.85
1995	468.99	449.22	768.64	383.93	282.68	613.31	471.01	674.78	846.03	452.77	310.46
1996	484.79	459.20	774.00	393.41	294.52	635.21	483.23	698.54	842.35	466.46	326.52
1997	504.71	474.12	748.44	415.24	307.73	657.69	502.81	715.82	870.62	483.63	344.45
1998	521.88	492.06	710.85	425.99	317.80	672.70	515.52	738.29	911.68	495.81	351.56
1999	540.29	506.20	763.01	442.13	334.50	689.19	531.88	749.06	908.63	517.08	363.15
2000	558.55	521.25	877.90	459.79	351.54	690.63	551.52	771.38	932.80	531.99	381.75

Note: Data include Alaska and Hawaii beginning in 1959.

Table 2-15. Employees on Total Nonfarm Payrolls by State, 1962–2000

(Thousands of persons.)

State	1962	1963	1964	1965	1966	1967	1968	1969	1970	1971	1972	1973	1974
Alabama	791.8	812.5	843.8	886.5	935.6	951.8	970.1	1 000.2	1 010.5	1 021.9	1 072.3	1 135.5	1 169.8
Alaska	58.9	62.1	65.4	70.5	73.1	76.9	79.9	86.8	93.1	97.8	103.5	110.0	127.9
Arizona	364.8	377.2	389.1	403.7	434.8	445.6	473.4	517.2	547.4	581.4	646.3	714.5	746.0
Arkansas	399.7	416.3	431.8	458.8	489.8	501.0	514.6	533.8	536.2	551.0	581.5	614.5	640.7
California	5 217.7	5 412.3	5 606.5	5 800.3	6 145.2	6 367.6	6 642.1	6 931.5	6 946.2	6 917.0	7 209.9	7 621.9	7 834.3
Colorado	557.5	571.7	583.2	598.9	631.2	655.8	686.6	720.7	750.2	787.0	869.4	936.0	959.7
Connecticut	949.8	969.3	991.2	1 032.9	1 095.4	1 130.1	1 158.0	1 194.1	1 197.5	1 164.3	1 190.4	1 238.7	1 264.0
Delaware	156.4	163.6	170.8	184.1	193.2	197.4	202.9	211.9	216.8	224.9	232.4	239.4	233.1
District of Columbia	527.2	542.5	551.5	572.5	587.0	594.7	582.8	575.0	566.7	566.6	572.0	573.7	580.1
Florida	1 387.8	1 447.4	1 526.5	1 619.1	1 726.8	1 816.4	1 932.3	2 069.9	2 152.1	2 276.4	2 513.1	2 778.6	2 863.8
Georgia	1 092.7	1 139.7	1 186.7	1 257.1	1 337.9	1 394.7	1 455.6	1 531.7	1 557.5	1 602.9	1 695.2	1 802.5	1 827.5
Hawaii	195.2	199.6	207.8	219.4	232.1	241.7	255.3	275.9	293.7	301.5	312.7	327.5	335.9
Idaho	164.6	164.7	168.6	177.6	184.8	187.7	192.9	201.4	207.8	217.1	236.5	251.7	266.8
Illinois	3 572.5	3 614.4	3 712.2	3 880.4	4 095.3	4 209.7	4 284.9	4 376.1	4 345.6	4 296.4	4 314.8	4 466.9	4 545.7
Indiana	1 461.3	1 498.7	1 545.7	1 631.1	1 737.2	1 777.0	1 817.4	1 880.3	1 849.0	1 841.1	1 921.9	2 028.1	2 031.4
Iowa	685.2	699.8	718.3	752.2	803.8	832.8	852.1	873.4	876.9	882.7	912.3	961.3	999.0
Kansas	573.5	574.2	587.2	600.4	634.3	652.8	672.1	686.4	678.8	677.8	717.5	763.3	790.0
Kentucky	673.7	702.9	721.7	758.9	803.8	836.5	868.6	895.5	910.1	931.5	988.3	1 038.6	1 065.9
Louisiana	790.1	810.3	849.4	898.4	957.9	997.3	1 020.5	1 032.7	1 033.6	1 055.9	1 128.6	1 176.1	1 220.8
Maine	279.5	279.6	285.1	295.4	309.2	316.9	323.2	330.0	332.2	332.3	343.7	354.8	361.5
Maryland	946.7	978.6	1 009.7	1 057.6	1 132.0	1 178.6	1 223.9	1 272.4	1 349.2	1 371.5	1 415.0	1 471.5	1 493.6
Massachusetts	1 942.7	1 943.2	1 958.1	2 015.8	2 097.4	2 147.9	2 187.9	2 249.4	2 243.5	2 211.4	2 251.7	2 333.5	2 353.7
Michigan	2 334.9	2 410.4	2 512.9	2 685.3	2 861.0	2 900.5	2 959.7	3 081.1	2 999.0	2 995.0	3 118.9	3 284.3	3 277.6
Minnesota	984.5	1 001.7	1 028.0	1 080.6	1 148.3	1 199.8	1 243.5	1 299.8	1 315.3	1 310.2	1 357.1	1 436.1	1 481.0
Mississippi	425.7	443.7	460.2	486.6	521.6	535.1	551.9	573.0	583.9	602.2	649.3	693.2	710.8
Missouri	1 357.2	1 383.5	1 418.3	1 478.3	1 554.1	1 595.5	1 631.3	1 672.1	1 668.0	1 660.8	1 700.1	1 770.6	1 789.5
Montana	169.7	172.6	174.2	179.2	184.6	188.0	192.5	195.5	199.1	204.8	215.3	224.2	234.0
Nebraska	396.4	401.9	408.9	418.7	434.1	449.3	458.8	474.4	484.3	490.8	517.0	541.3	562.1
Nevada	126.9	142.8	149.3	157.4	162.0	166.1	177.3	193.5	203.3	210.5	223.4	244.6	256.1
New Hampshire	207.9	208.8	212.8	220.8	235.2	244.0	251.8	259.2	258.5	259.9	278.5	297.8	300.3
New Jersey	2 095.8	2 129.4	2 168.7	2 259.0	2 359.1	2 421.5	2 485.2	2 569.6	2 606.2	2 607.6	2 672.5	2 759.7	2 783.0
New Mexico	242.6	248.6	255.7	262.5	271.7	272.6	276.6	287.5	292.6	305.7	327.5	346.0	360.2
New York	6 261.3	6 273.7	6 370.7	6 518.7	6 709.5	6 858.3	7 001.7	7 182.0	7 156.4	7 011.4	7 038.5	7 132.2	7 077.1
North Carolina	1 258.5	1 298.6	1 353.7	1 431.2	1 534.2	1 600.9	1 678.5	1 747.0	1 782.7	1 813.8	1 911.9	2 018.1	2 048.2
North Dakota	131.3	136.7	142.6	146.1	148.3	151.5	155.6	157.8	163.6	167.0	176.1	183.9	193.8
Ohio	3 099.2	3 145.2	3 216.3	3 364.3	3 537.3	3 619.8	3 750.8	3 887.3	3 880.7	3 839.6	3 938.4	4 112.9	4 169.4
Oklahoma	596.7	606.7	619.3	642.5	676.0	699.7	720.4	748.3	762.6	774.4	811.9	851.9	886.9
Oregon	529.0	549.5	573.9	608.4	640.4	652.1	679.2	708.5	710.5	729.1	774.7	816.2	838.2
Pennsylvania	3 694.9	3 694.8	3 777.1	3 917.5	4 077.1	4 171.3	4 263.5	4 374.9	4 351.6	4 291.3	4 400.0	4 506.5	4 514.6
Rhode Island	298.3	298.1	303.9	316.3	330.0	338.3	343.0	346.4	344.1	342.8	358.1	365.9	367.0
South Carolina	609.8	630.6	651.4	686.0	734.9	754.4	782.9	819.8	842.0	862.6	920.3	984.0	1 015.8
South Dakota	153.9	152.6	152.2	155.5	160.1	163.9	167.8	172.9	175.4	179.0	189.9	199.1	206.6
Tennessee	969.4	1 002.5	1 045.5	1 108.5	1 184.4	1 218.8	1 264.0	1 309.8	1 327.6	1 356.8	1 450.1	1 531.1	1 558.2
Texas	2 631.2	2 706.5	2 808.0	2 932.4	3 108.7	3 259.4	3 424.3	3 597.1	3 624.9	3 683.5	3 884.4	4 141.7	4 360.2
Utah	286.1	293.7	293.2	299.8	317.4	326.6	335.1	348.2	357.0	369.3	393.0	414.8	434.1
Vermont	110.5	111.5	113.7	121.3	130.8	136.3	140.3	145.5	147.9	148.1	153.6	161.3	162.8
Virginia	1 081.8	1 123.8	1 163.0	1 218.9	1 285.3	1 330.2	1 385.1	1 436.4	1 518.9	1 567.2	1 655.2	1 753.4	1 804.3
Washington	856.8	850.6	854.7	896.4	988.4	1 045.3	1 099.4	1 120.1	1 079.4	1 064.5	1 100.1	1 152.3	1 199.1
West Virginia	447.5	449.9	460.9	476.6	495.1	503.6	508.4	512.3	516.5	520.0	540.5	561.6	572.4
Wisconsin	1 207.2	1 233.5	1 270.9	1 331.7	1 394.1	1 430.5	1 472.1	1 525.1	1 530.4	1 525.4	1 580.8	1 660.5	1 703.4
Wyoming	95.5	96.2	97.2	96.6	97.2	99.0	102.9	106.9	108.3	111.0	117.3	126.1	136.5
Puerto Rico	...	...	...	...	...	...	...	...	...	...	...	...	...
Virgin Islands	...	...	...	...	...	...	...	...	...	...	...	...	...

See footnote at end of table.

Table 2-15. Employees on Total Nonfarm Payrolls by State, 1962–2000—*Continued*

(Thousands of persons.)

State	1975	1976	1977	1978	1979	1980	1981	1982	1983	1984	1985	1986	1987
Alabama	1 155.4	1 207.0	1 269.2	1 336.5	1 362.0	1 356.1	1 347.6	1 312.5	1 328.8	1 387.7	1 427.1	1 463.3	1 507.7
Alaska	161.8	171.7	163.3	163.5	166.9	169.4	186.1	200.4	214.3	225.7	230.7	220.7	210.1
Arizona	729.1	758.7	809.3	895.4	979.9	1 014.0	1 040.8	1 029.8	1 077.8	1 181.9	1 278.6	1 337.8	1 385.8
Arkansas	623.8	660.0	695.6	732.7	749.4	742.3	740.1	720.1	741.3	780.2	797.1	813.8	836.6
California	7 847.2	8 154.2	8 599.7	9 199.8	9 664.6	9 848.8	9 985.3	9 810.3	9 917.8	10 390.0	10 769.8	11 085.5	11 472.6
Colorado	963.5	1 003.4	1 058.1	1 150.0	1 218.0	1 251.1	1 295.2	1 316.6	1 327.2	1 402.3	1 418.7	1 408.3	1 412.6
Connecticut	1 223.4	1 239.7	1 282.3	1 346.1	1 398.0	1 426.8	1 438.3	1 428.5	1 444.2	1 517.3	1 558.2	1 598.4	1 638.2
Delaware	229.9	236.7	238.8	247.8	256.7	259.2	259.2	259.2	266.1	280.0	293.4	303.2	320.7
District of Columbia	576.5	575.8	578.7	596.3	612.5	616.1	611.0	597.9	596.6	613.8	629.0	640.0	655.6
Florida	2 746.4	2 784.3	2 933.2	3 180.6	3 381.2	3 576.2	3 736.0	3 761.9	3 905.4	4 204.2	4 410.0	4 599.4	4 848.1
Georgia	1 755.7	1 839.1	1 926.4	2 050.1	2 127.5	2 159.4	2 198.6	2 201.5	2 279.5	2 448.7	2 569.8	2 672.4	2 782.0
Hawaii	342.8	349.2	359.4	377.3	394.0	404.1	404.8	399.4	406.2	412.7	425.7	438.6	460.0
Idaho	273.0	291.0	307.4	331.3	338.0	330.0	327.8	312.2	317.9	330.5	336.0	328.2	333.4
Illinois	4 418.9	4 565.7	4 655.5	4 788.8	4 880.0	4 850.3	4 732.3	4 593.3	4 530.6	4 672.3	4 755.3	4 790.7	4 928.3
Indiana	1 941.7	2 023.8	2 114.0	2 205.5	2 236.3	2 129.5	2 114.4	2 028.0	2 029.5	2 122.3	2 168.6	2 221.8	2 304.9
Iowa	998.7	1 036.9	1 079.2	1 119.2	1 131.7	1 109.9	1 088.6	1 041.9	1 040.4	1 074.7	1 074.2	1 073.8	1 109.1
Kansas	801.2	834.8	871.0	912.5	946.8	944.7	949.7	921.4	921.6	960.8	967.9	984.8	1 005.1
Kentucky	1 057.6	1 103.1	1 148.3	1 209.9	1 245.4	1 210.0	1 196.0	1 160.7	1 152.3	1 213.8	1 250.3	1 274.1	1 328.2
Louisiana	1 249.5	1 314.4	1 364.6	1 463.5	1 517.4	1 578.9	1 630.5	1 607.0	1 565.2	1 601.5	1 591.2	1 518.5	1 483.6
Maine	356.9	375.3	387.8	405.6	415.9	418.3	419.2	415.5	425.0	445.7	458.4	477.4	501.1
Maryland	1 479.3	1 498.3	1 545.6	1 625.8	1 691.3	1 711.8	1 715.8	1 675.8	1 724.1	1 814.0	1 887.8	1 952.0	2 028.0
Massachusetts	2 273.1	2 323.5	2 416.0	2 526.3	2 603.5	2 654.3	2 671.8	2 642.0	2 696.5	2 855.8	2 930.0	2 988.8	3 065.8
Michigan	3 136.6	3 283.0	3 442.3	3 609.4	3 637.1	3 442.8	3 364.4	3 193.3	3 223.1	3 381.0	3 561.5	3 657.3	3 735.8
Minnesota	1 474.4	1 520.9	1 597.3	1 689.3	1 767.0	1 770.2	1 761.3	1 707.3	1 718.4	1 819.8	1 865.5	1 892.5	1 962.5
Mississippi	692.3	727.5	765.9	813.7	838.1	829.3	819.1	790.9	792.8	820.8	838.9	848.2	864.4
Missouri	1 740.6	1 797.8	1 861.8	1 953.1	2 011.1	1 969.8	1 956.3	1 922.4	1 937.0	2 032.7	2 094.7	2 142.6	2 197.8
Montana	238.1	251.1	264.8	280.4	283.8	280.4	281.8	273.7	276.0	281.1	279.1	275.4	274.1
Nebraska	557.8	572.1	593.7	609.9	631.2	627.6	623.2	609.8	610.8	635.4	650.5	652.5	667.2
Nevada	263.1	279.8	308.2	350.3	383.7	399.9	411.2	401.1	402.8	426.0	446.4	468.1	500.2
New Hampshire	292.8	313.4	337.1	350.6	[1] 378.5	385.4	394.6	394.4	409.5	441.5	466.0	490.1	512.8
New Jersey	2 699.9	2 753.7	2 836.9	2 961.9	3 027.2	3 060.4	3 098.9	3 092.7	3 165.1	3 329.2	3 414.1	3 488.1	3 576.3
New Mexico	370.2	390.0	415.4	444.3	461.0	465.4	475.5	473.6	479.5	502.8	520.2	525.9	529.3
New York	6 829.9	6 789.5	6 857.6	7 044.5	7 179.4	7 207.1	7 287.3	7 254.6	7 313.3	7 570.4	7 751.3	7 007.9	8 059.4
North Carolina	1 979.9	2 082.7	2 170.4	2 277.4	2 373.0	2 380.0	2 391.6	2 347.0	2 419.2	2 565.2	2 651.2	2 744.1	2 862.6
North Dakota	203.6	215.0	221.1	234.0	244.2	245.2	249.4	249.7	250.6	252.5	252.0	249.9	252.8
Ohio	4 016.2	4 094.6	4 230.1	4 394.9	4 484.8	4 367.4	4 317.7	4 124.3	4 092.5	4 260.2	4 372.9	4 471.4	4 582.6
Oklahoma	899.7	931.1	971.5	1 035.7	1 087.9	1 138.1	1 201.2	1 216.9	1 170.6	1 180.3	1 165.3	1 124.4	1 108.5
Oregon	837.4	878.5	936.9	1 009.2	1 056.0	1 044.6	1 018.7	961.1	966.7	1 006.9	1 030.0	1 058.5	1 100.1
Pennsylvania	4 435.8	4 512.8	4 565.2	4 716.2	4 806.1	4 753.1	4 728.9	4 580.1	4 524.3	4 654.8	4 730.3	4 790.9	4 915.1
Rhode Island	349.2	366.7	381.7	395.8	400.0	398.3	401.4	390.5	396.3	416.4	429.2	442.5	451.9
South Carolina	982.6	1 038.1	1 081.7	1 137.5	1 176.0	1 188.8	1 196.4	1 162.3	1 189.0	1 262.5	1 296.2	1 338.0	1 392.2
South Dakota	209.3	218.6	226.6	236.6	241.4	238.0	236.0	230.2	235.3	247.0	249.4	251.9	256.9
Tennessee	1 505.7	1 575.4	1 648.1	1 737.0	1 777.3	1 746.6	1 755.4	1 703.0	1 719.0	1 812.0	1 867.8	1 929.8	2 011.6
Texas	4 462.9	4 683.7	4 906.8	5 271.6	5 601.8	5 851.2	6 180.0	6 263.4	6 193.6	6 492.4	6 663.1	6 564.2	6 516.9
Utah	440.3	462.8	488.7	525.4	548.4	550.8	558.0	560.9	566.9	601.2	624.3	634.1	640.0
Vermont	162.1	168.4	178.4	190.6	197.9	200.1	204.3	202.9	206.4	214.9	224.7	234.4	245.6
Virginia	1 778.7	1 848.1	1 930.4	2 033.5	2 115.0	2 157.2	2 160.8	2 146.4	2 206.9	2 333.3	2 454.7	2 557.7	2 680.4
Washington	1 225.7	1 282.9	1 367.0	1 485.4	1 581.2	1 608.3	1 612.0	1 568.6	1 586.1	1 659.6	1 710.4	1 769.9	1 851.8
West Virginia	574.7	596.3	611.6	633.1	658.6	645.9	628.5	607.8	582.3	596.6	597.2	597.5	599.0
Wisconsin	1 676.8	1 725.9	1 798.9	1 887.0	1 960.2	1 938.1	1 923.2	1 866.7	1 867.3	1 949.2	1 983.1	2 023.9	2 089.6
Wyoming	146.0	156.5	170.5	187.4	200.7	210.2	223.5	217.7	202.5	204.3	206.9	196.3	182.6
Puerto Rico	. . .	. . .	. . .	. . .	. . .	693.1	679.7	641.6	645.6	684.2	692.5	728.0	763.8
Virgin Islands	33.1	31.3	32.2	33.8	36.1	37.3	37.7	36.5	36.4	36.6	36.9	37.7	39.6

See footnote at end of table.

Table 2-15. Employees on Total Nonfarm Payrolls by State, 1962–2000—*Continued*

(Thousands of persons.)

State	1988	1989	1990	1991	1992	1993	1994	1995	1996	1997	1998	1999	2000
Alabama	1 558.7	1 601.2	1 635.7	1 642.0	1 674.5	1 716.8	1 758.5	1 803.6	1 828.6	1 866.3	1 898.1	1 919.5	1 933.6
Alaska	213.7	227.0	238.1	242.8	247.2	252.9	259.3	262.0	263.6	268.7	275.0	277.8	284.0
Arizona	1 419.3	1 454.5	1 483.0	1 491.4	1 517.0	1 584.4	1 692.1	1 795.7	1 892.3	1 984.6	2 074.7	2 163.1	2 248.0
Arkansas	865.4	893.4	923.5	936.4	963.1	994.0	1 034.1	1 069.4	1 086.0	1 104.0	1 122.2	1 141.7	1 161.6
California	11 911.5	12 238.5	12 499.9	12 359.0	12 153.5	12 045.3	12 159.5	12 422.2	12 743.4	13 129.7	13 596.1	13 991.8	14 518.6
Colorado	1 436.1	1 482.3	1 520.9	1 545.0	1 596.9	1 670.7	1 755.9	1 834.4	1 900.4	1 979.5	2 057.0	2 131.8	2 214.8
Connecticut	1 667.4	1 665.6	1 623.5	1 555.2	1 526.2	1 531.1	1 543.7	1 561.5	1 583.6	1 612.6	1 643.4	1 669.1	1 693.4
Delaware	334.2	344.5	347.6	341.8	341.3	348.6	356.0	366.4	376.4	387.9	400.2	412.9	420.9
District of Columbia	673.6	680.6	686.1	677.3	673.6	670.3	658.8	642.6	623.1	618.4	613.6	627.4	646.8
Florida	5 066.6	5 260.9	5 387.4	5 294.3	5 358.7	5 571.4	5 799.4	[1]5 996.1	6 183.3	6 414.4	6 636.5	6 827.0	7 076.4
Georgia	2 875.9	2 941.1	2 991.8	2 937.5	2 987.2	3 109.2	3 265.9	3 402.3	3 527.4	3 614.4	3 740.8	3 883.1	3 993.3
Hawaii	478.1	505.5	528.4	539.1	542.8	538.8	536.2	532.8	530.7	531.6	531.3	535.0	551.5
Idaho	348.5	365.8	384.9	398.1	416.4	436.5	460.9	477.3	492.9	509.9	521.8	538.9	560.0
Illinois	5 097.5	5 213.9	5 288.3	5 231.5	5 234.9	5 330.5	5 462.9	5 593.1	5 684.7	5 772.1	5 898.5	5 958.3	6 029.0
Indiana	2 395.6	2 479.3	2 521.9	2 507.3	2 554.2	2 626.9	2 712.7	2 786.5	2 814.4	2 858.6	2 917.3	2 969.9	3 010.3
Iowa	1 156.2	1 200.1	1 226.3	1 238.1	1 252.6	1 278.6	1 319.9	1 358.1	1 383.4	1 407.0	1 442.8	1 468.6	1 478.4
Kansas	1 035.4	1 064.2	1 088.5	1 095.4	1 115.0	1 133.3	1 165.8	1 198.0	1 226.7	1 268.2	1 312.2	1 327.0	1 345.7
Kentucky	1 381.9	1 433.0	1 470.5	1 474.7	1 508.5	1 547.9	1 597.2	1 642.8	1 671.7	1 711.2	1 752.8	1 795.5	1 824.7
Louisiana	1 511.6	1 538.5	1 589.9	1 613.0	1 626.9	1 658.6	1 722.1	1 772.4	1 809.7	1 849.9	1 889.5	1 896.2	1 931.3
Maine	527.1	541.8	534.9	513.4	511.9	519.4	531.6	538.2	542.5	553.7	569.2	586.3	604.1
Maryland	2 102.3	2 155.2	2 171.2	2 099.8	2 081.3	2 102.4	2 145.8	2 182.7	2 211.2	2 267.1	2 324.4	2 386.5	2 449.1
Massachusetts	3 130.8	3 108.6	2 984.8	2 821.2	2 795.1	2 840.2	2 903.8	2 976.6	3 035.4	3 109.2	3 178.6	3 236.8	3 319.2
Michigan	3 819.2	3 922.3	3 969.6	3 891.1	3 927.4	4 005.8	4 146.8	4 273.9	4 360.7	4 448.2	4 510.1	4 582.0	4 679.3
Minnesota	2 028.1	2 086.8	2 126.7	2 136.8	2 184.9	2 242.7	2 310.4	2 378.6	2 433.3	2 490.8	2 555.1	2 613.0	2 669.0
Mississippi	896.2	919.3	936.6	937.5	960.3	1 002.3	1 055.5	1 074.5	1 088.9	1 107.1	1 133.7	1 153.2	1 157.1
Missouri	2 258.9	2 315.0	2 345.0	2 309.1	2 333.7	2 394.5	2 470.5	2 520.9	2 567.4	2 639.4	2 684.0	2 726.6	2 757.6
Montana	282.9	291.0	297.3	303.7	316.6	325.6	340.2	350.8	360.3	364.9	373.0	380.4	389.1
Nebraska	688.1	708.0	730.1	739.2	750.1	767.2	796.1	816.4	834.8	854.3	876.3	892.7	909.5
Nevada	537.6	581.2	620.9	628.7	638.7	671.4	738.0	786.1	843.0	890.7	925.9	982.9	1 028.7
New Hampshire	529.0	529.1	508.0	482.1	487.0	502.4	523.1	539.7	553.6	570.2	589.0	605.8	620.7
New Jersey	3 651.0	3 689.8	3 635.1	3 498.7	3 457.9	3 493.1	3 552.8	3 600.7	3 638.9	3 724.6	3 801.3	3 901.1	3 996.2
New Mexico	547.5	562.2	580.4	585.4	601.5	626.2	657.2	682.4	694.6	708.5	720.0	729.6	743.9
New York	8 186.9	8 246.8	8 212.4	7 886.7	7 730.3	7 759.8	7 831.4	7 892.2	7 938.7	8 067.1	8 236.7	8 455.4	8 632.3
North Carolina	2 986.6	3 073.9	3 117.7	3 072.2	3 125.5	3 244.7	3 358.9	3 459.5	3 546.5	3 663.2	3 773.8	3 870.4	3 946.8
North Dakota	256.7	260.4	265.9	270.6	277.2	284.8	294.9	301.8	308.7	314.1	319.5	323.9	327.3
Ohio	4 700.6	4 817.4	4 882.3	4 818.6	4 847.7	4 918.3	5 076.0	5 221.0	5 296.4	5 392.4	5 482.2	5 563.5	5 642.1
Oklahoma	1 131.5	1 163.8	1 195.9	1 211.0	1 221.7	1 247.0	1 279.5	1 316.1	1 353.5	1 392.5	1 441.2	1 461.9	1 484.9
Oregon	1 152.8	1 205.8	1 247.1	1 244.7	1 267.6	1 308.4	1 362.9	1 418.4	1 474.6	1 526.4	1 551.8	1 575.0	1 603.3
Pennsylvania	5 041.7	5 138.5	5 170.1	5 083.7	5 075.5	5 122.8	5 192.4	5 253.1	5 306.2	5 406.5	5 494.9	5 586.1	5 698.4
Rhode Island	459.4	461.9	451.2	421.5	424.8	430.0	434.2	440.1	441.6	450.0	458.0	465.5	475.7
South Carolina	1 449.0	1 499.7	1 545.0	1 513.4	1 527.7	1 570.1	1 607.2	1 646.1	1 675.2	1 720.2	1 783.3	1 830.6	1 876.7
South Dakota	266.1	276.0	288.7	296.4	308.7	318.7	332.0	343.5	348.7	354.9	363.2	373.2	379.1
Tennessee	2 092.1	2 167.2	2 193.2	2 183.6	2 245.0	2 328.5	2 423.0	2 499.0	2 533.4	2 584.0	2 638.5	2 685.4	2 737.5
Texas	6 677.8	6 840.0	7 095.4	7 174.7	7 269.1	7 481.5	7 750.9	8 022.5	8 256.1	8 608.0	8 940.1	9 159.2	9 444.3
Utah	660.0	691.1	723.6	745.2	768.7	809.8	859.7	907.7	954.5	993.8	1 023.3	1 048.6	1 077.1
Vermont	256.1	261.8	257.5	248.9	251.0	257.2	263.8	270.0	274.9	279.2	284.8	291.3	298.2
Virginia	2 772.5	2 861.9	2 896.3	2 828.9	2 848.4	2 918.9	3 003.6	3 069.7	3 136.0	3 231.8	3 320.0	3 412.4	3 507.2
Washington	1 941.4	2 046.8	2 143.0	2 177.4	2 222.4	2 253.0	2 304.3	2 346.9	2 415.6	2 514.2	2 594.9	2 648.7	2 716.8
West Virginia	609.8	614.7	630.1	629.1	640.0	652.6	674.6	687.8	698.6	707.8	719.2	726.0	735.6
Wisconsin	2 168.5	2 236.4	2 291.5	2 302.0	2 357.9	2 412.7	2 490.8	2 558.5	2 600.5	2 655.7	2 718.0	2 783.9	2 834.2
Wyoming	189.0	192.8	198.5	203.1	205.6	210.3	216.8	219.4	221.1	224.5	228.3	233.0	239.3
Puerto Rico	817.8	837.4	843.8	835.6	855.8	869.4	895.8	927.3	970.6	986.8	994.4	1 009.0	1 012.4
Virgin Islands	41.5	42.0	43.1	43.8	44.8	48.6	44.6	42.1	41.3	41.5	41.7	41.1	42.1

1. Data not continuous.

Table 2-16. Employees on Manufacturing Payrolls by State, 1962–2000

(Thousands of persons.)

State	1962	1963	1964	1965	1966	1967	1968	1969	1970	1971	1972	1973	1974
Alabama	242.2	249.4	259.2	279.2	296.9	300.6	310.0	327.3	327.2	322.7	333.4	350.9	353.7
Alaska	5.5	5.7	5.6	6.3	6.6	6.6	6.9	7.3	8.6	7.8	8.1	9.5	9.7
Arizona	55.2	58.0	59.5	64.9	77.7	79.1	84.9	94.2	91.2	89.2	98.7	110.2	112.9
Arkansas	114.0	119.4	126.7	135.9	149.7	153.4	159.0	169.1	168.6	172.5	185.2	200.4	203.9
California	1 382.5	1 394.3	1 389.4	1 411.2	1 531.3	1 594.0	1 639.7	1 661.3	1 558.0	1 473.2	1 542.7	1 660.7	1 701.3
Colorado	96.1	96.4	93.5	92.6	102.7	106.1	110.5	118.3	120.8	123.5	131.5	143.3	146.6
Connecticut	418.3	420.8	421.0	436.1	471.4	479.5	474.3	471.7	441.9	399.0	400.1	420.2	430.9
Delaware	56.1	59.1	61.9	67.8	71.0	71.7	72.9	73.6	71.1	68.8	69.4	73.7	70.8
District of Columbia	20.6	20.6	20.7	21.1	21.7	22.0	21.4	20.8	19.3	18.5	17.8	17.4	17.0
Florida	223.1	229.3	237.9	252.6	276.1	293.8	311.4	329.2	322.5	322.7	351.3	380.6	375.9
Georgia	350.5	363.8	378.9	403.9	431.5	438.9	452.9	477.6	467.1	461.7	476.6	494.5	483.7
Hawaii	25.0	25.0	25.2	24.5	24.2	24.7	23.8	25.2	25.6	25.2	24.9	23.8	22.7
Idaho	30.5	30.4	31.8	33.3	35.6	35.3	37.9	39.9	40.3	41.2	43.6	46.9	48.0
Illinois	1 214.0	1 218.6	1 253.3	1 318.4	1 410.5	1 409.6	1 404.0	1 417.4	1 358.6	1 282.4	1 284.2	1 353.5	1 345.1
Indiana	601.8	614.5	630.9	673.6	719.7	716.0	722.9	752.3	710.2	683.4	709.4	758.2	737.2
Iowa	174.8	179.0	183.5	192.9	212.1	219.3	223.1	225.4	216.0	209.8	222.9	241.3	249.9
Kansas	120.4	117.9	123.1	124.7	142.3	149.3	151.0	150.6	137.2	132.5	145.7	164.5	169.2
Kentucky	176.4	184.7	194.0	207.8	228.6	234.2	242.9	250.4	255.4	253.3	268.3	288.3	290.9
Louisiana	141.9	148.9	155.4	161.1	168.3	176.7	181.9	184.6	179.0	177.7	183.2	190.5	192.5
Maine	104.3	102.8	104.0	108.0	115.0	116.3	118.0	115.7	110.4	102.7	102.4	104.5	105.1
Maryland	258.6	260.4	258.2	264.8	279.8	283.3	280.6	281.7	271.4	252.4	248.8	257.0	254.5
Massachusetts	687.6	663.5	649.9	668.2	699.1	700.8	689.5	681.5	648.2	605.7	610.2	634.7	639.3
Michigan	952.2	989.6	1 032.0	1 112.4	1 179.6	1 148.8	1 172.5	1 203.8	1 081.1	1 059.2	1 097.4	1 178.8	1 114.0
Minnesota	239.1	242.1	246.4	261.6	287.4	302.2	314.7	331.4	318.7	298.8	310.2	331.2	340.7
Mississippi	128.0	134.5	140.4	153.0	166.6	167.4	175.5	182.5	182.1	189.5	207.7	221.0	220.0
Missouri	390.3	396.8	405.7	420.1	448.7	457.4	462.7	465.7	449.4	430.3	441.5	459.7	451.6
Montana	21.9	22.3	21.4	22.1	22.9	22.4	23.2	24.1	23.9	23.9	24.5	24.8	24.5
Nebraska	67.6	66.2	67.2	68.7	74.7	79.7	82.8	86.2	84.5	82.6	85.0	90.5	93.4
Nevada	6.0	6.8	6.9	7.1	7.1	6.8	7.1	8.2	8.6	8.8	9.8	11.8	12.3
New Hampshire	88.6	85.9	85.6	89.8	96.0	97.6	99.7	97.9	91.6	86.3	90.8	96.0	94.2
New Jersey	812.8	[illegible]	[illegible]	837.5	879.3	882.8	893.7	892.5	860.7	818.3	823.3	842.6	825.9
New Mexico	17.6	17.2	17.9	17.6	18.6	[illegible]	18.5	20.7	21.4	22.6	26.1	28.9	29.6
New York	1 837.9	1 804.1	1 794.8	1 838.1	1 894.5	1 885.7	1 879.0	1 870.8	1 760.6	[illegible]	[illegible]	[illegible]	1 574.6
North Carolina	525.6	537.0	557.1	590.6	638.1	657.5	686.1	714.0	713.0	716.2	756.8	796.9	789.6
North Dakota	7.0	7.8	8.4	8.7	8.9	8.6	8.9	9.0	9.9	10.2	10.8	12.6	14.7
Ohio	1 218.2	1 236.6	1 259.1	1 326.0	1 404.4	1 401.4	1 433.5	1 471.0	1 409.9	1 333.8	1 346.8	1 426.3	1 416.6
Oklahoma	90.4	90.9	96.6	103.0	113.3	116.4	121.7	129.9	134.1	132.7	141.1	151.9	156.7
Oregon	143.4	145.1	151.7	158.2	167.2	165.4	173.7	180.5	172.3	174.3	184.2	196.9	197.1
Pennsylvania	1 403.9	1 401.0	1 434.8	1 494.1	1 565.3	1 562.4	1 570.0	1 588.9	1 528.8	1 438.1	1 444.0	1 480.1	1 464.5
Rhode Island	118.9	115.5	116.0	121.0	127.6	127.4	127.4	127.9	120.9	115.2	121.0	125.6	126.0
South Carolina	260.1	269.6	277.7	293.0	313.7	319.0	327.3	341.5	340.3	337.2	354.3	374.9	375.9
South Dakota	14.0	14.8	13.3	13.5	14.3	15.4	15.9	15.9	15.8	16.5	18.4	19.8	20.9
Tennessee	331.6	344.7	361.5	386.6	424.2	434.8	454.3	469.0	463.8	459.5	489.2	519.4	513.3
Texas	502.1	516.5	540.5	572.1	622.1	661.9	709.4	750.2	734.3	710.5	738.7	790.2	831.3
Utah	54.3	55.5	52.5	50.0	51.2	50.9	51.9	54.8	56.0	56.5	60.5	65.1	70.4
Vermont	35.6	34.9	34.7	38.6	43.4	44.2	43.7	43.4	40.5	37.9	38.5	41.6	42.8
Virginia	292.4	297.5	308.6	322.5	340.0	346.0	362.7	371.0	366.0	366.2	387.8	401.8	401.9
Washington	232.6	224.0	219.3	227.0	265.2	277.1	286.9	278.5	239.5	214.7	224.1	244.2	253.6
West Virginia	122.6	124.2	126.2	129.2	133.0	133.2	132.4	131.0	126.5	122.9	123.3	129.0	132.1
Wisconsin	455.9	461.4	469.6	491.9	508.6	508.7	510.3	520.9	500.9	479.6	495.4	531.7	546.1
Wyoming	7.5	7.2	7.7	7.1	6.8	7.1	6.8	7.4	7.4	7.5	7.9	8.4	8.4
Puerto Rico	. . .	. . .	. . .	. . .	. . .	. . .	. . .	. . .	. . .	. . .	. . .	. . .	. . .
Virgin Islands	. . .	. . .	. . .	. . .	. . .	. . .	. . .	. . .	. . .	. . .	. . .	. . .	. . .

See footnote at end of table.

Table 2-16. Employees on Manufacturing Payrolls by State, 1962–2000—*Continued*

(Thousands of persons.)

State	1975	1976	1977	1978	1979	1980	1981	1982	1983	1984	1985	1986	1987
Alabama	321.9	340.2	354.3	368.9	374.9	363.1	362.0	337.8	340.9	359.8	358.1	358.6	368.8
Alaska	9.6	10.3	10.9	11.6	12.7	13.4	14.0	12.6	11.9	11.3	12.1	12.6	12.9
Arizona	99.8	105.6	113.9	126.9	144.1	154.4	160.6	154.5	155.8	172.8	181.6	184.6	187.4
Arkansas	179.2	195.1	209.3	217.5	217.8	209.1	209.7	195.2	200.3	213.0	209.6	211.8	219.6
California	1 593.7	1 659.8	1 737.8	1 884.6	2 012.7	2 018.2	2 032.3	1 957.7	1 927.0	2 004.1	2 024.2	2 039.1	2 060.1
Colorado	137.2	144.5	152.8	168.2	180.6	180.4	186.2	183.3	180.7	195.3	192.2	185.3	184.5
Connecticut	389.8	397.0	406.7	419.6	436.5	440.8	439.0	418.7	403.2	415.1	408.0	394.0	384.2
Delaware	65.7	68.2	67.6	69.0	70.2	70.9	71.0	67.9	68.2	70.6	72.2	68.7	70.5
District of Columbia	15.5	15.3	14.8	15.0	15.3	15.4	14.5	13.7	14.2	14.5	14.8	15.7	16.1
Florida	339.4	354.0	380.9	415.5	443.6	456.4	472.2	456.7	464.3	501.9	514.4	517.2	531.0
Georgia	439.3	476.3	494.1	515.8	528.5	519.2	524.6	500.3	511.1	546.5	557.1	564.6	571.2
Hawaii	23.7	23.4	23.2	23.7	24.0	23.3	23.0	22.4	22.4	21.9	21.9	22.0	21.9
Idaho	47.8	52.0	54.1	58.1	58.3	53.3	52.7	47.8	51.4	54.8	54.7	52.1	54.3
Illinois	1 199.8	1 215.2	1 241.3	1 276.0	1 271.6	1 208.2	1 131.4	1 013.4	955.8	997.0	970.7	925.8	940.2
Indiana	647.2	685.1	713.2	741.5	733.2	657.0	652.6	589.0	581.6	620.5	609.8	604.0	616.6
Iowa	230.4	234.0	245.6	252.5	259.8	244.8	236.5	209.8	202.3	211.9	204.7	201.7	213.5
Kansas	164.2	166.6	172.9	185.9	198.9	190.5	188.6	168.8	164.7	176.4	174.4	175.7	176.2
Kentucky	259.7	273.3	284.9	292.2	297.2	276.2	270.5	244.8	242.5	257.4	255.3	253.8	262.5
Louisiana	186.2	195.4	203.3	209.5	213.6	214.2	222.1	202.6	180.1	182.4	178.0	166.0	164.5
Maine	96.3	102.5	105.9	111.3	114.6	113.2	113.5	108.6	109.2	110.6	105.9	103.6	104.1
Maryland	230.0	232.4	235.1	241.5	246.9	236.7	231.7	215.3	214.1	219.4	217.2	210.2	208.4
Massachusetts	577.8	593.6	621.0	652.1	672.8	673.3	668.0	636.5	629.0	667.6	649.7	614.4	599.1
Michigan	983.7	1 061.7	1 128.4	1 179.6	1 160.2	998.9	979.0	876.9	880.5	962.8	1 002.4	1 000.4	972.5
Minnesota	313.0	321.7	339.3	360.4	381.6	371.2	364.0	346.8	346.4	373.8	375.4	369.1	376.4
Mississippi	201.8	218.9	230.1	235.3	235.2	221.8	220.3	203.2	204.7	218.7	221.6	223.7	228.6
Missouri	405.3	424.9	439.6	456.8	464.4	437.0	427.5	406.8	405.4	433.8	430.3	424.7	424.0
Montana	22.1	23.7	25.1	26.3	27.0	24.2	23.2	20.6	22.1	22.5	21.8	21.1	20.8
Nebraska	85.4	87.9	90.6	94.1	99.6	96.4	94.9	87.9	84.7	90.5	88.4	86.0	88.6
Nevada	12.2	13.0	15.1	17.8	19.4	19.2	20.1	18.8	19.1	21.0	21.9	22.3	23.3
New Hampshire	85.1	94.5	101.4	109.8	116.5	116.6	116.6	111.7	113.3	123.4	122.5	118.1	117.5
New Jersey	747.9	756.2	767.4	786.8	799.1	781.0	771.1	729.6	715.1	726.7	712.8	689.7	672.2
New Mexico	28.6	30.3	32.2	33.4	34.8	34.4	34.3	34.1	34.4	36.5	37.3	37.4	38.3
New York	1 421.9	1 438.9	1 459.6	1 481.2	1 492.8	1 445.1	1 433.3	1 352.5	1 302.4	1 326.3	1 293.1	1 251.6	1 217.9
North Carolina	715.5	756.3	780.9	807.2	826.8	820.0	820.7	782.2	796.1	835.6	828.6	832.8	856.0
North Dakota	16.2	16.2	15.3	15.7	16.7	15.6	15.3	14.9	14.8	15.5	15.4	15.3	15.8
Ohio	1 267.5	1 295.3	1 344.1	1 377.2	1 382.3	1 264.3	1 232.6	1 099.9	1 066.0	1 127.0	1 124.2	1 109.8	1 098.9
Oklahoma	150.7	156.1	163.2	172.7	184.4	191.3	200.0	180.6	166.2	175.0	172.0	160.4	156.8
Oregon	182.3	193.7	206.1	219.1	228.3	215.1	202.7	185.7	188.8	201.1	199.3	198.4	206.2
Pennsylvania	1 334.8	1 335.2	1 341.9	1 367.8	1 386.8	1 328.2	1 299.0	1 170.5	1 095.8	1 121.9	1 089.5	1 048.9	1 044.0
Rhode Island	112.7	122.9	128.8	134.4	132.6	128.2	127.7	116.6	116.2	121.7	119.2	118.9	116.3
South Carolina	339.9	371.0	380.2	391.1	399.5	391.9	390.2	364.3	362.4	377.6	365.4	365.2	374.0
South Dakota	19.8	22.2	23.4	24.9	27.5	26.1	25.9	24.8	26.0	29.2	27.5	28.2	29.3
Tennessee	459.0	486.1	507.5	526.0	524.7	502.1	506.9	466.7	468.6	497.1	492.4	490.5	497.4
Texas	815.9	862.3	893.5	962.8	1 021.9	1 056.9	1 115.3	1 045.2	963.7	1 004.3	998.6	951.1	932.0
Utah	67.5	70.7	74.5	80.3	86.8	87.7	89.6	85.7	85.5	94.0	94.0	92.0	92.1
Vermont	39.5	41.0	43.4	47.7	50.8	50.9	51.3	48.6	47.6	49.0	49.8	49.5	49.6
Virginia	371.5	387.7	400.8	409.4	413.8	413.8	414.0	397.2	403.6	421.3	423.4	424.7	428.9
Washington	244.0	247.4	260.0	284.7	309.6	308.7	305.2	289.0	278.4	288.1	295.6	305.0	318.4
West Virginia	121.1	124.4	123.8	126.6	126.1	117.2	111.5	98.1	89.8	91.5	89.5	86.8	86.2
Wisconsin	507.0	519.4	540.4	569.7	591.3	558.0	543.5	498.2	486.7	518.9	513.9	514.5	528.7
Wyoming	8.3	8.4	9.0	9.6	10.1	9.6	9.9	9.1	8.2	8.0	8.0	7.9	8.2
Puerto Rico	. . .	. . .	. . .	. . .	. . .	154.6	153.1	142.7	143.7	150.1	147.5	148.8	151.3
Virgin Islands	3.1	3.1	3.1	2.9	3.2	3.2	3.1	2.7	2.5	2.3	2.2	1.8	2.1

See footnote at end of table.

Table 2-16. Employees on Manufacturing Payrolls by State, 1962–2000—*Continued*

(Thousands of persons.)

State	1988	1989	1990	1991	1992	1993	1994	1995	1996	1997	1998	1999	2000
Alabama	380.6	385.6	384.5	379.3	380.7	384.2	386.4	391.8	382.6	380.5	377.8	367.6	360.9
Alaska	15.0	15.7	17.2	18.0	18.0	17.1	16.6	16.9	15.9	15.2	14.4	14.4	13.8
Arizona	189.0	188.2	185.3	176.1	173.2	176.5	186.4	194.0	199.9	207.4	216.0	211.7	214.9
Arkansas	226.3	231.0	232.8	233.7	237.0	244.3	254.0	259.3	253.8	252.9	253.5	252.1	251.3
California	2 096.7	2 107.0	2 068.8	1 970.9	1 890.5	1 805.1	1 777.3	1 794.2	1 851.8	1 914.0	1 951.0	1 923.0	1 944.1
Colorado	189.6	193.4	193.2	185.6	185.9	188.1	190.9	192.4	197.1	204.0	207.4	204.6	205.2
Connecticut	372.3	359.3	341.0	322.5	305.7	294.1	285.1	279.0	274.8	276.1	276.9	268.4	262.3
Delaware	70.3	73.1	71.8	70.1	67.4	65.6	63.5	61.5	57.9	57.8	59.7	59.8	58.6
District of Columbia	16.3	15.8	15.7	14.6	14.0	13.8	13.0	13.0	13.0	12.7	12.2	11.6	11.4
Florida	539.6	537.9	522.1	492.8	482.9	485.2	484.0	486.5	489.7	492.0	493.5	487.7	486.6
Georgia	574.3	568.3	561.1	541.0	545.2	558.2	577.3	586.9	585.4	588.6	594.6	596.7	587.3
Hawaii	22.0	21.5	21.1	20.5	19.7	19.2	17.8	17.0	16.7	16.6	16.4	16.5	17.2
Idaho	57.9	60.5	62.9	63.3	65.7	69.2	71.9	71.0	72.9	74.6	76.1	76.3	76.8
Illinois	975.2	986.6	982.7	940.8	919.3	933.1	952.1	962.2	969.7	973.1	974.8	954.9	944.4
Indiana	636.7	646.3	638.0	618.7	628.6	642.9	664.4	683.8	676.0	676.7	684.9	690.2	687.8
Iowa	226.4	234.8	236.4	232.5	230.2	236.1	244.9	250.3	248.7	253.3	261.3	261.0	261.1
Kansas	181.6	184.4	186.0	183.9	182.7	183.5	187.9	191.4	196.7	206.6	214.1	213.1	210.1
Kentucky	274.1	284.2	287.5	281.4	286.9	294.6	305.1	313.8	311.7	316.8	320.3	320.7	321.8
Louisiana	171.5	176.3	184.4	186.4	185.0	185.4	186.5	188.0	188.6	191.1	191.0	187.1	183.5
Maine	108.0	105.5	101.9	95.2	92.2	90.9	91.4	91.1	88.3	87.8	87.1	86.2	85.2
Maryland	210.2	209.8	205.9	191.7	183.7	180.2	178.2	176.0	175.0	176.9	178.2	177.9	179.7
Massachusetts	584.7	561.1	521.3	485.0	465.7	454.8	447.2	446.1	444.7	447.9	448.2	433.6	435.7
Michigan	955.4	971.3	943.6	896.7	900.6	908.3	951.5	979.7	971.7	966.3	969.7	981.8	979.8
Minnesota	394.1	399.8	400.8	395.2	397.1	406.5	414.7	425.8	429.6	435.0	441.2	439.0	439.9
Mississippi	238.8	243.6	246.5	246.9	251.9	255.7	261.0	257.8	245.6	241.8	245.5	243.9	233.9
Missouri	433.9	440.6	438.1	415.6	412.0	411.1	414.1	420.8	416.6	418.0	418.4	411.8	403.4
Montana	21.3	22.3	22.3	21.7	22.5	23.0	23.0	23.4	23.9	24.1	24.2	24.5	24.8
Nebraska	93.6	94.7	97.8	99.6	100.7	103.8	108.8	112.2	113.6	116.4	118.9	118.2	119.9
Nevada	24.9	25.4	26.2	25.9	26.1	29.5	33.7	36.6	38.7	40.7	41.9	42.6	44.4
New Hampshire	117.9	113.6	105.6	98.2	97.4	97.6	100.3	102.6	104.4	107.2	108.6	106.6	105.7
New Jersey	662.1	639.6	596.6	558.4	530.3	516.6	509.3	499.2	483.5	481.9	476.6	466.7	462.4
New Mexico	40.4	42.6	43.4	41.8	41.0	42.7	44.7	45.1	46.0	46.2	44.7	42.4	42.8
New York	1 212.5	1 189.0	1 101.4	1 050.6	1 014.4	980.5	956.1	941.7	924.4	920.8	911.7	890.3	874.2
North Carolina	867.5	871.1	861.5	826.1	834.4	847.8	859.9	864.2	844.9	833.7	824.2	801.0	782.1
North Dakota	16.4	16.5	17.4	17.9	18.3	19.5	21.4	21.3	21.6	23.4	24.0	24.1	25.0
Ohio	1 110.6	1 122.6	1 112.3	1 066.9	1 050.6	1 049.7	1 070.2	1 102.3	1 093.9	1 091.8	1 096.6	1 090.4	1 085.4
Oklahoma	161.4	164.4	168.8	168.8	163.8	168.6	169.8	170.7	174.1	180.9	185.9	183.8	182.2
Oregon	214.2	218.4	220.3	211.7	209.0	211.7	221.3	229.3	235.8	243.6	246.1	242.2	243.0
Pennsylvania	1 055.2	1 047.0	1 019.0	973.0	953.0	943.1	942.0	940.7	929.6	938.1	943.2	930.4	926.0
Rhode Island	112.4	108.3	99.7	91.7	89.5	88.1	86.8	84.9	82.1	79.8	78.0	74.8	72.9
South Carolina	385.0	389.6	383.3	369.2	371.0	374.8	377.4	377.2	366.0	362.7	362.1	344.6	347.2
South Dakota	31.6	32.3	34.4	35.0	37.0	39.6	43.5	46.6	47.8	49.4	49.7	50.1	50.0
Tennessee	511.9	524.5	520.3	502.7	514.5	528.4	538.9	538.9	519.3	517.6	514.7	511.0	508.4
Texas	962.6	979.1	997.4	981.0	969.6	987.6	1 009.0	1 032.8	1 056.2	1 083.9	1 107.2	1 084.4	1 086.1
Utah	99.0	103.1	107.3	105.8	106.9	110.7	116.7	124.2	129.5	133.0	132.5	132.0	131.2
Vermont	49.7	48.6	46.4	44.2	43.7	43.6	43.9	45.1	45.9	46.6	47.9	47.9	48.9
Virginia	427.4	429.6	426.4	412.0	407.4	405.1	404.3	402.9	400.0	405.2	403.4	395.7	388.8
Washington	341.6	361.6	369.4	351.9	347.7	340.8	336.9	332.4	344.7	370.0	379.5	364.2	350.3
West Virginia	87.0	87.8	87.5	83.2	82.2	82.9	81.6	82.4	81.9	81.6	82.4	81.6	80.7
Wisconsin	551.5	558.5	558.6	546.2	549.6	561.8	583.9	601.6	601.1	608.8	618.6	617.6	616.6
Wyoming	8.7	8.9	9.5	9.3	9.3	9.6	9.9	9.7	[1]10.8	10.8	11.0	11.1	11.4
Puerto Rico	154.5	157.3	154.9	151.6	151.7	150.2	151.0	153.7	153.3	152.3	147.6	143.4	140.9
Virgin Islands	2.4	2.3	2.4	2.7	2.8	2.8	2.9	2.5	2.3	2.2	2.4	2.4	2.5

1. Data not continuous.

Table 2-17. Employees on Government Payrolls by State, 1962–2000

(Thousands of persons.)

State	1962	1963	1964	1965	1966	1967	1968	1969	1970	1971	1972	1973	1974
Alabama	167.8	170.0	173.3	179.1	191.6	197.7	201.4	204.7	209.5	213.6	220.9	225.7	235.1
Alaska	25.0	27.1	28.1	29.7	30.8	31.8	32.2	33.3	35.6	37.9	40.5	41.5	43.8
Arizona	77.7	81.6	85.3	92.2	98.9	104.7	110.0	113.4	119.5	129.5	139.2	147.6	161.0
Arkansas	76.1	74.6	76.5	84.9	91.6	93.4	97.0	100.9	102.7	104.9	108.5	110.1	115.6
California	962.8	1 001.6	1 043.5	1 105.4	1 196.7	1 274.3	1 335.8	1 391.7	1 424.7	1 446.3	1 492.7	1 524.8	1 586.0
Colorado	123.5	128.6	132.0	137.7	148.2	157.7	162.4	166.9	177.2	184.7	190.8	197.2	204.0
Connecticut	98.7	103.3	109.0	115.9	122.5	131.5	140.0	150.9	157.9	160.9	165.2	167.7	171.0
Delaware	20.9	22.6	23.9	25.0	26.3	27.9	29.3	31.9	35.0	36.8	39.0	39.2	39.1
District of Columbia	240.8	249.5	251.3	262.7	274.6	278.0	264.6	254.4	249.7	256.7	260.2	259.6	265.3
Florida	247.4	262.5	278.7	301.2	326.2	342.3	361.8	377.9	397.8	419.1	437.9	469.9	510.5
Georgia	197.2	204.0	210.8	222.8	243.9	263.0	275.3	286.1	297.5	309.6	320.9	328.2	340.5
Hawaii	51.2	52.9	54.4	57.8	62.6	66.3	69.1	71.1	73.7	78.2	79.4	78.0	78.8
Idaho	36.4	37.8	38.1	39.6	41.9	44.3	45.2	46.8	49.1	51.3	54.5	56.2	59.7
Illinois	447.0	459.3	475.0	502.4	536.5	572.0	593.4	615.6	638.9	648.6	654.3	666.5	680.9
Indiana	201.3	209.7	219.2	232.2	254.1	271.4	285.3	280.9	286.4	296.3	301.4	303.8	308.0
Iowa	125.4	129.5	133.1	138.8	148.8	157.1	163.8	171.7	176.0	178.3	180.2	182.8	186.7
Kansas	118.9	120.6	126.2	130.2	137.0	143.2	146.0	149.6	153.3	155.1	162.8	166.5	164.0
Kentucky	120.2	125.2	128.4	135.2	145.2	155.5	163.3	166.1	172.1	180.5	188.5	194.3	198.5
Louisiana	154.4	158.3	163.4	171.7	185.4	197.4	201.8	208.2	213.2	216.0	227.9	233.2	241.6
Maine	50.3	51.5	52.9	54.3	57.4	59.5	61.6	64.3	66.4	68.7	69.4	70.7	72.9
Maryland	159.4	166.0	174.1	183.8	201.9	218.2	232.3	243.2	301.0	314.9	327.0	338.1	349.1
Massachusetts	261.7	267.5	272.7	278.5	286.2	297.1	302.5	310.7	319.9	330.6	343.1	351.6	354.3
Michigan	343.2	359.8	373.3	395.4	433.0	455.0	471.3	494.5	506.6	509.4	526.8	534.4	562.5
Minnesota	162.2	171.8	179.3	189.9	201.6	214.1	215.4	224.1	234.9	239.7	246.2	256.6	263.8
Mississippi	94.2	97.2	99.5	105.2	114.3	120.6	125.1	128.0	131.2	133.7	139.4	145.0	150.4
Missouri	198.0	202.9	210.6	225.4	244.7	260.3	269.1	276.1	284.1	292.9	297.5	306.9	312.9
Montana	41.1	43.0	44.7	45.9	48.1	51.8	53.3	52.1	52.6	54.3	55.4	55.4	58.2
Nebraska	85.4	87.7	89.1	92.5	93.3	97.6	97.4	100.9	104.7	109.1	114.3	116.9	121.4
Nevada	22.0	24.2	26.4	28.6	30.3	32.3	34.1	35.8	36.9	38.1	39.7	41.4	43.0
New Hampshire	27.0	28.0	29.0	30.1	31.4	33.4	34.4	35.5	37.3	38.8	41.2	43.4	45.6
New Jersey	262.8	272.1	280.0	295.4	312.0	329.2	344.4	360.1	374.8	388.0	405.3	417.1	439.9
New Mexico	67.7	70.3	71.8	75.4	81.0	83.4	85.0	86.3	89.2	92.3	96.0	99.5	102.5
New York	875.7	897.2	924.1	958.6	1 012.4	1 073.1	1 123.8	1 176.0	1 218.1	1 239.8	1 243.9	1 268.6	1 301.9
North Carolina	178.8	185.6	192.7	201.6	217.4	231.6	244.4	254.3	264.2	268.4	275.3	281.8	303.2
North Dakota	33.9	36.4	38.8	40.3	42.1	44.4	47.2	48.4	49.3	49.3	51.3	52.2	53.3
Ohio	424.2	431.7	440.3	458.6	483.0	509.5	528.3	544.8	565.5	577.2	589.1	597.8	613.1
Oklahoma	131.0	134.9	136.9	145.8	158.8	168.2	171.9	175.5	176.7	179.0	184.9	192.2	199.0
Oregon	103.4	107.9	111.3	118.2	125.3	132.4	136.1	140.8	146.7	152.0	157.5	160.3	168.5
Pennsylvania	465.1	474.8	488.6	508.4	536.1	567.2	588.1	609.4	618.7	629.2	651.9	658.7	682.0
Rhode Island	41.9	42.4	43.4	46.1	48.7	51.2	52.3	52.8	53.6	55.9	56.8	55.5	55.1
South Carolina	99.5	103.1	106.8	111.1	121.0	128.4	134.0	140.8	149.9	156.7	165.6	170.7	182.2
South Dakota	42.2	43.0	44.4	46.6	48.2	49.3	50.3	53.0	53.1	52.6	53.7	53.8	54.9
Tennessee	157.4	163.5	173.3	185.1	195.3	201.8	208.2	214.2	225.9	231.9	240.6	246.2	256.4
Texas	461.2	480.7	500.0	525.6	567.1	607.1	630.1	651.4	662.3	684.2	714.8	745.3	776.0
Utah	68.6	71.6	73.7	79.4	90.7	98.0	98.8	99.6	100.1	103.2	105.5	105.7	108.2
Vermont	18.2	18.9	19.5	20.3	21.2	22.3	23.4	24.4	26.2	27.2	28.2	28.7	29.3
Virginia	207.7	215.7	221.2	232.2	251.2	270.5	283.6	292.4	355.1	371.9	380.0	391.2	405.9
Washington	175.4	179.9	184.6	193.1	206.2	218.5	230.1	237.4	244.5	252.4	258.7	259.0	269.3
West Virginia	71.4	72.1	75.3	81.7	88.5	92.1	94.9	95.0	95.9	98.0	99.4	104.2	106.4
Wisconsin	174.6	181.7	190.4	201.0	215.2	230.3	244.6	255.3	265.5	270.2	275.8	276.3	276.9
Wyoming	22.8	23.8	24.6	25.6	26.9	28.4	28.1	28.1	28.4	29.4	30.5	31.3	32.4
Puerto Rico	...	...	...	...	...	...	...	...	...	...	...	...	...
Virgin Islands	...	...	...	...	...	...	...	...	...	...	...	...	...

See footnote at end of table.

Table 2-17. Employees on Government Payrolls by State, 1962–2000—*Continued*

(Thousands of persons.)

State	1975	1976	1977	1978	1979	1980	1981	1982	1983	1984	1985	1986	1987
Alabama	247.5	252.9	266.3	285.9	291.6	297.4	291.3	290.1	292.7	293.4	295.9	298.0	300.6
Alaska	47.7	48.2	50.1	51.6	54.4	55.0	57.1	59.6	63.0	66.5	68.3	68.0	65.8
Arizona	169.7	177.3	181.9	194.8	196.2	201.8	199.5	199.9	203.1	207.5	218.1	225.0	232.0
Arkansas	120.9	125.3	128.6	135.9	139.1	141.1	138.1	136.0	137.3	139.5	143.0	145.1	146.1
California	1 670.6	1 695.6	1 740.7	1 753.1	1 735.0	1 763.9	1 756.4	1 735.2	1 724.3	1 747.4	1 792.8	1 838.8	1 883.7
Colorado	216.6	219.5	221.1	234.0	238.8	243.6	241.7	238.6	240.7	244.4	248.9	256.0	262.2
Connecticut	178.7	175.1	175.6	179.2	181.3	[1]185.2	182.4	179.6	181.9	185.2	188.8	195.3	201.2
Delaware	40.3	40.6	41.4	42.8	44.4	45.2	44.5	43.8	43.4	43.7	44.8	46.1	46.6
District of Columbia	269.7	275.9	275.6	281.6	284.5	282.2	273.2	260.8	258.8	260.6	265.0	266.9	270.6
Florida	546.0	542.8	565.7	601.8	600.5	618.8	620.1	632.5	639.3	649.5	674.4	701.9	731.8
Georgia	354.8	366.1	384.0	407.9	418.7	429.2	431.1	434.0	437.6	442.0	448.7	462.2	476.6
Hawaii	82.0	84.8	85.7	87.1	86.5	89.0	89.0	90.3	91.3	91.8	93.3	93.9	96.1
Idaho	62.3	64.5	67.3	69.8	69.6	70.5	69.2	67.8	67.8	68.9	70.2	70.9	73.3
Illinois	714.5	717.2	717.8	728.0	739.8	749.4	734.5	717.9	701.6	687.9	697.8	714.8	724.5
Indiana	323.3	332.5	342.0	349.1	347.6	346.6	339.7	328.7	327.0	328.1	332.9	339.7	347.2
Iowa	192.0	197.0	202.5	208.2	204.5	207.4	203.1	202.0	203.4	204.5	206.8	207.3	210.2
Kansas	168.7	171.6	176.9	180.0	183.3	187.4	185.9	183.8	182.9	185.2	188.7	194.1	199.0
Kentucky	208.3	213.0	212.0	220.3	230.4	230.9	224.3	218.9	216.6	223.0	230.0	236.0	240.2
Louisiana	248.7	253.0	257.4	280.3	289.7	300.8	303.8	307.3	315.0	318.6	322.4	319.3	313.1
Maine	74.8	75.2	77.7	81.5	82.6	83.3	82.6	82.1	83.1	83.9	84.9	86.7	88.4
Maryland	366.1	372.1	378.1	401.9	418.7	434.8	415.9	393.2	379.6	387.9	393.6	391.6	392.9
Massachusetts	365.1	375.8	407.9	429.2	416.7	412.3	394.6	374.7	375.4	375.4	385.3	393.0	401.2
Michigan	583.1	594.5	596.7	611.4	621.0	627.8	598.4	577.8	569.8	567.2	580.7	598.6	611.6
Minnesota	271.5	276.0	286.3	292.8	295.6	300.6	299.0	289.6	286.6	293.7	301.2	307.9	313.8
Mississippi	153.5	156.2	163.9	181.8	192.2	194.5	185.9	180.0	181.1	183.2	188.5	189.5	191.1
Missouri	316.0	316.5	321.5	335.6	338.5	339.2	326.6	328.2	323.2	321.8	334.1	338.5	344.0
Montana	64.9	65.7	70.0	71.7	70.1	70.2	69.3	67.4	68.4	68.7	69.9	70.2	69.4
Nebraska	124.7	124.3	129.2	130.3	130.6	130.8	129.7	129.3	130.2	131.1	133.8	134.9	135.3
Nevada	45.6	46.8	49.2	52.2	54.7	57.0	57.1	58.2	58.0	58.9	60.5	61.6	64.1
New Hampshire	48.0	49.9	[1]53.8	54.3	[1]55.1	57.3	56.7	55.9	56.1	57.5	60.0	62.0	65.4
New Jersey	470.2	480.5	504.0	523.0	517.8	529.7	529.0	528.6	525.9	526.6	536.0	540.8	547.1
New Mexico	104.0	109.0	111.0	116.6	120.5	126.0	125.8	125.6	127.2	129.7	132.8	135.9	137.6
New York	1 328.7	1 273.6	1 270.8	1 315.1	1 311.3	1 314.4	1 300.3	1 280.7	1 290.6	1 318.2	1 353.0	1 382.0	1 402.1
North Carolina	328.3	347.9	367.6	386.4	397.2	409.9	403.7	400.3	407.1	413.7	420.5	430.9	442.3
North Dakota	54.5	56.2	57.5	60.0	60.6	60.9	60.5	60.3	61.3	62.2	63.6	64.4	64.6
Ohio	626.4	632.2	642.3	667.5	674.0	669.9	676.0	659.6	656.1	655.2	665.2	678.9	687.3
Oklahoma	206.3	207.0	212.4	218.4	224.0	228.5	235.7	237.2	245.2	241.4	245.7	246.8	245.4
Oregon	177.1	181.6	186.8	197.1	200.7	203.2	202.6	195.5	192.3	194.1	197.7	200.2	205.6
Pennsylvania	721.4	722.1	710.9	720.7	720.7	723.3	703.4	682.5	673.7	672.9	680.2	679.8	688.7
Rhode Island	56.6	57.0	58.2	59.8	59.3	59.2	58.5	57.8	56.9	57.4	57.7	58.0	58.2
South Carolina	199.8	203.3	213.7	223.8	228.8	236.4	233.0	228.1	230.3	237.3	244.8	251.4	258.0
South Dakota	55.7	55.9	56.6	58.1	58.3	58.6	57.8	56.6	56.9	57.2	57.9	58.8	58.9
Tennessee	271.3	283.1	291.2	305.6	313.9	317.2	311.7	297.5	294.1	296.1	304.2	312.4	321.2
Texas	815.8	847.0	875.5	923.7	953.2	978.1	1 000.8	1 023.6	1 042.0	1 063.5	1 088.9	1 118.8	1 142.7
Utah	110.3	112.2	115.8	121.0	123.2	125.0	125.1	126.4	128.8	131.5	137.8	141.2	141.5
Vermont	30.5	30.9	[1]34.3	35.1	35.8	37.0	36.2	36.0	36.3	36.5	37.4	38.2	39.0
Virginia	422.8	436.6	453.6	482.7	493.5	511.2	506.6	500.1	500.9	505.0	515.6	519.9	530.3
Washington	280.5	284.8	294.9	308.0	315.5	330.8	326.4	318.5	[1]324.0	334.5	342.8	348.9	357.2
West Virginia	108.1	109.6	111.0	120.3	130.1	133.1	130.2	126.8	127.8	130.7	127.5	128.9	128.2
Wisconsin	285.4	288.6	287.1	298.2	310.1	321.1	318.0	314.1	312.5	314.7	320.6	325.6	325.0
Wyoming	34.5	36.1	38.0	39.1	40.8	43.0	44.5	46.0	48.9	50.9	52.2	53.1	50.5
Puerto Rico	. . .	. . .	. . .	. . .	246.0	254.4	244.6	236.7	240.1	253.2	255.4	267.7	281.2
Virgin Islands	11.7	11.3	11.9	12.8	13.5	13.4	13.9	13.5	14.0	13.8	13.5	13.1	12.8

See footnote at end of table.

Table 2-17. Employees on Government Payrolls by State, 1962–2000—*Continued*

(Thousands of persons.)

State	1988	1989	1990	1991	1992	1993	1994	1995	1996	1997	1998	1999	2000
Alabama	309.5	317.9	326.7	332.6	337.9	340.7	346.0	343.2	342.9	346.2	347.1	350.7	352.7
Alaska	66.5	68.7	71.0	71.6	73.3	74.6	73.9	72.8	73.1	73.2	73.7	73.6	74.5
Arizona	237.2	246.4	258.9	271.1	276.7	[1]286.6	294.3	[1]310.5	317.9	328.2	341.5	354.1	366.6
Arkansas	150.0	154.2	159.3	163.2	167.1	169.8	173.0	177.1	180.3	183.4	185.2	187.4	191.2
California	1 934.1	1 998.7	2 074.8	2 090.6	2 095.6	2 080.6	2 093.2	2 107.0	2 113.3	2 140.7	2 166.1	2 239.3	2 321.2
Colorado	266.7	271.4	276.8	283.3	291.1	296.7	299.3	303.7	308.7	315.6	322.3	328.3	339.4
Connecticut	206.3	207.7	210.4	207.6	207.4	210.7	217.2	220.9	222.8	225.7	227.8	235.1	242.2
Delaware	47.5	47.1	47.9	48.0	48.6	49.7	50.4	50.8	52.4	53.2	54.4	55.1	56.6
District of Columbia	276.1	276.8	277.3	281.2	285.8	285.3	270.5	254.9	240.5	233.2	225.8	222.5	224.3
Florida	773.0	800.1	846.7	859.3	870.1	881.6	910.6	[1]918.4	928.4	942.2	954.8	965.6	994.0
Georgia	494.1	512.2	531.9	536.6	537.1	548.1	564.0	570.3	569.5	577.3	586.0	592.4	603.3
Hawaii	99.5	101.6	105.6	108.9	111.1	111.5	111.8	111.4	110.6	111.7	112.2	112.7	114.6
Idaho	76.0	77.9	81.3	84.3	88.1	90.4	92.9	95.7	97.0	100.0	102.6	105.2	108.5
Illinois	738.8	744.4	766.0	770.6	773.9	774.4	786.0	798.7	809.4	808.3	816.1	825.6	833.8
Indiana	354.5	366.6	378.6	379.9	387.6	391.3	390.7	391.7	391.0	392.0	399.2	402.6	412.2
Iowa	212.1	216.7	219.0	220.6	221.0	222.5	226.9	230.3	232.9	234.6	236.2	239.4	242.1
Kansas	204.4	209.1	214.4	219.0	225.7	229.5	233.4	236.7	233.5	235.5	239.8	239.6	245.3
Kentucky	246.1	253.3	260.2	267.3	273.3	276.6	280.6	286.9	288.8	290.9	294.7	301.1	308.7
Louisiana	312.6	315.7	326.2	332.3	339.5	342.0	351.5	358.3	361.8	364.2	367.3	370.3	374.8
Maine	91.6	94.1	95.8	95.9	95.7	95.4	94.1	93.2	92.8	93.0	94.6	96.7	99.9
Maryland	399.1	411.3	419.3	416.3	414.8	417.4	420.1	421.8	420.6	420.8	431.8	439.0	445.2
Massachusetts	411.3	408.8	402.2	389.9	382.6	387.5	390.0	395.1	400.0	404.6	411.6	417.4	424.2
Michigan	623.5	623.2	633.9	635.8	639.0	639.4	638.9	640.9	643.8	647.4	656.0	667.6	683.9
Minnesota	320.8	328.7	337.7	341.8	346.1	352.1	359.5	377.9	379.5	379.6	381.3	387.4	396.4
Mississippi	196.0	199.8	203.4	203.9	207.9	210.1	213.7	214.7	216.8	219.0	223.4	227.0	234.4
Missouri	351.8	359.3	369.7	370.7	370.7	376.8	384.9	390.0	400.8	412.8	414.1	421.3	425.7
Montana	70.7	70.3	71.4	71.9	74.2	74.1	76.3	76.9	77.0	77.4	78.6	78.8	80.6
Nebraska	137.8	139.7	143.4	145.6	147.6	149.0	151.6	150.8	151.4	152.2	150.9	151.4	154.2
Nevada	67.0	70.8	75.6	81.3	86.0	88.6	92.3	96.5	101.2	106.5	111.8	117.4	121.4
New Hampshire	68.7	71.2	72.7	72.4	73.1	74.4	76.2	76.2	77.9	78.8	79.8	81.5	82.9
New Jersey	556.2	564.2	576.7	571.6	571.9	570.7	573.4	573.4	570.6	570.3	571.7	577.6	588.8
New Mexico	141.6	144.9	149.7	152.3	156.1	159.1	163.1	166.5	171.5	177.0	178.5	180.2	183.1
New York	1 433.2	1 447.6	1 473.4	1 445.1	1 428.0	1 433.3	1 436.0	1 416.4	1 400.6	1 406.9	1 424.0	1 445.3	1 463.5
North Carolina	458.7	477.2	492.0	501.7	502.5	527.1	538.6	550.6	561.4	576.3	593.6	604.2	625.5
North Dakota	64.8	65.6	65.4	65.7	66.8	67.1	67.2	71.1	70.8	70.8	71.1	71.8	72.9
Ohio	693.8	706.4	722.2	727.9	735.1	735.6	741.0	748.7	752.3	757.9	763.4	772.2	784.3
Oklahoma	248.5	257.2	261.9	264.9	270.1	269.8	270.2	269.7	271.4	276.2	278.2	282.6	288.1
Oregon	211.2	215.6	223.5	226.4	231.0	232.6	234.7	240.2	246.6	249.5	255.3	261.3	266.0
Pennsylvania	694.6	697.9	706.3	701.9	699.9	709.0	713.6	719.2	719.8	711.8	706.0	710.1	726.9
Rhode Island	58.9	59.1	62.5	60.9	61.2	61.4	61.7	61.3	61.3	63.2	62.9	63.3	64.3
South Carolina	261.5	273.1	282.2	285.7	291.9	295.8	295.3	294.2	294.6	298.9	309.5	315.3	323.4
South Dakota	60.1	61.6	62.7	63.4	65.4	66.6	67.1	71.0	70.4	70.5	71.0	71.0	[1]70.3
Tennessee	328.4	344.3	351.4	363.2	356.9	362.0	370.7	373.1	381.6	380.3	385.5	390.1	399.3
Texas	1 175.5	1 206.6	1 263.4	1 287.5	1 334.3	1 376.0	1 413.7	1 445.7	1 457.7	1 483.3	1 504.2	1 534.8	1 566.3
Utah	142.7	146.3	150.5	153.9	156.9	159.5	161.4	163.6	166.8	172.3	176.7	179.5	185.1
Vermont	40.9	42.0	43.5	43.8	43.7	44.0	44.7	45.1	45.4	45.7	46.2	47.6	49.6
Virginia	544.4	562.6	578.4	580.5	589.4	597.8	603.2	597.6	596.2	596.6	602.0	611.3	622.8
Washington	368.8	379.9	397.6	411.6	423.6	430.0	437.2	444.4	450.6	458.0	465.9	474.3	483.5
West Virginia	129.3	125.9	127.4	127.7	132.3	132.8	136.5	136.4	138.7	139.1	140.8	140.9	143.3
Wisconsin	327.8	335.0	342.9	346.4	356.9	361.5	367.1	378.7	383.5	386.7	393.2	398.8	404.7
Wyoming	[1]54.1	54.3	55.3	55.8	56.8	57.2	58.2	57.8	58.1	58.1	58.5	59.4	60.8
Puerto Rico	298.5	298.1	294.6	290.6	295.8	289.9	300.1	304.6	316.5	310.1	307.5	291.3	286.2
Virgin Islands	13.2	13.6	13.6	13.4	13.9	13.9	13.8	13.6	14.1	13.7	13.8	13.4	13.1

1. Data not continuous.

Table 2-18. Average Weekly Hours of Production Workers on Manufacturing Payrolls by State, 1972–2000

(Thousands of persons.)

State	1972	1973	1974	1975	1976	1977	1978	1979	1980	1981	1982	1983	1984	1985
Alabama	41.0	41.0	40.5	39.5	40.6	40.5	40.6	40.7	40.1	39.9	38.5	40.7	41.0	40.8
Alaska	40.1	36.6	40.5	36.6	40.5	43.3	42.4	43.9	42.7	40.0	38.6	36.2	39.3	[1]40.7
Arizona	40.5	39.8	39.2	39.0	39.5	40.1	40.3	40.6	40.1	39.6	38.9	40.5	40.8	[1]40.9
Arkansas	40.2	39.9	39.2	38.8	39.6	39.7	39.3	39.6	39.3	39.4	38.6	40.1	40.5	40.2
California	40.1	40.3	39.7	39.4	39.7	40.1	40.1	39.9	39.5	39.6	39.2	40.0	40.3	40.2
Colorado	...	...	...	...	...	39.4	39.3	39.5	39.8	39.8	39.2	[1]39.9	40.9	40.2
Connecticut	41.5	42.1	41.4	40.5	40.8	41.5	42.0	42.0	41.8	41.6	40.5	41.3	42.5	41.9
Delaware	40.1	40.3	39.4	39.3	40.0	39.6	40.0	39.5	40.5	40.3	39.2	40.6	41.5	41.1
Florida	41.2	41.0	40.2	40.0	40.4	40.7	40.9	40.5	40.8	40.6	39.9	40.7	41.2	41.3
Georgia	41.0	40.5	39.8	39.5	40.1	40.5	40.1	40.4	40.2	40.1	38.6	41.1	41.0	40.6
Hawaii	39.5	39.9	39.4	39.1	39.0	38.0	38.6	38.3	37.8	38.5	37.9	38.6	38.1	37.4
Idaho	39.4	38.8	39.0	38.8	38.7	39.3	38.8	38.3	37.1	37.8	36.7	37.4	37.6	37.8
Illinois	41.0	41.2	40.4	39.7	40.4	40.6	40.1	40.7	39.8	40.0	39.2	40.6	40.6	40.6
Indiana	...	...	...	...	...	...	...	...	...	...	...	...	...	...
Iowa	...	...	...	...	39.9	40.1	40.1	40.5	39.6	39.5	38.7	39.8	40.2	40.2
Kansas	...	...	...	...	...	...	...	40.7	40.4	40.4	39.2	39.1	40.1	39.5
Kentucky	40.4	40.3	39.6	38.7	39.4	39.5	39.6	39.4	39.1	39.3	38.4	39.2	39.2	38.9
Louisiana	42.3	41.4	40.1	42.8	41.3	41.8	41.6	41.3	41.2	42.2	41.0	40.0	41.6	41.7
Maine	40.7	40.8	40.3	39.9	39.9	39.8	40.2	40.1	40.0	40.4	40.0	39.9	39.9	40.0
Maryland	40.2	40.5	39.9	39.1	39.6	39.9	39.9	40.0	39.6	39.9	39.2	40.0	41.0	40.3
Massachusetts	40.1	40.5	39.9	39.1	39.7	39.9	40.2	40.1	39.6	40.0	39.2	39.9	40.1	40.7
Michigan	...	...	...	...	42.7	43.3	43.0	41.2	40.1	40.5	40.2	42.5	43.2	43.1
Minnesota	40.7	41.0	39.9	39.2	39.8	40.0	40.2	40.0	39.4	39.4	39.1	39.7	40.3	40.3
Mississippi	41.1	40.3	39.3	39.3	40.0	40.1	39.9	39.6	39.3	39.3	38.1	40.1	40.6	40.6
Missouri	39.8	39.8	39.3	39.0	39.8	40.2	40.0	39.5	39.2	39.2	38.6	39.9	40.5	40.2
Montana	40.3	39.3	38.8	38.0	39.8	41.8	42.7	42.9	43.2	41.0	39.3	39.7	39.2	39.1
Nebraska	41.7	41.8	41.2	40.5	41.1	40.8	41.1	41.3	40.6	40.3	39.9	40.3	40.5	40.3
Nevada	40.2	40.0	38.8	38.2	38.9	38.8	38.5	38.5	38.2	38.6	37.3	38.8	39.8	40.4
New Hampshire	39.8	39.8	39.3	39.1	30.6	40.0	40.3	40.1	[1]39.8	39.9	39.6	40.5	41.0	40.7
New Jersey	40.9	41.4	40.7	39.9	40.4	41.1	40.8	41.2	40.7	40.6	39.9	40.6	41.1	40.8
New Mexico	40.1	39.4	38.4	39.0	[illegible]	[illegible]	39.2	39.5	39.8	39.5	39.2	30.7	39.9	39.8
New York	39.6	39.9	39.4	38.9	39.4	39.6	39.8	39.6	39.4	39.4	38.8	39.3	39.8	38.8
North Carolina	40.7	40.1	39.1	38.4	39.4	39.6	39.8	39.6	39.3	39.1	37.3	40.0	39.9	39.6
North Dakota	40.2	40.4	40.2	39.9	39.1	38.6	39.7	39.1	37.5	38.1	37.6	38.0	38.4	38.6
Ohio	41.6	42.3	41.2	40.3	41.4	42.0	42.1	41.5	40.6	40.9	40.1	41.4	42.3	42.0
Oklahoma	40.5	40.6	40.5	40.0	40.3	40.4	40.2	40.5	40.1	40.1	39.5	40.5	41.6	41.3
Oregon	39.4	39.3	38.8	38.4	38.9	38.6	39.0	38.5	38.1	37.5	37.9	38.9	39.2	38.7
Pennsylvania	39.8	40.2	30.6	38.8	39.2	[1]39.5	40.0	39.9	38.8	39.2	38.4	39.2	40.2	39.9
Rhode Island	39.5	39.3	39.2	38.9	39.5	39.1	38.9	39.1	39.3	39.3	38.8	39.0	40.9	40.2
South Carolina	41.4	40.5	39.8	39.4	40.4	40.6	40.8	40.8	40.3	40.4	38.2	40.6	40.8	40.4
South Dakota	43.3	42.6	41.7	40.7	39.9	39.3	41.7	41.9	40.9	41.6	41.1	41.6	42.1	41.8
Tennessee	40.6	40.4	39.9	39.8	40.3	40.2	39.6	39.7	39.7	39.9	38.6	40.5	40.9	41.0
Texas	...	...	...	...	40.9	41.1	41.3	41.1	41.2	41.3	40.0	40.9	41.7	41.2
Utah	38.5	38.8	38.7	38.1	39.2	40.0	39.5	39.0	39.1	39.7	38.5	39.4	39.9	40.1
Vermont	41.5	41.5	41.1	40.4	41.0	40.8	41.0	40.8	40.6	40.0	39.0	40.0	40.6	40.7
Virginia	40.8	40.6	39.8	39.2	39.9	39.9	39.8	39.7	39.3	39.7	38.4	39.7	40.3	40.1
Washington	39.6	39.2	38.9	38.7	39.1	39.2	39.3	38.6	38.4	38.8	38.5	38.9	38.8	39.0
West Virginia	40.0	40.0	39.6	39.0	39.2	39.5	39.6	39.6	39.2	39.4	38.8	39.6	40.3	39.9
Wisconsin	41.3	41.4	41.1	40.4	40.6	40.6	41.0	40.9	40.2	40.1	39.6	40.7	41.1	41.1
Wyoming	38.6	38.6	38.0	38.6	40.2	39.8	38.6	37.6	38.9	40.0	38.2	36.9	39.5	40.9
Puerto Rico	...	...	...	...	...	...	...	...	38.0	38.2	37.5	38.7	38.7	38.5
Virgin Islands	...	...	...	...	...	...	40.9	40.9	41.1	42.3	42.3	41.4	42.7	41.7

See footnote at end of table.

Table 2-18. Average Weekly Hours of Production Workers on Manufacturing Payrolls by State, 1972–2000—*Continued*

(Thousands of persons.)

State	1986	1987	1988	1989	1990	1991	1992	1993	1994	1995	1996	1997	1998	1999	2000
Alabama	41.1	41.4	41.4	41.2	41.0	40.8	41.2	41.2	41.9	41.6	41.7	41.9	42.2	42.1	41.9
Alaska	41.1	42.7	[1]42.1	44.4	44.9	46.4	45.5	45.0	47.4	47.8	46.5	46.7	49.9	45.3	44.3
Arizona	41.0	40.6	41.1	41.2	40.7	40.7	40.8	40.7	42.3	42.5	42.8	41.4	40.4	40.4	40.4
Arkansas	40.4	41.0	40.9	40.8	41.0	41.2	41.4	41.4	41.8	41.0	41.5	41.4	41.7	41.7	41.0
California	40.3	40.3	40.7	40.7	40.6	40.6	40.6	40.9	41.4	41.2	41.5	41.9	41.8	41.7	41.7
Colorado	39.9	40.2	40.4	40.2	41.2	40.4	40.5	41.2	41.3	41.0	41.2	41.8	41.5	41.5	41.7
Connecticut	41.8	42.1	42.2	42.2	42.0	41.8	41.7	42.1	42.8	42.8	42.5	42.6	42.7	42.4	42.6
Delaware	41.3	40.7	40.0	41.5	41.3	40.8	40.8	42.1	42.8	41.0	40.5	41.9	42.3	43.0	43.4
Florida	40.8	40.8	40.7	40.9	40.7	40.7	40.9	41.2	41.4	41.4	41.5	41.8	41.7	41.8	41.9
Georgia	40.9	41.6	41.4	41.1	40.9	41.0	41.4	41.7	42.4	42.3	42.3	42.4	41.8	41.7	41.2
Hawaii	38.9	39.4	40.0	40.0	40.3	39.8	40.0	39.8	38.3	37.5	38.1	37.9	37.3	39.3	38.3
Idaho	38.2	38.1	38.1	38.9	38.9	39.1	39.2	40.1	40.0	39.3	39.5	40.1	38.3	39.4	39.2
Illinois	40.9	41.6	42.3	41.9	41.4	41.2	41.0	41.5	41.9	41.7	41.7	42.2	41.8	41.9	41.5
Indiana	. . .	. . .	. . .	41.6	41.3	41.2	42.0	42.7	43.3	42.2	42.8	43.2	42.9	42.9	42.1
Iowa	40.6	41.3	41.4	40.8	40.5	40.5	41.3	41.6	42.4	41.9	42.0	42.6	41.9	41.4	41.6
Kansas	40.3	40.8	40.7	40.2	40.3	40.3	40.9	41.6	41.6	41.1	42.4	42.3	41.9	41.1	40.6
Kentucky	39.2	40.5	40.5	40.0	40.1	40.3	40.3	40.5	41.3	41.3	41.1	41.8	41.5	41.7	42.1
Louisiana	41.8	41.8	42.5	42.6	42.9	42.7	42.6	42.5	43.4	43.2	44.2	44.1	44.0	43.3	42.8
Maine	40.6	41.5	41.0	40.2	40.1	40.0	40.2	40.8	40.6	39.8	39.9	40.6	40.6	40.8	41.3
Maryland	40.5	40.8	41.5	41.1	40.8	40.6	40.8	41.1	41.5	41.5	41.0	41.4	41.6	41.4	40.8
Massachusetts	41.3	41.0	40.7	40.7	40.7	41.0	41.0	41.3	41.6	41.7	41.8	42.3	42.0	42.0	41.9
Michigan	42.6	42.2	43.3	42.9	41.8	41.5	41.8	43.1	44.9	44.3	43.9	44.1	43.3	44.2	43.6
Minnesota	40.6	40.9	40.8	40.5	40.3	40.4	40.8	41.1	41.6	41.5	41.4	41.5	41.3	41.2	40.8
Mississippi	40.2	40.3	40.3	40.0	39.4	39.7	40.3	41.0	41.7	41.0	41.3	41.5	41.4	41.3	40.7
Missouri	40.5	40.6	40.8	40.7	40.7	40.4	40.6	41.4	42.0	41.3	41.5	41.6	41.5	41.5	41.4
Montana	39.4	38.6	38.7	39.2	39.0	39.1	38.9	38.6	39.3	39.4	39.1	39.9	39.3	39.0	38.5
Nebraska	40.4	40.5	41.1	40.7	40.8	40.4	41.1	41.5	42.1	41.5	41.6	41.3	41.9	41.9	41.4
Nevada	40.2	40.3	39.7	40.9	40.7	40.6	40.7	41.4	41.1	41.4	41.6	42.9	42.0	41.3	42.4
New Hampshire	41.2	41.2	40.7	41.2	40.8	41.2	41.6	42.1	42.3	41.6	41.8	42.0	41.3	40.6	40.8
New Jersey	41.2	41.2	41.0	[1]41.0	41.4	41.4	41.5	41.5	41.8	41.8	41.8	42.0	41.8	41.7	41.9
New Mexico	39.5	39.7	40.5	40.0	40.7	40.1	40.0	40.9	40.9	39.9	40.2	39.8	38.6	39.0	38.2
New York	39.9	39.9	39.9	40.0	39.6	39.8	40.0	40.4	41.0	40.9	40.8	41.2	41.1	41.2	41.0
North Carolina	40.7	41.2	40.5	40.3	39.9	40.1	40.7	40.8	41.1	40.6	40.4	41.2	41.1	41.0	41.4
North Dakota	38.2	38.7	38.7	39.8	39.8	39.8	40.4	41.2	42.3	40.7	42.2	40.5	39.9	40.0	40.2
Ohio	42.1	42.6	43.0	42.7	42.4	42.2	42.2	43.0	43.9	43.4	43.3	43.6	42.9	42.9	42.9
Oklahoma	41.3	41.2	41.1	41.6	41.1	41.0	41.2	41.9	43.1	41.9	42.0	42.4	41.5	41.3	40.9
Oregon	39.0	39.2	39.3	39.4	39.3	39.4	39.5	39.5	40.4	40.1	40.2	40.9	40.7	40.4	40.0
Pennsylvania	40.2	40.9	41.1	41.0	40.7	40.4	40.8	41.2	41.6	41.3	[1]41.2	42.0	41.9	41.8	42.1
Rhode Island	40.4	40.0	39.7	39.3	39.7	40.0	40.1	39.8	40.3	40.5	40.0	40.9	40.6	39.9	40.4
South Carolina	41.1	41.7	41.1	41.3	41.0	41.3	41.7	41.6	41.8	41.9	41.8	42.2	42.6	42.6	42.5
South Dakota	42.1	41.7	42.5	41.8	40.6	41.2	41.2	41.3	42.0	41.8	41.5	41.9	42.6	42.9	43.1
Tennessee	41.2	41.6	41.6	40.8	38.6	39.6	40.3	40.8	40.9	40.4	40.6	41.2	40.5	40.6	40.2
Texas	41.4	41.6	41.7	41.8	41.8	42.1	42.5	42.8	43.1	42.8	43.0	43.5	43.7	43.5	43.3
Utah	40.0	39.5	40.3	40.0	39.8	39.9	40.3	39.6	40.6	39.8	40.3	40.2	40.4	40.0	39.8
Vermont	40.7	40.6	40.4	40.9	40.8	40.8	41.0	41.5	40.9	40.5	40.5	40.7	39.6	39.5	40.3
Virginia	40.4	41.1	40.8	40.9	40.4	40.5	41.0	41.0	41.7	41.6	41.5	42.2	42.3	42.4	42.3
Washington	39.4	39.9	40.1	39.4	40.6	39.9	40.0	40.2	40.5	40.8	40.8	40.6	40.8	40.9	40.7
West Virginia	40.3	40.6	40.6	40.7	40.7	40.6	40.6	40.9	41.3	41.8	41.2	41.7	41.6	41.6	41.3
Wisconsin	41.3	41.4	41.8	41.5	41.4	41.4	41.8	42.0	42.7	42.1	42.2	42.4	41.8	41.9	41.5
Wyoming	39.0	38.8	38.5	39.8	39.9	38.6	38.6	38.9	40.0	39.4	40.1	40.3	40.4	39.3	39.2
Puerto Rico	39.0	38.9	39.1	39.5	39.1	39.0	39.6	39.5	39.9	39.6	38.6	39.6	40.0	41.0	40.6
Virgin Islands	41.9	42.2	40.4	41.7	42.4	41.4	42.0	43.5	42.7	41.7	41.5	42.7	40.1	43.8	44.0

1. Data not continuous.

Table 2-19. Average Hourly Earnings of Production Workers on Manufacturing Payrolls by State, 1972–2000

(Dollars.)

State	1972	1973	1974	1975	1976	1977	1978	1979	1980	1981	1982	1983	1984	1985
Alabama	3.25	3.42	3.73	4.10	4.46	4.89	5.40	5.95	6.49	7.01	7.33	7.58	7.97	8.48
Alaska	5.92	5.97	7.10	8.09	7.82	9.12	8.86	9.14	10.22	11.42	11.74	12.33	12.25	[1]12.19
Arizona	3.85	4.03	4.40	4.85	5.19	5.55	6.03	6.62	7.29	8.02	8.73	8.99	9.09	[1]9.48
Arkansas	2.79	2.99	3.30	3.69	3.91	4.30	4.72	5.19	5.71	6.26	6.69	7.05	7.31	7.57
California	4.25	4.44	4.76	5.22	5.59	6.00	6.43	7.03	7.70	8.56	9.24	9.52	9.77	10.12
Colorado	...	...	...	...	...	5.80	6.21	6.93	7.63	8.28	8.63	[1]8.97	9.24	9.52
Connecticut	3.87	4.14	4.42	4.78	5.12	5.56	5.96	6.43	7.08	7.67	8.23	8.76	9.22	9.57
Delaware	4.04	4.29	4.62	5.02	5.51	5.94	6.58	7.04	7.58	8.28	8.64	9.19	9.28	9.86
Florida	3.20	3.45	3.76	4.11	4.36	4.63	5.07	5.48	5.98	6.53	7.02	7.33	7.62	7.86
Georgia	3.04	3.25	3.50	3.80	4.10	4.46	4.88	5.30	5.77	6.37	6.75	7.13	7.58	8.10
Hawaii	3.59	3.93	4.24	4.68	5.14	5.51	5.90	6.38	6.83	7.53	7.97	8.23	8.35	8.65
Idaho	3.69	4.05	4.41	4.77	5.29	5.82	6.53	6.92	7.55	8.23	8.62	8.98	9.34	9.41
Illinois	4.28	4.57	4.97	5.53	5.85	6.28	6.76	7.30	8.02	8.91	9.31	9.70	10.08	10.37
Indiana	...	...	...	...	...	...	...	...	...	...	...	...	...	...
Iowa	...	...	...	...	5.85	6.43	7.02	7.75	8.67	9.60	10.01	10.09	10.24	10.32
Kansas	...	...	...	...	...	...	...	6.71	7.37	8.05	8.80	9.23	9.38	9.45
Kentucky	3.70	4.00	4.36	4.77	5.15	5.69	6.26	6.77	7.34	7.86	8.38	8.79	9.28	9.53
Louisiana	3.68	3.98	4.40	4.88	5.33	5.75	6.42	6.97	7.74	8.58	9.38	9.79	10.06	10.43
Maine	3.03	3.23	3.51	3.81	4.16	4.52	4.91	5.42	6.00	6.66	7.22	7.61	8.05	8.40
Maryland	3.92	4.22	4.62	5.04	5.52	6.05	6.46	7.09	7.61	8.39	8.78	9.02	9.45	9.73
Massachusetts	3.65	3.89	4.16	4.48	4.79	5.13	5.54	5.98	6.51	7.01	7.58	8.01	8.50	9.00
Michigan	...	...	...	...	6.81	7.54	8.13	8.73	9.52	10.53	11.18	11.62	12.18	12.64
Minnesota	4.00	4.22	4.67	5.10	5.53	5.97	6.44	6.93	7.61	8.40	9.11	9.56	9.75	10.05
Mississippi	2.75	2.95	3.19	3.58	3.83	4.15	4.56	4.95	5.44	6.01	6.41	6.70	6.95	7.22
Missouri	3.78	4.05	4.39	4.80	5.20	5.75	6.21	6.70	7.26	7.90	8.46	8.89	9.31	9.57
Montana	4.11	4.53	5.05	5.53	5.93	6.53	7.81	8.44	8.78	9.09	9.86	10.44	10.76	10.95
Nebraska	3.55	3.75	4.15	4.63	4.93	5.39	5.83	6.53	7.38	8.01	8.47	8.76	8.93	9.02
Nevada	4.46	4.71	4.89	5.26	5.61	6.10	6.54	6.95	7.72	8.42	8.80	9.02	9.12	9.15
New Hampshire	3.20	3.39	3.65	3.97	4.26	4.56	4.94	5.37	[1]5.87	6.41	6.94	7.42	7.86	8.39
New Jersey	3.99	4.26	4.57	4.99	5.33	5.82	6.28	6.71	7.31	8.05	8.66	9.11	9.50	9.86
New Mexico	2.88	3.08	3.31	3.60	4.07	4.42	4.79	5.36	5.79	6.54	7.22	7.60	7.97	8.41
New York	3.98	4.20	4.53	4.91	5.27	5.67	6.08	6.57	7.18	7.84	8.35	8.84	9.22	9.07
North Carolina	2.77	2.99	3.28	3.52	3.79	4.10	4.47	4.87	5.37	5.94	6.35	6.68	7.01	7.29
North Dakota	3.31	3.55	3.83	4.31	4.75	5.19	5.55	5.98	6.56	7.12	7.50	7.73	7.86	8.05
Ohio	4.45	4.76	5.13	5.57	6.10	6.74	7.29	7.84	8.57	9.53	10.07	10.56	10.96	11.38
Oklahoma	3.49	3.69	4.01	4.45	4.83	5.31	5.81	6.53	7.36	8.20	8.69	9.21	9.64	9.86
Oregon	4.30	4.60	5.01	5.53	6.07	6.67	7.23	7.92	8.65	9.47	10.02	10.25	10.44	10.50
Pennsylvania	3.88	4.16	4.57	4.98	5.36	[1]5.85	6.37	6.97	7.59	8.30	8.63	8.95	9.28	9.57
Rhode Island	3.15	3.37	3.62	3.84	4.15	4.39	4.71	5.10	5.59	6.10	6.61	6.92	7.33	7.59
South Carolina	2.80	3.03	3.32	3.59	3.91	4.28	4.66	5.10	5.59	6.18	6.68	7.03	7.28	7.61
South Dakota	3.17	3.37	3.77	4.21	4.51	4.84	5.19	5.70	6.50	7.12	7.36	7.31	7.14	7.43
Tennessee	3.07	3.29	3.62	3.93	4.24	4.68	5.13	5.56	6.08	6.72	7.16	7.49	7.93	8.29
Texas	...	...	...	...	4.98	5.42	5.88	6.46	7.15	7.95	8.60	8.88	9.04	9.41
Utah	3.62	3.83	4.19	4.61	4.89	5.18	5.68	6.29	7.02	7.74	8.40	8.69	8.92	9.64
Vermont	3.28	3.50	3.78	4.07	4.40	4.70	5.10	5.53	6.14	6.79	7.35	7.66	8.03	8.41
Virginia	3.10	3.34	3.65	3.99	4.30	4.69	5.11	5.58	6.22	6.84	7.37	7.79	8.10	8.51
Washington	4.54	4.83	5.24	5.82	6.36	6.83	7.56	8.39	9.41	10.44	11.23	11.42	11.57	11.63
West Virginia	3.87	4.14	4.53	4.93	5.42	6.06	6.68	7.41	8.08	8.80	9.40	9.74	9.93	10.24
Wisconsin	4.15	4.45	4.81	5.26	5.69	6.16	6.69	7.27	8.03	8.80	9.37	9.78	10.03	10.26
Wyoming	3.45	4.03	4.52	4.92	5.43	5.70	6.18	6.68	7.01	7.89	8.62	8.73	9.14	9.64
Puerto Rico	...	...	...	...	...	...	...	...	4.02	4.39	4.64	4.83	5.02	5.19
Virgin Islands	...	...	...	...	...	...	6.12	6.70	7.18	8.50	9.76	10.03	9.51	9.44

See footnote at end of table.

Table 2-19. Average Hourly Earnings of Production Workers on Manufacturing Payrolls by State, 1972–2000—*Continued*

(Dollars.)

State	1986	1987	1988	1989	1990	1991	1992	1993	1994	1995	1996	1997	1998	1999	2000
Alabama	8.64	8.76	8.95	9.10	9.39	9.72	9.99	10.35	10.75	11.14	11.55	11.86	12.11	12.54	12.94
Alaska	11.62	11.79	[1]11.98	12.01	12.46	11.40	10.75	11.14	10.96	11.00	11.14	11.78	11.09	12.16	12.45
Arizona	9.88	9.97	9.85	9.92	10.21	10.70	10.96	11.06	11.17	11.16	11.49	11.67	12.17	12.70	12.77
Arkansas	7.76	7.88	8.07	8.26	8.51	8.81	9.05	9.36	9.65	10.05	10.41	10.78	11.12	11.55	11.98
California	10.36	10.75	10.80	11.16	11.48	11.87	12.19	12.38	12.44	12.55	12.84	13.24	13.66	13.95	14.25
Colorado	9.82	10.05	10.38	10.44	10.94	11.33	11.32	12.01	12.26	12.51	12.83	13.31	13.74	14.19	14.76
Connecticut	10.07	10.46	10.78	11.21	11.53	11.99	12.46	13.01	13.53	13.71	14.01	14.46	14.83	15.33	15.69
Delaware	10.05	10.67	[1]11.49	12.36	12.39	12.20	12.35	13.29	13.92	14.20	14.02	14.81	15.36	15.91	16.54
Florida	8.02	8.16	8.39	8.67	8.98	9.30	9.59	9.76	9.97	10.18	10.55	10.95	11.43	11.83	12.28
Georgia	8.35	8.49	8.65	8.87	9.17	9.56	9.86	10.09	10.34	10.71	11.19	11.64	12.03	12.51	13.01
Hawaii	8.86	9.30	9.84	10.37	10.99	11.39	11.61	11.98	12.22	12.82	12.79	13.11	13.16	13.49	13.58
Idaho	9.66	9.75	10.00	10.21	10.60	11.11	11.42	11.88	11.88	11.46	12.15	12.46	12.80	13.42	14.17
Illinois	10.67	10.85	10.98	11.21	11.44	11.68	11.84	12.04	12.25	12.64	13.03	13.35	13.75	14.05	14.39
Indiana	...	...	...	11.70	12.03	12.43	12.79	13.17	13.55	13.91	14.33	14.79	14.97	15.26	15.83
Iowa	10.35	10.62	10.56	10.82	11.27	11.62	11.92	12.22	12.45	12.73	13.13	13.57	13.91	14.20	14.66
Kansas	9.76	9.97	10.24	10.68	10.94	11.24	11.60	11.99	12.15	12.39	12.88	13.45	13.84	14.44	14.98
Kentucky	9.86	10.02	10.16	10.37	10.70	11.00	11.28	11.47	11.81	12.22	12.70	13.17	13.82	14.27	14.82
Louisiana	10.60	10.90	10.94	11.13	11.61	11.86	12.19	12.66	13.11	13.43	13.65	14.14	14.63	15.18	15.57
Maine	8.65	8.77	9.31	9.92	10.59	11.08	11.40	11.63	11.91	12.39	12.71	13.12	13.49	13.94	14.28
Maryland	9.91	10.11	10.71	11.19	11.57	11.92	12.50	12.83	13.15	13.49	13.73	14.14	14.31	14.62	14.99
Massachusetts	9.24	9.77	10.40	10.87	11.39	11.81	12.15	12.36	12.59	12.79	13.05	13.42	13.80	14.24	14.65
Michigan	12.80	12.97	13.31	13.51	13.86	14.52	14.81	15.36	16.13	16.31	16.67	17.18	17.61	18.38	19.20
Minnesota	10.20	10.37	10.59	10.95	11.23	11.52	11.92	12.23	12.58	12.79	13.16	13.63	13.92	14.34	14.99
Mississippi	7.46	7.59	7.83	8.03	8.37	8.67	8.91	9.16	9.41	9.76	10.18	10.41	10.73	11.17	11.64
Missouri	9.83	10.00	10.24	10.49	10.74	10.86	11.24	11.55	11.77	12.17	12.57	12.98	13.38	13.93	14.40
Montana	10.94	10.61	10.68	11.15	11.51	11.57	12.18	12.40	12.49	12.94	13.00	13.29	13.76	14.17	14.34
Nebraska	9.26	9.33	9.38	9.53	9.66	9.84	10.22	10.46	10.94	11.19	11.51	12.10	12.32	12.77	12.93
Nevada	9.36	9.76	10.08	10.33	11.05	11.04	11.55	11.65	11.83	12.62	13.59	14.17	14.42	13.92	13.84
New Hampshire	8.77	9.29	9.97	10.37	10.83	10.84	11.22	11.62	11.74	11.94	12.23	12.55	12.79	13.17	13.41
New Jersey	10.12	10.40	10.86	[1]11.2	11.76	12.17	12.57	12.98	13.36	13.56	13.85	14.24	14.58	15.11	15.47
New Mexico	8.75	8.74	8.87	8.74	9.04	9.40	9.68	9.74	10.13	10.68	10.99	11.74	12.47	12.53	13.34
New York	9.92	10.09	10.43	10.67	11.11	11.43	11.72	11.97	12.19	12.50	12.78	13.19	13.47	13.87	14.24
North Carolina	7.54	7.84	8.12	8.42	8.79	9.19	9.49	9.81	10.19	10.56	10.97	11.41	11.84	12.32	12.79
North Dakota	8.19	8.43	8.36	8.80	9.27	9.25	9.60	9.86	10.19	10.75	10.95	11.29	11.40	11.94	12.66
Ohio	11.56	11.73	12.00	12.26	12.64	13.12	13.49	14.05	14.40	14.42	14.70	15.30	15.79	16.26	16.72
Oklahoma	9.80	10.14	10.35	10.48	10.73	11.09	11.38	11.42	11.42	11.52	11.78	12.36	12.61	12.70	13.17
Oregon	10.57	10.56	10.60	10.81	11.15	11.53	11.97	12.18	12.31	12.75	13.01	13.39	14.07	14.61	15.08
Pennsylvania	9.74	9.98	10.33	10.66	11.04	11.46	11.78	12.11	12.49	12.81	[1]13.40	13.78	14.06	14.19	14.60
Rhode Island	7.90	8.20	8.64	9.06	9.45	9.73	9.92	10.20	10.35	10.62	10.95	11.31	11.61	11.98	12.18
South Carolina	7.92	8.10	8.30	8.54	8.84	9.17	9.48	9.80	10.00	10.16	10.25	10.35	10.52	10.67	10.96
South Dakota	7.75	7.92	8.09	8.30	8.48	8.79	8.84	8.89	9.19	9.36	9.59	9.96	10.22	10.58	10.71
Tennessee	8.58	8.78	8.96	9.22	9.55	9.92	10.13	10.33	10.50	10.78	11.30	11.71	12.06	12.50	12.92
Texas	9.65	9.85	9.97	10.25	10.47	10.84	10.92	11.02	11.13	11.47	11.81	12.03	12.14	12.25	12.37
Utah	9.98	9.96	10.11	10.14	10.32	10.77	11.09	11.10	11.28	11.62	12.21	12.85	13.07	13.39	13.69
Vermont	8.83	9.12	9.47	9.99	10.52	11.00	10.62	12.09	11.96	12.21	12.42	12.70	13.03	13.65	14.23
Virginia	8.83	9.14	9.37	9.69	10.07	10.43	11.52	10.85	11.24	11.72	12.19	12.51	12.90	13.37	13.82
Washington	11.65	11.73	11.90	12.12	12.61	13.13	13.59	14.01	14.86	14.73	14.73	15.16	15.76	16.14	16.76
West Virginia	10.38	10.55	10.81	11.17	11.53	11.77	12.11	12.27	12.60	12.64	12.96	13.17	13.72	14.09	14.60
Wisconsin	10.35	10.55	10.61	10.77	11.11	11.47	11.85	12.17	12.41	12.76	13.14	13.66	14.02	14.50	14.85
Wyoming	9.68	9.75	[1]10.27	10.58	10.83	10.98	11.10	11.53	11.79	11.96	13.17	14.54	14.93	15.40	15.76
Puerto Rico	5.31	5.43	5.56	5.77	6.04	6.32	6.63	6.98	7.22	7.41	7.70	7.99	8.41	8.93	9.37
Virgin Islands	9.60	9.40	9.86	10.87	11.85	12.52	13.68	14.97	15.16	15.82	17.00	18.09	18.60	18.89	22.08

1. Data not continuous.

Table 2-20. Average Weekly Earnings of Production Workers on Manufacturing Payrolls by State, 1972–2000

(Dollars.)

State	1972	1973	1974	1975	1976	1977	1978	1979	1980	1981	1982	1983	1984	1985
Alabama	133.25	140.22	151.06	161.95	181.08	198.04	219.24	242.16	260.25	279.70	282.20	308.51	326.77	345.98
Alaska	237.39	239.40	287.55	296.09	316.71	394.90	375.66	401.25	436.49	456.80	453.16	446.35	481.42	[1]496.13
Arizona	155.92	160.39	172.48	189.15	205.00	222.56	243.01	268.77	292.33	317.59	339.60	364.10	370.87	[1]387.73
Arkansas	112.16	119.30	129.36	143.17	154.84	170.71	185.50	205.52	224.40	246.64	258.23	282.71	296.06	304.31
California	170.43	178.93	188.97	205.67	221.92	240.60	257.84	280.50	304.15	338.98	362.21	380.80	393.73	406.82
Colorado	...	...	...	...	...	228.52	244.05	273.74	303.67	329.54	338.30	[1]357.90	377.92	382.70
Connecticut	160.61	174.29	182.99	193.59	208.90	230.74	250.32	270.06	295.94	319.07	333.32	361.79	391.85	400.98
Delaware	162.00	172.89	182.03	197.29	220.40	235.22	263.20	278.08	306.99	333.68	338.69	373.11	385.12	405.25
Florida	131.84	141.45	151.15	164.40	176.14	188.44	207.36	221.94	243.98	265.12	280.10	298.33	313.94	324.62
Georgia	124.64	131.63	139.30	150.10	164.41	180.63	195.69	214.12	231.95	255.44	260.55	293.04	310.78	328.86
Hawaii	141.81	156.81	167.06	182.99	200.46	209.38	227.74	244.35	258.17	289.90	302.06	317.68	318.14	323.51
Idaho	145.39	157.14	171.99	185.08	204.72	228.73	253.36	265.04	280.11	311.09	316.35	335.85	351.18	355.70
Illinois	175.55	187.85	200.69	219.13	236.11	254.91	271.42	296.66	319.20	356.23	364.86	393.59	409.35	421.02
Indiana	...	...	...	...	...	...	...	...	...	...	...	...	...	...
Iowa	...	...	...	...	233.42	257.84	281.50	313.88	343.33	379.20	387.39	401.58	411.65	414.86
Kansas	...	...	...	...	...	...	...	273.10	297.75	325.22	344.96	360.89	376.14	373.28
Kentucky	149.48	161.20	172.66	184.60	202.91	224.75	247.90	266.74	286.99	308.90	321.79	344.57	363.78	370.72
Louisiana	155.66	164.77	176.44	208.86	220.13	240.35	267.07	287.86	318.89	362.08	384.58	391.60	418.50	434.93
Maine	123.32	131.78	141.45	152.02	165.98	179.90	197.38	217.34	240.00	269.06	288.80	303.64	321.20	336.00
Maryland	157.58	170.91	184.34	197.06	218.59	241.40	257.75	283.60	301.36	334.76	344.18	360.80	387.45	392.12
Massachusetts	146.37	157.55	165.98	175.17	190.16	204.69	222.71	239.80	257.80	280.40	297.14	319.60	340.85	366.30
Michigan	...	...	...	...	290.97	326.27	349.50	359.72	381.87	426.27	449.33	494.02	526.18	544.78
Minnesota	162.80	173.02	186.33	199.92	220.09	238.80	258.89	277.20	299.83	330.96	356.20	379.53	392.93	405.02
Mississippi	113.03	118.89	125.37	140.69	153.20	166.42	181.94	196.02	213.79	236.19	244.22	268.67	282.17	293.13
Missouri	150.44	161.19	172.53	187.20	206.96	231.15	248.40	264.65	284.59	318.37	326.56	354.71	377.06	384.71
Montana	165.63	178.03	195.94	210.14	236.01	272.95	333.49	362.08	379.30	372.69	387.50	414.47	421.79	428.15
Nebraska	148.07	156.78	170.98	187.66	202.57	219.91	239.61	269.69	299.63	322.80	337.95	353.03	361.67	363.51
Nevada	179.29	188.40	189.73	200.93	218.23	236.68	251.79	267.58	294.90	325.01	328.24	349.98	362.98	369.66
New Hampshire	127.36	134.92	143.44	155.23	100.70	182.40	199.08	215.34	[1]233.63	255.76	274.82	300.51	322.26	341.47
New Jersey	163.35	176.41	186.11	199.68	215.71	239.20	256.22	276.45	297.07	327.16	345.53	369.87	390.45	402.20
New Mexico	115.49	121.35	127.10	141.57	160.77	171.88	187.77	211.72	230.44	258.33	200.02	301.72	318.00	334.72
New York	157.61	167.58	178.48	191.00	207.64	224.53	241.98	260.17	282.89	308.90	323.98	347.41	366.96	384.87
North Carolina	112.74	119.90	128.25	135.17	149.33	162.36	177.91	192.85	211.04	232.25	236.86	267.20	279.70	288.68
North Dakota	133.06	143.42	153.97	171.97	185.73	200.33	220.34	233.82	246.00	271.27	282.00	293.74	301.82	310.73
Ohio	185.12	201.35	211.36	224.47	252.54	283.08	306.91	325.36	347.94	389.78	403.81	437.18	463.61	477.96
Oklahoma	141.34	149.81	162.40	178.00	194.65	214.52	233.56	264.46	295.14	328.82	343.26	373.01	401.02	407.22
Oregon	169.42	180.78	194.39	212.35	236.12	257.46	281.97	304.92	329.57	355.13	379.76	398.73	409.25	406.35
Pennsylvania	154.42	167.23	180.97	193.22	210.11	[1]231.08	254.80	278.10	294.49	325.36	331.39	350.84	373.06	381.84
Rhode Island	124.43	132.44	141.90	149.04	163.93	171.65	183.22	199.41	219.69	239.73	255.16	269.88	299.80	305.11
South Carolina	115.92	122.72	132.14	141.45	157.96	173.77	190.13	208.08	225.28	249.67	255.18	285.30	297.07	307.44
South Dakota	137.26	143.56	157.21	171.35	179.95	190.21	216.42	238.83	265.85	296.19	302.50	304.10	300.59	310.57
Tennessee	124.64	132.92	144.44	156.41	170.87	188.14	203.15	220.73	241.38	268.13	276.38	303.34	324.34	339.72
Texas	...	...	...	...	203.68	222.76	242.84	265.51	294.58	328.34	344.00	363.19	376.97	387.69
Utah	139.56	148.62	162.02	175.77	191.69	207.15	224.36	245.31	274.48	307.28	323.40	342.39	355.91	386.56
Vermont	136.12	145.25	155.36	164.43	180.40	191.76	209.10	225.62	249.28	271.60	286.65	306.40	326.02	342.29
Virginia	126.48	135.60	145.27	156.41	171.57	187.13	203.38	221.53	244.45	271.55	283.01	309.26	326.43	341.25
Washington	179.78	189.34	203.84	225.23	248.68	267.74	297.11	323.85	361.34	405.07	432.36	444.24	448.92	453.57
West Virginia	154.80	165.60	179.39	192.27	212.46	239.37	264.53	293.44	316.74	346.72	364.72	385.70	400.18	408.58
Wisconsin	171.04	183.99	197.43	212.25	230.91	250.06	274.21	297.00	323.10	352.55	370.87	398.05	412.23	421.69
Wyoming	133.10	155.58	171.71	190.36	218.11	226.82	238.55	251.17	272.69	315.60	329.28	322.21	361.03	394.28
Puerto Rico	...	...	...	...	...	...	...	...	152.76	167.77	174.00	186.92	194.27	199.82
Virgin Islands	...	...	...	...	...	...	250.31	274.03	295.10	359.55	412.85	415.24	405.41	393.65

See footnote at end of table.

Table 2-20. Average Weekly Earnings of Production Workers on Manufacturing Payrolls by State, 1972–2000—*Continued*

(Dollars.)

State	1986	1987	1988	1989	1990	1991	1992	1993	1994	1995	1996	1997	1998	1999	2000
Alabama	355.10	362.66	370.53	374.92	384.99	396.58	411.59	426.42	450.43	463.42	481.64	496.93	511.04	527.93	542.19
Alaska	477.58	503.43	[1]504.36	533.24	559.45	528.96	489.13	501.30	519.50	525.80	518.01	550.13	553.39	550.85	551.54
Arizona	405.08	404.78	404.84	408.70	415.55	435.49	447.17	450.14	472.49	474.30	491.77	483.14	491.67	513.08	515.91
Arkansas	313.50	323.08	330.06	337.01	348.91	362.97	374.67	387.50	403.37	412.05	432.02	446.29	463.70	481.64	491.18
California	417.51	433.23	439.56	454.21	466.09	481.92	494.91	506.34	515.02	517.06	532.86	554.76	570.99	581.72	594.23
Colorado	391.82	404.01	419.35	419.69	450.73	457.73	458.46	494.81	506.34	512.91	528.60	556.36	570.21	588.89	615.49
Connecticut	420.93	440.37	454.92	473.06	484.26	501.18	519.58	547.72	579.08	586.79	595.43	616.00	633.24	649.99	668.39
Delaware	415.07	434.27	459.60	512.94	511.71	497.76	503.88	559.50	595.78	582.20	567.81	620.54	649.73	684.13	717.84
Florida	327.22	332.93	341.47	354.60	365.49	378.51	392.23	402.11	412.76	421.45	437.83	457.71	476.63	494.49	514.53
Georgia	341.52	353.18	358.11	364.56	375.05	391.96	408.20	420.75	438.42	453.03	473.34	493.54	502.85	521.67	536.01
Hawaii	344.65	366.42	393.60	414.80	442.90	453.32	464.40	476.80	468.03	480.75	487.30	496.87	490.87	530.16	520.11
Idaho	369.01	371.48	381.00	397.16	412.34	434.40	447.66	476.39	475.20	450.38	479.93	499.65	490.24	528.75	555.46
Illinois	436.40	451.36	464.45	469.70	473.62	481.22	485.44	499.66	513.28	527.09	543.35	563.37	574.75	588.70	597.19
Indiana	...	...	...	486.72	496.84	512.12	537.18	562.36	586.72	587.00	613.32	638.93	642.21	654.65	666.44
Iowa	420.21	438.61	437.18	441.46	456.44	470.61	492.30	508.35	527.88	533.39	551.46	578.08	582.83	587.88	609.86
Kansas	393.33	406.78	416.77	429.34	440.88	452.97	474.44	498.78	505.44	509.23	546.11	568.94	579.90	593.48	608.19
Kentucky	386.51	405.81	411.48	414.80	429.07	443.30	454.58	464.54	487.75	504.69	521.97	550.51	573.53	595.06	623.92
Louisiana	443.08	455.62	464.95	474.14	498.07	506.42	519.29	538.05	568.97	580.18	603.33	623.57	643.72	657.29	666.40
Maine	351.19	363.96	381.71	398.78	424.66	443.20	458.28	474.50	483.55	493.12	507.13	532.67	547.69	568.75	589.76
Maryland	401.36	412.49	444.47	459.91	472.06	483.95	510.00	527.31	545.73	559.84	562.93	585.40	595.30	605.27	611.59
Massachusetts	381.61	400.57	423.28	442.41	463.57	484.21	498.15	510.47	523.74	533.34	545.49	567.67	579.60	598.08	613.84
Michigan	545.28	547.33	576.32	579.58	579.35	602.58	619.06	662.02	724.24	722.53	731.81	757.64	762.51	812.40	837.12
Minnesota	414.12	424.13	432.07	443.48	452.57	465.41	486.34	502.65	523.33	530.79	544.82	565.65	574.90	590.81	611.59
Mississippi	299.89	305.88	315.55	321.20	329.78	344.20	359.07	375.56	392.40	400.16	420.43	432.02	444.22	461.32	473.75
Missouri	398.12	406.00	417.79	426.94	437.12	438.74	456.34	478.17	494.34	502.62	521.66	539.97	555.27	578.10	596.16
Montana	431.04	409.55	413.32	437.08	448.89	452.39	473.80	478.64	490.86	509.84	508.30	530.27	540.77	552.63	552.09
Nebraska	374.10	377.87	385.52	387.87	394.13	397.54	420.04	434.09	460.57	464.39	478.82	499.73	516.21	535.06	535.30
Nevada	376.27	393.33	400.18	422.50	449.74	448.22	470.09	482.31	486.21	522.47	565.34	607.89	605.64	574.90	586.82
New Hampshire	361.32	382.75	405.78	427.24	441.86	446.61	466.75	489.20	496.60	496.70	511.21	527.10	528.23	534.70	547.13
New Jersey	416.94	428.48	445.26	[1]458.0	486.86	503.84	521.66	538.67	558.45	566.81	578.93	598.08	609.44	630.09	648.19
New Mexico	345.63	346.98	359.24	349.60	367.93	376.94	387.20	398.37	414.32	426.13	441.80	467.25	481.34	488.67	509.59
New York	395.81	402.59	416.16	426.80	439.96	454.91	468.80	483.59	499.79	511.25	521.42	543.43	553.62	571.44	583.84
North Carolina	306.88	323.01	328.86	339.33	350.72	368.52	386.24	400.25	418.81	428.74	443.19	470.09	486.62	505.12	529.51
North Dakota	312.86	326.24	323.53	350.24	368.95	368.15	387.84	406.23	431.04	437.53	462.09	457.25	454.86	477.60	508.93
Ohio	486.68	499.70	516.00	523.50	535.94	553.66	569.28	604.15	632.16	625.83	636.51	667.08	677.39	697.55	717.29
Oklahoma	404.74	417.77	425.39	435.97	441.00	454.69	468.86	478.50	492.20	482.69	494.76	524.06	523.32	524.51	538.65
Oregon	412.23	413.95	416.58	425.91	438.20	454.28	472.82	481.11	497.32	511.28	523.00	547.65	572.65	590.24	603.20
Pennsylvania	391.55	408.18	424.56	437.06	449.33	462.98	480.62	498.93	519.58	529.05	[1]552.08	578.76	589.11	593.14	614.66
Rhode Island	319.16	328.00	343.01	356.06	375.17	389.20	397.79	405.96	417.11	430.11	438.00	462.58	471.37	478.00	492.07
South Carolina	325.51	337.77	341.13	352.70	362.44	378.72	395.32	407.68	418.00	425.70	428.45	436.77	448.15	454.54	465.80
South Dakota	326.28	330.26	343.83	346.94	344.29	362.15	364.21	367.16	385.98	391.25	397.99	417.32	435.37	453.88	461.60
Tennessee	353.50	365.25	372.74	376.18	368.63	392.83	408.24	421.46	429.45	435.51	458.78	482.45	488.43	507.50	519.38
Texas	399.51	409.76	415.75	428.45	437.65	456.36	464.10	471.66	479.70	490.92	507.83	523.31	530.52	532.88	535.62
Utah	399.20	393.42	407.43	405.60	410.74	429.72	446.93	439.56	457.97	462.48	492.06	516.57	528.03	535.60	544.86
Vermont	359.38	370.27	382.59	408.59	429.22	448.80	472.32	501.74	489.16	494.51	503.01	516.89	515.99	539.18	573.47
Virginia	356.73	375.65	382.30	396.32	406.83	422.42	435.42	444.85	468.71	487.55	505.89	527.92	545.67	566.89	584.59
Washington	459.01	468.03	477.19	477.53	511.97	523.89	543.60	563.20	601.83	600.98	600.98	615.50	643.01	660.13	682.13
West Virginia	418.31	428.33	438.89	454.62	469.27	477.86	491.67	501.84	520.38	528.35	533.95	549.19	570.75	586.14	602.98
Wisconsin	427.46	436.77	443.50	446.96	459.95	474.86	495.33	511.14	529.91	537.20	554.51	579.18	586.04	607.55	616.28
Wyoming	377.52	378.30	[1]395.40	421.08	432.12	423.83	428.46	448.52	471.60	471.22	528.12	585.96	603.17	605.22	617.79
Puerto Rico	207.09	211.23	217.40	227.92	236.16	246.48	262.55	275.71	288.08	293.44	297.22	316.40	336.40	366.13	380.42
Virgin Islands	402.24	396.68	398.34	453.28	502.44	518.33	574.56	651.20	647.33	659.69	705.50	772.44	745.86	827.38	971.52

1. Data not continuous.

PART THREE

PROJECTIONS OF LABOR FORCE AND EMPLOYMENT BY INDUSTRY AND OCCUPATION

PROJECTIONS OF LABOR FORCE AND EMPLOYMENT BY INDUSTRY AND OCCUPATION

HIGHLIGHTS

This is the latest in a series of projections published every 2 years for the U.S. economy, providing information on future job growth by industry and occupation. The projections for 2008 result from the application of a set of assumptions about the demographics of the future population, economic trends, both domestic and international, and changes in the structure of industry.

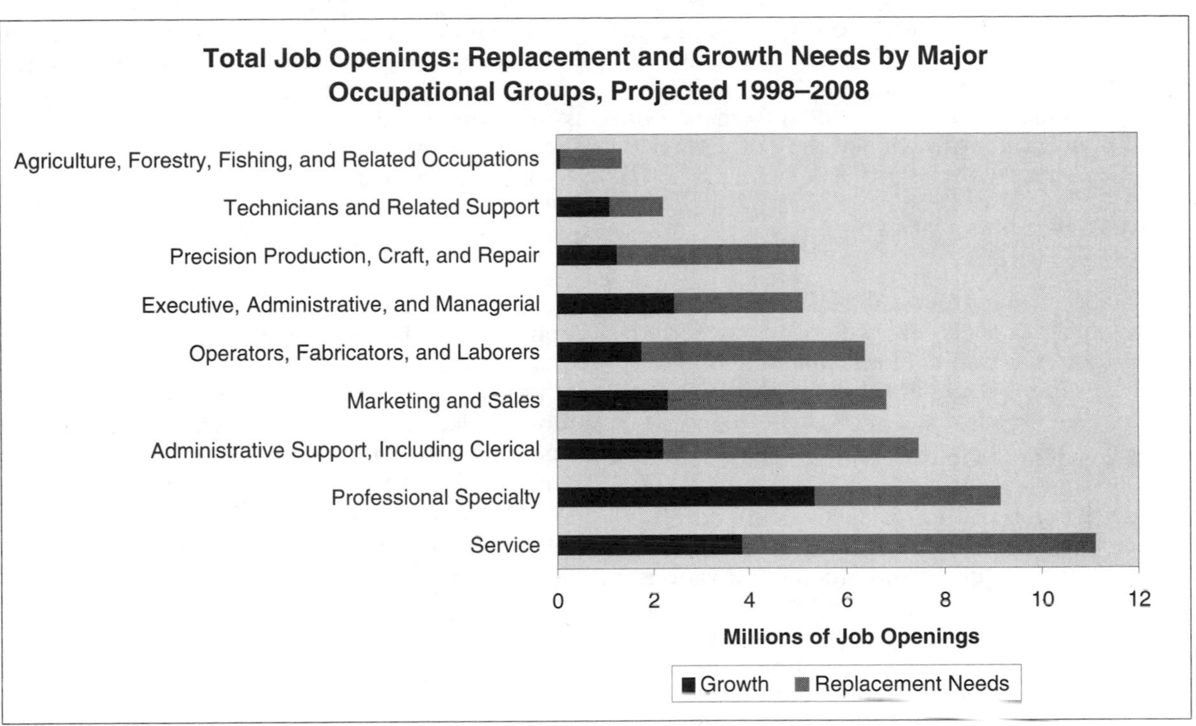

Job openings occur as a result of growth and replacement needs. The relative importance of the two factors varies by occupational group. "Professional specialties," which includes teachers as well as computer occupations, is the only group where growth is expected to exceed replacement. For the services sector, replacement needs are projected to be almost twice that generated by growth. Replacement needs are generally greatest in those occupations with relatively low pay.

OTHER HIGHLIGHTS:

- The total labor force is projected to grow 1.2 percent per year between 1998 and 2008, the same as 1988–1998 but slower than in earlier decades. However, the labor force of Hispanic origin is expected to grow 3.2 percent per year, constituting almost one-third of the total labor force increase. (Table 3-1)
- Service industries are projected to grow the fastest by 2008, accounting for over one-half of the employment increase. Within service industries, health services, social services, and business services constitute 70 percent of these new jobs. Within business services, computer and data processing services is projected to be the fastest growing industry at an 8 percent annual rate of employment growth. (Table 3-2)
- The industries with the most rapidly declining employment are projected to be crude petroleum, apparel, and coal mining at annual rate of -6.0 percent, -4.4 percent and -4.2 percent respectively. (Table 3-2)
- From 1998 to 2008, professional specialty occupations are projected to increase the fastest at 27 percent, and add the most jobs (5.3 million). On the other hand, the agriculture, forestry, fishing and related occupations group is projected to grow the least (1.6 percent), and add 0.1 million new jobs over the period. (Table 3-3)

NOTES AND DEFINITIONS

Concepts, Definitions, and Procedures

Long-term projections of likely employment conditions in the U.S. economy have been developed by the Bureau of Labor Statistics since 1957. These projections cover the future size and composition of the labor force, the aggregate economy, detailed estimates of industrial production, and industrial and occupational employment. The resulting data serve many users who need information on likely patterns of economic growth and their effects on employment. Beginning with the projections for 1996–2006, projections have been developed for a 10-year period and published every 2 years.

To carry out the projection process, the BLS makes many underlying assumptions concerning general economic and social conditions and sets ranges of acceptability for the key results of the various stages of the projection process.

Projecting employment in industry and occupational detail requires an integrated projection of the total economy and its various sectors. BLS projections are developed in a series of six steps, each of which is based on separate projections procedures and models and various related assumptions. The six steps or analytical phases are (1) labor force, (2) aggregate economy, (3) final demand (GDP) by sector and product, (4) inter-industry relationships (input-output), (5) industry output and employment, and (6) occupational employment. Each phase is solved separately, with the results of each used as input for the next phase, and with some results feeding back to earlier steps. In each phase, many iterations are made to ensure internal consistency as assumptions and results are reviewed and revised.

Labor force projections are determined by projections of the future age, sex, and racial composition of the population and by trends in labor force participation rates—the percent of the specified group in the population who will be working or seeking work. The population projections, prepared by the U.S. Bureau of the Census, are based on trends in birth rates, death rates, and net migration. With the population projections in hand, BLS analyzes and projects changes in labor force participation rates for more than 100 age, sex, and race or Hispanic origin groups.

Projections of labor force participation rates for each group are developed by first estimating a trend rate of change based on participation rate behavior during the prior 15-year period. Second, the rate is modified when the time-series projections for the specific group appear inconsistent with the results of cross-sectional and cohort analyses. This second step ensures consistency in the projections across various groups. Finally, the size of the labor force is derived by applying the participation rates to the population projections. The results are again reviewed for consistency.

Aggregate *economic performance*—the second phase of the BLS projections process—develops projections of the gross domestic product (GDP) and major categories of demand and income. These results provide control totals that are consistent with each other and with the various assumptions and conditions of the projection scenario. The values generated for each demand sector and subsector are then used in the next phase in developing detailed projections for personal consumption, business investment, foreign trade, and government.

These projections are accomplished using a macroeconomic model. The model basically consists of sets of equations that correlate various aspects of the economy with each other. It provides internally consistent, moderately detailed projections for each set of given assumptions and goals. *Employment Outlook 1998–2008* projections were based upon a long-term macro model developed by Data Resources, Inc. This model has approximately 400 equations that determine those factors affecting growth in the U.S. economy. This model is driven by a set of over 200 exogenous variables, the values of which are specified by BLS.

Final demand. The BLS projection then proceeds from the aggregate to the industrial level. For the industry output projections, the economy is disaggregated into about 190 producing sectors that cover the U.S. industrial structure, both public and private. The framework for this procedure is an input-output model. The initial input-output data used by BLS are prepared by the Bureau of Economic Analysis, U.S. Department of Commerce.

The development of projections of industry output begins with aggregate demand projections from the Data Resources model. In this model, projections are made for seven major categories of consumption, six categories of investment, 13 end-use categories of foreign trade, and three categories of government spending. A further disaggregation of the values from the model is then undertaken. For example, personal consumption expenditures are estimated for approximately 90 detailed categories.

Provision is made to allow for shifts in the commodity makeup of a given demand category. This is accomplished by projecting "bridge tables" relating individual types of demand to the actual industries supplying the goods. The bridge table is a percent distribution for each given demand category, such as the personal consumption or investment category, among each of the sectors in the BLS input-output model. In projecting changes in these bridge tables, expected changes in technology, consumer tastes or buying patterns, the commodity pattern of exports and imports, the future composition of business investment, and other structural factors are considered.

Input-output. The next stage in the projections process is the estimation of the intermediate flows of goods and services required to produce the projected GDP. Only final sales are counted in the GDP to avoid repeated counting of intermediate inputs. An industry's total employment, however, depends on its total output, whether sold to another industry, or used as a final good. The total output of each industry is projected using an inter-industry or input-output model. This model mathematically solves for all levels of intermediate inputs given industry relationships and final demand.

The BLS input-output model consists of two basic matrices for each year, a "use" and a "make" table. The principal table is the "use" table. This table shows the purchase of commodities by each industry as inputs into its production process. Projecting this table must take into account changes in the input pattern or the way in which goods or services are produced by each industry. In general, two types of changes in these input patterns are made in developing a future input-output table: (a) Those made to the inputs of a specific industry (as, for example, the changes in inputs in the publishing industry); and, (b) those made to the inputs of a specific commodity in all or most industries (as for example increased use of business services across a wide spectrum of industries). The "make" table shows the commodity output of each industry. It allocates commodity output to the industry to which it is primary and to all other industries where the commodity is produced as a secondary product. The "use" table is the basis for the direct requirements table of coefficients showing the inputs required to produce one dollar of that industry's output. The "make" table is used to create a "market shares" table, which shows the values of the "make" table as coefficients. The coefficient tables are used to calculate the total requirements tables that show the direct and indirect requirements to produce a dollar's worth of final demand. Projection tables are based on historical tables and on studies of specific industries.

Industry Employment. The projected level of industry employment is based on the projected levels of industry output as well as other factors such as expected technological changes and their impact on labor productivity. After the initial industry output is calculated, employment is derived from a model of the industry-level employment requirements. The employment projections by industry are constrained by the requirement that they sum to the aggregate employment level as determined by the aggregate projections. Employment for wage and salary workers is based on the Current Employment Statistics (payroll) survey, which counts jobs, whereas self-employed, unpaid family worker, agricultural, and private household data are based on the Current Population Survey (household survey), which counts workers. In these projections, there were additional secondary jobs as self-employed and unpaid family workers were included for the first time. Job totals for historical periods, therefore, differ from the official employment estimates of the Bureau of Labor Statistics.

Employment by Occupation. The model used to develop the occupational employment projections is an industry-occupation matrix showing the distribution of employment for 264 industries and for more than 520 detailed occupations. Occupational staffing patterns for the industries are based on data collected by state employment security agencies and analyzed by the BLS.

Staffing patterns of industries in the base-year industry-occupation matrix are projected to the target year to account for changes expected to occur in technology, shifts in production mix, and other factors. For example, one would expect greater employment of computer specialists as computer technology spreads across industries. In projecting the staffing patterns, the changes introduced into the input-output model for expected change are also analyzed to account for the impact of that technological change on future occupational staffing patterns of industries. The projected industry total employment data are applied to the projected industry staffing patterns, yielding employment by occupation for each industry. These data are aggregated across all industries to yield total occupational employment for the projected year.

Final Review. An important element of the projection system is its comprehensive structure. To ensure the internal consistency of this large structure, the BLS procedure encompasses detailed review and analysis of the results at each stage for reasonableness and for consistency with the results from other stages of the BLS projections. The final results reflect innumerable interactions among staff members who focus on particular variables in the model. Because of this review, the projection process at BLS converges to an internally consistent set of employment projections across a substantial number of industries and occupations.

Sources of Additional Information

A complete presentation of the projections including analysis of results and additional tables and a comprehensive description of the methodology is found in the *Monthly Labor Review,* November 1999. A more detailed description of methods is contained in the *BLS Handbook of Methods,* BLS Bulletin 2490, April 1997, Chapter 13 and BLS Bulletin 2521, *Occupational Projections and Training Data,* May 2000. Once the target year is reached, BLS evaluates the projections and these evaluations generally appear in articles in the *Monthly Labor Review.*

Table 3-1. Civilian Labor Force by Sex, Age, Race, and Hispanic Origin, 1978, 1988, 1998, and Projected 2008

Sex, age, race, and Hispanic origin	Level (thousands)				Change (thousands)			Percent change			Percent distribution				Annual growth rate (percent)		
	1978	1988	1998	2008	1978-1988	1988-1998	1998-2008	1978-1988	1988-1998	1998-2008	1978	1988	1998	2008	1978-1988	1988-1998	1998-2008
TOTAL, 16 YEARS AND OVER	102 251	121 669	137 673	154 576	19 418	16 004	16 903	19.0	13.2	12.3	100.0	100.0	100.0	100.0	1.8	1.2	1.2
16 to 24	25 022	22 536	21 894	25 210	-2 486	-642	3 316	-9.9	-2.8	15.1	24.5	18.5	15.9	16.3	-1.0	-0.3	1.4
16 to 19	9 652	8 031	8 256	9 396	-1 621	225	1 140	-16.8	2.8	13.8	9.4	6.6	6.0	6.1	-1.8	0.3	1.3
20 to 24	15 370	14 505	13 638	15 814	-865	-867	2 176	-5.6	-6.0	16.0	15.0	11.9	9.9	10.2	-0.6	-0.6	1.5
25 to 54	62 414	84 041	98 718	104 133	21 627	14 677	5 415	34.7	17.5	5.5	61.0	69.1	71.7	67.4	3.0	1.6	0.5
25 to 34	26 703	35 503	32 813	32 398	8 800	-2 690	-415	33.0	-7.6	-1.3	26.1	29.2	23.8	21.0	2.9	-0.8	-0.1
35 to 44	18 821	29 435	37 536	34 945	10 614	8 101	-2 591	56.4	27.5	-6.9	18.4	24.2	27.3	22.6	4.6	2.5	-0.7
45 to 54	16 891	19 104	28 368	36 790	2 213	9 264	8 422	13.1	48.5	29.7	16.5	15.7	20.6	23.8	1.2	4.0	2.6
55 and over	14 814	15 092	17 062	25 233	278	1 970	8 171	1.9	13.1	47.9	14.5	12.4	12.4	16.3	0.2	1.2	4.0
55 to 64	11 744	11 808	13 215	20 588	64	1 407	7 373	0.5	11.9	55.8	11.5	9.7	9.6	13.3	0.1	1.1	4.5
65 and over	3 070	3 284	3 847	4 645	214	563	798	7.0	17.1	20.7	3.0	2.7	2.8	3.0	0.7	1.6	1.9
65 to 74	2 627	2 814	3 179	3 849	187	365	670	7.1	13.0	21.1	2.6	2.3	2.3	2.5	0.7	1.2	1.9
75 and over	444	471	668	796	27	197	128	6.1	41.9	19.1	0.4	0.4	0.5	0.5	0.6	3.6	1.8
Men, 16 Years And Over	59 620	66 927	73 959	81 132	7 307	7 032	7 173	12.3	10.5	9.7	58.3	55.0	53.7	52.5	1.2	1.0	0.9
16 to 24	13 476	11 752	11 464	13 049	-1 724	-288	1 585	-12.8	-2.5	13.8	13.2	9.7	8.3	8.4	-1.4	-0.2	1.3
16 to 19	5 149	4 159	4 244	4 769	-990	85	525	-19.2	2.0	12.4	5.0	3.4	3.1	3.1	-2.1	0.2	1.2
20 to 24	8 327	7 594	7 221	8 279	-733	-373	1 059	-8.8	-4.9	14.7	8.1	6.2	5.2	5.4	-0.9	-0.5	1.4
25 to 54	37 057	46 382	53 002	54 496	9 325	6 620	1 494	25.2	14.3	2.8	36.2	38.1	38.5	35.3	2.3	1.3	0.3
25 to 34	15 814	19 742	17 796	17 145	3 928	-1 946	-651	24.8	-9.9	-3.7	15.5	16.2	12.9	11.1	2.2	-1.0	-0.4
35 to 44	11 159	16 074	20 242	18 345	4 915	4 168	-1 897	44.0	25.9	-9.4	10.9	13.2	14.7	11.9	3.7	2.3	-1.0
45 to 54	10 083	10 566	14 963	19 006	483	4 397	4 043	4.8	41.6	27.0	9.9	8.7	10.9	12.3	0.5	3.5	2.4
55 and over	9 088	8 793	9 493	13 587	-295	700	4 095	-3.2	8.0	43.1	8.9	7.2	6.9	8.8	-0.3	0.8	3.7
55 to 64	7 151	6 831	7 253	10 797	-320	422	3 544	-4.5	6.2	48.9	7.0	5.6	5.3	7.0	-0.5	0.6	4.1
65 and over	1 936	1 960	2 240	2 790	24	280	551	1.2	14.3	24.6	1.9	1.6	1.6	1.8	0.1	1.3	2.2
65 to 74	1 634	1 657	1 826	2 287	23	169	461	1.4	10.2	25.2	1.6	1.4	1.3	1.5	0.1	1.0	2.3
75 and over	302	304	413	503	2	109	90	0.7	35.9	21.8	0.3	0.2	0.3	0.3	0.1	3.1	2.0
Women, 16 Years And Over	42 631	54 742	63 714	73 444	12 111	8 972	9 729	28.4	16.4	15.3	41.7	45.0	46.3	47.5	2.5	1.5	1.4
16 to 24	11 546	10 783	10 430	12 161	-763	-353	1 732	-6.6	-3.3	16.6	11.3	8.9	7.6	7.9	-0.7	-0.3	1.5
16 to 19	4 503	3 872	4 012	4 627	-631	140	615	-14.0	3.6	15.3	4.4	3.2	2.9	3.0	-1.5	0.4	1.4
20 to 24	7 043	6 910	6 418	7 535	-133	-492	1 117	-1.9	-7.1	17.4	6.9	5.7	4.7	4.9	-0.2	-0.7	1.6
25 to 54	25 358	37 659	45 716	49 637	12 301	8 057	3 921	48.5	21.4	8.6	24.8	31.0	33.2	32.1	4.0	2.0	0.8
25 to 34	10 888	15 761	15 017	15 253	4 873	-744	236	44.8	-4.7	1.6	10.6	13.0	10.9	9.9	3.8	-0.5	0.2
35 to 44	7 662	13 361	17 294	16 600	5 699	3 933	-694	74.4	29.4	-4.0	7.5	11.0	12.6	10.7	5.7	2.6	-0.4
45 to 54	6 807	8 537	13 405	17 784	1 730	4 868	4 379	25.4	57.0	32.7	6.7	7.0	9.7	11.5	2.3	4.6	2.9
55 and over	5 727	6 301	7 569	11 645	574	1 268	4 077	10.0	20.1	53.9	5.6	5.2	5.5	7.5	1.0	1.9	4.4
55 to 64	4 593	4 977	5 962	9 791	384	985	3 829	8.4	19.8	64.2	4.5	4.1	4.3	6.3	0.8	1.8	5.1
65 and over	1 134	1 324	1 607	1 854	190	283	247	16.8	21.4	15.4	1.1	1.1	1.2	1.2	1.6	2.0	1.4
65 to 74	993	1 157	1 352	1 562	164	195	209	16.5	16.9	15.5	1.0	1.0	1.0	1.0	1.5	1.6	1.4
75 and over	141	167	255	293	26	88	38	18.4	52.7	14.8	0.1	0.1	0.2	0.2	1.7	4.3	1.4
White, 16 Years And Over	89 634	104 756	115 415	126 665	15 122	10 659	11 251	16.9	10.2	9.7	87.7	86.1	83.8	81.9	1.6	1.0	0.9
Men	52 955	58 317	63 034	67 664	5 362	4 717	4 630	10.1	8.1	7.3	51.8	47.9	45.8	43.8	1.0	0.8	0.7
Women	36 679	46 439	52 380	59 001	9 760	5 941	6 621	26.6	12.8	12.6	35.9	38.2	38.0	38.2	2.4	1.2	1.2
Black, 16 Years And Over	10 432	13 205	15 982	19 101	2 773	2 777	3 119	26.6	21.0	19.5	10.2	10.9	11.6	12.4	2.4	1.9	1.8
Men	5 435	6 596	7 542	8 877	1 161	946	1 335	21.4	14.3	17.7	5.3	5.4	5.5	5.7	2.0	1.3	1.6
Women	4 997	6 609	8 441	10 224	1 612	1 832	1 783	32.3	27.7	21.1	4.9	5.4	6.1	6.6	2.8	2.5	1.9
Asian And Other, 16 Years And Over [1]	2 190	3 721	6 278	8 809	1 531	2 557	2 531	69.9	68.7	40.3	2.1	3.1	4.6	5.7	5.4	5.4	3.4
Men	1 237	2 019	3 383	4 591	782	1 364	1 208	63.2	67.5	35.7	1.2	1.7	2.5	3.0	5.0	5.3	3.1
Women	953	1 702	2 895	4 219	749	1 193	1 323	78.6	70.1	45.7	0.9	1.4	2.1	2.7	6.0	5.5	3.8
Hispanic Origin, 16 Years And Over [2]	...	8 982	14 317	19 585	...	5 335	5 268	...	59.4	36.8	...	7.4	10.4	12.7	...	4.8	3.2
Men	...	5 409	8 571	11 033	...	3 162	2 462	...	58.5	28.7	...	4.4	6.2	7.1	...	4.7	2.6
Women	...	3 573	5 746	8 552	...	2 173	2 806	...	60.8	48.8	...	2.9	4.2	5.5	...	4.9	4.1
Other Than Hispanic Origin, 16 Years And Over [2]	...	112 687	123 356	134 991	...	10 669	11 635	...	9.5	9.4	...	92.6	89.6	87.3	...	0.9	0.9
Men	...	61 518	65 388	70 099	...	3 870	4 711	...	6.3	7.2	...	50.6	47.5	45.3	...	0.6	0.7
Women	...	51 169	57 968	64 892	...	6 799	6 924	...	13.3	11.9	...	42.1	42.1	42.0	...	1.3	1.1
White Non-Hispanic, 16 Years And Over [2]	...	96 141	101 767	109 216	...	5 626	7 449	...	5.9	7.3	...	79.0	73.9	70.7	...	0.6	0.7
Men	...	53 122	54 833	57 756	...	1 710	2 924	...	3.2	5.3	...	43.7	39.8	37.4	...	0.3	0.5
Women	...	43 018	46 935	51 459	...	3 916	4 525	...	9.1	9.6	...	35.4	34.1	33.3	...	0.9	0.9

1. The "Asian and Other" group includes Asians and Pacific Islanders and American Indians and Alaska Natives. The historical data are derived by subtracting "Black" from the "Black and Other" group; projections are made directly, not by subtraction.
2. Data by Hispanic origin are not available before 1980.

Table 3-2. Employment and Output by Industry, 1988, 1998, and Projected 2008

Industry	Employment							Output				
	Jobs (thousands)			Change (thousands)		Average annual rate of change (percent)		Billions of chained (1992) dollars			Average annual rate of change (percent)	
	1988	1998	2008	1988-1998	1998-2008	1988-1998	1998-2008	1988	1998	2008	1988-1998	1998-2008
TOTAL [1, 2, 3]	120 010	140 514	160 795	20 503	20 281	1.6	1.4	10 204	13 322	18 241	2.7	3.2
NONFARM WAGE AND SALARY [4]	104 570	124 887	144 526	20 316	19 640	1.8	1.5	9 558	12 420	17 145	2.7	3.3
Mining	713	590	475	-123	-115	-1.9	-2.1	183	175	197	-0.4	1.2
Metal mining	50	50	37	1	-13	0.1	-3.0	9	11	15	2.3	3.7
Coal mining	151	92	59	-59	-32	-4.9	-4.2	26	29	31	1.2	0.7
Crude petroleum, natural gas, and gas liquids	201	143	77	-58	-66	-3.4	-6.0	117	99	109	-1.6	0.9
Oil and gas field services	199	196	205	-3	9	-0.2	0.5	18	19	21	0.7	1.2
Nonmetallic minerals, except fuels	112	109	96	-3	-13	-0.3	-1.2	15	17	20	1.3	1.5
Construction	5 098	5 985	6 535	887	550	1.6	0.9	661	697	792	0.5	1.3
Manufacturing	19 314	18 772	18 684	-542	-89	-0.3	(5)	2 904	3 861	5 650	2.9	3.9
Durable manufacturing	11 363	11 170	11 277	-193	107	-0.2	0.1	1 506	2 241	3 813	4.1	5.5
Lumber and wood products	767	813	811	46	-2	0.6	(5)	94	100	104	0.7	0.4
Logging	88	79	82	-9	2	-1.0	0.3	22	18	20	-2.1	1.2
Sawmills and planing mills	204	183	162	-21	-21	-1.1	-1.2	24	27	25	1.1	-0.7
Millwork, plywood, and structural members	273	308	315	34	7	1.2	0.2	28	30	30	0.7	-0.1
Wood containers and miscellaneous wood products	134	144	147	10	4	0.7	0.3	13	16	18	2.2	1.3
Wood buildings and mobile homes	68	99	105	31	6	3.8	0.6	7	10	11	3.4	1.4
Furniture and fixtures	527	530	546	4	15	0.1	0.3	46	63	71	3.3	1.2
Household furniture	308	283	266	-25	-16	-0.8	-0.6	22	29	28	2.7	-0.4
Partitions and fixtures	79	93	109	13	16	1.6	1.6	7	9	11	2.7	2.6
Office and miscellaneous furniture and fixtures	140	155	170	15	15	1.0	0.9	17	25	32	4.2	2.3
Glass and glass products	157	151	140	-6	-11	-0.4	-0.8	18	22	26	2.1	1.7
Hydraulic cement	20	17	14	-2	-4	-1.1	-2.3	4	5	4	0.9	-1.2
Stone, clay, and miscellaneous mineral products	176	166	147	-11	-18	-0.6	-1.2	19	20	22	0.6	0.8
Concrete, gypsum, and plaster products	214	229	230	15	1	0.7	(5)	26	29	33	1.3	1.1
Primary metal industries	770	712	643	-59	-69	-0.8	-1.0	145	162	216	1.1	3.0
Blast furnaces and basic steel products	278	232	177	-47	-55	-1.8	-2.7	64	69	91	0.8	2.7
Iron and steel foundries	136	131	134	-5	3	-0.4	0.2	13	15	21	1.4	3.4
Primary nonferrous smelting and refining	44	39	32	-5	-8	-1.2	-2.1	12	12	15	-0.3	2.1
All other primary metals	45	47	46	3	-2	0.6	-0.4	9	11	17	2.4	3.9
Nonferrous rolling and drawing	179	170	157	-9	-13	-0.5	-0.8	39	44	60	1.1	3.2
Nonferrous foundries	88	93	98	5	6	0.5	0.6	8	10	14	3.1	2.8
Fabricated metal products	1 428	1 501	1 519	72	18	0.5	0.1	172	217	260	2.4	1.8
Metal cans and shipping containers	53	37	25	-16	-12	-3.6	-3.8	13	14	16	0.7	0.8
Cutlery, hand tools, and hardware	139	126	108	-13	-18	0.9	-1.5	16	20	23	2.4	1.3
Plumbing and nonelectric heating equipment	62	68	57	6	-1	-0.8	-0.1	7	8	8	1.1	0.1
Fabricated structural metal products	423	464	500	41	36	0.9	0.8	46	50	60	2.1	0.7
Screw machine products, bolts, rivets, etc.	99	107	105	7	-2	0.7	-0.2	10	14	14	3.5	0.6
Metal forgings and stampings	227	257	250	30	-7	1.2	0.3	32	44	51	3.1	1.4
Metal coating, engraving, and allied services	119	144	165	25	21	1.9	1.3	10	16	27	4.8	5.0
Ordanance and ammunition	77	41	34	-36	-7	-6.1	-1.8	9	5	6	-6.3	2.9
Miscellaneous fabricated metal products	200	268	275	38	7	1.6	0.3	30	41	55	3.2	3.1
Industrial machinery and equipment	2 089	2 203	2 197	114	-6	0.5	(5)	238	574	1 541	9.2	10.4
Engines and turbines	92	84	69	-9	-15	-1.0	-1.9	19	24	29	2.2	1.0
Farm and garden machinery	102	104	95	2	-9	0.2	-0.9	15	22	28	3.9	2.5
Construction and related machinery	222	253	270	31	17	1.3	0.6	30	41	52	3.2	2.5
Metalworking machinery and equipment	327	352	324	25	-28	0.7	-0.8	26	33	40	2.4	2.0
Special industry machinery	159	179	187	20	8	1.2	0.4	21	33	51	4.8	4.3
General industrial machinery and equipment	232	269	273	37	4	1.5	0.1	30	38	53	2.5	3.4
Computer and office equipment	459	379	369	-80	-11	-1.9	-0.3	50	446	1 723	24.6	14.5
Refrigeration and service industry machinery	186	200	216	14	16	0.7	0.8	28	40	49	3.3	2.1
Industrial machinery, n.e.c.	309	382	393	73	11	2.2	0.3	24	41	58	5.7	3.6
Electronic and other electronic equipment	1 764	1 704	1 773	-60	69	-0.3	0.4	193	401	870	7.6	8.1
Electric distribution equipment	101	82	70	-18	-13	-2.0	-1.7	11	13	17	1.5	2.7
Electrical industrial apparatus	178	153	122	-25	-31	-1.5	-2.3	19	27	37	3.6	3.2
Household appliances	137	117	96	-21	-20	-1.6	-1.9	17	19	21	1.6	0.8
Electric lighting and wiring equipment	198	183	157	-15	-26	-0.8	-1.5	21	24	28	1.2	1.6
Household audio and video equipment	84	82	67	-2	-14	-0.2	-1.9	9	16	20	6.3	2.4
Communications equipment	275	282	302	7	21	0.3	0.7	38	78	169	7.6	8.1
Electronic components and accessories	622	660	820	38	160	0.6	2.2	55	203	571	13.9	10.9
Miscellaneous electrical equipment	170	146	139	-24	-7	-1.5	-0.5	25	27	31	1.0	1.3
Transportation equipment	2 036	1 884	1 988	-152	104	-0.8	0.5	392	480	603	2.1	2.3
Motor vehicles and equipment	856	990	940	133	-50	1.5	-0.5	238	324	375	3.2	1.5
Aerospace	892	615	750	-276	135	-3.6	2.0	126	120	179	-0.5	4.1
Ship and boat building and repairing	196	166	160	-30	-6	-1.6	-0.4	17	16	18	-0.7	1.0
Railroad equipment	31	37	42	6	5	1.8	1.3	4	8	10	6.8	3.1
Miscellaneous transportation equipment	62	76	96	14	20	2.1	2.3	7	13	21	6.2	5.2

See footnotes and *Note* at end of table.

Table 3-2. Employment and Output by Industry, 1988, 1998, and Projected 2008—*Continued*

Industry	Employment: Jobs (thousands) 1988	Jobs 1998	Jobs 2008	Change (thousands) 1988-1998	Change 1998-2008	Average annual rate of change (percent) 1988-1998	Average annual rate 1998-2008	Output: Billions of chained (1992) dollars 1988	1998	2008	Average annual rate of change (percent) 1988-1998	1998-2008
Instruments and related products	1 031	868	887	-164	19	-1.7	0.2	123	154	222	2.2	3.7
Search and navigation equipment	316	162	143	-155	-19	-6.5	-1.2	41	33	41	-2.1	2.1
Measuring and controlling devices	324	304	300	-20	-4	-0.6	-0.1	31	45	73	3.9	4.8
Medical equipment, instruments, and supplies	231	279	335	48	56	1.9	1.8	28	51	80	6.3	4.5
Opthalmic goods	39	35	36	-4	1	-1.1	0.3	2	3	5	5.6	5.1
Photographic equipment and supplies	109	81	69	-28	-12	-2.9	-1.6	21	20	24	-0.1	1.6
Watches, clocks and parts	12	7	5	-5	-2	-5.4	-3.7	2	1	(5)	-3.2	-11.7
Miscellaneous manufacturing industries	383	393	382	10	-10	0.3	-0.3	38	50	61	2.8	2.0
Jewelry, silverware, and plated ware	53	50	42	-3	-8	-0.6	-1.8	6	8	8	1.9	(5)
Toys and sporting goods	103	106	95	2	-11	0.2	-1.1	11	15	17	3.3	1.6
Manufactured products, n.e.c.	226	237	246	11	9	0.5	0.4	21	28	36	2.8	2.7
Nondurable manufacturing	7 951	7 602	7 406	-349	-196	-0.4	-0.3	1 398	1 633	1 909	1.6	1.6
Food and kindred products	1 626	1 686	1 721	60	35	0.4	0.2	373	442	497	1.7	1.2
Meat products	399	494	570	95	76	2.2	1.4	84	102	121	2.0	1.7
Dairy products	158	140	124	-18	-16	-1.2	-1.2	50	54	57	0.7	0.6
Preserved fruits and vegetables	236	229	217	-7	-13	-0.3	-0.6	42	49	54	1.5	0.9
Grain mill products and fats and oils	156	158	159	3	1	0.2	0.1	54	61	71	1.2	1.5
Bakery products	212	206	197	-5	-10	-0.3	-0.5	27	29	29	0.8	-0.1
Sugar and confectionery products	100	97	93	-3	-4	-0.3	-0.4	21	26	28	2.0	0.6
Beverages	199	182	165	-17	-18	-0.9	-1.0	63	80	93	2.4	1.5
Miscellaneous food and kindred products	166	178	197	11	19	0.7	1.0	32	41	45	2.6	0.9
Tobacco products	54	41	30	-14	-11	-2.9	-3.1	41	41	45	0.1	1.0
Textile mill products	728	598	501	-130	-97	-1.9	-1.7	68	85	95	2.2	1.2
Weaving, finishing, yarn, and thread mills	400	320	251	-80	-69	-2.2	-2.4	36	40	42	1.2	0.4
Knitting mills	215	159	128	-55	-32	-2.9	-2.2	14	21	26	4.4	2.1
Carpets and rugs	61	64	74	3	10	0.5	1.4	12	14	17	1.5	2.0
Miscellaneous textile goods	53	55	49	2	-6	0.4	-1.1	7	10	12	3.2	1.4
Apparel and other textile products	1 085	763	586	-322	-177	-3.5	-2.6	67	76	78	1.2	0.3
Apparel	888	547	350	-341	-197	-4.7	-4.4	52	55	52	0.6	-0.6
Miscellaneous fabricated textile products	197	216	236	19	20	0.9	0.9	16	21	26	2.8	2.2
Paper and allied products	689	675	674	-14	(5)	-0.2	(5)	128	146	172	1.3	1.7
Pulp, paper, and paperboard mills	244	215	187	-29	-28	-1.3	-1.4	54	55	64	0.3	1.4
Paperboard containers and boxes	206	219	236	13	17	0.6	0.7	29	36	44	1.9	2.1
Converted paper products except containers	239	241	252	2	11	0.1	0.4	44	55	64	2.1	1.6
Printing and publishing	1 543	1 565	1 545	22	-20	0.1	-0.1	170	181	197	0.7	0.8
Newspapers	473	443	401	-30	-42	-0.7	-1.0	42	32	28	-2.7	-1.4
Periodicals	127	138	150	12	12	0.9	0.8	23	25	27	0.7	0.7
Books	115	127	139	12	12	1.0	0.9	21	24	28	1.5	1.7
Miscellaneous publishing	79	91	97	13	6	1.5	0.7	10	12	16	2.5	2.6
Commercial printing and business forms	589	623	624	34	1	0.6	(5)	61	72	83	1.7	1.5
Greeting cards	24	29	32	5	3	1.9	0.9	3	4	4	3.1	0.1
Blankbooks and bookbinding	75	64	62	-11	-2	-1.6	-0.3	5	6	5	2.6	-1.9
Service industries for the printing trade	62	50	41	-12	-9	-2.1	-2.0	5	6	5	1.3	-0.7
Chemicals and allied products	1 057	1 043	1 043	-15	(5)	-0.1	(5)	284	332	415	1.6	2.2
Industrial chemicals	279	253	236	-25	-17	-1.0	-0.7	88	78	83	-1.2	0.6
Plastic materials and synthetics	177	157	141	-20	-16	-1.2	-1.1	47	56	78	1.8	3.4
Drugs	228	279	309	51	30	2.1	1.0	54	84	117	4.6	3.3
Soap, cleaners, and toilet goods	159	156	165	-4	10	-0.2	0.6	43	56	64	2.6	1.3
Paints and allied products	63	52	45	-11	-7	-1.9	-1.5	16	18	19	1.2	0.7
Agricultural chemicals	52	52	49	(5)	-3	(5)	-0.6	16	19	23	1.9	1.8
Miscellaneous chemical products	100	94	98	-6	4	-0.7	0.4	20	23	32	1.3	3.5
Petroleum and coal products	160	140	117	-20	-23	-1.3	-1.8	158	169	183	0.6	0.8
Petroleum refining	121	96	75	-25	-21	-2.3	-2.5	145	153	165	0.5	0.8
Miscellaneous petroleum and coal products	39	44	42	5	-2	1.2	-0.5	14	16	19	1.6	1.4
Rubber and miscellaneous plastic products	866	1 009	1 130	143	121	1.5	1.1	100	151	221	4.2	3.9
Tires and inner tubes	84	79	66	-5	-13	-0.6	-1.8	12	14	17	2.0	1.9
Rubber products and plastic hose and footwear	76	189	199	13	9	0.7	0.5	17	22	33	2.9	3.9
Miscellaneous plastic products, n.e.c.	606	740	865	135	125	2.0	1.6	72	114	171	4.8	4.1
Leather and leather products	143	83	59	-60	-24	-5.3	-3.3	10	9	8	-2.0	-1.2
Footwear, except rubber and plastic	89	38	25	-51	-13	-8.3	-4.1	5	3	3	-4.8	0.4
Luggage, handbags, and leather products, n.e.c.	54	45	34	-8	-11	-1.6	-2.7	5	5	4	0.1	-2.2
Transportation, Communications, And Utilities	5 512	6 600	7 541	1 088	941	1.8	1.3	837	1 115	1 502	2.9	3.0
Transportation	3 301	4 276	4 951	975	675	2.6	1.5	339	493	729	3.8	4.0
Railroad transportation	298	231	185	-67	-46	-2.5	-2.2	35	44	53	2.5	1.8
Local and interurban passenger transit	309	468	622	159	154	4.2	2.9	17	21	27	2.1	2.7
Trucking and warehousing	1 351	1 745	1 944	394	199	2.6	1.1	142	230	353	4.9	4.4
Trucking and courier services, except air transportation	1 240	1 579	1 744	338	166	2.4	1.0	134	216	331	4.9	4.4
Warehousing and storage	111	166	200	55	34	4.1	1.9	8	14	22	5.1	4.5
Water transportation	171	180	190	9	10	0.5	0.5	32	30	36	-0.8	1.9
Air transportation	850	1 183	1 400	333	217	3.4	1.7	80	128	203	4.8	4.7
Pipelines, except natural gas	19	14	13	-5	-1	-2.8	-1.0	8	7	9	-0.6	1.5
Transportation services	302	455	597	153	142	4.2	2.7	25	33	48	2.8	3.9
Passenger transportation arrangement	171	219	268	48	48	2.5	2.0	10	16	22	4.8	3.2
Miscellaneous transportation services	131	236	329	105	94	6.0	3.4	15	17	26	1.2	4.5

See footnotes and *Note* at end of table.

Table 3-2. Employment and Output by Industry, 1988, 1998, and Projected 2008—*Continued*

Industry	Employment							Output				
	Jobs (thousands)			Change (thousands)		Average annual rate of change (percent)		Billions of chained (1992) dollars			Average annual rate of change (percent)	
	1988	1998	2008	1988-1998	1998-2008	1988-1998	1998-2008	1988	1998	2008	1988-1998	1998-2008
Communications	1 280	1 470	1 768	190	299	1.4	1.9	218	329	519	4.2	4.6
Telephone and telegraph communications and communication service	942	1 042	1 285	100	244	1.0	2.1	166	264	434	4.7	5.1
Cable and pay television services	111	181	230	70	49	5.0	2.4	23	32	48	3.6	4.1
Radio and television broadcasting	227	247	253	20	6	0.8	0.2	29	34	39	1.4	1.5
Utilities	931	855	822	-76	-33	-0.9	-0.4	280	292	268	0.4	-0.9
Electric utilities	452	364	311	-87	-53	-2.1	-1.6	164	191	209	1.6	0.9
Gas utilities	164	136	117	-28	-20	-1.8	-1.5	67	52	52	-2.5	-0.1
Combined utilities	194	159	131	-36	-27	-2.0	-1.9	30	28	31	-0.8	0.9
Water and sanitation	121	196	263	74	67	4.9	3.0	19	21	24	1.0	1.2
Wholesale Trade	6 030	6 831	7 330	802	499	1.3	0.7	497	820	1 178	5.1	3.7
Retail Trade	19 023	22 296	25 363	3 273	3 067	1.6	1.3	793	1 065	1 393	3.0	2.7
Retail trade, excluding eating and drinking places	12 765	14 536	16 281	1 771	1 745	1.3	1.1	578	813	1 098	3.5	3.1
Eating and drinking places	6 258	7 760	9 082	1 502	1 321	2.2	1.6	215	253	297	1.6	1.6
Finance, Insurance And Real Estate	6 629	7 408	8 367	778	960	1.1	1.2	1 079	1 330	1 788	2.1	3.0
Depository institutions	2 255	2 042	2 100	-213	58	-1.0	0.3	275	273	382	-0.1	3.4
Nondepository institutions; holding and investment offices	573	906	1 141	334	235	4.7	2.3	63	86	146	3.1	5.4
Security and commodity brokers	447	645	900	198	255	3.7	3.4	57	176	361	12.0	7.5
Insurance carriers	1 435	1 597	1 751	162	154	1.1	0.9	158	180	207	1.3	1.4
Insurance agents, brokers and service	640	746	825	107	79	1.6	1.0	73	46	41	-4.6	-1.0
Real estate	1 280	1 471	1 650	190	179	1.4	1.2	458	569	707	2.2	2.2
Royalties	. . .	. . .	. . .	. . .	. . .	. . .	. . .	43	81	150	6.6	6.3
Owner-occupied dwellings	. . .	. . .	. . .	. . .	. . .	. . .	. . .	420	528	633	2.3	1.8
Services [4]	24 866	37	48 543	11 720	11 957	3.9	2.9	1 702	2 413	3 556	3.6	4.0
Hotels	1 494	1 719	2 030	225	311	1.4	1.7	87	85	93	-0.3	1.0
Other lodging places	46	57	58	11	1	2.2	0.2	5	5	6	0.9	1.5
Personal services	1 056	1 195	1 317	139	122	1.2	1.0	66	77	96	1.6	2.2
Laundry, cleaning, and shoe repair	420	440	467	20	27	0.5	0.8	20	23	28	1.2	2.0
Personal services, n.e.c.	175	234	266	59	32	2.9	1.3	20	25	34	2.1	3.1
Beauty and barber shops	371	411	474	40	63	1.0	1.2	19	22	25	1.5	1.4
Funeral service and crematories	79	99	110	20	11	2.3	1.0	7	8	10	1.9	1.9
Business services	4 638	8 584	13 146	3 946	4 562	6.3	4.4	273	559	1 093	7.4	6.9
Advertising	229	268	323	39	55	1.6	1.9	23	34	47	4.0	3.2
Service to buildings	780	950	1 187	170	237	2.0	2.3	24	37	50	4.4	3.0
Miscellaneous equipment rental and leasing	180	258	369	79	111	3.7	3.6	23	32	52	3.2	5.0
Personnel supply services	1 350	3 230	4 623	1 879	1 393	9.1	3.7	30	78	129	10.2	5.1
Computer and data processing services	673	1 599	3 472	926	1 872	9.0	8.1	77	219	584	11.1	10.3
Miscellaneous business services	1 426	2 278	3 172	853	893	4.8	3.4	95	158	229	5.2	3.8
Auto repair, services and garages	834	1 144	1 550	311	406	3.2	3.1	90	140	240	4.4	5.6
Automotive rentals, without drivers	161	200	250	39	50	2.2	2.3	16	50	122	12.4	9.3
Automobile parking, repair, and services	672	944	1 300	272	356	3.5	3.2	75	89	116	1.7	2.7
Miscellaneous repair shops	350	382	406	32	24	0.9	0.6	38	37	38	-0.2	0.2
Electrical repair shops	108	113	127	5	13	0.5	1.1	12	14	16	1.2	1.7
Watch, jewelry, and furniture repair	29	29	26	(5)	-3	(5)	-1.1	2	2	2	1.1	-0.1
Miscellaneous repair shops and related services	213	240	253	27	13	1.2	0.5	24	21	20	-1.1	-0.5
Motion pictures	341	573	636	233	62	5.3	1.0	37	42	68	1.5	4.9
Motion pictures	238	408	451	171	43	5.6	1.0	33	35	58	0.7	5.1
Video tape rental	103	165	185	62	20	4.8	1.1	4	7	10	6.8	3.2
Amusement and recreation services	977	1 601	2 108	624	507	5.1	2.8	63	102	150	4.9	3.9
Producers, orchestras, and entertainers	122	176	225	54	49	3.7	2.5	14	22	33	4.5	4.2
Bowling centers	92	82	70	-10	-12	-1.2	-1.5	4	3	2	-2.7	-2.2
Commercial sports	91	127	160	35	34	3.3	2.4	12	13	13	0.5	0.6
Amusement and recreation services, n.e.c.	671	1 217	1 653	545	436	6.1	3.1	33	65	102	6.8	4.7
Health services	7 106	9 846	12 667	2 741	2 821	3.3	2.6	503	637	795	2.4	2.2
Offices of health practitioners	1 937	2 949	4 098	1 012	1 150	4.3	3.3	211	249	313	1.7	2.3
Nursing and personal care facilities	1 311	1 762	2 213	451	451	3.0	2.3	41	62	74	4.3	1.8
Hospitals, private	3 294	3 926	4 337	632	411	1.8	1.0	210	254	312	1.9	2.1
Health services, n.e.c.	564	1 209	2 018	645	809	7.9	5.3	42	72	96	5.7	2.8
Legal services	845	973	1 200	128	228	1.4	2.1	112	126	154	1.2	2.1
Educational services	1 567	2 177	2 690	610	513	3.3	2.1	72	100	136	3.4	3.1
Social services	1 552	2 644	3 678	1 092	1 034	5.5	3.4	60	95	137	4.7	3.7
Individual and miscellaneous social services	565	923	1 223	358	300	5.0	2.9	25	42	63	5.4	4.2
Job training and related services	241	369	484	129	114	4.4	2.7	7	11	16	4.6	3.8
Child day care services	356	605	800	248	196	5.4	2.8	16	21	27	2.9	2.5
Residential care	389	747	1 171	357	424	6.7	4.6	13	21	30	5.4	3.7
Museums, botanical, and zoological gardens	58	93	131	35	39	4.8	3.6	3	5	7	5.2	3.7
Membership organizations	1 740	2 361	2 600	621	239	3.1	1.0	67	87	104	2.6	1.9
Engineering, management, and other services	2 263	3 237	4 328	975	1 091	3.6	2.9	230	326	464	3.6	3.6
Engineering and architectural services	730	905	1 140	175	235	2.2	2.3	81	100	142	2.1	3.6
Research and testing services	492	614	861	122	247	2.2	3.4	30	53	101	5.9	6.7
Management and public relations	508	1 034	1 500	526	466	7.4	3.8	63	114	157	6.0	3.3
Accounting, auditing, and other services	532	684	827	153	143	2.6	1.9	56	61	69	1.0	1.2

See footnotes and *Note* at end of table.

Table 3-2. Employment and Output by Industry, 1988, 1998, and Projected 2008—*Continued*

Industry	Employment							Output				
	Jobs (thousands)			Change (thousands)		Average annual rate of change (percent)		Billions of chained (1992) dollars			Average annual rate of change (percent)	
	1988	1998	2008	1988-1998	1998-2008	1988-1998	1998-2008	1988	1998	2008	1988-1998	1998-2008
Government	17 386	19 819	21 688	2 433	1 869	1.3	0.9	891	979	1 111	1.0	1.3
Federal Government	2 971	2 686	2 550	-285	-136	-1.0	-0.5	333	307	310	-0.8	0.1
Federal enterprises	1 024	987	993	-37	6	-0.4	0.1	59	74	91	2.4	2.0
U.S. Postal Service	831	867	895	36	28	0.4	0.3	46	58	72	2.3	2.2
Federal electric utilities	38	30	20	-8	-10	-2.3	-4.1	6	7	8	2.0	1.7
Federal government enterprises, n.e.c.	156	90	78	-66	-12	-5.3	-1.4	7	10	11	3.0	0.7
Federal general government	1 947	1 699	1 557	-248	-142	-1.4	-0.9	216	172	162	-2.3	-0.6
Federal government capital services	...	...	...	...	...	...	...	58	61	58	0.5	-0.5
State and local government	14 415	17 133	19 138	2 718	2 005	1.7	1.1	558	673	801	1.9	1.8
State and local enterprises	880	910	958	30	48	0.3	0.5	91	110	131	1.9	1.8
Local government passenger transit	201	212	214	11	2	0.5	0.1	6	6	7	0.2	2.1
State and local electric utilities	82	86	90	4	4	0.4	0.4	19	23	26	1.8	1.4
State and local government enterprises, n.e.c.	597	612	654	15	42	0.2	0.7	66	82	98	2.1	1.8
State and local general government	13 535	16 223	18 181	2 688	1 958	1.8	1.1	467	563	670	1.9	1.8
State and local government hospitals	1 065	983	948	-82	-35	-0.8	-0.4	34	40	47	1.7	1.5
State and local government education	7 343	8 998	10 195	1 655	1 197	2.1	1.3	222	263	305	1.7	1.5
State and local general government, n.e.c.	5 127	6 242	7 038	1 115	796	2.0	1.2	171	203	236	1.7	1.5
State and local government capital services	...	...	...	...	...	...	...	40	57	83	3.6	3.8
AGRICULTURE [6]	3 355	3 576	3 526	221	-51	0.6	-0.1	212	267	308	2.3	1.4
Agricultural production	2 292	2 106	1 729	-186	-377	-0.8	-2.0	170	219	255	2.6	1.5
Agricultural services	960	1 385	1 724	425	340	3.7	2.2	34	36	42	0.4	1.5
Veterinary services	126	217	282	91	65	5.6	2.7	8	9	11	1.8	1.5
Landscape and horticultural services	506	768	993	262	224	4.3	2.6	17	17	19	-0.1	1.5
Agricultural services, n.e.c.	328	400	450	72	51	2.0	1.2	10	10	12	0.2	1.7
Forestry, fishing, hunting and trapping	103	86	73	-17	-13	-1.8	-1.6	9	12	12	2.7	-0.7
PRIVATE HOUSEHOLD WAGE AND SALARY	1 153	962	759	-191	-203	-1.8	-2.3	10	11	10	0.9	-0.8
NONAGRICULTURAL SELF-EMPLOYED AND UNPAID FAMILY [7, 8]	8 731	9 029	9 925	298	896	0.3	1.0	...	...	...	...	...
SECONDARY WAGE AND SALARY JOBS IN AGRICULTURE (EXCEPT AGRICULTURAL SERVICES); FORESTRY, FISHING, HUNTING, AND TRAPPING; PRIVATE HOUSEHOLDS [8, 9]	211	163	158	-48	-0.5	-2.5	-0.3	...	...	...	...	...
SECONDARY JOB AS A SELF-EMPLOYED WORKER OR UNPAID FAMILY WORKER [8, 10]	1 990	1 897	1 901	-94	5	-0.5	(5)	...	...	...	...	...

Note: n.e.c. = not elsewhere classified.

1. Differs from historical employment totals. See "Notes and Definitions."
2. Output subcategories do not necessarily add to higher categories as a by-product of chain-weighting.
3. This is the first time the Total category includes second jobs: wage and salary and second jobs: self-employed and unpaid family.
4. Excludes SIC 074, 075, 078 (agricultural services) and 99 (nonclassifiable establishments). The data therefore are not exactly comparable with data published in 'Employment and Earnings'.
5. Value less than 0.05.
6. Excludes government wage and salary workers, and includes private sector for SIC 08 and 09 (forestry, fishing, hunting, and trapping).
7. Excludes SIC 08, 09 (forestry, fishing, hunting, and trapping).
8. Comparable estimate of output growth is not available.
9. Workers who hold a secondary wage and salary job in agriculture (except agricultural services); forestry, fishing, hunting, and trapping; and private households.
10. Wage and salary workers who hold a secondary wage and salary job as a self-employed or unpaid family worker.

Table 3-3. Employment by Occupation, 1998 and Projected 2008

(Thousands of jobs, percent.)

Occupation	Employment				Change 1998–2008		Total job openings due to growth and replacement 1998–2008
	Number		Percent distribution		Number	Percent	
	1998	2008	1998	2008			
TOTAL, ALL OCCUPATIONS	140 514	160 795	100.0	100.0	20 281	14.4	54 622
Executive, Administrative, And Managerial Occupations	14 770	17 196	10.5	10.7	2 426	16.4	5 107
Managerial and administrative occupations	10 139	11 823	7.2	7.4	1 684	16.6	3 484
Administrative services managers	364	430	0.3	0.3	66	18.1	130
Advertising, marketing, promotions, public relations, and sales managers	485	597	0.3	0.4	112	23.0	179
Communication, transportation, and utilities operations managers	196	234	0.1	0.1	38	19.3	72
Construction managers	270	308	0.2	0.2	38	14.0	85
Education administrators	447	505	0.3	0.3	58	13.0	171
Engineering, natural science, and computer and information systems managers	326	468	0.2	0.3	142	43.5	199
Financial managers	693	791	0.5	0.5	97	14.0	207
Food service and lodging managers	595	691	0.4	0.4	97	16.3	201
Funeral directors and morticians	28	32	(2)	(2)	4	16.1	9
General managers and top executives	3 362	3 913	2.4	2.4	551	16.4	1 140
Government chief executives and legislators	80	82	0.1	0.1	2	2.8	22
Human resources managers	230	274	0.2	0.2	45	19.4	98
Industrial production managers	208	207	0.1	0.1	-2	-0.9	36
Medical and health services managers	222	297	0.2	0.2	74	33.3	114
Postmasters and mail superintendents	26	27	(2)	(2)	1	3.0	5
Property, real estate, and community association managers	315	359	0.2	0.2	43	13.7	86
Purchasing managers	176	188	0.1	0.1	13	7.1	52
All other managers and administrators	2 114	2 420	1.5	1.5	305	14.4	678
Management support occupations	4 631	5 374	3.3	3.3	743	16.0	1 623
Accountants and auditors	1 080	1 202	0.8	0.7	122	11.3	289
Assessors and real estate appraisers	70	78	0.1	(2)	8	11.4	23
Assessors	22	25	(2)	(2)	3	11.8	8
Real estate appraisers	48	53	(2)	(2)	5	11.2	15
Budget analysts	59	67	(2)	(2)	8	13.7	21
Buyers and purchasing agents	371	396	0.3	0.2	25	6.8	120
Purchasing agents and buyers, farm	29	30	(2)	(2)	1	5.0	9
Purchasing agents, except wholesale, retail, and farm products	224	248	0.2	0.2	24	10.8	82
Wholesale and retail buyers, except farm products	118	118	0.1	0.1	(2)	-0.4	29
Construction and building inspectors	68	79	(2)	(2)	11	15.7	28
Cost estimators	152	171	0.1	0.1	20	13.0	38
Credit analysts	42	50	(2)	(2)	8	19.9	18
Employment interviewers, private or public employment service	66	74	(2)	(2)	8	12.9	20
Human resources, training, and labor relations specialists	367	433	0.3	0.3	66	17.9	163
Inspectors and compliance officers, except construction	176	195	0.1	0.1	19	10.5	51
Insurance claims adjusters, appraisers, examiners, and investigators	239	284	0.2	0.2	45	18.6	84
Insurance claims adjusters, examiners, and investigators	229	272	0.2	0.2	43	18.7	81
Claims examiners, property and casualty insurance	49	55	(2)	(2)	6	12.5	14
Insurance adjusters, examiners, and investigators	180	217	0.1	0.1	37	20.4	67
Insurance appraisers, auto damage	10	12	(2)	(2)	2	16.0	3
Insurance underwriters	97	100	0.1	0.1	3	2.7	30
Loan counselors and officers	227	276	0.2	0.2	48	21.2	98
Management analysts	344	442	0.2	0.3	98	28.4	125
Tax examiners, collectors, and revenue agents	62	66	(2)	(2)	3	5.4	17
Tax preparers	79	95	0.1	0.1	15	19.3	33
All other management support workers	1 130	1 366	0.8	0.8	236	20.9	459
Professional Specialty Occupations	19 802	25 145	14.1	15.6	5 343	27.0	9 148
Engineers	1 462	1 752	1.0	1.1	290	19.9	610
Aerospace engineers	53	58	(2)	(2)	5	8.8	13
Chemical engineers	48	53	(2)	(2)	5	9.5	15
Civil engineers	195	236	0.1	0.1	41	20.9	78
Electrical and electronics engineers	357	450	0.3	0.3	93	25.9	169
Industrial engineers, except safety engineers	126	142	0.1	0.1	16	12.8	34
Materials engineers	20	21	(2)	(2)	2	9.0	6
Mechanical engineers	220	256	0.2	0.2	36	16.4	79
Mining engineers, including mine safety engineers	4	4	(2)	(2)	-1	-12.6	1
Nuclear engineers	12	12	(2)	(2)	1	5.8	3
Petroleum engineers	12	12	(2)	(2)	(2)	-3.6	3
All other engineers	415	509	0.3	0.3	94	22.6	208
Architects and surveyors	163	185	0.1	0.1	23	13.8	50
Architects, except landscape and naval	99	118	0.1	0.1	19	18.9	33
Landscape architects	22	25	(2)	(2)	3	14.5	6
Surveyors, cartographers, and photogrammetrists	41	42	(2)	(2)	1	1.4	10
Life scientists	173	219	0.1	0.1	45	26.2	87
Agricultural and food scientists	21	24	(2)	(2)	2	10.9	8
Biological scientists	81	109	0.1	0.1	28	35.0	45
Conservation scientists and foresters	39	46	(2)	(2)	7	17.9	17
Medical scientists	31	39	(2)	(2)	8	24.6	17
All other life scientists	1	1	(2)	(2)	(2)	16.5	(2)

See footnotes at end of table.

Table 3-3. Employment by Occupation, 1998 and Projected 2008—*Continued*

(Thousands of jobs, percent.)

Occupation	Employment				Change 1998–2008		Total job openings due to growth and replacement 1998–2008
	Number		Percent distribution		Number	Percent	
	1998	2008	1998	2008			
Computer, mathematical, and operations research occupations	1 653	3 182	1.2	2.0	1 529	92.5	1 664
Actuaries	16	17	(2)	(2)	1	7.1	3
Computer systems analysts, engineers, and scientists	1 530	3 052	1.1	1.9	1 522	99.4	1 625
Computer engineers and scientists	914	1 858	0.7	1.2	944	103.4	1 010
Computer engineers	299	622	0.2	0.4	323	107.9	341
Computer support specialists	429	869	0.3	0.5	439	102.3	466
Database administrators	87	155	0.1	0.1	67	77.2	82
All other computer scientists	97	212	0.1	0.1	115	117.5	121
Systems analysts	617	1 194	0.4	0.7	577	93.6	616
Statisticians	17	17	(2)	(2)	(2)	2.3	3
Mathematicians and all other mathematical scientists	14	13	(2)	(2)	-1	-5.5	2
Operations research analysts	76	83	0.1	0.1	7	8.7	32
Physical scientists	200	229	0.1	0.1	29	14.7	77
Atmospheric scientists	8	10	(2)	(2)	1	14.6	3
Chemists	96	110	0.1	0.1	13	13.9	35
Geologists, geophysicists, and oceanographers	44	51	(2)	(2)	7	15.5	18
Physicists and astronomers	18	18	(2)	(2)	(2)	2.2	5
All other physical scientists	33	41	(2)	(2)	8	22.7	16
Religious workers	304	356	0.2	0.2	53	17.3	106
Clergy	149	169	0.1	0.1	20	13.4	49
Directors, religious activities and education	112	140	0.1	0.1	28	25.1	46
All other religious workers	43	48	(2)	(2)	5	10.7	11
Social scientists	321	365	0.2	0.2	44	13.8	107
Economists and marketing research analysts	70	83	(2)	0.1	13	18.4	27
Psychologists	166	185	0.1	0.1	19	11.4	49
Urban and regional planners	35	41	(2)	(2)	6	17.4	13
All other social scientists	50	56	(2)	(2)	6	12.7	17
Social and recreation workers	1 303	1 797	0.9	1.1	494	37.9	749
Recreation worker	241	287	0.2	0.2	46	19.2	110
Residential counselors	190	278	0.1	0.2	88	46.3	131
Social and human service assistants	268	410	0.2	0.3	141	52.7	211
Social workers	604	822	0.4	0.5	218	36.1	296
Lawyers and judicial workers	752	871	0.5	0.5	119	15.8	205
Judges, magistrates, and other judicial workers	71	73	0.1	(2)	2	2.9	13
Lawyers	681	798	0.5	0.5	117	17.2	192
Teachers, librarians, and counselors	6 939	8 248	4.9	5.1	1 309	18.9	2 832
Teachers, preschool and kindergarten	529	645	0.4	0.4	116	22.0	229
Teachers, preschool	346	437	0.2	0.3	92	26.5	165
Teachers, kindergarten	184	208	0.1	0.1	25	13.4	64
Teachers, elementary school	1 754	1 959	1.2	1.2	205	11.7	610
Teachers, secondary school	1 426	1 749	1.0	1.1	322	22.6	778
Teachers, special education	406	543	0.3	0.3	137	33.8	172
College and university faculty	865	1 061	0.6	0.7	195	22.6	435
Other teachers and instructors	956	1 139	0.7	0.7	183	19.1	284
Farm and home management advisors	10	10	(2)	(2)	(2)	2.2	1
Instructors and coaches, sports and physical training	359	460	0.3	0.3	102	28.4	140
Adult and vocational education teachers	588	669	0.4	0.4	81	13.8	143
Instructors, adult (nonvocational) education	168	203	0.1	0.1	35	20.9	53
Teachers and instructors, vocational education and training...	420	466	0.3	0.3	46	11.0	90
All other teachers and instructors	644	739	0.5	0.5	95	14.7	183
Librarians, archivists, curators, and related workers	175	186	0.1	0.1	10	5.8	55
Archivists, curators, museum technicians, and conservators	23	26	(2)	(2)	3	12.6	9
Librarians	152	159	0.1	0.1	7	4.8	46
Counselors	182	228	0.1	0.1	46	25.0	87
Health diagnosing occupations	892	1 049	0.6	0.7	157	17.6	312
Chiropractors	46	57	(2)	(2)	11	22.8	20
Dentists	160	165	0.1	0.1	5	3.1	38
Optometrists	38	42	(2)	(2)	4	10.6	12
Physicians	577	699	0.4	0.4	122	21.2	212
Podiatrists	14	15	(2)	(2)	1	10.5	4
Veterinarians	57	71	(2)	(2)	14	24.7	26
Health assessment and treating occupations	2 860	3 531	2.0	2.2	671	23.5	1 158
Dietitians and nutritionists	54	64	(2)	(2)	10	19.1	21
Pharmacists	185	199	0.1	0.1	14	7.3	64
Physician assistants	66	98	(2)	0.1	32	48.0	43
Registered nurses	2 079	2 530	1.5	1.6	451	21.7	794
Therapists	476	640	0.3	0.4	164	34.6	236
Occupational therapists	73	98	0.1	0.1	25	34.2	36
Physical therapists	120	161	0.1	0.1	41	34.0	59
Radiation therapists	12	14	(2)	(2)	2	16.7	4
Recreational therapists	39	44	(2)	(2)	5	13.4	11
Respiratory therapists	86	123	0.1	0.1	37	42.6	50
Speech-language pathologists and audiologists	105	145	0.1	0.1	40	38.5	56
All other therapists	40	54	(2)	(2)	14	35.7	20

See footnotes and *Note* at end of table.

Table 3-3. Employment by Occupation, 1998 and Projected 2008—*Continued*

(Thousands of jobs, percent.)

Occupation	Employment				Change 1998–2008		Total job openings due to growth and replacement 1998–2008
	Number		Percent distribution		Number	Percent	
	1998	2008	1998	2008			
Writers, artists, and entertainers	1 996	2 409	1.4	1.5	413	20.7	834
Actors, directors, and producers	160	198	0.1	0.1	38	23.8	74
Announcers	60	58	(2)	(2)	-3	-4.3	14
Artists and commercial artists	308	388	0.2	0.2	79	25.7	143
Athletes, coaches, umpires, and related workers	52	66	(2)	(2)	14	27.9	33
Dancers and choreographers	29	33	(2)	(2)	4	13.6	10
Designers	423	532	0.3	0.3	110	25.9	171
Designers, except interior designers	335	426	0.2	0.3	91	27.1	140
Interior designers	53	68	(2)	(2)	15	27.2	22
Merchandise displayers and window dressers	34	38	(2)	(2)	4	12.7	9
Musicians, singers, and related workers	273	314	0.2	0.2	41	14.8	93
News analysts, reporters, and correspondents	67	68	(2)	(2)	2	2.8	22
Photographers and camera operators	161	176	0.1	0.1	15	9.2	39
Camera operators, television, motion picture, video	11	15	(2)	(2)	3	29.0	5
Photographers	149	161	0.1	0.1	12	7.7	34
Public relations specialists	122	152	0.1	0.1	30	24.6	62
Writers and editors, including technical writers	341	424	0.2	0.3	83	24.4	173
All other professional workers	785	952	0.6	(2)	166	21.2	355
Technicians And Related Support Occupations	4 949	6 048	3.5	3.8	1 098	22.2	2 202
Health technicians and technologists	2 447	3 063	1.7	1.9	616	25.2	1 122
Cardiovascular technologists and technicians	21	29	(2)	(2)	8	39.4	13
Clinical laboratory technologists and technicians	313	366	0.2	0.2	53	17.0	93
Dental hygienists	143	201	0.1	0.1	58	40.5	90
EKG technicians	12	10	(2)	(2)	-3	-23.1	3
Electroneurodiagnostic technologists	5	6	(2)	(2)	(2)	5.9	2
Emergency medical technicians and paramedics	150	197	0.1	0.1	47	31.6	84
Licensed practical and licensed vocational nurses	692	828	0.5	0.5	136	19.7	284
Medical records and health information technicians	92	133	0.1	0.1	41	43.9	63
Nuclear medicine technologists	14	16	(2)	(2)	2	11.6	4
Opticians, dispensing	71	81	0.1	0.1	10	13.8	19
Pharmacy technicians	109	126	0.1	0.1	17	15.7	44
Psychiatric technicians	66	73	(2)	(2)	7	10.9	16
Radiologic technologists and technicians	162	194	0.1	0.1	32	20.1	55
Surgical technologists	54	77	(2)	(2)	23	41.8	36
Veterinary technologists and technicians	32	37	(2)	(2)	5	16.2	12
All other health professionals and paraprofessionals	510	688	0.4	0.4	178	35.0	302
Engineering and science technicians and technologists	1 351	1 525	1.0	0.9	175	12.9	485
Engineering technicians	771	897	0.5	0.6	126	16.3	301
Electrical and electronic technicians and technologists	335	391	0.2	0.2	56	16.8	125
All other engineering technicians and technologists	437	506	0.3	0.3	70	15.9	176
Drafters	283	301	0.2	0.2	18	6.4	86
Science and mathematics technicians	227	243	0.2	0.2	16	7.0	68
Surveying and mapping technicians	69	84	(2)	0.1	15	21.8	31
Technicians, except health and engineering and science	1 152	1 460	0.8	0.9	308	26.7	595
Aircraft pilots and flight engineers	94	99	0.1	0.1	6	5.9	26
Air traffic controllers	30	30	(2)	(2)	1	2.3	9
Broadcast and sound technicians	37	39	(2)	(2)	2	6.0	12
Computer programmers	648	839	(2)	0.5	191	29.5	392
Legal assistants and technicians, except clerical	252	346	0.2	0.2	94	37.4	117
Paralegals and legal assistants	136	220	0.1	0.1	84	62.0	96
Title examiners, abstractors, and searchers	30	29	(2)	(2)	(2)	-0.6	2
All other legal assistants, including law clerks	86	96	0.1	0.1	10	11.6	18
Library technicians	72	85	0.1	0.1	13	18.2	33
All other technicians	20	21	(2)	(2)	1	4.1	6
Marketing And Sales Occupations	15 341	17 627	10.9	11.0	2 287	14.9	6 810
Cashiers	3 198	3 754	2.3	2.3	556	17.4	1 950
Counter and rental clerks	469	577	0.3	0.4	108	23.1	311
Insurance sales agents	387	396	0.3	0.2	9	2.2	97
Marketing and sales worker supervisors	2 584	2 847	1.8	1.8	263	10.2	601
Models, demonstrators, and product promoters	92	121	0.1	0.1	30	32.3	54
Parts salespersons	300	303	0.2	0.2	4	1.2	90
Real estate agents and brokers	347	382	0.2	0.2	34	9.8	104
Brokers, real estate	63	71	(2)	(2)	8	13.5	21
Sales agents, real estate	285	310	0.2	0.2	26	9.0	83
Retail salespersons	4 056	4 620	2.9	2.9	563	13.9	1 938
Sales engineers	79	92	0.1	0.1	12	15.7	28
Securities, commodities, and financial services sales agents	303	427	0.2	0.3	124	41.0	147

See footnotes and *Note* at end of table.

Table 3-3. Employment by Occupation, 1998 and Projected 2008—*Continued*

(Thousands of jobs, percent.)

Occupation	Employment, Number, 1998	Employment, Number, 2008	Percent distribution, 1998	Percent distribution, 2008	Change 1998–2008, Number	Change 1998–2008, Percent	Total job openings due to growth and replacement 1998–2008
Travel agents	138	163	0.1	0.1	25	18.4	54
All other sales and related workers	3 388	3 945	2.4	2.5	558	16.5	1 436
Administrative Support Occupations, Including Clerical	24 461	26 659	17.4	16.6	2 198	9.0	7 463
Adjusters, investigators, and collectors	1 237	1 540	0.9	1.0	302	24.4	497
Adjustment clerks	479	642	0.3	0.4	163	34.0	194
Bill and account collectors	311	420	0.2	0.3	110	35.3	192
Insurance claims, examining and policy processing clerks	339	377	0.2	0.2	38	11.3	88
Insurance claims clerks	160	183	0.1	0.1	23	14.5	50
Insurance examining clerks	10	11	(2)	(2)	2	17.3	3
Insurance policy processing clerks	170	183	0.1	0.1	13	7.9	35
Welfare eligibility workers and interviewers	109	100	0.1	0.1	-8	-7.6	23
Communications equipment operators	297	252	0.2	0.2	-46	-15.4	65
Telephone operators	261	220	0.2	0.1	-41	-15.6	57
Central office operators	23	19	(2)	(2)	-4	-16.6	5
Directory assistance operators	23	16	(2)	(2)	-7	-31.1	5
Switchboard operators	214	185	0.2	0.1	-30	-13.9	47
All other communications equipment operators	36	32	(2)	(2)	-5	-13.6	8
Computer operators	251	187	0.2	(2)	-64	-25.5	36
Peripheral equipment operators	27	17	(2)	(2)	-10	-37.6	4
Computer operators, except peripheral equipment	224	170	0.2	0.1	-54	-24.1	32
Information clerks	1 910	2 296	1.4	1.4	386	20.2	817
Hotel, motel, and resort desk clerks	159	180	0.1	0.1	21	13.5	82
Interviewing clerks, except personnel and social welfare	128	158	0.1	0.1	30	23.3	71
New accounts clerks, banking	111	127	0.1	0.1	16	14.7	52
Receptionists and information clerks	1 293	1 599	0.9	1.0	305	23.6	553
Reservation and transportation ticket agents and travel clerks	219	232	0.2	0.1	13	6.0	59
Mail clerks and messengers	247	270	0.2	0.2	23	9.2	81
Couriers and messengers	120	130	0.1	0.1	11	8.8	39
Mail clerks, except mail machine operators and postal service	128	140	0.1	0.1	12	9.5	42
Postal clerks and mail carriers	405	434	0.3	0.3	30	7.3	135
Postal mail carriers	332	357	0.2	0.2	25	7.4	118
Postal service clerks	73	78	0.1	(2)	5	6.8	17
Material recording, scheduling, dispatching, and distributing occupations	4 183	4 382	3.0	2.7	199	4.8	895
Dispatchers	248	278	0.2	0.2	30	12.2	70
Dispatchers, except police, fire, and ambulance	163	186	0.1	0.1	23	14.4	50
Dispatchers, police, fire, and ambulance	85	92	0.1	0.1	7	8.0	21
Meter readers, utilities	50	51	(2)	(2)	(2)	0.4	13
Procurement clerks	58	49	(2)	(2)	-9	-14.8	9
Production, planning, and expediting clerks	248	249	0.2	0.2	1	0.4	30
Shipping, receiving, and traffic clerks	1 000	1 031	0.7	0.6	31	3.1	198
Stock clerks and order fillers	2 331	2 462	1.7	1.5	131	5.6	504
Weighers, measurers, checkers, and samplers, record keeping	51	51	(2)	(2)	1	1.5	14
All other material recording, scheduling, and distribution workers	196	210	0.1	0.1	13	6.8	58
Records processing occupations	3 731	3 775	2.7	2.3	44	1.2	943
Advertising clerks	14	14	(2)	(2)	1	4.4	4
Brokerage clerks	77	98	0.1	0.1	22	28.4	32
Correspondence clerks	25	28	(2)	(2)	3	12.2	9
File clerks	272	298	0.2	0.2	26	9.6	121
Financial records processing occupations	2 698	2 653	1.9	1.7	-44	-1.6	561
Billing, cost, and rate clerks	342	392	0.2	0.2	50	14.6	118
Billing and posting clerks and machine operators	107	104	0.1	0.1	-3	-2.6	21
Bookkeeping, accounting, and auditing clerks	2 078	1 997	1.5	1.2	-81	-3.9	388
Payroll and time keeping clerks	172	161	0.1	0.1	-11	-6.2	34
Library assistants and bookmobile drivers	127	148	0.1	0.1	21	16.5	82
Order clerks	362	378	0.3	0.2	17	4.6	103
Human resources assistants, except payroll and time keeping	142	145	0.1	0.1	3	2.0	30
Statement clerks	16	12	(2)	(2)	-3	-22.3	2
Secretaries, stenographers, and typists	3 764	3 744	2.7	2.3	-19	-0.5	703
Court reporters, medical transcriptionists, and stenographers	110	121	0.1	0.1	11	9.7	29
Secretaries	3 195	3 258	2.3	2.0	63	2.0	585
Legal secretaries	285	322	0.2	0.2	37	13.0	83
Medical secretaries	219	246	0.2	0.2	26	12.0	62
Secretaries, except legal and medical	2 690	2 691	1.9	1.7	(2)	(2)	439
Word processors and typists	459	365	0.3	0.2	-93	-20.4	89

See footnotes and *Note* at end of table.

Table 3-3. Employment by Occupation, 1998 and Projected 2008—*Continued*

(Thousands of jobs, percent.)

Occupation	Employment				Change 1998–2008		Total job openings due to growth and replacement 1998–2008
	Number		Percent distribution		Number	Percent	
	1998	2008	1998	2008			
Other clerical and administrative support workers	8 436	9 780	6.0	6.1	1 344	15.9	3 290
Bank tellers	560	529	0.4	0.3	-31	-5.5	240
Court, municipal, and license clerks	100	112	0.1	0.1	12	11.6	28
Court clerks	51	57	(2)	(2)	6	10.8	14
License clerks	24	27	(2)	(2)	3	13.1	7
Municipal clerks	25	28	(2)	(2)	3	11.9	7
Credit and loan authorizers, checkers, and clerks	254	271	0.2	0.2	17	6.7	47
Credit authorizers	17	15	(2)	(2)	-2	-10.7	2
Credit checkers	41	42	(2)	(2)	1	1.5	3
Loan and credit clerks	179	200	0.1	0.1	21	11.8	40
Loan interviewers	16	14	(2)	(2)	-3	-17.0	2
Data entry keyers	435	474	0.3	0.3	39	9.0	72
Duplicating, mail, and other office machine operators	197	201	0.1	0.1	4	1.9	62
Office and administrative support supervisors and managers	1 611	1 924	1.1	1.2	313	19.4	675
Office clerks, general	3 021	3 484	2.1	2.2	463	15.3	1 300
Proofreaders and copy markers	41	34	(2)	(2)	-7	-17.1	13
Statistical clerks	72	69	0.1	(2)	-3	-4.5	10
Teacher assistants	1 192	1 567	0.8	1.0	375	31.5	512
All other clerical and administrative support workers	953	1 116	0.7	0.7	162	17.0	332
Service Occupations	22 548	26 401	16.0	16.4	3 853	17.1	11 112
Cleaning and building service occupations, except private household	3 623	4 031	2.6	2.5	408	11.3	1 164
Institutional cleaning supervisors	87	97	0.1	0.1	9	10.5	30
Janitors and cleaners, including maids and housekeeping cleaners	3 184	3 549	2.3	2.2	365	11.5	1 027
Pest control workers	52	65	(2)	(2)	13	25.4	25
All other cleaning and building service workers	300	320	0.2	0.2	20	6.7	83
Food preparation and service occupations	8 735	9 831	6.2	6.1	1 096	12.6	5 159
Chefs, cooks, and other kitchen workers	3 306	3 748	2.4	2.3	442	13.4	1 669
Cooks, except short order	1 373	1 560	1.0	1.0	187	13.6	545
Bakers, bread and pastry	171	200	0.1	0.1	28	16.6	73
Cooks, institution or cafeteria	418	431	0.3	0.3	12	2.9	121
Cooks, restaurant	783	929	0.6	0.6	146	18.7	351
Cooks, short order and fast food	677	801	0.5	0.5	124	18.4	301
Food preparation workers	1 256	1 387	0.9	0.9	131	10.4	823
Food and beverage service occupations	5 150	5 778	3.7	3.6	628	12.2	3 356
Bartenders	404	412	0.3	0.3	8	1.0	181
Dining room and cafeteria attendants and bar helpers	405	422	0.3	0.3	16	4.0	140
Food counter, fountain, and related workers	2 025	2 272	1.4	1.4	247	12.2	1 476
Hosts and hostesses, restaurant, lounge, or coffee shop	297	351	0.2	0.2	54	18.2	145
Waiters and waitresses	2 019	2 322	1.4	1.4	303	15.0	1 415
All other food preparation and service workers	280	306	0.2	0.2	26	9.4	134
Health service occupations	2 309	2 984	1.6	1.9	676	29.3	1 064
Ambulance drivers and attendants, EMTs	19	26	(2)	(2)	7	35.0	11
Dental assistants	229	325	0.2	0.2	97	42.2	131
Medical assistants	252	398	0.2	0.2	146	57.8	208
Nursing and psychiatric aides	1 461	1 794	1.0	1.1	332	22.7	536
Nursing aides, orderlies, and attendants	1 367	1 692	1.0	1.1	325	23.8	515
Psychiatric aides	95	102	0.1	0.1	7	7.7	20
Occupational therapy assistants and aides	19	26	(2)	(2)	7	39.8	12
Pharmacy aides	61	71	(2)	(2)	10	15.9	25
Physical therapy assistants and aides	82	118	0.1	0.1	36	43.7	56
All other health service workers	185	226	0.1	0.1	41	22.3	85
Personal service occupations	2 934	3 828	2.1	2.4	894	30.5	1 413
Amusement and recreation attendants	337	439	0.2	0.3	102	30.2	163
Baggage porters and bellhops	40	45	(2)	(2)	5	13.7	13
Child care workers	905	1 141	0.6	0.7	236	26.1	325
Barbers, cosmetologists, and related workers	723	796	0.5	0.5	73	10.0	264
Barbers	54	50	(2)	(2)	-4	-7.3	15
Hairdressers, hairstylists, and cosmetologists	605	667	0.4	0.4	62	10.2	218
Manicurists	49	62	(2)	(2)	13	26.0	25
Shampooers	15	17	(2)	(2)	2	14.5	6
Flight attendants	99	129	0.1	0.1	30	30.1	51
Personal care and home health aides	746	1 179	0.5	0.7	433	58.1	567
Ushers, lobby attendants, and ticket takers	84	99	0.1	0.1	15	17.6	30
Private household workers	928	751	0.7	0.5	-178	-19.1	276
Child care workers, private household	306	209	0.2	0.1	-97	-31.7	140
Cleaners and servants, private household	600	530	0.4	0.3	-71	-11.8	131
Cooks, private household	5	2	(2)	(2)	-2	-51.3	1
Housekeepers and butlers	17	10	(2)	(2)	-7	-42.4	4

See footnotes and *Note* at end of table.

Table 3-3. Employment by Occupation, 1998 and Projected 2008—*Continued*

(Thousands of jobs, percent.)

Occupation	Employment				Change 1998–2008		Total job openings due to growth and replacement 1998–2008
	Number		Percent distribution		Number	Percent	
	1998	2008	1998	2008			
Protective service occupations	2 769	3 486	2.0	2.2	717	25.9	1 490
Fire fighting occupations	314	334	0.2	0.2	20	6.4	103
Firefighters	239	251	0.2	0.2	11	4.7	70
Firefighting and prevention supervisors	60	66	(2)	(2)	6	10.7	26
Fire inspection occupations	15	17	(2)	(2)	2	17.2	6
Law enforcement occupations	1 147	1 501	0.8	0.9	354	30.8	643
Correctional officers	383	532	0.3	0.3	148	38.7	253
Police and detectives	727	929	0.5	0.6	202	27.8	382
Detectives and criminal investigators	79	96	0.1	0.1	17	21.0	38
Police and detective supervisors	111	124	0.1	0.1	13	12.0	45
Police patrol officers	446	586	0.3	0.4	141	31.6	260
Sheriffs and deputy sheriffs	91	123	0.1	0.1	31	34.2	40
Other law enforcement occupations	37	40	(2)	(2)	3	9.4	8
Other protective service workers	1 308	1 651	0.9	1.0	343	26.2	743
Crossing guards	54	57	(2)	(2)	2	4.0	18
Guards	1 027	1 321	0.7	0.8	294	28.6	550
Private detectives and investigators	61	76	(2)	(2)	15	24.3	30
All other protective service workers	166	198	0.1	0.1	32	19.0	145
All other service workers	1 249	1 490	0.9	0.9	241	19.3	546
Agriculture, Forestry, Fishing, And Related Occupations	4 435	4 506	3.2	2.8	71	1.6	1 356
Farm operators and managers	1 483	1 309	1.1	0.8	-174	-11.7	232
Farmers	1 308	1 135	0.9	0.7	-173	-13.2	203
Farm managers	175	174	0.1	0.1	-1	-0.8	29
Farm workers	851	794	0.6	0.5	-57	-6.6	262
Fishers and fishing vessel operators	51	40	(2)	(2)	-11	-21.8	10
Captains and other officers, fishing vessels	11	9	(2)	(2)	-2	-18.6	2
Fishers	40	31	(2)	(2)	-9	-22.7	8
Forestry, conservation, and logging occupations	120	116	0.1	0.1	-4	-3.1	27
Forest and conservation workers	33	33	(2)	(2)	(2)	0.7	7
Timber cutting and logging occupations	87	83	0.1	0.1	-4	-4.6	20
Fallers and buckers	18	16	(2)	(2)	-2	-11.5	5
Logging equipment operators	56	55	(2)	(2)	-1	-2.0	12
All other timber cutting and related logging workers	13	12	(2)	(2)	-1	-6.0	3
Landscaping, grounds keeping, nursery, greenhouse, and lawn service occupations	1 285	1 548	0.9	1.0	262	20.4	626
Laborers, landscaping and grounds keeping	1 130	1 364	0.8	0.8	234	20.7	572
Lawn service managers	86	104	0.1	0.1	17	20.0	24
Nursery and greenhouse managers	5	6	(2)	(2)	1	15.1	1
Pruners	45	50	(2)	(2)	5	12.1	19
Sprayers/applicators	19	23	(2)	(2)	4	23.6	10
Supervisors, farming, forestry, and agricultural related occupations	92	97	0.1	0.1	6	6.2	18
Veterinary assistants and nonfarm animal caretakers	181	223	0.1	0.1	42	23.2	68
Animal caretakers, except farm	137	166	0.1	0.1	30	21.6	49
Veterinary assistants	45	57	(2)	(2)	12	28.0	19
All other agricultural, forestry, fishing and related workers	373	379	0.3	0.2	6	1.7	113
Precision Production, Craft, And Repair Occupations	15 619	16 871	11.1	10.5	1 252	8.0	5 051
Blue-collar worker supervisors	2 198	2 394	1.6	1.5	196	8.9	803
Construction trades	4 628	5 018	3.3	3.1	390	8.4	1 425
Boilermakers	18	19	(2)	(2)	(2)	1.6	5
Bricklayers, block masons, and stonemasons	157	176	0.1	0.1	19	12.3	51
Carpenters	1 071	1 145	0.8	0.7	74	6.9	361
Carpet, floor, and tile installers and finishers	138	147	0.1	0.1	8	6.0	40
Carpet installers	85	88	0.1	(2)	3	3.6	21
Hard tile setters	29	31	(2)	(2)	3	8.7	10
All other carpet, floor, and tile installers and finishers	25	28	(2)	(2)	3	11.0	9
Ceiling tile installers and acoustical carpenters	16	17	(2)	(2)	1	8.9	6
Concrete finishers, cement masons, and terrazzo workers	139	148	0.1	0.1	9	6.1	25
Construction equipment operators	321	346	0.2	0.2	25	7.7	76
Grader, bulldozer, and scraper operators	122	129	0.1	0.1	7	5.7	17
Operating engineers	126	135	0.1	0.1	10	7.9	32
Paving, surfacing, and tamping equipment operators	74	82	0.1	0.1	8	10.6	27
Drywall installers and finishers	163	175	0.1	0.1	12	7.5	34
Electricians	656	724	0.5	0.5	68	10.3	202
Elevator installers and repairers	30	33	(2)	(2)	4	12.2	11
Glaziers	44	46	(2)	(2)	2	3.9	13
Hazardous materials removal workers	38	45	(2)	(2)	7	19.3	16
Highway maintenance workers	155	173	0.1	0.1	17	11.1	54
Insulation workers	67	72	(2)	(2)	5	7.5	26
Painters and paperhangers	476	517	0.3	0.3	41	8.6	162
Pipe layers and pipe laying fitters	57	60	(2)	(2)	3	4.9	16
Plasterers and stucco masons	40	47	(2)	(2)	7	17.1	17
Plumbers, pipe fitters, and steam fitters	426	449	0.3	0.3	22	5.3	76
Roofers	158	177	0.1	0.1	19	12.0	73
Sheet metal workers and duct installers	230	262	0.2	0.2	32	14.1	89
Structural and reinforcing metal workers	81	87	0.1	0.1	6	8.0	28
All other construction trades workers	146	155	0.1	0.1	8	5.7	43

See footnotes and *Note* at end of table.

Table 3-3. Employment by Occupation, 1998 and Projected 2008—*Continued*

(Thousands of jobs, percent.)

Occupation	Employment				Change 1998–2008		Total job openings due to growth and replacement 1998–2008
	Number		Percent distribution		Number	Percent	
	1998	2008	1998	2008			
Extractive and related workers, including blasters	244	255	0.2	0.2	11	4.5	83
Oil and gas extraction occupations	69	63	(2)	(2)	-6	-9.0	17
Roustabouts, oil and gas	30	23	(2)	(2)	-6	-21.1	7
All other oil and gas extraction occupations	40	40	(2)	(2)	(2)	(2)	10
Mining, quarrying, and tunneling occupations	23	18	(2)	(2)	-4	-19.1	6
All other extraction and related workers	152	173	0.1	0.1	21	14.1	60
Mechanics, installers, and repairers	5 176	5 763	3.7	3.6	588	11.4	1 842
Electrical and electronic equipment mechanics, installers, and repairers	409	472	0.3	0.3	63	15.4	180
Computer, automated teller, and office machine repairers	138	184	0.1	0.1	46	33.7	70
Data processing equipment repairers	79	117	0.1	0.1	37	47.0	49
Office machine and cash register servicers	58	67	(2)	(2)	9	15.6	22
Telecommunications equipment mechanics, installers, and repairers	125	138	0.1	0.1	13	10.0	60
Radio mechanics	7	7	(2)	(2)	(2)	-1.4	2
Telephone equipment installers and repairers	69	75	(2)	(2)	6	8.8	37
Central office and PBX installers and repairers	44	59	(2)	(2)	14	32.3	29
Station installers and repairers, telephone	24	16	(2)	(2)	-8	-33.8	8
All other telecommunications equipment mechanics, installers, and repairers	49	56	(2)	(2)	7	13.3	21
Miscellaneous electrical and electronic equipment mechanics, installers, and repairers	146	150	0.1	0.1	4	2.7	50
Electronic home entertainment equipment repairers	36	31	(2)	(2)	-4	-11.9	10
Electronics repairers, commercial and industrial equipment	72	81	0.1	0.1	9	12.7	29
All other electrical and electronic equipment mechanics, installers, and repairers	39	38	(2)	(2)	-1	-2.4	10
Machinery mechanics, installers, and repairers	1 850	1 967	1.3	1.2	117	6.3	537
Industrial machinery mechanics	535	559	0.4	0.3	24	4.4	144
Maintenance repairers, general utility	1 232	1 327	0.9	0.8	95	7.7	370
Millwrights	82	81	0.1	0.1	-2	-1.9	22
Vehicle and mobile equipment mechanics and repairers	1 612	1 828	1.1	1.1	216	13.4	618
Aircraft mechanics and service technicians	133	147	0.1	0.1	14	10.4	40
Automotive body and related repairers	227	263	0.2	0.2	36	15.8	102
Automotive mechanics and service technicians	790	922	0.6	0.6	132	16.7	328
Bus and truck mechanics and diesel engine specialists	255	280	0.2	0.2	25	9.8	81
Farm equipment mechanics	49	47	(2)	(2)	-3	-5.2	13
Mobile heavy equipment mechanics	106	116	0.1	0.1	10	9.3	38
Motorcycle, boat, and small engine mechanics	52	54	(2)	(2)	2	4.7	16
Motorcycle mechanic	14	14	(2)	(2)	1	3.9	4
Small engine mechanics	38	40	(2)	(2)	2	5.0	12
Other mechanics, installers, and repairers	1 305	1 496	0.9	0.9	191	14.7	507
Bicycle repairers	11	13	(2)	(2)	2	22.6	5
Camera and photographic equipment repairers	9	10	(2)	(2)	1	8.2	3
Coin, vending, and amusement machine servicers and repairers	27	31	(2)	(2)	4	15.6	10
Heating, air conditioning, and refrigeration mechanics and installers	286	334	0.2	0.2	48	16.9	101
Home appliance and power tool repairers	51	54	(2)	(2)	3	5.6	18
Line installers and repairers	279	335	0.2	0.2	56	19.9	137
Electrical power line installers and repairers	99	100	0.1	0.1	1	1.1	24
Telephone and cable TV line installers and repairers	180	235	0.1	0.1	55	30.3	113
Locksmiths and safe repairers	27	30	(2)	(2)	3	10.0	10
Medical equipment repairers	11	12	(2)	(2)	1	13.5	4
Musical instrument repairers and tuners	13	13	(2)	(2)	1	6.5	4
Precision instrument repairers	33	32	(2)	(2)	-1	-4.0	8
Riggers	11	11	(2)	(2)	(2)	0.5	3
Tire repairers and changers	83	92	0.1	0.1	9	10.4	45
Watch repairers	8	8	(2)	(2)	(2)	-4.2	2
All other mechanics, installers, and repairers	455	520	0.3	0.3	65	14.3	157
Production occupations, precision	2 971	3 010	2.1	1.9	39	1.3	774
Assemblers, precision	422	442	0.3	0.3	20	4.6	118
Aircraft assemblers, precision	17	20	(2)	(2)	3	19.3	7
Electrical and electronic equipment assemblers, precision	201	213	0.1	0.1	12	6.0	56
Electromechanical equipment assemblers, precision	50	52	(2)	(2)	3	5.7	14
Fitters, structural metal, precision	17	15	(2)	(2)	-2	-13.0	4
Machine builders and other precision machine assemblers	74	76	0.1	(2)	1	1.7	19
All other precision assemblers	64	66	(2)	(2)	2	3.7	18
Food workers, precision	310	303	0.2	0.2	-7	-2.4	78
Bakers, manufacturing	55	60	(2)	(2)	5	8.5	12
Butchers and meat cutters	216	201	0.2	0.1	-15	-7.1	51
All other precision food and tobacco workers	39	42	(2)	(2)	3	8.5	15
Inspectors, testers, and graders, precision	689	667	0.5	0.4	-22	-3.2	153
Metal workers, precision	707	734	0.5	0.5	27	3.8	176
Jewelers and precious stone and metalworkers	30	28	(2)	(2)	-2	-6.0	7
Machinists	426	452	0.3	0.3	26	6.2	111
Numerical control machine tool programmers	8	9	(2)	(2)	1	6.1	3
Ship fitters	9	8	(2)	(2)	(2)	-4.5	2
Tool and die makers	138	136	0.1	0.1	-2	-1.5	26
All other precision metal workers	97	101	0.1	0.1	4	4.0	27
Printing workers, precision	138	137	0.1	0.1	-1	-1.0	44
Bookbinders	7	6	(2)	(2)	-1	-15.2	2
Prepress printing workers, precision	115	114	0.1	0.1	(2)	-0.4	39
Camera operators	9	6	(2)	(2)	-3	-31.4	2
Compositors and type setters, precision	14	11	(2)	(2)	-3	-18.9	2
Desktop publishing specialists	26	44	(2)	(2)	19	72.6	23
Film strippers, printing	23	15	(2)	(2)	-8	-33.0	4
Job printers	17	18	(2)	(2)	1	4.3	4
Paste-up workers	9	4	(2)	(2)	-5	-51.2	2
Photoengravers	3	1	(2)	(2)	-1	-51.5	(2)
Plate makers	15	14	(2)	(2)	-1	-5.2	2
All other printing workers, precision	17	17	(2)	(2)	(2)	0.2	3

See footnotes and *Note* at end of table.

Table 3-3. Employment by Occupation, 1998 and Projected 2008—*Continued*

(Thousands of jobs, percent.)

Occupation	Employment Number 1998	Employment Number 2008	Percent distribution 1998	Percent distribution 2008	Change 1998–2008 Number	Change 1998–2008 Percent	Total job openings due to growth and replacement 1998–2008
Textile, apparel, and furnishings workers, precision	234	226	0.2	0.1	-8	-3.3	49
Custom tailors and sewers	74	67	0.1	(2)	-6	-8.4	14
Patternmakers and layout workers, fabric and apparel	16	15	(2)	(2)	-1	-3.8	3
Shoe and leather workers and repairers, precision	23	19	(2)	(2)	-4	-17.6	5
Upholsterers	66	67	(2)	(2)	1	0.9	14
All other precision textile, apparel, and furnishings workers	55	58	(2)	(2)	2	4.4	13
Woodworkers, precision	229	236	0.2	0.1	7	2.9	42
Cabinetmakers and bench carpenters	123	129	0.1	0.1	6	5.2	20
Furniture finishers	38	38	(2)	(2)	(2)	-1.0	9
Wood machinists	40	41	(2)	(2)	1	3.2	6
All other precision wood workers	27	27	(2)	(2)	-1	-2.5	7
Other precision workers	242	266	0.2	0.2	25	10.2	85
Dental laboratory technicians, precision	44	44	(2)	(2)	(2)	1.0	9
Ophthalmic laboratory technicians	23	24	(2)	(2)	1	4.7	4
Photographic process workers, precision	18	19	(2)	(2)	1	7.0	8
All other precision workers	157	179	0.1	0.1	22	14.0	64
Plant and system occupations	403	431	0.3	0.3	28	6.9	153
Chemical plant and system operators	43	48	(2)	(2)	5	11.0	18
Electric power generating plant operators, distributors, and dispatchers	45	44	(2)	(2)	-1	-1.6	15
Power distributors and dispatchers	14	12	(2)	(2)	-2	-12.2	4
Power generating and reactor plant operators	31	32	(2)	(2)	1	3.1	11
Gas and petroleum plant and system occupations	38	33	(2)	(2)	-5	-12.6	12
Stationary engineers	31	29	(2)	(2)	-2	-5.7	7
Water and liquid waste treatment plant and system operators	98	112	0.1	0.1	14	14.2	37
All other plant and system operators	148	164	0.1	0.1	16	11.1	64
Operators, Fabricators, And Laborers	18 588	20 341	13.2	12.7	1 753	9.4	6 374
Machine setters, set-up operators, operators, and tenders	5 139	5 230	3.7	3.3	91	1.8	1 456
Numerical control machine tool operators and tenders, metal and plastic	88	108	0.1	0.1	20	22.6	39
Combination machine tool setters, set-up operators, operators, and tenders, metal and plastic	107	122	0.1	0.1	15	13.8	38
Machine tool cut and form setters, operators, and tenders, metal and plastic	726	690	0.5	0.4	-36	-4.9	188
Drilling and boring machine tool setters and set-up operators, metal and plastic	42	34	(2)	(2)	-8	-18.3	9
Grinding, lapping, and buffing machine tool setters and set-up operators, metal and plastic	75	68	0.1	(2)	-7	-9.6	20
Lathe and turning machine tool setters and set-up operators, metal and plastic	72	66	0.1	(2)	-6	-8.4	16
Machine forming operators and tenders, metal and plastic	163	157	0.1	0.1	-6	-3.9	41
Machine tool cutting operators and tenders, metal and plastic	109	88	0.1	0.1	-22	-19.9	28
Punching machine setters and set-up operators, metal and plastic	47	44	(2)	(2)	-4	-7.5	9
All other machine tool setters, set-up operators, metal and plastic	218	235	0.2	0.1	17	7.7	65
Metal fabricating machine setters, operators, and related workers	167	178	0.1	0.1	10	6.2	51
Metal fabricators, structural metal products	46	49	(2)	(2)	3	7.5	14
Soldering and brazing machine operators and tenders	12	13	(2)	(2)	1	8.2	4
Welding machine setters, operators, and tenders	110	116	0.1	0.1	6	5.4	34
Metal and plastic processing machine setters, operators, and related workers	478	528	0.3	0.3	50	10.5	169
Electrolytic plating machine setters, set-up operators, operators, and tenders, metal and plastic	45	49	(2)	(2)	4	9.6	16
Foundry mold assembly and shake out workers	9	10	(2)	(2)	(2)	2.5	3
Furnace operators and tenders	23	22	(2)	(2)	-1	-5.0	4
Heat treating, annealing, and tempering machine operators and tenders, metal and plastic	23	22	(2)	(2)	-1	-4.1	6
Metal molding machine setters, set-up operators, operators, and tenders	58	63	(2)	(2)	5	9.0	20
Plastic molding machine setters, set-up operators, operators, and tenders	171	196	0.1	0.1	25	14.7	68
All other metal and plastic machine setters, operators, and related workers	148	166	0.1	0.1	18	11.9	55
Printing, binding, and related workers	406	410	0.3	0.3	4	1.1	106
Bindery machine operators and set-up operators	90	100	0.1	0.1	10	11.5	26
Prepress printing workers, production	20	11	(2)	(2)	-9	-44.7	3
Photoengraving and lithographic machine operators and tenders	7	6	(2)	(2)	-1	-15.0	1
Type setting and composing machine operators and tenders	13	5	(2)	(2)	(2)	-59.8	2
Printing press operators	225	225	0.2	0.1	(2)	0.2	61
Letterpress operators	10	8	(2)	(2)	-2	-18.2	2
Offset lithographic press operators	63	54	(2)	(2)	-9	-14.7	14
Printing press machine setters, operators and tenders	142	154	0.1	0.1	12	8.3	43
All other printing press setters and set-up operators	10	9	(2)	(2)	(2)	-4.5	2
Screen printing machine setters and set-up operators	28	29	(2)	(2)	1	3.0	7
All other printing, binding, and related workers	43	45	(2)	(2)	2	4.1	10
Textile and related setters, operators, and related workers	851	687	0.6	0.4	-164	-19.3	133
Extruding and forming machine operators and tenders, synthetic or glass fibers	33	35	(2)	(2)	3	7.9	8
Pressing machine operators and tenders, textile, garment, and related materials	69	66	(2)	(2)	-3	-4.0	11
Sewing machine operators, garment	369	257	0.3	0.2	-112	-30.3	50
Sewing machine operators, nongarment	137	140	0.1	0.1	3	2.5	22
Textile bleaching and dyeing machine operators and tenders	24	22	(2)	(2)	-2	-9.0	4
Textile draw-out and winding machine operators and tenders	192	141	0.1	0.1	-50	-26.3	32
Textile machine setters and set-up operators	28	26	(2)	(2)	-3	-9.6	5
Woodworking machine setters, operators, and other related workers	143	130	0.1	0.1	-14	-9.4	37
Head sawyers and sawing machine operators and tenders, setters and set-up operators	64	61	(2)	(2)	-4	-5.7	19
Woodworking machine operators and tenders, setters and set-up operators	79	69	0.1	(2)	-10	-12.5	18

See footnotes and *Note* at end of table.

Table 3-3. Employment by Occupation, 1998 and Projected 2008—*Continued*

(Thousands of jobs, percent.)

Occupation	Employment				Change 1998–2008		Total job openings due to growth and replacement 1998–2008
	Number		Percent distribution		Number	Percent	
	1998	2008	1998	2008			
Other machine setters, set-up operators, operators, and tenders	2 172	2 377	1.5	1.5	205	9.4	693
Boiler operators and tenders, low pressure	16	14	(2)	(2)	-2	-11.0	3
Cement and gluing machine operators and tenders	32	27	(2)	(2)	-5	-15.6	8
Chemical equipment controllers, operators and tenders	100	111	0.1	0.1	11	11.4	35
Cooking and roasting machine operators and tenders, food and tobacco	31	28	(2)	(2)	-3	-8.5	6
Crushing, grinding, mixing, and blending machine operators and tenders	150	154	0.1	0.1	4	2.8	39
Cutting and slicing machine setters, perators and tenders	96	102	0.1	0.1	6	6.4	29
Dairy processing equipment operators, including setters	15	12	(2)	(2)	-3	-20.4	4
Electronic semiconductor processors	63	92	(2)	0.1	29	45.2	38
Extruding and forming machine setters, operators, and tenders	126	132	0.1	0.1	6	5.0	36
Furnace, kiln, oven, drier, or kettle operators and tenders	25	24	(2)	(2)	-0.1	-5.6	4
Laundry and dry-cleaning machine operators and tenders, except pressing	167	184	0.1	0.1	16	9.8	57
Motion picture projectionists	9	7	(2)	(2)	-2	-21.8	2
Packaging and filling machine operators and tenders	377	425	0.3	0.3	49	12.9	147
Painting and coating machine operators	171	186	0.1	0.1	15	8.8	52
Coating, painting, and spraying machine operators, tenders, setters, and set-up operators	129	140	0.1	0.1	11	8.7	39
Painters, transportation equipment	42	46	(2)	(2)	4	9.0	13
Paper goods machine setters and set-up operators	62	59	(2)	(2)	-3	-4.1	13
Photographic processing machine operators and tenders	46	41	(2)	(2)	-5	-11.4	18
Separating, filtering, clarifying, precipitating, and still machine operators and tenders	28	26	(2)	(2)	-2	-7.2	7
Shoe sewing machine operators and tenders	7	4	(2)	(2)	-2	-35.8	1
Tire building machine operators	18	17	(2)	(2)	(2)	-1.4	3
All other machine operators, tenders, setters, and set-up operators	635	732	0.5	0.5	97	15.2	191
Hand workers, including assemblers and fabricators	3 092	3 382	2.2	2.1	290	9.4	967
Cannery workers	50	44	(2)	(2)	-6	-12.0	13
Coil winders, tapers, and finishers	22	22	(2)	(2)	1	2.5	4
Cutters and trimmers, hand	42	39	(2)	(2)	-4	-8.3	10
Electrical and electronic assemblers	246	265	0.2	0.2	19	7.7	63
Grinder sand polishers, hand	81	84	0.1	0.1	3	4.3	25
Machine assemblers	67	71	(2)	(2)	4	5.5	16
Meat, poultry, and fish cutters and trimmers, hand	143	178	0.1	0.1	35	24.2	63
Painting, coating, and decorating workers, hand	39	46	(2)	(2)	7	17.7	16
Pressers, hand	13	12	(2)	(2)	-2	-11.4	4
Sewers, hand	10	8	(2)	(2)	-1	-14.8	2
Solderers and brazers	35	40	(2)	(2)	5	14.4	13
Welders and cutters	368	398	0.3	0.2	31	8.3	124
All other assemblers, fabricators, and hand workers	1 976	2 175	1.4	1.4	198	10.0	610
Transportation and material moving machine and vehicle operators	5 215	5 960	3.7	3.7	745	14.3	1 609
Motor vehicle operators	4 084	4 723	2.9	2.9	639	15.6	1 272
Bus drivers	638	(2)	0.5	0.5	108	17.0	223
Bus drivers, transit and intercity	203	235	0.1	0.1	32	15.8	69
Bus drivers, school	435	511	0.3	0.3	76	17.6	154
Taxi drivers and chauffeurs	132	158	0.1	0.1	26	20.0	48
Truck drivers	3 274	3 782	2.3	2.4	507	15.5	994
Driver/sales workers	305	319	0.2	0.2	14	4.7	75
Truck drivers light and heavy	2 970	3 463	2.1	2.2	493	16.6	919
All other motor vehicle operators	40	37	(2)	(2)	-3	-8.5	7
Rail transportation workers	85	75	0.1	(2)	-10	-11.4	31
Locomotive engineers	33	35	(2)	(2)	2	4.8	13
Railroad brake, signal, and switch operators	14	7	(2)	(2)	-7	-47.8	5
Railroad conductors and yard masters	25	24	(2)	(2)	-2	-6.7	9
Subway and streetcar operators	3	4	(2)	(2)	(2)	7.1	1
All other rail transportation workers	8	5	(2)	(2)	-3	-35.6	3
Water transportation and related workers	56	58	(2)	(2)	3	4.7	24
Able seamen, ordinary seamen, and marine oilers	23	24	(2)	(2)	1	5.1	10
Captains and pilots, water vessels	19	19	(2)	(2)	1	3.0	8
Mates, ship, boat, and barge	8	9	(2)	(2)	1	7.9	4
Ship engineers	6	7	(2)	(2)	(2)	4.3	3
Material moving equipment operators	808	883	0.6	0.5	74	9.2	208
Crane and tower operators	49	49	(2)	(2)	(2)	0.5	11
Excavation and loading machine operators	106	122	0.1	0.1	16	15.3	36
Hoist and winch operators	11	11	(2)	(2)	1	6.0	3
Industrial truck and tractor operators	415	454	0.3	0.3	38	9.2	87
All other material moving equipment operators	228	247	0.2	0.2	19	8.3	71
All other transportation and material moving equipment operators	183	222	0.1	0.1	39	21.5	75
Helpers, laborers, and material movers, hand	5 142	5 768	3.7	3.6	626	12.2	2 342
Cleaners of vehicles and equipment	288	360	0.2	0.2	72	25.0	163
Freight, stock, and material movers, hand	822	834	0.6	0.5	12	1.5	314
Hand packers and packagers	984	1 197	0.7	0.7	213	21.7	456
Helpers, construction trades	576	618	0.4	0.4	42	7.3	307
Machine feeders and offbearers	213	211	0.2	0.1	-2	-0.9	64
Parking lot attendants	86	113	0.1	0.1	27	31.2	42
Refuse and recyclable material collectors	99	103	0.1	0.1	4	3.9	42
Service station attendants	141	139	0.1	0.1	-2	-1.2	62
All other helpers, laborers, and material movers, hand	1 934	2 194	1.4	1.4	260	13.4	893

Note: Detail may not equal total or 100 percent due to rounding.

1. Total job openings represent the sum of employment increases and net replacements. If employment change is negative, job openings due to growth are zero and total job openings equal net replacements.
2. Value less than 0.05 percent.

PART FOUR

PRODUCTIVITY AND COSTS

PRODUCTIVITY AND COSTS

HIGHLIGHTS

This part covers the two kinds of productivity measures produced by BLS, output per hour or labor productivity and multifactor productivity. Multifactor productivity is designed to measure the joint influence on economic growth of technological change, efficiency improvements, returns to scale and other factors. For some measures there is a lag in available data.

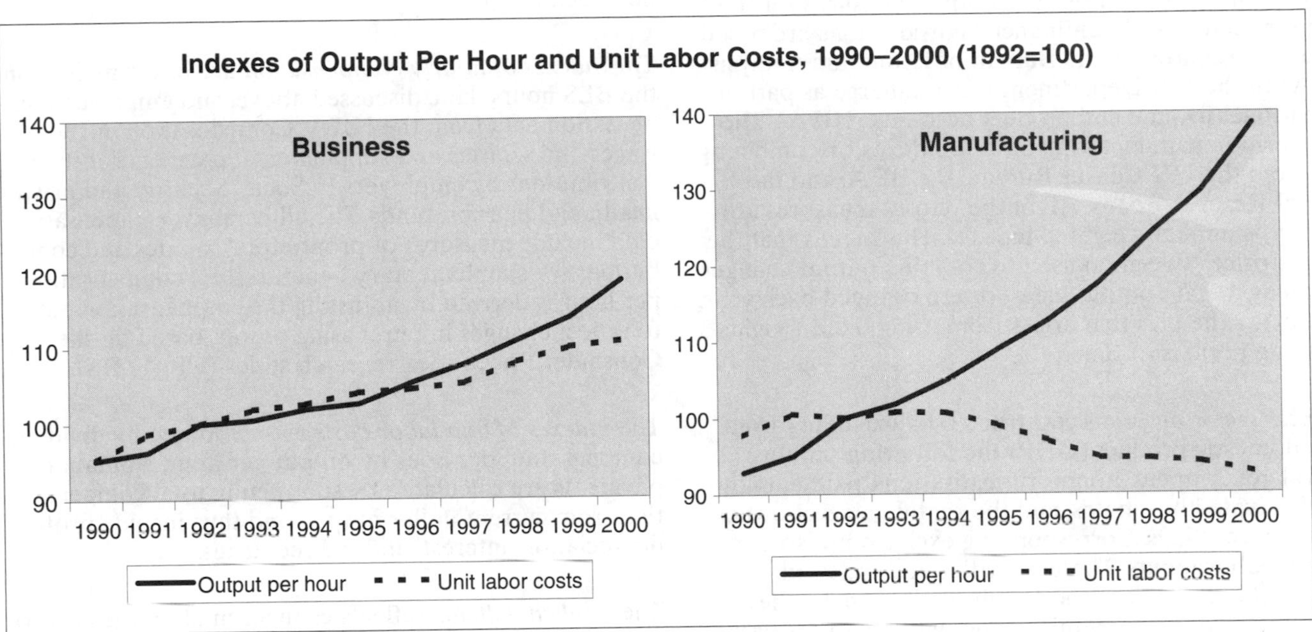

In 2000, the increase in output per hour in the manufacturing sector continued to exceed that in the business sector, (6.9 and 4.2 percent respectively). However, the increase in unit labor costs in the business sector slowed somewhat while unit costs in manufacturing continued to decline.

OTHER HIGHLIGHTS:

- During the period 1995 to 2000, the increase in manufacturing productivity reflected a 27 percent increase in output, while hours worked actually declined 0.8 percent. (Table 4-1)
- In the period from 1990 to 1999, the largest increases by far in output per hour in the manufacturing sector were recorded by computer equipment (33.3 percent), electronic components (26 percent) and communications equipment (11.4 percent). (Table 4-2)
- From 1996 to 1999, the increase in multifactor productivity for durable goods was much higher (14.6 percent) than nondurable (2.5 percent). Industrial machinery and electronics industries led the growth of durables. (Table 4-5)
- For the period 1996–1999, output increases for manufacturing and total private business were similar, but multifactor productivity in manufacturing rose 9.4 percent compared with 3.5 percent for business. (Table 4-4)

NOTES AND DEFINITIONS

Concepts and Definitions

The measures of output per hour for the business, nonfarm business, and manufacturing sectors describe the relationship between real output and the labor time involved in its production. The output measures for the business sectors and nonfinancial corporations are based on series prepared by the Bureau of Economic Analysis (BEA) of the U.S. Department of Commerce as part of the national income and product accounts (NIPA). The BLS derives manufacturing output indexes by combining data from the U.S. Census Bureau, the BEA, and the Federal Reserve Board. All of the output measures are chain-type annual-weighted indexes. This means that the relative prices (weights) used to combine output changes into an aggregate output measure are changed each year, minimizing the bias that arises from using fixed weights over long periods of time.

Business sector output is constructed by excluding from gross domestic product (GDP) the following outputs: general government, nonprofit institutions, paid employees of private households, and the rental value of owner-occupied dwellings. Corresponding exclusions also are made in labor inputs. These activities are excluded because theoretical or practical difficulties make the computation of meaningful productivity measures based on them impossible. Business output accounted for about 77 percent of GDP in 1996 and nonfinancial corporations about 53 percent. Manufacturing indexes are constructed by deflating current-dollar industry value of production data with deflators from the BEA. These deflators are based on data from the BLS producer price program and other sources. To avoid duplication, intrasector transactions are removed when industry shipments are aggregated.

Productivity measures show the changes from period to period in the amount of goods and services produced per hour. Although these measures relate output to hours of persons engaged in a sector, they do not measure only the specific contributions of labor, capital, or any other factor of production. Rather, they reflect the joint effects of many influences, including changes in technology; capital investment; level of output; utilization of capacity, energy, and materials; the organization of production; managerial skill; and the characteristics and effort of the work force.

Measures of labor input are based mainly on the monthly BLS survey of nonagricultural establishments. From this are drawn measures of employment and average weekly hours paid for employees of these establishments. Weekly hours paid are adjusted to hours at work using the BLS Hours at Work survey, conducted for this purpose. Supplementary information for farm workers, the self-employed, and unpaid family workers is obtained from the monthly survey of households, the Current Population Survey. Without these supplementary data, labor input would be seriously understated in the business sectors.

The indexes of hourly compensation are based mainly on the BLS hours data, discussed above, and employee compensation data from the NIPA. Compensation includes wages and salaries and supplemental payments such as contributions by employers to Social Security and private health and pension funds. The all persons' compensation data include measures of proprietors' salaries and contributions for supplementary benefits. Real compensation per hour is derived by adjusting the compensation data to reflect changes in purchasing power, based on the Consumer Price Index research series (CPI-U-RS).

The *indexes of unit labor costs* are computed by dividing compensation per hour by output per hour. Nonlabor payments are calculated by subtracting total compensation from current dollar output, and thus include profits, depreciation, interest, and indirect taxes.

The *implicit deflator* reflects changes in all of the costs of production and distribution (unit labor costs plus unit nonlabor payments). To construct the implicit price deflator, the current-dollar measure of output in a sector is divided by the real output series.

Multifactor Productivity

The *measures of output per unit of combined labor and capital input* (multifactor productivity) and related measures are produced for the private business and private nonfarm business sectors. The *private business and private nonfarm business* sectors for which multifactor productivity indexes are prepared *exclude* government enterprises, and thus differ from the business and nonfarm business sectors described above.

Multifactor productivity measures refer to the ratio of an output index to an index of combined labor and capital services inputs. *Multifactor productivity growth* reflects the amount of output growth that cannot be accounted for by the growth of weighted labor and capital inputs as they have been measured. The weights are associated cost shares; *labor's* share is the ratio of compensation to current-dollar output. *Capital's* share is equal to the ratio of capital cost to current-dollar output. As is the case with the output measures, the weights are updated annually.

Capital services measure the services derived from the stock of physical assets and software. Physical assets included are fixed business equipment, structures, inventories, and land. Structures include nonresidential structures and residential capital that is rented out by profit-making firms or persons. Software includes pre-packaged, custom and own-account software. Financial assets are excluded, as are owner-occupied residential structures. The aggregate capital measures are obtained by weighting the capital stocks for each asset type within each of 53 industries using estimated rental prices for each asset type. Data on investments in physical assets and gross product originating by industry, used in measuring the rental prices, are obtained from BEA.

Labor input in private business and private nonfarm business is obtained by weighting the hours worked by all persons, classified by education, work experience, and gender, by their shares of labor compensation. Additional information concerning data sources and methods of measuring labor composition can be found in BLS Bulletin 2426 (December 1993), "Labor Composition and U.S. Productivity Growth, 1948–90."

The *manufacturing multifactor productivity index* is derived by dividing an output index by a weighted index of combined hours, capital services, energy, materials and purchased business services. Weights (shares of total costs) are updated annually. The labor hours for the manufacturing measure are directly added and thus do not include the effect of changing labor composition, unlike those used for business multifactor productivity. The manufacturing sector coverage is the same in the multifactor and labor productivity series.

Output per Hour and Related Series in Selected Industries

The BLS industry productivity program produces annual indexes of labor productivity, labor compensation, and unit labor costs for selected 2-, 3- and 4-digit industries. These data series cover 54 percent of employment in the private, non-farm business sector, and 100 percent of manufacturing and retail trade. The data sources used in the industry measures differ from those used in the productivity and cost measures for the major sectors.

Output per hour and related indexes for manufacturing and nonmanufacturing industries are updated annually and published in a news release and on the BLS World Wide Web site at http://stats.bls.gov.

Output per hour indexes are obtained by dividing an output index by an index of aggregate hours. Although the measures relate output to one input—labor time—they do not measure the specific contribution of labor or any other factor of production. Rather, they reflect the joint effect of a number of interrelated influences, such as changes in technology, capital investment per worker, and capacity utilization. Caution is necessary when analyzing year-to-year changes in output per hour; the annual changes can be irregular and therefore not necessarily indicative of long-term trends. Conversely, long-term trends are not necessarily applicable to any 1 year or period in the future.

An *output index* for an industry is calculated with a Tornqvist index formula that aggregates the growth rates of the industry products between two periods with weights based on the products' shares in industry value of production. The weight for each product equals its average value share in the two periods. The formula yields the ratio of output in a given period to that in the previous period. The ratios for successive years must be chained together to form a time series. The quantities of products used in the output index are measured either with deflated values of production or with actual quantities. For most industries, output indexes are developed in two stages. First, comprehensive data from the economic censuses conducted by the Bureau of the Census every 5 years are used to develop benchmark indexes for the census years. Second, less comprehensive data are used to prepare annual indexes. The latter indexes are adjusted to the benchmark indexes by means of linear interpolation. For the period following the last census year, annual indexes are linked to the most recent benchmark index.

Indexes of labor input are employee hours indexes or all person hours indexes. In manufacturing industries, employee hours are used. In nonmanufacturing industries where self-employed workers play a significant role, all person hours are used. For most industries, the hours series are based on hours paid. Total hours are calculated by multiplying the number of workers by average weekly hours. Employee hours are treated as homogenous and additive with no distinction made between hours of different groups. Annual indexes are developed by dividing the aggregate hours for each year by the base period aggregate.

Indexes of unit labor costs are calculated as the ratio of total labor compensation to real output, or equivalently, as the ratio of hourly compensation to labor productivity (output per hour). Unit labor costs measure the cost of labor input required to produce one unit of output.

Indexes of total compensation measure the change in the total costs to the employer of securing the services of labor. Compensation is defined as payroll plus supplemental payments. Payroll includes salaries, wages, commissions, dismissal pay, bonuses, vacation and sick leave pay, and compensation in kind. Supplemental payments are divided into legally required expenditures and payments for voluntary programs. The legally required expenditures include employers' contributions to Social

Security, unemployment insurance taxes, and workers' compensation. Payments for voluntary programs include all programs not specifically required by legislation, such as the employer portion of private health insurance and pension plans.

Sources of Additional Information

Productivity concepts and methodology are described in the BLS *Handbook of Methods,* BLS Bulletin 2490, April 1997. Additional information on industry productivity is found in BLS news release USDL 01-40 for output per hour, and 01-82 for multifactor productivity.

Table 4-1. Indexes of Productivity and Related Data, 1947–2000

(1992=100.)

Year	Business											
	Output per hour of all persons	Output	Hours of all persons	Compen-sation per hour	Real compen-sation per hour	Unit labor costs	Unit nonlabor payments	Implicit price deflator	Employ-ment	Output per person	Compen-sation in current dollars	Nonlabor payments in current dollars
1947	31.8	20.7	65.0	6.8	39.6	21.4	18.9	20.5	54.7	37.8	4.4	3.9
1948	33.3	21.8	65.5	7.4	39.8	22.2	21.0	21.7	55.4	39.3	4.8	4.6
1949	34.0	21.6	63.3	7.5	40.9	22.0	20.8	21.5	54.1	39.8	4.7	4.5
1950	36.9	23.7	64.1	8.0	43.3	21.8	21.8	21.8	54.7	43.3	5.2	5.2
1951	38.0	25.2	66.1	8.8	44.0	23.2	24.0	23.5	56.3	44.6	5.8	6.0
1952	39.2	26.0	66.2	9.4	45.9	23.9	23.4	23.7	56.7	45.8	6.2	6.1
1953	40.7	27.2	67.0	10.0	48.5	24.5	22.9	23.9	57.6	47.3	6.7	6.2
1954	41.6	26.9	64.6	10.3	49.8	24.8	22.8	24.1	56.1	47.9	6.7	6.1
1955	43.3	29.0	67.0	10.6	51.3	24.4	24.3	24.4	57.8	50.2	7.1	7.0
1956	43.4	29.5	68.0	11.3	53.9	26.0	23.7	25.2	59.0	49.9	7.7	7.0
1957	44.7	30.0	67.0	12.0	55.6	26.9	24.4	26.0	59.0	50.8	8.1	7.3
1958	46.0	29.4	63.9	12.6	56.5	27.3	25.0	26.5	56.7	51.9	8.0	7.4
1959	47.9	31.9	66.6	13.1	58.4	27.4	25.5	26.7	58.5	54.5	8.7	8.1
1960	48.8	32.5	66.6	13.7	59.9	28.0	25.2	27.0	58.8	55.2	9.1	8.2
1961	50.6	33.1	65.5	14.2	61.8	28.1	25.5	27.2	58.1	57.0	9.3	8.5
1962	52.9	35.2	66.6	14.9	63.9	28.1	26.3	27.4	58.9	59.9	9.9	9.3
1963	55.0	36.8	67.0	15.4	65.4	28.0	26.9	27.6	59.2	62.2	10.3	9.9
1964	57.5	39.2	68.1	16.2	67.9	28.2	27.5	27.9	60.3	64.9	11.0	10.8
1965	59.6	41.9	70.4	16.8	69.3	28.2	28.6	28.4	62.1	67.5	11.8	12.0
1966	62.0	44.8	72.3	17.9	71.9	28.9	29.3	29.1	64.0	70.0	13.0	13.1
1967	63.4	45.6	72.0	19.0	73.7	29.9	29.7	29.9	64.9	70.3	13.7	13.6
1968	65.4	47.9	73.4	20.4	76.2	31.3	30.6	31.0	66.5	72.1	15.0	14.7
1969	65.7	49.4	75.2	21.9	77.4	33.3	30.9	32.4	68.6	72.0	16.4	15.3
1970	67.0	49.4	73.7	23.5	78.8	35.1	31.6	33.9	68.4	72.1	17.3	15.6
1971	69.9	51.3	73.3	25.0	80.3	35.8	34.4	35.3	68.4	75.0	18.4	17.6
1972	72.2	54.7	75.7	26.6	82.7	36.8	35.8	36.5	70.7	77.4	20.1	19.6
1973	74.6	58.6	78.5	28.9	84.5	38.8	37.7	38.4	73.6	79.5	22.7	22.0
1974	73.2	57.6	78.6	31.7	83.4	40.0	40.0	42.1	74.0	77.0	24.9	23.1
1975	75.8	57.0	75.2	34.9	84.3	46.1	46.1	46.1	72.5	78.6	26.3	26.3
1976	78.5	60.9	77.6	38.0	86.8	48.4	48.6	48.5	74.7	81.5	29.5	29.6
1977	79.8	64.3	80.6	41.0	87.9	51.4	51.5	51.4	77.9	82.6	33.1	33.2
1978	80.7	68.3	84.7	44.6	89.4	55.3	54.8	55.1	82.1	83.2	37.8	37.5
1979	80.7	70.6	87.5	48.9	89.7	60.7	58.3	59.8	85.3	82.8	42.8	41.2
1980	80.4	69.8	86.8	54.2	89.4	67.4	61.5	65.2	85.5	81.6	47.0	42.9
1981	82.0	71.7	87.4	59.4	89.5	72.4	69.2	71.2	86.4	82.9	51.9	49.6
1982	81.7	69.6	85.2	63.8	90.9	78.2	70.3	75.3	84.9	81.9	54.4	48.9
1983	84.6	73.3	86.6	66.5	91.0	78.6	76.4	77.8	85.7	85.6	57.6	56.0
1984	87.0	79.7	91.6	69.5	91.3	79.8	80.4	80.0	90.0	88.6	63.6	64.1
1985	88.7	83.1	93.6	72.9	92.7	82.1	82.2	82.2	92.3	90.0	68.2	68.3
1986	91.4	86.1	94.2	76.7	95.8	83.9	82.8	83.5	93.8	91.9	72.2	71.3
1987	91.9	89.2	97.0	79.7	96.3	86.7	83.6	85.6	96.2	92.7	77.3	74.5
1988	93.0	92.9	100.0	83.5	97.3	89.8	85.7	88.3	99.1	93.8	83.4	79.6
1989	93.9	96.2	102.4	85.8	95.9	91.3	91.8	91.5	101.2	95.1	87.9	88.4
1990	95.2	97.6	102.6	90.7	96.5	95.3	93.9	94.8	102.0	95.7	93.0	91.7
1991	96.3	96.5	100.2	95.0	97.5	98.7	97.0	98.1	100.5	96.0	95.2	93.6
1992	100.0	100.0	100.0	100.0	100.0	100.0	100.0	100.0	100.0	100.0	100.0	100.0
1993	100.5	103.1	102.6	102.5	99.9	101.9	102.5	102.2	102.0	101.1	105.1	105.7
1994	101.9	108.1	106.2	104.5	99.7	102.6	106.4	104.0	105.1	102.8	111.0	115.1
1995	102.6	111.5	108.7	106.7	99.3	104.1	109.4	106.0	107.7	103.5	116.0	122.0
1996	105.4	116.4	110.4	110.1	99.8	104.5	113.3	107.7	109.9	105.9	121.6	131.8
1997	107.8	122.5	113.6	113.5	100.7	105.3	117.1	109.7	112.4	109.0	129.0	143.4
1998	110.8	128.6	116.1	119.6	104.6	108.0	115.1	110.6	115.0	111.9	138.9	148.0
1999	113.8	134.8	118.4	125.1	107.1	109.9	115.1	111.8	117.0	115.2	148.1	155.2
2000	118.6	142.4	120.0	131.4	108.9	110.7	119.1	113.8	118.9	119.7	157.7	169.6

Table 4-1. Indexes of Productivity and Related Data, 1947–2000—*Continued*

(1992=100.)

Year	Nonfarm business											
	Output per hour of all persons	Output	Hours of all persons	Compen-sation per hour	Real compen-sation per hour	Unit labor costs	Unit nonlabor payments	Implicit price deflator	Employ-ment	Output per person	Compen-sation in current dollars	Nonlabor payments in current dollars
1947	36.7	20.3	55.3	7.3	42.5	19.9	18.0	19.2	47.3	42.9	4.0	3.7
1948	37.7	21.2	56.2	7.9	42.7	21.0	19.6	20.5	48.3	43.9	4.5	4.1
1949	39.0	21.0	53.9	8.2	44.6	21.0	20.2	20.7	46.8	44.9	4.4	4.2
1950	41.7	23.1	55.6	8.7	46.7	20.8	21.1	20.9	48.0	48.2	4.8	4.9
1951	42.7	24.9	58.2	9.4	47.1	22.1	22.7	22.3	50.2	49.5	5.5	5.6
1952	43.6	25.6	58.8	10.0	48.8	22.8	22.4	22.7	50.9	50.4	5.9	5.7
1953	44.6	26.9	60.2	10.5	51.2	23.6	22.4	23.2	52.5	51.3	6.3	6.0
1954	45.5	26.4	58.1	10.9	52.5	23.9	22.5	23.4	50.9	51.9	6.3	5.9
1955	47.4	28.6	60.4	11.3	54.7	23.8	23.9	23.8	52.5	54.5	6.8	6.8
1956	47.0	29.1	61.9	12.0	57.1	25.5	23.3	24.7	54.0	53.9	7.4	6.8
1957	48.2	29.7	61.6	12.7	58.5	26.3	24.0	25.4	54.3	54.7	7.8	7.1
1958	49.3	29.1	58.9	13.2	59.2	26.7	24.4	25.9	52.3	55.6	7.8	7.1
1959	51.3	31.6	61.6	13.7	61.1	26.7	25.2	26.2	54.2	58.3	8.4	8.0
1960	51.9	32.1	61.9	14.3	62.8	27.5	24.6	26.5	54.7	58.7	8.9	7.9
1961	53.7	32.8	61.1	14.8	64.4	27.6	25.0	26.7	54.2	60.5	9.1	8.2
1962	56.1	35.0	62.4	15.4	66.3	27.5	26.0	26.9	55.2	63.4	9.6	9.1
1963	58.1	36.6	63.1	16.0	67.7	27.5	26.5	27.1	55.9	65.6	10.1	9.7
1964	60.6	39.1	64.6	16.7	69.9	27.6	27.3	27.5	57.2	68.4	10.8	10.7
1965	62.4	41.9	67.1	17.2	71.1	27.6	28.2	27.8	59.2	70.8	11.6	11.8
1966	64.6	44.9	69.5	18.2	73.1	28.2	28.9	28.5	61.6	72.9	12.7	13.0
1967	65.8	45.7	69.4	19.3	75.1	29.4	29.4	29.4	62.6	73.0	13.4	13.4
1968	67.8	48.1	70.9	20.7	77.4	30.6	30.4	30.5	64.3	74.8	14.7	14.6
1969	67.9	49.5	73.0	22.2	78.4	32.6	30.5	31.9	66.6	74.3	16.2	15.1
1970	68.9	49.5	71.8	23.7	79.5	34.4	31.3	33.3	66.7	74.2	17.0	15.5
1971	71.8	51.4	71.5	25.3	81.1	35.2	33.9	34.7	66.8	76.9	18.1	17.4
1972	74.2	54.9	74.0	26.9	83.5	36.2	34.9	35.8	69.0	79.6	19.9	19.2
1973	76.6	58.9	76.9	29.1	85.1	38.0	35.3	37.0	72.0	81.7	22.4	20.8
1974	75.3	58.0	77.0	32.0	84.2	42.4	38.0	40.8	73.2	79.2	24.6	22.1
1975	77.4	57.0	73.7	35.2	84.9	45.5	44.6	45.1	71.0	80.2	25.9	25.4
1976	80.3	61.1	76.1	38.2	87.2	47.6	47.5	47.6	73.4	83.3	29.1	29.0
1977	81.5	64.6	79.2	41.3	88.5	50.7	50.6	50.6	76.6	84.2	32.7	32.7
1978	82.6	68.8	83.3	45.0	90.2	54.5	53.4	54.1	80.9	85.0	37.5	36.7
1979	82.2	70.9	86.3	49.3	90.3	59.9	56.5	58.7	84.3	84.2	42.5	40.1
1980	82.0	70.2	85.6	54.6	90.0	66.5	60.5	64.3	84.6	83.0	46.7	42.5
1981	83.0	71.6	86.2	59.9	90.2	72.1	67.7	70.5	85.5	83.8	51.6	48.5
1982	82.5	69.4	84.1	64.3	91.6	77.9	69.4	74.8	84.0	82.6	54.1	48.1
1983	86.3	73.8	85.6	67.1	91.7	77.8	76.2	77.2	84.8	87.1	57.4	56.2
1984	88.1	80.0	90.7	70.0	92.0	79.4	79.3	79.4	89.3	89.6	63.5	63.4
1985	89.3	83.0	93.0	73.2	93.1	82.0	81.6	81.9	91.8	90.4	68.1	67.8
1986	92.0	86.2	93.8	77.0	96.3	83.7	82.4	83.2	93.4	92.3	72.2	71.1
1987	92.3	89.3	96.7	80.0	96.6	86.6	83.2	85.4	96.0	93.0	77.3	74.2
1988	93.5	93.3	99.8	83.6	97.5	89.4	85.4	87.9	99.0	94.3	83.4	79.7
1989	94.2	96.5	102.4	85.8	95.9	91.1	91.3	91.2	101.2	95.4	87.9	88.1
1990	95.3	97.8	102.7	90.5	96.3	95.0	93.6	94.5	102.1	95.8	92.9	91.5
1991	96.4	96.6	100.2	95.0	97.5	98.5	97.1	98.0	100.5	96.1	95.1	93.8
1992	100.0	100.0	100.0	100.0	100.0	100.0	100.0	100.0	100.0	100.0	100.0	100.0
1993	100.5	103.3	102.9	102.2	99.6	101.7	103.0	102.2	102.2	101.2	105.1	106.4
1994	101.8	108.2	106.2	104.3	99.5	102.5	106.9	104.1	105.2	102.8	110.9	115.7
1995	102.8	111.8	108.8	106.6	99.2	103.7	110.4	106.1	107.8	103.7	116.0	123.5
1996	105.4	116.7	110.7	109.8	99.5	104.2	113.5	107.6	110.2	105.9	121.6	132.5
1997	107.5	122.7	114.1	113.1	100.3	105.2	118.0	109.8	112.8	108.7	129.0	144.7
1998	110.4	129.0	116.8	119.0	104.0	107.7	116.3	110.8	115.6	111.6	139.0	150.0
1999	113.2	135.1	119.3	124.2	106.4	109.7	116.8	112.3	117.8	114.7	148.2	157.8
2000	118.1	142.8	120.9	130.5	108.1	110.5	121.0	114.3	119.8	119.2	157.8	172.8

Table 4-1. Indexes of Productivity and Related Data, 1947–2000—*Continued*

(1992=100.)

Year	Nonfinancial corporations												
	Output per employee hour	Output	Employee hours	Compen-sation per hour	Real compen-sation per hour	Unit labor costs	Unit nonlabor costs	Unit profits	Implicit price deflator	Employ-ment	Output per employee	Compen-sation in current dollars	Nonlabor payments in current dollars
1947	...	...	...	...	...	...	...	...	...	...	...	...	...
1948	...	...	...	...	...	...	...	...	...	...	...	...	...
1949	...	...	...	...	...	...	...	...	...	...	...	...	...
1950	...	...	...	...	...	...	...	...	...	...	...	...	...
1951	...	...	...	...	...	...	...	...	...	...	...	...	...
1952	...	...	...	...	...	...	...	...	...	...	...	...	...
1953	...	...	...	...	...	...	...	...	...	...	...	...	...
1954	...	...	...	...	...	...	...	...	...	...	...	...	...
1955	...	...	...	...	...	...	...	...	...	...	...	...	...
1956	...	...	...	...	...	...	...	...	...	...	...	...	...
1957	...	...	...	...	...	...	...	...	...	...	...	...	...
1958	51.8	25.5	49.3	14.4	64.7	27.8	23.5	47.3	28.4	44.1	57.9	7.1	7.5
1959	54.4	28.4	52.3	14.9	66.7	27.5	22.6	55.1	28.6	46.2	61.6	7.8	8.8
1960	55.4	29.4	53.0	15.6	68.3	28.1	23.3	50.2	28.8	47.2	62.3	8.2	8.9
1961	57.3	30.0	52.4	16.1	70.0	28.1	23.8	50.3	28.9	46.7	64.3	8.4	9.2
1962	59.7	32.5	54.5	16.7	71.9	28.0	23.4	54.6	29.1	48.3	67.3	9.1	10.2
1963	61.7	34.4	55.8	17.2	73.1	27.9	23.3	57.8	29.3	49.4	69.7	9.6	11.1
1964	64.1	36.9	57.5	18.0	75.2	28.0	23.3	60.2	29.6	50.8	72.5	10.3	12.0
1965	65.8	39.9	60.7	18.5	76.3	28.1	23.1	64.8	30.0	53.4	74.8	11.2	13.5
1966	66.7	42.7	64.0	19.5	78.1	29.2	23.2	64.7	30.7	56.4	75.6	12.5	14.4
1967	67.7	43.8	64.7	20.6	80.0	30.4	24.6	60.5	31.5	58.1	75.4	13.3	14.8
1968	70.0	46.6	66.5	22.1	82.6	31.6	26.2	60.3	32.7	60.1	77.5	14.7	16.3
1969	70.0	48.4	69.2	23.6	83.6	33.7	28.3	54.4	34.1	62.9	77.0	16.3	16.9
1970	70.4	48.0	68.2	25.3	84.6	35.9	31.9	44.4	35.6	63.1	76.0	17.2	16.8
1971	73.3	49.9	68.0	26.9	86.2	36.7	33.4	50.2	37.0	63.3	78.8	18.3	18.8
1972	75.3	53.8	71.5	28.4	88.3	37.8	33.5	54.1	38.1	66.2	81.2	20.3	20.8
1973	76.1	57.0	74.9	30.7	89.8	40.4	35.1	55.5	40.3	69.7	81.7	23.0	23.0
1974	74.4	56.0	75.2	33.6	88.0	46.2	40.5	49.2	44.4	71.1	78.7	25.3	23.9
1975	77.2	55.1	71.3	37.0	89.3	47.9	45.9	64.1	48.8	68.4	80.5	26.4	27.8
1976	79.7	59.5	74.6	40.0	91.4	50.2	45.9	72.3	51.0	71.5	83.2	29.8	31.3
1977	81.6	63.8	78.2	43.1	92.5	52.9	47.4	79.4	53.8	75.2	84.8	33.7	35.5
1978	82.1	68.1	82.9	46.8	93.8	57.0	50.0	82.5	57.4	80.2	84.8	38.8	39.7
1979	81.5	70.2	86.1	51.1	93.7	62.7	55.1	76.7	62.0	83.8	83.7	44.0	42.5
1980	81.1	69.2	85.3	56.4	93.1	69.6	65.1	68.8	68.4	84.0	82.3	48.2	45.7
1981	82.6	71.5	86.5	61.6	92.9	74.6	74.8	82.4	75.3	85.4	83.7	53.3	54.9
1982	83.4	70.0	83.9	66.0	94.1	79.2	82.3	75.0	79.6	83.5	83.8	55.4	56.2
1983	85.9	73.3	85.3	68.4	93.5	79.6	81.5	91.2	81.1	84.1	87.1	58.3	61.6
1984	88.2	80.2	91.0	71.2	93.6	80.7	81.1	108.6	83.2	89.3	89.9	64.8	70.7
1985	89.9	83.8	93.2	74.4	94.6	82.7	82.4	104.2	84.5	92.1	91.1	69.4	73.8
1986	91.7	85.9	93.7	78.0	97.5	85.1	85.7	88.0	85.5	93.6	91.7	73.1	74.1
1987	94.7	90.7	95.8	81.7	98.7	86.2	85.3	98.1	87.0	95.2	95.3	78.2	80.4
1988	95.9	95.8	99.9	84.2	98.1	87.7	87.4	108.0	89.4	99.0	96.7	84.0	88.7
1989	94.7	97.4	102.8	86.3	96.5	91.1	94.6	97.3	92.5	101.6	95.9	88.7	92.8
1990	95.4	98.3	103.0	90.8	96.7	95.2	98.0	94.3	95.8	102.5	95.9	93.5	95.4
1991	97.7	97.5	99.8	95.3	97.8	97.5	102.1	93.0	98.3	100.3	97.2	95.1	97.3
1992	100.0	100.0	100.0	100.0	100.0	100.0	100.0	100.0	100.0	100.0	100.0	100.0	100.0
1993	100.7	103.0	102.3	102.0	99.5	101.3	100.2	113.2	102.1	101.8	101.2	104.4	106.7
1994	103.1	109.6	106.3	104.2	99.4	101.0	101.3	131.7	103.7	105.3	104.1	110.8	119.5
1995	104.2	114.2	109.6	106.2	98.8	101.9	102.2	139.0	105.1	108.6	105.1	116.3	127.4
1996	107.5	119.9	111.5	109.0	98.7	101.4	100.6	152.2	105.5	111.2	107.9	121.5	136.4
1997	108.4	127.0	117.1	110.3	97.8	101.8	100.9	156.9	106.2	116.1	109.4	129.2	146.3
1998	112.3	134.9	120.2	115.9	101.3	103.2	101.2	148.9	106.6	119.2	113.2	139.2	153.0
1999	116.2	142.9	123.0	121.1	103.7	104.2	102.5	147.6	107.4	121.9	117.2	148.9	162.9
2000	121.1	151.6	125.2	126.8	105.1	104.8	105.6	149.2	108.8	124.5	121.8	158.8	177.0

Table 4-1. Indexes of Productivity and Related Data, 1947–2000—*Continued*

(1992=100.)

Year	Manufacturing											
	Output per hour of all persons	Output	Hours of all persons	Compen-sation per hour	Real compen-sation per hour	Unit labor costs	Unit nonlabor payments	Implicit price deflator	Employ-ment	Output per person	Compen-sation in current dollars	Nonlabor payments in current dollars
1947	...	...	...	...	...	...	...	...	...	...	...	...
1948	...	...	...	...	...	...	...	...	...	...	...	...
1949	33.5	26.5	79.1	8.3	45.1	24.6	23.5	24.0	80.1	33.1	6.5	6.2
1950	34.0	29.1	85.5	8.7	46.8	25.5	23.9	24.5	84.3	34.5	7.4	7.0
1951	33.8	31.1	92.1	9.5	47.7	28.3	25.8	26.8	90.6	34.3	8.8	8.0
1952	35.2	32.9	93.3	10.2	49.9	28.9	25.3	26.7	91.8	35.8	9.5	8.3
1953	36.4	35.7	98.1	10.7	52.2	29.5	24.7	26.6	96.8	36.8	10.5	8.8
1954	37.3	33.4	89.6	11.2	54.2	30.1	25.0	27.0	90.1	37.1	10.1	8.3
1955	38.8	36.7	94.6	11.7	56.5	30.1	25.4	27.2	93.1	39.4	11.0	9.3
1956	38.6	37.1	96.0	12.4	59.3	32.1	25.6	28.1	95.0	39.0	11.9	9.5
1957	39.4	37.2	94.5	13.2	60.8	33.4	26.5	29.2	94.7	39.3	12.4	9.9
1958	40.0	34.7	86.6	13.8	61.8	34.4	27.0	29.9	87.9	39.4	11.9	9.4
1959	40.9	37.8	92.5	14.3	63.7	34.9	27.4	30.3	91.9	41.1	13.2	10.3
1960	41.8	38.5	92.1	14.9	65.2	35.6	26.8	30.2	92.6	41.5	13.7	10.3
1961	42.8	38.4	89.7	15.3	66.5	35.7	26.8	30.3	90.0	42.6	13.7	10.3
1962	44.2	41.3	93.4	15.9	68.3	36.0	26.7	30.3	92.8	44.4	14.8	11.0
1963	45.7	43.1	94.4	16.4	69.4	35.8	26.8	30.3	93.5	46.1	15.4	11.6
1964	47.4	45.7	96.4	17.0	71.4	36.0	26.8	30.3	94.9	48.2	16.4	12.2
1965	48.5	49.5	102.0	17.4	71.8	35.9	27.4	30.7	99.3	49.8	17.8	13.6
1966	49.1	53.3	108.6	18.2	73.0	37.1	28.0	31.5	105.4	50.6	19.8	14.9
1967	50.9	54.9	108.0	19.2	74.6	37.7	28.4	32.0	106.7	51.5	20.7	15.6
1968	52.7	57.7	109.6	20.7	77.1	39.2	28.6	32.7	108.5	53.2	22.6	16.5
1969	53.5	59.4	110.9	22.2	78.5	41.4	29.0	33.8	110.6	53.7	24.6	17.2
1970	54.2	56.5	104.4	23.7	79.4	43.8	29.3	35.0	106.3	53.2	24.8	16.6
1971	57.8	58.2	100.5	25.2	80.7	43.5	31.6	36.2	102.2	56.9	25.3	18.4
1972	60.3	63.3	105.1	26.5	82.3	43.9	33.4	37.4	105.0	60.3	27.8	21.1
1973	61.4	67.8	110.4	28.5	83.4	46.4	36.5	40.3	110.5	61.4	31.5	24.8
1974	61.2	66.1	107.9	31.6	83.4	51.7	44.6	47.3	110.1	60.0	34.2	29.5
1975	64.3	62.5	97.2	35.5	85.6	55.2	51.6	53.0	100.6	62.1	34.5	32.2
1976	67.0	68.2	101.9	38.4	87.7	57.4	53.9	55.3	104.2	65.4	39.2	36.8
1977	69.7	73.9	106.1	41.8	89.6	60.0	57.8	58.7	108.2	68.4	44.4	42.8
1978	70.4	77.8	110.6	45.2	90.6	64.2	61.7	62.7	112.7	69.0	50.0	48.0
1979	69.8	78.7	112.7	49.6	90.9	71.1	69.1	69.8	115.6	68.1	55.9	54.3
1980	70.1	75.3	107.5	55.6	91.6	79.3	80.2	79.9	111.6	67.5	59.7	60.4
1981	70.7	75.6	107.0	61.1	92.1	86.3	87.7	87.1	111.0	68.1	65.3	66.3
1982	74.2	72.7	97.9	67.0	95.4	90.2	89.3	89.6	103.5	70.2	65.6	64.9
1983	76.7	75.9	98.9	68.8	94.1	89.7	90.2	90.0	101.8	74.6	68.1	68.5
1984	79.5	83.7	105.3	71.2	93.6	89.6	92.7	91.5	106.8	70.4	75.0	77.6
1985	82.3	86.0	104.6	75.1	95.5	91.3	90.8	91.0	106.0	81.2	78.5	78.1
1986	85.9	88.5	103.0	78.5	98.1	91.3	85.0	87.5	104.5	84.7	80.8	75.2
1987	88.3	91.6	103.8	80.7	97.5	91.4	87.8	89.2	104.7	87.5	83.8	80.5
1988	90.2	96.1	106.6	84.0	97.9	93.1	90.9	91.8	106.6	90.2	89.5	87.4
1989	90.3	96.6	107.1	86.6	96.8	96.0	95.3	95.6	107.0	90.3	92.8	92.1
1990	92.9	97.3	104.8	90.8	96.6	97.8	99.8	99.0	105.4	92.3	95.1	97.1
1991	95.0	95.4	100.4	95.6	98.1	100.6	99.0	99.6	101.8	93.8	96.0	94.4
1992	100.0	100.0	100.0	100.0	100.0	100.0	100.0	100.0	100.0	100.0	100.0	100.0
1993	101.9	103.3	101.4	102.7	100.2	100.8	100.9	100.9	100.1	103.2	104.2	104.2
1994	105.0	108.7	103.6	105.6	100.8	100.7	102.8	102.0	101.3	107.3	109.4	111.8
1995	109.0	113.4	104.0	107.9	100.4	99.0	106.9	103.9	102.5	110.7	112.2	121.2
1996	112.8	117.0	103.7	109.3	99.0	96.9	109.9	104.9	102.2	114.5	113.4	128.5
1997	117.6	124.1	105.5	111.4	98.8	94.7	110.0	104.1	103.2	120.2	117.5	136.5
1998	124.0	130.4	105.2	117.3	102.6	94.6	104.2	100.5	104.0	125.4	123.4	135.9
1999	129.6	135.2	104.3	122.0	104.5	94.1	105.5	101.1	102.3	132.1	127.3	142.6
2000	138.5	142.9	103.2	128.4	106.4	92.7	...	...	101.6	140.7	132.5	...

Table 4-2. Average Annual Percent Change in Output per Hour and Related Series: Manufacturing Industries, 1990–1999

Industry	SIC Code	1999 Employment [1] (thousands)	Average annual percent change, 1990–1999				
			Output per hour	Output	Employee hours	Total compensation	Unit labor costs
Meat products	201	504	0.6	3.0	2.4	5.3	2.2
Dairy products	202	143	0.7	0.2	-0.5	2.2	2.0
Preserved fruits and vegetables	203	226	2.6	1.6	-0.9	2.7	1.0
Grain mill products	204	125	2.4	2.1	-0.3	2.6	0.5
Bakery products	205	202	1.7	1.3	-0.3	3.8	2.4
Sugar and confectionery products	206	92	2.6	1.7	-0.9	2.4	0.8
Fats and oils	207	29	3.1	1.9	-1.2	2.5	0.5
Beverages	208	183	1.4	1.6	0.2	2.3	0.7
Miscellaneous food and kindred products	209	174	1.8	1.4	-0.4	2.9	1.5
Cigarettes	211	26	2.0	-1.5	-3.5	-0.4	1.1
Broadwoven fabric mills, cotton	221	66	3.4	0.1	-3.1	-0.6	-0.7
Broadwoven fabric mills, manmade	222	58	5.0	2.0	-2.8	1.1	-0.9
Narrow fabric mills	224	20	2.7	0.9	-1.8	3.0	2.1
Knitting mills	225	141	3.4	-0.6	-3.9	-0.6	0.1
Textile finishing, except wool	226	61	2.1	1.9	-0.3	3.1	1.2
Carpets and rugs	227	65	0.5	1.2	0.6	2.7	1.5
Yarn and thread mills	228	84	4.9	3.0	-1.8	1.3	-1.7
Miscellaneous textile goods	229	55	1.7	2.7	1.0	4.1	1.4
Men's and boys' furnishings	232	157	7.0	0.6	-6.0	-1.5	-2.0
Women's and misses' outerwear	233	205	5.9	1.0	-4.7	-1.7	-2.7
Women's and children's undergarments	234	26	12.4	1.9	-9.4	-5.8	-7.6
Hats, caps, and millinery	235	14	2.2	0.8	-1.4	3.5	2.8
Miscellaneous apparel and accessories	238	31	1.7	-2.2	-3.8	-1.6	0.6
Miscellaneous fabricated textile products	239	215	2.9	3.7	0.8	5.7	1.9
Sawmills and planing mills	242	182	2.6	2.0	-0.6	3.8	1.8
Millwork, plywood, and structural members	243	323	-0.9	1.9	2.8	5.4	3.4
Wood containers	244	57	-0.6	1.9	2.5	5.3	3.4
Wood buildings and mobile homes	245	103	-0.7	5.5	6.3	9.2	3.5
Miscellaneous wood products	249	86	3.1	3.2	0.1	4.0	0.8
Household furniture	251	290	2.3	2.6	0.2	3.7	1.1
Office furniture	252	75	1.6	3.3	1.6	3.4	0.1
Public building and related furniture	253	52	6.5	12.0	5.2	10.4	-1.5
Partitions and fixtures	254	90	3.2	5.1	1.9	6.9	1.7
Miscellaneous furniture and fixtures	259	41	1.9	3.1	1.2	4.6	1.4
Pulp mills	261	12	-3.0	-4.7	-1.8	-5.9	-1.2
Paper mills	262	146	2.0	-0.2	-2.2	0.8	1.0
Paperboard mills	263	48	3.0	1.8	-1.1	3.2	1.3
Paperboard containers and boxes	265	219	1.3	2.0	0.7	4.0	2.0
Miscellaneous converted paper products	267	243	2.6	2.7	0.1	3.9	1.2
Newspapers	271	442	-0.5	-1.3	-0.8	2.5	3.8
Periodicals	272	144	2.3	3.4	1.1	7.9	4.4
Books	273	125	1.0	1.5	0.6	5.2	3.6
Miscellaneous publishing	274	91	3.7	4.7	1.0	10.3	5.3
Commercial printing	275	570	1.3	1.7	0.4	3.7	1.9
Manifold business forms	276	43	-2.6	-4.2	-1.7	-1.1	3.3
Greeting cards	277	26	0.4	0.7	0.3	0.7	(2)
Blankbooks and bookbinding	278	63	2.4	1.2	-1.2	1.7	0.5
Printing trade services	279	49	2.2	-0.6	-2.7	-0.4	0.2
Industrial inorganic chemicals	281	72	5.3	2.3	-2.9	0.6	-1.6
Plastics materials and synthetics	282	155	4.2	2.6	-1.5	1.6	-1.0
Drugs	283	295	0.1	2.6	2.5	5.7	3.0
Soaps, cleaners, and toilet goods	284	160	1.3	1.5	0.2	2.8	1.2
Paints and allied products	285	52	1.9	0.2	-1.6	3.1	2.9
Industrial organic chemicals	286	127	1.0	-1.1	-2.1	2.5	3.6
Agricultural chemicals	287	55	0.2	0.3	0.1	1.5	1.2
Miscellaneous chemical products	289	91	3.1	2.2	-0.9	3.2	1.0
Petroleum refining	291	89	5.0	1.3	-3.5	2.5	1.2
Asphalt paving and roofing materials	295	31	1.9	3.3	1.4	2.9	-0.4
Miscellaneous petroleum and coal products	299	14	-0.5	1.4	1.9	2.8	1.4

See footnotes and *Note* at end of table.

Table 4-2. Average Annual Percent Change in Output per Hour and Related Series: Manufacturing Industries, 1990–1999—*Continued*

Industry	SIC Code	1999 Employment [1] (thousands)	Average annual percent change, 1990–1999				
			Output per hour	Output	Employee hours	Total compensation	Unit labor costs
Tires and inner tubes	301	80	3.9	3.2	-0.7	3.1	(2)
Hose and belting and gaskets and packing	305	74	1.9	4.3	2.3	4.9	0.6
Fabricated rubber products, n.e.c.	306	107	2.9	3.4	0.5	3.8	0.4
Miscellaneous plastics products, n.e.c.	308	740	3.3	5.3	2.0	5.6	0.3
Footwear, except rubber	314	33	3.0	-5.8	-8.5	-4.3	1.7
Flat glass	321	16	4.7	3.6	-1.1	0.6	-2.9
Glass and glassware, pressed or blown	322	64	3.6	0.7	-2.8	0.7	(2)
Products of purchased glass	323	64	4.2	5.5	1.3	5.4	-0.1
Cement, hydraulic	324	17	2.4	2.4	(2)	3.4	1.0
Structural clay products	325	32	1.4	0.6	-0.8	1.4	0.8
Pottery and related products	326	38	2.3	2.6	0.3	2.9	0.3
Concrete, gypsum, and plaster products	327	240	1.3	3.3	2.1	5.4	2.0
Miscellaneous nonmetallic mineral products	229	73	2.1	1.8	-0.3	3.0	1.2
Blast furnace and basic steel products	331	228	3.5	1.6	-1.8	0.5	-1.1
Iron and steel foundries	332	128	1.9	2.0	0.1	2.5	0.4
Primary nonferrous metals	333	37	2.8	0.5	-2.2	-0.1	-0.6
Nonferrous rolling and drawing	335	168	3.2	3.1	(2)	3.1	(2)
Nonferrous foundries (castings)	336	95	2.6	4.7	2.1	4.7	(2)
Miscellaneous primary metal products	339	28	3.2	3.6	0.5	3.2	-0.5
Metal cans and shipping containers	341	36	3.5	0.1	-3.3	-1.2	-1.2
Cutlery, handtools, and hardware	342	122	2.7	2.1	-0.6	2.8	0.6
Plumbing and heating, except electric	343	59	2.4	2.8	0.4	4.1	1.2
Fabricated structural metal products	344	484	1.5	3.1	1.6	4.5	1.3
Metal forgings and stampings	346	254	3.5	5.2	1.7	3.5	-1.7
Metal services, n.e.c.	347	143	2.3	4.4	2.1	4.9	0.4
Ordnance and accessories, n.e.c.	348	41	1.3	-5.1	-6.3	-6.0	-1.0
Miscellaneous fabricated metal products	349	271	1.4	3.0	1.6	4.2	1.1
Engines and turbines	351	86	4.0	3.9	-0.1	1.6	-2.2
Farm and garden machinery	352	99	0.8	(2)	-0.8	2.5	2.5
Construction and related machinery	353	244	2.8	3.6	0.8	3.6	(2)
Metalworking machinery	354	338	2.3	2.6	0.3	3.6	1.1
Special industry machinery	355	169	2.9	3.5	0.6	3.6	0.1
General industrial machinery	356	255	1.0	1.4	0.4	3.2	1.8
Computer and office equipment	357	370	33.3	30.8	-1.9	1.7	-22.3
Refrigeration and service machinery	358	214	1.9	4.5	2.5	4.4	(2)
Industrial machinery, n.e.c.	359	367	2.5	4.2	1.6	4.7	0.5
Electric distribution equipment	361	83	3.6	2.0	-1.6	2.6	0.6
Electrical industrial apparatus	362	151	4.7	3.4	-1.3	3.5	0.1
Household appliances	363	118	4.0	3.7	-0.3	3.6	-0.1
Electric lighting and wiring equipment	364	183	3.2	3.2	(2)	2.9	-0.2
Communications equipment	366	267	11.4	11.4	(2)	5.5	-5.3
Electronic components and accessories	367	636	26.0	27.5	1.2	5.1	-17.6
Miscellaneous electrical equipment and supplies	369	151	5.0	4.1	-0.8	2.0	-2.0
Motor vehicles and equipment	371	1 019	3.2	6.4	3.1	5.1	-1.3
Aircraft and parts	372	495	3.9	-0.1	-3.9	-0.8	-0.7
Ship and boat building and repairing	373	166	0.9	-0.3	-1.2	0.2	0.5
Railroad equipment	374	37	4.2	5.5	1.2	4.6	-0.9
Motorcycles, bicycles, and parts	375	20	2.9	7.7	4.6	12.5	4.5
Guided missiles, space vehicles, parts	376	88	3.5	-4.8	-8.0	-6.0	-1.2
Search and navigation equipment	381	166	2.4	-3.5	-5.8	-3.1	0.4
Measuring and controlling devices	382	294	4.1	3.0	-1.1	2.4	-0.6
Medical instruments and supplies	384	283	3.6	5.3	1.6	6.2	0.9
Ophthalmic goods	385	34	7.4	4.8	-2.3	3.3	-1.5
Photographic equipment and supplies	386	74	3.5	0.3	-3.1	-0.6	-0.9
Jewelry, silverware, and plated ware	391	50	3.4	3.0	-0.3	2.3	-0.7
Musical instruments	393	17	-1.3	1.6	3.0	5.8	4.1
Toys and sporting goods	394	105	1.5	1.9	0.3	3.2	1.3
Pens, pencils, office, and art supplies	395	31	1.0	-0.4	-1.4	1.8	2.3
Costume jewelry and notions	396	20	4.0	-2.2	-5.9	-0.2	2.0
Miscellaneous manufactures	399	173	0.5	3.0	2.5	4.4	1.3

Note: n.e.c. = not elsewhere classified.

1. Employment figures are based primarily on the data from the BLS Current Employment Statistics (CES) program.
2. Value less than 0.05.

Table 4-3. Average Annual Percent Change in Output per Hour and Related Series: Mining and Service Producing Industries, 1990–1999

Industry	SIC Code	1999 Employment[1] (thousands)	Average annual percent change, 1990–1999				
			Output per hour[2]	Output	Employee hours[3]	Output per hour[2]	Unit labor costs
MINING							
Copper ores	102	14	0.3	-0.1	-0.4	3.7	3.7
Gold and silver ores	104	14	5.6	1.2	-4.2	0.4	-0.7
Coal mining	12	85	5.5	-0.4	-5.6	-3.2	-2.8
Bituminous coal and lignite mining	122	80	5.5	-0.4	-5.6	-3.2	-2.7
Oil and gas extraction	13	293	2.7	-0.9	-3.5	1.9	2.8
Crude petroleum and natural gas	131	133	3.5	-0.9	-4.2	1.1	2.0
Nonmetallic minerals, except fuels	14	112	0.8	1.1	0.3	3.7	2.5
Crushed and broken stone	142	45	0.3	1.8	1.5	4.7	2.9
TRANSPORTATION							
Railroad transportation	4011	203	4.9	2.7	-2.1	0.8	-1.9
Trucking, except local	4213	901	1.9	3.9	1.9	5.1	1.2
U.S. Postal Service[4]	43	873	0.7	1.8	1.2	4.0	2.2
Air transportation	4512, 13, 22 (PTS)	711	1.7	4.2	2.4	4.8	0.6
COMMUNICATION AND UTILITIES							
Telephone communications	481	1 070	5.9	7.9	2.0	7.1	-0.8
Radio and television broadcasting stations	483	248	-0.3	0.6	1.0	5.1	4.4
Cable and other pay television stations	484	201	-1.4	4.8	6.3	12.4	7.3
Electric utilities	491, 3 (PT)	480	4.4	1.8	-2.5	1.9	0.1
Gas utilities	492, 3 (PT)	169	3.6	1.5	-2.0	2.5	1.0
RETAIL TRADE							
Building materials, hardware, garden supply and mobile homes	52	1 030	4.2	6.4	2.2	6.1	-0.3
Lumber and other building materials dealers	521	625	3.5	7.2	3.6	7.3	0.1
Paint, glass, and wallpaper stores	523	71	4.8	3.8	-1.0	2.6	-1.2
Hardware stores	525	173	2.9	2.3	-0.6	3.0	0.8
Retail nurseries, lawn and garden supply stores	526	109	6.7	6.8	0.1	3.8	-2.8
General merchandise stores	53	2 778	4.9	6.4	1.4	4.5	-1.8
Department stores	531	2 431	4.8	6.8	1.9	5.1	-1.6
Variety stores	533	141	8.4	5.7	-2.5	0.3	-5.7
Miscellaneous general merchandise stores	539	207	5.7	4.8	-0.9	1.1	-3.5
Food stores	54	3 617	-0.3	0.3	0.6	3.6	3.3
Grocery stores	541	3 154	-0.1	0.3	0.5	3.4	3.1
Meat and fish (seafood) markets	542	58	(6)	-0.4	-0.4	1.6	1.9
Retail bakeries	546	212	-0.9	1.0	2.0	5.7	4.7
Automotive dealers and gasoline service stations	55	2 449	2.0	2.8	0.7	5.4	2.5
New and used car dealers	551	1 079	0.5	2.1	1.6	6.3	4.1
Auto and home supply stores	553	424	1.3	2.8	1.6	4.7	1.8
Gasoline service stations	554	681	3.5	2.4	-1.1	2.4	0.1
Apparel and accessory stores	56	1 233	5.3	4.7	-0.6	3.4	-1.3
Men's and boy's wear stores	561	85	3.3	0.7	-2.5	0.5	-0.2
Women's clothing stores	562	293	6.7	2.0	-4.4	-0.3	-2.3
Family clothing stores	565	433	4.2	8.0	3.6	7.7	-0.3
Shoe stores	566	215	3.8	2.3	-1.5	2.5	0.3
Furniture, home furnishings, and equipment stores	57	1 197	6.7	9.1	2.2	6.6	-2.3
Furniture and homefurnishings stores	571	626	2.8	4.1	1.3	5.2	1.0
Household appliance stores	572	81	6.5	4.1	-2.3	0.5	-3.4
Radio, television, computer, and music stores	573	491	11.2	16.3	4.6	9.7	-5.6
Eating and drinking places[5]	58	8 174	(6)	2.2	2.2	5.8	3.6
Miscellaneous merchandise stores	59	3 613	3.3	4.9	1.5	5.7	0.7
Drug and proprietary stores	591	672	2.2	3.2	1.0	5.3	2.0
Liquor stores	592	144	0.9	0.2	-0.7	3.2	3.0
Used merchandise stores	593	208	6.5	11.3	4.5	7.9	-3.1
Miscellaneous shopping goods stores	594	1 203	3.4	5.0	1.5	5.2	0.3
Nonstore retailers	596	593	8.0	10.7	2.5	8.5	-2.0
Fuel dealers	598	100	3.5	1.9	-1.6	1.6	-0.2
Retail stores, n.e.c.	599	693	3.9	5.6	1.7	5.1	-0.4
FINANCE AND SERVICES							
Commercial banks	602	1 476	2.6	1.9	-0.7	5.7	3.8
Hotels and motels	701	1 809	1.8	3.1	1.2	5.7	2.5
Personal services	72	1 815	1.2	2.1	0.9	4.7	2.5
Laundry, cleaning, and garment services	721	525	2.0	2.0	0.1	3.5	1.5
Photographic studios, portrait	722	90	0.8	3.4	2.7	4.3	0.9
Beauty shops	723	731	1.7	2.6	0.9	5.2	2.5
Barber shops	724	57	3.6	0.8	-2.7	-0.1	-0.9
Funeral services and crematories	726	107	1.0	0.9	-0.1	4.1	3.2
Automotive repair shops	753	900	1.9	3.1	1.2	4.8	1.6
Motion picture theaters	783	138	-0.7	1.5	2.3	4.7	3.1

1. Employment figures are based primarily on data from the BLS Current Employment Statistics (CES) program and the Current Population Survey (CPS). Other sources are the Association of American Railroads, the Department of Transportation, and the U.S. Postal Service.
2. Output per employee hour is measured in mining, transportation, communications, and SICs 531, 551, 602, and 783. Output per hour of all persons is used for all other trade and services industries. All persons include self-employed and unpaid family workers as well as employees. In SIC 4213 and 4512, 13, 22 (pts), output per employee hour is based on output per employee with the assumption of constant average weekly hours.
3. Employee hours are measured in mining, transportation, communications, and SICs 531, 551, 602, and 783. Hours of all persons are used for all other trade and service industries. All persons include self-employed and unpaid family workers as well as employees. In SIC 4213 and 4512, 13, 22 (pts), employee hours are based on employees with the assumption of constant average weekly hours.
4. The United States Postal Service, SIC 43, is also designated in the *Standard Industrial Classification Manual* and is identical to the three-digit SIC group Number, SIC 431, and the four-digit SIC Industry Number, SIC 4311. Employee hours in SIC 43 are based on the number of full-time equivalent (FTE) employee years, as reported in the U.S. Postal Service budget. FTE employee years are computed by dividing total hours of full-time, part-time, and intermittent workers by the number of hours in a standard work year. The output and hours for SIC 43 reflect the federal fiscal year.
5. Eating and drinking places, SIC 58, is also designated in the *Standard Industrial Classification Manual* and is identical to the three-digit SIC Group Number, SIC 581.
6. Value less than 0.05.

Table 4-4. Indexes of Multifactor Productivity and Related Measures, Selected Years, 1950–1999

(1996=100.)

Industry	1950	1955	1960	1965	1970	1975	1980	1985	1986	1987	1988
PRIVATE BUSINESS											
Productivity											
Output per hour of all persons	35.0	40.9	45.6	55.9	63.0	71.5	75.8	83.9	86.5	87.0	88.1
Output per unit of capital services	111.0	114.7	111.1	122.4	112.3	103.4	102.7	99.2	98.8	98.9	100.2
Multifactor productivity	55.9	61.9	65.3	76.4	80.3	85.2	88.6	92.4	93.8	94.1	94.7
Output	20.5	24.9	27.5	35.6	42.0	48.5	59.4	71.0	73.6	76.3	79.6
Inputs											
Labor input	50.3	53.7	54.0	58.0	61.0	62.4	71.9	79.6	80.5	83.1	86.3
Capital services	18.4	21.7	24.8	29.1	37.4	46.9	57.9	71.5	74.6	77.1	79.4
Combined units of labor and capital inputs	36.6	40.3	42.2	46.7	52.3	57.0	67.1	76.9	78.5	81.1	84.0
Capital per hour of all persons	31.5	35.6	41.1	45.7	56.1	69.1	73.8	84.6	87.6	88.0	87.9
PRIVATE NONFARM BUSINESS											
Productivity											
Output per hour of all persons	39.1	44.6	48.7	58.6	64.9	73.0	77.3	84.4	87.1	87.5	88.6
Output per unit of capital services	120.7	125.3	120.8	132.0	119.6	108.2	106.9	101.1	100.4	100.2	101.5
Multifactor productivity	60.9	66.3	69.2	79.8	82.9	87.4	90.8	93.3	94.7	94.8	95.5
Output	19.7	24.4	27.2	35.5	41.9	48.4	59.6	70.8	73.5	76.2	79.7
Inputs											
Labor input	43.7	48.6	50.1	55.4	59.3	60.9	70.7	78.8	79.8	82.5	85.9
Capital services	16.4	19.5	22.5	26.9	35.1	44.7	55.7	70.0	73.2	76.0	78.5
Combined units of labor and capital inputs	32.4	36.8	39.3	44.4	50.6	55.3	65.6	75.9	77.6	80.4	83.5
Capital per hour of all persons	32.4	35.6	40.3	44.4	54.3	67.4	72.3	83.5	86.7	87.3	87.3
MANUFACTURING											
Productivity											
Output per hour of all persons	30.1	34.4	37.1	43.1	48.1	57.0	62.1	73.0	76.2	78.4	80.0
Output per unit of capital services	127.7	129.6	118.8	130.6	111.5	99.2	96.5	95.6	95.9	97.2	100.2
Multifactor productivity	62.8	66.9	68.3	77.7	79.2	78.9	81.3	89.2	90.7	93.5	95.2
Output	24.9	31.4	32.9	42.3	48.3	53.4	64.4	73.6	75.7	78.4	82.2
Inputs											
Hours at work of all persons	82.5	91.2	88.8	98.3	100.5	93.8	103.7	100.8	99.3	99.9	102.8
Capital services	19.5	24.2	27.7	32.4	43.4	53.9	66.7	76.9	78.9	80.6	82.0
Energy	28.3	39.4	48.0	62.6	79.8	82.1	86.4	81.0	81.7	86.8	90.2
Non-energy materials	25.5	31.5	32.1	34.7	37.7	51.8	63.0	71.8	73.5	70.7	72.0
Purchased business services	18.1	23.3	25.9	34.1	44.6	53.1	67.3	62.9	67.0	71.3	77.7
Combined units of all inputs	39.6	46.9	48.2	54.5	61.0	67.7	79.2	82.5	83.5	83.8	86.4

Table 4-4. Indexes of Multifactor Productivity and Related Measures, Selected Years, 1950–1999—*Continued*

(1996=100.)

Industry	1989	1990	1991	1992	1993	1994	1995	1996	1997	1998	1999
PRIVATE BUSINESS											
Productivity											
Output per hour of all persons	89.0	90.2	91.3	94.8	95.4	96.6	97.3	100.0	102.2	105.1	107.9
Output per unit of capital services	100.8	99.5	96.3	97.8	98.6	100.3	99.7	100.0	100.3	99.6	98.1
Multifactor productivity	95.3	95.4	94.5	96.6	97.1	98.1	98.4	100.0	101.2	102.6	103.5
Output	82.4	83.6	82.6	85.7	88.5	92.8	95.8	100.0	105.2	110.6	115.8
Inputs											
Labor input	88.9	89.4	88.3	89.3	91.8	95.6	98.0	100.0	103.5	106.1	108.9
Capital services	81.8	84.0	85.8	87.6	89.8	92.5	96.0	100.0	104.9	111.0	118.1
Combined units of labor and capital inputs	86.5	87.6	87.5	88.7	91.1	94.6	97.3	100.0	104.0	107.7	111.9
Capital per hour of all persons	88.3	90.6	94.8	96.9	96.7	96.3	97.6	100.0	101.9	105.5	110.0
PRIVATE NONFARM BUSINESS											
Productivity											
Output per hour of all persons	89.3	90.3	91.4	94.8	95.3	96.5	97.5	100.0	102.0	104.7	107.3
Output per unit of capital services	101.8	100.3	96.8	98.1	98.9	100.4	99.9	100.0	100.0	99.3	97.6
Multifactor productivity	95.8	95.7	94.8	96.7	97.2	98.1	98.6	100.0	101.0	102.4	103.0
Output	82.4	83.5	82.5	85.5	88.4	92.6	95.8	100.0	105.1	110.6	115.8
Inputs											
Labor input	88.5	89.2	88.0	89.0	91.8	95.4	97.8	100.0	103.6	106.4	109.5
Capital services	81.0	83.3	85.2	87.1	89.4	92.3	95.9	100.0	105.1	111.3	118.7
Combined units of labor and capital inputs	86.0	87.3	87.1	88.4	91.0	94.4	97.2	100.0	104.1	108.0	112.4
Capital per hour of all persons	87.7	90.0	94.4	96.6	96.4	96.2	97.6	100.0	101.9	105.5	110.0
MANUFACTURING											
Productivity											
Output per hour of all persons	80.0	82.3	84.2	88.7	90.3	93.1	96.6	100.0	104.3	109.9	114.9
Output per unit of capital services	98.9	97.2	93.3	95.7	96.8	99.6	100.5	100.0	101.8	102.3	100.8
Multifactor productivity	93.4	93.3	92.4	94.0	94.9	97.3	99.2	100.0	103.5	106.3	109.4
Output	82.6	83.2	81.6	85.5	88.3	93.0	97.0	100.0	106.1	111.5	115.6
Inputs											
Hours at work of all persons	103.2	101.1	96.8	96.4	97.8	99.9	100.3	100.0	101.7	101.4	100.6
Capital services	83.6	85.6	87.4	89.3	91.3	93.3	96.4	100.0	104.2	109.0	114.6
Energy	90.5	93.4	93.5	93.4	96.9	100.2	102.3	100.0	97.1	100.3	103.2
Non-energy materials	75.1	77.6	78.6	83.9	86.9	90.3	92.9	100.0	101.5	108.7	109.1
Purchased business services	82.7	81.7	84.4	91.7	94.2	96.2	100.5	100.0	104.8	103.4	102.0
Combined units of all inputs	88.4	89.2	88.3	91.0	93.1	95.6	97.7	100.0	102.6	104.9	105.7

Table 4-5. Indexes of Multifactor Productivity and Related Measures, Manufacturing Industries, 1985–1999

(1996=100.)

Industry	1985	1986	1987	1988	1989	1990	1991	1992	1993	1994	1995	1996	1997	1998	1999
NONDURABLE GOODS															
Output per hour of all persons	79.8	82.0	83.7	84.9	84.5	86.6	88.3	92.1	92.6	94.4	97.2	100.0	104.1	106.7	108.3
Output per unit of capital services	100.5	101.5	103.8	105.2	103.5	102.6	99.6	101.8	101.2	102.1	101.6	100.0	101.3	98.8	95.7
Multifactor productivity	98.5	99.2	100.8	102.0	99.7	98.8	98.1	98.5	98.6	99.5	100.6	100.0	101.9	102.2	102.5
Sector output	78.1	80.6	84.0	86.5	87.0	88.7	88.6	93.0	94.7	97.3	99.3	100.0	104.1	105.2	105.9
Hours of all persons at work	98.0	98.3	100.3	101.9	102.9	102.5	100.3	101.0	102.2	103.1	102.1	100.0	100.0	98.6	97.7
Capital services	77.7	79.5	80.9	82.2	84.0	86.5	88.9	91.3	93.6	95.3	97.7	100.0	102.8	106.5	110.7
Energy	76.4	77.5	80.8	83.3	85.2	89.4	90.4	92.4	96.3	98.8	102.1	100.0	96.0	97.3	98.7
Non-energy materials	73.9	76.5	78.1	77.9	80.0	83.0	83.8	90.0	91.6	95.3	95.2	100.0	103.1	105.1	105.0
Purchased business services	58.9	62.7	66.2	73.6	80.6	87.2	89.9	97.4	98.8	97.0	101.7	100.0	104.5	102.6	101.3
Combined units of all inputs	79.3	81.3	83.3	84.9	87.3	89.8	90.3	94.4	96.0	97.8	98.7	100.0	102.1	102.9	103.3
Food And Kindred Products															
Output per hour of all persons	89.1	89.1	89.6	92.0	89.5	90.2	93.4	98.3	98.5	98.9	100.9	100.0	102.3	106.3	105.5
Output per unit of capital services	101.7	100.8	100.1	102.1	100.4	100.9	100.6	103.4	103.3	103.0	104.1	100.0	101.7	100.9	99.0
Multifactor productivity	103.8	102.4	102.9	106.5	102.3	101.0	101.9	101.4	102.8	100.6	104.6	100.0	101.1	101.2	103.3
Sector output	81.9	83.2	84.6	87.2	86.9	89.3	91.0	95.8	97.5	98.5	101.9	100.0	103.4	106.6	107.9
Hours of all persons at work	91.9	93.3	94.4	94.8	97.1	99.0	97.4	97.5	99.0	99.6	100.9	100.0	101.1	100.2	102.2
Capital services	80.5	82.6	84.5	85.4	86.6	88.6	90.5	92.7	94.4	95.6	97.8	100.0	101.7	105.7	108.9
Energy	78.7	81.5	84.3	86.8	87.7	88.2	91.1	93.1	95.8	99.8	104.7	100.0	99.8	103.4	104.5
Non-energy materials	77.1	79.1	80.6	78.9	81.9	85.5	86.0	92.8	92.5	97.4	95.5	100.0	102.8	107.3	104.9
Purchased business services	62.0	69.4	63.9	71.0	79.8	87.4	93.6	102.5	103.9	101.9	101.4	100.0	101.9	102.0	98.2
Combined units of all inputs	78.9	81.3	82.2	81.9	85.0	88.4	89.3	94.5	94.9	97.9	97.4	100.0	102.2	105.3	104.4
Textile Mill Products															
Output per hour of all persons	70.2	71.3	72.7	73.6	76.5	78.9	79.7	85.7	89.0	91.2	95.1	100.0	100.9	103.6	110.2
Output per unit of capital services	84.6	88.2	94.8	94.5	96.3	93.5	93.0	100.3	104.0	105.1	101.7	100.0	98.9	95.5	91.1
Multifactor productivity	83.6	85.4	86.5	89.2	89.8	90.6	90.8	94.7	96.3	96.9	98.4	100.0	101.5	101.0	106.8
Sector output	77.1	80.4	86.6	86.4	88.3	86.2	85.8	93.0	97.7	101.5	100.5	100.0	100.7	99.2	97.8
Hours of all persons at work	109.8	112.8	119.1	117.4	115.4	109.2	107.6	108.5	109.7	111.3	105.7	100.0	99.8	95.7	88.8
Capital services	91.1	91.1	91.3	91.4	91.7	92.2	92.2	92.7	93.9	96.6	98.8	100.0	101.8	103.9	107.4
Energy	79.5	82.9	91.2	91.3	91.9	88.5	90.5	94.5	98.7	104.6	106.1	100.0	95.3	93.4	92.3
Non-energy materials	87.4	89.0	95.7	88.5	91.2	88.7	87.1	92.4	97.6	102.0	99.8	100.0	99.0	100.9	93.0
Purchased business services	55.3	57.7	63.4	71.0	80.4	81.0	86.5	97.4	101.0	105.1	103.7	100.0	95.8	88.8	76.1
Combined units of all inputs	92.2	94.2	100.1	96.8	98.3	95.2	94.5	98.2	101.5	104.8	102.2	100.0	99.2	98.2	91.6
Apparel And Related Products															
Output per hour of all persons	72.7	75.0	76.0	76.2	72.4	75.1	75.6	81.4	85.3	90.0	95.5	100.0	113.5	117.2	128.0
Output per unit of capital services	102.5	102.9	105.6	102.2	99.1	97.5	97.9	102.3	101.3	102.8	99.4	100.0	107.7	101.8	100.5
Multifactor productivity	96.1	97.1	98.2	98.1	96.6	96.2	94.4	94.0	94.5	96.8	98.7	100.0	102.5	103.5	105.3
Sector output	88.6	91.0	93.5	92.3	87.8	87.0	86.3	93.4	96.3	100.8	101.6	100.0	106.9	103.2	103.6
Hours of all persons at work	121.9	121.3	123.0	121.1	121.2	115.8	114.1	114.8	112.9	112.1	106.3	100.0	94.1	88.1	81.0
Capital services	86.5	88.4	88.6	90.3	88.5	89.2	88.2	91.3	95.0	98.1	102.2	100.0	99.2	101.4	103.1
Energy	62.3	66.4	69.0	69.6	60.8	60.1	61.4	95.9	106.3	103.8	110.4	100.0	80.8	78.3	78.9
Non-energy materials	93.4	96.1	98.6	93.9	85.1	84.0	83.8	92.9	97.2	101.2	100.8	100.0	111.7	107.8	110.9
Purchased business services	31.8	33.0	31.9	40.2	48.0	59.3	71.6	93.3	97.2	100.7	102.8	100.0	107.1	99.2	94.2
Combined units of all inputs	92.2	93.8	95.3	94.1	90.8	90.4	91.4	99.4	101.8	104.2	103.0	100.0	104.3	99.7	98.4
Paper And Allied Products															
Output per hour of all persons	81.4	86.7	86.6	88.4	88.2	88.4	90.7	93.1	94.9	98.5	99.2	100.0	101.3	104.7	105.8
Output per unit of capital services	103.2	104.7	105.4	107.2	104.7	100.8	98.2	100.1	101.2	104.7	103.3	100.0	100.3	99.2	99.4
Multifactor productivity	97.8	100.1	99.7	100.7	98.3	97.4	98.2	99.5	103.0	104.1	98.2	100.0	102.7	102.1	103.3
Sector output	78.8	82.4	84.6	87.8	89.1	89.6	90.2	94.1	96.3	100.6	100.4	100.0	102.3	103.4	105.2
Hours of all persons at work	96.8	95.1	97.7	99.3	101.1	101.3	99.5	101.1	101.5	102.1	101.2	100.0	100.9	98.7	99.4
Capital services	76.4	78.7	80.3	82.0	85.1	88.8	91.9	94.0	95.2	96.1	97.2	100.0	102.0	104.2	105.8
Energy	76.9	80.3	84.0	85.4	87.8	93.2	93.9	95.8	98.1	100.2	103.9	100.0	99.8	101.0	103.1
Non-energy materials	76.8	79.8	81.7	83.3	87.0	87.5	86.9	90.2	87.7	93.5	103.1	100.0	98.2	103.1	103.9
Purchased business services	58.0	63.8	70.0	80.5	90.3	90.5	91.1	95.7	90.8	94.3	113.6	100.0	96.3	96.3	91.7
Combined units of all inputs	80.5	82.4	84.8	87.2	90.7	92.0	91.9	94.5	93.5	96.6	102.3	100.0	99.6	101.3	101.8

Table 4-5. Indexes of Multifactor Productivity and Related Measures, Manufacturing Industries, 1985–1999—*Continued*

(1996=100.)

Industry	1985	1986	1987	1988	1989	1990	1991	1992	1993	1994	1995	1996	1997	1998	1999
Printing And Publishing															
Output per hour of all persons	103.4	104.3	106.6	101.5	99.5	98.0	96.8	100.4	98.4	97.0	97.2	100.0	103.1	102.6	102.2
Output per unit of capital services	142.2	138.8	138.2	131.1	122.6	117.2	108.0	107.2	105.1	104.1	102.1	100.0	98.8	90.1	80.2
Multifactor productivity	114.7	113.2	113.2	111.2	109.9	107.2	104.7	106.0	102.1	102.6	100.9	100.0	100.3	98.6	97.8
Sector output	93.4	96.6	101.1	101.4	100.0	99.7	95.2	97.6	97.9	98.5	99.2	100.0	105.4	103.8	103.3
Hours of all persons at work	90.3	92.6	94.9	99.9	100.5	101.7	98.3	97.2	99.6	101.4	102.1	100.0	102.2	101.1	101.1
Capital services	65.7	69.6	73.2	77.3	81.6	85.1	88.2	91.1	93.2	94.5	97.2	100.0	106.7	115.2	128.7
Energy	65.3	70.4	82.2	87.9	88.1	91.9	91.0	91.8	94.7	98.5	102.9	100.0	72.5	71.5	71.0
Non-energy materials	82.8	87.5	91.7	89.0	85.6	87.8	85.9	87.7	94.4	90.7	92.5	100.0	106.3	105.9	103.6
Purchased business services	71.8	77.6	85.8	85.7	85.7	87.4	83.0	87.5	91.8	91.9	99.8	100.0	111.9	109.6	105.8
Combined units of all inputs	81.4	85.3	89.4	91.2	91.1	93.0	91.0	92.1	96.0	95.9	98.3	100.0	105.1	105.2	105.6
Chemical And Allied Products															
Output per hour of all persons	72.9	78.3	85.1	86.5	86.1	87.5	87.5	89.1	89.2	94.9	97.9	100.0	107.2	107.5	107.9
Output per unit of capital services	96.4	98.9	107.0	110.7	109.8	108.6	103.2	103.4	100.8	102.3	101.6	100.0	103.0	99.7	95.3
Multifactor productivity	92.7	96.7	102.7	101.8	99.7	100.0	97.1	96.7	95.3	98.2	99.1	100.0	103.0	103.8	102.9
Sector output	71.2	74.6	82.1	86.2	87.8	90.2	89.5	92.6	93.0	96.6	98.5	100.0	106.6	107.8	108.3
Hours of all persons at work	97.7	95.3	96.5	99.7	102.0	103.1	102.3	104.0	104.2	101.8	100.6	100.0	99.4	100.3	100.4
Capital services	73.8	75.4	76.7	77.8	80.0	83.1	86.7	89.6	92.2	94.4	96.9	100.0	103.5	108.1	113.6
Energy	74.4	72.6	78.3	81.8	84.3	89.2	88.9	89.7	94.1	96.1	98.6	100.0	93.4	94.6	94.4
Non-energy materials	73.4	74.6	77.6	83.4	86.7	86.9	89.1	93.9	96.7	99.9	98.6	100.0	107.9	103.3	106.0
Purchased business services	53.9	56.2	62.0	74.0	83.0	88.0	91.6	98.4	99.0	98.6	103.9	100.0	105.5	104.6	98.8
Combined units of all inputs	76.8	77.2	79.9	84.6	88.1	90.2	92.1	95.7	97.5	98.4	99.4	100.0	103.5	103.8	105.3
Petroleum Refining And Related Products															
Output per hour of all persons	68.7	76.6	79.4	83.4	84.1	83.8	83.4	85.7	91.1	92.2	97.0	100.0	105.5	107.9	110.0
Output per unit of capital services	92.4	99.1	102.8	105.6	106.2	106.1	103.4	102.6	102.6	99.8	99.2	100.0	102.5	106.6	106.3
Multifactor productivity	96.1	98.6	98.7	99.4	99.2	98.6	98.7	99.5	100.2	99.8	99.9	100.0	100.9	104.1	103.2
Sector output	83.8	89.0	91.0	92.9	92.9	93.4	92.6	94.6	97.3	96.6	97.6	100.0	102.7	105.3	103.9
Hours of all persons at work	121.9	116.1	114.5	111.3	110.5	111.4	111.1	110.4	106.9	104.8	100.6	100.0	97.3	97.6	94.5
Capital services	90.7	89.9	88.5	88.0	87.5	88.0	89.6	92.2	94.9	96.8	98.4	100.0	100.1	98.7	97.8
Energy	103.0	104.1	91.5	95.2	95.2	107.9	106.0	101.8	104.9	101.1	104.0	100.0	98.6	98.9	105.1
Non-energy materials	84.5	90.0	92.6	94.5	94.4	94.3	93.1	94.9	97.8	97.0	97.8	100.0	102.5	105.2	103.1
Purchased business services	73.5	55.0	70.0	72.7	82.3	100.1	93.2	86.4	81.7	83.7	88.8	100.0	103.1	72.4	89.1
Combined units of all inputs	87.1	90.2	92.2	93.5	93.7	94.8	93.8	95.1	97.1	96.8	97.7	100.0	101.7	101.1	100.7
Rubber And Miscellaneous Plastic Products															
Output per hour of all persons	73.3	74.1	78.3	78.8	79.6	81.9	83.1	90.4	91.7	94.6	95.8	100.0	104.1	106.6	110.2
Output per unit of capital services	94.3	93.4	99.0	100.2	99.2	97.2	91.8	100.3	102.9	106.6	102.5	100.0	99.3	96.1	92.6
Multifactor productivity	88.4	88.4	90.0	90.5	92.3	92.4	93.6	95.6	96.3	97.9	98.1	100.0	102.2	103.1	103.7
Sector output	60.3	62.1	67.5	70.1	71.9	73.4	71.9	81.2	86.7	94.3	96.4	100.0	106.0	109.3	114.2
Hours of all persons at work	82.3	83.8	86.2	89.0	90.4	89.6	86.6	89.8	94.5	99.7	100.6	100.0	101.8	102.6	103.6
Capital services	63.9	66.5	68.2	70.0	72.5	75.5	78.3	80.9	84.3	88.5	94.1	100.0	106.8	113.8	123.2
Energy	67.1	70.2	75.6	78.8	81.3	81.7	80.2	83.8	90.6	96.9	101.8	100.0	103.6	106.8	111.8
Non-energy materials	64.9	67.1	73.2	74.9	74.0	76.0	72.2	83.2	88.8	95.9	97.1	100.0	103.8	106.8	112.1
Purchased business services	45.6	47.3	54.2	60.5	63.9	68.2	69.0	82.6	87.4	95.4	100.5	100.0	106.7	104.4	107.3
Combined units of all inputs	68.2	70.3	75.0	77.5	77.9	79.4	76.9	84.9	90.0	96.3	98.3	100.0	103.7	106.0	110.1

Table 4-5. Indexes of Multifactor Productivity and Related Measures, Manufacturing Industries, 1985–1999—*Continued*

(1996=100.)

Industry	1985	1986	1987	1988	1989	1990	1991	1992	1993	1994	1995	1996	1997	1998	1999
DURABLE GOODS															
Output per hour of all persons	68.2	71.8	74.5	76.2	76.3	78.3	79.5	84.7	87.5	91.4	95.8	100.0	105.1	113.7	121.6
Output per unit of capital services	91.9	91.3	92.1	96.1	94.7	92.3	87.5	90.6	93.4	98.0	99.8	100.0	102.3	105.2	104.9
Multifactor productivity	82.2	84.2	87.7	89.5	88.5	89.0	88.2	90.6	92.2	95.6	98.1	100.0	104.6	109.3	114.6
Sector output	70.1	71.8	74.2	78.8	78.9	78.4	75.1	79.0	82.8	89.3	94.9	100.0	108.2	117.6	124.7
Hours of all persons at work	102.7	100.1	99.7	103.4	103.5	100.1	94.5	93.3	94.7	97.6	99.1	100.0	102.9	103.4	102.6
Capital services	76.3	78.6	80.6	82.0	83.4	84.9	85.9	87.1	88.7	91.1	95.1	100.0	105.7	111.7	118.9
Energy	88.7	88.7	96.0	100.9	98.5	99.3	98.0	95.0	97.9	102.4	102.9	100.0	98.2	103.9	108.6
Non-energy materials	72.0	72.7	67.9	70.9	73.1	73.7	72.8	77.7	82.5	86.6	92.4	100.0	102.4	114.1	116.0
Purchased business services	67.0	71.4	76.5	81.9	84.8	82.3	78.9	86.0	89.5	95.4	99.3	100.0	105.1	104.3	102.8
Combined units of all inputs	85.2	85.3	84.6	88.0	89.2	88.1	85.2	87.1	89.8	93.4	96.7	100.0	103.4	107.6	108.8
Lumber And Wood Products															
Output per hour of all persons	101.5	106.5	108.1	105.6	102.6	103.9	106.1	106.3	100.1	99.5	99.7	100.0	98.7	99.2	101.0
Output per unit of capital services	84.8	92.3	101.1	101.9	100.7	99.5	93.1	97.9	98.2	102.0	102.2	100.0	97.0	100.7	103.0
Multifactor productivity	102.0	105.9	110.8	111.8	111.0	111.8	111.5	110.8	101.9	101.2	102.5	100.0	98.5	97.8	97.8
Sector output	87.7	94.9	102.2	101.0	97.9	96.3	88.9	92.3	92.2	97.2	99.6	100.0	99.8	103.4	107.0
Hours of all persons at work	86.4	89.1	94.5	95.7	95.4	92.6	83.8	86.8	92.1	97.7	99.9	100.0	101.1	104.2	105.9
Capital services	103.4	102.8	101.0	99.1	97.2	96.8	95.4	94.2	93.8	95.3	97.5	100.0	102.8	102.7	103.9
Energy	71.7	77.9	88.0	92.9	90.9	92.0	91.9	85.4	94.8	100.6	104.1	100.0	89.1	92.7	96.2
Non-energy materials	87.3	92.3	93.8	88.6	83.2	80.4	73.2	78.4	85.5	93.4	94.4	100.0	100.9	109.4	116.4
Purchased business services	47.4	55.7	59.7	58.0	62.8	63.0	60.4	69.5	100.3	102.6	98.0	100.0	104.5	103.7	107.3
Combined units of all inputs	86.0	89.6	92.2	90.4	88.2	86.1	79.7	83.3	90.5	96.1	97.2	100.0	101.3	105.7	109.4
Furniture And Fixtures															
Output per hour of all persons	81.7	84.1	86.8	85.5	85.5	87.7	88.1	91.7	93.5	93.9	98.2	100.0	107.3	111.4	112.8
Output per unit of capital services	99.9	102.5	104.2	100.6	99.6	96.4	90.2	96.7	99.4	100.3	101.1	100.0	107.1	110.8	109.1
Multifactor productivity	97.4	96.9	98.4	97.5	96.9	96.5	96.2	98.8	100.5	99.3	99.9	100.0	103.5	103.9	104.7
Sector output	78.6	82.5	87.2	87.1	87.7	86.4	80.9	87.4	92.0	95.0	98.7	100.0	111.1	119.0	123.5
Hours of all persons at work	96.3	98.1	100.4	101.9	102.7	98.6	91.8	95.3	98.4	101.2	100.5	100.0	103.5	106.8	109.4
Capital services	78.7	80.5	83.7	86.6	88.1	89.7	89.6	90.4	92.5	94.7	97.6	100.0	103.7	107.4	113.2
Energy	71.3	76.2	89.5	92.6	97.0	91.2	90.3	91.1	96.3	98.5	103.8	100.0	102.5	109.3	113.6
Non-energy materials	70.6	75.7	78.8	79.5	81.2	82.4	77.7	83.4	86.7	92.1	97.4	100.0	109.6	120.3	124.3
Purchased business services	90.5	103.0	111.8	108.4	106.1	101.6	90.4	93.4	95.3	97.8	101.3	100.0	112.3	117.9	118.4
Combined units of all inputs	80.7	85.1	88.6	89.3	90.5	89.6	84.0	88.5	91.5	95.7	98.8	100.0	107.3	114.5	118.0
Stone, Clay, Glass, And Concrete															
Output per hour of all persons	85.7	89.0	91.3	90.3	90.0	92.2	91.0	95.8	95.9	96.2	97.4	100.0	104.0	108.2	110.9
Output per unit of capital services	80.8	84.1	86.3	88.0	87.2	86.8	80.8	86.3	89.9	95.1	96.8	100.0	98.2	98.8	96.8
Multifactor productivity	89.4	92.7	94.3	94.4	95.5	96.3	94.2	98.6	97.2	99.0	99.8	100.0	104.0	103.3	104.0
Sector output	82.8	86.3	88.4	90.2	89.6	88.8	81.8	85.7	87.6	91.9	94.5	100.0	103.4	108.5	112.3
Hours of all persons at work	96.6	96.9	96.9	99.9	99.6	96.3	89.8	89.5	91.3	95.5	97.0	100.0	99.5	100.3	101.2
Capital services	102.4	102.7	102.5	102.5	102.8	102.3	101.2	99.3	97.4	96.6	97.6	100.0	105.4	109.8	116.0
Energy	95.3	100.4	102.7	104.5	101.7	101.7	97.1	99.7	100.7	98.8	104.4	100.0	99.3	104.4	107.8
Non-energy materials	87.8	87.1	87.4	88.3	85.0	84.1	78.9	79.2	85.3	88.2	89.8	100.0	97.5	109.0	112.6
Purchased business services	72.7	78.2	85.3	88.0	87.9	86.8	81.6	85.5	87.9	90.3	94.0	100.0	97.4	102.2	103.7
Combined units of all inputs	92.6	93.1	93.8	95.5	93.9	92.1	86.8	87.0	90.1	92.8	94.6	100.0	99.5	105.1	108.0
Primary Metal Industries															
Output per hour of all persons	76.0	81.3	85.2	87.8	85.3	85.4	86.1	91.5	95.3	96.1	97.8	100.0	101.1	106.2	107.6
Output per unit of capital services	73.8	75.1	81.9	90.0	88.5	86.4	82.1	86.1	91.3	97.1	98.4	100.0	101.7	103.6	102.9
Multifactor productivity	92.0	98.1	97.1	96.1	94.6	96.4	96.8	100.0	103.5	102.3	99.9	100.0	100.4	104.1	108.1
Sector output	81.4	80.9	86.4	93.6	91.0	88.5	83.7	86.6	90.9	96.2	97.6	100.0	102.7	105.9	106.9
Hours of all persons at work	107.2	99.5	101.4	106.7	106.7	103.6	97.2	94.7	95.4	100.1	99.9	100.0	101.6	99.7	99.3
Capital services	110.3	107.7	105.5	104.0	102.9	102.4	101.9	100.7	99.6	99.1	99.2	100.0	101.0	102.2	103.9
Energy	103.8	95.8	99.2	111.9	103.6	105.6	107.3	100.0	99.3	110.6	100.0	100.0	95.9	98.7	99.5
Non-energy materials	74.8	69.2	78.3	87.9	86.5	80.6	75.6	77.9	80.1	87.3	94.9	100.0	103.6	104.2	99.4
Purchased business services	73.2	70.9	84.0	100.6	101.2	93.0	81.4	83.9	85.1	93.6	101.6	100.0	103.6	98.1	89.0
Combined units of all inputs	88.5	82.5	89.0	97.5	96.2	91.8	86.5	86.7	87.9	94.1	97.7	100.0	102.3	101.7	98.9

Table 4-5. Indexes of Multifactor Productivity and Related Measures, Manufacturing Industries, 1985–1999—*Continued*

(1996=100.)

Industry	1985	1986	1987	1988	1989	1990	1991	1992	1993	1994	1995	1996	1997	1998	1999
Fabricated Metal Products															
Output per hour of all persons	84.7	87.7	91.4	90.3	87.2	87.8	87.6	92.8	94.5	96.6	98.2	100.0	103.3	106.5	106.9
Output per unit of capital services	97.6	95.1	95.2	98.0	95.3	92.3	87.1	91.6	94.5	99.9	100.1	100.0	103.4	104.7	101.9
Multifactor productivity	95.5	96.3	99.2	99.9	97.2	95.9	93.9	95.7	96.6	99.9	100.4	100.0	101.2	101.1	100.1
Sector output	83.4	83.4	85.1	87.7	85.3	83.4	79.1	83.7	86.9	93.5	96.8	100.0	106.4	110.7	111.5
Hours of all persons at work	98.4	95.1	93.1	97.1	97.8	95.0	90.3	90.2	92.0	96.8	98.6	100.0	103.0	103.9	104.3
Capital services	85.4	87.7	89.4	89.5	89.5	90.4	90.8	91.3	92.0	93.6	96.7	100.0	102.9	105.7	109.4
Energy	80.7	81.6	90.6	94.4	94.0	93.4	92.2	89.4	93.8	97.2	103.3	100.0	98.4	102.1	103.1
Non-energy materials	81.7	81.5	79.6	80.4	79.8	80.2	78.3	84.0	87.7	91.1	94.0	100.0	107.4	115.6	119.1
Purchased business services	79.8	80.3	85.2	89.9	90.7	88.1	83.2	89.5	91.0	94.8	99.2	100.0	106.9	108.5	104.5
Combined units of all inputs	87.3	86.6	85.8	87.8	87.7	87.0	84.2	87.4	90.0	93.6	96.4	100.0	105.1	109.5	111.3
Industrial And Commercial Machinery															
Output per hour of all persons	49.7	53.2	55.9	60.3	61.0	62.6	62.4	69.3	74.3	81.5	89.7	100.0	108.5	121.0	132.3
Output per unit of capital services	75.5	73.4	75.0	82.0	80.9	79.1	73.3	77.2	81.7	88.4	95.2	100.0	104.3	105.0	98.9
Multifactor productivity	69.0	71.3	76.0	80.1	80.7	81.6	79.6	83.9	86.3	91.0	95.1	100.0	106.9	115.4	124.4
Sector output	50.1	50.4	52.3	59.2	60.5	60.7	57.6	62.4	68.5	77.8	89.1	100.0	113.0	126.4	132.9
Hours of all persons at work	100.8	94.9	93.7	98.1	99.2	97.0	92.4	90.1	92.2	95.4	99.3	100.0	104.1	104.5	100.5
Capital services	66.4	68.7	69.8	72.2	74.8	76.8	78.6	80.8	83.8	88.0	93.6	100.0	108.3	120.3	134.4
Energy	86.6	87.4	92.6	95.6	99.8	99.7	98.4	90.6	93.3	100.2	103.0	100.0	97.1	108.6	114.1
Non-energy materials	54.8	53.9	50.5	56.3	57.2	57.4	56.7	61.3	68.7	76.6	88.7	100.0	107.7	113.9	111.4
Purchased business services	72.2	74.0	75.2	80.4	80.6	76.2	70.7	74.0	79.8	88.9	95.7	100.0	100.4	99.0	88.1
Combined units of all inputs	72.7	70.8	68.8	73.8	75.0	74.4	72.4	74.3	79.4	85.5	93.6	100.0	105.7	109.5	106.8
Electrical And Electronic Equipment															
Output per hour of all persons	38.4	40.7	44.4	46.5	48.0	51.0	54.9	61.9	67.1	75.6	88.8	100.0	113.6	127.0	151.5
Output per unit of capital services	67.6	65.7	65.7	68.0	67.5	66.6	66.4	71.6	76.0	84.4	94.1	100.0	105.3	110.9	118.9
Multifactor productivity	60.1	61.8	65.8	67.9	69.5	71.2	73.0	76.4	79.5	86.7	94.4	100.0	108.2	114.7	129.1
Sector output	41.5	42.6	45.3	48.3	49.3	50.1	50.7	56.0	61.5	71.7	86.4	100.0	115.1	129.5	150.8
Hours of all persons at work	108.2	104.6	101.9	104.0	102.7	98.1	92.4	90.4	91.7	94.8	97.3	100.0	101.3	102.0	99.5
Capital services	61.4	64.9	68.9	71.1	73.0	75.2	76.4	78.2	80.9	84.9	91.8	100.0	109.3	116.8	126.8
Energy	75.2	77.9	87.7	88.8	91.1	92.3	91.1	90.0	95.5	98.0	102.8	100.0	105.1	117.2	136.8
Non-energy materials	45.5	45.2	44.0	46.5	45.8	46.6	48.1	55.2	62.0	68.3	83.5	100.0	107.6	126.9	132.8
Purchased business services	55.7	58.7	62.1	64.5	63.5	60.9	57.9	66.9	70.7	82.1	95.0	100.0	111.9	105.3	110.7
Combined units of all inputs	60.1	68.9	68.0	71.2	70.9	70.4	69.5	73.2	77.3	82.7	91.5	100.0	106.3	112.9	116.8
Transportation Equipment															
Output per hour of all persons	72.9	75.9	78.0	78.8	78.7	80.5	80.3	87.8	92.9	97.8	98.0	100.0	106.6	116.5	122.3
Output per unit of capital services	95.2	94.4	93.0	95.6	94.0	90.8	84.4	90.1	94.2	100.6	100.8	100.0	107.0	110.6	111.0
Multifactor productivity	102.2	102.2	103.6	102.8	100.1	98.9	97.8	97.9	100.3	101.8	101.3	100.0	102.6	105.9	106.6
Sector output	78.4	81.6	83.2	88.1	88.2	86.4	81.0	86.5	90.5	97.2	98.3	100.0	111.2	121.8	129.4
Hours of all persons at work	107.7	107.5	106.7	111.8	112.1	107.4	100.9	98.6	97.4	99.3	100.3	100.0	104.3	104.6	105.8
Capital services	82.4	86.4	89.5	92.1	93.8	95.2	96.1	96.0	96.1	96.6	97.5	100.0	103.9	110.2	116.6
Energy	76.8	79.1	102.1	98.6	96.4	96.9	93.8	97.2	102.5	103.0	105.4	100.0	99.7	108.0	117.3
Non-energy materials	63.7	67.0	66.7	71.9	74.2	74.9	70.3	79.4	83.5	91.3	94.0	100.0	111.6	122.1	131.6
Purchased business services	57.1	66.7	71.4	81.3	90.7	91.1	91.3	102.0	100.8	105.5	102.5	100.0	107.5	111.9	116.6
Combined units of all inputs	76.7	79.8	80.3	85.7	88.1	87.4	82.9	88.4	90.3	95.5	97.0	100.0	108.4	115.0	121.4
Instruments And Related Products															
Output per hour of all persons	64.7	68.7	73.6	74.0	74.3	77.4	80.7	87.2	88.2	91.5	95.5	100.0	99.1	103.1	106.6
Output per unit of capital services	116.6	116.0	125.0	125.6	116.6	111.6	106.0	104.3	100.6	98.9	99.1	100.0	101.1	93.6	89.8
Multifactor productivity	90.7	92.0	95.2	99.0	96.4	98.7	98.7	99.7	98.5	99.4	99.1	100.0	99.0	100.4	103.0
Sector output	77.5	79.9	84.9	88.3	87.8	89.1	89.3	92.7	92.5	92.5	94.9	100.0	102.0	105.1	107.0
Hours of all persons at work	119.9	116.3	115.5	119.2	118.1	115.2	110.7	106.4	104.9	101.0	99.3	100.0	102.9	102.0	100.4
Capital services	66.5	68.9	68.0	70.3	75.3	79.9	84.2	88.9	91.9	93.5	95.8	100.0	100.9	112.4	119.3
Energy	98.5	101.9	96.2	100.2	99.8	104.3	100.6	99.4	100.5	99.3	104.1	100.0	99.6	102.2	104.1
Non-energy materials	61.1	65.3	68.7	66.1	69.0	69.6	72.5	79.1	80.9	82.6	89.8	100.0	104.7	110.1	110.1
Purchased business services	80.1	82.3	89.6	89.4	94.8	92.6	92.8	99.8	104.5	103.8	104.3	100.0	99.1	94.3	91.3
Combined units of all inputs	85.5	86.9	89.2	89.2	91.1	90.3	90.5	93.0	93.9	93.1	95.7	100.0	103.1	104.7	103.9
Miscellaneous Manufacturing															
Output per hour of all persons	84.2	85.5	89.4	90.3	87.7	90.9	90.0	90.6	92.1	91.0	97.3	100.0	96.9	99.7	103.2
Output per unit of capital services	85.2	88.2	90.2	95.3	92.2	92.5	90.1	91.3	94.9	95.4	97.9	100.0	100.0	98.9	98.5
Multifactor productivity	98.5	97.9	100.3	103.4	101.7	100.5	96.7	94.3	95.0	96.1	99.2	100.0	100.3	99.9	101.9
Sector output	76.9	79.6	83.4	88.8	86.9	87.6	84.5	87.6	92.5	94.2	96.8	100.0	102.2	103.6	106.2
Hours of all persons at work	91.3	93.1	93.4	98.3	99.2	96.3	93.9	96.6	100.4	103.5	99.5	100.0	105.4	103.9	102.9
Capital services	90.3	90.3	92.5	93.2	94.3	94.6	93.8	95.9	97.4	98.7	98.9	100.0	102.1	104.8	107.8
Energy	68.2	73.7	90.8	92.7	95.1	96.3	94.1	85.4	96.4	97.1	108.2	100.0	101.6	102.8	105.4
Non-energy materials	65.5	68.8	69.6	71.4	70.6	76.0	79.7	88.8	95.0	94.1	95.1	100.0	99.2	105.2	107.3
Purchased business services	72.8	83.2	92.1	95.3	91.1	90.3	86.0	92.5	97.6	95.4	97.9	100.0	100.4	96.5	93.0
Combined units of all inputs	78.1	81.3	83.2	85.8	85.5	87.1	87.4	92.8	97.4	98.0	97.6	100.0	101.8	103.6	104.2

PART FIVE

COMPENSATION OF EMPLOYEES

COMPENSATION OF EMPLOYEES

HIGHLIGHTS

This part covers three related topics: employment cost index for total compensation (ECI), covering wages and salaries and benefits; employee participation in various benefit plans; and occupational employment and wages derived from the Occupational Employment Statistics Survey (OES). All the surveys from which these data are derived are now components of the National Compensation Survey. (See article on p. xvii)

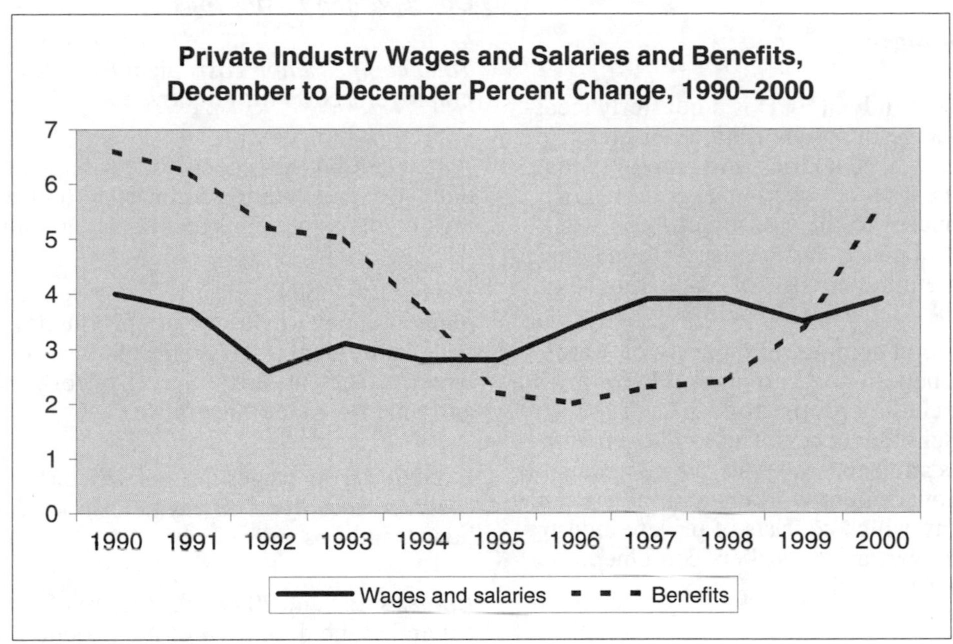

In 2000, the benefits component of the total Employment Cost Index (ECI) for private business increased substantially more than the wage and salary component, 5.6 percent and 3.9 percent respectively. The rise in benefits was the sharpest since 1991, after several years of more subdued growth.

OTHER HIGHLIGHTS:

- Industries with more than average increases in wages and salaries included construction (5.3 percent), aircraft manufacturing (5.6 percent), food stores (5 percent) and nursing homes (5.8 percent). (Table 5-1)
- Employer costs per hour worked for state and local governments were higher than for private industry in March 2000, by 42 percent for wages and salaries and 58 percent for benefits. (Tables 5-5, 5-6)
- Legally required benefits per hour for state and local employees make up 20 percent of total benefits. For private industry, required benefits are 31 percent and represent the largest non-wage and salaries employee cost. (Tables 5-5, 5-6)
- The largest major occupation group in the new SOC which accounts for 17.7 percent of total employees, is in office and administrative support occupations. (Table 5-11)
- In 1999, the top mean hourly wage is for the legal group, which exceeds the mean for the education group by 85 percent. (Table 5-11)
- Over half of the lowest earning groups (healthcare support, personal care, and food preparation) earn less than $8.50 per hour in 1999. (Table 5-13)

NOTES AND DEFINITIONS

EMPLOYMENT COST INDEX

Note: The employment cost index will be part of the National Compensation Survey (NCS). See article describing NCS on p. xvii.

Collection and Coverage

The Employment Cost Index (ECI) is a quarterly measure of the rate of change in compensation per hour worked and includes wages, salaries, and employer costs of employee benefits. It uses a fixed market basket of labor—similar in concept to the Consumer Price Index's fixed market basket of goods and services—to measure change over time in employer costs of employing labor.

Statistical series on total compensation costs, on wages and salaries, and on benefit costs are available for private nonfarm workers excluding proprietors, the self-employed, and household workers. The total compensation costs and wages and salaries series are also available for state and local government workers and for the civilian nonfarm economy, which consists of private industry and state and local government workers combined. Federal workers are excluded.

The ECI probability sample consists of about 4,400 private nonfarm establishments providing about 23,000 occupational observations and 1,000 state and local government establishments providing 6,000 occupational observations selected to represent total employment in each sector. On average, each reporting unit provides wage and compensation information on five well-specified occupations. The occupations are defined narrowly enough so that all workers in the job carry out the same task at roughly the same level of skill. Data are collected each quarter for the pay period including the 12th day of March, June, September, and December.

From June 1986 to March 1995 fixed employment weights from the 1980 Census of Population were used each quarter to calculate the civilian and private indexes and the index for state and local governments. Employment counts for 1990 were introduced in March 1995. Prior to June 1986, the employment weights are from the 1970 Census of Population. These fixed weights, also used to derive all of the industry and occupation series indexes, ensure that changes in these indexes reflect only changes in compensation, not employment shifts among industries or occupations with different levels of wages and compensation. For the bargaining status, region, and metropolitan/nonmetropolitan area series, however, employment data by industry and occupation are not available from the census. Instead, the 1980 employment weights are reallocated within these series each quarter based on the current sample. Therefore, these indexes are not strictly comparable to those for the aggregate, industry, and occupation series.

Concepts and Definitions

Total compensation costs include wages, salaries, and the employer's costs for employee benefits.

Wages and salaries consist of earnings before payroll deductions, including production bonuses, incentive earnings, commissions, and cost-of-living adjustments.

Benefits include the cost to employers for paid leave, supplemental pay (including nonproduction bonuses), insurance, retirement and savings plans, and legally required benefits (such as Social Security, workers' compensation, and unemployment insurance).

Excluded from wages and salaries and employee benefit costs are such items as payment-in-kind, free room and board, and tips.

Bonuses. In June 2000, the Bureau of Labor Statistics expanded the definition of nonproduction bonuses in the ECI to better represent the compensation packages offered to employees. In addition to the traditional types of nonproduction bonuses, such as attendance bonuses and lump sum payments, the ECI will include hiring and referral bonuses. Hiring bonuses are payments made by the employer to induce an individual to accept employment; referral bonuses are made by the employer to an employee for recommending an applicant who is hired by the establishment.

As part of its ongoing research program, the Bureau of Labor Statistics currently is conducting research on stock option plans. This research will be completed in stages. BLS has begun testing the incidence of stock option plans across all industries and occupations. The prevalence of these plans, based on test results and the potential impact on compensation costs, will determine the next stage of research. The results of the pilot incidence survey were published in October 2000.

Sources of Additional Information

Additional information on Employment Cost Index methodology and data is available in BLS Bulletin 2532, September 2000. The quarterly publication, *Compensation and Working Conditions*, contains articles on the new National Compensation Survey.

Table 5-1. Employment Cost Index, Private Industry Workers[1], Total Compensation and Wages and Salaries by Occupation and Industry, 1987–2000

(June 1989=100, not seasonally adjusted.)

Series and year	Total compensation					Wages and salaries				
	Indexes				Percent change for 12 months ended December	Indexes				Percent change for 12 months ended December
	March	June	September	December		March	June	September	December	
PRIVATE INDUSTRY WORKERS										
1987	91.0	91.6	92.5	93.1	3.3	92.0	92.6	93.5	94.1	3.3
1988	94.5	95.7	96.6	97.6	4.8	95.0	96.1	97.0	98.0	4.1
1989	98.8	100.0	101.2	102.3	4.8	99.0	100.0	101.2	102.0	4.1
1990	103.9	105.2	106.2	107.0	4.6	103.2	104.5	105.4	106.1	4.0
1991	108.5	109.8	111.0	111.7	4.4	107.3	108.4	109.3	110.0	3.7
1992	113.1	113.9	114.8	115.6	3.5	110.9	111.6	112.2	112.9	2.6
1993	117.1	118.0	119.1	119.8	3.6	113.9	114.6	115.7	116.4	3.1
1994	121.0	122.0	123.0	123.5	3.1	117.2	118.1	119.1	119.7	2.8
1995	124.5	125.4	126.2	126.7	2.6	120.6	121.5	122.4	123.1	2.8
1996	127.9	129.0	129.8	130.6	3.1	124.4	125.6	126.5	127.3	3.4
1997	131.7	132.8	133.9	135.1	3.4	128.6	129.7	131.0	132.3	3.9
1998	136.3	137.5	139.0	139.8	3.5	133.7	134.9	136.6	137.4	3.9
1999	140.4	142.0	143.3	144.6	3.4	138.1	139.7	141.0	142.2	3.5
2000	146.8	148.5	149.9	150.9	4.4	143.9	145.4	146.8	147.7	3.9
Private industry workers, excluding sales occupations										
1987	91.0	91.7	92.7	93.4	3.5	92.1	92.7	93.8	94.5	3.6
1988	94.9	95.9	96.9	97.7	4.6	95.4	96.3	97.3	98.0	3.7
1989	99.0	100.0	101.2	102.1	4.5	99.1	100.0	101.1	101.9	4.0
1990	103.9	105.1	106.3	107.1	4.9	103.2	104.4	105.4	106.2	4.2
1991	108.6	109.8	111.1	112.0	4.6	107.4	108.4	109.4	110.2	3.8
1992	113.3	114.1	115.1	115.9	3.5	111.1	111.8	112.5	113.2	2.7
1993	117.5	118.5	119.5	120.2	3.7	114.2	115.0	115.9	116.6	3.0
1994	121.4	122.3	123.4	123.9	3.1	117.5	118.3	119.4	120.0	2.9
1995	125.0	125.7	126.5	127.1	2.6	121.0	121.8	122.6	123.4	2.8
1996	128.3	129.2	130.2	130.8	2.9	124.7	125.7	126.8	127.5	3.3
1997	131.9	133.0	134.1	135.2	3.4	128.6	129.9	131.2	132.4	3.8
1998	136.4	[illegible]	[illegible]	139.4	3.1	133.7	134.8	136.3	136.9	3.4
1999	140.5	141.9	143.2	144.5	3.7	[illegible]	[illegible]	140.8	142.0	3.7
2000	146.5	148.2	149.8	150.9	4.4	143.5	145.1	146.5	147.6	3.9
WORKERS BY OCCUPATIONAL GROUP										
White-Collar Occupations										
1987	90.6	91.2	92.1	92.7	3.7	91.4	91.9	93.0	93.4	3.7
1988	93.9	95.1	96.2	97.3	5.0	94.4	95.6	96.7	97.8	4.7
1989	98.9	100.0	101.4	102.4	5.2	99.0	100.0	101.4	102.4	4.7
1990	104.1	105.5	106.7	107.4	4.9	103.6	104.9	106.0	106.6	4.1
1991	109.0	110.3	111.4	112.2	4.5	107.9	109.1	110.1	110.7	3.8
1992	113.4	114.2	115.1	115.9	3.3	111.7	112.3	112.9	113.7	2.7
1993	117.4	118.3	119.4	120.2	3.7	114.7	115.5	116.7	117.5	3.3
1994	121.5	122.5	123.5	124.1	3.2	118.3	119.3	120.2	120.8	2.8
1995	125.3	126.2	127.0	127.6	2.8	121.7	122.7	123.6	124.3	2.9
1996	129.0	130.0	131.1	131.7	3.2	125.8	127.0	128.0	128.7	3.5
1997	133.1	134.1	135.2	136.7	3.8	130.2	131.3	132.7	134.2	4.3
1998	138.1	139.4	141.1	142.0	3.9	135.7	137.0	139.0	139.9	4.2
1999	142.4	144.1	145.6	146.9	3.5	140.3	142.1	143.5	144.8	3.5
2000	149.3	151.1	152.6	153.6	4.6	146.6	148.3	149.7	150.6	4.0
White-collar occupations, excluding sales occupations										
1987	90.6	91.3	92.5	93.2	4.3	91.4	92.0	93.4	94.0	4.3
1988	94.5	95.5	96.7	97.5	4.6	95.0	95.9	97.1	98.0	4.3
1989	99.0	100.0	101.3	102.2	4.8	99.2	100.0	101.2	102.1	4.2
1990	104.2	105.4	106.9	107.7	5.4	103.7	104.8	106.2	106.9	4.7
1991	109.2	110.4	111.8	112.7	4.6	108.2	109.2	110.5	111.3	4.1
1992	113.8	114.6	115.8	116.6	3.5	112.1	112.8	113.7	114.4	2.8
1993	118.3	119.2	120.2	121.0	3.8	115.7	116.4	117.4	118.2	3.3
1994	122.4	123.3	124.4	125.1	3.4	119.0	119.9	121.0	121.7	3.0
1995	126.3	127.0	127.8	128.6	2.8	122.8	123.4	124.3	125.2	2.9
1996	129.9	130.7	132.0	132.5	3.0	126.7	127.6	129.0	129.4	3.4
1997	133.7	134.8	135.9	137.4	3.7	130.8	132.0	133.4	134.8	4.2
1998	138.8	139.9	141.3	141.9	3.3	136.3	137.5	139.1	139.7	3.6
1999	143.0	144.5	146.0	147.3	3.8	141.0	142.5	143.9	145.2	3.9
2000	149.4	151.3	152.9	154.1	4.6	146.7	148.5	149.9	151.1	4.1

See footnotes at end of table.

Table 5-1. Employment Cost Index, Private Industry Workers[1], Total Compensation and Wages and Salaries by Occupation and Industry, 1987–2000—*Continued*

(June 1989=100, not seasonally adjusted.)

Series and year	Total compensation					Wages and salaries				
	Indexes				Percent change for 12 months ended December	Indexes				Percent change for 12 months ended December
	March	June	September	December		March	June	September	December	
Professional specialty and technical occupations										
1987	90.3	90.8	92.1	92.9	4.0	91.0	91.5	92.8	93.8	4.6
1988	94.3	95.4	96.9	97.5	5.0	94.7	95.9	97.4	97.9	4.4
1989	99.0	100.0	101.8	102.9	5.5	99.3	100.0	101.6	102.5	4.7
1990	104.9	105.8	107.5	108.7	5.6	104.1	104.8	106.5	107.5	4.9
1991	110.1	111.1	112.8	113.9	4.8	108.6	109.5	111.1	112.0	4.2
1992	115.3	116.4	118.0	119.0	4.5	113.0	114.0	115.3	116.0	3.6
1993	120.4	121.3	122.2	122.9	3.3	117.1	117.9	118.9	119.5	3.0
1994	124.6	125.3	126.3	126.8	3.2	120.4	121.3	122.2	123.0	2.9
1995	127.7	128.4	129.3	129.9	2.4	123.7	124.4	125.3	126.1	2.5
1996	131.6	132.6	133.3	133.7	2.9	127.8	128.8	129.6	129.9	3.0
1997	134.6	135.9	136.7	137.8	3.1	131.0	132.4	133.7	134.8	3.8
1998	138.8	140.1	141.6	142.6	3.5	135.9	137.1	138.7	139.7	3.6
1999	142.9	144.1	145.2	146.7	2.9	140.7	141.8	142.6	144.1	3.1
2000	148.4	150.7	152.2	153.7	4.8	145.1	147.3	148.6	150.2	4.2
Executive, administrative, and managerial occupations										
1987	91.6	92.2	93.5	93.9	4.4	92.1	92.6	94.1	94.5	4.3
1988	94.7	95.7	96.6	97.8	4.2	95.0	95.9	96.7	98.0	3.7
1989	99.1	100.0	100.9	101.5	3.8	99.3	100.0	100.8	101.5	3.6
1990	103.7	105.3	106.6	107.2	5.6	103.3	104.9	106.2	106.9	5.3
1991	108.9	110.3	111.5	112.3	4.8	108.2	109.4	110.6	111.4	4.2
1992	112.7	113.1	113.9	114.5	2.0	111.6	112.0	112.5	113.2	1.6
1993	116.5	117.2	118.1	118.9	3.8	114.7	115.3	116.2	117.0	3.4
1994	120.3	121.3	122.6	123.3	3.7	117.8	118.8	120.0	120.5	3.0
1995	124.9	125.4	126.2	126.9	2.9	121.9	122.5	123.4	124.4	3.2
1996	128.0	128.8	130.9	131.3	3.5	125.9	126.8	128.9	129.3	3.9
1997	133.0	133.9	135.2	137.4	4.6	131.0	132.1	133.6	135.8	5.0
1998	139.4	140.0	141.9	141.8	3.2	137.8	138.7	140.9	140.5	3.5
1999	143.7	145.8	147.7	149.1	5.1	141.9	144.3	146.4	147.6	5.1
2000	151.1	152.7	154.4	155.3	4.2	149.2	150.7	152.3	153.0	3.7
Sales occupations										
1987	90.0	90.5	90.5	90.2	1.2	91.3	91.6	91.6	90.9	0.9
1988	91.4	93.6	94.1	96.3	6.8	91.9	94.3	94.8	96.9	6.6
1989	98.3	100.0	101.9	103.3	7.3	98.6	100.0	102.1	103.7	7.0
1990	103.6	105.6	105.9	106.0	2.6	103.3	105.3	105.4	105.2	1.4
1991	108.0	109.8	109.8	109.6	3.4	106.8	108.5	108.2	107.9	2.6
1992	111.6	112.2	111.8	112.6	2.7	109.7	110.1	109.7	110.7	2.6
1993	112.9	113.8	115.6	116.5	3.5	110.5	111.6	113.8	114.7	3.6
1994	117.2	118.8	119.2	119.6	2.7	114.8	116.2	116.5	116.7	1.7
1995	120.2	122.4	123.2	123.2	3.0	116.9	119.3	120.5	120.4	3.2
1996	124.8	126.9	126.7	128.1	4.0	122.0	124.4	123.9	125.9	4.6
1997	130.1	130.7	132.2	133.5	4.2	127.8	128.3	129.8	131.4	4.4
1998	135.3	137.3	140.4	142.6	6.8	133.1	135.2	138.8	141.3	7.5
1999	139.6	142.6	144.1	145.3	1.9	137.3	140.5	142.1	143.3	1.4
2000	148.9	150.3	151.2	151.4	4.2	146.7	147.9	149.0	148.7	3.8
Administrative support occupations, including clerical occupations										
1987	90.0	90.8	91.8	92.6	4.0	91.1	91.9	93.0	93.7	4.1
1988	94.4	95.3	96.6	97.3	5.1	95.1	95.8	97.2	97.8	4.4
1989	98.9	100.0	101.2	102.3	5.1	99.1	100.0	101.1	102.2	4.5
1990	104.2	105.3	106.4	107.3	4.9	103.6	104.7	105.7	106.4	4.1
1991	108.6	109.9	111.0	111.9	4.3	107.6	108.6	109.6	110.4	3.8
1992	113.6	114.4	115.5	116.4	4.0	111.6	112.4	113.2	114.0	3.3
1993	118.1	119.2	120.3	121.2	4.1	115.2	116.1	117.1	118.0	3.5
1994	122.5	123.5	124.5	125.1	3.2	119.0	119.9	120.9	121.6	3.1
1995	126.5	127.3	128.1	129.0	3.1	122.9	123.5	124.3	125.3	3.0
1996	130.1	130.8	132.0	132.5	2.7	126.5	127.3	128.5	129.2	3.1
1997	133.7	134.7	135.9	137.0	3.4	130.6	131.7	132.9	133.9	3.6
1998	138.2	139.6	140.6	141.4	3.2	135.3	136.7	137.9	138.9	3.7
1999	142.6	143.7	145.0	146.2	3.4	140.4	141.4	142.7	143.8	3.5
2000	149.0	150.6	152.3	153.4	4.9	146.0	147.5	149.1	150.1	4.4

See footnotes at end of table.

Table 5-1. Employment Cost Index, Private Industry Workers[1], Total Compensation and Wages and Salaries by Occupation and Industry, 1987–2000—*Continued*

(June 1989=100, not seasonally adjusted.)

Series and year	Total compensation					Wages and salaries				
	Indexes				Percent change for 12 months ended December	Indexes				Percent change for 12 months ended December
	March	June	September	December		March	June	September	December	
Blue-Collar Occupations										
1987	91.3	92.1	92.9	93.7	3.1	92.8	93.5	94.3	95.2	3.0
1988	95.4	96.4	97.1	97.9	4.5	95.9	96.8	97.4	98.2	3.2
1989	98.8	100.0	101.1	101.9	4.1	99.0	100.0	101.0	101.6	3.5
1990	103.5	104.7	105.6	106.4	4.4	102.7	103.8	104.6	105.2	3.5
1991	107.9	109.0	110.2	111.0	4.3	106.4	107.3	108.0	108.8	3.4
1992	112.5	113.4	114.3	115.0	3.6	109.7	110.4	111.1	111.6	2.6
1993	116.6	117.7	118.7	119.3	3.7	112.5	113.2	114.1	114.8	2.9
1994	120.3	121.2	122.3	122.6	2.8	115.6	116.5	117.5	118.0	2.8
1995	123.5	124.4	125.1	125.6	2.4	119.0	120.1	120.8	121.4	2.9
1996	126.6	127.6	128.1	129.0	2.7	122.5	123.7	124.3	125.1	3.0
1997	129.6	130.8	131.7	132.3	2.6	126.0	127.3	128.3	129.1	3.2
1998	133.1	134.3	135.2	135.9	2.7	130.2	131.3	132.4	133.2	3.2
1999	136.9	138.2	139.4	140.5	3.3	134.3	135.6	136.8	137.7	3.4
2000	142.6	144.1	145.5	146.4	4.2	139.1	140.5	141.9	142.8	3.7
Precision production, craft, and repair occupations										
1987	92.0	92.7	93.7	94.4	3.1	92.8	93.5	94.5	95.1	2.8
1988	95.8	96.8	97.3	98.0	3.8	95.9	96.8	97.2	97.9	2.9
1989	98.7	100.0	101.2	102.0	4.1	98.8	100.0	101.0	101.6	3.8
1990	103.4	104.7	105.6	106.2	4.1	102.5	103.6	104.4	104.9	3.2
1991	108.0	109.2	110.5	111.0	4.5	106.3	107.0	107.8	108.4	3.3
1992	112.2	113.1	114.3	115.0	3.6	109.3	110.1	111.0	111.5	2.9
1993	116.6	117.6	118.7	118.9	3.4	112.4	113.2	114.2	114.7	2.9
1994	120.2	121.2	122.5	122.5	3.0	115.5	116.5	117.8	117.9	2.8
1995	123.4	124.4	125.4	125.7	2.6	118.8	119.9	121.0	121.4	3.0
1996	126.5	127.7	128.2	129.1	2.7	122.4	123.7	124.2	125.1	3.0
1997	129.6	130.9	131.7	131.9	2.2	125.8	127.4	128.2	128.7	2.9
1998	132.9	134.4	135.4	136.1	3.2	129.8	131.2	132.3	133.0	3.3
1999	137.2	138.4	139.6	140.6	3.3	134.3	135.6	136.7	137.5	3.4
2000	142.3	144.1	145.8	146.7	4.3	138.9	140.6	142.0	142.8	3.9
Machine operators, assemblers, and inspectors										
1987	90.2	91.1	91.6	92.8	3.3	92.3	93.2	93.8	95.1	3.5
1988	94.7	95.8	96.5	97.6	5.2	95.6	96.5	97.1	98.1	3.2
1989	98.9	100.0	100.9	101.8	4.3	99.0	100.0	100.6	101.6	3.6
1990	103.7	105.0	105.9	106.9	5.0	103.0	104.2	104.9	105.8	4.1
1991	108.3	109.4	110.5	111.6	4.4	107.1	108.0	108.7	109.8	3.8
1992	113.9	114.6	115.0	115.8	3.8	110.9	111.6	111.7	112.4	2.4
1993	117.8	119.0	120.0	120.8	4.3	113.2	113.8	114.7	115.6	2.8
1994	121.3	122.2	122.9	123.4	2.2	116.2	117.2	118.0	118.8	2.8
1995	124.2	124.8	125.1	126.2	2.3	119.6	120.9	121.4	122.3	2.9
1996	127.1	128.1	128.7	129.5	2.6	123.4	124.5	125.4	126.4	3.4
1997	130.0	131.2	132.2	133.0	2.7	127.2	128.5	129.5	130.6	3.3
1998	133.6	134.7	135.7	136.8	2.9	131.6	132.7	133.8	134.9	3.3
1999	137.3	138.4	139.9	141.4	3.4	135.7	136.7	138.3	139.5	3.4
2000	144.0	145.0	146.0	146.8	3.8	140.7	141.6	142.9	143.7	3.0
Transportation and material moving occupations										
1987	91.6	92.6	93.3	93.9	3.0	93.6	94.4	95.0	95.5	2.4
1988	95.3	97.0	97.9	98.2	4.6	96.1	97.4	98.4	98.6	3.2
1989	99.0	100.0	101.2	101.4	3.3	99.3	100.0	101.2	101.2	2.6
1990	103.1	104.3	104.9	105.5	4.0	102.0	103.1	103.6	104.1	2.9
1991	106.3	107.6	108.3	109.0	3.3	104.5	105.6	106.1	106.7	2.5
1992	110.4	111.4	112.5	113.0	3.7	107.4	108.3	109.3	109.7	2.8
1993	113.9	115.2	115.9	117.0	3.5	110.0	111.2	111.7	112.6	2.6
1994	118.5	119.1	120.3	120.6	3.1	113.5	114.0	115.2	115.6	2.7
1995	121.8	122.4	122.9	123.0	2.0	117.0	117.8	118.5	118.6	2.6
1996	123.9	124.7	124.9	125.2	1.8	120.0	120.6	121.0	121.1	2.1
1997	126.1	126.8	128.0	128.9	3.0	122.3	123.0	124.1	125.1	3.3
1998	129.3	129.9	130.7	130.7	1.4	125.9	126.4	127.6	127.8	2.2
1999	131.6	133.6	134.4	135.2	3.4	129.1	131.0	131.9	132.7	3.8
2000	137.5	138.6	139.9	141.1	4.4	134.1	135.2	136.5	137.6	3.7

See footnotes at end of table.

Table 5-1. Employment Cost Index, Private Industry Workers[1], Total Compensation and Wages and Salaries by Occupation and Industry, 1987–2000—*Continued*

(June 1989=100, not seasonally adjusted.)

Series and year	Total compensation					Wages and salaries				
	Indexes				Percent change for 12 months ended December	Indexes				Percent change for 12 months ended December
	March	June	September	December		March	June	September	December	
Handlers, equipment cleaners, helpers, and laborers										
1987	91.3	91.7	92.5	93.5	2.7	92.6	93.2	94.0	95.0	3.0
1988	95.5	96.2	97.0	97.7	4.5	96.3	96.9	97.6	98.3	3.5
1989	98.8	100.0	101.3	102.2	4.6	99.1	100.0	101.1	102.0	3.8
1990	103.6	104.7	105.7	106.7	4.4	103.0	104.4	105.3	106.2	4.1
1991	108.1	109.3	110.4	111.4	4.4	107.3	108.5	109.2	109.9	3.5
1992	112.6	113.4	114.6	115.3	3.5	110.6	111.3	112.1	112.6	2.5
1993	116.8	117.6	118.4	119.1	3.3	113.6	114.3	114.9	115.7	2.8
1994	120.2	121.4	122.7	122.9	3.2	116.6	117.3	117.9	118.9	2.8
1995	124.1	125.3	125.9	126.8	3.2	120.1	121.2	121.5	122.6	3.1
1996	128.5	129.3	130.0	131.3	3.5	124.2	125.1	125.8	127.1	3.7
1997	132.8	133.4	134.2	135.8	3.4	128.4	129.3	130.2	131.8	3.7
1998	137.0	137.6	138.5	139.2	2.5	133.2	133.7	135.1	135.8	3.0
1999	141.0	142.3	143.2	144.4	3.7	137.3	138.3	139.4	140.4	3.4
2000	146.4	148.1	149.4	150.4	4.2	141.8	143.6	145.0	146.2	4.1
Service Occupations										
1987	91.9	92.3	92.8	93.3	2.4	93.3	93.6	94.1	94.5	2.4
1988	94.6	95.6	97.1	98.2	5.3	95.5	96.4	97.7	98.7	4.4
1989	99.2	100.0	101.1	102.5	4.4	99.4	100.0	100.9	102.3	3.6
1990	103.9	104.9	105.7	107.3	4.7	103.1	104.2	104.9	106.4	4.0
1991	108.3	109.9	111.5	112.4	4.8	106.9	108.3	109.8	110.6	3.9
1992	113.5	114.2	115.4	115.9	3.1	111.2	111.6	112.5	112.9	2.1
1993	117.2	118.0	118.9	119.5	3.1	113.5	114.1	114.9	115.3	2.1
1994	120.6	121.0	121.8	122.9	2.8	116.3	116.8	117.6	118.8	3.0
1995	123.4	124.0	124.7	125.2	1.9	119.4	120.0	120.8	121.4	2.2
1996	125.8	126.5	127.4	128.9	3.0	122.2	123.0	124.1	125.7	3.5
1997	129.8	130.9	133.1	134.1	4.0	126.6	127.6	129.9	131.1	4.3
1998	135.3	136.0	137.3	138.0	2.9	132.1	133.0	134.4	135.3	3.2
1999	139.5	140.6	141.0	142.6	3.3	136.7	137.8	138.0	139.6	3.2
2000	143.9	145.4	146.6	148.1	3.9	141.0	142.5	143.5	144.9	3.8
Production And Nonsupervisory Occupations										
1987	90.6	91.3	92.1	92.8	3.3	91.9	92.5	93.4	93.9	3.2
1988	94.3	95.5	96.6	97.5	5.1	94.8	96.0	97.0	97.9	4.3
1989	98.8	100.0	101.4	102.4	5.0	99.0	100.0	101.3	102.2	4.4
1990	103.8	105.1	106.0	106.9	4.4	103.2	104.3	105.2	105.9	3.6
1991	108.4	109.6	110.8	111.5	4.3	107.0	108.1	109.0	109.6	3.5
1992	113.0	113.8	114.8	115.5	3.6	110.6	111.3	112.0	112.6	2.7
1993	116.9	117.9	119.0	119.7	3.6	113.4	114.2	115.3	115.9	2.9
1994	120.7	121.6	122.6	123.1	2.8	116.6	117.5	118.5	119.1	2.8
1995	124.1	125.0	125.8	126.3	2.6	119.9	121.0	121.8	122.4	2.8
1996	127.5	128.6	129.2	130.0	2.9	123.7	124.9	125.6	126.5	3.3
1997	131.1	132.1	133.2	134.2	3.2	127.7	128.8	130.1	131.2	3.7
1998	135.3	136.6	138.0	139.0	3.6	132.3	133.6	135.2	136.4	4.0
1999	139.3	140.8	141.9	143.1	2.9	136.8	138.2	139.3	140.4	2.9
2000	145.3	146.9	148.4	149.5	4.5	142.1	143.7	145.0	146.0	4.0
WORKERS BY INDUSTRY DIVISION										
Goods-Producing Industries[2]										
1987	91.5	92.1	92.9	93.8	3.1	92.8	93.4	94.3	95.2	3.1
1988	95.5	96.5	97.1	97.9	4.4	96.1	96.9	97.5	98.2	3.2
1989	98.9	100.0	101.1	102.1	4.3	99.1	100.0	101.0	102.0	3.9
1990	103.9	105.2	106.2	107.0	4.8	103.1	104.2	105.1	105.8	3.7
1991	108.5	109.8	111.0	111.9	4.6	107.0	108.0	108.7	109.7	3.7
1992	113.5	114.3	115.3	116.1	3.8	110.7	111.4	112.1	112.8	2.8
1993	118.0	119.1	119.9	120.6	3.9	113.8	114.5	115.3	116.1	2.9
1994	121.8	123.0	123.9	124.3	3.1	116.9	118.0	118.9	119.6	3.0
1995	125.3	125.9	126.5	127.3	2.4	120.4	121.4	122.1	122.9	2.8
1996	128.2	129.3	130.1	130.9	2.8	123.9	125.1	126.1	126.8	3.2
1997	131.4	132.7	133.6	134.1	2.4	127.5	128.9	129.9	130.6	3.0
1998	135.1	136.2	137.1	137.8	2.8	132.0	133.2	134.3	135.2	3.5
1999	138.9	139.9	141.1	142.5	3.4	136.3	137.3	138.5	139.7	3.3
2000	144.8	146.6	147.9	148.8	4.4	141.3	143.0	144.3	145.2	3.9

See footnotes at end of table.

Table 5-1. Employment Cost Index, Private Industry Workers[1], Total Compensation and Wages and Salaries by Occupation and Industry, 1987–2000—*Continued*

(June 1989=100, not seasonally adjusted.)

Series and year	Total compensation: Indexes, March	June	September	December	Percent change for 12 months ended December	Wages and salaries: Indexes, March	June	September	December	Percent change for 12 months ended December
Goods-producing industries, excluding sales occupations										
1987	91.5	92.1	92.9	93.8	3.1	92.9	93.4	94.3	95.2	3.3
1988	95.4	96.5	97.1	97.9	4.4	95.9	96.9	97.4	98.2	3.2
1989	98.9	100.0	101.1	102.2	4.4	99.1	100.0	101.0	102.0	3.9
1990	103.9	105.1	106.1	107.0	4.7	103.0	104.2	105.0	105.7	3.6
1991	108.4	109.6	110.9	111.8	4.5	106.9	107.9	108.7	109.7	3.8
1992	113.4	114.1	115.2	115.9	3.7	110.5	111.2	112.0	112.6	2.6
1993	117.8	118.8	119.6	120.1	3.6	113.5	114.2	114.9	115.6	2.7
1994	121.4	122.5	123.5	124.0	3.2	116.4	117.4	118.4	119.1	3.0
1995	124.9	125.6	126.1	127.0	2.4	119.9	120.9	121.6	122.4	2.8
1996	128.0	129.0	129.8	130.5	2.8	123.5	124.6	125.7	126.3	3.2
1997	131.1	132.3	133.1	133.6	2.4	127.0	128.3	129.3	130.0	2.9
1998	134.5	135.6	136.5	137.2	2.7	131.3	132.5	133.6	134.4	3.4
1999	138.3	139.3	140.5	141.8	3.3	135.5	136.6	137.8	138.9	3.3
2000	144.2	145.9	147.2	148.2	4.5	140.5	142.1	143.4	144.6	4.1
Goods-producing industries, white-collar occupations										
1987	. . .	92.3	93.1	94.0	. . .	. . .	92.9	94.0	94.9	. . .
1988	95.6	96.4	97.2	97.8	4.0	96.2	96.9	97.6	98.3	3.6
1989	99.0	100.0	101.2	101.9	4.2	99.2	100.0	101.0	101.9	3.7
1990	104.1	105.3	106.7	107.4	5.4	103.5	104.6	105.7	106.3	4.3
1991	108.8	110.1	111.2	112.3	4.6	107.4	108.5	109.5	110.4	3.9
1992	113.6	114.5	115.5	116.7	3.9	111.7	112.5	113.2	114.2	3.4
1993	118.6	119.6	120.5	121.1	3.8	115.4	116.4	117.3	118.2	3.5
1994	123.0	124.3	125.1	125.9	4.0	119.1	120.3	121.1	122.0	3.2
1995	127.2	127.6	128.1	129.0	2.5	123.0	123.8	124.4	125.3	2.7
1996	130.0	131.0	132.2	132.9	3.0	126.2	127.3	128.6	129.1	3.0
1997	133.5	134.8	135.6	136.2	2.5	130.0	131.4	132.3	132.9	2.9
1998	137.7	138.8	139.7	140.2	2.9	135.0	136.3	137.4	138.2	4.0
1999	141.7	142.7	143.9	145.5	3.7	100.1	140.5	141.7	143.0	3.5
2000	148.1	150.1	151.3	151.9	4.4	145.0	146.8	147.9	148.7	4.0
Goods-producing industries, white-collar occupations, excluding sales occupations										
1987	. . .	92.2	93.0	93.9	. . .	. . .	92.9	93.9	94.8	. . .
1988	95.4	96.4	97.1	97.7	4.0	96.0	96.9	97.6	98.2	3.6
1989	99.0	100.0	101.2	102.0	4.4	99.2	100.0	101.0	102.0	3.9
1990	103.9	105.2	106.4	107.1	5.0	103.3	104.4	105.6	106.2	4.1
1991	108.5	110.0	111.1	112.2	4.8	107.2	108.5	109.5	110.5	4.0
1992	113.2	113.9	115.1	116.2	3.6	111.3	112.0	112.9	113.7	2.9
1993	118.1	119.0	119.7	119.9	3.2	114.9	115.6	116.4	116.8	2.7
1994	121.9	123.2	124.1	125.0	4.3	117.7	118.8	119.8	120.8	3.4
1995	126.2	126.7	127.2	128.2	2.6	121.8	122.5	123.2	124.2	2.8
1996	129.4	130.2	131.5	132.1	3.0	125.3	126.3	127.7	128.1	3.1
1997	132.6	133.8	134.5	135.0	2.2	128.9	130.0	130.9	131.6	2.7
1998	136.3	137.4	138.3	138.8	2.8	133.3	134.6	135.7	136.4	3.6
1999	140.4	141.3	142.5	143.9	3.7	137.8	138.8	140.1	141.3	3.6
2000	146.5	148.4	149.6	150.5	4.6	143.2	144.9	146.0	147.2	4.2
Goods-producing industries, blue-collar occupations										
1987	. . .	92.1	92.8	93.8	. . .	. . .	93.6	94.4	95.3	. . .
1988	95.4	96.6	97.1	98.0	4.5	95.9	96.9	97.3	98.1	2.9
1989	98.9	100.0	101.1	102.3	4.4	99.0	100.0	101.0	101.9	3.9
1990	103.9	105.1	106.0	106.9	4.5	102.9	104.1	104.7	105.5	3.5
1991	108.4	109.7	110.8	111.6	4.4	106.8	107.6	108.3	109.2	3.5
1992	113.4	114.1	115.1	115.8	3.8	110.1	110.7	111.4	111.9	2.5
1993	117.6	118.7	119.6	120.2	3.8	112.8	113.4	114.1	114.9	2.7
1994	121.1	122.2	123.1	123.4	2.7	115.6	116.6	117.5	118.1	2.8
1995	124.1	124.9	125.5	126.3	2.4	118.8	119.9	120.7	121.4	2.8
1996	127.1	128.3	128.9	129.6	2.6	122.4	123.7	124.5	125.3	3.2
1997	130.2	131.4	132.4	132.8	2.5	126.0	127.3	128.4	129.2	3.1
1998	133.5	134.6	135.5	136.3	2.6	130.1	131.3	132.3	133.3	3.2
1999	137.1	138.3	139.4	140.7	3.2	134.3	135.4	136.6	137.6	3.2
2000	142.8	144.4	145.8	146.8	4.3	139.0	140.5	142.0	143.1	4.0

See footnotes at end of table.

Table 5-1. Employment Cost Index, Private Industry Workers[1], Total Compensation and Wages and Salaries by Occupation and Industry, 1987–2000—*Continued*

(June 1989=100, not seasonally adjusted.)

Series and year	Total compensation					Wages and salaries				
	Indexes				Percent change for 12 months ended December	Indexes				Percent change for 12 months ended December
	March	June	September	December		March	June	September	December	
Construction										
1987	91.5	92.7	93.4	94.0	3.6	92.5	93.2	94.1	94.8	3.3
1988	95.2	96.4	97.2	98.0	4.3	95.7	97.0	97.7	98.3	3.7
1989	99.0	100.0	101.2	102.4	4.5	99.1	100.0	101.1	101.7	3.5
1990	103.1	104.3	105.2	105.6	3.1	102.0	102.9	103.5	103.7	2.0
1991	107.4	108.5	109.3	109.9	4.1	105.1	105.9	106.3	106.8	3.0
1992	110.6	111.7	113.1	113.8	3.5	107.2	107.9	108.7	108.9	2.0
1993	114.9	116.0	116.8	116.5	2.4	109.5	110.4	111.3	111.1	2.0
1994	118.6	120.2	121.4	120.8	3.7	112.2	113.6	114.6	114.7	3.2
1995	121.1	122.0	123.1	123.4	2.2	114.8	115.7	116.8	117.4	2.4
1996	124.3	125.3	125.9	126.4	2.4	118.3	119.6	120.4	120.8	2.9
1997	127.2	128.7	129.7	129.7	2.6	122.0	123.6	124.7	124.9	3.4
1998	130.6	132.7	133.4	134.3	3.5	126.0	128.1	128.5	129.3	3.5
1999	135.6	136.9	137.9	138.7	3.3	130.7	131.9	133.0	133.6	3.3
2000	140.8	143.2	145.1	146.7	5.8	136.0	138.0	139.4	140.7	5.3
Manufacturing										
1987	91.1	91.6	92.5	93.4	3.0	92.7	93.3	94.2	95.2	3.4
1988	95.3	96.2	96.9	97.6	4.5	96.0	96.8	97.3	98.1	3.0
1989	98.9	100.0	101.1	102.0	4.5	99.0	100.0	100.9	101.9	3.9
1990	104.0	105.3	106.4	107.2	5.1	103.3	104.5	105.4	106.2	4.2
1991	108.6	110.0	111.2	112.2	4.7	107.4	108.4	109.3	110.3	3.9
1992	114.0	114.7	115.7	116.5	3.8	111.5	112.2	112.9	113.7	3.1
1993	118.6	119.7	120.6	121.3	4.1	114.7	115.5	116.3	117.3	3.2
1994	122.5	123.5	124.4	125.1	3.1	118.0	119.0	120.0	120.8	3.0
1995	126.2	126.9	127.3	128.3	2.6	121.9	122.9	123.5	124.3	2.9
1996	129.3	130.4	131.3	132.1	3.0	125.4	126.5	127.7	128.4	3.3
1997	132.6	133.8	134.6	135.3	2.4	129.1	130.3	131.3	132.2	3.0
1998	136.4	137.2	138.2	138.9	2.7	133.7	134.6	136.0	136.8	3.5
1999	139.9	140.9	142.1	143.6	3.4	137.9	139.0	140.2	141.5	3.4
2000	146.0	147.5	148.7	149.3	4.0	142.9	144.4	145.7	146.5	3.5
Manufacturing, white-collar occupations										
1987	. . .	92.2	93.1	94.1	. . .	. . .	93.0	94.0	95.0	. . .
1988	95.7	96.4	97.1	97.7	3.8	96.2	96.9	97.5	98.2	3.4
1989	99.0	100.0	101.1	101.9	4.3	99.2	100.0	100.9	101.8	3.7
1990	104.1	105.3	106.8	107.4	5.4	103.7	104.7	105.9	106.4	4.5
1991	108.8	110.2	111.3	112.4	4.7	107.6	108.8	109.8	110.7	4.0
1992	113.6	114.6	115.5	116.6	3.7	111.9	112.9	113.6	114.6	3.5
1993	118.7	119.7	120.5	121.3	4.0	116.0	116.9	117.7	118.8	3.7
1994	122.7	123.9	124.9	126.0	3.9	119.5	120.6	121.7	122.7	3.3
1995	127.4	128.0	128.7	129.5	2.8	123.9	124.7	125.3	126.1	2.8
1996	130.5	131.6	132.8	133.6	3.2	127.1	128.2	129.6	130.1	3.2
1997	133.9	135.2	135.8	136.7	2.3	130.6	131.9	132.8	133.6	2.7
1998	138.2	139.1	140.1	140.5	2.8	135.6	136.8	138.3	139.0	4.0
1999	141.8	143.0	144.3	145.8	3.8	140.1	141.4	142.7	144.0	3.6
2000	148.2	150.2	151.4	151.5	3.9	145.8	147.7	148.7	149.2	3.6
Manufacturing, white-collar occupations, excluding sales occupations										
1987	. . .	92.1	93.0	93.9	. . .	. . .	92.9	93.9	94.8	. . .
1988	95.5	96.3	97.1	97.7	4.0	96.0	96.8	97.4	98.0	3.4
1989	99.0	100.0	101.1	101.9	4.3	99.1	100.0	100.9	101.9	4.0
1990	104.0	105.1	106.4	107.0	5.0	103.4	104.4	105.6	106.2	4.2
1991	108.3	109.9	111.1	112.2	4.9	107.2	108.6	109.7	110.7	4.2
1992	113.0	113.8	115.0	115.9	3.3	111.4	112.2	113.0	114.0	3.0
1993	118.0	118.8	119.5	119.9	3.5	115.3	115.9	116.7	117.2	2.8
1994	121.3	122.5	123.6	124.9	4.2	118.0	119.1	120.2	121.4	3.6
1995	126.1	126.6	127.4	128.3	2.7	122.4	123.2	123.9	124.8	2.8
1996	129.5	130.5	131.8	132.5	3.3	126.0	127.0	128.4	128.9	3.3
1997	132.8	133.8	134.5	135.3	2.1	129.3	130.5	131.3	132.2	2.6
1998	136.5	137.3	138.3	138.7	2.5	133.8	135.0	136.3	137.1	3.7
1999	140.1	141.3	142.5	143.8	3.7	138.3	139.6	140.8	142.0	3.6
2000	146.2	148.2	149.3	149.7	4.1	143.7	145.6	146.6	147.5	3.9

See footnotes at end of table.

Table 5-1. Employment Cost Index, Private Industry Workers[1], Total Compensation and Wages and Salaries by Occupation and Industry, 1987–2000—*Continued*

(June 1989=100, not seasonally adjusted.)

Series and year	Total compensation					Wages and salaries				
	Indexes				Percent change for 12 months ended December	Indexes				Percent change for 12 months ended December
	March	June	September	December		March	June	September	December	
Manufacturing, blue-collar occupations										
1987	...	91.3	92.0	93.1	...	...	93.5	94.4	95.4	...
1988	95.1	96.1	96.7	97.6	4.8	96.0	96.8	97.2	98.1	2.8
1989	98.8	100.0	101.1	102.1	4.6	98.9	100.0	100.9	102.0	4.0
1990	104.0	105.2	106.2	107.2	5.0	103.1	104.4	105.1	106.1	4.0
1991	108.5	109.8	111.1	112.0	4.5	107.3	108.2	109.0	110.0	3.7
1992	114.2	114.8	115.7	116.4	3.9	111.1	111.7	112.4	113.1	2.8
1993	118.5	119.6	120.5	121.3	4.2	113.9	114.5	115.2	116.2	2.7
1994	122.3	123.2	124.0	124.5	2.6	116.9	117.8	118.7	119.5	2.8
1995	125.3	126.0	126.3	127.5	2.4	120.4	121.6	122.2	123.1	3.0
1996	128.4	129.5	130.2	131.1	2.8	124.2	125.4	126.3	127.3	3.4
1997	131.7	132.8	133.7	134.3	2.4	128.0	129.2	130.2	131.2	3.1
1998	135.0	135.9	136.8	137.7	2.5	132.3	133.1	134.3	135.3	3.1
1999	138.5	139.4	140.5	142.1	3.2	136.3	137.2	138.4	139.7	3.3
2000	144.4	145.6	146.7	147.8	4.0	140.8	142.0	143.4	144.6	3.5
Manufacturing, durable goods										
1987	91.3	92.0	92.6	93.5	2.6	93.0	93.7	94.5	95.5	3.1
1988	95.6	96.5	97.0	97.7	4.5	96.2	96.9	97.4	98.0	2.6
1989	99.0	100.0	101.1	102.2	4.6	99.0	100.0	100.7	101.9	4.0
1990	104.0	105.1	106.3	107.2	4.9	103.2	104.3	105.3	106.1	4.1
1991	108.5	109.9	111.2	112.1	4.6	107.3	108.3	109.2	110.2	3.9
1992	114.1	114.8	115.8	116.7	4.1	111.2	111.8	112.7	113.4	2.9
1993	119.0	120.0	121.0	121.9	4.5	114.4	115.1	115.9	117.2	3.4
1994	122.9	123.8	125.1	125.8	3.2	117.8	118.7	119.8	120.8	3.1
1995	127.0	127.7	128.2	129.0	2.5	121.9	122.9	123.6	124.3	2.9
1996	129.7	131.2	131.9	132.6	2.8	125.1	126.5	127.7	128.4	3.3
1997	133.0	134.1	135.0	135.7	2.3	129.0	130.1	131.2	131.9	2.7
1998	136.5	137.4	138.5	139.2	2.6	133.4	134.5	135.9	136.9	3.8
1999	139.9	141.0	142.3	144.0	3.4	137.9	139.1	140.4	141.8	3.6
2000	146.5	148.3	149.4	150.1	4.2	143.0	144.7	146.1	147.3	3.9
Aircraft manufacturing (SIC 3721)										
1988	...	...	...	98.8	...	...	...	...	98.8	...
1989	99.2	100.0	101.0	103.6	4.9	99.4	100.0	100.6	102.2	3.4
1990	105.4	107.0	108.5	108.6	4.8	103.2	104.9	105.7	107.0	4.7
1991	110.2	111.8	113.1	114.8	5.7	108.4	109.8	110.9	112.6	5.2
1992	116.9	119.0	120.1	122.9	7.1	113.6	115.2	116.0	117.2	4.1
1993	124.1	124.5	126.7	125.2	1.9	117.9	118.8	120.5	121.6	3.8
1994	126.2	127.1	128.7	129.2	3.2	122.4	123.3	124.0	124.8	2.6
1995	130.6	131.0	131.5	133.8	3.6	125.7	126.5	127.4	128.1	2.6
1996	136.9	138.2	138.2	137.4	2.7	129.0	130.3	130.6	130.9	2.2
1997	137.3	138.4	137.8	136.9	-0.4	132.0	133.5	133.3	134.0	2.4
1998	137.2	138.9	139.3	140.6	2.7	135.1	136.9	137.2	138.3	3.2
1999	140.5	142.4	143.7	146.9	4.5	139.4	141.5	142.7	143.6	3.8
2000	151.2	154.3	156.0	155.3	5.7	146.3	148.6	150.0	151.6	5.6
Aircraft manufacturing (SIC 3721), white-collar occupations										
1988	...	...	...	98.8	...	...	...	...	98.7	...
1989	99.1	100.0	100.8	102.8	4.0	99.3	100.0	100.4	101.5	2.8
1990	104.6	105.9	107.2	106.8	3.9	102.3	103.8	104.2	105.0	3.4
1991	108.1	109.7	110.5	112.0	4.9	106.0	107.4	107.9	108.9	3.7
1992	114.2	116.3	117.0	119.0	6.3	110.0	111.6	112.2	113.1	3.9
1993	120.5	121.2	123.2	121.8	2.4	113.9	115.2	116.7	117.3	3.7
1994	122.7	123.8	125.3	125.3	2.9	118.1	119.1	119.8	120.2	2.5
1995	126.7	127.2	127.8	129.0	3.0	121.0	121.6	122.7	123.2	2.5
1996	132.4	133.9	133.8	133.7	3.6	124.1	125.9	126.1	126.5	2.7
1997	133.5	134.9	134.6	134.3	0.4	127.8	129.6	129.3	129.8	2.6
1998	134.7	137.1	137.4	137.4	2.3	131.2	133.7	133.9	134.5	3.6
1999	137.3	139.5	139.8	141.7	3.1	135.5	138.0	138.3	139.1	3.4
2000	146.6	150.7	151.8	151.2	6.7	142.1	145.2	146.0	146.2	5.1

See footnotes at end of table.

Table 5-1. Employment Cost Index, Private Industry Workers[1], Total Compensation and Wages and Salaries by Occupation and Industry, 1987–2000—*Continued*

(June 1989=100, not seasonally adjusted.)

Series and year	Total compensation					Wages and salaries				
	Indexes				Percent change for 12 months ended December	Indexes				Percent change for 12 months ended December
	March	June	September	December		March	June	September	December	
Aircraft manufacturing (SIC 3721), blue-collar occupations										
1988	...	...	...	98.9	...	...	...	...	98.9	...
1989	99.5	100.0	101.4	104.7	5.9	99.6	100.0	100.9	103.3	4.4
1990	106.6	108.6	110.1	110.9	5.9	104.6	106.7	107.8	110.0	6.5
1991	113.2	114.7	116.7	118.8	7.1	112.0	113.5	115.4	118.0	7.3
1992	120.8	122.8	124.2	128.2	7.9	119.0	120.5	121.5	123.3	4.5
1993	129.2	129.2	131.5	129.8	1.2	123.9	124.1	126.1	127.9	3.7
1994	130.9	131.5	133.2	134.2	3.4	128.7	129.4	130.2	131.7	3.0
1995	135.7	136.1	136.3	140.5	4.7	132.7	133.6	134.1	135.1	2.6
1996	143.3	144.1	144.4	142.3	1.3	136.1	136.4	137.0	137.1	1.5
1997	142.3	142.8	141.8	139.6	-1.9	137.7	138.8	138.4	139.6	1.8
1998	139.6	140.1	140.8	144.4	3.4	140.1	140.5	141.0	143.2	2.6
1999	144.3	145.7	149.0	154.4	6.9	144.5	145.5	148.9	149.9	4.7
2000	157.8	158.5	161.4	160.4	3.9	151.8	152.1	155.1	159.3	6.3
Manufacturing, nondurable goods										
1987	90.7	91.2	92.3	93.4	3.8	92.2	92.5	93.8	94.7	3.7
1988	94.8	95.6	96.5	97.5	4.4	95.8	96.5	97.2	98.2	3.7
1989	98.8	100.0	101.2	101.9	4.5	99.0	100.0	101.1	101.8	3.7
1990	104.1	105.5	106.6	107.4	5.4	103.6	104.8	105.7	106.3	4.4
1991	108.8	110.1	111.2	112.3	4.6	107.6	108.6	109.4	110.6	4.0
1992	113.8	114.7	115.4	116.3	3.6	111.8	112.8	113.2	114.3	3.3
1993	117.9	119.0	119.7	120.3	3.4	115.5	116.3	116.9	117.5	2.8
1994	121.7	122.8	123.2	123.8	2.9	118.3	119.5	120.3	120.8	2.8
1995	124.7	125.4	125.7	127.0	2.6	121.9	122.9	123.3	124.4	3.0
1996	128.3	128.9	130.0	131.0	3.1	125.8	126.5	127.6	128.5	3.3
1997	131.7	133.0	133.7	134.5	2.7	129.3	130.6	131.4	132.6	3.2
1998	135.9	136.7	137.6	138.2	2.8	134.2	134.9	136.0	136.8	3.2
1999	139.6	140.4	141.5	142.8	3.3	138.0	138.7	139.7	140.9	3.0
2000	144.9	146.0	147.5	147.7	3.4	142.7	143.9	145.0	145.4	3.2
Service-Producing Industries[3]										
1987	90.5	91.2	92.1	92.6	3.7	91.5	92.1	93.1	93.4	3.4
1988	93.8	95.1	96.2	97.3	5.1	94.3	95.5	96.7	97.8	4.7
1989	98.8	100.0	101.3	102.3	5.1	99.1	100.0	101.4	102.2	4.5
1990	103.8	105.2	106.2	107.0	4.6	103.3	104.6	105.7	106.3	4.0
1991	108.5	109.8	111.0	111.6	4.3	107.5	108.7	109.7	110.2	3.7
1992	112.8	113.6	114.4	115.2	3.2	111.1	111.7	112.3	113.0	2.5
1993	116.4	117.3	118.5	119.3	3.6	113.9	114.7	115.9	116.6	3.2
1994	120.4	121.2	122.3	122.8	2.9	117.3	118.2	119.2	119.7	2.7
1995	123.9	124.9	125.8	126.2	2.8	120.7	121.6	122.6	123.2	2.9
1996	127.6	128.6	129.5	130.2	3.2	124.7	125.8	126.7	127.5	3.5
1997	131.6	132.5	133.8	135.3	3.9	129.0	130.1	131.5	133.1	4.4
1998	136.7	137.8	139.6	140.5	3.8	134.4	135.6	137.6	138.4	4.0
1999	140.9	142.8	144.1	145.3	3.4	138.9	140.8	142.1	143.3	3.5
2000	147.4	149.1	150.6	151.7	4.4	145.0	146.5	147.9	148.9	3.9
Service-producing industries, excluding sales occupations										
1987	90.6	91.4	92.5	93.1	4.0	91.5	92.2	93.5	94.0	4.0
1988	94.3	95.4	96.7	97.5	4.7	94.9	95.8	97.1	98.0	4.3
1989	98.9	100.0	101.2	102.1	4.7	99.2	100.0	101.2	101.8	3.9
1990	103.9	105.1	106.4	107.3	5.1	103.4	104.5	105.8	106.6	4.7
1991	108.7	109.9	111.3	112.1	4.5	107.7	108.7	110.0	110.7	3.8
1992	113.2	114.0	115.1	115.9	3.4	111.5	112.2	113.0	113.7	2.7
1993	117.3	118.3	119.3	120.2	3.7	114.8	115.6	116.6	117.4	3.3
1994	121.4	122.1	123.3	123.8	3.0	118.3	119.0	120.2	120.7	2.8
1995	125.0	125.8	126.6	127.2	2.7	121.8	122.5	123.4	124.2	2.9
1996	128.4	129.2	130.3	130.9	2.9	125.6	126.5	127.6	128.3	3.3
1997	132.2	133.3	134.5	136.1	4.0	129.7	130.9	132.3	133.9	4.4
1998	137.4	138.5	140.0	140.6	3.3	135.2	136.2	137.9	138.5	3.4
1999	141.7	143.3	144.6	145.9	3.8	139.8	141.4	142.6	143.8	3.8
2000	147.7	149.4	151.1	152.2	4.3	145.3	146.9	148.3	149.4	3.9

See footnotes at end of table.

Table 5-1. Employment Cost Index, Private Industry Workers[1], Total Compensation and Wages and Salaries by Occupation and Industry, 1987–2000—*Continued*

(June 1989=100, not seasonally adjusted.)

Series and year	Total compensation					Wages and salaries				
	Indexes				Percent change for 12 months ended December	Indexes				Percent change for 12 months ended December
	March	June	September	December		March	June	September	December	
Service-producing industries, white-collar occupations										
1987	...	90.7	91.8	92.1	...	...	91.6	92.6	92.9	...
1988	93.4	94.7	95.9	97.2	5.5	93.7	95.1	96.3	97.5	5.0
1989	98.8	100.0	101.4	102.6	5.6	99.0	100.0	101.5	102.5	5.1
1990	104.2	105.5	106.7	107.4	4.7	103.6	105.0	106.1	106.8	4.2
1991	109.1	110.4	111.5	112.1	4.4	108.1	109.3	110.3	110.7	3.7
1992	113.4	114.1	114.9	115.7	3.2	111.7	112.2	112.8	113.6	2.6
1993	116.9	117.8	119.0	119.8	3.5	114.5	115.2	116.5	117.3	3.3
1994	121.0	121.9	122.9	123.4	3.0	118.0	118.9	119.9	120.4	2.6
1995	124.6	125.6	126.5	127.1	3.0	121.3	122.3	123.2	124.0	3.0
1996	128.5	129.6	130.6	131.1	3.1	125.6	126.8	127.8	128.5	3.6
1997	132.7	133.7	134.9	136.6	4.2	130.1	131.2	132.6	134.3	4.5
1998	138.0	139.3	141.2	142.2	4.1	135.7	137.0	139.2	140.1	4.3
1999	142.3	144.3	145.8	147.0	3.4	140.3	142.3	143.8	145.0	3.5
2000	149.3	151.0	152.6	153.7	4.6	146.9	148.5	150.0	150.9	4.1
Service-producing industries, white-collar occupations, excluding sales occupations										
1987	...	90.9	92.3	92.9	...	...	91.7	93.1	93.7	...
1988	94.1	95.1	96.6	97.5	5.0	94.5	95.5	96.9	97.9	4.5
1989	99.0	100.0	101.4	102.3	4.9	99.2	100.0	101.3	102.1	4.3
1990	104.4	105.6	107.1	108.0	5.6	103.8	105.0	106.4	107.2	5.0
1991	109.5	110.6	112.1	113.0	4.6	108.5	109.5	110.9	111.6	4.1
1992	114.1	114.9	116.1	116.8	3.4	112.4	113.1	114.0	114.7	2.8
1993	118.4	119.3	120.4	121.4	3.9	116.0	116.8	117.8	118.7	3.5
1994	122.7	123.4	124.6	125.1	3.0	119.6	120.4	121.5	122.1	2.9
1995	126.4	127.1	128.0	128.7	2.9	123.2	123.8	124.7	125.6	2.9
1996	130.0	130.9	132.2	132.6	3.0	127.2	128.1	129.5	129.9	3.4
1997	134.0	135.1	136.3	138.1	4.1	131.5	132.7	134.2	135.9	4.6
1998	139.5	140.6	142.2	142.9	3.4	137.0	138.4	140.2	140.7	3.5
1999	143.8	145.5	147.0	148.3	3.9	142.0	143.7	145.1	146.4	4.1
2000	150.3	152.1	153.9	155.1	4.6	147.8	149.6	151.2	152.3	4.0
Service-producing industries, blue-collar occupations										
1987	...	92.2	93.0	93.8	...	...	93.2	94.1	94.8	...
1988	95.2	96.2	97.1	97.5	3.9	95.9	96.7	97.5	98.0	3.4
1989	98.7	100.0	101.1	101.1	3.7	99.0	100.0	100.9	100.9	3.0
1990	102.6	103.9	104.8	105.4	4.3	102.1	103.3	104.2	104.7	3.8
1991	106.6	107.6	108.7	109.4	3.8	105.6	106.5	107.3	107.8	3.0
1992	110.4	111.6	112.4	113.2	3.5	108.7	109.7	110.3	111.0	3.0
1993	114.3	115.5	116.6	117.2	3.5	111.9	112.9	114.1	114.6	3.2
1994	118.4	119.1	120.6	120.7	3.0	115.5	116.2	117.5	117.6	2.6
1995	122.1	123.1	123.9	124.0	2.7	119.2	120.3	121.1	121.4	3.2
1996	125.2	126.0	126.4	127.3	2.7	122.7	123.5	123.8	124.8	2.8
1997	128.2	129.2	130.0	130.9	2.8	126.0	127.2	127.9	128.9	3.3
1998	132.1	133.2	134.3	134.8	3.0	130.2	131.1	132.4	132.9	3.1
1999	136.2	137.8	139.1	139.8	3.7	134.4	135.9	137.0	137.8	3.7
2000	141.8	143.1	144.5	145.3	3.9	139.1	140.3	141.6	142.2	3.2
Service-producing industries, service occupations										
1987	...	92.4	92.9	93.4	...	...	93.6	94.1	94.4	...
1988	94.6	95.6	97.1	98.4	5.4	95.3	96.3	97.7	98.8	4.7
1989	99.3	100.0	101.1	102.5	4.2	99.4	100.0	100.8	102.3	3.5
1990	103.9	105.0	105.8	107.4	4.8	103.2	104.3	105.0	106.5	4.1
1991	108.4	109.9	111.6	112.5	4.7	107.0	108.4	110.0	110.7	3.9
1992	113.4	114.1	115.2	115.7	2.8	111.3	111.7	112.6	112.9	2.0
1993	116.8	117.7	118.6	119.1	2.9	113.5	114.1	114.9	115.2	2.0
1994	120.2	120.7	121.3	122.5	2.9	116.3	116.7	117.3	118.7	3.0
1995	123.0	123.6	124.2	124.8	1.9	119.3	119.8	120.7	121.3	2.2
1996	125.3	126.1	127.1	128.6	3.0	122.0	122.8	124.0	125.6	3.5
1997	129.5	130.6	132.7	133.9	4.1	126.5	127.5	129.8	131.0	4.3
1998	135.0	135.8	137.0	137.8	2.9	132.1	133.0	134.2	135.2	3.2
1999	139.3	140.5	140.8	142.4	3.3	136.7	137.8	138.0	139.6	3.3
2000	143.6	145.1	146.3	147.9	3.9	141.1	142.5	143.5	144.8	3.7

See footnotes at end of table.

Table 5-1. Employment Cost Index, Private Industry Workers[1], Total Compensation and Wages and Salaries by Occupation and Industry, 1987–2000—*Continued*

(June 1989=100, not seasonally adjusted.)

Series and year	Total compensation					Wages and salaries				
	Indexes				Percent change for 12 months ended December	Indexes				Percent change for 12 months ended December
	March	June	September	December		March	June	September	December	
Transportation and public utilities										
1987	92.9	93.9	94.4	94.8	3.0	94.7	95.6	96.1	96.2	2.1
1988	95.8	96.8	97.5	97.5	2.8	97.0	97.9	98.7	98.6	2.5
1989	98.7	100.0	100.7	101.2	3.8	99.5	100.0	100.7	101.2	2.6
1990	103.0	103.3	104.2	105.1	3.9	102.6	103.2	104.1	104.6	3.4
1991	106.0	107.7	109.0	109.7	4.4	105.4	106.6	107.7	108.4	3.6
1992	111.1	111.9	112.9	113.5	3.5	109.7	110.6	111.2	111.8	3.1
1993	114.8	116.0	116.8	117.5	3.5	112.9	114.0	114.7	115.4	3.2
1994	119.2	119.8	121.4	122.1	3.9	116.4	117.2	118.9	119.6	3.6
1995	124.0	124.7	126.0	126.6	3.7	121.2	122.0	122.9	123.7	3.4
1996	127.9	128.4	129.3	130.4	3.0	124.6	125.0	125.9	127.0	2.7
1997	131.3	131.7	132.9	134.2	2.9	128.2	128.8	130.1	131.3	3.4
1998	135.8	137.1	138.5	139.3	3.8	132.1	132.8	134.3	135.1	2.9
1999	139.7	140.9	141.8	142.3	2.2	135.4	136.8	137.5	137.9	2.1
2000	143.9	145.7	147.4	148.3	4.2	138.5	140.0	141.3	142.3	3.2
Transportation										
1987	92.4	93.7	93.8	94.0	2.7	94.9	96.1	96.5	96.3	1.7
1988	95.3	96.9	97.6	97.3	3.5	97.1	98.2	99.0	98.7	2.5
1989	98.8	100.0	100.5	100.8	3.6	99.4	100.0	100.6	100.7	2.0
1990	102.8	103.0	103.8	104.6	3.8	102.3	102.3	103.3	103.5	2.8
1991	105.2	106.8	107.8	108.6	3.8	104.3	105.5	106.6	107.0	3.4
1992	109.9	110.5	111.7	111.8	2.9	108.3	109.2	109.8	109.9	2.7
1993	112.8	114.1	114.8	115.7	3.5	110.8	112.0	112.6	113.4	3.2
1994	117.1	117.7	119.7	120.3	4.0	114.2	114.8	116.7	117.5	3.6
1995	122.3	123.0	124.7	125.1	4.0	119.0	119.8	121.0	121.6	3.5
1996	126.9	127.7	128.2	129.2	3.3	122.9	123.2	123.8	124.7	2.5
1997	130.6	130.9	132.1	133.4	3.3	126.5	126.9	128.5	129.5	3.8
1998	134.0	134.9	136.7	137.3	2.9	130.1	130.4	132.4	132.9	2.6
1999	136.8	138.1	138.7	139.5	1.6	132.3	133.7	134.4	134.9	1.5
2000	140.4	141.8	142.8	143.9	3.2	134.9	136.2	137.4	138.6	2.7
Public utilities										
1987	93.5	94.3	95.2	95.7	3.2	94.4	95.1	95.7	96.2	2.6
1988	96.4	96.7	97.3	97.7	2.1	97.0	97.6	98.3	98.7	2.6
1989	98.8	100.0	101.0	101.7	4.1	99.5	100.0	101.1	101.8	3.1
1990	103.2	103.8	104.8	105.7	3.9	103.0	104.1	105.0	106.0	4.1
1991	107.0	108.8	110.4	111.2	5.2	106.9	108.0	109.0	110.0	3.8
1992	112.6	113.7	114.4	115.6	4.0	111.4	112.4	113.0	114.1	3.7
1993	117.4	118.3	119.2	119.9	3.7	116.4	116.4	117.2	117.9	3.3
1994	121.7	122.6	123.6	124.4	3.8	119.1	120.1	121.4	122.3	3.7
1995	126.1	126.8	127.5	128.5	3.3	123.9	124.5	125.2	126.1	3.1
1996	128.9	129.1	130.4	131.7	2.5	126.5	127.1	128.4	129.8	2.9
1997	132.0	132.5	133.7	135.1	2.6	130.1	130.9	132.0	133.5	2.9
1998	137.9	139.7	140.7	141.9	5.0	134.5	135.7	136.5	137.8	3.2
1999	143.4	144.6	145.7	146.1	3.0	139.2	140.6	141.5	141.8	2.9
2000	148.6	150.9	153.5	154.1	5.5	143.2	144.9	146.4	147.1	3.7
Communications										
1987	...	...	95.6	96.3	...	...	...	96.4	97.1	...
1988	96.7	96.9	97.5	97.5	1.2	97.6	98.1	98.9	99.0	2.0
1989	98.5	100.0	101.0	101.6	4.2	99.9	100.0	101.1	101.8	2.8
1990	103.1	103.1	104.2	105.2	3.5	103.1	104.1	105.0	106.1	4.2
1991	106.0	108.0	109.9	110.7	5.2	106.5	107.6	108.5	109.6	3.3
1992	111.8	112.7	113.4	114.7	3.6	110.8	111.7	112.2	113.5	3.6
1993	116.5	117.5	118.5	119.2	3.9	114.7	115.6	116.5	117.1	3.2
1994	121.0	122.1	122.9	124.0	4.0	118.4	119.5	121.0	122.1	4.3
1995	126.3	126.6	127.4	128.3	3.5	124.3	124.6	125.3	126.2	3.4
1996	128.0	127.5	129.1	131.1	2.2	126.1	126.5	128.2	130.3	3.2
1997	130.2	130.5	131.8	134.0	2.2	129.8	130.6	131.8	134.0	2.8
1998	136.6	139.2	140.5	141.7	5.7	134.4	135.8	136.7	138.0	3.0
1999	143.3	144.9	146.1	146.0	3.0	139.4	141.1	141.9	142.2	3.0
2000	148.4	150.9	153.9	154.7	6.0	143.4	145.0	146.7	147.4	3.7

See footnotes at end of table.

Table 5-1. Employment Cost Index, Private Industry Workers[1], Total Compensation and Wages and Salaries by Occupation and Industry, 1987–2000—*Continued*

(June 1989=100, not seasonally adjusted.)

Series and year	Total compensation					Wages and salaries				
	Indexes				Percent change for 12 months ended December	Indexes				Percent change for 12 months ended December
	March	June	September	December		March	June	September	December	
Electric, gas, and sanitary services										
1987	. . .	. . .	. . .	95.0	. . .	. . .	. . .	. . .	94.9	. . .
1988	96.0	96.7	97.1	98.0	3.2	96.1	96.9	97.3	98.2	3.5
1989	99.2	100.0	101.0	101.7	3.8	99.0	100.0	101.0	101.7	3.6
1990	103.2	104.6	105.5	106.2	4.4	103.0	104.2	105.0	105.7	3.9
1991	108.3	109.8	111.0	111.7	5.2	107.3	108.6	109.5	110.5	4.5
1992	113.7	115.0	115.9	116.7	4.5	112.2	113.3	114.2	114.8	3.9
1993	118.6	119.4	120.2	120.8	3.5	116.3	117.4	118.2	118.8	3.5
1994	122.7	123.2	124.4	124.8	3.3	119.9	120.9	121.9	122.4	3.0
1995	125.9	127.0	127.7	128.7	3.1	123.4	124.4	125.2	125.9	2.9
1996	130.1	131.1	132.0	132.4	2.9	127.0	127.7	128.5	129.0	2.5
1997	134.2	134.9	136.0	136.4	3.0	130.4	131.2	132.2	132.9	3.0
1998	139.6	140.3	141.0	142.1	4.2	134.7	135.6	136.3	137.4	3.4
1999	143.4	144.2	145.1	146.1	2.8	138.9	140.0	140.9	141.3	2.8
2000	148.9	151.0	152.9	153.4	5.0	143.0	144.7	145.9	146.6	3.8
Wholesale and retail trade										
1987	90.7	92.1	92.6	92.8	3.1	91.4	92.9	93.4	93.4	3.0
1988	94.0	95.8	96.8	97.6	5.2	94.3	96.2	97.2	97.9	4.8
1989	98.9	100.0	101.6	102.6	5.1	99.1	100.0	101.6	102.7	4.9
1990	103.5	105.0	105.6	106.2	3.5	103.3	104.6	105.1	105.6	2.8
1991	107.4	109.2	110.3	110.7	4.2	106.6	108.4	109.4	109.6	3.8
1992	111.4	112.5	113.0	113.7	2.7	109.9	111.2	111.5	112.3	2.5
1993	114.7	115.9	116.4	117.1	3.0	113.0	114.2	114.7	115.4	2.8
1994	117.6	119.4	120.5	120.6	3.0	115.5	117.4	118.3	118.4	2.6
1995	121.7	122.8	123.8	124.2	3.0	119.4	120.6	121.6	122.3	3.3
1996	125.5	126.4	127.5	128.0	3.5	123.9	124.8	125.8	127.0	3.8
1997	130.1	131.2	132.4	132.9	3.3	128.5	129.7	130.0	131.6	3.6
1998	134.7	135.8	137.6	138.2	4.0	133.3	134.6	136.6	137.0	4.1
1999	138.9	141.1	142.0	143.5	3.8	137.7	139.6	140.7	142.0	3.6
2000	145.6	147.3	148.3	149.4	4.1	143.8	145.5	146.4	147.4	3.8
Wholesale and retail trade, excluding sales occupations										
1987	91.5	92.6	93.3	93.8	3.4	92.2	93.2	94.1	94.5	3.4
1988	94.9	96.2	97.3	98.2	4.7	95.3	96.6	97.5	98.4	4.1
1989	99.2	100.0	101.3	102.0	3.9	99.4	100.0	101.1	101.9	3.6
1990	103.0	104.5	105.4	106.1	4.0	102.6	104.2	104.9	105.5	3.5
1991	107.7	109.1	110.1	110.8	4.4	106.8	108.3	109.2	109.6	3.9
1992	111.5	112.7	113.5	114.1	3.0	110.1	111.4	112.1	112.6	2.7
1993	115.4	116.2	117.0	118.0	3.4	113.6	114.4	115.2	116.1	3.1
1994	118.6	119.8	120.9	120.9	2.5	116.5	117.8	118.7	118.8	2.3
1995	122.4	123.1	124.1	125.0	3.4	120.2	120.9	121.9	123.2	3.7
1996	125.9	126.4	128.0	129.0	3.2	124.4	124.9	126.5	127.7	3.7
1997	130.4	131.9	133.0	134.0	3.9	129.3	131.1	132.2	133.2	4.3
1998	135.5	136.3	138.1	138.8	3.6	134.7	135.6	137.6	138.2	3.8
1999	139.9	141.9	142.8	144.3	4.0	139.5	141.1	141.8	143.3	3.7
2000	146.4	148.1	149.6	150.6	4.4	145.2	146.8	148.2	149.0	4.0
Wholesale trade										
1987	89.7	91.1	91.6	92.2	3.9	90.5	92.1	92.5	93.0	4.1
1988	93.0	94.7	95.6	96.1	4.2	93.3	95.1	96.1	96.4	3.7
1989	98.5	100.0	102.6	104.5	8.7	99.0	100.0	102.8	105.2	9.1
1990	104.8	105.4	105.8	106.5	1.9	104.6	105.2	105.5	106.2	1.0
1991	107.8	109.6	110.7	111.1	4.3	107.3	109.2	110.4	110.3	3.9
1992	112.5	113.5	113.2	114.4	3.0	111.4	112.5	111.9	113.5	2.9
1993	115.3	116.4	116.6	117.8	3.0	113.9	115.1	115.1	116.4	2.6
1994	117.9	119.7	120.6	121.5	3.1	116.2	118.3	118.9	119.9	3.0
1995	123.2	124.8	126.1	127.0	4.5	120.9	122.7	123.9	125.5	4.7
1996	127.5	129.3	129.9	130.9	3.1	126.1	128.0	128.5	129.6	3.3
1997	132.9	133.8	134.6	135.1	3.2	131.4	132.2	133.0	133.6	3.1
1998	137.7	138.6	140.8	142.8	5.7	136.2	137.1	139.3	141.3	5.8
1999	142.7	144.6	146.3	148.5	4.0	140.7	142.3	144.3	146.5	3.7
2000	150.0	151.8	152.1	154.4	4.0	147.4	149.4	149.6	151.6	3.5

See footnotes at end of table.

Table 5-1. Employment Cost Index, Private Industry Workers[1], Total Compensation and Wages and Salaries by Occupation and Industry, 1987–2000—*Continued*

(June 1989=100, not seasonally adjusted.)

Series and year	Total compensation					Wages and salaries				
	Indexes				Percent change for 12 months ended December	Indexes				Percent change for 12 months ended December
	March	June	September	December		March	June	September	December	
Wholesale trade, excluding sales occupations										
1987	91.7	92.3	93.4	94.1	3.6	92.7	93.3	94.4	95.2	3.7
1988	95.2	96.2	97.2	97.7	3.8	95.7	96.7	97.7	98.3	3.3
1989	98.9	100.0	101.8	102.6	5.0	99.2	100.0	101.7	102.5	4.3
1990	103.7	105.0	105.4	106.2	3.5	103.2	104.7	105.2	105.9	3.3
1991	108.2	109.6	110.3	111.2	4.7	107.9	109.2	109.8	110.5	4.3
1992	112.5	113.5	114.1	114.9	3.3	111.5	112.7	113.3	114.1	3.3
1993	116.0	116.8	117.6	118.7	3.3	114.7	115.5	116.3	117.5	3.0
1994	119.3	120.3	121.3	122.0	2.8	117.8	118.8	119.6	120.2	2.3
1995	124.4	125.1	126.2	127.1	4.2	122.2	122.9	123.7	125.7	4.6
1996	127.4	128.7	130.0	130.9	3.0	126.3	127.6	128.9	129.8	3.3
1997	132.6	133.7	134.5	135.4	3.4	131.8	132.8	133.9	135.0	4.0
1998	137.0	138.2	140.0	141.2	4.3	136.5	137.8	139.6	140.8	4.3
1999	142.4	144.0	145.8	147.4	4.4	141.9	143.0	144.8	146.4	4.0
2000	149.6	151.1	152.7	154.9	5.1	147.9	149.7	151.3	153.2	4.6
Retail trade										
1987	91.3	92.5	93.0	93.0	2.4	91.9	93.3	93.8	93.7	2.6
1988	94.5	96.3	97.3	98.4	5.8	94.8	96.6	97.7	98.5	5.1
1989	99.1	100.0	101.1	101.6	3.3	99.1	100.0	101.0	101.6	3.1
1990	103.0	104.8	105.5	106.0	4.3	102.7	104.4	105.0	105.3	3.6
1991	107.3	109.0	110.1	110.5	4.2	106.2	108.0	109.0	109.2	3.7
1992	110.8	112.1	112.9	113.4	2.6	109.3	110.6	111.3	111.8	2.4
1993	114.5	115.6	116.2	116.8	3.0	112.6	113.8	114.5	115.0	2.9
1994	117.5	119.2	120.4	120.1	2.8	115.2	117.0	118.0	117.8	2.4
1995	120.9	121.8	122.6	122.7	2.2	118.7	119.6	120.5	120.6	2.4
1996	124.5	124.8	126.2	127.4	3.8	122.8	123.1	124.4	125.8	4.3
1997	128.5	129.7	131.1	131.7	3.4	127.1	128.5	129.9	130.6	3.8
1998	133.1	134.4	135.9	135.6	3.0	131.9	133.3	135.2	134.8	3.2
1999	136.8	139.1	140.0	140.7	3.8	136.2	138.3	138.9	139.6	3.6
2000	143.2	144.8	146.2	146.6	4.2	142.1	143.5	144.8	145.2	4.0
General merchandise stores										
1988	...	97.2	98.5	99.6	...	...	95.6	97.0	98.2	...
1989	100.5	100.0	100.4	101.5	1.9	99.2	100.0	100.3	101.4	3.3
1990	102.6	105.7	105.9	106.9	5.3	102.4	105.2	105.6	106.5	5.0
1991	108.3	110.1	111.2	111.1	3.9	107.8	110.0	110.9	110.6	3.8
1992	111.7	112.9	113.3	113.3	2.0	111.1	111.7	111.7	111.8	1.1
1993	114.1	114.7	115.5	116.3	2.6	112.4	113.4	114.5	115.0	2.9
1994	115.3	118.0	118.7	119.3	2.6	114.0	116.4	116.5	117.5	2.2
1995	120.1	120.7	121.0	121.7	2.0	117.9	118.6	119.0	120.1	2.2
1996	122.4	123.6	124.6	126.3	3.8	121.0	121.7	122.6	124.7	3.8
1997	126.4	127.7	128.6	130.0	2.9	125.0	126.2	126.7	128.4	3.0
1998	131.2	133.0	133.2	134.0	3.1	129.4	131.5	132.2	133.0	3.6
1999	135.0	135.6	137.2	138.3	3.2	133.7	134.3	135.6	136.7	2.8
2000	139.7	141.0	142.2	144.4	4.4	137.8	138.5	139.7	142.2	4.0
Food stores										
1987	...	...	94.5	95.5	...	...	...	95.8	96.7	...
1988	96.3	96.8	97.1	98.2	2.8	97.3	97.8	98.2	99.0	2.4
1989	99.8	100.0	100.8	101.7	3.6	100.0	100.0	100.4	101.7	2.7
1990	103.2	104.6	105.7	106.4	4.6	102.8	104.3	105.1	105.8	4.0
1991	107.5	109.3	110.3	111.7	5.0	106.9	108.7	109.4	110.4	4.3
1992	112.6	113.6	114.2	115.1	3.0	110.9	112.3	112.9	113.7	3.0
1993	115.9	117.2	117.1	118.3	2.8	114.6	115.4	114.9	115.9	1.9
1994	119.6	120.6	120.3	120.0	1.4	117.0	117.8	117.4	117.3	1.2
1995	120.8	120.7	121.8	122.4	2.0	117.8	117.6	118.6	119.1	1.5
1996	123.6	124.4	127.0	128.4	4.9	120.5	121.2	123.1	124.7	4.7
1997	128.2	128.2	129.8	129.4	0.8	124.8	124.7	126.7	127.0	1.8
1998	131.3	132.9	133.7	132.7	2.6	129.0	130.5	131.7	130.5	2.8
1999	134.3	135.7	137.0	138.1	4.1	131.8	132.8	133.9	134.9	3.4
2000	140.1	142.5	143.4	144.5	4.6	136.7	139.5	140.2	141.6	5.0

See footnotes at end of table.

Table 5-1. Employment Cost Index, Private Industry Workers[1], Total Compensation and Wages and Salaries by Occupation and Industry, 1987–2000—*Continued*

(June 1989=100, not seasonally adjusted.)

Series and year	Total compensation					Wages and salaries				
	Indexes				Percent change for 12 months ended December	Indexes				Percent change for 12 months ended December
	March	June	September	December		March	June	September	December	
Finance, insurance, and real estate										
1987	90.9	90.0	90.2	90.4	2.0	91.9	90.6	90.8	90.6	1.2
1988	91.5	92.8	92.9	96.2	6.4	91.5	92.9	92.9	96.3	6.3
1989	98.3	100.0	100.4	101.4	5.4	98.3	100.0	100.6	101.3	5.2
1990	102.6	104.4	105.4	105.5	4.0	101.8	103.5	104.9	104.8	3.5
1991	108.3	109.5	109.7	110.0	4.3	107.0	108.1	108.0	108.4	3.4
1992	111.7	110.8	111.1	111.3	1.2	109.5	108.2	108.2	108.3	-0.1
1993	112.6	113.1	115.7	116.4	4.6	109.3	109.3	112.3	112.9	4.2
1994	117.7	117.7	118.5	118.9	2.1	113.7	113.2	113.8	114.2	1.2
1995	120.2	121.8	122.7	123.1	3.5	115.0	117.0	118.0	118.4	3.7
1996	124.5	126.3	126.7	126.0	2.4	119.8	121.9	122.2	122.2	3.2
1997	128.6	129.4	130.5	134.5	6.7	124.5	125.3	126.4	130.6	6.9
1998	136.7	138.4	141.0	142.5	5.9	132.6	134.8	138.1	139.8	7.0
1999	141.5	145.8	147.6	148.3	4.1	137.2	142.4	144.5	145.2	3.9
2000	152.0	153.1	155.2	155.7	5.0	148.7	149.5	151.7	151.7	4.5
Finance, insurance and real estate, excluding sales occupations										
1987	90.8	91.1	92.0	92.6	4.2	91.3	91.5	92.5	92.9	3.7
1988	93.8	94.6	95.4	97.1	4.9	93.8	94.5	95.3	97.1	4.5
1989	98.5	100.0	100.1	101.0	4.0	98.4	100.0	100.2	100.9	3.9
1990	103.5	104.7	106.3	106.7	5.6	103.0	103.9	105.8	106.1	5.2
1991	108.6	109.5	110.6	111.4	4.4	107.6	108.4	109.5	110.4	4.1
1992	112.5	112.2	112.5	113.0	1.4	110.6	109.9	109.9	110.2	-0.2
1993	114.9	116.4	117.5	118.2	4.6	112.0	113.1	114.0	114.6	4.0
1994	119.7	120.3	121.5	121.8	3.0	115.5	116.0	117.2	117.4	2.4
1995	123.7	124.6	125.4	125.7	3.2	119.3	120.2	121.1	121.3	3.3
1996	127.5	128.5	129.7	129.2	2.8	123.4	124.5	126.0	125.3	3.3
1997	131.5	132.4	133.5	137.6	6.5	127.2	128.1	129.3	133.6	6.6
1998	140.2	141.3	140.2	143.3	4.1	135.9	137.5	139.7	139.6	4.5
1999	145.6	148.8	151.0	151.0	5.8	141.0	144.8	147.5	148.0	6.0
2000	154.2	155.5	157.4	158.4	4.5	150.2	151.5	153.3	154.1	4.1
Banking, savings and loan, and other credit agencies										
1987	89.8	90.7	91.4	92.3	5.5	89.8	90.9	91.7	92.4	5.4
1988	95.3	96.0	97.0	97.8	6.0	95.2	96.0	97.0	97.8	5.8
1989	98.8	100.0	100.6	100.7	3.0	98.8	100.0	101.1	100.9	3.2
1990	102.1	104.1	104.4	105.8	5.1	101.6	103.6	103.9	105.4	4.5
1991	107.4	107.0	107.5	107.4	1.5	106.6	105.9	106.4	106.3	0.9
1992	110.2	110.0	111.0	111.4	3.7	108.2	107.7	108.6	109.0	2.5
1993	114.6	116.0	116.9	117.8	5.7	112.1	112.9	113.7	114.5	5.0
1994	118.7	119.4	120.8	120.5	2.3	114.7	115.0	116.5	116.2	1.5
1995	123.5	124.1	124.8	124.4	3.2	119.2	119.7	120.4	120.1	3.4
1996	126.9	128.2	130.3	128.0	2.9	122.7	124.2	126.8	123.8	3.1
1997	130.6	131.6	133.1	140.6	9.8	125.9	126.8	128.9	138.3	11.7
1998	143.3	145.3	148.4	146.7	4.3	140.9	143.2	147.0	144.4	4.4
1999	148.8	155.4	159.3	159.8	8.9	146.1	154.5	159.2	159.6	10.5
2000	162.7	164.2	165.8	166.5	4.2	162.0	163.3	165.0	165.7	3.8
Insurance										
1987	. . .	89.6	90.3	91.9	. . .	. . .	90.0	90.8	92.4	. . .
1988	92.6	95.0	95.8	97.0	5.5	93.1	95.4	96.2	97.4	5.4
1989	98.3	100.0	99.9	101.0	4.1	98.5	100.0	99.6	100.8	3.5
1990	103.2	105.2	106.5	106.0	5.0	102.3	104.1	105.8	105.1	4.3
1991	107.4	109.5	109.5	110.7	4.4	105.7	107.8	107.5	108.6	3.3
1992	113.2	114.7	114.9	115.2	4.1	111.2	112.7	112.7	112.7	3.8
1993	114.3	116.1	117.4	119.7	3.9	111.2	112.9	113.9	116.6	3.5
1994	119.9	120.5	121.5	122.3	2.2	116.0	116.8	117.7	118.6	1.7
1995	123.5	124.6	124.9	125.9	2.9	119.8	120.8	121.1	122.2	3.0
1996	127.6	128.2	129.3	129.6	2.9	123.6	124.1	125.4	126.0	3.1
1997	131.9	132.1	133.1	134.8	4.0	127.9	128.0	128.7	130.2	3.3
1998	137.4	138.9	141.9	141.7	5.1	133.1	134.8	138.7	138.5	6.4
1999	141.7	144.0	144.5	145.8	2.9	137.4	139.8	140.2	141.5	2.2
2000	149.9	151.3	154.8	155.2	6.4	145.5	146.6	150.7	150.8	6.6

See footnotes at end of table.

Table 5-1. Employment Cost Index, Private Industry Workers [1], Total Compensation and Wages and Salaries by Occupation and Industry, 1987–2000—*Continued*

(June 1989=100, not seasonally adjusted.)

Series and year	Total compensation: Indexes: March	June	September	December	Percent change for 12 months ended December	Wages and salaries: Indexes: March	June	September	December	Percent change for 12 months ended December
Insurance, excluding sales occupations										
1987	...	90.9	91.9	92.3	...	...	91.6	92.6	93.0	...
1988	93.8	95.3	96.5	97.3	5.4	94.4	95.8	97.0	97.6	4.9
1989	98.6	100.0	101.0	101.8	4.6	98.5	100.0	100.9	101.5	4.0
1990	104.5	106.1	106.8	107.6	5.7	103.8	105.2	105.9	106.5	4.9
1991	108.7	110.3	111.4	112.5	4.6	107.1	108.7	109.4	110.5	3.8
1992	113.9	115.7	116.1	117.2	4.2	111.7	113.4	113.8	114.9	4.0
1993	118.6	120.6	121.8	122.7	4.7	115.8	117.6	118.3	119.2	3.7
1994	124.4	125.0	126.0	126.5	3.1	120.6	121.4	122.3	122.7	2.9
1995	127.6	129.0	129.6	130.2	2.9	123.8	125.2	125.7	126.3	2.9
1996	132.1	132.7	133.4	133.5	2.5	128.0	128.6	129.3	129.7	2.7
1997	136.0	136.6	137.4	138.6	3.8	131.6	132.2	132.9	133.7	3.1
1998	140.0	140.9	141.6	142.5	2.8	134.7	135.7	136.6	137.9	3.1
1999	144.5	145.4	146.2	147.0	3.2	139.1	139.9	140.9	141.6	2.7
2000	149.4	150.5	152.2	153.1	4.1	143.2	144.1	145.7	146.5	3.5
Service industries										
1987	89.0	89.5	91.3	92.2	5.1	89.9	90.5	92.5	93.2	5.4
1988	93.6	94.5	96.4	97.5	5.7	94.2	94.9	96.9	97.8	4.9
1989	99.0	100.0	101.8	102.9	5.5	99.1	100.0	101.6	102.5	4.8
1990	105.0	106.5	108.1	109.3	6.2	104.2	105.7	107.1	108.3	5.7
1991	110.8	111.5	113.1	114.0	4.3	109.5	110.0	111.5	112.2	3.6
1992	115.3	116.4	117.8	118.9	4.3	113.2	114.0	115.2	116.1	3.5
1993	120.1	120.9	122.3	123.1	3.5	117.0	117.6	118.9	119.6	3.0
1994	124.4	124.9	125.9	126.6	2.8	120.8	121.3	122.2	123.0	2.8
1995	127.5	128.2	128.9	129.4	2.2	123.9	124.4	125.3	126.0	2.4
1996	130.7	131.7	132.7	133.4	3.1	127.6	128.7	129.7	130.5	3.6
1997	134.6	135.7	137.0	138.5	3.8	131.8	133.0	134.7	136.2	4.4
1998	139.3	140.3	141.8	142.7	3.0	137.2	138.3	140.0	140.8	3.4
1999	143.5	144.6	146.1	147.6	3.4	142.2	143.2	144.5	146.0	3.7
2000	149.4	151.2	152.9	154.1	4.4	147.4	149.1	150.6	151.8	4.0
Business services										
1987	88.5	89.5	91.7	92.5	6.1	89.1	90.2	92.8	93.5	6.7
1988	93.8	94.9	96.2	97.2	5.1	94.3	95.1	96.5	97.4	4.2
1989	98.1	100.0	100.7	101.3	4.2	98.4	100.0	100.9	101.2	3.9
1990	103.6	105.3	106.3	107.4	6.0	103.0	105.1	105.7	107.4	6.1
1991	110.3	110.4	110.0	111.1	3.4	109.6	109.5	108.9	110.0	2.4
1992	112.5	113.6	115.2	115.9	4.3	111.0	111.7	113.3	113.9	3.5
1993	116.5	117.4	118.1	118.6	2.3	114.2	114.6	115.3	115.7	1.6
1994	121.3	122.1	122.4	123.0	3.7	118.8	119.4	119.9	120.4	4.1
1995	124.5	125.3	125.7	126.3	2.7	122.1	122.9	123.6	124.3	3.2
1996	128.9	129.2	130.2	131.8	4.4	126.9	127.7	128.5	130.1	4.7
1997	133.3	134.2	136.3	138.6	5.2	131.4	132.4	134.9	137.3	5.5
1998	139.5	140.7	143.5	145.9	5.3	137.6	139.2	141.8	144.1	5.0
1999	147.5	148.7	150.7	151.9	4.1	145.4	146.3	148.5	149.8	4.0
2000	154.2	156.3	157.5	158.4	4.3	152.0	154.1	155.3	156.0	4.1
Health services										
1987	88.8	89.4	90.4	91.5	4.3	89.2	89.8	91.1	92.1	4.7
1988	92.6	94.1	95.6	97.0	6.0	92.7	94.4	96.0	97.3	5.6
1989	98.9	100.0	101.9	103.7	6.9	99.1	100.0	101.9	103.5	6.4
1990	105.8	107.1	109.0	110.8	6.8	105.3	106.3	108.1	109.7	6.0
1991	112.6	113.5	115.3	116.5	5.1	111.1	111.9	113.5	114.6	4.5
1992	117.9	118.9	120.6	121.8	4.5	115.6	116.3	117.9	118.9	3.8
1993	123.0	124.0	125.0	126.0	3.4	119.8	120.7	121.7	122.6	3.1
1994	126.7	127.1	127.9	128.7	2.1	123.1	123.5	124.3	125.4	2.3
1995	129.7	130.3	131.3	132.2	2.7	126.2	126.7	127.5	128.4	2.4
1996	132.6	133.5	134.2	134.5	1.7	129.3	130.1	130.8	131.4	2.3
1997	135.5	135.9	137.0	138.1	2.7	132.5	133.2	134.3	135.4	3.0
1998	138.2	138.7	139.0	139.0	0.7	136.2	136.5	137.5	137.4	1.5
1999	140.5	141.4	142.6	144.2	3.7	138.7	139.6	140.6	142.2	3.5
2000	145.8	147.5	149.0	150.6	4.4	143.5	145.3	146.6	148.1	4.1

See footnotes at end of table.

Table 5-1. Employment Cost Index, Private Industry Workers[1], Total Compensation and Wages and Salaries by Occupation and Industry, 1987–2000—*Continued*

(June 1989=100, not seasonally adjusted.)

Series and year	Total compensation					Wages and salaries				
	Indexes				Percent change for 12 months ended December	Indexes				Percent change for 12 months ended December
	March	June	September	December		March	June	September	December	
Hospitals										
1987	87.8	88.3	89.9	91.0	4.8	88.2	88.8	90.4	91.5	5.1
1988	92.2	93.6	95.2	96.6	6.2	92.5	94.0	95.6	96.9	5.9
1989	98.8	100.0	101.9	103.5	7.1	98.9	100.0	101.9	103.3	6.6
1990	105.4	106.6	108.9	110.7	7.0	105.0	106.0	108.2	109.8	6.3
1991	112.2	113.2	114.9	116.1	4.9	110.8	111.6	113.2	114.4	4.2
1992	117.7	118.5	120.2	121.6	4.7	115.4	115.9	117.3	118.3	3.4
1993	122.7	123.4	124.5	125.6	3.3	119.3	119.9	121.0	122.0	3.1
1994	126.7	127.1	127.7	128.6	2.4	122.8	123.3	123.9	124.8	2.3
1995	128.9	129.7	130.3	131.3	2.1	125.4	125.9	126.6	127.7	2.3
1996	132.2	132.8	133.4	133.7	1.8	128.5	129.1	129.7	130.3	2.0
1997	134.0	134.4	135.4	136.5	2.1	130.7	131.2	132.2	133.2	2.2
1998	136.7	138.2	139.1	139.9	2.5	133.6	134.7	135.8	136.5	2.5
1999	141.2	142.1	143.0	144.6	3.4	137.6	138.3	139.3	140.9	3.2
2000	145.8	147.5	149.2	151.1	4.5	141.8	143.3	144.9	146.8	4.2
Nursing homes										
1993	...	...	...	...	3.9	...	...	...	...	3.7
1994	...	...	...	...	3.3	...	...	...	...	3.6
1995	...	...	...	...	3.4	...	...	...	...	3.3
1996	...	...	...	...	2.6	...	...	...	...	2.8
1997	...	...	...	...	2.6	...	...	...	...	3.1
1998	...	...	...	...	3.2	...	...	...	...	3.7
1999	...	...	...	...	4.2	...	...	...	...	4.4
2000	...	...	...	...	6.1	...	...	...	...	5.8
Educational services										
1988	...	...	...	98.3	...	...	...	...	98.8	...
1989	99.1	100.0	103.9	104.2	6.0	99.1	100.0	103.7	103.9	5.2
1990	105.4	105.9	110.2	111.4	6.9	104.7	105.0	109.2	110.2	6.1
1991	111.9	111.5	114.9	115.7	3.9	110.3	109.7	113.0	113.7	3.2
1992	115.8	116.3	119.3	120.0	3.7	113.4	113.6	116.5	117.1	3.0
1993	120.5	120.6	123.8	124.1	3.4	117.5	117.4	120.7	120.9	3.2
1994	124.5	125.4	128.2	128.4	3.5	121.2	122.2	124.9	125.1	3.5
1995	128.8	130.3	133.2	133.7	4.1	125.6	125.9	128.6	129.4	3.4
1996	134.4	134.8	137.5	138.0	3.2	130.1	130.4	133.3	133.8	3.4
1997	138.5	138.8	141.6	142.6	3.3	134.5	134.8	137.8	138.4	3.4
1998	143.4	143.9	147.0	147.7	3.6	139.1	139.6	142.8	143.5	3.7
1999	148.3	148.7	152.2	153.0	3.6	143.9	144.2	147.5	148.2	3.3
2000	154.0	154.9	158.8	159.9	4.5	148.9	149.6	153.4	154.3	4.1
Colleges and universities										
1988	...	...	...	98.2	...	...	...	...	98.7	...
1989	99.0	100.0	103.3	103.8	5.7	99.1	100.0	103.3	103.7	5.1
1990	105.2	105.7	109.8	110.6	6.6	104.4	104.8	108.7	109.3	5.4
1991	111.3	112.0	115.5	116.3	5.2	109.6	110.2	113.7	114.2	4.5
1992	116.8	117.4	120.3	120.8	3.9	114.2	114.5	117.3	117.6	3.0
1993	121.5	121.5	125.0	125.3	3.7	118.0	117.7	121.3	121.6	3.4
1994	125.7	126.0	128.5	128.8	2.8	122.0	122.2	124.5	124.9	2.7
1995	129.3	131.3	134.6	135.2	5.0	125.5	125.9	129.0	130.1	4.2
1996	135.9	136.2	138.6	139.1	2.9	130.6	130.9	133.4	133.8	2.8
1997	139.5	139.9	142.5	143.7	3.3	134.6	135.0	137.8	138.7	3.7
1998	144.3	144.8	147.8	148.5	3.3	139.1	139.7	142.8	143.6	3.5
1999	149.2	149.6	152.6	153.3	3.2	144.1	144.4	147.2	147.9	3.0
2000	154.6	155.5	158.6	159.2	3.8	148.9	149.4	152.5	152.9	3.4
Nonmanufacturing Industries										
1987	90.9	91.5	92.4	92.9	3.6	91.7	92.3	93.3	93.7	3.4
1988	94.1	95.4	96.5	97.5	5.0	94.5	95.8	96.9	97.8	4.4
1989	98.8	100.0	101.3	102.3	4.9	99.1	100.0	101.4	102.2	4.5
1990	103.8	105.1	106.2	106.9	4.5	103.2	104.5	105.4	106.1	3.8
1991	108.5	109.7	110.9	111.5	4.3	107.3	108.4	109.3	109.8	3.5
1992	112.7	113.5	114.4	115.1	3.2	110.7	111.3	111.9	112.6	2.6
1993	116.3	117.2	118.4	119.0	3.4	113.4	114.2	115.4	116.0	3.0
1994	120.3	121.2	122.3	122.6	3.0	116.8	117.7	118.7	119.1	2.7
1995	123.7	124.6	125.5	125.9	2.7	120.0	120.9	121.9	122.5	2.9
1996	127.2	128.2	129.1	129.8	3.1	123.9	125.1	125.9	126.8	3.5
1997	131.1	132.1	133.3	134.7	3.8	128.2	129.3	130.7	132.1	4.2
1998	136.0	137.2	138.9	139.7	3.7	133.4	134.7	136.5	137.4	4.0
1999	140.3	142.0	143.4	144.5	3.4	137.9	139.7	141.0	142.1	3.4
2000	146.7	148.4	150.0	151.1	4.6	143.9	145.5	146.9	147.9	4.1

See footnotes at end of table.

Table 5-1. Employment Cost Index, Private Industry Workers[1], Total Compensation and Wages and Salaries by Occupation and Industry, 1987–2000—*Continued*

(June 1989=100, not seasonally adjusted.)

Series and year	Total compensation					Wages and salaries				
	Indexes				Percent change for 12 months ended December	Indexes				Percent change for 12 months ended December
	March	June	September	December		March	June	September	December	
Nonmanufacturing, white-collar occupations										
1987	...	90.8	91.8	92.2	...	...	91.7	92.7	93.0	...
1988	93.4	94.8	95.9	97.2	5.4	93.8	95.2	96.4	97.6	4.9
1989	98.8	100.0	101.4	102.6	5.6	99.1	100.0	101.5	102.5	5.0
1990	104.1	105.5	106.7	107.4	4.7	103.6	105.0	106.1	106.7	4.1
1991	109.1	110.4	111.5	112.1	4.4	108.0	109.2	110.2	110.6	3.7
1992	113.4	114.1	114.9	115.7	3.2	111.6	112.1	112.8	113.5	2.6
1993	117.0	117.9	119.0	119.9	3.6	114.4	115.2	116.4	117.2	3.3
1994	121.1	122.1	123.1	123.5	3.0	117.9	118.9	119.7	120.2	2.6
1995	124.7	125.6	126.5	127.0	2.8	121.1	122.1	123.1	123.8	3.0
1996	128.5	129.5	130.5	131.1	3.2	125.4	126.6	127.6	128.3	3.6
1997	132.7	133.6	134.9	136.5	4.1	129.9	131.0	132.4	134.1	4.5
1998	137.9	139.2	141.1	142.0	4.0	135.5	136.8	138.9	139.8	4.3
1999	142.3	144.1	145.6	146.9	3.5	140.1	142.0	143.5	144.7	3.5
2000	149.2	151.0	152.6	153.7	4.6	146.5	148.2	149.6	150.6	4.1
Nonmanufacturing, white-collar occupations, excluding sales occupations										
1987	...	91.0	92.3	92.9	...	...	91.7	93.1	93.7	...
1988	94.1	95.3	96.6	97.5	5.0	94.5	95.6	97.0	97.9	4.5
1989	99.0	100.0	101.4	102.3	4.9	99.2	100.0	101.3	102.0	4.2
1990	104.3	105.6	107.0	108.0	5.6	103.8	105.0	106.3	107.2	5.1
1991	109.5	110.6	112.1	112.9	4.5	108.5	109.4	110.7	111.5	4.0
1992	114.1	114.9	116.0	116.9	3.5	112.3	113.0	113.9	114.6	2.8
1993	118.5	119.4	120.4	121.4	3.8	115.8	116.6	117.6	118.5	3.4
1994	122.8	123.6	124.7	125.1	3.0	119.4	120.2	121.3	121.8	2.8
1995	126.4	127.1	128.0	128.6	2.8	122.9	123.5	124.4	125.4	3.0
1996	130.0	130.8	132.1	132.5	3.0	126.9	127.8	129.2	129.6	3.3
1997	134.0	135.1	136.2	137.9	4.1	131.2	132.4	133.8	135.5	4.6
1998	139.3	140.5	142.0	142.7	3.5	136.9	138.1	139.8	140.3	3.5
1999	143.7	145.3	146.8	148.1	3.8	141.6	143.2	144.6	145.9	4.0
2000	150.2	152.0	153.8	155.1	4.7	147.4	149.1	150.7	151.9	4.1
Nonmanufacturing, blue-collar occupations										
1987	...	92.9	93.7	94.5	...	...	93.5	94.3	95.0	...
1988	95.7	96.8	97.6	98.1	3.8	95.9	96.9	97.7	98.1	3.3
1989	98.8	100.0	101.1	101.7	3.7	99.0	100.0	101.0	101.3	3.3
1990	102.9	104.1	105.0	105.6	3.8	102.2	103.2	104.0	104.3	3.0
1991	107.2	108.2	109.2	109.8	4.0	105.5	106.3	107.1	107.5	3.1
1992	110.7	111.8	112.8	113.4	3.3	108.2	109.1	109.7	110.2	2.5
1993	114.6	115.6	116.6	117.1	3.3	111.1	111.9	113.0	113.4	2.9
1994	118.2	119.1	120.5	120.5	2.9	114.2	115.1	116.4	116.4	2.6
1995	121.5	122.5	123.5	123.7	2.7	117.5	118.5	119.4	119.8	2.9
1996	124.6	125.6	125.9	126.7	2.4	120.9	122.0	122.4	123.1	2.8
1997	127.5	128.6	129.4	130.1	2.7	124.1	125.5	126.4	127.1	3.2
1998	131.0	132.4	133.4	134.0	3.0	128.2	129.5	130.5	131.1	3.1
1999	135.2	136.8	138.0	138.7	3.5	132.4	134.0	135.1	135.8	3.6
2000	140.6	142.3	143.9	144.8	4.4	137.4	138.9	140.3	140.9	3.8
Nonmanufacturing, service occupations										
1987	...	92.4	92.8	93.3	...	...	93.6	94.1	94.4	...
1988	94.6	95.6	97.1	98.3	5.4	95.4	96.3	97.7	98.8	4.7
1989	99.2	100.0	101.0	102.4	4.2	99.4	100.0	100.8	102.3	3.5
1990	103.9	105.0	105.8	107.4	4.9	103.2	104.3	105.0	106.5	4.1
1991	108.4	109.9	111.7	112.5	4.7	107.1	108.4	110.0	110.7	3.9
1992	113.4	114.1	115.2	115.7	2.8	111.3	111.7	112.6	112.9	2.0
1993	116.8	117.7	118.6	119.1	2.9	113.4	114.1	114.8	115.1	1.9
1994	120.2	120.7	121.3	122.4	2.8	116.3	116.7	117.3	118.6	3.0
1995	123.0	123.5	124.2	124.7	1.9	119.2	119.8	120.6	121.2	2.2
1996	125.3	126.0	127.0	128.6	3.1	122.0	122.7	123.9	125.5	3.5
1997	129.4	130.5	132.7	133.8	4.0	126.4	127.4	129.7	130.9	4.3
1998	134.9	135.7	136.9	137.7	2.9	132.0	132.9	134.1	135.1	3.2
1999	139.2	140.4	140.7	142.3	3.3	136.5	137.7	137.9	139.5	3.3
2000	143.5	145.1	146.3	147.8	3.9	140.9	142.4	143.4	144.7	3.7

1. Excludes farm and household workers.
2. Includes mining, construction, and manufacturing.
3. Includes transportation, communication, and public utilities; wholesale and retail trade; finance, insurance, and real estate; and service industries.

Table 5-2. Employment Cost Index, State and Local Government Workers, Total Compensation and Wages and Salaries by Occupation and Industry, 1987–2000

(June 1989=100, not seasonally adjusted.)

Series and year	Total compensation					Wages and salaries				
	Indexes				Percent change for 12 months ended December	Indexes				Percent change for 12 months ended December
	March	June	September	December		March	June	September	December	
STATE AND LOCAL GOVERNMENT WORKERS, TOTAL										
1987	89.8	90.0	92.1	93.0	4.5	91.0	91.2	93.3	94.1	4.2
1988	94.2	94.5	97.1	98.2	5.6	95.0	95.2	97.7	98.7	4.9
1989	99.4	100.0	103.3	104.3	6.2	99.5	100.0	103.1	103.9	5.3
1990	105.8	106.5	109.4	110.4	5.8	105.1	105.7	108.6	109.4	5.3
1991	111.8	112.0	113.9	114.4	3.6	110.6	110.9	112.8	113.2	3.5
1992	115.2	115.7	117.9	118.6	3.7	113.8	114.2	115.9	116.6	3.0
1993	119.3	119.6	121.4	121.9	2.8	117.2	117.4	119.3	119.7	2.7
1994	122.6	123.1	125.0	125.6	3.0	120.4	120.7	122.8	123.4	3.1
1995	126.4	126.9	128.7	129.3	2.9	124.3	124.6	126.6	127.3	3.2
1996	129.9	130.2	131.9	132.7	2.6	127.8	128.1	130.1	130.9	2.8
1997	133.2	133.3	135.0	135.7	2.3	131.4	131.5	133.6	134.4	2.7
1998	136.5	136.9	139.0	139.8	3.0	135.1	135.4	137.6	138.5	3.1
1999	140.5	141.0	143.1	144.6	3.4	139.0	139.6	142.2	143.5	3.6
2000	145.5	145.9	147.8	148.9	3.0	144.3	144.7	147.2	148.3	3.3
WORKERS, BY OCCUPATIONAL GROUP										
White-Collar Occupations										
1987	89.4	89.6	91.9	92.8	4.6	90.7	90.8	93.1	94.1	4.6
1988	94.0	94.3	97.0	98.3	5.9	94.8	95.0	97.6	98.8	5.0
1989	99.5	100.0	103.6	104.6	6.4	99.6	100.0	103.4	104.2	5.5
1990	106.1	106.7	109.9	110.9	6.0	105.5	106.0	109.2	109.9	5.5
1991	112.2	112.3	114.2	114.6	3.3	111.0	111.2	113.1	113.5	3.3
1992	115.4	115.8	118.1	118.9	3.8	114.0	114.3	116.2	116.9	3.0
1993	119.5	119.6	121.5	121.9	2.5	117.5	117.6	119.6	119.9	2.6
1994	122.6	122.9	124.9	125.5	3.0	120.6	120.9	122.9	123.6	3.1
1995	126.2	126.6	128.6	129.1	2.9	124.4	124.6	126.8	127.4	3.1
1996	129.6	129.9	131.0	132.5	2.6	127.9	128.2	130.3	131.1	2.9
1997	132.9	133.0	134.8	135.5	2.3	131.4	[illegible]	133.7	134.5	2.6
1998	136.1	136.2	138.4	139.3	2.8	135.0	135.2	137.6	138.5	3.0
1999	139.8	140.2	142.6	144.0	3.4	138.9	139.3	142.1	143.4	3.5
2000	144.9	145.3	147.3	148.3	3.0	144.1	144.5	147.1	148.0	3.2
Professional specialty and technical occupations										
1989	. . .	100.0	103.8	104.7	. . .	. . .	100.0	103.7	104.4	. . .
1990	106.4	107.0	110.3	111.2	6.2	105.8	106.3	109.8	110.6	5.9
1991	112.3	112.4	114.5	115.0	3.4	111.5	111.7	113.8	114.2	3.3
1992	115.5	116.0	118.5	119.2	3.7	114.5	114.8	117.0	117.6	3.0
1993	119.6	119.7	121.7	122.0	2.3	118.1	118.2	120.4	120.7	2.6
1994	122.5	122.7	125.0	125.5	2.9	121.1	121.3	123.6	124.2	2.9
1995	126.0	126.3	128.4	128.8	2.6	124.8	125.0	127.4	128.0	3.1
1996	129.1	129.5	131.6	132.3	2.7	128.3	128.6	131.1	131.7	2.9
1997	132.5	132.5	134.6	135.1	2.1	131.9	132.0	134.4	135.1	2.6
1998	135.6	135.6	137.7	138.5	2.5	135.5	135.6	137.9	138.7	2.7
1999	138.8	139.3	142.0	143.2	3.4	138.9	139.4	142.5	143.6	3.5
2000	144.1	144.5	146.6	147.4	2.9	144.3	144.7	147.4	148.2	3.2
Executive, administrative, and managerial occupations										
1989	. . .	100.0	103.1	104.1	. . .	. . .	100.0	102.8	103.7	. . .
1990	105.7	106.4	109.3	110.1	5.8	104.9	105.7	108.4	108.9	5.0
1991	112.2	112.0	113.3	113.7	3.3	110.6	110.7	112.0	112.3	3.1
1992	115.0	115.2	116.8	117.8	3.6	113.3	113.5	114.7	115.5	2.8
1993	119.0	119.2	121.0	121.6	3.2	116.5	116.6	118.2	118.8	2.9
1994	122.8	123.4	124.7	125.3	3.0	119.8	120.3	121.6	122.4	3.0
1995	126.9	127.4	129.1	129.9	3.7	124.1	124.3	126.0	126.9	3.7
1996	130.7	131.0	132.0	132.9	2.3	127.7	128.0	129.3	130.2	2.6
1997	134.1	134.4	135.6	136.4	2.6	131.3	131.7	133.1	134.1	3.0
1998	137.5	137.9	140.4	141.6	3.8	135.1	135.6	138.0	139.3	3.9
1999	142.6	142.8	144.5	146.1	3.2	140.1	140.5	142.7	144.3	3.6
2000	147.0	147.2	149.2	150.7	3.1	144.9	145.1	147.3	148.8	3.1

See footnote at end of table.

Table 5-2. Employment Cost Index, State and Local Government Workers, Total Compensation and Wages and Salaries by Occupation and Industry, 1987–2000—*Continued*

(June 1989=100, not seasonally adjusted.)

Series and year	Total compensation					Wages and salaries				
	Indexes				Percent change for 12 months ended December	Indexes				Percent change for 12 months ended December
	March	June	September	December		March	June	September	December	
Administrative support occupations, including clerical occupations										
1989	. . .	100.0	102.9	103.9	. . .	. . .	100.0	102.4	103.0	. . .
1990	105.4	106.0	108.7	110.2	6.1	104.4	104.8	107.2	107.9	4.8
1991	111.8	111.7	113.5	114.0	3.4	109.4	109.7	111.4	111.8	3.6
1992	115.4	115.7	117.5	118.5	3.9	112.7	112.9	114.1	114.9	2.8
1993	119.2	119.6	121.0	121.6	2.6	115.4	115.9	117.2	117.8	2.5
1994	122.7	123.3	124.9	125.6	3.3	118.9	119.4	120.9	121.7	3.3
1995	126.3	126.9	128.4	129.1	2.8	122.5	122.9	124.4	125.1	2.8
1996	130.0	130.4	131.8	133.0	3.0	125.8	126.1	127.7	129.0	3.1
1997	133.3	133.5	135.3	136.1	2.3	129.2	129.5	131.4	132.3	2.6
1998	136.9	137.2	139.5	140.3	3.1	133.0	133.3	135.4	136.5	3.2
1999	141.4	141.3	143.0	145.0	3.4	137.4	137.5	139.6	141.7	3.8
2000	145.9	146.5	148.3	149.4	3.0	142.4	143.0	145.0	146.2	3.2
Blue-Collar Occupations										
1987	92.0	92.4	93.7	94.3	3.4	92.8	93.3	94.7	95.1	3.4
1988	95.4	95.4	97.0	97.5	3.4	96.1	96.1	97.8	98.2	3.3
1989	99.3	100.0	102.1	103.7	6.4	99.5	100.0	101.9	103.3	5.2
1990	105.5	106.3	108.2	108.7	4.8	104.3	105.3	107.2	107.7	4.3
1991	110.4	110.9	112.4	112.9	3.9	109.1	110.0	111.1	111.6	3.6
1992	114.2	115.3	116.9	117.8	4.3	112.5	113.7	115.0	115.6	3.6
1993	118.3	118.7	120.5	121.4	3.1	116.2	116.5	118.4	119.0	2.9
1994	122.3	122.7	124.2	124.7	2.7	119.7	120.1	121.8	122.5	2.9
1995	125.4	126.3	127.2	128.0	2.6	123.1	123.8	124.8	125.7	2.6
1996	129.0	129.5	130.3	131.2	2.5	126.6	127.0	127.9	128.8	2.5
1997	132.1	132.3	133.3	134.2	2.3	129.6	129.8	131.2	132.3	2.7
1998	135.0	135.2	136.8	137.8	2.7	133.1	133.5	135.1	136.0	2.8
1999	138.8	139.5	140.9	142.5	3.4	136.9	137.6	139.4	140.7	3.5
2000	143.7	144.2	145.9	147.2	3.3	141.5	142.1	143.9	145.1	3.1
Service Occupations										
1987	90.2	90.7	92.2	92.9	4.3	91.7	92.1	93.5	93.9	3.6
1988	94.4	95.1	97.9	98.2	5.7	95.1	95.9	98.4	98.7	5.1
1989	99.2	100.0	102.8	103.6	5.5	99.3	100.0	102.4	102.9	4.3
1990	104.8	105.3	108.1	109.2	5.4	103.9	104.2	106.7	107.6	4.6
1991	111.0	111.3	113.4	114.0	4.4	109.3	110.1	112.0	112.7	4.7
1992	115.0	115.6	117.4	118.0	3.5	113.2	113.7	114.9	115.5	2.5
1993	119.1	119.7	121.4	122.1	3.5	116.3	117.1	118.3	118.9	2.9
1994	123.1	123.9	126.0	126.6	3.7	119.7	120.4	122.7	123.3	3.7
1995	127.6	128.8	130.1	131.0	3.5	124.6	125.2	126.6	127.3	3.2
1996	131.9	132.3	133.6	134.5	2.7	128.1	128.6	130.1	131.0	2.9
1997	135.6	135.6	137.0	137.8	2.5	132.4	132.4	134.2	135.2	3.2
1998	139.4	141.0	143.0	143.4	4.1	136.5	137.2	139.2	140.0	3.6
1999	144.3	145.3	146.7	148.6	3.6	141.1	142.1	144.1	145.7	4.1
2000	149.5	149.7	151.5	152.9	2.9	146.4	146.6	149.6	151.2	3.8
WORKERS, BY INDUSTRY DIVISION										
Service Industries										
1987	89.0	89.2	91.7	92.5	4.4	90.3	90.5	93.0	93.8	4.2
1988	93.8	94.0	97.0	98.5	6.5	94.6	94.9	97.7	98.9	5.4
1989	99.5	100.0	103.8	104.7	6.3	99.6	100.0	103.6	104.3	5.5
1990	106.1	106.8	110.2	111.3	6.3	105.5	106.0	109.5	110.3	5.8
1991	112.4	112.6	114.8	115.3	3.6	111.3	111.5	113.7	114.1	3.4
1992	115.8	116.2	118.8	119.6	3.7	114.4	114.7	116.9	117.5	3.0
1993	120.0	120.2	122.2	122.6	2.5	118.1	118.2	120.3	120.6	2.6
1994	123.1	123.4	125.6	126.1	2.9	121.1	121.3	123.6	124.2	3.0
1995	126.7	127.1	129.2	129.6	2.8	124.9	125.1	127.6	128.2	3.2
1996	130.0	130.3	132.4	133.1	2.7	128.6	128.9	131.2	131.9	2.9
1997	133.2	133.3	135.4	136.0	2.2	132.1	132.2	134.7	135.3	2.6
1998	136.5	136.6	139.0	139.7	2.7	135.7	135.9	138.4	139.2	2.9
1999	140.0	140.5	143.2	144.5	3.4	139.5	139.9	142.9	144.0	3.4
2000	145.2	145.5	148.0	148.9	3.0	144.6	144.9	147.9	148.7	3.3

See footnote at end of table.

Table 5-2. Employment Cost Index, State and Local Government Workers, Total Compensation and Wages and Salaries by Occupation and Industry, 1987–2000—*Continued*

(June 1989=100, not seasonally adjusted.)

Series and year	Total compensation					Wages and salaries				
	Indexes				Percent change for 12 months ended December	Indexes				Percent change for 12 months ended December
	March	June	September	December		March	June	September	December	
Service industries, excluding schools										
1987	89.8	90.3	91.4	92.2	3.7	91.5	92.0	93.2	93.9	3.6
1988	94.7	94.8	96.5	97.8	6.1	95.4	95.5	97.3	98.2	4.6
1989	99.1	100.0	102.5	103.2	5.5	99.1	100.0	102.5	103.0	4.9
1990	105.4	106.4	108.8	110.2	6.8	105.4	106.4	108.8	109.6	6.4
1991	112.2	111.7	113.7	114.4	3.8	111.4	111.4	113.5	114.2	4.2
1992	115.1	115.6	117.5	118.6	3.7	114.8	115.2	116.4	117.4	2.8
1993	119.6	120.0	121.4	121.9	2.8	118.4	118.7	120.1	120.4	2.6
1994	122.8	123.3	124.9	125.6	3.0	121.3	121.9	123.2	124.0	3.0
1995	126.4	127.7	128.9	129.4	3.0	125.0	125.5	126.9	127.4	2.7
1996	130.3	130.8	131.9	132.0	2.0	128.2	128.7	130.1	130.5	2.4
1997	132.5	132.9	134.4	135.3	2.5	131.2	131.6	133.3	134.4	3.0
1998	136.1	136.2	138.7	138.8	2.6	135.4	135.5	137.8	138.2	2.8
1999	139.6	140.3	142.6	143.8	3.6	139.0	139.6	142.1	143.2	3.6
2000	145.2	145.8	147.6	148.8	3.5	144.3	144.8	146.7	147.9	3.3
Health services										
1987	89.5	90.1	92.0	93.0	4.7	89.9	90.5	92.3	93.2	4.4
1988	94.0	94.4	96.5	97.3	4.6	93.8	94.4	96.7	97.7	4.8
1989	98.8	100.0	103.1	104.2	7.1	98.9	100.0	102.7	103.7	6.1
1990	106.2	106.9	109.9	111.1	6.6	105.5	106.1	108.9	109.7	5.8
1991	112.6	112.2	113.9	114.9	3.4	111.1	111.7	113.0	114.0	3.9
1992	115.9	116.8	118.6	119.4	3.9	114.9	115.7	116.7	117.4	3.0
1993	120.2	120.7	122.2	123.1	3.1	118.1	118.8	120.4	121.0	3.1
1994	124.2	125.2	127.2	127.7	3.7	121.9	122.9	124.7	125.3	3.6
1995	128.4	129.8	131.0	131.6	3.1	126.0	126.6	127.9	128.6	2.6
1996	132.5	133.1	134.0	134.1	1.9	129.3	129.9	131.1	131.4	2.2
1997	134.5	134.9	136.0	137.2	2.3	132.1	132.6	133.9	135.3	3.0
1998	137.9	138.0	140.2	140.7	2.6	136.3	136.5	138.7	139.2	2.9
1999	141.2	142.0	144.2	145.8	3.6	139.7	140.4	142.8	144.2	3.6
2000	147.3	147.9	150.0	151.6	4.0	145.3	145.7	147.7	149.3	3.5
Hospitals										
1988	94.0	94.8	97.0	97.6	. . .	94.0	94.8	97.0	97.9	. . .
1989	98.6	100.0	103.2	104.5	7.1	98.7	100.0	102.9	103.8	6.0
1990	106.0	107.0	109.8	111.4	6.6	105.0	105.9	108.6	109.8	5.8
1991	112.2	112.1	114.1	115.2	3.4	110.7	111.3	112.9	114.1	3.9
1992	115.9	116.7	118.6	119.4	3.6	114.5	115.2	116.5	117.1	2.6
1993	120.0	120.4	122.0	123.3	3.3	117.6	118.2	119.9	120.7	3.1
1994	123.7	124.5	127.0	127.7	3.6	121.2	122.0	124.2	125.1	3.6
1995	128.4	129.9	131.1	131.7	3.1	125.8	126.3	127.6	128.4	2.6
1996	132.6	133.2	134.2	134.3	2.0	129.1	129.7	130.9	131.3	2.3
1997	134.8	135.2	136.3	137.6	2.5	131.9	132.4	133.7	135.2	3.0
1998	138.4	138.4	140.7	141.2	2.6	136.3	136.5	138.6	139.1	2.9
1999	141.7	142.7	144.8	146.3	3.6	139.7	140.6	142.8	144.1	3.6
2000	147.9	148.4	150.7	152.0	3.9	145.3	145.6	147.7	149.2	3.5
Educational services										
1989	99.5	100.0	104.1	104.9	. . .	99.6	100.0	103.8	104.5	. . .
1990	106.2	106.8	110.3	111.4	6.2	105.5	106.0	109.7	110.5	5.7
1991	112.4	112.6	114.9	115.3	3.5	111.3	111.5	113.8	114.1	3.3
1992	115.7	116.1	118.9	119.7	3.8	114.3	114.6	116.9	117.6	3.1
1993	120.0	120.1	122.3	122.7	2.5	118.0	118.1	120.3	120.6	2.6
1994	122.9	123.1	125.5	126.0	2.7	120.9	121.1	123.6	124.2	3.0
1995	126.5	126.8	129.0	129.4	2.7	124.8	124.9	127.7	128.3	3.3
1996	129.7	130.0	132.3	133.0	2.8	128.5	128.8	131.3	132.0	2.9
1997	133.1	133.2	135.4	135.9	2.2	132.1	132.2	134.8	135.3	2.5
1998	136.3	136.5	138.8	139.6	2.7	135.7	135.8	138.4	139.3	3.0
1999	139.9	140.3	143.1	144.4	3.4	139.5	139.8	142.9	144.0	3.4
2000	145.0	145.2	147.9	148.7	3.0	144.5	144.8	148.0	148.7	3.3

See footnote at end of table.

Table 5-2. Employment Cost Index, State and Local Government Workers, Total Compensation and Wages and Salaries by Occupation and Industry, 1987–2000—*Continued*

(June 1989=100, not seasonally adjusted.)

Series and year	Total compensation					Wages and salaries				
	Indexes				Percent change for 12 months ended December	Indexes				Percent change for 12 months ended December
	March	June	September	December		March	June	September	December	
Schools										
1987	88.7	88.9	91.8	92.7	4.9	90.0	90.0	92.9	93.9	4.7
1988	93.4	93.7	97.2	98.7	6.5	94.4	94.6	97.7	99.1	5.5
1989	99.6	100.0	104.4	105.3	6.7	99.7	100.0	104.0	104.7	5.7
1990	106.4	106.9	110.6	111.6	6.0	105.5	105.9	109.7	110.5	5.5
1991	112.5	112.9	115.2	115.6	3.6	111.2	111.5	113.7	114.0	3.2
1992	116.0	116.4	119.2	119.9	3.7	114.3	114.6	117.0	117.5	3.1
1993	120.2	120.3	122.5	122.9	2.5	117.9	118.0	120.3	120.7	2.7
1994	123.2	123.4	125.9	126.3	2.8	121.0	121.2	123.8	124.3	3.0
1995	126.8	127.1	129.4	129.8	2.8	125.0	125.1	127.8	128.4	3.3
1996	130.0	130.3	132.6	133.4	2.8	128.7	128.9	131.4	132.2	3.0
1997	133.4	133.5	135.7	136.2	2.1	132.2	132.3	134.9	135.5	2.5
1998	136.6	136.7	139.1	139.9	2.7	135.8	136.0	138.5	139.5	3.0
1999	140.2	140.6	143.5	144.7	3.4	139.6	140.0	143.1	144.2	3.4
2000	145.3	145.5	148.2	149.0	3.0	144.7	144.9	148.1	148.9	3.3
Elementary and secondary schools										
1987	88.6	88.7	92.1	92.9	5.0	89.7	89.8	93.1	93.9	4.7
1988	93.5	93.8	97.4	99.1	6.7	94.3	94.5	97.8	99.3	5.8
1989	99.6	100.0	104.6	105.5	6.5	99.7	100.0	104.2	104.9	5.6
1990	106.5	107.1	111.1	112.1	6.3	105.5	105.9	110.1	110.9	5.7
1991	112.9	113.0	115.7	116.2	3.7	111.6	111.7	114.3	114.7	3.4
1992	116.6	117.1	119.9	120.7	3.9	114.9	115.3	117.9	118.5	3.3
1993	120.7	120.8	123.0	123.6	2.4	118.7	118.8	121.1	121.6	2.6
1994	123.7	123.8	126.3	126.5	2.3	121.7	121.8	124.5	124.9	2.7
1995	127.1	127.4	129.8	130.1	2.8	125.5	125.8	128.7	129.2	3.4
1996	130.2	130.5	132.6	133.1	2.3	129.3	129.5	132.0	132.4	2.5
1997	133.1	133.3	135.5	135.8	2.0	132.4	132.6	135.3	135.7	2.5
1998	136.1	136.2	138.8	139.3	2.6	136.0	136.1	138.7	139.3	2.7
1999	139.6	140.0	142.9	144.1	3.4	139.5	139.9	143.1	144.1	3.4
2000	144.5	144.7	147.3	148.1	2.8	144.5	144.6	147.9	148.5	3.1
Colleges and universities										
1989	99.6	100.0	103.4	104.7	. . .	99.6	100.0	102.9	104.1	. . .
1990	106.1	106.3	109.2	110.2	5.3	105.6	105.9	108.4	109.2	4.9
1991	111.3	112.5	113.4	113.5	3.0	110.2	111.0	112.0	112.0	2.6
1992	114.0	114.1	116.9	117.2	3.3	112.3	112.3	114.1	114.3	2.1
1993	118.4	118.5	120.8	120.7	3.0	115.5	115.6	117.8	117.7	3.0
1994	121.5	122.0	124.5	125.5	4.0	118.6	119.2	121.5	122.5	4.1
1995	126.0	126.1	128.0	128.7	2.5	123.2	122.9	125.0	125.9	2.8
1996	129.4	129.9	132.5	134.0	4.1	126.8	127.1	129.8	131.2	4.2
1997	134.3	134.1	136.3	137.2	2.4	131.5	131.4	133.6	134.6	2.6
1998	137.9	138.1	140.1	141.5	3.1	135.2	135.5	137.7	139.6	3.7
1999	141.7	142.1	144.8	146.5	3.5	139.6	139.8	142.6	144.4	3.4
2000	147.4	147.6	150.5	151.7	3.5	144.9	145.6	148.3	149.5	3.5
Public Administration [1]										
1987	91.3	91.6	92.7	93.8	4.6	92.6	92.9	93.9	94.7	4.1
1988	95.2	95.8	97.5	97.8	4.3	95.8	96.4	98.1	98.4	3.9
1989	99.2	100.0	102.5	103.2	5.5	99.4	100.0	102.1	102.8	4.5
1990	105.1	105.5	107.8	108.7	5.3	104.3	104.6	106.5	107.3	4.4
1991	110.8	110.9	112.2	112.6	3.6	109.1	109.5	110.6	110.9	3.4
1992	114.0	114.6	115.8	116.3	3.3	111.9	112.4	113.1	113.6	2.4
1993	117.6	118.0	119.3	120.0	3.2	114.4	114.9	115.9	116.6	2.6
1994	121.5	122.2	123.7	124.2	3.5	117.9	118.5	119.9	120.6	3.4
1995	125.4	126.1	127.4	128.3	3.3	121.9	122.3	123.2	124.1	2.9
1996	129.2	129.6	130.7	131.8	2.7	124.9	125.3	126.6	127.7	2.9
1997	133.0	133.0	134.1	135.1	2.5	128.9	129.0	130.3	131.4	2.9
1998	136.4	137.4	138.9	139.9	3.6	132.7	133.2	134.8	135.9	3.4
1999	140.8	141.5	142.4	144.4	3.2	136.9	137.8	139.5	141.5	4.1
2000	145.7	146.1	146.9	148.3	2.7	142.5	142.9	144.6	146.1	3.3

1. Includes executive, legislative, judicial, administrative, and regulatory activities of state and local governments, SICs 91 through 96.

Table 5-3. Employment Cost Index, Benefits, by Occupation, Industry, and Bargaining Status, 1987–2000

(June 1989=100, not seasonally adjusted.)

Series and year	Indexes				Percent change for 12 months ended December
	March	June	September	December	
CIVILIAN WORKERS [1]					
1987	88.0	88.6	89.6	90.5	3.7
1988	93.2	94.3	95.7	96.8	7.0
1989	98.6	100.0	101.9	103.2	6.6
1990	105.9	107.2	108.9	110.1	6.7
1991	112.2	113.6	115.4	116.3	5.6
1992	118.6	119.6	121.4	122.5	5.3
1993	125.0	126.2	127.4	128.1	4.6
1994	130.1	131.0	132.3	132.5	3.4
1995	133.8	134.5	135.2	135.5	2.3
1996	136.2	136.9	137.7	138.2	2.0
1997	138.9	139.6	140.3	141.1	2.1
1998	142.0	143.0	144.0	144.7	2.6
1999	145.3	146.6	147.9	149.5	3.3
2000	152.6	154.3	155.8	156.9	4.9
PRIVATE INDUSTRY [2]					
1987	88.2	89.0	89.6	90.5	3.4
1988	93.4	94.7	95.7	96.7	6.9
1989	98.4	100.0	101.4	102.6	6.1
1990	105.5	106.9	108.3	109.4	6.6
1991	111.6	113.5	115.2	116.2	6.2
1992	118.6	119.7	121.2	122.2	5.2
1993	125.2	126.7	127.7	128.3	5.0
1994	130.7	131.7	132.8	133.0	3.7
1995	134.5	135.1	135.6	135.9	2.2
1996	136.6	137.4	138.1	138.6	2.0
1997	139.4	140.1	140.8	141.8	2.3
1998	142.6	143.7	144.5	145.2	2.4
1999	145.8	147.3	148.6	150.2	3.4
2000	153.8	155.7	157.6	158.6	5.6
White-collar occupations					
1987	88.2	88.9	89.7	90.5	3.7
1988	92.0	94.0	95.0	96.2	6.3
1989	98.3	100.0	101.4	102.6	6.7
1990	105.6	107.1	108.6	109.7	6.9
1991	112.1	113.8	115.3	116.4	6.1
1992	118.4	119.4	121.0	122.0	4.8
1993	124.7	125.9	126.8	127.6	4.6
1994	130.5	131.6	132.8	133.3	4.5
1995	135.2	136.0	136.6	136.7	2.6
1996	137.7	138.4	139.5	139.7	2.2
1997	140.8	141.5	142.0	143.4	2.6
1998	144.7	145.6	146.6	147.4	2.8
1999	147.9	149.4	151.0	152.5	3.5
2000	156.3	158.5	160.4	161.5	5.9
Blue-collar occupations					
1987	88.2	89.1	89.8	90.7	3.4
1988	94.2	95.7	96.5	97.4	7.4
1989	98.6	100.0	101.4	102.6	5.3
1990	105.2	106.6	107.9	109.0	6.2
1991	111.0	112.8	114.9	115.7	6.1
1992	118.7	119.7	121.2	122.2	5.6
1993	125.5	127.3	128.4	128.9	5.5
1994	130.5	131.5	132.7	132.5	2.8
1995	133.3	133.6	134.1	134.7	1.7
1996	135.2	136.1	136.2	137.0	1.7
1997	137.2	138.0	138.8	139.0	1.5
1998	139.1	140.4	141.0	141.6	1.9
1999	142.2	143.6	144.8	146.2	3.2
2000	150.0	151.6	153.1	154.1	5.4

See footnotes at end of table.

Table 5-3. Employment Cost Index, Benefits, by Occupation, Industry, and Bargaining Status, 1987–2000—*Continued*

(June 1989=100, not seasonally adjusted.)

Series and year	Indexes				Percent change for 12 months ended December
	March	June	September	December	
Service occupations					
1987	88.2	88.4	88.7	89.7	2.4
1988	92.1	93.4	95.1	96.8	7.9
1989	98.7	100.0	101.6	103.0	6.4
1990	106.0	107.0	108.1	109.9	6.7
1991	112.3	114.5	116.5	117.8	7.2
1992	120.0	121.6	123.7	124.6	5.8
1993	127.7	129.3	130.5	131.5	5.5
1994	132.9	133.1	134.2	134.7	2.4
1995	135.0	135.6	135.7	136.0	1.0
1996	135.7	136.3	136.2	137.4	1.0
1997	138.3	139.6	141.4	142.0	3.3
1998	143.3	143.7	144.7	144.8	2.0
1999	146.3	147.6	148.4	149.9	3.5
2000	150.8	152.7	154.4	156.4	4.3
Goods-Producing Industries [3]					
1987	88.7	89.4	90.0	90.9	2.9
1988	94.4	95.7	96.5	97.3	7.0
1989	98.7	100.0	101.5	102.6	5.4
1990	105.7	107.2	108.7	109.9	7.1
1991	111.9	113.9	115.8	116.7	6.2
1992	119.7	120.6	122.3	123.4	5.7
1993	127.3	129.0	130.0	130.3	5.6
1994	132.7	133.9	134.8	134.8	3.5
1995	135.9	135.9	136.2	137.1	1.7
1996	137.7	138.6	138.8	139.7	1.9
1997	139.9	140.9	141.5	141.5	1.3
1998	141.5	142.5	143.0	143.2	1.2
1999	144.3	145.2	146.3	148.2	3.4
2000	152.3	154.2	155.7	156.2	5.4
Manufacturing					
1987	87.5	88.2	88.8	89.8	2.6
1988	93.7	94.9	95.8	96.6	7.6
1989	98.8	100.0	101.6	102.3	5.9
1990	105.5	106.9	108.4	109.5	7.0
1991	111.2	113.3	115.3	116.1	6.0
1992	119.3	120.1	121.5	122.6	5.6
1993	126.8	128.6	129.7	130.0	6.0
1994	132.0	133.0	133.9	134.3	3.3
1995	135.4	135.2	135.5	136.7	1.8
1996	137.5	138.5	138.8	139.8	2.3
1997	139.9	141.0	141.4	141.7	1.4
1998	141.7	142.4	142.6	142.7	0.7
1999	143.6	144.5	145.7	147.8	3.4
2000	152.3	153.9	154.9	154.8	4.7
Aircraft manufacturing (SIC 3721)					
1988	. . .	. . .	. . .	99.0	. . .
1989	99.1	100.0	102.0	106.5	7.6
1990	110.1	111.4	114.5	111.9	5.1
1991	114.2	116.0	117.7	119.7	7.0
1992	124.1	127.3	128.9	135.1	12.9
1993	137.6	137.0	140.1	133.1	-1.5
1994	134.4	135.3	138.7	138.4	4.0
1995	141.0	140.8	140.5	146.1	5.6
1996	154.2	155.4	154.8	151.6	3.8
1997	148.6	148.8	147.6	143.0	-5.7
1998	141.7	143.1	143.8	145.3	1.6
1999	142.6	144.3	145.6	153.9	5.9
2000	161.9	166.6	168.7	163.1	6.0

See footnotes at end of table.

Table 5-3. Employment Cost Index, Benefits, by Occupation, Industry, and Bargaining Status, 1987–2000—*Continued*

(June 1989=100, not seasonally adjusted.)

Series and year	Indexes				Percent change for 12 months ended December
	March	June	September	December	
Aircraft manufacturing (SIC 3721), white-collar occupations					
1988	...	...	...	99.1	...
1989	98.9	100.0	101.7	105.7	6.7
1990	109.9	110.9	114.3	111.2	5.2
1991	113.1	115.1	116.4	119.2	7.2
1992	124.0	127.5	128.4	133.0	11.6
1993	136.2	135.4	138.7	132.5	-0.4
1994	133.5	134.7	138.0	137.3	3.6
1995	140.1	140.2	139.9	142.5	3.8
1996	152.0	152.9	152.1	150.9	5.9
1997	146.8	147.3	146.8	144.8	-4.0
1998	142.9	145.0	145.5	143.9	-0.6
1999	141.3	142.7	142.9	147.6	2.6
2000	156.8	163.6	165.4	162.8	10.3
Aircraft manufacturing (SIC 3721), blue-collar occupations					
1988	...	...	...	98.8	...
1989	99.2	100.0	102.3	107.4	8.7
1990	110.5	112.2	114.6	112.8	5.0
1991	115.5	117.1	119.3	120.4	6.7
1992	124.2	127.2	129.5	137.7	14.4
1993	139.3	139.0	141.9	133.5	-3.1
1994	135.0	135.6	139.0	139.2	4.3
1995	141.6	140.9	140.6	150.8	8.3
1996	156.7	158.4	158.4	152.2	0.9
1997	150.9	150.4	148.2	139.6	-8.3
1998	139.0	139.5	140.7	146.6	5.0
1999	144.2	146.3	149.5	163.0	11.2
2000	169.2	170.5	173.3	162.7	-0.2
Service-Producing Industries [1]					
1987	87.8	88.6	89.4	90.2	3.9
1988	92.5	93.8	94.9	96.1	6.5
1989	98.2	100.0	101.4	102.6	6.8
1990	105.3	106.6	107.9	109.0	6.2
1991	111.4	113.0	114.6	115.7	6.1
1992	117.7	118.8	120.4	121.2	4.8
1993	123.4	124.6	125.7	126.7	4.5
1994	128.9	129.7	131.2	131.5	3.8
1995	133.2	134.1	134.8	134.7	2.4
1996	135.5	136.2	137.2	137.4	2.0
1997	138.5	139.2	139.8	141.4	2.9
1998	142.7	143.8	144.9	145.7	3.0
1999	146.1	147.9	149.4	150.7	3.4
2000	154.0	156.0	157.9	159.4	5.8
Nonmanufacturing Industries					
1987	88.7	89.5	90.3	91.0	4.0
1988	93.2	94.5	95.5	96.8	6.4
1989	98.2	100.0	101.4	102.8	6.2
1990	105.4	106.9	108.2	109.3	6.3
1991	111.9	113.5	115.1	116.2	6.3
1992	118.2	119.4	121.0	122.0	5.0
1993	124.2	125.5	126.5	127.4	4.4
1994	129.9	130.8	132.2	132.3	3.8
1995	133.9	134.7	135.4	135.3	2.3
1996	136.0	136.7	137.5	137.9	1.9
1997	138.9	139.5	140.2	141.5	2.6
1998	142.7	143.9	145.0	145.8	3.0
1999	146.3	148.0	149.4	150.7	3.4
2000	154.0	156.1	158.1	159.7	6.0

See footnotes at end of table.

Table 5-3. Employment Cost Index, Benefits, by Occupation, Industry, and Bargaining Status, 1987–2000—*Continued*

(June 1989=100, not seasonally adjusted.)

Series and year	Indexes				Percent change for 12 months ended December
	March	June	September	December	
Union Workers					
1987	89.0	89.7	90.2	91.1	3.2
1988	94.9	96.1	96.9	97.5	7.0
1989	98.6	100.0	101.3	102.1	4.7
1990	104.6	105.6	106.7	108.2	6.0
1991	110.1	112.1	113.9	115.2	6.5
1992	119.2	120.0	121.7	122.5	6.3
1993	126.6	128.5	129.7	130.6	6.6
1994	131.9	132.9	133.3	133.7	2.4
1995	134.8	135.5	136.6	138.0	3.2
1996	139.1	140.0	139.9	140.7	2.0
1997	140.2	140.9	142.2	142.0	0.9
1998	142.1	143.8	145.0	145.5	2.5
1999	145.8	146.9	148.3	149.7	2.8
2000	153.7	155.5	157.4	157.5	5.2
Nonunion Workers					
1987	88.0	88.7	89.5	90.3	3.7
1988	92.6	94.0	95.1	96.3	6.6
1989	98.4	100.0	101.5	102.9	6.9
1990	105.8	107.4	108.9	109.9	6.8
1991	112.3	114.0	115.7	116.6	6.1
1992	118.4	119.5	121.0	122.1	4.7
1993	124.6	125.9	126.9	127.4	4.3
1994	130.1	131.1	132.6	132.7	4.2
1995	134.2	134.8	135.2	135.1	1.8
1996	135.8	136.5	137.4	137.8	2.0
1997	138.9	139.7	140.2	141.5	2.7
1998	142.5	143.4	144.2	144.9	2.4
1999	145.6	147.1	148.5	150.0	3.5
2000	153.6	155.5	157.3	158.6	5.7
STATE AND LOCAL GOVERNMENT					
1989	. . .	100.0	103.9	105.3	. . .
1990	107.5	108.3	111.3	112.7	7.0
1991	114.6	114.4	116.4	117.1	3.9
1992	118.5	119.3	122.3	123.4	5.4
1993	124.2	124.5	126.2	127.0	2.9
1994	127.9	128.5	130.3	130.5	2.8
1995	131.1	132.2	133.6	133.9	2.6
1996	134.7	135.1	136.1	136.8	2.2
1997	137.4	137.4	138.2	138.6	1.3
1998	139.7	140.3	142.1	142.7	3.0
1999	143.6	144.0	145.0	146.7	2.8
2000	148.2	148.5	149.0	150.2	2.4

1. Includes private industry and state and local government workers and excludes farm, household, and federal government workers.
2. Excludes farm and household workers.
3. Includes mining, construction, and manufacturing.
4. Includes transportation, communication, and public utilities; wholesale and retail trade; finance, insurance, and real estate; and service industries.

Table 5-4. Employment Cost Index, Private Industry Workers[1], Total Compensation and Wages and Salaries by Bargaining Status, Industry, Region[2], and Area Size, 1987–2000

(June 1989=100, not seasonally adjusted.)

Series and year	Total compensation					Wages and salaries				
	Indexes				Percent change for 12 months ended December	Indexes				Percent change for 12 months ended December
	March	June	September	December		March	June	September	December	
UNION WORKERS, TOTAL										
1987	92.5	93.0	93.6	94.5	2.7	94.3	94.8	95.3	96.4	2.7
1988	96.1	97.0	97.7	98.2	3.9	96.8	97.5	98.2	98.5	2.2
1989	99.0	100.0	100.9	101.8	3.7	99.2	100.0	100.6	101.6	3.1
1990	103.3	104.1	105.1	106.2	4.3	102.6	103.3	104.2	105.1	3.4
1991	107.5	108.8	110.1	111.1	4.6	106.2	107.1	108.0	108.9	3.6
1992	113.1	114.0	115.2	115.9	4.3	109.8	110.8	111.7	112.3	3.1
1993	117.8	119.1	120.0	120.9	4.3	113.1	113.9	114.8	115.7	3.0
1994	121.9	123.0	123.8	124.2	2.7	116.5	117.6	118.6	119.1	2.9
1995	125.1	125.8	126.8	127.7	2.8	119.8	120.6	121.5	122.2	2.6
1996	128.5	129.7	130.1	130.8	2.4	122.8	124.2	124.8	125.4	2.6
1997	131.0	131.8	133.2	133.5	2.1	126.0	126.9	128.3	128.9	2.8
1998	134.0	135.3	136.8	137.5	3.0	129.6	130.7	132.4	133.1	3.3
1999	138.0	139.0	140.2	141.2	2.7	133.6	134.7	135.7	136.5	2.6
2000	143.0	144.4	146.1	146.9	4.0	137.2	138.5	140.0	141.2	3.4
Union workers, blue-collar occupations										
1987	. . .	92.7	93.2	94.2	. . .	. . .	94.5	95.0	96.2	. . .
1988	96.1	97.0	97.6	98.3	4.4	96.5	97.2	97.8	98.4	2.3
1989	98.9	100.0	100.9	101.7	3.5	99.1	100.0	100.7	101.5	3.2
1990	103.0	104.1	104.8	105.9	4.1	102.2	103.2	103.8	104.8	3.3
1991	107.4	108.6	109.7	110.7	4.5	105.8	106.7	107.3	108.2	3.2
1992	112.9	113.8	114.8	115.5	4.3	109.1	109.9	110.8	111.3	2.9
1993	117.4	118.7	119.7	120.6	4.4	112.0	112.8	113.7	114.5	2.9
1994	121.2	122.4	123.1	123.4	2.3	115.1	116.2	117.3	117.6	2.7
1995	124.0	124.8	125.7	126.3	2.4	118.2	119.1	120.0	120.3	2.3
1996	126.8	128.0	128.3	128.9	2.1	120.9	122.0	122.8	123.4	2.6
1997	128.9	129.9	131.2	131.6	2.1	123.6	124.7	126.0	126.7	2.7
1998	131.8	133.3	134.6	135.3	2.8	127.2	128.5	129.9	130.6	3.1
1999	135.6	136.7	137.8	138.9	2.7	131.2	132.5	133.6	134.5	3.0
2000	141.1	142.5	144.3	145.0	4.4	135.2	136.5	138.2	139.2	3.5
Union workers, goods-producing industries[3]										
1987	91.8	92.3	92.9	94.2	3.0	93.7	94.3	94.8	96.3	2.9
1988	96.2	97.1	97.7	98.4	4.5	96.5	97.2	97.8	98.4	2.2
1989	98.9	100.0	100.9	101.9	3.6	99.0	100.0	100.6	101.6	3.3
1990	103.3	104.5	105.1	106.3	4.3	102.3	103.5	104.0	105.0	3.3
1991	107.9	109.2	110.3	111.3	4.7	106.2	107.1	107.7	108.7	3.5
1992	114.0	114.6	115.7	116.4	4.6	109.6	110.2	111.1	111.7	2.8
1993	118.7	120.0	121.0	121.9	4.7	112.2	113.0	113.8	114.8	2.8
1994	122.5	123.8	124.4	124.7	2.3	115.4	116.7	117.5	117.9	2.7
1995	125.2	125.9	126.7	127.5	2.2	118.4	119.3	120.2	120.6	2.3
1996	127.9	129.0	129.2	129.8	1.8	121.3	122.5	123.2	123.6	2.5
1997	130.0	131.2	132.3	132.5	2.1	124.1	125.4	126.6	127.1	2.8
1998	132.7	134.3	135.6	136.5	3.0	127.9	129.4	131.0	131.7	3.6
1999	136.8	138.2	139.2	140.8	3.2	132.3	133.8	134.9	136.1	3.3
2000	143.3	144.8	146.8	147.3	4.6	137.2	138.4	140.2	141.3	3.8
Union workers, service-producing industries[4]										
1987	93.4	94.0	94.4	95.0	2.5	95.2	95.5	96.0	96.5	2.0
1988	95.9	96.9	97.6	97.9	3.1	97.1	97.8	98.8	98.8	2.4
1989	99.1	100.0	100.8	101.7	3.9	99.6	100.0	100.7	101.7	2.9
1990	103.2	103.6	104.9	106.0	4.2	102.9	103.1	104.4	105.2	3.4
1991	107.1	108.3	109.8	110.9	4.6	106.1	107.0	108.4	109.2	3.8
1992	111.9	113.2	114.6	115.2	3.9	110.1	111.5	112.5	113.1	3.6
1993	116.7	117.7	118.6	119.6	3.8	114.2	115.1	116.0	116.8	3.3
1994	121.0	121.8	122.9	123.6	3.3	118.0	118.7	120.1	120.6	3.3
1995	124.8	125.6	126.8	127.9	3.5	121.6	122.3	123.2	124.2	3.0
1996	129.0	130.3	131.0	131.7	3.0	124.8	126.2	126.8	127.6	2.7
1997	131.9	132.4	134.0	134.5	2.1	128.2	128.8	130.4	131.2	2.8
1998	135.3	136.2	138.0	138.5	3.0	131.8	132.2	134.1	134.8	2.7
1999	139.2	139.7	141.0	141.4	2.1	135.4	135.8	136.8	137.2	1.8
2000	142.5	143.9	145.2	146.4	3.5	137.6	138.9	140.1	141.5	3.1

See footnotes at end of table.

Table 5-4. Employment Cost Index, Private Industry Workers[1], Total Compensation and Wages and Salaries by Bargaining Status, Industry, Region[2], and Area Size, 1987–2000—*Continued*

(June 1989=100, not seasonally adjusted.)

Series and year	Total compensation: Indexes, March	June	September	December	Percent change for 12 months ended December	Wages and salaries: Indexes, March	June	September	December	Percent change for 12 months ended December
Union workers, manufacturing industries										
1987	90.6	91.1	91.6	93.1	2.9	93.5	93.9	94.5	96.2	3.0
1988	95.5	96.4	97.0	97.8	5.0	96.4	97.0	97.5	98.3	2.2
1989	99.0	100.0	100.8	102.0	4.3	99.0	100.0	100.5	101.7	3.5
1990	103.6	104.7	105.3	106.6	4.5	102.6	103.8	104.3	105.5	3.7
1991	108.1	109.5	110.6	111.7	4.8	106.7	107.5	108.3	109.4	3.7
1992	114.8	115.2	116.1	116.9	4.7	110.4	110.9	111.7	112.5	2.8
1993	119.8	121.1	121.9	123.0	5.2	113.2	113.9	114.6	115.9	3.0
1994	123.6	124.8	125.3	125.8	2.3	116.6	117.8	118.5	119.2	2.8
1995	126.3	126.6	127.1	128.1	1.8	119.8	120.5	121.3	122.0	2.3
1996	128.8	129.8	129.8	130.6	2.0	122.9	123.9	124.5	125.2	2.6
1997	130.8	131.7	133.0	133.3	2.1	125.6	126.5	127.8	128.6	2.7
1998	133.6	134.6	136.0	136.9	2.7	129.6	130.4	132.2	133.0	3.4
1999	137.0	138.1	139.1	141.0	3.0	133.6	134.7	135.8	137.5	3.4
2000	144.5	145.4	147.1	147.4	4.5	138.8	139.7	141.4	142.6	3.7
Union workers, manufacturing, blue-collar occupations										
1987	...	90.9	91.5	93.0	...	...	93.8	94.4	96.2	...
1988	95.5	96.4	96.9	97.8	5.2	96.4	97.0	97.5	98.3	2.2
1989	99.0	100.0	100.9	101.9	4.2	99.0	100.0	100.6	101.8	3.6
1990	103.5	104.6	105.1	106.5	4.5	102.6	103.8	104.2	105.4	3.5
1991	108.1	109.4	110.6	111.6	4.8	106.6	107.5	108.2	109.3	3.7
1992	114.7	115.1	116.0	116.8	4.7	110.3	110.8	111.6	112.4	2.8
1993	119.6	121.0	121.8	122.9	5.2	113.1	113.8	114.4	115.7	2.9
1994	123.5	124.6	125.1	125.6	2.2	116.4	117.6	118.3	118.9	2.8
1995	126.1	126.4	126.8	127.8	1.8	119.5	120.2	121.0	121.6	2.3
1996	128.3	129.4	129.5	130.1	1.8	122.4	123.5	124.2	125.0	2.8
1997	130.5	131.4	132.6	133.0	2.2	125.4	126.2	127.6	128.4	2.7
1998	133.1	134.2	135.5	136.4	2.6	129.0	130.0	131.4	132.4	3.1
1999	136.5	137.5	138.5	140.4	2.9	133.0	134.1	135.1	136.8	3.3
2000	143.9	144.8	146.5	147.0	4.7	137.8	138.7	140.4	141.7	3.6
Union workers, nonmanufacturing industries										
1987	94.0	94.7	95.2	95.8	2.7	95.1	95.5	96.0	96.5	2.1
1988	96.6	97.5	98.3	98.5	2.8	97.0	97.9	98.8	98.8	2.4
1989	98.9	100.0	100.8	101.6	3.1	99.4	100.0	100.7	101.5	2.7
1990	103.0	103.7	104.9	105.9	4.2	102.5	103.0	104.1	104.8	3.3
1991	107.1	108.3	109.7	110.6	4.4	105.8	106.7	107.9	108.6	3.6
1992	111.8	113.1	114.5	115.1	4.1	109.4	110.7	111.7	112.2	3.3
1993	116.3	117.4	118.5	119.3	3.6	113.0	113.9	114.9	115.5	2.9
1994	120.5	121.5	122.6	123.0	3.1	116.4	117.3	118.6	119.0	3.0
1995	124.0	125.0	126.2	127.1	3.3	119.9	120.6	121.6	122.3	2.8
1996	128.0	129.2	129.9	130.4	2.6	122.8	124.3	124.9	125.5	2.6
1997	130.6	131.5	132.9	133.2	2.1	126.1	127.1	128.6	129.1	2.9
1998	133.9	135.3	136.9	137.4	3.2	129.6	130.8	132.4	133.1	3.1
1999	138.1	139.2	140.3	140.8	2.5	133.7	134.6	135.6	135.9	2.1
2000	141.7	143.4	145.0	146.2	3.8	136.4	137.8	139.2	140.4	3.3
NONUNION WORKERS, TOTAL										
1987	90.5	91.1	92.1	92.7	3.7	91.3	92.0	93.0	93.5	3.7
1988	94.0	95.3	96.3	97.4	5.1	94.5	95.6	96.6	97.7	4.5
1989	98.8	100.0	101.4	102.4	5.1	99.0	100.0	101.3	102.1	4.5
1990	104.1	105.5	106.6	107.3	4.8	103.4	104.8	105.8	106.4	4.2
1991	108.8	110.1	111.2	111.9	4.3	107.6	108.7	109.7	110.3	3.7
1992	113.1	113.8	114.7	115.5	3.2	111.2	111.8	112.4	113.1	2.5
1993	116.8	117.7	118.8	119.5	3.5	114.1	114.8	115.9	116.6	3.1
1994	120.7	121.7	122.7	123.2	3.1	117.4	118.3	119.2	119.8	2.7
1995	124.3	125.2	126.0	126.5	2.7	120.8	121.8	122.6	123.3	2.9
1996	127.7	128.7	129.7	130.4	3.1	124.8	125.9	126.9	127.7	3.6
1997	131.8	132.8	133.9	135.3	3.8	129.1	130.3	131.6	133.0	4.2
1998	136.7	137.8	139.3	140.1	3.5	134.5	135.7	137.4	138.3	4.0
1999	140.8	142.5	143.8	145.2	3.6	139.0	140.7	142.0	143.3	3.6
2000	147.4	149.1	150.6	151.6	4.4	145.1	146.7	148.1	149.0	4.0

See footnotes at end of table.

Table 5-4. Employment Cost Index, Private Industry Workers[1], Total Compensation and Wages and Salaries by Bargaining Status, Industry, Region[2], and Area Size, 1987–2000—*Continued*

(June 1989=100, not seasonally adjusted.)

Series and year	Total compensation					Wages and salaries				
	Indexes				Percent change for 12 months ended December	Indexes				Percent change for 12 months ended December
	March	June	September	December		March	June	September	December	
Nonunion workers, blue-collar occupations										
1987	. . .	91.6	92.6	93.3	. . .	. . .	92.6	93.7	94.2	. . .
1988	94.6	96.0	96.6	97.5	4.5	95.3	96.4	97.0	97.8	3.8
1989	98.7	100.0	101.3	102.1	4.7	98.8	100.0	101.2	101.7	4.0
1990	103.9	105.3	106.3	106.8	4.6	103.0	104.3	105.1	105.5	3.7
1991	108.3	109.4	110.6	111.2	4.1	106.8	107.7	108.5	109.2	3.5
1992	112.2	113.0	113.9	114.6	3.1	110.1	110.8	111.3	111.9	2.5
1993	115.9	116.9	117.8	118.2	3.1	112.8	113.6	114.4	115.0	2.8
1994	119.6	120.4	121.7	121.9	3.1	115.9	116.7	117.7	118.3	2.9
1995	123.0	123.9	124.5	125.1	2.6	119.5	120.7	121.4	122.1	3.2
1996	126.3	127.3	127.8	128.9	3.0	123.6	124.7	125.2	126.3	3.4
1997	129.9	131.2	131.8	132.6	2.9	127.5	128.9	129.7	130.6	3.4
1998	133.8	134.7	135.5	136.3	2.8	132.0	132.9	134.0	134.8	3.2
1999	137.6	139.0	140.3	141.4	3.7	136.2	137.5	138.7	139.7	3.6
2000	143.4	144.9	146.1	147.2	4.1	141.4	142.9	144.1	144.9	3.7
Nonunion workers, goods-producing industries[3]										
1987	91.3	92.0	92.9	93.6	3.1	92.3	92.9	94.0	94.7	3.4
1988	95.1	96.2	96.9	97.7	4.4	95.8	96.8	97.3	98.1	3.6
1989	98.9	100.0	101.3	102.3	4.7	99.1	100.0	101.1	102.1	4.1
1990	104.2	105.5	106.7	107.4	5.0	103.5	104.5	105.5	106.1	3.9
1991	108.8	110.1	111.3	112.2	4.5	107.3	108.3	109.2	110.1	3.8
1992	113.3	114.1	115.1	116.0	3.4	111.2	111.9	112.6	113.3	2.9
1993	117.7	118.6	119.4	119.9	3.4	114.4	115.2	116.0	116.7	3.0
1994	121.5	122.6	123.6	124.1	3.5	117.6	118.6	119.5	120.3	3.1
1995	125.2	125.9	126.4	127.2	2.5	121.3	122.2	122.9	123.8	2.9
1996	128.3	129.4	130.4	131.3	3.2	124.9	126.1	127.3	128.0	3.4
1997	132.0	133.2	134.0	134.7	2.6	128.9	130.2	131.2	132.0	3.1
1998	135.9	[illegible]	[illegible]	[illegible]	[illegible]	133.6	134.7	135.7	136.5	3.4
1999	139.7	140.5	141.8	143.1	3.5	137.8	[illegible]	[illegible]	[illegible]	[illegible]
2000	145.4	147.2	148.4	149.3	4.3	142.9	144.7	145.8	146.8	4.0
Nonunion workers, service-producing industries[4]										
1987	89.9	90.6	91.6	92.1	4.0	90.8	91.4	92.5	92.9	3.8
1988	93.4	94.7	95.9	97.2	5.5	93.8	95.1	96.3	97.6	5.1
1989	98.7	100.0	101.5	102.4	5.3	98.9	100.0	101.4	102.2	4.7
1990	103.9	105.5	106.5	107.2	4.7	103.4	104.9	105.9	106.5	4.2
1991	108.8	110.1	111.2	111.8	4.3	107.8	108.9	109.9	110.4	3.7
1993	116.3	117.2	118.4	119.2	3.5	113.8	114.6	115.9	116.6	3.2
1994	120.3	121.1	122.2	122.7	2.9	117.2	118.1	119.0	119.5	2.5
1995	123.8	124.8	125.6	126.0	2.7	120.5	121.5	122.4	123.0	2.9
1996	127.3	128.3	129.2	129.9	3.1	124.6	125.7	126.6	127.5	3.7
1997	131.5	132.5	133.7	135.3	4.2	129.1	130.2	131.6	133.2	4.5
1998	136.7	138.0	139.7	140.6	3.9	134.6	135.9	137.9	138.8	4.2
1999	141.1	143.0	144.4	145.7	3.6	139.3	141.3	142.6	143.9	3.7
2000	148.0	149.6	151.2	152.3	4.5	145.8	147.3	148.7	149.6	4.0
Nonunion workers, manufacturing industries										
1987	91.3	92.0	93.0	93.6	3.2	92.4	93.0	94.1	94.7	3.4
1988	95.2	96.1	96.8	97.6	4.3	95.8	96.7	97.2	98.0	3.5
1989	98.8	100.0	101.2	102.1	4.6	98.9	100.0	101.0	102.0	4.1
1990	104.2	105.5	106.9	107.6	5.4	103.6	104.8	105.9	106.5	4.4
1991	108.8	110.2	111.5	112.4	4.5	107.7	108.8	109.7	110.7	3.9
1992	113.6	114.5	115.5	116.4	3.6	111.9	112.7	113.4	114.2	3.2
1993	118.1	119.0	120.0	120.6	3.6	115.4	116.1	117.0	117.9	3.2
1994	122.0	122.9	124.0	124.8	3.5	118.6	119.5	120.5	121.5	3.1
1995	126.1	126.9	127.3	128.3	2.8	122.7	123.8	124.3	125.2	3.0
1996	129.3	130.5	131.7	132.5	3.3	126.3	127.5	128.8	129.6	3.5
1997	133.1	134.4	135.1	135.9	2.6	130.3	131.7	132.6	133.5	3.0
1998	137.2	138.0	138.9	139.4	2.6	135.1	136.2	137.3	138.2	3.5
1999	140.7	141.7	143.0	144.4	3.5	139.4	140.5	141.7	142.9	3.4
2000	146.5	148.2	149.2	149.9	3.8	144.4	146.1	147.2	148.0	3.6

See footnotes at end of table.

Table 5-4. Employment Cost Index, Private Industry Workers[1], Total Compensation and Wages and Salaries by Bargaining Status, Industry, Region[2], and Area Size, 1987–2000—*Continued*

(June 1989=100, not seasonally adjusted.)

Series and year	Total compensation					Wages and salaries				
	Indexes				Percent change for 12 months ended December	Indexes				Percent change for 12 months ended December
	March	June	September	December		March	June	September	December	
Nonunion workers, manufacturing, blue-collar occupations										
1987	...	91.8	92.8	93.2	...	...	93.1	94.2	94.4	...
1988	94.6	95.7	96.4	97.4	4.5	95.4	96.3	96.8	97.8	3.6
1989	98.7	100.0	101.4	102.4	5.1	98.7	100.0	101.2	102.2	4.5
1990	104.4	105.9	107.2	107.9	5.4	103.6	105.0	106.0	106.7	4.4
1991	109.0	110.3	111.7	112.5	4.3	107.9	108.8	109.7	110.7	3.7
1992	113.8	114.6	115.5	116.2	3.3	111.9	112.5	113.1	113.7	2.7
1993	117.5	118.4	119.4	119.9	3.2	114.6	115.2	116.0	116.7	2.6
1994	121.2	121.9	123.0	123.5	3.0	117.5	118.1	119.1	120.0	2.8
1995	124.5	125.5	125.7	127.0	2.8	121.2	122.6	123.1	124.2	3.5
1996	128.1	129.3	130.3	131.4	3.5	125.4	126.7	127.8	128.8	3.7
1997	132.2	133.5	134.2	134.8	2.6	129.8	131.2	132.0	133.0	3.3
1998	136.0	136.7	137.4	138.3	2.6	134.4	135.1	136.2	137.2	3.2
1999	139.5	140.2	141.6	142.9	3.3	138.5	139.2	140.5	141.6	3.2
2000	144.4	145.8	146.7	148.0	3.6	142.8	144.2	145.4	146.6	3.5
Nonunion workers, nonmanufacturing industries										
1987	90.1	90.7	91.8	92.2	3.7	90.9	91.6	92.7	93.0	3.7
1988	93.5	94.9	96.0	97.3	5.5	94.0	95.3	96.4	97.7	5.1
1989	98.8	100.0	101.4	102.4	5.2	99.0	100.0	101.4	102.3	4.7
1990	104.0	105.4	106.5	107.2	4.7	103.3	104.8	105.7	106.3	3.9
1991	108.8	110.1	111.2	111.7	4.2	107.6	108.7	109.6	110.1	3.6
1992	112.9	113.5	114.3	115.1	3.0	110.9	111.4	112.0	112.7	2.4
1993	116.3	117.2	118.3	119.0	3.4	113.5	114.3	115.5	116.1	3.0
1994	120.2	121.1	122.2	122.5	2.9	116.9	117.8	118.7	119.1	2.6
1995	123.6	124.5	125.3	125.7	2.6	120.0	121.0	121.9	122.6	2.9
1996	127.0	128.0	128.9	129.6	3.1	124.2	125.2	126.1	127.0	3.6
1997	131.1	132.2	133.4	134.9	4.1	128.5	129.7	131.1	132.6	4.4
1998	136.3	137.5	139.1	140.0	3.8	134.0	135.3	137.1	138.0	4.1
1999	140.6	142.4	143.8	145.1	3.6	138.6	140.5	141.8	143.0	3.6
2000	147.4	149.1	150.7	151.8	4.6	145.0	146.6	148.0	148.9	4.1
WORKERS BY REGION										
Northeast										
1987	88.4	89.1	90.2	91.3	5.1	89.1	89.9	91.0	91.9	4.9
1988	92.4	93.8	95.0	96.7	5.9	92.7	94.0	95.1	96.9	5.4
1989	98.7	100.0	101.8	102.9	6.4	98.7	100.0	101.8	102.9	6.2
1990	104.4	105.3	106.5	107.6	4.6	104.0	104.8	105.9	106.9	3.9
1991	109.4	110.6	111.7	112.5	4.6	108.3	109.4	110.3	110.9	3.7
1992	113.9	114.5	115.5	116.4	3.5	111.7	112.2	113.0	113.7	2.5
1993	117.8	119.1	120.2	120.7	3.7	114.6	115.7	116.8	117.3	3.2
1994	121.6	122.8	124.0	124.3	3.0	117.8	118.8	120.0	120.2	2.5
1995	125.6	126.6	127.4	127.8	2.8	121.3	122.1	123.1	123.6	2.8
1996	128.9	129.7	130.6	131.1	2.6	124.9	126.0	127.0	127.7	3.3
1997	132.2	133.1	134.0	135.0	3.0	128.8	129.8	130.7	131.6	3.1
1998	136.0	137.0	138.7	139.5	3.3	132.6	133.8	135.4	136.4	3.6
1999	140.5	141.5	143.2	144.3	3.4	137.1	138.2	139.9	140.9	3.3
2000	146.3	147.6	149.3	150.3	4.2	142.3	143.7	145.3	146.0	3.6
South										
1987	91.7	92.4	93.1	94.0	3.1	92.9	93.6	94.4	95.0	2.8
1988	95.1	96.7	97.4	98.1	4.4	95.7	97.2	97.9	98.4	3.6
1989	99.0	100.0	101.2	102.2	4.2	99.2	100.0	101.2	102.1	3.8
1990	104.0	105.7	106.3	106.9	4.6	103.5	105.2	105.7	106.1	3.9
1991	108.4	109.8	110.7	111.2	4.0	107.4	108.5	109.2	109.6	3.3
1992	112.5	113.3	114.1	114.8	3.2	110.8	111.5	112.0	112.7	2.8
1993	116.2	117.0	118.1	118.8	3.5	113.6	114.3	115.3	116.0	2.9
1994	120.0	120.8	121.8	122.5	3.1	116.6	117.4	118.5	119.1	2.7
1995	123.7	124.3	125.2	125.6	2.5	120.0	120.8	121.8	122.4	2.8
1996	127.0	127.8	128.8	129.7	3.3	124.1	125.1	126.0	127.0	3.8
1997	130.8	131.5	132.5	134.6	3.8	128.5	129.4	130.6	133.0	4.7
1998	135.5	136.4	137.6	138.1	2.6	134.0	134.9	136.5	136.7	2.8
1999	139.1	140.7	141.8	143.0	3.5	137.9	139.4	140.2	141.5	3.5
2000	145.0	146.7	147.6	148.6	3.9	143.0	144.6	145.3	146.3	3.4

See footnotes at end of table.

Table 5-4. Employment Cost Index, Private Industry Workers[1], Total Compensation and Wages and Salaries by Bargaining Status, Industry, Region[2], and Area Size, 1987–2000—*Continued*

(June 1989=100, not seasonally adjusted.)

Series and year	Total compensation					Wages and salaries				
	Indexes				Percent change for 12 months ended December	Indexes				Percent change for 12 months ended December
	March	June	September	December		March	June	September	December	
Midwest										
1987	91.6	92.4	93.1	93.5	2.9	93.1	93.9	94.7	94.9	2.9
1988	95.4	96.2	97.0	97.9	4.7	95.9	96.5	97.4	98.2	3.5
1989	98.9	100.0	101.0	101.9	4.1	99.1	100.0	100.8	101.6	3.5
1990	103.5	104.8	106.3	107.1	5.1	102.6	103.7	105.1	105.8	4.1
1991	108.5	109.7	111.2	112.2	4.8	106.9	107.7	108.9	109.9	3.9
1992	113.8	114.6	115.3	116.1	3.5	110.7	111.3	111.8	112.5	2.4
1993	117.9	119.3	120.1	121.2	4.4	113.5	114.6	115.2	116.5	3.6
1994	122.8	123.6	124.6	125.0	3.1	117.5	118.3	119.5	120.1	3.1
1995	125.8	126.9	127.7	128.3	2.6	120.9	122.2	123.0	123.6	2.9
1996	129.5	130.7	131.3	132.1	3.0	125.1	126.2	126.9	127.7	3.3
1997	133.3	134.7	136.2	136.9	3.6	129.0	130.4	132.2	133.0	4.2
1998	138.3	139.6	140.9	141.4	3.3	134.7	136.0	137.5	138.0	3.8
1999	141.7	143.6	145.0	146.3	3.5	138.9	141.0	142.4	143.6	4.1
2000	148.9	150.7	152.2	153.3	4.8	145.3	147.1	148.6	149.6	4.2
West										
1987	92.5	92.6	93.7	94.1	2.7	93.2	93.2	94.6	94.9	2.6
1988	95.4	96.3	97.0	97.7	3.8	95.9	96.7	97.7	98.2	3.5
1989	98.8	100.0	101.0	101.8	4.2	99.1	100.0	100.8	101.4	3.3
1990	103.3	104.5	105.6	106.3	4.4	102.5	104.0	104.8	105.4	3.9
1991	107.5	108.9	110.0	110.9	4.3	106.4	107.6	108.6	109.4	3.8
1992	111.9	112.9	114.1	114.9	3.6	110.2	111.1	112.2	112.8	3.1
1993	116.2	116.4	117.8	118.1	2.8	113.6	113.7	115.3	115.7	2.6
1994	119.4	120.5	121.3	121.7	3.0	116.6	117.9	118.1	119.0	2.9
1995	122.6	123.4	123.9	125.0	2.7	119.9	120.9	121.4	122.7	3.1
1996	125.9	127.3	128.3	128.9	3.1	123.3	124.8	125.8	126.5	3.1
1997	130.3	131.4	132.5	133.4	3.5	127.7	128.9	130.2	131.2	3.7
1998	135.2	136.6	138.5	140.0	4.9	132.9	134.5	136.7	138.4	5.5
1999	140.3	142.1	143.3	144.7	3.4	138.2	140.2	141.3	142.6	3.0
2000	147.0	148.8	150.8	151.8	4.0	144.7	146.3	148.2	149.2	4.6
WORKERS BY AREA SIZE										
Metropolitan areas										
1987	90.6	91.2	92.1	92.7	3.3	91.8	92.3	93.2	93.9	3.4
1988	94.2	95.3	96.3	97.4	5.1	94.7	95.7	96.7	97.8	4.2
1989	98.8	100.0	101.4	102.2	4.9	99.0	100.0	101.3	102.1	4.4
1990	103.9	105.1	106.3	107.1	4.8	103.3	104.4	105.4	106.1	3.9
1991	108.5	109.8	111.0	111.8	4.4	107.3	108.4	109.3	110.1	3.8
1992	113.1	113.9	114.8	115.6	3.4	110.9	111.6	112.3	112.9	2.5
1993	117.1	118.1	119.1	119.8	3.6	113.9	114.7	115.8	116.5	3.2
1994	120.9	121.9	122.9	123.4	3.0	117.2	118.1	119.1	119.7	2.7
1995	124.5	125.4	126.2	126.8	2.8	120.6	121.6	122.4	123.2	2.9
1996	128.0	129.1	130.0	130.6	3.0	124.6	125.8	126.7	127.4	3.4
1997	131.7	132.8	133.9	135.1	3.4	128.7	129.9	131.1	132.3	3.8
1998	136.4	137.5	139.1	139.8	3.5	133.8	135.1	136.9	137.7	4.1
1999	140.4	142.0	143.3	144.7	3.5	138.3	139.9	141.2	142.5	3.5
2000	146.9	148.6	150.1	151.0	4.4	144.1	145.7	147.1	148.0	3.9
Other areas										
1987	93.3	94.1	94.9	95.4	3.1	93.6	94.5	95.5	96.0	3.3
1988	96.6	98.0	98.5	98.9	3.7	96.8	98.4	98.7	98.9	3.0
1989	99.4	100.0	100.8	102.0	3.1	99.6	100.0	100.7	101.9	3.0
1990	103.6	105.2	106.0	106.8	4.7	103.0	104.6	105.3	106.0	4.0
1991	108.4	109.9	110.7	111.2	4.1	107.2	108.4	109.0	109.4	3.2
1992	113.1	113.7	114.8	115.6	4.0	110.7	111.2	112.0	112.8	3.1
1993	117.0	117.8	118.7	119.7	3.5	113.5	114.4	115.0	115.8	2.7
1994	121.3	122.5	123.2	123.5	3.2	117.0	118.1	118.6	119.0	2.8
1995	124.8	125.3	126.1	126.5	2.4	120.5	121.3	122.1	122.4	2.9
1996	127.2	128.0	128.7	130.2	2.9	123.4	124.2	125.0	126.5	3.3
1997	131.4	132.4	133.8	135.3	3.9	127.7	128.8	130.4	132.0	4.3
1998	135.9	137.1	138.2	139.4	3.0	132.5	133.4	134.7	136.0	3.0
1999	140.5	141.8	143.1	143.6	3.0	137.1	138.4	139.8	140.2	3.1
2000	146.0	147.7	148.8	150.3	4.7	142.2	143.7	144.7	146.0	4.1

1. Excludes farm and household workers.
2. The regional coverage is as follows: Northeast: Connecticut, Maine, Massachusetts, New Hampshire, New Jersey, New York, Pennsylvania, Rhode Island, and Vermont; South: Alabama, Arkansas, Delaware, District of Columbia, Florida, Georgia, Kentucky, Louisiana, Maryland, Mississippi, North Carolina, Oklahoma, South Carolina, Tennessee, Texas, Virginia, and West Virginia; Midwest: Illinois, Indiana, Iowa, Kansas, Michigan, Minnesota, Missouri, Nebraska, North Dakota, Ohio, South Dakota, and Wisconsin; and West: Alaska, Arizona, California, Colorado, Hawaii, Idaho, Montana, Nevada, New Mexico, Oregon, Utah, Washington, and Wyoming.
3. Includes mining, construction, and manufacturing.
4. Includes transportation, communication, and public utilities; wholesale and retail trade; finance, insurance, and real estate; and service industries.

Table 5-5. Employer Compensation Costs per Hour Worked and Percent of Total Compensation, Private Industry, by Major Industry Group, March 2000

(Dollars, percent of total cost.)

Compensation component	All workers in private industry		Goods-producing industries[1]		Service-producing industries[2]		Manufacturing industries		Nonmanufacturing industries	
	Cost	Percent	Cost	Percent	Cost	Percent	Cost	Percent	Cost	Percent
TOTAL COMPENSATION	$19.85	100.0	$23.55	100.0	$18.72	100.0	$23.41	100.0	$19.12	100.0
WAGES AND SALARIES	14.49	73.0	16.25	69.0	13.95	74.5	16.01	68.4	14.18	74.2
TOTAL BENEFITS	5.36	27.0	7.30	31.0	4.77	25.5	7.40	31.6	4.94	25.8
Paid Leave	1.28	6.4	1.51	6.4	1.20	6.4	1.74	7.4	1.18	6.2
Vacation pay	0.63	3.2	0.76	3.2	0.59	3.2	0.86	3.7	0.58	3.0
Holiday pay	0.44	2.2	0.56	2.4	0.40	2.1	0.65	2.8	0.40	2.1
Sick leave	0.15	0.8	0.11	0.5	0.16	0.9	0.13	0.6	0.15	0.8
Other leave pay	0.06	0.3	0.08	0.3	0.05	0.3	0.10	0.4	0.05	0.3
Supplemental Pay	0.60	3.0	1.02	4.3	0.47	2.5	1.04	4.4	0.51	2.7
Premium pay[3]	0.24	1.2	0.54	2.3	0.15	0.8	0.58	2.5	0.17	0.9
Shift pay	0.05	0.3	0.08	0.3	0.04	0.2	0.10	0.4	0.04	0.2
Nonproduction bonuses	0.31	1.6	0.41	1.7	0.29	1.5	0.36	1.5	0.30	1.6
Insurance	1.19	6.0	1.77	7.5	1.02	5.4	1.85	7.9	1.06	5.5
Life insurance	0.04	0.2	0.06	0.3	0.04	0.2	0.06	0.3	0.04	0.2
Health insurance	1.09	5.5	1.62	6.9	0.92	4.9	1.69	7.2	0.96	5.0
Short-term disability[4]	0.04	0.2	0.06	0.3	0.03	0.2	0.07	0.3	0.03	0.2
Long-term disability	0.03	0.2	0.03	0.1	0.03	0.2	0.03	0.1	0.03	0.2
Retirement And Savings	0.59	3.0	0.83	3.5	0.51	2.7	0.75	3.2	0.56	2.9
Defined benefit plans	0.23	1.2	0.41	1.7	0.18	1.0	0.34	1.5	0.21	1.1
Defined contribution plans	0.36	1.8	0.43	1.8	0.34	1.8	0.41	1.8	0.35	1.8
Legally Required Benefits	1.67	8.4	2.09	8.9	1.54	8.2	1.92	8.2	1.62	8.5
Social security[5]	1.20	6.0	1.38	5.9	1.15	6.1	1.38	5.9	1.17	6.1
OASDI	0.97	4.9	1.12	4.8	0.92	4.9	1.11	4.7	0.94	4.9
Medicare	0.24	1.2	0.27	1.1	0.23	1.2	0.27	1.2	0.23	1.2
Federal unemployment insurance	0.03	0.2	0.03	0.1	0.03	0.2	0.03	0.1	0.03	0.2
State unemployment insurance	0.10	0.5	0.12	0.5	0.09	0.5	0.11	0.5	0.10	0.5
Workers' compensation	0.33	1.7	0.56	2.4	0.27	1.4	0.40	1.7	0.32	1.7
Other Benefits[6]	0.03	0.2	0.07	0.3	(7)	(8)	0.09	0.4	(7)	(8)

Note: The sum of individual items may not equal totals due to rounding.

1. Includes mining, construction, and manufacturing.
2. Includes transportation, communication, and public utilities; wholesale and retail trade; finance, insurance, and real estate; and service industries.
3. Includes premium pay for work in addition to the regular work schedule (such as overtime, weekends, and holidays).
4. Short-term disability (previously called sickness and accident insurance) includes all insured, self-insured, and state-mandated plans that provide benefits for each disability, including unfunded plans.
5. The total employer's cost for Social Security consists of an OASDI portion and a Medicare portion. OASDI is the acronym for Old-Age, Survivors, and Disability Insurance.
6. Includes severance pay and supplemental unemployment benefits.
7. Cost per hour worked is $0.01 or less.
8. Less than 0.05 percent.

Table 5-6. Employer Compensation Costs per Hour Worked and Percent of Total Compensation, State and Local Government, by Selected Characteristics, March 2000

(Dollars, percent of total cost.)

Compensation component	All workers		White-collar occupations [1]		Service occupations [1]		Service industries [1]	
	Cost	Percent	Cost	Percent	Cost	Percent	Cost	Percent
TOTAL COMPENSATION	$29.05	100.0	$32.17	100.0	$22.05	100.0	$30.61	100.0
WAGES AND SALARIES	20.57	70.8	23.36	72.6	14.29	64.8	22.37	73.1
TOTAL BENEFITS	8.48	29.2	8.81	27.4	7.76	35.2	8.25	27.0
Paid Leave	2.26	7.8	2.33	7.2	2.06	6.3	2.04	6.7
Vacation pay	0.77	2.7	0.72	2.2	0.88	4.0	0.55	1.8
Holiday pay	0.73	2.5	0.77	2.4	0.66	3.0	0.68	2.2
Sick leave	0.58	2.0	0.65	2.0	0.38	1.7	0.62	2.0
Other leave pay	0.18	0.6	0.19	0.6	0.14	0.6	0.18	0.6
Supplemental Pay	0.25	0.9	0.14	0.4	0.53	2.4	0.16	0.5
Premium pay [2]	0.12	0.4	0.04	0.1	0.28	1.3	0.05	0.2
Shift pay	0.06	0.2	0.04	0.1	0.12	0.5	0.05	0.2
Nonproduction bonuses	0.07	0.2	0.06	0.2	0.13	0.6	0.05	0.2
Insurance	2.38	8.2	2.51	7.8	2.01	9.1	2.44	8.0
Life insurance	0.05	0.2	0.06	0.2	0.04	0.2	0.05	0.2
Health insurance	2.27	7.8	2.40	7.5	1.89	8.6	2.33	7.6
Short-term disability [3]	0.03	0.1	0.02	0.1	0.05	0.2	0.02	0.1
Long-term disability	0.03	0.1	0.04	0.1	0.02	0.1	0.03	0.1
Retirement And Savings	1.84	6.3	1.96	6.1	1.73	7.8	1.84	6.0
Defined benefit plans	1.64	5.6	1.73	5.4	1.65	7.5	1.64	5.4
Defined contribution plans	0.20	0.7	0.23	0.7	0.08	0.4	0.20	0.7
Legally Required Benefits	1.70	5.9	1.82	5.7	1.38	6.3	1.73	5.7
Social security [4]	1.35	4.6	1.54	4.8	0.89	4.0	1.47	4.8
OASDI	1.05	3.6	1.19	3.7	0.69	3.1	1.14	3.7
Medicare	0.30	1.0	0.35	1.1	0.21	1.0	0.33	1.1
Federal unemployment insurance	(5)	(6)	(5)	(6)	(5)	(6)	(5)	(6)
State unemployment insurance	0.03	0.1	0.03	0.1	0.04	0.2	0.03	0.1
Workers' compensation	0.31	1.1	0.25	0.8	0.45	2.0	0.22	0.7
Other Benefits [7]	0.05	0.2	0.05	0.2	0.06	0.3	0.05	0.2

Note: The sum of individual items may not equal totals due to rounding.

1. In state and local governments there are two major occupational groups: White-collar occupational groups, largely professional occupations, including teachers; and service occupations, including police and firefighters; and one major industry group, services. The service industries, which include health and educational services, employ a large part of the state and local government workforce.
2. Includes premium pay for work in addition to the regular work schedule (such as overtime, weekends, and holidays).
3. Short-term disability (previously called sickness and accident insurance) includes all insured, self-insured, and state-mandated plans that provide benefits for each disability, including unfunded plans.
4. The total employer's cost for Social Security consists of an OASDI portion and a Medicare portion. OASDI is the acronym for Old-Age, Survivors, and Disability Insurance.
5. Cost per hour worked is $0.01 or less.
6. Less than 0.05 percent.
7. Includes severance pay and supplemental unemployment benefits.

NOTES AND DEFINITIONS

EMPLOYEE BENEFITS SURVEY

Note: The Employee Benefits Survey will be part of the National Compensation Survey. See article describing NCS on p. xvii. The following applies to the data in this volume prior to the introduction of the combined survey.

Collection and Coverage

Employee benefits data are obtained from an annual survey of the incidence and provisions of selected benefits provided by employers. The survey collects data from a sample of approximately 6,000 private sector and state and local government establishments. The data are presented as a percentage of employees who participate in a certain benefit, or as an average benefit provision (for example, the average number of paid holidays provided to employees per year).

The survey covers paid leave benefits such as lunch and rest periods; holidays and vacations; personal, funeral, jury duty, military, parental, and sick leave; sickness and accident, long-term disability, and life insurance; medical, dental, and vision care plans; defined benefit and defined contribution plans; flexible benefits plans; reimbursement accounts; and unpaid parental leave.

Concepts and Definitions

Employer-provided benefits are benefits that are financed either wholly or partly by the employer. They may be sponsored by a union or other third party, as long as there is some employer financing. However, also included are some benefits that are fully paid for by the employee, but the premiums for which are available at group rates.

Participants are workers who are covered by a benefit, whether or not they use that benefit. If the benefit plan is financed wholly by employers and requires employees to complete a minimum length of service for eligibility, the workers are considered participants whether or not they have met the requirement. If workers are required to contribute towards the cost of a plan, they are considered participants only if they elect the plan and agree to make the required contributions.

Defined benefit pension plans use pre-determined formulas to calculate a retirement benefit, and obligate the employer to provide those benefits. Benefits are generally based on salary, years of service, or both.

Defined contribution plans generally specify the level of employer and employee contributions to a plan, but not the formula for determining eventual benefits. Instead, individual accounts are set up for participants, and benefits are based on amounts credited to these accounts.

Tax-deferred savings plans are a type of defined contribution plan that allows participants to contribute a portion of their salary to an employer-sponsored plan and defer income taxes until withdrawal.

Flexible benefit plans allow employees to choose among several benefits, such as life insurance, medical care, and vacation days, and among several levels of care within a given benefit.

Notes on the Data

Surveys of employees in medium and large establishments conducted over the 1979–86 period included establishments that employed at least 50, 100, or 250 workers, depending on the industry; most service industries were excluded. The survey conducted in 1987 covered only state and local governments with 50 or more employees. The surveys conducted in 1988 and 1989 included medium and large establishments with 100 workers or more in all private industries. All surveys conducted over the 1979–89 period excluded establishments in Alaska and Hawaii, as well as part-time employees.

Beginning in 1990, surveys of state and local governments and small establishments are conducted in even-numbered years and surveys of medium and large establishments are conducted in odd-numbered years. The small establishment survey includes all private nonfarm establishments with fewer than 100 workers, while the state and local government survey includes all governments, regardless of the number of workers. All three surveys include full- and part-time workers, and workers in all 50 states and the District of Columbia.

Sources of Additional Information

Additional data and further information on methodology are available for medium and large establishments in BLS news release USDL 99-02 (January 1999), for small establishments in BLS release 98-240 (June 1998), and for state and local governments in Bulletin 2531 (December 2000).

Table 5-7. Percent of Full-Time Employees Participating in Employer-Provided Benefit Programs[1], Medium and Large Private Establishments, Selected Years, 1980–1997

(Percent, days, dollars.)

Benefit program	1980	1981	1982	1983	1984	1985	1986	1988	1989	1991	1993	1995	1997
TIME-OFF PLANS													
Participants With													
Paid funeral leave	. . .	. . .	. . .	. . .	. . .	88	88	85	84	80	83	80	81
Average days per occurrence	. . .	. . .	. . .	. . .	. . .	3.2	3.2	3.2	3.3	3.3	3.0	3.3	3.7
Paid holidays	99	99	99	99	99	98	99	96	97	92	91	89	89
Average days per year	10.1	10.2	10.0	9.8	9.8	10.1	10.0	9.4	9.2	10.2	9.4	9.1	9.3
Paid personal leave	20	23	24	25	23	26	25	24	22	21	21	22	20
Average days per year	. . .	. . .	3.8	3.7	3.6	3.7	3.7	3.3	3.1	3.3	3.1	3.3	3.5
Paid vacation	100	99	99	100	99	99	100	98	97	96	97	96	95
Paid sick leave[2]	62	65	67	67	67	67	70	69	68	67	65	58	56
Unpaid maternity leave	. . .	. . .	. . .	. . .	. . .	. . .	. . .	33	37	37	60	. . .	. . .
Unpaid paternity leave	. . .	. . .	. . .	. . .	. . .	. . .	. . .	16	18	26	53	. . .	. . .
Unpaid family leave	. . .	. . .	. . .	. . .	. . .	. . .	. . .	. . .	. . .	. . .	. . .	84	93
INSURANCE PLANS													
Participants In Medical Care Plans	97	97	97	96	97	96	95	90	92	83	82	77	76
Participants with coverage for													
Home health care	. . .	. . .	. . .	37	46	56	66	76	75	81	86	78	85
Extended care facilities	58	60	62	58	62	67	70	79	80	80	82	73	78
Mental health care	98	99	99	99	99	99	99	98	97	98	98	97	. . .
Alcohol abuse treatment	. . .	. . .	50	53	61	68	70	80	97	97	98	98	. . .
Drug abuse treatment	. . .	. . .	37	43	52	61	66	74	96	96	98	97	. . .
Participants with employee contribution required for													
Self coverage	26	27	27	33	36	36	43	44	47	51	61	67	69
Average monthly contribution	. . .	. . .	. . .	$10.13	$11.93	$12.05	$12.80	$19.29	$25.31	$26.60	$31.55	$33.92	$39.14
Family coverage	46	49	51	54	58	56	63	64	66	69	76	78	80
Average monthly contribution	. . .	. . .	. . .	$32.51	$35.93	$38.33	$41.40	$60.07	$72.10	$96.97	$107.42	$118.33	$130.07
Medical care in HMOs	. . .	. . .	. . .	. . .	. . .	. . .	. . .	19	17	17	23	27	33
Medical care in PPOs	. . .	. . .	. . .	. . .	. . .	. . .	. . .	7	10	16	26	34	40
Medical care in fee-for-service plans	. . .	. . .	. . .	. . .	. . .	. . .	. . .	74	74	67	50	37	27
Participants In Life Insurance Plans	96	96	96	96	96	96	96	92	94	94	91	87	87
Participants with													
Accidental death and dismemberment insurance	69	72	72	72	74	70	73	70	71	71	76	77	74
Survivor income benefits	. . .	. . .	. . .	. . .	. . .	13	10	8	7	6	5	7	6
Retiree protection available	. . .	64	64	66	64	62	59	49	42	44	41	37	33
Participants in long-term disability insurance plans	40	41	43	45	47	48	48	42	45	40	41	42	43
Participants in short-term disability plans[3]	54	50	51	49	51	52	49	46	43	45	44	53	55
RETIREMENT PLANS													
Participants In Defined Benefit Pension Plans	84	84	84	82	82	80	76	63	63	59	56	52	50
Participants with													
Normal retirement prior to age 65	55	56	58	64	63	67	64	59	62	55	52	52	52
Early retirement available	98	98	97	97	97	97	96	98	97	98	95	96	95
Ad hoc pension increase in last five years	. . .	. . .	. . .	51	47	41	35	26	22	7	6	4	10
Terminal earnings formula	53	50	52	54	54	57	57	55	64	56	61	58	56
Benefit coordinated with Social Security	45	43	45	55	56	61	62	62	63	54	48	51	49
Participants In Defined Contribution Plans	. . .	. . .	. . .	. . .	. . .	53	60	45	48	48	49	55	57
Participants In Plans With Tax-Deferred Savings Arrangements	. . .	. . .	. . .	. . .	. . .	26	33	36	41	44	43	54	55
OTHER BENEFITS													
Employees Eligible For													
Flexible benefit plans	. . .	. . .	. . .	. . .	. . .	. . .	2	5	9	10	12	12	13
Reimbursement accounts[4]	. . .	. . .	. . .	. . .	. . .	. . .	5	12	23	36	52	38	32
Premium conversion plans	. . .	. . .	. . .	. . .	. . .	. . .	. . .	. . .	. . .	. . .	. . .	5	7

1. Except for family leave, benefits paid for entirely by the employee were excluded from the tabulations.
2. The definition for paid sick leave was changed for the 1995 and 1997 surveys. Paid sick leave now includes only plans that either specify a maximum number of days per year or unlimited days.
3. The definition for short-term disability (previously called sickness and accident insurance) was changed for the 1995 and 1997 surveys. Short-term disability now includes all insured, self-insured, and state-mandated plans available on a per-disability basis, as well as the unfunded per-disability plans previously reported as sick leave. Sickness and accident insurance, reported in years prior to this survey, included only insured, self-insured, and state-mandated plans providing per-disability benefits at less than full pay.
4. Prior to 1995, reimbursement accounts included premium conversion plans, which specifically allow medical plan participants to pay required plan premiums with pretax dollars. Also, reimbursement accounts that were part of flexible benefit plans were tabulated separately.

Table 5-8. Percent of Full-Time Employees Participating in Selected Employee Benefit Programs[1] by Class of Employee, Medium and Large Private Establishments, 1997

Benefit program	All employees	Professional, technical, and related employees[2]	Clerical and sales employees[3]	Blue-collar and service employees[4]
PAID TIME OFF				
Holidays	89	89	91	88
Vacations	95	96	97	94
Personal leave	20	23	33	13
Funeral leave	81	84	85	76
Jury duty leave	87	92	89	83
Military leave	47	60	50	38
Family leave	2	3	3	1
UNPAID TIME OFF				
Family leave	93	95	96	91
DISABILITY BENEFITS				
Paid sick leave[5]	56	73	73	38
Short-term disability[6]	55	54	52	58
Long-term disability insurance	43	62	52	28
INSURANCE				
Medical care	76	79	78	74
Dental care	59	64	59	56
Vision care	26	28	25	24
Life insurance	87	94	91	81
RETIREMENT				
All retirement[7]	79	89	81	72
Defined benefit plans	50	52	49	50
Defined contribution plans[8]	57	70	63	46
Savings and thrift	39	49	45	30
Deferred profit sharing	13	15	15	12
Employee stock ownership	4	6	6	3
Money purchase pension	8	12	6	6
Tax-deferred savings arrangements				
With employer contributions	46	56	51	38
Without employer contributions	9	11	8	8

1. Except for unpaid family leave and certain tax-deferred earnings arrangements, employers pay some or all of the costs for each benefit.
2. Includes professional, technical, executive, and administrative occupations.
3. Includes clerical, administrative support, and sales occupations.
4. Includes production, craft, repair, laborer, and service occupations.
5. The definitions of paid sick leave and short-term disability (previously called sickness and accident insurance) were changed after 1994. Paid sick leave now includes only plans with an unlimited or specific number of days per year.
6. Short-term disability now includes all insured, self-insured, and state-mandated plans that provide benefits for each disability, including unfunded plans reported as sick leave in 1994.
7. Includes defined benefit and defined contribution plans. Some employees participate in both types, but are counted just once in all retirement.
8. Total participation is less than the sum of individual plan types because some employees participate in two or more types of plans.

Table 5-9. Percent of Full-Time Employees Participating in Employer-Provided Benefit Programs[1], Small Private Establishments and State and Local Government, Selected Years, 1987–1998

(Percent, dollars.)

Benefit program	Small private establishments				State and local government				
	1990	1992	1994	1996	1987	1990	1992	1994	1998
TIME-OFF PLANS									
Participants With									
Paid funeral leave	47	50	50	51	56	63	65	62	65
Average days per occurrence	2.9	3.0	3.1	3.0	3.7	3.7	3.7	3.7	3.7
Paid holidays	84	82	82	80	81	74	75	73	73
Average days per year[1]	9.5	9.2	7.5	7.6	10.9	13.6	14.2	11.5	11.4
Paid personal leave	11	12	13	14	38	39	38	38	38
Average days per year	2.8	2.6	2.6	3.0	2.7	2.9	2.9	3.0	3.1
Paid vacation	88	88	88	86	72	67	67	66	67
Paid sick leave[2]	47	53	50	50	97	95	95	94	96
Unpaid maternity leave	17	18	...	...	57	51	59	...	...
Unpaid paternity leave	8	7	...	...	30	33	44	...	...
Unpaid family leave	...	...	47	48	...	...	...	93	95
INSURANCE PLANS									
Participants In Medical Care Plans	69	71	66	64	93	93	90	87	86
Participants with coverage for									
Home health care	79	80	...	...	76	82	87	84	90
Extended care facilities	83	84	...	...	78	79	84	81	78
Mental health care	98	98	...	...	98	99	99	99	...
Alcohol abuse treatment	97	95	...	...	87	99	99	99	...
Drug abuse treatment	94	94	...	...	86	98	99	98	...
Participants with employee contribution required for									
Self coverage	42	47	52	52	35	38	43	47	51
Self coverage contribution	$25.13	$36.51	$40.97	$42.63	$15.74	$25.53	$28.97	$30.20	$31.94
Family coverage	67	73	76	75	71	65	72	71	75
Family coverage contribution	$109.34	$150.54	$159.63	$181.53	$71.89	$117.59	$139.23	$149.70	$152.46
Medical care in HMOs	14	14	19	...	24	22	27	30	39
Medical care in PPOs	13	18	24	...	7	17	29	30	35
Medical care in fee-for-service plans	74	68	55	...	67	61	43	38	25
Participants In Life Insurance Plans	64	64	61	62	85	88	89	87	89
Participants with									
Accidental death and dismemberment insurance	78	76	79	77	67	67	74	64	58
Survivor income benefits	1	1	2	1	1	1	1	2	1
Retiree protection available	19	25	20	13	55	45	46	46	...
Participants in long-term disability insurance plans	19	23	20	22	31	27	28	30	34
Participants in sickness and accident insurance plans	6	26	26	...	14	21	22	21	...
Participants in short-term disability plans[3]	...	...	...	29	...	...	...	...	20
RETIREMENT PLANS									
Participants In Defined Benefit Pension Plans	20	22	15	15	93	90	87	91	90
Participants with									
Normal retirement prior to age 65	54	50	...	47	92	89	92	92	77
Early retirement available	95	95	...	92	90	88	89	87	87
Ad hoc pension increase in last five years	7	4	...	...	33	16	10	13	...
Terminals earnings formula	58	54	...	53	100	100	100	99	99
Benefit coordinated with Social Security	49	46	...	44	18	8	10	4	7
Participants In Defined Contribution Plans	31	33	34	38	9	9	9	9	14
Participants In Plans With Tax-Deferred Savings Arrangements	17	24	23	28	28	45	45	24	35
OTHER BENEFITS									
Employees Eligible For									
Flexible benefit plans	1	2	3	4	5	5	5	5	5
Reimbursement accounts[4]	8	14	19	12	5	31	50	64	42
Premium conversion	...	...	...	7	...	...	...	...	9

1. Methods used to calculate the average number of paid holidays were revised in 1994 to count partial days more precisely. Average holidays for 1994 are not comparable with those reported in 1990 and 1992.
2. The definitions for paid sick leave and short-term disability (previously called sickness and accident insurance) were changed for the 1998 survey. Paid sick leave now only includes plans that either specify a maximum number of days per year or unlimited days.
3. Short-term disability (previously called sickness and accident insurance) now includes all insured, self-insured, and state-mandated plans available on a per-disability basis, as well as the unfunded per-disability plans previously reported as sick leave. Sickness and accident insurance, reported in years prior to this survey, included only insured, self-insured, and state-mandated plans providing per-disability benefits at less than full pay.
4. Prior to 1998, reimbursement accounts included premium conversion plans, which specifically allow medical plan participants to pay required plan premiums with pretax dollars. Also, reimbursement accounts that were part of flexible benefit plans were tabulated separately.

Table 5-10. Percent of Full-Time Employees Participating[1] in Employer-Provided Benefit Programs[2] by Class of Employee, Small Private Establishments, 1996, and State and Local Government, 1998

Benefit program	Small private establishments, 1996				State and local government, 1998			
	All employees	Professional, technical, and related employees[3]	Clerical and sales employees[4]	Blue-collar and service employees[5]	All employees	White-collar employees, except teachers	Teachers	Blue-collar and service employees
PAID TIME OFF								
Holidays	80	86	89	71	73	86	31	92
Vacations	86	90	95	79	67	83	10	92
Personal leave	14	21	18	8	38	31	55	31
Funeral leave	51	60	60	42	65	62	61	71
Jury duty leave	59	74	68	47	95	95	96	95
Military leave	18	25	23	12	76	81	60	82
Sick leave[6]	50	66	64	35	96	94	97	97
Family leave	2	3	3	3	4	3	4	5
INSURANCE								
Short-term disability insurance[7]	29	32	33	25	20	20	15	24
Long-term disability insurance	22	39	30	10	34	36	38	28
Medical care	64	76	69	56	86	86	86	86
Dental care	31	40	35	34	60	59	62	60
Life insurance	62	72	68	54	89	90	88	88
RETIREMENT								
All retirement[8]	46	56	53	37	98	98	98	98
Defined benefit pension	15	12	16	15	90	89	92	91
Defined contribution plans[9]	38	51	46	28	14	15	11	14
Savings and thrift	23	32	29	16	5	5	1	6
Deferred profit sharing	12	13	17	9	...	...	...	...
Employee stock ownership	1	2	2	1	...	...	...	...
Money purchase pension	4	6	3	3	10	11	9	10
Simplified employee pension	1	1	1	1	(10)	(10)	...	(10)
Tax-deferred earnings arrangement with employer contribution	24	30	31	17	...	...	...	...
Tax-deferred earnings arrangements without employer contribution	4	8	4	3	...	...	...	...
401(k) plans with employer contribution	...	...	...	...	...	...	...	...
OTHER BENEFITS								
Flexible benefits plans	4	6	6	2	5	6	4	4
Reimbursement accounts	12	18	16	7	42	46	39	38
Premium conversion plans	7	7	7	7	9	7	9	10
Child care	2	4	2	1	7	12	4	5

1. Only current employee are counted as participants. Participants in insurance and retirement benefits have met minimum length-of-service requirements and paid any required employee share of the benefit cost. Participants in all other benefits include all employees in occupations offered the benefit.
2. Employee benefit programs in this survey almost always include those sponsored by employers, who pay some share of the cost. Except for unpaid family leave, postretirement medical care and life insurance, dependent life insurance, supplement life insurance, and some salary reduction plans, benefits for which the employees pay the full cost are excluded from the survey.
3. Includes professional, technical, executive, and administrative occupations.
4. Includes clerical, administrative support, and sales occupations.
5. Includes production, craft, repair, laborer, and service occupations.
6. The definitions for paid sick leave and short-term disability (previously called sickness and accident insurance) were changed for the 1995 survey. Paid sick leave now only includes plans that either specify a maximum number of days per year or unlimited days.
7. Short-term disability now includes all insured, self-insured, and state-mandated plans available on a per-disability basis as well as the unfunded per-disability plans previously reported as the sick leave. Sickness and accident insurance, reported in years prior to the 1995 survey, only included insured, self-insured, and state-mandated plans providing per-disability benefits at less than full pay.
8. Includes defined benefit pension plans and defined contribution retirement plans. The total is less than the sum of the individual items because many employees participated in both types of plans.
9. The total is less than the sum of the individual items because some employees participated in more than one type of plans.
10. Value less than 0.05.

NOTES AND DEFINITIONS

OCCUPATIONAL EMPLOYMENT AND WAGES

Note: The Occupational Employment Statistics (OES) Survey will be part of the National Compensation Survey (NCS). See article describing NCS on p. xvii.

Collection and Coverage

Employment and wage data for 1999 from the OES survey are the first estimates using the new Office of Management and Budget (OMB) Standard Occupational Classification (SOC) system. (The new SOC system was also described in an article in the third edition of this Handbook). The new SOC system is to be used by all Federal statistical agencies for reporting occupational data.

The OES program provides occupational employment and wage data at the major group and detailed occupation level. Due to the OES survey's transition to the new SOC system, data for 1999 are not directly comparable with previous years' OES occupational employment and wage data. Approximately one-half of the detailed occupations were unchanged under the new SOC system, with the other half being new SOC occupations or occupations that are slightly different from similar occupations in the old OES classification system. The 1999 OES survey data are benchmarked to a fourth-quarter 1999 reference period. Due to the shift to the new SOC system, employment estimates are based only on the data collected in the 1999 survey. Wage estimates for detailed occupations that changed under the SOC also are based only on data collected in the 1999 survey, while wage estimates for detailed occupations that were unaffected by the SOC are based on data collected in the 1997, 1998, and 1999 surveys. Before combining, data from earlier years are updated to 1999 levels using changes from the Employment Cost Index.

The OES survey is a Federal-State cooperative program between BLS and State Employment Security Agencies (SESAs). BLS provides the procedures and technical support, while SESAs collect the data.

The OES survey is an annual mail survey measuring occupational employment and wage rates for wage and salary workers in nonfarm establishments, by industry. (The military are not covered.) The OES program samples and contacts approximately 400,000 establishments each year and, over 3 years, contacts approximately 1.2 million establishments. The reference period for each year's survey is the fourth quarter of that year. While estimates can be made from a single year of data, the OES survey has been designed to produce estimates using the full 3 years of sample. The full sample allows the production of estimates at fine levels of geography, industry, and occupational detail.

Concepts and definitions

Employment is defined as the number of workers who can be classified as full-time or part-time employees, including workers on paid vacations or other types of leave; workers on unpaid short-term absences; salaried officers, executives, and staff members of incorporated firms; employees temporarily assigned to other units; and employees for whom the reporting unit is their permanent duty station regardless of whether that unit prepares their paycheck. The survey excludes the self-employed, owners/partners of unincorporated firms, and unpaid family workers. Employees are reported in the occupation in which they are working, not necessarily for which they were trained. The OES survey currently uses the SIC system to classify all establishments.

Wages in the OES survey are straight-time gross pay, exclusive of premium pay. Base rates, cost-of-living allowances, guaranteed pay, hazardous-duty pay, incentive pay including commissions and production bonuses, tips, and on-call pay are included. Excluded are back pay, jury duty pay, overtime pay, severance pay, shift differentials, nonproduction bonuses, and tuition reimbursements.

The OES survey collects wage data in 12 intervals. Employers report the number of employees in an occupation per each wage range. The wage intervals used for the 1999 survey are those shown in Table 5-13, except that there are two separate intervals under $8.50 and three over $43.75. The mean wage is the estimated total wages for an occupation divided by its weighted survey employment. With the exception of the upper open-ended wage interval ($70.00 and over), a mean wage value is calculated for each wage interval based on occupational wage data collected by the Office of Compensation and Working Conditions. The mean wage value for the upper open-ended wage interval is its lower bound. These interval mean wage values are then attributed to all workers reported in the interval. For each occupation, total weighted wages in each interval are summed across all intervals and divided by the occupation's weighted survey employment. The median wage is the wage at the midpoint of the distribution of wages.

Annual wages have been calculated by multiplying the hourly mean wage by a year-round full-time hours figure of 2080 hours. For those occupations where there is not an hourly mean wage published, the annual wage has been directly calculated from the reported survey data.

An *establishment* is defined as an economic unit that processes goods or provides services, such as a factory, mine, or store. The establishment is generally at a single physical location and is engaged primarily in one type of economic activity. The OES survey currently uses thc Standard Industrial Classification (SIC) system to classify all establishments.

Additional Information

For additional data including area data see BLS news release UDL 00-368 and BLS Bulletins and articles in *Compensation and Working Conditions.*

Table 5-11. Employment and Wages by Major Occupational Group, New Series, 1999

(Number, percent, dollars.)

Occupational group	Occupations		Employment		Mean hourly wage
	Number	Percent	Number	Percent	
Total	769	100.0	127 274 000	100.0	
Management	30	3.9	8 063 410	6.3	$31.13
Business and financial operations	28	3.6	4 361 980	3.4	22.16
Computer and mathematical	16	2.1	2 620 080	2.1	26.41
Architecture and engineering	35	4.6	2 506 380	0.2	24.81
Life, physical, and social science	39	5.1	909 530	0.7	21.95
Community and social services	14	1.8	1 404 540	1.1	15.21
Legal	9	1.2	858 320	0.7	32.10
Education, training, and library	58	7.5	7 344 830	5.8	17.33
Arts, design, entertainment, sports, and media	37	4.8	1 551 600	1.2	18.10
Healthcare practitioner and technical	45	5.9	6 001 950	4.7	21.76
Healthcare support	15	0.2	2 970 780	2.3	9.51
Protective service	20	2.6	2 958 730	2.3	14.26
Food preparation and serving related	16	2.1	9 687 970	7.6	7.50
Building and grounds cleaning and maintenance	9	1.2	4 274 200	3.4	9.09
Personal care and service	33	4.3	2 556 920	0.2	9.76
Sales and related	21	2.7	12 938 130	10.2	13.01
Office and administrative support	56	7.3	22 562 480	17.7	12.17
Farming, fishing, and forestry	13	1.7	463 360	0.4	8.65
Construction and extraction	58	7.5	5 938 860	4.7	16.18
Installation, maintenance, and repair	53	6.9	5 140 210	0.4	15.77
Production	112	14.6	12 620 920	9.9	12.21
Transportation and material moving	52	6.8	9 538 820	7.5	11.84

Note: Data for 1999 are based on the new Standard Occupational Classification System (SOC), and are not directly comparable with previous years' data. See "Notes and Definitions" for information on revised SOC.

Table 5-12. Distribution of Occupations and Employment by Occupational Division, Old Series, 1997–1998

(Number, percent.)

Occupational division	Occupations		Employment	
	Number	Percent	Number	Percent
1997				
Total	777	100.0	121 592 210	100.0
Managerial	20	2.6	8 192 170	6.7
Professional	214	27.5	25 594 320	21.0
Sales	22	2.8	14 319 050	11.8
Clerical	77	9.9	21 251 910	17.5
Service	64	8.2	19 610 730	16.1
Agricultural	20	2.6	1 515 370	1.2
Production	360	46.3	31 108 660	25.6
1998				
Total	777	100.0	124 704 630	100.0
Managerial	20	2.6	8 320 910	6.7
Professional	214	27.5	26 427 600	21.2
Sales	22	2.8	14 814 380	11.9
Clerical	77	9.9	21 665 320	17.4
Service	64	8.2	19 942 840	16.0
Agricultural	20	2.6	1 566 630	1.3
Production	360	46.3	31 966 950	25.6

Note: See "Notes and Definitions" for information on revised Standard Occupational Classification System (SOC).

Table 5-13. Distribution of Employment by Wage Range and Occupational Group, New Series, 1999

(Percentage distribution.)

Occupational group	Total	Wage range								
		Under $8.50	$8.50 to $10.74	$10.75 to $13.49	$13.50 to $16.99	$17.00 to $21.49	$21.50 to $27.24	$27.25 to $34.49	$34.50 to $43.74	$43.75 and over
Management	100.0	2.1	2.7	5.4	9.2	13.0	16.5	16.7	14.4	19.9
Business and financial operations	100.0	2.8	4.1	9.7	18.6	21.6	20.1	12.8	6.2	4.2
Computer and mathematical	100.0	0.9	2.0	5.2	10.7	17.2	23.0	20.8	13.4	6.8
Architecture and engineering	100.0	1.4	3.0	6.5	11.9	18.6	22.9	19.7	11.4	4.6
Life, physical, and social science	100.0	4.3	5.3	10.6	16.9	19.4	19.3	13.0	6.8	4.3
Community and social services	100.0	11.5	14.8	20.7	20.9	16.9	10.4	3.7	0.8	0.2
Legal	100.0	2.5	3.6	8.2	13.1	12.7	11.5	10.0	10.7	27.7
Education, training, and library	100.0	16.3	9.0	11.4	17.7	19.3	14.4	7.8	2.9	1.3
Arts, design, entertainment, sports, and media	100.0	18.2	11.0	3.6	14.6	14.3	11.7	7.3	5.6	3.6
Healthcare practitioner and technical	100.0	5.5	7.1	11.4	17.6	21.9	17.3	8.7	3.8	6.6
Healthcare support	100.0	44.6	28.7	16.7	7.3	2.0	0.5	0.1	. . .	. . .
Protective service	100.0	26.9	14.4	14.5	13.6	13.9	10.5	4.6	1.3	0.2
Food preparation and serving related	100.0	77.5	13.1	5.7	2.5	0.9	0.2	0.1	. . .	. . .
Building and grounds cleaning and maintenance	100.0	56.8	19.9	12.1	7.0	3.0	0.9	0.2	0.1	. . .
Personal care and service	100.0	60.3	16.0	8.9	6.0	4.0	2.3	1.2	0.7	0.7
Sales and related	100.0	47.0	13.1	10.2	9.1	7.1	5.2	3.5	2.2	2.7
Office and administrative support	100.0	23.0	23.8	22.5	16.1	10.0	3.1	0.9	0.3	0.1
Farming, fishing, and forestry	100.0	67.7	13.1	7.7	6.6	3.0	1.2	0.5	0.1	. . .
Construction and extraction	100.0	10.6	14.8	17.4	18.9	16.7	13.6	6.2	1.4	0.2
Installation, maintenance, and repair	100.0	10.7	13.4	17.7	21.2	19.2	12.9	3.7	0.9	0.3
Production	100.0	28.0	22.0	19.0	14.6	8.8	5.8	1.3	0.4	0.1
Transportation and material moving	100.0	35.0	19.9	16.6	13.3	9.2	3.9	1.0	0.4	0.7

Note: Data for 1999 are based on the new Standard Occupational Classification System (SOC), and are not directly comparable with previous years' data. See "Notes and Definitions" for information on revised SOC.

Table 5-14. Distribution of Mean Wage of Occupations by Occupational Division, Old Series, 1997–1998

(Percentage distribution.)

Occupational division	Total	Wage range								
		Under $8.50	$8.50 to $9.99	$10.00 to $11.24	$11.25 to $13.24	$13.25 to $15.74	$15.75 to $19.24	$19.25 to $24.24	$24.25 to $43.24	$43.25 to $60.00
1997										
Managerial	100.0	...	...	...	5.0	15.0	5.0	30.0	45.0	...
Professional	100.0	0.5	3.7	3.7	6.5	9.8	23.4	17.8	33.6	0.9
Sales	100.0	13.6	13.6	9.1	9.1	4.5	22.7	13.6	13.6	...
Clerical	100.0	7.8	24.7	19.5	33.8	7.8	5.2	1.3	...	...
Service	100.0	46.9	14.1	7.8	6.3	9.4	7.8	6.3	1.6	...
Agricultural	100.0	30.0	10.0	20.0	35.0	5.0	...	...	...	...
Production	100.0	5.8	11.7	16.1	21.9	21.1	16.7	6.1	0.6	...
1998										
Managerial	100.0	...	...	...	...	20.0	5.0	15.0	60.0	...
Professional	100.0	0.5	2.8	4.2	4.7	10.3	18.7	31.3	26.6	0.9
Sales	100.0	13.6	13.6	4.5	13.6	...	18.2	18.2	18.2	...
Clerical	100.0	5.2	19.5	15.6	44.2	7.8	5.2	2.6	...	...
Service	100.0	43.8	12.5	10.9	9.4	7.8	4.7	9.4	1.6	...
Agricultural	100.0	30.0	5.0	15.0	40.0	10.0	...	...	...	...
Production	100.0	4.7	8.9	15.0	23.3	23.6	16.9	6.9	0.6	...

Note: See "Notes and Definitions" for information on revised Standard Occupational Classification System (SOC).

Table 5-15. Employment and Wages by Occupation, 1999

(Number of persons, dollars.)

Occupational division and occupation	Employment	Mean hourly wages	Mean annual wages[1]	Median hourly wages
MANAGEMENT OCCUPATIONS				
Chief executives	597 060	$48.67	$101 240	$52.08
General and operations managers	2 305 610	31.69	65 910	27.23
Legislators	49 330	11.92	24 790	6.50
Advertising and promotions managers	100 600	28.32	58 910	24.30
Marketing managers	202 710	34.14	71 010	32.18
Sales managers	367 640	33.44	69 560	30.59
Public relations managers	67 210	27.77	57 770	24.77
Administrative services managers	363 530	23.36	48 580	20.78
Computer and information systems managers	280 820	35.79	74 430	34.97
Financial managers	646 050	33.22	69 100	30.62
Human resources managers[2]	227 810	27.34	56 880	25.55
Industrial production managers[2]	213 510	29.56	61 480	28.64
Purchasing managers[2]	137 950	24.61	51 200	22.31
Transportation, storage, and distribution managers	123 450	26.03	54 140	24.51
Farm, ranch, and other agricultural managers	5 450	20.80	43 260	17.94
Construction managers	240 490	28.92	60 160	26.75
Education administrators, preschool and child care center/program	35 380	18.63	38 750	15.81
Education administrators, elementary and secondary school	186 220	(3)	65 480	(3)
Education administrators, postsecondary	95 690	28.93	60 170	26.52
Engineering managers	248 210	39.21	81 560	38.52
Food service managers	287 940	16.04	33 360	14.92
Funeral directors[2]	23 740	20.56	42 770	17.75
Gaming managers	4 590	26.40	54 900	22.51
Lodging managers	28 170	16.34	33 980	14.49
Medical and health services managers	230 640	27.93	58 090	25.82
Natural sciences managers	36 920	34.84	72 470	33.75
Postmasters and mail superintendents	26 930	21.78	45 300	21.16
Property, real estate, and community association managers	143 040	19.68	40 940	16.73
Social and community service managers	88 340	19.41	40 370	17.74
BUSINESS AND FINANCIAL OPERATIONS OCCUPATIONS				
Agents and business managers of artists, performers, and athletes	7 280	33.53	69 740	25.00
Purchasing agents and buyers, farm products	21 550	21.08	43 840	16.94
Wholesale and retail buyers, except farm products[2]	133 070	19.12	39 770	16.52
Purchasing agents, except wholesale, retail, and farm products[2]	224 110	20.44	42 510	19.01
Claims adjusters, examiners, and investigators	154 770	20.17	41 960	18.69
Insurance appraisers, auto damage[2]	19 310	19.81	41 200	19.22
Compliance officers, except agriculture, construction, health and safety, and transportation	123 280	20.17	41 960	18.50
Cost estimators[2]	201 500	22.12	46 000	20.36
Emergency management specialists	11 390	19.87	41 330	17.84
Employment, recruitment, and placement specialists	181 710	18.94	39 400	16.52
Compensation, benefits, and job analysis specialists	78 310	20.09	41 800	18.98
Training and development specialists	186 940	19.96	41 510	18.54
Management analysts	300 600	28.05	58 350	25.91
Meeting and convention planners	32 820	17.27	35 930	16.24
Accountants and auditors[2]	843 160	21.31	44 320	19.16
Appraisers and assessors of real estate[2]	52 520	20.04	41 670	18.12
Budget analysts[2]	61 740	23.64	49 170	22.41
Credit analysts[2]	61 580	20.28	42 180	17.96
Financial analysts	142 820	27.09	56 340	23.65
Personal financial advisors	79 970	31.10	64 680	25.26
Insurance underwriters[2]	93 970	21.61	44 940	19.69
Financial examiners	27 630	28.01	58 270	24.63
Loan counselors	22 320	17.25	35 880	14.95
Loan officers	200 180	21.74	45 210	18.72
Tax examiners, collectors, and revenue agents[2]	64 960	19.36	40 270	17.75
Tax preparers[2]	58 100	15.37	31 970	13.04
COMPUTER AND MATHEMATICAL OPERATIONS OCCUPATIONS				
Computer and information scientists, research	26 280	32.30	67 180	31.38
Computer programmers[2]	528 600	26.42	54 960	24.55
Computer software engineers, applications	287 600	31.62	65 780	30.45
Computer software engineers, systems software	209 030	31.84	66 230	31.07
Computer support specialists	402 840	18.95	39 410	17.54
Computer systems analysts	428 210	27.85	57 920	26.91
Database administrators[2]	101 460	25.26	52 550	23.83
Network and computer systems administrators	204 680	24.08	50 090	22.98
Network systems and data communications analysts	98 330	26.78	55 710	25.24
Actuaries	12 560	34.56	71 880	31.88

See footnotes at end of table.

Table 5-15. Employment and Wages by Occupation, 1999—*Continued*

(Number of persons, dollars.)

Occupational division and occupation	Employment	Mean hourly wages	Mean annual wages[1]	Median hourly wages
Mathematicians	3 450	32.68	67 970	32.86
Operations research analysts	43 760	25.89	53 850	23.35
Statisticians [2]	14 620	24.35	50 650	22.65
Mathematical technicians [2]	1 560	21.01	43 710	17.44
ARCHITECTURE AND ENGINEERING OCCUPATIONS				
Architects, except landscape and naval [2]	71 040	25.68	53 410	23.67
Landscape architects [2]	13 870	21.40	44 510	19.24
Cartographers and photogrammetrists	6 150	19.74	41 060	19.20
Surveyors	50 150	17.50	36 400	16.61
Aerospace engineers [2]	71 790	31.03	64 550	31.35
Agricultural engineers [2]	2 260	26.85	55 840	26.25
Biomedical engineers	6 450	25.21	52 430	24.36
Chemical engineers [2]	28 630	30.89	64 250	31.84
Civil engineers [2]	209 100	26.76	55 660	25.83
Computer hardware engineers	60 420	32.19	66 960	31.12
Electrical engineers	149 210	29.58	61 520	29.15
Electronics engineers, except computer	106 830	30.49	63 410	29.96
Environmental engineers	51 450	27.43	57 050	26.39
Health and safety engineers, except mining safety engineers and inspectors	40 470	25.81	53 680	25.16
Industrial engineers	155 910	27.62	57 450	26.81
Marine engineers and naval architects [2]	4 450	28.16	58 580	27.89
Materials engineers [2]	21 730	28.54	59 370	28.29
Mechanical engineers [2]	202 910	27.41	57 010	26.85
Mining and geological engineers, including mining safety engineers	7 160	29.76	61 900	28.03
Nuclear engineers [2]	9 580	35.04	72 870	35.87
Petroleum engineers [2]	9 640	34.99	72 780	35.71
Architectural and civil drafters	92 790	17.40	36 190	16.37
Electrical and electronics drafters	39 890	18.82	39 150	17.93
Mechanical drafters	65 960	18.57	38 620	17.37
Aerospace engineering and operations technicians	17 270	23.38	48 630	21.39
Civil engineering technicians [2]	91 040	16.95	35 270	16.35
Electrical and electronic engineering technicians	242 160	18.94	39 390	18.45
Electro-mechanical technicians	40 310	17.91	37 250	16.79
Environmental engineering technicians	18 640	16.86	35 060	15.58
Industrial engineering technicians [2]	51 690	20.83	43 320	19.41
Mechanical engineering technicians	57 560	19.50	40 560	18.41
Surveying and mapping technicians [2]	47 330	14.07	29 260	12.87
LIFE, PHYSICAL, AND SOCIAL SCIENCE OCCUPATIONS				
Agricultural and food scientists [2]	9 720	21.69	45 110	20.56
Biochemists and biophysicists	11 810	27.01	56 170	25.15
Microbiologists	15 630	24.37	50 690	22.21
Zoologists and wildlife biologists	11 120	20.87	43 400	20.12
Conservation scientists	12 240	21.78	45 310	21.64
Foresters	10 090	20.34	42 300	19.73
Epidemiologists	2 270	23.57	49 020	22.03
Medical scientists, except epidemiologists	21 200	26.87	55 880	23.93
Astronomers	680	36.47	75 860	36.96
Physicists	10 290	36.61	76 140	36.63
Atmospheric and space scientists [2]	7 170	25.76	53 580	25.60
Chemists [2]	73 840	24.80	51 580	23.07
Materials scientists	8 200	28.39	59 060	27.33
Environmental scientists and specialists, including health	53 610	22.60	47 000	20.99
Geoscientists, except hydrologists and geographers	20 940	29.33	61 000	26.18
Hydrologists	6 890	26.26	54 620	25.53
Economists	14 490	29.59	61 550	27.92
Market research analysts	67 670	25.33	52 680	22.89
Survey researchers	21 990	10.84	22 540	8.36
Clinical, counseling, and school psychologists	92 460	23.90	49 720	22.75
Industrial-organizational psychologists	1 780	34.23	71 200	33.59
Sociologists	1 320	22.74	47 310	20.78
Urban and regional planners [2]	28 730	22.44	46 670	21.41
Anthropologists and archeologists	3 220	17.79	37 010	16.89
Geographers	720	21.37	44 450	19.98
Historians	1 510	19.88	41 350	18.35
Political scientists	4 280	35.03	72 860	35.71
Agricultural and food science technicians	15 050	14.09	29 310	12.75
Biological technicians	39 580	15.42	32 060	14.66
Chemical technicians	78 730	17.35	36 080	16.46

See footnotes at end of table.

Table 5-15. Employment and Wages by Occupation, 1999—*Continued*

(Number of persons, dollars.)

Occupational division and occupation	Employment	Mean hourly wages	Mean annual wages[1]	Median hourly wages
Geological and petroleum technicians	10 830	19.58	40 730	17.43
Nuclear technicians [2]	2 640	24.81	51 600	24.00
Environmental science and protection technicians, including health	26 240	16.47	34 270	15.63
Forensic science technicians	5 340	18.37	38 200	17.40
Forest and conservation technicians	17 140	14.11	29 340	13.20
COMMUNITY AND SOCIAL SERVICE OCCUPATIONS				
Substance abuse and behavioral disorder counselors	57 290	13.73	28 560	12.82
Educational, vocational, and school counselors [2]	190 930	19.95	41 490	19.22
Marriage and family therapists	18 530	17.14	35 660	16.14
Mental health counselors	62 910	14.15	29 430	12.80
Rehabilitation counselors	93 130	12.75	26 520	11.37
Child, family, and school social workers	262 570	15.25	31 720	14.42
Medical and public health social workers	101 680	17.02	35 400	16.16
Mental health and substance abuse social workers	72 730	14.98	31 150	14.08
Health educators	41 620	16.81	34 960	15.49
Probation officers and correctional treatment specialists	78 930	18.28	38 030	17.37
Social and human service assistants	242 530	10.94	22 760	10.30
Clergy [2]	26 000	15.48	32 210	14.50
Directors, religious activities and education [2]	14 960	13.73	28 550	12.77
LEGAL OCCUPATIONS				
Lawyers	464 250	43.44	90 360	42.81
Administrative law judges, adjudicators, and hearing officers	27 250	24.80	51 580	21.23
Arbitrators, mediators, and conciliators	6 260	33.80	70 310	25.49
Judges, magistrate judges, and magistrates	23 150	32.29	67 150	32.72
Paralegals and legal assistants	175 870	17.57	36 550	16.39
Court reporters	17 460	18.29	38 040	17.78
Law clerks [2]	26 060	14.08	29 280	12.94
Title examiners, abstractors, and searchers [2]	38 730	14.84	30 880	13.38
EDUCATION, TRAINING, AND LIBRARY OCCUPATIONS				
Business teachers, postsecondary [2]	63 110	(3)	53 800	(3)
Computer science teachers, postsecondary [2]	30 760	(3)	49 420	(3)
Mathematical science teachers, postsecondary [2]	38 850	(3)	49 750	(3)
Architecture teachers, postsecondary [2]	3 730	(3)	55 200	(3)
Engineering teachers, postsecondary [2]	25 960	(3)	64 510	(3)
Agricultural sciences teachers, postsecondary [2]	8 180	(3)	59 600	(3)
Biological science teachers, postsecondary	33 790	(3)	54 930	(3)
Forestry and conservation science teachers, postsecondary	1 830	(3)	53 320	(3)
Atmospheric, earth, marine, and space sciences teachers, postsecondary	7 930	(3)	58 250	(3)
Chemistry teachers, postsecondary [2]	17 860	(3)	53 010	(3)
Environmental science teachers, postsecondary	3 790	(3)	54 120	(3)
Physics teachers, postsecondary [2]	11 230	(3)	59 740	(3)
Anthropology and archeology teachers, postsecondary	3 850	(3)	56 220	(3)
Area, ethnic, and cultural studies teachers, postsecondary [2]	3 000	(3)	52 800	(3)
Economics teachers, postsecondary [2]	11 100	(3)	58 730	(3)
Geography teachers, postsecondary [2]	3 330	(3)	53 410	(3)
Political science teachers, postsecondary [2]	10 480	(3)	53 920	(3)
Psychology teachers, postsecondary [2]	24 690	(3)	53 170	(3)
Sociology teachers, postsecondary	12 490	(3)	50 090	(3)
Health specialties teachers, postsecondary [2]	72 130	(3)	66 470	(3)
Nursing instructors and teachers, postsecondary [2]	35 360	(3)	47 830	(3)
Education teachers, postsecondary [2]	35 030	(3)	46 200	(3)
Library science teachers, postsecondary [2]	3 870	(3)	49 860	(3)
Criminal justice and law enforcement teachers, postsecondary [2]	7 830	(3)	43 580	(3)
Law teachers, postsecondary	8 250	(3)	70 860	(3)
Social work teachers, postsecondary [2]	5 660	(3)	46 690	(3)
Art, drama, and music teachers, postsecondary [2]	51 710	(3)	46 700	(3)
Communications teachers, postsecondary [2]	15 960	(3)	46 220	(3)
English language and literature teachers, postsecondary [2]	51 030	(3)	46 260	(3)
Foreign language and literature teachers, postsecondary [2]	20 140	(3)	46 930	(3)
History teachers, postsecondary [2]	16 950	(3)	50 800	(3)
Philosophy and religion teachers, postsecondary [2]	13 380	(3)	48 700	(3)
Graduate teaching assistants	124 750	(3)	20 840	(3)
Home economics teachers, postsecondary [2]	4 970	(3)	48 580	(3)
Recreation and fitness studies teachers, postsecondary	14 970	(3)	43 590	(3)
Vocational education teachers, postsecondary	129 780	18.10	37 650	17.04
Preschool teachers, except special education [2]	339 310	9.43	19 610	8.41
Kindergarten teachers, except special education [2]	158 250	(3)	36 770	(3)
Elementary school teachers, except special education [2]	1 357 340	(3)	39 560	(3)
Middle school teachers, except special and vocational education [2]	570 010	(3)	39 690	(3)

See footnotes at end of table.

Table 5-15. Employment and Wages by Occupation, 1999—*Continued*

(Number of persons, dollars.)

Occupational division and occupation	Employment	Mean hourly wages	Mean annual wages[1]	Median hourly wages
Vocational education teachers, middle school	17 450	(3)	41 090	(3)
Secondary school teachers, except special and vocational education	947 010	(3)	41 430	(3)
Vocational education teachers, secondary school	107 330	(3)	41 710	(3)
Special education teachers, preschool, kindergarten, and elementary school	203 690	(3)	40 400	(3)
Special education teachers, middle school	86 850	(3)	38 600	(3)
Special education teachers, secondary school	119 870	(3)	42 070	(3)
Adult literacy, remedial education, and GED teachers and instructors	56 880	15.77	32 800	14.92
Self-enrichment education teachers	125 650	14.37	29 900	12.54
Archivists, curators, and museum technicians [2]	16 760	16.42	34 160	14.79
Librarians [2]	137 760	19.84	41 270	19.19
Library technicians	98 030	11.28	23 450	10.84
Audio-visual collections specialists	9 690	15.88	33 030	14.18
Farm and home management advisors [2]	9 530	18.74	38 980	17.24
Instructional coordinators	76 870	21.06	43 800	20.06
Teacher assistants [2]	1 115 820	(3)	17 400	(3)
ART, DESIGN, ENTERTAINMENT, SPORTS, AND MEDIA OCCUPATIONS				
Art directors	19 190	29.65	61 680	25.81
Fine artists, including painters, sculptors, and illustrators	13 240	17.00	35 370	14.51
Multi-media artists and animators	30 530	19.87	41 330	17.82
Commercial and industrial designers	38 350	23.03	47 910	22.15
Fashion designers	9 600	25.28	52 580	21.96
Floral designers	59 410	9.12	18 980	8.66
Graphic designers	119 820	17.41	36 210	15.95
Interior designers [2]	29 690	18.44	38 360	16.03
Merchandise displayers and window trimmers [2]	51 530	10.37	21 560	9.36
Set and exhibit designers	8 290	14.57	30 310	13.62
Actors	84 790	(3)	50 620	(3)
Producers and directors	39 200	(3)	47 230	(3)
Athletes and sports competitors	10 620	(3)	69 440	(3)
Coaches and scouts	65 820	(3)	32 010	(3)
Umpires, referees, and other sports officials	8 150	(3)	23 510	(3)
Dancers	14 910	11.90	24 750	9.42
Choreographers	11 170	15.56	32 370	12.95
Music directors and composers	6 310	(3)	34 750	(3)
Musicians and singers	46 440	(3)	37 510	(3)
Announcers [2]	50 410	12.33	25 640	8.95
News analysts, reporters and correspondents [2]	64 590	16.96	35 270	13.37
Public relations specialists [2]	118 280	19.61	40 780	17.63
Editors	95 210	20.20	42 030	18.01
Technical writers	46 680	22.57	46 940	21.32
Writers and authors	45 670	21.88	45 500	19.62
Interpreters and translators	13 640	14.16	29 450	12.94
Audio and video equipment technicians	39 090	16.36	34 020	13.51
Broadcast technicians	25 570	13.33	27 740	11.33
Radio operators [2]	3 290	12.48	25 950	11.20
Sound engineering technicians	9 380	16.87	35 090	13.98
Photographers [2]	66 070	12.36	25 710	10.01
Camera operators, television, video, and motion picture [2]	17 330	15.26	31 730	11.94
Film and video editors [2]	12 770	21.34	44 380	18.84
HEALTHCARE PRACTITIONERS AND TECHNICAL OCCUPATIONS				
Chiropractors	11 540	34.10	70 930	27.92
Dentists	69 360	51.03	106 130	53.21
Dietitians and nutritionists [2]	41 320	17.96	37 350	17.54
Optometrists	21 400	37.38	77 750	37.10
Pharmacists [2]	226 300	30.31	63 030	32.16
Anesthesiologists	25 910	59.51	123 780	(4)
Family and general practitioners	134 490	50.04	104 090	54.34
Internists, general	48 740	59.27	123 280	(4)
Obstetricians and gynecologists	18 780	65.11	135 430	(4)
Pediatricians, general	18 940	54.21	112 760	58.65
Psychiatrists	17 870	49.84	103 660	55.69
Surgeons	48 450	65.22	135 660	(4)
Physician assistants [2]	56 750	24.35	50 650	25.54
Podiatrists	4 470	48.12	100 090	51.00
Registered nurses [2]	2 205 430	21.38	44 470	20.33
Audiologists	12 950	21.96	45 670	20.51
Occupational therapists [2]	78 950	24.96	51 910	23.73
Physical therapists [2]	131 050	28.05	58 350	27.08
Radiation therapists [2]	12 340	20.84	43 360	20.04
Recreational therapists [2]	30 190	14.08	29 280	13.47

See footnotes at end of table.

Table 5-15. Employment and Wages by Occupation, 1999—*Continued*

(Number of persons, dollars.)

Occupational division and occupation	Employment	Mean hourly wages	Mean annual wages[1]	Median hourly wages
Respiratory therapists[2]	80 230	17.72	36 860	17.38
Speech-language pathologists	85 920	22.99	47 820	22.03
Veterinarians	39 250	31.76	66 060	28.19
Medical and clinical laboratory technologists[2]	145 750	18.90	39 310	18.52
Medical and clinical laboratory technicians[2]	142 090	13.67	28 430	12.89
Dental hygienists[2]	90 050	23.15	48 150	22.69
Cardiovascular technologists and technicians[2]	41 490	16.00	33 280	15.46
Diagnostic medical sonographers	29 280	21.04	43 760	20.35
Nuclear medicine technologists[2]	17 880	20.40	42 430	19.66
Radiologic technologists and technicians	177 850	17.07	35 510	16.47
Emergency medical technicians and paramedics[2]	172 360	11.19	23 280	10.21
Dietetic technicians[2]	29 190	10.09	21 000	9.39
Pharmacy technicians[2]	196 430	9.64	20 050	9.11
Psychiatric technicians[2]	54 560	11.30	23 510	10.56
Respiratory therapy technicians	33 990	16.07	33 430	15.14
Surgical technologists[2]	64 810	13.25	27 560	12.84
Veterinary technologists and technicians	47 470	10.30	21 430	9.89
Licensed practical and licensed vocational nurses[2]	688 510	13.95	29 020	13.39
Medical records and health information technicians	142 720	11.13	23 150	10.37
Opticians, dispensing[2]	58 860	12.11	25 190	11.10
Orthotists and prosthetists	3 330	21.45	44 610	17.94
Occupational health and safety specialists and technicians	34 840	19.99	41 590	18.94
Athletic trainers	16 670	(3)	33 650	(3)
HEALTHCARE SUPPORT OCCUPATIONS				
Home health aides[2]	577 530	9.04	18 810	8.21
Nursing aides, orderlies, and attendants[2]	1 308 740	8.59	17 860	8.29
Psychiatric aides[2]	51 100	10.76	22 390	10.32
Occupational therapist assistants	17 290	15.97	33 230	15.79
Occupational therapist aides	9 250	10.92	22 710	9.34
Physical therapist assistants	48 600	16.20	33 690	15.90
Physical therapist aides	44 340	9.69	20 160	9.05
Massage therapists	21 910	13.82	28 740	11.01
Dental assistants[2]	175 160	11.60	24 130	11.24
Medical assistants	281 480	10.89	22 650	10.40
Medical equipment preparers	29 070	10.20	21 220	9.70
Medical transcriptionists	97 260	11.86	24 660	11.67
Pharmacy aides[2]	48 270	9.14	19 010	8.76
Veterinary assistants and laboratory animal caretakers	53 680	8.03	16 710	7.60
PROTECTIVE SERVICE OCCUPATIONS				
First-line supervisors, managers of correctional officers	28 300	20.30	42 230	18.70
First-line supervisors, managers of police and detectives[2]	111 600	26.01	54 100	25.31
First-line supervisors, managers of fire fighting and prevention workers[2]	57 300	23.60	49 100	23.24
Fire fighters[2]	252 730	16.38	34 070	15.80
Fire inspectors and investigators[2]	10 050	19.98	41 550	19.26
Forest fire inspectors and prevention specialists[2]	1 630	14.57	30 300	12.98
Bailiffs[2]	12 620	14.40	29 950	14.13
Correctional officers and jailers[2]	381 250	14.94	31 070	13.66
Detectives and criminal investigators[2]	83 340	22.90	47 620	22.09
Fish and game wardens[2]	8 220	20.16	41 940	18.05
Parking enforcement workers[2]	7 660	12.00	24 970	11.71
Police and sheriff's patrol officers[2]	581 860	18.61	38 710	18.06
Transit and railroad police[2]	4 590	20.32	42 260	19.72
Animal control workers	8 300	11.47	23 850	10.62
Private detectives and investigators	30 690	14.48	30 120	12.60
Gaming surveillance officers and gaming investigators	12 780	10.43	21 700	9.78
Security guards[2]	1 088 470	8.95	18 610	8.07
Crossing guards[2]	68 310	8.59	17 870	7.70
FOOD PREPARATION AND SERVING RELATED OCCUPATIONS				
Chefs and head cooks	118 070	13.48	28 040	11.88
First-line supervisors, managers of food preparation and serving workers	545 700	11.47	23 860	10.59
Cooks, fast food[2]	418 400	6.54	13 610	6.24
Cooks, institution and cafeteria[2]	438 660	8.38	17 420	7.89
Cooks, restaurant[2]	656 540	8.52	17 730	8.05
Cooks, short order[2]	163 160	7.48	15 560	7.14
Food preparation workers	878 650	7.57	15 740	7.23
Bartenders[2]	358 450	7.07	14 700	6.52
Combined food preparation and serving workers, including fast food[2]	1 950 970	6.64	13 810	6.30
Counter attendants, cafeteria, food concession, and coffee shop[2]	407 960	6.83	14 210	6.46

See footnotes at end of table.

Table 5-15. Employment and Wages by Occupation, 1999—*Continued*

(Number of persons, dollars.)

Occupational division and occupation	Employment	Mean hourly wages	Mean annual wages[1]	Median hourly wages
Waiters and waitresses[2]	2 039 950	6.46	13 430	6.07
Food servers, nonrestaurant[2]	192 850	7.77	16 170	7.09
Dining room and cafeteria attendants and bartender helpers[2]	425 600	6.70	13 940	6.33
Dishwashers	538 360	6.78	14 090	6.57
Hosts and hostesses, restaurant, lounge, and coffee shop[2]	380 850	7.13	14 840	6.73
BUILDING AND GROUNDS CLEANING AND MAINTENANCE OCCUPATIONS				
First-line supervisors, managers of housekeeping and janitorial workers[2]	202 460	11.67	24 270	10.61
First-line supervisors, managers of landscaping, lawn service, and groundskeeping workers	91 330	15.87	33 000	14.31
Janitors and cleaners, except maids and housekeeping cleaners[2]	2 090 560	8.76	18 220	7.90
Maids and housekeeping cleaners[2]	913 470	7.46	15 530	7.03
Pest control workers[2]	40 240	11.60	24 120	11.16
Landscaping and groundskeeping workers	739 460	9.32	19 380	8.48
Pesticide handlers, sprayers, and applicators, vegetation[2]	23 440	11.29	23 490	10.81
Tree trimmers and pruners[2]	47 890	11.43	23 770	10.73
PERSONAL CARE AND SERVICE OCCUPATIONS				
Gaming supervisors	26 890	16.96	35 270	16.46
Slot key persons	13 220	11.38	23 660	10.28
First-line supervisors, managers of personal service workers	84 610	14.02	29 150	12.47
Animal trainers[2]	5 900	12.39	25 770	11.09
Nonfarm animal caretakers	84 760	8.25	17 160	7.50
Gaming dealers	87 390	6.79	14 120	6.20
Gaming and sports book writers and runners	8 390	7.74	16 090	7.53
Motion picture projectionists[2]	8 610	10.28	21 390	7.33
Ushers, lobby attendants, and ticket takers[2]	88 590	6.76	14 050	6.26
Amusement and recreation attendants	190 600	7.17	14 920	6.55
Costume attendants	5 860	11.28	23 470	9.93
Locker room, coatroom, and dressing room attendants	22 960	(5)	(5)	(5)
Embalmers[2]	6 670	15.05	31 300	14.09
Funeral attendants[2]	24 970	8.33	17 320	7.70
Barbers[2]	14 150	10.08	20 970	8.91
Hairdressers, hairstylists, and cosmetologists	314 750	10.00	20 800	8.33
Makeup artists, theatrical and performance	1 170	12.11	25 180	10.60
Manicurists and pedicurists[2]	23 540	7.73	16 080	6.70
Shampooers[2]	13 580	6.72	13 970	6.29
Skin care specialists	11 910	10.16	21 130	8.87
Baggage porters and bellhops[2]	59 580	8.23	17 110	6.84
Concierges	16 440	10.78	22 420	9.44
Tour guides and escorts	35 780	9.66	20 100	8.46
Travel guides	4 180	13.07	27 190	12.00
Flight attendants[2]	123 310	(3)	47 910	(3)
Transportation attendants, except flight attendants and baggage porters[2]	22 780	9.89	20 570	8.13
Child care workers[2]	377 110	7.42	15 430	6.91
Personal and home care aides[2]	300 500	7.72	16 060	7.50
Fitness trainers and aerobics instructors	127 310	13.12	27 300	10.84
Recreation workers	245 180	8.89	18 500	7.90
Residential advisors	43 260	9.90	20 590	9.21
SALES AND RELATED OCCUPATIONS				
First-line supervisors, managers of retail sales workers	1 237 050	15.11	31 430	12.91
First-line supervisors, managers of non-retail sales workers	302 870	25.66	53 380	21.57
Cashiers[2]	3 162 090	7.35	15 290	6.68
Gaming change persons and booth cashiers	40 390	8.88	18 470	8.60
Counter and rental clerks[2]	392 560	8.02	16 690	7.16
Parts salespersons[2]	265 380	12.22	25 410	10.92
Retail salespersons[2]	3 729 040	9.24	19 210	7.66
Advertising sales agents[2]	142 830	19.91	41 400	15.93
Insurance sales agents	241 730	22.93	47 690	18.61
Securities, commodities, and financial services sales agents	249 660	34.44	71 640	28.63
Travel agents[2]	111 130	11.86	24 660	11.25
Sales representatives, wholesale and manufacturing, technical and scientific products[2]	341 930	25.07	52 140	22.09
Sales representatives, wholesale and manufacturing, except technical and scientific products[2]	1 315 900	20.80	43 260	17.91
Demonstrators and product promoters[2]	95 160	10.30	21 420	8.56
Models[2]	5 220	10.15	21 110	8.37
Real estate brokers	26 760	29.90	62 190	24.22
Real estate sales agents[2]	107 680	17.78	36 990	13.25
Sales engineers[2]	93 620	27.95	58 130	26.13
Telemarketers	485 650	10.15	21 100	8.91
Door-to-door sales workers, news and street vendors, and related workers	36 130	13.91	28 940	11.51

See footnotes at end of table.

Table 5-15. Employment and Wages by Occupation, 1999—*Continued*

(Number of persons, dollars.)

Occupational division and occupation	Employment	Mean hourly wages	Mean annual wages[1]	Median hourly wages
OFFICE AND ADMINISTRATIVE SUPPORT OCCUPATIONS				
First-line supervisors, managers of office and administrative support workers [2]	1 312 630	17.36	36 110	15.93
Switchboard operators, including answering service [2]	248 570	9.51	19 780	9.11
Telephone operators [2]	50 820	12.88	26 800	13.66
Bill and account collectors [2]	383 090	11.95	24 860	11.32
Billing and posting clerks and machine operators [2]	551 410	11.48	23 880	11.00
Bookkeeping, accounting, and auditing clerks [2]	1 619 870	12.14	25 250	11.53
Gaming cage workers	20 100	9.85	20 480	9.57
Payroll and timekeeping clerks [2]	196 660	12.89	26 800	12.37
Procurement clerks [2]	76 970	12.62	26 250	12.23
Tellers [2]	453 140	8.81	18 330	8.60
Brokerage clerks [2]	72 930	14.99	31 180	13.79
Correspondence clerks	46 160	11.48	23 880	11.05
Court, municipal, and license clerks [2]	93 910	12.84	26 700	12.11
Credit authorizers, checkers, and clerks	82 900	12.34	25 660	11.51
Customer service representatives	1 789 620	12.19	25 360	11.30
Eligibility interviewers, government programs	107 650	14.08	29 290	13.15
File clerks [2]	266 890	8.94	18 590	8.38
Hotel, motel, and resort desk clerks [2]	152 040	7.79	16 200	7.54
Interviewers, except eligibility and loan [2]	164 310	10.25	21 320	9.66
Library assistants, clerical	89 050	9.14	19 010	8.49
Loan interviewers and clerks	145 400	12.79	26 600	12.12
New accounts clerks [2]	69 790	10.81	22 480	10.63
Order clerks	376 430	11.51	23 950	10.78
Human resources assistants, except payroll and timekeeping [2]	174 110	13.05	27 140	12.59
Receptionists and information clerks [2]	987 680	9.55	19 870	9.26
Reservation and transportation ticket agents and travel clerks	222 340	12.47	25 930	10.74
Cargo and freight agents [2]	52 690	13.38	27 830	12.37
Couriers and messengers [2]	134 370	9.04	18 810	8.36
Police, fire, and ambulance dispatchers [2]	79 140	12.26	25 500	11.77
Dispatchers, except police, fire, and ambulance [2]	171 560	14.14	29 420	13.00
Meter readers, utilities [2]	46 090	13.16	27 370	12.45
Postal service clerks	80 330	18.37	38 220	18.64
Postal service mail carriers	352 550	17.60	36 610	18.21
Postal service mail sorters, processors, and processing machine operators	234 820	14.47	30 100	14.86
Production, planning, and expediting clerks [2]	298 770	15.24	31 700	14.47
Shipping, receiving, and traffic clerks [2]	886 230	10.62	22 080	9.99
Stock clerks and order fillers [2]	1 800 840	9.45	19 650	8.35
Weighers, measurers, checkers, and samplers, recordkeeping [2]	83 840	12.34	25 670	10.96
Executive secretaries and administrative assistants	1 316 290	14.84	30 870	14.21
Legal secretaries [2]	272 090	15.48	32 200	15.04
Medical secretaries [2]	247 950	11.51	23 940	10.95
Secretaries, except legal, medical, and executive	1 582 080	11.60	24 130	11.18
Computer operators [2]	198 500	13.54	28 170	12.70
Data entry keyers [2]	520 220	10.13	21 070	9.77
Word processors and typists [2]	271 310	11.67	24 270	11.29
Desktop publishers	37 040	14.98	31 170	14.12
Insurance claims and policy processing clerks	268 650	15.38	32 000	13.93
Mail clerks and mail machine operators, except postal service [2]	198 440	9.33	19 400	8.76
Office clerks, general	2 561 300	10.31	21 450	9.77
Office machine operators, except computer [2]	101 490	10.34	21 510	9.71
Proofreaders and copy markers [2]	25 970	10.46	21 750	9.37
Statistical assistants [2]	24 450	12.49	25 970	11.55
FARMING, FISHING, AND FORESTRY OCCUPATIONS				
First-line supervisors, managers of farming, fishing, and forestry workers	20 360	15.88	33 030	14.59
Farm labor contractors	11 260	8.72	18 140	6.71
Agricultural inspectors	10 520	14.46	30 080	13.89
Animal breeders	1 420	12.04	25 050	10.65
Graders and sorters, agricultural products [2]	62 380	7.46	15 520	6.76
Agricultural equipment operators [2]	17 630	8.48	17 640	7.67
Farmworkers and laborers, crop, nursery, and greenhouse [2]	215 080	6.80	14 150	6.42
Farmworkers, farm and ranch animals	34 510	7.96	16 560	7.40
Forest and conservation workers [2]	11 780	9.67	20 120	8.21
Fallers	9 420	14.44	30 040	13.44
Logging equipment operators [2]	33 230	12.17	25 310	11.43
Log graders and scalers [2]	5 500	12.59	26 180	11.61

See footnotes at end of table.

Table 5-15. Employment and Wages by Occupation, 1999—*Continued*

(Number of persons, dollars.)

Occupational division and occupation	Employment	Mean hourly wages	Mean annual wages[1]	Median hourly wages
CONSTRUCTION AND EXTRACTION OCCUPATIONS				
First-line supervisors, managers of construction trades and extraction workers	476 770	21.98	45 720	20.71
Boilermakers [2]	29 160	18.51	38 500	18.09
Brickmasons and blockmasons	98 530	19.90	41 380	19.36
Stonemasons [2]	8 640	16.46	34 240	15.36
Carpenters	771 030	16.55	34 420	15.35
Carpet installers [2]	37 750	15.26	31 750	13.23
Floor layers, except carpet, wood, and hard tiles	11 310	15.04	31 280	13.96
Floor sanders and finishers [2]	6 400	12.91	26 860	11.88
Tile and marble setters	27 330	17.84	37 100	17.08
Cement masons and concrete finishers	151 760	15.01	31 210	13.68
Terrazzo workers and finishers	4 570	15.45	32 130	15.03
Construction laborers	763 450	12.75	26 510	10.85
Paving, surfacing, and tamping equipment operators [2]	58 410	13.99	29 090	12.45
Pile-driver operators [2]	4 940	20.00	41 600	19.93
Operating engineers and other construction equipment operators [2]	324 350	16.71	34 760	15.31
Drywall and ceiling tile installers	118 300	16.39	34 090	15.34
Tapers [2]	36 950	17.04	35 430	16.02
Electricians	611 920	20.28	42 180	19.13
Glaziers	49 630	14.75	30 680	13.33
Insulation workers [2]	56 850	14.02	29 170	12.52
Painters, construction and maintenance	260 880	14.08	29 280	12.86
Paperhangers	10 070	15.78	32 830	15.34
Pipelayers [2]	53 530	14.08	29 290	12.67
Plumbers, pipefitters, and steamfitters [2]	413 170	18.63	38 750	17.41
Plasterers and stucco masons [2]	50 060	15.70	32 650	14.48
Reinforcing iron and rebar workers [2]	27 760	17.79	37 000	16.03
Roofers [2]	115 280	14.36	29 870	12.94
Sheet metal workers [2]	231 690	15.92	33 110	14.09
Structural iron and steel workers [2]	85 520	18.16	37 780	17.19
Helpers-brickmasons, blockmasons, stonemasons, and tile and marble setters [2]	56 660	12.03	25 020	10.61
Helpers-carpenters [2]	104 910	10.20	21 210	9.61
Helpers-electricians	100 460	10.41	21 650	9.89
Helpers-painters, paperhangers, plasterers, and stucco masons [2]	30 790	9.73	20 230	8.95
Helpers-pipelayers, plumbers, pipefitters, and steamfitters [2]	81 410	10.25	21 320	9.62
Helpers-roofers [2]	27 340	8.80	18 310	8.41
Construction and building inspectors [2]	67 010	19.11	39 740	18.55
Elevator installers and repairers [2]	25 010	22.95	47 740	22.38
Fence erectors [2]	15 540	10.67	22 200	9.95
Hazardous materials removal workers [2]	34 750	15.22	31 650	14.05
Highway maintenance workers [2]	139 540	12.85	26 730	12.44
Rail-track laying and maintenance equipment operators [2]	8 620	17.81	37 050	17.67
Septic tank servicers and sewer pipe cleaners [2]	12 820	13.86	28 820	13.03
Segmental pavers	2 890	12.45	25 900	11.35
Derrick operators, oil and gas [2]	13 720	14.24	29 630	12.84
Rotary drill operators, oil and gas [2]	9 500	17.81	37 040	15.71
Service unit operators, oil, gas, and mining [2]	11 630	12.39	25 780	11.29
Earth drillers, except oil and gas [2]	19 650	15.02	31 240	13.75
Explosives workers, ordnance handling experts, and blasters [2]	4 180	16.08	33 450	15.52
Continuous mining machine operators [2]	10 090	16.53	34 370	15.73
Mine cutting and channeling machine operators [2]	(5)	17.15	35 680	17.57
Mining machine operators, all other [2]	5 120	16.77	34 880	16.08
Rock splitters, quarry [2]	2 140	11.49	23 900	11.12
Roof bolters, mining [2]	4 170	17.71	36 840	17.48
Roustabouts, oil and gas [2]	29 860	11.18	23 260	10.08
Helpers-extraction workers	27 730	10.62	22 090	9.83
INSTALLATION, MAINTENANCE, AND REPAIR OCCUPATIONS				
First-line supervisors, managers of mechanics, installers, and repairers	386 170	21.65	45 040	20.54
Computer, automated teller, and office machine repairers	130 090	15.04	31 290	14.26
Radio mechanics [2]	4 570	16.33	33 960	15.49
Telecommunications equipment installers and repairers, except line installers	172 700	19.77	41 130	20.37
Avionics technicians	15 560	19.75	41 090	19.63
Electric motor, power tool, and related repairers	35 270	14.81	30 800	13.97
Electrical and electronics installers and repairers, transportation equipment	14 700	15.54	32 310	15.23
Electrical and electronics repairers, commercial and industrial equipment	71 530	17.39	36 160	17.15
Electrical and electronics repairers, powerhouse, substation, and relay	20 580	21.87	45 490	22.92
Electronic equipment installers and repairers, motor vehicles	14 250	12.29	25 560	11.50

See footnotes at end of table.

Table 5-15. Employment and Wages by Occupation, 1999—*Continued*

(Number of persons, dollars.)

Occupational division and occupation	Employment	Mean hourly wages	Mean annual wages[1]	Median hourly wages
Electronic home entertainment equipment installers and repairers	26 090	12.99	27 020	12.03
Security and fire alarm systems installers	38 350	14.81	30 810	13.96
Aircraft mechanics and service technicians	125 970	18.88	39 280	18.90
Automotive body and related repairers	179 960	16.21	33 720	15.06
Automotive glass installers and repairers	20 520	13.34	27 740	13.26
Automotive service technicians and mechanics [2]	587 320	14.49	30 130	13.62
Bus and truck mechanics and diesel engine specialists [2]	273 320	15.29	31 800	14.77
Farm equipment mechanics [2]	40 490	11.91	24 770	11.42
Mobile heavy equipment mechanics, except engines [2]	113 540	16.24	33 790	15.75
Rail car repairers [2]	7 230	17.83	37 080	18.09
Motorboat mechanics	18 450	13.52	28 120	13.01
Motorcycle mechanics [2]	11 390	12.26	25 510	11.61
Outdoor power equipment and other small engine mechanics	26 550	11.38	23 660	10.86
Bicycle repairers [2]	8 080	8.08	16 810	7.72
Recreational vehicle service technicians	13 100	12.49	25 980	11.86
Tire repairers and changers [2]	99 880	8.96	18 630	8.37
Mechanical door repairers	9 620	14.77	30 710	14.68
Control and valve installers and repairers, except mechanical door	31 040	19.77	41 120	19.96
Heating, air conditioning, and refrigeration mechanics and installers [2]	187 850	15.40	32 040	14.50
Home appliance repairers	33 050	14.43	30 020	13.95
Industrial machinery mechanics	176 070	17.41	36 210	16.56
Maintenance and repair workers, general [2]	1 201 690	12.95	26 930	11.99
Maintenance workers, machinery [2]	107 180	15.29	31 800	14.57
Millwrights [2]	80 390	18.90	39 320	18.76
Refractory materials repairers, except brickmasons [2]	3 320	15.54	32 320	14.99
Electrical power-line installers and repairers [2]	99 090	20.91	43 490	20.97
Telecommunications line installers and repairers [2]	158 990	17.21	35 790	16.35
Camera and photographic equipment repairers [2]	5 330	15.20	31 630	14.27
Medical equipment repairers [2]	19 640	17.02	35 390	16.45
Musical instrument repairers and tuners [2]	4 500	12.42	25 830	11.63
Watch repairers [2]	3 870	12.65	26 320	11.79
Coin, vending, and amusement machine servicers and repairers	35 900	12.33	25 650	11.94
Commercial divers	2 400	33.86	70 420	27.17
Fabric menders, except garment	2 980	11.62	24 100	9.53
Locksmiths and safe repairers [2]	11 300	13.47	28 020	12.00
Manufactured building and mobile home installers	13 200	10.86	22 580	10.07
Riggers [2]	15 850	15.59	32 420	15.12
Signal and track switch repairers [2]	3 720	19.90	41 400	18.91
Helpers-installation, maintenance, and repair workers [2]	145 610	10.03	20 860	9.14
PRODUCTION OCCUPATIONS				
First-line supervisors, managers of production and operating workers	760 050	19.83	41 250	18.61
Aircraft structure, surfaces, rigging, and systems assemblers [2]	18 070	17.65	36 720	17.83
Coil winders, tapers, and finishers [2]	56 350	10.45	21 740	9.65
Electrical and electronic equipment assemblers	387 430	10.50	21 840	9.84
Electromechanical equipment assemblers	69 830	11.46	23 830	10.69
Engine and other machine assemblers	85 570	13.41	27 900	13.23
Structural metal fabricators and fitters	94 390	13.21	27 470	12.62
Fiberglass laminators and fabricators	49 750	11.34	23 600	10.20
Team assemblers	1 302 820	10.67	22 200	9.95
Timing device assemblers, adjusters, and calibrators	10 270	10.67	22 190	9.90
Bakers [2]	176 080	9.61	19 990	8.82
Butchers and meat cutters	138 870	11.97	24 890	11.20
Meat, poultry, and fish cutters and trimmers [2]	159 890	8.35	17 370	8.08
Slaughterers and meat packers	116 970	9.13	18 980	9.18
Food and tobacco roasting, baking, and drying machine operators and tenders	19 830	11.58	24 080	9.83
Food batchmakers	64 760	10.22	21 260	9.64
Food cooking machine operators and tenders	44 340	10.45	21 730	9.85
Computer-controlled machine tool operators, metal and plastic	168 170	13.66	28 420	13.07
Numerical tool and process control programmers	24 180	17.45	36 300	17.27
Extruding and drawing machine setters, operators, and tenders, metal and plastic	108 570	11.65	24 220	11.25
Forging machine setters, operators, and tenders, metal and plastic	60 970	12.99	27 020	11.91
Rolling machine setters, operators, and tenders, metal and plastic	47 580	13.49	28 060	12.95
Cutting, punching, and press machine setters, operators, and tenders, metal and plastic	353 300	11.37	23 640	10.67
Drilling and boring machine tool setters, operators, and tenders, metal and plastic	75 140	12.60	26 220	11.89
Grinding, lapping, polishing, and buffing machine tool setters, operators, and tenders, metal and plastic	127 920	12.14	25 250	11.54

See footnotes at end of table.

Table 5-15. Employment and Wages by Occupation, 1999—*Continued*

(Number of persons, dollars.)

Occupational division and occupation	Employment	Mean hourly wages	Mean annual wages[1]	Median hourly wages
Lathe and turning machine tool setters, operators, and tenders, metal and plastic	83 940	14.18	29 490	13.65
Milling and planing machine setters, operators, and tenders, metal and plastic	35 830	13.44	27 960	12.70
Machinists	419 800	14.69	30 540	14.30
Metal-refining furnace operators and tenders [2]	19 350	13.75	28 590	12.94
Pourers and casters, metal [2]	15 600	12.94	26 920	12.34
Model makers, metal and plastic	12 520	16.89	35 130	16.15
Patternmakers, metal and plastic	8 340	14.53	30 230	13.45
Foundry mold and coremakers	34 840	11.99	24 950	11.39
Molding, coremaking, and casting machine setters, operators, and tenders, metal and plastic	179 640	10.81	22 480	9.81
Multiple machine tool setters, operators, and tenders, metal and plastic [2]	103 620	12.89	26 820	12.00
Tool and die makers [2]	132 350	19.12	39 770	18.60
Welders, cutters, solderers, and brazers [2]	410 040	13.40	27 870	12.58
Welding, soldering, and brazing machine setters, operators, and tenders [2]	68 680	13.17	27 400	12.29
Heat treating equipment setters, operators, and tenders, metal and plastic [2]	36 300	13.00	27 030	12.13
Lay-out workers, metal and plastic	17 990	14.65	30 470	13.90
Plating and coating machine setters, operators, and tenders, metal and plastic [2]	58 350	11.45	23 810	10.76
Tool grinders, filers, and sharpeners [2]	28 150	13.97	29 060	13.19
Bindery workers	106 560	10.90	22 660	9.74
Bookbinders [2]	10 010	11.59	24 110	10.36
Job printers [2]	45 850	13.17	27 390	12.55
Prepress technicians and workers	109 350	14.90	30 990	13.90
Printing machine operators [2]	208 980	13.86	28 830	12.94
Laundry and dry-cleaning workers	217 350	7.58	15 760	7.25
Pressers, textile, garment, and related materials [2]	93 320	7.77	16 170	7.49
Sewing machine operators [2]	403 770	8.05	16 750	7.57
Shoe and leather workers and repairers	15 610	8.67	18 040	8.04
Shoe machine operators and tenders	11 450	8.62	17 920	8.63
Sewers, hand	23 910	9.48	19 720	8.06
Tailors, dressmakers, and custom sewers [2]	32 310	10.22	21 260	9.29
Textile bleaching and dyeing machine operators and tenders	44 450	9.14	19 020	9.09
Textile cutting machine setters, operators, and tenders	39 870	9.45	19 650	8.98
Textile knitting and weaving machine setters, operators, and tenders	79 440	10.17	21 150	10.00
Textile winding, twisting, and drawing out machine setters, operators, and tenders	83 360	10.25	21 320	9.91
Extruding and forming machine setters, operators, and tenders, synthetic and glass fibers	35 810	11.94	24 840	11.97
Fabric and apparel patternmakers [2]	16 920	13.52	28 120	10.63
Upholsterers [2]	45 380	11.58	24 090	10.98
Cabinetmakers and bench carpenters	136 910	11.20	23 300	10.46
Furniture finishers [2]	38 040	10.41	21 650	9.86
Model makers, wood	4 910	13.14	27 330	11.84
Patternmakers, wood	5 820	14.77	30 710	14.48
Sawing machine setters, operators, and tenders, wood [2]	54 760	10.22	21 250	9.71
Woodworking machine setters, operators, and tenders, except sawing	103 650	10.02	20 840	9.65
Nuclear power reactor operators [2]	3 240	27.19	56 550	26.73
Power distributors and dispatchers [2]	14 080	22.89	47 600	22.60
Power plant operators	34 310	20.73	43 110	21.30
Stationary engineers and boiler operators	56 350	18.78	39 070	18.54
Water and liquid waste treatment plant and system operators [2]	81 830	15.07	31 350	14.46
Chemical plant and system operators [2]	64 320	18.91	39 330	18.88
Gas plant operators [2]	16 740	20.71	43 080	20.89
Petroleum pump system operators, refinery operators, and gaugers [2]	34 370	20.58	42 810	21.55
Chemical equipment operators and tenders [2]	51 080	16.61	34 560	16.58
Separating, filtering, clarifying, precipitating, and still machine setters, operators, and tenders [2]	33 470	13.61	28 310	13.23
Crushing, grinding, and polishing machine setters, operators, and tenders	49 690	12.31	25 600	11.71
Grinding and polishing workers, hand [2]	49 510	11.18	23 260	10.15
Mixing and blending machine setters, operators, and tenders	114 540	12.67	26 360	12.26
Cutters and trimmers, hand	33 590	10.94	22 750	9.78
Cutting and slicing machine setters, operators, and tenders [2]	85 060	11.44	23 800	10.87
Extruding, forming, pressing, and compacting machine setters, operators, and tenders [2]	74 100	12.01	24 990	11.44
Furnace, kiln, oven, drier, and kettle operators and tenders [2]	29 640	13.42	27 910	12.52
Inspectors, testers, sorters, samplers, and weighers [2]	577 650	13.05	27 140	11.68
Jewelers and precious stone and metal workers [2]	28 690	12.67	26 360	11.19
Dental laboratory technicians [2]	42 940	14.06	29 240	12.46
Medical appliance technicians [2]	13 610	13.02	27 080	10.97
Ophthalmic laboratory technicians [2]	34 590	10.42	21 680	9.49
Packaging and filling machine operators and tenders	379 760	9.99	20 790	9.01
Coating, painting, and spraying machine setters, operators, and tenders [2]	101 610	11.46	23 840	10.86
Painters, transportation equipment [2]	45 920	15.36	31 940	14.13
Painting, coating, and decorating workers [2]	34 780	10.43	21 700	9.56
Photographic process workers [2]	26 170	11.11	23 110	9.92
Photographic processing machine operators [2]	50 270	9.58	19 920	8.59

See footnotes at end of table.

Table 5-15. Employment and Wages by Occupation, 1999—*Continued*

(Number of persons, dollars.)

Occupational division and occupation	Employment	Mean hourly wages	Mean annual wages[1]	Median hourly wages
Semiconductor processors [2]	42 110	13.24	27 540	12.45
Cementing and gluing machine operators and tenders [2]	32 440	10.69	22 240	10.23
Cleaning, washing, and metal pickling equipment operators and tenders	18 850	10.38	21 590	9.41
Cooling and freezing equipment operators and tenders [2]	6 200	10.35	21 520	9.36
Etchers and engravers [2]	9 420	10.76	22 380	9.50
Molders, shapers, and casters, except metal and plastic	34 310	11.04	22 960	10.47
Paper goods machine setters, operators, and tenders [2]	118 830	13.24	27 540	12.82
Tire builders [2]	16 680	17.30	35 980	17.93
Helpers-production workers	584 060	8.98	18 680	8.37
TRANSPORTATION AND MATERIAL MOVING OCCUPATIONS				
Aircraft cargo handling supervisors	8 090	18.55	38 590	17.02
First-line supervisors, managers of helpers, laborers, and material movers, hand	138 210	16.86	35 080	15.88
First-line supervisors, managers of transportation and material-moving machine and vehicle operators	175 260	20.02	41 650	18.80
Airline pilots, copilots, and flight engineers	88 040	(3)	98 280	(3)
Commercial pilots	18 780	(3)	56 240	(3)
Air traffic controllers	22 620	35.19	73 190	35.61
Airfield operations specialists	4 510	14.27	29 670	13.15
Ambulance drivers and attendants, except emergency medical technicians [2]	13 520	9.63	20 030	8.40
Bus drivers, transit and intercity [2]	160 210	12.72	26 450	11.67
Bus drivers, school [2]	463 860	9.83	20 460	9.57
Driver, sales workers [2]	385 210	10.83	22 520	9.71
Truck drivers, heavy and tractor-trailer	1 558 400	15.34	31 900	14.74
Truck drivers, light or delivery services	1 085 050	11.31	23 530	10.33
Taxi drivers and chauffeurs [2]	119 630	8.75	18 200	7.89
Locomotive engineers [2]	19 940	23.10	48 050	21.19
Locomotive firers [2]	890	24.32	50 570	22.35
Rail yard engineers, dinkey operators, and hostlers [2]	5 070	17.43	36 260	17.44
Railroad brake, signal, and switch operators [2]	14 500	19.21	39 950	18.47
Railroad conductors and yardmasters [2]	36 680	21.24	44 180	19.44
Sailors and marine oilers [2]	27 200	12.41	25 820	11.97
Captains, mates, and pilots of water vessels [2]	20 660	19.93	41 460	19.00
Motorboat operators [2]	4 000	13.42	27 910	12.74
Ship engineers [2]	6 800	22.02	45 800	21.31
Bridge and lock tenders [2]	6 970	13.46	28 000	14.30
Parking lot attendants [2]	109 340	7.38	15 350	6.89
Service station attendants [2]	109 050	7.58	15 770	7.11
Traffic technicians	5 000	15.70	32 650	14.56
Transportation inspectors [2]	22 440	20.66	42 980	20.29
Conveyor operators and tenders [2]	57 180	11.67	24 280	11.08
Crane and tower operators [2]	53 830	16.21	33 710	15.29
Dredge operators [2]	1 910	13.73	28 550	12.96
Excavating and loading machine and dragline operators [2]	62 360	15.13	31 460	13.73
Loading machine operators, underground mining [2]	2 930	14.66	30 500	14.59
Hoist and winch operators [2]	7 900	15.03	31 260	14.18
Industrial truck and tractor operators [2]	590 710	12.33	25 650	11.49
Cleaners of vehicles and equipment [2]	302 380	8.00	16 650	7.26
Laborers and freight, stock, and material movers, hand	2 035 640	9.50	19 750	8.75
Machine feeders and offbearers [2]	176 400	10.04	20 890	9.40
Packers and packagers, hand [2]	1 114 330	7.83	16 280	7.20
Gas compressor and gas pumping station operators [2]	6 940	17.26	35 900	17.87
Pump operators, except wellhead pumpers [2]	13 480	16.95	35 250	15.70
Wellhead pumpers [2]	14 710	16.09	33 460	16.19
Refuse and recyclable material collectors [2]	135 320	12.03	25 020	11.19
Shuttle car operators [2]	2 830	16.33	33 960	17.00
Tank car, truck, and ship loaders	20 830	14.09	29 310	12.43

1. Annual wages have been calculated by multiplying the hourly mean wage by a "year-round, full-time" hours figure of 2,080 hours; for those occupations where there is not an hourly mean wage published, the annual wage has been directly calculated from the reported survey data.
2. Wage rates are calculated using three years of data, 1997, 1998, and 1999.
3. Hourly wage rates for occupations where workers typically work fewer than 2,080 hours per year are not available.
4. Represents a wage above $70.01 per hour.
5. Data not released due to high relative standard error.

PART SIX

PRICES AND LIVING CONDITIONS

PRICES AND LIVING CONDITIONS

HIGHLIGHTS

This part covers one of the most important aspects of the state of the economy, the movement of prices. Three price indexes are covered: prices received by producers, prices paid by consumers, and prices involved in foreign trade.

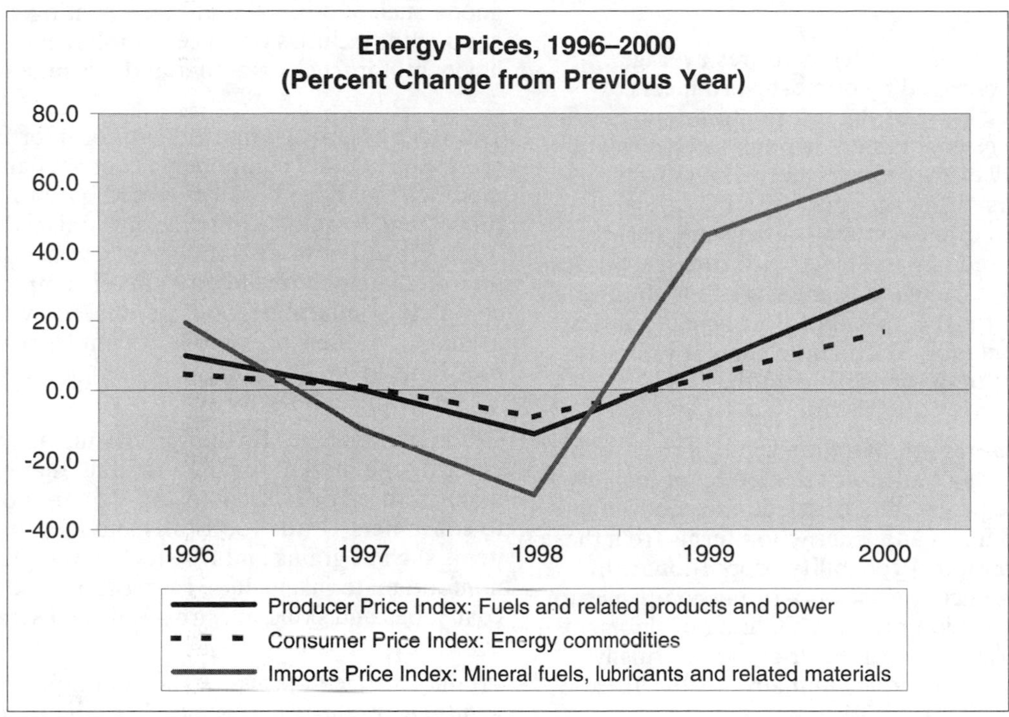

The three indexes related to energy, while not identical in coverage, show how domestic producer prices are related to import prices and consumer prices to both. Energy played a significant part in the 2000 increases in consumer and producer prices, the largest since 1990. The Consumer Price Index (CPI) rose 3.4 percent, and Producer Price Index for Finished Goods (PPI) rose 3.8 percent from 1999 to 2000.

OTHER HIGHLIGHTS:

- The CPI for all items less energy increased 2.4 percent in 2000 from the previous year. (Table 6-5)
- Increases in energy in 2000 also led to larger increases in housing (3.5 percent) and transportation (6.5 percent) than the recent trend in these components. (Table 6-4)
- Medical care costs continued to increase in 2000 (4 percent) faster than the CPI for all items (3.4 percent). (Table 6-4)
- In 2000, the purchasing power of the dollar had its biggest drop since 1995, declining by -3.2 percent to a value of $0.58 when the dollar's value in 1982–1984 is taken to be $1.00. This was the result of the increase in energy prices accompanied by price increases of rent of shelter and medical care. (Tables 6-5, 6-6)

NOTES AND DEFINITIONS

PRODUCER PRICE INDEX

Coverage

The *Producer Price Index* (PPI) measures average changes in prices received by domestic producers of goods and services. Most of the information used in calculating the indexes is obtained through the systematic sampling of nearly every industry in the manufacturing and mining sectors of the economy. The PPI program also includes data from other sectors—agriculture, fishing, forestry, services, and gas and electricity. Because producer price indexes are designed to measure only the change in prices received for the output of domestic industries, *imports are not included.* The sample currently contains about 80,000 price quotations per month.

Producer price indexes are based on selling prices reported by establishments of all sizes selected by probability sampling, with the probability of selection proportionate to size. Individual items and transaction terms from these firms are also chosen by probability proportionate to size. BLS strongly encourages cooperating companies to supply actual transaction prices at the time of shipment to minimize the use of list prices. Prices are normally reported monthly by mail questionnaire for the Tuesday of the week containing the 13th.

Price data are always provided on a voluntary and confidential basis; only BLS employees, sworn to secrecy, are allowed access to individual company price reports. The Bureau publishes price indexes instead of unit dollar prices. All producer price indexes are routinely subject to revision once, 4 months after original publication, to reflect the availability of late reports and corrections by respondents.

There are three primary systems of indexes within the PPI program: (1) stage-of-processing indexes; (2) indexes for the net output of industries and their products; and (3) commodity indexes. The commodity-based *stage-of-processing* structure organizes products by class of buyer and degree of fabrication. The entire output of various industries is sampled to derive price indexes for the net output of industries and their products. The commodity structure organizes products by similarity of end-use or material composition.

Within the commodity stage-of-processing system, finished goods are commodities that will not undergo further processing and are ready for sale to the final demand user, either an individual consumer or a business firm. Consumer foods include unprocessed foods, such as eggs and fresh vegetables, as well as processed foods, such as bakery products and meats. Other finished consumer goods include durable goods, such as automobiles, household furniture, and appliances; and nondurable goods, such as apparel and home heating oil. Capital equipment includes producer durable goods, such as heavy motor trucks, tractors, and machine tools.

The stage-of-processing category for intermediate materials, supplies, and components consists partly of commodities that have been processed but require further processing. Examples of such semi-finished goods include flour, cotton, yarn, steel mill products, and lumber. The intermediate goods category also encompasses physically complete nondurable goods purchased by business firms as inputs for their operations. Examples include diesel fuel, belts and belting, paper boxes, and fertilizers.

Crude materials for further processing are products entering the market for the first time that have not been manufactured or fabricated and that are not sold directly to consumers. Crude foodstuffs and feedstuffs include items such as grains and livestock. Examples of crude nonfood materials include raw cotton, crude petroleum, coal, hides and skins, and iron and steel scrap.

Producer price indexes for the net output of industries and their products are grouped according to the Standard Industrial Classification (SIC) and the Census product code extensions of the SIC. Industry price indexes are compatible with other economic time series organized by SIC codes, such as data on employment, wages, and productivity.

Net output values of shipments are used as weights for industry indexes. Net output values refer to the value of shipments from establishments in one industry shipped to establishments classified in another industry. However, *weights for commodity price indexes* are based on gross shipment values, including shipment values between establishments within the same industry. As a result, commodity aggregate indexes, such as the *all commodities index,* are affected by the multiple counting of price change at successive stages of processing, which can lead to exaggerated or misleading signals about inflation. Stage-of-processing indexes partially correct this defect, but industry indexes consistently correct this weakness at all levels of aggregation. Therefore, industry and stage-of-processing indexes are more appropriate than commodity aggregate indexes for economic analysis of general price trends.

Weights for most traditional commodity groupings of the PPI, as well as all indexes calculated from traditional commodity groupings (such as stage-of-processing indexes), currently reflect 1992 values of shipments as reported in the *Census of Manufactures* and other sources. Major industry group indexes, which are based on the SIC system, are currently calculated using 1992 net output weights. BLS is in the process of updating weights to take effect in 2002. The source data will be the most recent data from the Census of Manufactures and the Bureau of Economic Analysis. The new North American Industry Classification System (NAICS) is scheduled to be introduced in the PPI in 2004.

Sources of Additional Information

Additional information is published monthly by the BLS in the *Producer Price Index Detailed Report.* For information on the underlying concepts and methodology of the Producer Price Index, see chapter 14, "Producer Prices," in BLS Handbook of Methods (April 1997), Bulletin 2490. Reprints are available from the Bureau of Labor Statistics on request.

Table 6-1. Producer Price Indexes by Stage of Processing, 1947–2000

(1982=100.)

Year	Crude materials for further processing				Intermediate materials, supplies, and components						Finished goods		
	Total	Food-stuffs and feedstuffs	Nonfood materials, except fuel, including crude petroleum	Fuel, excluding crude petroleum	Total	Materials and compo-nents for construc-tion	Materials and compo-nents for manufac-turing	Pro-cessed fuels and lubricants	Contain-ers	Supplies	Total	Consum-er goods	Capital equip-ment
1947	31.7	45.1	24.0	7.5	23.3	22.5	24.9	14.4	23.4	28.5	26.4	28.6	19.8
1948	34.7	48.8	26.7	8.9	25.2	24.9	26.8	16.4	24.4	29.8	28.5	30.8	21.6
1949	30.1	40.5	24.3	8.8	24.2	24.9	25.7	14.9	24.5	28.0	27.7	29.4	22.7
1950	32.7	43.4	27.8	8.8	25.3	26.2	26.9	15.2	25.2	29.0	28.2	29.9	23.2
1951	37.6	50.2	32.0	9.0	28.4	28.7	30.5	15.9	29.6	32.6	30.8	32.7	25.5
1952	34.5	47.3	27.8	9.0	27.5	28.5	29.3	15.7	28.0	32.6	30.6	32.3	25.9
1953	31.9	42.3	26.6	9.3	27.7	29.0	29.7	15.8	28.0	31.0	30.3	31.7	26.3
1954	31.6	42.3	26.1	8.9	27.9	29.1	29.8	15.8	28.5	31.7	30.4	31.7	26.7
1955	30.4	38.4	27.5	8.9	28.4	30.3	30.5	15.8	28.9	31.2	30.5	31.5	27.4
1956	30.6	37.6	28.6	9.5	29.6	31.8	32.0	16.3	31.0	32.0	31.3	32.0	29.5
1957	31.2	39.2	28.2	10.1	30.3	32.0	32.7	17.2	32.4	32.3	32.5	32.9	31.3
1958	31.9	41.6	27.1	10.2	30.4	32.0	32.8	16.2	33.2	33.1	33.2	33.6	32.1
1959	31.1	38.8	28.1	10.4	30.8	32.9	33.3	16.2	33.0	33.5	33.1	33.3	32.7
1960	30.4	38.4	26.9	10.5	30.8	32.7	33.3	16.6	33.4	33.3	33.4	33.6	32.8
1961	30.2	37.9	27.2	10.5	30.6	32.2	32.9	16.8	33.2	33.7	33.4	33.6	32.9
1962	30.5	38.6	27.1	10.4	30.6	32.1	32.7	16.7	33.6	34.5	33.5	33.7	33.0
1963	29.9	37.5	26.7	10.5	30.7	32.2	32.7	16.6	33.2	35.0	33.4	33.5	33.1
1964	29.6	36.6	27.2	10.5	30.8	32.5	33.1	16.2	32.9	34.7	33.5	33.6	33.4
1965	31.1	39.2	27.7	10.6	31.2	32.8	33.6	16.5	33.5	35.0	34.1	34.2	33.8
1966	33.1	42.7	28.3	10.9	32.0	33.6	34.3	16.8	34.5	36.5	35.2	35.4	34.6
1967	31.3	40.3	26.5	11.3	32.2	34.0	34.5	16.9	35.0	36.8	35.6	35.6	35.8
1968	31.8	40.9	27.1	11.5	33.0	35.7	35.3	16.5	35.9	37.1	36.6	36.5	37.0
1969	33.9	44.1	28.4	12.0	34.1	37.7	36.5	16.6	37.2	37.8	38.0	37.9	38.3
1970	35.2	45.2	29.1	13.8	35.4	38.3	38.0	17.7	39.0	39.7	39.3	39.1	40.1
1971	36.0	46.1	29.4	15.7	36.8	40.8	38.9	19.5	40.8	40.8	40.5	40.2	41.7
1972	39.9	51.5	32.3	16.8	38.2	43.0	40.4	20.1	42.7	42.5	41.8	41.5	42.8
1973	54.5	72.6	42.9	18.6	42.4	46.5	44.1	22.2	45.2	51.7	45.6	46.0	44.2
1974	61.4	76.4	54.5	24.8	52.5	55.0	56.0	33.6	53.3	56.8	52.6	53.1	50.5
1975	61.6	77.4	50.0	30.6	58.0	60.1	61.7	39.4	60.0	61.8	58.2	58.2	58.2
1976	63.4	76.8	54.9	34.5	60.9	64.1	64.0	42.3	63.1	65.8	60.8	60.4	62.1
1977	65.5	77.5	56.3	42.0	64.9	69.3	67.4	47.7	65.9	69.3	64.7	64.3	66.1
1978	73.4	87.3	61.9	48.2	69.5	76.5	72.0	49.9	71.0	72.9	69.8	69.4	71.3
1979	85.9	100.0	75.5	57.3	78.4	84.2	80.9	61.6	79.4	80.2	77.6	77.5	77.5
1980	95.3	104.6	91.8	69.4	90.3	91.3	91.7	85.0	89.1	89.9	88.0	88.6	85.8
1981	103.0	103.9	109.8	84.8	98.6	97.9	98.7	100.6	96.7	96.9	96.1	96.6	94.6
1982	100.0	100.0	100.0	100.0	100.0	100.0	100.0	100.0	100.0	100.0	100.0	100.0	100.0
1983	101.3	101.8	98.8	105.1	100.6	102.8	101.2	95.4	100.4	101.8	101.6	101.3	102.8
1984	103.5	104.7	101.0	105.1	103.1	105.6	104.1	95.7	105.9	104.1	103.7	103.3	105.2
1985	95.8	94.8	94.3	102.7	102.7	107.3	103.3	92.8	109.0	104.4	104.7	103.8	107.5
1986	87.7	93.2	76.0	92.2	99.1	108.1	102.2	72.7	110.3	105.6	103.2	101.4	109.7
1987	93.7	96.2	88.5	84.1	101.5	109.8	105.3	73.3	114.5	107.7	105.4	103.6	111.7
1988	96.0	106.1	85.9	82.1	107.1	116.1	113.2	71.2	120.1	113.7	108.0	106.2	114.3
1989	103.1	111.2	95.8	85.3	112.0	121.3	118.1	76.4	125.4	118.1	113.6	112.1	118.8
1990	108.9	113.1	107.3	84.8	114.5	122.9	118.7	85.9	127.7	119.4	119.2	118.2	122.9
1991	101.2	105.5	97.5	82.9	114.4	124.5	118.1	85.3	128.1	121.4	121.7	120.5	126.7
1992	100.4	105.1	94.2	84.0	114.7	126.5	117.9	84.5	127.7	122.7	123.2	121.7	129.1
1993	102.4	108.4	94.1	87.1	116.2	132.0	118.9	84.7	126.4	125.0	124.7	123.0	131.4
1994	101.8	106.5	97.0	82.4	118.5	136.6	122.1	83.1	129.7	127.0	125.5	123.3	134.1
1995	102.7	105.8	105.8	72.1	124.9	142.1	130.4	84.2	148.8	132.1	127.9	125.6	136.7
1996	113.8	121.5	105.7	92.6	125.7	143.6	128.6	90.0	141.1	135.9	131.3	129.5	138.3
1997	111.1	112.2	103.5	101.3	125.6	146.5	128.3	89.3	136.0	135.9	131.8	130.2	138.2
1998	96.8	103.9	84.5	86.7	123.0	146.8	126.1	81.1	140.8	134.8	130.7	128.9	137.6
1999	98.2	98.7	91.1	91.2	123.2	148.9	124.6	84.6	142.5	134.2	133.0	132.0	137.6
2000	120.6	100.2	118.0	136.9	129.2	150.7	128.1	102.0	151.6	136.9	138.0	138.2	138.8

Table 6-2. Producer Price Indexes by Commodity Groups, 1913–2000

(1982=100.)

Year	All commodities	Farm products	Processed foods and feeds	Industrial commodities: Total	Textile products and apparel	Hides, leather, and related products	Fuels and related products and power	Chemicals and related products	Rubber and plastics products	Lumber and wood products	Pulp, paper, and allied products	Metals and metal products	Machinery and equipment	Furniture and household durables	Nonmetallic mineral products	Transportation equipment	Miscellaneous products
1913	12.0	18.0	...	11.9	...	...	...	...	...	...	...	...	...	...	...	...	...
1914	11.8	17.9	...	11.3	...	...	...	...	...	...	...	...	...	...	...	...	...
1915	12.0	18.0	...	11.6	...	...	...	...	...	...	...	...	...	...	...	...	...
1916	14.7	21.3	...	15.0	...	...	...	...	...	...	...	...	...	...	...	...	...
1917	20.2	32.6	...	19.5	...	...	...	...	...	...	...	...	...	...	...	...	...
1918	22.6	37.4	...	21.1	...	...	...	...	...	...	...	...	...	...	...	...	...
1919	23.9	39.8	...	22.0	...	...	...	...	...	...	...	...	...	...	...	...	...
1920	26.6	38.0	...	27.4	...	...	...	...	...	...	...	...	...	...	...	...	...
1921	16.8	22.3	...	17.8	...	...	...	...	...	...	...	...	...	...	...	...	...
1922	16.7	23.7	...	17.4	...	...	...	...	...	...	...	...	...	...	...	...	...
1923	17.3	24.9	...	17.8	...	...	...	...	...	...	...	...	...	...	...	...	...
1924	16.9	25.2	...	17.0	...	...	...	...	...	...	...	...	...	...	...	...	...
1925	17.8	27.7	...	17.5	...	...	...	...	...	...	...	...	...	...	...	...	...
1926	17.2	25.3	...	17.0	...	17.1	10.3	...	47.1	9.3	...	13.7	...	28.6	16.4	...	...
1927	16.5	25.1	...	16.0	...	18.4	9.1	...	35.7	8.8	...	12.9	...	27.9	15.7	...	...
1928	16.7	26.7	...	15.8	...	20.7	8.7	...	28.3	8.5	...	12.9	...	27.2	16.2	...	...
1929	16.4	26.4	...	15.6	...	18.6	8.6	...	24.6	8.8	...	13.3	...	27.0	16.0	...	...
1930	14.9	22.4	...	14.5	...	17.1	8.1	...	21.5	8.0	...	12.0	...	26.5	15.9	...	...
1931	12.6	16.4	...	12.8	...	14.7	7.0	...	18.3	6.5	...	10.8	...	24.4	14.9	...	...
1932	11.2	12.2	...	11.9	...	12.5	7.3	...	15.9	5.6	...	9.9	...	21.5	13.9	...	...
1933	11.4	13.0	...	12.1	...	13.8	6.9	16.2	16.7	6.7	...	10.2	...	21.6	14.7	...	...
1934	12.9	16.5	...	13.3	...	14.8	7.6	17.0	19.5	7.8	...	11.2	...	23.4	15.7	...	...
1935	13.8	19.8	...	13.3	...	15.3	7.6	17.7	19.6	7.5	...	11.2	...	23.2	15.7	...	...
1936	13.9	20.4	...	13.5	...	16.3	7.9	17.8	21.1	7.9	...	11.4	...	23.6	15.8	...	...
1937	14.9	21.8	...	14.5	...	17.9	8.0	18.6	24.9	9.0	...	13.1	...	26.1	16.1	...	...
1938	13.5	17.3	...	13.9	...	15.8	7.9	17.7	24.4	8.5	...	12.6	...	25.5	15.6	...	...
1939	13.3	16.5	...	13.9	...	16.3	7.5	17.6	25.4	8.7	...	12.5	14.8	25.4	15.3	...	...
1940	13.5	17.1	...	14.1	...	17.2	7.4	17.9	23.7	9.6	...	12.5	14.9	26.0	15.3	...	...
1941	15.1	20.8	...	15.1	...	18.4	7.9	19.5	25.5	11.5	...	12.8	15.1	27.6	15.7	...	...
1942	17.0	26.7	...	16.2	...	20.1	8.1	21.7	29.7	12.5	...	13.0	15.4	29.9	16.3	...	...
1943	17.8	30.9	...	16.5	...	20.1	8.3	21.9	30.5	13.2	...	12.9	15.2	29.7	16.4	...	...
1944	17.9	31.2	...	16.7	...	19.9	8.6	22.2	30.1	14.3	...	12.9	15.1	30.5	16.7	...	...
1945	18.2	32.4	...	17.0	...	20.1	8.7	22.3	29.2	14.5	...	13.1	15.1	30.5	17.4	...	...
1946	20.8	37.5	...	18.6	...	23.3	9.3	24.1	29.3	16.6	...	14.7	16.6	32.4	18.5	...	...
1947	25.6	45.1	33.0	22.7	50.6	31.7	11.1	32.1	29.2	25.8	25.1	18.2	19.3	37.2	20.7	...	26.6
1948	27.7	48.5	35.3	24.6	52.8	32.1	13.1	32.8	30.2	29.5	26.2	20.7	20.9	39.4	22.4	...	27.7
1949	26.3	41.9	32.1	24.1	48.3	30.4	12.4	30.0	29.2	27.3	25.1	20.9	21.9	40.1	23.0	...	28.2
1950	27.3	44.0	33.2	25.0	50.2	32.9	12.6	30.4	35.6	31.4	25.7	22.0	22.6	40.9	23.5	...	28.6
1951	30.4	51.2	36.9	27.6	56.0	37.7	13.0	34.8	43.7	34.1	30.5	24.5	25.3	44.4	25.0	...	30.3
1952	29.6	48.4	36.4	26.9	50.5	30.5	13.0	33.0	39.6	33.2	29.7	24.5	25.3	43.5	25.0	...	30.2
1953	29.2	43.8	34.8	27.2	49.3	31.0	13.4	33.4	36.9	33.1	29.6	25.3	25.9	44.4	26.0	...	31.0
1954	29.3	43.2	35.4	27.2	48.2	29.5	13.2	33.8	37.5	32.5	29.6	25.5	26.3	44.9	26.6	...	31.3
1955	29.3	40.5	33.8	27.8	48.2	29.4	13.2	33.7	42.4	34.1	30.4	27.2	27.2	45.1	27.3	...	31.3
1956	30.3	40.0	33.8	29.1	48.2	31.2	13.6	33.9	43.0	34.6	32.4	29.6	29.3	46.3	28.5	...	31.7
1957	31.2	41.1	34.8	29.9	48.3	31.2	14.3	34.6	42.8	32.8	33.0	30.2	31.4	47.5	29.6	...	32.6
1958	31.6	42.9	36.5	30.0	47.4	31.6	13.7	34.9	42.8	32.5	33.4	30.0	32.1	47.9	29.9	...	33.3
1959	31.7	40.2	35.6	30.5	48.1	35.9	13.7	34.8	42.6	34.7	33.7	30.6	32.8	48.0	30.3	...	33.4

Table 6-2. Producer Price Indexes by Commodity Groups, 1913–2000—*Continued*

(1982=100.)

Year	All commodities	Farm products	Processed foods and feeds	Industrial commodities													
				Total	Textile products and apparel	Hides, leather, and related products	Fuels and related products and power	Chemicals and related products	Rubber and plastics products	Lumber and wood products	Pulp, paper, and allied products	Metals and metal products	Machinery and equipment	Furniture and household durables	Nonmetallic mineral products	Transportation equipment	Miscellaneous products
1960	31.7	40.1	35.6	30.5	48.6	34.6	13.9	34.8	42.7	33.5	34.0	30.6	33.0	47.8	30.4	. . .	33.6
1961	31.6	39.7	36.2	30.4	47.8	34.9	14.0	34.5	41.1	32.0	33.0	30.5	33.0	47.5	30.5	. . .	33.7
1962	31.7	40.4	36.5	30.4	48.2	35.3	14.0	33.9	39.9	32.2	33.4	30.2	33.0	47.2	30.5	. . .	33.9
1963	31.6	39.6	36.8	30.3	48.2	34.3	13.9	33.5	40.1	32.8	33.1	30.3	33.1	46.9	30.3	. . .	34.2
1964	31.6	39.0	36.7	30.5	48.5	34.4	13.5	33.6	39.6	33.5	33.0	31.1	33.3	47.1	30.4	. . .	34.4
1965	32.3	40.7	38.0	30.9	48.8	35.9	13.8	33.9	39.7	33.7	33.3	32.0	33.7	46.8	30.4	. . .	34.7
1966	33.3	43.7	40.2	31.5	48.9	39.4	14.1	34.0	40.5	35.2	34.2	32.8	34.7	47.4	30.7	. . .	35.3
1967	33.4	41.3	39.8	32.0	48.9	38.1	14.4	34.2	41.4	35.1	34.6	33.2	35.9	48.3	31.2	. . .	36.2
1968	34.2	42.3	40.6	32.8	50.7	39.3	14.3	34.1	42.8	39.8	35.0	34.0	37.0	49.7	32.4	. . .	37.0
1969	35.6	45.0	42.7	33.9	51.8	41.5	14.6	34.2	43.6	44.0	36.0	36.0	38.2	50.7	33.6	40.4	38.1
1970	36.9	45.8	44.6	35.2	52.4	42.0	15.3	35.0	44.9	39.9	37.5	38.7	40.0	51.9	35.3	41.9	39.8
1971	38.1	46.6	45.5	36.5	53.3	43.4	16.6	35.6	45.2	44.7	38.1	39.4	41.4	53.1	38.2	44.2	40.8
1972	39.8	51.6	48.0	37.8	55.5	50.0	17.1	35.6	45.3	50.7	39.3	40.9	42.3	53.8	39.4	45.5	41.5
1973	45.0	72.7	58.9	40.3	60.5	54.5	19.4	37.6	46.6	62.2	42.3	44.0	43.7	55.7	40.7	46.1	43.3
1974	53.5	77.4	68.0	49.2	68.0	55.2	30.1	50.2	56.4	64.5	52.5	57.0	50.0	61.8	47.8	50.3	48.1
1975	58.4	77.0	72.6	54.9	67.4	56.5	35.4	62.0	62.2	62.1	59.0	61.5	57.9	67.5	54.4	56.7	53.4
1976	61.1	78.8	70.8	58.4	72.4	63.9	38.3	64.0	66.0	72.2	62.1	65.0	61.3	70.3	58.2	60.5	55.6
1977	64.9	79.4	74.0	62.5	75.3	68.3	43.6	65.9	69.4	83.0	64.6	69.3	65.2	73.2	62.6	64.6	59.4
1978	69.9	87.7	80.6	67.0	78.1	76.1	46.5	68.0	72.4	96.9	67.7	75.3	70.3	77.5	69.6	69.5	66.7
1979	78.7	99.6	88.5	75.7	82.5	96.1	58.9	76.0	80.5	105.5	75.9	86.0	76.7	82.8	77.6	75.3	75.5
1980	89.8	102.9	95.9	88.0	89.7	94.7	82.8	89.0	90.1	101.5	86.3	95.0	86.0	90.7	88.4	82.9	93.6
1981	98.0	105.2	98.9	97.4	97.6	99.3	100.0	298.4	96.4	102.8	94.8	99.6	94.4	95.9	96.7	94.3	96.1
1982	100.0	100.0	100.0	100.0	100.0	100.0	100.0	100.0	100.0	100.0	100.0	100.0	100.0	100.0	100.0	100.0	100.0
1983	101.3	102.4	101.8	101.1	100.3	103.2	95.9	100.3	100.8	107.9	103.3	101.8	102.7	103.4	101.6	102.8	104.8
1984	103.7	105.5	105.4	103.3	102.7	109.0	94.8	102.9	102.3	108.0	110.3	104.8	105.1	105.7	105.4	105.2	107.0
1985	103.2	95.1	103.5	103.7	102.9	108.9	91.4	103.7	101.9	106.6	113.3	104.4	107.2	107.1	108.6	107.9	109.4
1986	100.2	92.9	105.4	100.0	103.2	113.0	69.8	102.6	101.9	107.2	116.1	103.2	108.8	108.2	110.0	110.5	111.6
1987	102.8	95.5	107.9	102.6	105.1	120.4	70.2	106.4	103.0	112.8	121.8	107.1	110.4	109.9	110.0	112.5	114.9
1988	106.9	104.9	112.7	106.3	109.2	131.4	66.7	116.3	109.3	118.9	130.4	118.7	113.2	113.1	111.2	114.3	120.2
1989	112.2	110.9	117.8	111.6	112.3	136.3	72.9	123.0	112.6	126.7	137.8	124.1	117.4	116.9	112.6	117.7	126.5
1990	116.3	112.2	121.9	115.8	115.0	141.7	82.3	123.6	113.6	129.7	141.2	122.9	120.7	119.2	114.7	121.5	134.2
1991	116.5	105.7	121.9	116.5	116.3	138.9	81.2	125.6	115.1	132.1	142.9	120.2	123.0	121.2	117.2	126.4	140.8
1992	117.2	103.6	122.1	117.4	117.8	140.4	80.4	125.9	115.1	146.6	145.2	119.2	123.4	122.2	117.3	130.4	145.3
1993	118.9	107.1	124.0	119.0	118.0	143.7	80.0	128.2	116.0	174.0	147.3	119.2	124.0	123.7	120.0	133.7	145.4
1994	120.4	106.3	125.5	120.7	118.3	148.5	77.8	132.1	117.6	180.0	152.5	124.8	125.1	126.1	124.2	137.2	141.9
1995	124.7	107.4	127.0	125.5	120.8	153.7	78.0	142.5	124.3	178.1	172.2	134.5	126.6	128.2	129.0	139.7	145.4
1996	127.7	122.4	133.3	127.3	122.4	150.5	85.8	142.1	123.8	176.1	168.7	131.0	126.5	130.4	131.0	141.7	147.7
1997	127.6	112.9	134.0	127.7	122.6	154.2	86.1	143.6	123.2	183.8	167.9	131.8	125.9	130.8	133.2	141.6	150.9
1998	124.4	104.6	131.6	124.8	122.9	148.0	75.3	143.9	122.6	179.1	171.7	127.8	124.9	131.3	135.4	141.2	156.0
1999	125.5	98.4	131.1	126.5	121.1	146.0	80.5	144.2	122.5	183.6	174.1	124.6	124.3	131.7	138.9	141.8	166.6
2000	132.7	99.5	133.1	134.8	121.4	151.5	103.5	151.0	125.5	178.2	183.7	128.1	124.0	132.6	142.5	143.8	170.8

Table 6-3. Producer Price Indexes for the Net Output of Selected Industries, 1987–2000

(December 1984=100, unless otherwise indicated.)

Industry	1987	1988	1989	1990	1991	1992	1993	1994	1995	1996	1997	1998	1999	2000
MINING INDUSTRIES														
Metal mining	100.1	100.7	100.3	93.4	82.2	76.6	69.7	81.4	101.4	92.1	85.8	73.2	70.3	73.8
Iron ores	81.8	80.9	81.5	82.2	82.7	82.8	82.1	82.1	91.0	95.7	95.3	94.5	94.0	93.9
Copper ores (06/88=100)	. . .	. . .	129.5	112.8	99.5	96.6	79.1	106.9	157.1	117.0	110.4	76.8	71.3	88.7
Lead and zinc ores (12/85=100)	. . .	. . .	. . .	. . .	. . .	. . .	82.2	93.5	103.1	109.4	138.6	107.0	111.8	118.8
Gold and silver ores	96.0	96.1	82.9	81.2	71.3	68.0	69.1	75.9	77.1	78.6	67.9	61.1	58.2	57.0
Metal mining services (12/85=100)	100.6	102.5	107.2	108.6	108.7	108.8	111.2	111.3	111.4	112.5	116.7	122.2	120.2	109.0
Miscellaneous metal ores (12/85=100)	100.7	87.9	57.9	58.0	49.2	33.9	32.6	32.9	33.6	31.9	29.9	27.6	25.9	26.4
Coal mining (12/85=100)	96.0	94.6	94.3	96.5	96.3	94.0	93.3	93.2	91.6	91.4	92.2	89.5	87.3	84.8
Bituminous coal and lignite (12/93=100)	. . .	. . .	. . .	. . .	. . .	. . .	. . .	99.1	97.3	97.0	98.0	95.0	92.6	89.8
Anthracite mining (12/93=100)	. . .	. . .	. . .	. . .	. . .	. . .	. . .	99.4	98.2	98.1	98.3	99.0	98.1	97.2
Coal mining services (06/91=100)	. . .	. . .	. . .	. . .	. . .	96.1	98.0	97.6	98.3	101.6	100.6	100.6	100.2	100.8
Oil and gas extraction (12/85=100)	74.3	68.5	75.7	82.7	77.9	76.5	76.2	71.1	66.6	84.8	87.5	68.3	78.5	126.8
Crude petroleum, natural gas, and natural gas liquids (06/96=100)	. . .	. . .	. . .	. . .	. . .	. . .	. . .	. . .	. . .	. . .	115.6	86.1	102.6	174.3
Oil and gas field services (12/85=100)	87.7	90.9	91.2	95.7	99.1	95.5	100.6	103.8	107.1	108.8	120.7	125.5	116.2	122.6
Mining and quarrying of non-metallic minerals, except fuels	105.1	108.0	111.2	113.7	116.3	117.5	118.8	120.5	123.8	127.1	128.8	132.2	134.0	137.0
Dimension stone (06/85=100)	106.3	108.3	110.5	113.4	116.7	118.2	120.3	123.4	126.4	132.2	138.1	142.2	145.9	153.4
Crushed and broken stone, including riprap	110.3	111.8	113.6	115.7	118.7	120.6	123.4	126.3	130.7	133.2	135.4	138.8	142.1	147.3
Sand and gravel	108.9	113.0	115.5	119.6	123.1	125.3	129.1	134.0	137.6	141.6	145.4	152.1	157.4	163.1
Clay, ceramic, and refractory minerals	102.3	105.1	108.3	109.8	110.9	111.3	112.8	113.1	115.3	116.6	117.5	117.5	116.2	117.0
Chemical and fertilizer mineral mining	96.4	99.6	104.7	106.7	108.5	108.3	104.3	102.1	104.2	108.6	107.6	110.1	108.0	106.8
Non-metallic minerals (except fuels) services (06/85=100)	108.0	103.0	102.9	102.7	98.5	98.1	98.0	96.1	100.0	103.4	104.7	104.7	106.5	107.2
Miscellaneous nonmetallic minerals, except fuels	109.6	112.8	115.1	117.9	122.9	126.9	131.1	132.3	136.0	139.8	143.2	146.6	148.0	148.8
MANUFACTURING INDUSTRIES														
Food and kindred products	102.6	107.1	112.2	116.2	116.5	116.9	118.7	120.1	121.7	127.1	127.9	126.3	126.3	128.5
Meat products	101.7	103.9	110.0	118.1	114.8	110.0	113.6	110.7	109.3	114.6	116.1	109.2	108.9	115.0
Dairy products	99.4	100.1	108.0	113.5	111.0	113.7	114.1	115.6	115.8	125.0	123.9	133.1	133.8	129.9
Canned and preserved fruits and vegetables	104.1	108.9	114.5	119.5	119.5	121.5	121.2	123.7	125.5	129.7	129.9	130.1	131.7	132.1
Grain mill products	97.8	111.3	116.4	114.5	115.9	119.1	120.5	124.9	125.9	139.9	133.0	122.5	117.3	117.5
Bakery products	107.3	115.2	123.5	128.7	133.7	139.1	142.7	145.3	149.6	154.4	158.2	160.0	162.0	166.0
Sugar and confectionery products	104.7	106.0	110.2	112.5	117.4	117.0	118.7	120.4	123.3	127.7	129.3	128.8	129.4	127.5
Fats and oils	89.4	109.4	104.6	98.8	93.3	93.1	100.4	105.0	103.0	111.1	113.9	102.1	86.9	85.1
Beverages	104.1	105.8	109.0	112.0	116.4	117.9	118.5	118.8	123.1	125.5	126.3	127.2	129.8	134.4
Miscellaneous food preparations and kindred products	108.7	110.2	114.2	116.7	118.4	117.7	118.3	125.4	131.1	128.5	135.1	135.3	136.1	138.7
Tobacco manufactures	126.5	141.8	161.4	183.2	207.5	230.2	218.0	187.8	193.2	199.1	210.8	243.1	325.7	345.8
Cigarettes (12/82=100)	133.5	150.8	173.1	197.6	225.0	250.5	235.2	198.9	204.3	210.5	223.3	260.4	356.7	379.3
Cigars (12/82=100)	116.0	121.2	130.5	141.4	160.0	159.1	166.4	172.9	186.5	201.8	228.5	242.7	259.6	268.8
Chewing and smoking tobacco and snuff (12/82=100)	137.4	145.5	154.1	166.2	182.3	199.2	214.2	229.5	240.0	253.8	265.3	282.1	303.1	318.1
Tobacco stemming and redrying (06/84=100)	95.5	97.7	98.9	103.9	107.6	107.5	108.7	109.4	112.2	109.7	106.5	104.2	104.7	109.0
Textile mill products	102.6	106.8	109.3	111.6	112.5	113.6	113.6	113.6	116.5	118.2	118.8	118.6	116.3	116.7
Cotton broadwoven fabric (12/80=100)	101.9	107.6	107.2	109.3	109.6	112.8	112.2	113.5	118.6	119.1	118.5	117.4	114.2	110.6
Synthetic fiber and silk broadwoven fabric (06/81=100)	103.7	110.1	112.3	115.6	115.2	115.9	114.6	109.9	112.4	113.0	115.0	114.8	108.6	108.6
Wool weaving and finishing (06/85=100)	101.1	109.8	119.4	118.5	116.3	114.7	113.8	113.3	113.5	114.2	115.0	115.3	113.2	114.6
Narrow fabric mills (06/84=100)	101.3	103.1	108.1	111.7	113.2	114.6	115.6	116.8	119.7	121.2	122.7	123.8	124.3	125.3
Knitting mills	103.3	105.5	107.4	109.9	110.9	112.8	113.3	113.0	115.7	116.6	117.0	116.6	114.0	113.9
Dyeing and finishing textiles, except wool fabrics and knit goods	107.2	111.6	114.8	117.0	119.9	122.6	125.1	125.5	127.8	129.0	129.2	130.2	131.4	132.2
Floor covering mills	102.5	105.8	107.6	108.9	109.7	109.4	108.7	110.0	111.6	114.1	115.7	116.3	115.4	117.8
Yarn and thread mills	101.9	104.9	106.4	109.7	110.7	109.9	107.0	107.4	112.1	113.6	114.1	112.1	106.9	105.5
Miscellaneous textile goods	100.9	106.6	112.4	115.0	117.0	116.3	116.5	118.1	122.9	126.4	125.6	124.9	123.4	124.1
Apparel and other finished products made from fabrics and similar materials	103.9	107.2	110.2	113.3	116.0	118.0	119.2	119.7	120.6	122.3	123.4	124.8	125.3	125.7
Men's and boys' suits and coats (12/80=100)	125.2	131.6	140.3	145.7	149.2	151.8	151.9	154.0	155.8	158.1	160.2	166.8	168.5	168.2
Men's, youths' and boys' furnishings, work clothing and allied garments	103.1	106.9	110.1	113.0	116.2	119.7	121.9	122.7	124.0	125.5	125.7	126.1	126.0	125.6
Women's, misses', and juniors' outerwear	104.5	107.7	110.8	114.0	116.7	117.5	117.8	117.0	116.2	116.1	116.8	117.7	118.3	118.4
Women's, misses', children's, and infants' undergarments	104.6	107.3	109.4	111.2	112.9	115.3	116.8	118.3	118.9	119.3	120.1	121.0	122.1	123.3
Hats, caps, and millinery (06/85=100)	102.4	104.9	109.8	115.1	118.2	122.9	126.0	129.5	130.8	132.7	135.0	136.4	138.6	141.0
Girls', children's, and infants' outerwear	101.7	103.4	106.3	110.7	113.1	114.6	115.8	115.4	118.1	118.9	118.9	118.6	119.5	120.7
Fur goods (12/83=100)	120.1	115.9	104.9	98.7	100.5	102.6	101.4	107.5	103.8	119.4	127.3	128.5	134.4	141.5
Miscellaneous apparel and accessories (06/85=100)	102.9	106.9	110.8	115.2	117.6	119.3	120.6	120.8	123.2	125.7	128.0	130.4	131.0	131.3
Miscellaneous fabricated textile products	102.7	105.6	107.9	110.8	113.4	115.1	116.6	117.7	119.6	124.2	126.4	128.8	128.7	129.5
Lumber and wood products, except furniture	105.3	109.2	115.3	117.0	119.4	129.7	148.3	154.4	154.1	153.5	158.9	157.0	161.8	158.1
Logging camps and logging contractors (12/81=100)	100.4	112.8	128.0	135.6	135.0	151.3	186.4	192.6	194.3	185.7	191.2	188.1	182.7	177.5
Sawmills and planing mills	106.7	110.2	114.6	113.7	115.3	131.3	161.8	165.2	154.8	155.7	166.9	157.2	162.2	153.9
Millwork, veneer, plywood, and structural wood members	105.3	107.5	114.1	115.4	118.3	128.4	142.8	148.7	150.5	148.3	151.7	151.8	158.6	155.1
Wood containers (06/85=100)	101.3	103.8	109.7	113.9	115.8	123.5	141.7	147.5	148.6	147.7	151.5	155.5	156.0	156.6
Wood buildings and mobile homes	103.6	107.9	112.1	115.5	118.9	121.5	129.5	139.8	147.8	151.5	155.0	157.5	162.1	165.7
Miscellaneous wood products	104.7	108.6	113.3	114.9	118.0	123.4	132.8	140.9	144.9	145.1	145.9	147.6	152.8	149.6
Furniture and fixtures	106.4	111.4	115.6	119.1	121.6	122.9	125.4	129.7	133.3	136.2	138.2	139.7	141.3	143.3
Household furniture	105.9	110.1	114.0	117.2	119.9	121.6	124.8	128.7	132.2	134.7	136.4	138.4	140.3	142.5
Office furniture	108.1	115.0	119.0	123.4	125.8	125.3	127.3	132.9	137.5	140.7	142.5	142.3	143.0	144.5
Public building and related furniture	108.2	111.9	115.9	118.4	119.4	120.9	123.5	128.4	130.0	133.7	135.9	136.0	136.9	138.6
Partitions, shelving, lockers, and office and store fixtures	108.8	113.7	117.5	120.9	123.1	124.7	126.9	131.9	135.3	138.0	140.7	142.0	143.5	145.6
Miscellaneous furniture and fixtures	102.9	109.5	116.3	120.6	123.4	125.5	125.6	127.3	130.4	133.3	134.8	137.4	139.0	141.7

Table 6-3. Producer Price Indexes for the Net Output of Selected Industries, 1987–2000—*Continued*

(December 1984=100, unless otherwise indicated.)

Industry	1987	1988	1989	1990	1991	1992	1993	1994	1995	1996	1997	1998	1999	2000
Paper and allied products	104.9	113.7	120.8	121.9	121.1	121.2	120.2	123.7	146.7	138.6	133.5	136.2	136.4	145.8
Pulp mills (12/82=100)	117.0	141.7	161.3	153.8	121.8	118.5	105.8	116.5	182.4	135.5	131.0	125.1	122.7	143.4
Paper mill products except building paper (06/81=100)	115.5	127.4	134.6	134.0	131.0	126.6	126.6	128.6	164.8	152.2	143.2	144.5	139.7	148.8
Paperboard mills (12/82=100)	126.2	141.6	149.9	146.0	140.7	142.6	138.3	152.6	203.1	169.7	158.2	165.1	166.9	192.2
Paperboard containers and boxes	104.3	111.7	117.2	117.7	116.6	118.5	118.0	123.7	148.5	140.4	132.9	141.1	144.1	157.1
Converted paper and paperboard products, except containers and boxes (06/93=100)	...	...	...	...	...	...	...	100.7	110.1	109.5	108.7	108.2	108.2	111.7
Printing, publishing, and allied industries	112.2	118.2	124.7	130.5	136.4	140.8	145.6	149.7	159.0	165.6	169.1	174.0	177.6	182.9
Newspaper publishing (12/79=100)	181.7	193.9	206.9	220.4	235.7	248.7	259.5	269.5	286.7	306.9	317.7	328.7	339.3	351.3
Periodical publishing (12/79=100)	173.8	183.8	194.0	205.7	217.8	227.9	233.3	239.1	246.3	253.1	263.2	276.9	284.9	292.6
Books	111.9	117.7	125.3	132.3	138.7	143.7	147.8	153.4	162.3	169.4	174.0	178.9	184.7	190.2
Miscellaneous publishing (06/84=100)	116.4	123.1	128.2	133.8	142.0	148.3	154.6	160.6	167.1	174.5	181.1	187.7	194.5	201.3
Commercial printing	107.1	110.7	115.7	118.7	120.8	121.9	124.9	126.3	133.4	136.6	137.2	140.0	140.3	142.8
Manifold business forms (12/83=100)	112.1	120.3	124.9	124.6	123.9	121.0	128.6	134.0	163.9	168.4	165.8	167.0	170.5	185.8
Greeting cards (12/85=100)	102.8	108.4	114.4	120.3	125.3	131.3	139.4	145.7	156.5	162.7	164.9	169.2	174.3	177.7
Blankbooks, looseleaf binders, and bookbinding and related work (06/85=100)	107.2	111.9	119.6	124.8	132.3	135.4	139.0	142.9	150.1	155.6	158.7	159.6	159.8	163.0
Service industries for the printing trade (06/85=100)	103.4	106.1	108.4	109.3	110.7	112.3	113.5	114.1	115.2	116.1	116.4	117.2	117.7	119.0
Chemicals and allied products	103.6	113.0	119.6	121.0	124.4	125.8	127.2	130.0	143.4	145.8	147.1	148.7	149.7	156.7
Industrial inorganic chemicals	101.4	104.0	115.1	116.6	117.5	116.5	115.0	115.4	126.3	135.0	134.5	132.7	127.8	132.0
Plastic materials and synthetic resins, rubber, and non-glass fibers	99.6	114.7	118.0	114.9	113.2	110.0	110.6	113.8	127.8	123.1	124.4	115.9	115.4	128.0
Drugs	119.6	128.1	137.9	146.7	156.2	165.7	172.4	174.8	178.7	181.2	184.8	203.1	210.1	215.7
Soap, detergents, and cleaning preparations, perfumes, cosmetics and other toilet preparations	105.5	109.6	114.1	115.8	118.1	120.6	122.8	123.0	125.0	126.6	127.3	128.7	130.3	132.5
Paints and allied products (06/83=100)	107.2	111.7	119.5	125.0	130.3	132.3	133.5	136.0	143.1	147.6	152.3	155.1	157.6	160.7
Industrial organic chemicals	98.4	114.2	122.3	120.2	123.3	123.1	122.7	125.9	158.1	164.0	163.9	160.1	161.4	177.3
Agricultural chemicals	97.8	106.9	109.4	108.2	111.9	110.0	109.7	119.6	129.7	133.4	131.9	128.5	123.2	124.9
Miscellaneous chemical products	99.8	106.8	114.2	117.4	122.1	123.7	127.2	131.2	137.1	138.5	140.3	141.7	141.5	143.0
Petroleum refining and related products	70.5	67.7	75.7	91.4	83.1	80.3	77.6	74.8	77.2	87.4	85.6	66.3	76.8	112.8
Petroleum refining (06/85=100)	68.6	65.4	73.6	90.1	80.9	78.3	75.2	72.2	74.5	85.3	83.1	62.3	73.6	111.6
Paving and roofing materials	92.5	94.1	93.5	94.3	96.1	94.0	95.0	94.9	98.1	99.4	102.2	102.0	102.8	113.5
Miscellaneous products of petroleum and coal	98.6	104.3	114.4	123.6	131.1	128.4	129.9	130.6	136.3	140.9	142.0	142.5	142.1	150.3
Rubber and miscellaneous plastics products	100.9	106.7	110.2	111.3	113.7	114.2	115.4	117.1	123.3	123.1	122.8	122.1	122.2	124.6
Tires and inner tubes (06/81=100)	95.1	99.5	102.9	103.0	105.0	106.0	106.2	106.4	108.5	105.2	103.4	102.0	100.4	100.4
Rubber and plastics footwear (12/80=100)	111.7	114.6	120.2	121.5	122.0	122.8	124.1	125.5	126.9	128.3	127.1	128.0	129.1	131.2
Gaskets, packing, and sealing devices and rubber and plastics hose and belting (06/95=100)	...	...	...	...	...	...	...	...	...	102.7	104.4	105.5	106.0	107.1
Fabricated rubber products, n.e.c. (12/88=100)	...	...	102.4	105.0	107.5	108.6	110.3	111.9	115.6	118.3	119.8	120.2	119.9	120.5
Miscellaneous plastics products (06/93=100)	...	...	...	...	...	...	...	101.9	108.3	108.0	107.6	106.8	107.1	109.8
Leather and leather products	106.6	113.4	118.0	122.6	124.8	127.0	129.0	130.6	134.1	134.7	137.1	137.1	136.5	137.9
Leather tanning and finishing (06/81=100)	137.5	158.7	161.6	168.0	158.9	156.1	160.9	171.9	183.9	172.4	176.9	171.6	168.8	174.6
Boot and shoe cut stock and findings	107.9	114.6	116.7	119.6	122.3	123.3	124.4	125.0	129.6	132.4	133.3	133.8	133.8	135.2
Footwear, except rubber	106.3	112.1	117.5	122.2	125.2	128.1	130.3	131.6	135.3	137.5	139.5	140.5	139.3	139.7
Leather gloves and mittens (06/85=100)	101.6	108.1	112.0	117.6	118.6	120.1	120.7	125.8	131.5	137.4	138.7	140.8	141.3	141.3
Luggage	98.7	104.1	109.0	113.4	116.2	118.8	119.9	120.3	120.3	121.1	123.2	124.7	126.5	127.6
Handbags and other personal leather goods	105.8	111.6	114.2	118.1	121.3	122.4	123.5	121.5	122.8	122.8	123.5	124.1	124.6	124.7
Leather goods, n.e.c. (06/85=100)	105.7	113.5	117.7	122.1	123.7	123.4	125.1	127.2	131.7	135.6	140.6	141.0	142.5	144.5
Stone, clay, glass, and concrete products	104.5	105.8	107.9	110.0	112.3	112.8	115.4	119.6	124.3	125.8	127.4	129.3	132.6	134.7
Flat glass (12/80=100)	113.6	115.1	112.8	109.2	105.4	104.9	106.1	113.0	116.6	108.9	104.1	99.5	95.9	97.3
Glass and glassware, pressed or blown	107.2	107.6	110.5	113.8	117.4	118.4	119.7	121.8	125.0	125.0	123.2	121.8	121.0	122.6
Products of purchased glass (06/83=100)	110.0	113.4	116.7	117.6	118.8	120.4	122.1	123.7	126.8	126.3	127.1	127.5	128.4	131.6
Hydraulic cement (06/82=100)	100.9	101.2	101.1	102.7	105.8	105.4	111.0	118.7	127.2	132.9	138.1	144.2	149.1	148.6
Structural clay products	106.0	109.6	111.8	114.2	115.6	117.1	119.7	121.9	124.4	126.1	127.5	129.0	131.4	135.1
Pottery and related products	104.4	109.2	113.1	117.0	119.6	120.6	122.7	125.2	129.3	130.0	131.8	133.5	138.1	139.7
Concrete, gypsum, and plaster products	103.6	103.3	104.4	106.1	108.0	108.6	111.7	117.7	123.5	126.5	130.5	134.5	140.0	143.1
Cut stone and stone products	109.8	116.2	120.1	122.7	128.0	129.3	130.7	131.7	134.0	135.8	138.4	141.7	143.3	144.8
Abrasives, asbestos, and miscellaneous nonmetallic mineral products	103.1	105.7	109.1	111.5	114.2	113.3	116.0	119.2	123.6	125.6	126.2	127.4	131.3	130.9
Primary metal industries	101.0	113.0	118.8	116.5	113.1	111.7	111.4	117.0	128.2	123.7	124.7	120.9	115.8	119.8
Blast furnaces, steel works, and rolling and finishing mills	97.5	105.1	108.5	106.5	104.5	102.4	104.3	109.1	114.9	111.3	112.0	110.0	102.3	104.4
Iron and steel foundries	101.2	104.9	108.3	111.5	113.2	114.6	115.8	118.3	124.0	127.6	129.2	129.7	130.4	132.1
Primary smelting and refining of nonferrous metals (12/80=100)	100.5	127.2	134.6	123.4	103.6	98.4	90.3	106.7	134.2	115.5	115.5	98.5	93.6	103.0
Secondary nonferrous metals (06/80=100)	84.5	100.6	101.4	97.0	84.7	81.8	77.2	90.2	102.1	94.0	94.5	85.9	84.8	88.4
Rolling, drawing and extruding of nonferrous metals	104.7	127.8	138.4	132.7	127.5	126.2	122.8	129.4	151.0	143.0	144.8	137.8	133.7	142.8
Nonferrous foundries (castings)	103.2	112.0	119.5	121.1	120.9	121.7	122.7	125.7	132.8	131.4	133.8	132.7	131.6	133.5
Miscellaneous primary metal products (06/85=100)	105.2	112.2	116.1	115.9	116.1	116.3	115.9	119.0	124.4	126.2	126.7	126.1	126.0	126.5
Fabricated metal products, except machinery and transportation equipment	102.1	107.4	112.6	115.1	116.6	117.2	118.2	120.3	124.8	126.2	127.6	128.7	129.1	130.3
Metal cans and shipping containers	100.4	101.5	103.8	105.9	107.2	106.3	103.1	101.7	109.4	103.9	102.7	102.3	100.7	101.0
Cutlery, hand tools, and general hardware	102.3	106.1	111.7	116.5	120.7	123.2	125.7	127.9	131.3	133.8	135.2	136.5	137.8	139.9
Heating equipment, except electric and warm air; and plumbing fixtures	108.3	114.7	121.7	127.2	131.7	135.3	138.0	140.8	147.6	153.2	156.2	157.7	159.6	162.0
Fabricated structural metal products	102.5	110.7	116.3	117.9	118.1	117.7	118.8	122.6	129.6	131.8	134.0	136.1	137.1	138.5
Screw machine products, and bolts, nuts, screws, rivets, and washers	101.1	104.7	109.9	113.3	114.9	115.4	116.3	117.6	120.0	121.6	122.6	122.7	121.8	122.9
Metal forgings and stampings	99.0	102.4	107.1	109.4	109.5	109.7	109.8	110.5	111.9	112.9	113.9	114.0	112.9	113.2
Coating, engraving, and allied services	106.7	110.7	116.0	117.9	119.3	120.1	121.8	123.5	125.8	127.2	128.4	129.2	132.0	132.7
Ordnance and accessories, except vehicles and guided missiles (06/85=100)	105.5	108.2	111.2	112.6	116.4	120.2	124.3	125.5	127.6	129.5	129.2	130.5	133.3	135.1
Miscellaneous fabricated metal products	103.9	110.8	117.2	120.5	122.9	124.1	125.8	128.7	133.4	135.6	137.9	139.5	140.3	141.9

Table 6-3. Producer Price Indexes for the Net Output of Selected Industries, 1987–2000—*Continued*

(December 1984=100, unless otherwise indicated.)

Industry	1987	1988	1989	1990	1991	1992	1993	1994	1995	1996	1997	1998	1999	2000
Machinery, except electrical	103.2	106.4	110.7	113.9	116.4	116.7	116.8	117.5	119.0	119.2	118.5	117.7	117.3	117.5
Engines and turbines	102.7	105.0	109.8	116.5	121.4	123.8	125.8	128.3	130.8	132.3	133.6	133.9	135.7	136.6
Farm and garden machinery and equipment	100.8	102.9	107.6	111.1	114.3	116.9	118.7	120.9	123.4	126.1	127.4	128.1	129.1	130.1
Construction, mining, and materials handling machinery and equipment	102.6	105.9	109.8	113.5	117.5	120.1	122.9	125.0	128.1	131.4	133.7	136.0	138.0	139.4
Metalworking machinery and equipment	104.2	...	111.5	116.1	120.3	122.8	125.4	128.4	...	135.4	138.4	141.2	142.2	143.9
Special industry machinery, except metalworking machinery	108.5	112.6	117.5	121.6	125.6	128.4	132.1	134.2	137.3	140.5	143.0	145.4	147.2	148.7
General industrial machinery and equipment	104.1	...	...	119.6	124.3	127.4	130.6	133.4	137.8	141.7	144.7	146.9	149.3	151.7
Office, computing, and accounting machines	...	...	...	...	...	...	...	...	70.5	63.4	55.9	48.8	44.0	41.3
Refrigeration and service industry machinery	104.2	107.8	112.4	116.0	117.6	119.4	120.9	122.3	125.3	127.9	129.6	131.5	132.2	132.0
Miscellaneous machinery, except electrical	102.6	104.6	109.3	112.3	113.4	113.9	116.1	118.8	121.9	123.6	125.5	127.0	127.7	129.6
Electrical and electronic machinery, equipment, and supplies	103.3	104.6	107.1	108.9	110.1	110.8	112.0	112.7	113.3	113.2	111.6	110.4	109.5	108.3
Electric transmission and distribution equipment	103.1	105.8	113.2	118.7	122.0	122.8	123.4	125.8	129.5	130.5	131.3	133.6	135.9	138.5
Electrical industrial apparatus	104.5	108.5	113.5	117.5	120.7	122.9	125.7	127.1	130.1	132.7	134.9	136.6	137.2	137.8
Household appliances	99.7	100.4	102.9	105.2	106.0	106.8	108.1	108.7	108.8	109.7	108.3	107.5	107.2	106.2
Electric lighting and wiring equipment	105.0	108.3	113.4	116.3	118.6	119.8	122.1	123.2	126.6	128.1	129.4	129.4	128.7	128.4
Radio and television receiving equipment, except communication types	99.6	97.5	96.9	94.5	95.2	94.2	92.6	92.4	91.5	91.4	89.5	88.9	87.1	85.4
Communication equipment (12/85=100)	103.5	103.9	105.8	107.5	108.5	109.7	111.7	113.3	113.9	115.0	115.7	115.0	113.0	110.4
Electronic components and accessories	102.6	104.0	105.1	104.9	104.9	104.6	105.3	104.8	102.5	99.3	95.1	91.9	90.1	88.8
Miscellaneous electrical machinery, equipment, and supplies	103.2	105.4	107.8	109.8	110.6	110.9	110.4	110.7	111.9	112.8	113.0	112.4	112.5	112.4
Transportation equipment	105.9	107.8	112.1	115.6	119.8	123.0	126.3	130.1	132.2	134.2	134.1	133.6	134.5	136.8
Motor vehicles and motor vehicle equipment	106.4	107.7	110.7	113.0	117.4	120.5	123.8	127.5	129.1	130.4	129.0	127.7	128.3	129.2
Aircraft and parts (06/85=100)	102.8	105.5	112.1	117.7	122.3	126.6	130.1	134.0	137.3	140.8	142.7	143.4	144.8	149.9
Ship and boat building and repairing	108.5	111.0	116.0	120.1	122.7	125.7	129.9	133.0	135.0	138.2	142.0	144.1	145.6	149.0
Railroad equipment (06/84=100)	101.9	103.7	110.0	114.2	117.3	118.7	119.8	122.6	127.6	129.7	127.4	127.6	128.2	128.6
Motorcycles, bicycles, and parts	101.1	104.3	107.8	109.9	111.8	114.4	116.9	119.0	122.2	123.4	123.3	124.2	125.5	127.8
Miscellaneous transportation equipment	104.8	106.2	110.4	112.5	114.1	115.2	117.1	118.1	120.3	121.9	123.0	124.2	125.0	128.3
Measuring and controlling instruments; photographic, medical, optical goods; watches, clocks	105.1	107.0	110.8	114.6	116.8	118.7	120.8	122.1	124.0	125.1	125.6	126.0	125.7	126.2
Engineering and scientific instruments (12/85=100)	104.5	108.1	112.7	116.9	120.5	121.4	123.0	124.6	127.4	128.3	130.0	132.5	132.5	132.0
Measuring and controlling instruments	106.0	107.9	111.7	116.3	120.1	123.3	126.1	127.9	129.9	131.5	133.5	134.4	134.8	136.6
Surgical, medical, and dental instruments and supplies	109.0	111.5	115.9	120.7	124.1	127.9	131.9	133.4	134.1	134.9	134.4	135.0	135.6	136.7
Opthalmic goods (12/83=100)	110.2	112.1	115.1	117.0	117.6	121.0	123.4	124.9	126.4	124.7	124.3	123.7	123.5	123.3
Photographic equipment and supplies (12/83=100)	104.2	105.3	109.3	112.2	111.9	112.1	112.1	111.7	113.8	114.9	113.5	109.7	106.7	106.2
Watches, clocks and watchcases (06/83=100)	104.2	105.3	108.2	110.5	113.6	114.7	115.9	116.6	118.9	119.2	118.3	118.4	119.4	120.8
Miscellaneous manufacturing industries (12/85=100)	103.8	107.5	111.8	114.9	117.5	119.6	121.5	123.3	125.9	127.8	129.0	129.7	130.3	130.9
Jewelry, silverware, and plated ware (12/85=100)	108.1	112.5	115.3	119.3	121.0	121.6	123.5	124.7	126.3	128.0	128.0	127.1	126.4	127.1
Musical instruments (06/85=100)	106.4	110.4	115.7	119.5	123.7	128.3	134.4	140.2	147.5	152.9	157.1	161.1	163.6	166.6
Toys and amusement, sporting, and athletic goods (12/85=100)	102.5	105.0	110.6	113.0	115.3	117.3	117.9	119.2	120.7	122.2	123.7	124.2	123.8	123.0
Pens, pencils, and other office and artists' materials (12/85=100)	102.9	106.3	110.4	114.3	118.0	120.8	121.4	123.2	127.4	[illegible]	129.8	130.9	132.0	132.0
Costume jewelry, costume novelties, buttons, and miscellaneous notions (12/85=100)	100.7	103.1	107.7	111.0	113.8	116.0	117.1	117.9	119.1	120.7	122.4	122.2	123.5	124.8
Miscellaneous manufacturing industries (12/85=100)	103.1	106.9	111.4	114.4	117.3	119.6	122.8	125.1	128.5	130.3	131.6	132.9	134.5	136.1
SERVICE INDUSTRIES														
Railroad transportation (12/96=100)	...	...	...	...	...	...	...	...	...	...	100.5	101.7	101.3	102.6
Motor freight transportation and warehousing (06/93=100)	...	...	...	...	...	...	...	101.9	104.5	106.3	108.9	111.6	114.8	119.4
Trucking and courier services, except air (06/93=100)	...	...	...	...	...	...	...	101.9	104.5	106.4	109.1	111.9	115.0	119.7
Public warehousing and storage (06/93=100)	...	...	...	...	...	...	...	101.3	103.0	103.6	104.6	106.0	109.0	111.2
United States Postal Service (06/89=100)	86.5	96.6	100.0	100.0	117.9	119.8	119.8	119.8	132.2	132.3	132.3	132.3	135.3	135.2
Water transportation (12/92=100)	...	...	...	...	...	...	99.7	100.0	103.0	103.7	104.2	105.6	113.0	122.6
Deep sea foreign transportation of freight (12/96=100)	...	...	...	...	...	...	...	...	...	...	99.0	102.0	116.4	134.7
Deep sea domestic transportation of freight (12/96=100)	...	...	...	...	...	...	...	...	...	...	99.9	97.2	99.8	104.2
Freight transportation, Great Lakes-St Lawrence Seaway (12/96=100)	...	...	...	...	...	...	...	...	...	...	101.3	102.2	102.3	102.2
Water transportation of freight, n.e.c. (12/96=100)	...	...	...	...	...	...	...	...	...	...	99.5	100.3	104.3	110.3
Transportation by air (12/92=100)	...	...	...	...	...	...	105.6	108.5	113.7	121.1	125.3	124.5	130.8	147.7
Air transportation, scheduled and air courier services (12/89=100)	...	...	...	110.2	121.2	114.2	125.4	129.1	135.9	145.5	150.8	149.3	157.3	180.1
Air transportation, nonscheduled (12/96=100)	...	...	...	...	...	...	...	...	...	...	97.8	99.2	102.2	107.3
Airports, flying fields, and airport terminal services (12/96=100)	...	...	...	...	...	...	...	...	...	...	102.5	105.2	108.6	114.2
Pipelines, except natural gas (12/86=100)	97.9	94.8	94.4	95.8	96.1	96.4	96.6	102.6	110.8	104.6	98.8	99.2	98.3	102.3
Arrangement of transportation of freight and cargo (12/96=100)	...	...	...	...	...	...	...	...	...	...	99.4	97.7	97.3	98.3
Telephone communications (06/99=100)	...	...	...	...	...	...	...	...	...	...	...	...	...	96.4
Cable and other pay television services (12/96=100)	...	...	...	...	...	...	...	...	...	...	103.3	107.3	110.9	115.4
Food stores (12/99=100)	...	...	...	...	...	...	...	...	...	...	...	...	...	103.8
Grocery stores (12/99=100)	...	...	...	...	...	...	...	...	...	...	...	...	...	104.2
Meat and fish (seafood) markets (12/99=100)	...	...	...	...	...	...	...	...	...	...	...	...	...	99.5
Fruit and vegetable markets (12/99=100)	...	...	...	...	...	...	...	...	...	...	...	...	...	98.9
Candy, nut, and confectionery stores (12/99=100)	...	...	...	...	...	...	...	...	...	...	...	...	...	102.8
Retail bakeries (12/99=100)	...	...	...	...	...	...	...	...	...	...	...	...	...	99.3
Miscellaneous food stores (12/99=100)	...	...	...	...	...	...	...	...	...	...	...	...	...	102.3
New car dealers (12/99=100)	...	...	...	...	...	...	...	...	...	...	...	...	...	99.7
Life insurance carriers (12/98=100)	...	...	...	...	...	...	...	...	...	...	...	...	100.4	99.2
Property and casualty insurance 12/98=100)	...	...	...	...	...	...	...	...	...	...	...	...	100.7	101.9
Real estate agents and managers (12/96=100)	...	...	...	...	...	...	...	...	...	...	101.3	103.0	104.9	108.3
Hotels and motels (12/96=100)	...	...	...	...	...	...	...	...	...	...	104.2	108.1	112.7	116.2
Personnel supply services (12/96=100)	...	...	...	...	...	...	...	...	...	...	101.0	103.2	105.2	107.3
Health services (12/94=100)	...	...	...	...	...	...	...	...	102.4	104.6	106.1	107.7	109.9	112.8
Offices and clinics of doctors of medicine (12/96=100)	...	...	...	...	...	...	...	...	...	...	101.0	103.2	105.5	107.3
Hospitals (12/92=100)	...	...	...	...	...	...	102.5	106.2	110.0	112.6	113.6	114.4	116.4	119.4
Home health care services (12/96=100)	...	...	...	...	...	...	...	...	...	...	103.3	106.2	107.1	111.1
Legal services (12/96=100)	...	...	...	...	...	...	...	...	...	...	102.5	106.1	108.7	112.5
Engineering, architectural, and surveying services (12/96=100)	...	...	...	...	...	...	...	...	...	...	102.2	105.1	108.5	111.8
Accounting, auditing, and bookkeeping services (12/96=100)	...	...	...	...	...	...	...	...	...	...	101.5	103.9	107.5	110.8

NOTES AND DEFINITIONS

CONSUMER PRICE INDEX

Coverage

The *Consumer Price Index* (CPI) measures the average change in prices of goods and services that urban consumers purchase for day-to-day living. The weights used in calculating the index, which remain fixed for relatively long periods, are based on actual expenditures reported in the Consumer Expenditure Surveys. The quantities and qualities of the sample items in the "market basket" remain essentially the same between consecutive pricing periods, so that the index measures only the effect of price change on the cost of living. The index does not measure changes in the total amount families spend for living. Geographic area indexes measure price changes over time in individual areas, not relative differences in prices or living costs between areas.

Periodic Updating

The index for the years 1913–1935 used as the basis for its weights, a study of 1917–1919 spending by households of wage earners and clerical workers. Since then, there have been six updatings, bringing the "market basket" of goods and services up to date, revising the weights, and improving the sampling methods. In the past 20 years, several major changes have been introduced into the CPI.

The 1978 revision of the CPI updated the CPI for Urban Wage Earners and Clerical Workers (CPI-W), and introduced a new index for All Urban Consumers (CPI-U), which includes salaried workers, the self-employed, the retired, and the unemployed, as well as wage earners and clerical workers. The CPI-W now represents the spending patterns of 32 percent of the population; the CPI-U, 87 percent. For years before 1978, changes in the CPI-U are based on changes in the CPI-W. The 1978 revision also instituted sampling for all levels of the index down to the selection of items within each retail outlet.

Starting with the index for January 1983, BLS changed the way the CPI-U measures homeowners' costs; the CPI-W included the same change starting in January 1985. The change converted the homeownership component from an asset approach, which included both the investment and consumption aspects of homeownership, to a flow-of-services approach, which measures only the cost of shelter services consumed by homeowners. The new approach uses a rental equivalence method to calculate homeowner shelter costs by estimating the implicit rent owners would have to pay to rent the homes they live in. The old method calculated homeowner costs as home purchase, mortgage interest costs, property taxes, property insurance, and maintenance and repair.

The 1987 major revision of both the CPI-U and the CPI-W introduced weights based upon data from the 1982, 1983, and 1984 Consumer Expenditure Surveys. The 1998 CPI revision, which went into effect with the index for January 1998, uses expenditure data from the 1993–95 Consumer Expenditure Surveys and population data from the 1990 Decennial Census.

Current Methodology

The CPI selected 87 pricing areas, comprising 38 different index areas, from around the United States. BLS resamples the outlets and items in its sample on a five-year rotating basis. Before rotating the sample, the Bureau of the Census conducts a Point of Purchase Survey for BLS. This survey determines location of the retail outlets where consumers buy goods and services in various categories; it also determines how much they spend on each category in each reported outlet. BLS then draws outlet samples from the Point-of-Purchase Survey information. BLS field agents visit the selected retail outlets and sample within the item categories using checklists, which exhaustively define these categories of goods and services. The original selection of the specific items to be priced in a specific retail store is generally done by a data collector using the checklist in systematic stages that take into account in each stage sales information provided by the respondent. Outlets may be located outside of their pricing area to represent out-of-town purchases.

After the initial selection, the same item (or a close substitute) is priced from period to period so that, as far as possible, differences in reported prices are measures of price change only. All taxes directly associated with the purchase or continued use of the items priced are included in the indexes. Foods, fuels, rents, and a few other items are priced monthly in all areas. Prices of most other commodities and services are obtained monthly in the three largest areas and every other month in the remaining areas, half in the odd months and half in the even months. Between scheduled survey dates, prices are held at the level of their last pricing. BLS agents also collect data for a sample of rental units drawn from the Decennial Census of Population and Housing. This sample is heavily augmented with renter-occupied housing units in areas where there are many owner-occupied units. This survey is the basis for the Rent and Owners' equivalent rent components of the CPI.

BLS calculates basic indexes (elementary aggregates) for the 211 item strata in each of the 38 index areas. Basic indexes are combined with weights based on the 1993–95 Consumer Expenditure Surveys and the Census of Population.

BLS publishes CPI indexes for a variety of commodities and services, by region, by size of city, for cross-classifications of regions and population size classes, and for 26 metropolitan areas.

The purchasing power of the consumer dollar for any given date is calculated as the reciprocal of the index for that date, expressed in dollars, with the dollar's value in 1982–84 equal to $1.00. It shows changes in the value of the dollar resulting from changes in prices of consumer goods and services. The purchasing power of the dollar with reference to other bases can be calculated by dividing the index for the desired base date by the index for the current date and expressing the result in dollars.

The relative importance figures are percentage distributions of the cost or value weights used in the index calculation. At the time of their introduction, after a major weight revision, the cost weights represent average expenditures for specific classes of goods and services by consumers. However, in the subsequent pricing periods, the value weights and the corresponding relative importance figures change as prices change differentially; i.e., the relative importance increases for an item or group having a greater than average price increase and decreases for one having a less than average price increase. Since the index measures only price change, the cost weights eventually become unrepresentative of actual expenditures and must be revised on the basis of new surveys of consumer expenditures.

Future Plans

Since the CPI traditionally measured price changes for a fixed market basket of goods and services, it was criticized as overstating inflation in that it did not account for the fact that consumers can substitute (buy more or less) as relative prices change. In 1999, the CPI began using a geometric mean formula to average the prices within most CPI item categories. This formula assumes a modest degree of substitution within CPI item categories as relative prices change.

In 2002, the CPI plans to create an additional index using a "superlative" formula, to address consumer substitution across CPI item categories. This superlative index will be a new index; it will not replace the CPI-U and CPI-W.

Historically, the weights in the CPI have been updated about every 10 years. Beginning in 2002, the CPI plans to update its expenditure weights every two years, to keep the weights more up-to-date with consumer spending patterns.

Sources of Additional Information

The entire December 1996 issue of the *Monthly Labor Review* was devoted to a description and discussion of issues related to the 1998 CPI Revision. Further changes in methodology are described in BLS press releases. A press release dated April 1998, "Planned Change In The Consumer Price Index Formula," describes the geometric mean methodology and one dated December 1998, "Future Schedule for Expenditure Weight Updates in the Consumer Price Index" announces the new biennial timetable for weight revision. A detailed description of the CPI before 1978 is contained in *The Consumer Price Index: History and Techniques,* BLS Bulletin 1517 (1966). For further information see *The Consumer Price Index: Concepts and Content Over the Years,* BLS Report 517 (1977). *The Consumer Price Index Detailed Report* is published monthly and contains occasional articles.

Table 6-4. Consumer Price Indexes, All Urban Consumers (CPI-U): U.S. City Average, Major Groups, 1967–2000

(1982–1984=100, unless otherwise indicated.)

Year	All items	Food and beverages	Housing	Apparel	Transportation	Medical care	Recreation [1]	Education and communi-cation [1]	Other goods and services
1967	33.4	35.0	30.8	51.0	33.3	28.2	...	...	35.1
1968	34.8	36.2	32.0	53.7	34.3	29.9	...	...	36.9
1969	36.7	38.1	34.0	56.8	35.7	31.9	...	...	38.7
1970	38.8	40.1	36.4	59.2	37.5	34.0	...	...	40.9
1971	40.5	41.4	38.0	61.1	39.5	36.1	...	...	42.9
1972	41.8	43.1	39.4	62.3	39.9	37.3	...	...	44.7
1973	44.4	48.8	41.2	64.6	41.2	38.8	...	...	46.4
1974	49.3	55.5	45.8	69.4	45.8	42.4	...	...	49.8
1975	53.8	60.2	50.7	72.5	50.1	47.5	...	...	53.9
1976	56.9	62.1	53.8	75.2	55.1	52.0	...	...	57.0
1977	60.6	65.8	57.4	78.6	59.0	57.0	...	...	60.4
1978	65.2	72.2	62.4	81.4	61.7	61.8	...	...	64.3
1979	72.6	79.9	70.1	84.9	70.5	67.5	...	...	68.9
1980	82.4	86.7	81.1	90.9	83.1	74.9	...	...	75.2
1981	90.9	93.5	90.4	95.3	93.2	82.9	...	...	82.6
1982	96.5	97.3	96.9	97.8	97.0	92.5	...	...	91.1
1983	99.6	99.5	99.5	100.2	99.3	100.6	...	...	101.1
1984	103.9	103.2	103.6	102.1	103.7	106.8	...	...	107.9
1985	107.6	105.6	107.7	105.0	106.4	113.5	...	...	114.5
1986	109.6	109.1	110.9	105.9	102.3	122.0	...	...	121.4
1987	113.6	113.5	114.2	110.6	105.4	130.1	...	...	128.5
1988	118.3	118.2	118.5	115.4	108.7	138.6	...	...	137.0
1989	124.0	124.9	123.0	118.6	114.1	149.3	...	...	147.7
1990	130.7	132.1	128.5	124.1	120.5	162.8	...	...	159.0
1991	136.2	136.8	133.6	128.7	123.8	177.0	...	...	171.6
1992	140.3	138.7	137.5	131.9	126.5	190.1	...	...	183.3
1993	144.5	141.6	141.2	133.7	130.4	201.4	90.7	85.5	192.9
1994	148.2	144.9	144.8	133.4	134.3	211.0	92.7	88.8	198.5
1995	152.4	148.9	148.5	132.0	139.1	220.5	94.5	92.2	206.9
1996	156.9	153.7	152.8	131.7	143.0	228.2	97.4	95.3	215.4
1997	160.5	157.7	156.8	132.9	144.3	234.6	99.6	98.4	224.8
1998	163.0	161.1	160.4	133.0	141.6	242.1	101.1	100.3	237.7
1999	166.6	164.6	163.9	131.3	144.4	250.6	102.0	101.2	258.3
2000	172.2	168.4	169.6	129.6	153.3	260.8	103.3	102.5	271.1

1. December 1997=100.

Table 6-5. Consumer Price Indexes, All Urban Consumers (CPI-U): U.S. City Average, Commodity, Service, and Special Groups, 1967–2000

(1982–1984=100, unless otherwise indicated.)

Year	All items	All items less food	All items less shelter	All items less medical care	All items less energy	All items less food and energy	Commodities	Commodities less food and beverages	Energy commodities	Commodities less food and energy	Nondurables
1967	33.4	33.4	35.2	33.7	34.4	34.7	36.8	38.3	23.9	41.3	35.7
1968	34.8	34.9	36.7	35.1	35.9	36.3	38.1	39.7	24.4	42.9	37.1
1969	36.7	36.8	38.4	37.0	38.0	38.4	39.9	41.4	25.2	44.7	38.9
1970	38.8	39.0	40.3	39.2	40.3	40.8	41.7	43.1	25.6	46.7	40.8
1971	40.5	40.8	42.0	40.8	42.0	42.7	43.2	44.7	26.1	48.5	42.1
1972	41.8	42.0	43.3	42.1	43.4	44.0	44.5	45.8	26.4	49.7	43.5
1973	44.4	43.7	46.2	44.8	46.1	45.6	47.8	47.3	29.1	51.1	47.5
1974	49.3	48.0	51.4	49.8	50.6	49.4	53.5	52.4	40.4	55.0	54.0
1975	53.8	52.5	56.0	54.3	55.1	53.9	58.2	57.3	43.4	60.1	58.3
1976	56.9	56.0	59.3	57.2	58.2	57.4	60.7	60.2	45.4	63.2	60.5
1977	60.6	59.6	63.1	60.8	61.9	61.0	64.2	63.6	48.7	66.5	64.0
1978	65.2	63.9	67.4	65.4	66.7	65.5	68.8	67.3	51.0	70.5	68.6
1979	72.6	71.2	74.2	72.9	73.4	71.9	76.6	75.2	68.7	76.4	77.2
1980	82.4	81.5	82.9	82.8	81.9	80.8	86.0	85.7	95.2	83.5	87.6
1981	90.9	90.4	91.0	91.4	90.1	89.2	93.2	93.1	107.6	90.0	95.2
1982	96.5	96.3	96.2	96.8	96.1	95.8	97.0	96.9	102.9	95.3	97.8
1983	99.6	99.7	99.8	99.6	99.6	99.6	99.8	100.0	99.0	100.2	99.7
1984	103.9	104.0	103.9	103.7	104.3	104.6	103.2	103.1	98.1	104.4	102.5
1985	107.6	108.0	107.0	107.2	108.4	109.1	105.4	105.2	98.2	107.1	104.8
1986	109.6	109.8	108.0	108.8	112.6	113.5	104.4	101.4	77.2	108.6	103.5
1987	113.6	113.6	111.6	112.6	117.2	118.2	107.7	104.0	80.2	111.8	107.5
1988	118.3	118.3	115.9	117.0	122.3	123.4	111.5	107.3	80.8	115.8	111.8
1989	124.0	123.7	121.6	122.4	128.1	129.0	116.7	111.6	87.9	119.6	118.2
1990	130.7	130.3	128.2	128.8	134.7	135.5	122.8	117.0	101.2	123.6	126.0
1991	136.2	136.1	133.5	133.8	140.9	142.1	126.6	120.4	99.1	128.8	130.3
1992	140.3	140.8	137.0	137.5	145.4	147.3	129.1	123.2	98.3	132.5	132.8
1993	144.5	145.1	141.4	141.2	150.0	152.2	131.5	125.3	97.3	135.2	135.1
1994	148.2	149.0	144.8	144.7	154.1	156.5	133.8	126.0	97.6	107.1	136.8
1995	152.4	153.1	148.6	148.6	158.7	161.2	136.4	128.9	98.8	139.3	139.3
1996	156.9	157.5	152.8	152.8	163.1	165.6	139.9	131.5	105.7	141.3	143.5
1997	160.5	161.1	155.9	156.3	167.1	169.5	141.8	132.2	105.7	142.3	146.4
1998	163.0	163.4	157.2	158.6	170.9	173.4	141.9	130.5	92.1	143.2	146.9
1999	166.6	167.0	160.2	162.0	174.4	177.0	144.4	132.5	100.0	144.1	151.2
2000	172.2	173.0	165.7	167.3	178.6	181.3	149.2	137.7	129.5	144.9	158.2

See footnotes at end of table.

Table 6-5. Consumer Price Indexes, All Urban Consumers (CPI-U): U.S. City Average, Commodity, Service, and Special Groups, 1967–2000—*Continued*

(1982–1984=100, unless otherwise indicated.)

Year	Nondurables less food	Nondurables less food and apparel	Services						Services less medical care	Energy	Services less energy
			Total [1]	Rent of shelter [2]	Gas (piped) and electricity	Transportation services	Medical care services	Other services			
1967	37.6	32.6	28.8	...	23.7	32.6	26.0	36.0	29.3	23.8	29.3
1968	39.1	33.7	30.3	...	23.9	33.9	27.9	38.1	30.8	24.2	30.9
1969	40.9	34.9	32.4	...	24.3	36.3	30.2	40.0	32.9	24.8	33.2
1970	42.5	36.3	35.0	...	25.4	40.2	32.3	42.2	35.6	25.5	36.0
1971	44.0	37.6	37.0	...	27.1	43.4	34.7	44.4	37.5	26.5	38.0
1972	45.0	38.6	38.4	...	28.5	44.4	35.9	45.6	38.9	27.2	39.4
1973	46.9	40.3	40.1	...	29.9	44.7	37.5	47.7	40.6	29.4	41.1
1974	52.9	46.9	43.8	...	34.5	46.3	41.4	51.3	44.3	38.1	44.8
1975	57.0	51.5	48.0	...	40.1	49.8	46.6	55.1	48.3	42.1	48.8
1976	59.5	54.1	52.0	...	44.7	56.9	51.3	58.4	52.2	45.1	52.7
1977	62.5	57.2	56.0	...	50.5	61.5	56.4	62.1	55.9	49.4	56.5
1978	65.5	60.4	60.8	...	55.0	64.4	61.2	66.4	60.7	52.5	61.3
1979	74.6	71.2	67.5	...	61.0	69.5	67.2	71.9	67.5	65.7	68.2
1980	88.4	87.1	77.9	...	71.4	79.2	74.8	78.7	78.2	86.0	78.5
1981	96.7	96.8	88.1	...	81.9	88.6	82.8	86.1	88.7	97.7	88.7
1982	98.3	98.2	96.0	...	93.2	96.1	92.6	93.5	96.4	99.2	96.3
1983	100.0	100.0	99.4	102.7	101.5	99.1	100.7	100.0	99.2	99.9	99.2
1984	101.7	101.8	104.6	107.7	105.4	104.8	106.7	106.5	104.4	100.9	104.5
1985	104.1	104.1	109.9	113.9	107.1	110.0	113.2	113.0	109.6	101.6	110.2
1986	98.5	96.9	115.4	120.2	105.7	116.3	121.9	119.4	114.6	88.2	116.5
1987	101.8	100.3	120.2	125.9	103.8	121.9	130.0	125.7	119.1	88.6	122.0
1988	105.8	104.0	125.7	132.0	104.6	128.0	138.3	132.6	124.3	89.3	127.9
1989	111.7	111.3	131.9	138.0	107.5	135.6	148.9	140.9	130.1	94.3	134.4
1990	119.9	120.9	139.2	145.5	109.3	144.2	162.7	150.2	136.8	102.1	142.3
1991	124.5	125.7	146.3	152.1	112.6	151.2	177.1	159.8	143.3	102.5	149.8
1992	127.6	128.9	152.0	157.3	114.8	155.7	190.5	168.5	148.4	103.0	155.9
1993	129.3	130.7	157.9	162.0	118.5	162.9	202.9	177.0	153.6	104.2	161.9
1994	129.7	131.6	163.1	167.0	119.2	168.6	213.4	185.4	158.4	104.6	167.6
1995	130.9	134.1	168.7	172.4	119.2	175.9	224.2	193.3	163.5	105.2	173.7
1996	134.5	139.5	174.1	178.0	122.1	180.5	232.4	201.4	168.7	110.1	179.4
1997	136.3	141.8	179.4	183.4	125.1	185.0	239.1	209.6	173.9	111.5	185.0
1998	134.6	139.2	184.2	189.6	121.2	187.9	246.8	216.9	178.4	102.9	190.6
1999	139.4	147.5	188.8	195.0	120.9	190.7	255.1	223.1	182.7	106.6	195.7
2000	149.1	162.9	195.3	201.3	128.0	196.1	266.0	229.9	188.9	124.6	202.1

1. Includes tenants and household insurance, water, sewer, trash, and household operations services, not shown separately
2. December 1982=100.

Table 6-6. Consumer Price Indexes, All Urban Consumers (CPI-U): U.S. City Average, Selected Groups, and Purchasing Power of the Consumer Dollar, 1913–2000

(1982–1984=100, unless otherwise indicated.)

Year	All items	Food	Rent of primary residence	Owners' equivalent rent of primary residence [1]	Apparel	Purchasing power of the consumer dollar [2]
1913	9.9	10.0	21.0	. . .	14.9	10.077
1914	10.0	10.2	21.0	. . .	15.0	9.942
1915	10.1	10.0	21.1	. . .	15.3	9.843
1916	10.9	11.3	21.3	. . .	16.8	9.152
1917	12.8	14.5	21.2	. . .	20.2	7.793
1918	15.1	16.7	21.5	. . .	27.3	6.635
1919	17.3	18.6	23.3	. . .	36.2	5.779
1920	20.0	21.0	27.4	. . .	43.1	4.989
1921	17.9	15.9	31.5	. . .	33.2	5.585
1922	16.8	14.9	32.4	. . .	27.0	5.962
1923	17.1	15.4	33.2	. . .	27.1	5.857
1924	17.1	15.2	34.4	. . .	26.8	5.845
1925	17.5	16.5	34.6	. . .	26.3	5.701
1926	17.7	17.0	34.2	. . .	25.9	5.647
1927	17.4	16.4	33.7	. . .	25.3	5.755
1928	17.1	16.3	32.9	. . .	25.0	5.833
1929	17.1	16.5	32.1	. . .	24.7	5.833
1930	16.7	15.6	31.2	. . .	24.2	5.986
1931	15.2	12.9	29.6	. . .	22.0	6.563
1932	13.7	10.7	26.5	. . .	19.5	7.317
1933	13.0	10.4	22.9	. . .	18.8	7.712
1934	13.4	11.6	21.4	. . .	20.6	7.464
1935	13.7	12.4	21.4	. . .	20.8	7.281
1936	13.9	12.6	21.9	. . .	21.0	7.213
1937	14.4	13.1	22.9	. . .	22.0	6.961
1938	14.1	12.1	23.7	. . .	21.9	7.093
1939	13.9	11.8	23.7	. . .	21.6	7.195
1940	14.0	12.0	23.7	. . .	21.8	7.126
1941	14.7	13.1	24.2	. . .	22.8	6.780
1942	16.3	15.4	24.7	. . .	26.7	6.132
1943	17.3	17.1	24.7	. . .	27.8	5.779
1944	17.6	16.9	24.8	. . .	29.8	5.680
1945	18.0	17.3	24.8	. . .	31.4	5.552
1946	19.5	19.8	25.0	. . .	34.4	5.115
1947	22.3	24.1	25.8	. . .	39.9	4.474
1948	24.1	26.1	27.5	. . .	42.5	4.151
1949	23.8	25.0	28.7	. . .	40.8	4.193
1950	24.1	25.4	29.7	. . .	40.3	4.151
1951	26.0	28.2	30.9	. . .	43.9	3.846
1952	26.5	28.7	32.2	. . .	43.5	3.765
1953	26.7	28.3	33.9	. . .	43.1	3.735
1954	26.9	28.2	35.1	. . .	43.1	3.717
1955	26.8	27.8	35.6	. . .	42.9	3.732
1956	27.2	28.0	36.3	. . .	43.7	3.678
1957	28.1	28.9	37.0	. . .	44.5	3.549
1958	28.9	30.2	37.6	. . .	44.6	3.457
1959	29.1	29.7	38.2	. . .	45.0	3.427

See footnotes at end of table.

Table 6-6. Consumer Price Indexes, All Urban Consumers (CPI-U): U.S. City Average, Selected Groups, and Purchasing Power of the Consumer Dollar, 1913–2000—*Continued*

(1982–1984=100, unless otherwise indicated.)

Year	All items	Food	Rent of primary residence	Owners' equivalent rent of primary residence [1]	Apparel	Purchasing power of the consumer dollar [2]
1960	29.6	30.0	38.7	...	45.7	3.373
1961	29.9	30.4	39.2	...	46.1	3.340
1962	30.2	30.6	39.7	...	46.3	3.304
1963	30.6	31.1	40.1	...	46.9	3.265
1964	31.0	31.5	40.5	...	47.3	3.220
1965	31.5	32.2	40.9	...	47.8	3.166
1966	32.4	33.8	41.5	...	49.0	3.080
1967	33.4	34.1	42.2	...	51.0	2.993
1968	34.8	35.3	43.3	...	53.7	2.873
1969	36.7	37.1	44.7	...	56.8	2.726
1970	38.8	39.2	46.5	...	59.2	2.574
1971	40.5	40.4	48.7	...	61.1	2.466
1972	41.8	42.1	50.4	...	62.3	2.391
1973	44.4	48.2	52.5	...	64.6	2.251
1974	49.3	55.1	55.2	...	69.4	2.029
1975	53.8	59.8	58.0	...	72.5	1.859
1976	56.9	61.6	61.1	...	75.2	1.757
1977	60.6	65.5	64.8	...	78.6	1.649
1978	65.2	72.0	69.3	...	81.4	1.532
1979	72.6	79.9	74.3	...	84.9	1.380
1980	82.4	86.8	80.9	...	90.9	1.215
1981	90.9	93.6	87.9	...	95.3	1.098
1982	96.5	97.4	94.6	...	97.8	1.035
1983	99.6	99.4	100.1	102.5	100.2	1.003
1984	103.9	103.2	105.3	107.3	102.1	0.961
1985	107.6	105.6	111.8	113.2	105.0	0.928
1986	109.6	109.0	118.3	119.4	105.9	0.913
1987	113.6	113.5	123.1	124.8	110.6	0.880
1988	118.3	118.2	127.8	131.1	115.4	0.846
1989	124.0	125.1	132.8	137.4	118.6	0.807
1990	130.7	132.4	138.4	144.8	124.1	0.766
1991	136.2	136.3	143.3	150.4	128.7	0.734
1992	140.3	137.9	146.9	155.5	131.9	0.713
1993	144.5	140.9	150.3	160.5	133.7	0.692
1994	148.2	144.3	154.0	165.8	133.4	0.675
1995	152.4	148.4	157.8	171.3	132.0	0.656
1996	156.9	153.3	162.0	176.8	131.7	0.638
1997	160.5	157.3	166.7	181.9	132.9	0.623
1998	163.0	160.7	172.1	187.8	133.0	0.614
1999	166.6	164.1	177.5	192.9	131.3	0.600
2000	172.2	167.8	183.9	198.7	129.6	0.581

1. December 1982=100.
2. Purchasing power in 1982–1984= $1.00.

Table 6-7. Consumer Price Indexes, Urban Wage Earners and Clerical Workers (CPI-W): U.S. City Average, Major Groups, 1913–2000

(1982–1984=100, unless otherwise indicated.)

Year	All items	Food and beverages	Housing	Apparel	Transportation	Medical care	Recreation [1]	Education and communi-cation [1]	Other goods and services
1913	10.0	...	...	15.0	...	...	...	...	...
1914	10.1	...	...	15.1	...	...	...	...	...
1915	10.2	...	...	15.4	...	...	...	...	...
1916	11.0	...	...	16.9	...	...	...	...	...
1917	12.9	...	...	20.3	...	...	...	...	...
1918	15.1	...	...	27.5	...	...	...	...	...
1919	17.4	...	...	36.4	...	...	...	...	...
1920	20.1	...	...	43.3	...	...	...	...	...
1921	18.0	...	...	33.4	...	...	...	...	...
1922	16.9	...	...	27.2	...	...	...	...	...
1923	17.2	...	...	27.2	...	...	...	...	...
1924	17.2	...	...	26.9	...	...	...	...	...
1925	17.6	...	...	26.4	...	...	...	...	...
1926	17.8	...	...	26.0	...	...	...	...	...
1927	17.5	...	...	25.5	...	...	...	...	...
1928	17.2	...	...	25.1	...	...	...	...	...
1929	17.2	...	...	24.8	...	...	...	...	...
1930	16.8	...	...	24.3	...	...	...	...	...
1931	15.3	...	...	22.1	...	...	...	...	...
1932	13.7	...	...	19.6	...	...	...	...	...
1933	13.0	...	...	18.9	...	...	...	...	...
1934	13.5	...	...	20.7	...	...	...	...	...
1935	13.8	...	...	20.9	14.1	10.2	...	...	...
1936	13.9	...	...	21.1	14.2	10.3	...	...	...
1937	14.4	...	...	22.1	14.5	10.4	...	...	...
1938	14.2	...	...	22.0	14.6	10.4	...	...	...
1939	14.0	...	...	21.7	14.2	10.4	...	...	...
1940	14.1	...	...	21.9	14.1	10.4	...	...	...
1941	14.8	...	...	23.0	14.6	10.5	...	...	...
1942	16.4	...	...	26.8	15.9	10.8	...	...	...
1943	17.4	...	...	28.0	15.8	11.3	...	...	...
1944	17.7	...	...	30.0	15.8	11.6	...	...	...
1945	18.1	...	...	31.5	15.8	11.9	...	...	...
1946	19.6	...	...	34.6	16.6	12.6	...	...	...
1947	22.5	...	...	40.1	18.4	13.6	...	...	...
1948	24.2	...	...	42.7	20.4	14.5	...	...	...
1949	24.0	...	...	41.0	22.0	14.9	...	...	...
1950	24.2	...	...	40.5	22.6	15.2	...	...	...
1951	26.1	...	...	44.1	24.0	15.9	...	...	...
1952	26.7	...	...	43.7	25.6	16.8	...	...	...
1953	26.9	...	...	43.3	26.3	17.4	...	...	...
1954	27.0	...	...	43.3	25.9	17.9	...	...	...

See footnote at end of table.

Table 6-7. Consumer Price Indexes, Urban Wage Earners and Clerical Workers (CPI-W): U.S. City Average, Major Groups, 1913–2000—*Continued*

(1982–1984=100, unless otherwise indicated.)

Year	All items	Food and beverages	Housing	Apparel	Transportation	Medical care	Recreation [1]	Education and communication [1]	Other goods and services
1955	26.9	...	...	43.1	25.6	18.3	...	...	...
1956	27.3	...	...	44.0	26.1	19.0	...	...	...
1957	28.3	...	...	44.7	27.6	19.8	...	...	...
1958	29.1	...	...	44.8	28.4	20.7	...	...	...
1959	29.3	...	...	45.2	29.6	21.6	...	...	...
1960	29.8	...	...	45.9	29.6	22.4	...	...	...
1961	30.1	...	...	46.3	30.0	23.0	...	...	...
1962	30.4	...	...	46.6	30.6	23.6	...	...	...
1963	30.8	...	...	47.1	30.8	24.2	...	...	...
1964	31.2	...	...	47.5	31.2	24.7	...	...	...
1965	31.7	...	...	48.0	31.7	25.3	...	...	...
1966	32.6	...	...	49.2	32.2	26.4	...	...	...
1967	33.6	35.0	31.1	51.2	33.1	28.3	...	...	35.4
1968	35.0	36.2	32.3	54.0	34.1	30.0	...	...	37.2
1969	36.9	38.0	34.3	57.1	35.5	32.1	...	...	39.1
1970	39.0	40.1	36.7	59.5	37.3	34.1	...	...	41.3
1971	40.7	41.3	38.3	61.4	39.2	36.3	...	...	43.3
1972	42.1	43.1	39.8	62.7	39.7	37.5	...	...	45.1
1973	44.7	48.8	41.5	65.0	41.0	39.0	...	...	46.9
1974	49.6	55.5	46.2	69.8	45.5	42.6	...	...	50.2
1975	54.1	60.2	51.1	72.9	49.8	47.7	...	...	54.4
1976	57.2	62.0	54.2	75.6	54.7	52.3	...	...	57.6
1977	60.9	65.7	57.9	79.0	58.6	57.3	...	...	60.9
1978	65.6	72.1	62.9	81.7	61.5	62.1	...	...	64.8
1979	73.1	79.9	70.7	85.2	70.4	68.0	...	...	69.4
1980	82.9	86.9	81.7	90.9	82.9	75.6	...	...	75.6
1981	91.4	93.6	91.1	95.6	93.0	83.5	...	...	82.5
1982	96.9	97.3	97.7	97.8	97.0	92.5	...	...	90.9
1983	99.8	99.5	100.0	100.2	99.2	100.5	...	...	101.3
1984	103.3	103.2	102.2	102.0	103.8	106.9	...	...	107.9
1985	106.9	105.5	106.6	105.0	106.4	113.6	...	...	114.2
1986	108.6	108.9	109.7	105.8	101.7	122.0	...	...	120.9
1987	112.5	113.3	112.8	110.4	105.1	130.2	...	...	127.8
1988	117.0	117.9	116.8	114.9	108.3	139.0	...	...	136.5
1989	122.6	124.6	121.2	117.9	113.9	149.6	...	...	147.4
1990	129.0	131.8	126.4	123.1	120.1	162.7	...	...	158.9
1991	134.3	136.5	131.2	127.4	123.1	176.5	...	...	171.7
1992	138.2	138.3	135.0	130.7	125.8	189.6	...	...	183.3
1993	142.1	141.2	138.5	132.4	129.4	200.9	91.2	86.0	192.2
1994	145.6	144.4	142.0	132.2	133.4	210.4	93.0	89.1	196.4
1995	149.8	148.3	145.4	130.9	138.8	219.8	94.7	92.3	204.2
1996	154.1	153.2	149.6	130.9	142.8	227.6	97.5	95.4	212.2
1997	157.6	157.2	153.4	132.1	143.6	234.0	99.7	98.5	221.6
1998	159.7	160.4	156.7	131.6	140.5	241.4	100.9	100.4	236.1
1999	163.2	163.8	160.0	130.1	143.4	249.7	101.3	101.5	261.9
2000	168.9	167.7	165.4	128.3	152.8	259.9	102.4	102.7	276.5

1. December 1997=100.

Table 6-8. Consumer Price Indexes, All Urban Consumers (CPI-U): U.S. City Average, by Expenditure Category, 1986–2000

(1982–1984=100, unless otherwise indicated.)

Expenditure category	1986	1987	1988	1989	1990	1991	1992	1993	1994	1995	1996	1997	1998	1999	2000
ALL ITEMS	109.6	113.6	118.3	124.0	130.7	136.2	140.3	144.5	148.2	152.4	156.9	160.5	163.0	166.6	172.2
Food And Beverages	109.1	113.5	118.2	124.9	132.1	136.8	138.7	141.6	144.9	148.9	153.7	157.7	161.1	164.6	168.4
Food	109.0	113.5	118.2	125.1	132.4	136.3	137.9	140.9	144.3	148.4	153.3	157.3	160.7	164.1	167.8
Food at home	107.3	111.9	116.6	124.2	132.3	135.8	136.8	140.1	144.1	148.8	154.3	158.1	161.1	164.2	167.9
Cereals and bakery products	110.9	114.8	122.1	132.4	140.0	145.8	151.5	156.6	163.0	167.5	174.0	177.6	181.1	185.0	188.3
Meats, poultry, fish, and eggs	104.5	110.5	114.3	121.3	130.0	132.6	130.9	135.5	137.2	138.8	144.8	148.5	147.3	147.9	154.5
Dairy and related products	103.3	105.9	108.4	115.6	126.5	125.1	128.5	129.4	131.7	132.8	142.1	145.5	150.8	159.6	160.7
Fruits and vegetables	109.4	119.1	128.1	138.0	149.0	155.8	155.4	159.0	165.0	177.7	183.9	187.5	198.2	203.1	204.6
Nonalcoholic beverages and beverage materials	110.4	107.5	107.5	111.3	113.5	114.1	114.3	114.6	123.2	131.7	128.6	133.4	133.0	134.3	137.8
Other food at home	109.4	110.5	113.1	119.1	123.4	127.3	128.8	130.5	135.6	140.8	142.9	147.3	150.8	153.5	155.6
Sugar and sweets	109.0	111.0	114.0	119.4	124.7	129.3	133.1	133.4	135.2	137.5	143.7	147.8	150.2	152.3	154.0
Fats and oils	106.5	108.1	113.1	121.2	126.3	131.7	129.8	130.0	133.5	137.3	140.5	141.7	146.9	148.3	147.4
Other foods	109.2	113.8	118.0	125.5	131.2	137.1	140.1	143.7	147.5	151.1	156.2	161.2	165.5	168.9	172.2
Other miscellaneous foods [1]	. . .	. . .	. . .	. . .	. . .	. . .	. . .	. . .	. . .	. . .	. . .	. . .	102.6	104.9	107.5
Food away from home	112.5	117.0	121.8	127.4	133.4	137.9	140.7	143.2	145.7	149.0	152.7	157.0	161.1	165.1	169.0
Other food away from home [1]	. . .	. . .	. . .	. . .	. . .	. . .	. . .	. . .	. . .	. . .	. . .	. . .	101.6	105.2	109.0
Alcoholic beverages	111.1	114.1	118.6	123.5	129.3	142.8	147.3	149.6	151.5	153.9	158.5	162.8	165.7	169.7	174.7
Housing	110.9	114.2	118.5	123.0	128.5	133.6	137.5	141.2	144.8	148.5	152.8	156.8	160.4	163.9	169.6
Shelter	115.8	121.3	127.1	132.8	140.0	146.3	151.2	155.7	160.5	165.7	171.0	176.3	182.1	187.3	193.4
Rent of primary residence	118.3	123.1	127.8	132.8	138.4	143.3	146.9	150.3	154.0	157.8	162.0	166.7	172.1	177.5	183.9
Lodging away from home [1]	. . .	. . .	. . .	. . .	. . .	. . .	. . .	. . .	. . .	. . .	. . .	. . .	109.0	112.3	117.5
Owners' equivalent rent of primary residence [2]	119.4	124.8	131.1	137.4	144.8	150.4	155.5	160.5	165.8	171.3	176.8	181.9	187.8	192.9	198.7
Tenants' and household insurance [1]	. . .	. . .	. . .	. . .	. . .	. . .	. . .	. . .	. . .	. . .	. . .	. . .	99.8	101.3	103.7
Fuels and utilities	104.1	103.0	104.4	107.8	111.6	115.3	117.8	121.3	122.8	123.7	127.5	130.8	128.5	128.8	137.9
Fuels	99.2	97.3	98.0	100.9	104.5	106.7	108.1	111.2	111.7	111.5	115.2	117.9	113.7	113.5	122.8
Fuel oil and other household fuels	77.6	77.9	78.1	81.7	99.3	94.6	90.7	90.3	88.8	88.1	99.2	99.8	90.0	91.4	129.7
Gas (piped) and electricity	105.7	103.8	104.6	107.5	109.3	112.6	114.8	118.5	119.2	119.2	122.1	125.1	121.2	120.9	128.0
Water and sewer and trash collection services [1]	. . .	. . .	. . .	. . .	. . .	. . .	. . .	. . .	. . .	. . .	. . .	. . .	101.6	104.0	106.5
Household furnishings and operation	105.2	107.1	109.4	111.2	113.3	116.0	118.0	119.3	121.0	123.0	124.7	125.4	126.6	126.7	128.2
Household operations [1]	. . .	. . .	. . .	. . .	. . .	. . .	. . .	. . .	. . .	. . .	. . .	. . .	101.5	104.5	110.5
Apparel	105.9	110.6	115.4	118.6	124.1	128.7	131.9	133.7	133.4	132.0	131.7	132.9	133.0	131.3	129.6
Men's and boys' apparel	106.2	109.1	113.4	117.0	120.4	124.2	126.5	127.5	126.4	126.2	127.7	130.1	131.8	131.1	129.7
Women's and girls' apparel	104.0	110.4	114.9	116.4	122.6	127.6	130.4	132.6	130.9	126.9	124.7	126.1	126.0	123.3	121.5
Infants' and toddlers' apparel	111.8	112.1	110.4	110.1	125.8	120.9	120.3	127.1	128.1	127.2	129.7	129.0	126.1	129.0	130.6
Footwear	101.9	105.1	109.9	114.4	117.4	120.9	125.0	125.0	126.0	125.4	126.6	127.6	128.0	125.7	123.8
Transportation	102.3	105.4	108.7	114.1	120.5	123.8	126.5	130.4	134.3	139.1	143.0	144.3	141.6	144.4	153.3
Private transportation	101.2	104.2	107.6	112.9	118.8	121.9	124.6	127.5	131.4	136.3	140.0	141.0	137.9	140.5	149.1
New and used motor vehicles [1]	. . .	. . .	. . .	. . .	. . .	. . .	. . .	91.8	95.5	99.4	101.0	100.5	100.1	100.1	100.8
New vehicles	110.6	114.4	116.5	119.2	121.4	126.0	129.2	132.7	137.6	141.0	143.7	144.3	143.4	142.0	142.8
Used cars and trucks	108.8	113.1	118.0	120.4	117.6	118.1	123.2	133.9	141.7	156.5	157.0	151.1	150.6	152.0	155.8
Motor fuel	77.1	80.2	80.9	88.5	101.2	99.4	99.0	98.0	98.5	100.0	106.3	106.2	92.2	100.7	129.3
Gasoline (all types)	77.0	80.1	80.8	88.5	101.0	99.2	99.0	97.7	98.2	99.8	105.9	105.8	91.6	100.1	128.6
Motor vehicle parts and equipment	95.4	96.1	97.9	100.2	100.9	102.2	103.1	101.6	101.4	102.1	102.2	101.9	101.1	100.5	101.5
Motor vehicle maintenance and repair	110.3	114.8	119.7	124.9	130.1	136.0	141.3	145.9	150.2	154.0	158.4	162.7	167.1	171.9	177.3
Public transportation	117.0	121.1	123.3	129.5	142.6	148.9	151.4	167.0	172.0	175.9	181.9	186.7	190.3	197.7	209.6
Medical Care	122.0	130.1	138.6	149.3	162.8	177.0	190.1	201.4	211.0	220.5	228.2	234.6	242.1	250.6	260.8
Medical care commodities	122.8	131.0	139.9	150.8	163.4	176.8	188.1	195.0	200.7	204.5	210.4	215.3	221.8	230.7	238.1
Medical care services	121.9	130.0	138.3	148.9	162.7	177.1	190.5	202.9	213.4	224.2	232.4	239.1	246.8	255.1	266.0
Professional services	120.8	128.8	137.5	146.4	156.1	165.7	175.8	184.7	192.5	201.0	208.3	215.4	222.2	229.2	237.7
Hospital and related services	123.1	131.6	143.9	160.5	178.0	196.1	214.0	231.9	245.6	257.8	269.5	278.4	287.5	299.5	317.3
Recreation [1]	. . .	. . .	. . .	. . .	. . .	. . .	. . .	90.7	92.7	94.5	97.4	99.6	101.1	102.0	103.3
Video and audio [1]	. . .	. . .	. . .	. . .	. . .	. . .	. . .	96.5	95.4	95.1	96.6	99.4	101.1	100.7	101.0
Education And Communication [1]	. . .	. . .	. . .	. . .	. . .	. . .	. . .	85.5	88.8	92.2	95.3	98.4	100.3	101.2	102.5
Education [1]	. . .	. . .	. . .	. . .	. . .	. . .	. . .	78.4	83.3	88.0	92.7	97.3	102.1	107.0	112.5
Educational books and supplies	128.1	138.1	148.1	158.0	171.3	180.3	190.3	197.6	205.5	214.4	226.9	238.4	250.8	261.7	279.9
Tuition, other school fees, and childcare	129.6	140.0	151.0	162.7	175.7	191.4	208.5	225.3	239.8	253.8	267.1	280.4	294.2	308.4	324.0
Communication [1]	. . .	. . .	. . .	. . .	. . .	. . .	. . .	96.7	97.6	98.8	99.6	100.3	98.7	96.0	93.6
Information and information processing [1]	. . .	. . .	. . .	. . .	. . .	. . .	. . .	97.7	98.6	98.7	99.5	100.4	98.5	95.5	92.8
Telephone services [1]	. . .	. . .	. . .	. . .	. . .	. . .	. . .	. . .	. . .	. . .	. . .	. . .	100.7	100.1	98.5
Information and information processing other than telephone services [3]	. . .	. . .	. . .	96.3	93.5	88.6	83.7	78.8	72.0	63.8	57.2	50.1	39.9	30.5	25.9
Personal computers and peripheral equipment [1]	. . .	. . .	. . .	. . .	. . .	. . .	. . .	. . .	. . .	. . .	. . .	. . .	78.2	53.5	41.1
Other Goods And Services	121.4	128.5	137.0	147.7	159.0	171.6	183.3	192.9	198.5	206.9	215.4	224.8	237.7	258.3	271.1
Tobacco and smoking products	124.7	133.6	145.8	164.4	181.5	202.7	219.8	228.4	220.0	225.7	232.8	243.7	274.8	355.8	394.9
Personal care	111.9	115.1	119.4	125.0	130.4	134.9	138.3	141.5	144.6	147.1	150.1	152.7	156.7	161.1	165.6
Personal care products	111.3	113.9	118.1	123.2	128.2	132.8	136.5	139.0	141.5	143.1	144.3	144.2	148.3	151.8	153.7
Personal care services	112.5	116.2	120.7	126.8	132.8	137.0	140.0	144.0	147.9	151.5	156.6	162.4	166.0	171.4	178.1
Miscellaneous personal services	125.1	133.8	140.3	148.1	158.4	168.8	177.5	186.1	195.9	205.9	215.6	226.1	234.7	243.0	252.3

1. December 1997=100.
2. December 1982=100.
3. December 1988=100.

Table 6-9. Relative Importance of Components in the Consumer Price Index, U.S. City Average, New Series, December 1997–December 2000

(Percent of all items.)

Index and year	All items	Food and beverages	Housing	Apparel	Transportation	Medical care	Recreation	Education and communication	Other goods and services
All URBAN CONSUMERS (CPI-U)									
December 1997	100.0	16.3	39.6	4.9	17.6	5.6	6.1	5.5	4.3
December 1998	100.0	16.4	39.8	4.8	17.0	5.7	6.1	5.5	4.6
December 1999	100.0	16.3	39.6	4.7	17.5	5.8	6.0	5.4	4.7
December 2000	100.0	16.2	40.0	4.4	17.6	5.8	5.9	5.3	4.8
URBAN WAGE EARNERS AND WORKERS (CPI-W)									
December 1997	100.0	17.9	36.5	5.3	19.8	4.6	6.0	5.4	4.5
December 1998	100.0	18.0	36.7	5.2	19.2	4.7	5.9	5.4	5.0
December 1999	100.0	17.9	36.5	5.0	19.7	4.7	5.8	5.3	5.1
December 2000	100.0	17.8	36.8	4.8	19.9	4.7	5.7	5.2	5.2

Table 6-10. Relative Importance of Components in the Consumer Price Index, U.S. City Average, Old Series, December 1997 and Dates of Major Weight Revisions

(Percent of all items.)

Index and year	All items	Food and beverages	Housing	Apparel and upkeep	Transportation	Medical care	Entertainment	Other goods and services
ALL URBAN CONSUMERS (CPI-U)								
December 1977	100.0	18.8	43.9	5.8	18.0	5.0	4.1	4.4
December 1982	100.0	20.1	37.7	5.2	21.8	6.0	4.2	5.0
December 1995	100.0	17.3	41.3	5.3	17.0	7.4	4.4	7.1
December 1997	100.0	17.5	41.5	5.3	16.6	7.4	4.3	7.4
URBAN WAGE EARNERS AND CLERICAL WORKERS (CPI-W)								
1935-1939	100.0	35.4	33.7	11.0	8.1	4.1	2.8	4.9
December 1952	100.0	32.2	33.5	9.4	11.3	4.8	4.0	4.8
December 1963	100.0	25.2	34.9	10.6	14.0	5.7	3.9	5.7
December 1977	100.0	20.5	40.7	5.8	20.2	4.5	3.9	4.4
December 1984	100.0	21.3	34.9	5.0	24.1	5.6	3.9	5.2
December 1995	100.0	19.3	38.9	5.5	19.0	6.3	4.0	7.0
December 1997	100.0	19.4	39.0	5.3	18.6	6.3	4.0	7.3

Table 6-11. Consumer Price Indexes, All Urban Consumers, All Items, Selected Areas, Selected Years, 1955–2000

(1982–1984=100, unless otherwise indicated.)

Area	1955	1960	1965	1970	1975	1980	1981	1982	1983	1984	1985	1986	1987
NORTHEAST													
New York-Northern New Jersey-Long Island	27.1	30.2	32.6	41.2	57.6	82.1	90.1	95.3	99.8	104.8	108.7	112.3	118.0
Philadelphia-Wilmington-Atlantic City	27.9	30.6	32.8	40.8	56.8	83.6	92.1	96.6	99.4	104.1	108.8	111.5	116.8
Boston-Brockton-Nashua	26.4	29.8	32.5	40.2	55.8	82.6	91.8	95.5	99.8	104.7	109.4	112.2	117.1
Pittsburgh	26.3	29.7	31.4	38.1	52.4	81.0	89.3	94.4	101.1	104.5	106.9	108.2	111.4
NORTH CENTRAL													
Chicago-Gary-Kenosha	27.5	30.4	31.7	38.9	52.8	82.2	90.0	96.2	100.0	103.8	107.7	110.0	114.5
Detroit-Ann Arbor-Flint	27.7	29.7	31.2	39.5	53.9	85.3	93.2	97.0	99.8	103.2	106.8	108.3	111.7
St. Louis	27.0	29.5	31.7	38.8	52.6	82.5	90.1	96.6	100.1	103.3	107.1	108.6	112.2
Cleveland-Akron	25.7	28.3	29.6	37.2	50.2	78.9	87.2	94.0	101.2	104.8	107.8	109.4	112.7
Minneapolis-St. Paul	25.9	28.3	30.1	37.4	51.2	78.9	88.6	97.4	99.5	103.1	107.0	108.4	111.6
Milwaukee-Racine	27.1	29.2	31.0	37.5	50.8	81.4	90.7	95.9	100.2	103.8	107.0	107.4	111.5
Cincinnati-Hamilton	26.6	29.1	30.5	37.4	51.8	82.1	87.9	94.9	100.8	104.3	106.6	107.6	111.9
Kansas City	26.5	29.3	32.2	39.0	53.2	83.6	90.5	95.0	100.5	104.5	107.7	108.7	113.1
SOUTH													
Baltimore	26.7	29.8	31.6	39.1	55.2	83.7	91.5	95.6	99.9	104.5	108.2	110.9	114.2
Washington	27.4	29.7	31.9	39.8	54.7	82.9	90.5	95.5	99.8	104.6	109.0	112.2	116.2
Washington-Baltimore [1]	...	...	...	...	...	...	...	...	...	...	...	...	...
Dallas-Fort Worth	...	...	29.9	37.6	50.4	81.5	90.8	96.0	99.7	104.3	108.2	109.9	112.9
Houston-Galveston-Brazoria	25.7	27.8	29.6	36.4	51.4	82.7	91.0	97.3	100.0	102.7	104.9	103.9	106.5
Atlanta	27.1	29.6	31.2	38.6	53.6	80.3	90.2	96.0	99.9	104.1	108.9	112.2	116.5
Miami-Fort Lauderdale	...	...	...	...	...	81.1	90.5	96.7	99.9	103.5	106.5	107.9	111.8
Tampa-St. Petersburg-Clearwater [2]	...	...	...	...	...	...	...	...	...	...	...	...	100.0
New Orleans [2]	...	...	...	...	...	...	...	...	...	...	...	...	100.0
WEST													
Los Angeles-Riverside-Orange County	26.7	30.0	32.4	38.7	53.3	83.7	91.9	97.3	99.1	103.6	108.4	111.9	116.7
San Francisco-Oakland-San Jose	24.9	28.6	30.8	37.7	51.8	80.4	90.8	97.6	98.4	104.0	108.4	111.6	115.4
Seattle-Tacoma-Bremerton	25.9	28.8	31.0	37.4	51.1	82.7	91.8	97.7	99.3	103.0	105.6	106.7	109.2
San Diego	...	...	28.2	34.1	47.6	79.4	90.1	96.2	99.0	104.8	110.4	113.5	117.5
Portland-Salem	26.8	29.8	32.3	38.7	53.5	87.2	95.0	98.0	99.1	102.8	106.7	108.2	110.9
Honolulu	...	...	34.4	41.5	56.3	83.0	91.7	97.2	99.3	103.5	106.8	109.4	114.9
Anchorage	...	...	35.3	41.1	57.1	85.5	92.4	97.4	99.2	103.3	105.8	107.8	108.2
Denver-Boulder-Greeley	...	...	28.8	34.5	48.4	78.4	87.2	95.1	100.5	104.3	107.1	107.9	110.8

Area	1988	1989	1990	1991	1992	1993	1994	1995	1996	1997	1998	1999	2000
NORTHEAST													
New York-Northern New Jersey-Long Island	123.7	130.6	138.5	144.8	150.0	154.5	158.2	162.2	166.9	170.8	173.6	177.0	182.5
Philadelphia-Wilmington-Atlantic City	122.4	128.3	135.8	142.2	146.6	150.2	154.6	158.7	162.8	166.5	168.2	171.9	176.5
Boston-Brockton-Nashua	124.2	131.3	138.9	145.0	148.6	152.9	154.9	158.6	163.3	167.9	171.7	176.0	183.6
Pittsburgh	114.9	120.1	126.2	131.3	136.0	139.9	144.6	149.2	153.2	157.0	159.2	162.5	168.0
NORTH CENTRAL													
Chicago-Gary-Kenosha	119.0	125.0	131.7	137.0	141.1	145.4	148.6	153.3	157.4	161.7	165.0	168.4	173.8
Detroit-Ann Arbor-Flint	116.1	122.3	128.6	133.1	135.9	139.6	144.0	148.6	152.5	156.3	159.8	163.9	169.8
St. Louis	115.7	121.8	128.1	132.1	134.7	137.5	141.3	145.2	149.6	152.9	154.5	157.6	163.1
Cleveland-Akron	116.7	122.7	129.0	134.2	136.8	140.3	144.4	147.9	152.0	156.1	159.8	162.5	168.0
Minneapolis-St. Paul	117.2	122.0	127.0	130.4	135.0	139.2	143.6	147.0	151.9	155.4	158.3	163.3	170.1
Milwaukee-Racine	115.9	120.8	126.2	132.2	137.1	142.1	147.0	151.0	154.7	157.7	160.3	163.7	168.6
Cincinnati-Hamilton	116.1	120.9	126.5	131.4	134.1	137.8	142.4	146.2	149.6	152.1	155.1	159.2	164.8
Kansas City	117.4	121.6	126.0	131.2	134.3	138.1	141.3	145.3	151.6	155.8	157.8	160.1	166.6
SOUTH													
Baltimore	119.3	124.5	130.8	136.4	140.1	143.1	146.9	150.7	154.2	...	...	...	...
Washington	121.0	128.0	135.6	141.2	144.7	149.3	152.2	155.3	159.6	...	...	...	...
Washington-Baltimore [1]	...	...	...	...	...	...	...	...	...	100.8	102.1	104.2	107.6
Dallas-Fort Worth	116.1	119.5	125.1	130.8	133.9	137.3	141.2	144.9	148.8	151.4	153.6	158.0	164.7
Houston-Galveston-Brazoria	109.5	114.1	120.6	125.1	129.1	133.4	137.9	139.8	142.7	145.4	146.8	148.7	154.2
Atlanta	120.4	126.1	131.7	135.9	138.5	143.4	146.7	150.9	156.0	158.9	161.2	164.8	170.6
Miami-Fort Lauderdale	116.8	121.5	128.0	132.3	134.5	139.1	143.6	148.9	153.7	158.4	160.5	162.4	167.8
Tampa-St. Petersburg-Clearwater [2]	103.7	107.2	111.7	116.4	119.2	124.0	126.5	129.7	131.6	134.0	137.5	140.6	145.7
New Orleans [2]	102.7	107.2	111.5	116.0	120.2	124.7	129.0	133.4	138.4	...	...	...	...
WEST													
Los Angeles-Riverside-Orange County	122.1	128.3	135.9	141.4	146.5	150.3	152.3	154.6	157.5	160.0	162.3	166.1	171.6
San Francisco-Oakland-San Jose	120.5	126.4	132.1	137.9	142.5	146.3	148.7	151.6	155.1	160.4	165.5	172.5	180.2
Seattle-Tacoma-Bremerton	112.8	118.1	126.8	134.1	139.0	142.9	147.8	152.3	157.5	163.0	167.7	172.8	179.2
San Diego	123.4	130.6	138.4	143.4	147.4	150.6	154.5	156.8	160.9	163.7	166.9	172.8	182.8
Portland-Salem	114.7	120.4	127.4	133.9	139.8	144.7	148.9	153.2	158.6	164.0	167.1	172.6	178.0
Honolulu	121.7	128.7	138.1	148.0	155.1	160.1	164.5	168.1	170.7	171.9	171.5	173.3	176.3
Anchorage	108.6	111.7	118.6	124.0	128.2	132.2	135.0	138.9	142.7	144.8	146.9	148.4	150.9
Denver-Boulder-Greeley	113.7	115.8	120.9	125.6	130.3	135.8	141.8	147.9	153.1	158.1	161.9	166.6	173.2

1. November 1996=100.
2. 1987=100.

NOTES AND DEFINITIONS

EXPORT AND IMPORT PRICE INDEXES

Collection and Coverage

United States export and import price indexes cover transactions in nonmilitary goods between the United States and the rest of the world. The export price indexes provide a measure of price change for U.S. products sold to other countries, and the import price indexes provide a measure of price change for goods purchased from other countries by U.S. residents.

Prices used in constructing the indexes are initially collected through personal visits by BLS field representatives; thereafter, the prices generally are collected each month by mail questionnaire or telephone. To the extent possible, products are priced at the U.S. border for exports and at both the foreign border and the U.S. border for imports. For a given product, however, only one price basis series is used in constructing the index. For most products, prices refer to transactions completed during the first week of the month. Indexes published here are based on the Standard Industrial Trade Classification System (SITC), a United Nations product classification system. The SITC is especially useful for international comparisons. These indexes are also published by End Use Category as well as the Harmonized System nomenclature.

Prices are collected according to the specification method. The specifications for each product include detailed descriptions of the physical and functional characteristics of the product. The terms of transaction include information on the number of units bought or sold, discount, credit terms, packaging, class of buyer or seller, etc. When there are changes in either the specifications or terms of transaction of a product, the dollar value of each change is deleted from the total price change in order to obtain the "pure price change." Once this value is determined, a linking procedure is employed which allows for continued repricing of the item.

At the elementary level, the price changes for individual items within a given Company/Classification Group cell are generally averaged together using equal weights in order to produce an index at the cell level. These cells are then averaged together using the relative importance of a given company's trade in the product area, in order to produce an index at the Classification Group level. These Classification Group indexes are then averaged together using weights derived from these company weights in order to produce the lowest level publication strata. Successively higher levels of publication strata are then averaged together using their relative importance based on 1995 U.S. trade values.

A limited number of import price indexes based on locality of origin indexes are also produced. BLS also publishes indexes for selected categories of internationally traded services calculated on an international basis.

Sources of Additional Information

Concepts and methodology are described in the *BLS Handbook of Methods,* BLS Bulletin 2490, April 1997, Chapter 15, and in monthly press releases.

Table 6-12. U.S. Export Price Indexes for Selected Categories of Goods, by Standard International Trade Classification, 1986–2000

(1995=100, unless otherwise indicated.)

Categories	Relative importance [1]	1986				1987				1988			
		March	June	September	December	March	June	September	December	March	June	September	December
ALL COMMODITIES	100.00	80.5	80.1	79.3	80.2	81.1	82.8	83.3	84.9	86.4	88.7	90.5	90.3
Food And Live Animals	7.02	79.5	79.4	70.3	73.7	71.4	73.5	70.9	77.4	77.9	84.6	97.1	93.5
Meat and meat preparations	1.29	70.3	72.2	76.4	78.6	78.9	83.2	81.5	80.2	84.3	89.9	94.0	89.4
Fish, crustaceans, aquatic invertebrates and preparations thereof	0.58	66.0	71.5	73.7	76.3	77.1	82.9	86.4	91.3	92.8	95.6	115.9	114.7
Cereals and cereal preparations	2.28	81.6	79.2	59.0	64.4	60.8	63.1	60.3	68.8	71.0	77.5	96.4	90.7
Vegetables, fruit and nuts, fresh or dried	1.29	71.6	78.8	83.2	85.2	83.6	81.5	73.4	72.9	70.7	75.7	79.8	80.0
Feeding stuff for animals (not including unmilled cereals)	0.70	94.5	90.4	97.6	94.3	92.2	97.5	96.9	114.4	106.0	124.5	126.8	123.7
Miscellaneous edible products and preparations	0.41	89.3	88.4	89.9	90.9	91.2	91.6	91.3	91.4	93.2	93.6	95.8	95.5
Beverages And Tobacco	1.54	67.0	67.6	67.5	71.2	71.2	72.9	73.2	74.2	76.1	76.8	77.7	77.5
Tobacco and tobacco manufactures	1.27	66.8	67.3	67.3	71.1	71.1	72.8	73.2	74.2	76.1	76.8	77.7	77.5
Crude Materials, Inedible, Except Fuels	5.44	59.3	59.8	58.3	59.9	61.8	67.0	69.4	73.3	76.1	81.9	82.4	79.5
Hides, skins and furskins, raw	0.34	70.5	76.0	70.3	75.2	85.6	97.1	95.9	102.0	111.2	108.3	101.7	88.8
Oil seeds and oleaginous fruits	0.94	87.1	86.3	85.7	83.7	79.4	89.3	83.6	96.3	101.6	125.7	136.0	119.3
Cork and wood	0.91	37.6	37.5	38.1	40.0	41.2	43.1	52.5	54.1	55.7	55.5	55.6	55.1
Pulp and waste paper	1.01	38.7	43.2	47.9	48.1	53.6	55.7	56.8	59.6	63.6	66.7	67.5	67.6
Textile fibers and their waste	0.74	65.9	64.4	48.0	59.8	64.3	73.9	76.6	73.4	70.7	72.3	66.3	68.1
Crude fertilizers and crude minerals	0.32	102.1	100.6	100.1	99.0	96.4	96.1	93.6	93.6	94.8	96.3	96.9	96.8
Metalliferous ores and metal scrap	0.79	58.7	57.3	58.7	56.6	57.8	62.6	68.7	73.6	77.1	85.4	84.8	88.0
Mineral Fuels, Lubricants And Related Materials	3.09	94.4	86.7	87.4	87.8	91.8	93.4	95.4	93.1	89.5	92.7	89.8	89.6
Coal, coke and briquettes	0.74	100.3	99.4	98.9	97.4	98.0	93.3	96.2	95.0	95.9	97.4	98.3	98.8
Petroleum, petroleum products and related materials	2.35	...	...	...	...	...	...	...	91.9	83.4	89.4	82.0	81.2
Animal And Vegetable Oils, Fats And Waxes	0.28	68.0	62.0	56.9	65.7	67.6	72.1	71.8	74.7	84.9	89.1	92.9	83.7
Chemicals And Related Products, n.e.s.	10.76	73.9	72.6	70.9	70.5	73.8	79.0	79.8	83.6	87.4	90.1	92.6	93.0
Organic chemicals	2.63	67.8	64.1	63.1	63.6	70.2	81.5	80.0	85.1	93.0	99.6	105.6	103.9
Inorganic chemicals	0.85	...	...	...	...	...	...	...	...	...	...	...	...
Dyeing, tanning and coloring materials	0.49	...	...	...	...	...	...	...	...	...	...	...	...
Medicinal and pharmaceutical products	1.23	84.0	84.8	84.6	84.2	84.4	84.7	85.4	88.0	91.3	88.8	88.5	89.8
Essential oils; polishing and cleansing preparations	0.77	72.6	74.9	74.4	74.2	75.1	75.2	76.4	77.2	79.1	80.9	85.6	87.1
Fertilizers [2]	0.46	...	...	...	...	...	...	...	...	...	...	...	...
Plastics in primary forms	1.78	...	...	...	...	...	...	...	...	...	...	...	...
Plastics in nonprimary forms	0.83	...	...	...	...	...	...	...	...	...	...	...	...
Chemical materials and products, n.e.s.	1.72	76.0	76.9	73.7	73.5	73.6	73.8	73.3	74.2	75.8	76.8	78.6	79.6
Manufactured Goods Classified Chiefly By Material	10.07	71.6	72.4	73.3	73.6	75.2	76.2	78.0	78.6	80.8	83.2	84.5	85.2
Rubber manufactures, n.e.s.	0.69	74.7	74.2	74.6	74.9	75.7	76.0	77.1	77.3	78.1	80.7	81.2	81.9
Cork and wood manufactures other than furniture	0.30	...	...	...	...	...	...	...	...	...	...	...	...
Paper, paperboard, and articles of paper pulp, paper or paperboard	1.63	62.6	65.2	67.9	68.9	71.4	72.8	74.8	76.2	78.5	80.3	81.1	81.6
Textile yarn, fabrics, and made-up articles, n.e.s.	1.34	76.8	78.0	77.2	77.2	78.3	78.6	78.9	79.7	80.7	81.8	82.3	84.6
Nonmetallic mineral manufactures, n.e.s.	1.33	72.6	73.5	75.2	77.5	76.6	78.0	79.2	79.9	81.4	81.9	83.0	83.8
Iron and steel	1.05	...	...	...	...	...	...	...	...	...	...	...	...
Nonferrous metals	1.48	69.5	68.7	70.2	68.4	71.1	75.3	82.0	82.9	89.3	95.7	99.4	100.0
Manufactures of metals, n.e.s.	2.10	75.5	75.7	75.8	75.8	76.3	76.1	76.9	77.7	78.5	80.9	82.6	83.3
Machinery And Transport Equipment	49.78	87.2	87.2	87.4	88.0	88.0	88.2	88.4	88.7	89.3	90.1	90.8	91.6
Power generating machinery and equipment	4.72	75.5	75.5	75.6	76.5	77.1	76.5	77.3	77.6	78.9	79.9	80.0	80.6
Machinery specialized for particular industries	4.84	78.2	78.0	78.0	78.2	77.7	77.8	78.1	78.4	79.4	80.5	81.4	82.4
Metalworking machinery	1.00	74.8	74.9	75.7	76.5	77.7	78.4	79.2	79.4	80.3	81.4	81.5	84.0
General industrial machinery, equipment, and parts, n.e.s.	5.22	76.1	76.6	77.3	77.9	78.6	78.9	78.9	79.5	80.5	81.5	82.5	83.2
Computer equipment and office machines	5.39	139.4	138.1	137.9	137.1	134.0	134.1	133.5	133.3	133.6	133.5	135.1	134.5
Telecommunications and sound recording and reproducing apparatus and equipment	3.72	83.9	83.7	84.3	85.7	86.2	85.8	85.7	86.2	86.9	88.5	88.1	88.9
Electrical machinery and equipment	10.65	89.6	89.4	89.8	90.3	91.6	92.0	92.3	91.7	92.8	93.1	94.8	95.2
Road vehicles	9.37	83.8	84.4	84.6	85.8	85.6	85.9	86.2	86.9	86.8	87.1	87.5	88.7
Miscellaneous Manufactured Articles	11.35	80.6	81.5	81.5	81.8	82.4	82.9	83.1	83.2	84.2	85.1	85.8	87.1
Furniture and parts thereof	0.66	82.5	83.1	83.3	83.8	86.4	87.1	87.1	89.1	90.0	90.2	90.4	92.5
Articles of apparel and clothing accessories	1.20	...	...	...	...	...	...	...	...	...	...	...	...
Professional, scientific and controlling instruments and apparatus, n.e.s.	3.86	71.0	71.8	71.7	72.1	72.7	73.5	74.1	74.6	76.6	77.4	78.4	79.3
Photographic apparatus, equipment and supplies and optical goods, n.e.s.	0.95	95.8	96.5	96.3	96.0	96.5	96.3	93.1	92.1	91.7	94.1	93.5	93.9
Miscellaneous manufactured articles, n.e.s.	4.21	89.2	89.8	89.6	90.2	90.4	90.1	91.1	91.0	90.7	91.6	91.6	93.5

See footnotes and *Note* at end of table.

Table 6-12. U.S. Export Price Indexes for Selected Categories of Goods, by Standard International Trade Classification, 1986–2000—*Continued*

(1995=100, unless otherwise indicated.)

Categories	1989				1990				1991			
	March	June	September	December	March	June	September	December	March	June	September	December
ALL COMMODITIES	91.6	91.6	90.9	90.8	91.2	91.5	92.2	92.7	92.8	92.5	92.0	92.1
Food And Live Animals	96.2	94.5	90.3	88.6	87.9	89.0	83.6	81.1	83.8	86.0	85.2	87.2
Meat and meat preparations	91.2	88.0	81.9	80.3	86.4	84.9	85.3	88.4	88.7	87.9	89.0	86.4
Fish, crustaceans, aquatic invertebrates and preparations thereof	111.4	104.7	90.3	87.1	86.6	83.6	85.6	84.0	83.5	80.4	74.8	80.2
Cereals and cereal preparations	96.4	94.7	90.3	89.8	87.5	90.6	80.5	75.0	77.2	80.7	80.7	85.7
Vegetables, fruit and nuts, fresh or dried	79.0	82.4	82.6	80.0	83.1	83.6	80.9	80.3	93.3	99.5	92.7	85.8
Feeding stuff for animals (not including unmilled cereals)	121.4	113.5	109.9	101.6	95.8	93.2	94.7	98.4	99.0	95.5	100.5	101.2
Miscellaneous edible products and preparations	97.5	98.3	98.1	98.8	99.8	100.4	100.2	101.5	100.3	100.9	100.2	100.4
Beverages And Tobacco	81.3	81.6	83.6	83.3	84.9	86.4	87.1	89.5	91.5	92.0	92.5	94.2
Tobacco and tobacco manufactures	81.5	81.8	83.8	83.5	85.1	86.6	87.4	89.6	91.6	92.1	92.5	94.2
Crude Materials, Inedible, Except Fuels	83.5	83.7	81.4	79.9	80.1	80.4	80.6	78.7	78.6	76.3	73.3	71.6
Hides, skins and furskins, raw	95.2	97.3	101.5	102.5	105.0	105.1	97.3	92.3	84.1	81.5	71.7	80.3
Oil seeds and oleaginous fruits	122.4	114.1	98.0	96.2	96.2	97.0	103.2	103.0	103.7	99.2	97.7	93.4
Cork and wood	58.3	63.3	65.9	65.6	67.0	66.4	64.5	62.5	63.5	63.7	64.5	64.4
Pulp and waste paper	71.6	71.9	71.8	72.0	69.3	64.7	62.4	62.1	60.3	56.0	51.0	50.7
Textile fibers and their waste	70.2	76.0	77.2	76.5	77.0	81.8	80.3	79.9	83.4	85.3	77.9	71.1
Crude fertilizers and crude minerals	100.9	101.4	101.4	99.9	100.8	101.9	102.2	102.2	103.2	102.9	100.4	100.6
Metalliferous ores and metal scrap	95.7	91.9	88.0	81.0	81.0	83.4	88.2	81.5	80.5	74.4	72.8	68.7
Mineral Fuels, Lubricants And Related Materials	92.2	97.1	99.2	102.8	102.5	100.1	116.6	120.2	102.9	98.7	98.7	99.8
Coal, coke and briquettes	99.1	99.8	101.2	101.9	101.8	103.2	103.6	103.7	103.4	101.7	101.7	101.8
Petroleum, petroleum products and related materials	86.9	96.9	99.9	107.0	104.4	99.9	134.2	137.7	103.1	95.3	95.5	97.4
Animal And Vegetable Oils, Fats And Waxes	82.7	79.9	76.7	79.4	81.5	86.6	83.1	85.0	82.1	78.9	79.4	77.2
Chemicals And Related Products, n.e.s.	93.0	90.4	87.2	85.3	85.5	85.6	88.2	91.9	90.9	87.5	86.1	85.5
Organic chemicals	103.0	99.9	92.3	88.0	84.7	81.7	86.5	91.4	87.6	81.4	77.1	77.1
Inorganic chemicals	...	...	...	...	...	...	...	...	...	...	...	...
Dyeing, tanning and coloring materials	...	...	...	...	...	...	...	...	...	...	...	...
Medicinal and pharmaceutical products	91.1	91.0	91.4	90.6	91.8	91.9	92.1	92.0	92.4	92.6	94.1	94.2
Essential oils; polishing and cleansing preparations	89.2	88.8	87.1	87.5	89.0	90.3	90.5	90.8	90.9	91.0	91.7	91.3
Fertilizers [2]	...	...	...	...	...	...	...	...	...	...	...	...
Plastics in primary forms	...	...	...	...	...	...	...	...	...	...	...	...
Plastics in nonprimary forms	...	...	...	...	...	...	...	...	...	...	...	...
Chemical materials and products, n.e.s.	81.9	82.6	82.7	83.2	85.2	85.9	87.5	89.4	91.2	90.0	89.0	88.9
Manufactured Goods Classified Chiefly By Material	86.6	87.0	86.8	86.6	86.8	86.9	87.3	87.2	87.4	87.1	86.9	86.8
Rubber manufactures, n.e.s.	83.8	83.8	84.2	84.6	84.8	84.9	85.8	87.9	89.4	90.1	90.4	90.8
Cork and wood manufactures other than furniture	...	...	...	...	...	...	...	...	...	...	...	...
Paper, paperboard, and articles of paper pulp, paper or paperboard	82.5	83.2	82.7	81.5	81.4	81.1	81.6	81.8	81.4	81.1	80.4	80.6
Textile yarn, fabrics, and made-up articles, n.e.s.	86.4	87.4	87.7	88.6	90.2	89.7	89.7	90.6	92.6	93.7	93.3	93.6
Nonmetallic mineral manufactures, n.e.s.	86.4	87.8	88.9	89.6	91.6	91.1	91.0	91.9	92.5	92.5	92.6	93.4
Iron and steel	...	...	...	...	...	...	...	...	...	...	...	...
Nonferrous metals	101.1	97.2	93.6	90.6	87.5	88.4	90.6	86.3	82.3	77.7	77.1	75.1
Manufactures of metals, n.e.s.	84.6	85.6	86.0	86.7	87.7	88.0	88.2	88.9	90.1	90.6	90.8	91.2
Machinery And Transport Equipment	92.3	92.8	93.4	94.0	94.8	95.3	95.6	96.2	97.6	98.3	98.7	99.0
Power generating machinery and equipment	82.5	83.2	84.4	84.6	85.8	86.5	86.8	87.4	89.6	90.7	91.4	91.9
Machinery specialized for particular industries	83.4	84.6	85.4	86.6	87.9	88.0	88.7	89.9	90.8	91.6	91.6	92.1
Metalworking machinery	85.0	86.2	86.4	87.1	87.9	89.0	89.1	91.2	93.1	95.1	95.3	95.7
General industrial machinery, equipment, and parts, n.e.s.	85.0	85.5	86.2	87.0	88.4	89.2	89.8	90.2	92.2	92.7	93.4	93.4
Computer equipment and office machines	133.7	132.3	132.3	132.2	132.1	132.0	131.8	130.2	130.4	129.4	127.8	126.4
Telecommunications and sound recording and reproducing apparatus and equipment	90.3	91.0	92.0	92.6	92.3	94.1	94.6	95.0	97.4	100.0	101.4	102.3
Electrical machinery and equipment	95.6	95.9	96.3	96.3	97.1	96.8	96.6	96.9	96.9	97.4	99.2	99.9
Road vehicles	89.0	89.5	90.3	91.3	91.6	92.1	92.6	93.6	94.4	94.7	95.0	95.6
Miscellaneous Manufactured Articles	87.8	88.9	89.5	90.5	90.9	91.7	93.1	94.5	95.7	96.5	96.8	97.3
Furniture and parts thereof	92.6	95.0	94.9	96.4	97.6	99.0	98.8	100.7	102.5	103.2	103.4	103.1
Articles of apparel and clothing accessories	...	...	...	...	...	...	...	...	...	...	...	...
Professional, scientific and controlling instruments and apparatus, n.e.s.	80.5	82.3	83.3	84.5	85.4	86.9	88.9	90.9	91.9	93.1	93.3	94.2
Photographic apparatus, equipment and supplies and optical goods, n.e.s.	92.6	93.3	93.4	95.0	92.3	91.8	93.1	95.5	95.9	95.7	95.5	96.5
Miscellaneous manufactured articles, n.e.s.	94.8	94.6	94.9	95.8	96.4	96.9	97.5	98.1	99.8	100.0	100.6	100.5

See footnotes and *Note* at end of table.

Table 6-12. U.S. Export Price Indexes for Selected Categories of Goods, by Standard International Trade Classification, 1986–2000—*Continued*

(1995=100, unless otherwise indicated.)

Categories	1992				1993				1994			
	March	June	September	December	March	June	September	December	March	June	September	December
ALL COMMODITIES	92.5	92.8	93.0	92.7	92.9	93.2	93.2	93.7	94.5	94.8	95.4	97.2
Food And Live Animals	90.6	87.8	85.8	85.3	84.9	83.5	87.3	92.0	92.7	88.7	87.4	91.1
Meat and meat preparations	90.4	91.5	90.2	92.0	93.7	96.2	92.2	92.4	95.3	92.5	92.9	94.0
Fish, crustaceans, aquatic invertebrates and preparations thereof	86.7	83.3	81.4	77.0	78.5	82.0	76.9	75.0	80.1	83.3	90.0	94.2
Cereals and cereal preparations	91.2	87.4	82.6	81.8	80.7	75.7	80.0	92.7	93.4	84.9	80.1	86.6
Vegetables, fruit and nuts, fresh or dried	87.0	82.0	82.5	84.4	84.9	84.4	96.7	93.7	91.9	89.8	89.8	92.9
Feeding stuff for animals (not including unmilled cereals)	97.4	97.6	100.3	99.2	95.5	96.2	102.7	105.0	101.9	101.4	99.3	94.7
Miscellaneous edible products and preparations	99.7	100.6	101.4	101.6	100.3	100.8	100.5	96.8	98.2	98.3	99.4	99.5
Beverages And Tobacco	94.8	95.5	96.3	97.2	98.0	98.4	99.2	98.1	98.6	98.7	98.4	98.6
Tobacco and tobacco manufactures	94.8	95.5	96.4	97.3	98.2	98.3	99.1	98.0	98.5	98.6	98.3	98.4
Crude Materials, Inedible, Except Fuels	72.7	74.7	75.1	74.8	77.6	79.6	78.3	78.9	83.7	86.4	87.1	93.4
Hides, skins and furskins, raw	78.8	80.8	82.8	86.8	82.1	79.1	82.9	86.0	91.3	94.3	103.9	110.4
Oil seeds and oleaginous fruits	95.1	98.3	92.0	92.1	95.6	97.8	108.7	111.9	112.2	112.7	96.1	91.8
Cork and wood	68.5	71.7	78.0	81.4	95.5	105.1	96.8	95.6	99.6	97.3	97.1	98.6
Pulp and waste paper	51.4	53.4	54.4	51.2	46.3	45.4	43.1	43.5	49.2	61.1	67.9	82.0
Textile fibers and their waste	67.8	68.6	65.6	65.2	67.7	66.6	64.7	66.2	78.5	83.7	81.2	88.2
Crude fertilizers and crude minerals	101.4	101.5	101.3	97.3	96.6	96.7	99.0	99.1	97.1	97.3	97.9	98.1
Metalliferous ores and metal scrap	71.7	71.1	71.7	68.6	69.2	70.1	70.1	71.2	75.7	76.2	83.7	97.3
Mineral Fuels, Lubricants And Related Materials	91.2	95.0	96.3	94.7	96.0	96.6	94.0	89.9	92.0	96.0	96.2	98.1
Coal, coke and briquettes	100.6	99.8	99.1	99.8	98.1	96.8	96.7	96.9	98.2	96.8	96.2	97.0
Petroleum, petroleum products and related materials	82.3	92.0	94.9	90.8	93.0	96.0	91.5	83.8	87.0	95.7	96.6	98.5
Animal And Vegetable Oils, Fats And Waxes	77.0	79.7	80.1	83.2	82.2	82.7	84.8	88.8	92.5	92.5	97.7	111.0
Chemicals And Related Products, n.e.s.	85.3	85.5	85.3	84.2	84.3	84.4	83.7	83.8	84.7	86.9	91.2	95.9
Organic chemicals	77.0	78.8	80.0	78.0	77.6	77.9	76.4	75.5	76.3	79.8	85.2	93.4
Inorganic chemicals	. . .	. . .	. . .	86.4	84.6	83.7	81.1	81.1	78.4	81.5	86.8	88.9
Dyeing, tanning and coloring materials	. . .	. . .	. . .	. . .	. . .	. . .	. . .	97.7	99.5	97.3	98.3	98.4
Medicinal and pharmaceutical products	95.2	95.8	95.8	96.0	97.3	98.5	98.8	99.6	100.2	99.8	99.3	98.9
Essential oils; polishing and cleansing preparations	92.9	93.5	92.5	92.4	93.5	93.4	94.0	94.6	95.9	98.4	98.9	98.6
Fertilizers [2]	. . .	. . .	. . .	. . .	. . .	. . .	. . .	. . .	. . .	. . .	. . .	. . .
Plastics in primary forms	. . .	. . .	. . .	74.7	74.6	76.4	75.8	75.1	76.0	79.6	90.8	100.1
Plastics in nonprimary forms	. . .	. . .	. . .	92.1	91.8	89.2	89.9	89.8	90.5	91.7	93.4	96.6
Chemical materials and products, n.e.s.	89.5	89.5	90.0	90.0	91.3	91.9	92.0	92.0	94.1	94.6	94.8	96.4
Manufactured Goods Classified Chiefly By Material	87.3	87.6	87.9	87.8	88.6	87.7	88.2	87.8	89.7	90.9	92.8	96.5
Rubber manufactures, n.e.s.	90.6	90.6	91.2	91.5	92.5	93.1	93.5	93.3	93.5	93.7	94.6	94.9
Cork and wood manufactures other than furniture	. . .	. . .	. . .	93.4	102.1	92.4	96.1	98.7	98.9	101.5	103.7	106.3
Paper, paperboard, and articles of paper pulp, paper or paperboard	80.3	80.2	79.7	79.3	78.2	76.5	75.7	75.9	76.4	78.4	83.0	90.5
Textile yarn, fabrics, and made-up articles, n.e.s.	95.0	95.1	95.4	95.7	95.7	96.2	96.2	95.4	96.1	96.1	95.4	95.6
Nonmetallic mineral manufactures, n.e.s.	93.6	94.6	94.8	94.9	95.1	96.4	97.5	96.7	97.8	98.1	98.4	99.3
Iron and steel	. . .	. . .	. . .	. . .	. . .	. . .	. . .	90.5	92.4	93.4	94.3	95.9
Nonferrous metals	76.5	77.5	77.6	75.1	75.5	71.7	73.4	69.7	77.5	81.6	87.1	98.2
Manufactures of metals, n.e.s.	91.3	91.4	92.0	92.9	93.4	92.7	93.5	94.1	94.9	94.7	95.1	97.0
Machinery And Transport Equipment	99.4	99.7	99.9	99.9	99.6	99.8	99.5	99.7	99.7	99.4	99.0	99.0
Power generating machinery and equipment	93.2	94.9	94.8	95.0	95.8	95.9	96.3	96.8	97.6	97.7	98.5	99.3
Machinery specialized for particular industries	92.9	93.5	94.0	94.7	95.3	95.8	96.3	96.8	96.8	97.3	97.4	97.4
Metalworking machinery	96.9	97.4	97.4	97.3	98.9	99.1	98.9	98.9	98.7	98.8	98.0	98.8
General industrial machinery, equipment, and parts, n.e.s.	94.7	94.9	95.3	95.8	96.4	96.8	97.4	97.9	98.3	98.4	98.8	98.8
Computer equipment and office machines	125.6	124.5	123.6	120.8	116.8	115.3	112.9	111.3	108.6	106.5	103.7	102.7
Telecommunications and sound recording and reproducing apparatus and equipment	101.0	101.8	102.2	102.3	101.5	102.9	102.1	102.1	101.1	100.9	100.3	100.0
Electrical machinery and equipment	101.0	100.3	100.8	100.7	99.8	100.2	99.5	100.2	100.4	99.9	98.6	98.3
Road vehicles	95.7	96.2	96.4	96.8	97.2	97.3	97.3	97.6	98.2	98.4	98.6	99.2
Miscellaneous Manufactured Articles	98.0	98.3	98.5	98.6	98.8	99.0	99.0	98.9	98.8	99.1	99.5	99.4
Furniture and parts thereof	104.1	103.8	103.4	103.8	101.4	99.7	99.6	99.9	100.0	100.3	100.9	99.6
Articles of apparel and clothing accessories	. . .	. . .	. . .	. . .	. . .	. . .	. . .	98.9	99.0	99.8	99.7	100.1
Professional, scientific and controlling instruments and apparatus, n.e.s.	95.2	95.6	95.5	95.6	96.4	96.9	97.6	97.5	98.0	98.2	99.0	99.1
Photographic apparatus, equipment and supplies and optical goods, n.e.s.	96.4	95.4	96.2	96.8	95.9	98.0	98.2	98.5	98.8	99.0	100.3	99.8
Miscellaneous manufactured articles, n.e.s.	100.9	101.8	102.3	102.1	101.6	101.2	100.4	100.3	99.3	99.6	99.4	99.4

See footnotes and *Note* at end of table.

Table 6-12. U.S. Export Price Indexes for Selected Categories of Goods, by Standard International Trade Classification, 1986–2000—*Continued*

(1995=100, unless otherwise indicated.)

Categories	1995				1996				1997			
	March	June	September	December	March	June	September	December	March	June	September	December
ALL COMMODITIES	99.1	100.5	100.5	100.5	100.6	101.4	99.9	99.3	99.7	99.3	99.0	98.2
Food And Live Animals	92.4	97.4	105.6	110.0	114.5	122.0	107.3	101.9	103.4	98.5	99.5	96.7
Meat and meat preparations	96.9	99.9	103.7	105.8	98.1	101.6	98.5	97.8	96.4	95.3	95.2	94.6
Fish, crustaceans, aquatic invertebrates and preparations thereof	102.9	103.2	101.7	92.8	87.9	89.4	93.4	96.8	89.1	85.3	99.1	93.1
Cereals and cereal preparations	86.0	95.4	107.1	120.2	131.0	145.6	109.3	100.5	104.9	92.3	95.0	94.4
Vegetables, fruit and nuts, fresh or dried	95.8	96.2	110.0	99.7	103.1	105.7	106.8	101.0	101.2	101.6	97.6	92.0
Feeding stuff for animals (not including unmilled cereals)	92.8	98.3	100.4	114.8	121.4	122.5	127.0	120.0	125.3	127.2	120.8	113.5
Miscellaneous edible products and preparations	99.3	101.3	100.4	101.8	102.5	103.2	102.8	103.7	103.3	103.5	105.0	104.9
Beverages And Tobacco	99.6	99.9	100.4	100.2	100.5	100.6	100.5	100.4	100.2	100.8	101.0	100.6
Tobacco and tobacco manufactures	99.5	100.0	100.5	100.3	100.4	100.6	100.5	100.4	100.1	100.9	101.0	100.4
Crude Materials, Inedible, Except Fuels	101.9	104.1	98.9	96.3	91.0	90.3	90.8	88.7	93.2	93.4	91.6	87.8
Hides, skins and furskins, raw	109.6	103.4	90.0	91.1	91.1	95.7	109.4	113.7	115.6	100.8	100.1	102.6
Oil seeds and oleaginous fruits	93.6	96.6	102.9	113.7	119.5	127.0	131.7	114.9	133.1	134.6	120.2	116.5
Cork and wood	102.4	102.1	96.8	97.3	98.1	94.7	96.3	97.6	96.0	93.2	90.9	85.6
Pulp and waste paper	100.9	111.6	101.8	86.3	59.5	56.8	58.1	55.9	58.6	65.9	68.2	66.8
Textile fibers and their waste	105.7	106.9	97.8	98.5	92.4	91.1	86.7	83.5	85.2	83.4	83.9	80.0
Crude fertilizers and crude minerals	100.1	99.4	100.4	99.7	98.8	96.8	96.6	97.2	96.9	97.8	97.9	97.4
Metalliferous ores and metal scrap	104.3	104.2	98.5	91.7	90.5	89.3	85.6	85.7	89.7	91.7	94.4	83.9
Mineral Fuels, Lubricants And Related Materials	97.7	102.0	100.4	102.0	106.9	109.1	112.5	116.8	111.4	110.9	111.8	112.8
Coal, coke and briquettes	97.6	100.3	101.5	101.6	102.6	103.1	101.5	101.8	102.2	102.0	101.9	101.3
Petroleum, petroleum products and related materials	97.5	103.6	99.7	102.9	111.4	113.7	121.0	128.5	119.5	119.4	121.8	119.0
Animal And Vegetable Oils, Fats And Waxes	102.5	96.5	97.1	98.7	89.3	95.4	101.7	93.0	98.5	94.7	94.9	106.5
Chemicals And Related Products, n.e.s.	101.3	102.6	98.7	96.5	97.0	97.1	96.3	96.1	96.8	96.5	95.5	94.9
Organic chemicals	101.8	106.8	97.9	92.1	90.4	87.8	85.0	84.9	86.1	84.9	83.7	83.5
Inorganic chemicals	100.8	99.3	100.0	100.6	103.8	104.4	101.6	101.8	99.3	99.4	98.7	99.2
Dyeing, tanning and coloring materials	99.8	100.3	100.9	100.5	100.7	100.8	100.8	102.1	102.4	102.0	102.7	102.7
Medicinal and pharmaceutical products	99.7	100.6	100.6	100.1	102.1	101.8	101.9	101.8	100.9	101.6	101.2	100.9
Essential oils; polishing and cleansing preparations	99.5	99.6	100.0	100.9	99.9	100.8	101.7	101.5	102.2	102.9	103.7	101.9
Fertilizers [2]	...	...	...	...	...	...	...	100.0	96.2	96.1	95.0	94.2
Plastics in primary forms	106.0	104.8	94.5	89.5	91.4	95.5	96.1	93.8	97.8	97.1	93.7	93.1
Plastics in nonprimary forms	98.1	100.9	101.1	100.4	100.6	99.9	98.0	97.4	98.7	99.1	98.9	98.7
Chemical materials and products, n.e.s.	98.5	100.0	100.8	100.7	100.9	102.0	102.8	103.1	103.5	103.9	103.6	101.9
Manufactured Goods Classified Chiefly By Material	99.2	100.8	100.7	99.5	98.7	97.9	97.1	97.0	97.5	98.2	98.7	98.5
Rubber manufactures, n.e.s.	99.4	99.8	101.3	102.5	102.2	102.8	102.7	103.0	102.7	103.2	101.9	102.1
Cork and wood manufactures other than furniture	101.6	100.0	99.8	97.4	92.3	91.8	90.1	90.8	92.7	90.8	91.3	91.9
Paper, paperboard, and articles of paper pulp, paper or paperboard	96.5	103.3	101.9	97.4	92.6	87.3	87.5	84.9	83.1	83.5	85.0	85.1
Textile yarn, fabrics, and made-up articles, n.e.s.	97.4	101.1	100.9	102.0	103.1	103.8	103.1	102.4	101.7	103.3	103.3	103.1
Nonmetallic mineral manufactures, n.e.s.	99.9	100.1	100.1	101.0	102.0	101.2	102.2	103.9	104.0	104.3	106.1	107.1
Iron and steel	98.6	100.8	100.8	101.5	101.5	102.7	101.5	101.7	103.4	102.8	102.9	103.1
Nonferrous metals	101.7	99.7	100.4	95.2	93.0	93.4	88.7	88.3	91.7	93.4	93.2	91.0
Manufactures of metals, n.e.s.	99.3	100.1	100.6	101.1	102.4	101.5	101.5	101.6	103.2	104.4	104.3	104.4
Machinery And Transport Equipment	99.5	100.0	100.2	100.5	100.6	100.9	100.5	100.5	100.5	100.6	100.1	99.8
Power generating machinery and equipment	99.2	99.4	99.7	101.4	103.2	104.3	104.3	104.6	105.6	106.0	106.2	106.2
Machinery specialized for particular industries	98.9	99.9	100.9	101.3	102.0	102.7	103.1	102.9	103.7	104.2	104.5	104.9
Metalworking machinery	99.7	100.0	100.6	100.6	101.6	102.3	102.5	102.4	104.8	104.3	104.5	105.7
General industrial machinery, equipment, and parts, n.e.s.	99.9	99.4	100.7	100.4	101.7	102.5	102.7	103.1	104.1	105.2	105.2	105.4
Computer equipment and office machines	101.2	100.8	98.9	97.6	95.4	93.7	90.4	87.9	86.7	84.7	83.7	81.6
Telecommunications and sound recording and reproducing apparatus and equipment	100.0	100.3	99.8	99.0	101.1	101.1	100.2	100.7	99.9	99.6	99.2	98.7
Electrical machinery and equipment	99.0	100.7	100.9	100.3	99.8	99.1	97.9	97.5	96.7	96.5	95.1	94.4
Road vehicles	99.7	99.8	100.0	100.9	100.9	101.0	101.0	101.4	101.8	101.8	101.7	102.0
Miscellaneous Manufactured Articles	99.7	99.9	100.0	100.2	100.7	100.8	100.9	101.3	101.5	101.7	101.8	101.8
Furniture and parts thereof	99.4	100.1	100.3	100.6	102.2	101.5	101.9	102.0	102.6	103.6	103.5	103.8
Articles of apparel and clothing accessories	99.9	99.0	100.9	99.1	99.5	100.3	100.7	100.9	101.4	101.3	103.5	103.5
Professional, scientific and controlling instruments and apparatus, n.e.s.	99.6	100.1	100.2	100.2	101.2	101.6	101.9	102.7	103.8	103.4	103.4	103.5
Photographic apparatus, equipment and supplies and optical goods, n.e.s.	100.3	100.5	99.3	99.1	99.2	98.5	98.7	99.2	98.4	99.0	98.6	98.0
Miscellaneous manufactured articles, n.e.s.	99.7	99.7	99.7	100.6	100.7	100.6	100.4	100.6	100.1	100.6	100.4	100.2

See footnotes and *Note* at end of table.

Table 6-12. U.S. Export Price Indexes for Selected Categories of Goods, by Standard International Trade Classification, 1986–2000—*Continued*

(1995=100, unless otherwise indicated.)

Categories	1998				1999				2000			
	March	June	September	December	March	June	September	December	March	June	September	December
ALL COMMODITIES	96.9	96.1	94.8	94.8	94.2	94.5	94.8	95.2	96.3	96.3	96.6	96.3
Food And Live Animals	92.5	90.9	86.7	89.5	87.8	89.2	86.6	85.6	86.8	87.4	85.9	88.7
Meat and meat preparations	92.1	97.8	96.3	89.9	90.0	91.5	97.5	100.9	99.4	109.3	105.2	105.9
Fish, crustaceans, aquatic invertebrates and preparations thereof	82.9	80.7	95.9	95.7	105.8	118.5	97.1	98.9	95.3	96.9	96.4	94.8
Cereals and cereal preparations	90.4	82.6	70.2	78.9	75.8	75.9	72.7	68.5	74.4	71.6	67.8	75.8
Vegetables, fruit and nuts, fresh or dried	91.7	98.4	99.2	99.7	94.9	98.5	94.3	91.2	88.6	87.8	91.9	88.9
Feeding stuff for animals (not including unmilled cereals)	101.1	95.0	88.5	92.2	90.7	86.7	87.7	91.3	92.0	94.1	93.0	98.1
Miscellaneous edible products and preparations	104.8	105.0	106.3	106.8	106.8	107.0	107.4	107.6	106.6	106.8	106.9	107.1
Beverages And Tobacco	100.2	99.9	99.7	100.7	101.2	101.2	101.5	101.9	101.9	101.7	101.6	101.6
Tobacco and tobacco manufactures	100.2	99.7	99.4	100.4	101.2	101.2	101.7	102.1	102.1	101.8	101.9	101.9
Crude Materials, Inedible, Except Fuels	84.2	82.0	77.9	76.3	74.0	74.9	77.7	78.9	83.2	84.4	83.7	82.6
Hides, skins and furskins, raw	90.1	84.8	83.5	85.7	81.5	79.0	86.5	90.5	87.7	86.7	100.5	103.3
Oil seeds and oleaginous fruits	108.4	102.6	91.8	95.6	78.3	79.2	85.0	79.6	86.0	86.3	83.8	85.0
Cork and wood	84.0	82.0	82.2	81.4	81.5	82.0	82.8	85.0	87.2	86.7	86.9	85.9
Pulp and waste paper	65.0	64.0	62.7	57.7	62.0	66.0	75.2	80.9	90.0	97.6	90.7	85.9
Textile fibers and their waste	77.9	79.3	76.3	70.6	69.7	68.6	64.4	62.5	68.6	69.6	72.2	73.2
Crude fertilizers and crude minerals	97.1	97.0	96.9	95.1	93.6	93.5	93.3	94.1	93.5	93.3	91.5	90.6
Metalliferous ores and metal scrap	79.7	76.6	69.7	67.9	69.8	70.7	73.5	78.4	80.9	78.2	78.7	74.7
Mineral Fuels, Lubricants And Related Materials	106.2	103.2	93.4	93.7	93.1	102.0	115.3	126.6	152.1	144.9	166.3	157.4
Coal, coke and briquettes	101.0	100.1	99.4	99.4	99.3	98.3	97.6	97.5	96.1	93.8	93.1	93.0
Petroleum, petroleum products and related materials	110.5	106.8	90.8	92.2	90.9	107.6	128.6	140.1	179.2	168.2	203.3	183.6
Animal And Vegetable Oils, Fats And Waxes	100.8	107.9	102.7	99.7	82.6	76.6	78.8	78.0	70.8	67.1	61.7	58.7
Chemicals And Related Products, n.e.s.	93.6	92.6	91.8	91.0	90.5	91.2	92.3	93.6	94.4	95.5	94.4	93.0
Organic chemicals	79.3	77.1	75.1	74.2	73.7	75.2	78.8	83.8	85.9	88.8	86.9	83.5
Inorganic chemicals	102.0	103.5	103.2	103.4	103.0	101.0	98.7	98.0	98.0	99.6	98.2	99.7
Dyeing, tanning and coloring materials	102.1	100.7	99.6	100.1	101.4	101.1	101.0	100.0	99.3	99.5	99.4	99.4
Medicinal and pharmaceutical products	102.3	101.6	101.6	100.6	100.4	100.6	99.8	100.3	100.2	99.7	100.2	100.1
Essential oils; polishing and cleansing preparations	101.5	101.4	102.7	101.6	101.5	101.9	102.1	103.4	103.0	102.8	103.4	103.2
Fertilizers [2]	92.0	96.1	97.9	95.9	94.0	89.6	84.9	73.4	72.4	72.1	79.0	76.6
Plastics in primary forms	91.7	88.9	87.6	85.6	84.4	88.4	92.1	95.0	95.5	98.1	92.8	90.0
Plastics in nonprimary forms	99.7	97.9	97.3	95.4	96.4	97.2	97.6	98.0	100.1	99.3	99.3	98.3
Chemical materials and products, n.e.s.	100.5	100.6	100.0	101.2	100.4	99.6	99.2	99.1	99.6	99.1	99.2	99.9
Manufactured Goods Classified Chiefly By Material	98.3	97.9	96.8	96.4	96.4	96.8	97.5	98.3	99.7	100.3	101.1	100.5
Rubber manufactures, n.e.s.	102.1	101.9	102.4	106.0	106.8	105.5	106.9	108.5	103.6	104.4	104.7	103.8
Cork and wood manufactures other than furniture	92.2	89.6	92.7	92.7	95.8	96.6	93.5	93.0	93.4	93.1	91.6	92.7
Paper, paperboard, and articles of paper pulp, paper or paperboard	84.7	83.8	81.3	81.3	80.9	83.4	86.3	87.2	88.4	89.8	90.0	89.1
Textile yarn, fabrics, and made-up articles, n.e.s.	103.6	103.2	101.3	101.0	99.6	99.2	98.7	98.7	98.4	98.6	98.5	96.8
Nonmetallic mineral manufactures, n.e.s.	107.0	106.7	106.8	107.3	106.5	106.3	106.1	105.8	106.2	106.5	106.1	105.6
Iron and steel	100.7	100.5	99.8	97.0	95.6	94.5	94.6	94.7	96.8	98.1	96.9	96.4
Nonferrous metals	91.2	88.1	85.5	83.9	84.0	85.0	88.0	92.3	101.9	100.1	105.0	104.9
Manufactures of metals, n.e.s.	105.0	107.0	106.7	106.4	108.2	108.7	107.4	107.2	107.0	109.4	110.1	109.7
Machinery And Transport Equipment	99.3	98.7	98.2	98.2	97.9	97.6	97.2	97.2	97.3	97.3	97.4	97.4
Power generating machinery and equipment	106.8	107.1	107.0	108.5	109.4	109.6	110.1	111.0	111.8	112.0	112.4	113.7
Machinery specialized for particular industries	105.0	105.2	105.5	105.2	105.7	106.1	105.9	104.7	106.1	106.5	106.3	106.6
Metalworking machinery	107.8	108.4	108.5	108.9	109.0	108.8	108.8	108.5	108.5	107.6	108.5	108.2
General industrial machinery, equipment, and parts, n.e.s.	105.8	106.1	106.4	106.5	107.2	107.3	107.6	107.9	108.0	108.2	108.2	108.5
Computer equipment and office machines	79.8	76.5	74.8	74.4	73.0	71.6	70.2	70.2	68.7	68.2	67.8	67.6
Telecommunications and sound recording and reproducing apparatus and equipment	98.6	98.7	98.2	97.6	97.5	96.9	96.9	96.7	96.6	96.9	96.8	96.3
Electrical machinery and equipment	93.1	92.1	91.2	90.6	89.3	88.6	87.6	86.7	86.3	85.7	85.8	85.4
Road vehicles	101.8	101.9	102.0	102.1	102.2	102.5	102.4	103.1	104.0	103.9	104.1	104.0
Miscellaneous Manufactured Articles	101.4	100.8	100.6	100.6	101.0	101.0	101.2	101.3	100.9	101.0	101.5	101.6
Furniture and parts thereof	104.4	104.0	104.1	104.2	104.2	104.7	105.5	105.3	105.2	105.9	105.5	106.9
Articles of apparel and clothing accessories	103.8	103.8	102.5	100.9	101.1	100.3	100.4	100.1	96.7	96.4	95.6	96.1
Professional, scientific and controlling instruments and apparatus, n.e.s.	103.6	103.8	103.8	104.1	105.0	105.2	105.4	105.3	105.7	105.8	106.5	106.6
Photographic apparatus, equipment and supplies and optical goods, n.e.s.	95.5	93.7	92.5	94.4	95.1	94.4	95.7	97.3	95.0	95.2	98.7	98.3
Miscellaneous manufactured articles, n.e.s.	99.4	98.1	98.3	98.1	98.0	98.3	98.2	98.2	98.5	98.6	98.8	98.7

Note: n.e.s. = not elsewhere specified.

1. Percent of total, relative importance in December 1999, based on 1995 trade values.
2. December 1996=100.

Table 6-13. U.S. Import Price Indexes for Selected Categories of Goods, by Standard International Trade Classification, 1986–2000

(1995=100, unless otherwise indicated.)

Categories	Relative importance [1]	1986				1987				1988			
		March	June	September	December	March	June	September	December	March	June	September	December
ALL COMMODITIES	100.00	74.6	74.7	76.4	77.2	80.4	83.1	83.8	85.1	86.0	88.3	87.1	88.8
Food And Live Animals	3.67	86.3	81.5	85.0	82.9	79.8	82.2	82.8	85.4	86.6	86.5	85.6	86.8
Meat and meat preparations	0.33	84.1	81.8	88.9	93.1	89.5	92.1	97.5	96.7	95.0	91.2	94.8	92.6
Fish, crustaceans, aquatic invertebrates and preparations thereof	1.05	66.0	68.2	70.4	73.5	75.2	77.7	80.5	80.9	81.8	79.8	77.7	78.2
Vegetables, fruit and nuts, fresh or dried	1.07	67.0	68.7	72.8	71.6	70.0	75.6	75.5	79.8	79.2	82.6	85.0	87.7
Coffee, tea, cocoa, spices and manufactures thereof	0.35	132.8	108.3	112.2	97.0	83.1	80.3	78.6	83.7	87.2	86.3	80.7	83.7
Beverages And Tobacco	0.87	69.7	71.0	70.1	72.0	72.7	76.1	75.7	76.5	78.3	78.4	77.8	78.4
Beverages	0.74	69.6	70.8	71.7	73.1	74.8	76.2	76.6	77.5	79.2	80.0	79.3	80.0
Crude Materials, Inedible, Except Fuels	2.68	64.6	66.6	68.5	68.2	72.0	72.7	75.3	76.4	80.8	86.2	84.7	89.6
Cork and wood	0.91	64.1	65.7	67.7	66.0	71.5	69.4	73.9	68.5	70.8	70.2	69.1	67.9
Woodpulp and recovered paper	0.45	47.0	50.1	53.9	58.3	63.4	65.9	66.6	70.4	75.4	80.1	84.7	87.2
Metalliferous ores and metal scrap	0.60	66.1	71.7	73.6	69.7	72.4	73.4	75.8	81.3	89.1	98.8	101.5	121.1
Crude animal and vegetable materials, n.e.s. [2]	0.25	...	...	...	...	...	...	...	...	...	...	...	...
Mineral Fuels, Lubricants And Related Materials	15.15	88.8	75.1	76.1	81.5	98.3	108.2	108.4	98.0	88.4	92.5	84.2	82.2
Petroleum, petroleum products and related materials	12.13	83.7	70.2	71.7	78.9	96.7	106.8	107.9	97.2	86.7	91.2	82.7	80.5
Gas, natural and manufactured	2.91	...	...	...	...	...	...	...	...	...	...	...	109.2
Chemicals And Related Products, n.e.s.	5.39	74.9	74.5	74.5	73.9	76.6	78.3	78.9	82.2	85.3	86.9	89.0	91.3
Organic chemicals	1.63	82.1	77.9	75.6	74.6	81.9	85.0	83.7	87.8	90.2	91.5	94.9	98.2
Inorganic chemicals	0.63	99.5	99.5	100.1	97.7	93.5	92.8	92.8	93.1	95.1	95.3	96.1	99.3
Dyeing, tanning and coloring materials	0.25	...	...	...	...	...	...	...	...	...	...	...	...
Medicinal and pharmaceutical products	0.88	56.2	57.1	59.4	58.3	61.6	63.3	63.8	64.8	69.4	72.0	74.6	75.1
Essential oils; polishing and cleansing preps	0.28	62.5	65.1	65.1	65.5	72.0	72.1	73.0	75.4	77.0	77.3	78.1	79.9
Plastics in primary forms	0.37	...	...	...	...	...	...	...	...	...	...	...	...
Plastics in nonprimary forms	0.49	...	...	...	...	...	...	...	...	...	...	...	...
Chemical materials and products, n.e.s.	0.63	70.7	71.6	72.4	73.3	74.8	76.5	78.4	81.1	90.1	96.5	99.7	101.7
Manufactured Goods Classified Chiefly By Material	12.41	67.2	68.2	69.6	70.2	71.5	74.1	76.6	78.9	81.9	87.0	87.1	88.9
Rubber manufactures, n.e.s.	0.67	82.4	83.3	83.9	83.8	85.8	86.1	85.0	86.1	87.2	88.6	89.8	91.4
Cork and wood manufactures other than furniture	0.51	62.7	64.5	65.4	68.2	68.5	72.2	74.5	74.5	77.8	80.3	79.1	77.9
Paper and paperboard, cut to size	1.64	66.2	66.4	66.6	69.1	69.1	69.1	72.7	74.0	77.3	78.0	78.8	79.0
Textile yarn, fabrics, made-up articles, n.e.s., and related products	1.31	71.7	72.8	74.1	74.5	76.2	77.2	79.1	81.8	82.8	83.2	82.2	83.2
Nonmetallic mineral manufactures, n.e.s.	2.05	59.9	61.9	65.3	66.0	67.5	71.0	73.0	74.7	76.9	79.9	78.2	79.5
Iron and steel	1.89	72.1	71.9	72.7	73.3	74.7	77.5	79.5	82.9	87.3	92.5	94.4	95.1
Nonferrous metals	2.31	64.1	64.7	67.6	66.4	67.0	73.5	79.1	82.3	86.8	104.4	103.9	110.6
Manufactures of metals, n.e.s.	1.87	69.9	71.9	71.8	72.2	74.7	75.2	76.4	78.6	80.7	84.6	85.0	87.2
Machinery And Transport Equipment	42.95	74.2	76.5	78.3	79.3	81.5	83.1	83.1	85.3	86.9	88.3	87.9	90.1
Power generating machinery and equipment [2]	2.94	...	...	...	...	...	...	...	...	...	...	...	...
Machinery specialized for particular industries	2.53	59.9	61.9	64.9	65.1	69.0	72.0	71.1	75.2	77.7	79.3	76.1	79.8
Metalworking machinery	0.77	62.5	62.2	64.7	66.5	69.5	70.5	71.7	74.6	77.0	78.4	76.9	79.3
General industrial machinery, equipment, and machine parts, n.e.s.	3.27	61.3	64.1	66.1	66.7	70.5	72.2	71.8	75.6	77.4	79.3	77.0	79.5
Computer equipment and office machines	5.19	108.0	112.4	113.2	112.2	113.3	117.4	118.3	121.9	121.7	123.1	122.3	122.3
Telecommunications and sound recording and reproducing apparatus and equipment	4.02	94.2	97.5	100.0	99.8	101.3	101.0	101.0	102.7	103.4	104.2	104.4	105.8
Electrical machinery and equipment	8.66	74.2	76.6	78.3	79.0	80.9	83.4	82.9	85.1	88.0	89.4	90.7	93.1
Road vehicles	14.54	70.3	72.1	73.5	75.5	77.2	78.4	78.5	79.8	81.7	83.1	82.7	85.1
Miscellaneous Manufactured Articles	16.56	73.4	74.5	76.5	77.0	79.9	82.2	82.7	85.0	86.7	87.7	86.7	88.3
Prefabricated buildings; plumbing, heat and lighting fixtures, n.e.s.	0.36	71.5	73.5	75.1	75.0	75.5	79.1	78.6	81.9	83.5	85.8	84.2	86.1
Furniture and parts thereof	1.17	75.9	77.3	78.8	78.9	82.3	82.7	83.5	84.2	86.8	88.0	88.2	90.5
Travel goods, handbags and similar containers	0.49	73.6	73.9	74.6	75.3	76.9	77.3	78.5	82.1	85.0	86.9	87.7	87.0
Articles of apparel and clothing accessories	5.61	79.8	80.0	80.8	81.6	84.6	86.8	89.0	89.3	91.9	91.3	92.8	93.2
Footwear	1.73	75.7	76.3	78.2	79.3	81.1	84.6	84.1	87.8	88.6	91.6	90.4	91.2
Professional, scientific and controlling instruments and apparatus, n.e.s.	1.50	64.3	67.7	70.4	70.3	75.4	78.0	76.1	79.6	80.4	81.8	77.9	81.5
Photographic apparatus, equipment and supplies and optical goods, n.e.s.	1.27	72.2	74.3	77.1	77.7	80.8	82.3	79.7	83.2	84.4	84.5	81.9	85.3
Miscellaneous manufactured articles, n.e.s.	4.43	68.5	69.9	72.9	72.9	75.8	78.3	79.1	82.3	83.6	85.5	82.9	85.0

See footnotes and *Note* at end of table.

Table 6-13. U.S. Import Price Indexes for Selected Categories of Goods, by Standard International Trade Classification, 1986–2000—*Continued*

(1995=100, unless otherwise indicated.)

Categories	1989				1990				1991			
	March	June	September	December	March	June	September	December	March	June	September	December
ALL COMMODITIES	90.8	91.0	89.8	91.1	91.9	90.3	95.9	97.8	94.5	92.8	92.8	93.7
Food And Live Animals	86.6	84.5	80.5	82.2	84.7	84.9	86.6	88.2	88.2	88.1	87.2	88.1
Meat and meat preparations	94.8	93.5	105.7	114.3	111.1	116.3	119.6	118.4	118.8	122.8	117.5	113.9
Fish, crustaceans, aquatic invertebrates and preparations thereof	78.4	75.7	75.1	75.4	77.7	77.9	81.8	84.7	87.6	86.7	85.9	86.0
Vegetables, fruit and nuts, fresh or dried	84.8	84.6	81.8	88.0	90.2	86.5	82.7	90.1	87.8	90.9	91.4	95.1
Coffee, tea, cocoa, spices and manufactures thereof	84.3	78.9	57.7	53.0	60.2	61.3	64.3	60.7	60.8	57.4	57.0	57.2
Beverages And Tobacco	78.9	79.1	81.4	82.6	84.1	86.1	87.3	89.6	94.8	96.1	96.0	97.1
Beverages	80.5	80.5	82.0	82.8	84.7	86.4	87.7	89.2	94.9	96.0	95.5	96.6
Crude Materials, Inedible, Except Fuels	91.5	90.3	85.8	85.1	83.2	82.4	80.3	77.5	76.9	77.5	74.6	74.3
Cork and wood	70.6	70.8	71.5	70.3	71.7	72.5	71.9	67.0	68.3	76.2	72.4	73.9
Woodpulp and recovered paper	92.2	94.8	94.9	94.6	93.3	91.5	88.3	82.9	76.2	70.4	63.3	61.7
Metalliferous ores and metal scrap	120.5	125.2	108.1	104.1	99.1	94.7	91.7	90.6	90.5	88.0	88.2	87.6
Crude animal and vegetable materials, n.e.s. [2]	...	...	...	...	...	...	...	...	...	...	...	...
Mineral Fuels, Lubricants And Related Materials	97.4	107.0	100.3	108.0	109.3	92.9	148.2	157.9	111.7	105.8	108.0	107.5
Petroleum, petroleum products and related materials	96.5	106.7	99.7	107.3	108.0	91.7	150.3	159.2	110.9	105.5	108.0	106.9
Gas, natural and manufactured	112.2	111.5	110.0	120.0	130.9	112.7	118.5	142.0	126.3	111.1	109.6	118.6
Chemicals And Related Products, n.e.s.	92.3	90.0	87.9	88.8	88.8	88.3	89.4	92.0	91.8	90.3	89.9	90.1
Organic chemicals	100.3	97.2	94.0	96.1	97.3	96.7	98.5	103.2	100.3	97.1	94.7	95.7
Inorganic chemicals	96.2	89.4	88.5	88.9	87.2	87.5	88.7	92.0	92.8	91.6	89.6	86.7
Dyeing, tanning and coloring materials	...	...	...	...	...	...	...	...	...	...	...	...
Medicinal and pharmaceutical products	79.4	78.7	76.6	76.8	78.1	78.2	79.1	81.1	80.7	79.3	80.7	83.8
Essential oils; polishing and cleansing preps	79.8	79.8	77.9	82.8	80.4	81.4	81.9	84.1	83.0	82.8	85.3	84.6
Plastics in primary forms	...	...	...	...	...	...	...	...	...	...	...	...
Plastics in nonprimary forms	...	...	...	...	...	...	...	...	...	...	...	...
Chemical materials and products, n.e.s.	100.6	98.5	97.6	98.0	97.6	93.4	92.0	90.6	90.1	88.5	88.7	90.5
Manufactured Goods Classified Chiefly By Material	90.4	89.5	89.0	88.2	88.0	88.8	90.6	89.8	90.2	88.6	87.8	88.0
Rubber manufactures, n.e.s.	91.9	92.3	93.5	93.8	94.7	95.1	95.2	96.3	96.1	95.9	95.5	96.5
Cork and wood manufactures other than furniture	79.5	81.2	81.8	81.6	82.2	83.9	85.3	82.8	81.7	82.4	83.4	83.8
Paper and paperboard, cut to size	79.5	79.6	78.9	78.3	77.5	79.9	80.4	80.8	82.5	80.4	79.0	78.6
Textile yarn, fabrics, made-up articles, n.e.s., and related products	83.2	84.3	84.0	84.8	86.1	86.8	88.7	90.0	91.5	90.6	92.0	93.4
Nonmetallic mineral manufactures, n.e.s.	82.7	83.8	85.0	85.8	88.3	89.5	90.0	90.9	92.5	92.7	92.8	93.7
Iron and steel	96.4	97.1	97.2	95.1	93.5	91.5	90.5	91.7	91.5	91.2	90.3	90.6
Nonferrous metals	113.0	103.7	98.5	94.2	90.1	93.7	103.1	93.1	91.4	84.5	81.2	78.8
Manufactures of metals, n.e.s.	88.2	88.4	88.8	89.2	90.4	89.7	91.0	91.8	92.5	91.8	91.3	92.6
Machinery And Transport Equipment	90.2	89.6	89.4	90.3	90.9	90.2	91.1	93.2	94.3	92.8	92.9	94.3
Power generating machinery and equipment [2]	...	...	...	...	...	...	...	...	...	...	...	...
Machinery specialized for particular industries	78.9	77.1	77.1	78.5	83.3	84.1	87.3	90.9	92.3	87.9	87.6	90.1
Metalworking machinery	78.6	76.8	79.2	79.3	81.4	82.3	83.6	86.3	87.0	83.9	83.9	86.3
General industrial machinery, equipment, and machine parts, n.e.s.	79.8	78.9	79.2	80.3	83.3	84.4	87.6	90.2	91.0	87.7	87.8	90.3
Computer equipment and office machines	123.2	122.9	120.7	121.4	120.5	119.2	118.2	119.6	118.4	116.1	114.8	115.1
Telecommunications and sound recording and reproducing apparatus and equipment	106.0	106.1	105.4	104.4	103.4	102.0	100.7	101.3	100.2	99.6	99.0	99.5
Electrical machinery and equipment	93.9	93.3	92.7	92.9	93.5	92.0	93.2	94.2	95.5	93.7	93.3	94.7
Road vehicles	85.0	84.3	84.3	85.8	85.4	84.3	85.2	87.8	89.5	88.7	89.2	90.5
Miscellaneous Manufactured Articles	88.4	88.3	88.8	89.8	91.9	92.1	93.5	94.9	95.0	93.7	93.9	95.3
Prefabricated buildings; plumbing, heat and lighting fixtures, n.e.s.	87.9	89.0	90.0	92.4	96.0	95.3	97.3	98.6	95.2	94.9	94.8	96.0
Furniture and parts thereof	89.1	88.9	91.1	91.0	92.9	93.7	94.8	96.7	97.2	95.7	96.0	96.7
Travel goods, handbags and similar containers	86.8	88.0	89.8	90.2	91.0	91.2	90.2	92.0	92.0	92.5	92.3	93.2
Articles of apparel and clothing accessories	94.2	95.3	96.1	96.7	96.8	97.6	97.5	96.6	96.6	95.9	96.4	97.0
Footwear	89.9	90.3	90.9	92.5	95.9	97.2	98.9	100.7	100.9	99.1	98.8	99.5
Professional, scientific and controlling instruments and apparatus, n.e.s.	81.0	78.3	78.2	78.7	82.2	83.5	86.2	90.8	91.9	87.5	87.2	89.6
Photographic apparatus, equipment and supplies and optical goods, n.e.s.	85.1	83.6	82.5	84.1	85.9	86.1	88.9	90.6	90.8	88.0	88.3	90.4
Miscellaneous manufactured articles, n.e.s.	85.2	85.0	85.3	86.5	90.1	88.8	90.9	92.8	92.8	92.3	92.5	95.0

See footnotes and *Note* at end of table.

Table 6-13. U.S. Import Price Indexes for Selected Categories of Goods, by Standard International Trade Classification, 1986–2000—*Continued*

(1995=100, unless otherwise indicated.)

Categories	1992				1993				1994			
	March	June	September	December	March	June	September	December	March	June	September	December
ALL COMMODITIES	93.4	94.3	95.4	93.9	94.2	94.4	93.9	93.0	93.5	95.8	96.7	**97.9**
Food And Live Animals	89.8	84.3	84.9	85.9	84.1	87.0	88.1	87.9	88.8	93.9	102.2	**102.2**
Meat and meat preparations	112.8	110.4	109.6	107.6	111.5	115.6	113.9	109.3	112.3	105.9	106.9	**106.6**
Fish, crustaceans, aquatic invertebrates and preparations thereof	86.9	86.9	88.3	86.0	86.6	86.9	87.8	91.9	93.9	97.6	99.5	**103.0**
Vegetables, fruit and nuts, fresh or dried	107.1	89.4	89.0	91.2	84.9	96.0	93.1	88.8	87.5	89.6	87.5	**98.4**
Coffee, tea, cocoa, spices and manufactures thereof	52.3	47.6	47.4	55.8	52.2	50.0	60.5	62.6	63.5	84.5	124.6	**106.2**
Beverages And Tobacco	98.0	98.4	99.4	98.1	97.7	97.7	97.0	97.8	97.5	98.2	98.4	**98.5**
Beverages	97.5	97.9	99.2	97.6	97.6	98.2	97.5	97.8	97.7	98.1	98.8	**98.8**
Crude Materials, Inedible, Except Fuels	77.2	77.5	78.7	78.3	84.1	77.1	78.3	82.7	85.1	86.3	87.7	**92.6**
Cork and wood	81.8	82.7	83.8	85.9	115.0	92.2	100.4	120.5	118.1	113.2	110.0	**105.9**
Woodpulp and recovered paper	63.7	66.2	69.2	65.8	58.3	56.7	53.8	52.0	54.8	62.4	71.2	**80.7**
Metalliferous ores and metal scrap	87.3	85.7	86.7	85.1	84.2	83.0	81.8	78.2	84.8	84.2	86.8	**91.4**
Crude animal and vegetable materials, n.e.s. [2]	...	...	...	...	...	...	...	...	...	...	...	...
Mineral Fuels, Lubricants And Related Materials	96.5	110.1	110.9	101.9	104.4	101.6	93.4	81.0	81.9	96.9	93.5	**95.7**
Petroleum, petroleum products and related materials	96.1	110.4	110.8	100.8	103.8	100.8	92.0	78.7	79.8	96.4	92.4	**94.8**
Gas, natural and manufactured	102.1	105.5	113.7	119.3	112.7	113.8	115.5	118.6	114.2	105.4	110.1	**111.3**
Chemicals And Related Products, n.e.s.	90.7	91.2	91.8	91.5	91.5	92.1	91.5	90.8	90.8	92.0	94.7	**97.5**
Organic chemicals	95.6	95.4	95.1	93.0	92.6	93.2	93.0	91.5	91.3	93.8	98.5	**103.0**
Inorganic chemicals	87.2	86.0	85.7	90.5	90.6	89.5	89.3	89.1	88.5	89.5	91.3	**95.6**
Dyeing, tanning and coloring materials	...	...	...	92.7	91.9	93.6	92.6	92.6	93.6	94.0	95.0	**95.3**
Medicinal and pharmaceutical products	84.7	85.0	87.4	87.1	88.2	93.0	91.6	92.2	92.9	93.0	94.7	**95.4**
Essential oils; polishing and cleansing preps	86.6	87.6	87.8	87.8	89.6	90.8	89.1	90.1	88.5	88.8	90.5	**92.9**
Plastics in primary forms	...	...	...	91.7	92.5	90.7	91.4	91.4	92.5	92.8	93.2	**94.4**
Plastics in nonprimary forms	...	...	...	88.0	87.4	87.6	86.9	85.8	83.9	86.6	90.5	**94.3**
Chemical materials and products, n.e.s.	94.5	97.6	101.4	100.5	99.2	98.4	96.6	95.0	95.9	95.0	98.3	**96.8**
Manufactured Goods Classified Chiefly By Material	88.5	88.8	89.4	87.9	88.3	88.6	88.2	87.3	88.7	90.2	92.0	**95.0**
Rubber manufactures, n.e.s.	97.4	97.2	98.5	90.4	99.1	99.0	98.3	98.4	96.8	97.6	96.7	**97.5**
Cork and wood manufactures other than furniture	87.4	90.3	92.4	89.8	97.6	100.8	101.7	100.0	102.0	105.7	98.7	**96.5**
Paper and paperboard, cut to size	76.1	75.0	75.5	75.4	76.6	77.0	76.0	75.0	74.8	76.1	79.1	**83.8**
Textile yarn, fabrics, made-up articles, n.e.s., and related products	94.0	93.2	95.8	94.4	94.4	95.0	94.0	93.2	93.9	95.7	96.7	**96.9**
Nonmetallic mineral manufactures, n.e.s.	93.9	94.7	95.5	95.2	95.8	96.8	96.7	96.8	96.7	97.4	98.5	**99.1**
Iron and steel	90.0	89.6	88.4	88.4	88.6	90.2	90.0	89.9	90.7	91.0	92.9	**94.7**
Nonferrous metals	82.0	84.2	84.2	78.0	76.0	72.8	72.1	68.7	76.3	81.0	86.4	**98.0**
Manufactures of metals, n.e.s.	93.3	93.5	95.2	93.6	93.8	94.8	94.7	94.3	94.2	94.9	96.2	**96.6**
Machinery And Transport Equipment	94.5	94.5	95.7	94.9	94.9	95.9	96.4	97.0	97.2	97.6	98.2	**98.7**
Power generating machinery and equipment [2]	...	...	...	...	...	...	...	...	...	...	...	...
Machinery specialized for particular industries	91.0	91.0	95.6	92.1	91.6	92.9	92.5	92.7	93.5	94.7	96.3	**97.2**
Metalworking machinery	86.5	86.7	88.9	87.8	87.6	89.9	90.3	90.8	91.0	91.9	94.0	**95.0**
General industrial machinery, equipment, and machine parts, n.e.s.	90.5	90.6	93.3	91.5	91.0	92.4	92.4	93.1	93.6	94.1	95.2	**96.4**
Computer equipment and office machines	115.4	114.2	114.6	113.5	111.8	109.7	108.2	106.9	105.4	104.0	102.7	**101.2**
Telecommunications and sound recording and reproducing apparatus and equipment	99.1	99.0	99.0	99.3	99.0	99.9	100.9	100.0	99.2	99.2	99.4	**99.6**
Electrical machinery and equipment	94.5	95.2	96.1	94.7	95.2	96.9	98.7	98.2	98.4	98.9	99.3	**99.3**
Road vehicles	90.6	90.4	91.1	91.3	91.5	92.8	93.3	95.5	95.9	96.6	97.3	**98.6**
Miscellaneous Manufactured Articles	96.4	96.6	98.2	97.2	97.0	97.9	97.9	97.8	97.8	98.2	98.5	**98.7**
Prefabricated buildings; plumbing, heat and lighting fixtures, n.e.s.	97.0	98.2	99.7	98.6	97.5	98.8	98.9	98.6	98.0	96.4	97.5	**96.5**
Furniture and parts thereof	97.4	97.7	100.1	98.3	97.8	98.4	97.8	97.3	97.8	98.2	98.5	**98.8**
Travel goods, handbags and similar containers	94.3	97.6	98.1	95.9	96.2	96.9	97.2	96.4	96.3	95.9	97.1	**97.4**
Articles of apparel and clothing accessories	98.0	98.8	98.6	99.0	98.6	99.2	99.3	98.9	98.8	99.2	99.0	**99.3**
Footwear	100.1	100.7	102.2	99.5	98.8	99.4	98.5	98.3	97.8	98.4	99.1	**99.3**
Professional, scientific and controlling instruments and apparatus, n.e.s.	89.7	89.4	94.9	92.2	92.7	94.7	93.9	94.6	95.6	96.8	97.6	**98.5**
Photographic apparatus, equipment and supplies and optical goods, n.e.s.	91.0	90.4	93.6	92.1	92.1	93.9	94.8	95.6	95.4	95.9	97.3	**97.2**
Miscellaneous manufactured articles, n.e.s.	96.7	96.1	98.0	97.1	97.1	98.1	98.3	98.2	98.3	98.3	98.6	**98.7**

See footnotes and *Note* at end of table.

Table 6-13. U.S. Import Price Indexes for Selected Categories of Goods, by Standard International Trade Classification, 1986–2000—*Continued*

(1995=100, unless otherwise indicated.)

Categories	1995				1996				1997			
	March	June	September	December	March	June	September	December	March	June	September	December
ALL COMMODITIES	99.4	100.8	100.3	100.4	101.0	100.1	101.3	101.9	99.4	98.2	97.8	96.6
Food And Live Animals	103.8	100.1	98.4	96.6	95.2	94.7	96.6	94.6	101.8	103.7	101.3	99.6
Meat and meat preparations	103.1	99.1	95.6	97.9	92.1	90.4	100.8	98.9	103.5	101.9	103.9	104.2
Fish, crustaceans, aquatic invertebrates and preparations thereof	102.8	101.6	98.0	95.0	95.4	97.5	97.0	98.2	99.7	103.6	104.5	105.6
Vegetables, fruit and nuts, fresh or dried	99.9	97.0	100.4	105.8	101.8	98.3	106.5	101.8	111.1	101.7	103.4	102.5
Coffee, tea, cocoa, spices and manufactures thereof	113.2	102.4	96.3	82.5	83.9	83.5	78.9	75.0	98.6	118.4	100.0	92.1
Beverages And Tobacco	99.3	99.7	100.6	102.0	102.6	103.6	104.9	105.2	106.9	107.5	107.8	108.6
Beverages	99.6	99.9	100.5	100.8	100.9	101.4	102.4	102.9	103.3	104.0	104.3	105.2
Crude Materials, Inedible, Except Fuels	98.1	99.8	103.5	101.2	96.4	94.3	97.0	96.3	99.0	97.4	96.6	93.5
Cork and wood	101.4	92.7	102.9	96.1	99.2	113.6	126.0	120.6	126.2	122.5	121.2	113.1
Woodpulp and recovered paper	93.2	103.2	105.8	108.6	78.6	62.1	66.6	66.2	64.9	65.8	68.2	68.7
Metalliferous ores and metal scrap	100.2	100.0	103.2	101.8	101.9	101.7	97.4	97.5	103.0	105.8	104.5	102.3
Crude animal and vegetable materials, n.e.s.[2]	...	...	...	...	...	...	...	100.0	105.2	97.3	103.1	107.0
Mineral Fuels, Lubricants And Related Materials	100.6	105.1	97.8	100.6	112.5	110.6	123.4	135.5	113.9	104.6	107.0	103.3
Petroleum, petroleum products and related materials	100.6	105.4	97.8	100.7	112.8	111.0	124.3	133.9	113.1	104.0	105.5	100.1
Gas, natural and manufactured	100.2	101.2	96.8	100.8	112.3	108.2	115.7	157.5	125.9	113.3	123.7	133.4
Chemicals And Related Products, n.e.s.	99.4	100.7	100.4	100.3	100.4	98.8	99.0	99.1	97.8	96.4	96.2	95.2
Organic chemicals	101.0	99.2	99.6	98.8	99.2	98.4	98.9	99.4	99.8	95.8	97.1	95.3
Inorganic chemicals	100.5	101.6	101.3	100.7	101.9	99.8	100.4	103.5	101.5	99.0	99.7	97.3
Dyeing, tanning and coloring materials	98.6	100.6	100.6	101.7	103.2	102.1	102.6	100.4	96.9	97.9	94.0	96.9
Medicinal and pharmaceutical products	96.2	101.2	101.0	102.4	100.7	99.7	101.3	99.0	96.0	96.3	95.7	96.8
Essential oils; polishing and cleansing preps	95.7	101.1	101.9	102.6	103.8	100.3	100.2	100.1	98.2	97.0	96.9	97.5
Plastics in primary forms	97.9	100.5	99.5	102.2	102.5	97.2	93.5	95.0	91.6	91.6	92.6	92.0
Plastics in nonprimary forms	101.7	103.9	99.8	94.1	88.8	87.1	86.7	86.7	86.1	88.6	86.9	82.8
Chemical materials and products, n.e.s.	97.0	99.2	102.1	104.7	107.9	107.6	108.0	105.8	104.6	103.5	103.2	103.1
Manufactured Goods Classified Chiefly By Material	97.5	99.8	102.1	101.4	100.5	99.2	97.0	95.5	96.0	96.8	96.8	96.0
Rubber manufactures, n.e.s.	98.0	100.1	101.3	101.7	100.1	100.2	99.6	98.5	97.4	97.6	95.1	95.5
Cork and wood manufactures other than furniture	98.5	99.7	97.2	97.9	98.5	101.3	100.7	98.8	99.2	99.0	99.4	99.1
Paper and paperboard, cut to size	91.1	99.6	107.9	108.8	106.5	100.9	93.1	86.2	85.0	87.5	88.8	88.5
Textile yarn, fabrics, made-up articles, n.e.s., and related products	98.1	101.0	101.0	100.8	100.6	100.1	100.3	100.5	100.5	100.5	100.0	99.3
Nonmetallic mineral manufactures, n.e.s.	99.4	99.9	100.3	100.5	101.6	101.5	102.3	103.0	103.2	102.6	102.1	101.7
Iron and steel	96.9	99.6	103.1	100.7	98.6	97.7	97.7	97.1	96.2	96.3	96.3	96.3
Nonferrous metals	100.6	98.6	100.8	97.1	95.1	93.8	86.7	84.6	91.1	95.1	96.9	92.1
Manufactures of metals, n.e.s.	98.4	100.5	100.5	101.2	101.3	100.4	101.1	101.0	99.5	99.0	98.1	98.5
Machinery And Transport Equipment	99.1	100.6	100.3	100.3	99.5	98.6	98.6	98.1	96.5	95.7	94.8	94.0
Power generating machinery and equipment[2]	...	...	...	...	...	...	...	100.0	99.5	99.2	98.8	99.0
Machinery specialized for particular industries	98.5	101.1	100.2	102.0	102.7	101.1	101.3	101.5	99.7	99.3	98.4	99.1
Metalworking machinery	96.6	102.1	101.5	102.1	101.5	101.3	101.6	101.3	97.8	98.3	97.3	98.7
General industrial machinery, equipment, and machine parts, n.e.s.	97.6	100.7	100.9	101.6	101.0	100.5	101.4	100.7	98.5	98.3	97.2	97.3
Computer equipment and office machines	100.3	100.4	99.6	98.1	95.2	91.7	89.9	88.2	84.4	81.2	78.2	76.8
Telecommunications and sound recording and reproducing apparatus and equipment	99.5	100.5	100.4	99.6	98.3	97.3	96.5	95.8	94.4	93.4	92.6	91.7
Electrical machinery and equipment	99.6	101.6	99.7	98.9	97.6	95.5	94.9	92.7	90.8	90.2	89.2	86.6
Road vehicles	99.2	100.0	100.5	100.9	100.5	100.4	101.0	100.8	100.8	100.8	101.3	101.5
Miscellaneous Manufactured Articles	99.4	100.4	100.3	100.8	100.8	100.7	100.7	100.3	100.1	100.2	99.8	99.7
Prefabricated buildings; plumbing, heat and lighting fixtures, n.e.s.	100.1	100.4	101.1	102.5	101.5	99.5	101.5	99.2	96.0	96.2	95.2	96.3
Furniture and parts thereof	99.2	100.7	100.5	101.1	100.7	100.8	100.8	101.8	102.4	102.9	102.4	103.1
Travel goods, handbags and similar containers	97.9	100.0	102.0	100.8	101.1	101.1	101.2	100.7	101.4	101.2	101.0	100.4
Articles of apparel and clothing accessories	99.9	100.1	100.1	100.6	101.0	101.5	101.2	101.1	101.7	102.6	102.8	102.8
Footwear	99.3	100.0	100.4	100.9	101.4	101.3	101.0	100.9	101.0	101.1	100.8	101.2
Professional, scientific and controlling instruments and apparatus, n.e.s.	98.5	100.5	100.7	100.3	100.6	99.3	100.3	99.8	97.4	97.1	96.9	96.3
Photographic apparatus, equipment and supplies and optical goods, n.e.s.	97.6	101.4	100.8	100.8	99.4	97.4	97.8	96.9	95.3	94.4	93.6	93.1
Miscellaneous manufactured articles, n.e.s.	99.9	100.3	99.9	101.0	100.8	100.9	100.9	100.3	99.8	99.4	98.6	98.1

See footnotes and *Note* at end of table.

Table 6-13. U.S. Import Price Indexes for Selected Categories of Goods, by Standard International Trade Classification, 1986–2000—*Continued*

(1995=100, unless otherwise indicated.)

Categories	1998				1999				2000			
	March	June	September	December	March	June	September	December	March	June	September	December
ALL COMMODITIES	93.6	92.6	91.6	90.4	90.9	92.4	95.2	96.8	99.3	99.6	101.0	100.0
Food And Live Animals	97.9	98.0	95.5	95.2	93.2	93.3	91.5	94.7	93.1	91.3	91.2	92.4
Meat and meat preparations	101.2	98.3	97.2	91.8	94.0	94.5	99.4	98.4	99.1	99.1	99.0	97.3
Fish, crustaceans, aquatic invertebrates and preparations thereof	107.1	109.4	103.7	100.1	103.3	104.3	103.1	106.8	108.0	109.1	112.6	109.1
Vegetables, fruit and nuts, fresh or dried	95.7	103.5	106.7	110.6	101.7	103.2	101.6	103.6	101.2	95.7	97.8	104.5
Coffee, tea, cocoa, spices and manufactures thereof	94.0	82.1	77.4	75.0	71.0	69.4	61.4	70.6	61.0	59.5	54.5	50.8
Beverages And Tobacco	109.2	109.6	109.7	109.9	110.4	110.4	112.2	112.0	111.7	113.0	113.6	113.2
Beverages	105.8	106.3	106.4	106.6	106.9	107.2	109.1	108.7	108.5	110.1	110.7	110.5
Crude Materials, Inedible, Except Fuels	91.1	87.7	85.7	84.1	86.3	90.3	91.7	92.2	94.3	90.7	88.9	88.5
Cork and wood	110.6	101.2	107.3	106.9	113.2	122.3	121.7	118.7	118.6	110.1	99.7	101.7
Woodpulp and recovered paper	64.2	66.1	60.8	57.8	57.6	60.6	66.0	68.2	72.4	80.1	82.0	83.4
Metalliferous ores and metal scrap	100.4	98.6	92.9	92.8	89.9	91.9	94.3	99.0	104.0	100.7	101.6	98.8
Crude animal and vegetable materials, n.e.s. [2]	110.0	113.1	105.2	99.4	109.4	101.7	111.1	111.9	111.9	92.7	103.0	97.1
Mineral Fuels, Lubricants And Related Materials	80.3	77.6	77.5	64.6	73.2	92.7	126.5	141.2	165.4	172.0	189.0	180.2
Petroleum, petroleum products and related materials	76.1	73.4	74.0	58.7	70.2	91.3	125.7	141.4	166.6	171.0	187.6	163.9
Gas, natural and manufactured	114.7	111.9	106.4	110.7	97.4	106.5	142.2	150.2	170.5	195.4	218.1	331.8
Chemicals And Related Products, n.e.s.	93.5	93.6	91.8	91.1	90.8	90.6	91.3	92.0	92.8	94.1	95.4	94.9
Organic chemicals	92.1	92.3	91.3	89.7	90.3	90.2	91.8	92.9	94.5	99.0	101.0	100.6
Inorganic chemicals	94.8	97.8	93.9	90.9	88.6	86.7	86.6	88.0	88.8	91.5	92.5	94.2
Dyeing, tanning and coloring materials	94.9	94.9	94.8	96.5	94.3	91.9	90.2	89.7	88.4	86.1	87.9	86.9
Medicinal and pharmaceutical products	95.8	95.3	94.6	95.7	96.7	96.2	97.0	97.3	97.3	96.8	96.7	95.7
Essential oils; polishing and cleansing preps	94.4	94.8	93.8	95.2	93.5	92.4	92.3	90.2	89.7	89.6	88.8	85.5
Plastics in primary forms	94.4	94.0	91.6	91.3	92.0	93.6	93.8	94.0	93.9	94.3	95.3	95.8
Plastics in nonprimary forms	81.5	79.1	74.1	73.7	73.1	75.6	77.9	79.7	80.4	80.8	80.8	78.6
Chemical materials and products, n.e.s.	101.7	101.4	100.6	99.4	97.9	97.4	98.1	99.5	100.6	99.7	101.1	100.6
Manufactured Goods Classified Chiefly By Material	94.7	94.0	92.7	91.7	91.8	92.0	92.6	93.9	98.0	97.6	97.9	97.3
Rubber manufactures, n.e.s.	94.7	95.0	94.3	94.4	94.5	94.3	95.0	94.4	92.3	91.0	91.7	91.8
Cork and wood manufactures other than furniture	92.9	92.8	95.8	95.2	100.5	104.6	103.7	99.8	103.2	96.3	93.0	91.3
Paper and paperboard, cut to size	87.9	87.5	87.0	86.1	85.8	83.7	83.7	86.2	87.1	89.1	91.4	92.2
Textile yarn, fabrics, made-up articles, n.e.s., and related products	97.9	97.2	96.7	96.4	95.6	94.7	94.9	94.8	95.6	94.7	94.8	94.6
Nonmetallic mineral manufactures, n.e.s.	100.6	100.6	100.1	100.6	101.3	100.9	101.1	101.2	100.8	100.5	100.8	100.2
Iron and steel	94.9	93.0	90.1	87.2	85.0	85.7	86.2	89.0	93.5	96.8	93.8	91.2
Nonferrous metals	91.2	90.9	86.3	83.0	85.9	87.7	91.1	95.6	115.1	110.7	114.4	114.4
Manufactures of metals, n.e.s.	97.3	96.5	96.6	96.6	95.9	96.1	95.8	95.9	96.1	95.7	95.4	95.0
Machinery And Transport Equipment	92.9	91.8	90.9	91.2	90.9	90.3	89.9	89.7	89.6	89.6	89.3	89.0
Power generating machinery and equipment [2]	99.9	97.9	97.2	97.9	98.7	98.3	98.4	99.1	99.4	100.2	99.7	99.9
Machinery specialized for particular industries	98.1	97.6	96.7	98.4	98.3	97.6	97.6	97.8	97.3	96.1	95.9	95.3
Metalworking machinery	97.6	96.9	96.6	97.6	96.1	94.6	94.3	95.2	93.9	92.6	94.0	93.5
General industrial machinery, equipment, and machine parts, n.e.s.	96.6	96.7	96.6	98.4	98.4	97.6	97.4	97.0	97.0	96.2	96.1	95.4
Computer equipment and office machines	73.0	70.4	68.7	66.7	64.4	63.1	61.6	61.7	61.0	60.0	59.8	58.7
Telecommunications and sound recording and reproducing apparatus and equipment	90.8	89.4	88.9	88.3	88.4	87.6	87.1	85.6	84.9	84.6	84.1	83.6
Electrical machinery and equipment	85.5	84.5	83.2	84.1	83.8	82.7	82.5	82.1	82.2	83.3	82.6	82.2
Road vehicles	101.5	101.1	100.7	101.5	101.9	102.3	102.2	102.3	102.6	102.8	102.6	102.8
Miscellaneous Manufactured Articles	99.2	98.6	98.3	98.2	98.3	97.8	97.9	97.9	97.6	96.9	97.0	96.9
Prefabricated buildings; plumbing, heat and lighting fixtures, n.e.s.	96.7	96.0	95.5	94.3	93.3	93.0	91.2	92.9	94.2	92.7	92.9	92.7
Furniture and parts thereof	102.9	100.2	100.1	100.3	100.2	98.7	98.4	97.8	98.1	97.3	97.9	97.3
Travel goods, handbags and similar containers	99.5	101.1	100.1	101.0	100.7	101.8	102.5	101.7	102.1	101.3	101.4	101.3
Articles of apparel and clothing accessories	102.7	102.7	102.9	102.1	102.2	101.8	102.2	101.9	101.6	100.7	100.8	101.0
Footwear	100.7	100.7	100.9	100.9	101.1	100.7	100.8	100.8	100.7	100.3	100.9	100.6
Professional, scientific and controlling instruments and apparatus, n.e.s.	95.0	94.9	94.5	95.0	94.6	94.1	94.5	95.0	93.8	93.5	93.6	93.0
Photographic apparatus, equipment and supplies and optical goods, n.e.s.	91.8	91.0	90.1	91.1	91.8	91.3	91.4	92.5	91.8	91.6	91.4	90.7
Miscellaneous manufactured articles, n.e.s.	97.5	96.2	95.2	95.5	95.6	95.0	95.0	94.9	94.5	94.0	93.7	93.9

Note: n.e.s. = not elsewhere specified.

1. Percent of total, relative importance in December 1999, based on 1995 trade values.
2. December 1996=100.

Table 6-14. U.S. Import Price Indexes for Selected Categories of Goods, by Locality of Origin, 1991–2000

(1995=100, unless otherwise indicated.)

Category and year	Percent of U.S. imports 1995	Months			
		March	June	September	December
DEVELOPED COUNTRIES	55.6	...	...	...	...
1991	...	90.5	88.7	88.8	89.8
1992	...	90.0	90.4	91.8	90.9
1993	...	91.4	92.3	92.4	92.6
1994	...	93.1	94.3	95.7	97.0
1995	...	98.3	100.7	100.9	100.9
1996	...	100.6	99.7	100.3	100.3
1997	...	98.3	97.4	97.3	97.0
1998	...	95.5	94.9	94.2	94.7
1999	...	95.0	95.7	97.3	98.5
2000	...	100.5	101.0	101.8	102.3
Manufactured Goods	52.2	...	...	...	...
1991	...	89.9	88.4	88.4	89.6
1992	...	90.1	90.0	91.3	90.7
1993	...	91.0	92.0	92.4	92.8
1994	...	93.3	94.1	95.6	97.0
1995	...	98.1	100.7	101.0	101.0
1996	...	100.3	99.3	99.5	98.8
1997	...	97.7	97.1	97.0	96.8
1998	...	96.0	95.7	94.9	95.5
1999	...	95.8	95.9	96.3	97.1
2000	...	98.3	98.0	98.4	98.0
Nonmanufactured Goods	3.1	...	...	...	...
1991	...	97.7	94.6	94.8	95.4
1992	...	94.4	97.0	98.3	96.9
1993	...	98.2	97.0	94.0	89.4
1994	...	88.6	97.9	97.9	97.5
1995	...	100.9	102.9	99.2	100.4
1996	...	109.0	110.0	115.6	128.3
1997	...	111.5	104.8	105.6	104.2
1998	...	90.2	86.4	87.1	84.8
1999	...	86.5	99.0	119.7	126.6
2000	...	141.0	155.5	163.5	179.8
DEVELOPING COUNTRIES	42.7	...	...	...	...
1991	...	96.4	95.8	96.1	95.9
1992	...	94.5	97.1	97.3	96.8
1993	...	96.6	95.8	94.6	91.8
1994	...	92.4	96.6	97.3	98.1
1995	...	100.0	101.2	99.9	100.1
1996	...	102.3	101.5	103.8	105.3
1997	...	103.1	101.9	101.2	99.0
1998	...	94.7	93.0	91.7	89.0
1999	...	89.9	92.6	96.8	99.3
2000	...	102.3	102.9	105.0	102.0
Manufactured Goods	35.4	...	...	...	...
1991	...	97.3	97.2	97.0	97.3
1992	...	97.6	97.8	97.8	97.5
1993	...	96.8	96.7	96.4	95.9
1994	...	96.4	97.2	97.9	98.5
1995	...	99.2	100.6	100.5	100.3
1996	...	100.7	100.3	99.8	100.4
1997	...	100.3	99.7	99.0	97.4
1998	...	95.7	94.5	93.0	92.1
1999	...	91.4	91.5	91.6	91.8
2000	...	92.3	92.3	92.8	92.7
Nonmanufactured Goods	7.1	...	...	...	...
1991	...	95.6	94.0	95.2	94.0
1992	...	90.0	96.5	97.3	93.9
1993	...	95.7	92.6	87.1	76.5
1994	...	76.7	94.0	95.6	96.5
1995	...	102.5	103.7	97.4	99.2
1996	...	108.6	106.3	119.3	124.6
1997	...	111.8	107.1	106.4	101.5
1998	...	84.2	80.9	80.3	69.0
1999	...	78.1	93.8	118.4	131.5
2000	...	147.3	151.0	161.0	143.5

See footnote at end of table.

Table 6-14. U.S. Import Price Indexes for Selected Categories of Goods, by Locality of Origin, 1991–2000—*Continued*

(1995=100, unless otherwise indicated.)

Category and year	Percent of U.S. imports 1995	Months			
		March	June	September	December
CANADA	18.9	...	...	...	...
1991	...	93.3	93.4	93.0	93.3
1992	...	92.5	93.5	93.7	92.3
1993	...	92.5	91.9	91.2	91.1
1994	...	91.5	93.3	94.3	96.6
1995	...	98.6	100.4	101.5	101.4
1996	...	100.9	100.0	100.3	101.8
1997	...	99.7	99.1	99.7	98.4
1998	...	96.4	96.0	95.6	94.9
1999	...	95.0	96.9	100.0	101.3
2000	...	104.1	106.7	109.6	113.0
Manufactured Goods	16.5	...	...	...	...
1991	...	93.9	93.8	93.7	94.3
1992	...	93.6	93.2	93.1	92.1
1993	...	92.3	91.5	91.1	91.6
1994	...	92.1	93.0	94.3	96.6
1995	...	98.7	100.2	101.5	101.3
1996	...	99.7	98.7	98.4	98.1
1997	...	98.7	98.7	99.1	98.0
1998	...	97.4	97.3	97.0	96.2
1999	...	96.3	96.8	97.6	98.5
2000	...	99.6	99.7	102.1	102.5
Nonmanufactured Goods	2.2	...	...	...	...
1991	...	93.9	94.5	93.4	93.0
1992	...	92.2	96.4	97.1	95.2
1993	...	96.2	95.6	92.2	87.7
1994	...	86.7	96.9	95.3	95.7
1995	...	98.0	102.1	101.4	102.8
1996	...	111.5	112.2	118.0	133.8
1997	...	110.9	105.6	108.1	105.3
1998	...	92.7	89.8	89.6	89.3
1999	...	[illegible]	101.9	121.9	120.0
2000	...	141.8	164.4	170.6	197.3
EUROPEAN UNION	17.0	...	...	...	...
1991	...	96.3	92.6	92.7	95.0
1992	...	95.2	96.0	98.7	94.1
1993	...	93.2	93.9	93.0	92.7
1994	...	92.8	94.1	95.9	97.2
1995	...	98.7	100.5	100.8	101.5
1996	...	102.4	102.1	102.8	103.0
1997	...	101.6	101.1	100.2	101.2
1998	...	100.0	99.9	99.8	100.5
1999	...	99.9	100.1	100.9	101.4
2000	...	101.9	101.1	101.1	100.0
Manufactured Goods	16.4	...	...	...	...
1991	...	94.8	92.1	92.0	94.4
1992	...	95.1	95.7	98.9	93.8
1993	...	93.0	93.7	93.0	92.8
1994	...	92.9	93.8	95.8	97.1
1995	...	98.6	100.4	100.9	101.5
1996	...	102.3	101.8	102.4	102.3
1997	...	101.0	100.8	100.1	101.0
1998	...	100.4	100.6	100.5	101.5
1999	...	100.9	100.6	100.8	100.8
2000	...	100.8	99.9	99.6	98.6
Nonmanufactured Goods	0.5	...	...	...	...
1991	...	106.4	99.4	100.4	102.2
1992	...	101.2	102.3	103.8	102.7
1993	...	103.7	100.8	97.5	93.7
1994	...	93.6	101.8	99.6	99.7
1995	...	100.9	103.2	98.6	101.2
1996	...	109.2	111.7	118.7	127.0
1997	...	123.7	113.9	106.0	108.7
1998	...	90.9	81.3	81.5	74.0
1999	...	74.3	92.2	112.7	122.9
2000	...	139.1	142.6	149.5	147.2

See footnote at end of table.

Table 6-14. U.S. Import Price Indexes for Selected Categories of Goods, by Locality of Origin, 1991–2000—*Continued*

(1995=100, unless otherwise indicated.)

Category and year	Percent of U.S. imports 1995	Months			
		March	June	September	December
LATIN AMERICA [1]	14.1	...	...	...	...
1997	...	...	...	...	100.0
1998	...	94.7	94.3	93.2	90.3
1999	...	91.8	95.8	101.9	105.9
2000	...	111.1	113.3	116.3	111.8
Manufactured Goods [1]	10.4	...	...	...	...
1997	...	...	...	...	100.0
1998	...	97.6	97.8	96.5	96.2
1999	...	94.7	96.3	97.4	98.9
2000	...	101.1	102.5	104.5	105.3
Nonmanufactured Goods [1]	3.5	...	...	...	...
1997	...	...	...	...	100.0
1998	...	85.9	84.3	84.0	73.3
1999	...	83.8	94.9	116.0	127.4
2000	...	141.6	146.3	152.3	132.3
JAPAN	16.6	...	...	...	...
1991	...	85.1	84.1	84.6	85.7
1992	...	86.3	86.0	86.8	88.0
1993	...	88.8	90.9	93.2	94.0
1994	...	94.8	95.3	96.4	97.3
1995	...	97.8	101.3	100.9	100.0
1996	...	99.1	97.6	97.1	95.9
1997	...	94.2	93.0	92.5	91.0
1998	...	89.9	88.5	87.2	88.3
1999	...	88.5	88.4	88.9	89.7
2000	...	89.7	90.1	90.0	90.0
ASIAN NEWLY INDUSTRALIZED COUNTRIES	10.9	...	...	...	...
1991	...	99.5	99.4	99.5	100.0
1992	...	100.4	100.6	100.7	100.6
1993	...	100.4	100.1	100.1	99.8
1994	...	99.7	99.5	99.3	99.3
1995	...	99.9	100.2	100.4	99.8
1996	...	99.6	98.8	97.6	96.9
1997	...	96.3	95.3	94.0	92.0
1998	...	89.8	86.9	85.1	84.3
1999	...	83.7	83.3	83.2	83.3
2000	...	83.2	82.5	82.6	82.1

1. December 1997=100.

Table 6-15. U.S. Import and Export Price Indexes and Percent Changes for Selected Categories of Services, December 1999–December 2000

(1995=100, unless otherwise indicated.)

Category	Trade 1995 (millions of dollars)	Index		Percent change				
				Annual	Quarterly			
		September 2000	December 2000	December 1999 to December 2000	December 1999 to March 2000	March 2000 to June 2000	June 2000 to September 2000	September 2000 to December 2000
IMPORTS								
Air Freight	3 188	88.5	87.4	-3.6	-2.0	-0.6	0.1	-1.2
Atlantic	1 278	81.8	80.7	-8.2	-3.9	3.4	0.2	-1.3
Pacific	1 674	93.0	91.5	-2.1	-1.3	0.8	(1)	-1.6
Air Passenger Fares	11 127	109.1	103.2	1.0	0.4	5.2	1.1	-5.4
Atlantic	4 922	114.6	104.0	3.7	2.3	9.4	2.1	-9.2
Pacific	2 340	91.5	85.9	-7.1	-3.4	2.0	0.3	-6.1
Latin American/Caribbean	3 021	115.6	122.3	11.3	2.5	2.6	0.1	5.8
Crude Oil Tanker Freight	1 346	144.8	. . .	. . .	26.8	18.0	24.6	. . .
Ocean Liner Freight	9 868	142.8	142.8	2.4	-2.2	4.9	-0.1	(1)
U.S. East Coast	4 271	111.1	111.3	2.9	-0.8	3.5	(1)	0.2
from Atlantic	1 952	96.4	96.4	-3.7	-1.9	-1.8	(1)	(1)
from Pacific	1 774	129.9	130.3	6.9	(1)	6.6	(1)	0.3
U.S. West Coast	5 596	167.1	167.1	2.3	-2.9	5.5	-0.2	(1)
EXPORTS								
Air Freight (12/96 = 100)	2 562	92.6	92.6	1.0	(1)	1.2	-0.2	(1)
Air Passenger Fares	17 272	115.5	111.9	4.8	0.5	5.6	1.9	-3.1
Atlantic	4 120	114.2	107.1	10.8	2.0	11.3	4.1	-6.2
Pacific	10 700	102.8	98.3	-0.3	-2.1	5.3	1.2	-4.4
Latin American/Caribbean	1 392	127.0	133.6	12.0	5.0	0.9	0.2	5.2
Canadian	1 006	196.6	193.3	0.5	1.2	-0.1	1.1	-1.7

1. Value less than 0.05.

PART SEVEN

CONSUMER EXPENDITURES

CONSUMER EXPENDITURES

HIGHLIGHTS

The principal objective of the Consumer Expenditure Survey is to collect information on the buying habits of American households. The unique aspect of the survey is that the expenditures can be shown for the different demographic characteristics of the population such as income, age, family size, regions, etc. These data are used in a variety of research projects by government, business, and academic analysts. Another very important use of the survey is to provide expenditure weights for the periodic revisions of the Consumer Price Index.

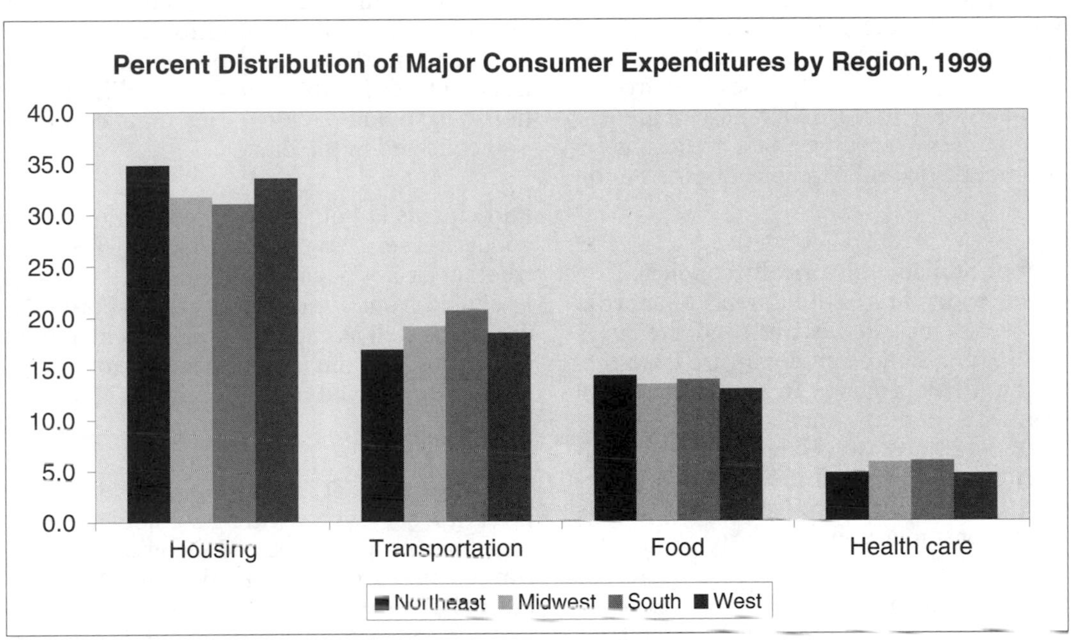

These four components average over 70 percent of total annual expenditures. Housing is the largest spending component in all regions, and is notoriously high in the Northeast (35 percent) and West (34 percent) regions. The share of transportation is higher in the South (18 percent) as a result of larger vehicle purchases and consumption of gasoline.

OTHER HIGHLIGHTS:

- Payments for pensions and social security are about 9.4 percent of total expenditures for the 25–64 years working age group and only 2.4 percent for the over 65 group in 1999. On the other hand, the out-of-pocket health care share for the over 65 group is over 11 percent and more than double the share for the 25–64 working age group. (Table 7-3)
- The highest quintile (20 percent) income group accounts for almost 40 percent of aggregate expenditures in 1999. (Table 7-2)
- In 1999, average annual expenditures by single men were 15 percent higher than those of single women. While the share of health care in total annual expenditure is about 4.0 percent for single men, this share jumps to almost double at 7.4 percent for single women. (Tables 7-16, 7-17)
- In 1999, the share of education in total annual expenditures in the urban areas is more than double that in rural areas, at 1.8 percent and 0.8 percent respectively. (Table 7-7)

NOTES AND DEFINITIONS

Purpose, Collection, and Coverage

The buying habits of American consumers change over time as a result of changes in relative prices, real income, family size and composition, and other determinants of people's tastes and preferences. The introduction into the marketplace of new products and the emergence of new concepts in retailing also influence consumer buying habits. As the only national survey that can relate family expenditures to demographic characteristics, data from the Consumer Expenditure Survey (CEX) are of great importance to researchers. The survey data are also used to revise the Consumer Price Index market baskets and item samples.

The Bureau of Labor Statistics historically conducted surveys of consumer expenditures at intervals of approximately 10 years. The last such survey was conducted in 1972–73. In late 1979, in a significant departure from previous surveys, BLS initiated a survey to be conducted on a continuous basis, with rotating panels of respondents. The regular flow of data that results from this design substantially enhances the usefulness of the survey by providing more timely information on consumption patterns of different kinds of consumer units.

The current CEX is similar to its 1972–73 predecessor in that it consists of two separate components, each with its own questionnaire and sample: (1) an interview panel survey in which each consumer unit in the sample is visited by an interviewer every 3 months over a 12-month period, and (2) a diary, or record-keeping, survey, completed by other consumer units for two consecutive one-week periods. The Bureau of the Census, under contract to BLS, collects the data for both components of the survey. Beginning in 1999, the sample was increased to from 5,000 to 7,500 households.

The Interview survey is designed to collect data on the types of expenditures that respondents can be expected to recall for a period of 3 months or longer. These include relatively large expenditures—such as those for property, travel, automobiles, and major appliances—and expenditures that occur on a regular basis—such as rent, utilities, insurance premiums, and clothing. The interview also obtains "global estimates" of food expenditures both for food at home and food away from home. For food-at-home expenditures, respondents are asked to estimate the usual weekly expenditure at the grocery store, and how much of the expenditure was for nonfood items. Nonfood items are then subtracted from the total expenditure. Convenience and specialty stores are also included in the food-at-home estimates. The Interview survey collects approximately 95 percent of total expenditures. Excluded from the interview survey are nonprescription drugs, household supplies, and personal care products.

The Diary survey is designed to collect expenditures on frequently purchased items that are more difficult to recall over longer periods of time. Respondents keep detailed records of expenses for food and beverages at home and meals in eating-places away from home. Expenditures for tobacco, drugs—including nonprescription drugs—and personal care supplies and services are also collected in the diary.

Participants in both surveys record dollar amounts for goods and services purchased during the reporting period whether or not payment is made at the time of purchase. Excluded from both surveys are business-related expenditures as well as expenditures for which the family is reimbursed. At the initial interview for each survey, information is collected on demographic and family characteristics.

The tables present integrated data from the Diary and Interview surveys, providing a complete accounting of consumer expenditures and income, which neither survey component alone is designed to do. Data on some expenditure items are collected only in either the Diary or Interview survey. For example, the Diary does not collect data for expenditures on overnight travel, or information on reimbursements, as the Interview does. Examples of expenditures for which any reimbursements (e.g., from insurance) are netted out include those for medical care; auto repair; and construction, repairs, alterations, and maintenance of property.

For items unique to one or the other survey, the choice of which survey to use as the source of data is obvious. However, there is considerable overlap in coverage between the surveys. Because of this, integrating the data presents the problem of determining the appropriate survey component. When data are available from both survey sources, the more reliable of the two is selected as determined by statistical methods. As a result, some items are selected from the Interview survey and others from the Diary survey.

Data Included in this Book

The data in this edition are for the calendar year 1998 for a single characteristic or for an average of 1997 and 1998 for the tables cross-classified by two characteristics. Income values from the survey are derived from "complete income reporters" only. Complete income reporters are defined as consumer units that provide values for at least one of the major sources of their income: wages and salaries; self-employment income; retirement income; dividends and interest; and welfare benefits. Some consumer units are defined as complete income reporters even though they may not have provided a full accounting of all income from all sources.

Consumer units are classified by quintiles of income before taxes; age of reference person; size of consumer unit; region; composition of consumer unit; number of earners in consumer unit; housing tenure; race; type of area (urban or rural); and occupation.

Concepts and Definitions

A *consumer unit* comprises either (1) all members of a particular household who are related by blood, marriage, adoption, or other legal arrangements; (2) a person living alone or sharing a household with others or living as a roomer in a private home or lodging house or in permanent living quarters in a hotel or motel, but who is financially independent; or (3) two or more persons living together who pool their income to make joint expenditure decisions. Financial independence is determined by the three major expense categories: housing, food, and other living expenses. To be considered financially independent, at least two of the three major expense categories have to be provided by the respondent. The terms "family," "household," and "consumer unit" are used interchangeably in descriptions of the CEX.

The *"householder"* or *"reference person"* is the first member of the consumer unit mentioned by the respondent as owner or renter of the premises at the time of the initial interview.

Expenditures are averages for consumer units with the specified characteristics, regardless of whether a particular unit incurred an expense for that specific item or service during the record-keeping period. An individual consumer unit may have spent substantially more or substantially less than the average. The less frequently an item or service is purchased, the greater the difference between the average for all consumer units and the average of those purchasing. Income, age of family members, taste, personal preferences, and geographic location are among the factors that influence expenditures and should be considered when relating averages to individual circumstances.

Expenditures reported are the direct out-of-pocket expenditures of consumer units. Indirect expenditures may be significant for some expenditure categories, for example, utilities. Rental contracts may include some or all utilities, and renters with such contracts would record little or no direct expense for utilities. Therefore, caution should be exercised in making comparisons of expenditures for utilities by consumers of various income classes and types of housing.

Earner is a consumer unit member who reported having worked at least 1 week during the 12 months prior to the interview date.

Sources of Additional Information

A 2-year report, published biennially by the BLS, includes analytical articles, tables of integrated Diary and Interview survey data, a glossary, a description of survey methods, and a survey source of data for the integrated tables. Also see BLS news release 00-369.

Table 7-1. Consumer Expenditures, Averages by Income Before Taxes, 1999

Item	All consumer units	Complete reporting of income									
		Complete reporting of income, total	Less than $5,000	$5,000 to $9,999	$10,000 to $14,999	$15,000 to $19,999	$20,000 to $29,999	$30,000 to $39,999	$40,000 to $49,999	$50,000 to $69,999	$70,000 and over
NUMBER OF CONSUMER UNITS (THOUSANDS)	108 465	81 692	3 909	7 588	8 639	6 995	11 560	9 453	7 381	10 999	15 168
CONSUMER UNIT CHARACTERISTICS											
Average Income Before Taxes[1]	$43 951	$43 951	$1 633	$7 631	$12 338	$17 311	$24 467	$34 353	$44 321	$58 473	$113 441
Age Of Reference Person	47.9	47.9	39.1	55.3	55.8	50.9	48.8	45.8	44.7	43.9	45.8
Average Number In Consumer Unit											
Persons	2.5	2.5	1.9	1.7	2.0	2.2	2.5	2.5	2.6	2.9	3.1
Children under 18	0.7	0.7	0.5	0.4	0.5	0.6	0.7	0.7	0.7	0.8	0.9
Persons 65 and over	0.3	0.3	0.2	0.5	0.5	0.5	0.4	0.3	0.2	0.1	0.1
Earners	1.3	1.4	0.9	0.5	0.7	0.9	1.1	1.4	1.6	1.9	2.1
Vehicles	1.9	2.0	1.0	0.9	1.3	1.5	1.8	2.1	2.3	2.5	2.8
PERCENT HOMEOWNER	65	64	29	43	54	53	61	63	67	77	88
With mortgage	38	38	13	8	15	18	28	37	46	59	72
Without mortgage	27	26	16	35	39	34	33	26	20	18	16
AVERAGE ANNUAL EXPENDITURES	$36 995	$39 143	$17 983	$14 921	$19 710	$24 367	$28 916	$35 048	$40 826	$49 606	$76 742
Food	5 031	5 216	2 873	2 576	2 917	3 821	4 322	5 060	5 823	6 527	8 725
Food at home	2 915	3 010	1 804	1 817	1 993	2 520	2 697	2 918	3 457	3 724	4 328
Cereals and bakery products	448	461	271	301	306	385	395	440	518	581	667
Meats, poultry, fish, and eggs	749	758	492	507	526	671	709	742	854	913	1 023
Dairy products	322	338	204	190	220	266	296	334	383	428	499
Fruits and vegetables	500	515	323	307	361	440	471	486	591	598	753
Other food at home	896	938	514	510	580	758	825	916	1 112	1 204	1 386
Food away from home	2 116	2 206	1 069	759	923	1 301	1 625	2 142	2 365	2 803	4 398
Alcoholic Beverages	318	348	271	100	180	205	267	292	345	443	696
Housing	12 057	12 314	6 403	5 737	7 106	8 323	9 419	10 863	12 643	14 873	23 067
Shelter	7 016	7 061	3 887	3 265	4 011	4 601	5 304	6 323	7 404	8 306	13 381
Owned dwellings	4 525	4 506	1 281	1 170	1 718	1 923	2 745	3 556	4 375	5 945	10 739
Rented dwellings	2 027	2 081	2 357	1 965	2 128	2 480	2 300	2 469	2 674	1 850	1 325
Other lodging	465	475	249	130	165	198	260	297	355	511	1 317
Utilities, fuels, and public services	2 377	2 368	1 311	1 506	1 825	1 944	2 159	2 298	2 491	2 795	3 412
Household operations	666	717	267	221	300	442	377	385	624	801	1 898
Housekeeping supplies	498	549	238	258	285	347	451	515	575	784	945
Household furnishings and equipment	1 499	1 619	700	488	684	990	1 127	1 343	1 549	2 188	3 431
Apparel And Services	1 743	1 871	993	699	893	1 356	1 553	1 904	1 677	2 139	3 625
Transportation	7 011	7 222	3 117	2 240	3 697	4 576	5 485	6 973	8 352	9 380	13 363
Vehicle purchases (net outlay)	3 305	3 407	1 453	947	1 797	2 110	2 500	3 239	4 138	4 317	6 437
Gasoline and motor oil	1 055	1 071	552	425	603	736	928	1 124	1 246	1 451	1 666
Other vehicle expenses	2 254	2 335	951	707	1 119	1 478	1 781	2 296	2 610	3 145	4 322
Public transportation	397	408	161	162	178	252	276	314	358	468	939
Health Care	1 959	2 042	935	1 162	1 641	1 921	2 019	1 970	2 023	2 391	2 870
Health insurance	923	945	343	604	810	876	969	965	1 032	1 065	1 220
Medical services	558	579	359	206	290	452	517	552	522	748	1 016
Drugs	370	398	180	299	432	503	430	351	331	419	459
Medical supplies	109	119	54	53	110	91	102	102	138	159	174
Entertainment	1 891	1 978	908	643	969	1 014	1 323	1 681	1 882	2 754	4 121
Personal Care Products And Services	408	447	233	219	209	294	385	452	500	525	794
Reading	159	169	68	68	102	106	132	147	166	209	330
Education	635	593	863	354	267	255	309	347	425	602	1 430
Tobacco Products And Smoking Supplies	300	315	259	223	257	295	305	336	376	391	328
Miscellaneous	867	936	359	348	377	579	705	875	948	1 102	1 951
Cash Contributions	1 181	1 341	299	245	504	608	845	1 057	1 118	1 847	3 270
Personal Insurance And Pensions	3 436	4 352	401	306	590	1 014	1 849	3 092	4 548	6 421	12 172
Life and other personal insurance	394	408	139	119	168	169	264	342	349	517	970
Pensions and Social Security	3 042	3 944	262	187	423	844	1 585	2 750	4 199	5 904	11 202

1. Components of income and taxes are derived from "complete income reporters" only.

Table 7-2. Consumer Expenditures, Averages by Quintiles of Income Before Taxes, 1999

Item	All consumer units	Complete reporting of income						Incomplete reporting of income
		Complete reporting of income, total	Lowest 20 percent	Second 20 percent	Third 20 percent	Fourth 20 percent	Highest 20 percent	
NUMBER OF CONSUMER UNITS (THOUSANDS)	108 465	81 692	16 307	16 351	16 332	16 341	16 361	26 773
CONSUMER UNIT CHARACTERISTICS								
Average Income Before Taxes[1]	$43 951	$43 951	$7 264	$18 033	$31 876	$52 331	$110 105	(1)
Age Of Reference Person	47.9	47.9	51.6	51.6	46.5	44.1	45.9	47.8
Average Number In Consumer Unit								
Persons	2.5	2.5	1.8	2.2	2.5	2.8	3.1	2.6
Children under 18	0.7	0.7	0.4	0.6	0.7	0.8	0.8	0.7
Persons 65 and over	0.3	0.3	0.4	0.5	0.3	0.2	0.1	0.3
Earners	1.3	1.4	0.7	0.9	1.3	1.8	2.0	1.3
Vehicles	1.9	2.0	1.0	1.6	2.0	2.4	2.8	1.8
PERCENT HOMEOWNER	65	64	43	55	63	73	88	67
With mortgage	38	38	11	19	35	54	72	37
Without mortgage	27	26	31	36	28	19	17	30
AVERAGE ANNUAL EXPENDITURES	$36 995	$39 143	$16 750	$24 840	$33 029	$45 998	$75 015	$30 787
Food	5 031	5 216	2 715	3 773	4 799	6 218	8 568	4 581
Food at home	2 915	3 010	1 834	2 472	2 832	3 637	4 273	2 683
Cereals and bakery products	448	461	292	372	424	555	661	418
Meats, poultry, fish, and eggs	749	758	504	655	713	911	1 008	726
Dairy products	322	338	199	267	319	411	492	285
Fruits and vegetables	500	515	318	436	487	589	744	462
Other food at home	896	938	520	742	887	1 171	1 369	793
Food away from home	2 116	2 206	882	1 301	1 968	2 580	4 295	1 897
Alcoholic Beverages	318	348	161	224	280	385	687	245
Housing	12 057	12 314	6 197	8 440	10 424	13 892	22 589	11 341
Shelter	7 016	7 061	3 584	4 720	5 990	7 890	13 110	6 877
Owned dwellings	4 525	4 506	1 355	2 069	3 322	5 274	10 496	4 582
Rented dwellings	2 027	2 081	2 076	2 421	2 392	2 200	1 316	1 861
Other lodging	465	475	153	229	277	416	1 298	433
Utilities, fuels, and public services	2 377	2 368	1 549	1 971	2 272	2 670	3 377	2 406
Household operations	666	717	248	391	389	740	1 818	508
Housekeeping supplies	498	549	248	384	486	697	928	377
Household furnishings and equipment	1 499	1 619	569	981	1 288	1 896	3 356	1 173
Apparel And Services	1 743	1 871	788	1 339	1 760	1 985	3 478	1 427
Transportation	7 011	7 222	2 790	4 752	6 384	8 998	13 170	6 374
Vehicle purchases (net outlay)	3 305	3 407	1 218	2 277	2 899	4 346	6 287	2 995
Gasoline and motor oil	1 055	1 071	505	759	1 079	1 350	1 661	1 004
Other vehicle expenses	2 254	2 335	902	1 461	2 119	2 898	4 291	2 010
Public transportation	397	408	164	255	286	403	931	365
Health Care	1 959	2 042	1 248	1 912	1 960	2 222	2 862	1 716
Health insurance	923	945	600	899	959	1 049	1 217	854
Medical services	558	579	266	447	522	650	1 009	492
Drugs	370	398	307	472	372	375	463	293
Medical supplies	109	119	75	93	106	148	173	77
Entertainment	1 891	1 978	812	1 083	1 555	2 405	4 030	1 636
Personal Care Products And Services	408	447	217	304	428	507	778	315
Reading	159	169	78	112	144	185	328	129
Education	635	593	459	265	335	520	1 385	765
Tobacco Products And Smoking Supplies	300	315	236	291	329	390	329	255
Miscellaneous	867	936	353	576	800	1 069	1 878	668
Cash Contributions	1 181	1 341	301	637	1 045	1 574	3 145	692
Personal Insurance And Pensions	3 436	4 352	395	1 126	2 786	5 647	11 788	643
Life and other personal insurance	394	408	133	209	311	450	936	353
Pensions and Social Security	3 042	3 944	262	917	2 475	5 197	10 852	290

1. Components of income and taxes are derived from "complete income reporters" only.

Table 7-3. Consumer Expenditures, Averages by Age of Reference Person, 1999

Item	All consumer units	Under 25 years	25 to 34 years	35 to 44 years	45 to 54 years	55 to 64 years	65 years and over
NUMBER OF CONSUMER UNITS (THOUSANDS)	108 465	8 164	19 332	24 405	20 903	13 647	22 015
CONSUMER UNIT CHARACTERISTCS							
Average Income Before Taxes[1]	$43 951	$18 276	$42 470	$53 579	$59 822	$49 436	$26 581
Age Of Reference Person	47.9	21.4	29.7	39.5	49.2	59.1	74.8
Average Number In Consumer Unit							
Persons	2.5	1.8	2.9	3.2	2.7	2.2	1.7
Children under 18	0.7	0.4	1.1	1.3	0.6	0.2	0.1
Persons 65 and over	0.3	(2)	(2)	(2)	(2)	0.1	1.4
Earners	1.3	1.3	1.5	1.7	1.8	1.3	0.4
Vehicles	1.9	1.1	1.7	2.1	2.5	2.2	1.5
PERCENT HOMEOWNER	65	13	45	67	77	80	80
With mortgage	38	7	37	54	54	40	16
Without mortgage	27	6	8	13	22	40	64
AVERAGE ANNUAL EXPENDITURES	$36 995	$21 704	$36 158	$42 792	$46 511	$39 394	$26 521
Food	5 031	3 354	5 140	6 109	5 945	5 056	3 511
Food at home	2 915	1 828	2 890	3 537	3 340	2 920	2 266
Cereals and bakery products	448	271	432	561	509	433	357
Meats, poultry, fish, and eggs	749	469	751	897	878	761	563
Dairy products	322	195	322	410	354	305	255
Fruits and vegetables	500	283	475	572	563	525	450
Other food at home	896	610	910	1 097	1 037	895	641
Food away from home	2 116	1 526	2 250	2 572	2 605	2 136	1 245
Alcoholic Beverages	318	369	365	384	320	330	172
Housing	12 057	6 585	12 519	14 215	14 513	12 093	8 944
Shelter	7 016	4 140	7 612	8 606	8 534	6 660	4 576
Owned dwellings	4 525	596	3 935	6 110	6 203	4 812	2 971
Rented dwellings	2 027	3 296	3 447	2 121	1 532	1 206	1 182
Other lodging	465	248	230	375	799	642	423
Utilities, fuels, and public services	2 377	1 166	2 249	2 586	2 819	2 608	2 145
Household operations	666	181	772	830	606	476	746
Housekeeping supplies	498	221	441	604	574	570	423
Household furnishings and equipment	1 499	877	1 445	1 590	1 980	1 779	1 054
Apparel And Services	1 743	1 192	2 047	2 053	2 048	1 722	1 070
Transportation	7 011	5 037	7 150	8 041	9 010	7 330	4 385
Vehicle purchases (net outlay)	3 305	2 859	3 500	3 807	4 117	3 406	1 911
Gasoline and motor oil	1 055	708	1 066	1 259	1 349	1 093	644
Other vehicle expenses	2 254	1 253	2 249	2 565	3 085	2 339	1 443
Public transportation	397	217	335	411	459	492	387
Health Care	1 959	551	1 170	1 631	2 183	2 450	3 019
Health insurance	923	233	597	746	942	1 063	1 554
Medical services	558	184	351	531	754	751	601
Drugs	370	97	162	254	368	497	706
Medical supplies	109	36	60	101	118	139	158
Entertainment	1 891	1 149	1 776	2 254	2 367	2 175	1 238
Personal Care Products And Services	408	254	381	471	475	449	333
Reading	159	70	116	157	210	195	163
Education	635	1 277	453	637	1 125	552	139
Tobacco Products And Smoking Supplies	300	220	295	370	395	329	148
Miscellaneous	867	353	727	946	1 089	1 021	790
Cash Contributions	1 181	182	585	1 067	1 415	1 750	1 627
Personal Insurance And Pensions	3 436	1 110	3 433	4 455	5 415	3 941	980
Life and other personal insurance	394	61	238	418	616	533	333
Pensions and Social Security	3 042	1 049	3 195	4 037	4 799	3 408	647

1. Components of income and taxes are derived from "complete income reporters" only.
2. Value less than 0.05.

Table 7-4. Consumer Expenditures, Averages by Size of Consumer Unit, 1999

Item	All consumer units	One person	Two or more persons	Two persons	Three persons	Four persons	Five or more persons
NUMBER OF CONSUMER UNITS (THOUSANDS)	108 465	31 550	76 915	33 798	17 200	15 039	10 878
CONSUMER UNIT CHARACTERISTICS							
Average Income Before Taxes[1]	$43 951	$25 247	$51 895	$47 779	$52 334	$59 551	$53 340
Age Of Reference Person	47.9	51.2	46.5	52.8	42.9	40.5	41.3
Average Number In Consumer Unit							
Persons	2.5	1.0	3.1	2.0	3.0	4.0	5.6
Children under 18	0.7	. . .	0.9	0.1	0.8	1.6	2.8
Persons 65 and over	0.3	0.3	0.3	0.5	0.1	0.1	0.1
Earners	1.3	0.6	1.6	1.2	1.8	2.0	2.2
Vehicles	1.9	1.0	2.3	2.1	2.3	2.6	2.6
PERCENT HOMEOWNER	65	49	71	73	68	75	68
With mortgage	38	19	46	36	49	60	53
Without mortgage	27	31	25	37	19	15	15
AVERAGE ANNUAL EXPENDITURES	$36 995	$22 373	$42 961	$38 856	$42 848	$49 096	$47 564
Food	5 031	2 685	5 975	5 085	5 770	7 021	7 716
Food at home	2 915	1 449	3 504	2 843	3 412	4 098	4 966
Cereals and bakery products	448	222	539	423	535	658	754
Meats, poultry, fish, and eggs	749	340	913	743	875	1 020	1 377
Dairy products	322	155	389	307	377	469	567
Fruits and vegetables	500	264	594	509	563	678	805
Other food at home	896	468	1 068	861	1 063	1 273	1 462
Food away from home	2 116	1 236	2 471	2 243	2 357	2 923	2 750
Alcoholic Beverages	318	286	331	378	314	291	259
Housing	12 057	8 206	13 632	12 171	13 620	15 953	14 991
Shelter	7 016	5 142	7 785	6 952	7 804	9 068	8 567
Owned dwellings	4 525	2 307	5 434	4 608	5 342	6 936	6 073
Rented dwellings	2 027	2 517	1 826	1 745	2 003	1 599	2 108
Other lodging	465	317	[illegible]	599	459	504	386
Utilities, fuels, and public services	2 377	1 551	2 716	2 432	2 732	3 017	3 160
Household operations	666	469	747	489	809	1 189	837
Housekeeping supplies	498	238	603	542	551	726	711
Household furnishings and equipment	1 499	807	1 782	1 756	1 723	1 953	1 717
Apparel And Services	1 743	933	2 069	1 645	1 982	2 698	2 690
Transportation	7 011	3 536	8 437	7 427	8 726	9 486	9 665
Vehicle purchases (net outlay)	3 305	1 507	4 043	3 525	4 172	4 584	4 702
Gasoline and motor oil	1 055	565	1 256	1 065	1 280	1 440	1 556
Other vehicle expenses	2 254	1 215	2 680	2 333	2 869	3 046	2 952
Public transportation	397	250	458	505	405	415	455
Health Care	1 959	1 336	2 214	2 475	1 946	2 070	2 024
Health insurance	923	614	1 049	1 177	903	996	958
Medical services	558	346	644	648	607	677	647
Drugs	370	304	397	514	333	274	304
Medical supplies	109	72	124	136	104	123	115
Entertainment	1 891	1 040	2 238	2 037	2 291	2 638	2 236
Personal Care Products And Services	408	254	470	434	474	519	516
Reading	159	122	175	185	171	182	136
Education	635	421	722	507	795	1 013	874
Tobacco Products And Smoking Supplies	300	189	346	301	372	387	385
Miscellaneous	867	663	950	890	1 054	979	937
Cash Contributions	1 181	1 013	1 250	1 521	1 070	919	1 147
Personal Insurance And Pensions	3 436	1 689	4 153	3 798	4 264	4 941	3 988
Life and other personal insurance	394	133	502	454	475	643	497
Pensions and Social Security	3 042	1 556	3 651	3 345	3 790	4 298	3 491

1. Components of income and taxes are derived from "complete income reporters" only.

Table 7-5. Consumer Expenditures, Averages by Composition of Consumer Unit, 1999

Item	All consumer units	Husband and wife consumer units: Total	Husband and wife consumer units: Husband and wife only	Husband and wife with children: Total	Husband and wife with children: Oldest child under 6 years	Husband and wife with children: Oldest child 6 to 17 years	Husband and wife with children: Oldest child 18 years or over	Other husband and wife consumer units	One parent, at least one child under 18 years	Single person and other consumer units
NUMBER OF CONSUMER UNITS (THOUSANDS)	108 465	56 429	23 406	28 535	5 304	15 378	7 853	4 488	6 571	45 465
CONSUMER UNIT CHARACTERISTICS										
Average Income Before Taxes[1]	$43 951	$59 126	$54 062	$63 666	$57 922	$63 558	$68 094	$56 519	$25 685	$28 281
Age Of Reference Person	47.9	48.2	56.8	41.2	31.7	39.5	50.9	48.4	36.3	49.2
Average Number In Consumer Unit										
Persons	2.5	3.2	2.0	3.9	3.5	4.1	3.9	4.9	2.9	1.6
Children under 18	0.7	0.9	. . .	1.6	1.5	2.1	0.6	1.5	1.8	0.2
Persons 65 and over	0.3	0.3	0.7	0.1	(2)	(2)	0.2	0.4	(2)	0.3
Earners	1.3	1.7	1.2	2.0	1.6	1.8	2.6	2.4	1.1	0.9
Vehicles	1.9	2.6	2.4	2.7	2.1	2.6	3.2	2.9	1.2	1.3
PERCENT HOMEOWNER	65	81	84	79	67	79	86	76	39	49
With mortgage	38	52	40	63	60	65	60	50	29	22
Without mortgage	27	28	44	16	8	14	26	26	10	28
AVERAGE ANNUAL EXPENDITURES	$36 995	$47 149	$42 133	$51 154	$46 085	$51 453	$54 214	$47 942	$27 900	$25 835
Food	5 031	6 372	5 380	7 034	5 379	7 472	7 415	7 419	4 526	3 507
Food at home	2 915	3 695	3 000	4 146	3 360	4 381	4 287	4 528	2 942	1 987
Cereals and bakery products	448	567	446	653	503	713	646	656	509	299
Meats, poultry, fish, and eggs	749	939	771	1 031	769	1 078	1 152	1 264	770	520
Dairy products	322	419	329	484	407	521	465	481	301	211
Fruits and vegetables	500	633	548	680	560	716	702	793	457	348
Other food at home	896	1 136	906	1 297	1 120	1 353	1 322	1 334	904	610
Food away from home	2 116	2 677	2 380	2 888	2 020	3 090	3 129	2 891	1 584	1 520
Alcoholic Beverages	318	337	388	299	261	322	276	309	144	321
Housing	12 057	14 789	12 964	16 349	17 168	16 411	15 736	14 376	10 105	8 970
Shelter	7 016	8 411	7 270	9 416	10 074	9 473	8 859	7 976	5 875	5 449
Owned dwellings	4 525	6 405	5 335	7 381	7 563	7 570	6 888	5 779	2 648	2 463
Rented dwellings	2 027	1 370	1 195	1 460	2 244	1 418	1 012	1 707	3 088	2 688
Other lodging	465	637	740	575	267	485	959	490	139	298
Utilities, fuels, and public services	2 377	2 860	2 585	3 015	2 570	3 009	3 326	3 312	2 194	1 805
Household operations	666	848	534	1 126	2 142	1 066	559	717	696	436
Housekeeping supplies	498	676	622	727	535	770	793	632	356	310
Household furnishings and equipment	1 499	1 994	1 953	2 066	1 848	2 093	2 201	1 739	984	971
Apparel And Services	1 743	2 169	1 679	2 520	2 078	2 696	2 496	2 517	1 946	1 202
Transportation	7 011	9 289	8 066	10 214	9 368	9 585	12 029	9 785	4 694	4 521
Vehicle purchases (net outlay)	3 305	4 421	3 700	4 946	4 855	4 727	5 435	4 372	2 260	2 072
Gasoline and motor oil	1 055	1 376	1 146	1 522	1 281	1 454	1 819	1 643	720	704
Other vehicle expenses	2 254	2 977	2 549	3 289	2 904	2 988	4 153	3 223	1 484	1 470
Public transportation	397	515	580	457	328	417	621	547	230	275
Health Care	1 959	2 522	2 908	2 200	1 705	2 154	2 630	2 553	1 003	1 401
Health insurance	923	1 201	1 390	1 049	905	993	1 255	1 185	481	641
Medical services	558	736	747	718	517	741	811	791	306	373
Drugs	370	443	612	303	199	291	402	452	165	311
Medical supplies	109	141	159	130	84	129	162	125	51	77
Entertainment	1 891	2 519	2 275	2 784	2 111	3 140	2 549	2 095	1 367	1 193
Personal Care Products And Services	408	506	471	541	450	552	597	460	362	299
Reading	159	201	215	197	160	201	214	150	71	121
Education	635	829	528	1 115	317	1 030	1 822	582	426	424
Tobacco Products And Smoking Supplies	300	324	269	342	239	344	406	500	239	279
Miscellaneous	867	1 019	911	1 063	1 090	965	1 206	1 321	824	686
Cash Contributions	1 181	1 463	1 787	1 197	808	1 198	1 457	1 462	368	949
Personal Insurance And Pensions	3 436	4 812	4 291	5 301	4 951	5 382	5 380	4 413	1 827	1 962
Life and other personal insurance	394	602	548	644	398	703	693	616	170	170
Pensions and Social Security	3 042	4 210	3 743	4 658	4 553	4 679	4 687	3 798	1 657	1 792

1. Components of income and taxes are derived from "complete income reporters" only.
2. Value less than 0.05.

Table 7-6. Consumer Expenditures, Averages by Number of Earners, 1999

Item	All consumer units	Single consumers		Consumer units of two or more persons			
		No earner	One earner	No earner	One earner	Two earners	Three or more earners
NUMBER OF CONSUMER UNITS (THOUSANDS)	108 465	11 965	19 585	9 810	21 647	35 123	10 336
CONSUMER UNIT CHARACTERISTICS							
Average Income Before Taxes[1]	$43 951	$16 231	$30 236	$22 281	$40 719	$61 923	$68 409
Age Of Reference Person	47.9	68.9	40.4	65.4	45.7	42.0	45.8
Average Number In Consumer Unit							
Persons	2.5	1.0	1.0	2.3	3.0	3.1	4.4
Children under 18	0.7	...	...	0.4	1.1	0.9	1.2
Persons 65 and over	0.3	0.7	0.1	1.3	0.3	0.1	0.1
Earners	1.3	...	1.0	...	1.0	2.0	3.3
Vehicles	1.9	0.8	1.1	1.8	1.9	2.4	3.2
PERCENT HOMEOWNER	65	63	41	75	65	73	79
With mortgage	38	9	24	16	38	55	60
Without mortgage	27	54	16	58	27	17	19
AVERAGE ANNUAL EXPENDITURES	$36 995	$17 272	$25 497	$27 645	$36 459	$47 785	$54 698
Food	5 031	2 084	3 056	4 154	5 342	6 307	7 895
Food at home	2 915	1 452	1 447	2 790	3 271	3 566	4 487
Cereals and bakery products	448	241	211	439	505	548	677
Meats, poultry, fish, and eggs	749	342	338	734	854	918	1 201
Dairy products	322	163	151	308	368	396	493
Fruits and vegetables	500	283	252	529	560	589	754
Other food at home	896	424	496	780	985	1 115	1 361
Food away from home	2 116	632	1 609	1 365	2 071	2 742	3 408
Alcoholic Beverages	318	118	389	195	245	401	385
Housing	12 057	7 024	8 929	9 105	12 484	15 044	15 534
Shelter	7 016	3 745	5 995	4 676	7 125	8 779	8 737
Owned dwellings	4 525	1 879	2 568	2 854	4 620	6 369	6 413
Rented dwellings	2 027	1 655	3 043	1 371	2 043	1 873	1 639
Other lodging	465	211	383	451	462	537	685
Utilities, fuels, and public services	2 377	1 578	1 535	2 295	2 555	2 759	3 310
Household operations	666	870	224	446	664	922	611
Housekeeping supplies	498	258	225	477	536	639	734
Household furnishings and equipment	1 499	573	950	1 211	1 605	1 944	2 142
Apparel And Services	1 743	718	1 066	1 136	1 849	2 254	2 784
Transportation	7 011	2 170	4 370	4 999	6 427	9 603	11 947
Vehicle purchases (net outlay)	3 305	860	1 902	2 351	2 954	4 771	5 457
Gasoline and motor oil	1 055	355	693	730	1 044	1 358	1 852
Other vehicle expenses	2 254	773	1 485	1 541	2 041	2 972	4 109
Public transportation	397	182	291	377	389	502	529
Health Care	1 959	1 928	974	3 160	2 098	1 994	2 312
Health insurance	923	944	412	1 576	974	944	1 066
Medical services	558	415	304	664	612	636	722
Drugs	370	475	200	753	409	303	356
Medical supplies	109	94	58	167	103	111	168
Entertainment	1 891	701	1 248	1 494	2 030	2 469	2 590
Personal Care Products And Services	408	217	277	306	409	504	637
Reading	159	108	131	150	149	189	200
Education	635	152	586	200	546	789	1 357
Tobacco Products And Smoking Supplies	300	147	214	186	317	365	494
Miscellaneous	867	767	600	658	757	1 050	1 290
Cash Contributions	1 181	1 020	1 008	1 544	844	1 370	1 411
Personal Insurance And Pensions	3 436	117	2 649	357	2 960	5 446	5 861
Life and other personal insurance	394	109	148	324	449	509	756
Pensions and Social Security	3 042	[2]8	2 417	[2]33	2 511	4 937	5 105

1. Components of income and taxes are derived from "complete income reporters" only.
2. Data are likely to have large sampling errors.

Table 7-7. Consumer Expenditures, Averages by Housing Tenure, Type of Area, Race and Hispanic Origin of Reference Person, 1999

Item	All consumer units	Housing tenure		Type of area		Race of reference person		Hispanic origin of reference person	
		Homeowner	Renter	Urban	Rural	White and Other	Black	Hispanic	Non-Hispanic
NUMBER OF CONSUMER UNITS (THOUSANDS)	108 465	70 469	37 996	95 174	13 291	95 293	13 172	9 111	99 354
CONSUMER UNIT CHARACTERISTICS									
Average Income Before Taxes[1]	$43 951	$53 056	$27 514	$45 597	$32 414	$45 688	$30 427	$33 803	$44 955
Age Of Reference Person	47.9	52.1	40.1	47.5	50.9	48.3	44.9	41.2	48.5
Average Number In Consumer Unit									
Persons	2.5	2.6	2.3	2.5	2.5	2.5	2.7	3.5	2.4
Children under 18	0.7	0.7	0.7	0.7	0.6	0.6	0.9	1.3	0.6
Persons 65 and over	0.3	0.4	0.2	0.3	0.4	0.3	0.2	0.2	0.3
Earners	1.3	1.4	1.2	1.4	1.3	1.4	1.3	1.6	1.3
Vehicles	1.9	2.3	1.2	1.9	2.4	2.0	1.3	1.6	2.0
PERCENT HOMEOWNER	65	100	. . .	63	82	68	47	44	67
With mortgage	38	59	. . .	38	37	39	29	30	39
Without mortgage	27	41	. . .	24	45	28	17	14	28
AVERAGE ANNUAL EXPENDITURES	$36 995	$42 753	$26 310	$37 871	$30 817	$38 323	$27 340	$33 044	$37 356
Food	5 031	5 580	4 009	5 145	4 262	5 149	4 146	5 493	4 986
Food at home	2 915	3 205	2 376	2 949	2 688	2 948	2 665	3 556	2 854
Cereals and bakery products	448	495	361	455	405	454	405	495	444
Meats, poultry, fish, and eggs	749	808	638	758	687	732	878	1 097	716
Dairy products	322	357	257	323	319	334	233	377	317
Fruits and vegetables	500	549	407	509	436	508	439	663	484
Other food at home	896	995	713	905	841	921	710	924	894
Food away from home	2 116	2 376	1 633	2 196	1 574	2 201	1 482	1 937	2 132
Alcoholic Beverages	318	320	313	335	202	339	158	269	322
Housing	12 057	13 647	9 105	12 550	8 526	12 380	9 707	11 001	12 154
Shelter	7 016	7 552	6 022	7 429	4 057	7 225	5 501	6 778	7 038
Owned dwellings	4 525	6 926	71	4 720	3 127	4 780	2 675	3 186	4 647
Rented dwellings	2 027	56	5 681	2 211	705	1 936	2 683	3 420	1 899
Other lodging	465	569	270	498	226	509	142	171	491
Utilities, fuels, and public services	2 377	2 796	1 600	2 376	2 391	2 374	2 403	2 124	2 401
Household operations	666	837	348	710	349	695	457	470	684
Housekeeping supplies	498	606	298	499	491	516	362	445	503
Household furnishings and equipment	1 499	1 856	836	1 536	1 237	1 570	984	1 184	1 529
Apparel And Services	1 743	1 926	1 403	1 818	1 224	1 725	1 877	2 071	1 712
Transportation	7 011	8 118	4 959	6 973	7 288	7 275	5 106	6 801	7 031
Vehicle purchases (net outlay)	3 305	3 807	2 375	3 221	3 909	3 434	2 374	3 362	3 300
Gasoline and motor oil	1 055	1 209	768	1 036	1 187	1 096	757	1 116	1 049
Other vehicle expenses	2 254	2 645	1 528	2 289	2 007	2 333	1 683	1 979	2 279
Public transportation	397	456	289	427	185	412	292	344	402
Health Care	1 959	2 441	1 065	1 934	2 134	2 078	1 093	1 119	2 036
Health insurance	923	1 151	498	905	1 050	972	564	534	958
Medical services	558	706	283	561	534	602	239	313	580
Drugs	370	447	226	359	445	388	235	211	385
Medical supplies	109	136	58	109	106	116	56	62	113
Entertainment	1 891	2 298	1 135	1 921	1 674	2 022	936	1 245	1 950
Personal Care Products And Services	408	471	291	419	337	409	401	404	409
Reading	159	193	98	164	126	170	81	71	168
Education	635	672	565	688	250	666	410	366	659
Tobacco Products And Smoking Supplies	300	294	312	287	391	313	208	172	312
Miscellaneous	867	1 030	564	872	834	908	570	637	888
Cash Contributions	1 181	1 544	507	1 209	982	1 269	541	678	1 227
Personal Insurance And Pensions	3 436	4 219	1 985	3 555	2 586	3 620	2 107	2 718	3 502
Life and other personal insurance	394	525	152	402	343	406	308	191	413
Pensions and Social Security	3 042	3 693	1 833	3 153	2 243	3 214	1 799	2 528	3 089

1. Components of income and taxes are derived from "complete income reporters" only.

Table 7-8. Consumer Expenditures, Averages by Region of Residence, 1999

Item	All consumer units	Northeast	Midwest	South	West
NUMBER OF CONSUMER UNITS (THOUSANDS)	108 465	20 979	25 765	37 816	23 906
CONSUMER UNIT CHARACTERISTICS					
Average Income Before Taxes[1]	$43 951	$48 307	$41 983	$40 387	$47 494
Age Of Reference Person	47.9	49.3	48.4	47.6	46.6
Average Number In Consumer Unit					
Persons	2.5	2.5	2.5	2.5	2.6
Children under 18	0.7	0.6	0.7	0.7	0.7
Persons 65 and over	0.3	0.3	0.3	0.3	0.3
Earners	1.3	1.4	1.4	1.3	1.4
Vehicles	1.9	1.6	2.1	1.9	2.0
PERCENT HOMEOWNER	65	63	69	67	59
With mortgage	38	35	39	38	40
Without mortgage	27	28	30	29	19
AVERAGE ANNUAL EXPENDITURES	$36 995	$38 403	$36 302	$33 303	$42 335
Food	5 031	5 480	4 865	4 615	5 462
Food at home	2 915	3 084	2 740	2 729	3 245
Cereals and bakery products	448	487	428	416	485
Meats, poultry, fish, and eggs	749	830	655	739	793
Dairy products	322	361	307	290	355
Fruits and vegetables	500	564	438	451	584
Other food at home	896	843	912	832	1 029
Food away from home	2 116	2 396	2 126	1 887	2 216
Alcoholic Beverages	318	367	324	256	365
Housing	12 057	13 366	11 525	10 338	14 199
Shelter	7 016	8 256	6 491	5 540	8 827
Owned dwellings	4 525	5 313	4 451	3 541	5 468
Rented dwellings	2 027	2 423	1 599	1 645	2 743
Other lodging	465	520	441	354	616
Utilities, fuels, and public services	2 377	2 455	2 401	2 445	2 178
Household operations	666	658	587	555	933
Housekeeping supplies	498	502	541	458	512
Household furnishings and equipment	1 499	1 496	1 506	1 339	1 749
Apparel And Services	1 743	1 817	1 591	1 598	2 070
Transportation	7 011	6 466	6 939	6 863	7 802
Vehicle purchases (net outlay)	3 305	2 706	3 382	3 466	3 495
Gasoline and motor oil	1 055	907	1 038	1 069	1 180
Other vehicle expenses	2 254	2 315	2 169	2 043	2 625
Public transportation	397	538	349	286	503
Health Care	1 959	1 804	2 087	1 956	1 962
Health insurance	923	840	1 009	926	896
Medical services	558	568	559	524	600
Drugs	370	292	405	412	334
Medical supplies	109	103	114	93	132
Entertainment	1 891	1 828	2 067	1 567	2 269
Personal Care Products And Services	408	404	401	385	457
Reading	159	195	166	117	189
Education	635	939	568	452	728
Tobacco Products And Smoking Supplies	300	318	346	302	232
Miscellaneous	867	827	854	778	1 057
Cash Contributions	1 181	1 100	1 151	1 132	1 362
Personal Insurance And Pensions	3 436	3 494	3 418	2 946	4 181
Life and other personal insurance	394	403	378	411	379
Pensions and Social Security	3 042	3 092	3 041	2 535	3 801

1. Components of income and taxes are derived from "complete income reporters" only.

Table 7-9. Consumer Expenditures, Averages by Occupation of Reference Person, 1999

Item	All consumer units	Self-employed workers	Wage and salary earners						Retired	All other, including not reporting
			Total wage and salary earners	Managers and Professionals	Technical sales and clerical workers	Service workers	Construction workers and mechanics	Operators fabricators and laborers		
NUMBER OF CONSUMER UNITS (THOUSANDS)	108 465	6 077	71 180	24 961	20 248	9 389	4 900	11 681	19 665	11 544
CONSUMER UNIT CHARACTERISTICS										
Average Income Before Taxes[1]	$43 951	$56 480	$50 710	$71 439	$42 965	$32 159	$47 750	$35 179	$24 217	$26 886
Age Of Reference Person	47.9	49.7	41.1	43.2	39.8	40.4	40.8	39.9	72.6	46.5
Average Number In Consumer Unit										
Persons	2.5	2.5	2.7	2.6	2.5	2.7	3.1	3.0	1.7	2.8
Children under 18	0.7	0.6	0.8	0.7	0.7	0.8	1.0	1.0	0.1	0.9
Persons 65 and over	0.3	0.2	0.1	0.1	0.1	0.1	0.1	0.1	1.2	0.2
Earners	1.3	1.7	1.7	1.7	1.7	1.7	1.9	1.8	0.2	0.7
Vehicles	1.9	2.2	2.1	2.2	1.9	1.7	2.7	2.1	1.6	1.5
PERCENT HOMEOWNER	65	79	62	72	57	47	69	57	81	51
With mortgage	38	47	45	56	41	30	50	38	17	27
Without mortgage	27	32	17	16	15	17	19	19	64	24
AVERAGE ANNUAL EXPENDITURES	$36 995	$47 496	$40 603	$53 159	$36 595	$28 870	$37 351	$31 607	$26 284	$27 357
Food	5 031	6 143	5 495	6 591	5 091	4 284	5 461	4 873	3 424	4 253
Food at home	2 915	3 286	3 074	3 402	2 858	2 659	3 310	2 987	2 241	2 866
Cereals and bakery products	448	497	470	530	440	411	493	434	355	444
Meats, poultry, fish, and eggs	749	827	787	802	717	746	928	843	562	786
Dairy products	322	371	338	382	314	284	353	321	252	320
Fruits and vegetables	500	566	515	602	470	443	507	472	436	476
Other food at home	896	1 026	965	1 086	916	775	1 029	917	637	840
Food away from home	2 116	2 857	2 421	3 189	2 233	1 625	2 152	1 886	1 183	1 387
Alcoholic Beverages	318	394	370	499	300	284	296	319	177	188
Housing	12 057	14 249	13 113	17 230	12 088	9 710	11 646	9 461	8 988	9 613
Shelter	7 016	8 071	7 850	10 467	7 258	5 820	6 805	5 353	4 560	5 501
Owned dwellings	4 525	5 908	5 071	7 470	4 384	2 876	4 708	3 051	3 026	2 984
Rented dwellings	2 027	1 474	2 292	2 151	2 520	2 696	1 758	2 100	1 110	2 240
Other lodging	465	688	487	846	354	248	340	202	425	278
Utilities, fuels, and public services	2 377	2 748	2 434	2 784	2 292	2 068	2 460	2 214	2 147	2 228
Household operations	666	777	674	1 037	607	318	539	357	770	380
Housekeeping supplies	498	729	510	637	511	347	450	399	436	411
Household furnishings and equipment	1 499	1 924	1 645	2 305	1 419	1 156	1 392	1 137	1 075	1 093
Apparel And Services	1 743	2 326	1 953	2 510	1 812	1 462	1 457	1 627	1 073	1 258
Transportation	7 011	8 066	7 924	9 768	7 225	5 860	8 116	6 776	4 469	5 157
Vehicle purchases (net outlay)	3 305	3 460	3 795	4 657	3 505	2 732	3 742	3 333	1 934	2 539
Gasoline and motor oil	1 055	1 184	1 188	1 297	1 085	985	1 475	1 175	672	819
Other vehicle expenses	2 254	2 873	2 529	3 168	2 302	1 836	2 595	2 088	1 475	1 557
Public transportation	397	549	412	646	332	308	304	180	388	242
Health Care	1 959	2 755	1 655	2 155	1 456	1 193	1 541	1 354	3 026	1 595
Health insurance	923	1 295	771	973	712	551	772	615	1 521	644
Medical services	558	805	521	713	417	359	450	448	660	481
Drugs	370	516	265	331	239	221	225	221	686	406
Medical supplies	109	138	99	137	88	62	94	71	160	64
Entertainment	1 891	2 498	2 060	2 768	1 828	1 337	1 791	1 648	1 444	1 285
Personal Care Products And Services	408	569	443	558	400	356	382	373	303	284
Reading	159	216	162	249	140	92	119	88	165	105
Education	635	985	756	1 132	672	510	538	384	116	587
Tobacco Products And Smoking Supplies	300	341	326	225	306	343	497	491	165	349
Miscellaneous	867	1 086	899	1 194	798	549	997	692	809	649
Cash Contributions	1 181	2 233	1 089	1 788	913	500	769	507	1 564	543
Personal Insurance And Pensions	3 436	5 634	4 359	6 492	3 568	2 390	3 742	3 014	559	1 492
Life and other personal insurance	394	601	423	654	322	240	324	293	275	313
Pensions and Social Security	3 042	5 033	3 936	5 838	3 246	2 149	3 418	2 721	284	1 179

1. Components of income and taxes are derived from "complete income reporters" only.

Table 7-10. Consumer Expenditures, Averages for Age Groups by Income Before Taxes, 1998–1999: Reference Person Under Age 25

Item	Complete reporting of income							
	Complete reporting of income, total	Less than $5,000	$5,000 to $9,999	$10,000 to $14,999	$15,000 to $19,999	$20,000 to $29,999	$30,000 to $39,999	$40,000 and over
NUMBER OF CONSUMER UNITS (THOUSANDS)	6 214	1 461	1 089	871	687	961	526	618
CONSUMER UNIT CHARACTERISTICS								
Average Income Before Taxes[1]	$17 547	$2 769	$7 174	$12 071	$17 162	$24 321	$34 391	$54 033
Age Of Reference Person	21.4	20.4	20.9	21.5	21.9	22.3	22.1	22.6
Average Number In Consumer Unit								
Persons	1.8	1.3	1.5	1.6	1.9	2.1	2.3	2.8
Children under 18	0.4	0.2	0.3	0.3	0.4	0.4	0.5	0.6
Persons 65 and over	(2)	(2)	(2)	(2)	(2)	(2)	(2)	(2)
Earners	1.3	1.0	1.0	1.1	1.4	1.5	1.7	2.0
Vehicles	1.1	0.5	0.7	1.0	1.2	1.5	1.8	2.2
PERCENT HOMEOWNER	10	3	5	4	8	14	25	30
With mortgage	7	(3)	1	1	5	10	20	26
Without mortgage	3	3	4	3	3	4	5	4
AVERAGE ANNUAL EXPENDITURES	$21 532	$11 596	$13 520	$18 138	$21 806	$27 698	$30 577	$43 178
Food	3 231	1 981	2 547	2 668	3 161	3 577	4 494	4 996
Food at home	1 585	843	1 247	1 278	1 837	1 723	2 184	2 485
Cereals and bakery products	234	127	191	203	254	236	317	380
Meats, poultry, fish, and eggs	370	164	293	305	382	444	511	602
Dairy products	186	123	143	146	226	192	266	263
Fruits and vegetables	254	135	190	193	349	293	358	345
Other food at home	541	294	431	432	625	558	732	895
Food away from home	1 646	1 139	1 300	1 390	1 325	1 855	2 309	2 511
Alcoholic Beverages	375	298	190	342	364	462	493	581
Housing	6 457	3 280	4 189	5 510	7 298	8 007	9 453	12 948
Shelter	4 001	2 106	2 776	3 450	4 821	5 016	5 832	7 364
Owned dwellings	467	112	98	61	237	635	1 137	1 951
Rented dwellings	3 291	1 610	2 435	3 233	4 326	4 209	4 544	5 211
Other lodging	243	384	242	156	258	173	151	202
Utilities, fuels, and public services	1 130	542	741	1 074	1 301	1 485	1 713	2 044
Household operations	204	94	80	167	258	219	335	535
Housekeeping supplies	218	94	140	152	186	239	242	544
Household furnishings and equipment	904	443	452	667	732	1 048	1 331	2 462
Apparel And Services	1 239	685	837	1 151	1 107	1 606	1 448	2 222
Transportation	4 838	2 211	1 872	4 322	4 888	7 312	7 027	11 224
Vehicle purchases (net outlay)	2 640	1 162	659	2 556	2 702	4 419	3 302	6 344
Gasoline and motor oil	700	393	471	605	685	906	1 130	1 294
Other vehicle expenses	1 293	442	599	986	1 311	1 791	2 347	3 259
Public transportation	205	215	144	175	190	197	249	328
Health Care	532	193	206	362	639	771	979	1 245
Health insurance	236	52	74	152	263	359	516	615
Medical services	173	76	67	82	198	290	278	418
Drugs	92	46	43	107	147	82	137	160
Medical supplies	31	[4]19	23	[4]21	32	39	48	52
Entertainment	1 105	676	797	1 117	887	1 212	1 530	2 247
Personal Care Products And Services	281	171	188	233	261	348	342	496
Reading	69	51	56	62	75	70	103	114
Education	1 234	1 555	1 729	978	1 211	1 207	689	491
Tobacco Products And Smoking Supplies	220	115	128	219	239	301	315	405
Miscellaneous	336	107	155	215	277	653	487	760
Cash Contributions	238	77	171	158	164	251	291	870
Personal Insurance And Pensions	1 375	197	456	801	1 235	1 921	2 926	4 578
Life and other personal insurance	59	[4]22	[4]42	[4]17	44	88	102	168
Pensions and Social Security	1 316	175	414	784	1 190	1 833	2 825	4 409

1. Components of income and taxes are derived from "complete income reporters" only.
2. Value less than 0.05.
3. Value less than 0.5.
4. Data are likely to have large sampling errors.

Table 7-11. Consumer Expenditures, Averages for Age Groups by Income Before Taxes, 1998–1999: Reference Person Age 25–34

Item	Complete reporting of income									
	Complete reporting of income, total	Less than $5,000	$5,000 to $9,999	$10,000 to $14,999	$15,000 to $19,999	$20,000 to $29,999	$30,000 to $39,999	$40,000 to $49,999	$50,000 to $69,999	$70,000 and over
NUMBER OF CONSUMER UNITS (THOUSANDS)	18 558	591	870	1 038	1 040	2 528	2 404	2 122	3 433	4 533
CONSUMER UNIT CHARACTERISTICS										
Average Income Before Taxes[1]	$52 216	$1 152	$7 662	$12 638	$17 447	$24 584	$34 497	$44 313	$58 412	$108 269
Age Of Reference Person	39.5	39.1	39.4	39.5	39.2	39.3	39.4	39.6	39.6	39.8
Average Number In Consumer Unit										
Persons	3.2	2.8	2.4	3.0	3.0	3.1	3.0	3.2	3.4	3.6
Children under 18	1.3	1.2	0.9	1.4	1.4	1.3	1.2	1.3	1.4	1.4
Persons 65 and over	(2)	(2)	(2)	(2)	(2)	(2)	(2)	(2)	(2)	(2)
Earners	1.7	1.2	0.9	1.2	1.4	1.5	1.7	1.8	2.0	2.0
Vehicles	2.2	1.4	1.1	1.2	1.6	1.8	2.2	2.4	2.6	2.8
PERCENT HOMEOWNER	68	45	30	37	41	57	62	68	81	90
With mortgage	57	29	16	23	28	42	51	58	72	82
Without mortgage	11	16	13	14	13	15	11	10	9	8
AVERAGE ANNUAL EXPENDITURES	$44 920	$23 949	$18 379	$20 390	$25 450	$28 479	$34 910	$40 994	$50 010	$75 542
Food	6 179	4 167	4 391	3 538	4 532	4 471	5 003	5 821	6 989	9 017
Food at home	3 541	2 778	3 033	2 332	2 947	2 837	2 976	3 518	3 953	4 599
Cereals and bakery products	562	427	516	391	438	447	456	528	649	738
Meats, poultry, fish, and eggs	894	757	917	672	851	748	776	907	971	1 060
Dairy products	407	282	311	278	319	318	342	396	472	538
Fruits and vegetables	562	480	419	333	441	472	497	568	575	763
Other food at home	1 115	833	870	658	899	852	906	1 119	1 287	1 500
Food away from home	2 638	1 389	1 359	1 206	1 585	1 634	2 026	2 303	3 035	4 418
Alcoholic Beverages	397	321	252	119	155	253	283	369	415	707
Housing	14 346	8 662	7 031	7 902	8 563	9 952	10 883	12 397	14 998	24 046
Shelter	8 479	5 279	4 043	4 823	5 188	5 711	6 541	7 385	8 693	14 261
Owned dwellings	6 000	2 655	1 228	1 524	2 095	2 971	3 880	4 724	6 760	12 107
Rented dwellings	2 083	2 433	2 767	3 241	2 957	2 611	2 487	2 408	1 533	1 195
Other lodging	396	[3]191	[3]48	57	137	129	174	254	401	958
Utilities, fuels, and public services	2 648	1 970	1 723	1 946	1 963	2 322	2 355	2 574	2 869	3 435
Household operations	817	300	272	159	349	285	373	537	743	1 967
Housekeeping supplies	629	292	334	310	323	382	473	522	810	1 027
Household furnishings and equipment	1 773	820	659	665	738	1 252	1 140	1 378	1 883	3 356
Apparel And Services	2 219	1 724	1 065	1 351	1 648	1 411	2 000	2 065	2 172	3 531
Transportation	8 296	4 308	2 345	3 109	5 027	5 404	6 732	8 124	9 643	13 398
Vehicle purchases (net outlay)	3 935	1 726	[3]1 026	1 226	2 446	2 480	2 889	3 853	4 656	6 599
Gasoline and motor oil	1 260	859	532	639	883	970	1 205	1 356	1 463	1 672
Other vehicle expenses	2 704	1 532	673	1 060	1 539	1 758	2 371	2 639	3 174	4 269
Public transportation	398	191	114	184	159	197	267	277	350	859
Health Care	1 728	954	616	834	924	1 250	1 438	1 723	2 097	2 582
Health insurance	787	382	278	305	434	607	727	800	896	1 172
Medical services	564	335	179	196	257	383	428	525	722	896
Drugs	266	193	125	219	200	203	207	307	335	325
Medical supplies	112	[3]44	[3]33	114	34	58	77	91	145	188
Entertainment	2 419	1 130	938	936	1 020	1 259	1 616	2 227	2 992	4 286
Personal Care Products And Services	499	453	318	269	219	285	458	414	547	818
Reading	170	108	45	62	63	114	125	150	199	295
Education	614	177	106	180	407	262	345	572	601	1 286
Tobacco Products And Smoking Supplies	375	445	405	446	432	372	387	393	449	261
Miscellaneous	1 048	488	299	451	605	648	1 015	1 095	1 240	1 578
Cash Contributions	1 070	[3]522	[3]136	330	390	459	923	755	1 210	2 105
Personal Insurance And Pensions	5 559	491	431	862	1 466	2 339	3 701	4 889	6 458	11 632
Life and other personal insurance	429	[3]285	69	88	190	196	301	325	478	861
Pensions and Social Security	5 130	206	362	775	1 275	2 143	3 400	4 564	5 981	10 771

1. Components of income and taxes are derived from "complete income reporters" only.
2. Value less than 0.05.
3. Data are likely to have large sampling errors.

Table 7-12. Consumer Expenditures, Averages for Age Groups by Income Before Taxes, 1998–1999: Reference Person Age 35–44

Item	Complete reporting of income									
	Complete reporting of income, total	Less than $5,000	$5,000 to $9,999	$10,000 to $14,999	$15,000 to $19,999	$20,000 to $29,999	$30,000 to $39,999	$40,000 to $49,999	$50,000 to $69,999	$70,000 and over
NUMBER OF CONSUMER UNITS (THOUSANDS)	18 558	591	870	1 038	1 040	2 528	2 404	2 122	3 433	4 533
CONSUMER UNIT CHARACTERISTICS										
Average Income Before Taxes[1]	$52 216	$1 152	$7 662	$12 638	$17 447	$24 584	$34 497	$44 313	$58 412	$108 269
Age Of Reference Person	40.0	39.0	39.0	40.0	39.0	39.0	39.0	40.0	40.0	40.0
Average Number In Consumer Unit										
Persons	3.0	3.0	2.0	3.0	3.0	3.0	3.0	3.0	3.0	4.0
Children under 18	1.0	1.0	1.0	1.0	1.0	1.0	1.0	1.0	1.0	1.0
Persons 65 and over	(2)	(2)	(2)	(2)	(2)	(2)	(2)	(2)	(2)	(2)
Earners	2.0	1.0	1.0	1.0	1.0	2.0	2.0	2.0	2.0	2.0
Vehicles	2.0	1.0	1.0	1.0	2.0	2.0	2.0	2.0	3.0	3.0
PERCENT HOMEOWNER	68	45	30	37	41	57	62	68	81	90
With mortgage	57	29	16	23	28	42	51	58	72	82
Without mortgage	11	16	13	14	13	15	11	10	9	8
AVERAGE ANNUAL EXPENDITURES	$44 920	$23 949	$18 379	$20 390	$25 450	$28 479	$34 910	$40 994	$50 010	$75 542
Food	6 179	4 167	4 391	3 538	4 532	4 471	5 003	5 821	6 989	9 017
Food at home	3 541	2 778	3 033	2 332	2 947	2 837	2 976	3 518	3 953	4 599
Cereals and bakery products	562	427	516	391	438	447	456	528	649	738
Meats, poultry, fish, and eggs	894	757	917	672	851	748	776	907	971	1 060
Dairy products	407	282	311	278	319	318	342	396	472	538
Fruits and vegetables	562	480	419	333	441	472	497	568	575	763
Other food at home	1 115	833	870	658	899	852	906	1 119	1 287	1 500
Food away from home	2 638	1 389	1 359	1 206	1 585	1 634	2 026	2 303	3 035	4 418
Alcoholic Beverages	397	321	252	119	155	253	283	369	415	707
Housing	14 346	8 662	7 031	7 902	8 563	9 052	10 883	12 397	14 008	24 046
Shelter	8 479	5 279	4 043	4 823	5 188	5 711	6 541	7 385	8 693	14 201
Owned dwellings	6 000	2 655	1 228	1 524	2 095	2 971	3 880	4 724	6 760	12 107
Rented dwellings	2 083	2 433	2 767	3 241	2 957	2 611	2 487	2 408	1 533	1 195
Other lodging	396	[3]191	[3]48	57	137	129	174	254	401	958
Utilities, fuels, and public services	2 648	1 970	1 723	1 946	1 963	2 322	2 355	2 574	2 869	3 435
Household operations	817	300	272	159	349	285	373	537	743	1 967
Housekeeping supplies	629	292	334	310	323	382	473	522	810	1 027
Household furnishings and equipment	1 773	820	659	665	738	1 252	1 140	1 378	1 883	3 356
Apparel And Services	2 219	1 724	1 065	1 351	1 648	1 411	2 000	2 065	2 172	3 531
Transportation	8 296	4 308	2 345	3 109	5 027	5 404	6 732	8 124	9 643	13 398
Vehicle purchases (net outlay)	3 935	[3]1 726	1 026	1 226	2 446	2 480	2 889	3 853	4 656	6 599
Gasoline and motor oil	1 260	859	532	639	883	970	1 205	1 356	1 463	1 672
Other vehicle expenses	2 704	1 532	673	1 060	1 539	1 758	2 371	2 639	3 174	4 269
Public transportation	398	191	114	184	159	197	267	277	350	859
Health Care	1 728	954	616	834	924	1 250	1 438	1 723	2 097	2 582
Health insurance	787	382	278	305	434	607	727	800	896	1 172
Medical services	564	335	179	196	257	383	428	525	722	896
Drugs	266	193	125	219	200	203	207	307	335	325
Medical supplies	112	[3]44	[3]33	114	34	58	77	91	145	188
Entertainment	2 419	1 130	938	936	1 020	1 259	1 616	2 227	2 992	4 286
Personal Care Products And Services	499	453	318	269	219	285	458	414	547	818
Reading	170	108	45	62	63	114	125	150	199	295
Education	614	177	106	180	407	262	345	572	601	1 286
Tobacco Products And Smoking Supplies	375	445	405	446	432	372	387	393	449	261
Miscellaneous	1 048	488	299	451	605	648	1 015	1 095	1 240	1 578
Cash Contributions	1 070	522	136	330	390	459	923	755	1 210	2 105
Personal Insurance And Pensions	5 559	491	431	862	1 466	2 339	3 701	4 889	6 458	11 632
Life and other personal insurance	429	285	69	88	190	196	301	325	478	861
Pensions and Social Security	5 130	206	362	775	1 275	2 143	3 400	4 564	5 981	10 771

1. Components of income and taxes are derived from "complete income reporters" only.
2. Value less than 0.05.
3. Data are likely to have large sampling errors.

Table 7-13. Consumer Expenditures, Averages for Age Groups by Income Before Taxes, 1998–1999: Reference Person Age 45–54

Item	Complete reporting of income									
	Complete reporting of income, total	Less than $5,000	$5,000 to $9,999	$10,000 to $14,999	$15,000 to $19,999	$20,000 to $29,999	$30,000 to $39,999	$40,000 to $49,999	$50,000 to $69,999	$70,000 and over
NUMBER OF CONSUMER UNITS (THOUSANDS)	15 468	455	739	779	783	1 540	1 849	1 594	2 794	4 934
CONSUMER UNIT CHARACTERISTICS										
Average Income Before Taxes[1]	$59 263	$-1 529	$7 644	$12 328	$17 433	$24 702	$34 355	$44 360	$58 925	$111 780
Age Of Reference Person	49.1	49.5	49.7	49.2	49.0	48.9	49.3	49.1	49.1	49.1
Average Number In Consumer Unit										
Persons	2.7	2.0	2.0	2.1	2.4	2.6	2.3	2.6	2.9	3.1
Children under 18	0.6	0.5	0.5	0.4	0.5	0.7	0.4	0.5	0.7	0.7
Persons 65 and over	(2)	(2)	(2)	(2)	0.1	(2)	(2)	(2)	(2)	(2)
Earners	1.8	0.9	0.7	1.1	1.2	1.5	1.6	1.8	2.1	2.3
Vehicles	2.5	1.3	1.1	1.6	1.6	2.0	2.3	2.4	2.8	3.2
PERCENT HOMEOWNER	76	41	34	52	51	60	70	79	86	93
With mortgage	56	22	12	30	24	39	47	61	65	77
Without mortgage	20	19	22	22	28	20	23	18	20	16
AVERAGE ANNUAL EXPENDITURES	$48 912	$21 936	$18 035	$22 126	$23 722	$30 140	$36 269	$40 659	$50 582	$77 186
Food	6 347	3 316	3 431	3 341	3 553	4 778	5 234	5 859	6 982	8 934
Food at home	3 593	2 264	2 457	2 181	2 528	3 302	3 182	3 502	4 095	4 370
Cereals and bakery products	534	339	346	321	368	489	464	529	576	676
Meats, poultry, fish, and eggs	926	622	759	601	771	841	857	897	1 119	1 021
Dairy products	379	239	277	230	258	345	331	350	420	476
Fruits and vegetables	614	376	385	371	463	586	507	607	683	764
Other food at home	1 142	687	690	658	668	1 040	1 024	1 120	1 297	1 433
Food away from home	2 754	1 052	974	1 160	1 026	1 476	2 052	2 358	2 887	4 563
Alcoholic Beverages	353	284	146	226	149	193	257	299	333	582
Housing	14 531	8 352	6 721	7 607	8 212	9 819	11 449	12 484	14 281	21 888
Shelter	8 392	4 890	3 887	4 204	4 735	5 736	6 297	7 245	7 946	12 869
Owned dwellings	6 050	2 175	1 357	1 861	1 790	3 070	3 912	5 074	6 154	10 436
Rented dwellings	1 566	2 502	2 391	2 184	2 775	2 504	2 051	1 703	1 163	775
Other lodging	776	213	139	159	170	161	335	469	629	1 658
Utilities, fuels, and public services	2 813	2 009	1 775	1 903	2 107	2 241	2 469	2 681	2 954	3 570
Household operations	564	228	100	301	140	196	262	447	483	1 084
Housekeeping supplies	647	269	272	435	238	490	662	585	818	836
Household furnishings and equipment	2 115	956	686	763	991	1 156	1 759	1 525	2 081	3 529
Apparel And Services	2 313	1 375	738	1 090	874	1 878	2 062	1 875	2 206	3 621
Transportation	9 005	3 310	3 248	4 379	5 278	5 609	6 701	7 390	10 134	13 528
Vehicle purchases (net outlay)	4 090	[3]1 126	[3]1 543	2 219	2 638	2 525	2 748	3 195	4 797	6 150
Gasoline and motor oil	1 342	746	609	791	841	991	1 147	1 319	1 529	1 756
Other vehicle expenses	3 068	1 293	819	1 220	1 675	1 896	2 495	2 545	3 379	4 663
Public transportation	506	145	277	149	124	197	311	330	429	959
Health Care	2 243	1 452	904	1 229	1 339	1 522	1 888	2 225	2 391	3 107
Health insurance	921	629	340	418	551	607	841	1 047	1 024	1 203
Medical services	776	455	242	385	306	462	562	599	795	1 246
Drugs	415	286	271	370	441	329	405	463	418	469
Medical supplies	131	81	51	56	40	123	80	116	154	189
Entertainment	2 350	965	612	1 072	813	1 279	1 876	1 682	2 533	3 845
Personal Care Products And Services	560	543	369	312	271	442	416	473	580	812
Reading	219	108	64	66	83	102	141	175	232	370
Education	1 018	386	144	83	161	343	508	445	1 085	2 045
Tobacco Products And Smoking Supplies	380	340	444	444	435	423	390	423	354	338
Miscellaneous	1 152	586	305	732	630	778	800	939	1 125	1 841
Cash Contributions	1 652	[3]174	355	455	523	609	827	1 260	1 412	3 249
Personal Insurance And Pensions	6 790	746	554	1 091	1 401	2 366	3 722	5 129	6 931	13 024
Life and other personal insurance	612	382	177	262	203	222	370	363	514	1 168
Pensions and Social Security	6 178	363	378	829	1 199	2 144	3 352	4 767	6 417	11 856

1. Components of income and taxes are derived from "complete income reporters" only.
2. Value less than 0.05.
3. Data are likely to have large sampling errors.

Table 7-14. Consumer Expenditures, Averages for Age Groups by Income Before Taxes, 1998–1999: Reference Person Age 55–64

Item	Complete reporting of income									
	Complete reporting of income, total	Less than $5,000	$5,000 to $9,999	$10,000 to $14,999	$15,000 to $19,999	$20,000 to $29,999	$30,000 to $39,999	$40,000 to $49,999	$50,000 to $69,999	$70,000 and over
NUMBER OF CONSUMER UNITS (THOUSANDS)	9 768	417	1 024	912	803	1 410	1 049	961	1 161	2 032
CONSUMER UNIT CHARACTERISTICS										
Average Income Before Taxes[1]	$46 870	$2 102	$7 647	$12 455	$17 221	$24 669	$34 478	$44 481	$58 787	$119 082
Age Of Reference Person	59.3	59.5	60.4	59.8	59.6	60.0	59.0	59.0	58.7	58.5
Average Number In Consumer Unit										
Persons	2.1	1.6	1.7	2.0	2.0	2.0	2.2	2.2	2.4	2.5
Children under 18	0.2	[2]0.1	0.2	0.3	0.2	0.1	0.2	0.1	0.2	0.2
Persons 65 and over	0.1	[2]0.1	[2]0.1	0.1	0.2	0.1	0.1	0.1	0.1	0.1
Earners	1.3	0.7	0.5	0.8	0.9	1.1	1.4	1.5	1.8	2.0
Vehicles	2.2	1.3	1.2	1.9	1.7	2.3	2.1	2.6	2.6	2.9
PERCENT HOMEOWNER	78	54	54	63	65	82	83	84	87	94
With mortgage	39	17	14	19	22	32	42	44	51	66
Without mortgage	39	37	40	43	43	51	41	40	35	28
AVERAGE ANNUAL EXPENDITURES	$40 457	$21 778	$15 719	$20 442	$21 673	$28 571	$35 759	$40 725	$49 237	$78 680
Food	5 097	2 885	2 444	2 938	3 154	4 096	4 852	5 349	6 115	8 720
Food at home	2 957	2 104	1 779	2 078	2 078	2 677	2 915	3 254	3 370	4 308
Cereals and bakery products	430	312	260	304	305	355	436	479	483	638
Meats, poultry, fish, and eggs	782	642	523	579	552	737	726	893	845	1 108
Dairy products	317	198	195	233	234	274	319	338	389	441
Fruits and vegetables	536	418	281	357	359	478	545	581	622	804
Other food at home	893	535	520	606	627	832	889	963	1 031	1 317
Food away from home	2 139	781	665	860	1 076	1 419	1 937	2 095	2 745	4 411
Alcoholic Beverages	342	241	74	168	140	239	246	257	546	676
Housing	12 188	8 702	6 158	7 371	7 480	8 823	11 054	11 590	14 641	21 745
Shelter	6 647	4 641	3 148	3 926	3 945	4 451	6 336	5 966	7 891	12 407
Owned dwellings	4 730	2 454	1 515	1 688	1 931	3 101	4 668	4 174	5 818	10 090
Rented dwellings	1 250	1 985	1 450	1 933	1 719	1 007	1 341	1 343	1 140	649
Other lodging	667	202	182	305	295	344	327	448	934	1 668
Utilities, fuels, and public services	2 565	1 935	1 794	1 993	2 010	2 313	2 466	2 644	2 848	3 584
Household operations	482	447	128	187	145	288	271	369	473	1 235
Housekeeping supplies	586	279	329	318	466	487	528	634	748	918
Household furnishings and equipment	1 908	1 400	759	948	914	1 284	1 454	1 983	2 581	3 602
Apparel And Services	1 664	675	768	571	729	1 273	1 257	1 550	1 764	3 767
Transportation	7 336	2 921	2 311	3 723	4 012	5 301	7 752	7 945	9 264	13 520
Vehicle purchases (net outlay)	3 221	[2]916	[2]812	[2]1 434	[2]1 469	2 138	4 034	3 708	3 866	6 135
Gasoline and motor oil	1 106	583	451	750	873	1 014	1 098	1 196	1 501	1 597
Other vehicle expenses	2 439	1 265	856	1 258	1 517	1 903	2 266	2 539	3 039	4 450
Public transportation	569	158	193	280	153	245	355	502	859	1 337
Health Care	2 394	1 645	1 280	1 803	2 258	2 261	2 224	2 379	2 721	3 423
Health insurance	1 040	639	542	729	994	1 126	1 028	1 052	1 185	1 387
Medical services	739	644	411	510	597	529	627	684	881	1 233
Drugs	482	301	278	488	598	479	431	454	491	602
Medical supplies	134	[2]61	48	75	70	128	138	190	164	202
Entertainment	2 168	1 665	736	988	936	1 613	1 599	1 909	2 291	4 713
Personal Care Products And Services	452	146	185	243	274	383	466	422	518	840
Reading	204	117	76	84	93	156	208	197	243	394
Education	432	[2]275	[2]45	251	107	160	275	210	393	1 268
Tobacco Products And Smoking Supplies	345	406	262	351	353	315	399	339	347	361
Miscellaneous	1 152	834	737	496	672	1 248	1 124	1 076	1 366	1 803
Cash Contributions	1 784	664	359	726	408	620	1 183	1 863	2 880	4 204
Personal Insurance And Pensions	4 899	603	282	729	1 056	2 083	3 119	5 631	6 249	13 248
Life and other personal insurance	630	214	134	293	252	453	468	1 247	782	1 095
Pensions and Social Security	4 268	389	149	436	804	1 630	2 651	4 385	5 467	12 153

1. Components of income and taxes are derived from "complete income reporters" only.
2. Data are likely to have large sampling errors.

Table 7-15. Consumer Expenditures, Averages for Age Groups by Income Before Taxes, 1998–1999: Reference Person Age 65 and Over

Item	Complete reporting of income, total	Complete reporting of income								
		Less than $5,000	$5,000 to $9,999	$10,000 to $14,999	$15,000 to $19,999	$20,000 to $29,999	$30,000 to $39,999	$40,000 to $49,999	$50,000 to $69,999	$70,000 and over
NUMBER OF CONSUMER UNITS (THOUSANDS)	17 348	504	3 314	3 816	2 548	3 169	1 578	782	883	754
CONSUMER UNIT CHARACTERISTICS										
Average Income Before Taxes[1]	$25 274	$2 326	$7 878	$12 307	$17 493	$24 329	$34 448	$44 493	$58 926	$134 453
Age Of Reference Person	74.6	74.1	76.5	76.1	74.3	74.0	73.3	72.1	72.1	71.4
Average Number In Consumer Unit										
Persons	1.7	1.4	1.3	1.4	1.8	1.9	2.0	2.1	2.3	2.5
Children under 18	0.1	(2)	0.1	(2)	0.1	0.1	0.1	[3]0.1	0.1	0.2
Persons 65 and over	1.4	1.2	1.1	1.2	1.5	1.6	1.6	1.5	1.5	1.5
Earners	0.4	0.3	0.2	0.2	0.3	0.5	0.6	0.8	1.1	1.4
Vehicles	1.6	1.1	0.8	1.2	1.5	1.9	2.1	2.4	2.7	2.8
PERCENT HOMEOWNER	79	60	61	76	85	89	86	93	92	95
With mortgage	16	13	7	14	15	16	19	23	28	41
Without mortgage	64	47	54	62	69	72	67	70	64	55
AVERAGE ANNUAL EXPENDITURES	$26 861	$18 178	$13 088	$19 229	$24 248	$28 753	$32 414	$40 402	$51 188	$79 558
Food	3 647	2 682	1 950	2 598	3 512	4 115	5 120	5 654	6 238	8 067
Food at home	2 351	1 690	1 477	1 889	2 421	2 607	3 208	3 266	3 692	3 913
Cereals and bakery products	372	247	252	303	378	420	529	474	586	548
Meats, poultry, fish, and eggs	589	450	371	454	629	653	793	798	905	1 018
Dairy products	260	213	153	218	264	287	340	369	443	436
Fruits and vegetables	453	321	278	382	442	510	624	605	686	788
Other food at home	677	460	424	532	708	737	922	1 021	1 072	1 122
Food away from home	1 296	992	473	710	1 091	1 508	1 912	2 388	2 547	4 154
Alcoholic Beverages	199	135	48	107	164	227	284	513	359	694
Housing	8 882	6 466	5 427	7 257	8 376	9 212	9 786	11 538	13 221	24 527
Shelter	4 506	3 999	2 806	4 036	4 217	4 584	5 083	5 700	6 351	10 748
Owned dwellings	2 947	2 184	1 356	2 467	2 807	3 236	3 272	4 185	4 765	8 038
Rented dwellings	1 149	1 596	1 359	1 328	1 154	923	1 192	744	778	724
Other lodging	410	219	90	241	256	425	620	771	808	1 985
Utilities, fuels, and public services	2 171	1 575	1 630	1 857	2 132	2 359	2 480	2 752	2 863	3 811
Household operations	665	189	337	379	520	546	476	879	1 031	4 637
Housekeeping supplies	439	254	201	332	434	546	515	630	671	1 134
Household furnishings and equipment	1 100	449	453	654	1 072	1 177	1 232	1 576	2 305	4 197
Apparel And Services	1 040	598	509	566	1 020	1 065	1 196	1 347	2 005	4 403
Transportation	4 337	2 830	1 693	3 233	3 773	4 987	4 877	8 367	8 762	11 279
Vehicle purchases (net outlay)	1 824	[3]1 264	680	1 493	1 521	1 973	1 599	4 197	3 759	5 005
Gasoline and motor oil	652	429	318	490	592	773	844	1 081	1 139	1 377
Other vehicle expenses	1 460	960	546	1 071	1 285	1 761	1 983	2 378	3 106	3 176
Public transportation	401	177	140	179	374	481	451	711	757	1 721
Health Care	3 103	2 219	1 851	2 504	3 654	3 640	3 867	3 826	4 143	4 612
Health insurance	1 589	1 057	1 029	1 323	1 671	1 894	2 027	1 963	2 008	2 394
Medical services	625	575	272	423	836	720	823	772	1 149	938
Drugs	724	471	471	627	918	871	797	730	834	999
Medical supplies	165	116	78	131	229	156	220	362	152	280
Entertainment	1 175	505	416	842	1 012	1 202	1 365	1 833	2 519	4 348
Personal Care Products And Services	366	286	175	274	329	418	532	595	612	842
Reading	173	99	75	133	163	198	234	257	323	398
Education	123	[3]44	29	44	41	131	159	146	535	674
Tobacco Products And Smoking Supplies	156	189	120	123	139	147	138	267	282	316
Miscellaneous	790	835	359	498	647	796	888	934	1 116	3 818
Cash Contributions	1 791	355	284	806	1 034	1 855	2 590	3 116	6 101	8 553
Personal Insurance And Pensions	1 079	935	151	243	383	762	1 378	2 010	4 972	7 027
Life and other personal insurance	349	422	135	195	272	403	520	491	769	1 058
Pensions and Social Security	730	513	16	48	111	359	858	1 520	4 202	5 969

1. Components of income and taxes are derived from "complete income reporters" only.
2. Value less than 0.05.
3. Data are likely to have large sampling errors.

Table 7-16. Consumer Expenditures, Averages for Single Men by Income Before Taxes, 1998–1999

Item	All single men	Complete reporting of income, total	Complete reporting of income: Less than $5,000	$5,000 to $9,999	$10,000 to $14,999	$15,000 to $19,999	$20,000 to $29,999	$30,000 to $39,999	$40,000 and over
NUMBER OF CONSUMER UNITS (THOUSANDS)	13 258	10 530	1 101	1 593	1 429	975	1 606	1 360	2 466
CONSUMER UNIT CHARACTERISTICS									
Average Income Before Taxes[1]	$28 509	$28 509	$1 297	$7 568	$12 122	$17 284	$24 496	$33 857	$67 782
Age Of Reference Person	43.9	43.9	32.9	48.5	50.3	45.3	42.9	41.5	43.5
Average Number In Consumer Unit									
Persons	1.0	1.0	1.0	1.0	1.0	1.0	1.0	1.0	1.0
Children under 18	(2)	(2)	(2)	(2)	(3)	(3)	(3)	(3)	(3)
Persons 65 and over	0.2	0.2	0.1	0.3	0.4	0.3	0.2	0.1	0.1
Earners	0.7	0.8	0.8	0.5	0.6	0.7	0.8	0.9	0.9
Vehicles	1.2	1.3	0.8	0.8	1.2	1.1	1.6	1.6	1.6
PERCENT HOMEOWNER	40	40	15	27	39	33	42	48	58
With mortgage	20	20	3	5	7	7	21	35	42
Without mortgage	20	20	12	21	32	26	21	14	15
AVERAGE ANNUAL EXPENDITURES	$23 739	$25 254	$12 943	$11 847	$17 434	$17 891	$22 804	$28 421	$46 219
Food	3 019	3 201	2 143	1 940	2 370	2 678	3 249	3 558	4 692
Food at home	1 348	1 433	880	1 126	1 295	1 397	1 621	1 398	1 770
Cereals and bakery products	198	207	119	178	211	212	241	192	233
Meats, poultry, fish, and eggs	341	360	189	283	318	383	396	327	465
Dairy products	140	151	105	130	147	162	171	128	173
Fruits and vegetables	221	236	121	181	218	202	283	228	306
Other food at home	448	478	345	353	401	438	531	523	593
Food away from home	1 672	1 768	1 263	814	1 076	1 281	1 628	2 160	2 923
Alcoholic Beverages	475	521	332	201	317	436	572	485	890
Housing	7 962	8 136	4 499	4 465	5 990	6 271	7 679	8 967	13 887
Shelter	5 277	5 297	2 013	2 933	3 799	3 983	4 996	5 973	9 098
Owned dwellings	2 124	2 121	410	659	1 100	944	1 845	2 607	4 750
Rented dwellings	2 792	2 777	2 113	2 148	2 417	2 950	2 946	3 143	3 309
Other lodging	362	398	390	126	199	89	204	223	1 039
Utilities, fuels, and public services	1 443	1 475	839	1 006	1 258	1 379	1 525	1 706	2 065
Household operations	240	267	98	55	328	156	199	209	564
Housekeeping supplies	197	224	101	112	196	169	227	231	356
Household furnishings and equipment	806	874	548	359	409	584	733	848	1 805
Apparel And Services	806	874	304	402	370	399	924	1 276	1 619
Transportation	4 040	4 221	2 514	1 615	3 281	3 244	3 968	5 364	7 129
Vehicle purchases (net outlay)	1 683	1 753	[4]1 035	516	1 511	1 306	1 461	2 377	3 034
Gasoline and motor oil	700	723	503	393	621	632	770	968	965
Other vehicle expenses	1 373	1 457	728	549	990	1 139	1 518	1 716	2 582
Public transportation	285	287	248	156	160	169	219	303	548
Health Care	960	1 024	337	748	1 237	851	1 025	1 020	1 446
Health insurance	448	469	157	377	548	451	458	508	614
Medical services	291	318	109	169	321	215	335	336	526
Drugs	173	184	53	176	290	156	178	144	214
Medical supplies	48	53	[4]17	26	78	[4]28	54	32	91
Entertainment	1 302	1 324	681	628	935	804	1 108	1 504	2 499
Personal Care Products And Services	140	152	82	65	109	85	173	193	242
Reading	112	121	65	58	101	85	118	123	213
Education	493	506	1 093	760	380	529	501	111	368
Tobacco Products And Smoking Supplies	270	279	206	261	282	311	300	371	246
Miscellaneous	711	750	311	185	585	531	652	1 022	1 399
Cash Contributions	1 229	1 408	133	189	872	575	487	1 112	4 167
Personal Insurance And Pensions	2 219	2 737	242	332	605	1 092	2 049	3 312	7 421
Life and other personal insurance	152	159	35	75	80	120	151	149	342
Pensions and Social Security	2 066	2 577	207	257	524	971	1 898	3 164	7 079

1. Components of income and taxes are derived from "complete income reporters" only.
2. Value less than 0.05.
3. No data reported.
4. Data are likely to have large sampling errors.

Table 7-17. Consumer Expenditures, Averages for Single Women by Income Before Taxes, 1998–1999

Item	All single women	Complete reporting of income, total	Less than $5,000	$5,000 to $9,999	$10,000 to $14,999	$15,000 to $19,999	$20,000 to $29,999	$30,000 to $39,999	$40,000 and over
		Complete reporting of income							
NUMBER OF CONSUMER UNITS (THOUSANDS)	17 859	14 046	1 335	3 414	2 914	1 537	1 824	1 282	1 740
CONSUMER UNIT CHARACTERISTICS									
Average Income Before Taxes[1]	$20 779	$20 779	$2 559	$7 624	$12 168	$17 286	$24 447	$34 184	$64 340
Age Of Reference Person	55.8	55.8	39.6	63.2	65.8	57.2	52.0	46.6	46.4
Average Number In Consumer Unit									
Persons	1.0	1.0	1.0	1.0	1.0	1.0	1.0	1.0	1.0
Children under 18	(2)	(2)	(2)	(2)	(3)	(3)	(3)	(3)	(3)
Persons 65 and over	0.4	0.4	0.2	0.6	0.7	0.5	0.3	0.1	0.1
Earners	0.5	0.5	0.7	0.3	0.3	0.6	0.7	0.9	0.9
Vehicles	0.8	0.9	0.6	0.6	0.8	1.0	1.1	1.1	1.1
PERCENT HOMEOWNER	52	52	19	47	61	58	52	53	66
With mortgage	18	18	6	6	11	16	21	35	50
Without mortgage	35	34	13	42	50	42	32	18	16
AVERAGE ANNUAL EXPENDITURES	$20 575	$21 775	$12 016	$12 441	$17 597	$21 140	$24 713	$29 444	$46 763
Food	2 398	2 497	1 661	1 957	2 194	2 606	2 690	3 102	4 054
Food at home	1 488	1 540	1 038	1 372	1 504	1 701	1 566	1 563	2 177
Cereals and bakery products	233	241	160	229	254	253	233	237	306
Meats, poultry, fish, and eggs	333	334	206	337	327	376	311	278	466
Dairy products	163	170	119	148	174	191	183	173	219
Fruits and vegetables	291	299	210	253	298	349	319	299	406
Other food at home	469	497	343	405	450	530	521	575	781
Food away from home	910	956	623	585	689	905	1 124	1 539	1 877
Alcoholic Beverages	156	163	146	76	137	97	140	310	382
Housing	8 025	8 256	4 257	5 015	6 992	8 010	9 351	11 034	16 884
Shelter	4 762	4 807	2 712	2 704	4 031	4 576	5 441	7 017	9 753
Owned dwellings	2 242	2 255	598	1 026	1 908	2 105	2 220	3 334	5 893
Rented dwellings	2 274	2 297	1 940	1 575	1 932	2 248	2 974	3 376	3 135
Other lodging	246	255	174	104	190	222	247	307	725
Utilities, fuels, and public services	1 619	1 637	927	1 376	1 630	1 686	1 785	1 828	2 363
Household operations	470	531	86	316	350	600	396	243	1 884
Housekeeping supplies	293	326	152	204	303	364	405	394	604
Household furnishings and equipment	882	955	381	415	679	784	1 324	1 551	2 280
Apparel And Services	1 051	1 156	919	559	628	1 071	1 458	1 562	2 949
Transportation	2 985	3 085	1 537	1 551	2 593	3 242	3 515	5 195	5 973
Vehicle purchases (net outlay)	1 252	1 286	[4]536	653	1 225	1 353	1 259	2 439	2 323
Gasoline and motor oil	433	441	321	265	362	487	575	610	703
Other vehicle expenses	1 036	1 084	547	475	789	1 149	1 418	1 805	2 254
Public transportation	264	275	133	158	218	253	264	341	693
Health Care	1 515	1 585	753	1 330	1 989	2 082	1 524	1 339	1 860
Health insurance	692	707	288	693	961	844	637	571	680
Medical services	391	422	252	211	401	665	480	462	699
Drugs	350	365	177	356	524	471	293	239	342
Medical supplies	83	91	35	69	102	102	114	67	139
Entertainment	840	906	783	429	739	844	1 127	1 099	1 937
Personal Care Products And Services	335	361	201	237	321	424	339	567	639
Reading	128	137	71	69	121	137	176	209	253
Education	349	359	963	266	206	194	211	303	677
Tobacco Products And Smoking Supplies	117	121	112	104	118	144	150	97	130
Miscellaneous	639	696	293	403	528	578	866	674	1 807
Cash Contributions	775	888	127	237	648	802	1 294	642	2 979
Personal Insurance And Pensions	1 261	1 566	192	208	383	909	1 873	3 312	6 238
Life and other personal insurance	136	147	56	94	136	132	240	177	236
Pensions and Social Security	1 125	1 419	136	114	248	777	1 633	3 136	6 003

1. Components of income and taxes are derived from "complete income reporters" only.
2. Value less than 0.05.
3. No data reported.
4. Data are likely to have large sampling errors.

Table 7-18. Consumer Expenditures, Averages by Selected Metropolitan Statistical Areas, 1998–1999: Northeast Region

Item	Complete reporting of income				
	All consumer units in the Northeast	New York	Philadelphia	Boston	Pittsburgh
NUMBER OF CONSUMER UNITS (THOUSANDS)	20 933	7 633	1 912	2 456	1 094
CONSUMER UNIT CHARACTERISTICS					
Average Income Before Taxes[1]	$46 809	$55 680	$48 442	$51 409	$36 860
Age Of Reference Person	49.0	48.3	49.9	46.9	52.2
Average Number In Consumer Unit					
Persons	2.5	2.7	2.6	2.4	2.2
Children under 18	0.6	0.7	0.7	0.6	0.5
Persons 65 and over	0.3	0.3	0.3	0.3	0.4
Earners	1.3	1.4	1.4	1.4	1.2
Vehicles	1.7	1.4	1.8	1.6	1.8
PERCENT HOMEOWNER	62	53	73	62	68
AVERAGE ANNUAL EXPENDITURES	$37 950	$43 998	$40 147	$39 234	$34 511
Food	5 314	6 265	4 753	4 904	4 981
Food at home	3 001	3 374	2 596	2 486	2 803
Cereals and bakery products	474	525	381	382	465
Meats, poultry, fish, and eggs	808	983	768	659	715
Dairy products	342	375	291	285	331
Fruits and vegetables	539	628	474	508	447
Other food at home	838	863	681	653	846
Food away from home	2 313	2 891	2 157	2 417	2 177
Alcoholic Beverages	368	405	350	519	280
Housing	13 229	16 182	14 783	14 612	9 993
Shelter	8 150	10 554	9 239	9 480	4 946
Owned dwellings	5 209	6 404	6 615	6 111	3 080
Rented dwellings	2 390	3 544	1 875	2 396	1 587
Other lodging	550	606	750	973	278
Utilities, fuels, and public services	2 457	2 592	2 841	2 419	2 426
Household operations	581	758	518	667	398
Housekeeping supplies	474	497	477	363	688
Household furnishings and equipment	1 567	1 781	1 709	1 684	1 535
Apparel And Services	1 831	2 327	1 433	1 671	2 331
Transportation	6 503	6 972	7 896	6 312	5 795
Vehicle purchases (net outlay)	2 761	2 655	3 865	2 645	2 443
Gasoline and motor oil	901	877	869	923	862
Other vehicle expenses	2 266	2 523	2 706	2 143	2 184
Public transportation	575	917	457	600	307
Health Care	1 788	1 863	1 781	1 686	1 932
Entertainment	1 821	2 007	1 721	1 937	1 631
Personal Care Products And Services	399	485	295	344	522
Reading	198	216	192	226	181
Education	877	975	1 088	1 252	467
Tobacco Products And Smoking Supplies	309	304	260	292	296
Miscellaneous	857	924	927	710	986
Cash Contributions	994	1 021	1 093	1 138	1 408
Personal Insurance And Pensions	3 461	4 052	3 576	3 631	3 710
Life and other personal insurance	424	464	543	396	1 078
Pensions and Social Security	3 037	3 588	3 033	3 235	2 632

1. Components of income and taxes are derived from "complete income reporters" only.

Table 7-19. Consumer Expenditures, Averages by Selected Metropolitan Statistical Areas, 1998–1999: South Region

Item	Complete reporting of income							
	All consumer units in the South	Washington, D.C.	Baltimore	Atlanta	Miami	Tampa	Dallas-Fort Worth	Houston
NUMBER OF CONSUMER UNITS (THOUSANDS)	37 577	1 852	941	1 725	1 402	1 019	2 035	1 700
CONSUMER UNIT CHARACTERISTICS								
Average Income Before Taxes[1]	$39 371	$65 387	$48 355	$49 483	$45 233	$40 101	$52 874	$50 313
Age Of Reference Person	47.6	46.5	48.7	45.6	49.2	50.8	44.6	44.8
Average Number In Consumer Unit								
Persons	2.5	2.6	2.5	2.6	2.6	2.3	2.6	2.8
Children under 18	0.7	0.7	0.7	0.7	0.7	0.5	0.7	0.9
Persons 65 and over	0.3	0.3	0.3	0.2	0.4	0.4	0.2	0.2
Earners	1.3	1.5	1.3	1.5	1.4	1.2	1.5	1.5
Vehicles	1.9	1.9	1.7	2.0	1.6	1.7	1.9	1.9
PERCENT HOMEOWNER	67	64	66	68	64	70	59	56
AVERAGE ANNUAL EXPENDITURES	$33 135	$46 801	$39 782	$38 727	$38 099	$32 928	$44 224	$43 038
Food	4 533	5 358	5 165	4 449	4 791	4 750	6 490	5 624
Food at home	2 660	2 907	2 967	2 390	2 884	2 741	3 512	2 948
Cereals and bakery products	401	412	441	365	465	398	535	409
Meats, poultry, fish, and eggs	725	696	799	649	905	786	910	819
Dairy products	282	291	312	234	326	295	384	294
Fruits and vegetables	438	602	502	415	497	438	601	522
Other food at home	815	906	913	727	692	825	1 082	904
Food away from home	1 873	2 451	2 198	2 060	1 908	2 009	2 979	2 676
Alcoholic Beverages	253	419	371	240	306	405	329	412
Housing	10 303	16 386	13 484	13 740	13 966	11 040	13 227	13 108
Shelter	5 467	10 477	8 164	8 136	8 446	6 255	7 358	7 166
Owned dwellings	3 465	6 505	5 751	5 397	5 384	3 832	4 393	4 122
Rented dwellings	1 641	3 052	1 784	2 230	2 744	1 873	2 662	2 572
Other lodging	361	921	629	508	319	550	302	472
Utilities, fuels, and public services	2 482	2 640	2 356	3 054	2 724	2 457	2 909	2 882
Household operations	553	815	606	793	1 017	639	797	762
Housekeeping supplies	473	473	661	340	407	449	538	489
Household furnishings and equipment	1 328	1 981	1 697	1 417	1 372	1 240	1 624	1 809
Apparel And Services	1 610	2 279	1 660	1 712	1 734	1 330	2 492	1 950
Transportation	6 738	8 171	6 347	8 058	7 425	5 986	7 835	9 569
Vehicle purchases (net outlay)	3 354	3 914	2 801	3 814	2 840	2 602	3 687	5 039
Gasoline and motor oil	1 052	1 040	1 012	1 074	1 085	900	1 272	1 243
Other vehicle expenses	2 033	2 463	2 100	2 824	3 054	2 074	2 468	2 853
Public transportation	298	755	435	346	446	411	407	435
Health Care	1 971	2 202	1 581	1 835	1 481	2 294	2 148	1 919
Entertainment	1 574	2 261	2 104	1 692	1 780	1 471	2 011	1 847
Personal Care Products And Services	393	640	462	343	408	292	528	537
Reading	121	244	129	177	88	118	163	130
Education	431	856	671	545	433	392	535	490
Tobacco Products And Smoking Supplies	288	228	243	198	204	284	301	346
Miscellaneous	750	1 038	2 090	727	608	707	794	959
Cash Contributions	1 122	1 366	1 122	1 488	1 059	834	2 251	1 388
Personal Insurance And Pensions	3 048	5 353	4 354	3 523	3 815	3 026	5 121	4 758
Life and other personal insurance	414	674	433	503	341	324	545	478
Pensions and Social Security	2 635	4 679	3 921	3 020	3 474	2 702	4 575	4 280

1. Components of income and taxes are derived from "complete income reporters" only.

Table 7-20. Consumer Expenditures, Averages by Selected Metropolitan Statistical Areas, 1998–1999: Midwest Region

Item	Complete reporting of income								
	All consumer units in the Midwest	Chicago	Detroit	Milwaukee	Minneapolis-St. Paul	Cleveland	Cincinnati	St. Louis	Kansas City
NUMBER OF CONSUMER UNITS (THOUSANDS)	25 556	3 055	1 995	686	1 242	1 200	838	993	768
CONSUMER UNIT CHARACTERISTICS									
Average Income Before Taxes[1]	$41 447	$47 591	$47 539	$43 855	$58 032	$47 202	$44 872	$43 121	$49 495
Age Of Reference Person	48.2	48.3	47.2	49.0	47.0	49.7	47.5	50.8	43.8
Average Number In Consumer Unit									
Persons	2.5	2.6	2.6	2.5	2.5	2.5	2.4	2.5	2.5
Children under 18	0.7	0.8	0.8	0.7	0.6	0.7	0.6	0.7	0.7
Persons 65 and over	0.3	0.3	0.3	0.4	0.3	0.3	0.3	0.4	0.2
Earners	1.4	1.4	1.3	1.4	1.5	1.3	1.4	1.4	1.5
Vehicles	2.1	1.6	2.0	2.0	2.6	2.0	1.9	1.9	2.2
PERCENT HOMEOWNER	69	64	71	63	68	71	62	75	63
AVERAGE ANNUAL EXPENDITURES	$35 352	$38 153	$38 097	$36 862	$48 445	$37 676	$37 376	$36 101	$36 870
Food	4 802	5 092	5 580	4 344	5 778	4 940	4 994	5 270	5 115
Food at home	2 733	2 802	3 126	2 473	3 050	2 892	2 605	3 193	3 254
Cereals and bakery products	430	423	504	363	435	437	397	499	437
Meats, poultry, fish, and eggs	671	731	845	538	656	833	600	912	916
Dairy products	304	285	329	281	382	302	312	314	332
Fruits and vegetables	442	514	510	391	535	465	384	536	565
Other food at home	887	849	939	900	1 042	854	912	931	1 005
Food away from home	2 069	2 290	2 454	1 871	2 728	2 048	2 389	2 078	1 861
Alcoholic Beverages	304	411	346	356	507	295	356	222	244
Housing	11 195	13 730	13 023	13 147	14 975	11 945	12 071	11 300	11 419
Shelter	6 269	8 406	7 603	8 249	8 812	6 942	6 932	6 432	6 537
Owned dwellings	4 282	5 624	5 478	5 538	6 065	4 920	4 330	4 536	4 192
Rented dwellings	1 558	2 238	1 668	2 326	2 029	1 469	2 153	1 589	1 979
Other lodging	429	545	458	384	719	547	449	308	366
Utilities, fuels, and public services	2 401	2 647	2 607	2 277	2 284	2 523	2 341	2 680	2 597
Household operations	542	520	673	590	1 003	410	797	744	619
Housekeeping supplies	508	567	558	500	659	554	433	328	378
Household furnishings and equipment	1 475	1 590	1 582	1 531	2 217	1 515	1 568	1 115	1 290
Apparel And Services	1 607	1 888	2 056	1 319	1 979	1 777	1 595	1 911	1 708
Transportation	6 617	6 233	7 162	7 271	8 847	7 133	6 857	7 014	7 789
Vehicle purchases (net outlay)	3 081	2 779	2 854	3 643	4 175	3 471	3 108	3 582	3 948
Gasoline and motor oil	1 036	928	1 054	1 022	1 172	916	1 029	970	1 155
Other vehicle expenses	2 159	1 958	2 835	2 140	2 891	2 304	2 388	2 168	2 383
Public transportation	341	568	419	466	610	442	332	294	303
Health Care	2 048	1 951	1 701	2 050	2 262	1 661	2 280	1 985	2 043
Entertainment	1 984	1 771	2 123	1 676	2 498	2 294	1 851	1 641	1 649
Personal Care Products And Services	385	429	532	270	526	481	369	342	307
Reading	168	151	178	182	247	201	183	140	144
Education	583	938	399	469	767	632	691	508	642
Tobacco Products And Smoking Supplies	331	266	403	413	344	321	402	233	302
Miscellaneous	855	778	813	981	1 402	1 345	948	867	920
Cash Contributions	1 120	1 248	676	1 085	1 454	928	1 752	1 290	917
Personal Insurance And Pensions	3 355	3 267	3 106	3 300	6 859	3 723	3 029	3 377	3 671
Life and other personal insurance	387	392	394	359	419	416	371	361	401
Pensions and Social Security	2 968	2 875	2 712	2 941	6 440	3 307	2 658	3 016	3 270

1. Components of income and taxes are derived from "complete income reporters" only.

Table 7-21. Consumer Expenditures, Averages by Selected Metropolitan Statistical Areas, 1998–1999: West Region

Item	Complete reporting of income									
	All consumer units in the West	Los Angeles	San Francisco	San Diego	Portland	Seattle	Honolulu	Anchorage	Phoenix	Denver
NUMBER OF CONSUMER UNITS (THOUSANDS)	23 758	5 483	2 781	945	1 053	1 337	298	92	1 220	1 131
CONSUMER UNIT CHARACTERISTICS										
Average Income Before Taxes[1]	$45 736	$51 552	$59 224	$49 988	$47 414	$52 304	$53 537	$59 391	$44 090	$52 948
Age Of Reference Person	46.5	47.0	47.3	49.0	47.2	48.1	51.9	42.5	46.1	44.7
Average Number In Consumer Unit										
Persons	2.6	2.8	2.5	2.5	2.5	2.5	2.9	2.6	2.5	2.4
Children under 18	0.7	0.8	0.6	0.6	0.7	0.6	0.7	0.8	0.7	0.6
Persons 65 and over	0.3	0.3	0.3	0.3	0.2	0.3	0.4	0.1	0.3	0.2
Earners	1.4	1.4	1.4	1.2	1.4	1.4	1.5	1.5	1.3	1.5
Vehicles	2.0	1.9	1.9	2.0	2.2	2.5	1.7	2.6	1.8	2.2
PERCENT HOMEOWNER	59	53	59	53	59	66	57	58	60	67
AVERAGE ANNUAL EXPENDITURES	$40 647	$43 192	$51 015	$44 179	$43 331	$44 065	$42 474	$50 955	$40 167	$44 413
Food	5 312	5 204	6 963	5 292	5 855	6 080	6 300	6 267	4 981	5 172
Food at home	3 132	3 013	4 214	2 849	3 557	3 486	3 423	3 922	2 670	2 793
Cereals and bakery products	466	435	660	444	539	545	501	524	371	432
Meats, poultry, fish, and eggs	761	815	1 047	671	770	805	935	977	607	593
Dairy products	341	319	409	304	397	362	298	408	334	318
Fruits and vegetables	562	563	794	530	670	641	690	699	454	439
Other food at home	1 001	881	1 304	901	1 182	1 133	999	1 313	904	1 012
Food away from home	2 180	2 192	2 749	2 443	2 298	2 594	2 877	2 345	2 311	2 378
Alcoholic Beverages	372	297	516	462	430	541	406	508	437	490
Housing	13 756	15 934	18 058	16 266	13 847	14 905	14 676	17 375	12 891	15 417
Shelter	8 515	10 087	11 885	10 457	8 708	9 393	10 079	10 531	7 723	9 728
Owned dwellings	5 230	5 804	7 376	6 101	5 568	6 166	6 156	6 169	4 689	6 120
Rented dwellings	2 709	3 671	3 818	3 756	2 601	2 461	3 403	3 367	2 538	2 296
Other lodging	575	612	691	600	539	766	520	995	496	1 312
Utilities, fuels, and public services	2 179	2 267	2 193	1 977	2 160	2 262	2 032	2 614	2 459	2 200
Household operations	781	1 256	1 128	989	675	666	514	958	669	860
Housekeeping supplies	513	469	620	514	506	693	554	700	479	482
Household furnishings and equipment	1 768	1 856	2 232	2 327	1 799	1 890	1 497	2 573	1 562	2 147
Apparel And Services	1 863	2 158	2 444	2 018	1 687	1 932	1 995	1 957	2 057	1 958
Transportation	7 423	7 551	8 186	8 550	8 117	7 650	5 354	9 284	8 212	8 233
Vehicle purchases (net outlay)	3 180	2 976	3 164	3 988	4 123	2 867	999	3 812	4 035	3 116
Gasoline and motor oil	1 129	1 157	1 232	1 177	1 103	1 216	1 060	1 300	1 016	1 107
Other vehicle expenses	2 585	2 860	2 954	2 748	2 373	2 843	2 262	3 191	2 697	3 380
Public transportation	530	558	836	637	519	725	1 033	981	464	631
Health Care	1 869	1 757	1 792	1 850	1 837	1 931	2 188	2 324	2 007	1 915
Entertainment	2 139	1 905	2 395	2 684	2 283	3 060	2 083	3 562	2 036	2 570
Personal Care Products And Services	449	472	558	544	424	522	638	524	455	419
Reading	181	144	257	191	198	256	193	312	182	234
Education	676	668	875	398	728	618	1 147	576	535	632
Tobacco Products And Smoking Supplies	217	177	192	166	256	311	217	419	251	288
Miscellaneous	1 058	1 305	1 136	847	826	1 087	978	1 480	958	1 325
Cash Contributions	1 342	1 352	2 056	842	2 036	873	1 410	1 225	1 538	969
Personal Insurance And Pensions	3 990	4 269	5 587	4 070	4 807	4 299	4 890	5 141	3 627	4 791
Life and other personal insurance	355	349	330	452	462	427	687	574	336	427
Pensions and Social Security	3 636	3 920	5 257	3 618	4 345	3 872	4 203	4 568	3 290	4 363

1. Components of income and taxes are derived from "complete income reporters" only.

PART EIGHT

OCCUPATIONAL SAFETY AND HEALTH

OCCUPATIONAL SAFETY AND HEALTH

HIGHLIGHTS

This part includes data on work-related illnesses and injuries and fatal work injuries based on the Annual Survey of Occupational Injuries and Illnesses and Census of Fatal Occupational Injuries. Data are classified by industry, occupation, worker characteristics, and major exposure.

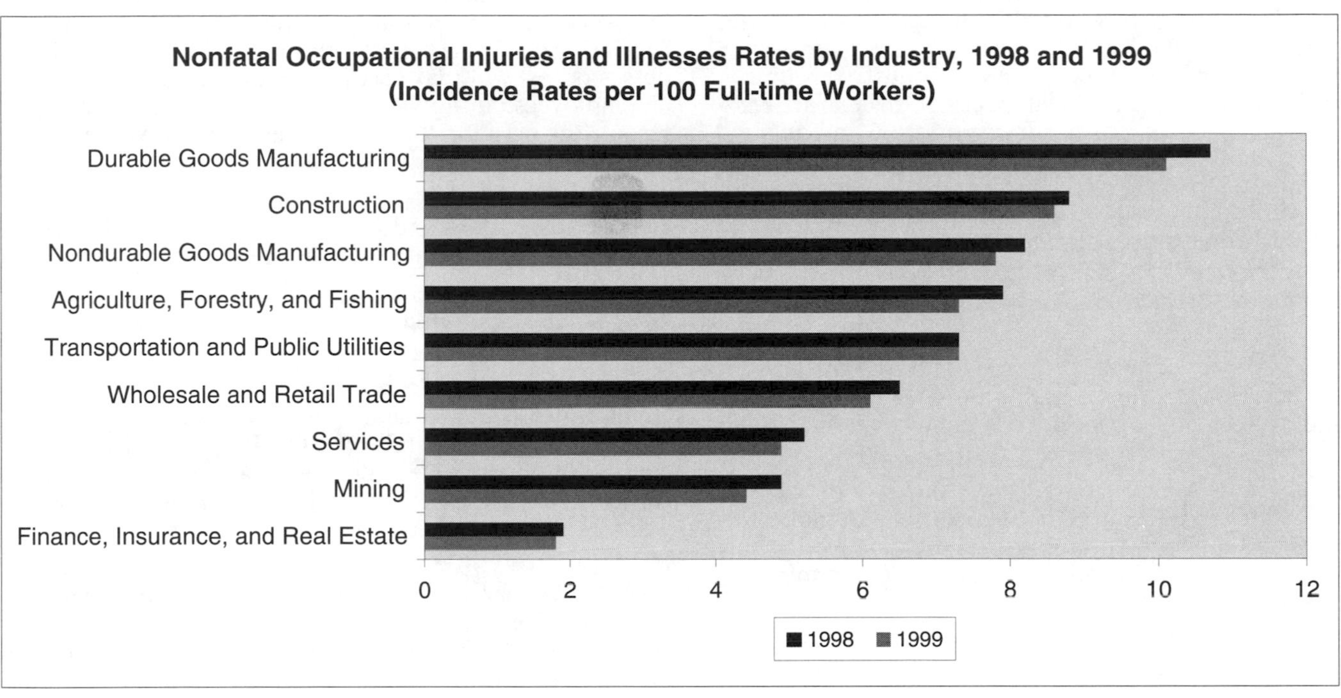

Incidence rates for nonfatal occupational injuries and illnesses continued to decline for all major industries except for transportation and public utilities which stayed the same. The durable goods manufacturing industry continued to have the highest rate.

OTHER HIGHLIGHTS:

- In 1999, 17 workers on average were fatally injured each day. Highway crashes were the greatest single cause, constituting 25 percent of the total occupational fatalities. (Tables 8-4, 8-5)
- Transportation and material moving was the occupational group with the largest number of fatal injuries (22 percent). Truck drivers constituted the highest proportion of fatal occupational injuries in 1999 at 15 percent, and averaged 2.4 fatalities each day. Also truck drivers had the highest share of nonfatal occupational injuries and illness at 8 percent in 1999. (Tables 8-3, 8-5)
- In 1999, while women represented 7 percent of total fatal injuries, this rate jumps to 33 percent for nonfatal occupational injuries and illnesses. (Tables 8-2, 8-4)
- The age group of 25–44 years constituted 55 percent of the nonfatal occupational injuries and 44 percent of the fatal occupational injuries. (Tables 8-2, 8-4)

NOTES AND DEFINITIONS

Collection and Coverage

The Annual Survey of Occupational Injuries and Illnesses is designed to collect data on injuries and illnesses based on records that employers maintain under the Occupational Safety and Health Act of 1970. The survey sample selected by BLS consists of approximately 250,000 units in the following private industry groups: agriculture, forestry, and fishing; oil and gas extraction; construction; manufacturing; transportation and public utilities; wholesale and retail trade; finance, insurance, and real estate; and services (except private households). Excluded from the survey are self-employed individuals; farmers with fewer than 11 employees; employers regulated by other federal safety and health laws; and federal, state, and local government agencies.

Mining and railroad data are furnished to BLS by the Mine Safety and Health Administration and the Federal Railroad Administration and are included in the tabulations.

Federal grants covering a portion of the operating cost permit states to develop estimates of occupational injuries and illnesses and to provide the data from which BLS produces national results and provides technical assistance to the state agencies.

Industry data are classified according to the Standard Industrial Classification.

Concepts and Definitions

Nonfatal Occupational Injuries and Illnesses

Recordable occupational injuries and illnesses are: (1) nonfatal occupational illnesses; or (2) nonfatal occupational injurics that involve one or more of the following: loss of consciousness, restriction of work or motion, transfer to another job, or medical treatment (other than first aid). The annual survey measures only nonfatal injuries and illnesses. To better address fatalities, BLS implemented the Census of Fatal Occupational Injuries (see below).

Occupational injury is any injury—such as a cut, fracture, sprain, amputation, and so forth—that results from a work accident or from exposure involving a single incident in the work environment.

Occupational illness is an abnormal condition or disorder, other than one resulting from an occupational injury, caused by exposure to environmental factors associated with employment. It includes acute and chronic illness or disease that may be caused by inhalation, absorption, ingestion, or direct contact. Long-term latent illnesses can be difficult to relate to the workplace and are believed to be understated in this survey.

Lost workday cases are cases that involve days away from work, days of restricted work activity, or both.

The data are presented in the form of incidence rates, defined as the number of injuries and illnesses or cases of lost workdays per 100 full-time employees. The formula is (N/EH) x 200,000, where N=number of injuries and illnesses or lost workday cases, EH=total hours worked by all employees during the calendar year, and 200,000 represents the base for 100 full-time equivalent workers (working 40 hours per week, 50 weeks per year).

Comparable data for individual states are available from the BLS Office of Safety, Health, and Working Conditions.

Fatal Occupational Injuries

Beginning in 1992, BLS has collected a comprehensive count of work-related deaths in the Census of Fatal Occupational Injuries (CFOI). The BLS fatality census covers not only private wage and salary workers, but also workers on small farms, the self-employed and family workers, and public sector workers.

The CFOI program is a cooperative venture between the state and federal governments. The program collects and cross checks fatality information from multiple sources, including death certificates, state and federal workers' compensation reports, Occupational Safety and Health Administration and Mine Safety and Health Administration records, medical examiner and autopsy reports, media accounts, state motor vehicle fatality records, and follow-up questionnaires to employers.

Fatality counts from the BLS Census are combined with annual average employment from the Current Population Survey to produce a fatal work injury rate.

For a fatality to be included in the CFOI, the decedent must have been employed at the time of the event and present at the site of the incident as a job requirement. Because of the latency period of many occupational illnesses and the resulting difficulty associated with linking illnesses to work, it is difficult to compile a complete count of all fatal illnesses in a given year. Thus, information on illness related deaths is excluded from the basic fatality count.

Sources of Additional Information

For more extensive definitions and description of collection methods see BLS news release USDL 01-71 for illnesses, USDL 00-236 for fatalities, and occasional articles in *Compensation and Working Conditions.*

Table 8-1. Nonfatal Occupational Injuries and Illnesses Incidence Rates by Industry and Case Types, 1989–1999

(Incidence rates per 100 full-time workers.)

Industry and type of case	1989	1990	1991	1992	1993	1994	1995	1996	1997	1998	1999
PRIVATE INDUSTRY [1, 2]											
Total cases	8.6	8.8	8.4	8.9	8.5	8.4	8.1	7.4	7.1	6.7	6.3
Lost workday cases	4.0	4.1	3.9	3.9	3.8	3.8	3.6	3.4	3.3	3.1	3.0
Agriculture, Forestry, And Fishing [2]											
Total cases	10.9	11.6	10.8	11.6	11.2	10.0	9.7	8.7	8.4	7.9	7.3
Lost workday cases	5.7	5.9	5.4	5.4	5.0	4.7	4.3	3.9	4.1	3.9	3.4
Mining [3]											
Total cases	8.5	8.3	7.4	7.3	6.8	6.3	6.2	5.4	5.9	4.9	4.4
Lost workday cases	4.8	5.0	4.5	4.1	3.9	3.9	3.9	3.2	3.7	2.9	2.7
Construction											
Total cases	14.3	14.2	13.0	13.1	12.2	11.8	10.6	9.9	9.5	8.8	8.6
Lost workday cases	6.8	6.7	6.1	5.8	5.5	5.5	4.9	4.5	4.4	4.0	4.2
General building contractors											
Total cases	13.9	13.4	12.0	12.2	11.5	10.9	9.8	9.0	8.5	8.4	8.0
Lost workday cases	6.5	6.4	5.5	5.4	5.1	5.1	4.4	4.0	3.7	3.9	3.7
Heavy construction, except building											
Total cases	13.8	13.8	12.8	12.1	11.1	10.2	9.9	9.0	8.7	8.2	7.8
Lost workday cases	6.5	6.3	6.0	5.4	5.1	5.0	4.8	4.3	4.3	4.1	3.8
Special trade contractors											
Total cases	14.6	14.7	13.5	13.8	12.8	12.5	11.1	10.4	10.0	9.1	8.9
Lost workday cases	6.9	6.9	6.3	6.1	5.8	5.8	5.0	4.8	4.7	4.1	4.4
Manufacturing											
Total cases	13.1	13.2	12.7	12.5	12.1	12.2	11.6	10.6	10.3	9.7	9.2
Lost workday cases	5.8	5.8	5.6	5.4	5.3	5.5	5.3	4.9	4.8	4.7	4.6
Durable goods											
Total cases	14.1	14.2	13.6	13.4	13.1	13.5	12.8	11.0	11.0	10.7	10.1
Lost workday cases	6.0	6.0	5.7	5.5	5.4	5.7	5.6	5.1	5.1	5.0	4.8
Lumber and wood products											
Total cases	18.4	18.1	16.8	16.3	15.9	15.7	14.9	14.2	13.5	13.2	13.0
Lost workday cases	9.4	8.8	8.3	7.6	7.6	7.7	7.0	6.8	6.5	6.8	6.7
Furniture and fixtures											
Total cases	16.1	16.9	15.9	14.8	14.6	15.0	13.9	12.2	12.0	11.4	11.5
Lost workday cases	7.2	7.8	7.2	6.6	6.5	7.0	6.4	5.4	5.8	5.7	5.9
Stone, clay, and glass products											
Total cases	15.5	15.4	14.8	13.6	13.8	13.2	12.3	12.4	11.8	11.8	10.7
Lost workday cases	7.4	7.3	6.8	6.1	6.3	6.5	5.7	6.0	5.7	6.0	5.4
Primary metal industries											
Total cases	18.7	19.0	17.7	17.5	17.0	16.8	16.5	15.0	15.0	14.0	12.9
Lost workday cases	8.1	8.1	7.4	7.1	7.3	7.2	7.2	6.8	7.2	7.0	6.3
Fabricated metal products											
Total cases	18.5	18.7	17.4	16.8	16.2	16.4	15.8	14.4	14.2	13.9	12.6
Lost workday cases	7.9	7.9	7.1	6.6	6.7	6.7	6.9	6.2	6.4	6.5	6.0
Industrial machinery and equipment											
Total cases	12.1	12.0	11.2	11.1	11.1	11.6	11.2	9.9	10.0	9.5	8.5
Lost workday cases	4.8	4.7	4.4	4.2	4.2	4.4	4.4	4.0	4.1	4.0	3.7
Electronic and other electric equipment											
Total cases	9.1	9.1	8.6	8.4	8.3	8.3	7.6	6.8	6.6	5.9	5.7
Lost workday cases	3.9	3.8	3.7	3.6	3.5	3.6	3.3	3.1	3.1	2.8	2.8
Transportation equipment											
Total cases	17.7	17.8	18.3	18.7	18.5	19.6	18.6	16.3	15.4	14.6	13.7
Lost workday cases	6.8	6.9	7.0	7.1	7.1	7.8	7.9	7.0	6.6	6.6	6.4
Instruments and related products											
Total cases	5.6	5.9	6.0	5.9	5.6	5.9	5.3	5.1	4.8	4.0	4.0
Lost workday cases	2.5	2.7	2.7	2.7	2.5	2.7	2.4	2.3	2.3	1.9	1.8
Miscellaneous manufacturing industries											
Total cases	11.1	11.3	11.3	10.7	10.0	9.9	9.1	9.5	8.9	8.1	8.4
Lost workday cases	5.1	5.1	5.1	5.0	4.6	4.5	4.3	4.4	4.2	3.9	4.0

See footnotes and *Note* at end of table.

Table 8-1. Nonfatal Occupational Injuries and Illnesses Incidence Rates by Industry and Case Types, 1989–1999—*Continued*

(Incidence rates per 100 full-time workers.)

Industry and type of case	1989	1990	1991	1992	1993	1994	1995	1996	1997	1998	1999
Nondurable goods											
Total cases	11.6	11.7	11.5	11.3	10.7	10.5	9.9	9.2	8.8	8.2	7.8
Lost workday cases	5.5	5.6	5.5	5.3	5.0	5.1	4.9	4.6	4.4	4.3	4.2
Food and kindred products											
Total cases	18.5	20.0	19.5	18.8	17.6	17.1	16.3	15.0	14.5	13.6	12.7
Lost workday cases	9.3	9.9	9.9	9.5	8.9	9.2	8.7	8.0	8.0	7.5	7.3
Tobacco products											
Total cases	8.7	7.7	6.4	6.0	5.8	5.3	5.6	6.7	5.9	6.4	5.5
Lost workday cases	3.4	3.2	2.8	2.4	2.3	2.4	2.6	2.8	2.7	3.1	2.2
Textile mill products											
Total cases	10.3	9.6	10.0	9.9	9.7	8.7	8.2	7.8	6.7	6.7	6.4
Lost workday cases	4.2	4.0	4.4	4.2	4.1	4.0	4.1	3.6	3.1	3.4	3.2
Apparel and other textile products											
Total cases	8.6	8.8	9.2	9.5	9.0	8.9	8.2	7.4	7.0	6.2	5.8
Lost workday cases	3.8	3.9	4.2	4.0	3.8	3.9	3.6	3.3	3.1	2.6	2.8
Paper and allied products											
Total cases	12.7	12.1	11.2	11.0	9.9	9.6	8.5	7.9	7.3	7.1	7.0
Lost workday cases	5.8	5.5	5.0	5.0	4.6	4.5	4.2	3.8	3.7	3.7	3.7
Printing and publishing											
Total cases	6.9	6.9	6.7	7.3	6.9	6.7	6.4	6.0	5.7	5.4	5.0
Lost workday cases	3.3	3.3	3.2	3.2	3.1	3.0	3.0	2.8	2.7	2.8	2.6
Chemicals and allied products											
Total cases	7.0	6.5	6.4	6.0	5.9	5.7	5.5	4.8	4.8	4.2	4.4
Lost workday cases	3.2	3.1	3.1	2.8	2.7	2.8	2.7	2.4	2.3	2.1	2.3
Petroleum and coal products											
Total cases	6.6	6.6	6.2	5.9	5.2	4.7	4.8	4.6	4.3	3.9	4.1
Lost workday cases	3.3	3.1	2.9	2.8	2.5	2.3	2.4	2.5	2.2	1.8	1.8
Rubber and miscellaneous plastics products											
Total cases	16.2	16.2	15.1	14.5	13.9	14.0	12.9	12.3	11.9	11.2	10.1
Lost workday cases	8.0	7.8	7.2	6.8	6.5	6.7	6.5	6.3	5.8	5.8	5.5
Leather and leather products											
Total cases	13.6	12.1	12.5	12.1	12.1	12.0	11.4	10.7	10.6	9.8	10.3
Lost workday cases	6.5	5.9	5.9	5.4	5.5	5.3	4.8	4.5	4.3	4.5	5.0
Transportation And Public Utilities [3]											
Total cases	9.2	9.6	9.3	9.1	9.5	9.3	9.1	8.7	8.2	7.3	7.3
Lost workday cases	5.3	5.5	5.4	5.1	5.4	5.5	5.2	5.1	4.8	4.3	4.4
Wholesale And Retail Trade											
Total cases	8.0	7.9	7.6	8.4	8.1	7.9	7.5	6.8	6.7	6.5	6.1
Lost workday cases	3.6	3.5	3.4	3.5	3.4	3.4	3.2	2.9	3.0	2.8	2.7
Wholesale trade											
Total cases	7.7	7.4	7.2	7.6	7.8	7.7	7.5	6.6	6.5	6.5	6.3
Lost workday cases	4.0	3.7	3.7	3.6	3.7	3.8	3.6	3.4	3.2	3.3	3.3
Retail trade											
Total cases	8.1	8.1	7.7	8.7	8.2	7.9	7.5	6.9	6.8	6.5	6.1
Lost workday cases	3.4	3.4	3.3	3.4	3.3	3.3	3.0	2.8	2.9	2.7	2.5
Finance, Insurance, And Real Estate											
Total cases	2.0	2.4	2.4	2.9	2.9	2.7	2.6	2.4	2.2	1.9	1.8
Lost workday cases	0.9	1.1	1.1	1.2	1.2	1.1	1.0	0.9	0.9	0.7	0.8
Services											
Total cases	5.5	6.0	6.2	7.1	6.7	6.5	6.4	6.0	5.6	5.2	4.9
Lost workday cases	2.7	2.8	2.8	3.0	2.8	2.8	2.8	2.6	2.5	2.4	2.2

Note: Because of rounding, components may not add to totals.

1. Totals include data for industries not shown separately.
2. Exclude farms with fewer than 11 employees.
3. Data conforming to OSHA definitions for mining operators in coal, metal, and nonmetal mining and for employers in railroad transportation are provided to BLS by the Mine Safety and Health Administration, U.S. Department of Labor; and the Federal Railroad Administration, U.S. Department of Transportation. Independent mining contractors are excluded from the coal, metal, and nonmetal mining industries.

Table 8-2. Number of Nonfatal Occupational Injuries and Illnesses Involving Days Away from Work[1] by Selected Worker Characteristics and Industry Division, Private Industry, 1999

(Numbers in thousands.)

Characteristic	Total cases[2]	Goods producing				Service producing				
		Agriculture, forestry, and fishing[2]	Mining[3]	Construction	Manufacturing	Transportation and public utilities[3]	Wholesale trade	Retail trade	Finance, insurance, and real estate	Services
TOTAL CASES	1 702.5	34.9	11.3	193.8	403.6	196.7	136.1	291.6	39.5	394.9
Sex										
Men	1 129.2	28.6	11.0	188.6	301.6	149.8	116.0	161.1	18.1	154.3
Women	558.1	6.2	0.3	4.6	100.4	39.6	19.3	128.8	21.3	237.7
Age[4]										
14 to 15 years	0.9	...	...	...	(5)	...	...	0.3	...	0.5
16 to 19 years	58.2	1.3	0.2	5.0	8.0	3.4	2.8	26.1	0.6	10.9
20 to 24 years	197.8	5.4	0.8	27.0	42.0	16.4	15.5	47.4	3.5	39.8
25 to 34 years	457.6	10.5	2.5	58.2	109.1	54.4	39.4	73.9	8.9	100.6
35 to 44 years	483.5	9.7	3.4	59.2	118.4	61.8	41.7	67.4	10.8	111.0
45 to 54 years	310.5	4.7	3.3	28.3	81.9	39.8	23.1	42.0	8.7	78.6
55 to 64 years	138.4	2.1	0.8	10.6	36.4	15.2	9.3	21.6	4.4	38.1
65 and over	22.5	0.4	(5)	0.8	3.2	1.9	1.3	6.3	1.0	7.6
Occupation										
Managerial and professional specialty	94.7	0.5	0.3	2.1	5.6	3.2	4.9	10.8	5.5	61.8
Technical, sales, and administrative support	249.4	1.5	0.1	2.5	22.8	27.6	20.6	91.6	16.0	66.7
Service	289.5	0.5	(5)	0.5	7.2	12.3	1.4	79.6	7.5	180.4
Farming, forestry, and fishing	42.9	27.4	...	0.4	2.8	0.3	1.7	1.0	2.9	6.5
Precision production, craft, and repair	298.0	1.3	5.3	114.6	72.3	26.5	16.3	30.7	5.0	25.8
Operators, fabricators, and laborers	719.7	3.5	5.2	72.6	290.9	126.5	90.2	76.8	2.1	51.8
Length Of Service With Employer										
Less than 3 months	230.0	7.4	1.5	41.2	45.5	16.2	17.1	47.1	3.7	50.4
3 to 11 months	308.3	8.0	1.6	43.2	65.3	23.7	24.5	62.9	6.6	72.5
1 to 5 years	549.7	11.3	3.8	63.0	126.0	53.4	50.5	94.1	15.0	132.6
More than 5 years	413.8	6.4	3.8	33.1	130.6	50.0	35.0	50.5	10.1	94.3
Not reported	200.7	1.9	0.6	13.3	36.2	53.5	9.0	37.0	4.1	45.1
Race Or Ethnic Origin										
White, non-Hispanic	859.6	14.0	2.2	121.5	219.3	68.8	78.0	149.4	19.2	187.1
Black, non-Hispanic	155.1	1.3	0.1	9.6	35.4	15.6	11.6	22.2	3.9	55.5
Hispanic	182.9	14.6	1.1	28.8	46.4	8.9	16.4	26.9	3.8	36.0
Asian or Pacific Islander	25.3	0.2	(5)	1.3	6.1	1.6	1.9	6.0	1.1	7.2
American Indian or Alaskan Native	6.8	0.1	...	1.1	1.5	0.4	0.8	0.7	0.3	1.8
Not reported	472.7	4.6	7.8	31.6	94.9	101.4	27.4	86.6	11.2	107.3

Note: Because of rounding and nonclassifiable responses, components may not add to totals.

1. Days-away-from-work cases include those which result in days away from work with or without restricted work activity.
2. Exclude farms with fewer than 11 employees.
3. Data conforming to OSHA definitions for mining operators in coal, metal, and nonmetal mining and for employers in railroad transportation are provided to BLS by the Mine Safety and Health Administration, U.S. Department of Labor; and the Federal Railroad Administration, U.S. Department of Transportation. Independent mining contractors are excluded from the coal, metal, and nonmetal mining industries.
4. Information is not shown separately for injured workers under age 14; they accounted for fewer than 50 cases.
5. Value less than 50 cases.

Table 8-3. Number and Percent Distribution of Nonfatal Occupational Injuries and Illnesses Involving Days Away from Work[1] by Selected Occupation and Number of Days Away from Work, Private Industry, 1999

(Numbers, percent, days.)

Occupation	Total cases (thousands)[2]	Percent of total cases	Percent of days-away-from-work-cases involving: 1 day	2 days	3 to 5 days	6 to 10 days	11 to 20 days	21 to 30 days	31 days and over	Median days away from work
TOTAL CASES	1 702.5	100.0	16.0	12.9	20.5	13.3	11.4	6.3	19.6	6
Truck drivers	141.1	100.0	11.0	11.1	18.9	14.1	13.4	6.8	24.7	8
Laborers, nonconstruction	89.1	100.0	17.7	12.4	20.2	14.7	11.2	6.1	17.6	5
Nursing aides, orderlies	75.7	100.0	16.5	14.6	24.2	13.4	10.4	4.3	16.6	5
Construction laborers	46.5	100.0	15.5	12.5	20.2	13.7	9.4	7.2	21.6	6
Janitors and cleaners	43.4	100.0	16.8	12.2	21.6	15.4	11.0	5.7	17.3	5
Assemblers	40.0	100.0	17.0	11.9	16.9	14.0	11.0	7.1	22.1	7
Carpenters	35.0	100.0	14.3	13.2	17.9	12.8	10.1	7.2	24.5	7
Cooks	28.0	100.0	16.2	15.5	26.4	14.8	8.0	5.7	13.4	4
Stock handlers and baggers	27.3	100.0	14.2	16.3	25.3	14.5	10.5	5.7	13.5	5
Registered nurses	25.7	100.0	17.5	15.5	23.2	14.8	9.8	4.6	14.7	4
Supervisors and proprietors	25.4	100.0	13.5	13.8	22.5	11.2	11.2	7.9	20.0	6
Miscellaneous food preparation	24.9	100.0	19.2	14.7	21.9	14.2	13.0	3.1	13.8	4
Welders and cutters	24.7	100.0	23.7	12.7	17.5	12.2	10.2	6.8	16.9	5
Cashiers	22.8	100.0	15.0	14.2	23.2	12.9	11.5	6.1	17.0	5
Sales workers, other commodities	21.9	100.0	16.6	12.3	23.8	9.8	13.0	5.9	18.6	5
Maids and housemen	21.4	100.0	14.7	13.9	22.5	15.6	9.3	4.7	19.3	5
Groundskeepers and gardeners, except farm	18.9	100.0	14.4	13.6	19.9	12.8	11.3	6.1	21.9	6
Electricians	17.9	100.0	17.5	10.3	19.2	12.5	14.2	5.3	21.0	7
Shipping and receiving clerks	16.6	100.0	19.7	13.2	20.2	12.4	10.2	7.7	16.5	5
Mechanics, automobile	16.5	100.0	18.3	11.9	23.8	11.9	9.2	6.6	18.3	5
Driver-sales workers	14.5	100.0	11.2	12.4	23.1	14.1	11.0	7.3	20.9	6
Kitchen workers	14.1	100.0	17.6	15.5	25.5	13.1	9.5	5.2	13.6	4
Industrial truck operators	13.9	100.0	18.4	11.6	18.5	10.8	12.9	6.6	21.1	6
Waiters and waitresses	13.2	100.0	15.3	16.0	21.9	13.7	11.2	5.0	16.8	5
Plumbers and pipefitters	12.4	100.0	13.7	13.1	19.5	14.4	10.7	7.0	21.6	6
Repairers, industrial machinery	11.9	100.0	16.6	11.5	16.4	11.5	13.4	8.3	22.3	8
Licensed practical nurses	11.7	100.0	15.3	12.3	24.5	15.5	7.4	4.9	19.9	5
Mechanics, bus, truck, stationary engine	11.6	100.0	17.7	11.9	17.2	11.8	8.6	8.5	24.3	7
Farm workers	11.5	100.0	10.9	13.0	22.1	14.8	11.6	6.3	21.3	6
Packaging, filling machine operators	11.5	100.0	16.1	14.7	18.6	13.8	9.9	6.8	20.1	6
Stock and inventory clerks	11.4	100.0	14.7	16.7	20.2	10.4	11.9	7.1	19.0	5
Supervisors, production workers	10.7	100.0	18.0	16.1	18.3	12.5	12.3	5.8	17.1	5
Health aides, except nursing	10.1	100.0	15.8	15.9	28.5	11.7	9.0	6.0	13.1	5
Hand packers and packagers	9.8	100.0	21.2	12.7	20.4	11.3	11.6	4.8	18.0	5
Butchers and meat cutters	9.8	100.0	19.4	14.7	18.6	16.0	10.8	4.6	15.9	5
Guards and police, except public	9.1	100.0	14.1	12.5	19.1	10.6	12.3	5.5	26.0	7
Attendants, public transportation	9.0	100.0	4.9	9.7	20.5	16.1	15.9	7.8	25.1	10
Heating, air conditioning, and refrigeration mechanics	8.9	100.0	15.9	10.4	17.8	11.4	10.5	10.4	23.5	10
Machinists	8.7	100.0	20.1	10.8	18.4	12.7	10.8	7.2	20.0	6
Helpers, construction trades	8.7	100.0	22.6	11.2	21.0	10.6	13.4	5.4	15.7	5

Note: Because of rounding and nonclassifiable responses, percentages may not add to 100.

1. Days-away-from-work cases include those which result in days away from work with or without restricted work activity.
2. Exclude farms with fewer than 11 employees.

Table 8-4. Fatal Occupational Injuries and Employment by Selected Worker Characteristics, 1999

Characteristics	Fatalities		Employment [1] (thousands)		Most frequent event [2] (percent of total)
	Number	Percent	Number	Percent	
TOTAL	6 023	100	134 666	100	Highway (25%)
Employee Status					
Wage and salary workers	4 884	81	124 445	92	Highway (27%)
Self-employed [3]	1 139	19	10 221	8	Homicides (14%)
Sex And Age					
Men	5 582	93	72 457	54	Highway (24%)
Women	441	7	62 209	46	Highway (34%)
Both sexes, by age [4]					
Under 16 years	26	. . .	. . .	. . .	Highway (35%)
16 to 17 years	46	1	2 796	2	Highway (28%)
18 to 19 years	122	2	4 494	3	Highway (26%)
20 to 24 years	450	7	13 242	10	Highway (26%)
25 to 34 years	1 171	19	31 280	24	Highway (24%)
35 to 44 years	1 499	25	36 983	28	Highway (24%)
45 to 54 years	1 326	22	28 671	21	Highway (25%)
55 to 64 years	814	14	13 317	10	Highway (25%)
65 and over	559	9	3 883	3	Highway (23%)
Race					
White	4 990	83	113 023	84	Highway (26%)
Black	626	10	15 284	11	Highway (23%)
Asian or Pacific Islander	57	1	. . .	. . .	Homicides (46%)
American Indian, Aleut, Eskimo	191	3	. . .	. . .	Highway (18%)
Other	159	3	. . .	. . .	Highway (20%)
Hispanic Origin					
Hispanic [5]	725	12	13 811	12	Highway (21%)

Note: Totals may include subcategories not shown separately. Percentages may not add to totals because of rounding. (. . .) indicate less than 0.5 percent or data that are not available or that do not meet publication criteria.

1. Employment is an annual average of employed civilians 16 years of age and older, plus resident armed forces, from the Current Population Survey, 1999.
2. "Highway" includes deaths to vehicle occupants resulting from traffic incidents that occur on the public roadway, shoulder, or surrounding area. It excludes incidents occurring entirely off the roadway, such as in parking lots and on farms. Incidents involving trains and deaths to pedestrians or other nonpassengers are excluded from both categories.
3. Includes paid and unpaid family workers and may include owners of incorporated businesses or members of partnerships.
4. There were 10 fatalities for which age was not reported.
5. Persons identified as Hispanic may be of any race. Hispanic employment does not include resident armed forces.

Table 8-5. Fatal Occupational Injuries by Occupation and Major Event or Exposure, 1999

Occupation [1]	Fatalities		Major event or exposure [2] (percent)			
	Number	Percent	Highway [3]	Homicide	Struck by object	Fall to lower level
TOTAL	6 023	100	25	11	10	11
Managerial And Professional Specialty	597	10	24	19	4	7
Executive, administrative and managerial	371	6	22	26	5	8
Professional specialty	226	4	27	8	3	6
Technical, Sales, And Administrative Support	610	10	27	32	2	3
Technicians and related support occupations	158	3	16	...	3	3
Airplane pilots and navigators	94	2	...	...	...	...
Sales occupations	356	6	28	49	2	2
Supervisors and proprietors, sales occupations	140	2	13	62	4	2
Sales workers, retail and personal services	144	2	27	51	...	...
Cashiers	55	1	...	80	...	...
Administrative support occupations including clerical	96	2	44	19	...	4
Service Occupations	468	8	20	33	1	9
Protective service occupations	261	4	26	32	1	3
Firefighting and fire prevention occupations, including supervisors	57	1	18	...	...	5
Police and detectives including supervisors	132	2	39	36	...	...
Guards, including supervisors	72	1	10	50	...	4
Farming, Forestry, And Fishing	897	15	13	2	21	5
Farming operators and managers	362	6	13	1	15	3
Farmers except horticultural	233	4	13	...	17	3
Managers, farms, except horticultural	118	2	13	...	10	4
Other agricultural and related occupations	335	6	18	4	14	8
Farm workers including supervisors	206	3	22	4	9	4
Forestry and logging occupations	122	2	6	...	67	3
Fishers, hunters and trappers	78	1	...	...	...	...
Fishers including vessel captains and officers	78	1	...	...	...	...
Precision Production, Craft, And Repair	1 142	19	11	3	12	28
Mechanics and repairers	353	6	12	7	19	13
Construction trades	633	11	11	1	7	39
Carpenters and apprentices	103	2	6	...	13	48
Electricans and apprentices	105	2	15	...	4	12
Painters	38	1	...	...	...	68
Roofers	59	1	5	...	...	85
Structural metal workers	43	1	...	...	19	77
Operators, Fabricators, And Laborers	2 194	36	37	5	10	8
Machine operators, assemblers, and inspectors	216	4	5	4	14	15
Transportation and material moving occupations	1 320	22	56	6	7	2
Motor vehicle operators	1 063	18	67	8	5	2
Truck drivers	898	15	70	2	6	2
Driver-sales workers	42	1	79	10	...	...
Taxicab drivers and chauffeurs	74	1	28	69	...	...
Material moving equipment operators	205	3	14	...	14	5
Handlers, equipment cleaners, helpers, and laborers	658	11	11	4	14	17
Construction laborers	341	6	11	...	14	25
Laborers, except construction	193	3	11	6	16	10
Military [4]	80	1	24	...	4	...

Note: Totals for major categories may include subcategories not shown separately. Percentages may not add to totals because of rounding. There were 35 fatalities for which there was insufficient information to determine an occupation classification. (. . .) indicate less than 0.5 percent or data that are not available or that do not meet publication criteria.

1. Based on the 1990 Occupational Classification System developed by the Bureau of the Census.
2. The figure shown is the percent of the total fatalities for that occupational group.
3. "Highway" includes deaths to vehicle occupants resulting from traffic incidents that occur on the public roadway, shoulder, or surrounding area. It excludes incidents occurring entirely off the roadway, such as in parking lots and on farms; incidents involving trains; and deaths to pedestrians or other nonpassengers.
4. Resident armed forces.

PART NINE

LABOR MANAGEMENT RELATIONS

LABOR MANAGEMENT RELATIONS

HIGHLIGHTS

This part is concerned with historical trends in union membership and earnings and in work stoppages (strikes and lockouts).

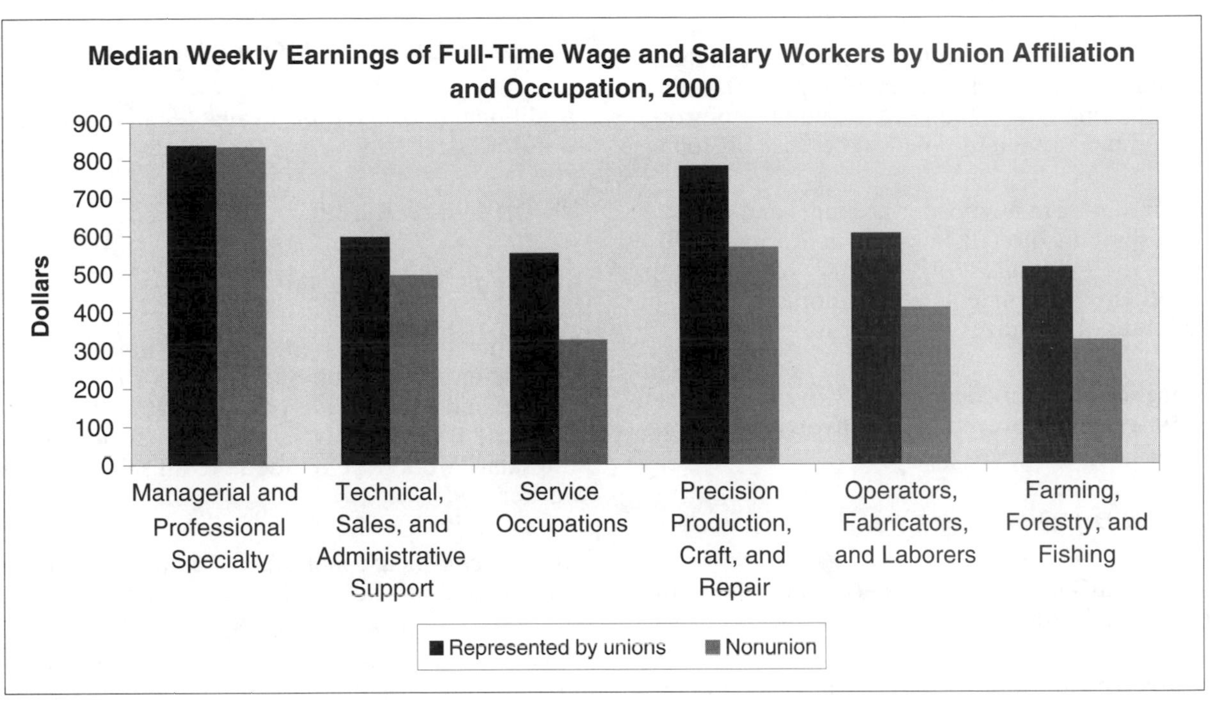

In all major occupational groups, median earnings of full-time wage and salary workers are higher for those employees represented by unions than for nonunion members. However, the difference varies by occupation, being least for managerial and professional specialties and greater for lower-paid workers.

OTHER HIGHLIGHTS:

- While median weekly earnings of members of unions exceed those of non-union members by 28 percent in the year 2000, the difference has declined from 35 percent in 1995. (Table 9-4)
- Union membership continued to be higher among men (15.2 percent) than women (11.5 percent) in 2000, but with a positive growth rate of women members of 3.9 percent from 1995 compared with -3.5 percent for men. Within both sexes, workers aged 45–64 years were most likely to be union members, with the rate of growth for women at 16 percent from 1995, almost 4 times that rate for men at 4 percent. (Table 9-2)
- Black men had the highest union membership rate (19.1 percent) among major demographic groups. While Blacks and Whites have recorded negative rates of growth for union membership since 1995 of -1.2 percent and -0.4 percent respectively, Hispanics reported a positive rate of 14.5 percent during that period. (Table 9-2)
- In 2000, New York had the highest rate of members in unions (25.5 percent), while North Carolina had the lowest rate at 3.6 percent. Members of unions in California, New York and Illinois constitute almost one-third of all U.S. union members. (Table 9-6)

NOTES AND DEFINITIONS

WORK STOPPAGES

Collection and Coverage

Data on work stoppages measure the number and duration of major strikes or lockouts (involving 1,000 workers or more) occurring during the year, the number of workers involved, and the amount of time lost because of stoppage.

Data are largely from newspaper accounts and cover only establishments directly involved in a stoppage. They do not measure the indirect or secondary effect of stoppages on other establishments whose employees are idle owing to material shortages or lack of service.

The current series is not comparable with the one terminated in 1981, which covered strikes involving six workers or more.

Concepts and Definitions

Stoppages are strikes and lockouts involving 1,000 workers or more and lasting a full shift or longer.

Workers involved are workers directly involved in the stoppage.

Number of days idle is the aggregate number of workdays lost by workers involved in the stoppages.

Days of idleness as a percent of estimated working time is aggregate workdays lost as a percent of the aggregate number of standard workdays in the period multiplied by total employment (excluding forestry, fisheries, and private household workers) in the period.

Sources of Additional Information

Additional information is available in BLS news release USDL 01-41.

UNION MEMBERSHIP

Collection, Coverage, and Definitions

The estimates of union membership are obtained from the Current Population Survey (CPS). The union membership and earnings data are tabulated from one-quarter of the CPS monthly sample and are limited to wage and salary workers. Excluded are all self-employed workers.

Union members are members of a labor union or an employee association similar to a union.

Represented by unions refers to union members as well as workers who have no union affiliation but whose jobs are covered by a union contract.

Sources of Additional Information

Additional information is available in BLS news release USDL 01-21, *Union Membership (Annual).*

Table 9-1. Work Stoppages Involving 1,000 Workers or More, 1947–2000

Year	Stoppages beginning in the year [1]		Days idle during the year [1]	
	Number	Workers involved (thousands)	Number (thousands)	Percent of estimated total working time [2]
1947	270	1 629	25 720	. . .
1948	245	1 435	26 127	0.22
1949	262	2 537	43 420	0.38
1950	424	1 698	30 390	0.26
1951	415	1 462	15 070	0.12
1952	470	2 746	48 820	0.38
1953	437	1 623	18 130	0.14
1954	265	1 075	16 630	0.13
1955	363	2 055	21 180	0.16
1956	287	1 370	26 840	0.20
1957	279	887	10 340	0.07
1958	332	1 587	17 900	0.13
1959	245	1 381	60 850	0.43
1960	222	896	13 260	0.09
1961	195	1 031	10 140	0.07
1962	211	793	11 760	0.08
1963	181	512	10 020	0.07
1964	246	1 183	16 220	0.11
1965	268	999	15 140	0.10
1966	321	1 300	16 000	0.10
1967	381	2 192	31 320	0.18
1968	392	1 855	35 367	0.20
1969	412	1 576	29 397	0.16
1970	381	2 468	52 761	0.29
1971	298	2 516	35 538	0.19
1972	250	975	16 764	0.09
1973	317	1 400	16 260	0.08
1974	424	1 796	31 809	0.16
1975	235	965	17 563	0.09
1976	231	1 519	23 962	0.12
1977	298	1 212	21 258	0.10
1978	219	1 006	23 774	0.11
1979	235	1 021	20 409	0.09
1980	187	795	20 844	0.09
1981	145	729	16 908	0.07
1982	96	656	9 061	0.04
1983	81	909	17 461	0.08
1984	62	376	8 499	0.04
1985	54	324	7 079	0.03
1986	69	533	11 861	0.05
1987	46	174	4 481	0.02
1988	40	118	4 381	0.02
1989	51	452	16 996	0.07
1990	44	185	5 926	0.02
1991	40	392	4 584	0.02
1992	35	364	3 989	0.01
1993	35	182	3 981	0.01
1994	45	322	5 020	0.02
1995	31	192	5 771	0.02
1996	37	273	4 889	0.02
1997	29	339	4 497	0.01
1998	34	387	5 116	0.02
1999	17	73	1 996	0.01
2000	39	394	20 419	0.06

1. The number of stoppages and workers relate to stoppages that began in the year. Days of idleness include all stoppages in effect. Workers are counted more than once if they are involved in more than one stoppage during the year.
2. Working time is for all employees, except those in private households, forestry, and fisheries.

Table 9-2. Union Affiliation of Employed Wage and Salary Workers by Selected Characteristics, 1995–2000

(Numbers in thousands, percent.)

Characteristics	1995					1996					1997				
	Total employed	Members of unions[1]		Represented by unions[2]		Total employed	Members of unions[1]		Represented by unions[2]		Total employed	Members of unions[1]		Represented by unions[2]	
		Total	Percent of employed	Total	Percent of employed		Total	Percent of employed	Total	Percent of employed		Total	Percent of employed	Total	Percent of employed
SEX AND AGE															
TOTAL, 16 YEARS AND OVER	110 038	16 360	14.9	18 346	16.7	111 960	16 269	14.5	18 158	16.2	114 533	16 110	14.1	17 923	15.6
16 to 24 years	18 205	1 022	5.6	1 199	6.6	18 106	991	5.5	1 146	6.3	18 571	968	5.2	1 140	6.1
25 years and over	91 833	15 337	16.7	17 148	18.7	93 854	15 278	16.3	17 012	18.1	95 962	15 142	15.8	16 783	17.5
25 to 34 years	29 761	3 596	12.1	4 090	13.7	29 564	3 536	12.0	3 994	13.5	29 408	3 434	11.7	3 870	13.2
35 to 44 years	29 800	5 254	17.6	5 883	19.7	30 619	5 132	16.8	5 716	18.7	31 461	4 987	15.9	5 571	17.7
45 to 54 years	20 623	4 483	21.7	4 964	24.1	21 641	4 626	21.4	5 106	23.6	22 714	4 645	20.5	5 092	22.4
55 to 64 years	9 202	1 801	19.6	1 980	21.5	9 527	1 795	18.8	1 984	20.8	9 871	1 894	19.2	2 045	20.7
65 years and over	2 448	203	8.3	231	9.4	2 503	189	7.5	211	8.4	2 509	182	7.3	205	8.2
Men, 16 Years And Over	57 669	9 929	17.2	10 868	18.8	58 473	9 859	16.9	10 761	18.4	59 825	9 763	16.3	10 619	17.7
16 to 24 years	9 531	640	6.7	721	7.6	9 392	627	6.7	709	7.5	9 666	612	6.3	691	7.1
25 years and over	48 137	9 289	19.3	10 146	21.1	49 080	9 232	18.8	10 052	20.5	50 159	9 150	18.2	9 928	19.8
25 to 34 years	16 094	2 220	13.8	2 469	15.3	15 930	2 205	13.8	2 434	15.3	15 832	2 132	13.5	2 359	14.9
35 to 44 years	15 505	3 169	20.4	3 460	22.3	15 921	3 100	19.5	3 368	21.2	16 430	3 068	18.7	3 346	20.4
45 to 54 years	10 521	2 679	25.5	2 885	27.4	10 936	2 739	25.0	2 960	27.1	11 471	2 718	23.7	2 908	25.4
55 to 64 years	4 779	1 117	23.4	1 209	25.3	4 978	1 079	21.7	1 166	23.4	5 101	1 130	22.1	1 198	23.5
65 years and over	1 238	105	8.5	123	9.9	1 315	109	8.3	124	9.5	1 324	103	7.8	118	8.9
Women, 16 Years And Over	52 369	6 430	12.3	7 479	14.3	53 488	6 410	12.0	7 397	13.8	54 708	6 347	11.6	7 304	13.4
16 to 24 years	8 673	382	4.4	478	5.5	8 714	364	4.2	437	5.0	8 906	355	4.0	449	5.0
25 years and over	43 696	6 048	13.8	7 001	16.0	44 773	6 046	13.5	6 960	15.5	45 802	5 992	13.1	6 855	15.0
25 to 34 years	13 667	1 377	10.1	1 621	11.9	13 634	1 331	9.8	1 560	11.4	13 575	1 302	9.6	1 512	11.1
35 to 44 years	14 295	2 085	14.6	2 423	16.9	14 698	2 032	13.8	2 349	16.0	15 030	1 919	12.8	2 225	14.8
45 to 54 years	10 101	1 804	17.9	2 078	20.6	10 705	1 887	17.6	2 146	20.0	11 242	1 927	17.1	2 184	19.4
55 to 64 years	4 423	685	15.5	771	17.4	4 549	716	15.7	818	18.0	4 770	764	16.0	847	17.8
65 years and over	1 210	98	8.1	108	8.9	1 187	80	6.7	87	7.3	1 184	80	6.7	87	7.3
RACE, HISPANIC ORIGIN, AND SEX															
White, 16 Years And Over	92 760	13 149	14.2	14 747	15.9	94 306	13 232	14.0	14 761	15.7	96 104	13 088	13.6	14 538	15.1
Men	49 162	8 178	16.6	8 960	18.2	49 961	8 216	16.4	8 961	17.9	50 941	8 171	16.0	8 859	17.4
Women	43 598	4 971	11.4	5 787	13.3	44 345	5 016	11.3	5 800	13.1	45 163	4 917	10.9	5 679	12.6
Black,16 Years And Over	12 644	2 519	19.9	2 819	22.3	12 909	2 441	18.9	2 733	21.2	13 346	2 394	17.9	2 688	20.1
Men	6 005	1 353	22.5	1 460	24.3	6 031	1 303	21.6	1 428	23.7	6 201	1 251	20.2	1 378	22.2
Women	6 639	1 167	17.6	1 358	20.5	6 878	1 138	16.5	1 305	19.0	7 145	1 143	16.0	1 309	18.3
Hispanic, 16 Years And Over	10 401	1 357	13.0	1 535	14.8	10 800	1 394	12.9	1 573	14.6	11 881	1 407	11.8	1 602	13.5
Men	6 223	871	14.0	969	15.6	6 455	881	13.7	971	15.0	7 153	904	12.6	1 023	14.3
Women	4 178	486	11.6	565	13.5	4 345	513	11.8	602	13.9	4 728	503	10.6	579	12.2
FULL- OR PART-TIME STATUS[3]															
Full-Time Workers	89 282	14 790	16.6	16 531	18.5	90 918	14 762	16.2	16 429	18.1	93 578	14 619	15.6	16 227	17.3
Part-Time Workers	20 550	1 537	7.5	1 781	8.7	20 810	1 477	7.1	1 697	8.2	20 710	1 449	7.0	1 653	8.0

See footnotes and *Note* at end of table.

Table 9-2. Union Affiliation of Employed Wage and Salary Workers by Selected Characteristics, 1995–2000—*Continued*

(Numbers in thousands, percent.)

Characteristics	1998					1999					2000				
	Total employed	Members of unions[1]		Represented by unions[2]		Total employed	Members of unions[1]		Represented by unions[2]		Total employed	Members of unions[1]		Represented by unions[2]	
		Total	Percent of employed	Total	Percent of employed		Total	Percent of employed	Total	Percent of employed		Total	Percent of employed	Total	Percent of employed
SEX AND AGE															
TOTAL, 16 YEARS AND OVER	116 730	16 211	13.9	17 918	15.4	118 963	16 477	13.9	18 182	15.3	120 786	16 258	13.5	17 944	14.9
16 to 24 years	19 164	1 014	5.3	1 151	6.0	19 606	1 110	5.7	1 239	6.3	20 166	1 010	5.0	1 152	5.7
25 years and over	97 566	15 198	15.6	16 767	17.2	99 358	15 367	15.5	16 943	17.1	100 620	15 248	15.2	16 792	16.7
25 to 34 years	29 121	3 332	11.4	3 711	12.7	28 657	3 415	11.9	3 785	13.2	28 406	3 369	11.9	3 720	13.1
35 to 44 years	31 865	5 013	15.7	5 511	17.3	32 438	4 918	15.2	5 428	16.7	32 470	4 822	14.9	5 293	16.3
45 to 54 years	23 579	4 737	20.1	5 220	22.1	24 665	4 881	19.8	5 377	21.8	25 651	4 815	18.8	5 305	20.7
55 to 64 years	10 427	1 923	18.4	2 110	20.2	10 880	1 932	17.8	2 107	19.4	11 204	1 998	17.8	2 193	19.6
65 years and over	2 574	193	7.5	214	8.3	2 718	221	8.1	247	9.1	2 889	243	8.4	281	9.7
Men, 16 Years And Over	60 973	9 850	16.2	10 638	17.4	61 914	9 949	16.1	10 758	17.4	62 853	9 578	15.2	10 355	16.5
16 to 24 years	9 927	637	6.4	719	7.2	10 116	716	7.1	781	7.7	10 440	618	5.9	697	6.7
25 years and over	51 046	9 213	18.0	9 919	19.4	51 797	9 232	17.8	9 977	19.3	52 412	8 960	17.1	9 657	18.4
25 to 34 years	15 656	2 112	13.5	2 301	14.7	15 330	2 142	14.0	2 325	15.2	15 197	2 030	13.4	2 207	14.5
35 to 44 years	16 768	3 055	18.2	3 264	19.5	17 020	2 993	17.6	3 241	19.0	17 028	2 871	16.9	3 077	18.1
45 to 54 years	11 874	2 771	23.3	2 982	25.1	12 395	2 800	22.6	3 026	24.4	12 898	2 739	21.2	2 956	22.9
55 to 64 years	5 404	1 177	21.8	1 265	23.4	5 622	1 186	21.1	1 267	22.5	5 770	1 191	20.6	1 268	22.0
65 years and over	1 343	98	7.3	108	8.0	1 431	111	7.7	118	8.2	1 519	129	8.5	148	9.8
Women, 16 Years And Over	55 757	6 362	11.4	7 280	13.1	57 050	6 528	11.4	7 425	13.0	57 933	6 680	11.5	7 590	13.1
16 to 24 years	9 237	377	4.1	432	4.7	9 489	393	4.1	458	4.8	9 726	392	4.0	455	4.7
25 years and over	46 520	5 985	12.9	6 848	14.7	47 560	6 135	12.9	6 966	14.6	48 207	6 288	13.0	7 135	14.8
25 to 34 years	13 464	1 219	9.1	1 410	10.5	13 327	1 273	9.6	1 460	11.0	13 209	1 340	10.1	1 513	11.5
35 to 44 years	15 097	1 958	13.0	2 248	14.9	15 418	1 924	12.5	2 187	14.2	15 441	1 951	12.6	2 215	14.3
45 to 54 years	11 705	1 967	16.8	2 238	19.1	12 270	2 081	17.0	2 351	19.2	12 752	2 077	16.3	2 348	18.4
55 to 64 years	5 023	746	[illegible]	[illegible]	[illegible]	5 250	740	14.2	839	16.0	5 434	807	14.9	925	17.0
65 years and over	1 231	95	7.7	106	8.6	1 287	110	8.5	129	10.0	1 370	114	8.3	133	9.7
RACE, HISPANIC ORIGIN, AND SEX															
White, 16 Years And Over	97 531	13 118	13.5	14 460	14.8	99 147	13 349	13.5	14 668	14.8	100 455	13 094	13.0	14 453	14.4
Men	51 700	8 166	15.8	8 788	17.0	52 492	8 246	15.7	8 896	16.9	53 105	7 911	14.9	8 541	16.1
Women	45 831	4 952	10.8	5 673	12.4	46 655	5 103	10.9	5 771	12.4	47 350	5 183	10.9	5 912	12.5
Black,16 Years And Over	13 894	2 460	17.7	2 739	19.7	14 346	2 463	17.2	2 757	19.2	14 544	2 489	17.1	2 744	18.9
Men	6 452	1 337	20.7	1 458	22.6	6 585	1 348	20.5	1 464	22.2	6 701	1 282	19.1	1 388	20.7
Women	7 443	1 123	15.1	1 282	17.2	7 760	1 116	14.4	1 293	16.7	7 843	1 208	15.4	1 356	17.3
Hispanic, 16 Years And Over	12 374	1 471	11.9	1 634	13.2	12 810	1 525	11.9	1 684	13.1	13 609	1 554	11.4	1 740	12.8
Men	7 360	937	12.7	1 017	13.8	7 457	966	13.0	1 052	14.1	7 884	972	12.3	1 063	13.5
Women	5 015	534	10.6	617	12.3	5 353	559	10.4	632	11.8	5 725	582	10.2	677	11.8
FULL- OR PART-TIME STATUS[3]															
Full-Time Workers	95 595	14 825	15.5	16 323	17.1	97 626	14 974	15.3	16 501	16.9	99 917	14 822	14.8	16 306	16.3
Part-Time Workers	20 862	1 354	6.5	1 559	7.5	21 065	1 459	6.9	1 634	7.8	20 619	1 395	6.8	1 593	7.7

Note: Data refer to the sole or principal job of full- and part-time workers. Excluded are all self-employed workers regardless of whether or not their businesses are incorporated. Detail for the above race and Hispanic-origin groups will not sum to totals because data for the Other races group are not presented and Hispanics are included in both the White and Black population groups. Beginning in January 2000, data reflect new composite estimation procedures and revised population controls used in the household survey.

1. Data refer to members of a labor union or an employee association similar to a union.
2. Data refer to members of a labor union or an employee association similar to a union as well as workers who report no union affiliation but whose jobs are covered by a union or an employee association contract.
3. The distinction between full- and part-time workers is based on hours usually worked. Data will not sum to totals because full- or part-time status on the principal job is not identifiable for a small number of multiple jobholders.

Table 9-3. Union Affiliation of Wage and Salary Workers by Occupation and Industry, 1998–2000

(Thousands of persons, percent.)

Characteristics	1998					1999					2000				
	Total em- ployed	Members of unions[1]		Represented by unions[2]		Total em- ployed	Members of unions[1]		Represented by unions[2]		Total em- ployed	Members of unions[1]		Represented by unions[2]	
		Total	Percent of em- ployed	Total	Percent of em- ployed		Total	Percent of em- ployed	Total	Percent of em- ployed		Total	Percent of em- ployed	Total	Percent of em- ployed
OCCUPATION															
Managerial And Professional Specialty	33 102	4 252	12.8	5 015	15.2	34 693	4 594	13.2	5 352	15.4	35 378	4 536	12.8	5 277	14.9
Executive, administrative, and managerial	15 473	812	5.2	1 017	6.6	16 000	903	5.6	1 138	7.1	16 434	875	5.3	1 075	6.5
Professional specialty	17 629	3 440	19.5	3 998	22.7	18 693	3 691	19.7	4 215	22.5	18 944	3 661	19.3	4 202	22.2
Technical, Sales, And Administrative Support	35 379	3 239	9.2	3 677	10.4	35 514	3 191	9.0	3 609	10.2	36 124	3 119	8.6	3 521	9.7
Technicians and related support	4 150	433	10.4	498	12.0	4 188	461	11.0	523	12.5	4 279	431	10.1	500	11.7
Sales occupations	13 378	544	4.1	620	4.6	13 451	549	4.1	613	4.6	13 677	481	3.5	533	3.9
Administrative support, including clerical	17 851	2 262	12.7	2 558	14.3	17 874	2 182	12.2	2 474	13.8	18 167	2 207	12.1	2 487	13.7
Service Occupations	16 594	2 209	13.3	2 398	14.5	16 829	2 151	12.8	2 336	13.9	16 953	2 234	13.2	2 441	14.4
Protective service	2 399	991	41.3	1 048	43.7	2 427	927	38.2	991	40.8	2 384	938	39.4	1 003	42.1
Service, except protective service	14 195	1 218	8.6	1 350	9.5	14 403	1 224	8.5	1 346	9.3	14 569	1 295	8.9	1 438	9.9
Precision Production, Craft, And Repair	12 274	2 708	22.1	2 834	23.1	12 474	2 800	22.4	2 929	23.5	12 716	2 783	21.9	2 910	22.9
Operators, Fabricators, And Laborers	17 443	3 713	21.3	3 894	22.3	17 514	3 627	20.7	3 830	21.9	17 642	3 498	19.8	3 687	20.9
Machine operators, assemblers, and inspectors	7 498	1 603	21.4	1 672	22.3	7 255	1 490	20.5	1 572	21.7	7 043	1 366	19.4	1 442	20.5
Transportation and material moving occupations	4 935	1 204	24.4	1 267	25.7	5 041	1 148	22.8	1 216	24.1	5 182	1 195	23.1	1 260	24.3
Handlers, equipment cleaners, helpers, and laborers	5 010	906	18.1	956	19.1	5 218	989	18.9	1 042	20.0	5 417	938	17.3	984	18.2
Farming, Forestry, And Fishing	1 938	90	4.6	100	5.2	1 940	113	5.8	125	6.4	1 974	89	4.5	109	5.5
INDUSTRY															
Agriculture Wage And Salary Workers	1 739	26	1.5	31	1.8	1 721	43	2.5	48	2.8	1 821	38	2.1	45	2.5
Private Nonagricultural Wage And Salary Workers	96 590	9 280	9.6	10 073	10.4	98 304	9 376	9.5	10 168	10.3	99 989	9 110	9.1	9 924	9.9
Mining	589	72	12.2	79	13.4	531	57	10.6	60	11.4	499	54	10.9	57	11.4
Construction	5 946	1 056	17.8	1 093	18.4	6 230	1 187	19.1	1 224	19.6	6 666	1 220	18.3	1 268	19.0
Manufacturing	19 763	3 127	15.8	3 315	16.8	19 323	3 024	15.6	3 209	16.6	19 167	2 832	14.8	2 999	15.6
Durable goods	11 999	1 990	16.6	2 097	17.5	11 824	1 941	16.4	2 063	17.5	11 688	1 791	15.3	1 894	16.2
Nondurable goods	7 763	1 138	14.7	1 218	15.7	7 499	1 083	14.4	1 146	15.3	7 480	1 041	13.9	1 105	14.8
Transportation and public utilities	7 147	1 843	25.8	1 931	27.0	7 317	1 865	25.5	1 956	26.7	7 508	1 805	24.0	1 920	25.6
Transportation	4 316	1 108	25.7	1 156	26.8	4 450	1 136	25.5	1 186	26.7	4 573	1 135	24.8	1 203	26.3
Communications and public utilities	2 831	735	26.0	775	27.4	2 866	729	25.4	770	26.9	2 935	670	22.8	717	24.4
Wholesale and retail trade	24 230	1 283	5.3	1 387	5.7	24 671	1 278	5.2	1 406	5.7	25 133	1 194	4.7	1 315	5.2
Wholesale trade	4 425	259	5.9	275	6.2	4 573	248	5.4	281	6.1	4 766	243	5.1	265	5.6
Retail trade	19 805	1 024	5.2	1 113	5.6	20 098	1 030	5.1	1 126	5.6	20 366	951	4.7	1 049	5.2
Finance, insurance, and real estate	7 420	150	2.0	195	2.6	7 588	156	2.1	191	2.5	7 488	121	1.6	156	2.1
Services	31 493	1 750	5.6	2 073	6.6	32 645	1 809	5.5	2 121	6.5	33 528	1 884	5.6	2 208	6.6
Government Workers	18 401	6 905	37.5	7 815	42.5	18 938	7 058	37.3	7 966	42.1	18 976	7 110	37.5	7 976	42.0
Federal	3 269	1 105	33.8	1 299	39.7	3 264	1 047	32.1	1 275	39.0	3 233	1 033	32.0	1 186	36.7
State	5 150	1 431	27.8	1 667	32.4	5 233	1 527	29.2	1 781	34.0	5 464	1 641	30.0	1 867	34.2
Local	9 982	4 370	43.8	4 849	48.6	10 440	4 484	42.9	4 911	47.0	10 278	4 436	43.2	4 923	47.9

Note: Data refer to the sole or principal job of full- and part-time workers. Excluded are all self-employed workers regardless of whether or not their businesses are incorporated. Beginning in January 2000, data reflect revised population controls used in the household survey.

1. Data refer to members of a labor union or an employee association similar to a union.
2. Data refer to members of a labor union or an employee association similar to a union as well as workers who report no union affiliation but whose jobs are covered by a union or an employee association contract.

Table 9-4. Median Weekly Earnings of Full-Time Wage and Salary Workers by Union Affiliation, Occupation, and Industry, 1995–2000

(Dollars.)

Characteristics	1995				1996				1997			
	Total	Members of unions [1]	Represented by unions [2]	Non-union	Total	Members of unions [1]	Represented by unions [2]	Non-union	Total	Members of unions [1]	Represented by unions [2]	Non-union
TOTAL, 16 YEARS AND OVER	$479	$602	$598	$447	$490	$615	$610	$462	$503	$640	$632	$478
OCCUPATION												
Managerial And Professional Specialty	703	745	737	694	718	758	749	708	738	776	766	731
Executive, administrative, and managerial	684	727	722	681	699	742	745	694	725	757	752	721
Professional specialty	718	750	741	707	730	762	750	721	750	782	769	742
Technical, Sales, And Administrative Support	426	522	516	414	441	532	524	427	456	550	541	441
Technicians and related support	558	629	619	542	573	664	661	554	582	677	675	566
Sales occupations	454	457	466	453	474	451	459	475	482	467	469	483
Administrative support, including clerical	399	517	510	383	405	524	516	389	419	545	534	404
Service Occupations	299	484	477	275	305	490	484	282	313	516	505	293
Protective service	528	678	676	399	538	693	686	413	550	724	713	418
Service, except protective service	274	366	359	264	283	379	379	271	293	398	393	283
Precision Production, Craft, And Repair	519	688	684	478	540	703	698	494	548	724	718	501
Operators, Fabricators, And Laborers	380	524	519	338	391	528	522	353	401	572	561	365
Machine operators, assemblers, and inspectors	368	509	504	328	380	512	508	345	390	533	524	356
Transportation and material moving occupations	476	612	606	420	476	610	601	425	498	658	642	451
Handlers, equipment cleaners, helpers and laborers	319	480	473	297	330	481	477	308	329	509	506	310
Farming, Forestry, And Fishing	287	404	404	280	294	439	423	288	295	505	475	290
INDUSTRY												
Agricultural Wage And Salary Workers	291	(3)	(3)	289	306	(3)	(3)	305	306	(3)	(3)	305
Private Nonagricultural Wage And Salary Workers	462	573	567	443	475	584	579	458	490	610	603	476
Mining	667	684	682	663	693	698	699	690	680	717	717	668
Construction	487	741	730	442	504	748	742	464	518	771	760	484
Manufacturing	494	548	544	479	507	560	558	494	517	595	592	503
Durable goods	517	576	573	503	533	588	587	517	548	619	616	523
Nondurable goods	454	506	504	438	466	510	507	453	484	536	529	470
Transportation and public utilities	590	676	673	545	596	680	676	555	617	718	714	580
Transportation	523	659	651	488	527	656	649	491	573	702	697	513
Communications and public utilities	675	690	690	661	693	707	705	684	709	746	743	690
Wholesale and retail trade	370	466	454	363	380	450	444	375	391	457	451	387
Wholesale trade	492	541	524	489	503	566	551	500	525	545	536	524
Retail trade	333	425	419	325	343	408	408	338	352	419	415	347
Finance, insurance, and real estate	501	477	490	502	521	534	533	520	546	487	501	548
Services	444	489	491	440	456	501	498	451	475	517	512	470
Government Workers	575	638	633	500	592	657	651	518	605	681	671	530
Federal	...	...	...	...	672	677	679	663	684	689	687	678
State	...	...	...	...	557	610	605	514	584	628	621	540
Local	...	...	...	...	580	671	661	473	592	697	682	479

See footnotes and *Note* at end of table.

Table 9-4. Median Weekly Earnings of Full-Time Wage and Salary Workers by Union Affiliation, Occupation, and Industry, 1995–2000—*Continued*

(Dollars.)

Characteristics	1998				1999				2000			
	Total	Members of unions [1]	Represented by unions [2]	Nonunion	Total	Members of unions [1]	Represented by unions [2]	Nonunion	Total	Members of unions [1]	Represented by unions [2]	Nonunion
TOTAL, 16 YEARS AND OVER	$523	$659	$653	$499	$549	$672	$667	$516	$576	$696	$691	$542
OCCUPATION												
Managerial And Professional Specialty	759	789	774	756	797	826	819	792	836	840	834	836
Executive, administrative, and managerial	755	801	789	753	792	823	829	789	840	834	854	839
Professional specialty	763	787	772	759	800	826	817	794	832	841	829	832
Technical, Sales, And Administrative Support	477	575	569	463	488	583	580	477	506	598	590	497
Technicians and related support	599	708	688	590	618	714	711	608	648	748	741	635
Sales occupations	502	496	492	502	523	513	519	523	550	526	522	552
Administrative support, including clerical	438	563	558	418	447	574	564	429	469	588	579	453
Service Occupations	327	557	542	305	336	536	529	314	355	554	542	327
Protective service	598	736	732	450	592	737	728	477	623	786	771	502
Service, except protective service	305	403	402	295	311	412	409	303	324	423	419	316
Precision Production, Craft, And Repair	572	753	747	514	594	755	747	546	613	784	778	570
Operators, Fabricators, And Laborers	415	585	580	381	429	591	584	398	446	605	602	411
Machine operators, assemblers, and inspectors	406	559	556	375	423	572	566	394	436	575	572	408
Transportation and material moving occupations	510	655	644	468	513	668	657	478	540	694	690	502
Handlers, equipment cleaners, helpers and laborers	351	514	514	326	363	507	499	340	378	555	551	355
Farming, Forestry, And Fishing	302	471	462	299	331	512	514	322	334	516	506	325
INDUSTRY												
Agricultural Wage And Salary Workers	315	(3)	(3)	314	340	(3)	(3)	337	347	(3)	(3)	344
Private Nonagricultural Wage And Salary Workers	509	626	620	496	525	634	628	513	555	664	657	537
Mining	684	733	723	673	734	710	731	735	768	746	748	774
Construction	534	790	783	496	552	778	772	509	584	814	810	529
Manufacturing	551	606	603	532	576	614	611	561	595	630	628	587
Durable goods	581	629	625	566	594	628	625	584	618	662	659	610
Nondurable goods	507	565	562	495	529	584	579	518	553	594	594	537
Transportation and public utilities	624	731	724	586	651	748	742	613	679	768	762	639
Transportation	570	704	695	519	596	727	718	551	615	744	741	582
Communications and public utilities	727	763	760	699	751	773	770	738	776	808	798	766
Wholesale and retail trade	410	480	476	405	421	499	492	418	444	518	514	439
Wholesale trade	562	611	604	557	573	584	570	573	595	607	608	593
Retail trade	373	442	439	369	391	472	463	387	403	495	490	399
Finance, insurance, and real estate	577	545	554	578	598	582	587	599	620	596	593	621
Services	498	540	548	494	517	554	563	515	543	567	574	540
Government Workers	620	694	688	558	641	714	709	585	665	730	726	609
Federal	694	690	693	696	729	721	723	737	745	736	738	755
State	596	646	638	563	615	683	677	578	633	685	681	606
Local	612	712	702	501	623	726	720	525	650	746	738	562

Note: Data refer to the sole or principal job of full-time workers. Excluded are all self-employed workers regardless of whether or not their businesses are incorporated. Beginning in January 2000, data reflect new composite estimation procedures and revised population controls used in the household survey.

1. Data refer to members of a labor union or an employee association similar to a union.
2. Data refer to members of a labor union or an employee association similar to a union as well as workers who report no union affiliation but whose jobs are covered by a union or an employee association contract.
3. Data not shown where base is less than 50,000 workers.

Table 9-5. Wage and Salary Employees Who Were Union or Employee Association Members, 1977–2000

Year	Wage and salary employees who were union or employee association members (thousands)	Total wage and salary employment (thousands)	Union or association members as a percent of wage and salary employment
1977	19 335	81 334	23.8
1978	19 548	84 968	23.0
1979	20 986	87 117	24.1
1980	20 095	87 480	23.0
1981	. . .	. . .	. . .
1982	. . .	. . .	. . .
1983 [1]	17 717	88 290	20.1
1984	17 340	92 194	18.8
1985	16 996	94 521	18.0
1986	16 975	96 903	17.5
1987	16 913	99 303	17.0
1988	17 002	101 407	16.8
1989	16 980	103 480	16.4
1990	16 740	103 905	16.1
1991	16 568	102 786	16.1
1992	16 390	103 688	15.8
1993	16 598	105 087	15.8
1994 [2]	16 748	107 989	15.5
1995	16 360	110 038	14.9
1996	16 269	111 960	14.5
1997	16 110	114 533	14.1
1998	16 211	116 730	13.9
1999	16 477	118 963	13.9
2000	16 258	120 786	13.5

1. Annual average data beginning in 1983 are not directly comparable with the May data for 1977–1980.
2. Data beginning in 1994 are not strictly comparable with data for 1993 and earlier years because of the introduction of a major redesign of the Current Population Survey questionnaire and collection methodology and the introduction of 1990 census-based population controls.

Table 9-6. Union Affiliation of Employed Wage and Salary Workers by State, 1999–2000

(Numbers in thousands, percent.)

State	1999					2000				
	Total employed	Members of unions [1]		Represented by unions [2]		Total employed	Members of unions [1]		Represented by unions [2]	
		Total	Percent of employed	Total	Percent of employed		Total	Percent of employed	Total	Percent of employed
U.S. TOTAL	118 963	16 477	13.9	18 182	15.3	120 786	16 258	13.5	17 944	14.9
Alabama	1 833	201	11.0	225	12.3	1 878	181	9.6	198	10.5
Alaska	251	51	20.4	59	23.6	259	57	21.9	64	24.8
Arizona	2 047	137	6.7	168	8.2	2 015	130	6.4	148	7.3
Arkansas	1 058	79	7.5	91	8.6	1 052	61	5.8	71	6.7
California	13 811	2 286	16.6	2 527	18.3	14 359	2 295	16.0	2 546	17.7
Colorado	1 927	181	9.4	199	10.4	1 923	173	9.0	193	10.0
Connecticut	1 455	264	18.2	279	19.2	1 508	246	16.3	262	17.4
Delaware	339	47	13.8	53	15.5	353	47	13.3	52	14.6
District of Columbia	245	32	13.1	38	15.4	244	36	14.7	40	16.5
Florida	6 263	410	6.5	543	8.7	6 399	434	6.8	554	8.7
Georgia	3 483	253	7.3	313	9.0	3 632	228	6.3	267	7.4
Hawaii	494	114	23.2	124	25.0	497	124	24.8	129	26.0
Idaho	527	48	9.2	59	11.3	533	41	7.6	48	9.0
Illinois	5 514	993	18.0	1 054	19.1	5 639	1 046	18.6	1 101	19.5
Indiana	2 704	424	15.7	454	16.8	2 687	418	15.6	461	17.1
Iowa	1 334	184	13.8	209	15.7	1 333	182	13.6	215	16.1
Kansas	1 224	119	9.7	141	11.5	1 200	109	9.0	135	11.2
Kentucky	1 656	192	11.6	213	12.9	1 729	208	12.0	235	13.6
Louisiana	1 795	145	8.1	180	10.0	1 711	122	7.1	155	9.0
Maine	544	84	15.4	93	17.1	556	78	14.0	92	16.6
Maryland	2 444	367	15.0	438	17.9	2 423	353	14.6	406	16.7
Massachusetts	2 875	465	16.2	492	17.1	2 841	406	14.3	445	15.7
Michigan	4 490	963	21.5	1 009	22.5	4 513	938	20.8	985	21.8
Minnesota	2 302	444	19.3	471	20.5	2 307	419	18.2	434	18.8
Mississippi	1 086	67	6.2	94	8.6	1 120	68	6.0	104	9.3
Missouri	2 458	353	14.4	376	15.3	2 567	338	13.2	365	14.2
Montana	362	55	15.3	62	17.2	369	51	13.9	58	15.7
Nebraska	748	66	8.8	92	12.2	775	65	8.4	89	11.5
Nevada	823	161	19.5	172	20.9	881	151	17.1	165	18.8
New Hampshire	565	60	10.6	69	12.2	576	60	10.4	67	11.6
New Jersey	3 609	741	20.5	807	22.4	3 668	762	20.8	801	21.8
New Mexico	660	65	9.9	78	11.8	692	56	8.1	70	10.1
New York	7 490	1 897	25.3	1 986	26.5	7 683	1 958	25.5	2 036	26.5
North Carolina	3 359	109	3.2	132	3.9	3 404	124	3.6	148	4.4
North Dakota	268	25	9.3	27	10.1	272	18	6.5	21	7.8
Ohio	5 008	896	17.9	955	19.1	5 071	879	17.3	955	18.8
Oklahoma	1 403	124	8.8	140	10.0	1 384	94	6.8	108	7.8
Oregon	1 420	216	15.2	234	16.5	1 457	234	16.1	251	17.2
Pennsylvania	5 152	896	17.4	960	18.6	5 149	870	16.9	926	18.0
Rhode Island	433	77	17.7	81	18.8	438	80	18.2	83	18.8
South Carolina	1 716	61	3.5	65	3.8	1 740	70	4.0	89	5.1
South Dakota	332	20	6.0	26	7.8	329	18	5.5	22	6.7
Tennessee	2 411	181	7.5	213	8.8	2 387	212	8.9	239	10.0
Texas	8 725	520	6.0	611	7.0	8 755	505	5.8	645	7.4
Utah	935	60	6.4	70	7.5	945	69	7.3	85	9.0
Vermont	273	26	9.7	29	10.8	274	28	10.3	34	12.4
Virginia	3 107	204	6.6	249	8.0	3 199	179	5.6	227	7.1
Washington	2 585	535	20.7	610	23.6	2 593	471	18.2	516	19.9
West Virginia	702	107	15.2	113	16.1	718	103	14.3	111	15.5
Wisconsin	2 505	452	18.1	476	19.0	2 533	446	17.6	473	18.7
Wyoming	212	19	9.1	23	10.8	216	18	8.3	22	10.0

Note: Data refer to the sole or principal job of full- and part-time workers. Excluded are all self-employed workers regardless of whether or not their businesses are incorporated.

1. Data refer to members of a labor union or an employee association similar to a union.
2. Data refer to members of a labor union or an employee association similar to a union as well as workers who report no union affiliation but whose jobs are covered by a union or an employee association contract.

PART TEN

FOREIGN LABOR AND PRICE STATISTICS

FOREIGN LABOR AND PRICE STATISTICS

HIGHLIGHTS

This part compares several summary statistics of labor force status, manufacturing productivity and consumer prices from the U.S. with other countries. Different concepts and methodologies make comparisons difficult and BLS makes such adjustments as it can to reconcile some of the data. There are lags in receipt of the data from other countries, so comparisons here are based on the latest available data.

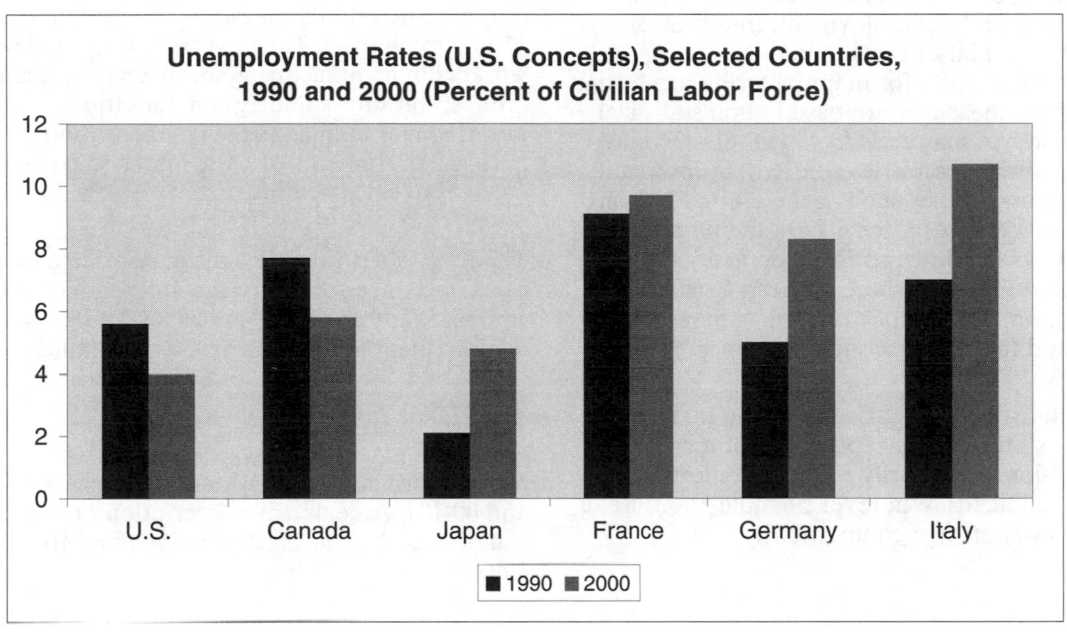

The United States had the lowest unemployment rate among the major industrial countries at 4.0 percent in 2000, followed by Japan at 4.8 percent. The United States and Canada have reduced unemployment since 1990, while major industrial countries in Asia and Europe showed increases.

OTHER HIGHLIGHTS:

- The United States increased employment by 8.3 percent 1995 to 2000, while employment in Japan was slightly less (-0.2 percent) in 2000 than in 1995. (Table 10-1)
- Output per hour in manufacturing increased in 1999 from the previous year in most of the major industrial countries. The United States had the highest rate of increase at 6.5 percent, followed by the United Kingdom at 4.5 percent. For the United States, this reflected a high rate (5.8 percent) of output increase achieved with a 0.9 percent decline in hours. In the United Kingdom, on the other hand, output was unchanged while hours dropped 4.2 percent, more than any other country shown. (Table 10-2)
- In the United States, compensation costs per hour for production workers in manufacturing were $19.20 per hour in 1999, a 2.9 percent increase from the 1998 level. This U.S. cost level was lower than in 10 of the other 28 countries shown for 1999. In Europe, costs declined 1.5 percent, whereas they increased 6.3 percent in the Asian newly industrialized economies. (Table 10-3)

NOTES AND DEFINITIONS

Collection and Coverage

From its inception, BLS has conducted a program of research and statistical analysis to compare labor conditions in the United States and selected foreign countries. The principal comparative measures cover the labor force, employment and unemployment; trends in labor productivity and unit labor costs in manufacturing; and hourly compensation costs for manufacturing production workers. All of the measures are based upon statistical data and other source materials from (a) the statistical agencies of the foreign countries studied; (b) international and supranational bodies such as the United Nations, the International Labour Office (ILO), the Organization for Economic Cooperation and Development (OECD), and the Statistical Office of the European Communities (EUROSTAT), which attempt to obtain comparable country data; and (c) other secondary sources.

International statistical comparisons should be used cautiously because statistical concepts and methods in each country are fashioned primarily to meet domestic rather than international needs. Wherever possible, the Bureau adjusts the data to improve comparability.

The first table provides the Bureau's comparative measures of the civilian labor force participation rate, employment, and unemployment approximating U.S. concepts. The second table provides trend indexes of manufacturing labor productivity (output per hour), hourly compensation, unit labor costs (labor compensation per unit of output), and related measures for the United States and 11 other countries. The next table is limited to production workers in manufacturing for 29 countries and 6 country groups, and shows hourly compensation costs in U.S. dollars. Changes in unadjusted compensation costs reflect both the movements of costs in national currencies and changes in exchange rates.

The final tables provide consumer price index levels and rates of change for selected countries. No adjustments for comparability are made in the total indexes except to convert them to a uniform base year (1982–84=100).

Additional Information

More information is in BLS news releases USDL 01-78 and 00-121. An extensive description of the methodology can be found in the *BLS Handbook of Methods,* April 1997.

Table 10-1. Employment Status of the Working-Age Population, Approximating U.S. Concepts, 10 Countries, 1965–2000

(Numbers in thousands, percent.)

Year and category	United States	Canada[1]	Australia	Japan	France	Germany [2]	Italy	Netherlands	Sweden	United Kingdom
CIVILIAN LABOR FORCE PARTICIPATION RATE										
1965	58.9	56.5	59.9	64.4	57.4	58.7	51.4	...	64.1	62.4
1966	59.2	57.3	60.6	64.6	57.3	58.2	50.0	...	64.2	62.3
1967	59.6	57.6	61.2	64.8	57.4	57.0	50.2	...	63.3	62.0
1968	59.6	57.6	61.2	64.9	57.1	56.9	49.7	...	63.8	61.6
1969	60.1	57.9	61.4	64.6	57.3	57.0	49.3	...	63.8	61.4
1970	60.4	57.8	62.1	64.5	57.5	56.9	49.0	...	64.0	61.1
1971	60.2	58.1	62.2	64.3	57.4	56.5	48.7	...	64.2	60.4
1972	60.4	58.6	62.3	63.8	57.2	56.2	47.7	...	64.1	60.8
1973	60.8	59.7	62.6	64.0	57.3	56.3	47.6	53.4	64.1	62.4
1974	61.2	60.5	63.0	63.1	57.4	55.7	47.7	53.5	64.8	62.2
1975	61.2	61.1	63.2	62.4	57.2	55.0	47.7	54.5	65.9	62.6
1976	61.6	[3]62.5	62.7	62.4	57.5	54.6	48.0	54.1	66.0	62.7
1977	62.3	62.8	62.7	62.5	57.8	54.4	48.2	54.2	65.9	62.7
1978	63.2	63.6	61.9	62.8	57.7	54.4	47.8	54.0	66.1	62.8
1979	63.7	64.4	61.6	62.7	57.8	54.5	48.0	54.2	66.6	62.5
1980	63.8	64.9	62.1	62.6	57.5	54.7	48.2	55.4	66.9	62.5
1981	63.9	65.6	61.9	62.6	57.5	54.7	48.3	56.7	66.8	62.3
1982	64.0	64.8	61.7	62.7	57.5	54.6	47.7	56.6	66.8	61.9
1983	64.0	65.1	61.4	63.1	57.2	[3]54.3	47.5	[3]55.7	66.7	61.6
1984	64.4	65.4	61.5	62.7	57.2	54.4	47.3	55.7	66.6	62.3
1985	64.8	65.9	61.6	62.3	56.8	54.7	47.2	55.5	66.9	62.4
1986	65.3	66.3	62.8	62.1	56.7	54.9	[3]47.8	56.0	67.0	62.5
1987	65.6	66.7	63.0	61.9	56.5	55.0	47.6	56.3	[3]66.4	62.9
1988	65.9	67.0	63.3	61.9	56.2	55.1	47.4	[3]54.7	66.9	63.5
1989	66.5	67.4	64.0	62.2	56.1	55.2	47.3	54.8	67.3	64.0
1990	[3]66.5	67.3	64.6	62.6	55.9	55.3	47.2	56.1	67.4	64.1
1991	66.2	66.7	64.1	63.2	55.9	[3]58.9	[3]47.7	56.8	67.0	63.7
1992	66.4	65.9	63.9	63.4	[3]55.8	58.3	47.5	57.7	65.7	63.1
1993	66.3	65.5	63.6	63.3	55.6	58.0	[3]47.9	58.2	64.5	62.8
1994	[3]66.6	65.2	63.9	63.1	55.5	57.6	47.3	59.0	63.7	62.5
1995	66.6	64.9	64.6	62.9	55.3	57.3	47.1	58.9	64.1	62.7
1996	66.8	64.7	64.6	63.0	55.5	57.4	47.1	60.3	64.0	62.7
1997	67.1	65.0	64.3	63.2	55.3	57.7	47.2	60.6	63.3	62.8
1998	67.1	65.4	64.4	62.8	55.7	57.7	47.6	61.4	62.8	62.7
1999	67.1	65.8	64.2	62.4	56.0	[4]57.9	47.8	61.5	[4]63.2	[4]62.9
2000	67.2	65.9	64.7	[4]62.0	...	...	...	...	...	...
UNEMPLOYMENT RATE										
1965	4.5	3.6	1.3	1.2	1.6	0.3	3.5	...	1.2	2.1
1966	3.8	3.4	1.6	1.4	1.6	0.3	3.7	...	1.6	2.3
1967	3.8	3.8	1.9	1.3	2.1	1.3	3.4	...	2.1	3.3
1968	3.6	4.5	1.8	1.2	2.7	1.1	3.5	...	2.2	3.2
1969	3.5	4.4	1.8	1.1	2.3	0.6	3.5	...	1.9	3.1
1970	4.9	5.7	1.6	1.2	2.5	0.5	3.2	...	1.5	3.1
1971	5.9	6.2	1.9	1.3	2.8	0.6	3.3	...	2.6	3.9
1972	5.6	6.2	2.6	1.4	2.9	0.7	3.8	...	2.7	4.2
1973	4.9	5.5	2.3	1.3	2.8	0.7	3.7	3.1	2.5	3.2
1974	5.6	5.3	2.7	1.4	2.9	1.6	3.1	3.6	2.0	3.1
1975	8.5	6.9	4.9	1.9	4.2	3.4	3.4	5.1	1.6	4.6
1976	7.7	[3]6.8	4.8	2.0	4.6	3.4	3.9	5.4	1.6	5.9
1977	7.1	7.8	5.6	2.0	5.2	3.4	4.1	4.9	1.8	6.4
1978	6.1	8.1	6.3	2.3	5.4	3.3	4.1	5.1	2.2	6.3
1979	5.8	7.2	6.3	2.1	6.1	2.9	4.4	5.1	2.1	5.4
1980	7.1	7.2	6.1	2.0	6.5	2.8	4.4	6.0	2.0	7.0
1981	7.6	7.3	5.8	2.2	7.6	4.0	4.9	8.9	2.5	10.5
1982	9.7	10.6	7.2	2.4	8.3	5.6	5.4	10.2	3.1	11.3
1983	9.6	11.5	10.0	2.7	8.6	[3]6.9	5.9	[3]11.4	3.5	11.8
1984	7.5	10.9	9.0	2.8	10.0	7.1	5.9	11.5	3.1	11.7
1985	7.2	10.2	8.3	2.6	10.5	7.2	6.0	9.6	2.8	11.2
1986	7.0	9.2	8.1	2.8	10.6	6.6	[3]7.5	10.0	2.6	11.2
1987	6.2	8.4	8.1	2.9	10.8	6.3	7.9	10.0	[3]2.2	10.3
1988	5.5	7.3	7.2	2.5	10.3	6.3	7.9	[3]7.7	1.9	8.6
1989	5.3	7.0	6.2	2.3	9.6	5.7	7.8	7.0	1.6	7.2
1990	[3]5.6	7.7	6.9	2.1	9.1	5.0	7.0	6.2	1.8	6.9
1991	6.8	9.8	9.6	2.1	9.6	[3]5.6	[3]6.9	5.9	3.1	8.8
1992	7.5	10.6	10.8	2.2	[3]10.4	6.7	7.3	5.6	5.6	10.1
1993	6.9	10.7	10.9	2.5	11.8	7.9	[3]10.2	6.5	9.3	10.5
1994	[3]6.1	9.4	9.7	2.9	12.3	8.5	11.2	7.2	9.6	9.7
1995	5.6	8.5	8.5	3.2	11.8	8.2	11.8	7.1	9.1	8.7
1996	5.4	8.7	8.6	3.4	12.5	8.9	11.7	6.3	9.9	8.2
1997	4.9	8.2	8.6	3.4	12.4	9.9	11.9	5.3	10.1	7.0
1998	4.5	7.5	8.0	4.1	11.8	9.3	12.0	4.0	8.4	6.3
1999	4.2	6.8	7.2	4.7	11.2	8.7	11.5	3.4	7.1	[4]6.1
2000	4.0	5.8	6.6	[4]4.8	[4]9.7	[4]8.3	[4]10.7	...	[4]5.9	...

See footnotes at end of table.

Table 10-1. Employment Status of the Working-Age Population, Approximating U.S. Concepts, 10 Countries, 1965–2000—*Continued*

(Numbers in thousands, percent.)

Year and category	United States	Canada[1]	Australia	Japan	France	Germany[2]	Italy	Netherlands	Sweden	United Kingdom
EMPLOYED										
1965	71 088	6 944	4 628	46 210	19 340	26 290	19 210	...	3 700	24 700
1966	72 895	7 242	4 785	47 200	19 530	26 220	18 890	...	3 736	24 760
1967	74 372	7 451	4 928	48 180	19 650	25 390	19 130	...	3 693	24 470
1968	75 920	7 593	5 046	49 100	19 640	25 400	19 080	...	3 737	24 370
1969	77 902	7 832	5 188	49 570	19 990	25 790	18 940	...	3 778	24 390
1970	78 678	7 919	5 388	50 140	20 270	26 100	19 080	...	3 850	24 330
1971	79 367	8 104	5 517	50 480	20 420	26 220	19 020	...	3 854	23 970
1972	82 153	8 344	5 601	50 590	20 540	26 280	18 710	...	3 856	24 120
1973	85 064	8 761	5 765	51 910	20 840	26 590	18 870	5 050	3 873	24 610
1974	86 794	9 125	5 891	51 710	21 030	26 240	19 280	5 100	3 956	24 680
1975	85 846	9 284	5 866	51 530	20 860	25 540	19 400	5 070	4 056	24 560
1976	88 752	[3]9 680	5 946	52 020	21 030	25 400	19 500	5 100	4 082	24 360
1977	92 017	9 822	6 000	52 720	21 220	25 430	19 670	5 210	4 093	24 400
1978	96 048	10 115	6 038	53 370	21 320	25 650	19 720	5 260	4 109	24 610
1979	98 824	10 550	6 111	54 040	21 390	26 080	19 930	5 350	4 174	24 940
1980	99 303	10 857	6 284	54 600	21 440	26 490	20 200	5 520	4 226	24 670
1981	100 397	11 184	6 416	55 060	21 330	26 450	20 280	5 550	4 219	23 800
1982	99 526	10 850	6 415	55 620	21 390	26 150	20 250	5 520	4 213	23 560
1983	100 834	10 940	6 300	56 550	21 380	[3]25 770	20 320	[3]5 420	4 218	23 470
1984	105 005	11 209	6 494	56 870	21 200	25 830	20 390	5 490	4 249	23 930
1985	107 150	11 516	6 697	57 260	21 150	26 010	20 490	5 650	4 293	24 290
1986	109 597	11 866	6 974	57 740	21 240	26 380	[3]20 610	5 740	4 326	24 470
1987	112 440	12 209	7 129	58 320	21 320	26 590	20 590	5 850	[3]4 340	25 010
1988	114 968	12 591	7 398	59 310	21 520	26 800	20 870	[3]5 880	4 410	25 850
1989	117 342	12 866	7 720	60 500	21 850	27 200	20 770	5 990	4 480	26 510
1990	[3]118 793	12 961	7 859	61 710	22 080	27 950	21 080	6 230	4 513	26 740
1991	117 718	12 747	7 676	62 920	22 120	[3]36 920	[3]21 360	6 380	4 447	26 090
1992	118 492	12 672	7 637	63 620	22 020	36 420	21 230	6 540	4 265	25 530
1993	120 259	12 770	7 680	63 810	21 740	36 030	[3]20 270	6 590	4 028	25 340
1994	[3]123 060	13 027	7 921	63 860	21 730	35 890	19 940	6 680	3 992	25 550
1995	124 900	13 271	8 235	63 890	21 910	35 900	19 820	6 730	4 056	26 000
1996	126 708	13 380	8 344	64 200	21 960	35 680	19 920	6 970	4 019	26 280
1997	[3]129 558	13 705	8 429	64 900	22 090	35 570	19 990	7 110	3 973	26 740
1998	[3]131 463	14 068	8 597	64 450	22 520	35 830	20 210	7 360	4 034	27 050
1999	[3]133 488	14 456	8 785	63 920	22 970	36 170	20 460	7 490	4 117	[4]27 330
2000	[3]135 208	14 827	9 043	[4]63 790	...	...	...	...	...	...
UNEMPLOYED										
1965	3 366	263	61	570	310	70	690	...	44	540
1966	2 875	251	76	650	320	70	730	...	59	570
1967	2 975	296	94	630	420	340	670	...	80	830
1968	2 817	358	94	590	550	290	700	...	85	810
1969	2 832	362	96	570	480	170	680	...	73	770
1970	4 093	476	91	590	530	140	640	...	59	770
1971	5 016	535	107	640	580	160	640	...	101	980
1972	4 882	553	150	730	610	190	740	...	107	1 070
1973	4 365	515	136	680	590	190	720	160	98	820
1974	5 156	514	162	730	630	420	620	190	80	790
1975	7 929	690	302	1 000	910	890	690	270	67	1 180
1976	7 406	[3]709	298	1 080	1 020	890	790	290	66	1 540
1977	6 991	826	358	1 100	1 160	900	840	270	75	1 660
1978	6 202	888	405	1 240	1 220	870	850	280	94	1 650
1979	6 137	824	408	1 170	1 390	780	920	290	88	1 420
1980	7 637	847	409	1 140	1 490	770	920	350	86	1 850
1981	8 273	881	394	1 260	1 760	1 090	1 040	540	108	2 790
1982	10 678	1 286	495	1 360	1 930	1 560	1 160	630	137	3 000
1983	10 717	1 424	697	1 560	2 020	[3]1 900	1 270	[3]700	151	3 140
1984	8 539	1 366	641	1 610	2 360	1 970	1 280	710	136	3 180
1985	8 312	1 303	603	1 560	2 470	2 010	1 310	600	125	3 060
1986	8 237	1 204	613	1 670	2 520	1 860	[3]1 680	640	117	3 080
1987	7 425	1 116	629	1 730	2 570	1 800	1 760	650	[3]97	2 860
1988	6 701	991	576	1 550	2 460	1 810	1 790	[3]490	84	2 420
1989	6 528	975	508	1 420	2 320	1 640	1 760	450	72	2 070
1990	[3]7 047	1 076	585	1 340	2 210	1 460	1 590	410	84	1 990
1991	8 628	1 381	814	1 360	2 350	[3]2 210	[3]1 580	400	144	2 520
1992	9 613	1 496	925	1 420	[3]2 550	2 620	1 680	390	255	2 880
1993	8 940	1 530	939	1 660	2 900	3 110	[3]2 300	460	415	2 970
1994	[3]7 996	1 359	856	1 920	3 060	3 320	2 510	520	426	2 730
1995	7 404	1 229	766	2 100	2 920	3 200	2 640	510	404	2 480
1996	7 236	1 271	783	2 250	3 130	3 500	2 650	470	440	2 340
1997	[3]6 739	1 230	791	2 300	3 130	3 910	2 690	400	445	2 020
1998	[3]6 210	1 148	750	2 790	3 020	3 690	2 750	310	368	1 820
1999	[3]5 880	1 058	685	3 170	2 890	3 460	2 670	260	313	[4]1 760
2000	[3]5 655	918	638	[4]3 200	...	...	...	...	...	...

1. There is a break in the published series as of 1966, resulting from sampling changes and a raising of the lower age limit from 14 to 15. The effect was to lower the as-published unemployment rate by about 0.4 percentage point.
2. Unified Germany for 1991 onward. Prior to 1991, data relate to the former West Germany.
3. Break in series.
4. Preliminary.

Table 10-2. Indexes of Manufacturing Productivity and Related Measures, 12 Countries, 1970 and 1985–1999

(1992=100.)

Item and year	United States	Canada	Japan	Belgium	Denmark	France	Germany [1]	Italy	Netherlands	Norway	Sweden	United Kingdom
OUTPUT PER HOUR [2]												
1970	...	56.6	37.5	32.9	52.7	43.0	52.0	37.9	38.1	58.3	52.2	44.7
1985	86.0	92.4	76.5	87.0	96.7	79.1	89.1	82.6	89.0	90.2	86.2	72.3
1986	86.0	90.0	76.1	87.8	91.1	80.4	89.6	83.8	90.8	89.0	87.5	74.8
1987	92.9	90.6	80.2	88.9	90.6	81.8	88.1	85.7	91.6	93.3	89.2	79.4
1988	96.9	90.9	83.9	92.0	94.1	87.5	91.5	86.7	93.7	92.2	90.5	82.3
1989	95.7	93.7	88.5	96.9	99.6	91.9	94.6	89.4	97.1	94.6	93.2	86.1
1990	96.9	95.7	94.4	96.8	99.1	93.5	99.0	92.5	98.6	96.6	94.6	88.3
1991	97.9	95.3	99.0	99.1	99.6	96.9	101.9	95.2	99.6	97.5	95.5	92.1
1992	100.0	100.0	100.0	100.0	100.0	100.0	100.0	100.0	100.0	100.0	100.0	100.0
1993	102.1	104.5	101.7	102.5	104.5	100.6	100.6	102.9	101.4	100.6	107.3	104.0
1994	107.3	109.9	103.3	108.4	...	108.5	107.9	105.6	112.7	101.4	119.4	106.8
1995	113.8	111.0	111.0	113.2	...	114.5	111.2	109.3	117.7	102.0	121.9	104.3
1996	117.0	109.5	116.1	117.1	...	115.0	115.1	109.5	119.7	102.0	124.5	102.3
1997	121.2	112.8	121.0	126.8	...	122.6	121.8	111.5	121.9	103.0	132.9	103.0
1998	126.8	112.5	121.2	128.8	...	124.0	127.1	111.1	124.6	103.9	136.7	102.9
1999	135.1	115.2	125.8	128.9	...	128.9	...	112.9	127.3	103.9	140.8	107.5
OUTPUT												
1970	...	60.6	39.2	57.6	68.0	64.1	70.9	45.8	59.5	89.9	80.7	90.3
1985	90.0	98.3	76.7	89.1	103.5	87.3	88.3	83.3	86.1	108.5	102.9	89.0
1986	88.6	99.4	75.5	89.1	103.5	87.3	89.7	85.5	88.3	108.1	104.0	90.1
1987	96.4	103.9	79.0	88.8	99.3	87.2	88.0	88.7	89.5	110.7	106.6	94.4
1988	103.2	110.1	85.3	93.3	100.8	92.2	90.9	94.5	92.8	105.3	109.8	101.4
1989	102.4	112.6	90.9	99.1	104.3	97.2	94.0	98.1	96.9	101.3	110.9	105.4
1990	101.6	108.6	97.1	101.0	102.7	99.1	99.1	99.6	100.1	100.2	110.1	105.3
1991	98.3	99.0	102.0	100.7	101.7	99.8	102.8	99.2	100.6	98.3	104.1	100.0
1992	100.0	100.0	100.0	100.0	100.0	100.0	100.0	100.0	100.0	100.0	100.0	100.0
1993	103.5	104.6	96.3	97.0	99.0	95.7	91.8	96.4	98.2	102.7	101.9	101.4
1994	111.1	113.2	94.9	101.4	109.3	100.3	93.5	102.2	104.2	106.7	117.1	106.1
1995	118.4	118.1	98.9	104.2	114.7	104.9	93.7	107.2	107.8	109.0	128.4	107.8
1996	121.3	119.8	103.0	106.6	109.7	104.6	92.5	105.6	108.4	110.1	131.1	108.2
1997	127.9	128.1	106.5	113.8	112.6	109.7	95.8	108.3	111.2	115.7	138.6	109.6
1998	133.3	133.1	100.2	116.3	115.3	111.5	100.7	110.3	114.9	117.6	144.6	110.1
1999	141.0	141.3	101.0	117.7	111.5	114.2	...	111.4	118.4	114.0	150.7	110.1
TOTAL HOURS												
1970	104.4	107.1	104.4	174.7	129.0	149.0	136.3	120.9	156.2	154.3	154.7	202.1
1985	104.6	106.4	100.3	102.4	107.0	110.4	99.1	100.8	96.7	120.2	119.4	123.1
1986	103.0	110.5	99.2	101.5	113.7	108.6	100.1	102.1	97.3	121.6	118.9	120.5
1987	103.8	114.7	98.5	100.0	109.6	106.6	99.9	103.5	97.7	118.6	119.5	118.9
1988	106.6	121.2	101.7	101.5	107.2	105.4	99.3	108.9	99.0	114.3	121.4	123.2
1989	107.1	120.2	102.7	102.3	104.7	105.8	99.3	109.7	99.8	107.1	119.0	122.4
1990	104.8	113.5	102.9	104.3	103.7	105.9	100.1	107.7	101.5	103.7	116.4	119.3
1991	100.4	103.9	103.1	101.5	102.1	103.0	100.9	104.2	101.0	100.8	109.0	108.6
1992	100.0	100.0	100.0	100.0	100.0	100.0	100.0	100.0	100.0	100.0	100.0	100.0
1993	101.4	100.1	94.7	94.7	94.8	95.1	91.3	93.6	96.9	102.1	94.9	97.5
1994	103.6	103.0	91.9	93.6	...	92.4	86.7	96.7	92.4	105.2	98.1	99.4
1995	104.0	106.4	89.1	92.0	...	91.6	84.3	98.0	91.6	106.8	105.3	103.3
1996	103.7	109.4	88.7	91.1	...	91.0	80.4	96.5	90.5	107.9	105.3	105.8
1997	105.5	113.5	88.0	89.7	...	89.5	78.6	97.1	91.2	112.3	104.3	106.4
1998	105.2	118.3	82.7	90.3	...	89.9	79.3	99.3	92.2	113.2	105.8	107.0
1999	104.3	122.7	80.3	91.3	...	88.6	...	98.6	93.0	109.8	107.1	102.5
COMPENSATION PER HOUR NATIONAL CURRENCY BASIS [2, 3]												
1970	23.7	17.0	16.4	13.7	13.3	10.3	20.7	4.7	20.2	11.8	10.7	6.3
1985	75.1	71.8	72.4	75.3	71.7	72.8	70.0	60.8	81.8	63.4	58.6	53.1
1986	78.5	72.8	76.0	77.3	73.2	75.8	72.8	63.3	85.0	69.1	63.4	57.6
1987	80.7	74.6	77.8	79.7	80.1	78.6	76.0	66.8	87.8	78.4	67.6	64.8
1988	84.0	77.4	79.1	81.1	82.9	81.6	79.1	69.3	87.7	83.3	71.8	67.7
1989	86.6	82.5	84.0	85.9	87.7	86.0	83.2	75.9	88.5	87.2	79.4	72.9
1990	90.8	88.3	90.5	90.1	92.7	90.6	89.4	84.4	90.8	92.3	87.8	80.9
1991	95.6	95.0	96.4	97.3	95.9	96.2	95.1	93.6	95.2	97.5	95.5	90.5
1992	100.0	100.0	100.0	100.0	100.0	100.0	100.0	100.0	100.0	100.0	100.0	100.0
1993	102.7	102.0	102.8	104.8	104.6	103.0	105.9	107.5	103.7	101.5	97.1	104.3
1994	105.6	103.7	104.9	106.1	...	105.6	111.7	107.8	108.2	104.4	99.8	106.5
1995	107.9	106.0	108.3	109.2	...	108.4	117.7	112.8	110.6	109.2	106.3	107.0
1996	109.3	105.1	109.2	110.9	...	110.2	123.7	120.3	113.2	113.6	114.1	107.1
1997	111.4	108.2	112.9	114.7	...	113.0	126.6	125.4	116.2	118.7	119.1	110.3
1998	117.3	111.2	115.8	116.4	...	114.9	127.6	123.0	119.8	126.2	124.1	114.6
1999	122.0	113.0	115.5	116.8	...	119.3	...	126.5	123.5	133.4	127.1	119.7

See footnotes at end of table.

Table 10-2. Indexes of Manufacturing Productivity and Related Measures, 12 Countries, 1970 and 1985–1999—*Continued*

(1992=100.)

Item and year	United States	Canada	Japan	Belgium	Denmark	France	Germany[1]	Italy	Netherlands	Norway	Sweden	United Kingdom
COMPENSATION PER HOUR U.S. CURRENCY BASIS [2,3]												
1970	23.7	19.7	5.8	8.9	10.7	9.9	8.9	9.2	9.8	10.3	12.0	8.6
1985	75.1	63.5	38.5	40.8	40.9	42.9	37.2	39.2	43.3	45.8	39.7	39.0
1986	78.5	63.3	57.2	55.6	54.6	57.9	52.4	52.3	61.1	58.0	51.8	47.8
1987	80.7	68.0	68.2	68.6	70.6	69.2	66.0	63.5	76.2	72.3	62.1	60.2
1988	84.0	76.0	78.2	70.9	74.3	72.5	70.4	65.5	78.0	79.3	68.2	68.3
1989	86.6	84.1	77.1	70.1	72.3	71.4	69.1	68.1	73.4	78.4	71.6	67.7
1990	90.8	91.5	79.1	86.6	90.4	88.0	86.4	86.8	87.7	91.7	86.4	81.7
1991	95.6	100.1	90.8	91.5	90.5	90.2	89.4	92.9	89.4	93.3	91.9	90.5
1992	100.0	100.0	100.0	100.0	100.0	100.0	100.0	100.0	100.0	100.0	100.0	100.0
1993	102.7	95.5	117.3	97.4	97.4	96.2	100.0	84.2	98.1	88.8	72.6	88.7
1994	105.6	91.7	130.1	102.1	. . .	100.8	107.6	82.4	104.6	91.9	75.3	92.4
1995	107.9	93.3	146.2	119.1	. . .	115.1	128.3	85.3	121.2	107.1	86.7	95.6
1996	109.3	93.1	127.2	115.1	. . .	114.1	128.4	96.1	118.0	109.3	99.1	94.7
1997	111.4	94.4	118.3	103.0	. . .	102.5	114.0	90.7	104.6	104.1	90.7	102.3
1998	117.3	90.6	112.0	103.0	. . .	103.1	113.3	87.3	106.2	103.8	90.9	107.5
1999	122.0	91.9	128.8	99.2	. . .	102.6	. . .	85.8	105.0	106.2	89.5	109.6
UNIT LABOR COSTS NATIONAL CURRENCY BASIS [2,3]												
1970	. . .	30.1	43.8	41.7	25.2	24.0	39.8	12.4	52.9	20.3	20.6	14.1
1985	87.3	77.7	94.6	86.5	74.2	92.0	78.6	73.5	91.8	70.2	68.0	73.5
1986	91.2	81.0	99.9	88.0	80.4	94.3	81.2	75.6	93.7	77.7	72.4	77.0
1987	86.9	82.4	97.0	89.7	88.4	96.1	86.3	78.0	95.9	84.1	75.8	81.6
1988	86.7	85.2	94.3	88.1	88.2	93.3	86.5	79.9	93.6	90.4	79.4	82.3
1989	90.5	88.0	94.9	88.7	88.1	93.6	87.9	84.9	91.1	92.2	85.1	84.7
1990	93.7	92.3	95.9	93.0	93.6	96.8	90.3	91.3	92.1	95.6	92.9	91.7
1991	97.6	99.7	97.4	98.1	96.3	99.3	93.3	98.4	95.5	100.0	100.0	98.2
1992	100.0	100.0	100.0	100.0	100.0	100.0	100.0	100.0	100.0	100.0	100.0	100.0
1993	100.6	97.6	101.1	102.3	100.1	102.4	105.3	104.4	102.3	100.9	90.5	100.3
1994	98.5	94.3	101.5	97.9	93.0	97.3	103.6	102.1	96.0	102.9	83.5	99.7
1995	94.8	95.5	97.6	96.4	93.8	94.7	105.9	103.2	94.0	107.0	87.2	102.6
1996	93.5	95.9	94.0	94.7	100.9	95.9	107.5	109.9	94.5	111.4	91.7	104.8
1997	91.9	95.9	93.3	90.5	102.0	92.2	103.9	112.4	95.3	115.2	89.6	107.1
1998	92.5	98.8	95.5	90.3	102.8	92.7	100.4	110.8	96.1	121.5	90.8	111.4
1999	90.3	98.1	91.8	90.6	108.9	92.6	. . .	112.0	97.0	128.4	90.3	111.4
UNIT LABOR COSTS U.S. CURRENCY BASIS [2,3]												
1970	. . .	34.8	15.5	27.0	20.3	23.0	17.1	24.4	25.7	17.6	23.1	19.2
1985	87.3	68.7	50.3	46.9	42.3	54.2	41.7	47.5	48.7	50.8	46.1	54.0
1986	91.2	70.4	75.2	63.4	60.0	72.1	58.5	62.4	67.3	65.3	59.2	64.0
1987	86.9	75.1	85.0	77.2	77.9	84.6	74.9	74.1	83.2	77.5	69.6	75.8
1988	86.7	83.6	93.2	77.0	79.0	82.9	76.9	75.6	83.2	86.1	75.4	83.0
1989	90.5	89.8	87.1	72.3	72.6	77.6	73.0	76.2	75.5	82.9	76.8	78.6
1990	93.7	95.6	83.8	89.5	91.3	94.1	87.3	93.8	88.9	95.0	91.3	92.6
1991	97.6	105.1	91.7	92.3	90.8	93.1	87.8	97.6	89.8	95.7	96.3	98.3
1992	100.0	100.0	100.0	100.0	100.0	100.0	100.0	100.0	100.0	100.0	100.0	100.0
1993	100.6	91.4	115.4	95.1	93.2	95.0	99.4	81.8	96.8	88.3	67.7	85.3
1994	98.5	83.4	125.9	94.2	88.3	92.9	99.8	78.1	92.8	90.7	63.1	86.5
1995	94.8	84.1	131.7	105.2	101.1	100.6	115.5	78.0	103.0	105.0	71.1	91.7
1996	93.5	85.0	109.6	98.3	105.0	99.2	111.6	87.8	98.6	107.1	79.6	92.6
1997	91.9	83.6	97.7	81.2	93.1	83.6	93.5	81.3	85.9	101.0	68.3	99.3
1998	92.5	80.5	92.4	80.0	92.6	83.2	89.1	78.6	85.2	100.0	66.5	104.5
1999	90.3	79.8	102.4	76.9	94.1	79.6	. . .	75.9	82.4	102.2	63.6	102.0
EXCHANGE RATE [4]												
1970	100.0	115.8	35.4	64.7	80.5	95.7	42.8	196.5	48.6	86.9	112.3	135.6
1985	100.0	88.5	53.2	54.2	57.0	58.9	53.1	64.5	53.0	72.3	67.7	73.5
1986	100.0	87.0	75.3	72.0	74.6	76.4	72.0	82.6	71.8	84.0	81.7	83.1
1987	100.0	91.1	87.7	86.1	88.2	88.0	86.9	95.0	86.8	92.2	91.8	92.8
1988	100.0	98.2	98.9	87.4	89.6	88.8	88.9	94.6	88.9	95.2	94.9	100.8
1989	100.0	102.1	91.8	81.6	82.5	83.0	83.0	89.8	82.9	89.9	90.2	92.7
1990	100.0	103.6	87.4	96.2	97.5	97.2	96.6	102.8	96.6	99.4	98.4	101.0
1991	100.0	105.5	94.2	94.0	94.3	93.7	94.0	99.3	93.9	95.7	96.3	100.1
1992	100.0	100.0	100.0	100.0	100.0	100.0	100.0	100.0	100.0	100.0	100.0	100.0
1993	100.0	93.7	114.1	93.0	93.1	93.4	94.4	78.3	94.6	87.5	74.7	85.0
1994	100.0	88.4	124.1	96.2	95.0	95.4	96.3	76.5	96.7	88.1	75.5	86.7
1995	100.0	88.1	134.9	109.1	107.8	106.2	109.1	75.6	109.6	98.1	81.6	89.4
1996	100.0	88.6	116.5	103.8	104.1	103.5	103.8	79.9	104.3	96.2	86.8	88.4
1997	100.0	87.3	104.7	89.8	91.3	90.7	90.0	72.3	90.1	87.7	76.2	92.7
1998	100.0	81.5	96.8	88.5	90.1	89.7	88.8	70.9	88.7	82.3	73.3	93.8
1999	100.0	81.3	111.5	84.9	86.4	86.0	85.1	67.8	85.0	79.6	70.4	91.6

1. Former West Germany.
2. The data relate to employees (wage and salary earners) in Belgium, Denmark, and Italy, and to all employed persons (employees and self-employed workers) in the other countries.
3. Compensation adjusted to include changes in employment taxes that are not compensation to employees, but are labor costs to employers.
4. Index of value of foreign currency relative to the U.S. dollar.

Table 10-3. Hourly Compensation Costs in U.S. Dollars for Production Workers in Manufacturing, 29 Countries and Selected Areas, Selected Years, 1975–1999

Country or area	1975	1980	1985	1990	1991	1992	1993	1994	1995	1996	1997	1998	1999
United States	$6.36	$9.87	$13.01	$14.91	$15.58	$16.09	$16.51	$16.87	$17.19	$17.70	$18.27	$18.66	$19.20
Canada	5.96	8.67	10.95	15.95	17.28	17.17	16.55	15.88	16.10	16.64	16.47	15.60	15.60
Mexico	1.47	2.21	1.59	1.58	1.84	2.17	2.40	2.47	1.51	1.54	1.78	1.84	2.12
Australia	5.62	8.47	8.20	13.07	13.53	13.02	12.49	14.12	15.27	16.88	16.58	14.92	15.89
Hong Kong SAR [1]	0.76	1.51	1.73	3.20	3.58	3.92	4.29	4.61	4.82	5.14	5.42	5.47	5.44
Israel	2.25	3.79	4.06	8.55	8.79	9.09	8.82	9.19	10.54	11.32	12.04	12.02	11.91
Japan	3.00	5.52	6.34	12.80	14.67	16.38	19.21	21.35	23.82	21.00	19.54	18.29	20.89
Korea	0.32	0.96	1.23	3.71	4.61	5.22	5.64	6.40	7.29	8.22	7.86	5.39	6.71
New Zealand	3.15	5.22	4.38	8.17	8.20	7.76	7.85	8.76	9.91	10.81	10.81	9.01	9.14
Singapore	0.84	1.49	2.47	3.78	4.35	4.95	5.25	6.29	7.33	8.32	8.24	7.77	7.18
Sri Lanka	0.28	0.22	0.28	0.35	0.40	0.40	0.42	0.45	0.48	0.48	0.46	0.47	...
Taiwan	0.40	1.00	1.50	3.93	4.36	5.09	5.24	5.56	5.94	5.95	5.90	5.27	5.62
Austria	4.51	8.88	7.58	17.75	18.09	20.29	20.16	21.55	25.32	24.80	21.97	22.21	21.83
Belgium	6.41	13.11	8.97	19.17	19.75	22.05	21.44	23.07	26.65	25.97	22.88	23.20	22.82
Denmark	6.28	10.83	8.13	18.04	18.39	20.20	19.11	20.30	24.07	24.11	22.03	22.69	22.96
Finland	4.61	8.24	8.16	21.03	21.25	19.92	16.63	19.06	24.10	23.41	21.32	21.66	21.10
France	4.52	8.94	7.52	15.49	15.65	17.47	16.79	17.63	20.01	19.93	17.99	18.28	17.98
Germany, Former West	6.31	12.25	9.53	21.88	22.63	25.38	25.19	26.70	31.58	31.20	27.68	27.52	26.93
Germany, Unified	...	...	...	...	...	...	24.44	25.86	30.65	30.26	26.84	26.76	26.18
Greece	1.69	3.73	3.66	6.76	6.95	7.60	7.23	7.73	9.17	9.59	9.20	8.91	...
Ireland	3.03	5.95	5.92	11.66	11.91	13.12	11.90	12.42	13.61	13.91	13.61	13.39	13.57
Italy	4.67	8.15	7.63	17.45	18.32	19.35	15.80	15.89	16.22	17.75	17.57	17.11	16.60
Luxembourg	6.50	12.03	7.81	16.74	17.14	19.10	18.74	20.33	23.35	22.55	...	...	...
Netherlands	6.58	12.06	8.75	18.06	18.13	20.10	19.94	20.73	24.12	23.22	20.98	21.17	20.94
Norway	6.77	11.59	10.37	21.47	21.63	23.03	20.21	20.97	24.38	25.05	23.72	23.50	23.91
Portugal	1.58	2.06	1.53	3.77	4.24	5.17	4.50	4.60	5.37	5.58	5.38	5.48	...
Spain	2.53	5.89	4.66	11.38	12.29	13.50	11.62	11.54	12.88	13.51	12.24	12.14	12.11
Sweden	7.18	12.51	9.66	20.93	22.15	24.59	17.69	18.62	21.44	24.07	22.22	22.02	21.58
Switzerland	6.09	11.09	9.66	20.86	21.69	23.23	22.63	24.91	29.30	28.34	24.19	24.38	23.56
United Kingdom	3.37	7.56	6.27	12.70	13.74	14.37	12.41	12.80	13.67	14.09	15.47	16.43	16.56
TRADE-WEIGHTED MEASURES [2, 3]													
All 28 foreign economies	3.83	6.60	6.75	12.36	13.35	14.27	14.34	15.00	16.36	16.09	15.30	14.72	15.24
OECD [4]	4.25	7.30	7.40	13.49	14.56	15.52	15.57	16.25	17.72	17.36	16.45	15.85	16.44
OECD less Mexico, Korea [5]	4.82	8.30	8.48	15.54	16.73	17.79	17.80	18.55	20.36	19.88	18.79	18.21	18.80
Europe [6]	5.10	9.90	7.96	17.31	17.96	19.67	18.31	19.24	21.97	22.07	20.43	20.61	20.31
European Union [6]	5.03	9.83	7.85	17.09	17.74	19.46	18.09	18.97	21.60	21.74	20.22	20.40	20.12
Asian NIEs [7]	0.52	1.17	1.65	3.72	4.30	4.91	5.20	5.78	6.41	6.92	6.83	5.83	6.20

1. Hong Kong Special Administration Region of China.
2. The trade weights used to compute the average compensation cost measures for selected country or economic groups are relative importances derived from the sum of the U.S. imports of manufactured products for consumption (customs value) and the U.S. exports of domestic manufactured products (free alongside ship value) in 1992 for each country or area and each economic group.
3. Data for Germany relate to the former West Germany only.
4. Organization for Economic Cooperation and Development.
5. Mexico joined the OECD in 1994; Korea joined in 1996.
6. The European Union (EU) consists of Austria, Belgium, Denmark, Finland, France, Germany, Greece, Ireland, Italy, Luxembourg, the Netherlands, Portugal, Spain, Sweden, and the United Kingdom. Europe includes the EU countries plus Norway and Switzerland.
7. The Asian NIEs consists of the four newly industrializing economies of Hong Kong, Korea, Singapore, and Taiwan.

Table 10-4. Consumer Price Indexes, 16 Countries, 1950 and 1955–2000

(1982–1984=100.)

Year	Consumer price index [1]															
	United States [2]	Canada [3]	Japan	Australia [4]	Austria	Belgium [5]	Denmark [6]	France [7]	Germany [8]	Italy	Netherlands	Norway [9]	Spain	Sweden	Switzerland [10]	United Kingdom
1950	24.1	21.6	14.8	12.6	. . .	24.0	12.3	11.1	. . .	. . .	. . .	13.6	5.5	13.3	33.2	9.8
1955	26.8	24.4	20.2	18.9	. . .	26.6	15.0	14.5	. . .	10.8	. . .	18.4	6.3	17.5	36.0	12.8
1956	27.2	24.8	20.3	20.1	. . .	27.4	15.8	14.8	. . .	11.1	. . .	19.1	6.7	18.4	36.6	13.5
1957	28.1	25.6	20.9	20.7	. . .	28.2	16.1	15.3	. . .	11.3	. . .	19.6	7.4	19.2	37.3	14.0
1958	28.9	26.3	20.8	20.9	. . .	28.6	16.3	17.6	. . .	11.6	. . .	20.6	8.4	20.0	38.0	14.4
1959	29.1	26.6	21.1	21.3	. . .	29.0	16.5	18.7	. . .	11.6	. . .	21.0	9.0	20.2	37.7	14.5
1960	29.6	26.9	21.8	22.1	32.6	29.1	16.7	19.4	41.6	11.7	. . .	21.1	9.1	21.0	38.2	14.6
1961	29.9	27.1	23.0	22.6	33.8	29.3	17.4	20.0	42.6	12.0	. . .	21.6	9.2	21.5	38.9	15.1
1962	30.2	27.4	24.6	22.6	35.3	29.8	18.8	21.0	43.8	12.6	. . .	22.8	9.7	22.5	40.6	15.8
1963	30.6	27.9	26.4	22.7	36.2	30.4	19.8	22.0	45.1	13.6	. . .	23.4	10.6	23.2	42.0	16.1
1964	31.0	28.4	27.4	23.2	37.6	31.7	20.5	22.7	46.2	14.4	. . .	24.7	11.3	23.9	43.3	16.6
1965	31.5	29.1	29.5	24.1	39.5	32.9	21.8	23.3	47.8	15.0	. . .	25.7	12.8	25.1	44.8	17.4
1966	32.4	30.2	31.0	24.9	40.3	34.3	23.3	23.9	49.4	15.3	. . .	26.6	13.6	26.8	46.9	18.1
1967	33.4	31.3	32.3	25.7	41.9	35.3	25.0	24.6	50.1	15.6	. . .	27.8	14.5	27.9	48.8	18.5
1968	34.8	32.5	34.0	26.3	43.1	36.3	27.0	25.7	50.8	15.8	. . .	28.7	15.2	28.4	50.0	19.4
1969	36.7	34.0	35.8	27.1	44.4	37.6	27.9	27.3	51.8	16.3	40.6	29.6	15.5	29.2	51.3	20.5
1970	38.8	35.1	38.5	28.2	46.4	39.1	29.8	28.8	53.5	17.1	42.1	32.8	16.4	31.3	53.1	21.8
1971	40.5	36.2	40.9	29.9	48.5	40.8	31.5	30.3	56.2	17.9	45.3	34.8	17.7	33.6	56.6	23.8
1972	41.8	37.9	42.9	31.6	51.6	43.0	33.6	32.2	59.2	18.9	48.9	37.3	19.2	35.6	60.4	25.5
1973	44.4	40.7	47.9	34.6	55.5	46.0	36.7	34.6	63.2	20.9	52.9	40.1	21.4	38.0	65.7	27.9
1974	49.3	45.2	59.1	39.9	60.8	51.9	42.3	39.3	67.6	25.0	58.1	43.8	24.8	41.7	72.1	32.3
1975	53.8	50.1	66.0	45.9	65.9	58.5	46.4	43.9	71.7	29.3	63.8	49.0	29.0	45.8	76.9	40.1
1976	56.9	53.8	72.2	52.1	70.8	63.8	50.5	48.2	74.8	34.1	69.6	53.5	34.1	50.5	78.2	46.8
1977	60.6	58.1	78.1	58.5	74.6	68.4	56.1	52.7	77.4	40.3	74.1	58.3	42.4	56.3	79.2	54.2
1978	65.2	63.3	81.4	63.1	77.3	71.4	61.8	57.5	79.4	45.3	77.2	63.1	50.8	61.9	80.1	58.7
1979	72.6	69.1	84.4	68.8	80.2	74.6	67.7	63.6	82.4	52.4	80.5	66.1	58.8	66.4	83.0	66.6
1980	82.4	76.1	90.9	75.8	85.3	79.6	76.1	72.3	86.7	64.0	86.1	73.3	67.9	75.5	86.3	78.5
1981	90.9	85.6	95.4	83.2	91.1	85.6	85.0	82.0	92.2	75.4	91.9	83.3	77.8	84.6	91.9	87.9
1982	96.5	94.9	98.0	92.4	96.0	93.1	93.6	91.6	97.1	87.8	97.2	92.7	89.0	91.9	97.1	95.4
1983	99.6	100.4	99.8	101.8	99.2	100.3	100.0	100.5	100.3	100.7	99.8	100.5	99.9	100.0	100.0	99.8
1984	103.9	104.7	102.1	105.8	104.8	106.6	106.4	107.9	102.7	111.5	103.0	106.8	111.1	108.1	102.9	104.8
1985	107.6	108.9	104.2	112.9	108.2	111.8	111.4	114.2	104.8	121.8	105.3	112.9	120.9	116.0	106.4	111.1
1986	109.6	113.4	104.8	123.2	110.0	113.3	115.4	117.2	104.7	129.0	105.6	121.0	131.5	121.0	107.2	114.9
1987	113.6	118.4	104.9	133.7	111.6	115.0	120.0	120.9	104.9	135.1	105.1	131.6	138.5	126.1	108.8	119.7
1988	118.3	123.2	105.7	142.9	113.8	116.4	125.5	124.2	106.3	141.9	106.1	140.4	145.1	133.4	110.8	125.6
1989	124.0	129.3	108.1	154.1	116.6	120.0	131.5	128.6	109.2	150.8	107.1	146.8	155.0	142.0	114.3	135.4
1990	130.7	135.5	111.4	165.3	120.5	124.1	135.0	133.0	112.1	160.5	109.9	152.8	165.4	156.7	120.5	148.2
1991	136.2	143.1	115.1	170.7	124.4	128.1	138.2	137.2	116.2	170.6	113.3	158.0	175.2	171.5	127.5	156.9
1992	140.3	145.3	117.0	172.4	129.5	131.2	141.1	140.6	120.9	179.4	116.9	161.7	185.6	175.6	132.7	162.7
1993	144.5	147.9	118.5	175.5	134.1	134.8	142.9	143.5	125.2	187.5	120.0	165.4	194.1	183.9	137.0	165.3
1994	148.2	148.2	119.3	178.8	138.2	138.0	145.8	145.9	128.6	195.0	123.3	167.7	203.3	187.8	138.3	169.3
1995	152.4	151.4	119.2	187.1	141.3	140.1	148.8	148.4	130.7	205.1	125.7	171.8	212.8	192.4	140.8	175.2
1996	156.9	153.8	119.3	192.0	143.9	142.9	151.9	151.3	132.4	213.4	128.2	174.0	220.3	193.5	141.9	179.4
1997	160.5	156.2	121.5	192.5	145.8	145.3	155.3	153.2	134.8	217.7	131.0	178.5	224.8	194.8	142.5	185.1
1998	163.0	157.7	122.2	194.1	147.1	146.7	158.2	154.3	136.0	222.0	133.6	182.5	228.8	194.2	142.7	191.4
1999	166.6	160.5	121.8	197.0	147.9	148.3	162.0	155.0	136.9	225.7	136.5	186.7	234.2	195.1	143.8	194.3
2000	172.2	164.8	121.0	205.8	151.4	152.1	166.8	157.7	139.7	231.4	140.0	192.5	242.1	196.9	146.0	200.1

1. The indexes are calculated by rebasing the official indexes of each country to the official U.S. base year. Because of the rebasing to 1982-84, the indexes may differ from official indexes published by national statistical agencies.
2. Urban worker households prior to 1978.
3. All households from January 1995, all urban households from September 1978 to December 1994, and middle-income urban households prior to September 1978. In February 1994, excise and duty taxes on cigarettes were reduced by the federal government and three provinces.
4. Urban worker households prior to September 1998.
5. Excluding rent and several other services prior to 1976.
6. Excluding rent prior to 1964.
7. Paris only prior to 1962. Urban worker households prior to 1993.
8. Former West Germany.
9. Urban worker households prior to 1960.
10. Urban worker households prior to May 1993.

Table 10-5. Consumer Price Indexes, 16 Countries, Percent Change from Previous Year, 1956–2000

Year	Percent change in consumer price index [1]															
	United States [2]	Canada [3]	Japan	Australia [4]	Austria	Belgium [5]	Denmark [6]	France [7]	Germany [8]	Italy	Netherlands	Norway [9]	Spain	Sweden	Switzerland [10]	United Kingdom
1956	1.5	1.5	0.4	6.3	...	2.9	5.3	1.9	...	3.4	...	3.7	5.9	5.0	1.5	4.9
1957	3.3	3.2	3.1	2.7	...	3.1	2.2	3.5	...	1.3	...	2.7	10.8	4.3	1.9	3.7
1958	2.8	2.6	-0.5	1.1	...	1.3	0.7	15.1	...	2.8	...	4.8	13.4	4.4	1.8	3.0
1959	0.7	1.1	1.1	1.9	...	1.2	1.8	6.1	...	-0.4	...	2.2	7.3	0.8	-0.7	0.6
1960	1.7	1.2	3.7	4.0	...	0.3	1.2	3.6	...	2.3	...	0.3	1.2	4.1	1.4	1.0
1961	1.0	0.9	5.3	2.6	3.6	1.0	4.2	3.3	...	2.1	...	2.6	1.1	2.1	1.9	3.4
1962	1.0	1.2	6.8	-0.3	4.4	1.4	7.5	4.8	...	4.7	...	5.3	5.7	4.8	4.3	4.3
1963	1.3	1.8	7.6	0.5	2.7	2.1	5.3	4.8	2.9	7.5	...	2.5	8.8	2.9	3.4	2.0
1964	1.3	1.8	3.8	2.4	3.8	4.2	3.6	3.4	2.4	5.9	...	5.7	7.0	3.4	3.1	3.3
1965	1.6	2.4	7.6	4.0	5.0	4.1	6.5	2.5	3.1	4.6	...	4.3	13.2	5.0	3.4	4.8
1966	2.9	3.7	5.1	3.0	2.2	4.2	6.7	2.7	3.7	2.3	...	3.2	6.2	6.4	4.7	3.9
1967	3.1	3.5	4.0	3.2	4.0	2.9	7.5	2.7	1.7	3.7	...	4.4	6.4	4.2	4.0	2.5
1968	4.2	4.1	5.3	2.7	2.8	2.8	8.0	4.5	1.5	1.4	...	3.5	4.9	1.9	2.4	4.7
1969	5.5	4.5	5.2	2.9	3.1	3.7	3.5	6.4	1.9	2.7	...	3.1	2.2	2.7	2.5	5.4
1970	5.7	3.3	7.7	3.9	4.4	3.9	6.5	5.2	3.4	4.9	3.7	10.6	5.7	7.0	3.6	6.4
1971	4.4	2.9	6.3	6.1	4.7	4.3	5.8	5.5	5.3	4.8	7.6	6.2	8.2	7.4	6.6	9.4
1972	3.2	4.8	4.9	5.9	6.3	5.5	6.6	6.2	5.5	5.7	8.0	7.2	8.3	6.0	6.7	7.1
1973	6.2	7.5	11.7	9.5	7.6	7.0	9.3	7.3	6.9	10.8	8.1	7.5	11.5	6.8	8.7	9.2
1974	11.0	10.9	23.2	15.1	9.5	12.7	15.2	13.7	7.0	19.1	9.8	9.4	15.7	9.9	9.8	16.0
1975	9.1	10.8	11.7	15.1	8.4	12.8	9.6	11.8	6.0	17.0	9.9	11.7	17.0	9.8	6.7	24.2
1976	5.8	7.5	9.4	13.5	7.3	9.2	9.0	9.6	4.3	16.8	9.0	9.1	17.6	10.3	1.7	16.5
1977	6.5	8.0	8.1	12.3	5.5	7.1	11.1	9.4	3.7	17.0	6.4	9.1	24.5	11.4	1.3	15.8
1978	7.6	9.0	4.2	7.9	3.6	4.4	10.1	9.1	2.7	12.1	4.2	8.1	19.8	10.0	1.1	8.3
1979	11.3	9.1	3.7	9.1	3.7	4.5	9.6	10.8	4.1	14.8	4.3	4.8	15.7	7.2	3.6	13.4
1980	13.5	10.1	7.7	10.2	6.4	6.6	12.3	13.6	5.4	21.2	7.0	10.9	15.5	13.7	4.0	18.0
1981	10.3	12.5	4.9	9.7	6.8	7.6	11.7	13.4	6.3	17.8	6.7	13.6	14.6	12.1	6.5	11.9
1982	6.2	10.8	2.8	11.2	5.4	8.7	10.1	11.8	5.3	16.5	5.7	11.3	14.5	8.6	5.6	8.6
1983	3.2	5.8	1.9	10.1	3.3	7.7	6.9	9.6	3.3	14.7	2.7	8.4	12.2	8.9	2.9	4.6
1984	4.3	4.4	2.3	4.0	5.6	6.3	6.0	7.4	2.4	10.8	3.2	6.2	11.3	8.1	3.0	5.0
1985	3.6	4.0	2.0	6.7	3.2	4.9	4.7	5.8	2.1	9.2	2.3	5.7	8.8	7.3	3.4	6.1
1986	1.9	4.1	0.6	9.1	1.7	1.3	3.6	2.7	-0.1	5.9	0.2	7.2	8.8	4.3	0.7	3.4
1987	3.6	4.4	0.1	8.5	1.4	1.6	4.0	3.1	0.2	4.7	-0.4	8.7	5.3	4.2	1.5	4.2
1988	4.1	4.1	0.7	6.9	2.0	1.2	4.6	2.7	1.3	5.0	0.9	6.7	4.8	5.8	1.8	4.9
1989	4.8	5.0	2.3	7.9	2.5	3.1	4.8	3.6	2.8	6.3	1.0	4.6	6.8	6.5	3.2	7.8
1990	5.4	4.8	3.1	7.3	3.3	3.5	2.6	3.4	2.7	6.5	2.6	4.1	6.7	10.4	5.4	9.5
1991	4.2	5.6	3.3	3.2	3.3	3.2	2.4	3.2	3.7	6.3	3.1	3.4	6.0	9.4	5.8	5.9
1992	3.0	1.5	1.6	1.0	4.1	2.4	2.1	2.4	4.0	5.2	3.2	2.3	5.9	2.4	4.0	3.7
1993	3.0	1.8	1.3	1.8	3.6	2.8	1.2	2.1	3.6	4.5	2.6	2.3	4.6	4.7	3.3	1.6
1994	2.6	0.2	0.7	1.9	3.0	2.4	2.0	1.7	2.7	4.0	2.7	1.4	4.8	2.1	0.9	2.4
1995	2.8	2.1	-0.1	4.6	2.2	1.5	2.1	1.7	1.6	5.2	2.0	2.4	4.6	2.5	1.8	3.5
1996	3.0	1.6	0.1	2.6	1.9	2.1	2.1	2.0	1.3	4.0	2.0	1.3	3.6	0.5	0.8	2.4
1997	2.3	1.6	1.8	0.3	1.3	1.6	2.2	1.2	1.9	2.0	2.2	2.6	2.0	0.7	0.5	3.1
1998	1.6	0.9	0.6	0.9	0.9	1.0	1.9	0.7	0.9	2.0	2.0	2.3	1.8	-0.3	0.1	3.4
1999	2.2	1.7	-0.3	1.5	0.6	1.1	2.5	0.5	0.7	1.7	2.2	2.3	2.3	0.5	0.8	1.5
2000	3.4	2.7	-0.7	4.5	2.3	2.5	3.0	1.7	2.0	2.5	2.6	3.1	3.4	0.9	1.5	3.0

1. The figures may differ from official percent changes published by national statistical agencies due to rounding. In the case of Sweden, the official percent changes are not calculated from the published index.
2. Urban worker households prior to 1978.
3. All households from January 1995, all urban households from September 1978 to December 1994, and middle-income urban households prior to September 1978. In February 1994, excise and duty taxes on cigarettes were reduced by the federal government and three provinces. In 1994, the consumer price index excluding tobacco increased 1.5 percent.
4. Urban worker households prior to September 1998.
5. Excluding rent and several other services prior to 1976.
6. Excluding rent prior to 1964.
7. Paris only prior to 1962. Urban worker households prior to 1993.
8. Former West Germany.
9. Urban worker households prior to 1960.
10. Urban worker households prior to May 1993.

INDEX

B

C

D

DEFINITIONS

M

P

U

W

Y